The Law and Practice of International Territorial Administration

International actors have played an active role in the administration of territories over the past two centuries. This book analyses the genesis and law and practice of international territorial administration, covering all experiments from the Treaty of Versailles to contemporary engagements such as the conflict in Iraq. The book discusses the background, legal framework and practice of international territorial administration, including its relationship to related paradigms (internationalisation, Mandate administration, Trusteeship administration and occupation). This is complemented by a discussion of four common legal issues which arise in the context of this activity: the status of the territory under administration, the status and accountability of administering authorities, the exercise of regulatory powers by international administrations and the relationship between international and domestic actors. Alongside surveys of the existing approaches and conceptual choices, the book also includes relevant case-law and practice and lessons learned for future engagements.

DR CARSTEN STAHN is a reader in Public International Law and International Criminal Justice at the School of Law, Swansea University. He was Legal Advisor at the International Criminal Court and is visiting Research Fellow at the Grotius Centre for International Legal Studies, Leiden University. He has also worked as a research fellow at the Max Planck Institute of Comparative Public Law and International Law in Heidelberg (Germany) and as a research assistant at the Institute of European Law and International Law of Humboldt University Berlin. Dr Stahn is Managing Editor of the *Criminal Law Forum*, Senior ICC Editor of the *Leiden Journal of International Law* and Correspondent of the *Netherlands International Law Review*.

CAMBRIDGE STUDIES IN INTERNATIONAL AND COMPARATIVE LAW

Established in 1946, this series produces high-quality scholarship in the fields of public and private international law and comparative law. Although these are distinct legal sub-disciplines, developments since 1946 confirm their interrelation.

Comparative law is increasingly used as a tool in the making of law at national, regional and international levels. Private international law is now often affected by international conventions, and the issues faced by classical conflicts rules are frequently dealt with by substantive harmonisation of law under international auspices. Mixed international arbitrations, especially those involving state economic activity, raise mixed questions of public and private international law, while in many fields (such as the protection of human rights and democratic standards, investment guarantees and international criminal law) international and national systems interact. National constitutional arrangements relating to "foreign affairs," and to the implementation of international norms, are a focus of attention.

The Board welcomes works of a theoretical or interdisciplinary character, and those focusing on the new approaches to international or comparative law or conflicts of law. Studies of particular institutions or problems are equally welcome, as are translations of the best work published in other languages.

A list of books in the series can be found at the end of this volume.

The Law and Practice of International Territorial Administration
Versailles to Iraq and Beyond

Carsten Stahn

CAMBRIDGE UNIVERSITY PRESS
Cambridge, New York, Melbourne, Madrid, Cape Town, Singapore, São Paulo, Delhi

Cambridge University Press
The Edinburgh Building, Cambridge CB2 8RU, UK

Published in the United States of America by Cambridge University Press, New York

www.cambridge.org
Information on this title: www.cambridge.org/9780521878005

First published 2008

Printed in the United Kingdom at the University Press, Cambridge

A catalogue record for this publication is available from the British Library

Library of Congress Cataloguing in Publication data
Stahn, Carsten, 1971–
The law and practice of international territorial administration : Versailles to Iraq and
beyond / Carsten Stahn.
    p. cm.
Includes bibliographical references and index.
ISBN 978-0-521-87800-5 (hardback)
1. Internationalized territories.   2. International trusteeships.   I. Title.
KZ3673.S73 2008
341.4′2–dc22   2008003209

ISBN 978-0-521-87800-5 hardback

Contents

Foreword		*page* xvii
Preface		xxi
Selected table of cases		xxiv
List of abbreviations		xxix
Table of engagements		xxxiii

Introduction		1
1	Why a study of the law and practice of international territorial administration?	3
	1.1 Ending misconceptions	6
	1.2 International territorial administration – a governance issue	17
	1.3 International territorial administration and peacemaking	22
	1.4 International territorial administration and the development of the international legal system	29
2	Contents and methodology	40

Part I	**The historical and social context of international territorial administration**	43

Introduction		43
1	International territorial administration – a definition	43
2	International territorial administration and related policy institutions	45
	2.1 Protectorates and protected states	46

	2.2 Condominiums	48
	2.3 Twentieth-century paradigms	49
1	**The concept of internationalisation**	**50**
	1 Territorial internationalisation	51
	1.1 The concept of "international(ised) territories"	51
	1.2 The relationship between territorial internationalisation and international territorial administration	52
	2 Functional internationalisation	64
	2.1 Patterns of functional internationalisation	64
	2.2 The functional internationalisation of territories under domestic jurisdiction	65
	3 Non-internationalised forms of territorial administration	70
	4 Conclusion	71
2	**The Mandate System of the League of Nations**	**73**
	1 Origin	74
	2 The choice in favour of indirect administration	76
	3 Challenges of the mandate system: a modern retrospection	78
	3.1 Governance issues	79
	3.2 Accountability issues	83
	3.3 Status questions	86
3	**The United Nations Trusteeship System**	**92**
	1 Genesis	92
	2 A leap forward	93
	3 The Trusteeship System from the perspective of international territorial administration	96
	3.1 Trusteeship administration as international territorial administration	96
	3.2 Trusteeship administration as a role model for international territorial administration	106
4	**Post-war occupation**	**115**
	1 Occupation and territorial administration – two distinct concepts	115
	1.1 The rationale of the laws of occupation	116

1.2 Limitations of occupation authority   119
2 The use of occupation as a framework for
  territorial administration   123
  2.1 Treaty-based occupation   123
  2.2 Post-surrender occupation   125
3 The development of the laws of occupation in the
  post-war era   140
  3.1 The decline of the *debellatio* doctrine   141
  3.2 The transformation of the concept of
       occupation   141

5   UN territorial administration and the tradition of
       peace-maintenance   147
       1 Peacekeeping and international territorial
         administration   147
       2 Conceptual developments   149
         2.1 A changing conception of trusteeship   150
         2.2 A new normative underpinning of territorial
              governance   151

       Conclusion: international territorial
       administration – an independent device with a
       certain normative heritage   155

Part II The practice of international territorial
         administration: a retrospective   159

       Introduction   159

6   International territorial administration as a means
       of dispute settlement – the post-war experiments
       of the League of Nations and the United Nations   162
       1 Precedents in the era of the League of Nations   163
         1.1 The administration of the Saar Territory by
              the League of Nations   163
         1.2 The League's administration of the Free City of
              Danzig   173
         1.3 The League's engagement in Memel   185
       2 United Nations experiments in neutralisation
         after World War II   187

2.1 The Permanent Statute of the Free Territory of
    Trieste   188
2.2 United Nations proposals for the
    internationalisation of Jerusalem   195
3 Conclusion   203
3.1 Dichotomies of the first experiments in
    territorial administration   204
3.2 Lessons   206

7   **From the post-war period to the end of the Cold
    War: the use of international territorial
    administration as an *ad hoc* device**   207
    1 Governance assistance missions   208
    1.1 Post-war decolonisation   208
    1.2 Referendum and election assistance   219
    1.3 Conclusion   232
    2 (Co-)governance missions   232
    2.1 The Leticia intervention – a precedent of
        ad hoc UN governance   233
    2.2 The United Nations Operation in the Congo
        (ONUC)   236
    2.3 The United Nations Temporary Executive
        Authority (UNTEA)   246
    2.4 The United Nations Council for Namibia   252
    2.5 The United Nations Operation in Somalia
        (UNOSOM II)   259

8   **The systematisation of international governance**   266
    1 The United Nations Transitional Authority in
      Cambodia (UNTAC)   269
    1.1 A consensual origin   270
    1.2 A balanced statebuilding mandate   271
    1.3 "Looking big, acting small" – challenges in
        implementation   274
    1.4 Assessment   278
    2 The United Nations Transitional Administration
      for Eastern Slavonia (UNTAES)   279
    2.1 A dual function   280
    2.2 The institutional design   282
    2.3 Practice   283

2.4 Assessment 285
3 Bosnia and Herzegovina: a special case of
international administration 287
3.1 The international administration of Bosnia
and Herzegovina 287
3.2 The European Union Administration of the
City of Mostar (EUAM) 301
4 The United Nations Interim Administration in
Kosovo (UNMIK) 308
4.1 Origin 309
4.2 A tripartite function 310
4.3 Fostering people's rights 324
4.4 Trials and errors 326
4.5 Assessment 330
5 The United Nations Transitional Administration in
East Timor (UNTAET) 332
5.1 Historical background 334
5.2 UNTAET – a reprise of UNMIK 337
5.3 Beyond UNMIK 341
5.4 Critique 343
5.5 Assessment 346

9 The "light footprint" and beyond 348
1 The United Nations Assistance Mission in
Afghanistan (UNAMA) 352
1.1 Background 352
1.2 The choice in favour of a light footprint – a
deliberate decision 354
1.3 Role and function of UNAMA 357
1.4 Assessment 360
2 The international administration of Iraq 363
2.1 Background 365
2.2 The light footprint: a power bargain 367
2.3 The scope of UN involvement 368
2.4 The practice of the CPA 371
2.5 Assessment 380
3 Multidimensional peace operations after Iraq 381
3.1 The United Nations Mission in Liberia (UNMIL) 382
3.2 The United Nations Organisation Mission in
the Democratic Republic of Congo (MONUC) 385

3.3 The United Nations Operation in Côte d'Ivoire
(UNOCI)   388
4 The end of the era of comprehensive governance
missions?   393

10   A conceptualisation of the practice   395
1 Models of administration   395
1.1 Direct v. indirect administration.   395
1.2 Exclusive v. shared forms of authority   397
1.3 Creation by consent and/or by unilateral act   399
2 Functions of international territorial
administration   401
2.1 The resolution of territorial disputes   401
2.2 Decolonisation   403
2.3 Statebuilding   404
2.4 The nexus to intervention   406
3 International territorial administration
and trusteeship   410

Part III   The foundations of international territorial
administration   413

Introduction   413

11   The legality of international territorial administration 415
1 The authority to administer territories under the
Charter of the United Nations   415
1.1 The drafting history of the UN Charter   416
1.2 Institutional practice   416
1.3 Territorial authority and systemic
coherence   419
2 Legal basis in the UN Charter   423
2.1 Security Council action   423
2.2 General Assembly action   436
2.3 The Trusteeship Council   439
2.4 The Secretary-General   441
2.5 Other institutional options   444
3 Authorisation of multinational administrations   447
3.1 Authorisation of states to administer
territories   447

3.2 Authorisation of international organisations
     to administer territories   450
3.3 Practice   451
4 Limits of international authority   454
   4.1 The nexus to international peace and
        security   454
   4.2 Limits to territorial administration under
        specific Charter provisions   455
   4.3 Limitations arising from the law of occupation   467
   4.4 Universally recognised human rights standards   479
   4.5 Territorial administration and democratic
        governance   510

12   The legitimacy of international territorial
      authority   517
      1 Features of international territorial authority   517
      2 Models of legitimation   518
         2.1 Legitimacy by consent   519
         2.2 Alternatives to consent   522
      Conclusion   530

Part IV A typology of problems arising within the context
         of international territorial administration   533

      Introduction   533

13   The legal status of the administered territory   535
      1 Status concepts   535
         1.1 Notions developed in legal doctrine   535
         1.2 A re-conceptualisation   538
      2 Treatment of the status question in practice   544
         2.1 Status decisions   544
         2.2 Legal personality of the territory   553
         2.3 External representation   564
      3 Conclusion   577

14   The status of international administering
      authorities   579
      1 The conceptual move: from external to internal
         responsibility   580

2 International territorial administrations and
  privileges and immunities   581
  2.1 Sources of privileges and immunities   581
  2.2 Privileges and immunities in the practice of
      territorial administration   583
  2.3 A critique of existing approaches   587
3 International administrations and institutional
  accountability   598
  3.1 Approaches in international practice   598
  3.2 A re-conceptualisation   615

15   **The exercise of regulatory authority within the
      framework of international administrations**   645
      1 Lawmaking by international administrations   647
        1.1 Institutional diversity   648
        1.2 The legal nature of regulatory acts of
            international administrations   648
        1.3 General authority problems   653
        1.4 Regulatory problems in specific fields   678
        1.5 Conclusions   706
      2 Involvement in constitution-making   707
        2.1 General parameters   707
        2.2 International practice   708

16   **The relationship with domestic actors**   717
      1 From the rule of territory to rule for
        the people   718
      2 Techniques of realising self-government and
        political participation   719
        2.1 Consultation   720
        2.2 Restoration of domestic authority, including
            devolution of authority   723
        2.3 Disengagement and beyond   726
        2.4 Lessons learned   729

Part V **International territorial administration at the
        verge of the twenty-first century: achievements,
        challenges and lessons learned**   731

        Introduction   731

17   **Strong on concept, imperfect in practice:**
      international territorial administration
      as a policy device   733
      1 On the record – a response to some
        criticisms   733
        1.1 International territorial administration and
            (ir-)relevance   733
        1.2 International territorial administration and
            (in-)efficiency   735
        1.3 International territorial administration and
            UN involvement   737
      2 Lessons learned   741
        2.1 The transitional nature of international
            territorial authority   741
        2.2 The role of domestic support   741
        2.3 Institutional design of the mission   743
        2.4 Clarification of the legal framework   744
        2.5 Framing the mandate   746
        2.6 Exercise of authority   747
        2.7 Enhancing sustainability   749

18   **International territorial administration**
      and normative change in the international
      legal order   751
      1 International territorial administration and
        neutrality *vis-à-vis* the internal realm of a
        constituency   751
        1.1 The classical principle of neutrality   752
        1.2 From neutrality to the agenda for
            democratisation   753
        1.3 The other side of interference   754
      2 International territorial administration and the
        theorisation of state sovereignty   754
        2.1 The disaggregation of sovereignty   755
        2.2 Sovereignty and conditions for self-rule and
            independence   756
      3 International territorial administration and the
        theorisation of governance   758

3.1 International territorial administration and
      communitarism   758
3.2 From territoriality to functionality: towards a
      common pool of governance obligations   760

Bibliography   764
Index   806

Foreword

The present work on the international administration of specific territories deals not only with the latest examples of UN operations launched by the Security Council under Chapter VII of the UN Charter, but endeavours to confront the reader with the wider panorama of all regimes of internationalisation since the time of the League of Nations. It is on this broad basis that the author succeeds in establishing a balance sheet which shows all of the achievements, but also all of the failures that have occurred in processes of internationalisation implemented since the end of World War I. Notwithstanding the wealth of information displayed, the reader of the book does not lose the requisite orientation. It is indeed not the aim of the author to give primarily an historical account. He intends instead to define the legal premises upon which, under the conditions of an emerging world of common values, any international territorial regime must be founded.

From the inter-war period, Danzig and the Saar are the most prominent examples of internationalised territories. The UN Charter does not provide for a mandate of the world organisation to assume governmental functions in a given country, either permanently or for a limited period of time. Nonetheless, as from its beginning, the world organisation was faced with territorial disputes as heated as those surrounding Jerusalem and Trieste, attempting to reduce national and religious tensions by sophisticated regimes of internationalisation – vainly, as we know with hindsight. As for future developments, the drafters of the Charter had hoped that any people reaching independent statehood would be able to govern itself in a responsible manner. No special powers were set aside for emergency situations during which a nation might fall into chaos and self-destruction. The Trusteeship Council was to lead the peoples still under the trusteeship system to independence. After that occurrence, it was not supposed to play any further role with a view to helping an infant state find its way on the international stage. Given that the General Assembly has been denied true powers of decision, it was the Security Council which had to fill in the gap left by the lack of imagination of the drafters. Today, it has become an established proposition that the Security Council is authorised to take any measures whatsoever in instances where temporarily an international regime constitutes the only viable solution for a territorial conflict.

It is at that point, however, that difficult questions arise. On the one hand, it is certain that the Security Council enjoys a large measure of discretion in making use of the powers conferred on it by Chapter VII. On the other hand, it pertains to an organisation which has not been endowed with sovereign powers. The Security Council must first of all respect the limitations specified in the UN Charter itself. On the other hand, if it interferes in the interest of the populations concerned it should not deny to those populations the enjoyment of fundamental human rights which the UN has set out to promote and respect. In an ideal world, a UN administration would of course apply in favour of all the persons concerned the full gamut of the human rights enshrined in the major human rights treaties established at worldwide level. This is easier said than done. When the UN is called to perform governmental functions in a given territory or country, the reason is mostly a general breakdown of law and order. Even with the best of intentions, measures must be taken which can easily be criticised as being not in full conformity with the human rights requirements of the International Bill of Rights. In particular, judicial machinery cannot be available as from the very first day of such an emergency operation. Clearly, therefore, compromises must be struck which it is never easy to justify.

Another conundrum is posed by the principle of democratic self-government. Necessarily, an internationalisation process introduces elements of alien domination, albeit by a well-minded custodian. The UN is normally called to intervene in situations where a human community has deprived itself of its capability to rule on its own destiny. In fact, for a democracy to thrive, its members must be prepared to respect the rights of minorities which did not approve of decisions taken by the majority. In many instances, it will be incumbent upon a UN administration first of all to instil in the majority the sense of responsibility which makes life acceptable for all the members of society. In the case of Jerusalem, the desired institutional equilibrium was not reached; in any event, the proposals by the UN were rejected by the parties concerned. In Kosovo, steps are still being taken with a view to preparing all of the groups of the population for a peaceful coexistence – which requires not only elaborate institutions, but also a spirit of tolerance which cannot be produced *ad hoc* and *ex nihilo*. Should the UN administration withdraw even under circumstances which do not augur well for the future? This problem is, as everyone knows, even worse in Iraq which, notwithstanding the unlawful invasion by US and UK forces, was placed under UN authority as a measure of last resort. Once the evil had been done, it could not be made to disappear by the usual means provided for in the rules on state responsibility. A hasty withdrawal as "reparation" would have made matters worse.

Carsten Stahn is fully aware of the intricacies of the many contradictions which are involved in the topic he deals with. Although recognising the hard facts of life, he nonetheless advocates resolving the many ensuing conflicts by complying with the rule of law to the greatest possible extent. In particular, he shows that a UN administration which makes determinations on the destiny of individual human beings cannot shield behind the traditional rule of immunity which otherwise protects the UN against attempts to encroach upon its rights and privileges as a subject of international law. Where the UN steps down to regulate, as a governing authority, the destiny of a human community, it must accept the rules which in the modern world of today shape the relationship between governmental institutions and the persons subject to their jurisdiction. That the king can do no wrong is not an adage suitable to our time.

It stands to reason that the UN is not ideally qualified to assume governmental functions. Since it is composed of 192 states, that variety will also be reflected in any administrative apparatus established by it and the corresponding procedures. However, the international community has not yet come up with better recipes. It may be, though, that in the future the new Peacebuilding Commission, established in 2006, will elaborate appropriate mechanisms which correspond to a greater extent to the requirement of efficiency than the operations of the past. Whatever such prospects, Carsten Stahn has provided us with a nearly complete blueprint for the necessary structure of an interim administration which is destined to end as soon as the population in the territory concerned is able once again to take its fate into its own hands. Although no operation can be implemented exactly in consonance with plans established, the existence of such plans is an indispensable necessity. Whoever takes up such a challenge without sufficient pre-programming, will end up in a mess or in an outright disaster. Carsten Stahn's masterful book is therefore compulsory reading not only for scholars interested in the issue, but also for international officers entrusted with any relevant responsibilities.

Christian Tomuschat, Berlin

Preface

The phenomenon of the administration of territories by international actors has a long tradition in the history of international law. State-based forms of administration, such as the internationalisation of territories, Mandate administration, Trusteeship System administration or multinational forms of occupation have been studied in some detail throughout the twentieth century. The exercise of territorial authority by international entities, however, has received less attention. Experiments of this kind were addressed at particular moments in time in the pre-, inter- and post-war years and the 1990s. But scholarship has remained focused on classical questions of public international law (e.g. the legal basis of territorial administration, the status of territories, legal personality) and an analysis of specific phenomena (e.g. the engagements of the League of Nations in the Saar Territory and Danzig and individual United Nations missions).

This focus has slightly changed over the last decade. The topic of international territorial administration has grown into a discipline of legal scholarship, with an ever-increasing amount of literature on different aspects of this type of activity. International territorial administration is thus no longer perceived as the sum of some "*sui generis*" type of international engagement, but as a distinct form of international authority that may serve as tool of dispute settlement and conflict management. This type of authority shares some conceptual groundwork with related forms of administration, but it has at the same time its own distinct features and problems.

This book seeks to offer a problem-oriented analysis of the project of international territorial administration. It examines the law and practice of international territorial administration before the background of broader themes and debates in contemporary international law, such as the normative heritage of international law, issues of governance beyond the state, models of accountability and the theorisation of sovereignty and neutrality under the United Nations Charter. This perspective requires empirical and theoretical analysis. It is impossible to give a nuanced account of the existing practice without a study of the historical background of individual missions. Moreover, issues of legality and legitimacy are closely linked in this enterprise. Positivist legal research is thus combined here with considerations of legal policy and reference to scholarship and critiques from other disciplines.

The research for this work started during my activity as a Research Fellow at the MPI in Heidelberg (2000–2) and my academic year as a Doctoral Research Fellow of the Max Planck Society for the Advancement of Science at New York University. Both experiences have laid the foundation for this book and my perception of law and scholarship.

The initiative for this work goes back to Professor Jochen Frowein (Heidelberg), who pointed my attention to the legal problems of lawmaking by United Nations administrations shortly after the establishment of the United Nations missions in Kosovo and East Timor in 1999.

In fall 2005, this work was submitted as a doctoral thesis at the Faculty of Law at Humboldt University, Berlin. The thesis was defended by the author at Humboldt University on 19 April 2006. It was revised and finalised in its current form in March 2007. The work was supervised by Professor Christian Tomuschat who has been a mentor, supporter and critical observer of my work since my first steps in the field of international law. His comments, wisdom and guidance throughout the years have been invaluable. Equal gratitude is owed to Professor Frowein and Professor Rüdiger Wolfrum (Heidelberg), who have supported my academic development as a scholar during my years at the Max Planck Institute in Heidelberg and the time thereafter.

A great number of people have helped me develop and refine my thoughts on the topic, including my former teachers at New York University (Professor Joseph Weiler, Professor Benedict Kingsbury and Professor Tomas Franck) and Professor Gerd Seidel, who served as my supervisor at Humboldt University between 1997 and 1999.

I am further indebted to Judge Tuiloma Neroni Slade and Judge Ekaterina Trendafilova, who supported my academic work during my professional activity as legal officer in the Pre-Trial Division of the International Criminal Court and encouraged me to complete this book.

I also wish to express my gratitude to Professor James Crawford (Cambridge) and Professor John S. Bell (Cambridge) for accepting this work as part of the Cambridge Studies in International and Comparative Law. Thanks are also due to Cambridge University Press, in particular, to Finola O'Sullivan, Richard Woodham and Elisabeth Doyle, for their help in turning this manuscript into a book.

My deepest thanks are owed to my parents, Erdmuthe and Hartwig Stahn. Without their warm support and encouragement, this work would not have been possible. This book is dedicated to them.

Carsten Stahn

Selected table of cases

Badischer Staatsgerichtshof, Judgments of 15 January 1949, 27
   November 1948 and 31 August 1949, Archiv des öffentlichen Rechts
   (1949), 477,   137, 610, 611
Constitutional Court of Bosnia and Herzegovina, Decision U 5/98, Third
   Partial Decision, 1 July 2000 ("Constituent Peoples case"),   69, 712
Constitutional Court of Bosnia and Herzegovina, Decision U 16/00,
   2 February 2001,   613, 614
Constitutional Court of Bosnia and Herzegovina, Decision U 25/00,
   23 March 2001.   613, 614
Constitutional Court of Bosnia and Herzegovina, Decision U 9/00,
   3 November 2000 ("Law on State Border Service").   533, 561
Constitutional Court of Bosnia and Herzegovina, Decision U 21/01,
   22 June 2001 ("Mu. K. v. Commission for Real Property Claims").
   295
Constitutional Court of Bosnia and Herzegovina, Decision U 26/01,
   28 September 2001.   614
Constitutional Court of Bosnia and Herzegovina, Decision U 32/01,
   22 June 2001 ("Joint Stock Company Central Profit Banka Sarajevo
   v. Commission for Real Property Claims).   295
Constitutional Court of Bosnia and Herzegovina, Decision U 37/01
   (2 November 2001).   614, 635
Constitutional Court of Bosnia and Herzegovina, Decision U 8/04,
   25 June 2004 ("Framework Law on Higher Education").   291
Control Commission, Court of Appeals, *Dalldorf and Others* v. *Director of
   Prosecutions*, 31 December 1949, Annual Digest (1949), Case No. 159.
   135
Court of Appeal (East Timor), *Prosecutor* v. *Armando Dos Santos*, Case
   No. 16/2001 (15 July 2003).   669

Court of Appeal (East Timor), *The Prosecutor* v. *Augustinho da Costa*, Case No. 3/2003 (18 July 2003). 671

District Court Gjilan (Kosovo), *Case against Momcillo Trajkovic*, Judgment of 6 March 2001, Docket No. P Nr. 68/2000. 666

European Commission on Human Rights, *Hess* v. *Great Britain*, Application No. 6231/73, Decisions and Reports, Vol. 2, at 72. 480, 497

European Court of Human Rights, *Bankovic et al.* v. *Belgium, the Czech Republic, Denmark, France, Germany, Greece, Hungary, Iceland, Italy, Luxembourg, the Netherlands, Norway, Poland, Portugal, Spain, Turkey and the United Kingdom*, Application No. 52207/99, Decision of 12 December 2001. 486

European Court of Human Rights, *Behrami & Behrami* v. *France*, Application No, 71412/01, *Saramati* v. *France, Germany and Norway*, Application No. 78166/01, Decision of 31 May 2007. 424, 431, 449, 452, 500

European Court of Human Rights, *Bosphorus Hava Yolllari Turizm ve Ticaret Anonim Sirketi (Bosphorus Airways)* v. *Ireland*, Application No. 45036/98, Judgment of 30 June 2005. 498

European Court of Human Rights, *Issa and Others* v. *Turkey*, Judgment of 16 November 2004, Application No. 31821/96. 488, 489, 761

European Court of Human Rights, *Loizidou* v. *Turkey*, Judgment of 18 December 1996, Reports of Judgments and Decisions 1996-VI. 487

European Court of Human Rights, *Matthews* v. *United Kingdom*, Judgment of 18 February 1999, Application No. 24833/94. 501

European Court of Human Rights, *Waite and Kennedy* v. *Germany*, Application No. 26083/94, Judgment of 18 February 1999. 501, 590, 591

European Court of Justice, *Van Gend en Loos* v. *Nederlandse Administratie der Belastingen*, Case 26/62 (1963), ECR 1. 646

High Court of Justice, Queens's Bench Division, *Bici* v. *Ministry of Defence*, Judgment of 7 April 2004, 2004 EWHC 786. 500

High Court of Justice, Queen's Bench Division, Divisional Court, *Mazin Jumaa Gatteh Al Skeini and Others* v. *Secretary of State for Defence and the Redress Trust*, Judgment of 14 December 2004. 487, 488, 497, 498, 503, 562, 563

High Court of Justice, *Vallaj* v. *Special Adjudicator*, Queen's Bench Division, 21 December 2000 (Westlaw: 2000 WL 1881268). 494

House of Lords, *Al-Skeini and others* v. *Secretary of State for Defence*, Judgment of 13 June 2007, 2007 UKHL 26. 487, 503, 562, 563

Human Rights Chamber for Bosnia and Herzegovina, *Blentic* v. *Republic Srpska*, Decision of 5 November 1997, Case No. CH/96/17.   686

Human Rights Chamber, *Adnan Suljanovic, Edita Cisic and Adam Lelic* v. *Bosnia and Herzegovina and the Republika Srpska*, Decision of 14 May 1998, Cases Nos. CH/98/230 and 231.   605

Human Rights Chamber, *Bojkovski* v. *Bosnia and Herzegovina and Federation of Bosnia and Herzegovina*, Decision of 6 April 2001, Case No. CH/97/73.   295, 298, 612

Human Rights Chamber for Bosnia and Herzegovina, *Dragan Cavic against Bosnia and Herzegovina*, Decision of 18 December 1998, Case No. CH/98/1266.   614

Human Rights Chamber for Bosnia and Herzegovina, *Leko* v. *Federation of Bosnia and Herzegovina*, Decision of 9 March 2001, Case No. CH/00/6144.   295

Human Rights Chamber for Bosnia and Herzegovina, *Petrovic* v. *Federation of Bosnia and Herzegovina*, Decision of 9 March 2001, Case No. CH/00/6142.   295, 686

ICJ, *Reparation for Injuries in the Service of the United Nations*, Advisory Opinion, 11 April 1949, ICJ, Rep. 1949.   434, 556, 707

ICJ, *International Status of South-West Africa*, Advisory Opinion, 11 July 1950, ICJ Rep. 1950.   87, 88, 103, 112, 114, 547

ICJ, *Effect of Awards of Compensation Made by the United Nations Administrative Tribunal*, Advisory Opinion, 13 July 1954, ICJ Rep. 1954.   422, 589

ICJ, *Legal Consequences for States of the Continued Presence of South Africa in Namibia*, Advisory Opinion, 21 June 1971, ICJ Rep. 1971.   254, 418, 438

ICJ, *Certain Expenses of the United Nations*, Advisory Opinion, 20 July 1962, ICJ Rep. 1962.   433, 436, 438

ICJ, *Certain Phosphate Lands in Nauru (Nauru* v. *Australia)*, Preliminary Objections, Judgment, 26 June 1992, ICJ Rep. 1992.   110

ICJ, *Case Concerning Questions of Interpretation and Application of the 1971 Montreal Convention arising from the Aerial Incident at Lockerbie* (Libya v. United Kingdom), Provisional Measures, Order of 14 April 1992, ICJ Rep. 1992.   640

ICJ, *Case concerning East Timor (Portugal* v. *Australia)*, Advisory Opinion of 30 June 1995, ICJ Rep. 1995.   335

ICJ, *Legality of the Threat or Use of Nuclear Weapons*, Advisory Opinion, 8 July 1996, ICJ Rep. 1996.   469, 505, 554

ICJ, *Difference Relating to Immunity From Legal Process of a Special Rapporteur of the Commission on Human Rights*, Advisory Opinion, 29 April 1999, ICJ Rep. 1999. 583

ICJ, *Legal Consequences of the Construction of a Wall in the Occupied Palestinian Territory*, Advisory Opinion, 9 July 2004, ICJ Rep. 2004. 116, 461, 486, 505, 506

ICJ, *Case Concerning Armed Activities on the Territory of the Congo (Democratic Republic of Congo v. Uganda)*, Judgment of 19 December 2005, ICJ Rep. 2005. 116, 117, 470, 471

ICTR, *Prosecutor v. Kanyabashi*, Decision on Jurisdiction, Case No. ICTR-96-15-T, 18 June 1997. 426

ICTY, Appeals Chamber, *Prosecutor v. Tadic*, Decision on the Defence Motion for Interlocutory Appeal on Jurisdiction, Case No. IT-94-1-A, 2 October 1995. 425, 426, 470

ICTY, Trial Chamber, *Prosecutor v. Naletilic and Martinovic*, Case No. IT-98-34-T, 31 March 2003. 470, 471, 472

Inter-American Commission on Human Rights, *Coard et al. v. United States*, Case No. 10.951, Report No. 109/99 (29 September 1999). 485, 486

Media Appeals Board (Kosovo), *Beqaj & Dita v. Temporary Media Commissioner*, Decision of 16 September 2000. 608

Military Court Rhineland, *Auditeur Militaire v. Reinhardt and Others*, Annual Digest, Vol. 2 (1923-1924), Case No. 239, 441. 125

Ombudsperson Institution in Kosovo, Report, Registration No. 122/01, *Elife Murseli against The United Nations Missions in Kosovo* (10 December 2001). 591, 605

PCIJ, *Case of the S.S. Wimbledon*, 28 June 1923, Ser. A, No. 1 (1923). 421

PCIJ, *Settlers of German Origin in the Territory Ceded by Germany to Poland*, Advisory Opinion, 10 September 1923, Ser. B, No. 6 (1923). 492

PCIJ, *The Mavrommatis Palestine Concessions*, 26 March 1925, Ser. A, No. 5 (1925). 84

PCIJ, *Polish Postal Service in Danzig*, Advisory Opinion, 16 May 1925, Ser. B, No. 11 (1925). 178, 179

PCIJ, *Interpretation of article 3, paragraph 2, of the Treaty of Lausanne*, Advisory Opinion, 21 November 1925, Ser. B, No. 12 (1925). 85

PCIJ, *German Interests in Polish Upper Silesia*, 25 May 1926, Ser. A, No. 7 (1926). 533

PCIJ, *Jurisdiction of Courts of Danzig*, Advisory Opinion, 3 March 1928, Ser. B, No. 15 (1928). 179, 646

PCIJ, *Free City of Danzig and International Labour Organization*, Advisory Opinion, 26 August 1930, Ser. B, No. 18 (1930).   179, 576

PCIJ, *Access to German Minority Schools in Upper Silesia*, Advisory Opinion, 15 May 1931, Ser. A/B, No. 40 (1931).   70

PCIJ, *Access to, or Anchorage in, the Port of Danzig, of Polish War Vessels*, Advisory Opinion, 11 December 1931, Ser. A/B, No. 43 (1931).   175, 179

PCIJ, *Treatment of Polish Nationals and Other Persons of Polish Origin or Speech in the Danzig Territory*, Advisory Opinion of 4 February 1932, Ser. A/B, No. 44 (1932).   174, 175, 177, 179

PCIJ, *Interpretation of the Statute of the Memel Territory*, 11 August 1932, Ser. A/B, No. 49 (1932).   66, 67, 186

PCIJ, *Consistency of certain Danzig Legislative Decrees with the Constitution of the Free City*, 4 December 1935, Ser. A/B, No. 65 (1935).   176, 179, 610

PCIJ, *Lighthouses in Crete and Samos*, 8 October 1937, Ser. A/B, No. 71 (1937).   55, 56

Privy Council, *Jerusalem-Jaffa District Governor and another v. Suleiman Murra and Others*, LR (1926), AC 321 (*Urtas Springs* case).   85

Special Panel for Serious Crimes (East Timor), *Prosecutor v. Joao Sarmento Domingos Mendonca*, Case No. 18a/2001 (24 July 2003).   671

Superior Court of Rastatt, *Druckerei und Verlagsgesellschaft m.b.H. v. Schmidts*, American Journal of International Law, Vol. 48 (1952), 307.   137

Supreme Court of Canada, *Reference Re Secession of Quebec*, 20 August 1998, 37 ILM 1340.   462

Supreme Court of Kosovo, Special Chamber on Kosovo Trust Agency Matters, *Terrosistem case*, SCEL 04-0001 (9 June 2004).   609

Supreme Court of Kosovo, *Bota Sot* case, AC 37/2004 (20 August 2004).   666

Supreme Court of Kosovo, *Decision on Petition for Transfer of Luan Goci and Bashkim Berisha*, Pn-Kr 333/05 (30 January 2006).   575

List of abbreviations

AC	Appeal Cases (England and Wales)
AU	African Union
BiH	Bosnia and Herzegovina
CFSP	Common Foreign and Security Policy
COMKFOR	Commander of KFOR
CPA	Coalition Provisional Authority
CRPC	Commission for Real Property Claims of Displaced Persons and Refugees
DMU	Detention Management Unit
DPA	Dayton Peace Agreement
DRC	Democratic Republic of Congo
ECHR	European Convention on Human Rights
ESA	European Space Agency
EU	European Union
EUAM	European Union Administration of Mostar
EUFOR RD Congo	European Union Force Democratic Republic of Congo
FRETILIN	Revolutionary Front for an Independent East Timor
FRY	Federal Republic of Yugoslavia
FUNCINPEC	United National Front for an Independent, Neutral, Peaceful and Cooperative Cambodia
GA	General Assembly
HPCC	Housing and Property Claims Commission
HPD	Housing and Property Directorate
IAC	Interim Administrative Council
ICC	International Criminal Court

ICCPR	International Covenant on Civil and Political Rights
ICJ	International Court of Justice
ICR	International Civilian Representative
ICRC	International Committee of the Red Cross
ICTR	International Criminal Tribunal for Rwanda
ICTY	International Criminal Tribunal for the former Yugoslavia
IFOR	Implementation Force
ILA	International Law Association
ILC	International Law Commission
ILO	International Labour Organization
ILM	International Legal Materials
ISAF	International Security Assistance Force
INTERFET	International Force for East Timor
IWG	International Working Group
JIAS	Joint Interim Administrative Structure
KCAC	Kosovo Claims Appeals Commission
KFOR	Kosovo Force
KJPC	Kosovo Judicial and Prosecutorial Council
KPNLF	Khmer People's National Liberation Front
KTC	Kosovo Transitional Council
LNOJ	League of Nations Official Journal
LNTS	League of Nations Treaty Series
LON	League of Nations
MINURSO	United Nations Mission for the Referendum in Western Sahara
MINUSTAH	United Nations Stabilization Mission in Haiti
MONUC	United Nations Mission in the Democratic Republic of Congo
NATO	North Atlantic Treaty Organization
OECD	Organization for Economic Cooperation and Development
OHR	Office of the High Representative
ONUB	United Nations Operation in Burundi
ONUC	United Nations Operation in Congo
ONUSAL	United Nations Observer Mission in El Salvador
ONUVEN	United Nations Observer Mission for the Verification of the Elections in Nicaragua

ONUVEH	United Nations Observer Mission for the Verification of the Elections in Haiti
OSCE	Organization for Security and Cooperation in Europe
PCIJ	Permanent Court of International Justice
PIC	Peace Implementation Council
POLISARIO	Front for the Liberation of Saguia el Hamra and Rio de Oro
PSC	Peace and Security Council
SC	Security Council
SCAP	Supreme Commander for the Allied Powers
SFOR	Security Force
SG	Secretary-General
SNC	Supreme National Council
SOFA	Status of Forces Agreement
SRSG	Special Representative of the Secretary-General
TAL	Transitional Administrative Law
TNC	Transitional National Council
UK	United Kingdom
UN	United Nations
UNAMA	United Nations Assistance Mission in Afghanistan
UNAMI	United Nations Assistance Mission in Iraq
UNAVEM	United Nations Angola Verification Mission
UNCLOS	United Nations Convention on the Law of the Sea
UNEF	United Nations Emergency Force
UNFICYP	United Nations Peacekeeping Force in Cyprus
UNGOMAP	United Nations Good Offices Mission in Afghanistan
UNIFIL	United Nations Interim Force in Lebanon
UN-IPTF	United Nations International Police Task Force
UNITAF	Unified Task Force
UNMIBH	United Nations Mission in Bosnia and Herzegovina
UNMIK	United Nations Interim Administration in Kosovo
UNMIL	United Nations Mission in Liberia
UNMISET	United Nations Mission of Support in East Timor

UNOCI	United Nations Operation in Côte d'Ivoire
UNOGIL	United Nations Observation Group in Lebanon
UNOSOM	United Nations Operation in Somalia
UNOTIL	United Nations Office in Timor-Leste
UNTAC	United Nations Transitional Authority in Cambodia
UNTAES	United Nations Transitional Administration for Eastern Slavonia
UNTAET	United Transitional Administration in East Timor
UNTAG	United Nations Transition Group in Namibia
UNTEA	United Nations Temporary Executive Authority
UNTS	United Nations Treaty Series
UNYOM	United Nations Yemen Observation Mission
US	United States
WHO	World Health Organization
WTO	World Trade Organization

Table of engagements

(1920–2006)

I. Direct international territorial administration

League of Nations

Saar Territory
Free City of Danzig
Memel
Leticia

United Nations

Free Territory of Trieste
Jerusalem
Libya*
Eritrea*
United Nations Operation in the Congo (ONUC)
United Nations Temporary Executive Authority (UNTEA)
United Nations Council for Namibia
United Nations Transition Assistance Group (UNTAG)*
United Nations Mission for the Referendum in the Western Sahara
     (MINURSO)*
United Nations Transitional Authority in Cambodia (UNTAC)
United Nations Operation in Somalia (UNOSOM II)
United Nations Transitional Administration for Eastern Slavonia
     (UNTAES)
United Nations Interim Administration in Kosovo (UNMIK)
United Transitional Administration in East Timor (UNTAET)
United Nations Assistance Mission in Afghanistan (UNAMA)*
United Nations Assistance Mission in Iraq (UNAMI)*

United Nations Mission in Liberia (UNMIL)*
United Nations Mission in the Democratic Republic of Congo (MONUC)*
United Nations Operation in Côte d'Ivoire (UNOCI)*

European Union

Mostar (EUAM)

II. Indirect international territorial administration

Bosnia and Herzegovina (OHR)
Iraq (CPA)

* Governance assistance missions

Introduction

Die Pfosten sind, die Bretter aufgeschlagen,
Und Jedermann erwartet sich ein Fest.
Sie sitzen schon mit hohen Augenbrauen
Gelassen da und möchten gern erstaunen.

Allein sie haben schrecklich viel gelesen.
Wie machen wir's, dass alles frisch und neu
Und mit Bedeutung auch gefällig sei?
Johann Wolfgang von Goethe, Faust,
Vorspiel auf dem Theater*

The twentieth century has witnessed a proliferation of forms of international engagement in areas that were typically governed by states. The involvement of international actors in the administration of territory is one of them. The League of Nations assumed a significant role in territorial administration in the 1920s when undertaking functions of guarantee and administration under the Treaty of Versailles. This type of engagement gained new attention in the era of the United Nations (UN). Both the emergence of peacekeeping and the revitalisation of the collective security system after the end of the Cold War sparked a revival of experiments in international administration. Today, there is growing confidence that the UN can perform tasks of governance in post-conflict situations. The *Handbook on United Nations Multidimensional Peacekeeping Operations* includes international administration of territory as one of

---

* "The posts are now erected and the planks, And all look forward to a festal treat, Their places taken, they, with eyebrows rais'd, Sit patiently, and fain would be amaz'd, But then appalling the amount they've read. How make our entertainment striking, new, And yet significant and pleasing too?" Johann Wolfgang von Goethe, Faust, Prologue for the Theatre.

the functions of multidimensional peacekeeping.[1] However, the format and practice of these engagements is still subject to considerable debate. The enthusiasm about robust UN governance missions that prevailed at the time of the establishment of UN Interim Administration in Kosovo (UNMIK)[2] and the UN Transitional Administration in East Timor (UN-TAET)[3] at the end of the 1990s has been tempered by criticism of the UN's style of governance[4] and calls for a move to "a light footprint" agenda,[5] limiting the role of the UN to the provision of assistance to existing governing authorities and local actors.[6] At the same time, there are some doubts whether and to what extent tasks of territorial administration can be successfully managed without input and expertise from the UN (Iraq).[7]

Both, the historical tradition of territorial administration and its contemporary use as an organising model for the management of transitions from conflict to peace make it likely that the technique of international territorial administration (understood here as "the exercise of administering authority by an international entity for the benefit of a territory

---

[1] The *Handbook on United Nations Multidimensional Peacekeeping Operations* notes that peace operations may be required to "administer a territory for a transitional period, thereby carrying out all the functions that are normally the responsibility of a government". See United Nations, Department of Peacekeeping Operations, Peacekeeping Best Practices Unit, *Handbook on United Nations Multidimensional Peacekeeping Operations*, December 2003, at 2.

[2] See SC Resolution 1244 (1999) of 10 June 1999.

[3] See SC Resolution 1272 (1999) of 25 October 1999.

[4] Chopra compared the United Nations Transitional Administration in East Timor to a "pre-constitutional monarch[y] in a sovereign kingdom". See Jarat Chopra, *The UN's Kingdom of East Timor*, Survival, Vol. 42 (2000), 27, at 29. For a critical assessment of UN practice, see also Joel C. Beauvais, *Benevolent Despotism, A Critique of U.N. State-Building in East Timor*, NYU Journal of International Law and Politics, Vol. 33 (2001), 1101; David Marshall and Shelley Inglis, *Human Rights in Transition: The Disempowerment of Human Rights-Based Justice in the United Nations Mission in Kosovo*, Harvard Human Rights Journal, Vol. 16 (2003), 95.

[5] This expression was used by the Special Representative of the Secretary-General, Lakhdar Brahimi, see United Nations Assistance Mission in Afghanistan (UNAMA): Mission Structure, UN/IMTF Working Paper No. 2, 14 January 2002.

[6] See generally Simon Chesterman,*Walking Softly in Afghanistan: The Future of UN Statebuilding*, Survival, Vol. 44 (2002), 37–46.

[7] For a critical account of the dilemmas of the occupation, see Rüdiger Wolfrum, *Iraq – From Belligerent Occupation to Iraqi Exercise of Sovereignty: Foreign Power versus International Community Interference*, Max Planck Yearbook of United Nations Law, Vol. 9 (2005), 1; Nehal Bhuta, *The Antinomies of Transformative Occupation*, European Journal of International Law, Vol. 16 (2005), 721. The case for UN involvement is further confirmed by a comparative study of US and UN "Ways of Nation-Building". See James Dobbins et al., *The UN's Role in Nation-Building: From The Congo to Iraq* (2005), at 244.

that is temporarily placed under international supervision or assistance for a communitarian purpose"[8]) will be replicated in other contexts. However, future experiments of this kind require a thorough analysis of the existing law and practice. International administration has thus far been dominated by "piecemeal" approaches. One experiment has followed another, without a systematic analysis of the flaws and benefits of each engagement. International administration has been criticised for lacking planning and coherence.[9] It is thus important to revisit some of the shortcomings and achievements of the different individual experiments in this area throughout the twentieth century.[10]

1. Why a study of the law and practice of international territorial administration?

Such a retrospective is long overdue. Until now, the project of international territorial administration has only been reviewed in a cursory fashion in law and practice. The UN has not undertaken a comprehensive assessment of the practice, but confined itself to a review of individual missions. The "*Brahimi* Report" devoted only a few paragraphs to the topic of transitional administration, without addressing the substantial tensions and challenges underlying the practice.[11] The Report of the High-level Panel on Threats, Challenges and Change and the Outcome Document of the High-Level Plenary Meeting of the General Assembly in September 2005 recommended some further institutional reform, by favouring the establishment of a Peacebuilding Commission, but failed to list responsibilities in the field of transitional administration as one of the functions of the Commission.[12]

---

[8] For a closer analysis of this definition, see below Part I, Introduction.

[9] See Edward Mortimer, *International Administration of War-Torn Societies*, Global Governance, Vol. 10, No. 1 (January–March 2004), 7, at 10.

[10] See also David Harland, *Legitimacy and Effectiveness in International Administration*, Global Governance, Vol. 10, No. 1 (January–March 2004), at 15–19.

[11] See paras. 76–83 of the *Report of the Panel on United Nations Peace Operations* ("*Brahimi* Report"), UN Doc. A/55/305, S/2000/809 (21 August 2000). The report concluded with one key recommendation, namely to "evaluate the feasibility and utility of developing an interim criminal code, including any regional adaptations potentially required, for use by such operations pending the re-establishment of local rule of law and local enforcement capacity".

[12] See Report of the High-level Panel on Threats, Challenges and Change, *A More Secure World: Our Shared Responsibility*, UN Doc. A/59/565 (2 December 2004), paras. 262–4. See also GA Resolution 60/1 (World Summit Outcome) of 24 October 2005, paras. 97–105. Paragraph 98 of the resolution specifies that "[t]he Commission should focus attention

A similar picture prevails in legal doctrine. The issue of international territorial administration has long remained a "sleeping beauty" in terms of legal scholarship.[13] Although the body of literature is growing,[14]

on the reconstruction and institution-building efforts necessary for recovery from conflict and support the development of integrated strategies in order to lay the foundations for sustainable development".

[13] Numerous writings were dedicated to international administration under the Mandates System of the League of Nations or the UN Trusteeship System. See Quincy Wright, *Mandates under the League of Nations* (1930); Hessel Duncan Hall, *Mandates, Dependencies and Trusteeship* (1948); Ramendra N. Chowdhuri, *International Mandates and Trusteeship Systems: A Comparative Study* (1955); Charmian E. Toussaint, *The Trusteeship System of the United Nations* (1956). But few authors explicitly addressed the topic of the administration of territories by international organisations. Some works were dedicated to the practice of the internationalisation of territories. See Alessandro Marazzi, *I Territori Internazionalizzati* (1959); Méir Ydit, *Internationalised Territories: From the "Free City of Cracow" to the "Free City of Berlin"* (1961); Raimund Beck, *Die Internationalisierung von Territorien* (1962); Hurst Hannum, *Autonomy, Sovereignty and Self-Determination* (1996), 375. Later in-depth study was devoted to the analysis of single UN missions or singular problems arising in the context of the assumption of administering authority by the UN. See e.g. John V. Czerapowicz, *International Territorial Authority: Leticia and West New Guinea* (1975); Michael J. Kelly, *Restoring and Maintaining Order in Complex Peace Operations* (1999), 65–90. However, few attempts have been made to put the various fragments of the mosaic together.

[14] Contemporary writing on the topic started in the mid- to late 1990s when Ratner and Chopra addressed the practice of civil administration within in the broader context of works on peace-maintenance. See Steven R. Ratner, *The New UN Peacekeeping: Building Peace in Lands of Conflict After the Cold War* (1995); Jarat Chopra, *Peace Maintenance: The Evolution of International Political Authority* (1999). See also Frank-Erich Hufnagel, *UN-Friedensoperationen der zweiten Generation. Vom Puffer zur Neuen Treuhand* (1996). These works were later followed by research on UN missions of the late 1990s and several contributions directly focusing on the concept of "international territorial administration". See the articles by Ralph Wilde: *From Danzig to East Timor and Beyond: The Role of International Territorial Administration*, American Journal of International Law, Vol. 95 (2001), 583; *Representing International Territorial Administration: A Critique of Some Approaches*, European Journal of International Law, Vol. 15 (2004), 71; *From Bosnia to Kosovo and East Timor: The Changing Role of the United Nations in the Administration of Territory*, ILSA Journal of International & Comparative Law, Vol. 6 (2000), 467. See also Michael J. Matheson, *United Nations Governance of Postconflict Societies*, American Journal of International Law, Vol. 95 (2001), 76; Erika De Wet, *The Direct Administration of Territories by the United Nations and its Member States in the Post Cold War Era: Legal Bases and Implications for National Law*, Max Planck Yearbook of United Nations Law, Vol. 8 (2004), 291; Rüdiger Wolfrum, *International Administration in Post-Conflict Situations by the United Nations and Other International Actors*, Max Planck Yearbook of United Nations Law, Vol. 9 (2005), 649; Carsten Stahn, *The United Nations Transitional Administrations in Kosovo and East Timor: A First Analysis*, Max Planck Yearbook of United Nations Law, Vol. 5 (2001), 105; Carsten Stahn, *International Territorial Administration in the Former Yugoslavia: Origins, Developments and Challenges Ahead*, Zeitschrift für ausländisches öffentliches Recht und Völkerrecht, Vol. 61 (2001), 108; Alexandros Yannis, *Kosovo under International Administration: An Unfinished Conflict* (2001); Matthias Ruffert, *The*

several aspects of this phenomenon deserve further scholarly analysis, including issues such as the theorisation of governance[15] and

Administration of Kosovo and East Timor by the International Community, International & Comparative Law Quarterly, Vol. 50 (2001), 555; Christian Tomuschat, *Yugoslavia's Damaged Sovereignty over the Province of Kosovo*, in State, Sovereignty and International Governance (Gerard Kreijen et al. eds., 2002), 323; Michael Bothe and Thilo Marauhn, *UN Administration of Kosovo and East Timor: Concept, Legality and Limitations of Security Council Mandated Trusteeship Administration*, in Kosovo and the International Community (Christian Tomuschat ed., 2002), 217–42; Outi Korhonen, *International Governance in Post-Conflict Situations*, Leiden Journal of International Law, Vol. 14 (2001), 495. See also the more recent contributions by Kirsten Schmalenbach, *Die Haftung Internationaler Organisationen im Rahmen von friedenssichernden Manahmen und Territorialverwaltungen* (2004); Leopold von Carlowitz, *UNMIK Lawmaking Between Effective Peace Support and Internal Self-determination*, Archiv des Völkerrechts, Vol. 41 (2003), 336–93; Bernhard Knoll, *Beyond the "Mission Civilisatrice": The Specific Properties of a Normative Order within an "Internationalized" Territory*, Leiden Journal of International Law, Vol. 19 (2006), 275–304 and *From Benchmarking to Final Status? Kosovo and the Problem of an International Administration's Open-Ended Mandate*, European Journal of International Law, Vol. 16 (2005), 637; Kristen Boon, *Legislative Reform in Post-Conflict Zones: Jus Post Bellum and the Contemporary Occupant's Law-Making Powers*, McGill Law Journal, Vol. 50 (2005), 285; Mariano J. Aznar-Goméz, *Some Paradoxes on Human Rights Protection in Kosovo*, in Völkerrecht als Werteordnung, Festschrift für Christian Tomuschat (Pierre-Marie Dupuy et al. eds., 2006), 15–40 as well as the articles on specific missions in Global Governance, Vol. 10, No. 1, January–March 2004 and Max Planck Yearbook of United Nations Law, Vol. 9 (2005). Some monographs have addressed the topic of trusteeship. See Richard Caplan, *A New Trusteeship? The International Administration of War-torn Territories*, Adelphi Paper 341 (2002); William Bain, *Between Anarchy and Society: Trusteeship and the Obligations of Power* (2003). However, few systematic and comprehensive legal analyses of the role and functions of international organisations in the area of territorial administration exist. The existing literature includes: Outi Korhonen and Jutta Gras, *International Governance of Post-Conflict Situations* (2001); Outo Korhonen, Jutta, Gras and Katja Kreuz, *International Post-Conflict Situations: New Challenges for Co-Operative Governance* (2006), 55–244; Aspen Institute, *Honoring Human Rights Under International Mandates: Lessons from Bosnia, Kosovo and East Timor* (Alice H. Henkin ed., 2003); Simon Chesterman, *You, the People: The United Nations, Transitional Administration and State-Building* (2004); Richard Caplan, *International Governance of War-Torn Territories* (2005); Nigel D. White and Dirk Klaasen (eds.), *The UN, Human Rights and Post-Conflict Situations* (2005); Robert Kolb, Gabriele Porretto and Sylvain Vité, *L'Application du Droit International Humanitaire et des Droits de l'Homme aux Organisations Internationales: Forces de Paix et Administrations Civiles Transitoire* (2005); Michaela Salamun, *Democratic Governance in International Territorial Administration: Institutional Prerequisites for Democratic Governance in the Constitutional Documents of Territories Administered by International Organisations* (2005); Daniel Smyrek, *Internationally Administered Territories – International Protectorates? An Analysis of Sovereignty over Internationally Administered Territories with Special Reference to the Legal Status of Post-War Kosovo* (2006); Dominik Zaum, *The Sovereignty Paradox: The Norms and Politics of International Statebuilding* (2007); Ralph Wilde, *International Territorial Administration* (2008).

[15] See generally Joseph S. Nye and John D. Donahue (eds.), *Governance in a Globalizing World* (2000). See also below Part III, Chapter 12 and Part V, Chapter 18.

accountability[16] or the role of international administration in the transformation of the international legal order.[17]

1.1. Ending misconceptions

In contemporary scholarship, international territorial administration is often treated as a modern phenomenon,[18] which is misleading.[19] The wheel was not invented yesterday.[20] The idea of international territorial administration has a long-established tradition in international law and must be viewed in its evolutionary context.

1.1.1. International territorial administration and modernity

The concept of the internationalisation of territories[21] became established in the nineteenth century, when groups of states, usually victors after war, shared administering authority over territories, in order to settle competing claims among themselves or to establish multinational zones of power. The first experiment in territorial internationalisation[22]

---

[16] See below Part IV, Chapter 14.

[17] See generally Benedict Kingsbury, *The International Legal Order*, in Oxford Handbook of Legal Studies (Peter Cane and Mark Tushnet eds., 2003), 271, at 289; Bruno Simma, *From Bilateralism to Community Interest in International Law*, Recueil des Cours, Vol. 250 (1994), 219, at 243–9; Hermann Mosler, *The International Society as a Legal Community* (1980); Christian Tomuschat, *Obligations Arising for States without or against Their Will*, Recueil des Cours, Vol. 241 (1993), 195, at 219–36; Christian Tomuschat, *Die Internationale Gemeinschaft*, Archiv des Völkerrechts, Vol. 33 (1995), 1; Jochen Abr. Frowein, *Konstitutionalisierung des Völkerrechts*, in Völkerrecht und Internationales Privatrecht in einem sich globalisierenden internationalen System – Auswirkungen der Entstaatlichung transnationaler Rechtsbeziehungen (2000), 427.

[18] See, *inter alia*, Wendy S. Betts, Scott N. Carlson and Gregory Gisvold, *The Post-Conflict Transitional Administration of Kosovo and the Lessons-Learned in Efforts to establish a Judiciary and Rule of Law*, Michigan Journal of International Law, Vol. 22 (2001), 372; Dianne M. Criswell, *Durable Consent and a Strong International Peacekeeping Plan: The Success of UNTAET in Light of the Lessons Learned in Cambodia*, Pacific Rim Law and Policy Journal, Vol. 11 (2002), 577, Boon, *Legislative Reform in Post-Conflict Zones*, at 312–15.

[19] See also Ralph Wilde, *Taxonomies of International Peacekeeping: An Alternative Narrative*, ILSA Journal of International & Comparative Law, Vol. 9 (2003), 391, and *Representing International Territorial Administration*, at 75–80.

[20] See Ralph Wilde, *The United Nations as Government: The Tensions of an Ambivalent Role*, American Society of International Law, Vol. 97 (2003), 212, and *From Danzig to East Timor*, at 585–7.

[21] See Rüdiger Wolfrum, *Internationalisation*, in Encyclopedia of Public International Law, Vol. II (1995), 1395; James Crawford, *Creation of States in International Law*, 2nd edn (2006), 233–44.

[22] Waterway commissions, such as the Central Rhine Commission (1804) were created even before that time. See generally on the functional internationalisation of special international regimes, Rüdiger Wolfrum, *Die Internationalisierung Staatsfreier Räume* (1984), 284.

dates back to 1815, when the Final Act of the Congress of Vienna vested Austria, Prussia and Russia with the authority to supervise the local executive and legislative authorities of the "Free City of Cracow" (1815–46) through the Permanent Delegates of the Three Protecting Powers in the city.[23] This example was later followed by multinational administrations of the City of Shanghai (1845–1944),[24] the Island of Crete (1897–1909)[25] and the International Zone of Tangier (1923–57).[26] The notion of direct administration of territories by international organisations emerged in the first quarter of the twentieth century with the establishment of the League of Nations by the Treaty of Versailles. The creation of the League initiated a new era of territorial administration, by placing several territories under the direct authority of the League, instead of conferring administering power exclusively on a restricted group or a consortium of leading European Powers.

The Treaty of Versailles charged the League with a 15-year mandate to administer the Saar Basin through a Commission directly responsible to the League.[27] Similarly, the League assumed an open-ended mandate to guarantee and supervise the administration of the Free City of Danzig through a High Commissioner appointed by the League.[28] Furthermore, the League administered the Colombian Town of Leticia

---

[23] The legal basis for the Free City of Cracow was a Treaty between Austria, Prussia and Russia of 3 May 1815. Article 1 of the Treaty provided: "La ville de Cracovie avec son territoire sera envisagé à perpétuité comme cité libre, indépendant et strictement neutre, sous la protection des trois hautes parties contractants." For a full analysis, see Ydit, *Internationalised Territories*, at 95.

[24] For a full account, see Ydit, *Internationalised Territories*, at 127–53.

[25] See Gorges Streit, *La Question Crétoise sur le Point de Vue de Droit International*, Revue Génerale de Droit International Public, Vol. 1897, 61–104, 446–83 ; Vol. 1900, 5–52, 301–69; Vol. 1903, 222–82. See also Ydit, *Internationalised Territories*, at 109–26.

[26] See generally Graham H. Stuart, *The International City of Tangier* (1955); Ydit, *Internationalised Territories*, at 154–84.

[27] See Section IV of the Treaty of Versailles, Articles 45–50 and Annexes, Articles 1–40. The Governing Commission consisted of five members appointed by the Council of the League of Nations for one year. See generally Fritz Münch, *Saar Territory*, in Encyclopedia of Public International Law (Rudolf Bernhardt ed.), Vol. IV (2000), 271; Ydit, *Internationalised Territories*, at 48–50.

[28] See Section XI of the Treaty of Versailles, Articles 100–8. According to Article 103 of the Treaty of Versailles, the Constitution of Danzig was subject to approval by the Council of the League of Nations which assumed the responsibility of guaranteeing it. Furthermore, the League appointed a High Commissioner who was charged with the task of deciding, in the first instance, all disputes between Poland and the Government of Danzig. See generally Ian F. D. Morrow, *The International Status of the Free City of Danzig*, British Yearbook of International Law, Vol. 18 (1937), 114–6; Ydit, *Internationalised Territories*, at 185–230.

between 1933 and 1934[29] and exercised partial control over the Memel Harbor.[30] These early experiments in internationalisation count among the most inventive examples of international administration of territory. They introduced a significant conceptual leap, by removing territorial administration from the ambit of the exercise of administering power in the name of a single sovereign or a group of states,[31] and linking it to the concept of direct administration by and on behalf of an independent international institution with a distinct legal personality.[32]

The early experience of the League in the field of international territorial administration lost some of its impetus after the end of World War II. Attempts to apply the model of internationalisation to the disputed cities of Trieste[33] and Jerusalem[34] in the immediate aftermath of the creation of the UN Charter failed due to the onset of political rivalries brought on by the Cold War. Instead, the practice of international territorial administration gained new attention in the realm of the maintenance of international peace and security.[35] The UN came to exercise extensive executive powers in the absence of local authorities within the framework of the UN Operation in Congo (ONUC).[36] Furthermore, in 1962 the UN established the UN Temporary Executive Authority (UNTEA)[37] following a Dutch-Indonesian agreement requesting the UN

---

[29] See Francis P. Walters, A History of the League of Nations (1952), 525–6, 536–40; L. H. Woolsey, The Leticia Dispute Between Columbia and Peru, American Journal of International Law, Vol. 27 (1933), 317, Vol. 29 (1935), 94; Ydit, Internationalised Territories, at 59–62.

[30] Germany renounced its sovereignty over the Memel Territory in favour of the Allied and Associated Powers in Article 99 of the Treaty of Versailles. See John L. Knudson, A History of the League of Nations (1938), 185–6.

[31] See Chopra, Peace-Maintenance, at 38–9.

[32] The question whether the League had legal personality under international law has been subject to some dispute. Some authors denied its international legal personality. See Percy E. Corbett, What is the League of Nations, British Yearbook of International Law, Vol. 5 (1924), 119, 119–23. But most observers recognised the League as a juridical person, because it enjoyed the power to conclude treaties, to declare war and to administer territories. See Lassa Oppenheim, Le Caractère Essentiel de la Societé des Nations, Revue Générale de Droit International Public, Vol. 24 (1919), 234, at 244.

[33] For the background, see Leprette Jacques, Le Statut International de Trieste (1948); Ydit, Internationalised Territories, at 231–72.

[34] See the proposal for a Statute of the City of Jerusalem, drafted by the UN Trusteeship Council, 26 May 1950, in The Jerusalem Question and its Resolution: Selected Documents (Ruth Lapidoth and Moshe Hirsch eds., 1994), 117; Ydit, Internationalised Territories, at 273–315.

[35] See Ratner, The New UN Peacekeeping, at 97.

[36] For an assessment of the UN Operation in Congo, see Georges Abi-Saab, The United Nations Operation in the Congo, 1960–1964 (1978); Chopra, Peace-Maintenance, at 44–5.

[37] See William J. Durch, UN Temporary Executive Authority, in The Evolution of UN Peacekeeping (William J. Durch ed., 1994), 285; Rosalyn Higgins, United Nations

to supervise the transfer of West Irian, the western half of New Guinea, from Dutch rule to Indonesian authority after a short period of transitional UN administration.[38] Together with the UN Council for Namibia,[39] which was created in 1967 to "administer South West Africa until independence" after the termination of the South Africa's League of Nations Mandate over the territory, these undertakings constituted the hallmark of international territorial administration under the auspices of the UN until the end of the Cold War.

A more systematic revival of the technique of international territorial administration began only in the 1990s when the performance of administrative functions became, *inter alia*, an essential component of multidimensional peacekeeping, which placed the objectives of democratisation, human rights protection and the promotion of justice on an equal footing with the traditional aims of ensuring security and promoting development. The UN moved from the level of assistance missions in the cases of Namibia (UN Transition Group in Namibia, UNTAG)[40] and Western Sahara (UN Mission for the Referendum in Western Sahara, MINURSO)[41] to experiments in statebuilding or governance in Cambodia (UN Transitional Authority in Cambodia, UNTAC),[42] Somalia (UN Operation

Peacekeping 1946–1967, Documents and Commentary, Vol. 2 (1970), 93–100; Michla Pomerance, *Methods of Self-Determination and the Argument of "Primitiveness"*, Canadian Yearbook of International Law, Vol. 12 (1974), 38; Thomas M. Franck, *Nation Against Nation: What Happened to the U.N. Dream and What the U.S. Can Do About It* (1985), 76–82.

[38] See Article V of the Agreement Between the Republic of Indonesia and the Kingdom of the Netherlands Concerning West New Guinea (West Irian), 15 August 1962, UNTS Vol. 437, 274, 276.

[39] The General Assembly created the United Nations Council for Namibia in 1967. See GA Res. 2248 (S-V) of 19 May 1967. For an assessment, see Lawrence L. Herman, *The Legal Status of Namibia and the United Nations Council for Namibia*, Canadian Yearbook of International Law, Vol. 13 (1975), 306.

[40] The United Nations Transition Group in Namibia (UNTAG) was created in 1989. See generally Marrack Goulding and Ingrid Lehmann, *Case Study: The United Nations Operation in Namibia*, in United Nations, The Singapore Symposium: The Changing Role of the United Nations in Conflict Resolution and Peace-Keeping, 13–15 March 1991, 33–41; Virgina Page Fortna, *United Nations Transition Assistance Group*, in The Evolution of Peacekeeping, at 353.

[41] See SC Resolution 690 of 29 April 1991; Report of the Secretary-General, UN. Doc. S/22464 (1991); William J. Durch, *United Nations Mission for the Referendum in the Western Sahara*, in The Evolution of Peacekeeping, at 406; Chopra, *Peace-Maintenance*, at 161–98.

[42] The 1991 Paris Peace Agreements, which were signed by four Cambodian factions, entrusted the United Nations Transitional Authority in Cambodia (UNTAC) with key aspects of civil administration. See generally, Steven R. Ratner, *The Cambodia Settlement Agreements*, American Journal of International Law, Vol. 87 (1993), 1; Trevor Findlay, *Cambodia: The Legacy and Lessons of UNTAC* (1995); Michael W. Doyle, *UN Peacekeeping in Cambodia: UNTAC's Civil Mandate* (1995).

in Somalia, UNOSOM II),[43] Eastern Slavonia (UN Transitional Administration for Eastern Slavonia, UNTAES),[44] Kosovo (UN Interim Administration in Kosovo, UNMIK)[45] and East Timor (UN Transitional Administration in East Timor, UNTAET).[46]

Much of the contemporary analysis focuses on the UN Transitional Administrations in Kosovo and East Timor.[47] These two missions are, in particular, described as "unprecedented in scope and complexity",[48] because

---

[43] Security Council Resolution 814 (1993) charged UNOSOM II with a broad mandate, including the reconstruction of the Somali police and judicial system, the establishment of regional councils and the maintenance of law and order. For a survey, see Chopra, *Peace-Maintenance*, 124–60.

[44] On 15 January 1996, the Security Council created the United Nations Transitional Administration for Eastern Slavonia (UNTAES) in order to prepare the local population for the full transfer of authority to Croatian rule. See Michael Bothe, *The Peace Process in Eastern Slavonia*, International Peacekeeping, December 1995/January 1996, at 6, and *The New Mission in Eastern Slavonia*, at 11.

[45] Security Council Resolution 1244 (1999) authorised the Secretary-General to establish UNMIK. See on the background, Tomuschat, *Yugoslavia's Damaged Sovereignty*, at 324.

[46] Security Council Resolution 1272 (1999) created UNTAET. For the background, see J. Toole, *A False Sense of Security: Lessons Learned from the United Nations Organization and Conduct Mission in East Timor*, American University International Law Review, Vol. 16 (2000), 199.

[47] See Jochen Abr. Frowein, *Notstandsverwaltung von Gebieten durch die Vereinten Nationen*, in Völkerrecht und Deutsches Recht, Festschrift für W. Rudolf (H. W. Arndt et al. eds., 2001), 43; Tomuschat, *Yugoslavia's Damaged Sovereignty*, 323; Ruffert, *The Administration of Kosovo and East Timor*, 555; Bothe and Marauhn, *UN Administration of Kosovo and East Timor*, 217; Hans-Jörg Stromeyer, *Collapse and Reconstruction of a Judicial System: The United Nations Missions in Kosovo and in East Timor*, American Journal of International Law, Vol. 95 (2001), 46; Tobias H. Irmscher, *The Legal Framework for the Activities of the United Nations Interim Mission in Kosovo: The Charter, Human Rights, and the Law of Occupation*, German Yearbook of International Law, Vol. 44 (2001), 353, at 383; Evelyn Lagrange, *La Mission Intérimaire des Nations Unies au Kosovo, Nouvel Essai d'Administration Directe d'un Territoire*, Annuaire Française de Droit International, Vol. XLV (1999), 335–70; Thierry García, *La Mission d'Administration Intérimaire des Nations Unies au Kosovo*, Revue Génerale de Droit International Public, Vol. 104 (2000), 61; Boris Kondoch, *The United Nations Administration of East Timor*, Journal of Conflict and Security Law, Vol. 6 (2001), 245; Aspen Institute, *Honoring Human Rights Under International Mandates: Lessons from Bosnia, Kosovo and East Timor* (2003).

[48] Hans Corell, former UN Legal Counsel, noted at a keynote address on 1 December 2000: "Peace operations under the auspices of the United Nations have become quite different from what they were in the early years of the Organization. It is true that the United Nations also performed administrative functions in West Irian, in Namibia and in Cambodia. However, the two missions in Kosovo and East Timor are unprecedented." See also Matheson, *United Nations Governance of Postconflict Societies*, at 79. See also Alexandros Yannis, *The UN as Government in Kosovo*, Global Governance, Vol. 10 (2004), 67, at 71 ("sui generis and a novel arrangement"). See also Hans-Jörg Strohmeyer, *Making Multilateral Interventions Work: The U.N. and the Creation of Transitional Justice Systems in Kosovo and East Timor*, Fletcher Forum of World Affairs, Vol. 25 (2001),

of two factors: the scope of authority exercised by UNMIK and UNTAET; and the broad nature of their mandate. But this view requires some clarification. As has been convincingly shown by *Wilde*, both arguments are open to criticism.[49] It is, first, difficult to infer the "uniqueness" of UNMIK or UNTAET from a review of their specific powers. Both administrations were vested with exclusive administering authority by the UN. But this conglomeration of authority is not novel in the practice of the organisation. There have been previous cases in the history of the UN in which international institutions held plenary administering power over territories, including, in particular, the administration of West Irian, Namibia and Eastern Slavonia by the UN, and the administration of the Saar Territory by the League of Nations.[50]

It is also misleading to assume that UNMIK and UNTAET are unprecedented in terms of the complexity of their mandate.[51] The administration of East Timor marked a cornerstone in the practice of international territorial administration because the UN exercised governing authority independently of any other territorial sovereign. However, as has been correctly observed, it would be naive to believe that the challenges of the twenty-first and late twentieth centuries are more complex in nature than the problems which arose in the early twentieth century.[52] To distinguish modern operations from previous undertakings creates obvious tensions and inconsistencies. It is difficult to claim that the relatively short transitional administration of East Timor by UNTAET was more challenging than the 15-year administration of the Saar by the League of Nations Governing Commission,[53] which assumed "all the powers of government hitherto belonging to the German Empire, Prussia or Bavaria", including "full powers" to create administrative and representative bodies, to operate public services, to conduct foreign relations, to ensure the protection of nationals abroad and to establish a local police force.[54] Similarly, the UN administration of Kosovo does not necessarily pose more complex problems than the 20-year League supervision of the city of Danzig, which remained a constant source

107, at 109 ("unprecedented in the history of the United Nations"); Strohmeyer, *Collapse and Reconstruction of a Judicial System*, at 46 ("unprecedented in United Nations peacekeeping operations").

[49] See Wilde, *Taxonomies of International Peacekeeping*, at 393, Wilde, *The United Nations as Government*, at 212.

[50] See Wilde, *Taxonomies of International Peacekeeping*, at 394.

[51] But see James Traub, *Inventing East Timor*, Foreign Affairs, July/August 2000, at 74, 75.

[52] See Wilde, *Taxonomies of International Peacekeeping*, at 396.

[53] *Ibid.*, at 396.   [54] See Treaty of Versailles, Annex, Articles 16, 19 and 21.

of tension between Germany and Poland and proved to be one of the hardest "test case[s] for the safeguarding of democracy against totalitarian expansion".[55] Recently, the attribute of complexity was again used in the context of the management of the first democratic elections by MONUC in the Democratic Republic of Congo.[56]

Such comparisons are shaky. The argument of complexity should not be used as a criterion to distinguish traditional from modern missions in the history of international territorial administration.[57] Nor does complexity lend itself to the possibility of creating a hierarchy among different experiments in international territorial administration. Rather, each mission may more accurately be described as being individual in its own way.

1.1.2. International territorial administration and (multi-)functionalism

The second phenomenon, which has been rightly criticised in doctrine,[58] is the strong focus of the current literature on the process of statebuilding. In particular, the writings of the last decade display a strong tendency to analyse the phenomenon of territorial administration primarily from the perspective of state reconstruction.[59] Following its conceptual entrenchment in the realm of UN peacekeeping in the 1990s, international territorial administration was rarely analysed as a stand-alone concept, but was mostly viewed as a specific element of multidimensional peacekeeping. In the early and mid-1990s and, in particular, in the aftermath of Somalia, many authors examined the phenomenon of international territorial administration from the point of view of its capacity to contribute to the reconstruction of "failed states".[60] Later, several

---

[55] See Ydit, *Internationalised Territories*, at 223.   [56] See below Part II, Chapter 9.

[57] See also the convincing argument by Wilde, *From Danzig to East Timor*, at 586.

[58] See Wilde, *Taxonomies of International Peacekeeping*, at 395.

[59] The literature on the phenomenon of statebuilding is rapidly growing. See Michael Ignatieff, *Empire Lite: Nation Building in Bosnia, Kosovo and Afghanistan* (2003); Francis Fukuyama, *State Building: Governance and World Order in the Twenty-First Century* (2004); David Chandler, *Empire in Denial: The Politics of State-building* (2006); Zaum, *The Sovereignty Paradox*, 1–6.

[60] See G. B. Helman and Steven R. Ratner, *Saving Failed States*, Foreign Policy, Vol. 89 (1992–3), 12; Ruth Gordan, *Saving Failed States: Sometimes a Neo-colonialist Notion*, American University Journal of International Law & Policy, Vol. 12 (1997); Ruth Gordan, *Some Legal Problems with Trusteeship*, Cornell International Law Journal, Vol. 28 (1995), 301. See more generally on a legal regime for "failed states", M. Herdegen and D. Thürer, *Der Wegfall effektiver Staatsgewalt im Völkerrecht: "The Failed State"*, Berichte der

contributions more directly addressed the nexus between contemporary UN practice and earlier undertakings in civil administration.[61] However, the great majority of work remained focused on the institutional and legal aspects of modern international administrative missions. Recently, a proposal was made to develop standard "Government out of a Box" response packages, in order to enable national and local governments to increase their capacity to govern.[62] This specific orientation has contributed to a statebuilding-centred[63] vision of international territorial administration,[64] which is not entirely misplaced, but is selective in view. A more nuanced account of the actual practice reveals that international territorial administration has traditionally served a number of different purposes than that of statebuilding.[65]

The filling of power vacuums is one important element of international territorial administration. It may, in particular, be ascribed to the specific UN missions in Congo (ONUC), Somalia (UNOSOM II), Cambodia (UNTAC) and East Timor (UNTAET). However, it is certainly not the only strategic function of international territorial administration. Historically, international institutions have exercised territorial powers for at least two other purposes, namely decolonisation and the resolution of territorial disputes.

Territorial dispute resolution is probably the oldest function of international territorial administration. The technique of

---

Deutschen Gesellschaft für Völkerrecht, Vol. 34 (1996), 49–85, 9–47; Daniel Thürer, *Der zerfallene Staat und das Völkerrecht*, Die Friedens-Warte, Vol. 74 (1999), 275–306.

[61] See Sally Morphet, *Organising Civil Administration in Peace-Maintenance*, in The Politics of Peace Maintenance, 41.

[62] The "Government out of a Box" project seeks to develop a service-tool for peacebuilding operations to facilitate the formation or re-establishment of a local civil service, including ready-made modules for managing and administering specific areas of activities such as health administrations or local civil registrations. See High-Level Workshop on State-Building and Strengthening of Civilian Administration in Post-Conflict Societies and Failed States, New York, *Government out of a Box – Some Ideas for Developing a Tool Box for Peace-Building* (21 June 2004).

[63] Statebuilding encompasses institutional support and domestic capacity building for the restoration or consolidation of governance. See also Asli U. Bali, *Justice under Occupation: Rule of Law and the Ethics of Nation-Building in Iraq*, Yale Journal of International Law, Vol. 30 (2005), 431, at 437.

[64] See most recently Dobbins, *The UN's Role in Nation-Building: From the Congo to Iraq*.

[65] See Chesterman, *You, The People*, at 48–98; Ralph Wilde, *International territorial administration and human rights*, in The UN, Human Rights and Post-conflict Situations (Nigel D. White and Dirk Klaasen eds., 2005), 149, at 152–60; Wilde, *From Danzig to East Timor*, at 587.

internationalisation has in this context been used for three main purposes, namely to:

- resolve a status question;
- insulate a territory from further dispute between competing states; or
- facilitate the transfer of a territory from one state to another.

All three functions have been exercised by the League or the UN throughout the history of international territorial administration. The intention to promote the adoption of a certain territorial status[66] was one of the main ambitions of the internationalisation of the Saar territory,[67] and currently underlies the administration of Kosovo.[68] Other missions, such as the administrations of Danzig[69] or Leticia,[70] were primarily guided by the objective of insulating the territories from hostilities between conflicting parties. Finally, the UN operations in West Irian (UNTEA) and Eastern Slavonia (UNTAES) were designed to facilitate the transfer of the respective territories through the establishment of a provisional buffer between the former territorial sovereign and the prospective successor state.

In several other cases, international territorial administration was used as a tool to further decolonisation. The establishment of MINURSO[71] and the UN Council for Namibia[72] were specifically driven

[66] But see Wilde, *From Danzig to East Timor*, at 592, who qualifies the administration of the Saar and UNMIK as responses to a "governance problem".

[67] The League was charged with the organisation of a referendum on the status of the Saar after the end of the 15-year administration, to determine whether the population of the Saar wanted the incorporation of the territory into Germany or France, or preferred the maintenance of the *status quo*. See Treaty of Versailles, Annex, Article 34.

[68] For the determination of the future status of Kosovo, see Andreas Zimmermann and Carsten Stahn, *Yugoslav Territory, United Nations Trusteeship or Sovereign State? Reflections on the Current and Future Legal Status of Kosovo*, Nordic Journal of International Law, Vol. 70 (2001), 423, at 451–9.

[69] Danzig was the subject of a dispute between Germany and Poland. Polish commercial interests in the territory collided with the city's German tradition and population. For the background of the dispute, see Knudson, *History of the League of Nations*, at 181–4.

[70] The Columbian town Leticia was seized by Peruvian troops in 1933. The one-year governance of the League facilitated the transition from Peruvian to Columbian rule. See Walters, *History of the League of Nations*, at 536–40.

[71] See also Chopra, *Peace-Maintenance*, at 164. MINURSO was charged with the task of guaranteeing the exercise of the self-determination of the indigenous population of the Western Sahara, torn between Morocco and the Front for the Liberation of Saguia el Hamra and Rio de Oro (POLISARIO). The overall implementation plan for MINURSO is contained in UN. Docs. S/21360 of 18 June 1990 and S/22464 of 19 April 1991.

[72] Namibia was subject to South Africa's League of Nations Mandate prior to its administration by the UN.

by this objective. Furthermore, the aim of ending colonial rule implicitly underlay the creation of two other UN administrations. UNTAET may not only be viewed as an exercise in statebuilding, but also as an example of decolonisation, as East Timor's transition to independence under the umbrella of the UN brought an end to its status as a non-self-governing territory.[73] The same may be said of UNTEA, as the administration and transfer of the territory to Indonesia by the UN was linked to the process of decolonisation of West Irian, which was supposed to end with a popular consultation determining the wishes of the Papuan people.[74]

These two last examples illustrate that the three main functions of international territorial administration are not exclusive, but are overlapping policy objectives. A specific mission may be designed to serve not only one, but several functions simultaneously. Such overlap occurs not only in the context of territorial dispute resolution and decolonisation (which are traditionally closely linked through the right to self-determination), but also in other cases. The administration of Kosovo, for example, may be characterised as an operation designed to address both the conflict over the final status of the territory and an internal vacuum requiring international reconstruction efforts. International territorial administration is therefore undoubtedly more than an *ad hoc* or default mechanism to address governance deficits in post-conflict situations. It is a multi-faceted policy device, dedicated to the resolution of territorial disputes, processes of decolonisation and the reconstruction of territories in situations of governance vacuums.

1.1.3. International territorial administration and progression

The third feature of modern analysis of international territorial administration, which has been aptly deconstructed, is its division of its history into successive "generations".[75] The imagery of "generations" has become a fashionable way of characterising the development of human rights

---

[73] Indonesia's sovereignty over East Timor has always been controversial. Portugal, the former administering power, acknowledged that Indonesia's occupation of East Timor entailed *de facto* limitations, but continuously insisted that East Timor's status was that of a Non-Self-Governing Territory. The question of the status of East Timor before the holding of the referendum was left open by the Agreement of 5 May 1999.

[74] Indonesia was obliged to organise a consultative process determining the will of the people with the assistance and participation of the UN. See Article 18 of the Agreement between Indonesia and the Netherlands.

[75] See Wilde, *Taxonomies of International Peacekeeping*, at 397; Wilde, *Representing International Territorial Administration*, at 75–7.

law and international peacekeeping since 1945.[76] However, it is misplaced in the context of international territorial administration. Building on the vocabulary used in the context of peacekeeping, attempts
have been made to qualify the UN missions in Kosovo and East Timor as
"third generation" operations.[77] However, the application of this analogy in the context of international territorial administration is flawed,
because it relies on the false assumption of the existence of a first and
a second generation, supposedly composed of the practice of the UN
after 1945 and the era of administration under the guidance of the
League of Nations. It is useful, to some extent, to distinguish experiments
in administration by ascribing them to particular periods in time.[78]
However, the use of the concept of "generations" of administration
is ill-advised.

It is difficult to establish that the evolution of international territorial administration incorporates clear patterns of successorship or continuation, which are at the heart of the idea of generational development. The early practice of the League was quite different from the
post-war practice of the UN. Any generation-based conception of international territorial administration is, in particular, open to the criticism
that some of the features of experiments of the alleged "first generation" (e.g. accountability structures) were arguably more developed than
corresponding structures of the "second generation".[79]

Secondly, the image of consecutive generations of international territorial administration is misleading, as it suggests a continuous progression. A process of development, however, can hardly be ascribed to the
different historical stages of international territorial administration. In
particular, the move from smaller or consent-based operations (of the
alleged "second generation") to more intrusive and comprehensive missions (of the alleged "third generation") is not necessarily the result of a
process of linear progression. The model of administration applied in the

---

[76] See on "third generation" rights generally Christian Tomuschat, *Solidarity Rights*
(Development, Peace, Environment, Humanitarian Assistance), in Encyclopedia of
Public International Law, Vol. IV (1992), 460.
[77] See Christopher David, *Russian and Chinese Opposition to NATO, Peacekeeping Operation in
Kosovo* (2002), 1, at www.usna.edu/NATAC/Papers/table04. For generational imagery, see
also Ratner, *The New UN Peacekeeping*, at 91.
[78] This attempt is undertaken below in Part II.
[79] This rather curious finding is shared by Ratner, who qualifies the League's governance
of the Saar Basin as "second-generation peacekeeping before its time". See Ratner, *The
New UN Peacekeeping*, at 91. For a comparative survey of accountability models, see
below Chapter 14.

cases of Kosovo and East Timor is not a universal formula. The template of each mission must be tailored according to the needs of the specific case. Missions like UNMIK and UNTAET cannot be regarded as the last stage in the historical evolution of international territorial administration.[80] A mission with a "light footprint" like the one in Afghanistan, for example, can be more effective in specific areas than an interventionist and long-term engagement, as in the case of Kosovo.

Moreover, the history of international territorial administration shows that each period contained a variety of missions (governance missions; co-governance missions; assistance missions). These missions were often unique in form and variable in success. This finding contradicts the theory of progression in the development of models of administration. Attempts to systematise the phenomenon of international territorial administration should therefore avoid a generation-based classification, and should rather rely on a division of the international practice into different categories of missions.[81]

1.2. International territorial administration – a governance issue

The role and function of international territorial administration also needs to be assessed in light of the transformation of the international legal system at the beginning of the twenty-first century. An account of the practice in international territorial administration is of interest to a range of contemporary issues, including the discourse on international governance.[82]

The idea of associating international territorial administration with the broader process of globalisation and governance may at first seem astonishing. Globalisation is usually related to socio-economic transformations at the macro level. Furthermore, it is mostly defined in opposition to the state, namely as a process of erosion of the powers of the state through loss of control over processes of market regulation, global trade and de-centralised international rulemaking. However, such a narrow understanding is simplistic. Globalisation is at least as much

---

[80] UNMIK and UNTAET are rather the tip of the iceberg, projecting the existence of a variety of other models of administrations.

[81] See below Part II, Chapter 10. See also previously Stahn, International Territorial Administration, at 129.

[82] See generally Günter Teubner (ed.), Global Law without a State (1997). For a treatment of international territorial administration as a governance issue, see Carsten Stahn, Governance Beyond the State: Issues of Legitimacy in International Territorial Administration, International Organizations Law Review, Vol. 1 (2005), Issue 2, at 9–56; Korhonen, Gras and Creutz, International Post-Conflict Situations, 12–39.

concerned with the eclipse of the state as with its transformation[83] – a process which is at the heart of international territorial administration. The label of international governance may easily be detached from its current focus on political and economic liberalisation at the universal and regional level and be transposed to the broader context of internationalised governance as such, including the administration of states by transnational institutions.[84]

There are compelling reasons to re-think international territorial administration from the perspective of international governance. International territorial administration has been conceived as a method of "strategic liberalisation",[85] because it pursues the overall goal of promoting peace through political and economic liberalisation in war-torn societies. This is reflected in the mandate of the international actors involved in peacebuilding activities, which goes far beyond the traditional objectives of the laws of occupation, obligating foreign powers to refrain from profoundly reshaping the internal political and legal system of the occupied territory.[86] International governing institutions have not only assumed direct responsibility for law and order in situations of transition; they have been vested with legislative and executive powers, such as the authority to repeal previous legislation, to rebuild and supervise the functioning of the domestic legal system or to appoint and dismiss public officials. In territories placed under exclusive international authority, international administrators have assumed responsibility for a whole array of economic tasks, including revenue-generation through customs and other taxes, the attraction of foreign investment, the creation of banking and fiscal authorities and the regulation of the budget.[87] These functions are traditionally embedded in a broader mandate

---

[83] See Tarak Barkawi and Mark Laffey, *The Imperial Peace: Democracy, Force and Globalization*, European Journal of International Relations, Vol. 5 (1999), 403, at 407.

[84] For a discussion, see also August Reinisch, *Governance Without Accountability*, German Yearbook of International Law, Vol. 44 (2001), 270, at 284.

[85] See Roland Paris, *Peacebuilding and the Limits of Liberal Internationalism*, International Security, Vol. 22 (1997), 54, at 58. See also Mohammed Ayoob, *Third World Perspectives on Humanitarian Intervention and International Administration*, Global Governance, Vol. 10 (2004), 99–118; Oliver P. Richmond, *The Globalization of Responses to Conflict and the Peacebuilding Consensus*, Cooperation and Conflict, Vol. 39 (2004), 129–50; and Knoll, *Beyond the "Mission Civilisatrice"*, 275.

[86] See Article 43 of the Hague Regulations and Article 64 of the Fourth Geneva Convention.

[87] See also para. 77 of the Brahimi Report. In the context of Kosovo, see, for instance, UNMIK Regulations No. 16/1999 of 6 November 1999 (*Central Fiscal Authority*) and No. 20/1999 of 15 November 1999 (*Banking and Payment Authority*).

to promote liberal rights and democratic state structures in post-conflict societies through various techniques, such as the integration of international human rights standards into the domestic legal system, the expansion of political participation mechanisms and the promotion of local self-government.

The underlying tenet of this practice is that the gradual establishment of a liberal democratic polity constitutes the best means to ensure stable peace, both within the administered territory and the states involved in the process of transition.[88] This project is sometimes not so far removed from the ideological heritage of liberal imperialism in the nineteenth century, which sought to defend colonial administration on the ground that it served "the mutual benefit" of Europe's industrial classes, "and of the native races in their progress to a higher plane" (the "dual mandate").[89] The very idea that a territory requires external guidance before being able to administer itself and its people shares some parallels with the normative heritage and moral justification of colonial administration which was based on the premise that a society needs to be educated and "civilised" before being able to be recognised as a sovereign and to join the community of nations.[90] Modern administrations are no longer preoccupied with the realisation of classical "standards of civilisation",[91] such as the right of people not to be cannibalised, enslaved or mutilated etc. However, they have used alternative concepts ("good governance", "rule of law", "capacity-building") to shape the law and institutions of societies along the guidelines of a Western liberal governing tradition. Moreover, they have set criteria for self-government when defining substantive benchmarks for devolution of power or the timing of access to independence.[92] Such a methodology causes novel

---

[88] For a contemporary critique, see also Roland Paris, *At War's End: Building Peace After Civil Conflict* (2004).

[89] See on liberal theory Uday Singh Metha, *Liberalism and Empire: A Study in Nineteenth Century British Liberal Thought* (1999). For an analysis of the ideological links between liberal imperialism and peacebuilding, see Bain, *Between Anarchy and Society*, at 192.

[90] Frederic Lugard, former British High Commissioner of Northern Nigeria, argued that the European presence in Africa serves a "dual mandate", namely "the mutual benefit of [Europe's] own industrial classes, and of the native races in their progress to a higher plane; that the benefit can be made reciprocal, and that it is the aim and desire of civilised administration to fulfil this dual mandate". See Frederic D. Lugard, *The Dual Mandate in British Tropical Africa* (1926), 617.

[91] See generally Gerrit W. Gong, *The Standard of 'Civilization' in International Society* (1984), 3; D. P. Fidler, *The Return of the Standard of Civilization*, Chicago Journal of International Law, Vol. 2 (2001), 137.

[92] See Knoll, *From Benchmarking to Final Status*, 637.

antinomies. The idea of "earning" self-government through compliance with internationally defined standards may conflict with the right of self-determination, as it is defined today.[93] Furthermore, it introduces certain normative distinctions, such as the idea of "able" and "less able", "knowing" and "less knowing" or "democratic" and "undemocratic" societies".[94] One of the critiques of international administration is that it raises some of the "fears" of globalisation, which is commonly perceived as a process of externally imposed decision-making threatening local values, cultures and traditions.[95]

Furthermore, it is worth revisiting the phenomenon of territorial administration in the context of the globalisation debate, because UN governance of territories marks, to some extent, a conceptual test case for other emerging governance regimes. UN territorial administration cannot be equated to "governance without government",[96] nor "governance without *demos*",[97] because international administrators usually exercise direct governmental powers over an entity with a strong identity-community. However, international territorial administration raises many of the most intriguing issues of the current global governance debate,[98] including the question of to what extent domestic and international governance institutions are subject to comparable democratic and procedural rule of law restraints in the exercise of regulatory powers.[99]

---

[93] See on the idea of earned sovereignty, Paul. R. Williams and Francesca J. Pecci, *Earned Sovereignty: Bridging the Gap between Sovereignty and Self-Determination*, Stanford Journal of International Law, Vol. 40 (2004), 347; Paul R. Williams, *Earned Sovereignty: The Road to Resolving the Conflict Over Kosovo's Final Status*, Denver Journal of International Law and Policy, Vol. 31 (2003), 387. For further discussion, see below Part IV, Chapter 18.

[94] See Nele Matz, *Civilization and the Mandate System under the League of Nations as Origin of Trusteeship*, Max Planck Yearbook of United Nations Law, Vol. 9 (2005), 47, at 69.

[95] For a cautious assessment, see Ian Johnstone, *UN Peace-Building: Consent, Coercion and the Crisis of State Failure*, in From Territorial Sovereignty to Human Security (Canadian Council on International Law, 2000), 186, at 196.

[96] See generally James N. Rosenau, Ernst-Otto Czempiel and Steve Smith, *Governance without Government: Order and Change in World Politics* (1992).

[97] The international level does not only lack elected decision-makers, but also a shared sense of community (*demos*). See Daniel Bodansky, *The Legitimacy of International Governance: A Coming Challenge for International Environmental Law*, American Journal of International Law, Vol. 93 (1999), 596, at 615–16.

[98] Note that international territorial administration can be viewed as being closer to traditional state-based forms of governance than comparable processes at the level of treaty regimes such as the EU or the WTO, because it replaces domestic actors in the exercise of public authority.

[99] See generally, Daniel C. Esty, *The World Trade Organization's Legitimacy Crisis*, World Trade Review, Vol. 1 (2002), 7; Robert O. Keohane and James S. Nye, Jr., *The Club Model of Multilateral Cooperation and Problems of Democratic Legitimacy*, in Efficiency, Equity and Legitimacy: The Multilateral Trading System at the Millennium (Roger Porter *et al.* eds., 2001), 264.

One would expect that international actors are generally bound by similar obligations as state actors when exercising governmental functions in a territory placed under their administration.[100] However, there is some evidence to the contrary. International legal practice has shown that there are double standards in the structural conception of "international governmental legitimacy", not only in the area of democratic legitimisation, but also in other fields such as accountability, institutional power-sharing and the rule of law. The practice in the field of UN governance missions illustrates, in particular, that international governing institutions have been perceived more as functional entities ruled by the laws and principles applicable to international organisations (e.g. in terms of privileges and immunities, legal obligations and intra-institutional power-sharing) than as state actors governed by standards of domestic law, even where they exercised governance functions in the role of a "surrogate state".[101] Domestic and international governing institutions are treated differently on at least three levels: the organisation of public power, the question of accountability and the applicability of human rights obligations to the administering authorities.[102] Some of these differences, such as the initial centralisation of power within the institution of the transitional administration, are rooted in the special circumstances of the post-conflict environment, in which international administrations usually operate. Others again appear to be rather arbitrary.

It is clear that features of national accountability and democratic theory cannot simply be transposed to internationalised governance within the framework of international territorial administration.[103] Such a transposition needs to take into account conflicting prerogatives and objectives, such as the functional immunity of international actors, the necessity for a neutral and independent decision-making authority in post-conflict societies and the limitations of classical majority rule in situations of transition. But the discrepancies between the governance practice of international administrations and existing standards of domestic governance raise some intriguing questions. There is, first, an

---

[100] See also Claudio Grossman and Daniel D. Bradlow, *Are We Being Propelled Towards a People-Centered Transnational Legal Order?*, American University Journal of International Law and Policy, Vol. 9 (1993), 1, at 21.

[101] See also Elizabeth Abraham, *The Sins of the Saviour: Holding the United Nations Accountable to International Human Rights Standards for Executive Order Detentions in its Mission in Kosovo*, American University Law Review, Vol. 52 (2003), 1291.

[102] See below Parts III and IV.

[103] See also Robert A. Dahl, *Can International Organizations Be Democratic? A Sceptic's View*, in Democracy's Edges (Ian Shapiro and Casioano Hacker-Cordón eds., 1999), 19, 23.

issue of legality, namely whether and to what extent such "double standards" can be reconciled with existing standards of international law.
Secondly, there is an issue of legitimacy,[104] which focuses on the question how governance within the field of international territorial administration can be justified on the basis of theories of the legitimisation of
public power (such as procedural rule-of-law principles and functional or
participatory models of legitimacy). These problems are often sidelined
by those who view international administration primarily as a pragmatic
and technocratic tool to address dilemmas of statebuilding.

1.3.   International territorial administration and peacemaking

Another area which deserves closer attention as a result of the practice
in the field of international territorial administration is the process of
peacemaking. The rise of international territorial administration as a
policy device invites new thinking on the organisation of post-conflict
peace.

1.3.1.   International territorial administration and the sustainability of peace

On more than one occasion, history has taught that an unjust peace carries the seeds of war. International territorial administration constitutes
an important instrument to develop an integrative and problem-solving
approach to peacemaking.[105] There is a growing recognition that conflict
termination cannot stop at the ending of wars, but requires additional
international assistance to allow a territory to return from a state of exceptionalism to the realms of normality.[106] The creation of international

---

[104] See below Part III, Chapter 12. The issue of the legitimacy of international
institutions has gained broadening attention in recent years. See Philippe Sands,
Turtles and Torturers: The Transformation of International Law, NYU Journal of
International Law and Policy, Vol. 33 (2001), 527, at 540; Chantal Thomas,
Constitutional Change and International Government, Hastings Law Journal, Vol. 52 (2000),
1, 41; Kal Raustiala, *Sovereignty and Multilateralism*, Chicago Journal of International
Law, Vol. 1 (2000), 401, at 416.

[105] See generally Michael Reisman, *Stopping Wars and Making Peace: Reflections on the
Ideology and Practice of Conflict Termination in Contemporary World Politics*, Tulane Journal
of International and Comparative Law, Vol. 6 (1998), 5, at 29.

[106] See *An Agenda for Peace, Preventive Diplomacy, Peacemaking and Peace-Keeping*, Report of the
Secretary-General, UN SCOR, 47th Sess., at 22, UN Doc. S/24111 (1992). Statistics have
found that half of the states emerging from conflict have lapsed back into violence
within five years. See *In Larger Freedom, Towards Development, Security and Human Rights
for All*, Report of the Secretary-General, 21 March 2005, Executive Summary, sub. II
("Freedom from Fear").

administrations is a cornerstone of modern peacemaking practice, insofar as it may help to reintegrate war-torn territories into the society of peaceful and law-abiding nations through a process involving the affected parties, international actors and private stakeholders.

Empirically, most undertakings in international territorial administration are related to some form of armed conflict. The early experiments of the League in the Saar, the City of Danzig and Memel territory were rooted in the peace settlements of World War I. Similarly, most UN international administrations were established in response to a conflict. International or internal armed conflicts gave rise to the UN operations in Congo (ONUC), Cambodia (UNTAC), Somalia (UNOSOM II), Eastern Slavonia (UNTAES), Kosovo (UNMIK), East Timor (UNTAET) and the more recent missions in Afghanistan (UNAMA), Iraq (UNAMI), Liberia (UNMIL), Democratic Republic of Congo (MONUC) and Ivory Coast (UNOCI). One of the most interesting aspects of this practice is that international territorial administrations have traditionally been deployed for two purposes: to deal with the consequences of conflict or to end conflict itself.

Most of the League's first missions (Saar, Danzig and Memel) were established for the first purpose, namely the intention to solve competing claims and security concerns of states after the cessation of hostilities. However, even the League used the technique of international territorial administration as a conflict resolution mechanism designed to end an ongoing conflict itself. The League acted proactively in the case of engagement in Leticia. The international administration for the City of Leticia was created by the League to resolve the causes of the conflict between Columbian and Peruvian forces, which had invaded the town and district of Leticia in September 1932 in violation of international agreements, including the League of Nations Covenant.[107] The Council of the League initiated peace negotiations between the parties upon request from the government of Colombia[108] and entrusted a special Commission with a one-year mandate to administer Leticia pending settlement of the dispute.

---

[107] The forcible intervention violated, *inter alia*, a Columbian-Peruvian border agreement of 24 March 1922, the Kellogg-Briand Pact and the League Covenant, to which Peru and Columbia were a party. See Ydit, *Internationalised Territories*, at 59–60.

[108] See Dispute Between Colombia and Peru: Appeal of the Columbian Government under Article 15 of the Covenant: Draft Report of the Council, provided for in Article 15, paragraph 4 of the Covenant, submitted by the Committee of the Council, 18 March 1933, League of Nations Official Journal 14 (1933), 516–23.

This conflict resolution function of international territorial administration was later more systematically developed in UN practice. The growing integration of civil administration mandates into peacekeeping and peace-enforcement operations has increased the use of international territorial administration as an instrument to resolve ongoing conflicts. The first peacekeeping operation in which patterns of territorial administration were exercised by UN actors to terminate conflict and prevent further hostilities was ONUC. The mission was established to restore order in Congo and to assist the Congolese government in the construction of a functioning civilian administration after the withdrawal of the Belgian colonial authorities.[109] It was later followed by a series of UN operations which deployed administrative and governance structures in order to end conflict or to prevent the resurgence of armed combat. UNOSOM was directly established in the conflict phase and assumed administering powers almost incidentally due to breakdown of local authorities.[110] Other missions, like UNTAC, UNMIK, UNTAET, UNAMA, UNMIL, MONUC or UNOCI, were created in the post-conflict phase or after a peace settlement and served the broader purpose of preventing a return to armed conflict through security management and statebuilding.

This last type of conflict resolution, which has become increasingly popular in the last decade, contributes to a more integrative and problem-solving approach to peacemaking. It strengthens the sustainability of peacemaking on several levels. The involvement of the UN in the negotiation of the terms of peace may contribute to a neutralisation of the bargaining process and ensure that the interests of relevant stakeholders are duly articulated. Further, statebuilding and reconstruction usually go hand in hand with domestic institution-building and power-sharing. Ideally, this process may encourage political dialogue and community-building and prevent inter-group dominance in the post-conflict phase. The presence of international support structures may facilitate the promotion of disarmament, human rights protection, the return of refugees and the establishment of the rule of law. Finally, international post-conflict engagement may have a certain distributive effect. The multinational nature of engagement may ensure to a wider distribution of the costs of reconstruction and help reconnect

---

[109] For a survey, see Ratner, *The New UN Peacekeeping*, at 105–9.

[110] UNOSOM II was originally conceived as an assistance mission, but subsequently confronted with governing tasks in the exercise of its mandate. See Chopra, *Peace-Maintenance*, at 141–2.

a domestic society to the network of transnational social and economic transactions.

1.3.2. International territorial administration and the justification of governance

Moreover, international territorial administration presents an alternative concept to foreign occupation.[111] State-based forms of administration have some tradition in international law. They were practised within the framework of the Mandate and the Trusteeship System.[112] Furthermore, Germany and Japan were governed under the framework of post-surrender occupation by the victorious allies in the aftermath 1945.[113]

Today, however, the idea of foreign occupation has become open to challenge in contemporary practice.[114] State occupations often carry a pejorative stigma that is less directly associated with UN peace operations, namely the image of unilateralism and coercion.[115] Moreover, occupation as a concept lacks some of the necessary legal tools to address the tensions arising in the context of post-conflict administration. The narrow focus of the law of occupation on the relationship between a military power and the former sovereign and its limited temporal scope of application are difficult to reconcile with the needs and dynamics of post-conflict reconstruction. Most importantly, the feasibility of occupation as a framework of governance may be questioned from a perspective of governmental legitimacy. The right to self-determination has evolved to embrace the right of "all peoples" to "freely determine, without external interference, their political status and to pursue their economic, social and cultural development". Emerging standards of democratic

---

[111] See Steven R. Ratner, *Foreign Occupation and International Territorial Administration, The Challenges of Convergence*, European Journal of International Law, Vol. 15 (2005), 695. In particular, the direct assumption of authority by the victorious states, which was practised after World War II and re-emerged in the case of Iraq, is increasingly exposed to criticisms. See also Henry H. Perritt, *Structures and Standards for Political Trusteeship*, UCLA Journal of International Law and Foreign Affairs, Vol. 8 (2003), 385; Michael Ottolenghi, *The Stars and Stripes in Al-Fardo Square: The Implications For International Law Of Belligerent Occupation*, Fordham Law Review, Vol. 72 (2004), 2177.

[112] For further analysis, see below Part I, Chapters 2 and 3.

[113] See below Part I, Chapter 4.

[114] For a survey of the demise of the law of occupation after 1945, see generally Eyal Benvenisti, *The International Law of Occupation* (2003); David Scheffer, *Beyond Occupation Law*, American Journal of International Law, Vol. 97 (2003), 842.

[115] See Ratner, *Foreign Occupation and International Territorial Administration*, at 711–12.

governance[116] make it difficult to justify the direct exercise of governmental powers by foreign authorities over the population of post-conflict societies over a longer period of time without consent or an official act of approval of the administered population.[117] The framework of occupation is ill-equipped to accommodate long-term processes of government, because it does not provide mechanisms of accountability of the occupying powers to the domestic population.[118]

Internationalised governing mechanisms have their own antinomies and pitfalls.[119] However, they present in some respects a more balanced institutional framework for post-conflict governance than historical models of foreign state administration.[120] They are typically embedded in a broader organisational system with internal mutual checks and balances, which are absent from the laws of occupation. Furthermore, they bring an element of impartiality into the post-conflict peace process that can not usually be guaranteed by either of the former parties to the conflict.[121]

1.3.3. Post-conflict administration as a corollary of intervention

Projects of international territorial administration also establish a link between intervention and post-conflict reconstruction. In contemporary international law, the justification for the use of armed force is often linked to the aim of establishing a just and sustainable peace.[122]

---

[116] See Thomas M. Franck, *The Emerging Right to Democratic Governance*, American Journal of International Law, Vol. 86 (1992), 91. For an elaboration of these claims, see Gregory H. Fox, *The Right to Political Participation in International Law*, Yale Journal of International Law, Vol. 17 (1992), 539; Gregory H. Fox and Georg Nolte, *Intolerant Democracies*, Harvard International Law Journal, Vol. 36 (1995), 1; and Christine Gerna, *Universal Democracy: an International Legal Right or a Pipe Dream of the West?*, NYU Journal of International Law and Policy, Vol. 27 (1995), 289.

[117] Knudson noted in 1938 that "[j]ustification for international interference in the internal affairs of a country becomes vital where conditions threaten 'to disturb international peace or the good understanding between nations upon which peace depends'". See Knudson, *History of the League of Nations*, at 173.

[118] See Yoram Dinstein, *International Law of Belligerent Occupation and Human Rights*, Israel Yearbook of Human Rights, Vol. 1 (1978), 104, at 116.

[119] See below Part I, Conclusion and Part V, Chapter 18.

[120] Concurring Perrit, *Structures and Standards for Political Trusteeship*, at 410.

[121] See also Fen Osler Hampson, *Making Peace Agreements Work: The Implementation and Enforcement of Peace Agreements between Sovereigns and Intermediate Sovereigns*, Cornell Journal of International Law, Vol. 30 (1997), 701, at 714.

[122] See generally Jordan Paust, *Use of Armed Force against Terrorists in Afghanistan, Iraq and Beyond*, Cornell Journal of International Law, Vol. 35 (2002), 533. See on self-defence and international terrorism, Carsten Stahn, *Nicaragua is dead, long live Nicaragua*, in

Military interventions are no longer exclusively justified by the purpose of thwarting security threats, but are guided by a range of post-conflict-oriented purposes, including, most notably, the promotion of human rights, democracy or self-determination.[123] The lawfulness of such (multifunctional) interventions is occasionally assessed by reference to the effects of the use of force in the post-conflict phase.[124]

The assumption of responsibility in the post-conflict phase has been viewed as a legitimating factor for intervention, or as a criterion of *ex post* validation.[125] Further, post-conflict reconstruction itself is increasingly viewed as a corollary of intervention. This point was made by the International Commission on Intervention and State Sovereignty. The Commission noted in its report on the "Responsibility to Protect":

> The responsibility to protect implies the responsibility not just to prevent and react, but to follow through and rebuild. This means if military intervention action is taken – because of a breakdown or abdication of a state's own capacity and authority in discharging its "responsibility to protect" – there should be a genuine commitment to helping to build a durable peace, and promoting good governance and sustainable development. Conditions of public safety and order have to be reconstituted by international agents acting in partnership with local authorities, with the goal of progressively transferring to them authority and responsibility to rebuild.[126]

The High-level Panel on Threats, Challenges and Change went a step further, by acknowledging "an emerging norm of collective international responsibility to protect".[127]

Pointing to international responses to "the successive humanitarian disasters in Somalia, Bosnia and Herzegovina, Rwanda, Kosovo and now Darfur, Sudan", the report noted that:

Terrorism as a Challenge for National and International Law: Security versus Liberty (C. Walter, S. Vöneky, V. Röben and F. Schorkopf eds., 2004), 827–77.

[123] Motives of this kind were at the heart of the humanitarian intervention in Kosovo and underpinned the operations in Afghanistan and Iraq.

[124] Theories of *ex post* legitimation have, in particular been advanced to validate the ECOWAS operations in Liberia and Sierra Leone. A similar argument was made in relation to *Operation Allied Force* in Kosovo. For further discussion, see below Part II, Chapter 10.

[125] See below Part II, Chapter 10.

[126] See Report of the International Commission on Intervention and State Sovereignty, *The Responsibility to Protect* (2001), at 39.

[127] See Report of the High-level Panel on Threats, Challenges and Changes, *A More Secure World: Our Shared Responsibility*, UN Doc A/59/565 (2 December 2004), para. 203. For a critical appraisal, see Carsten Stahn, *Responsibility to Protect: Political Rhetoric or Emerging Legal Norm*, American Journal of International Law, Vol. 101 (2007), 99–120.

[t]here is a growing recognition that the issue is not the "right to intervene" of any State, but the "responsibility to protect" of every State when it comes to people suffering from avoidable catastrophe ... [a]nd there is a growing acceptance that ... [this] responsibility should be taken up by the wider international community – with it spanning a continuum involving prevention, response to violence, if necessary, and rebuilding of shattered societies.[128]

The idea of a "collective responsibility to protect" after conflict was then, in a less assertive form, introduced into the Outcome document of the 2005 World Summit.[129] Heads of States and Government expressed their intention to "commit" themselves, *as necessary and appropriate*, to helping States build capacity to protect their populations from genocide, war crimes, ethnic cleansing and crimes against humanity and to assisting those which are under stress before crises and conflicts break out".[130]

The cautious phrasing of the Outcome document and the continuing reservations of states towards an obligation to respond after conflict[131] indicate that it is still difficult to speak of a "responsibility to rebuild" in the sense of a firm legal duty to act.[132] Nor is such an approach necessarily desirable from a policy perspective. The various experiences in the last decade have shown that "humanitarian" and "democratic" interventions have disturbing side-effects,[133] which stand in contrast to the objectives pursued.[134]

Nevertheless, the "responsibility to protect" concept has some merit from a systemic perspective. It places a new emphasis on considerations

---

[128] *Ibid.*, para. 201.

[129] See General Assembly Resolution 60/1 (*2005 World Summit Outcome*) of 24 October 2005.

[130] See para. 139 of GA Res. 60/1 of 24 October 2005. Emphasis added.

[131] Several states (Algeria, Belarus, Cuba, Egypt, Iran, Pakistan, Russian Federation, Venezuela) expressed reservations towards the inclusion of the concept of "responsibility to protect" into the Outcome Document. US Ambassador John Bolton stated in a letter dated 30 August 2005 that the US "would not accept that either the United Nations as a whole or the Security Council, or individual States have an obligation to intervene under international law". See Letter dated 30 August 2005, at 2, available at www.responsibilitytoprotect.org/index.php/government_statements/.

[132] For doubts as to the customary nature of the responsibility to protect, see also Gareth Evans, *The Responsibility to Protect and the Duty to Prevent*, American Society of International Law Proceedings, Vol. 98 (2004), 77, at 84.

[133] See among others Noam Chomsky, *The New Military Humanism: Lessons From Kosovo* (1999); David Kennedy, *The Dark Sides of Virtue: Reassessing International Humanitarianism* (2004); Adam Roberts, *The So-Called "Right" of Humanitarian Intervention*, Yearbook of International Humanitarian Law, Vol. 3 (2000), 3–53; Michael Reisman, *Why Regime Change is (Almost Always) a Bad Idea*, American Journal of International Law, Vol. 98 (2004), 516–25; Nathaniel Berman, *Intervention in a "Divided World": Axes of Legitimacy*, European Journal of International Law, Vol. 17 (2006), 743–69.

[134] Such interventions may actually defeat liberal goals by distorting local initiatives, reducing domestic dialogue and creating socio-economic dependencies. The "neo-imperial" features of intervention and statebuilding have been explored in

of sustainability in the contemporary understanding of intervention. It forces international actors to take into account the impact and effects of their decisions on the post-conflict phase, including modalities and institutional frameworks for peacemaking, when assessing the desirability and scope of intervention.[135] In this sense, the practice of international territorial administration may be conceived as an institutional framework for the organisation of post-conflict peace.[136]

1.4.   International territorial administration and the development of the international legal system

Lastly, any contemporary analysis of the phenomenon of international territorial administration would be incomplete without an assessment of its place and function in the international legal system. The practice of international territorial administration illustrates certain structural changes within the international legal system.

1.4.1.   International territorial administration and the executive function of the international community

Although the international legal order is in many ways still a minimalist system, it is continuing to develop into a normative legal framework in which various international organisations and institutions exercise law-making authority, executive tasks or judicial functions which govern the relationship between international and national actors.[137] The tendency to move from a decentralised and state-based mode of power-sharing

---

greater detail in the works by Michael Ignatieff, *Empire Lite: Nation Building on Bosnia, Kosovo and Afghanistan* (2003); Roland Paris, *At War's End: Building Peace After Civil Conflict* (2004), David Chandler, *Empire in Denial: The Politics of State-building* (2006).

[135] Post-conflict engagement would thus no longer be a purely discretionary element of foreign policy, but a structural element of responses that seek to the eliminate of the root causes of terror and conflict.

[136] International territorial administration may be said to form part of a broader category of "*jus post bellum*". See generally Brian Orend, *War and International Justice, A Kantian Perspective* (2000), 57; Brian Orend, *Jus Post Bellum*, Journal of Social Philosophy, Vol. 31 (2000), 117–37; Brian Orend, *The Morality of War* (2006), 160–90; and Gary J. Bass, *Jus Post Bellum*, Philosophy & Public Affairs, Vol. 32 (2004) 384–412. For an analysis of "*jus post bellum*" as a legal concept, see Carsten Stahn, *Jus Ad Bellum, Jus in Bello … Jus Post Bellum: Rethinking the Conception of the Law of Armed Force*, European Journal of International Law, Vol. 17 (2006), 921–43; Boon, *Legislative Reform in Post-Conflict Zones*, at 285.

[137] See also Christian Tomuschat, *General Course on Public International Law*, Recueil des Cours, Vol. 281 (1999), 13, at 305, 358 and 390, who uses the tripartite division "legislative function", "executive function" and "settlement of disputes" to describe the international community. See also Christian Tomuschat, *International Law and the Constitution of Mankind*, in International Law on the Eve of the Twenty-first Century (United Nations, 1997), 37, at 44–8.

á la Westphalia to a more centralised conception of governance[138] is not only reflected at the regional level, but also at the universal level. The Security Council has increasingly extended its function as a guarantor of law and order in the maintenance of peace and security[139] and acted in a (quasi-) legislative capacity on specific occasions.[140] Various judicial or quasi-judicial bodies such as the International Court of Justice, the International Tribunal for the Law of the Sea, the International Criminal Court or the World Trade Organization's dispute settlement mechanism provide an opportunity to settle disputes on the basis of law at the universal level.[141] Furthermore, an ever-increasing number of institutions exercise administering functions in the international legal system.[142] Some of the most classic examples are the Universal Postal Union, the International Olympic Committee and various environmental regimes. These institutions complement the decentralised executive capacity of states in the international legal system, which do not only act in the exercise of their powers, but also implement and enforce rules of international law in the absence of a unified international authority (*dédoublement fonctionnel*).[143]

---

[138] See generally on pre-Westphalian, Westphalian and post-Westphalian tendencies in international law, Rein Müllerson, *Ordering Anarchy, International Law in International Society* (2000), 102–110.

[139] For an assessment of the powers of the Council, see Tomuschat, *Obligations for States*, at 333–46.

[140] See SC Resolution 1540 of 28 April 2004 (*Non-proliferation of weapons of mass destruction*); SC Resolution 1373 of 28 September 2001 (*Threats to international Peace and Security by Terrorist Acts*). See generally Paul Szasz, *The Security Council Starts Legislating*, American Journal of International Law, Vol. 96 (2002), 901; Jurij Daniel Aston, *Die Bekämpfung abstrakter Gefahren für den Weltfrieden durch legislative Manahmen des Sicherheitsrats – Resolution 1373 (2001) im Kontext*, Zeitschrift für ausländisches öffentliches Recht und Völkerrecht, Vol. 62 (2002), 257; Stefan Talmon, *The Security Council as World Legislature*, American Journal of International Law, Vol. 99 (2005), 175. For a critical appraisal, see Gaetano Arangio-Ruiz, *On the Security Council's "Law-Making"*, Rivista di Diritto Internazionale, Vol. 83 (2000), 609. For a response, see Christian Tomuschat, *Peace Enforcement and Law Enforcement: Two Separate Chapters of International Law?*, in Studi di Diritto Internazionale in Onore di Geatano Arangio-Ruiz (2003), Vol. 3, 1745–69.

[141] See generally, Jonathan Charney, *Is International Law Threatened by Multiple International Tribunals?*, Recueil des Cours, Vol. 271 (1998), 101; Benedict Kingsbury, *Is the Proliferation of International Courts and Tribunals a Systemic Problem?*, NYU Journal of International Law and Politics, Vol. 31 (1999), 679.

[142] For a recent study, see Benedict Kingsbury, Nico Krisch & Richard B. Stewart, *The Emergence of Global Administrative Law*, Law & Contemporary Problems, Vol. 68 (2005), 15–61.

[143] According to Georges Scelle's doctrine of *dédoublement fonctionnel*, state officials exercise a double role: they act as state organs whenever they operate within their

International administration of territory may be conceived as a technique to help states to live up to their obligations under international law in situations of conflict and transition. Under contemporary international law, the state is not only the guardian of its own interests. It has positive obligations to secure the welfare of its citizens and to maintain law and order by virtue of its governance mandate.[144] The modern nation-state exercises, in fact, the function of an agent and "trustee for the human beings",[145] who are affected by the consequences of domestic and international authority. If a state loses effective authority and the capacity to guarantee the life, security and welfare of its people in a state of conflict, it fails not only in its role as a domestic governing institution, but also in its function as an executive agent of international obligations.[146] International territorial administration has developed into a default mechanism of the international community to address this "enforcement gap" through temporary assistance measures or the transitional exercise of governance functions by international actors.

The practice of international territorial administration is closely related to the process of the communitarisation of international law.[147] The exercise of territorial authority by international organisations is usually not only representative of the will and interests of a particular group of states, but is reflective of a broader engagement by the

---

domestic legal system; and they act as international agents when they operate within the international legal system. In this latter capacity, states assume the role of international enforcement agencies ("*agents exécutifs internationaux*"). See generally Georges Scelle, *Précis de Droit des Gens. Principes et Systématique*, Vol. I (1932) 43, 54–6, 217; Vol. II (1934) 10, 319, 450. For a recent treatment of Scelle's doctrine, see Antonio Cassese, *Remarks on Scelle's Doctrine of "Role Splitting" (Dédoublement Fonctionnel) in International Law*, European Journal of International Law, Vol. 1 (1990), 210–31.

[144] For an assessment of international law "as a comprehensive blueprint for social life", including international human rights obligations, standards of democracy and requirements of good governance, see Tomuschat, *General Course*, at 63.

[145] This understanding may be traced back to the contractual theories of John Locke, who characterised the state in terms of a relation of trust. See John Locke, *Two Treatises of Government* (1690), Peter Laslett ed. (1988) Chapter XIII, Section 149.

[146] This is, in particular evident, in the cases of collapsed states. See also Tomuschat, *Constitution of Mankind*, at 43.

[147] First traces of this school of thought may be found in the treatment of global commons by Hugo Grotius. Grotius postulated that certain areas, such as the sea, cannot become subject to private ownership, because they are so large that they "suffice for any possible use on the part of all peoples". See Hugo Grotius, *De Jure Belli Ac Pacis* (1625) (Francis W. Kelsey trans., Oxford, Clarendon Press 1925), Book, Chapter 2, Of Things Which Belong to Men in Common.

international community. This occurs, in particular, where international administrators exercise exclusive administering authority over a territory. Some precedents can be found in the practice of the internationalisation of natural resources, such as the administration of the international seabed, which was declared a common heritage of mankind under Part XI of the Convention on the Law of the Sea[148] and is currently administered by the International Sea-Bed Authority. International territorial administration, however, dissociates the phenomenon of community-based administration from the utilitarian concept of the exploitation and distribution of natural resources and places it at the service of the interests and needs of a territory's population.

The administration of territories by international actors marks an unusual model of international executive authority, as it involves the wielding of decision-making power with a direct effect on individuals. The institutionalisation of human rights law and international criminal law after 1945 has led to a rapid proliferation of legal mechanisms that regulate and adjudicate rights and obligations of individuals under international law. However, the exercise of normative authority with a direct effect on individuals is rare in the context of international administrative regimes.[149] The practice of international territorial administration is exceptional in this regard, because international administrators exercise such powers not by virtue of territorial sovereignty, but as mandatories of authority attributed to them by international law. International territorial administration is not merely a technique designed to regulate or administer a common space (such as waterways or Antarctica) or to facilitate the achievement of specific common goals, but a form of governance which determines the relations between a state, its people and

---

[148] Article 136 of the Convention on the Law of the Sea provides that "the Area and its resources are the common heritage of mankind". Following this logic, the Convention established a seabed authority and stated in Article 137 (2) that "[a]ll rights in the resources of the area are vested in mankind as a whole, on whose behalf the Authority shall act". After disputes over the use of the deep seabed, the Convention was completed in 1994 by an Agreement on the Implementation of Part XI of the United Nations Convention on the Law of the Sea, in ILM, Vol. 33 (1994), 1099. A similar approach underlies the Outer Space Treaty, which refers to the "common interest of all mankind" in the preamble and proclaims that the exploitation and use of outer space shall be carried out for the "benefit and in the interests of all countries". See Article 1 (1) of the Treaty on Principles Governing the Activities of States in the Exploration and Use of Outer Space, Including the Moon and Other Celestial Bodies, of 27 January 1967.

[149] The example of the European Union (EU) with its doctrines of supremacy and direct effect is still an exception on the international plane.

the international community. This finding has certain conceptual implications. It disconnects the notion of governance from the concept of the
sovereign state.[150] Furthermore, it embraces a functionalist understanding of sovereignty,[151] according to which the state is only one contender
among others to be considered when the allocation of governance is
made.

1.4.2. International territorial administration and legal theory

The historical evolution of international territorial administration artic-
ulates two fundamental structural changes which are symptomatic of
the transformation of the international legal system itself, namely: the
tendency to complement a dispute settlement-dominated understanding
of law with a problem-solving-oriented vision of legal rules and decision-
making; and the move from traditional realist approaches to law to a
broader cosmopolitan agenda.[152]

1.4.2.1. Dispute settlement versus managerial problem-solving

A substantial part of the contemporary international legal architecture
is shaped by a dispute settlement-focused conception of international
law. This view has a long-established historical tradition. Grotius' fundamental work *De Jure Belli ac Pacis* (1625) conceptualised the issues of war
and peace as a problem of managing disputes.[153] Furthermore, since the

---

[150] For a discussion of this issue within the area of European constitutionalism, see
Ingolf Pernice, *Multilevel Constitutionalism and the Treaty of Amsterdam: European
Constitution-Making Revisited?*, Common Market Law Review, Vol. 36 (1999), 703, at 709,
M. Morlok, *Grundfragen einer Verfassung auf europäischer Ebene*, in Staat und Verfassung
in Europa (P. Häberle ed., 2000), 73, at 74–5; Günther Hirsch, *EG: Kein Staat, aber eine
Verfassung?*, Neue Juristische Wochenschrift (2000), 46; Wolfram Hertel,
Supranationalität als Verfassungsprinzip (1999), 28; Dieter Grimm, *Does Europe need a
Constitution*, in The Question of Europe (P. Gowan and P. Anderson eds., 1997), 239, at
245–6; and Albrecht Randelzhofer, *Souveränität und Rechtsstaat: Anforderungen an eine
Europäische Verfassung*, in Der Rechtsstaat am Ende? (Noske ed., 1995), 123, at 124.

[151] Several North American scholars have argued that states are disaggregated into state
and private actors with distinct agendas and interests. See Harald Koh, *Transnational
Public Law Litigation*, Yale Law Journal, Vol. 100 (1991), 2372–402; Anne-Marie Slaughter,
International Law and International Relations, Recueil des Cours, Vol. 285 (2000), 13.

[152] For a general survey of theories on international law, see Anne Peters, *There is Nothing
more Practical than a Good Theory: An Overview of Contemporary Approaches to International
Law*, German Yearbook of International Law, Vol. 44 (2001), 25; Stefan Oeter,
International Law and the General Systems Theory, German Yearbook of International Law,
Vol. 44 (2001), 72.

[153] See Hugo Grotius' *De Jure Belli ac Pacis* (1625), which starts with the word
"controversiae" (disputes).

late nineteenth century, international law has been perceived as a body of rules that is developed and shaped by litigation and scholarship.[154] Principles such as the sources of international law under Article 38 of the Statute of the International Court of Justice, the hierarchy of norms, the status of international law in the domestic legal system and the identification of general principles of law have been shaped by the tradition of dispute resolution. Other concepts such as jurisdiction, diplomatic protection, state responsibility and responsibility of international organisations are embedded within the tradition of dispute settlement and consent.

However, this tradition of law fails to provide a conclusive answer to the needs of a progressively international society. The impact of private actors on the conduct of international relations has eclipsed the traditional focus on the state in international law[155] and prioritised the regulatory function of international law. The role of international law as a bargaining tool to be used in the definition of rights and obligations has been reduced by the emergence of numerous multilateral institutions in the aftermath of World War II, which have highlighted the existence of other systemic objectives, including the function of law to vindicate community interests. The New Haven School has called into question the exclusiveness of positivism through its insistence of the role of policy in the framing of law, and through its advocacy of decision-making positing community interests in world public order.[156] These various developments have laid the foundations for a more complex and

---

[154] See Kingsbury, *International Legal Order*, at 272.

[155] Note that there are some early examples in which private actors were involved in the governance of territories, for example, the International Association for the Congo, a private association which brought the Congo region under the auspices of the Belgian King Leopold II and a group of European investors. The Association's claim to govern the territory as an independent state was recognised by the great European Powers at the Berlin West Africa Conference of 1884–5. King Leopold II was recognised as the sovereign of the new state (The Congo Free State). The Congo Free State was administered by companies and internationals from Europe. For a survey, see L. H. Gann and Peter Duignan, *Rulers of Belgian Africa, 1884–1914* (1979).

[156] The New Haven School is, in particular, represented by the work of Myres S. McDougal, Harold D. Lasswell and W. Michael Reisman. The school understands law as "a process of decision characterized both by expectations of authority and by effective control". See Myres S. McDougal, Harold D. Lasswell and W. Michael Reisman, *The World Constitutive Process of Authoritative Decision*, in International Law Essays: A Supplement to International Law in Contemporary Practice (M. S. McDougal and W. M. Reisman eds., 1981), 191–286. For a critical review, see Sandra Voos, *Die Schule von New Haven – Darstellung und Kritik einer amerikanischen Völkerrechtslehre* (2000).

multifunctional conception of international law, which is not only guided by the pragmatic needs of dispute settlement, but pursues the broader goal of managerial problem-solving.

The transformation of international law from a means of dispute settlement to an instrument of problem-solving more generally is reflected in the evolution of international territorial administration. In particular, the early undertakings of the League were deeply embedded in the tradition of dispute settlement. The administration of the Saar Basin[157] and League's guarantee of the City of Danzig[158] were not exclusively tailored to address specific status problems or societal needs in the territories themselves, but rather part of a collective bargaining process over the post-war rights and obligations of Germany. Similar bargaining processes over post-war rights and obligations determined the internationalisation of the Memel Territory[159] and the proposed international administration of the City of Trieste after World War II.[160]

Today, international practice is more nuanced. The settlement of inter-state disputes remains one of the main functions of international territorial administration, as evidenced by the mandate of the UN administration in West Irian and Eastern Slavonia. In contemporary practice, however, this tradition is complemented by another strand of practice, which is more detached from the objectives of bilateral dispute settlement or inter-state bargaining, and is driven by the aim of managerial problem-solving. Due to changing conceptions of state sovereignty and non-intervention, the rise of liberal democracy and a new focus on "internal self-determination" and democratic entitlement, international territorial administration has become an instrument to secure collective and individual rights. In situations such as Congo, Somalia, Cambodia, Kosovo or Afghanistan, the UN exercised functions of governance and administration in order to secure the restoration or functioning of a viable domestic polity.[161] In such contexts, international administrations were forced to strike a balance between the responsibilities of international and local actors by virtue of law (e.g. relevant SC Resolutions and international obligations) rather than pragmatism. Moreover, the exercise of authority by international actors was coupled with the broader

---

[157] See also below Part II, Chapter 6.   [158] See below Part II, Chapter 6.
[159] See Hannum, *Autonomy, Sovereignty and Self-Determination*, at 379.
[160] See Ydit, *Internationalised Territories*, at 232, at 238–44.
[161] The establishment of UN missions in Libya and East Timor, however, is at least partly related to the settlement of inter-state disputes.

ambition of constructing a normative order. Traditional functions of dispute-settlement were thus replaced by or combined with managerial tasks of governance and administration (e.g. active problem-solving).

1.4.2.2. Realism, rationalism and cosmopolitanism

The practice of international territorial administration is shaped by the tensions between two major traditions of thought in contemporary international law: legal realism and cosmopolitan impulses.[162]

The realist tradition of international relations is founded upon the premise that the international legal system is primarily shaped by the power politics of competing states, which seek to maximise their influence and defined national interests within the constraints imposed by the power of other states. This vision contrasts with the cosmopolitan tradition of international law which is centred on the realisation of individual and societal interests in a global community of peoples,[163] and with *Grotian* rationalism,[164] which represents a middle way between the two, by continuing to treat the state as the centre unit of politics while promoting the advancement of justice and social change on the basis of a balancing of national interests.[165]

The view that the conduct of international relations reflects the patterns of a *Hobbesian* anarchy is today largely overcome by the growing regulation and institutionalisation of international law. However, a tension exists between cosmopolitanist approaches and intermediate responses that seek to temper emancipatory cosmopolitanism by the continuing need for state-action and inter-state power configuration.[166] The intellectual roots of cosmopolitanism were deeply shaped by the ideals of the

---

[162] See generally on traditions of thought in international relations Hedley Bull, *The Anarchical Society* (1977); Benedict Kingsbury and Adam Roberts, *Introduction: Grotian Thought in International Relations*, in Hugo Grotius and International Relations (Hedley Bull *et al.* eds., 1990), 51–64; Marin Wight, *International Theory: The Three Traditions* (Gabriele Wight & Brian Porter, eds., 1991).

[163] For a modern account of cosmopolitan theory, see Daniele Archibugi, *Immanuel Kant, Cosmopolitan Law and Peace*, European Journal of International Relations, Vol. 1 (1995), 429; David Held, *Democracy and the Global Order: From the Modern State to Cosmopolitan Governance* (1995), 271; Steve Charnovitz, *WTO Cosmopolitics*, NYU Journal of International Law and Politics, Vol. 34 (2002), 299.

[164] See Hersch Lauterpacht, *The "Grotian Tradition" in International Law*, British Yearbook of International Law, Vol. 23 (1946), 1; Martin Wight, *An Anatomy of International Thought*, Revue of International Studies, Vol. 13 (1987), 221; Benedict Kingsbury, *A Grotian Tradition of Theory and Practice?: Grotius, Law and Moral Scepticism in the Thought of Hedley Bull*, Quinnipiac Law Review, Vol. 17 (1997), 3.

[165] See Charles Covell, *Kant and the Law of Peace* (1998), at 144.

[166] See Kingsbury, *International Legal Order*, at 282.

Enlightenment,[167] and, in particular, the writings of *Kant*. The particularity of *Kant's* vision of international relations is that it was not focused on the relations between states, but on the relationship among human beings in a greater community of mankind. In his celebrated essay, "Perpetual Peace", *Kant* elaborated a normative basis for cosmopolitics by sketching the idea of a global civil society[168] and of a cosmopolitan law[169] that he regarded as the legal framework for the intercourse of human beings and states in an ideal universal state that extended to embrace all mankind.[170]

Contemporary theorists have taken up the *Kantian*-universalist tradition by embedding international law itself in an international society of societies[171] or by advocating a cosmopolitan model of democracy through the "opening of international governmental organisations to public scrutiny and the democratisation of international functional bodies"[172] or the development of a global public sphere of deliberative democracy, structured rules of participation and reasoned discourse.[173]

But the basic premise of cosmopolitanism, namely the ambition to construct a global order from the perspective of the individual human

---

[167] Earlier traces of cosmopolitanism can be found in the Stoic philosophy of the 4th century BC. See Charnovitz, *WTO Cosmopolitics*, at 301.

[168] See Immanuel Kant, *Perpetual Peace* (1927), Third Definitive Article for Perpetual Peace: "Thus the human race can gradually be brought closer and closer to a constitution establishing world citizenship." Kant granted a minimum of judicial recognition to each individual as a member, or citizen, of a world community. See James Bohman, *The Public Spheres of the World Citizen*, in Perpetual Peace: Essays on Kant's Cosmopolitan Ideal (James Bohman and Matthias Lutz-Bachmann eds., 1997), at 179, 181.

[169] Kant defines *ius cosmopoliticum* as the "constitution conforming to the law of world citizenship, so far as men and states are considered as a universal state of men, in their external mutual relationships". See Kant, *Perpetual Peace*, Section II, Note 3.

[170] See Kant, *Perpetual Peace*, Third Definitive Article for Perpetual Peace: "Since the narrower or wider community of the peoples of the earth has developed so far that a violation of rights in one place is felt throughout the word, the idea of a law of world citizenship is no high-flown or exaggerated notion. It is a supplement to the unwritten code of the civil and international law, indispensable for the maintenance of the public human rights and hence also of perpetual peace." It is even argued that Kant's cosmopolitan law would open a channel "to interfere in the internal affairs of each state in order to protect certain basic rights". See Archibugi, *Immanuel Kant, Cosmopolitan Law and Peace*, at 430.

[171] See Philip Allot, *Eunomia: New Order for a New World* (2001).

[172] See Held, *Democracy and the Global Order*, at 272–3.

[173] See Jürgen Habermas, *Between Facts and Norms: Contributions to a Discourse Theory of Law and Democracy* (1996).

being as the most basic unit of international analysis,[174] clashes with the need to preserve statism as a means of identifying diverging national interests, and avoiding "inter-state inequalities and doubtful claims of the powerful to be custodians of universal values".[175] *Grotian* ideas on inter-state bargaining, voluntarist lawmaking[176] and the communitarisation of international actors within the framework of a society of states[177] thus remain a persuasive starting point for the conceptualisation of the current international legal order. However, they are complemented by an increased tendency to shift state-like functions to regional and global institutions, to incorporate "the state" into a multilayered framework of transnational obligations or overlapping normative orders,[178] and to replace top-down approaches to governance by a perspective from below.[179]

Both the demise of realism and the search for a balance between rationalist and cosmopolitan conceptions of international law may be traced in the chronology of international territorial administration. The first era of international territorial administration under the authority of the League was overshadowed by the power politics of the Treaty of Versailles. The terms of the peace were essentially set by a bargaining process of the victors over the rights and obligations of the vanquished. This model of inter-state bargaining made it difficult to accommodate the pursuit of national interests in the broader goal of promoting cosmopolitan or community-based objectives,[180] as rational decision-making was hampered by underlying power struggles among the victors themselves and feelings of revenge towards the vanquished. Furthermore, the realisation of national political interests was not constrained by the authority

---

[174] See Charnovitz, *WTO Cosmopolitics*, at 310. For an assessment of this approach in Kant's thinking, see Fernando R. Téson, *The Kantian Theory of International Law*, Columbia Law Review, Vol. 92 (1992), 53, at 71.

[175] See Kingsbury, *International Legal Order*, at 286.

[176] The law of nations according to Grotius was derived from *jus gentium voluntarium* (the consent and practice of states) and natural law. The former gained in popularity because it coincided with the Renaissance theory of empiricism and with the contemporary theories of state sovereignty during the seventeenth century.

[177] See Covell, *Kant and the Law of Peace*, at 144.

[178] See Andreas L. Paulus, *Die Internationale Gemeinschaft im Völkerrecht* (2001).

[179] See Derk Bienen, Volker Rittberger and Wolfgang Wagner, *Democracy in the United Nations System: Cosmopolitan and Communitarian Principles*, in Re-Imagining Political Community: Studies in Cosmopolitan Democracy (Daniele Archibugi *et al.* eds., 1998), 287, 299; Markus Krajewski, *Democratic Legitimacy and Constitutional Perspectives of WTO Law*, Journal of World Trade, Vol. 35 (2001), 167, 181.

[180] In particular, the recognition of people's rights and interests was sacrificed to the realisation of security and strategic interests.

of common legal imperatives, because of a lack of established international legal rules governing the process of peacemaking.

Similar features characterised patterns of administration after World War II. Germany and Japan were not administered under the neutral supervision of the UN, but under the authority-based framework of occupation.[181] Moreover, the Charter rules were declared inapplicable to the process of peacemaking with the "enemy" powers.[182] The effect of the enemy state clause was that "in many cases there was not even a discussion before the organs of the UN of the legality of the measures taken by the victorious States".[183]

It was mainly in the aftermath of 1945 that international practice began to move away from a statist and national-interest driven application of international territorial administration. Collective institutions such as the UN Security Council and the General Assembly took on the role of deciding whether it was appropriate to place a territory under administration. International territorial administration became a multinational undertaking, involving the affected parties and neutral actors, such as international contact groups, regional organisations and non-governmental organisations (NGOs)[184] in the process of administration. Furthermore, the emergence of a body of substantive legal rules and principles guiding the conduct of governance (human rights obligations, self-determination etc.) tempered the dominance of traditional strategies of political realism (power balances, deterrence, diplomacy etc.).

Despite these conceptual changes, the practice of international territorial administration remained attached to the tradition of *Grotian* rationalism. Most UN missions were established upon request of the parties involved or with the consent of the (former) territorial sovereign,[185] even in those cases where the Security Council could have acted solely under

---

[181] See generally Robert Y. Jennings, *Government in Commission*, British Yearbook of International Law, Vol. 23 (1946); 112, 141; Maurice E. Bathurst and John L. Simpson, *Germany and the North Atlantic Community: A Legal Survey* (1956), 41–5; Nisuke Ando, *Surrender, Occupation, and Private Property in International Law* (1991).

[182] Article 107 of the Charter exempted the victorious powers from responsibility for actions taken "as a result" of the war. This included "attempts to reorder the legal relationship between states, e.g. through peace treaties". See Georg Ress, *On Article 107*, in Charter of the United Nations (B. Simma ed., 2002), 1333, para. 5.

[183] See Ress, *On Article 107*, 1333, at para. 4.

[184] See Carsten Stahn, *NGOs and International Peacekeeping – Issues, Prospects and Lessons Learned*, Zeitschrift für Ausländisches Öffentliches Recht und Völkerrecht, Vol. 61 (2001), p. 379-401.

[185] This includes the cases of the United Mission in Libya, ONUC, UNTEA, MINURSO, UNTAC, UNTAES, UNMIK, UNTAET and UNAMA.

Chapter VII. Furthermore, the use of international territorial administration as an instrument to fill governmental vacuums has encouraged
top-down approaches, focused on the (re-)construction or maintenance
of state power through international intervention.

Nevertheless, this focus on the empowerment of "the state" is coupled
with cosmopolitan impulses. The creation of international territorial administrations has rarely been determined by a specific national or sec-
toral interest alone. Such undertakings are usually driven by a broader
global interest in the maintenance of international peace and security.
In this sense, territorial administration conforms with the cosmopolitan
concept of the promotion and enforcement of a World Law ("Weltinnen-
recht"), constituted by an objective order of norms which applies to state
and non-state actors alike and thus forms the underpinning of a global
community.[186] Many administering mandates fit, at least in part, into
the cosmopolitan tradition of realising individual's or peoples' rights in
a given polity on the basis of common libertarian standards. The aim
of rethinking public rule from the angle of private actor interests and
democratisation is mostly a long-term objective of governance missions
and is at the heart of assistance missions. Moreover, the authority assumed by international administrators is exercised by representatives of
the international community for the benefit of the population of the
administered territory.[187] These features place international territorial
administration within the cosmopolitan traditions of overcoming the
limitations of states as organs of global democracy.

2. Contents and methodology

The four issues addressed in this introduction (myths and misconceptions about international territorial administration, the internationalisation of governance, the changing conception of peacemaking and the
development of the international legal system itself) are guiding themes
of this work. They recur in different forms in the individual parts of this
book, but they do not form the sole focus of it.

---

[186] See generally Jost Delbrück, *Prospects for a "World Internal law"?: Legal Developments in a
Changing International System*, Indiana Journal of Global Legal Studies, Vol. 9 (2002),
401.
[187] This finding may be traced back to Grotius, who argued that international
institutions such as international human rights treaty bodies are trustees of a global
interest. See Kingsbury, *International Legal Order*, at 285.

Part I addresses the historical and social context of international territorial administration. It traces the genesis of international territorial administration and serves to illustrate that modern forms of UN administration bear numerous traces of earlier models of governance and administration, such as the concept of internationalisation of territories, the Mandate System, the Trusteeship System and post-War occupation.

Part II analyses the practice of international organisations in the field of territorial administration in the twentieth century. Chapters 6 to 9 provide an assessment of the rise and fall of international territorial administration in the era of the League of Nations, the post-War years, the period of decolonisation, the 1990s and the most recent past. Each analysis contains a study of the governance and/or administration framework of the principal missions undertaken in each period in time, and a brief evaluation of their merits and failings. Chapter 10 concludes this assessment with a conceptualisation of the existing practice and an analysis of the different types and functions of international territorial administration.

Part III is devoted to the legal framework of territorial administration under the UN Charter. Chapter 11 revisits *Kelsen's* theory that "the Organisation is not authorised by the Charter to exercise sovereignty over a territory, which has not the legal status of a trust territory".[188] It begins with an analysis of the legal authority of the UN to administer territories, and the corresponding obligations of the organisation in the exercise of territorial authority, before examining the functional division between different UN bodies (Security Council, General Assembly, Trusteeship Council) in the field of territorial administration. Chapter 12 takes up the discussion of UN territorial administration as a governance device. It examines different concepts of procedural and substantive legitimacy that may be invoked to justify UN governance. The analysis includes a discussion of legitimacy *qua* consent, legitimacy through accountability, legitimacy based on emergency powers, functional legitimacy (e.g. expertise, neutrality and challenges to majority rule) and participatory legitimacy.

Part IV addresses four legal problems in greater detail: the legal status of the administered territory, the status of international administering authorities, the exercise of regulatory authority and the relationship with domestic actors. Chapter 13 examines different status models of

---

[188] See Hans Kelsen, *The Law of the United Nations: A Critical Appraisal of Its Fundamental Problems* (1964; reprinted 2000), at 651.

territories under international administration and the treatment of the status question in international legal practice (legal personality, external representation). Chapter 14 analyses the status of the UN as administering power. It discusses, in particular, to what extent international administrations are subject to internal and external forms of accountability, and how the existing *status quo* could be improved in practice through institutional reform or changes in practice. Chapter 15 critically reviews the regulatory activity of international administrations, including the nature of acts of international administrations, the scope of regulatory authority and practice in specific fields (property issues, detention, independence of the judiciary and constitution-framing). Chapter 16 examines the relationship between UN bodies and local actors and the role that international territorial administration has played in the realisation of claims of self-determination and self-government.

Part V revisits the findings of earlier chapters and draws lessons from practice. Chapter 17 replies to some of the criticisms raised against international territorial administration, before examining lessons for future operations. Chapter 18 assesses the role and place of the practice of international territorial administration in the transformation of the international legal system. It identifies three concrete areas where international territorial administration requires some fresh thinking: the treatment of the principles of neutrality and non-interference, the conception of the notion of sovereignty and the theorisation of governance.

The focus of analysis undertaken in this book lies in the examination of classical problems of international law, such as legal authority, institutional issues, status questions and legal responsibility. However, legal reasoning is in many cases interwoven with historical insights and patterns of political analysis. The following chapters examine international territorial administration, therefore, from a dual perspective: as a legal technique and as a policy device.

Part I

The historical and social context of international territorial administration

Peoples of transitional territories are generally inclined to place their trust in an international body rather than in the colonial overlord or another single power

Adrian Pelt, *Libyan Independence and the United Nations* (1970)

Introduction

International territorial administration has an established tradition in international law. This type of administration emerged in the context of internationalisation at the beginning of the twentieth century and was later developed under the umbrella of UN peace-maintenance. Part I of this book traces the historical emergence of international territorial administration in international law. It describes the evolution of territorial administration within the tradition of five legal paradigms that have shaped its current form: the concept of internationalisation, the Mandate System, the Trusteeship System, the practice of occupation and the development of UN peacekeeping. The analysis of the genesis of international territorial administration is designed to serve a dual purpose: to trace the origins of international territorial administration and to distinguish it from related forms of territorial administration practiced in the nineteenth and twentieth centuries.

1. International territorial administration – a definition

There is some confusion about the definition of the concept of international territorial administration. Scholars have adopted different approaches in doctrine. Chopra defined international administration as the exercise of international civil authority over a territory – a conception that distinguishes the practice of territorial administration from the assumption of military authority by a state or a group of states.[1] Other scholars conceive international territorial administration as a subset of the larger activity of foreign territorial administration. Wilde, for example, understands this paradigm as a policy device in which an international organisation exercises rights of supervision or control in the form of "a formally constituted, locally based management structure operating with respect to a particular territorial unit".[2] This definition covers various forms of the exercise of public authority by outside actors, including the international administration of camps hosting refugees or internally displaced persons.[3] Other commentators relate territorial administration more directly to the concept of statebuilding. Caplan, for example, defines international administration as an operation "whose purpose is to facilitate the emergence of a new state, or at least to promote substantial autonomy".[4] Chesterman uses the notion of "transitional administration" to describe operations in which international entities pursue "activities such as electoral assistance, human rights and rule of law technical assistance, security sector reform and certain forms of development assistance", while "assuming some or all of the powers of the state on a temporary basis".[5] The *Handbook on United Nations Multidimensional Peaekeeping Operations* associates UN transitional administration with "authority over the legislative, executive and judicial structures in the territory or country".[6]

This short survey indicates that the notion of international territorial administration may be defined in variety of ways, encompassing different forms of administration (e.g. administration by international organisations, administration by a collectivity of states) and different levels of engagement (governance, governance assistance). It shall be defined here as the exercise of administering authority (executive, legislative or judicial authority) by an international entity for the benefit of a territory that is temporarily placed under international supervision or assistance

---

[1] See Chopra, *Peace-Maintenance*, at 37.   [2] See Wilde, *From Danzig to East Timor*, at 585.
[3] *Ibid.*, at 584.   [4] See Caplan, *A New Trusteeship*, at 13–16.
[5] See Chesterman, *You, The People*, at 5.
[6] See Department of Peacekeeping Operations, *Handbook on United Nations Multidimensional Peacekeeping Operations*, at 20.

for a communitarian purpose.[7] This definition covers different forms of administration.[8] It describes territorial arrangements under which international organisations exercise direct authority over whole or part of the public affairs of administered territories ("direct international territorial administrations"). But it may also apply to certain decentralised forms of administration, under which international or multinational institutions with independent legal personality (e.g. the Office of the High Representative in Bosnia and Herzegovina or the Coalition Provisional Authority in Iraq) exercise territorial authority on behalf of or with the approval of an international organisation ("indirect international territorial administration"). The common structural bond of these undertakings is that the authority of the administering entity is held on a fiduciary basis, namely in the interests of the population of the territory and typically for a limited period of time.[9]

2. International territorial administration and related policy institutions

Territories under international administration are sometimes compared to historical territorial arrangements, such as protectorates, protected states or condominiums.[10] The motives behind this comparison are

---

[7] Management activities such as the administration of camps are not dealt with in this book as such activities differ from the engagements examined here. In such cases, it is difficult to establish that a territory is "placed" under administration. The focus of the activity is not a territorial arrangement but the management of the needs of people. Moreover, such engagements are not aimed at replacing or shaping structures of government in the classical sense. See also Wolfrum, *International Administration in Post-Conflict Situations*, at 656, note 20. For an argument in favour of a "human rights law governance" mandate for the United Nations High Commissioner for Refugees (UNHCR) in the light of its control over refugee camps, see Ralph Wilde, *Quis Custodiet Ipsos Custodes? Why and How UNHCR Governance of "Development" Refugee Camps Should be Subject to International Human Rights Law*, Yale Human Rights and Development Law Journal, Vol. 1 (1998), 107, at 112.

[8] For a more detailed classification, see below Part II, Chapter 10.

[9] For a discussion of international administration and trusteeship, see below Part II, Chapter 10.

[10] See Thomas D. Grant, *Extending Decolonization: How the United Nations Might Have Addressed Kosovo*, Georgia Journal of International and Comparative Law, Vol. 28 (1999), 9, at 49. Gordon argues that the establishment of trusteeship administration over a territory "parallels a protected State, which by agreement relinquishes part of its sovereignty and whose relationship with the protecting State is contractual". See Gordon, *Some Legal Problems with Trusteeship*, at 345.

evident. Territories under international administration may be, and have been, subject to considerable limitations of authority and local ownership by international intervention – a factor which evokes notions of political dominance and dependency. Nevertheless, the historical analogy is weak in legal terms. International territorial administration is a related, but distinct legal concept.

2.1. Protectorates and protected states

International territorial administration is founded on a different understanding from the concepts of protectorates and protected states.[11] Protectorates are a particular form of foreign state control under which one state (the protecting state) engages to protect another state or territory in exchange for the surrender of certain powers by the protected entity.[12] These types of arrangements may be traced back to Greek and Roman history and became a popular instrument of European power politics in the nineteenth century. The term "protectorate" itself covers a great variety of relationships, ranging from veiled annexation to agency relationships. Typically, a protectorate regime was based upon a treaty arrangement, by which vulnerable states placed themselves under the "protection" of European powers.[13] The protecting state assumed complete control over the external affairs of its counterpart, which retained ownership over its internal affairs. An international protectorate may thus be defined as:

a legal relationship between two States in which the superior State is bound by an international treaty or some other legal title to lend protection to the other, subordinate State and entitled to control its foreign relations.[14]

The notion of "protected states" is a variation of the protectorate concept. It describes more specifically an arrangement of protection, under which a protected entity maintains a sufficient degree of internal control and

---

[11] Concurring Wilde, *From Danzig to East Timor*, at 602; Markus Benzing, *Midwifing a New State: The United Nations in East Timor*, Max Planck Yearbook of United Nations Law, Vol. 9 (2005), 316, at 318.

[12] See James Crawford, *Creation of States in International Law* (1979), at 187–8 and 2nd edn (2006), at 287. See generally, Alfred M. Kamanda, *A Study of the Legal Status of Protectorates in Public International Law* (1961).

[13] See Lassa Oppenheim, *International Law: A Treatise* (ed. H. Lauterpacht, 6th edn, 1947), Vol. I (Peace), at 173–8.

[14] See J. H. W. Verzijl, *International Law in Historical Perspective*, Part II (International Persons) (1969), at 416.

influence over its external affairs to preserve its legal independence as a state.[15]

Although protectorates and protected states encompass a wide range of dependency relationships, they differ in several respects from transitional administrations. Both arrangements are traditionally based on alliances between states.[16] They have a bilateral focus, which is mostly based on mutual policy interests. This distinguishes them from frameworks of international territorial administration where protection is exercised in a multilateral context.[17]

Secondly, the establishment of a protectorate relationship is typically coupled with the takeover of foreign relations power by the protecting state with a view to preventing the protected entity from communicating with other states without the permission of the protecting state.[18] This specific concentration of interest on foreign relations distinguishes protectorates from international territorial administrations, which are usually not established with the particular aim of exercising control over the international relations of the administered territory.

Thirdly, the protectorate relationship and the status of a protected state are based on a treaty between the protecting state and the protected state, by which the terms of each individual relationship are determined.[19] International territorial administrations, by contrast, are not necessarily subject to a treaty arrangement based on the consent of the parties, but may be established on the basis of other legal acts (e.g. UN resolutions, decisions by regional organisations).

Lastly, the historical context of both policy institutions differs. The creation of protectorates and protected states was mainly a self-serving means of European power politics. These arrangements were used to protect "vulnerable states" against the power of nations that took control

---

[15] See Crawford, *Creation of States*, 2nd edn (2006), at 287 and 294.

[16] See Anthony Anghie, *Finding the Peripheries: Sovereignty and Colonialism in Nineteenth-Century International Law*, Harvard International Law Journal, Vol. 40 (1999), 1, at 55.

[17] See also Crawford, *Creation of States*, 2nd edn (2006), at 285, who describes the "internationalisation of a dependent entity" as a practice which may "be seen to have prefigured the administration of territory under United Nations authority".

[18] Although the establishment of a protectorate could also encompass the exercise of control over the internal affairs of the protected state, the focus was clearly on the assumption of external control. *Ibid.*, at 418.

[19] See Permanent Court of International Justice (PCIJ), Advisory Opinion, 7 February 1923, Series B. No. 4, at 27 ("The extent of the powers of a protecting State in the territory of a protected State depends, first, upon the Treaties between the protecting State and the protecting State establishing the Protectorate.").

of their external relations.[20] The aim of international territorial administration is not entirely absolved from utilitarian considerations. In fact, it is even sometimes argued that the realisation of some of its policy goals (e.g. statebuilding) requires a certain degree of "self-interest" in order to be successful.[21] Nevertheless, there is a qualitative difference. The exercise of "protective functions" within the framework of international administration is enshrined in the overall framework of the furtherance of broader community interest, namely peace-maintenance. It is thus misleading to present engagements of this kind as modern "protectorates".[22]

2.2. Condominiums

International territorial administrations also differ from power-sharing arrangements in the form of a condominium.[23] A condominium is a governing technique, under which two or more foreign powers exercise joint sovereignty over a single piece of territory through collective intermediate organs.[24] Condominiums were typically established in situations in which two sovereign states were unable to agree on a boundary dividing territories under their jurisdiction. They differ from modern experiments in international territorial administration in two respects: their conception of governance as sovereign ownership[25] and their self-centred power-sharing structure, which stands in contrast to the fiduciary and foreign interest-related character of projects of international territorial administration.

[20] This contradiction is pointed out by Anghie, Finding the Peripheries, at 55: "The protectorate was ostensibly a means of protecting vulnerable states from 'great power politics' by entrusting those same great powers to look after the interests of these vulnerable states."

[21] See Noah Feldman, What We Owe Iraq: War and the Ethics of Nation-Building (2004). Feldman argues, inter alia, that "self-interest" is important to sustain the engagement of nationbuilding.

[22] See, however, the analogy drawn by Oeter, who describes the undertakings in Bosnia and Kosovo as the "functional equivalent" of a protectorate. See Stefan Oeter, Die internationalen "Protektorate" in Bosnien-Herzegowina und im Kosovo – Entwicklung und rechtliche Folgeprobleme der UN-Friedensregime, in Krisensicherung und Humanitärer Schutz – Crisis Management and Humanitarian Protection, Festschrift für Dieter Fleck (Horst Fischer et al. eds., 2004), 427, at 451.

[23] Historical examples are the Prusso-Belgian Condominium of Moresnet (1830–1919), the Prusso-Austrian Condominium of Schleswig-Holstein (1889) and the Anglo-American Condominium of the Canton Enderbury Islands. See generally Abdalla El Erian, Condominium and Related Situations in International Law (1952), 91–132.

[24] See Ian Brownlie, Principles of Public International Law (1979), at 59 ("a joint exercise of state power within a particular territory by means of an autonomous local administration").

[25] See also Perritt, Structures and Standards for Political Trusteeship, at 417.

2.3. Twentieth-century paradigms

International territorial administration is more closely related to three other paradigms that emerged during the twentieth century, namely the Mandate System of the League of Nations, the UN Trusteeship System and post-surrender occupation after 1945. Each of these forms of administration shares at least two basic features with regimes of international territorial administration: the transitional character of foreign rule and the fiduciary nature of administering authority. Nevertheless, all three devices differ to some extent from the cases of international administration examined in this book.

One difference between international territorial administration and administration under the Mandate System, the Trusteeship System or post-surrender occupation is that the former primarily involves independent international institutions in the process of administration instead of mediating authority through state-centred forms of administration (such as under the Mandate system and the Trusteeship System) or bestowing a single or a group of states with powers of territorial administration (such as in the case of post-surrender occupation).

Secondly, international territorial administration is conceptually linked to the institutionalisation of peacemaking – a tradition that started with the era of Versailles and was later cultivated within the ambit of UN peace-maintenance. This normative basis distinguishes international territorial administration from the more specialised devices of Mandate and Trusteeship System administration, which were mainly used as a means of furthering decolonisation.

At the same time, international territorial administration differs from the framework of occupation. Unlike occupation, international territorial administration is primarily a disinterested technique of administration, involving neutral third actors (as opposed to the parties of a conflict) in the process of administration. Moreover, international territorial administration embraces processes of statebuilding and reconstruction – a function which is difficult to reconcile with the classic objectives of occupation.

The following chapters examine these distinctions. They demonstrate that international territorial administration is an independent administering device, which differs from related policy institutions in terms of its origin and legal basis, while carrying on some of their normative heritage.

1   The concept of internationalisation

International territorial administration has its origin in the practice of internationalisation. The notion of internationalisation formally emerged as a legal concept in the nineteenth and twentieth centuries,[1] and was originally used to define situations in which the territorial sovereignty of a state over strategically important areas, such as harbour cities, outlets to the sea, rivers and canals, was limited in favour of another state or a group of states. This narrow understanding was later overtaken by the growing institutionalisation and codification of international law in the aftermath of World Wars I and II. The emergence of organisations at an international level led to the increased involvement of international institutions in the administration of common spaces or international regimes.

Today, two main forms of internationalisation can be distinguished: territorial and functional internationalisation.[2] Territorial internationalisation is a device that removes a territory from the jurisdiction of a state and places it under an international institutional framework. Functional internationalisation, on the other hand, represents a broader technique which limits the jurisdiction of states over a certain space and submits it to international supervision and control.[3]

The practice of international territorial administration is rooted in both traditions. Territorial internationalisation has set a precedent for

---

[1] See Ydit, *Internationalised Territories*, at 11.

[2] See Louis Delbez, *Le Concept d'Internationalisation*, Révue Générale de Droit International Public, Vol. 38 (1967), 5, who distinguishes "l'internationalisation au sens large (fonctionnelle)" and "l'internationalisation au sens étroit (territoriale)". See on this distinction also Wolfrum, *Internationalisation*, at 1395.

[3] The restrictions may be related to the use of a specific state territory or of an area beyond national jurisdiction, such as the seabed or outer space. See Wolfrum, *Internationalisierung Staatsfreier Räume*, at 30 *et seq.*

the most concentrated forms of international territorial administration, namely models of governance and administration in which the exercise of state-like powers by an international organisation has coincided with the removal of jurisdiction of other entities over the territory.[4]

The label of functional internationalisation, by contrast, may be attached to forms of international administration where international organisations act as partners of local authorities in the exercise of specific governing functions, without assuming separate jurisdiction over the territory.[5]

1. Territorial internationalisation

International territorial administration is by its very nature most closely related to the process of territorial internationalisation. It emerged within the tradition of the internationalisation of territories – a legal concept developed in order to distinguish autonomous entities under international administration from systems of restricted sovereignty, such as protectorates, condominiums, Mandate territories and trusteeship territories.

1.1. The concept of "international(ised) territories"

The need to classify different types of territorial administration arose at the beginning of the twentieth century when the League of Nations began to institutionalise the practice of establishing autonomous territories with a special international status and legal personality. These entities, mostly called "Free Cities" or "Free Territories", did not fit into the category of condominiums,[6] nor were they formally placed under the Mandates System, or under protectorate status.[7]

Scholars have used several notions in order to categorise this phenomenon.[8] The most comprehensive study on the subject was conducted by Ydit, who dedicated an entire monograph to what he referred to as "internationalised territories".[9] Summing up the practice between

[4] Wolfrum, *Internationalisation*, at 1395.
[5] For a survey of the practice, see Jarat Chopra, *Introducing Peace-Maintenance*, in Politics of Peace-Maintenance (J. Chopra ed., 1998), 1, at 13–14.
[6] Their international status was not established for the exclusive benefit of the governing powers, but as part of a multilateral framework (charter, statute, constitution) that served the interests of the international community.
[7] See Wolfrum, *Internationalisation*, at 1395.
[8] See also Brownlie, *Principles of Public International Law*, at 60. For further discussion, see below Part IV, Chapter 14.
[9] See Ydit, *Internationalised Territories*, at 22–87.

1815 and 1960,[10] *Ydit* listed over fourteen attempts and experiments of internationalisation, including such diverse cases as the Free City of Cracow,[11] the proposed internationalisation of Constantinople,[12] the International Settlement of Shanghai,[13] the Congo Free State,[14] the Island of Crete,[15] Mount Athos,[16] Spitzbergen,[17] the Free City of Danzig[18] and the proposed internationalisations of Jerusalem[19] and Trieste.[20]

1.2. The relationship between territorial internationalisation and international territorial administration

The concept of the internationalisation of territories provided the historical framework from which international territorial administration emerged. The internationalisation of territories can be seen as influencing the development of territorial administration differently over three distinct periods of time. Before the emergence of the first undertakings of international territorial administration under the Treaty of Versailles, tasks of territorial administration were essentially carried out within the context of state-based frameworks of internationalisation, under which multinational institutions exercised legislative or executive authority over territories under common control.[21] These experiments paved the way for the first exercises of international governance under the auspices of the League of Nations and the UN after World War I and World War II, which were largely shaped by the use of internationalisation as a technique of territorial dispute resolution. Finally, in the aftermath of World War II, territorial internationalisation and territorial administration evolved more systematically towards becoming comprehensive devices of conflict management.[22]

---

[10] Ydit defined internationalised territories as "populated areas established for an unlimited duration as special State entities in which supreme sovereignty is vested in (or *de facto* exercised by) a group of States or in the organised international community, b. The local element in these territories is restricted in its sovereign powers by the provisions of an International Statute (Charter, Constitution, etc.) imposed upon it by the Powers holding supreme sovereignty over the territory". See Ydit, *Internationalised Territories*, at 21.

[11] *Ibid.*, at 95.   [12] *Ibid.*, at 22.   [13] *Ibid.*, at 127.   [14] *Ibid.*, at 24.   [15] *Ibid.*, at 109.

[16] *Ibid.*, at 33.   [17] *Ibid.*, at 34.   [18] *Ibid.*, at 185.   [19] *Ibid.*, at 273.   [20] *Ibid.*, at 231.

[21] Wilde speaks of "territorial administration by representative bodies". See Wilde, *From Danzig to East Timor*, at 602–3.

[22] Ydit draws a similar conclusion, noting that the concept of territorial internationalisation developed throughout history "from an action carried out by a consortium of certain Powers into an institution which nowadays quite without exception is implemented by the organisation of the international community, the 'United Nations', through its various agencies (the General Assembly, the Security Council, the Trusteeship Council, etc)". See Ydit, *Internationalised Territories*, at 320.

1.2.1. Multinational state administration – a precedent of international territorial administration

Prior to the establishment of the League of Nations, no clear distinction existed between internationalisation through arrangements of a group of states administering an area through shared institutions and other forms of internationalisation under the authority of international organisations.[23] Territorial internationalisation occurred mostly in the form of temporary administration of territory by a group of states. It was practised in two forms: the internationalisation of cities or strategic places and occupation.

In each of these cases, a group of jointly acting states assumed regulatory or executive authority over a territory under administration. But internationalisation was mainly a self-interested device. Instead of serving a broader communitarian purpose, territorial internationalisation was used as a mechanism to safeguard the individual or collective interests of the states in charge of administration, which were either military or economic in nature.

1.2.1.1. The administration of Cracow

The first notable attempt of multinational territorial internationalisation was in 1815 in the creation of the Free City of Cracow,[24] which was established by Article 6 of the Final Declaration of the Congress of Vienna as "in perpetuity a free, independent City, strictly neutral, under the protection of Russia, Austria and Prussia".[25] This regime constituted the first example of the tradition of internationalised Free Cities or Free Territories that would again gain prominence in the case of Danzig.[26]

The history of the administration reflects the realist background of the Cracow experiment. In the initial period from 1815 to 1830,

---

[23] See Chopra, *Peace-Maintenance*, at 39–40.

[24] See generally Verzijl, *International Persons*, at 502–3; Ydit, *Internationalised Territories*, at 95–108.

[25] The City of Cracow became a special treaty-based political entity, which gradually developed from a quasi-independent territory into a jointly governed dependency of the three protecting powers. The three powers elaborated a Constitution for the Free City of Cracow on 5 May 1815 and undertook to guarantee its terms under Article VII of the Additional Tripartite Treaty between Austria, Prussia and Russia of 3 May 1815. They exercised supervisory authority over the city through a Board of Delegates of the Three Protecting Powers, which was vested with the task of monitoring the development of the public affairs of Cracow and enjoyed right conjointly to veto local legislation contravening the purpose of the strict neutrality of the city.

[26] Note, however, that some authors regard the Free City of Cracow as a "collective protectorate". See Alfred Verdross, *Völkerrecht*, 4th edn (1959), 125.

the Board of Delegates of the Three Protecting Powers[27] refrained from interfering in the internal affairs of the City. However, from 1831 onwards, internationalisation became a mechanism of oppression which led to the dissolution of the internationalised status. The three powers (ab)used their special prerogatives to severely limit local self-government.[28] They enacted a new Constitution[29] which restricted the rights of local authorities by defining violations of the public order of the Free City as a threat to neutrality[30] and by granting the Board final decision-making power over legislative disputes and the interpretation of the new Constitution.[31] This regime ended with the incorporation of Cracow into the Austrian-Hungarian Monarchy by virtue of a Treaty of 6 November 1846 between Austria, Russia and Prussia.[32]

The two subsequent experiments in internationalisation were equally guided by self-interest. They were driven mainly by strategic interests of the great European powers in specific territories. One was the Allied occupation of the Island of Crete by UK, French, Italian, Russian, German and Austrian troops from 23 March 1897 to 29 April 1899, the other the proposed ten-year internationalisation of Albania.

1.2.1.2.   The de facto governance of the Island of Crete
The *de facto* governance of Crete (23 March 1897 to 29 April 1899) marked a case of joint military occupation after intervention.[33] It followed the concerted invasion of Crete by an alliance of European powers in 1897,

---

[27] The Board derived its authority from Article IV of the Additional Tripartite Treaty between Austria, Prussia and Russia of 3 May 1815, which granted Austria, Prussia and Russia special prerogatives to ensure by any means the strict neutrality of the Free City of Cracow.

[28] See Ydit, *Internationalised Territories*, at 100–5.

[29] See the Constitution of the Free City of Cracow of 30 May 1833.

[30] Article II of the 1833 Constitution read: "Tout acte public or clandestine, toute entreprise tendant à intervenir ou à troubler l'ordre public, établi dans les états sous la domination de l'un des trois souverains protecteurs, et toute participation à des pareilles entreprises ou à des actes de cette nature est une violation manifeste de cette stricte neutralité (de Cracovie), première condition de l'existence du pays, et sera par conséquence considérée, poursuivie et punie par les autorités."

[31] See Article XXVII of the Constitution of the Free City of Cracow of 30 May 1833.

[32] The Treaty emphasised that "since Cracow had become the headquarters of a Central Organisation which called itself 'Revolutionary Government', Cracow had infringed its obligations to preserve its strict neutrality in the Polish neutral struggle ... it became the focus of treason (Herd einer Verschwörung) which extended to all Polish territory, thus undermining the very reason of its independent existence".

[33] See generally Jean S. Dutowski, *Occupation de la Créte 1897–1909* (1952), Verzijl, *International Persons*, 387–9; Ydit, *Internationalised Territories*, 109–26.

which sought to prevent the separation of the island from the Ottoman Empire and its union with Greece.[34] The European powers did not intend to govern Crete within the framework of a fully fledged internationalisation scheme.[35] However, they established a multinational occupation regime, which came close to a removal of jurisdiction.[36] Although the flag of the Sultan continued to be flown in Crete until 1913, the Ottoman government exercised no governmental powers.[37] The overall authority over the island was assumed by a "Board of Ambassadors" of the occupying powers which exercised *de facto* powers through their local consuls and military contingents in Greece on the basis of the Paris Peace Treaty of 30 March 1896[38] and the Constitutional Charter signed by the Commission of the Consuls in Crete on 1 September 1896.[39]

The European powers divided Crete into four zones of occupation (each occupied by one of the protecting powers, the UK, France, Italy and Russia, under the authority of the Council of the Four Admirals) and the "international zone" of Canea which was placed under a mixed international occupation[40] – a model of administration which foreshadowed some of the traces of the Allied occupation of Germany and Austria

---

[34] The status of Crete during this period was discussed by the PCIJ in the case concerning *Lighthouses in Crete and Samos*. See PCIJ, Ser. A/B, No. 71 (1937). The Court found that "[n]otwithstanding its autonomy, Crete had not ceased to be part of the Ottoman Empire". *Ibid.*, at 103.

[35] See Ydit, *Internationalised Territories*, at 125.

[36] Ydit speaks of a "rudimentary form of an international administration not only in the field of an allied military occupation but especially through the establishment of the 'Commission of Consuls' [of the Four Powers] at Canea". See Ydit, *Internationalised Territories*, at 125.

[37] See also the dissenting opinion by Lord Hudson in the *Lighthouses in Crete and Samos* case (1937): "[T]he government of this island was entirely in the hands of the High Commissioner and the Cretans themselves, subject in certain respects to the approval of the four European States ... If it can be said that a theoretical sovereignty remained in the Sultan ... , it was a sovereignty shorn of the last vestige of power." See PCIJ, Ser. A/B, No. 71, at 127.

[38] Article VII of the Treaty stipulated: "Chacun des puissances signataires s'engage de son côté à respecter l'indépendance et l'intégrité territoriale de l'Empire Ottoman, garantissant en commun la stricte obligation de cet engagement et considéra en conséquence tout act de nature lui porter atteinte commune une question de l'intérêt général ... "

[39] The Charter authorised the Governor General of Crete to veto legislation adopted by the local General Assembly. Article 14 of the Charter vested the Board of Ambassadors and the Commission of European Consuls in Crete with the power to check and control the implementation of the Constitution. The Constitution had no time limit.

[40] See Dutowski, *Occupation de la Crète 1897–1909*, at 78 and 99.

after World War II.[41] In its external relations, Crete acted independently of the Ottoman Empire and acceded, *inter alia*, to the Universal Postal Union and the International Telegraphic Union.[42] In 1913, the Ottoman Empire formally surrendered its residual sovereignty to the European powers.[43]

1.2.1.3. *The Albanian Control Commission*

The same European powers that intervened in Crete also assumed responsibility for the settlement of Albania after the First Balkan War (17 October 1912 to 30 May 1913). The defeat of the Ottoman Empire by Serbia, Bulgaria, Montenegro and Greece had affected the balance of power between Russia, on the one hand, and the Austro-Hungarian Empire and Germany, on the other. The proposed international government of Albania by a conglomerate of states jointly exercising full international authority over the territory[44] was largely an attempt to restore this balance. The model of internationalisation emerged as a compromise between Austro-Hungarian and German interests and the plans of the UK, France and Italy at the London Ambassadorial Conference in July 1913. The Austrian-Hungarian Empire and Germany favoured the establishment of Albania as an independent state under international supervision while Italy, France and the UK recommended international administration of the territory. The dispute ended with the adoption of a model of administration, under which Albania was declared an independent state, but placed under the guarantee of the Great Powers (Austria, France, Germany, Russia and the UK).[45]

The compromise reflected in the Organisational Statute of Albania was one of the most far-reaching attempts in internationalisation at that

---

[41] The division of the island into four administrative zones reflects the formula chosen later in the case of the post-war governance of Germany. Furthermore, the mixed administration of the international zone of Canea by the Commission of Consuls of the Four Powers may be viewed as a precedent for the quadripartite administration of Berlin and Vienna.

[42] See dissenting opinion by Lord Hudson in *Lighthouses in Crete and Samos*, Ser. A/B, No. 71, at 127.

[43] For a full discussion of the legal status of Crete between 1899 and 1913, see Crawford, *Creation of States*, 2nd edn (2006), at 354–7.

[44] See generally Ydit, *Internationalised Territories*, at 31–2.

[45] The Conference of Ambassadors adopted a Statute for the Albanian State, under which Albania was freed from Turkish sovereignty and transformed into an autonomous principality under the guarantee of the European Powers. See Articles 1 and 2 of the Statute for Albania.

time.[46] Prince William von Wied, a German national, was appointed as governor of Albania. Furthermore, an International Control Commission (in which each of the five great powers as well as Albania was represented) assumed control over the civil and financial administration of Albania. The Commission was supposed to govern Albania for a period of ten years while enjoying sweeping powers, including, *inter alia*, the authority to reorganise Albania's state organisation and all branches of the administration. However, it was able to hold only a small number of sessions between 1913 and the outbreak of World War I, which resulted in the international members of the Commission leaving Albania.[47]

1.2.1.4. The International Zone of Tangier
After 1919, the tendency to establish multinational regimes of territorial internationalisation decreased due to the establishment of the League of Nations, which took on the predominant role in territorial internationalisation. The only famous example of multilateral territorial internationalisation in the era of the League of Nations is the International Zone of Tangier (1923–57),[48] which was largely a result of power struggles between the three great naval powers of France, Spain and the UK over the port of Tangier.

Following a compromise among the three powers in 1923, the Zone of Tangier was not incorporated in the French Protectorate over Morocco, nor was it formally separated from Morocco, but was turned into a neutral and demilitarised zone. The Sultan of Morocco formally retained sovereignty over Tangier[49] and jurisdiction over the native Muslim and Jewish population was exercised through a Moroccan representative (the *Mendoub*).[50] However, the main legislative and administrative powers over the territory were generally and permanently delegated to an

---

[46] Ydit, *Internationalised Territories*, at 31.
[47] For a discussion of the creation of Albania, see also Crawford, *Creation of States*, 2nd edn (2006), at 510–12.
[48] See the Statute of the International Zone of Tangier of 18 December 1923, in League of Nations, Treaty Series, Vol. 28, 542. See generally E. Rouard de Card, *Modifications du Statut de Tanger* (1928); Stuart, *The International City of Tangier*; Ydit, *Internationalised Territories*, at 154–83.
[49] See Article 1 of the Statute of Tangier. But the powers of the Sultan were curtailed by the French protectorate over Morocco.
[50] The *Mendoub*, a Moroccan commissar, administered the native population. He was charged to ensure that local people fulfilled their responsibilities towards the international administration (tax obligations, observance of the terms of Statute etc.). He also presided over the Legislative Assembly of Tangier and promulgated laws adopted by it, in the name of the Sultan. See Articles 29 and 34 of the Tangier Statute.

international administration that was principally in control of the signatory powers of the Tangier Statute.[51] The permanent nature of the delegation of authority to the international administration made it, in fact, comparable to a removal of jurisdiction.

The model of internationalisation of Tangier deviated from earlier examples of territorial internationalisation because it coupled military and strategic interests with economic ambitions, which culminated in a regime under which a broadly representative group of states (including not only France, Spain and the UK, but also Italy, the US, Belgium, the Netherlands and Portugal)[52] exercised responsibilities over the territory. However, it remained embedded within the realm of collective, but predominantly self-interested, multinational administration that characterised the early period of territorial internationalisation.[53]

1.2.1.5. Conclusion

The record of these early experiences in territorial internationalisation is mixed. None of the regimes of multinational administration succeeded in the long term. However, some administrations managed to bring peace and stability on an interim basis. The Free City model succeeded as an interim solution to reconcile the divergent interests of the Austrian, Russian and Polish populations. Similarly, the joint occupation of the Island of Crete marked a successful case of temporary occupation.[54] The international regime of the Zone of Tangier managed to replace Moroccan jurisdiction for several decades[55] with the international authority exercised by the signatory powers of the Statute of Tangier.[56]

---

[51] The signatories of the Tangier Statute constituted the International Control Commission which supervised the observance of the provisions of the Tangier Statute. The Control Commission was composed of the consuls of the signatory powers, and assumed the most significant executive powers.

[52] See for example the international composition of the Legislative Assembly, as reported by Ydit, *Internationalised Territories*, at 166.

[53] See also Chopra, *Peace-Maintenance*, at 39.

[54] The occupation endured until Prince George of Greece was appointed as General Governor of Crete and was entrusted with governmental authority under the Constitution of Crete on 29 April 1899.

[55] In World War II, the Zone of Tangier was occupied by Spain and incorporated into Spanish Morocco in 1940. However, the Tangier regime was revived at the end of the war by the Tangier Conference and continued to govern the status of the territory in a slightly modified form ("the Statute of 1945") until Tangiers's incorporation into Morocco by the Fedalla Protocol and the Charter of Tangier, which abolished the international status of the Zone of Tangier in 1956.

[56] See Delbez, *Le concept d'Internationalisation*, at 23 ("internationalisation intégrale"). See also Wolfrum, *Internationalisation*, 1395–6 ("example of territorial internationalization").

Only the international government of Albania failed as an experiment in administration, partly because of the outbreak of World War I and partly because the diplomacy and cooperation-based structure of the Albanian Control Commission was ill-equipped to address the political rivalries on the ground.[57]

1.2.2. The post-war eras – the naissance of international territorial administration as a device of territorial dispute resolution

In the post-war eras, the focus of internationalisation changed. Territorial internationalisation developed progressively into a mechanism designed for the pursuit of communitarian interests. Multilateral institutions like the League of Nations and the UN became involved in the process of internationalisation. Their engagement differed from the earlier practice in multinational administration because they performed tasks of internationalisation a priori as neutral actors, pursuing collective rather than individual interests. The technique of internationalisation, however, continued to be shaped by the political circumstances of the time. The assumption of authority by international organisations remained dominated by the strategic interests of the victorious powers and the overall objective of post-war dispute resolution – two features that characterise the first series of experiments of international territorial administration under the auspices of the League of Nations and the UN.

1.2.2.1. Versailles

The Treaty of Versailles started a new tradition of communitarian internationalisation. However, the context in which international authority was exercised still closely followed the tradition of the preservation of

---

[57] The Great Powers proved unable to agree on the sending of international troops to Albania, despite the urgent need to secure law and order through military presence in the territory. Furthermore, the territory still lacked unity: there was no uniform law; even the boundaries of the territory were still in dispute. Doubts about the viability of the Commission were expressed by Francis Bowes Sayre in 1918. He noted that: "[i]f there was ever a need for a strong, one-man government, it was in Albania in 1913. Instead of that there was set up a Commission of consuls, foreigners, and outsiders, all but one ignorant even of the Albanian language, representing sharply conflicting policies and interests. There could be but one result, no matter how excellent the Commission … It may show that an international Commission is not the happiest form for the fusing and unification of a disunited people." See Francis Bowes Sayre, *Experiments in International Administration* (1944), at 60, 62.

power structures and victors' interests. Territorial internationalisation was, in particular, used as a tool to rearrange the balance of power between Germany and its neighbours. It served mainly as a device to settle the territorial status of those territories that were of strategic interest in Europe's geopolitical architecture.

The best examples are the League's administrations of Danzig[58] and the Saar Basin.[59] Both territories were placed under the jurisdiction of the League by the Treaty of Versailles for two reasons: their special geographic location and the fact that the populations of these two areas were almost entirely German. Danzig was long disputed between East Prussia and Poland. The decision to place it under the League's guarantee under an internationalised framework originated as a result of the security interests of Poland and the strategic importance of Danzig as a harbour city with access to the Baltic sea. Similar reasons led to the internationalisation of the Saar Territory, the status of which had been disputed between Germany and France since the 1870 war.[60]

These strategic considerations coincided with a need to protect the interests of the inhabitants of the territory. Originally, the full transfer of Danzig and the Saar to Poland and France was considered as a means of reparation.[61] However, this transfer was difficult to reconcile with the interests of the German population of both territories. The option of internationalisation was the only practical compromise to resolve this conflict in accordance with the principles of self-determination and minority protection. Similar proposals[62] were

---

[58] The limitations of Polish sovereignty over Danzig justified the city's qualification as an internationalised territory. Danzig had its own nationality. Furthermore, according to the PCIJ: "[w]ith regard to Poland, the Danzig Constitution ... was, 'the Constitution of a foreign State'." See PICJ, *Treatment of Polish Nationals in the Danzig Territory*, Ser. A/B, No. 44 (1932), at 23–4. Concurring Crawford, *Creation of States*, 2nd edn (2006), at 238–40.

[59] For a qualification of the Saar Basin (1920–35) as an international(ised) territory, see Wolfrum, *Internationalisierung Staatsfreier Räume*, at 15; Delbez, *Le Concept d'Internationalisation*, at 19. See also Ydit, *Internationalised Territories*, at 45, who qualifies the Saar Territory as an "internationalised territory under the sovereignty of the LON", but does not address it, as it was not permanently internationalised.

[60] See Frank M. Russell, *The International Government of the Saar* (1926), at 116. For the French claims, see *ibid.*, at 121.

[61] See Knudson, *History of the League of Nations*, at 178.

[62] These proposals provided for the internationalisation of the city of Fiume on a similar basis as Danzig and the application of the "Saar formula" to Zara and the Dalmatian Coast. However, the proposals were finally dropped because alternative solutions were

made in relation to the Adriatic harbour of Fiume[63] and the Dalmatian coast.[64]

1.2.2.2. The aftermath of World War II

The first attempts at internationalisation after World War II under the auspices of the UN were equally shaped by a strong focus on power configurations and neutralisation. This is particularly evident in the case of the proposed internationalisation of Trieste,[65] which was mainly guided by the ambition of post-war dispute resolution. The territory of Trieste, similar to Danzig, had strategic importance as an ancient city and port. It was disputed between Italy and Yugoslavia. Italy claimed the territory because of its overwhelmingly Italian population. However, Yugoslavia also had an interest in Trieste because of its ties to central Eastern Europe and its economic importance. The proposal by France of 29 June 1946, suggesting the internationalisation of the city under the authority of the Security Council, constituted an attempt to break the impasse caused by the diverging geographical, ethnical, economic and historical arguments raised by Italy and Yugoslavia.

The UN proposal for the territorial internationalisation of Jerusalem as a *corpus separatum* was equally driven by the objective of neutralisation. It followed the footprints of the examples of Danzig and Trieste. After the establishment of the Jewish state on 14 May 1948, both Israel and Jordan claimed to have title over Jerusalem. Israel proclaimed the territory of Jerusalem (excluding the Old City) as an integral part of the newly founded state of Israel and appointed a military governor to the city. Similar steps were taken by Jordan, which declared the Arab

---

found. Italy and the Serb-Croat Slovene State thereupon reached a solution in their boundary treaty of Rapallo of 12 November 1920, pursuant to which Fiume was transformed into a non-internationalised Free State. See Articles 4 and 5 of the Treaty of Rapallo of 11 November 1920. On the background, see Verzijl, *International Persons*, at 503–4. The commune of Zara (Dalmatia) was recognised as forming part of Italy. See Article 2 of the Treaty of Rapallo.

[63] The proposal provided for the establishment of a League of Nations Commission, which would "have all powers of government within and relating to the area, including the appointment and dismissal of all functionaries and the creation of such administrative or representative bodies as it deems necessary". See the US Draft Proposal on the status of Fiume, in Ydit, *Internationalised Territories*, 53, at 54.

[64] The US proposal for Dalmatia noted that a League of Nations Commission should assume "all the powers over this territory and its inhabitants hitherto belonging to the Austrian Government". See Ydit, *Internationalised Territories*, at 55.

[65] For a survey, see Crawford, *Creation of States*, 2nd edn (2006), at 235–6.

section of Palestine as annexed territory under its occupation. The text of the proposed draft Statute for an international regime in Jerusalem[66] sought to overcome the territorial dispute through the model of internationalisation, which prohibited the declaration of Jerusalem as the capital of either a Jewish or an Arab state and prevented both sides from taking any steps which could alter the demographic *equilibrium* in the area.

1.2.3. The institutionalisation of territorial administration as a device of conflict management

International practice in the aftermath of the post-war period brought changes on two levels: territorial administration under the authority of a group of states developed from a mainstream device into a mechanism of exception; and the technique of internationalisation evolved more systematically from an instrument of territorial dispute resolution into a mechanism of conflict management serving broader goals of peacemaking rather than the interests of a selected group of states.

The first shift in focus was the result of the increasing institutionalisation of international law following World War II. Territorial internationalisation fell, to a greater extent, into the domain of international organisations, involving different actors such as the UN,[67] the EU (Mostar)[68] or the International Sea-Bed Authority[69] in processes of internationalisation. The phenomenon of multinational state administration, on the other hand, became an exceptional device used to address specific challenges of territorial internationalisation, such as the Allied

---

[66] See the Proposal for a Statute of the City of Jerusalem of 4 April 1950, drafted by the UN Trusteeship Council, reprinted in Lapidoth, *The Jerusalem Question and Its Resolution: Selected Documents*, at 117.

[67] See Wolfrum, *Internationalisation*, at 1396.

[68] The European Union Administration of Mostar (EUAM) turned Mostar into an area under European administration. For further analysis, see below Part II, Chapter 9.

[69] The seabed was an area outside national or any other jurisdiction before its internationalisation by Part XI of the United Nations Convention on the Law of the Sea (UNCLOS). The Convention limited the jurisdictional powers of states with respect to deep seabed activities. Furthermore, it charged the Sea-Bed Authority with the administration, control and execution of deep seabed mining, similar powers to those exercisable by a sovereign. See Article 156 of UNCLOS. The regime on deep seabed mining may therefore be considered as a case of territorial internationalisation. See Wolfrum, *Internationalisierung Staatsfreier Räume*, at 716.

administration of Germany after 1945[70] or the multi-headed administra-tion of Nauru[71] under the UN Trusteeship System.[72]

This change in the practice of internationalisation went hand in hand with a shift in function. In the post-1945 era, territorial internationalisa-tion was not only used as an instrument of neutralising or demilitarising areas of strategic importance, but also as a method of crisis management designed to end and prevent conflicts. An early precedent is the League's engagement in Leticia.[73] In this case, the League did not intervene as an organ of dispute settlement in the post-conflict phase but shaped the outcome of the peace process, by removing the city for a period of one year from the administrative control of Columbia and Peru, in order to end the hostilities between the two countries and facilitate a negotiated solution.[74]

The use of internationalisation as a crisis management technique resurfaced over half a century later again in the context of UN peace-maintenance. The notion of internationalisation was not officially in-voked in this context. However, UN missions with exclusive governing authority over the territories, such as the operations in Eastern Slavo-nia, Kosovo and East Timor come within this ambit[75] because they

[70] See below Part I, Chapter 4.
[71] See the Trusteeship Agreement for the Territory of Nauru, approved by the General Assembly on 1 November 1947, UNTS, Vol. 10, at 4. Article 2 of the Agreement provided that: "The Governments of Australia, New Zealand and the United Kingdom ... are hereby designated as the joint Authority which will exercise the administration of the Territory."
[72] Traces of internationalisation by a group of jointly acting states may also be found in the Antarctic Treaty regime, which was established to serve not only the interests of the contracting parties but also the common interests of the international community in the areas of demilitarisation and environmental protection. See Wolfrum, *Internationalisierung Staatsfreier Räume*, at 710.
[73] This intervention may be regarded as a precedent for a new tradition of internationalisation, because it involved the League in the actual management of a dispute. See below Part II, Chapter 7.
[74] During this period, a League of Nations Commission assumed plenary administration over the city. The Commission governed Leticia "in the name of the Government of Columbia" and took command of Columbian troops. See Article 2 of the Agreement relating to the Procedure for Putting into Effect the Recommendations Proposed by the Council of the League of Nations, 25 May 1933, Peru-Columbia, LNTS Vol. 138, 253 (Geneva Agreement). See also Hans Wehberg, *Theory and Practice of International Policing* (1935), at 17; Wilde, *From Danzig to East Timor*, at 588.
[75] Note that all three missions were not only created to solve a dispute between two or more states, but also involved the engagement of international administrators in tasks of statebuilding, reconstruction and the reconciliation of conflicts caused by the identity of certain local actors.

temporarily removed the respective territories from the domain of national jurisdiction and placed them under international administration in order to serve a broader community goal, namely the maintenance of international peace and security.[76]

Finally, international territorial administration and territorial internationalisation coincided in two other cases, which do not fit exclusively within the rubrics of neutralisation and dispute settlement, namely the UN administrations of West Irian and Namibia (under the UN Council for Namibia).[77] In both cases, a territorial dispute (between the Netherlands and Indonesia in the case of West Irian, and between the UN and South Africa in the case of Namibia) gave rise to the deployment of the operations. But the subsequent administration combined the objective of dispute resolution with a broader statebuilding and development mandate.

2. Functional internationalisation

The practice of international territorial administration is not only linked to the concept of territorial internationalisation, but also rooted in the tradition of functional internationalisation – a device which merely limits a state's territorial jurisdiction over an entity by an international institutional framework that serves specific community interests, such as the administration of common resources or spaces.[78]

2.1. Patterns of functional internationalisation

The most traditional form of functional internationalisation is the international administration of waterways through river commissions.[79] The understanding that waterways are common spaces which require international coordination and cooperation is quite old. It may be traced back to Grotius, who viewed waterways as a form of common patrimony

---

[76] The community interest may, in particular, be derived from the establishment of the missions under Chapter VII of the UN Charter.

[77] The UN authorities exercised plenary administering authority over the respective territories in both situations. A full case for internationalisation may be made in the context of UNTEA. However, a special terminology (de jure internationalisation) must be used to describe the specific situation of Namibia, because the UN was prevented from exercising any de facto authority over the territory due to South Africa's continued (illegal) presence in Namibia.

[78] See Wolfrum, Internationalisation, at 1397; Delbez, Le Concept d'Internationalisation, at 34 ("Il y a encore internationalisation quand l'organe commun ne dispose que de quelques droits déterminés, l'Etat territorial ayant pour le surplus conservé des droits attachés à la souveraineté") .

[79] See generally Richard R. Baxter, The Law of International Waterways (1964).

shared by all human beings.[80] The most classical example is the International Danube Commission, which administered the lower Danube River from 1856 to 1940, exercising independent legislative and administrative powers over the navigational use of the river, including the authority to levy charges, effect public works and regulate river traffic.[81] Later, the idea of functional internationalisation was applied to spaces which fall outside national jurisdiction, such as Spitzbergen (1910–14),[82] Antarctica[83] and Outer Space.[84]

However, functional internationalisation is not limited to the administration of natural resources or international commons. The concept also plays an important role in the context of the internationalisation of territories under domestic jurisdiction.

2.2. The functional internationalisation of territories under domestic jurisdiction

Territories may be said to be functionally internationalised in situations in which one or several specific functions of domestic jurisdiction are exercised by an international institution, while the territorial state maintains overall authority over that entity. Various examples of this kind have occurred in the history of international law. They complement the practice of territorial internationalisation.

2.2.1. The International Settlement of Shanghai

An early example of multinational functional internationalisation was the concessions regime of the International Settlement of Shanghai

---

[80] See Grotius, *De Jure Belli Ac Pacis*, Book III, Chapter II (De his quae hominibus communiter competent) XII, XIII.

[81] See generally, Henri Hajnal, *Le Droit du Danube International* (1929), 24. The Commission was established by Article 16 of the Paris Peace Treaty (1856). It was composed of delegates from the UK, France, Austria, Prussia, Sardinia and Turkey.

[82] Spitzbergen was considered *terra nullius* before the discovery of coal deposits in 1900. In 1912, Sweden, Norway and Russia adopted a draft Convention for the internationalisation of Spitzbergen. Furthermore, an international Commission was established to administer the territory. But the draft Convention was never ratified due to the outbreak of World War I. After the war, Spitzbergen was placed under Norwegian sovereignty by the Treaty of Paris of 9 February 1920. See Ydit, *Internationalised Territories*, at 34–9.

[83] The Antarctica Treaty regime did not lead to a renunciation of the territorial claims of the contracting parties, nor did it change the *status quo* of Antarctica in this regard. See Article IV of the Washington Treaty. For a denial of the claim of Antarctica's territorial internationalisation, see Wolfrum, *Internationalisierung Staatsfreier Räume*, at 94–5; Ydit, *Internationalised Territories*, at 77.

[84] See Wolfrum, *Internationalisierung Staatsfreier Räume*, at 269.

(1845–1944),[85] which gave personal extraterritorial privileges to foreigners residing in Shanghai. The settlement did not formally qualify as a case of international territorial administration, as it was exclusively conducted by a group of states representing a "wider but by no means universal set of interests".[86] But it may be viewed as a case of functional internationalisation for economic purposes, and as a precedent for international territorial administration. It led to the creation of a mixed international-national administration structure in Shanghai, which complemented Chinese jurisdiction and sovereignty over the city through a special international institutional regime safeguarding the interests of foreigners through a Municipal Council, a Consular Body and a Mixed Court.[87]

2.2.2.   The internationalisation of Memel

The first example of functional internationalisation under the authority of the League of Nations was the partial internationalisation of the Memel Territory after World War I. Memelland was established as an autonomous entity under the sovereignty of Lithuania in 1924,[88] after Germany renounced its sovereignty over the territory in Article 99 of the Treaty of Versailles. The territory was not internationalised in the same sense as the Free City of Danzig. It was essentially a Lithuanian province without international personality or influence over the conduct of Lithuania's foreign relations.[89] But traces of internationalisation were, in particular, reflected on two levels: the League's judicial competence over disputes concerning Memel's status[90] and the internationalisation

---

[85] For a full account, see Jean Escarra, *Le Régime des Concessions Étrangères en Chine*, Vol. 27 (1929-II), 1–146.

[86] See Chopra, *Peace-Maintenance*, at 39.

[87] For a detailed description, see Ydit, *Internationalised Territories*, at 134–9.

[88] See Article 2 of the Convention Concerning the Territory of Memel dated 8 May 1924, according to which Memel shall constitute "under the sovereigty of Lithuania, a unit enjoying legislative, judicial, administrative and financial autonomy". The Convention is reprinted in LNTS, Vol. 29, at 87.

[89] The Governor of Memel was appointed by Lithuania and enjoyed the power to veto local legislation. The PCIJ addressed the status of Memel in the case concerning the *Interpretation of the Statute of the Memel Territory*. In this case, the court equated Lithuania's rights concerning Memel to those of a sovereign state by applying the *Lotus* presumption in favour of Lithuania. See PCIJ, *Interpretation of the Statute of the Memel Territory*, Ser. A/B, No. 49 (1932), 313, at 314.

[90] Article 17 of the Memel Statute (concluded between Lithuania, the UK, France, Italy and Japan) allowed League members to take disputes concerning the Statute to the PCIJ, noting that any difference in opinion between Lithuania and the League Council

of the Memel Harbour Board.[91] These special features turned Memel, at least partially, into a functionally internationalised territory.[92]

2.2.3. The proposed "functional internationalisation" of Jerusalem

After World War II, the concept of functional internationalisation received broader support in international practice. The idea of functional internationalisation was formally raised in the debates over the administration of Jerusalem.[93] Sweden and the Netherlands tabled a proposal which replaced the ambitious model of territorial internationalisation with a more modest formula, limiting international intervention to the appointment of a UN High Commissioner who would exercise supervisory powers over issues concerning the Holy Places and interests of the international community in Jerusalem.[94] Sweden's efforts culminated in a draft resolution in the General Assembly of 5 December 1950 concerning the future status of Jerusalem[95] which left "jurisdiction and control of each part of the Jerusalem area" in the hands of the governments administering the city,[96] but empowered a UN-appointed High Commissioner to "modify, defer or suspend such laws, ordinances, regulations and administrative acts ... which [would] in his opinion impair the protection of and free access to Holy Places" and to "make such orders or regulations for the maintenance of public security as he deems

should be regarded as having the character of an international dispute under Article 13 of the League Covenant. Such a reference was made in the case concerning the *Interpretation of the Statute of the Memel Territory.*

[91] Annex II of the Memel Statute declared the Port of Memel as a "Port of international concern", to be administered by a special Harbour Board composed of one member appointed by Lithuania, one member appointed by Memel and one member appointed by the League. All changes concerning the port had to be approved by the Council of the League. Finally, the prerogatives of the League were protected by Article 15 of the Memel Statute which stated that the "rights of sovereignty over the Memel Territory or the exercise of such rights may not be transferred without the consent of the High Contracting Parties".

[92] See also Brownlie, *Principles of Public International Law*, at 60; Ydit, *Internationalised Territories*, at 50 ("international character of the Memel Territory").

[93] For a full discussion, see below Part II, Chapter 6.

[94] This proposal met the interests of Israel, which was willing to accept a functional internationalisation approach restricting the powers of the UN to the supervision of the Holy Places. See Ydit, *Internationalised Territories*, at 303–4.

[95] See Draft Resolution tabled by Sweden in the General Assembly concerning the future status of Jerusalem, 5 December 1950, UN Doc. A/AC.38.L.68, reprinted in Jerusalem Question and its Resolution, at 149.

[96] See Article IX of the Sweden's Draft Resolution.

necessary to ensure the protection of and free access to Holy Places".[97] However, the proposal was not adopted,[98] as the majority of states in the General Assembly called for a return to the model of territorial internationalisation as envisaged originally in the *corpus separatum* Statute of the Trusteeship Council.[99]

2.2.4.   Modern examples of functional internationalisation

The peacemaking practice of the UN revived the practice of the functional internationalisation of territories. It led, in particular, to the establishment of modern co-governance missions, in which international institutions exercise selected functions of domestic jurisdiction in cooperation with national institutions. These operations may be qualified as contemporary forms of functional internationalisation, dedicated to the accomplishment of specific tasks of post-conflict reconstruction. Two examples deserve to be mentioned, in particular: the cases of Cambodia and Bosnia-Herzegovina.[100]

2.2.4.1.   *Cambodia*

The first example is the power-sharing arrangement of the Cambodian Peace Accords, by which the four factions agreed to form the Supreme National Council (SNC) as the "unique legitimate body and source of authority in which ... the sovereignty, independence and unity of Cambodia ... [would be] embodied", but delegated to the UN Transitional Authority in Cambodia "all powers necessary to ensure the implementation" of the Comprehensive Peace Settlement.[101] This delegation incorporated an internationalisation of the Cambodian legal system for a

---

[97] See Article X of Sweden's Draft Resolution. The governments of the states administering Jerusalem were required to abide by requests of the UN High Commissioner. However, in cases of dispute, the matter would be referred for final decision to an arbitral tribunal. See Article IX (3) of the Resolution.

[98] See Ydit, *Internationalised Territories*, at 306.

[99] See Trusteeship Council, Proposal for a Statute for the City of Jerusalem, 4 April 1950.

[100] These cases differ from the situation of Cyprus which was placed under international guarantee. For a discussion of the Cyprian case, see Thomas D. Grant, *International Guaranteed Constitutive Order, Cyprus and Bosnia as Predicates for a New Non-traditional Actor in the Society of States*, Journal of Transnational Law and Policy, Vol. 8 (1998), 1; Crawford, *Creation of States*, 2nd edn (2006), 241–4.

[101] See Article 6 of the Agreement on the Political Settlement of the Cambodia Conflict. UNTAC was only required to comply with the SNC's "advice" if (1) the SNC adopted a unanimous decision, or if its President, Prince Sihanouk, spoke on behalf of the Council; and if (2) the advice was consistent with the objectives of the Agreement "as determined by the chief of UNTAC". If the SNC was unable to reach a decision, the UN Special Representative retained the prerogative to act as he wished. For further discussion, see below Part II, Chapter 8.

transitional period of eighteen months, driven by the overall goal of creating a peaceful and stable environment for the organisation of free and fair elections.[102]

2.2.4.2. Bosnia and Herzegovina

The second example of contemporary functional internationalisation is the internationalisation of Bosnia and Herzegovina's state system under the Dayton Accords.[103] The Dayton Peace Accords incorporated international structures into the domestic legal order. International institutions were established to serve two main purposes: to maintain the multi-ethnic constitutional structure of the country,[104] and to realise effective human rights protection.[105] The task of safeguarding of the complex federalist structure of Bosnia was conferred on two separate organs: the internationalised Constitutional Court;[106] and the Office of the High Representative (OHR),[107] which was mandated to act as the "final authority in theatre regarding interpretation of this Agreement

---

[102] See Korhonen, Gras and Creutz, *Internatiional Post-Conflict Situations*, at 233.

[103] For an analysis of the internationalisation of Bosnia, see Carsten Stahn, *Die Verfassungsrechtliche Pflicht zur Gleichstellung der drei Ethnischen Volksgruppen in den Bosnischen Teilrepubliken – Neue Hoffnung für das Friedensmodell von Dayton*, Zeitschrift für ausländisches öffentliches Recht und Völkerrecht, Vol. 60 (2000), 663, at 668–72. See also below Part II, Chapter 8.

[104] The institutionalisation of ethnicity is one of the main features of the Bosnian constitutional system. This is clearly reflected in the Preamble of the Bosnian Constitution, which defines Bosnians, Croats and Serbs as "constituent peoples" of Bosnia and Herzegovina (BiH), while "others" and "citizens" are mentioned only in passing. The emphasis on ethnicity has resulted in a constitutional structure that incorporates ethnic checks and balances into the decision-making structure of the national institutions.

[105] The institutionalisation of ethnicity in the Bosnian Constitution is countered by extensive human rights protections and explicit rejections of any discrimination on ethnic grounds. The dichotomy between individual rights and group rights was addressed in a decision of the Bosnian Constitutional Court of 1 July 2000, in which the Court held that the territorial delimitation of BiH into two entities does not constitute "a constitutional legitimation for ethnic domination, national homogenisation or a right to uphold the effects of ethnic cleansing". See Constitutional Court of Bosnia and Herzegovina, Decision U 5/98, Third Partial Decision, 1 July 2000. See below Part II, Chapter 9.

[106] The Court is composed of three international judges and six domestic judges (two Bosnians, two Serbs and two Croats). See Article of Annex IV to the Dayton Agreement. See generally on the Court, Louis Favoreu, *La Cour Constitutionelle de Bosnie-Herzégovine*, Mélanges P. Gélard (1999), 237.

[107] Article V of Annex 10 of the Dayton Peace Accord. The OHR derives its authority from three different sources: the parties to the Dayton Peace Accords, the international Peace Implementation Council and the Security Council.

on the Civilian Interpretation of the Peace Settlement".[108] Furthermore, a variety of international institutions (Human Rights Chamber, Ombudsperson Institution, Property Claims Commission) were charged with the guarantee and implementation of the numerous human rights provisions applicable in Bosnia and Herzegovina. These bodies transformed Bosnia and Herzegovina into an internationalised state.

3.   Non-internationalised forms of territorial administration

Although the practice of international territorial administration formally emerged in the framework of internationalisation, it is not identical to this tradition. International territorial assistance encompasses an additional group of international public authority which cannot be brought within the ambit of territorial or functional internationalisation: service-providing and assistance missions.

This practice has early precedents in the era of the League of Nations. The League played a role in assisting in the resolution of disputes that the Allied powers were unable to settle after the Treaty of Versailles. Between 1920 and 1921, the League intervened actively in the establishment of a special regime for Upper Silesia.[109] Moreover, the League

---

[108] See Laurent Pech, *La garantie internationale de la Constitution de Bosnie-Herzégovine*, Revue Française de Droit Constitutionnel, Vol. 42 (2000), 421, at 431–5.

[109] Article 88 of the Treaty of Versailles charged the Allied powers with the conduct of a plebiscite to terminate the German-Polish border dispute over the area. The plebiscite was held between 10 February and 13 March 1920 and ended with a 60 per cent majority in favour of Germany. In view of this result, the League decided to divide the territory. See Report by Viscount Ishii on the Request Addressed by the Supreme Council of the Principal Allied Powers to the Council of the League of Nations to Find a Solution of the Question of Upper Silesia, adopted by the Council on August 29, 1921, LNOJ 2 (1921), 1220–6. However, the socio-economic problems arising from the drawing of the frontier line led to the conclusion of a Convention concerning Upper Silesia of 15 March 1922 between Germany and Poland, which provided for a special regime for Upper Silesia, promoting economic integration in the area (through free cross-border traffic, free importation of coal producers and special interstate railways) and the protection of the cultural and linguistic rights of the Polish/German minorities. The League assumed an active role in the implementation of the Convention. It assisted in the execution of the partition and appointed the head of an arbitral panel designed to resolve private disputes. The League was also empowered to decide upon complaints regarding the treatment of minorities. Minorities were authorised to lodge a petition to the League Council against their own state authorities. This right was frequently exercised, especially by the German minority, and gave rise to decisions of the League Council and the Permanent Court of International Justice. See PCIJ, Advisory Opinion, *Access to German Minority Schools in Upper Silesia*, Series A/B (1931) No. 40, 4. See also Walters, *History of the League of Nations*, at 406–8, 447–8.

assumed an assistance function with respect to the disputed territories of Vilna[110] and Mosul,[111] and it elaborated plans for a deployment in Alexandretta (Syria),[112] involving the League in minority protection and the organisation of local elections.[113]

Later UN practice has institutionalised this approach through various missions of governance assistance, such as the engagements in Libya, Eritrea, Namibia (UNTAG), Western Sahara (MINURSO), Liberia (UNMIL) or Democratic Republic of Congo (MONUC).

These various missions are less prominent than the large-scale governance undertakings of the League of Nations or the UN. Nevertheless, they play an important systemic function in the history of territorial administration.[114] They represent assistance-based forms of crisis management that strike a balance between transformative interventionism and the preservation of local ownership and self-governance.

4. Conclusion

Internationalisation and international territorial administration are related, although not identical concepts. Most experiments in international territorial administration may either be viewed as cases of territorial internationalisation (Danzig, Saar, Leticia, Trieste, Jerusalem, West Irian, Eastern Slavonia, Kosovo, East Timor) or functional internationalisation (Memel, Cambodia). However, international territorial

---

[110] The status of the city of Vilna remained unresolved at Versailles. The League intervened to find a solution to the conflict between Poland and Lithuania. It recommended "public expression of opinion ... under the auspices and supervision of the League of Nations". See the Dispute between Lithuania and Poland, Report by M. Hymans, Acting President of the Council of the League of Nations, 28 October, 1920, Procès-Verbal of the Tenth Session of the Council, held in Brussels, 20 October 1920 to 28 October 1920, Annex 127, 281, 283 (1920). However, as Poland and Lithuania refused to cooperate, despite detailed planning by the League, the League then ended its engagement.

[111] The League sent a commission of inquiry to Mosul, an oil-rich territory which was the subject of a dispute between Iraq (the UK) and Turkey, to consider the feasibility of a plebiscite to draw a frontier. But the Commission rejected the idea of a plebiscite. The border was finally determined by an agreement between the UK and Turkey. See Ratner, *The New UN Peacekeeping*, 96–7.

[112] These plans never materialised, because France (Syria's mandatory power) and Turkey conducted their own elections which led to the integration of the territory into Turkey.

[113] See League of Nations, Question of Alexandretta and Antioch, 27 January and 29 May 1937, LNOJ 18 (1937), 118–23, 329–33.

[114] See also Chopra, *Peace-Maintenance*, at 40.

administration incorporates the additional and less intrusive category of governance assistance.

Moreover, one may observe that the concepts of internationalisation and territorial administration have undergone a transformation throughout time. The practice of the administration of territories by international organisations emerged in the context of the demilitarisation, neutralisation or internationalisation of historically disputed or strategically important areas after World War I, which led to the first great era of territorial administration under the auspices of the League of Nations, and later to the proposed internationalisations of Jerusalem and Trieste. In the aftermath of the post-war era, internationalisation was increasingly used as a tool of conflict management and liberalisation in the practice of the UN.[115]

---

[115] For further details, see below Part II, Chapters 7 and 8.

2 The Mandate System of the League of Nations

The Mandate System of the League of Nations is the second policy institution that influenced the development of territorial administration.[1] The Mandate System and the League's practice in territorial administration are formally two different devices. Article 22 of the League Covenant did not institute a direct form of international administration involving the League itself in the conduct of governance. Rather, the mandated territories were administered by mandatory states who acted on behalf of the League. The role of the League was restricted to the exercise of supervisory functions over the mandatories whose rights and obligations were enumerated in mandate agreements. These structural differences distinguish (indirect) administration under the Mandate System from (direct) administration by the League itself in the cases of Danzig, the Saar or Leticia. But the institutional practice of the Mandate System is nevertheless of interest for the analysis of the administration of territories by the UN, because both paradigms share some conceptual parallels.

One of the main objectives of the Mandate System was to promote the "well-being and development" of dependent people and to prevent their exploitation. This idea in reflected in Article 22 of the Covenant,

---

[1] Numerous scholarly works have been dedicated to this subject. See Wright, *Mandates Under the League of Nations*; Norman Bentwich, *The Mandates System* (1930); League of Nations, *The Mandates System, Origin – Principles – Application* (1945); Hall, *Mandates, Dependencies and Trusteeships*; Chowdhuri, *International Mandates*. For an account of specific mandates, see Isaak I. Dore, *The International Mandate System and Namibia* (1985); Christopher G. Weeramantry, *Nauru: Environmental Damage under International Trusteeship* (1992), 41–122. For a recent account, see Nele Matz, *Civilization and the Mandate System under the League of Nations as Origin of Trusteeship*, Max Planck Yearbook of United Nations Law, Vol. 9 (2005), 47–95.

which tied the exercise of administering powers to the legal concept of a "sacred trust of civilisation",[2] while subjecting Mandatory powers to certain reporting duties *vis-à-vis* the League.[3] The fiduciary nature of authority is not only a characteristic of the Mandate System, but a cardinal principle of subsequent experiments in territorial administration.[4]

Moreover, Mandate administration raised many of the theoretical and practical issues that arise in a slightly different form today, including status questions, accountability issues and problems concerning the relationship between the administration and local actors. These factors make it worthwhile to revisit the Mandate System in the context of the genesis of international territorial administration.[5]

1. Origin

The Mandate System was created in order to administer those colonies that had been under the control of two of the great powers defeated in World War I, Germany and the Ottoman Empire. The UK, France, Russia, Japan and Italy had originally planned to annex these colonies.[6] However, the plans conflicted with the interests of the only non-colonial power, the US. US President Wilson suggested the idea of pursuing a trust for these territories,[7] an idea which can be traced back to the General Act of the Berlin West Africa Conference (1884–5), which had promoted

---

[2] The concept of "sacred trust" can be traced back to Joseph Chamberlain, a British Colonial Secretary, who noted in 1998: "We, in our colonial policy, as fast we acquire new territories and develop it ... as trustees of civilisation for the commerce of the world. We offer in all these markets over which our flag floats the same opportunities ... that we offer to our own subjects and upon the same terms." See Chowdhuri, *International Mandates*, at 14. For the background to the concept of "sacred trust", see Toussaint, *Trusteeship System*, at 5–10.

[3] See Article 22, paras. 7 and 9.

[4] Note that both mandatory authority and modern UN governance are exercised on behalf of a broader collectivity, which may be referred to as the international community. See with respect to the Mandate System Sharon Korman, *Right of Conquest* (1996), at 142: "[The victorious powers] would be the bearers on behalf of the international community as a whole".

[5] For a recent assessment, see also Antony Anghie, *Colonialism and the Birth of International Institutions: Sovereignty, Economy, and the Mandate System of the League of Nations*, NYU Journal of International Law & Politics, Vol. 34 (2002), 513, at 622–3.

[6] See Dietrich Rauschning, *Mandates*, in Encyclopedia of Public International Law, Vol. III (1997), at 280.

[7] President Wilson sought a solution on the basis of the principles of non-annexation and self-determination, which he had postulated in his Fourteen Principles of 8 January 1914 and his Four Principles of 11 February 1918.

the idea that colonial rule over a foreign people must be exercised for the benefit of the local population.[8]

Concrete proposals for the design of the Mandate System were made by South African General Smuts in his pamphlet "The League of Nations: A Practical Suggestion", published on 16 December 1918.[9] Smuts proposed the application of the concept of international Mandates to all territories formerly belonging to the Russian, Ottoman and Austro-Hungarian Empires, who were "incapable of or deficient in power of self-government" and required "nursing towards political and economic independence".[10] He suggested the introduction of a system of administration by Mandatory powers subject "to the supervision and ultimate control of the League",[11] together with the adoption of the principles of self-determination, international accountability, non-militarisation and non-annexation.[12] Wilson endorsed this plan.[13]

This solution was a pragmatic compromise. It deviated from the practice of post-war annexation and conquest, by charging the League with the supervision of the Mandate administration and linking the authority of the Mandatory powers to the welfare and interests of the administered people, in order to prevent the exploitation of dependent territories. On the other hand, the Mandate System served as surrogate of conquest, because it granted the victorious powers the substance of control over the newly acquired territories.[14]

---

[8] The Berlin Conference of 1885 promoted the protection of native people through self-imposed restrictions by the European Powers. See Articles 6 and 9 of the General Act of the Berlin West Africa Conference. Article 9 provided that "each of the Powers binds itself to employ all the means at its disposal for putting an end to this [slave] trade and for punishing those who engage in it". But no colonial power was willing to place the supervision of dependent territories under international control. For a critique, see Chowdhuri, *International Mandates*, at 21: "To entrust the protection of native interest to individual States without supervision was 'a grave blunder as it left the natives completely at the mercy of individual governments and irresponsible trading Companies'."

[9] See Jan Smuts, *The League of Nations: A Practical Suggestion* (1918), in David H. Miller, *The Drafting of the Covenant* (1928), Vol. II, 23.

[10] See Smuts, *The League of Nations*, at 26. Smuts deliberately excluded the German colonies, which he considered suitable for annexation.

[11] *Ibid.*, at 31.   [12] *Ibid.*, at 29, 33.

[13] Note, however, that Wilson suggested its application not to the European territories, but to the Ottoman colonies in the Middle East and to the German territories in Africa and the Pacific. See Anghie, *Colonialism and the Birth of International Institutions*, at 523. He finally gained the acceptance of the other powers to apply "the principles of non-annexation, international accountability and consent of the governed in the Turkish dependencies". See Chowdhuri, *International Mandates*, at 47.

[14] See the critique by Korman, *Right of Conquest*, at 143; Inis L. Claude, *Swords into Plowshares: The Problems and Progress of International Organization* (1964), 323.

The division of the Mandates was carried out by the Principal Allied and Associated Powers (France, Italy, Japan, the UK and the US) themselves. The victors distinguished three different groups, according to their degree of advancement: (1) the communities formerly belonging to the Turkish Empire (A-Mandates), which comprised Palestine, Syria and Iraq; (2) central African peoples (B-Mandates); and (3) other territories, such as South West Africa and certain South Pacific Islands (C-Mandates).[15]

A-Mandates, which were deemed to be quasi-independent nations, were to be supported through "administrative advice and assistance by a Mandatory until such a time as they are able to stand alone".[16] B-Mandates were placed under full administrative control of the Mandatory powers.[17] C-Mandates were to "be best administered under the laws of Mandatory as integral portions of its territory".[18]

2. The choice in favour of indirect administration

The drafting history of Article 22 of the League Covenant reveals that some controversy existed among the Allies themselves as to the appropriate form of Mandate administration. One of the early drafts of the League Covenant prepared by President Wilson provided for the possibility of direct international administration by the League. His "first Paris draft" of 10 January 1919 granted the League complete power of supervision and intended to entrust the task of administration to "some single State or organised agency" or to the League itself.[19] This position was

---

[15] The territories were assigned by the Supreme Council of the Allied Powers within one year after the adoption of the League Covenant. The C-Mandates were distributed first. German South West Africa (Namibia) was entrusted to South Africa; the Island of Nauru to the British Empire; the Pacific Islands to New Zealand; and New Guinea to Australia. The B-Mandates were allocated among the UK, Belgium and France. German East Africa (Tanganyika) was administered by the UK; Ruanda-Urundi by Belgium; whereas the future of Togoland was to be jointly determined by the UK and France. The most advanced territories, the A-Mandates, were assigned last. The UK assumed authority over Iraq and Palestine. Syria-Lebanon was entrusted to France. See Chowdhuri, *International Mandates*, at 72.

[16] See Article 22, para. 4.   [17] See Article 22, para. 5.   [18] See Article 22, para. 6.

[19] The proposal read: "Any authority, control, or administration which may be necessary in respect of these peoples or territories other than their own self-determined and self-organized autonomy shall be the exclusive function of and shall be vested in the League of Nations and exercised or undertaken by or on behalf of it. It shall be lawful for the League of Nations to delegate its authority, control or administration of any such people or territory to some single State or organized agency which it may designate and appoint as its agent or mandatory." See Wilson's Second Draft or First Paris Draft, 10 January 919, in David H. Miller, *The Drafting of the Covenant* (1928), Vol. II, 88.

supported by Germany, which pleaded for international administration, because it hoped to exercise Mandatory powers upon delegation of authority by the League.[20] Most other nations, however, opposed the idea of direct League administration, invoking either the failure of experiments in international government in the past, or relying on pragmatic reasons in favour of national administration.

General Smuts rejected direct international administration on the ground that "the only successful administration of undeveloped or subject peoples ha[d] been carried on by states with long experience for this purpose, and staffs whose training and singleness of mind fit them for so difficult and special a task".[21] Smuts expressed concern about the idea of joint international administration undertaken by a group of states, noting that "[t]he administering personnel taken from different nations do not work smoothly or loyally together; the inhabitants of the territory are either confused or if they are sufficiently developed, make use of these differences by playing one set of nations off against the other".[22] Similar criticism about the efficiency of international or conjoint action in administrative matters was voiced by France, which noted that such efforts had usually failed in the past.[23] When Wilson's draft plan was finally discussed at the Paris Conference, Lloyd George dropped the option of direct international administration by the League, noting that "it was generally" agreed that former enemy colonies could not be directly internationally administered.[24] Instead, the principle of single mandatory administration "on behalf of the League" was adopted.

Overall, the decision not to place Mandates under direct international administration at the Paris Conference seems to have been based on three guiding factors. The Allies were reluctant to confer greater powers on the League, as they wanted to maintain unimpeded control over the

---

[20] See Jacob Stoyanovski, *La Théorie Générale des Mandats Internationaux* (1925), 8–10.

[21] See Smuts, *The League of Nations*, at 30.   [22] See Smuts, *The League of Nations*, at 30.

[23] See Chowdhuri, *International Mandates*, at 56–7. This pessimism was, *inter alia*, provoked by the failure of the International Control Commission for Albania. It was shared in doctrine. See Evelyn B. Cromer, *Modern Egypt* (1916), 303–4: "[The experiment of administrative internationalism] cannot be said to be encouraging to those who believe in the efficacy of international action in administrative matters. What has been proved is that international institutions possess admirable negative qualities. They are formidable checks to all action, and the reason why they are is that, when any other action is proposed, objections of one sort or another generally occur to some member of the international body."

[24] See Chowdhuri, *International Mandates*, at 56.

territories occupied or assigned to them.[25] This was later implicitly confirmed by Francis B. Sayre, the first President of the Trusteeship Council, who noted that the lack of popularity of direct forms of international administration was not so much the result of "any fundamental impossibilities in international government" but was rather a consequence of the unwillingness of states to grant international bodies any real power of control.[26]

Secondly, the choice of different models of administrations for the Mandate territories, on the one hand, and the Saar Basin and Danzig, on the other, may be explained by the difference in size. It was an audacious decision in the Treaty of Versailles to place two limited parts of former German territory under the direct control of the League. But to grant the League administering authority over Mandates would have placed entire countries such as Syria (including Lebanon) or Iraq under international control. Such a task would have clearly exceeded the capacities of the League.[27]

Finally, one must note that the League could not look back at any administrative record in the cases of Danzig, the Saar, Leticia and Memel when decisions were being made at Versailles. It was only after these experiences that the idea of direct international administration began to gain ground and broader acceptance in the international legal system.

3. Challenges of the Mandate System – a modern retrospection

The Mandate System added a new dimension to the League's role and function. It involved the League in the supervision of different stages of development and self-government of people. The administering functions exercised by the League in the context of direct administration under the Treaty of Versailles encompassed "classical" tasks of governance, supervision or maintenance of law and order. Mandate

---

[25] This understanding is reflected in a statement at the Eighteenth Session of the League of Nations Council with special reference to Palestine noting that "a mandate was a self-imposed limitation by the conquerors on the sovereignty which they exercised over the territory". In the general interests of mankind, the Allied and Associated Powers had imposed this limitation upon themselves, and had asked the League to assist them in seeing that this general policy was carried out". See Statement of Mr Balfour, League of Nations Official Journal (LNOJ), Vol. 3 (1922), 547.

[26] See Francis B. Sayre, *Experiments in International Administration* (1944), 147–50.

[27] Similar arguments were advanced by Smuts, *League of Nations*, at 30.

administration, by contrast, had a genuinely dynamic nature, as it charged the Mandatory powers with the promotion of the "development" and gradual self-government of peoples.[28] This obligation entailed the furtherance of native representation in governance, and in the case of the non-European territories of the former Ottoman Empire (the A-Mandates) an entitlement to independence.[29] The dynamic character of Mandate administration marked an innovation, because it entrusted the Mandatory powers and the League with a task of "creating sovereignty" under the framework of an internationally supervised regime.[30]

3.1. Governance issues

The process of promoting self-government caused certain governance problems. The machinery of the Mandate System was entrenched in the paternalistic tradition of imperial thinking.[31] It was guided by the belief that Western models of law and behaviour should be applied to non-European societies under "a new universalising mission in international law".[32] The exercise of administering authority was conceived as a form of "tutelage of backward people", aimed at the elevation of other races and cultures to the European standard. This understanding was reflected in the wording of Article 22 of the League Covenant which specified that "tutelage" of such peoples should be entrusted to "advanced nations who by reason of their resources, their experiences or their geographical position can best undertake this responsibility".[33] The fundamental assumption at the Paris Conference was that the peoples of the Mandated territories should adapt to the democratic way of life as it existed in the Western hemisphere, based on principles such as the liberty of person, free speech, economic

---

[28] See also Arthur J. R. Groom, *The Trusteeship Council: A Successful Demise*, in The United Nations at the Millennium (P. Taylor and A. J. R. Groom eds., 2000), 142, at 146.

[29] See Article 22, para. 4 of the Covenant: "Certain communities formerly belonging to the Turkish Empire have reached a stage of development where existence as independent nations can be provisionally recognized subject to the rendering of administrative advice and assistance by a Mandatory until such time as they are able to stand alone."

[30] See also Anghie, *Colonialism and the Birth of International Institutions*, at 544–5.

[31] For an excellent recent assessment, see Antony Anghie, *Imperialism, Sovereignty and the Making of International Law* (2005).

[32] See Anghie, *Colonialism and the Birth of International Institutions*, at 566. See also Wright, *Mandates under the League of Nations*, at 15–23.

[33] See Article 22, para. 2 of the Covenant.

liberalism and the rule of law.[34] However, these ambitions clashed with local cultures and traditions of non-European societies and the parallel need to promote the gradual self-government of people under tutelage. The tension between these two imperatives triggered numerous problems.

The Permanent Mandate Commission, which monitored the progress of Mandate people,[35] was required to formulate policies concerning the "well being and development" of people, the protection of natives and the promotion of self-government. The supervision by the Commission was strongly focused on the assessment of "economic development" of mandate territories. This preoccupation involved the Commission in the evaluation of social and labour policies. Mandatory powers relied on colonial techniques such as Lugard's idea of "indirect rule" (namely to "develop resources through the agency of the natives under European guidance, and not by direct ownership of those tropical lands"[36]), in order to enhance efficiency and economic development. Local procedures and practices (such as rituals, forced labour, tribal structures) could be a hindrance to economic progress. Indirect rule served to reconcile native procedures and institutions with economic progress and was endorsed by the Commission. A good example is the reform of the labour structure in the territory of Tanganyika, where the Mandatory power agreed with local chiefs to abolish the practices of "tribute" and "forced labour" in order to facilitate work on infrastructure projects. The Mandatory power introduced a new poll tax system under which native chiefs were paid to collect revenues for the administration. This reliance on native structures helped to create conditions for free labour and economic development and was subsequently endorsed by the

---

[34] See Hall, *Mandates, Dependencies and Trusteeships*, at 128. See also the catalogue of "General Conditions Which must be Fulfilled before the Mandates Regime Can be brought to an End in respect of a Country Placed under that Regime", in League of Nations, *The Mandates System*, at 118–20. The Mandates Commission suggested that a new state should ensure and guarantee: "(a) The effective protection of racial, linguistic and religious minorities... ; (c) The interests of foreigners in judicial, civil and criminal cases ... (d) Freedom of conscience and public worship and the free exercise of the religious, educational and medical activities of all denominations, subject to such measures as may be indispensable for the maintenance of public order ... "

[35] The Permament Mandates Commission was established to "receive and examine the annual reports of the Mandatories, and to advise the Council on all matters relating to the observance of the mandates". See Article 22, para. 9 of the Covenant.

[36] See Lugard, *The Dual Mandate*, at 506.

Commission.[37] In other cases, the Commission monitored labour policies in Mandate territories, in order to develop strategies to make native labour more efficient.[38]

A similar methodology was applied in the context of other aspects of social policy. Notions of self-determination and democratic governance were far less developed at that time, and certainly were not perceived as binding legal prerequisites for the conduct of foreign state administration. But pragmatism[39] and colonial wisdom led to respect of and deference to certain local rules. One of the first questions that Mandatory powers encountered was to determine to what extent they were obliged to respect native customs and institutions. The League never managed to reach full consensus on this question.[40] However, some basic principles are revealed in the reports of the Permanent Mandate Commission.[41] The Commission considered "the development of a sound administration of justice as a first task of the mandatory", but recognised at the same time that "native custom and conceptions of justice cannot be ignored".[42] It was decided "that certain native customs which conflict with humanitarian ideals should be abolished" (e.g. cannibalism), while others (e.g. "polygamy with an average of two wives") should be "tolerated as a vice capable of gradual correction".[43] Furthermore, it was understood that "a certain number of ancient customs, in which native life is founded" should be preserved "in the interests of peace of the territory"[44] and that domestic laws could be maintained, unless they were incompatible with modern standards of civilisation.

Other difficulties arose in the context of the treatment of local institutions. Article 22 of the League Covenant charged the Mandatory powers

---

[37] See also Anghie, *Globalization and its Discontents: International Institutions and the Colonial Origins of Law and Development*, www.nyulawglobal.org/documents/Anthony_Anghie.pdf, at 17.

[38] See Permanent Mandates Commission, 6th Sess. (1925), 47 *et seq.*

[39] See generally on the tradition of pragmatism in international law, David Kennedy, *The Disciplines of International Law and Policy*, Leiden Journal of International Law, Vol. 12 (1999), 9.

[40] See Wright, *Mandates under the League of Nations*, at 242.

[41] The Commission acted as a supervisory institution. For a recent account of the practice of the Permanent Mandate Commission, see Veronique Dimier, *On Good Colonial Government: Lessons from the League of Nations*, Global Society, Vol. 18, No. 3 (2004), 279–98.

[42] *Ibid.*, at 242.

[43] See Permanent Mandates Commission, *The Welfare and Development of the Natives in Mandated Territories*, Annexes to the Minutes of the Third Session, LON Doc. A.19 (Annexes) 1923 VI, at 282 (1923).

[44] *Ibid.*, at 283.

with the promotion of the well-being of the administered territories. However, it was not clear who was to decide what welfare meant. The members of the Permanent Mandates Commission were divided over the question of whether traditional native authorities should be retained in the political system of mandated territories. Some Commission members took the view that "the least perfect European administration was one hundred times better than a purely native administration", suggesting that "a European administrator ... could not have the welfare of the natives *as conceived by the natives themselves*, for its sole object".[45] Others argued that "the mandatory should endeavour to render the people able to stand alone",[46] coupling respect for local ownership with the conviction that some territories are "unsuited for European settlement".[47] The Commission adopted a compromise solution, recommending the maintenance of native structures, while allowing periods of transition from local rule which would be superseded by international governance structures acting in cooperation with advisory native Councils.[48] However, the degree of self-government remained dependent on the category of the mandate.[49]

This practice reflected the spirit of the time. Self-government was not yet recognised as an absolute standard, but viewed as part of a broader mission of civilisation that was determined by the goodwill of Western nations. The League quietly set some minimum standards of best practice and civilised behaviour concerning labour, land titles, education and

[45] See Permanent Mandates Commission, *The Interpretation of that Part of Article 22 of the Covenant Which Relates to the Well-Being and Development of the Peoples of Mandated Territories*, LON Doc. C.648 M.237 1925 VI, at 197.

[46] See response by Frederick Lugard to Andrade's statement, *Ibid.*, at 206.

[47] See Lugard, *The Dual Mandate*, at 506.

[48] See Anghie, *Colonialism and the Birth of International Institution*, at 596–7.

[49] Native representation or participation in government was required in A-Mandates (Iraq, Syria, Palestine), which were deemed to have reached a stage of development whereby their "existence as independent nations [could] be provisionally recognized". See Article 22(3) of the League Covenant. Mandatory powers of B-Mandates (German territories in Central Africa) and C-Mandates (South West Africa, Pacific territories), in contrast, enjoyed full power of administration and legislation. Mandatories of B-Mandates were responsible for the maintenance of order and good government, economic and social development and the prohibition of slave trade, traffic of arms and liquor. C-Mandates were regarded as "best administered under the laws of the Mandatory as integral portions of its territory". See Article 22 (6) of the League Covenant. If mechanisms of self-government were promoted in B- and C-Mandates, they mainly took the form of native advisory councils. See Wright, *Mandates under the League of Nations*, at 248.

health.[50] Violations of these standards could ultimately be sanctioned by condemnation.

3.2. Accountability issues

The accountability system of the Mandate regime was weak. It departed from the precedents set by colonialism by placing mandatory administration under institutionalised rules and even judicial control.[51] However, it was shaped by the resistance of Mandatory powers vis-à-vis independent international control and by internal disagreements over an ideal role for the League, which oscillated between supervision and cooperation. The greatest weakness of the accountability system was that it failed to provide a mechanism under which native institutions could independently trigger the responsibility of the Mandatory power. Supervision was essentially mediated through the administering state and could take three different forms.

The main mechanism was a reporting system under Article 22 of the Covenant, which obliged Mandatory powers to submit an annual report to the League Council that was then examined by the Permanent Mandates Commission. The Commission introduced a questionnaire with a detailed list of issues to be dealt with in annual reports by Mandatory powers.[52] It itself defined its task as "one of supervision and cooperation". It noted:

It is [the Commission's] duty, when carefully examining the reports of the mandatory Powers, to determine how far the principles of the Covenant and of the mandates have been truly applied in the administration of the different territories. But at the same time, it is its duty to do the utmost that lies in its power to assist the mandatory Governments in carrying out the important and difficult tasks which they are accomplishing on behalf of the League of Nations, and in which they render reports to the Council.[53]

---

[50] See Wright, *Mandates under the League of Nations*, at 249–59.

[51] The lack of international supervision was one of the most criticised shortcomings of the Berlin and Brussels Conferences of 1885 and 1890. See Norman D. Harris, *Intervention and Colonization in Africa* (1914), 33.

[52] The headings included: Status of the Territory; Status of the Native Inhabitants of the Territory; International Relations; General Administration; Public Finance; Direct Taxes; Indirect Taxes; Trade Statistics; Judicial Organization; Police; Defence of the Territory; Arms and Ammunition; Social, Moral and Material Condition of the Natives; Conditions and Regulation of Labour; Liberty of Conscience and Worship; Education; Public Health; Land Tenure; Forests; Mines; and Population.

[53] See Wright, *Mandates under the League of Nations*, at 196.

The Commission exercised its authority "less as a judge from whom critical pronouncements are expected", but more than a "collaborator".[54] It limited its supervision to legal comments in the form of recommendations, which were not binding on the Mandatories, but could acquire authoritative form through a resolution of the League's Council.[55] The Commission focused its comments on four main areas. It criticised any law or treaty adopted by the Mandatories that appeared to imply an assumption of sovereignty over the mandated territory. It ensured that the mandatory would not profit from the mandated territory through its administration.[56] It safeguarded the interests of the natives by censoring policies of oppression, and supervising land, labour, health and education standards.[57] Finally, the Commission monitored the mandatory's obligation to further economic development of the territory.[58] However, within this system, there was no direct channel of communication between representatives of the native population and League itself, which weakened the objectivity of the mechanism.

The second instrument of control was judicial supervision.[59] Each mandate agreement contained a provision which provided that "any dispute ... between the Mandatory and another member of the League of Nations relating to the interpretation or the application of the provisions of the mandate" could be submitted to the PCIJ. Judicial review was therefore equally mediated through the state. However, it played only a limited role in practice. The Permanent Court exercised its jurisdiction concerning mandates twice, regarding the Mandate of Palestine[60] and

---

[54] See League of Nations, Council, Min., sess. XIV, 178.
[55] This procedure was rarely used. One instance in which it was employed was the definition of terms concerning liquor traffic. See Wright, *Mandates under the League of Nations*, at 225.
[56] The Mandatory power was obliged to keep separate budgets and to hold land and property only as a trustee.
[57] See generally on standards of administration in different areas, Wright, *Mandates under the League of Nations*, at 219.
[58] *Ibid.*, at 214.
[59] See generally Nathan Feinberg, *La Juridiction de la Cour Permanente de Justice Internationale dans le Système des Mandats* (1930).
[60] This was the only contentious case. A Greek national, Mavrommatis, had been deprived of certain concessions granted by Turkey in Palestine in 1914 for the supply of water to Jerusalem. The Court upheld the contention of Mavrommatis, but dismissed his claim for lost profits. See PCIJ, Ser. A, No. 5, *The Mavrommatis Jerusalem Concessions*, 26 March 1925, 31–51.

the Mandate of Iraq.[61] In some cases, domestic courts considered the mandate to be directly enforceable in the mandated territory and examined the compatibility of domestic legal acts with the provisions of the mandate.[62] However, the scope of judicial review remained limited in such cases. The fulfilment of the mandate was considered to be a political rather than a legal responsibility. Courts were thus inclined to grant domestic authority broad discretion in the interpretation of the provisions of a mandate.[63]

The strongest form of supervision was instituted by the Permanent Mandates Commission *ex post*. It was a petition system, modelled on petition practice under UK colonial rule.[64] Its creation alone was an invention. Neither the League's rules on the Mandates Commission nor the Mandate treaties made any provision for the acceptance of petitions. The Commission attempted to establish a system by which native inhabitants could directly transmit complaints to the Commission itself. However, this suggestion met with opposition from the Mandatory powers, who claimed that such a mechanism would turn the Commission into "a tribunal controlling the administration of the area".[65] The Council of the League subsequently adopted a system, which permitted the Commission to receive petitions from inhabitants of the mandate territories, but only through the Mandatory, which was required to forward all petitions within six months, along with its observations.[66]

---

[61] The case was an advisory Opinion on the Mosul frontier between Iraq and Turkey. The Court observed that the decision of the League Council with respect to the border was binding on the parties. See PCIJ, *Interpretation of article 3, paragraph 2, of the Treaty of Lausanne*, Ser. B, No. 12, 21 November 1925, 33.

[62] The most famous case is the Urtas Springs case, in which the Judicial Committee of the Privy Council reviewed a decision of the Supreme Court of Palestine which had declared an Ordinance by the High Commissioner for Palestine incompatible with Article 2 of the Palestine Mandate (providing that the UK should be responsible for "safeguarding the civil and religious rights of the inhabitants of Palestine"). See Privy Council, *Jerusalem-Jaffa District Governor and another* v. *Suleiman Murra and Others*, LR (1926), AC 321. For a survey of this and other related cases concerning the Palestine Mandate, see ILC, Law of Treaties, Replies from Governments to Questionnaires, UN. Doc. A/CN.4/19, Yearbook of the ILC 1950, Vol. II, at 212–13.

[63] See also Quincy Wright, *Some Recent Cases on the Status of Mandated Areas*, American Journal of International Law, Vol. 20 (1926), 768, at 770.

[64] The initiative for the petition system came from the UK, whose colonial practice allowed a petition to the UK Secretary of State through the local governor. See Wright, *Mandates under the League of Nations*, at 174.

[65] See League of Nations, Records of the Third League Assembly, Plenary Meetings, XII, 20 September 1922, Vol. I, 163–6.

[66] See League of Nations, LNOJ IV Yr., March 1923, 200, at 298–300.

Overall, the right to petition represented an important tool of supervision. It provided a means of redress for individual and group grievances. Furthermore, it marked an additional source of information and power for the Commission. Petitions were, in particular, filed by minorities of different races in A-Mandates and by German settlers.[67] However, the efficiency of the system and its aptitude to safeguard individual rights and liberties were compromised by two shortcomings. The Commission was not vested with a right to hear petitioners in person, as it was feared that "such a procedure ... involv[ing] the hearing at the same time of a representative of the Mandatory Power ... would transform the Commission into a court of law".[68] Moreover, the Commission did not formally enjoy the right to undertake on-site inspections in the mandated territory. The absence of these powers rendered the petition system a rather toothless device.

3.3. Status questions

The particular status of administered territories under the Mandate System has given rise to two other conceptual problems which continue to be relevant to international territorial administration today: the issue of sovereignty and the question of the nature of administering authority.

3.3.1. The location of sovereignty

The issue of sovereignty over mandated territories was one of the most disputed questions among jurists at the time.[69] The construction of the Mandate System departed from the positivist idea of absolute state sovereignty which prevailed in nineteenth-century international law and was increasingly questioned in the inter-war period.[70] The question of who held sovereignty over mandated territories was vividly debated. Some authors attributed sovereignty to such different entities as the Principal Allied Powers, the Mandatory powers, the inhabitants

---

[67] See Hall, *Mandates, Dependencies and Trusteeships*, at 198.   [68] *Ibid.*, at 203.

[69] Wright speaks of "not less than ten theories" and "among fifty juridical discussions". See Wright, *Mandates under the League of Nations*, at 319. For a recent discussion, see Crawford, *Creation of States*, 2nd edn (2006), at 568–73.

[70] Scholars like Alvarez or Hudson claimed that international law is not merely a science governing inter-state relations, but a body of law in the service of the lives and needs of society. See Manley Hudson, *The Prospect for International Law in the Twentieth-Century*, Cornell Law Quarterly, Vol. 10 (1925), 419, at 434–5; Alejandro Alvarez, *The New International Law*, Grotius Society Transactions, Vol. 15 (1930), 35.

of mandated territories or the League of Nations, while others argued that sovereignty was suspended or even inapplicable to the Mandates System.[71]

Many of the proposed theories encountered serious objections. The theory that sovereignty was vested in a condominium of Allied powers (on the grounds that the Mandates were allocated by this body)[72] proved to be untenable, because the fact that Mandatory powers received their authority from the Principal Allied Powers did not mean that these entities continued to maintain sovereignty.[73] Similarly, it was difficult to establish that the Mandatory powers themselves exercised sovereignty over the administered territories, because the institution of the Mandate System served as means of detaching administering authority from sovereignty, in particular with respect to A- and B-Mandates.[74] The claim that sovereignty resided in the League was innovative in that it formally detached the concept of sovereignty from the notion of the state.[75] However, this theory did not adequately reflect the limited powers of the League.[76] Furthermore, concepts of divided or joint sovereignty held by the League and Mandatory powers were flawed, as none of them "owned" mandated territories.[77]

The most convincing theory was that "sovereignty" resided in the inhabitants of the mandated territories. This argument foreshadowed not only modern notions of popular sovereignty in international law, but also received some backing from the text of Article 22 of the Covenant which stated that mandatory territories "have reached a stage of development where their existence as independent nations may be provisionally recognised subject to the rendering of administrative advice and assistance by a mandatory until such time as they are able to stand alone".

---

[71] For a recent treatment of the concept of "suspended sovereignty", see Alexandros Yannis, *The Concept of Suspended Sovereignty in International Law*, European Journal of International Law, Vol. 13 (2002), 1037–52.

[72] For a full survey, see Wright, *Mandates under the League of Nations*, at 319.

[73] See Chowdhuri, *International Mandates*, at 232.

[74] The theory that Mandates were merely another form of sovereignty was emphatically opposed by the Mandates Commission. See Wright, *Mandates under the League of Nations*, at 326. It was also refuted by the International Court of Justice (ICJ) in its Advisory Opinion on the question of South West Africa (Namibia). See ICJ, *International Status of South West Africa*, ICJ Rep. 1950, 128–32.

[75] Opponents declared this theory unacceptable because the League "lacked the essential features of a sovereign state – territory, population and force". See Chowdhuri, *International Mandates*, at 231–2.

[76] The League could not alter the status of the Mandates. *Ibid.*, at 232.

[77] See also Crawford, *Creation of States*, 2nd edn (2006), at 573.

This theory was most vividly defended by Stoyanovsky, who argued that sovereignty resided in the people of the Mandated territories, whereas "the exercise of the attributes of sovereignty [was] provisionally confided to a power acting in the capacity of tutor to these minor peoples ... [and] guaranteed by an international control".[78] Nevertheless, the weakness of this approach was that the concept of self-determination was much less pronounced in the B- and C-Mandates than in the A-Mandates.[79]

It made much sense therefore to argue, as some authors did, that sovereignty was "dormant" under the Mandate System during the exercise of mandatory authority[80] or "inappropriate to the new conditions" created by the System.[81] This view was later officially taken by Lord McNair in the Advisory Opinion on the *South West Africa* Case. He noted:

> The Mandates System (and the "corresponding principles" of the International Trusteeship System) is a new institution – a new relationship between territory and its inhabitants on the one hand and the government which represents them internationally on the other ... The doctrine of sovereignty has no application to this new system. Sovereignty over a Mandated Territory is in abeyance; if and when the inhabitants of the Territory obtain recognition as an independent State ... sovereignty will revive and rest in the new State. What matters in considering this new institution is not where sovereignty lies but what are the rights and duties of the Mandatory in regard to the territory being administered by it.[82]

These last lines illustrate that the Mandate System introduced a new chapter in international law. Mandate administration dissociated the concepts of "sovereignty" and "governance". It instituted a special type of foreign state administration, under which states exercised non-sovereign powers over (not yet sovereign) people as agents of the League. Moreover, it opened a new perspective on the impact of international law on the "internal" realm of societies. The political and social conditions underlying the "interior" of a society were no longer screened from international attention, but monitored by the League which became involved in shaping the development, self-government or emerging statehood of mandated territories.[83]

---

[78] See Stoyanovsky, *Théorie Générale des Mandats Internationaux*, at 85–6.
[79] See Mark F. Lindley, *The Acquisition and Government of Backward Territory in International Law* (1926), 263–4.
[80] For a survey, see Chowdhuri, *International Mandates*, at 235.
[81] See the explanation given by the Dutch delegate, Beelaerts van Blokland, in his report to the League Council in 1927. League of Nations, LNOJ, VIII yr., 1118–19.
[82] See ICJ, Advisory Opinion, *South West Africa*, ICJ. Rep. 1950, 148–49.
[83] See Anghie, *International Institutions and the Colonial Origins of Law and Development*, at 8.

3.3.2. The nature of authority

The overarching conceptual principle which facilitated the dissociation of "sovereignty" and "governance" was the concept of a trust. This concept has its roots in medieval English property law. A trust is an institution whereby property is held or duties are undertaken by a person (trustee) for the benefit of another (cestui que trust). The trustee must act solely in the interests of cestui que trust, and may not accept a personal benefit from the trust administration aside from his commissions.[84]

This idea of trust was applied as a political concept in the context of colonial administration.[85] The eighteenth-century British politician Edmund Burke invoked the concept of trusteeship in the context of the dispute over the rights and responsibilities of the East India Company in British India. Burke argued in his speech on the East India Bill (1 December 1783) that the holding of political power over people entails special fiduciary obligations for the ruler, namely that "all privilege claimed or exercised in exclusion of them, being wholly artificial ... ought to be in some way or other exercised ultimately for their benefit".[86] In the nineteenth century, this idea gained recognition as a moral principle of colonial administration. The concept was reflected in the idea of the "dual mandate" of colonial administrators[87] and the General Act of the Berlin Conference, which recognised a certain responsibility of colonial powers vis-à-vis domestic societies.[88]

This idea was developed by the Mandate System.[89] Article 22 of the League institutionalised the concept of trusteeship.[90] It formalised the

[84] See Wright, Mandates under the League of Nations, at 385–6.

[85] See Alpheus H. Snow, The Question of Aborigines in the Law and Practice of Nations (1919), at 70.

[86] See Hansard, Parliamentary History of England, Parliamentary Debates, Vol. 23 (1783), 1316–17. Furthermore, Burke added "if this is true with regard to every species of political dominion ... , then such rights or privileges ... are all, in the strictest sense, a trust; and it is of the very essence of every trust to be rendered accountable; and even totally to cease, when it substantially varies from the purpose for which alone it could have a lawful existence".

[87] The concept of the "dual mandate" (Lugard) embraced the idea that colonial administration serves the "mutual benefit" of Africa and Europe alike.

[88] See Articles 6 and 9 of the General Act of the Berlin West Africa Conference. The signatories agreed, inter alia, to "care for the improvement of the conditions of the moral and material well-being" of the natives of the Congo Basin.

[89] For a discussion, see Robert H. Jackson, The Global Covenant (2000), at 303.

[90] The establishment of the Mandate System reflected certain intellectual tendencies at the beginning of the twentieth century which favoured greater supervision of colonial administration.

idea that Mandatory powers exercise fiduciary responsibilities *vis-à-vis* mandated "peoples". Moreover, it added a dimension of international accountability to the style of administration of dependent territories, which was, *inter alia*, aimed at preventing economic exploitation. This culminated in a closer definition of the concept of "trusteeship" in the context of Mandate administration. The League's conception of trusteeship was paternalistic in that it implied a right of Western powers to exercise tutelage of entire "peoples" and to govern C-Mandates as "integral parts" of their territory.[91] The Covenant also provided little guidance as to how administration was to be carried out in concrete terms.[92] Nevertheless, Article 22 established four structural principles, which characterise "trusteeship" as an international principle: the obligation to administrate mandate territories for the benefit of the native population; the principle of international accountability of the administering power; the temporary nature of foreign rule over certain territories ("until such time as they are able to stand alone"); and the exercise of administering authority on behalf of a broader community of states.[93]

This construction was innovative from a historical perspective, but ambiguous from a conceptual point view. The reference the notion of the "sacred trust" left some doubts as to whether "trusteeship" was understood as a "legal" concept or as a "moral" principle.[94] Furthermore, the terminology used in Article 22 of the League Covenant followed neither a pure common law nor a pure civil law tradition.[95] Instead, it mixed a

---

[91] See Article 22, para. 6.

[92] Some rudimentary guidance was provided with respect to A- and B- Mandates. See Article 22, paras. 4 and 5.

[93] For a survey of the historical development of these principles, see Toussaint, *Trusteeship System*, at 3–17.

[94] See in this latter sense Matz, *Civilization and the Mandate System under the League of Nations*, at 71.

[95] Article 22 of the League Covenant contained some constructional ambiguities. The phrase that "securities for the performance of this [sacred] trust [of civilization] should be embodied in the Covenant" suggested that "the League of Nations, as the embodiment of civilization" would be the trustee, while the subsequent phrase "the tutelage of this such peoples should be *entrusted* to advanced nations" appeared to indicate that mandatories acted as trustees. Furthermore, the common law concept of the trust was complemented by the Roman law concept of tutelage (*tutelle*) which suggested that Mandatory powers were entitled to define the interests of mandated territories until they were "able to stand by themselves".

conglomerate of different elements ("tutelage", "trust") to describe the special tripartite relationship between the League, the Mandatory powers and the mandated territories. This construction reflected the particular nature and historical circumstances of Mandate administration.[96] Its four elements laid the foundations for the formal development of the concept of trusteeship under the UN Charter.[97]

---

[96] Article 22 of the League Covenant used three related concepts in order to describe the special tripartite relationship between the League, the Mandatory powers and the mandated territories. The use of the terms "mandatory" and "mandate" characterised the relationship between the League and the administering powers. They implied that the administering states acted for and on behalf of the League, and under its supervision when exercising administering authority. The terms "tutelage" and "trust" defined the relations of the League and the Mandatory powers vis-à-vis the mandated territories. They illustrated that some form of moral justification had to be found for the imposition of foreign rule over native people. This justification was the fiduciary character of authority exercised for the benefit of "peoples not yet able to stand by themselves".

[97] See Groom, *The Trusteeship Council*, at 145–6.

3 The UN Trusteeship System

The UN Trusteeship System was built upon the premises of Mandate administration. It was specifically designed to further self-government and decolonisation. Moreover, it operated mainly on the principle of state-based administration.

At the same time, the Trusteeship System administration shared some more parallels with modern engagements in international territorial administration than the Mandate System. The Trusteeship system gave rise to two quasi-experiments of direct UN administration: the proposed UN administration of Jerusalem and *de jure* authority of the UN over Namibia – two examples of direct UN administration exercised after the termination of former Mandates (the UK Mandate over Palestine and South Africa's Mandate concerning South West Africa). Furthermore, the Trusteeship System corrected some of the failings of the League's system of administration and laid some foundations for the conceptualisation of territorial administration under the umbrella of peace-maintenance.

1. Genesis

The Trusteeship System has its origins in the negotiations held during World War II. Both the US and the Soviet Union pushed for the dismemberment of the old European empires, and organised bilateral talks on the issue of decolonisation as early as 1942.[1] The first proposal to establish an international forum for the control of colonial policy was prepared by the US Department of State. The draft, known as the "Declaration by the United Nations on National Independence", proposed

---

[1] See Dietrich Rauschning, *United Nations Trusteeship System*, in Encyclopedia of Public International Law, Vol. IV at 1193.

the creation of a truly international trusteeship administration, composed of UN representatives, interested nations and the trust territories,
which would operate through regional Councils in order to supervise the
protection of colonial territories.[2] However, this plan met with strong
opposition from UK Prime Minister Winston Churchill, who viewed the
suggestion as a device to undermine and eventually destroy the British
Empire.[3] The divergent positions remained irreconcilable[4] until the "Big
Three" Conference held in Yalta in February 1945, where the Soviet, US
and UK Foreign Ministers agreed on a modified formula, under which
trusteeship would only be applied to former League of Nation Mandates,
territories detached from the enemy as a result of the war, and territories "voluntarily" placed under the system.[5] This move safeguarded both
UK and French colonial interests and laid the basis for the adoption of
the Trusteeship System at the San Francisco Conference.[6]

2.   A leap forward

The Trusteeship System did not simply represent a continuation of the
Mandate System, but addressed some of the shortcomings of the League
of Nations' system of administration. The most important conceptual
change was the concerted effort of the UN to limit colonial rule through
two distinct mechanisms: the rules on the administration of non-self-
governing territories (Chapter XI of the UN Charter) and the Trusteeship
System (Chapters XII and XIII of the UN Charter).

Chapter XI of the Charter was essentially a concession to the European
colonial empires. It was adopted as a way of allowing for imperial
association which in the British Empire was interpreted in terms
of dependent colonies eventually becoming self-governing dominions.
Administering authority was therefore linked to the development of

---

[2] Furthermore, the draft required colonial powers to set fixed deadlines, for the
independence of colonial peoples. See Chowdhuri, *International Mandates*, at 32.
[3] See Groom, *The Trusteeship Council*, at 148.
[4] The subject of trusteeship administration was not mentioned in the Dumbarton Oaks
proposals (29 August – 7 October 1944), which envisaged the creation of the UN as a
universal organisation.
[5] See *Arrangements for International Trusteeship*, reprinted in Ruth B. Russell and Jeanette E.
Muther, *A History of the United Nations Charter: The Role of the United States 1940–1945* (1958),
at 1030.
[6] For the drafting history at San Francisco, see Russell and Muther, *History of the United
Nations Charter*, at 824–42.

self-government[7] rather than to immediate political independence.[8] The
UN Trusteeship System, by contrast, which was applied to former League
mandates, territories detached from enemy states after World War II
and territories voluntarily placed under the system under a trusteeship agreement,[9] set a strict decolonisation agenda right from the start.
Article 76 of the Charter referred to the progressive development of trust
territories "towards self-government or independence as may be appropriate to the particular circumstances of each territory". Thus, within
the context of Chapter XII, self-government *and* independence[10] became
equal objectives of the Trusteeship System.

Moreover, the Trusteeship System modified the imperfect system of
administration envisaged under the Mandate System. It broke with the
tradition of regarding colonial people as "uncivilised" or as belonging to
inferior races and cultures. The UN Charter repeated the concept of the
"sacred trust" in its Article 73, but deleted the League Covenant's unfortunate terminological use of notions such "tutelage", (un)"advanced
nations" and (in)ability "to stand by themselves under the strenuous
conditions of the modern world". Instead, the Charter used the more
neutral language of "political, economic, social and educational advancement",[11] "progressive development"[12] and "equal treatment".[13] Furthermore, it made express reference to the "freely expressed wishes of
the peoples concerned".[14] These notions reflected international opinion,

[7] Article 73 of the Charter refers to the "administration of territories whose people have
not yet attained a full measure of self-government" by colonial powers which
"recognise the principle that the interests of the inhabitants of those territories are
paramount, and accept as a sacred trust the obligation to promote the utmost ...
well-being of the inhabitants of these territories".
[8] However, Chapter XI made the advancement of all colonial territories a concern of the
international community and placed UN members under an international obligation
to promote the well-being of the inhabitants of non-self-governing territories. Later it
developed into one of the cornerstones of the UN practice of decolonisation which
culminated in the adoption of the Declaration of Independence to Colonial Countries
and Peoples and General Assembly Resolution 1541, allowing colonial people to
exercise their right to self-determination according to their "freely expressed will and
desire". See *Declaration on the Granting of Independence to Colonial Countries and Peoples*, GA
Res. 1514, UN. GAOR, 15th Sess., Supp. No. 16, UN Doc. A/4684 (1960). The Resolution
required "a speedy and unconditional end to colonialism". See also GA Res. 1541, UN
GAOR 15th Sess., Supp. No. 16, at 29, UN Doc. A/4684 (1960).
[9] See Article 77 of the UN Charter.
[10] The word "independence" does appear in Article 73 (b) of the Charter, which deals
with Non-Self-Governing-Territories.
[11] See Article 76 (b) of the UN Charter.   [12] *Ibid.*
[13] See Article 76 (d) of the UN Charter.   [14] See Article 76 (b) of the UN Charter.

moving from regarding colonial territories as "backward", to acknowledging the rights of equality and self-determination.

Similar shifts in thinking influenced the principles of administration. Unlike the League Covenant, Article 76 of the Charter enumerated in detail the objectives and principles guiding trusteeship administration.[15] Moreover, the UN Charter incorporated a number of significant changes in response to the lacunary system of supervision of the League.[16] The Mandates Commission, which had been formed by individual experts,[17] was replaced by the UN Trusteeship Council, a principal organ of the UN, composed of governmental officials. The Council was not only charged with the consideration of periodical reports submitted by the administering authorities, but was expressly authorised to exercise the two types of control which the Mandates Commission had been denied: the right to hear oral petitions from the inhabitants of the Trust Territories[18] and the power to undertake visiting missions to the territories.[19]

Most importantly, the UN Charter extended the form of exercise of administering authority. Article 81 of the Charter provided that the administering authority "may be one or more states or the Organisation itself".[20] This definition allowed for several forms of administration:

[15] Article 76 (a) charged the trusteeship authority with the maintenance of peace and security in the Trust Territories. The reference to the "wishes of people" in Article 76 (b) indicated that self-determination should play a role in deciding whether complete independence or self-government represented the final goal of political development. Moreover, it illustrated that the political advancement of territories itself should be based on democratic principles. See Chetlur Lakshiminarayan, *Analysis of the Principles and System of International Trusteeship in the Charter* (1951), 144. Furthermore, the objective of human rights protection gained a new level of recognition. This obligation was implemented in various trusteeship agreements, which specifically guaranteed rights such as freedom of speech, freedom of the press, freedom of assembly and freedom of religion. See Dietrich Rauschning, On *Article 76*, in Charter of the United Nations, at 1113, para. 33

[16] See Groom, *The Trusteeship Council*, at 154.

[17] See on these features of the Mandates Commission, Hall, *Mandates, Dependencies and Trusteeship*, at 158.

[18] See Article 88 (b) of the UN Charter. Rules 91–96 of the Rules of Procedure of the Trusteeship Council allowed oral petitions. See Rauschning, On *Article 87*, in Charter of the United Nations, 1133, para. 11.

[19] See Article 88 (c) of the UN Charter.

[20] Article 81 reads: "The trusteeship agreement shall in each case include the terms under which the trust territory will be administered and designate the authority which will exercise the administration of the trust territory. Such authority, hereinafter called the administering authority, may be one or more States or the Organization itself." For the drafting history, see Chowdhuri, *International Mandates*, at 58.

administration by a single state, joint administration by more than one state and direct administration by the UN.[21]

3. The Trusteeship System from the perspective of international territorial administration

Due to its institutionalisation in the UN Charter, the Trusteeship System shared more common features with modern patterns of international territorial administration than the Mandate System. However, administration under the Trusteeship System and direct territorial administration by the UN remained formally separate paradigms. Article 78 of the Charter limited the application of the Trusteeship System to the immediate context of decolonisation, by excluding its application to "territories which have become Members of the United Nations".[22] Furthermore, in practice trusteeship administration under Chapters XII and XIII of the Charter maintained its own distinct character.[23]

3.1. Trusteeship administration as international territorial administration

The construction of Chapters XII and XIII of the UN Charter itself left some doubts as to whether the option of direct administration by the UN was ever meant to gain a significant role under the Trusteeship System.

3.1.1. Drafting and construction of Article 81 of the UN Charter

The idea of incorporating the principle of direct international administration by the UN in the framework of Article 81 of the UN Charter stems from a Chinese proposal at San Francisco. It provided that the Trust "territories may be administered either directly by the Organisation through an agency of its own or indirectly by one or more of the United Nations

---

[21] The provision for direct administering authority by the UN was an important step, at least symbolically. It mitigated the scepticism *vis-à-vis* international territorial administration at the universal level, which had prevailed at Versailles.

[22] See Groom, *The Trusteeship Council*, at 172.

[23] With the exception of a small number of examples, trusteeship administration has essentially taken on the form of state-conducted administration, carried out under the mere supervision of the UN. Trusteeship authority was mostly exercised by a single state, or in the case of Nauru, by a group of states composed of the UK, Australia and New Zealand. See Articles 2 and 4 of the Trusteeship Agreement on Nauru, UNTS, Vol. 10, at 3. See also Rauschning, *On Article 81*, in Charter of the United Nations, at 1122, para. 2.

Members by agreement of the States concerned".[24] This proposal was vehemently criticised by South Africa, which argued that the adoption of
this provision would confer excessive powers on the UN as an organisation and would reduce the role of states under the Trusteeship System to
that of mere agents.[25] The dispute ended with the adoption of the current version of Article 81, which allows for direct administration by the
UN, but makes such administration dependent on an express choice by
the parties to the trusteeship agreement to place the territory under UN
supervision ("The trusteeship agreement shall *in each case*... designate
the authority which will exercise the administration of the trust
territory"[26]).

The Trusteeship System offered limited space for the exercise of administering powers by the UN itself. The trusteeship machinery was not set
up as a mechanism for conflict resolution, but as an instrument to implement commonly agreed decolonisation policies.[27] Furthermore, direct
UN administration the Trusteeship System was conceived as an exceptional paradigm.[28] The institutional framework of the Charter refrained
from establishing specific rules on the conduct of direct UN administration under Article 81.[29] The Trusteeship System failed to name the

---

[24] See UNCIO, Doc 2, G/26 (e), 10 May 1945, Vol. III, at 615–17.

[25] See UNCIO, Doc. 310 II/4, 15 May 1945, Vol. X, at 439.

[26] See Article 81 of the UN Charter, emphasis added.

[27] The philosophy of trusteeship administration was aptly characterised by a
representative of the US at San Francisco, who noted that "[t]erritories would be
placed in trust only after [territorial] claims were resolved, when the 'states concerned'
would agree among themselves on a trust agreement for a specific area and then
present it for approval by the international organization". See Russell and Muther,
History of the United Nations, at 835. Trusteeship administration was therefore from its
very inception only a fragment of the larger practice of UN territorial administration,
which has been used as a tool of conflict resolution and territorial settlement itself.

[28] This impression is confirmed by the Summary Report of the 11th meeting of
Committee II/4 at San Francisco, which contains the following statement about the
drafting process: "Opposition to the provision for direct international administration
was expressed, on the grounds both that this was likely to provide an unsatisfactory
system in itself, and that the reference to it was out of harmony with the apparent
intentions of the draft as a whole. But no motion in this sense was submitted." See
UNCIO Doc. 712, II/4/30, at 4. See also Toussaint, *Trusteeship System*, at 208 ("The
possibility of the Organization becoming an administering authority raises numerous
practical difficulties which would have the effect of changing the whole conception of
United Nations Trusteeship, if indeed it is feasible at all for the organization to
assume this administrative role").

[29] See also the criticism by Toussaint, *Trusteeship System*, at 210 ("The machinery of
supervision, which is such an essential element of the Trusteeship System, completely
breaks down when the administering authority is the Organisation itself"). For a more
favourable assessment, see Kelsen, *Law of the United Nations*, at 652–3.

institutions which would exercise administering authority if the organisation itself assumed tasks of territorial administration.[30] Both the Security Council[31] and the General Assembly[32] were vested with the power to establish subsidiary organs, enabling them to decentralise authority. However, no such authority was given to the Trusteeship Council.[33] This led to a controversy over the question of whether UN authority under Article 81 could be validly exercised by the Trusteeship Council through subordinated administrators or governors,[34] as suggested by the draft trusteeship agreement for Palestine[35] or the Statute for Jerusalem.[36]

Secondly, the Charter failed to specify the procedure under which supervision by the Trusteeship System would be carried out in instances where UN organs exercise administering authority. The UN essentially took on the role of a "judge in its own cause" in these situations.[37] In the case of the annual report under Article 87 (a) of the Charter, the organisation was technically obliged to report to itself, following the example of the British colonial tradition, under which local governors submitted reports to their own governmental representatives. Petitions submitted by inhabitants of trust territories turned into mechanisms of self-investigation running counter to the spirit of Article 87 (b), which distinguishes expressly the "the administering authority", on the one hand, and the supervisory organs (General Assembly, Trusteeship Council), on the other. Finally, visiting missions to trust territories under Article 87 (c) lost their supervisory effect in the case of direct UN administration.[38]

---

[30] The idea behind Article 81 was that administration would be exercised by "the General Assembly, the Security Council or the Trusteeship Council, authorised by the General Assembly". See Kelsen, Law of the United Nations, at 652.

[31] See Article 29 of the UN Charter.

[32] See Article 22 of the UN Charter.

[33] The Trusteeship has asserted authority to establish Special Committees under Rule 66 of the Council's Rules of Procedure. For a critical appraisal, see Toussaint, Trusteeship System, at 176.

[34] See Kelsen, Law of the United Nations, at 653, 834-836; Toussaint, Trusteeship System, at 209–210.

[35] Article 2 of the Trusteeship Agreement provided: "The United Nations, acting through the Trusteeship Council, is hereby designated as the Administering Authority." Article 11 added that administration would have to be exercised by a Governor General to be appointed by the Trusteeship Council.

[36] See Article 5 and Article 12 of the Trusteeship Council Proposal for the Statute of the City of Jerusalem, in Lapidoth, The Jerusalem Question, at 117.

[37] See Toussaint, Trusteeship System, at 211. See also Kelsen, Law of the United Nations, at 651.

[38] The conflict between UN authority, on the one hand, and meaningful intra-institutional supervision, on the other, is further evidenced by the Charter's

3.1.2.   Practice under Article 81?

It does not come as a surprise that the option of direct UN administration under Article 81 of the UN Charter remained largely a dead letter in practice. Usually, states were appointed as administering authorities.[39] Where direct UN trusteeship authority was invoked, it faced obstacles in practice.

The question as to whether the UN itself should become an administering authority was first discussed in the case of the former Italian colonies. The proposal to place these territories under direct UN trusteeship was made by the United States in 1946.[40] However, the US proposal failed to gain sufficient support. The idea was taken up again in 1949, when the future of the former Italian colonies was again discussed in the General Assembly. This time, the Soviet Union[41] and India[42] were supportive of the establishment of direct UN authority. A Soviet proposal provided that each colony should be administered under the authority of the Trusteeship Council with the help of a UN-appointed administrator and an Advisory Council, composed of seven UN members.[43] But this project was finally discarded.

3.1.2.1.   Jerusalem

Attempts to charge the UN with direct authority under Article 81 of the UN Charter continued with the proposed administration of Jerusalem

---

special regime for the administration of strategic trust territories. Article 83 (1) of the UN Charter charges the Security Council with all functions of the UN relating to strategic trust territories to the Security Council, but does not contain an explicit reference to Chapter XIII of the Charter, which introduces the Trusteeship System's method of supervision. But the Security Council finally charged the Trusteeship Council with the assumption of supervisory tasks in the administration of strategic areas in its Resolution 70 of 7 March 1949. The Trusteeship Council reported to the Security Council on the realisation of the objectives of trusteeship within the meaning of Article 76 of the Charter. Moreover, it dealt with petitions from strategic areas and submitted an annual report to the Security Council. See Rauschning, *On Article 83*, in Charter of the United Nations, at 1125–6, paras. 2–3.

[39] It is even controversial whether there was a case of direct administration by the organisation under Article 81 in UN practice. Toussaint noted in 1956: "There is no example of the Organisation becoming the administering authority of a trust territory, although it has been proposed at many times." See Toussaint, *Trusteeship System*, at 208. Rauschning also fails to name a case. See Rauschning, *On Article 81*, in Charter of the United Nations, 1122, paras. 3–4.

[40] See GAOR, 1st Sess., Second Part, Fourth Committee, Part 2, at 36.

[41] See GAOR, 3rd Sess., Second Part, First Committee, at 23.   [42] *Ibid.*, at 65.

[43] See GAOR, 3rd Sess., Second Part, First Committee, at 23, UN. Doc. A/C.I/433.

by the Trusteeship Council. UN administration took very precise forms on paper. However, it remained controversial in substance and was not implemented.

The idea of internationalising Jerusalem was suggested by the UN Special Committee on Palestine in a report of 31 August 1947. The Committee sought to base its plan on Chapter XII of the Charter. The Report noted that "[t]he International Trusteeship System is proposed as the most suitable instrument for meeting the special problems presented by Jerusalem, for the reason that the Trusteeship Council, as a principal organ of the United Nations, affords a convenient and effective means of ensuring both the desired international supervision and the political, economic and social well-being of the population of Jerusalem."[44] Accordingly, the Committee recommended that "Jerusalem ... be placed under an International Trusteeship System by means of a Trusteeship Agreement which shall designate the United Nations as the Administering Authority, in accordance with Article 81 of the Charter of the United Nations".[45]

This recommendation was adopted three months later by the UN General Assembly in its Resolution 181 (II) on the Future Government of Palestine (the "Partition Resolution") of 29 November 1947.[46] The Resolution failed to make explicit reference to Chapters XII or XIIII of the Charter, but stated:

The City of Jerusalem shall be established as a *corpus separatum* under a special international regime and shall be administered by the United Nations. The Trusteeship Council shall be designated to discharge the responsibilities of the Administering Authority on behalf of the United Nations.[47]

The Trusteeship Council was instructed to elaborate and approve a detailed Statute for the City. It adopted a Statute, which stated that "the Trusteeship Council, by virtue of the authority conferred upon it by the resolution of the General Assembly of the United Nations of November 29, 1947, shall discharge the responsibilities of the

---

[44] See UN Special Committee on Palestine, Proposal of 31 August 1947, Chapter VI, Part III (City of Jerusalem), GAOR 2nd Sess., 1947, Supp. No. 11, in Lapidoth, *The Jerusalem Question*, at 2–3.

[45] See UN Special Committee on Palestine, Recommendation No. 1, *ibid.*, at 3.

[46] See GA Res. 181 (II) on the Future Government of Palestine of 29 November 1947, GAOR 2nd Sess., 1947, Resolutions 16 September–29 November, 146–50, in Lapidoth, *The Jerusalem Question*, at 6.

[47] See Part III. A of GA Resolution 181 (II) of 29 November 1947.

United Nations for the administration of the City in accordance with this Statute".[48]

The legality of the Statute remained contentious. The Trusteeship Council itself had some difficulty in identifying a clear basis of its authority under the Charter. It derived its powers primarily from General Assembly Resolution 181 (II), but refrained from qualifying the international framework for Jerusalem as a case of trusteeship administration. The Council described the proposed framework for Jerusalem, in particular, as a *sui generis* type of international government ("special international regime") to be exercised "on behalf of the community of nations".[49]

This position was fiercely opposed by the newly established state of Israel. The Israeli delegation to the UN claimed that the organisation lacked the power to impose a permanent administrative and executive structure on Jerusalem.[50] In addition, the Government of Israel openly

---

[48] See Article 5 of the Statute for the City of Jerusalem, approved by the Trusteeship Council at its 81st meeting held on 4 April 1950. See also the previous draft of 21 April 1948, Trusteeship Council Resolution 34 (II), [Draft] Statute of Jerusalem, UN. Doc. T/118 Rev. 2, 21 April 1948.

[49] The Council expressed its position at the 6th meeting of its 2nd session in December 1947. It noted: "Although the General Assembly of the United Nations vested the Trusteeship Council with power to define, to constitute and to administer the international regime of the City of Jerusalem, it is obvious that the City is not a trust territory and that the provisions of Chapters XII and XIII of the Charter are not generally applicable to the case. Therefore, the Committee tried to avoid any arbitrary resemblance to the Trusteeship system; it considered rather that the legal status of this territory was a new one; Jerusalem would come, as it were, directly under the authority of the United Nations and it would be governed on behalf of the community of nations. Such would be the entirely original sense that might suitably be given to the term: Special International Regime. In this matter, therefore, the Trusteeship Council will be carrying out a special duty on behalf of the United Nations. This will be its authority for assuming first the constituent and later the supreme administrative authority over the City of Jerusalem. The Assembly Resolution will be the text on which it will have to base its action in this matter ... The reason for this juridical innovation may be found in the obligation laid upon the United Nations to ensure the protection of a City which is the holy place for three great religions." See Report of the Working Committee on Jerusalem, 6th meeting, 2nd Sess., 1 December 1947, UN Doc. T/122, in Kelsen, *Law of the United Nations*, at 687, note 8.

[50] It stated its position in a Memorandum on the Future of Jerusalem, submitted to the UN General Assembly on 15 November 1949, that: "[the UN] has no sovereignty [over Jerusalem] arising out of the mere fact of the termination of the Mandate on May 14, 1948 ... The United Nations has not acquired in Jerusalem such legal or administrative authority as it may acquire in certain territories under Chapter XII. No measures were ever taken under these articles of the Charter which define the maximal degree of partial and temporary political authority which the United Nations can exercise over any area in the world." Representatives of the Jewish population of Palestine proclaimed the establishment of the Jewish State on 14 May 1948.

questioned the applicability of Chapter XII to the specific situation in Jerusalem.[51]

A similar critique was in the same year voiced by Kelsen, who qualified the administering regime proposed under the Statute as an illegal framework adopted "outside the scope of the Trusteeship system". Kelsen argued that the Trusteeship Council was not competent to adopt the Statute and would not have been authorised to perform the function of an administering authority of the UN.[52]

A formal decision as to the legality of the Trusteeship Council's administration of Jerusalem was never required to be taken, as plans for a territorial internationalisation of the City were soon replaced by proposals for a functional internationalisation leading to the non-adoption of the General Assembly Resolution for the Implementation of the International Statute for Jerusalem at the fifth session of the General Assembly in 1950.[53] However, the criticism of the Trusteeship Council model in the case of Jerusalem illustrated the need to distinguish these two different strands of administration: Mandate/Trusteeship System administration, on the one hand, and general territorial administration, on the other.[54]

---

[51] The Permanent Representative of Israel to the UN addressed a letter to the Trusteeship Council on 26 May 1950, which stated: "Whatever its position in 1947, when it was a 'territory under mandate', Jerusalem no longer falls into any of the categories defined in Article 77, to which any form of international trusteeship may be applied. Moreover, the procedures of agreement required by Articles 79 and 81 have not been applied and are not feasible in this case. Apart from being legally ineligible for the operation of a trusteeship regime in the sense of Article 77, Jerusalem is by its very nature, the exact antithesis of any territory to which any system of tutelage may properly apply. For the object of the Trusteeship System is to promote the advancement of backward people towards self-government, and not to effect the transformation of mature and independent democracies into subject areas. Thus, the letter of the Charter, as well as its fundamental spirit, is subjected to comprehensive violation by this unconstitutional proposal." See Letter of the Permanent Representative of Israel to the UN, Abba Eban, addressed to the President of the Trusteeship Council, 26 May 1950, Question of an International Regime for the Jerusalem Area and the Protection of the Holy Places, in Lapidoth, *The Jerusalem Question*, 135, at 140.

[52] Kelsen based his findings on a strict interpretation of the institutional competences assigned under the Charter. See Kelsen, *Law of the United Nations*, at 685.

[53] See below Part II, Chapter 6. See also Ydit, *Internationalised Territories*, at 306–7.

[54] Trusteeship administration under Chapter XII and XIII of the Charter is designed to "promote the political, economic, social and educational advancement of the inhabitants of the trust territories and their progressive development towards self-government or independence as may be appropriate to the particular circumstances of each territory and its peoples and the freely expressed wishes of the peoples concerned". The proposed administration of Jerusalem did not fit into this category of mandate. It could hardly be claimed that the people of Jerusalem required

3.1.2.2. Namibia

The (virtual) UN administration of Namibia is the case in UN practice that most closely replicates the exercise of direct trusteeship authority by the organisation under Article 81.[55] The UN assumed authority over the territory following the revocation of South Africa's Mandate over the territory by General Assembly Resolution 2145 (XXI), which "[d]ecide[d] that South Africa has no ... right to administer the Territory and that henceforth South West Africa comes under the direct responsibility of the United Nations".[56]

However, the exact legal basis for the assumption of UN authority over the former Mandate remained ambiguous. None of the UN resolutions openly reached the conclusion that Namibia was administered by the UN as a trust territory under Article 81.[57] UN bodies were reluctant to make reference to the direct applicability of the Trusteeship provisions of the Charter to the situation in Namibia.[58] The General Assembly provided a rather weak justification in Resolution 2145, arguing that in these special "circumstances the United Nations must discharge ... responsibilities with respect to South West Africa".[59] This reference and

development through the Trusteeship Council. Moreover, it would have been difficult to apply Article 81 directly, because Israel refused to place Jerusalem voluntarily under the Trusteeship System by a trusteeship agreement under Article 77 (c) of the Charter. See the statement by the Ambassador of Israel, Abba Eban, in the UN Trusteeship Council, 20 February 1950, in Lapidoth, *The Jerusalem Question*, at 112–13.

[55] See generally Eckard Klein, Namibia, in Encyclopedia of Public International Law, Vol. 3 (1997), at 485; John Dugard, *The South West Africa/Namibia Dispute* (1973), at 409–38.

[56] See para. 4 of GA Res. 2145 of 27 October 1966, in Dugard, *The South West Africa/Namibia Dispute*, at 379–80.

[57] The resolutions listed numerous grounds for the exercise of direct administering powers by the UN, including the realisation of "the inalienable right of the people of South West Africa to freedom and independence in accordance with ... General Assembly resolution 1514 (XV) of 14 December 1960" (see para. 1 of the preamble of GA Res. 2145), the continuing responsibility of the UN "as the successor to the League of Nations" with "supervisory powers in respect of South West Africa" (see para. 2 of the preamble of GA Res. 2145) and the failure of South Africa "to fulfil its obligations in respect of the administration of the Mandated Territory" (see para. 3 of GA Res. 2145) through the institution of the apartheid system, resulting in the "disavow[al]" and termination of its Mandate (see para. 4 of GA Res. 2145).

[58] In its 1950 Advisory Opinion on the Legal Status of South West Africa, the ICJ concluded "that the provisions of Chapter XII of the Charter are applicable to the Territory of South-West Africa in the sense that they provide a means by which the Territory may be brought under the Trusteeship System", and that "the provisions of Chapter XII of the Charter do not impose on the Union of South Africa a legal obligation to place the Territory under the Trusteeship System". See ICJ, *International Status of South-West Africa, Advisory Opinion*, 11 July 1950, ICJ Rep. 1950, 128.

[59] See para. 5 of GA Res. 2145.

deliberations in the General Assembly[60] suggest that the organisation sought to justify its authority once again by a *sui generis* construction, conditioned by the exigencies of the situation.[61] This argument was a convenient solution for the UN, because it saved the organisation from the controversial step of applying Chapter XII authority in the absence of a trusteeship agreement.[62]

However, the authority exercised by the UN over Namibia was, at least, a *de facto* application of Article 81.[63] South Africa's Mandate over Namibia had been terminated by the General Assembly as a matter of law. The termination of the Mandate was upheld by a 1971 ruling of the ICJ[64] and reaffirmed by the Security Council, which declared South Africa's continued presence in Namibia illegal in its Resolution 276 (1970)[65] and

---

[60] The assumption of UN authority was justified on the basis of a general "principle of reversion of powers" by Latin American countries. The representative of Bolivia explained this theory as follows: "[I]f we agree that there is no trusteeship and no mandate – the first because the trusteeship agreement was never signed and the second because of the dissolution of the League of Nations – then it is obvious that the *sui generis* sovereignty exercised by delegation over the Territory reverts to the international community." See GAOR, 21st Sess., 1448th meeting, UN Doc. A/PV.1448, at 15.

[61] This construction appears to underlie the specific reasoning of the decisive fourth operative paragraph of Resolution 2145, which states "that the Mandate conferred upon his Britannic Majesty to be exercised on his behalf by the Government of the Union of South Africa is therefore terminated ... and that *henceforth* South West Africa comes under the direct responsibility of the United Nations" (emphasis added).

[62] In its 1971 Advisory Opinion on Namibia, the ICJ invoked Article 80 of the Charter to justify UN authority which states that "until such [trusteeship] agreements have been concluded, nothing in this Chapter shall be construed in or of itself to alter in any manner the rights whatsoever of any states or any peoples or the terms of existing international instruments to which Members of the United Nations may respectively be parties". The ICJ argued that "[s]ince a provision of the Charter – Article 80, paragraph 1 – had maintained the obligations of the Mandatory, the United Nations had become the appropriate forum for supervising the fulfilment of those obligations".

[63] See UN, UNTAG, Historical Background, at www.un.org/Depts/dpko/co_mission/ untagS.htm ("In 1967, the Assembly established the United Nations Council for South West Africa to administer the territory until independence. It thus became the only Territory for which the United Nations, rather than a Member State, assumed direct responsibility".) See also Henry J. Richardson, *Failed States, Self-Determination and Preventive Diplomacy: Colonialist Nostalgia and Democratic Expectations*, Temple International and Comparative Law Journal, Vol. 10 (1996), 1, at 4 ("grounded under Chapter XII of the Charter, with the UN as the trustee under Article 81"). Dissenting Rauschning, *United Nations Trusteeship System*, at 1195 ("Though provided for in Art. 81 ... the UN has never itself functioned as an administering authority in practice").

[64] See ICJ, Advisory Opinion, ICJ Rep. 1971, 21.

[65] See para. 2 of SC Res. 276 (1970), in Dugard, *The South West Africa/Namibia Dispute*, at 442.

stated that "all acts taken by the Government of South Africa on behalf of or concerning Namibia after the termination of the Mandate
are illegal and invalid".[66] South Africa had therefore lost its title to
govern Namibia. No indigenous government existed either. In the resulting legal vacuum, the UN was the only body which could legitimately assert a claim of authority over the territory. The legal niche in
which the situation fit most closely was the Trusteeship System.[67] There
was no trusteeship agreement, as contemplated by Articles 77 (c) and
81 of the UN Charter. However, it may be argued that South Africa's
persistent refusal to cooperate with the UN made the reliance on the

---

[66] See para. 2 of SC Res. 276 (1970).

[67] The strong resemblances between the role of the UN concerning Namibia under
Resolution 2248 and the exercise of trusteeship authority under Chapter XII of the
Charter were highlighted in 1975 by the Representative of the Netherlands to the UN.
The delegate made the following statement at the occasion of the adoption of General
Assembly Resolution 3295, which requested all UN member states "to take all
appropriate measures to ensure the full application of, and compliance with" Decree
No. 1 of the Council for Namibia: "[W]e have always held the General Assembly legally
entitled to revoke the mandate conferred by the League of Nations. The implications
of that act of revocation should be derived from the Charter provisions on the
trusteeship system, the new system under the Charter replacing the mandate system
of the League of Nations. Now, according to Article 81 of the Charter, the
administration of a trust territory can be exercised not only by one or more States but
also by the United Nations itself as administering authority. Further Article 85
provides that the functions of the United Nations with regard to trusteeship
agreements for all areas not designated as strategic shall be exercised by the General
Assembly. Consequently, in those cases where the UN itself functions as the
administering authority of a trust territory, it is the General Assembly which possesses
the legal powers necessary for the exercise of the administration. Such administrative
powers with regard to a specific territory are of an entirely different character than
the general powers concerning questions dealt with by the UN. They are, therefore, by
no means limited to the making of recommendations as provided for in Article 10 of
the Charter. In respect of Namibia, the General Assembly has delegated the exercise of
those executive powers to the UN Council for Namibia, In its resolution 2248 (S-V) the
General Assembly has entrusted to the Council the powers and functions to
administer the territory and, among other things, to promulgate such laws, decrees
and administrative regulations as are necessary for the administration of the territory.
My government holds the view that the General Assembly was legally fully competent
to do so." See Statement of J. H. Burgers, Representative of the Netherlands to the
United States in the Fourth Committee of the General Assembly, 21 October 1975, UN.
Doc A/C.4/SR.2151, at 15–16, reprinted in Federic L. Kirgis, *International Organizations in
Their Legal Setting* (1993), at 384. For a different view, see the Statement of the UK
Minister of State for Defence Procurement in 1988 before the House of Lords,
reprinted in Kirgis, *ibid.* ("I am afraid that decree number one of the United Nations
Council for Namibia was made outside the competence of the General Assembly which
set up that particular Council. Therefore we regard it as null and void").

formal requirement of a trusteeship agreement inappropriate or even inapplicable.[68]

3.2.   Trusteeship administration as a role model for international territorial administration

Both the cases of Jerusalem and Namibia show quite clearly that administration under the Trusteeship System and direct UN administration were largely treated as separate issues in the practice of the UN. The organisation displayed an almost natural instinct against the formal exercise of direct administering authority under the Trusteeship System. Even in circumstances where an analogous or even direct application of Chapter XII to exercises in international governance would have been conceivable, the UN avoided making extensive use of Article 81. Instead, the organisation developed case-specific justifications for the assumption of administering authority.

It is, however, useful to take a closer look at the structure and functioning of Trusteeship System administration from a conceptual perspective. This practice provides lessons for contemporary practice in at least three core areas: accountability, institutional diversity and status issues.

3.2.1.   Trusteeship System administration and the accountability of governance

The establishment of the Trusteeship System represented an important step forward in terms of accountability. The UN Charter instituted stringent forms of international control over the administration of trust territories. Measures taken by the administering powers were not considered as matters falling into the domestic jurisdiction of these states,[69] but

---

[68] South Africa was the only state which was "directly concerned" within the meaning of Article 79 of the Charter. One may assume that South Africa had forfeited its rights over the territory. See also ICJ Advisory Opinion, 1971, para. 91 ("One of the fundamental principles governing the international relationship thus established is that a party which disowns or does not fulfil its own obligations cannot be recognized as retaining the rights which it claims to derive from the relationship"). See also para. 95 ("[Resolution 2145] is to be viewed as the exercise of the right to terminate a relationship in case of a deliberate and persistent violation of obligations, which destroys the very object and purpose of that relationship").

[69] The supervision and limitation of the authority of administering powers by the UN deviated from the general prohibition on intervening in the internal affairs of its members under Article 2 (7) of the Charter and reflected quite clearly that Chapter XII administration was conceived as a different kind of authority than "domestic jurisdiction" of the administering states.

were judged according to the parameters of the Charter and the standards defined in the respective trusteeship agreements,[70] which were subject to approval by the UN.[71]

Trusteeship agreements contained provisions concerning economic development (maintenance of land, preservation of natural resources) and the promotion of human rights and fundamental freedoms, such as freedom of speech, freedom of the press, freedom of assembly. The Trusteeship Council monitored the implementation of these goals. The Council promoted, in particular, the advancement of democratic government from the beginning. As early as 1948, the Council requested the Administering Authorities of Ruanda-Urundi and Tanganyika to transform existing tribal structures into a modern electoral system.[72] Similar recommendations were made in 1949 in relation to the British Cameroons, Togoland and New Guinea.

Furthermore, the Charter introduced a mechanism to monitor compliance of administration practice with the provisions of the Charter and the trust agreements on a case-by-case basis. The most important instrument was the petition system. It allowed indigenous inhabitants to bring misconduct of the administering authorities directly to the attention of the UN Secretary General.[73] The Charter itself remained silent on the scope of review to be exercised by the UN over acts of the administering states. This gap was subsequently closed by the Rules of Procedure of the Trusteeship Council. Rule 81[74] allowed, in particular, "petitions against legislation on the grounds of its incompatibility with the provisions of

---

[70] See Toussaint, *Trusteeship System*, at 103.

[71] The "states directly concerned" formally drafted the trusteeship agreements. The content of these agreements was then subject to a second agreement between the administering authority and the General Assembly (or the Security Council). See Toussaint, *Trusteeship System*, at 78.

[72] See Brian Deiwert, *A New Trusteeship for World Peace and Security: Can an Old League of Nations Idea Be Applied to a Twenty-First Century Iraq?*, Indiana International & Comparative Law Review, Vol. 14 (2004), 771, at 790–1.

[73] See Rule 77 of the Rules of Procedure of the Trusteeship Council ("Petitioners may be inhabitants of the Trust Territories or other parties"). Rule 82 states: "Written petitions may be addressed directly to the Secretary-General or may be transmitted to him through the Administering Authority." See UN, *Rules of Procedure of the Trusteeship Council* (1958), UN. Doc T/1/Rev.5.

[74] Rule 81 introduced a local remedies rule for the admissibility of petitions. Rule 81 states: "Normally petitions shall be considered inadmissible if they are directed against judgments of competing courts of the Administering Authority or if they lay before the Council a dispute with which the courts have competence to deal."

the Charter of the United Nations or of the Trusteeship agreement, irrespective of whether decisions on cases arising under such legislation have previously been given by the courts of the Administering Authority".[75] The petition system was therefore not only a means of gaining information about trust territories, but also a mechanism to weigh and judge the conduct of the administering states.[76] It shed light on such delicate issues as the testing of hydrogen bombs in the strategic areas of Trusteeship of the Pacific Islands[77] and the Ewe and Togoland unification problem.[78]

The power of the Trusteeship Council and the General Assembly to "accept petitions and examine them" was complemented by an authorisation to arrange periodic visits to the respective trust territories "at times agreed upon with the administering authority".[79] Such visits were made for a number of purposes. Some missions were undertaken to analyse problems raised in annual reports or petitions,[80] while other visits served to investigate the steps taken by the administering powers towards the realisation of self-government or independence, or to receive and investigate petitions on the spot.[81] The recommendations that arose from the missions were mostly endorsed by the Trusteeship Council, which in turn requested the administering authorities to give "most careful consideration to the conclusions of the mission". The findings of visiting missions could have significant implications for trust territories. The report of the visiting mission to Tanganyika recommended a specific target date for the independence of the territory, arguing that "progress is bound to be slow and somewhat purposeless as long as the target [of statehood] is not in the foreseeable

---

[75] For an analysis, see Toussaint, *Trusteeship System*, at 192, who points out that Rule 81 "cannot limit the right of the General Assembly to accept and examine a petition which the rules seek to render inadmissible".

[76] See also Chowdhuri, *International Mandates*, at 208 ("In contrast to the [Permanent Mandates] Commission which regarded the petitions as additional sources of information, the [Trusteeship] Council considers them as a means for ascertaining facts and redressing the grievances of the people").

[77] See UN Doc. T/PET. 10/27, 26 April 1954, at 1; UN Doc. T/PET. 10/28, 6 May 1954, at 1. See Chowdhuri, *International Mandates*, at 209–11.

[78] See UN Doc. A/603, 1948, RTC, at 34–5.

[79] See Article 87 (c) of the Charter.

[80] Visting missions presented "the eyes and ears of the Trusteeship Council and the General Assembly". See Statement of British delegate Mathieson to the Fourth Committee of the General Assembly, UN. Doc. A/C.4/386, 1 December 1953, at 483–4.

[81] See Chowhuri, *International Mandates*, at 224.

future".[82] Similar findings were made by the visiting mission to Rwanda-Urundi, which noted that the people of the territory should "achieve self-government within an estimated period of 20 to 25 years".[83] The Administering Authority of Ruanda-Urundi was requested by the Council to abolish all traces of racial discrimination in its legislation.

The machinery of trusteeship supervision under Article 87 of the UN Charter was supported by the general power of the General Assembly under Article 10 of the Charter to make recommendations to the administering powers.[84] The Assembly used this authority on several occasions to shape policy decisions in the trusteeship territories.[85] The General Assembly requested, *inter alia*, that the Trusteeship Council recommend that administering powers fly the flag of the UN in all trust territories and examine the possibility of native participation in the administration of these territories.[86] By another resolution, the Assembly asked the administering authorities to establish a university in each of the trust territories, in order to further the educational advancement of their inhabitants.[87] The Assembly invited administering states to specify time estimates in their annual reports for the attainment of self-government or independence of the trust territories.[88] Moreover, reports of visiting missions to Western Samoa, Rwanda-Urundi, Togoland and British Cameroons led to the adoption of GA Resolutions 323 (IV) and 440 (V), by which the Assembly recommended the abolition of corporal punishment in UK-administered trust territories.

---

[82] See Trusteeship Council, Res. 648 (XII), 20 July 1953, UN.Doc. T/1075, 18 August 1953, at 4. See *Report of the UN Visiting Mission to Trust Territories in East Africa*, 1954, on Tanganyika, UN. Doc. T/1142/, 23 December 1954, 6, at 186. The Mission noted that there is a "need for a more precise statement than appears yet to have been made that a self-governing or independent Tanganyika will inevitably be a State primarily African in character". See also Visiting Mission to Trust Territories in East Africa, 1954, *Report on the Trust Territory of Rwanda-Urundi*, UN Doc. T/1141, 8 December 1954, at 50.

[83] See Chowdhuri, *International Mandates*, at 225.

[84] Note that the General Assembly and the Trusteeship Council lacked the authority to take binding decisions *vis-à-vis* the administering powers. Article 89 of the Charter speaks of decisions of the Trusteeship Council. But there is no provision obliging member states to carry out these decisions, as exists in the case of the Security Council. Article 10 of the Charter provides that the General Assembly may "make recommendations to the Members of the United Nations or to the Security Council". The implementation of the system therefore depended to a large degree on the good faith of the administering authorities.

[85] See generally Chowdhuri, *International Mandates*, at 159; Toussaint, *Trusteeship Council*, at 182.

[86] See GA Res. 325 (IV), 28 December 1949, UN Doc. A/1251, at 40.

[87] See GA Res. 225 (III), GAOR, 3rd Sess.   [88] See GA Res. 558 (VI), GAOR, 6th Sess.

However, the best example of accountability under the Trusteeship System is the case of the Island of Nauru. In this case, the General Assembly intervened to prevent the resettlement of the population of the territory for purposes of the exploitation of mineral resources. Australia sought to move the native population of the phosphate-rich island, in order to facilitate mining operations. The General Assembly blocked this objective, by reaffirming the "inalienable right of the people of Nauru to self-government and independence" and mandating Australia to restore the island "for habitation by the Nauruan people".[89] This initiative led to the creation of domestic legislative Council in 1966 and the acquisition of the phosphate industry by Nauru Local Government Council.[90]

Following independence, the issue of rehabilitation arose before the ICJ. Nauru claimed compensation for the exploitation of mineral deposits by its former Administering Power. The Court found that it had jurisdiction to hear the case.[91] The dispute was settled by an agreement by which Australia agreed to pay compensation.

3.2.2. Trusteeship System administration and institutional diversity

The institutional structure of the Trusteeship System combined expertise with the objective of representative decision-making.[92] The Trusteeship Council consisted of the administering authorities of the trust territories, who had experience in the conduct of trusteeship administration, and non-administering powers, who in turn brought impartiality and objectivity to the decision-making process.[93] Both categories of members were required to be equally represented in the Council.[94] The continuance of expertise was safeguarded by Article 86 (2) of the UN Charter, which obliged members of the Council to designate a "specially qualified person to represent it therein".

Secondly, the Trusteeship System favoured the idea of taking into account the interests of the inhabitants of the administered territories.[95]

---

[89] See GA Res. 2111 (XX), 1407th Plen. Meeting (1965).

[90] See Tom Parker, *The Ultimate Intervention: Revitalising the UN Trusteeship Council for the 21st Century*, Report Centre for European and Asian Studies (2003), at 28.

[91] See ICJ, *Certain Phosphate Lands in Nauru (Nauru v. Australia)*, Preliminary Objections, Judgment 26 June 1992, ICJ Rep. 1992, 240.

[92] See Geiger, *On Article 86*, in Charter of the United Nations, at 1130, para. 7. See also Parker, *Revitalising the UN Trusteeship Council for the 21st Century*, at 50.

[93] See Chowdhuri, *International Mandates*, at 184.   [94] See Article 86 (1) (c) of the Charter.

[95] The first attempt in this direction stems back to the San Francisco Conference, where the Chinese delegation proposed indigenous participation in the work of the

The Trusteeship Council first attempted to associate "suitable qualified indigenous inhabitants of the Trust Territories in the work of the Council, as part of their delegations or in any other manner which they might deem desirable".[96] Later, the General Assembly instructed visiting missions in its Resolution 853 (IX)[97] to consider expressions of public opinion spontaneously brought before it by the native population to "take the initiative in seeking out public opinion on all important problems and to undertake popular consultations in whatever forms it might deem appropriate", and to grant "a hearing in case of urgency to the qualified representatives of public opinion".[98] This step prompted administering powers to show greater willingness to include indigenous members in their delegations. In addition, the Charter created a balance between responsibility and power, by granting non-administering Security Council members a seat in the Council, without giving them veto power.[99]

3.2.3. Status issues

Last, but not least, Chapters XII and XIII of the UN Charter brought some structural innovations concerning the governance and administration of non-sovereign entities.

Trusteeship Council. See UNCIO, Doc. 2 G/26 (e), 10 May 1945, Vol. III. 617. In the end, the proposal failed to gain sufficient support for adoption, as it was regarded at the time as being too innovative in nature. However, China's move created an awareness of the issue. See also Chowdhuri, *International Mandates*, at 240. The Trusteeship Council itself adopted a compromise solution in the first years of its existence. It granted administering authorities the right to associate indigenous inhabitants in the work of the Council, but did not make local participation mandatory. Rules 74 and 75 of the Council's Rules of Procedure allowed administering powers to designate a native inhabitant as a special representative to the Council, who was entitled to participate without vote in the examination and discussion of annual reports. But this rule fell short of meeting the demands of other delegations, which took the position that "the population of the trust territories" should be given "the right ... to send their representatives to participate without vote" in the work of the Trusteeship Council. See the Soviet proposal for a "special representative" clause in the Council's Rule of Procedure, in George Thullen, *Problems of the Trusteeship System* (1964), at 94.

[96] See Trusteeship Council, Res. 466 (XI), UN Doc. T/1030, 20 August 1952, 3–4. But fierce controversies between administering and non-administering powers over the issue prevented the adoption of a common position. The problem was that a single representative from a trust territory could only reflect part of a general opinion, while the hearing of several representatives would turn the Trusteeship Council into a forum for internal political struggle. See Thullen, *Problems of the Trusteeship System*, at 94–101.

[97] See GA Res. 853 (IV), 14 December 1954, Doc. A/2890 (1955), at 29–30.

[98] See also Trusteeship Council, RTC. (1954), 31, UN Doc A/2680.

[99] See Article 86 (1) (b) of the Charter.

3.2.3.1. Sovereignty

Following the precedent set by Article 22 of the League Covenant, Chapter XII of the UN Charter formally separated sovereignty from territorial authority. The administering powers lacked sovereign ownership over the administered territory during the period of trusteeship administration. They acquired only a limited title over the trust territories[100] and derived their rights and obligations from trusteeship agreements, which could be terminated by the Security Council under Article 24 of the Charter.[101] The inhabitants of the trust territories depended on the assistance of the administering authorities to assume functions of self-government. However, the references to self-government, independence and "the freely expressed wishes of the peoples concerned" in Article 76 (b) of the Charter made it clear that sovereignty ultimately resided with the people. It is therefore justified to claim that the Trusteeship System introduced "a new species of international government, which [did] not fit into the old concept of sovereignty and [was] alien to it".[102]

3.2.3.2. Partial legal personality

Trust territories were typically administered under the laws of the administering powers.[103] Yet, they possessed an "international status".[104]

---

[100] See also the Statement of the representative of Ecuador at the 9th General Assembly: "We can no more speak of the sovereignty of an administering power than we can speak of guardian's ownership of his ward's property." See UN Doc. A/PV.485, 1 October 1954, 146. See also Chowdhuri, *International Mandates*, at 234.

[101] See in relation to Mandates, ICJ Advisory Opinion, *South West Africa* (1971), paras. 110–16. The Council used this authority in Resolution 276 to declare South Africa's presence in Namibia as unlawful after the revocation of its mandate by the General Assembly. The same argument can be made with respect to trusteeship agreements.

[102] See Lord McNair, ICJ Rep. 1950, at 150.

[103] See Article 5 of the Trusteeship Agreement for the Territory of Tanganyika ("full powers of legislation, administration and jurisdiction in Tanganyika, subject to the provisions of the United Nations Charter and of this agreement"), Article 5 of the Trusteeship Agreement for the Territory of Togoland, Article 5 of the Trusteeship Agreement for the Territory of Ruanda-Urundi, Article 3 of the Trusteeship Agreement for the Territory of Western Samoa, Article 4 of the Trusteeship Agreement for the Territory of New Guinea, reprinted in Hall, *Mandates, Dependencies and Trusteeships*, at 340–70. The trusteeship agreements contained at the same time an obligation to "take into consideration local laws and customs". See, for example, Article 8 of the Trusteeship Agreement for the Territory of Tanganyika, Article 7 of the Trusteeship Agreement for the French Cameroons and Togoland, Article 8 of the Trusteeship Agreement for the Territory of Ruanda-Urundi, Article 8 of the Trusteeship Agreement for the Territory of New Guinea.

[104] See with regard to Mandates, ICJ, *International Status of South-West Africa*, ICJ Rep. 1950, response to question c. It is even argued that trust territories possessed a limited degree of international legal personality. Rauschning, *On Article 75*, in Charter of the United Nations, at 1103, para. 15.

Trust territories and their inhabitants were in several respects treated as subjects of their own rather than integral parts of the administering state. Their separate identity resulted from "the international rules regulating the rights, powers and obligations relating to the administration of the Territory and the supervision of that administration".[105] Inhabitants of the trust territory enjoyed, in particular, certain "passive rights", which reflected their identity. They were not automatically regarded as nationals of the administering powers.[106] They enjoyed the right to be administered according to the terms of the trusteeship agreements, which incorporated numerous protections for their benefit, including human rights provisions, restrictions on the transfer or sale of native territory and duties of the administering powers to preserve certain local laws and customs.[107] Moreover, international treaties concluded or applied by the administering authorities in the period of trusteeship administration did not automatically continue to bind trust territories after the termination of their trusteeship status.[108] These particularities indicate that trust territories enjoyed partial international legal personality,[109] which reflects their special nature as "a new species of international government" (McNair).[110]

3.2.3.3. Authority in trust

Lastly, the Trusteeship System formalised the concept of trusteeship authority. The UN Charter abandoned the reference to the ambiguous concept of the "sacred trust of civilisation" used in the Covenant of the League of Nations and defined trusteeship as a legal concept.

---

[105] Ibid.

[106] See Rauschning, On Article 75, in Charter of the United Nations, at 1103, para. 15.

[107] See, for example, Articles 8 and 11 of the Trusteeship Agreement for the Territory of Tanganyika, Articles 7 and 10 of the Trusteeship Agreement for the French Cameroons and Togoland, Articles 11 and 14 of the Trusteeship Agreement for the Territory of Ruanda-Urundi and Articles 8, 12 and 13 of the Trusteeship Agreement for Western Samoa.

[108] Most of the trusteeship agreements contained a clause which authorised the administering powers to apply international conventions to trust territories which were in the interests of the population and consistent with the basic objectives of the trusteeship system. See Article 7 of the Trusteeship Agreement for the Territory of Tanganyika, Article 6 of the Trusteeship Agreement for the French Cameroons and Togoland, Article 7 of the Trusteeship Agreement for the Territory of Ruanda-Urundi and Article 7 of the Trusteeship Agreement for Western Samoa. However, trust territories neither become parties to the agreements nor were they obliged by the trusteeship agreements to abide by these obligations after the termination of trusteeship.

[109] See also Crawford, Creation of States, 2nd edn (2006), at 574.

[110] See also Parker, Revitalising the UN Trusteeship Council for the 21st Century, at 30.

Lord McNair identified three basic features of trusteeship authority, namely:

(1) that the control of the trustee, *tuteur* or *curateur* over the property is limited in one way or another; he is not in the position of the normal complete owner who can do what he likes to with his own, because he is precluded from administering the property for his own benefit; (2) that the trustee, *tuteur* or *curateur* is under some kind of legal obligation, based on confidence and conscience, to carry out the trust or mission confided to him for the benefit of some other person or for some public purpose; (3) that any attempt by one of these persons to absorb the property entrusted to him into his own patrimony would be illegal and would be prevented by law.[111]

The authority exercised by administering powers under the Trusteeship System was trusteeship authority *per excellence*. All three parameters were met by administration under the Trusteeship System. The authority of the administering powers was limited by the trusteeship agreements and Article 76 of the Charter, which allowed them to exercise jurisdiction and control over the administered territories, but prevented them from exercising ownership over the trust territories. The administration itself was carried out to serve the "interests of the inhabitants of the territory" and "humanity in general" and tied to the development of self-government.[112] Finally, violations of the obligations under the trusteeship agreements and the Charter were subject to accountability under the Trusteeship System[113] and judicial review by the ICJ.[114] "Trusteeship" was therefore no longer a moral responsibility under the UN Charter, but a legal principle of administration with clear-cut obligations for administering powers.

---

[111] See Separate Opinion of Judge McNair in the South-West Africa case, ICJ Rep. 1950, 146, at 149. See generally on the legal concept of the trust, Hans Albrecht Schwarz-Liebermann v. Wahlendorf, *Vormundschaft und Treuhand des römischen und englischen Privatrechts in ihrer Anwendbarkeit auf völkerrechtlicher Ebene* (1951), 88 *et seq.*

[112] See in relation to Mandates, ICJ, *Legal Consequences for States of the Continued Presence of South Africa in Namibia*, ICJ Rep. 1971, at 29.

[113] See Chapter XIII of the UN Charter.

[114] The Trusteeship Agreements contained a clause which stated: "If any dispute whatever should arise between the Administering Authority and another Member of the United Nations relating to the interpretation or the application of the provisions of the present Trusteeship Agreement, such dispute, if it cannot be settled by negotiation or other means, shall be submitted to the International Court of Justice provided for by Chapter XIV of the Charter of the United Nations." See, for example, Article 19 of the Trusteeship Agreement for the Territory of Tanganyika, Article 13 of the Trusteeship Agreement for the French Cameroons and Togoland, Article 19 of the Trusteeship Agreement for the Territory of Ruanda-Urundi and Article 16 of the Trusteeship Agreement for Western Samoa.

4 Post-war occupation

The third legal framework that has given rise to experiments in territorial administration is the law of occupation. The law of occupation is not specifically a framework for the administration of territory. Occupation is primarily a conflict-centred device that is designed to restore order and civil life and to balance certain interests after the cessation of hostilities. The authority of the occupant is limited by specific constraints emanating from the inviolability of the rights of the territorial sovereign and the limited regulatory powers of the occupant over the occupied territory.[1] Occupation has therefore only in exceptional circumstances served as a long-term instrument of territorial administration, namely either in conjunction with an additional peace settlement or in special historical circumstances (Germany, Japan, Palestine).

1. Occupation and territorial administration – two distinct concepts

The framework of occupation is based on two assumptions, which compromise its capacity to serve as a multilateral governing framework for the administration of territory. The rules of the law of occupation address a very particular conflict of interest, namely the relationship between the occupant, the local population and the ousted government.[2] Secondly, they offer limited leeway for the occupant to shape the internal structure of the territory under administration.[3]

---

[1] These special features of occupation were already emphasised by Grotius. See Grotius, *De jure belli ac pacis*, Book III, Chapter 6.

[2] See Benvenisti, *International Law of Occupation*, at 210.

[3] See Adam Roberts, *Transformative Military Occupation: Applying the Laws of War and Human Rights*, American Journal of International Law, Vol. 100 (2006), 580.

1.1.   The rationale of the laws of occupation

The structure of the law of occupation is not geared towards objective and long-term peacemaking. It is centred on the organisation of the relationship between the former parties to the conflict and the population of the occupied territory. This is reflected in the history of the laws of occupation.

Throughout the nineteenth century, occupation was mainly regarded as a by-product of war, in which the interaction between the enemy's army and the local population was reduced to an absolute minimum.[4] The concept of occupation was founded on utilitarian considerations. The occupying power assumed authority mainly to protect its own forces. The ousted sovereign conceded these powers to the occupant in order to protect its remaining rights over the territory against internal resistance, and in order to guarantee the local population a minimum standard of welfare.[5]

The introduction of the Regulations Respecting the Laws and Customs of War in 1907 brought about a slight shift in conception. The framework of the rules of occupation was based on the assumption that the occupying power would substitute its own authority over that of the ousted government.[6] Occupation was therefore directly conceived as a device

---

[4] Following the war doctrine prevailing at the time, armed hostilities were primarily conceived a duel between governments. The spirit of the time was expressed by Rousseau who noted in his "Contrat Social" that "war ... is not a relation of man to man, but a relation of states in which private persons are enemies only accidentally". The same understanding was later expressed by King William of Prussia, who defined the 1870 war between Germany and France as conduct of "war with the French soldiers, not with the French citizens". See Benvenisti, *International Law of Occupation*, at 27.

[5] See Eyal Benvenisti, *The Security Council and the Law on Occupation: Resolution 1483 on Iraq in Historical Perspective*, Israel Defense Forces Law Review, Vol. 1 (2003) 23. This minimalist conception of occupation coincided with the practice of short-term occupations, which was typical of the nineteenth century.

[6] This idea is reflected in Article 42 of the Hague Regulations which states that "the occupation extends only to the territory where such authority has been established" and Article 43, which refers to a situation in which "[t]he authority of the legitimate power ha[s] in fact passed into the hands of the occupant". See also ICJ, *Legal Consequences of the Construction of a Wall in the Occupied Palestinian Territory*, Advisory Opinion, 9 July 2004, ICJ Rep. 2004, p. 167, para. 78 and p. 172, para. 89, where Court held that occupation, under customary international law, as reflected in Article 42 of the Hague Regulations of 1907, extends only to territory where such authority has been established and can be exercised. See also ICJ, *Case Concerning Armed Activities on the Territory of the Congo (Democratic Republic of Congo v. Uganda)*, Judgment of 19 December 2005, para. 173.

of administration, namely as a form of control over territory which requires not only the establishment of authority by the intervening force (e.g. through the stationing of troops), but also the establishment of certain structures demonstrating the exercise of governmental authority over territory.[7] However, the Hague Regulations remained focused on the idea of the preservation of balance between the occupant and the occupied power[8] and left the exercise of managing powers for the benefit of the indigenous population largely at the discretion of the occupant. They did, in particular, not proscribe a catalogue of duties to be satisfied by the occupant, but merely obliged the occupant to "take all the measures in his power to restore and ensure, as far as possible, public order and [civil life]".[9]

The Fourth Geneva Convention strengthened the managerial responsibilities of occupying powers. The Convention placed the protection of civilians at the centre of the rules of occupation.[10] Occupation came to include concrete tasks of governance and administration.[11] Moreover, occupying powers became trustees bound to serve the interests and benefits of the territorial sovereign and its population when ruling foreign

[7] The applicability of the laws of occupation was not formally made dependent on the establishment of a direct system of military or civilian government. But these rules were interpreted as obliging occupants to institute a separate system of administration to execute the powers and duties allotted to them under the law of occupation. See, for example, (UK) War Office, *The Law of War on Land*, Part III of the Manual of Military Law (1958), at 145, para. 518. The degree of control to be exercised by an occupying power was specified by the ICJ in the *Case Concerning Armed Activities on the Territory of the Congo (Democratic Republic of Congo v. Uganda)*. The Court acknowledged that an occupation may be exercised without the establishment of a "structured military administration" through "indirect" forms of administration, for example, through control over foreign factions. However, the Court required proof that the intervening force takes measures to substitute the authority of the territorial sovereign. The Court clarified that the exercise of authority as occupying power must be accompanied by the exercise of (effective) control over the specific part of the territory, in order to trigger the obligations under Article 43 of the Hague Regulations. See ICJ, *Case Concerning Armed Activities on the Territory of the Congo*, paras. 173–7.

[8] See Article 43 of the 1907 Hague Regulations ("while respecting, unless absolutely prevented, the laws in force in the country"). See also Benvenisti, *International Law of Occupation*, at 6.

[9] See Article 43 of the Hague Regulations.

[10] See Jean S. Pictet, *Commentary, IV Geneva Convention* (1958), at 613 ("the Hague Regulations... are intended above all to serve as a guide to the armed forces, whereas the Fourth Convention aims principally at the protection of civilians").

[11] The Fourth Geneva Convention replaced the restrictive and disinterested model of occupant regulation by a broader authorisation enabling the occupying power to exercise the regulatory authority necessary to exercise its functions effectively. See Article 64 (2) of the Fourth Geneva Convention.

territory.[12] This change in focus is reflected in two important innovations, namely the codification of fundamental rights for the occupied
population[13] and the extension of the regulatory powers of the administering authorities.[14]

However, even in this context, territorial administration remained essentially an annex of occupation. The scope of application of the provisions of the Fourth Geneva Convention was centred on the immediate
aftermath of the cessation of hostilities, in particular the year after the
general close of military operations.[15] Moreover, the exercise of public
authority under the Convention continued to be shaped by the primary
aim of regulating the conflict of interest between the occupant, the
territorial sovereign and the local population. These two features distinguish it generally from the more objective and third-party dominated

[12] See Sir Arnold Wilson, *The Laws of War in Occupied Territory*, Transactions of the Grotius
Society, Vol. 18 (1933), 17, at 38. The structural connection between laws of occupation
and the principle of trusteeship was later reaffirmed by numerous other scholars. See
Gerhard von Glahn, *Law Among Nations: An Introduction to Public International Law*, 5th
edn (1986), at 686 ("[T]he occupant...exercises a temporary right of administration on
a sort of trusteeship basis"; Allan Gerson, *Trustee Occupant: The Legal Status of Israel's
Presence in the West Bank*, Harvard International Law Journal, Vol. 14 (1973), 1–49; Adam
Roberts, *What is Military Occupation?*, British Yearbook of International Law, Vol. 55
(1984), 249, at 295 ("the idea of 'trusteeship' is implicit in all occupation law");
Benvenisti, *International Law of Occupation*, at 6.
[13] Part III of the Convention dedicates an entire chapter to the protection of civilians.
The core provision of Part III is Article 27, which obligates the occupying power to
protect civilians against violence, to ensure the humane treatment of protected
persons and to protect their honour, family rights, religious convictions and customs.
Chapter III complements this protection by imposing positive obligations on
occupying powers, including the duty to facilitate the proper functioning of
institutions devoted to the care and education of children (Article 50), the obligation
to ensure the provision of food and medical supplies to the local population (Article
55) and to maintain medical and hospital establishments (Article 56).
[14] Article 64 (2) of the Convention broadened the regulatory authority of occupying
powers, by recognising the right of the occupant to modify existing domestic law in
order to fulfil its obligations under the Convention. The provision states: "The
Occupying Power may... subject the populations of the occupied territory to
provisions which are essential to enable the Occupying Power to fulfil its obligations
under the present Convention, to maintain the orderly government of the territory,
and to ensure the security of the Occupying Power, of the members and property of
the occupying forces or administration, and likewise of the establishments and lines
of communication used by them." The wording of the Convention extended the terms
of Article 43 of the Hague Regulations, which allowed only limited modifications of
the local laws "to restore and ensure, as far as possible, public order and civil life,
while respecting, unless absolutely prevented, the laws in force in the country".
[15] See Article 6 of the Fourth Geneva Convention.

framework of authority typical in the context of direct or indirect international territorial administration.

1.2.   Limitations of occupation authority

Secondly, the laws of occupation are not intended to provide a general framework for reconstruction and law reform. Occupation authority is restricted by specific limitations arising from the protection of the occupied territory and its people.[16]

The Hague Regulations limit the powers of occupying authorities under Article 43. This provision was originally adopted in order to protect smaller and weaker countries against the risks of socio-economic transformation under occupation. It reads:

> The authority of the legitimate power having in fact passed into the hands of the occupant, the latter shall take all the measures in his *power to restore and ensure, as far as possible, public order and safety*, while respecting, unless absolutely prevented, the laws in force in the country.[17]

This English translation ("public order and safety") is frequently criticised as deviating from the authentic French words (*"l'ordre et la vie publics"*) and read as an entitlement for the occupant to organise "public order and *civil life*".[18] However, the powers of the occupant are drafted as an exception ("unless absolutely prevented"[19]). Moreover, the occupying power is bound to preserve the existing *status quo* ("laws in force in the country"[20]), including laws and other general and abstract rules (Constitution, decrees, ordinances etc.) adopted by the former sovereign.[21] The right to modify the laws applicable in the occupied territory is therefore limited.

It is generally agreed that the occupant can enact new laws if required for reasons of military necessity, such as for the safety of the troops of the occupying powers, or the maintenance of order.[22] However, Article 43

---

[16] See Jean S. Pictet (ed.), *On Article 47*, in Commentary, IV Geneva Convention (1958), at 273.

[17] Emphasis added.

[18] See Marco Sassòli, *Legislation and Maintenance of Public Order and Civil Life by Occupying Powers*, European Journal of International Law, Vol. 16 (2005), 661, at 663-664.

[19] In French "*sauf empêchement absolu*".   [20] In French "*les lois en vigueur*".

[21] See Sassòli, *Legislation and Maintenance of Public Order and Civil Life*, at 668-9.

[22] See Yoram Dinstein, *Legislation under Article 43 of the Hague Regulations: Belligerent Occupation and Peacebuilding*, Program on Humanitarian Policy and Conflict Research, Occasional Paper, Fall 2004, No. 1, at 4 ("When a necessity arises, the Occupying Power is allowed to enact new legislation, repealing, suspending or modifying the preexisting legal system").

does not vest the occupying power with "general legislative competence".[23] It is disputed whether and to what extent occupants are entitled to invoke the welfare of the native population as a ground for
adopting new legislation under Article 43,[24] as the Hague Regulations
offer no reliable criteria to define the requirement to "respect" the existing laws "unless absolutely prevented". Some authorities read this term
essentially as a synonym for "military necessity",[25] while others recognise a right of the occupying power to "legislate for reasons other than
military necessity".[26]

At the same, it is generally understood that the occupying authority
is not entitled to "substitute a new indigenous governmental structure
or change internal boundaries, except, in the latter case, on a temporary
basis to protect the safety of [its] armed forces and to realise the purposes
of the war".[27] The obligation to respect "the laws in force in the country" extends to institutions of the occupied territory. The occupant is
therefore generally prevented from changing fundamental institutions
or the constitutional order of the occupied territory.[28]

The Fourth Geneva Convention displays similar caution towards the
enforcement of profound changes and new legal standards on the administered population. The Convention is built on the principle of
the inalienability of sovereignty through the use of force by the occupant. The concept of the inviolability of the rights of the occupied sovereign is contained in Article 47 of the Convention, which
states:

---

[23] See Christopher Greenwood, *The Administration of Occupied Territories*, in International
Law and the Administration of Occupied Territories (E. Playfair ed., 1992), 243, at 247.

[24] Von Glahn considers the benefit of the population a "secondary aim of any lawful
military occupation". See Gerhard von Glahn, *The Occupation of Enemy Territory* (1957), at
97. See also Arnold Duncan McNair and Arthur D. Watts, *The Legal Effects of War* (1966),
at 369. But the definition of the exact legal threshold differs among authors. For a
comprehensive survey, see Benvenisti, *International Law of Occupation*, at 14–15.

[25] See Michael Bothe, *Belligerent Occupation*, Max Planck Encyclopedia of Public
International Law, Vol. III (1997), at 765.

[26] See Sassòli, *Legislation and Maintenance of Public Order and Civil Life*, at 673–4. Dinstein
observes that "the common interpretation of Article 43 is that 'empêchement absolu'
is the equivalent of 'nécessité'". See Dinstein, *Legislation under Article 43 of the Hague
Regulations*, at 4.

[27] See von Glahn, *Occupation of Enemy Territory*, at 96. See also Greenwood, *The
Administration of Occupied Territories*, at 245.

[28] The denazification carried out by the US government in post-war Germany marks an
exception, which was justified on a different basis, namely the *debellatio* doctrine. See
also Sassòli, *Legislation and Maintenance of Public Order and Civil Life*, at 671–2.

Protected persons who are in occupied territory shall not be deprived, in any case or in any manner whatsoever, of the benefits of the present Convention by any change introduced, as a result of the occupation of a territory, into the institutions or government of the said territory, nor by any agreement concluded between the authorities of the occupied territories and the Occupying Power, nor by any annexation by the latter of the whole or part of the occupied territory.

The provision does not expressly prohibit the occupying power from effecting changes in the internal system or organisation of the occupied territory. However, it is intended to prevent radical transformations of the territory's structure and organisation which may deteriorate "the position of inhabitants" or which deprive protected persons "of the rights and safeguards provided for them".[29]

Further restrictions on the power of the occupant to amend the institutional system of the occupied territory are contained in Article 54 of the Convention, which allows occupying powers to remove public officials from office, but prohibits them from "alter[ing] the status of public officials or judges in the occupied territories". Moreover, Article 64 (1) of the Convention imposes express limits on the entitlement of the occupant to change existing penal laws, which is restricted to cases "where [these laws] constitute a threat to the [Occupying Power's] security or an obstacle to the application of the ... Convention".[30] Modifications of non-penal laws are subject to the specific conditions listed in Article 64 (2), which authorises changes only to maintain order, to protect the security of the occupying power or to implement essential obligations of the occupant under the Convention. The limited legislative powers of the occupant are summarised by the Commentary of the International Committee of the Red Cross on the Fourth Geneva Convention as follows:

(a) [The occupant] may promulgate provisions required for the application of the Convention in accordance with the obligations imposed on it by the latter in a number of spheres: child welfare, labour, food, hygiene and public health etc.

(b) It will have the right to enact provisions necessary to maintain the 'orderly government of the territory' in its capacity as the Power responsible for public law and order.

---

[29] See Pictet, *On Article 47*, Commentary IV Geneva Convention, at 274. See also Greenwood, *The Administration of Occupied Territories*, at 256.

[30] For a discussion, see Benvenisti, *International Law of Occupation*, at 101–3.

(c) It is, lastly authorized to promulgate penal provisions for its own protection.[31]

Last, but not least, the customary law of occupation contains specific principles to assess the impact of acts of occupation on the returning sovereign. It relies on reciprocal concepts, such as *postliminium*[32] and *uti possidetis*,[33] in order to determine whether and to what extent acts adopted by the occupying powers continue to apply in the aftermath of period of belligerent occupation. These principles balance the authority of the occupying power to exercise regulatory powers for the organisation of public life during the period of occupation against the right of the former sovereign to the preservation of the *status quo*.

This specific conception of authority has systemic implications for the status of the occupant. Since the authority of the occupant is based on this specific balancing of interest and deemed to be temporary in nature, the law of occupation does not contain elaborate forms of democratic accountability. The occupying power is called upon to act in the best interests of the citizens of the occupied territory and to satisfy certain positive duties. However, the exercise of authority is not measured by the standard of accountability that governs the ties between a government and its citizens in a democratic society. The occupant is not formally accountable to the people of the occupied territory, nor subject to express reporting requirements or power-sharing obligations.[34]

All of these factors establish quite clearly that the laws of occupation are, in principle, not intended to provide a governance structure for long-term processes of territorial administration, nor designed to promote a

---

[31] See Pictet, *On Article 64*, Commentary IV Geneva Convention, at 337. See also Dinstein, *Legislation under Article 43 of the Hague Regulations*, at 6–7, who notes that the concept of necessity under Article 64 of the Fourth Geneva Convention has three dimensions, namely "the need of the Occupying Power to remove any threat to its security", "the duty of the Occupying to discharge its duties under the Geneva Convention" and the necessity "to ensure the 'orderly government' of the occupied territory".

[32] Principles of *postliminium* come into play when "a conquered territory reverts, either during or at the end of the war, into the possession of the legitimate sovereign". They require a return to the *status quo* before occupation in relation to unlawful modifications under the regime of occupation. See Oppenheim, *International Law*, Vol. II, Disputes, War and Neutrality, 6th edn, at 483. See also Wolff Heintschel von Heinegg, *Factors in War to Peace Transitions*, Harvard Journal of Law and Public Policy, Vol. 27 (2004), 843, a 865–6.

[33] The principle of *uti possidetis* obliges the returning sovereign to respect lawful acts adopted during the occupation regime. See Oppenheim, *International Law*, Vol. II, 6th edn, at 482.

[34] See also Boon, *Legislative Reform in Post-Conflict Zones*, at 305.

law reform agenda involving substantial changes in the constitutional and institutional system of the occupied territory.[35]

2. The use of occupation as a framework for territorial administration

Foreign state occupation involved extensive administration and governance over a prolonged period of time only in two situations, namely treaty-based occupation and post-surrender occupation. Both types of administration have posed legal problems in practice. The exercise of public authority has, in particular, triggered disputes over the scope of powers of the occupant under the terms of the respective agreements or controversies over the applicability of the limitations under the Hague Regulations. These experiences confirm the general scepticism about the aptitude of the laws of occupation to serve as general framework for territorial governance.[36]

2.1. Treaty-based occupation

Treaty-based occupations usually provide greater scope for the exercise of regulatory authority by occupying powers. Contractual arrangements, such as armistice agreements[37] or peace agreements,[38] may alter the legal regime of occupation and expand the powers of occupants, so as

---

[35] Occupation is rather a tool to address short-term power vacuums arising in and after conflict, requiring targeted and provisional regulation of the relations between the occupying power, the ousted government and the local population. See Benvenisti, *International Law of Occupation*, at 211–13. See also Pitman B. Potter, *Legal Bases and Character of Military Occupation in Germany and Japan*, American Journal of International Law, Vol. 43 (1949), at 323.

[36] See also Dinstein, *Legislation under Article 43 of the Hague Regulations,* at 12 ("There is ... no valid legislation by an Ocuupying Power without necessity (as defined in Geneva Article 64). Moreover, any new legislation in the course of belligerent occupation should be subject to some qualifications ... and – whatever the good intentions of the occupying power – no fundamental changes ought to be permitted even on a provisional basis. These conclusions apply *to peacebuilding as much as to belligerent occupation*."). (Emphasis added.)

[37] Armistice occupation is an occupation agreed upon under the terms of an armistice agreement between the belligerents. The rights and duties of occupying powers derive from two different sources – the laws of occupation and the armistice agreement, which may alter the legal regime of occupation. Armistice occupation constitutes therefore a *sui generis* form of occupation, which has been called "mixed occupation" (*Mischbesetzung*). For a survey, see Michael Bothe, *Occupation After Armistice*, in Encyclopedia of Public International Law, Vol. III (1997), at 761.

[38] The key feature of peacetime occupation by consent is that foreign presence is based on the terms of a post-war agreement, "in which the States provide in advance for the

to allow the exercise of regulatory powers in different fields of public authority. However, neither armistice occupations[39] nor consent-based occupations[40] were particularly successful techniques of foreign state

occupation of all or part of the territory of one of them". See Roberts, What is Military Occupation?, at 277.

[39] Occupations following an armistice have traditionally been characterised by conflicts between the occupying power and the former sovereign over the scope of applicability of the Hague Regulations. The German occupation of Belgium (1914–18), one of most famous examples of armistice occupation, illustrates the various problems raised by the use of treaty-based occupation as a governance mechanism. See generally Jacques Pirenne and Maurice Vauthier, La Législation et l'Administration Allemandes en Belgique (1925), at 56. The German administering authorities recognised their obligation to observe the law of occupation. But they regulated a wide array of public and private affairs, including energy resources and industrial production, monetary politics, taxation, welfare legislation and, most of all, the division of Belgium into Flanders and Wallonia. Many of these measures not only abrogated or amended existing Belgian laws, but also sought to shape or change the political system of the country. German authorities tried to justify their acts on the basis of Article 43 of the Hague Regulations, arguing that legislative authority had passed from the Belgium sovereign to the German occupant with the transfer of authority to the German rulers. This broad interpretation of Article 43 was, however, rejected by the Belgian authorities, including the Belgian King, who expressly challenged the validity of the German occupation measures in a decree of 8 April 1917, claiming that Hague Regulations precluded occupants from effecting substantial changes in the local law. See Benvenisti, International Law of Occupation, at 45, note 66. The conflict ended only after Belgium's liberation in 1918, when the newly formed Belgian government revoked all German occupation orders on the ground that they were invalid under international law. Similar disputes characterised occupation policies during the armistice occupation of the Rhineland (1918–20). For a detailed account, see Ernst Fraenkel, Military Occupation and the Rule of Law (1944), at 2–68. See also Carl L. Heyland, Die Rechtsstellung der besetzten Rheinlande nach dem Versailler Friedensvertrag und dem Rheinlandsabkommen (1923). In this instance, the roles were reversed. This time, German authorities withdrew from their broad interpretation of occupying authority under Article 43 of the Hague Regulations and called for deference to domestic rules, whereas the Allied powers interpreted their powers widely, arguing that the terms of the armistice created an exception to the framework of Article 43 of the Hague Regulations. See Benvenisti, International Law of Occupation, at 49, 57.

[40] In the case of peacetime occupation by consent, the role of the laws of occupation is significantly reduced. The conditions of foreign rule are largely determined by the terms of the occupation agreement. The laws of occupation have, if at all, only a subsidiary function, namely to solve interpretational disputes or to close gaps where the agreement is silent. See Roberts, What is Military Occupation?, at 278; McNair and Watts, Legal Effects of War, at 418, 420. The most frequently cited example is the pacific occupation of the Rhineland carried out in accordance with the terms of the Treaty of Versailles. The conditions of the occupation were laid down in the Rhineland Agreement, signed on the same day as the Treaty of Versailles, 28 June 1919. However, the legal framework of the agreement was in many points ambiguous or lacunary. This shortcoming led to numerous disputes over the question of whether the Hague Regulations served as a limitation to the powers of the Inter-Allied Rhineland High

administration. The assumption of managerial functions by the occupant conflicted with the imperatives of the deference to local law and the preservation of domestic structures. Domestic actors invoked the language of the rules of occupation as a defence against the promotion of social and political change by the occupant in the occupied territory. This prompted occupants to deny the applicability of the laws of occupation and, ultimately, caused a decline in the use of treaty-based occupation as a device of administration.[41]

2.2. Post-surrender occupation

The second type of occupation under which states have exercised comprehensive public authority over foreign territory is "post-surrender occupation".[42] It describes a situation in which a country continues to remain under the *de facto* or *de jure* control of an occupant after its unconditional surrender or its collapse as an independent and organised entity (*debellatio*).[43] The most famous examples of post-surrender occupation are the Allied occupations of Germany and Japan after World War II. Both occupations were dominated by an ideological motive, namely the will to implant democracy in post-war Germany and Japan.[44] Due to this agenda, both undertakings shared more common bonds with experiments in territorial administration than with classic occupations,

---

Commission, which was authorised under Article 3 of the Rhineland Agreement "to issue ordinances so far as may be necessary for securing the maintenance, safety and requirements of the Allied and Associated Forces". See Kelly, *Restoring and Maintaining Order*, at 136–9. The Commission used this authority, in particular, to promulgate detailed regulations governing the local police and judiciary. These measures were openly contested by the German Government, which tended to argue that the Hague Regulations formed the source of the occupant's authority. See Fraenkel, *Military Occupation and the Rule of Law*, at 149–51; Roberts, *What is Military Occupation?*, at 277. Courts never found a breach of the Hague Regulations. But they did not fully exclude the applicability of the laws of occupation either. See Judgment of the Military Court of the Belgian Army of Occupation in the Rhineland in the case of *Auditeur Militaire* v. *Reinhardt and Others*, Annual Digest, Vol. 2 (1923–4), Case No. 239, 441, 442. This hybrid situation created confusion and raised doubts as to the feasibility of the Rhineland Occupation, which culminated in calls for a detailed and unified Occupation Statute. See Fraenkel, *Military Occupation and the Rule of Law*, at 230.

[41] See Benvenisti, *International Law of Occupation*, at 211–12.

[42] See Nisuke Ando, *Surrender, Occupation, and Private Property in International Law: An Evaluation of U.S. Practice in Japan* (1991), at 38, 65; Roberts, *What is Military Occupation?*, at 267; Benvenisti, *International Law of Occupation*, at 91.

[43] The *debellatio* doctrine claims that occupation transfers sovereignty if the enemy state has disintegrated. See generally Roberts, *What is Military Occupation?*, at 267.

[44] See John D. Montgomery, *Forced to Be Free* (1957), at 4. See also Roberts, *What is Military Occupation?*, at 268.

making them exceptional forms of post-war governance.[45] The model of post-surrender occupation worked comparatively well in the context of the historical circumstances of the time. However, it remained open to criticism from a legal point of view and was later ruled out by the provisions of the Fourth Geneva Convention.

2.2.1.   The post-war governance of Germany

The Allied Administration of Germany (1945–9)[46] instituted a transformative form of multinational post-war administration.[47] The administration was not only established to respond to a security threat, or to fill a provisional governance vacuum: Allied authority was conceived as an instrument to transform the political and social structure of the German state through constitutional reform, de-nazification, re-education and political and economic reconstruction. Its particular focus on state reconstruction distinguished Allied authority quite significantly from traditional forms of occupation authority.[48] However, this new regime posed a series of conceptual problems that were difficult to solve on the basis of the existing categories of international law.[49]

2.2.1.1.   Challenges of Allied occupation
The Allied powers assumed control over Germany by the "Declaration Regarding the Defeat of Germany of June, 5 1945", which stated that the Four Powers assumed "supreme authority with respect to Germany", without annexing the country.[50] US, UK and French military analysts had anticipated[51] during the war that Germany would still possess a

---

[45] The scope of regulatory authority exercised by the Allies and the unique nature of both undertakings exceeded the traditional rubric of the laws of occupation. See also Potter, *Legal Bases and Character of Military Occupation*, at 325, who aptly qualifies the administrations of Germany and Japan as "conduct of international territorial administration in disguise".

[46] See generally Theodor Schweisfurth, *Germany, Occupation After World War II*, Encyclopedia of Public International Law, at 582; Jennings, *Government in Commission*, 112–41; Wolfgang Friedmann, *The Allied Military Government of Germany* (1947); Wilhelm Grewe, *Ein Besatzungsstatut für Deutschland* (1948); Michel Virally, *L'Administration Internationale de L'Allemagne* (1948); Edward H. Litchfield, *Governing Postwar Germany* (1953). See also Chesterman, *You, The People*, at 25–36.

[47] See also Friedmann, *Allied Military Government of Germany*, at 13.

[48] See also Potter, *Legal Bases and Character of Military Occupation*, at 324.

[49] For a detailed analysis, see von Glahn, *Occupation of Enemy Territory*, at 273.

[50] See Schweisfurth, *Occupation After World War II*, at 584.

[51] The UK, the US and France set up specialist teams for the preparation of the military occupation of Germany nearly two years before the end of the war. However, the

viable institutional and economic system at the date of surrender, and that a German administration would replace the Nazi government and would govern the German state under Allied control.[52] However, this hope was shattered by the military events of the last nine months of the war. By the time the Allies assumed control, Germany was a paralysed country, with devastated cities, desolate industries and dilapidated transportation systems. Furthermore, the entire administrative apparatus had disintegrated during the last few months of the war. The Allied military government therefore faced the task of reconstructing Germany from scratch.[53] This reality was captured in the Potsdam Declaration of August 1945 which reads more like the founding Charter of a new political entity than an instrument instituting provisional military government. The opening lines stated:

The Allied armies are in occupation of the whole of Germany... It is the intention of the Allies that the German people be given the opportunity to prepare for the eventual reconstruction of their life on a democratic and peaceful basis...

These lines foreshadowed that Allied occupation would, as a Zurich court later stated, "correspond closely to a kind of fiduciary administration of the authority of the German states by the occupying powers",[54] exercised until such time as the Allies would decide that German authorities were prepared to resume responsibility.[55]

The text of the Declaration set out the framework and the objectives of post-war administration. Point 1 of the Declaration followed the Declaration of Berlin of 5 June 1945, by which the Allied powers

details of the planning remained controversial. Common purposes of military government were only clarified in February 1945, when Roosevelt, Churchill and Stalin issued the communiqué of the Yalta Conference: see Ando, *Surrender, Occupation, and Private Property*, at 61.

[52] The Allied leaders had counted on German resistance or an early surrender, misjudging "the complete nihilism of the Nazi leaders, their absolute indifference to the fate of their own country and people, once their own plans were frustrated and their regime doomed to collapse". See Friedmann, *Allied Military Government of Germany*, at 14.

[53] See also Friedmann, *Allied Military Government of Germany*, at 16.

[54] Reported by Edward H. Litchfield, *Political Objectives and Legal Bases of Occupation Government*, in Litchfield (ed.) *Governing Postwar Germany*, at 16. The text is reprinted in Schweizerische Juristen-Zeitung, Vol. 42 (1946), at 89.

[55] For a development of the concept of trusteeship administration with regard to Germany, see Max Rheinstein, *The Legal Status of Occupied Germany*, Michigan Law Review (1948), 23–40.

had assumed "supreme authority with respect to Germany, including all the powers possessed by the German Government, the High Command, and any state, municipal or local government or authority".[56] It stated that:

1. [S]upreme authority is exercised on instructions from their respective Governments, by the Commander-in-Chief of the armed forces of the United States of America, the United Kingdom, the Union of Soviet Socialist Republics, and the French Republic, each in his zone of occupation, and also jointly, in matters affecting Germany as a whole, in their capacity as members of the Control Council...

The subsequent paragraphs of the text determined the agenda of Allied administration, which covered every sphere of public and economic life. The Declaration defined the purposes of the occupation of Germany as follows:

(i)   [to] complete disarmament and demilitarisation of Germany and the elimination or control of all German industry that could be used for military production...
(iii) to destroy the National Socialist Party and its affiliated and supervised organisations, to dissolve all Nazi institutions, to ensure that they are not revived in any form...
(iv) to prepare for the eventual reconstruction of German political life on a democratic basis and for eventual peaceful co-operation in international life by Germany...

Paragraphs 4 to 18 determined the "political and economic principles to govern the treatment of Germany in the initial control period". They included, in particular, four principles: demilitarisation, de-nazification, democratisation and decentralisation ("the Four Ds"). The Potsdam Declaration provided, *inter alia*, that:

5. All Nazi laws which provided the basis of the Hitler regime or established discrimination on the grounds of race, creed, or political opinion shall be abolished...
6. All members of the Nazi Party who have been more than nominal participants in its activities and all other persons hostile to Allied purposes shall be removed from public and semi-public office, and from positions of responsibility in important private undertakings...
7. German education shall be so controlled as completely to eliminate Nazi and militarist doctrines and to make possible the successful development of democratic ideas.

[56] See Declaration of Berlin, 5 June 1945, para. 5.

8. The judicial system will be reorganised in accordance with the principles of democracy, of justice under law, and of equal rights for all citizens without distinction of race, nationality or religion.
9. The administration of affairs in Germany should be directed towards the decentralisation of the political structure and the development of local responsibility. To this end:-
    (i)   Local self-government shall be restored throughout Germany on democratic principles, and in particular, through elective councils as rapidly as is consistent with military security and the purposes of military occupation...
    (iii) Representative and elective principles shall be introduced into regional, provincial and state (Land) administration as rapidly as may be justified by the successful application of these principles in local self-government.
    (iv) For the time being no Central German Government shall be established. Notwithstanding this, however, certain essential central German administrative departments, headed by State Secretaries, shall be established, particularly in the fields of finance, transport, communications, foreign trade and industry. Such departments will act under the direction of the Control Council...
15. Allied controls shall be imposed upon the German economy...
    (a)   To carry out programmes of industrial disarmament and demilitarisation...
    (b)   To assure the production and maintenance of goods and service required to meet the needs of the occupying forces and displaced persons in Germany...
    (d)   to control German industry and all economic and financial transactions, including exports and imports with the aim of preventing Germany from developing a war...[57]

These sweeping ambitions went far beyond the traditional boundaries of belligerent occupation. The changes in the internal political structure of Germany, the reorganisation of the legal system, the transformation of the economic and social life and the objective of re-education could not be reconciled with the restrictive language of the Hague Regulations, which conceives occupation as a temporary measure that shall not interfere with the "constitutional and permanent aspects of the life of the country".[58] This contradiction was acknowledged by the Allies. A legal memorandum of the UK Foreign Office addressed the issue directly in March 1945. It noted:

---

[57] Reprinted in Friedmann, *Allied Military Government of Germany*, at 261.
[58] See Potter, *Legal Bases and Character of Military Occupation*, at 323. See also von Glahn, *Occupation of Enemy Territory*, at 276.

The truth is that the Allies are dealing with a situation without previous parallel; they are proposing to exercise their authority with respect to Germany in order to expel the Nazi system and its manifestations completely and utterly, and to continue this process indefinitely until it has succeeded. These objects, far ranging as they are, do not necessarily amount to annexation and the positive and complete transfer of sovereignty whether by cession or by conquest. But they do undoubtedly go far beyond the exercise of military occupation as limited by previous international law.[59]

The measures adopted by the Allies to implement the objectives of the Potsdam Declaration after Germany's unconditional surrender exceeded previous undertakings of administration under the umbrella of occupation.

The Allied Control Council assumed "supreme authority in matters affecting Germany as a whole".[60] The Council acted as a superstructure of allied government,[61] exercising control over military government in the four zones. The Council was composed of the military governors of the respective zones and met regularly to consider problems referred to it by its subordinate bodies and subjects. One of the main functions of the Council was to establish uniform regulations applicable to Germany as a whole. Control Council Proclamation No. 3 established fundamental principles of judicial reform to be applied throughout Germany.[62] Control Council Law No. 4 reorganised the German judicial system "on the basis of the principles of democracy, legality and equality before the law".[63] Directive No. 24 outlined the procedure to be followed for the removal from office of members of the Nazi Party.[64] The Council regulated various domestic affairs of common interest, including the creation of German Labour Courts, the institution of indirect and direct taxation, the implementation of property restitution, the control of

---

[59] See Opinion of the Lord Chancellor and the Law Officers of the Crown, March 1945, Public Record Office FO 371/50759 (U1949), quoted in Roberts, *What is Military Occupation?*, at 269.

[60] See para. 2 of Proclamation No. 1 Establishing the Control Council, 30 August 1945, in Friedmann, *Allied Military Government of Germany*, at 276.

[61] Originally, the Control Council was conceived to be the main organ of Allied government. But, from the outset, plans for a truly joint Allied government of Germany were compromised by conflict between the Four Powers as to the policies to be applied concerning Germany. The main responsibilities were therefore discharged by the military governors of the four zones. See Schweisfurth, *Occupation After World War II*, at 584.

[62] Text in Friedmann, *Allied Military Government of Germany*, at 294.

[63] *Ibid.*, at 295.   [64] *Ibid.*, at 308.

shipbuilding and reparation issues.[65] Moreover, the Council rearranged the German state system by abolishing "the Prussian State, together with its central government and all its agencies", in order to "assure further reconstruction of the political life of Germany on a democratic basis".[66]

The four military governors exercised "supreme authority" in their individual zones.[67] They held full legislative, executive and judicial powers in the initial phase of administration,[68] but gradually devolved power to municipal and state (*Länder*) authorities. They authorised German state and local authorities ("agent governments") to execute legislative and executive powers on behalf of the occupying powers in public institutions such as the Council of States (*Länderrat*).[69] In addition, they restored self-government on the municipal and state level.[70] However, all German governmental agencies and laws remained subject to the authority and limitations arising from "[a]ll international agreements regarding Germany", "[a]ll present and future quadripartite policy decisions, laws and regulations" and "the rights of an occupying power under international law to maintain an occupying force within the zone, to preserve peace and order, to reassume at any time full occupation powers in the event the purposes of the occupation are jeopardized".[71]

---

[65] For a survey, see Edward H. Litchfield, *Emergence of German Governments*, in Litchfield, *Governing Postwar Germany*, 19, at 24; Friedmann, *Allied Military Government of Germany*, at 50–3.

[66] See Constitutional Control Council Law No. 46 of 25 February 1947 ("Abolition of the State of Prussia"), in Friedmann, *Allied Military Government of Germany*, at 279.

[67] See also Friedmann, *Allied Military Government of Germany*, at 49.

[68] See, for example, Proclamation No. 1 of Supreme Commander Eisenhower, in Friedmann, *Allied Military Government of Germany*, at 277: "Supreme legislative, judicial and executive authority and powers within the occupied territory are vested in me as Supreme Commander of the Allied Forces and as Military Governor, and the Military Government is established to exercise these powers under my direction. All persons in the occupied territory will obey immediately and without question all the enactments and orders of the Military Government."

[69] For a full discussion of German Governments as agents of the occupying powers, see Litchfield, *Emergence of German Governments*, in Litchfield, *Governing Postwar Germany*, 19, at 25.

[70] *Ibid.*, at 34.

[71] See the Directive of the US Military Governor concerning the "Relationship between Military and Civil Government (U.S.) Subsequent to the adoption of Land Constitutions" of 30 September 1946, in Litchfield, *Governing Postwar Germany*, at 539. The example set in the US zone was followed in the French and Soviet Zones. See Litchfield, *Emergence of German Governments*, in Litchfield, *Governing Postwar Germany*, 19, at 36.

The military governors of the four zones actively used their far-reaching powers to secure the maintenance of public order and to implement the policies (the Four Ds) of the Potsdam Declaration. This resulted in the adoption of a variety of political, administrative and economic reforms,[72] ranging from the abrogation of Nazi law,[73] to territorial reorganisation[74] and the introduction of local government codes in the military zones.[75]

2.2.1.2. Legal issues

The legal justification of the Allied occupation of Germany was as unorthodox as its challenges.[76] The Allied powers justified their exercise of authority over Germany under international law. However, the legal arguments advanced by the Allies in support of this position were shaped by the historical circumstances of the situation. Theories of exception dominated not only the debate over the nature of Allied authority, but also the alleged exemption of Allied rule from the provisions of the Hague Regulations.

2.2.1.2.1. The legal status of Germany under occupation

The traditional law of occupation is based on the assumption that the occupied territory remains formally attached to a sovereign entity, which holds title over the territory. Germany, however, was a collapsed state that had declared its unconditional surrender. This led to conflicting

---

[72] One paradox of the post-war administration of Germany was the divergence of standards and conceptions of governance in the occupation zones. The quasi-autonomous powers of each military government in "its" respective zone and conflicting understandings of the Potsdam Declaration led to a fragmentation of policies and government in the four zones. Varying practices were employed in fields such police administration, the structure of local government and the role of citizen participation in welfare administration. See Litchfield, *Emergence of German Governments*, at 24. Furthermore, different interpretations of the concept of "democratisation" finally resulted in the establishment of fundamentally different socio-economic systems in the Soviet and Western zones. See Friedmann, *Allied Military Government of Germany*, at 37.

[73] See, for example, US Military Government Law No. 1 on the Abrogation of Nazi Law, in Friedmann, *Allied Military Government of Germany*, at 297. See also Military Government Law No. 2 Regulating German Courts, in von Glahn, *Occupation of Enemy Territory*, at 305; Military Government Law No. 6 Dispensing with Compliance with German Law, in von Glahn, *Occupation of Enemy Territory*, at 304.

[74] See Roger H. Wells, *State Government*, in Litchfield, *Governing Postwar Germany*, 84, at 87.

[75] See Wells, *State Government*, 57, at 67.

[76] See also Potter, *Legal Bases and Character of Military Occupation*, at 325.

theories about the nature of Allied authority and the status of Germany and to the search for new concepts to justify the Allied occupation.

The most radical claim was that Germany had ceased to exist as a subject of international law when the Allies assumed supreme authority.[77] According to this theory, Germany constituted *terra nullius* or a separate international entity, administered by the Four Powers as joint sovereigns in a sort of condominium. However, this thesis rested on weak grounds. The unconditional surrender of Germany did not extinguish Germany as a state:[78] the German Reich persisted as a subject of international law after 1945. Furthermore, it was contradictory to impose wartime responsibilities on Germany, on the one hand, while treating it as an extinct entity in terms of the laws of war, on the other.[79]

This reality was acknowledged by a second school of thought which continued to view the administration of Germany as a case of "foreign" state administration but held that the personality of Germany was in a state of suspension after the Reich's surrender. Proponents of this view argued that "the occupying powers, having conquered, but not annexed Germany exercised the powers of sovereignty in the Reich on a temporary

---

[77] The view that German sovereignty had vanished, and with it Germany's status as a separate unit in the family of nations was most vividly pronounced by Kelsen. He expressed his views in two articles, *The International Legal Status of Germany to be Established Immediately Upon Termination of the War*, American Journal of International Law, Vol. 38 (1944), 692, and *The Legal Status of Germany According to the Declaration of Berlin*, American Journal of International Law, Vol. 39 (1945), 518–26.

[78] Evidence of the continued existence of Germany as a state can be found in a number of official statements and court decisions. The UK Secretary of State for Foreign Affairs, for example, declared that under the Declaration of 5 June 1945: "Germany still exists as State and German nationality as a nationality, but the Allied Control Commission is the agency through which the Government of Germany is carried on." For court practice in this direction, see von Glahn, *Occupation of Enemy Territory*, at 279.

[79] See Kurt von Laun, *The Legal Status of Germany*, American Journal of International Law, Vol. 45 (1951), 274–81; Karl Doehring, *Peace Settlements After World War II*, in Encyclopedia of Public International Law, Vol. III, at 931; Christian Tomuschat, *How To Make Peace After War – The Potsdam Agreement of 1945 Revisited*, Die Friedenswarte, Vol. 72 (1997), 11, at 18; Christian Tomuschat, *Die Kapitulation: Wirkung und Nachwirkung aus völkerrechtlicher Sicht*, in 8. Mai 1945 – Befreiung oder Kapitulation (R. Schröder ed., 1997), 21. This approach was taken in 1952 by the Superior Restitution Court of Rastatt (French Zone, Germany) in the case of *Druckerei und Verlagsgesellschaft v. Schmidts*. The Court held that Germany had survived World War II as a subject of international law and noted that the Allied zone commanders legislated in two capacities, as exercising the supreme powers of the German government and as exercising the rights of military occupants, despite the end of hostilities. The Court added that the Allies were in this latter capacity bound by the rules of international law, including Article 43 of the Hague Regulations. An abstract of the case is reprinted in the American Journal of International Law, Vol. 48 (1955), p. 307.

basis, and that the international personality of the Reich had not ended by such foreign control but had been merely suspended".[80]

Finally, a third theory admitted that the post-war occupation of Germany reached the limits of the law existing at the time, arguing "international law had not developed as rapidly as the problems with which the victors of World War II were faced".[81] Proponents of this approach used the concept of "Allied legal sovereignty, in order to characterise the post-war governance of Germany".[82] Germany was regarded as a country under a *sui generis* regime of occupation.[83] Allied authority was justified by the argument that "legal sovereignty itself was held in trust, until such time as the trustees might decide that the possessors of political sovereignty were prepared to undertake its responsibilities in accordance with the Allied understanding of the Potsdam minima of 'life on a democratic and peaceful basis'".[84]

2.2.1.2.2.   The (in-)applicability of the Hague Regulations

Additional legal arguments had to be developed in order to explain the exemption of Allied occupation from the applicability of the strict regime of the Hague Regulations.[85]

The most popular theory was the *debellatio* doctrine, which held that the law of occupation ceases to apply in situations "in which a party

---

[80] See von Glahn, *Occupation of Enemy Territory*, at 276–7. Concurring Friedmann, *Allied Military Government of Germany*, at 67.

[81] See Litchfield, *Political Objectives and Legal Bases of Occupation Government* in Litchfield, *Governing Postwar Germany*, at 15; see also Potter, *Legal Bases and Character of Military Occupation*, at 325.

[82] See Litchfield, *Political Objectives and Legal Bases of Occupation Government* in Litchfield, *Governing Postwar Germany*, at 17. For a critique, see von Glahn, *Occupation of Enemy Territory*, at 285: "This view suffers from the flaw that no such concept as envisaged by the phrase 'Allied legal sovereignty' had existed previously in international law and no real explanation of the new term was supplied".

[83] This regime of occupation covered several periods: direct occupation government, a process of the devolution of power to domestic authorities and a final phase in which German institutions were created by and in the name of the German people.

[84] See Litchfield, *Political Objectives and Legal Bases of Occupation Government* in Litchfield, *Governing Postwar Germany*, at 16.

[85] Some acts of the Allied authorities such as the repeal of Nazi legislation or the performance of the de-nazification programme may have been permissible under Article 43 of the Hague Regulations, because Allied forces may be said to have been "absolutely prevented" from respecting the German legislation in force at the time. But major reforms such as the decentralisation of the German political structure, the democratisation of the judicial system or the reorganization of German education could not "by any stretch of imagination" be said to come within the restrictive language of the Hague Regulations, even though they were morally justified and necessary in the historic circumstances to remove the traces of an unjust regime. See von Glahn, *Occupation of Enemy Territory*, at 276.

to a conflict has been totally defeated in war, its national institutions have disintegrated, and none of its allies continue militarily to challenge the enemy on its behalf".[86] It was argued that measures taken in such circumstances were not measures of occupation, but acts of domestic jurisdiction, because they were adopted in the exercise of national sovereignty.[87] Allied military tribunals, in particular, relied on this theory,[88] which gave Allied forces significant discretion to adopt measures exceeding the powers of a traditional occupant.[89]

A similar argument was advanced by Virally, who took the view that the Allied presence in Germany should not be regarded as an occupation regime, but as a new form of "international administration", which differed from traditional categories of occupation and bore more resemblance to international mandates than the system of belligerent occupation.[90] Virally argued that this novel form of administration authorised the Allies to exercise broader powers than ordinary occupants.

However, even at the time, some doubts remained as to whether the *debellatio* doctrine or Virally's concept of "international administration"

---

[86] See Benvenisti, *International Law of Occupation*, at 92.

[87] This theory gained support from the Instrument of Surrender of 5 June 1945 which declared that the Allies assumed "supreme authority with respect to Germany, including all the powers possessed by the German government, the high command, and any state, municipal or local government or authority".

[88] A classical application of this reasoning can be found in a decision of the Control Commission Court of Appeal in the British Zone of 31 December 1949, which stated: "There was no Government in Germany after the occupation of the country by the Allied Forces. The so-called Dönitz Government never had any authority from the German people to represent them. With the collapse of German armed resistance there resulted ... the complete collapse of governmental structure and disintegration of administrative organization ... The Control Council and the Zone and Sector Commanders in their respective spheres are neither mere de facto authorities set up by a belligerent occupant with limited powers nor are they ruling the occupied territory adversely to any existing German Government, for there is no other German Government; but they are, for the time being, the supreme organs of Government in Germany. For these reasons we cannot agree that they are restricted by the limitations placed by the Hague Convention on a belligerent occupant." See Control Commission, Court of Appeal, *Dalldorf and Others v. Director of Prosecutions*, 31 December 1949, Annual Digest No. 159, 435, at 437–8. See also von Glahn, *Occupation of Enemy Territory*, at 281.

[89] The US Department of the Army took the position that the occupying powers were only prohibited from adopting acts which constitute crimes against peace or crimes against humanity. See Schweisfurth, *Occupation After World War II*, at 588.

[90] See Virally, *L'Administration Internationale de L'Allemagne*, at 23 and 26 ("Cette administration international constitue un régime original absolument indépendant de l'occupation militaire du temps de guerre et se rapproche, par boen de points, beaucoup plus des mandats internationaux que de l'occupatio bellica").

provided a convincing legal justification for the deviation from the Hague law,[91] as these theories seemed irreconcilable with the claim of the continuation of Germany as a subject of international law.

Other authorities construed alternative explanations for the deviation from the standards of the Hague Regulations. Wright, for instance, argued that the occupation regime applied to post-war Germany was justified because the Allies could have fully annexed Germany (*argumentum a majore ad minus*).[92] Other authors took the view that the Allied powers were authorised to exercise broader regulatory powers than ordinary occupation powers, because they exercised their authority in the capacity of trustees for the German state (trusteeship occupation).[93] Others again explained the situation by creating the concept of interventionist occupation (*occupatio interveniens*), arguing that the abrogation of Nazi laws and institutions and Allied statebuilding were justified, because they served exceptional humanitarian purposes.[94]

However, none of these theories managed to gain broader recognition beyond the special context of World War II. They were fiercely contested by a school of thought which criticised the indeterminacy of the criteria used by supporters of the doctrines of humanitarian or interventionist occupation, and which contended that the rules of the Hague Regulations continued to apply to Germany and the Allies even after the unconditional surrender of the Reich.[95] Moreover, this legal

---

[91] See Litchfield, *Political Objectives and Legal Bases of Occupation Government* in Litchfield, *Governing Postwar Germany*, at 11–12. ("In the summer of 1945 there were long discussions as to the applicability of the Hague Convention on the Laws and Customs of War. More than one year later US and UK political and legal directors in Berlin still debated the legal status of occupation legislation and its relationship to the body of German law then emerging from a variety of Allied-sponsored German agencies. Later negotiations concerning the Occupation Statute and its subsequent revisions raised many of the same questions. Much of the uncertainty resulted from the fact that existing international law did not cover the major portion of the occupation".) For a modern critique of the *debellatio* doctrine, see Benvenisti, *International Law of Occupation*, at 94–5.

[92] See Quincy Wright, *The Status of Germany and the Peace Proclamation*, American Journal of International Law, Vol. 46 (1952), 307.

[93] See Rheinstein, *Legal Status of Occupied Germany*, 23–40. For the notion of trusteeship occupation, see also Gerson, *Trustee Occupant*, 1.

[94] The concept of interventionist occupation (*occupatio interveniens*) is an interesting corollary of the doctrine of humanitarian intervention. See Schweisfurth, *Occupation After World War II*, at 588.

[95] See von Laun, *The Legal Status of Germany*, at 281, who claims that the Allies had no title for trusteeship and that "a trusteeship without obligations... amounts practically to a dictatorship".

criticism was later followed by conceptual doubts as to whether the framework of the laws of occupation should be extended so as to allow comprehensive patterns of "international territorial administration in disguise".[96]

The lesson to be drawn from these controversies is clear: the body of occupation law was stretched in order to give the post-war governance of Germany a legal basis. Furthermore, if claims as to the inapplicability of the restrictions of the laws of occupation had any legitimacy, then this was due to the exceptional historical situation of Germany in the post-war period.

2.2.1.2.3. The status of the occupying powers

The status of the Allied powers was exceptional. Allied authorities were largely absolved from domestic control. It was widely held that the Allied powers could act in two capacities, as exercising the supreme powers of the German government and as exercising the rights of military occupants.[97] As occupying authorities, the Allies were entitled to consider their own interests; as German authorities they were obliged to safeguard German interests.

But this theory was not consistently applied. If the notion of dual authority had been taken seriously, German courts should have been in a position to judge the validity of acts passed by the Allied powers in their capacity as German authorities.[98] Such a power of judicial review, however, was frequently excluded, irrespective of whether the concrete act in question was passed in the interests of the German population.[99] This approach stood in contrast to previous practice under the laws

---

[96] See Potter, *Legal Bases and Character of Military Occupation*, at 325.

[97] See Superior Court of Rastatt, *Druckerei und Verlagsgesellschaft m.b.H.* v. *Schmidts*, in American Journal of International Law, Vol. 48 (1952), 307; Grewe, *Besatzungsstatut*, at 82; Rheinstein, *The Legal Status of Occupied Germany*, at 27.

[98] See also von Laun, *The Legal Status of Germany*, at 284.

[99] German courts were unable to determine the validity or effects of Allied orders or laws. A good example of this inability can be found in Military Government Law No. 2 Regulating German Courts, which prohibited domestic courts from declaring military government law invalid. See Article VII of Military Government Law No. 2, in von Glahn, *Occupation of Enemy Territory*, at 306. See also Laws Nos. 13 and 28 of the Allied High Commission, Official Gazette, Allied High Commission, 1949/1950, at 54, 168 and 391. See for the non-reviewability of regulations which have been adopted on the basis of laws issued by the occupying powers, Badischer Staatsgerichtshof, Judgments of 15 January 1949, 27 November 1948 and 31 August 1949, in Archiv des öffentlichen Rechts (1949), 477.

of occupation, under which domestic courts had occasionally exercised judicial review over the acts of occupying powers.[100]

2.2.2.   The US occupation of Japan

The Allied administration of Japan bore many resemblances to the post-war governance of Germany. It also had two components, military government and civil administration, and marked the second example of post-surrender occupation after World War II. But the legal parameters which governed the Allied occupation of Japan were slightly different.

2.2.2.1.   Differences between the occupations of Germany and Japan

Unlike in the case of Germany, which had hardly any functioning institutions at the end of the war, Japan still possessed viable governmental structures at all levels, when the instrument of surrender was signed.[101] It is therefore difficult to speak of a case of *debellatio* in the proper sense.[102] Furthermore, the legal authority of Allied power did not flow from a unilateral act of the occupants, but was the result of an accord between Japan and the Allies, formed by the Potsdam Declaration, the Instrument of Surrender and the Japanese responses to it.[103] This particular feature gave the occupation a quasi-contractual nature.[104] Finally, throughout the period of occupation, Japan was not only governed by direct military government, but remained formally under the control of the Japanese government, which shared responsibilities with the US

---

[100] Such a right was asserted by several domestic courts during World War II. See Felice Morgenstern, *Validity of the Acts of the Belligerent Occupant*, British Yearbook of International Law, Vol. 28 (1951), 297, at 303. See also von Glahn, *Occupation of Enemy Territory*, at 110. For a recent account of judicial practice on the scope effect of Article 43 of the Hague Regulations, see Kaiyan Homi Kaikobad, *Problems of Belligerent Occupation: The Scope of Powers Exercised by the Coalition Provisional Authority in Iraq, April/May 2003–June 2004*, International & Comparative Law Quarterly, Vol. 54 (2005), 253, at 256–9. For a different view, see von Laun, *The Legal Status of Germany*, at 284, who refers to the existence of a "rule of international law that the courts of the occupied territory can pass judgment upon neither the validity of acts of the occupants nor their conformity with international law."

[101] See von Glahn, *Occupation of Enemy Territory*, at 286.

[102] See Benvenisti, *International Law of Occupation*, at 92.

[103] See Ando, *Surrender, Occupation, and Private Property*, at 93.   [104] *Ibid.*, at 98.

occupying power[105] and executed its (limited) authority[106] in accordance with the provisions of the Potsdam Declaration and the orders of the Supreme Commander for the Allied Powers (SCAP).[107]

2.2.2.2. Ambiguities of US reformism

Despite these differences, the US occupation of Japan shared many of the problems of the German model. The objectives of the occupation were very broadly defined by the Potsdam Declaration and the US Initial Post-Surrender Policy for Japan, which called for the demilitarisation and democratisation of the country, the removal from office of militarists and ultranationalists, economic reform and the promotion of individual rights and freedoms. The subsequent administration of defeated Japan changed the entire social structure of the country. The SCAP, US General Douglas McArthur, implemented a wide range of measures,[108] including the revision of the Constitution of Japan, the liquidation of big economic combines (*Zaibutsu* companies), the reform of the Japanese educational system, the purging of Japanese institutions from radical forces, the demilitarisation of industry and land reform.

Many of these measures required amendments to, and abrogation of, existing laws. However, not all changes were easy to justify on the basis of the authority of the SCAP as occupying power. Since the *debellatio* doctrine was not applicable in the case of Japan, a plausible argument could be made that the Hague Regulations continued to apply to the post-war occupation of Japan, complemented by the additional powers granted by the Japanese Instrument of Surrender and the Potsdam

---

[105] See the US Initial Post-Surrender Policy for Japan, 29 August 1945, reprinted in Ando, *Surrender, Occupation, and Private Property*, at 130, 132: "In view of the present character of Japanese society and the desire of the United States to attain its objectives with a minimum commitment of its forces and resources, the Supreme Commander will exercise his authority through Japanese governmental machinery and agencies, including the Emperor, to the extent that this satisfactorily furthers U.S. objectives... This policy, however, will be subject to the right and duty of the Supreme Commander... to act directly if the Emperor or other Japanese authority does not satisfactorily meet the requirements of the Supreme Commander in effectuating the surrender terms... This policy is to use the existing form of Government in Japan."

[106] The US SCAP held wide powers. See Ando, *Surrender, Occupation, and Private Property*, at 101.

[107] *Ibid.*, at 98.

[108] For a full account, see Edwin Martin, *The Allied Occupation of Japan* (1948).

Declaration.[109] It was, in particular, reasonable to assume that the Japanese Instrument of Surrender, which granted the SCAP the authority to demilitarise and democratise Japan,[110] could not be interpreted so as to justify deviations from the Hague Regulations' basic protections of persons and property of enemy civilians under military occupation. This left doubts as to whether the SCAP was authorised to interfere directly with private property rights, by liquidating *Zaibutsu* companies and expropriating farming land.[111] Moreover, it challenged the view that the US occupying authorities were entitled to eliminate the pension rights of "purged" Japanese militarists or ultranationalists – a measure which stood in open contradiction to the responsibility of the occupant to respect minimum property rights.[112]

3. The development of the laws of occupation in the post-war era

The experiences of the post-war occupations of Germany and Japan leave the observer with mixed feelings. The democratisation and economic reconstruction of Germany and Japan are among the greatest legacies of post-conflict reconstruction. However, the framework under which these objectives were achieved was vulnerable in legal terms and overshadowed by power politics (*Machtpolitik*).[113] It does not come as a surprise

---

[109] See von Glahn, *Occupation of Enemy Territory*, at 286; Ando, *Surrender, Occupation, and Private Property*, at 102.

[110] The Potsdam Declaration provided for the complete demilitarisation and democratisation of Japan. The Instrument of Surrender authorised the Allied Commander to take the steps necessary to implement the provisions of the Potsdam Declaration. The last sentence of the Instrument of Surrender read: "The authority of the Emperor and the Japanese Government to rule the state shall be subject to the Supreme Commander for the Allied Powers who will take such steps as he deems necessary to effectuate these terms of surrender."

[111] See Ando, *Surrender, Occupation, and Private Property*, at 106–8, 114–15.

[112] *Ibid.*, at 113. ("The non-payment of the pensions ought to be considered an abuse of power of the occupant in contravention of the principle of humanity".)

[113] Note that the process of making peace with the defeated powers at the end of the war and the establishment of the UN as a post-war collective security organisation were formally treated as separate processes. The UN Charter rules were declared inapplicable to the process of peacemaking with the "enemy" powers. Article 107 of the Charter exempted the victorious powers from responsibility for actions taken "as a result" of the war. This included "attempts to reorder the legal relationship between states, e.g. through peace treaties". See Ress, *On Article 107*, at 1333, para. 5. The effect of the enemy state clauses was that "in many cases there was not even a discussion before the organs of the UN of the legality of the measures taken by the victorious States". *Ibid.*, 1333, at para. 4.

that the model of post-surrender occupation was later largely abandoned in international legal practice.

3.1. The decline of the deballatio doctrine

Possible *lacunae* in the Hague Regulations were closed by the Fourth Geneva Convention. Article 2 of the Convention stated that the Convention shall apply to all cases of war and armed conflict and also to cases of partial or total occupation of a signatory's territory. This clearly includes occupation after surrender.[114] Article 6 of the same Convention adds that, "in the case of occupied territory, the application of the... Convention shall cease one year after the general close of military operations". However, some of the most important provisions continue to apply as the occupying power "exercises the functions of government" in the territory. One may thus infer that "post-surrender" occupants are today restricted by Article 6 of the Fourth Geneva Convention, "even under conditions approximating the German situation in 1945".[115]

3.2. The transformation of the concept of occupation

At the same time, the concept of occupation itself has encountered growing opposition in international practice.

3.2.1. The demise of the concept of occupation in legal practice

The argument that an occupying power may exercise unrestrained governmental power on foreign soil has become questionable in legal terms.[116] The concept of occupation carries a negative connotation,[117]

---

[114] Roberts identifies several situations, in which the Fourth Geneva Convention applies, namely where there is a military force whose presence in a territory is not regulated by a valid agreement, or whose activities involve an extensive range of contacts with the host country which are not adequately covered by an existing agreement and where the military force has displaced the territory's ordinary system of public order and government. See Roberts, *What is Military Occupation*, at 300–1.

[115] See von Glahn, *Occupation of Enemy Territory*, at 281. See also Benvenisti, *International Law of Occupation*, at 95.

[116] Unrestrained authority conflicts with principles of international human rights law, which prevents a defeated government from disposing the rights vested in its people, and the principle of self-determination, which opposes subjugation and social change imposed against the will of the native population. See Benvenisti, *International Law of Occupation*, at 94–5. See also Ando, *Surrender, Occupation, and Private Property*, at 124.

[117] The most explicit statement of this kind can be found in the Charter of Economic Rights and Duties of 12 December 1974, which provided that "[i]t is the right and duty of all States, individually and collectively, to eliminate colonialism, apartheid, racial discrimination, neo-colonialism *and all forms of foreign aggression, occupation and*

which has prevented international actors from invoking it in practice. States often refused to acknowledge that their presence on foreign soil amounted to an occupation.[118] Instead, they have tended to argue that their control over foreign territory was based on the invitation expressed by an indigenous government[119] or on the disputed status of the occupied territory. The UN systematically avoided referring to the applicability of the law of occupation in the context of UN administration.

Moreover, international practice seems to indicate that state-based forms of territorial administration must be built on greater consensus and legitimacy than pure military victory. Post-war practice has channelled reconstruction efforts under the heading of multilateralism – a claim that has been advocated since 1949.[120] Forms of foreign-state administration, by contrast, have become rare, and subject to the need of justification and legitimation. Even multinational administrations have been increasingly built on collective processes of bargaining and decision-making, such as the involvement of a representative group of states in the process of administration or Security Council approval.[121]

3.2.2.   Iraq – a contemporary model of post-war occupation

The post-war occupation of Iraq illustrates this development. It signals that if occupation is to serve as a framework for territorial administration at all, then this must be not along the lines of the precedent

---

domination, and the economic and social consequences thereof, as a prerequisite for development". See Article 16 (1) of GA Res. 3281 (XXIX) of 12 December 1974. Furthermore, in its Resolution 3171 of 17 December 1973, the General Assembly resolutely supported "the efforts of the developing countries and of the peoples of the territories under colonial and racial domination and foreign occupation in their struggle to regain effective control over their natural resources". See GA Res. 3171 of 17 December 1973, UN Doc. A/9400.

[118] The applicability of the Fourth Geneva Convention has been contested by Israel (West Bank), Indonesia (Est Timor), the Soviet Union (Afghanisatan), Iraq (Kuwait) and China (Tibet).

[119] See generally Georg Nolte, *Eingreifen auf Einladung* (1999).

[120] The need for a turnaround was expressed in the immediate aftermath of the war, when scholars pointed out that "it is perfectly certain that continued prolongation ... of the super-normal military occupation [in Germany and Japan], and the conduct of international territorial administration in disguise, will elicit insistent demands for adequate attention to this problem". See Potter, *Legal Bases and Character of Military Occupation*, at 325.

[121] Note that the Dayton Framework Agreement has been endorsed by the Security Council. For a discussion, see below Part II, Chapter 8.

of 1945, but under the umbrella of multilateral or international structures.[122]

Although peacemaking in Iraq required comprehensive reconstruction similar to the cases of Germany and Japan,[123] the process of statebuilding was not left to the parties and states participating in the conflict, but neutralised through the participation of a UN assistance mission and the endorsement of the Security Council.

Following the initial reluctance of the US and the UK to acknowledge their status as occupying powers ("This has been about liberation, not about occupation"),[124] the Security Council invented a new model of multilateral occupation[125] which integrated the basic structures of occupation into the ambit of peacemaking under Chapter VII.

The Security Council recognised the status of the US and the UK as occupying powers and their specific responsibilities under international law in its Resolution 1483 (2003).[126] Operative paragraph 4 of the resolution called upon the Authority (the US and the UK) to promote the welfare of the Iraqi people through the effective administration of the territory, including in particular "working towards the restoration of conditions of security and stability and the creation of conditions in which the Iraqi people can freely determine their own political future".[127] Operative paragraph 8 of the resolution set out the responsibilities of the UN Special Representative for Iraq, who was vested with the task of "working intensively with the Authority, the people of Iraq

---

[122] For an analysis, see Michael Kelly, *Iraq and the Law of Occupation: New Tests For an Old Law*, Yearbook of International Humanitarian Law, Vol. 6 (2003), 128–65; Adam Roberts, *The End of Occupation: Iraq 2004*, International & Comparative Law Quarterly, Vol. 54 (2005), 27; Roberts, *Transformative Military Occupation*; Marten Zwanenburg, *Existentialism in Iraq: Security Council Resolution 1483 and the Law of Occupation*, International Review of the Red Cross, Vol. 86 (2004), 745.

[123] See generally Scheffer, *Beyond Occupation Law*, at 844.

[124] See the statement by General Tommy Franks, The Independent, 17 April 2003. Accordingly, the UK and the US merely undertook to abide "by their obligations under international law, including those relating to the essential humanitarian needs of the people of Iraq". See Letter from the Permanent Representatives of the UK and the US addressed to the President of the Security Council, UN Doc. S/2003/538 of 8 May 2003.

[125] See also Benvenisti, *The Security Council and the Law on Occupation*, sub. III; Ottolenghi, *Stars and Stripes in Al-Fardo Square*, at 2218.

[126] The Council recognised "the specific authorities, responsibilities and obligations under applicable international law... [the US and the UK] as occupying powers under unified command ('the Authority')". See para. 13 of the preamble of SC Res. 1483 (2003) of 22 May 2003, UN Doc. S/RES/1483 (2003).

[127] See para. 4 of SC Res. 1483 (2003).

and others concerned to advance efforts to restore and establish national and local institutions for representative governance, including by working together to facilitate a process leading to an internationally recognised, representative government of Iraq".[128] Finally, operative paragraph 9 supported the establishment of an interim Iraqi administration.

This solution had a double effect. Resolution 1483 (2003) legitimated the continuing presence of the US and the UK on Iraqi soil,[129] which was contested in the aftermath of *Operation Iraqi Freedom*.[130] Moreover, it embodied modern principles of international law into the framework of the occupation. The resolution reaffirmed, in particular, that post-war occupation does not entail a transfer of sovereignty or title over the territory, but rather a mandate to build or restore domestic self-determination or self-government. The occupying powers were bound to promote the welfare of the local population, including equal rights and justice, while being subjected to a rudimentary form of public accountability *via* their duty to report to the Security Council.[131]

At the same time, Resolution 1483 (2003) contained a significant constructive weakness. It failed to address the tensions between the limits of the laws of the occupation and the challenges of statebuilding in a satisfactory way. Paragraph 5 of the resolution called upon "all concerned to comply fully with their obligations under international law, including in particular the Geneva Conventions 1949 and the Hague Regulations of 1907".[132] However, several responsibilities mentioned in the resolution went beyond the ordinary framework of the maintenance of law and order under the laws of occupation ("effective administration of the territory"; "creation of conditions in which the Iraqi

---

[128] See para. 8 (c) of SC Res. 1483 (2003).

[129] See also Rabinder Singh and Charlotte Kilroy, *In The Matter of the Legality of the Occupation of Iraq by UK Armed Forces*, An Opinion Given to the Campaign for Nuclear Disarmament, 23 July 2003, paras. 40–1. Paragraph 4 of the Resolution removed the foreign presence in Iraq from the twilight of illegal occupation, and transformed "the Authority" into a trustee of the interests of Iraqi people, and a guarantor of peace and security, acting under the general supervision of the Security Council.

[130] See below Part II, Chapter 9.

[131] The incorporation of these standards of administration (preservation of basic standards of self-determination, recognition of human rights obligations, provision for a minimum form of international accountability) tempered some of the contemporary objections against the concept of occupation. See also Benvenisti, *The Security Council and the Law on Occupation*, sub. III.

[132] See para. 5 of SC Res. 1483 (2003). See also Jordan J. Paust, *The U.S. as Occupying Power over Portions of Iraq and Relevant Responsibilities Under the Laws of War*, ASIL Insight, April 2003, at www.asil.org.

people can freely determine their own political future" (para. 4); establishment of "national and local institutions for representative governance" (para. 8.c)).[133]

The reference of the Council to two parallel legal regimes,[134] namely the law of occupation, on the one hand, and principles of statebuilding, on the other, left room for conflicting interpretations. Some authorities, including the Coalition Provisional Authority (CPA),[135] interpreted the resolution as an entitlement for the CPA to deviate from the narrow framing of the Geneva and Hague law, based in the derogatory nature of a Chapter VII Resolution under Article 103 of the Charter.[136] But this view remained controversial from a legal point of view.

One may have some doubts whether the language contained in Resolution 1483 (2003) ("calls upon") did in fact create a formal conflict of obligations which is required to trigger the application of conflict-rule under Article 103 of the Charter.[137] It is also uncertain whether the Council went so far as to authorise the CPA specifically to engage

---

[133] See also Roberts, *Transformative Military Occupation*, at 613.

[134] A joint application of these legal regimes is possible because the rules of the Hague and the Geneva law of occupation cannot be regarded as a uniform set of norms of *jus cogens* governing all forms of post-conflict military presence alike. Occupation law has only been applied on selected circumstances in state practice and international practice after 1945. See Benvenisti, *International Law of Occupation*, at 189–90. See also Scheffer, *Beyond Occupation Law*, at 852. This selective application speaks firmly against a qualification as *jus cogens*.

[135] The CPA derived its authority to adopt regulatory acts in the form of Regulations and Orders from two separate sources of authority: the "laws and usages of war", *and* "relevant Security Council resolutions", including Resolution 1483 (2003). Moreover, the US Administrator, L. Paul Bremer, on several occasions made express reference to SC Resolution 1483 (2003) when adopting measures that did not fall within the classical competences of occupying powers. Coalition Provisional Authority Order No. 22, which established a "New Iraqi Army as the first step toward the creation of a national defence force of the new Iraq", contains an explicit reference to the mandate of the coalition to "assist the people of Iraq to contribute to conditions of stability and security in Iraq". See para. 2 of the preamble of CPA Order No. 22 of 7 August 2003. Similarly, the Authority justified the introduction of a new Bank Law on the grounds that the Security Council "called upon the CPA to promote economic reconstruction and conditions for sustainable development". See para. 7 of the preamble of CPA Order No. 40 of 19 September 2003. Other regulatory measures contain similar cross-references. See Section 1 of CPA Regulation No. 6 (Governing Council of Iraq).

[136] See Thomas D. Grant, *Iraq: How to Reconcile Conflicting Obligations of Occupation and Reform* ASIL Insights, June 2003. See also von Heinegg, *Factors in War to Peace Transitions*, at 864.

[137] For a discussion, see Robert Kolb, *Does Article 103 of the Charter of the United Nations Apply to Decisions or also to Authorizations Adopted by the Security Council?*, Zeitschrift für ausländisches öffentliches Recht und Völkerrecht, Vol. 64 (2004), 21.

in efforts of statebuilding and long-term reconstruction.[138] As has been rightly pointed out in doctrine, Security Council Resolutions "must be interpreted whenever possible in a manner compatible with [international humanitarian law".[139] Due to the Council's continuous reference to the applicability of international humanitarian law, a broadening of the mandate of the CPA would have required a clear exemption of the latter from the restrictions of occupation law.[140] The Council failed to go so far. None of the respective resolutions exempted the CPA expressly from its limitations under international humanitarian law in the area of statebuilding. Nor did the mandate defined in Resolution 1483 entail a clear authorisation for reform by the CPA, as is suggested in the 2004 UK Military Manual.[141] Paragraphs 8 and 9 of Resolution 1483 (2003) envisaged direct cooperation between the CPA and the UN Special Representative ("in coordination with the Authority", "with the help of the authority") in matters of statebuilding. The law reform mandate was primarily addressed to the Special Representative of the Secretary-General. It is therefore logical to assume that the "primary responsibility for nation-building, judicial reform and economic reconstruction rest[ed] [in fact] with the UN Special Representative and *not* with the occupying powers".[142]

This ambiguity cast doubts about the scope of authority of the CPA and the feasibility of the Iraq occupation as a model for future administration.

---

[138] See Scheffer, *Beyond Occupation Law*, at 850.

[139] See Sassòli, *Legislation and maintenance of Public Order and Civil Life*, at 681.

[140] *Ibid.*, at 681. See also Gregory Fox, *The Occupation of Iraq*, Georgetown Journal of International Law, Vol. 36 (2005), 195, at 262.

[141] See UK Ministry of Defence, *The Manual of the Law of Armed Conflict* (2004), at para. 11.11, note 15.

[142] See Singh and Kilroy, *In The Matter of the Legality of the Occupation of Iraq by UK Armed Forces*, paras. 2, 55–7, who argue that the US and the UK were only vested with "facilitating", but not with "a decisive role" in the area of statebuilding. See also Fox, *The Occupation of Iraq*, at 261.

5 UN territorial administration and the tradition of peace-maintenance

The practice of peace-maintenance shaped the contemporary profile of international territorial administration. The demise of colonialism and the creation of the UN and other international organisations after World War II instituted a certain faith in multilateralist approaches towards peacemaking. International organisations were more regularly entrusted with tasks formerly exercised by states. The UN came to exercise functions of territorial administration under the umbrella of peace-maintenance. International administration became one of the components of "multi-dimensional" UN peacekeeping.[1] This practice removed engagements in territorial administration partly from their historical realist tradition as post-war devices of power alliances.

1. Peacekeeping and international territorial administration

The UN Charter does not make express provision for peacekeeping activities by the UN. The practice of the organisation was born out of pragmatism. The start of peacekeeping under the Charter dates back to 1948–9 when the UN deployed military personnel to monitor ceasefires between Israel and its neighbours and between India and Pakistan. Seven years later, on 4 November 1956, the UN General Assembly requested Secretary-General Dag Hammarskjöld to send a UN Emergency Force (UNEF) to the Sinai, in order to secure and supervise a ceasefire between Egypt and Israel.[2] This mission was followed by a series of other operations in which observer groups or military forces were deployed

---

[1] See Handbook on United Nations Multidimensional Peacekeeping Operations, at 20.
[2] This mission is often referred to as the formal date of birth of the first era of peacekeeping activities.

by the UN with the consent of the host state in order to monitor cease-fires or prevent hostilities among warring parties. These operations were embedded in the tradition of neutrality. The UN was involved because it was viewed as an impartial actor that could serve as a neutral buffer between competing parties to a conflict.[3]

These experiments were soon complemented by a second, more problem-solving oriented tradition of peace-maintenance with a broader focus on governmental assistance, non-military mandates and peace-building objectives such de-mining, election monitoring and assistance, the maintenance of law and order, police activities, human rights protection and the supervision of civil administration. In this tradition, the principle of neutrality remained a formal cornerstone of military engagement.[4] However, neutrality was interwoven with institutional and operational mandates that required the organisation to act in support of the interests of a certain state or group within society. This practice laid the foundations for the pursuance of engagements of territorial administration under the umbrella of peace-maintenance.

The first traces of this approach can be found in the early practice of the UN in the post-war era, when the organisation assisted Libya and Eritrea in their efforts to devise constitutional frameworks for independence or self-governance.[5] However, the first real test case of this practice was ONUC, which forced the UN to become deeply involved in the restoration of law and order and the internal affairs of the Congo due to the breakdown of local authority. The enforcement and governance functions performed by ONUC challenged the imperatives of neutrality and non-intervention, which had formerly marked the core principles of classical peacekeeping.

This proactive type of engagement grew into a formal technique of peacemaking after the end of the Cold War. The increase of internal armed conflicts and the emergence of the phenomenon of collapsed

---

[3] They include, *inter alia*, the UN Observation Group in Lebanon (UNOGIL), the UN Yemen Observation Mission (UNYOM), the UN Peacekeeping Force in Cyprus (UNFICYP), the second UN Emergency Force in the Sinai (UNEF II), the UN Interim Force in Lebanon (UNIFIL) and the first UN Operation in Somalia (UNOSOM I). See Ratner, *The New UN Peacekeeping*, at 11.

[4] The Report of the Panel on UN Peace Operations reaffirmed the UN's commitment to neutrality. See para. 48 of the Report where neutrality is qualified as a bedrock principle of peacekeeping.

[5] For a survey, see Ratner, *The New UN Peacekeeping*, at 115–16.

states[6] contributed to the deployment of complex peacebuilding operations. Rather than being deployed to reinforce an existing peace, UN operations became multi-operational undertakings, involved in a wide variety of statebuilding tasks, such as the reconstruction of governmental authority, judicial reform, refugee return, disarmament and election monitoring.[7] This new type of peacekeeping gave rise to different undertakings in territorial administration, ranging from small and unspectacular support missions to complex undertakings in civil governance. After a series of observer missions with electoral mandates in Haiti (ONUVEH), El Salvador (ONUSAL), Western Sahara (MINURSO) and Angola (UNAVEM II), the UN launched, in particular, five major statebuilding missions within seven years (UNTAC in Cambodia, 1992; UNOSOM in Somalia, 1993; UNTAES in Eastern Slavonia, 1996; UNMIK in Kosovo, 1999; UNTAET in East Timor, 1999). These missions engaged the UN actively in the exercise of governmental responsibilities, including executive and legislative powers.[8]

2. Conceptual developments

The expanding concept of peacekeeping and peace enforcement marked a niche in the UN Charter under which the UN could assume tasks of administration of territories outside the context of decolonisation.

---

[6] For a thoughtful critique of the notion of "failed state", see Henry J. Richardson, *Failed States, Self-Determination and Preventive Diplomacy: Colonialist Nostalgia and Democratic Expectations*, Temple International & Comparative Law Journal, Vol. 10 (1996), at 1.

[7] The conceptual basis for the transformation of peacekeeping from tool of peace-maintenance into an instrument to shape the legal, political and social system of states was provided by the principles of positive peace and post-conflict peacebuilding, which may be indirectly inferred from the preamble ("determined ... to promote social progress and better standards of life in larger freedom, and ... to employ international machinery for the promotion of the economic and social advancement of all peoples") and Article 1 of the UN Charter ("The Purposes of the United Nations are: ... 2. To develop friendly relations among nations based on respect for the principle of equal rights and self-determination of peoples, *and to take other appropriate measures to strengthen universal peace*; 3. To achieve international cooperation ... , in promoting and encouraging respect for human rights and for fundamental freedoms for all ... "). These two concepts shaped the perception that peacekeeping cannot halt at the restoration of the *status quo ante*, but must address the root causes of conflict, in order to prevent a return to violence. See Boutros Boutros-Ghali, *An Agenda for Peace, Preventive Diplomacy, Peacemaking and Peace-Keeping*, Report of the Secretary-General, UN SCOR, 47th Sess., at 22, UN Doc. S/24111 (1992).

[8] See also Handbook on United Nations Multidimensional Peacekeeping Operations, at 20, which distinguishes these types of administration from other multidimensional peacekeeping operations.

Chapters VI and VII of the Charter provided enough flexibility to justify the exercise of direct administering authority with regard to sovereign UN member states, thereby deviating from the strict restriction of Article 78 of the Charter, which limited the application of trusteeship administration to non-UN members.[9]

The embedding of territorial administration within the context of peace-maintenance provided not only a space for the development of territorial administration outside the confines of the UN Trusteeship System, but also triggered some fundamental changes in conception.

2.1. A changing conception of trusteeship

The ideological connotation of trusteeship evolved within the context of the peace-maintenance practice of the UN. The use of administering authority under the heading of peace-maintenance allowed territorial administration to avoid some of the stigmas of colonial predominance, exploitation and victors' benevolence. Concepts such as political "tutelage" or "civilisation" were formally banned from the vocabulary of international law in the second half of the twentieth century with the recognition of the right of self-determination of peoples and the sovereign equality of all states.[10] The UN Charter made it impossible to justify rule or title over foreign societies by annexation.[11] International institutions derived their authority to exercise governing or administrative functions on behalf of local actors from agency relationships or peacemaking objectives, such as the need to restore stable and peaceful relations among warring factions or to establish a certain territorial status through their administration.[12] Similarly, it has become inconceivable to justify trusteeship on the basis of a lack of education or sophistication of local populations. The exercise of fiduciary authority

---

[9] The Trusteeship System was obviously not designed to address such scenarios, since Article 78 of the Charter excluded the application of the Trusteeship System to sovereign states. See Jackson, *Global Covenant*, at 305. ("UN trusteeship was not intended to reverse the process and transfer already independent states back to a quasi-colonial status.")

[10] The reference to the concept of "civilised nations" in the definition of general principles of law under Article 38 of the ICJ Statute has become an "embarrassment" in contemporary international law. See Matz, *Civilization and the Mandate System under the League of Nations*, at 68.

[11] Article 2 (4) of the Charter prohibits the annexation of territory belonging to another state. The principle of self-determination prohibits the establishment of foreign rule by a state against the will of the people of a territory. *Ibid.*, at 57-8.

[12] See also generally on the case for a modern notion of trusteeship, Jackson, *Global Covenant*, at 305.

was therefore associated with solidarist motives, born out of the desire to provide emergency relief and assistance rather than intellectual tutelage.

These transformations have influenced the conception of trusteeship. The Mandate System associated the concept of trusteeship authority with the idea of stewardship of people. The concept of the "sacred trust" under Article 22 of the Covenant was based on the assumption that mandatory powers exercise trusteeship of the future of mandatory people. The Covenant charged mandatory powers with the promotion of "the well-being and development of... *peoples*"[13] and "tutelage of such *peoples*".[14]

The exercise of authority in governance missions under the umbrella of peace-maintenance is founded on a different understanding. International administrators are no longer deemed to be guardians of the "people" of a territory.[15] Their fiduciary responsibilities are comparable to those of a domestic interim government. They hold administering authority or "powers of government" on a temporary basis and in interest of the people of the territory.[16] However, they lack "ownership" over the territory and its people. Moreover, the terms of their authority are not discretionary, but predetermined by certain fixed parameters, such as the terms of a peace agreement or a specific UN mandate to restore peace and security, or to realise a certain social or legal *status quo*.

2.2.   A new normative underpinning of territorial governance

This change in the conception of authority coincides with a greater consolidation of some of the policies and values (democratisation, human rights protection, economic liberalisation) that territorial administration seeks to promote.

Some of the methods and techniques used by international administrators may be traced back to the colonial tradition. However, the evaluation and perception of such policies has changed.

In European colonial practice, respect for local tradition was an inherent part of governance and administration.[17] Although colonial powers

---

[13] See Article 22, para. 1.   [14] See Article 22, para. 2.

[15] See also the convincing argument by Feldman, who argues that nation-builders hold "authority to govern" in trust, rather than the people and the territory of a country. See Feldman, *What We Owe Iraq*, Chapter 2.

[16] A good example is the Saar administration, which held "powers of government" in trust. See below Part II, Chapter 7.

[17] See generally M. B. Hooker, *Legal Pluralism: An Introduction to Colonial and Neo-Colonial Laws* (1975), at 198.

held supremacy over the administered territories, they sought to seek a balance between the preservation of domestic traditions and the import of foreign law on the basis of practical concerns. This decision was driven by pragmatic reasons and economic interests. It was convenient and efficient to leave domestic structures and practices in place and lucrative to reform laws concerning commerce and trade.[18] A similar understanding prevailed in the era of the League of Nations and the Mandate System. Foreign governance and administration continued to be widely discretionary undertakings, guided mostly by pragmatism,[19] colonial experience and a rudimentary notion of self-determination.[20]

A different conception of governance gained ground in the second half of the twentieth century.[21] In the aftermath of World War II, international law began to develop a more systematic *corpus* of legal rules guiding the relationship between the territorial ruler and the population of an administered territory. The proliferation of human rights treaty law after 1945 posited the principle that states and governing organs are not self-centred and auto-regulating units, but organising frameworks for the accommodation of the rights of individuals. Human rights guarantees and procedures for holding governments accountable became increasingly part of a treaty-based law[22] or "regional *acquis*".[23] Furthermore, international law began to deviate from its traditional neutrality vis-à-vis the internal affairs of a state. Autocratic and oppressive structures of governance came under challenge in light of rights of political participation enshrined in Article 21 of the Universal Declaration of Human Rights and Article 25 of the International Covenant on Civil and Political Rights (ICCPR).[24] A broader notion of internal

---

[18] The principle of "indirect rule", for example, which formed a cardinal principle of British colonial policy, was defended by Lord Lugard on the ground that "the interests of a large native population shall not be subject to the will... of a small minority of educated and Europeanized natives who have nothing in common with them, and whose interests are often opposed to theirs". This idea to keep traditional African policies in place was supported by economic considerations. The less African society changed, the less it would cost to rule.

[19] See Anghie, *Colonialism and the Birth of International Institutions*, at 538–43.

[20] See Chopra, *Peace-Maintenance*, at 42.

[21] See also Boon, *Legislative Reform in Post-Conflict Zones*, at 297.

[22] See, for example, Human Rights Committee, General Comment No. 26, which established the principle of automatic succession into human rights treaties.

[23] See, for example, Articles 6 and 49 of the Treaty on the European Union.

[24] These provisions postulate the right of all persons to take part in government, as well as in "periodic elections which shall be by universal and equal suffrage". Both norms have been further developed by international practice within the UN and the Organization for Security and Co-operation in Europe (OSCE).

self-determination emerged after World War II, which linked the protection of a people under international law to the enjoyment of institutional rights (such as autonomy of federalist structures) in the domestic legal system.[25] Finally, standards of democratic governance and human rights protection were made a precondition of fiscal, trade and development benefits[26] or a building block of UN or regional action.[27]

These transformations have implications for the characterisation of projects of international territorial administration.

The growing recognition of people-centred rights made it necessary to re-think the relationship between foreign and domestic actors in processes of transitional administration. Today, it is no longer possible to justify practices such as the deference to domestic rule or respect of local customs solely by pragmatic or utilitarian considerations. The preservation of domestic decision-making power and local ownership is founded upon a different justification, namely the perception that domestic stakeholders are entitled to govern themselves by virtue of internally guaranteed protections (sovereignty, self-determination, autonomy) and political rights protected by law.[28]

---

[25] Self-determination is increasingly viewed as a principle requiring group interaction and representation within pluralistic states. For a survey of the constitutional options for the realisation of internal self-determination, see M. Suksi, *Constitutional Options for Self-determination: What Works?*, Paper prepared for the UNA-USA/IAI Conference on "Kosovo's final status", Rome, 12–14 December 1999, available at www.unausa.org/issues/kosovo.

[26] Intergovernmental organisations have linked foreign aid and membership in regional and international organisations to compliance with principles such as democracy, a multi-party system and free and fair elections. For the practice of the EU, see Frank Hoffmeister, *Menschenrechts- und Demokratieklauseln in den Vertraglichen Außenbeziehungen der Europäischen Gemeinschaft* (1998). Furthermore, in order to promote transparency and accountability, the World Bank conditions loans upon the adoption of fiscal and trade policies and labour, health care and environmental regulation. See Karl J. Irving, *The United Nations and Democratic Intervention: Is Swords into Ballot Boxes Enough?*, Denver Journal of International Law and Policy, Vol. 25 (1996), 41, at 49. The World Bank practice of promoting liberal democracy in post-conflict countries has emerged following the end of the Cold War. Before then, involvement in peace operations was considered a topic of inherently political character, running counter to the objectives of the Bank. In particular, the terms of Section 10 of Article IV of the Agreement on the International Bank for Reconstruction and Development were interpreted broadly. This provision reads: "The Bank and its officers shall not interfere in the political affairs of any member; nor shall they be influenced in their decisions by the political character of the member or members concerned. Only economic considerations shall be relevant to their decisions, and these considerations shall be weighed impartially ... "

[27] For a survey, see Irving, *United Nations and Democratic Intervention*, at 49–52.

[28] For a survey of contemporary practice. See below Part II, Chapter 9.

Moreover, territorial administration itself is no longer a mere strategic policy device. It became to some extent a "law enforcement" technique, namely a means to implement international legal standards and further commonly defined community interests.[29]

---

[29] See on the distinction between "peace enforcement" and "law enforcement" Tomuschat, *Peace Enforcement and Law Enforcement*, 1745, at 1748 *et seq*. See generally on the process of the communitarisation of international law, Simma, *From Bilateralism to Community Interest in International Law*, at 243–9; Tomuschat, *Obligations for States*, at 219–36.

Conclusion: international territorial administration – an independent device with a certain normative heritage

A survey of the historical and social evolution of international territorial administration shows that the exercise of territorial authority by international entities is mainly a twentieth-century phenomenon which gradually replaced previously established models of foreign state administration, such as protectorates, condominiums or regimes of belligerent occupation following territorial conquest.[1] It covers cases of territorial administration in which international organisations exercise administering authority or control over territories, either directly or through international institutions acting on their behalf or with their approval.

International territorial administration shares conceptual parallels with three major techniques of the governance devices of the twentieth century: The Mandate System, the Trusteeship System and post-surrender occupation. It draws, in particular, upon the concept of fiduciary authority inherent in the Mandate and the UN Trusteeship System and the temporal limitations inherent in trusteeship occupation. Nonetheless, international territorial administration constitutes an independent governance technique, both in form and in substance.

International administration is, to some extent, a counter-model to the classic concept of occupation. It is not a state-centred form of administration which is triggered by factual events (i.e. the exercise of effective authority over territory), but an arranged form of authority that is carried out by or under the auspices of international actors. This type of arrangement offered an institutional framework to carry out forms of administration that are difficult to reconcile with the rationale of occupation, namely missions that are aimed at the transformation of the political and legal order of the territory under administration.

---

[1] See also Wilde, *From Danzig to East Timor*, at 602–4.

These divergences are less pronounced in the case of the Mandate and the Trusteeship System. Both devices have a dynamic dimension. They were directly geared at the development of the territory under administration. Moreover, they bear some resemblance to indirect forms of administration, since the respective administering authorities acted formally on behalf of the League of Nations and, later, the UN. However, there is an important formal difference. Administering powers carried out their mandate as individual states, without being organised in the form of a collective entity with a separate identity of its own. Mandate administration and Trusteeship administration were therefore, strictly speaking, state-based, rather than indirect forms of international administration, under which separate international or multinational institutions exercise territorial authority on behalf of or with the approval of an international organisation.[2]

Secondly, experiments in international territorial administration have a slightly different conceptual underpinning from Mandate administration, Trusteeship administration or post-surrender occupation. All three systems of administration were established in order to achieve a balance between national interests and "other-regarding interests". This "dual objective" provided a justification for use of foreign state administration.[3] In all three cases, a system of foreign administration was deployed, because it provided a means to reconcile the strategic interests of victors of war and administering powers with certain benefits for the administered peoples ("civilisation", self-government, security). The logic is different in the context of projects of international territorial administration. In these contexts, "self-interest" is not irrelevant.[4] But it is embedded in or subordinated to the achievement of a broader community interest. Territorial authority was usually conferred on independent entities such as the League of Nations or the UN, or carried out under the

---

[2] It is also impossible to qualify the post-war occupation of Germany as an experiment in indirect territorial administration. The occupation of Germany was formally carried out under the collective framework of an international body – the quadripartite Control Council, which maintained authority concerning questions regarding Germany as a whole. However, the Council acted without a separate mandate or the approval of the UN.

[3] This rationale follows to some extent the logic of Lugard's "dual mandate" which sought to bring "self-" and "other-interest" into harmony, by declaring that colonial administration serves the "mutual benefit" Western nations and native races.

[4] Self-interest is often a motivation underlying national engagement in a multilateral framework, in particular in nation-building. See Feldman, *What We Owe Iraq*, Chapter 2.

collective umbrella of peace-maintenance, in order to limit the pursuit self-interest. This tradition differs from the practice of colonial administration,[5] Mandate administration[6] or Trusteeship administration,[7] where administering powers were entrusted with authority due to their links to the administered territory and where considerations of peace and security remained linked to the interests of administering powers.

Moreover, the nature of interests, which are to be protected through administration, has evolved over time. In many modern cases, UN engagement was motivated by human catastrophe and conflict rather than "ideology".[8] Consequently, international territorial administrations were rarely entrusted with trusteeship over "people" (as is anticipated in the Mandate System). They were entrusted with a more modest mandate, namely the temporary takeover of certain aspects public authority, which had to be exercised in the interest of the administered population.[9]

Nevertheless, engagements in international territorial administration carry some of the normative heritage that is associated with Mandate administration, Trusteeship administration or colonial administration. Some of the features of contemporary governance missions, namely the promotion of the virtues of liberalism and good governance, are sometimes not so different from the moral justification of nineteenth-century imperialism which sought to justify Western rule over colonial territories by ideas such as the welfare and education of natives or the economic development of societies. There are, of course, some differences. In a modern context, these goals are framed with different names. Moreover, they are implemented through international structures and mostly supported by some form of formal domestic consent. However, the exercise of authority continues to based on a similar rationale: an assumed deficit or a need of protection of domestic actors. International authority is exercised because domestic actors are deemed to be unable or less well

---

[5] The signatories of the General Act of the Berlin Conference established a system of neutrality, in order to facilitate trade and to ensure a peaceful administration of dependent territories. See Article X of the General Act of the Berlin Conference.

[6] In the context of Mandate administration, a system of neutrality was, *inter alia*, applied to B-Mandates.

[7] The Trusteeship System was tied to the concern for international peace and security. In this framework, the administering powers were vested with "the duty to ensure that the trust territory shall play its part in the maintenance of international peace and security". See Article 84 of the UN Charter.

[8] See also Boon, *Legislative Reform in Post-Conflict Zones*, at 297

[9] See also Feldman, *What We Owe Iraq*, Chapter 2.

equipped than international actors to perform certain tasks of government or public administration.

Contemporary practice is at the same time shaped by novel antinomies. Modern governance missions have revealed new forms of coercion. The exercise of public authority by international actors has been accompanied by extensive external regulation, preconceptions of the desirability of certain objectives and pressure concerning the implementation of internationally defined goals. Such policies have similar effects as traditional notions of trusteeship, namely to reduce "dialogue about what is thought to be good, right or just" for a specific society.[10] Further contradictions have arisen in the conduct of international administrations. Concepts such as "good governance" or the "rule of law" have been invoked by administrations in a one-sided fashion or to constrain the devolution of authority to domestic actors.

International territorial administration is thus not an exact replicate of the colonial paradigm. It has some of its own paradoxes and pitfalls, which will be explored further in Parts II and IV.

---

[10] In this sense, the project of international territorial administration bears resemblance to the concept of trusteeship. See Bain, *Between Anarchy and Society*, at 172.

Part II

The practice of international territorial administration: a retrospective

We must learn as well to eschew one size-fits-all formulas and the importation of foreign models, and instead, base our support on national assessments, national participation and national needs and aspirations
UN Secretary-General, *The rule of law and transitional justice in conflict and post-conflict societies (2004)*

Introduction

International entities have exercised functions of governance and territorial administration on a regular basis since 1919. This practice can be analysed in different ways. One way is to distinguish the different missions according to the degree of authority exercised by international actors. Following a classification proposed by Helman and Ratner in 1992,[1] one may distinguish at least three different models of involvement:

- governance assistance missions, in which governmental authority remains with the administered state while international agents help administer the territory;[2]
- co-governance or co-administration operations, in which international authorities provisionally exercise independent and binding authority in a specific area of governance, either through a delegation of power by domestic actors or under a UN mandate; and
- exclusive governance or administration missions, under which international actors are vested with the complete assumption of governmental functions until this authority is resumed by the former or a different territorial sovereign.[3]

[1] See Helman and Ratner, *Saving Failed States*, at 3.
[2] *Ibid.*, at 13. A typical task is the organisation of free elections, combined with a mandate to assist the national state in rebuilding its political or judicial system.
[3] *Ibid.*, at 14.

However, each mission must at the same time be viewed in its historical context. The practice of international territorial administration is therefore presented from a historical perspective here, namely in the context of its conceptual evolution. This evolution can be divided into four principal periods: the era of dispute settlement and neutralisation (Chapter 6), which determined the post-war experiments of the League of Nations and the UN after World War II; the phase of the Cold War (Chapter 7), in which territorial administration served mainly as an *ad hoc* device; the time of the revival and systematisation of territorial administration in 1990s (Chapter 8), under which international administration became a governance technique and a tool to address the root causes of conflict; and more recent practice (Chapter 9), which is characterised by a return to more limited models of administration safeguarding local ownership[4] and self-government.[5]

This practice highlights a shift in perception of international administration of territory. Traditionally, there was an implicit assumption that it is justified to bestow international institutions with powers of government and administration because they are neutral and impartial agents for the realisation of the interests at stake.[6] This equation needs to be refined in light of the practice in the twentieth century.[7] Practice has shown that it is difficult to maintain traditional perceptions of neutrality when international organisations assume the powers of states. The more international actors ventured into the field of domestic

---

[4] See below Part II, Chapter 9.

[5] All four eras of administration are very closely linked to the broader geopolitical context of their time. The era of dispute settlement was rooted in the historical tradition of World Wars I and II, when international law was still mainly conceived as a bilateral and state-centred system of rules designed to solve sovereignty or governance conflicts among competing international actors. The phase of *ad hoc*-ism was largely conditioned by the political parameters of the Cold War, which prevented large-scale international interventionism and limited international engagements to governance-assistance operations or co-governance operations by accident. The revival of territorial administration in the last decades coincided with the rise of multilateralism and the rediscovery of the collective security system in the 1990s, which encouraged the promotion of international governance structures and strategies of liberalisation.

[6] This perception is rooted in the premise that an international organisation "should conduct its institutional and operational activities in a manner which is objective and impartial and can be seen to be so". See International Law Association, *Accountability of International Organisations*, Final Report (Berlin, 2004), at 14. This factor is often viewed as a source of legitimacy. For a classical application of this argument, see Dobbins, *The UN's Role in Nation-Building*, at xxv.

[7] For a similar argument, see Wilde, *International Territorial Administration*, Chapter 3.

governance, the more they were forced to give up their status as neutral and impartial actors and to promote specific interests and values domestically.

Moreover, the parameters for assessing the desirability of international involvement have evolved. Experiments in international administration are no longer perceived to be legitimate simply because they are carried out by international actors. It is increasingly acknowledged that such undertakings are legitimate to the extent that they safeguard or enable domestic choices and decision-making power.[8]

Part II of this book traces the evolution of this thought. It presents an account of the profile and challenges of individual experiments in territorial administration over the last century. Moreover, it analyses both the different functions which international territorial administration has taken on in international practice and the internal contradictions which have emerged in this context.

---

[8] See Handbook on UN Multidimensional Peacekeeping Operations, at 21. ("The success of an interim or transitional administration is ultimately determined by its effectiveness in devolving powers held by the UN to local authorities.")

6 International territorial administration as a means of dispute settlement – the post-war experiments of the League of Nations and the United Nations

The first era of experiments in international territorial administration was deeply embedded in the tradition of dispute settlement. The understanding of law as a means of solving disputes among competing actors has a long-standing tradition in the history of international law.[1] It is reflected in the first era of experiments in territorial administration international civil governance after World War I (Saar Territory, Danzig, Memel) and World War II (Trieste and Jerusalem).

The early experiments of the League of Nations and the UN were predominantly guided by objectives of inter-state dispute settlement and neutralisation, due to their close connection to the process of conflict termination.[2] Moreover, they enjoyed a number of common features that distinguished them from later experiments in territorial administration. They were established *ex post*, that is after, rather than in response to, a specific conflict and state-centred in the sense that they mainly sought to reconcile diverging geographic and strategic interests of conflicting parties. Structures of international administration were deployed on the basis of a pragmatic case-by-case approach, under which international administrations served primarily as a means of neutralising conflict and guaranteeing peace. The strong focus on dispute settlement and

---

[1] Since the late nineteenth century, the development of the international legal system has been shaped by a dispute settlement-oriented conception of law, with a focus on the identification of recognised sources of law (treaties, customs, general principles of law) that may be invoked in international litigation, the development of concepts to bind states by law (acquiescence, opposability of legal rules between parties, *abus de droit*), a tendency to encourage legal-positivist doctrines and the creation of international institutions to resolve legal disputes. See generally Kingsbury, *International Legal Order*, at 271.

[2] See also Wolfrum, *International Administration in Post-Conflict Situations*, at 655.

impartial third-party mediation limited the managerial function of international institutions and gave higher priority to solving bilateral problems than to vindicating other kinds of community interest.

1. Precedents in the era of the League of Nations

The era of the League of Nations gave rise to three major experiments in territorial administration that come directly within the tradition of dispute settlement: the administration of the Saar territory, the League's guarantee of the City of Danzig and its engagement in Memel. All three undertakings were directly aimed the reconstruction of a new security architecture in central Europe after the defeat of Germany in World War I.

1.1. The administration of the Saar Territory by the League of Nations

The most comprehensive governance mission of the League, and one of the longest experiments in international territorial administration ever, was the administration of the Saar Territory by the League of Nations (1920–35).[3]

1.1.1. Features

The Saar administration may be counted as a comparatively successful undertaking in international administration, given the length and complexity of the League's mandate. However, the mission was visibly shaped by both the power configurations of post-war politics and by statist conceptions of governance.

1.1.1.1. A realist background

The international regime of the Saar Territory was laid down in Part III of the Treaty of Versailles which contained the "political clauses for Europe".[4] The idea of the temporary internationalisation of the territory itself emerged as a compromise between French security and compensation interests,[5] on the one hand, and Wilsonian claims for the

---

[3] For a comprehensive analysis, see Russell, *The International Government of the Saar*; Willem R. Bisschop, *The Saar Controversy* (1924).
[4] See Part III, Section IV of the Treaty of Versailles.
[5] France accepted Wilson's compromise of an internationalisation of the Saar Territory only "under the threat of the faltering of the entire peace conference over the Saarland issue". See Korhonen and Gras, *International Governance*, at 83.

consideration of self-determination in the delimitation of Europe's new borders, on the other.[6] France, which had suffered the destruction of its mines by Germany in World War I, demanded control over the Saar Territory as a matter of reparation.[7] It received the right to exploit the rich coal mines situated in the Saar Basin "as compensation for the destruction of the coal-mines in the north of France and as part payment toward the total reparation due from Germany for the damage resulting from the war".[8] But in order to safeguard the rights of the German inhabitants of the territory,[9] the Treaty of Versailles placed the territory under a fifteen-year government of the League of Nations, after which the inhabitants of the territory would "be called upon to indicate the sovereignty under which they desire to be placed".[10]

This compromise prevented the annexation of the Saar Territory and was a victory for the "moderates" at the Paris Conference. Nevertheless, it continued to be dominated by the *Zeitgeist* of the post-war era. The terms of the Saar formula were unilaterally determined by the victorious powers, without any German participation in the negotiations, or in the actual drafting of the Treaty.[11] Germany formally agreed to the framework of the Treaty, but only after expressing its criticism of the Saar regime[12] and following an ultimatum set by the Allied Powers, threatening Germany with invasion[13] – an argument that was later used by Hitler to declare the Treaty void because of "vitiated consent".[14]

---

[6] See generally Russell, *International Government of the Saar*, at 121.

[7] Russell notes that "the French did not demand outright annexation of ... the Saar region, but apparently envisaged a semi-independent state linked to France": Russell, *International Government of the Saar*, at 126.

[8] See Article 45 of the Treaty of Versailles.

[9] Wilson reportedly expressed himself as follows: "I have no right to hand over to her [France] people who do not want to go to her, or to give them a special government, even it is better for them, if they do not want it". See Russell, *International Government of the Saar*, at 129.

[10] See Article 49 of the Treaty of Versailles.

[11] Germany submitted a counter-proposal on 7 May 1919. However, it was rejected because the terms of the Treaty were considered to be non-negotiable. See generally, Alma Luckau, *The German Delegation at the Paris Peace Conference* (1941).

[12] See Russell, *International Government of the Saar*, at 132–3.

[13] The Entente threatened to advance further into German territory, if it refused to sign the Treaty.

[14] He stated in his famous speech to the German Reichstag of 1 September 1939 that: "the dictated Treaty of Versailles is not law. It will not do to blackmail a person at the point of a pistol with the threat of starvation for millions of people into signing a document and afterwards proclaim that this document with its forced signature was a solemn law". See Brian Tearney and Joan Scott (eds.), *World War II, Hitler's Speech to the Reichstag (September 1, 1939)*, in Western Societies: A Documentary History, Vol. 2 (1984), at 498.

1.1.1.2. A state-centred framework

The Treaty framework itself was, at least partly, an experiment in dispute resolution,[15] in the sense that it was centred on the accommodation of German and French prerogatives. The League acted as the formal government of the territory through a Governing Commission, composed of one citizen of France, one native inhabitant of the Saar Territory and three members from three countries other than France and Germany.[16] But the entire period of administration was shaped by conflict and mediation between German and French interests.

1.1.1.2.1. League governance – a balancing act between German and French interests

The Governing Commission was vested with "all the powers of government hitherto belonging to the German Empire, Prussia, or Bavaria, including the appointment and dismissal of officials, and the creation of such administrative and representative bodies as it may deem necessary".[17] However, the exercise of this authority was largely influenced by the undetermined future status of the territory, which precluded the League from adopting measures that could be interpreted as furthering German or French claims over the territory.[18] Germany had only renounced the "government of the territory" in favour of the League.[19] This forced the League to take a neutral and balanced position on controversial issues. Matters raising issues of sovereignty, in particular, had to be handled with great care, so as to allow the population freely to decide in the 1935 referendum whether it wanted "maintenance of the regime established by the ...Treaty [of Versailles] and by [its Annex]; or union with France; or union with Germany".[20] This constant act of balance between conflicting responsibilities turned the exercise of governance into a state- rather than people-centred undertaking.

---

[15] See Ratner, *The New UN Peacekeeping*, at 93.

[16] See Treaty of Versailles, Annex Saar Territory, Article 17.

[17] See Treaty of Versailles, Annex Saar Territory, Article 19.

[18] See the Statement by the French representative, Mr Hanotaux on 3 July 1923, reproduced in Russell, *The International Government of the Saar*, at 214–15: "According to this Treaty, there is one point which governs the whole situation, namely, that France has particular rights in the Saar ...France is the proprietor of mines; France has the right to exploit the mines without any obstacles or restriction being placed upon the use or exploitation of this property ...Moreover, the future destiny of the Territory is held in suspense pending the future plebiscite ...The League of Nations is the trustee of the Allied Powers for the maintenance of these two rights."

[19] See Article 49 of the Treaty of Versailles.

[20] See Treaty of Versailles, Annex Saar Territory, Article 19.

The same tension was reflected in the substantive provisions of the Saar regime, which established a middle ground between the maintenance of German-based administrative structures, on the one hand, and the protection of French interests, on the other. Politically, the inhabitants of the Saar were completely severed from Germany. They lost their right to Representatives in the Reichstag and the Prussian and Bavarian legislative, and were compelled to regard the Governing Commission as the legal authority for the protection of their interests both inside and outside the territory.[21] However, German law remained in force in the territory (subject to possible modification by the Governing Commission).[22] Judicial functions were, in principle,[23] left to the existing civil and criminal courts. Furthermore, inhabitants of the territory were entitled to retain their local assemblies, religious liberties, schools and language.[24] France, on the other hand, gained primarily economic concessions. In addition to its Treaty-based right to exploit the mines in the Saar Territory, France was entitled to substitute francs for German currency in making payments, purchases and contracts in connection with the mines.[25] Moreover, the Saar Basin was subjected to the French customs regime.[26]

Although the Governing Commission had the ultimate power concerning the interpretation of the provisions of the Saar regime, including its own powers,[27] the German government frequently intervened in the process of administration of the territory through written protests. The German government challenged the composition of the Commission, arguing that a majority of its members instead of being neutral, as the Treaty intended, were supporters of France.[28] Similarly, it protested to the League about the expulsion of German nationals by the Commission[29] and the decision of the Commission to entrust France with the protection abroad of the interests of the inhabitants of the Saar[30] – a measure which directly contravened the letter of the Treaty of Versailles.[31] Finally, the Governing Commission was criticised by German

---

[21] See Treaty of Versailles, Annex Saar Territory, Articles 21 and 30.
[22] See *ibid.*, Article 23.
[23] The Governing Commission established only a separate civil and criminal court of appeal. See Treaty of Versailles, Annex Saar Territory, Article 25.
[24] Treaty of Versailles, Annex Saar Territory, Article 28.   [25] *Ibid.*, Article 32.
[26] *Ibid.*, Article 31.   [27] See *ibid.*, Article 33.
[28] See Russell, *International Government of the Saar*, at 168.
[29] *Ibid.*, at 171–2.   [30] *Ibid.*, at 171.
[31] See Treaty of Versailles, Annex Saar Territory, Article 21. ("It will be the duty of the Governing Commission to ensure, by such means and under such conditions as it may

representatives for its educational policies[32] and for introducing the franc as the sole legal currency in the Saar Territory.[33] These complaints illustrate the degree to which the daily administration of the Saar was politicised by power struggles between German and French interests.

1.1.1.2.2. The limited scope of people's rights

The strong focus of the Saar regime on the reconciliation of state interests coincided with a limited degree of political participation rights and civil liberties afforded to the native inhabitants. Local actors had little impact on policy-shaping in their territory. The Governing Commission held quasi-absolutist powers.[34] It was not responsible to the people of the Saar Basin, but to the League of Nations.[35] Furthermore, the requirement for local consent in legislative matters was minimal. Consultation with the elected representatives of the inhabitants could be handled "in such a manner as the Commission may determine".[36] This situation improved slightly with the creation of an Advisory Council (Landesrat) by the Governing Commission in 1922, upon the initiative of the leaders of the political parties in the Saar Basin.[37] But the Council had little influence. It exercised only an advisory function in line with the cases stipulated in the Treaty (modification of the laws and regulations in force[38] and changes to the fiscal system[39]), and even this prerogative was not respected in all circumstances.[40] The Commission did not consider itself bound by the wishes of the pro-German local authorities, and

---

deem suitable, the protection abroad of the interests and inhabitants of the territory of the Saar Basin.")

[32] See Russell, International Government of the Saar, at 174.

[33] For a full account of the monetary problem, which was partly caused by a depreciation of the mark, see Bisschop, The Saar Controversy, at 61–7. See also Russell, International Government of the Saar, at 173.

[34] See Hannum, Autonomy, Sovereignty and Self-Determination, at 394.

[35] The members of the Commission were appointed by the Council of the League of Nations and could be removed by it. See Treaty of Versailles, Annex Saar Territory, Article 17.

[36] See Treaty of Versailles, Annex Saar Territory, Article 23.

[37] In a petition of 12 April 1922 to the League of Nations, representatives of the political parties of the Saar population had expressed their wish to be consulted in every case of legislation and regarding the budget. The establishment of the Advisory Council by decree of the Governing Commission of 24 March 1924 fell short of these demands. See Bisschop, The Saar Controversy, at 46–8.

[38] See Treaty of Versailles, Annex Saar Territory, Article 23.   [39] Ibid., Article 26.

[40] Local representatives were not consulted before the introduction of the franc as the main currency. See Russell, International Government of the Saar, at 173.

consulted Saar leaders only from time to time.[41] This autocratic style of governance led to dissatisfaction among local leaders,[42] and triggered protests, including the non-cooperation of the local Advisory Council with the Governing Commission.[43]

The civil liberties in the Treaty providing for the protection of local inhabitants against arbitrary action on the part of the Governing Commission were equally weak.[44] Article 30 of the governing framework for the Saar Territory placed the Governing Commission under a general duty "to provide in all cases for the protection of persons and property in the Saar Basin".[45] However, the only guarantees explicitly mentioned in the Treaty were religious liberties, educational rights, the right to vote in local elections[46] and the right to leave the territory.[47] Moreover, local inhabitants were left with few remedies to enforce their treaty-based rights against the international government.[48] Occasionally, domestic courts judged decrees of the Governing Commission as being *ultra vires*, because they were issued "without consulting the elected representatives of the people".[49] But generally, local inhabitants sought redress

---

[41] See Bisschop, *The Saar Controversy*, at 47.

[42] In a note of protest on 2 June 1923, the leaders of the political parties in the Saar Basin stated: "[T]he Advisory Council was to be crushed down into insignificance by all possible means. Even the very few rights left to it have been disregarded by the Governing Commission. Decrees affecting the population most intimately have been published without the Advisory Council having been heard at all, as, for instance, in the case of the notorious Provisional Decree and the decree *re* pickets. Where the Advisory Council has been heard, the Governing Commission has only carried out its proposals in matters of secondary importance, whilst in matters of the first importance it has never allowed itself to be influenced by its votes. Thus it has come about that the phrase which stands at the head of every decree: 'after consultation with the Elected Representatives of the people' is regarded by the people as an insult and designed to mislead. The people see in the autocratic administration of the finances by the Governing Commission a special contempt for their rights. The Governing Commission makes any real co-operation of the Advisory Council in the expenditure quite illusory by carefully giving its members a clear picture of how the money of the State is to be employed. The tax-payers have, however, even in the Saar Basin, a right to know how their money is employed. There is no excuse now that the period of transition has been passed through, for not respecting this acknowledged principle of every modern democratic State." See Bisschop, *The Saar Controversy*, at 86.

[43] See Hannum, *Autonomy, Sovereignty and Self-Determination*, at 394.

[44] The lack of adequate protection of the rights of the inhabitants was criticised by Germany in its observations to the Treaty of Versailles. See Russell, *International Government of the Saar*, at 133.

[45] See Treaty of Versailles, Annex Saar Territory, Article 30.   [46] See *ibid.*, Article 28.

[47] See *ibid.*, Article 29.   [48] See Bisschop, *The Saar Controversy*, at 30.

[49] One incident was reported in *The Times* on 25 June 1925, *German Flag in the Saar*: "A curious dispute has arisen in the Saar Territory between the Governing Commission

through petitions and memorials communicated by their representatives to the Council of the League of Nations.[50]

1.1.1.3. The neutralising function of the Governing Commission

The Governing Commission itself regarded its mandate under the Treaty of Versailles primarily as a neutralising mission. The terms of the Treaty left some leeway to link the power of government more closely to the needs and wishes of the population, as the Commission was bound to exercise its authority "in the capacity as a trustee"[51] and "in order to assure the rights and welfare of the population".[52] But the Commission placed a strong emphasis on the adoption of measures designed to emphasise the political autonomy of the Saar Territory.[53] It quickly used its powers to establish visible symbols of the Territory's independence, by designing a Saar Territory flag and its own postage stamps. It ordered that justice be rendered "in the name of the Governing Commission", as provided by Article 25 of the League's governing framework. Furthermore, in setting up a new administration, the Commission asked the Prussian and the Bavarian governments to place their former civil servants formally holding office in the Saar at its disposal, in order to relieve the administering structures of the Saar Basin from outside independence.[54] Mr Rault, the first President of the Commission, explained the general policy taken by the Saar administration explicitly in the Tenth Report of the Governing Commission. He noted:

The inhabitants of the Basin are to be placed in an exceptional situation for fifteen years. The special status accorded them in the Treaty of Peace was arranged in order to give them at a later date, the full and independent right

and the local judiciary. The display of the German Imperial red, white and black flag was prohibited by an ordinance of the Governing Commission dated June, 1924. The Courts of first instance refused to convict a citizen – the well known industrial, Hermann Röckling – who was accused of displaying the flag, and declared the ordinance to be null and void. The Public Prosecutor was ordered by the Commission to enter an appeal, and the Upper Courts have now decided that prohibition of the German Imperial flag is *ultra vires*, as it was issued 'without consulting the elected representatives of the people'; the flying of the flag is declared to be contrary neither to the laws of the Saar nor to the Treaty of Versailles."

[50] See generally, Russell, *International Government of the Saar*, at 200.

[51] See Article 49 of the Treaty of Versailles.   [52] See Article 46 of the Treaty of Versailles.

[53] It expressed this ambition in its first report, which noted: "It [the Governing Commission] is endeavouring to conform with the Treaty by making the Territory of the Saar an autonomous country independent of Germany." See Russell, *International Government of the Saar*, at 152.

[54] See Russell, *International Government of the Saar*, at 155.

of self-determination. In their own interest, and in order to assure the genuine character of the plebiscite of 1935, they must be immediately subjected to a completely autonomous regime. This autonomy would not have been complete if the political and the administrative bonds attaching the Saar Basin to the German Empire, to Prussia and to Bavaria had not been gradually broken, and if the population had continued to be to any extent or in any way dependent upon authorities outside the Basin, or if the policy adopted in the Territory had been influenced by the German, Prussian or Bavarian administration.[55]

This statement illustrates that the League's governance of the Saar was strongly shaped by the objective of neutralisation. The Governing Commission sought to weaken German influence and to strengthen international rule in the Saar Territory, in order to create a neutral and balanced environment for the exercise of the 1935 referendum on the future of the territory which was finally to solve the German-French dispute of interests over the Saar Basin.

1.1.1.4. The monitoring function of the League Council
With its plenary executive and legislative authority (including the power to operate public services, to conduct foreign relations and to establish a local police force), the Governing Commission enjoyed extremely wide powers in order to fulfil its mandate. However, it was subject to some basic scrutiny by the Council of the League of Nations. The Commission was required to report on its activities to the Council.[56] Furthermore, the German and the French governments and local representatives of the Saar inhabitants could address petitions and memorials to the Council. Both devices provided a minimal form of protection and checks and balances against abuses of the Commission, as the Council had the authority to block the re-election of the members of the Commission after their one-year term.[57] Although the Council decided that it "should not intervene in the administration of the Saar Basin except for reasons of the highest importance",[58] it exercised its supervisory function in extreme situations.

---

[55] *Ibid.*, at 156–7.
[56] Until 1935, the Commission filed three or four reports a year to the Council. See Ratner, *The New UN Peacekeeping*, at 92.
[57] See Treaty of Versailles, Annex Saar Territory, Article 17. The Council did not have the means to annul decisions of the Commission. The only sanction was publicity and the threat of non-re-election of a Commission member. See Bisschop, *The Saar Controversy*, at 30.
[58] See Saar Basin Governing Commission, Report presented by the Greek Representative, M. Caclamanos, and adopted by the Council of the League of Nations, 20 September 1920, LNOJ I (1920), 400, 403.

The most famous case is the intervention of the Council against a decree of the Commission which made it a criminal offence, punishable by imprisonment for five years, publicly to express criticism of the Treaty of Versailles or to insult or traduce the League of Nations.[59] The British government[60] requested an inquiry by the Council into the administration of the Saar, arguing that "as the League of Nations is the trustee for the Saar Basin and as the Governing Commission represents the League, it is the duty of the Council to make sure that the administration is being carried out in accordance with the Treaty of Versailles".[61] The Council summoned the Governing Commission to Geneva in 1923 for questioning – a measure which finally led to a review of the decree by the Commission.

In addition to its monitoring role, the Council exercised an organisational function in dispute settlement related to the exercise of the Treaty-mandated referendum. The Council created a plebiscite commission and a multinational force (reportedly the "first multinational military operation under the auspices of international organisation"[62]) to maintain order during the elections. Moreover it appointed a special rapporteur to facilitate negotiations between Germany and France over the plebiscite, which took place on 13 January 1935 and resulted in an overwhelming vote (90 per cent) in favour of immediate reunification with Germany.[63]

1.1.2. Assessment

The Saar regime as a whole presented a rather successful experiment in territorial administration.[64] The greatest legacy of the Saar model is that it instituted a new governance technique in international relations, by replacing the pre-war tradition of multinational state administration with a truly international form of government. This new government model presented several advantages over prior experiments

---

[59] Cases under the decree were to be tried before a special court appointed by the Governing Commission. See Russell, *International Government of the Saar*, at 210.

[60] The decree was, in particular, vehemently criticised by British officials, who qualified it as being "in entire defiance of the all the principles which all democratic countries and all free countries have been endeavouring to practice". See Statement of Mr Asquith, Sir John Simon, Lord Robert Cecil and others in the British House of Commons, 10 May 1923, reproduced in Russell, *International Government of the Saar*, at 211.

[61] See Russell, *International Government of the Saar*, at 213.

[62] See Ratner, *The New UN Peacekeeping*, at 93.   [63] *Ibid.*, at 93.

[64] The League itself considered the Saar mission as an "undeniable success". See Secretariat of the League of Nations, *The Aims, Methods and Activity in the League of Nations* (1935), at 125.

in territorial administration. The structural embodiment of governance within the institutional framework of the League of Nations turned the administration of the territory into a communitarian enterprise, which was open to public scrutiny and monitoring, and left little room for inter-state bargains, deals and intrigues in the running of the administration.[65] Furthermore, the institutionalisation of governance under the umbrella of the Saar Basin Governing Commission with members from disinterested states and representatives acting on behalf of the League of Nations rather than in the capacity of their own government, strengthened the case for impartiality in decision-making and provided the ground for the neutralisation of the conflict between German and French interests.

This new model of administration was difficult to categorise in legal terms.[66] Some authors claimed that Germany retained sovereignty over the Saar,[67] because Germany renounced only on the "government of the territory",[68] while others argued that sovereignty resided in the League,[69] which legislated and rendered justice in its own name and assumed responsibility for the protection of nationals abroad. The best explanation was, however, provided by representatives of the League itself, who expressed the views that sovereignty was "in abeyance for fifteen years" of League administration and that the situation of the Saar Basin marked "a new international legal conception – namely a territory over which there is no sovereignty".[70]

This experiment succeeded *grosso modo* as an instrument of dispute resolution, in so far as it managed to find a peaceful solution to the strategic conflict over the Saar.[71] The Saar compromise combined

---

[65] See also Russell, *International Government of the Saar*, at 239.

[66] See generally Henri Coursier, *Le Statut International de la Sarre* (1925), 33–7.

[67] See Ratner, *The New UN Peacekeeping*, at 92; Hannum, *Autonomy, Sovereignty and Self-Determination*, at 391.

[68] See Article 49 (1) of the Treaty of Versailles ("Germany renounces in favour of the League of Nations in the capacity of trustee (fidéicommissaire), the government of the territory ...").

[69] See Knudson, *History of the League of Nations*, at 179 ("The Commission exercised sovereign power in the Territory and governed under instructions from the Council in addition to the authority contained in the Treaty of Versailles"). See also Ydit, *Internationalised Territories*, at 45 ("internationalized territory under the sovereignty of the LON").

[70] See Letter from Eric Drummond, Secretary-General of the League of Nations, to Harold Nicolson, British diplomat, 15 December 1919, League of Nations Archive No. 11/2474/2432.

[71] See Ratner, *The New UN Peacekeeping*, at 93.

short-term interest-management with long-term dispute resolution. The Treaty of Versailles reconciled the conflict of interest between Germany and France in the immediate post-war period, by granting France the right to compensation through access and exploitation of the Saar coal mines, while formally preserving Germany's territorial title over the territory until the holding of the referendum. Moreover, the Saar formula offered a reasonable solution to the dispute over the Saar on a long-term basis, by laying the decision on the status of the territory in the hands of the freely expressed wishes of the local population.

The main deficit of the Saar model was its unfettered trust in the omnipotence of the Governing Commission.[72] The strong concentration of power within the Commission and the limited degree of local self-government dissociated international rule from the people. Due to its autocratic mode of governance, the Commission failed to win the respect and cooperation of local authorities. The lack of formal accountability[73] added to the general scepticism about the French bias of the majority of the members of the Commission in the eyes of the German population.[74] Both elements were counterproductive to the accomplishment of the goal of the mission, because they encouraged the rise of nationalism – a development running counter to the objective of neutralisation envisaged by the drafters of the Treaty of Versailles.

Despite these shortcomings and its realist background, the Saar administration can be presented as one of the most important undertakings in international administration, because it instituted a new culture of dispute settlement that was later revived and practised on a number of other occasions, most notably in the prominent case of the UN administration of Kosovo.

1.2. The League's administration of the Free City of Danzig

The League of Nations' engagement in Danzig[75] marked the second great experiment in international territorial administration under the Treaty

---

[72] See Russell, *International Government of the Saar*, at 239.
[73] The Council of the League of Nations, for instance, did not have the express authority to reverse controversial decisions of the Commission – a power that would have strengthened the framework of governance in terms of institutional accountability and legitimacy.
[74] The executive power of the Commission was given to a French member (M. Rault) by the Council. Furthermore, the majority of the original members of the Commission were known to be French in their sympathies. See Russell, *International Government of the Saar*, at 207.
[75] See generally John B. Mason, *The Danzig Dilemma* (1945).

of Versailles. Like the League's engagement in the Saar, the Danzig administration was deeply rooted in the tradition of dispute resolution.

1.2.1. Features

The internationalisation of the city was proposed by the drafters of the Treaty of Versailles in order to reconcile two competing interests, namely the historically founded claim of the predominantly German inhabitants of the territory for autonomous rule, on the one hand, and the strategic interest of the newly created Polish state to gain free and secure access to the sea, on the other.[76] This specific background gave the Danzig regime a bilateral, rather than a community-oriented, nature. The international authority of the League was not an instrument of promoting political and social transformation or reconstruction, but mainly a neutralising factor and a mechanism of dispute settlement between the population of Danzig and the Polish state. The administration of Danzig therefore presented an example of traditional third-party mediation and internationalisation.

1.2.1.1. Internationalisation – an imperfect compromise

The idea of transforming the formerly German Hansa city of Danzig into an independent city ("free city") within the customs zone of Poland but under the authority of the League was a political construct that remained a constant source of tension between Germany, Poland and the League throughout the period of administration from 1920 to 1939. Originally, neither Poland nor the inhabitants of Danzig supported the establishment of a politically neutralised entity with certain Polish privileges (foreign policy, economic and naval rights).[77] The people of Danzig intended to be either sovereign or fully autonomous, in order to facilitate their eventual reunification with Germany. Poland, by contrast, pleaded for the full placement of the city under Polish rule. Articles 100–102 of the Treaty of Versailles, however, placed the city directly under the protection of the League of Nations. This solution represented the most

---

[76] This ambition was recognised by President Wilson, point 13 of its Fourteen Points and in an address delivered to the US Senate on 22 January 1917. See Mason, *The Danzig Dilemma*, at 57.

[77] The PCIJ stated: "The separation of Danzig from Germany was contrary to the wishes of the German people. Almost the whole of the population of that city was German; and the Peace Conference, in order to assure Poland free and secure access to the sea, decided to make Danzig a Free City without incorporating it into Poland." See PCIJ, *Treatment of Polish Nationals and Other Persons of Polish Origin or Speech in the Danzig Territory*, Advisory Opinion of 4 February 1932, Ser. A/B, No. 44, 27–8.

acceptable compromise between Danzig's interest to remain "politically German" and yet economically to maintain trade with Poland. However, this solution was far from perfect. The people of Danzig continued to cultivate their German heritage in anticipation of a future unification with the Reich, and Poland never ceased its attempts to incorporate Danzig into its territory.

1.2.1.2.   The governing framework

The drafters of the Versailles Treaty sought to address these difficulties through three types of arrangement: provisions securing Danzig's internal and external status, rules establishing special relations between Danzig and Poland and the establishment of dispute settlement mechanisms conducted under the authority of the League of Nations.

The main contribution of the Treaty of Versailles was that it transformed Danzig into an independent legal entity under international law[78] that was neither part of Poland[79] nor part of Germany,[80] although the regulatory framework of the Treaty itself was quite minimal. Unlike in the case of the Saar, the Allied powers devoted little attention to the regulation of the internal system of the new entity. The Treaty left the main responsibilities for the governance of the city of Danzig in the hands of the people of Danzig. The League of Nations did not assume exclusive administering authority over the territory. It merely acted as a "guarantor" of the territory.[81]

Article 103 of the Treaty of Versailles charged "the duly appointed representatives of the Free City" with the elaboration of a Constitution of the City of Danzig,[82] which was to be approved by a League-appointed High Commissioner and "placed under the guarantee of the League of

---

[78] In its advisory opinion of 4 February 1932, the PCIJ stated: "In its [the Court's] opinion, the fact that the legal status of Danzig is *sui generis* does not authorize it [the Polish government] to depart from the ordinary rules governing relations between states and to establish new rules for the relations between Poland and Danzig. The general principles of international law apply to Danzig subject, however, to the treaty provisions binding upon the Free City and to decisions taken by the organs of the League under these provisions." See PCIJ, *Treatment of Polish Nationals and Other Persons of Polish Origin or Speech in the Danzig Territory*, at 23–4.

[79] See PCIJ, *Access to, or Anchorage in, the Port of Danzig, of Polish War Vessels*, Advisory Opinion of 11 December 931, Ser. A/B, No. 43, at 142 ("The port of Danzig is not Polish territory").

[80] Germany renounced its title over Danzig under Article 100 of the Treaty of Versailles.

[81] According to Article 3 of the Constitution of Danzig, sovereign power was formally vested in the people of the City.

[82] Constitution of the Free City of Danzig, reprinted in Mason, *The Danzig Dilemma*, at 332.

Nations". The League's first High Commissioner soon clarified the meaning of the term "guarantee", interpreting it so as to imply that the new Constitution of Danzig, and any subsequent amendments, had to obtain the approval of the League, and that the government in the city had to be conducted in accordance with the terms of the Constitution.[83] The Constitution of Danzig therefore became the first constitutional document which was formally approved by the League, guaranteed by it and which could not be amended without its consent.

But the League of Nations' engagement in the shaping of the daily constitutional life of the city remained limited. Danzig enjoyed "complete autonomy over its internal affairs, both *de jure* and *de facto*".[84] The High Commissioner had no direct authority over the executive and legislative institutions of the city. The Constitution vested the executive power in a local twelve-member Senate, which was responsible for the promulgation of laws, the drafting of the budget, the conduct of public administration, the nomination of public servants and the maintenance of public security.[85] Furthermore, legislative authority was exercised by the popular assembly (*Volkstag*), which was elected every four years under a system of proportional representation and empowered to enact any laws falling short of a constitutional amendment.[86] The High Commissioner merely assumed a "watchdog function" in the legislative and executive process involving responsibilities in the approval of constitutional amendments and the control of treaties (in)compatible with the City's status.[87]

The widespread regulatory autonomy granted to the Danzig authorities under the Treaty of Versailles was coupled with the stipulation of a number of privileged rights in favour of Poland. The legal relationship between Danzig and Poland was addressed by Article 104 of the Treaty of Versailles, which required the Allied Powers to negotiate a treaty between Poland and the Free City:

---

[83] See Mason, *The Danzig Dilemma*, at 67. The PCIJ endorsed the view that the function of the League was not limited to the supervision of violations of the Danzig Constitution. See PCIJ, *Consistency of Certain Danzig Legislative Decrees with the Constitution of the Free City*, Ser. A/B, No. 65 (1935), 57.

[84] See Hannum, *Autonomy, Sovereignty and Self-Determination*, at 379.

[85] See Article 25 *et seq.* of the Constitution of Danzig.

[86] See Article 6 *et seq.* of the Constitution of Danzig.

[87] See Article 49 of the Constitution of Danzig (constitutional amendments) and Article 6 of the Paris Convention between Danzig and Poland of Paris of 9 November 1920 (treaty vetoes). See also Ian F. D. Morrow, *The International Status of the Free City of Danzig*, British Yearbook of International Law, Vol. 18 (1937), 114–26.

to effect the inclusion of the Free City of Danzig within the Polish Customs frontiers, and to establish a free area in the port; to ensure to Poland without any restriction the free use and service of all waterways, docks, basins, wharves, and other works within the territory of the Free City necessary for Polish imports and exports; to ensure to Poland the control and administration ... of the whole railway system within the Free City ... and of postal, telegraphic and telephonic communications between Poland and the port of Danzig; ... to provide against discrimination within the Free City of Danzig to the detriment of citizens of Poland and other persons of Polish origin or speech; [and] to provide that the Polish Government shall undertake the conduct of the foreign relations of the Free City of Danzig as well as the diplomatic protection of citizens to that city when abroad.[88]

The details of these privileges were laid down in the Treaty of Paris of 9 November 1920 between the Free City and Poland which formed the main foundation for Danzig-Polish relationships.[89]

The agreement on the establishment of special Polish rights over Danzig was a fundamental part of the political compromise at Versailles. But it turned out to be detrimental to the objective of neutralisation. Throughout the history of the Free City, the issue of Polish privileges developed into a source of controversy and challenge among the parties to the Convention, and into a medium to voice the underlying tensions between the predominantly German population of Danzig and Polish interests. Both sides, Poland and the political *apparatus* of the city of Danzig, used the framework of the Paris Treaty as a tool of power politics in order to expand their influence over the city. Representatives of Danzig sought to uphold the greatest degree of autonomy and sovereignty over the city, whereas Poland made every effort to obtain as many privileges as possible in Danzig. This gave rise to a chain of controversies in every possible field of public affairs. Legal disputes were fought over the right of Poland to establish its own mail service in Danzig ("Mail Box Incident"), over Polish authority to store munitions in the harbour, over customs services, railway issues, minority protection and the legality of

[88] See Article 104 of the Treaty of Versailles.
[89] See Convention of Paris, Treaty Between Poland and the Free City of Danzig of 9 November, 1920, in Mason, *The Danzig Dilemma*, at 325. In its advisory opinion on the treatment of Polish nationals, the PCIJ stated: "As between Danzig and Poland, the Convention of Paris is the instrument which is directly binding on Danzig; but in the case of doubt as to the meaning of its provisions, recourse may be had to the Treaty of Versailles, not for the purpose of discarding the terms of the Convention, but with a view to elucidating their meaning." See PCIJ, *Treatment of Polish Nationals and Other Persons of Polish Origin or Speech in the Danzig Territory*, at 32.

the introduction of the Zloty as the single currency for railway charges.[90] This uninterrupted sequence of interest-guided litigation caused a "constant strain on the people" of Danzig[91] and on the League itself.

1.2.1.3. The mediation and dispute settlement function of the League of Nations
It became the main task of the League of Nations to serve as a neutral dispute settlement organ responsible for the resolution of the numerous legal controversies arising in the context of the administration of Danzig.

The League High Commissioner and the Council of the League of Nations were charged with this cumbersome task. Article 103 of the Treaty of Versailles entrusted the High Commissioner with the "duty of dealing in the first instance with all differences arising between Poland and the Free City of Danzig in regard to [the Versailles] Treaty or any arrangements or agreement thereunder". But Article 39 of the Treaty of Paris of 9 November 1920 significantly broadened this mandate, by providing that "any differences arising between Poland and the Free City of Danzig in regard to the present Treaty or any other subsequent agreements, arrangements, or conventions, *or to any matter affecting the relations between Poland and the Free City,* shall be submitted by one or the other party to the decision of the High Commissioner, who shall, if he deems it necessary, refer the matter to the Council of the League of Nations".[92] The High Commissioner was required to decide in each case whether a given dispute came within his authority. But his decision on admissibility was subject to an appeal to the Council of the League of Nations.

This jurisdiction led to widespread judicial activity in the League of Nations.[93] The High Commissioner rendered over eighty decisions in the period of the Danzig administration concerning treaty obligations between Danzig and Poland.[94] In addition, most of the decisions were appealed to the Council of the League (twenty-three by Poland and nineteen by Danzig). Referrals of the High Commissioner or appeals to its

---

[90] For a survey, see Ydit, *Internationalised Territories*, at 211–21.
[91] *Ibid.*, at 227.   [92] Emphasis added.
[93] The PCIJ reaffirmed the judicial character of the High Commissioner's function, noting that "[f]rom these provisions [Article 103 of the Treaty of Versailles and Article 39 of the Treaty of Paris] it is quite clear that the functions of the High Commissioner are of a judicial character and limited to deciding questions submitted by one or other of the parties". See PCIJ, *Polish Postal Service in Danzig*, Advisory Opinion of 16 May 1925, Ser. B, No. 11, at 26.
[94] Most decisions were made in the early period of administration between 1921 and 1924. See Mason, *The Danzig Dilemma*, at 83.

decisions involved the Council in over fifty proceedings,[95] and the Council in turn requested six advisory opinions from the PCIJ.[96]

This multi-layered system of League dispute settlement marked a progression from the Saar regime, because it provided the people of Danzig with an authoritative means of defending their political and legal autonomy.[97] Moreover, it set an early precedent for judicial review of decisions of international administrators by way of an advisory procedure.[98] The system, however, was overambitious in its design. The dispute settlement mechanism under the Treaty of Versailles and the Paris Treaty flooded the agenda of the League with Danzig questions,[99] and denaturised the function the Council of the League which had to decide "on every little two-penny-half-penny question about a steam ferry or whether a policeman was to sit in the water or on the land".[100] Moreover, the strong focus on detailed inter-party dispute settlement proved to be slightly unfortunate in policy terms, as it stimulated a culture of rivalry ("paragraph war"[101]) between the people of Danzig and Poland, in which the law was politicised and used to encourage conflict.[102]

[95] Ibid., at 86.
[96] These six cases were PCIJ, Polish Postal Services in Danzig, Advisory Opinion of 16 May 1925, Ser. B, No. 11; Jurisdiction of the Courts of Danzig, Advisory Opinion of 3 March 1928, Ser. B, No. 15; Free City of Danzig and International Labour Organization, Advisory Opinion of 26 August 1930, Ser. B, No. 38; Access to, or Anchorage in, the Port of Danzig, of Polish War Vessels, Advisory Opinion of 11 December 1931, Ser. A/B, No. 43; Treatment of Polish Nationals and Other Persons of Polish Origin or Speech in the Danzig Territory, Advisory Opinion of 4 February 1932, Ser. A.B, No. 44; Consistency of Certain Danzig Legislative Decrees with the Constitution of the Free City, Advisory Opinion of 4 December 1935, Ser. A/B, No. 65.
[97] Most disputed questions were submitted by Danzig in protest against Polish demands or actions. See Mason, The Danzig Dilemma, at 82.
[98] The PCIJ exercised restraint in reviewing the decisions of the High Commissioner. One example is the case concerning the jurisdiction of the courts of Danzig. In this case, the government of the Free City requested to nullify the decision of the High Commissioner regarding the jurisdiction of Danzig courts over railway and employment contract issues. The PCIJ merely responded by a finding that the decision of the High Commissionere was unfounded in law on the basis of the Court's interpretation of the applicable agreements.
[99] See Korhonen, Gras and Creutz, International Post-Conflict Situations, at 184.
[100] See the criticism of High Commissioner MacDonnell in a report to the Council in 1925, reprinted in Mason, The Danzig Dilemma, at 83. Mason notes that there were occasions on which the Council members "had to listen for hours to the most tedious details of a Danzig dispute, in spite of the preliminary work done by its Rapporteur and the League Secretariat". Ibid., at 306.
[101] See Ydit, Internationalised Territories, at 213.
[102] See also Mason, The Danzig Dilemma, at 304. ("Existing possibilities for honest disagreement over questions of rights and obligations in their mutual relationship were affected by an atmosphere of suspicion and distrust arising from opposite aims as well as an obvious unwillingness to compromise.")

The negative effects of this system were later attenuated through the introduction of additional mediation mechanisms by the High Commissioner, which promoted direct negotiations between the parties and facilitated the withdrawal of appeals.[103] However, this move was not a solution to the underlying flaw of the system, namely the fact that the League could not fully live up to the dispute settlement responsibilities that it had assumed in regard to Danzig under the Treaty of Versailles.[104]

1.2.1.4. The protective function of the League
In addition to its dispute settlement function and its role as a guarantor of the Constitution of Danzig, the League was vested with the task of protecting Danzig's international status. The functions of the guarantee of Danzig's Constitution and its protection were closely connected. The main idea behind the internationalisation of Danzig under the Treaty of Versailles was, in the words of the Rapporteur of the League Council, "that the Free City should form in the international organisation of Europe a community which must be protected against all undue interference on the part of any country, and which must have its own regular existence".[105] The modalities of protection were not spelled out by the Treaty. The vision of the League Council was that the League itself would ensure the defence of Danzig against external aggression, in collaboration with one or more members of the League and Poland, which was authorised to assume police powers in Danzig in the event that local authorities proved unable to fulfil this task, subject to the approval of the League Council or the High Commissioner.

But this security strategy was unable to cope with the growing nazification of Danzig in the mid-1930s and to prevent the city's subsequent incorporation into Germany. This failure may be explained on several grounds, which originate less from the shortcomings of the Danzig model itself than from its lack of enforcement by the League.

One weakness of the League's conception was that it relied too heavily on the potential cooperation and force of Poland. The League Council assumed that any expansion of German influence over Danzig would meet with fierce Polish resistance and that Poland itself would be strong enough to repel an invader.[106] This theory, however, failed to anticipate

---

[103] *Ibid.*, at 64–86.
[104] See also Korhonen, Gras and Creutz, *International Post-Conflict Situations*, at 184–5.
[105] See the Report of Rapporteur Viscount Ishii on the draft Constitution for Danzig, in Mason, *The Danzig Dilemma*, at 78.
[106] See Mason, *The Danzig Dilemma*, at 302.

Poland's rapprochement with Hitler (1934–9)[107] which facilitated the rise of Nazi government in Danzig[108] and limited the willingness of other League members to come to the defence of Poland in 1939,[109] which was the main benefactor of the Danzig arrangement.

Furthermore, the League itself reacted only very cautiously to assaults on its authority over Danzig.[110] Petitions by members of the oppressed opposition parties in Danzig against the nazification and *Gleichschaltung* of Danzig were treated only reluctantly by the Council of the League of Nations. When the Council dealt with the first petitions in January 1934, "[C]ouncil members were expressly blind to the nature and magnitude of the danger that threatened Danzig, and implicitly, the LON itself".[111] The League satisfied itself with assurances that Germany would respect the territorial status of Danzig. Even attempts of the Nazis to undermine the guardianship of the High Commissioner did not change the Council's passive attitude. After Germany forced the League's acting Commissioner to resign (the Leipzig "incident") and openly demanded the appointment of a new Commissioner who would refrain from any interference in Danzig's internal politics, the Council failed to act decisively, but merely appointed a committee to follow the situation in Danzig and expressed its confidence "that given wholehearted cooperation by the Government of the free City with the League's High Commissioner the internal situation would speedily be restored to normal".[112] Moreover, in the following years, other large-scale geopolitical events (the Spanish civil war (1936–9), Japan's invasion of China (1937), Hitler's preparation for the annexation of Austria and Czechoslovakia and Mussolini's occupation of Albania (1939)) captured the attention of the League and shifted the focus away from Danzig, which remained formally under the control of a weak High Commissioner[113] until 1 September 1939, when German troops invaded Danzig.

[107] See Ydit, *Internationalised Territories*, at 216-217.   [108] *Ibid.*, at 218–21.
[109] Mason notes that "Poland during this period made no effort to support the authority of the League and acquiesced in the violation of the Danzig constitution on the understanding that Nazi-dominated Danzig would respect certain rights of Poland in the Free City". See Mason, *The Danzig Dilemma*, at 301.
[110] See also Ratner, *The New UN Peacekeeping*, at 95. ("From 1937 onward ... the Council maintained only the 'pretence' of guardianship over Danzig.")
[111] See Ydit, *Internationalised Territories*, at 221.
[112] See League of Nations Official Journal (1936) Part II, 762–899. See also Ydit, *Internationalised Territories*, at 223.
[113] The last High Commissioner was Carl Jacob Burckhardt, a Swiss national who refrained from taking strong action against Nazi practices. See Ydit, *Internationalised Territories*, at 220–1.

1.2.2. Assessment

Like the Treaty of Versailles' arrangement for the Saar, the framework of the Free City of Danzig broke new ground in international law on several levels. The first novelty was the special international status of the territory. The internationalisation of Danzig transformed the city into a new territorial entity with a special legal status that triggered even more legal controversy than the classification of the status of the Saar. No fewer than five diverging theories were advanced in legal doctrine to explain the special status of the Free City of Danzig.[114]

A first theory held that "sovereignty" still belonged to the Principal Allied Powers to which Germany had ceded its rights in the Treaty of Versailles, as each of the three other authorities (the League of Nations, Poland and the Free City itself) possessed only limited powers over the territory of Danzig, but no general authority (*compétence globale*).[115] A second view took the position that Poland exercised "sovereignty" over Danzig, arguing that the Free City constituted an autonomous part of the territory of Poland, administered by the latter as a protectorate (*Verwaltungsprotektorat*).[116] Another group of authors claimed that the Free City of Danzig itself possessed sovereignty over its territory,[117] while being under the protectorate of the League of Nations.[118] A fourth theory refused to regard the Free City of Danzig as a state and qualified it as a protectorate of the League of Nations exercised in the form a joint association (*Verwaltungsgemeinschaft*) by the League and Poland.[119] Finally, a fifth – and in the opinion of this author the most convincing – view did not characterise Danzig as a protectorate of Poland or the League of Nations but considered it as a non-sovereign, international legal entity with a restricted capacity to determine its foreign relations and a part of its internal affairs.[120]

---

[114] See Verzijl, *International Persons*, at 517–19.

[115] See Geneviéve Levesque, *La Situation Internationale de Dantzig* (1924), 118, 120, 121.

[116] See Julijan Makowski, *La Situation Juridique de la Ville Libre de Dantzig*, Revue Générale de Droit International Public, Vol. 30 (1923), 169, at 194, 213.

[117] See Rudolf Pfeuffer, *Die Völkerrechtliche Stellung der Freien Stadt Danzig* (1921), 93. See also Ydit, *Internationalised Territories*, at 224.

[118] See Walther Schücking and Hans Wehberg, *Die Satzung des Völkerbundes* (1931), at 121–4.

[119] See Julius Hatschek, *Das Völkerrecht als System völkerrechtlich bedeutsamer Staatsakte* (1923), 44–6.

[120] See Malcolm L. Lewis, *The Free City of Danzig*, British Yearbook of International Law, Vol. V (1924), 89 ("entity *sui generis*"); Verzijl, *International Persons*, at 542 ("a non-sovereign state, to be recognized as a subject of international law with a greatly restricted capacity to act, burdened with certain state servitudes in favour of Poland"). See also Charles De Lannoy, *Le Règlement de la Question de Dantzig*, Revue de

The most interesting feature of the Danzig model, however, was not the question of the legal status of Danzig, but the Treaty of Versailles' new approach to territorial dispute settlement. Following the tradition of the Saar settlement, the drafters of the Danzig arrangement used the technique of internationalisation mainly as an instrument of neutralisation. But the means deployed to achieve this goal in the case of Danzig differed from the strategies used in the case of the Saar. The innovation of the Danzig formula was that it left the principal governing authority over the territory in the hands of the local authorities and sought to balance Danzig's autonomy and Polish interests through the use of the League as an organ of adjudication and mediation of dispute. This approach differed from the Saar experiment in the sense that it respected domestic self-government and kept international intervention to a moderate level. The League exercised classic regulatory authority only *ex ante*, namely in the process of the framing of Danzig's Constitution, in which the Council of the League required the Constituent Assembly of Danzig to revise the proposed text of Danzig Constitution along the lines of the Council's demands.[121] Afterwards, the League limited itself to the exercise of supervisory authority through mediation and adjudication – a function that the League performed "with great skill and lack of bias" within the confines of its possibilities.[122]

However, the Danzig model contained a number of flaws that compromised its capacity to serve as a long-term instrument of conflict resolution. The first shortcoming of the Treaty of Versailles was that it only regulated the relationship between Danzig and Poland in very general terms, making it necessary to clarify the respective rights and duties of both sides in greater detail through bilateral proceedings. This regulatory deficit invited disputes between Danzig and Poland and divided both parties more than was necessary.[123]

Secondly, the possibility for disputants to file appeals to the League Council was at odds with the limited capacity and the political function

Droit International et de Législation Comparée (1921), at 452 ("*aucune des catégories juridiques adoptées par le droit de gens*").

[121] The Council asked the Constitutive Assembly, *inter alia*, to provide that "amendments could not come into force without the consent of the League; that the League had the right to require authentic information at any time from the Danzig government on the public affairs of Danzig; that the Constitution should forbid the use of the Free City as a military or naval base, the erection of fortifications, and the manufacture of munitions or war materials in its territory except with the special consent of the League". See Mason, *The Danzig Dilemma*, at 300.

[122] See Ydit, *Internationalised Territories*, at 221. The League Council managed successfully to settle forty-nine disputes.

[123] See also Mason, *The Danzig Dilemma*, at 306.

of the Council. The authority to hear appeals from the decisions of the High Commissioner would have better been conferred to a permanent non-political arbitral body which could have devoted more time to the settlement of disputes, leaving policy matters to the Council.[124]

Finally, the strong weight given to the dispute settlement function of the League in the case of Danzig was unsatisfactory in the sense that it fell short of solving the root causes of conflict in Polish-German relations. A more proactive mandate charging the League with broader responsibilities in the executive or legislative functions might have prevented the passive approach that the League displayed in the period of the rise of the Nazi government in Danzig.

Nevertheless, it would be wrong to qualify the League supervision over Danzig as a failed experiment of international territorial administration.[125] During the first ten years of its existence, the Danzig experience proved to be quite a successful undertaking in international civil governance.[126] Deficient as it was, the framework of the Treaty of Versailles did ensure a peaceful coexistence between Germans and the Polish minority in Danzig.[127] The situation only began to decline in the mid-1930s, when the League adopted its policy of disengagement and passivity towards the rise of the Nazi government of Danzig. Even in this period, the Danzig model itself had a positive impact on the social life in the Free City. Danzig's internationalised constitutional system and its special protections for the Polish minority did serve to slow the process of its nazification.[128] The veto right of the High Commissioner prevented the Nazi government from legitimating discriminatory legislation through amendments to the Danzig Constitution.[129] The PCIJ ruled in an Advisory Opinion to the League Council that the amendment of the Danzig Penal Code by Nazi legislation constituted "an arbitrary

[124] See Jan F. D. Morrow, *The Peace Settlement in the German-Polish Borderlands* (1936), at 126, note 2.

[125] It is sometimes argued that the internationalisation of Danzig presents a failure in territorial administration, because it failed to prevent Danzig's *Anschluss* to Germany. See Korhonen, Gras and Creutz, *International Post-Conflict Situations*, at185; and Ydit, *Internationalised Territories*, at 221.

[126] See also Ratner, *The New UN Peacekeeping*, at 95.

[127] The Danzig population "acquiesced" as a result of the fact that it was "at least not ceded outright to Poland". See Ydit, *Internationalised Territories*, at 212.

[128] See Ydit, *Internationalised Territories*, at 218–20. The Nazis lacked the two-thirds majority in the *Volkstag* to amend the democratic Constitution of Danzig. Furthermore, they needed the approval of the Council of the League of Nations for amendments to Danzig's Constitution.

[129] See Ydit, *Internationalised Territories*, at 219.

encroachment of individual liberty on the part of the authorities of the State (of) Danzig".[130] The Nazi government even revoked some of its discriminatory decrees, in order to comply with the wishes of League.[131] The League's guarantee of Danzig marked therefore at least, a partly successful device of territorial administration.

1.3. The League's engagement in Memel

The League of Nations' engagement concerning the Memel territory[132] constituted the last undertaking in the series of experiments in territorial neutralisation exercised by the League in conjunction with the Treaty of Versailles. The territory was not internationalised to the same degree as the Saar Basin or the City of Danzig, although the League assumed responsibilities that helped to secure the autonomous status of the local, ethnically German population of Memelland vis-à-vis Lithuania, which had a strategic interest in the Port of Memel as an outlet to the Baltic Sea.[133] Conceptually, the case of Memel falls therefore into the same historical tradition of neutralisation as its two popular predecessors.

1.3.1. Memel – a non-Danzig by accident

Like the Saar Basin and Danzig, the Memel territory was part of Germany, until the latter renounced "in favour of the Principal Allied and Associated Powers all rights and title" over the territory pursuant to Article 99 of the Treaty of Versailles. But the Treaty did not directly place the territory under League supervision. A Conference of Ambassadors of the Allied Powers was charged with the elaboration of a framework for the status of the territory, which Germany undertook to accept in advance. The Allied Powers planned to internationalise Memelland along the lines of the Danzig model, granting Lithuania special right over the territory, while placing the territory under the supervision of a High Commissioner appointed by the League.[134] However, the course of history changed this schedule of events. After three years of Allied deliberations

---

[130] See PCIJ, *Consistency of Certain Danzig Legislative Decrees with the Constitution of the Free City*, 57. The true problem was that the various Nazi infringements leading up to the dismissal of the League's last High Commissioner in 1939 were not followed by sanctions.

[131] See Ydit, *Internationalised Territories*, at 222.

[132] See generally Hannum, *Autonomy, Sovereignty and Self-Determination*, at 379; Ydit, *Internationalised Territories*, at 48.

[133] See also Walters, *History of the League of Nations*, Vol. I (1952), at 303.

[134] See Ydit, *Internationalised Territories*, at 48.

about the details of the internationalisation, Lithuania occupied the then provisionally French-administered territory,[135] in order to enforce a solution to the Memel problem. The subsequent Lithuanian presence in and control of the territory forced the Allies to recognise full Lithuanian sovereignty over Memel, accompanied by a special autonomy status preserving "the traditional rights and culture of its inhabitants".[136]

1.3.2. The tripartite role of the League

The League of Nations assumed a tripartite role in the resolution of the Memel problem. The Council of the League assisted, first, in the elaboration of a legal framework for Memel. The Council appointed a special Commission of Experts, which was charged with the preparation of a draft Statute for the Memel Territory. The Statute proposed by the Commission was agreed upon by the Principal Allied Powers (Great Britain, France, Italy and Japan) and Lithuania, and placed within the framework of the Memel Convention, signed by the respective parties on 8 May 1924.[137] The Statute acknowledged Lithuania's territorial sovereignty over Memel, but transformed the territory into a special "unit enjoying legislative, judicial, administrative and financial autonomy".[138]

The League itself did not directly interfere in the administration of the territory. Memel was governed by a Directorate (composed of not more than five Memel citizens and a Governor appointed by Lithuania), a local Chamber of Representatives (*Landtag*) with legislative competences in the domain of local government.[139] However, the League exercised administrative authority regarding the Memel harbour and dispute settlement functions concerning Memel itself.

The Memel Convention granted the League special responsibilities in the field of dispute resolution. Article 17 of the treaty entitled "any member of the Council of the League of Nations ... to draw the attention of the Council to any infraction of the provisions of the Memel

---

[135] After the entry into force of the Versailles Treaty, Memel was occupied by French troops and administered by a French High Commissioner.

[136] See Memel Statute, preamble. See also generally Hannum, *Autonomy, Sovereignty and Self-Determination*, at 379, 383.

[137] The legal character of the Statute of Memel was discussed by the PCIJ. See PCIJ, *Interpretation of the Statute of the Memel Territory* (1932), Ser. A/B, No. 49, 300.

[138] See Article 2 of the Memel Convention.

[139] The competences included the organisation of local government, police powers and legislative powers. See Article 5 of the Memel Statute.

Convention".[140] This provision turned the League Council indirectly into a public guarantor of the Memel settlement. Furthermore, Article 13 of the Convention gave the Allied powers the right to submit disputes concerning the Memel Statute for final resolution to the PCIJ[141] – a move which reaffirmed Memel's status as a territory of international concern.

Moreover, the League enjoyed direct administering responsibilities concerning the port of Memel. The administration of the Memel harbour was entrusted to an "international Harbor Board", which had the duty to report annually to the Government of Lithuania and the League. The League was authorised to appoint one of the three Commissioners of the Memel port[142] and enjoyed veto rights concerning amendments of the harbour regime and transit traffic rights.

Overall, the powers of the League concerning Memel were much more limited than those afforded to it in Danzig and the Saar.[143] However, the case of Memel again illustrats the strong role that the concept of neutralisation played in the post-war settlements under the Treaty of Versailles.

2. United Nations experiments in neutralisation after World War II

The League of Nations' practice in territorial administration visibly shaped the plans for the takeover of governance by the UN in the cases of Trieste and Jerusalem after World War II. Both experiments remained primarily dominated by the objectives of neutralisation and impartial international supervision, which had characterised the League's undertakings in territorial administration after World War I. The strong focus on bilateral dispute settlement and strategic internationalisation distinguished them from the later practice of the UN. At the same time, both governing frameworks began to display some traces of innovation and reform: they began to deviate more directly from the idea of state-centred peacemaking and incorporated community-based structures in the settlement, which were designed to grant all states access to UN-administered territories. However, both arrangements continued to be influenced by the spirit of their time, in the sense that they relied on

---

[140] See Article 17 of the Memel Convention.
[141] See Article 13 of the Memel Convention.
[142] The Harbour Board consisted of one member appointed by Lithuania, one delegate of Memel and one neutral member appointed by the League.
[143] This is mainly a result of the fact that Memel became an integral part of Lithuania.

robust and authoritarian formulas of international governance without devoting systematic attention to issues such as democratic accountability and participatory self-determination.

2.1.   The Permanent Statute of the Free Territory of Trieste

The proposed UN internationalisation of Trieste[144] was directly related to the process of dispute settlement after World War II. Both Italy and Yugoslavia had historical interests and rights over the port of Trieste, which was shared by Italian, Slav and Austrian inhabitants and constituted an important commercial and strategic area for trade.[145]

2.1.1.   The historical context

Trieste was occupied by Yugoslav and New Zealand troops in the last phase of World War II. After the war, Tito's forces remained in Trieste. But the victorious powers took charge of the settlement of the disputed city and its surrounding territory. Trieste was provisionally divided into a British-American zone (Zone "A") and a Yugoslav zone (Zone "B") of occupation, while efforts were made to reconcile the competing claims of Italy and Yugoslavia.[146] Tito intended to incorporate Trieste into Yugoslavia, granting it the status of an independent Republic under the Yugoslav Federation with widely autonomous powers and a Free Port. Italy, on the other hand, sought to maintain its title over the territory and proposed the internationalisation of the harbour of Trieste. The Council of the Foreign Ministers of the victorious powers (the United States, Great Britain, the Soviet Union and France), which was charged with the conclusion of peace settlements with the former enemy states at the Potsdam Conference, suggested the fully fledged internationalisation of Trieste as a compromise solution between the two diverging positions in a resolution adopted on 3 July 1946.[147] The resolution provided that Trieste should be transformed into an autonomous and independent international entity placed under the guarantee of the UN Security Council. This idea met with opposition from both Italy and

---

[144] See generally, C. A. Caillier, *Le Problème de Trieste et de son Territoire Libre* (1956); Kelsen, *Law of the United Nations*, at 825

[145] See generally on the importance of the Port of Trieste, Ydit, *Internationalised Territories*, at 235.

[146] The acting US Foreign Secretary stated that "it is the firm policy of the United States that territorial changes should be made only after thorough study and after full consultation and deliberation between the various governments concerned". See Ydit, *Internationalised Territories*, at 238.

[147] *Ibid.*, at 241.

Yugoslavia, although it was subsequently taken up by the twenty-one participants of the Paris Peace Treaty Conference (29 July–15 October 1945), who clarified the framework of the proposed Statute for Trieste, and by the Security Council, which approved the Statute on 10 January 1947 by ten votes to one (Australia dissenting).[148] The new Statute of Trieste was then embodied in Annex VI and VII of the Peace Treaty with Italy, which was signed by Italy one month later on 10 February 1947.

2.1.2.   The governing framework of the Statute

Conceptually, the proposed governing framework for the territory of Trieste constituted both a (post)modern replication and a development of the Danzig arrangement.

2.1.2.1.   *Trieste – a variation of the theme of Danzig*

The main objectives of internationalisation were very similar to the objectives in the cases of Danzig and Trieste. The drafters of both arrangements used structures of international governance in order to balance competing state interests over strategically important areas, and in order to protect the rights of the local population against interference in their status, language and cultural rights.

2.1.2.1.1.   *The neutralising function of the Trieste settlement*

Like the Danzig model, the proposed international regime for Trieste served as an instrument of neutralisation. Italy agreed to terminate its "sovereignty over the area constituting the Free Territory of Trieste" under Article 21 of the 1947 Peace Treaty.[149] Upon its proposed independence, Trieste was to become a permanently internationalised entity. Article 3 of the Statute of the Free Territory declared Trieste a demilitarised and neutral zone and prohibited the domestic government from entering into arrangements that might jeopardise that neutrality. The Security Council was supposed to assume direct control over the territory. Article 2 of the Statute charged the Council with guaranteeing the "integrity and independence" of Trieste – a responsibility that obligated the Council to ensure both the "maintenance of public order and security" and "the observance of the ... Statute and in particular the protection

---

[148] See SC Res. 16 of 10 January 1947. Australia argued that the Council would transcend its powers under the Charter by assuming the guarantee of Trieste as proposed by the Statute. See Kelsen, *Law of the United Nations*, at 832.

[149] See Article 21 (2) of the Treaty of Peace with Italy.

of the basic human rights of the inhabitants". The territory itself was to be separated from Italian or Yugoslav rule and bound to receive "its own flag and coat of arms",[150] its own citizenship[151] and constitution,[152] legislative[153] and judicial authorities,[154] foreign relations power[155] and its own monetary system.[156] This special framework was designed to safeguard the rights of both the overwhelmingly Italian population and the Slav-German minorities.

2.1.2.1.2. The guarantee of the observance of the Statute by the international Governor of Trieste
The Statute of the Free Territory of Trieste also shared some parallels with the Danzig arrangement in terms of the system's model of supervision of governance. The Statute vested legislative and executive powers primarily with locally elected or appointed institutions (a popular Assembly[157] and a Council of Government[158]). However, this local structure of government was superseded by international control mechanisms, designed to ensure the observance of the Statute by the domestic governing institutions.

Article 17 of the Statute entrusted the Governor of Trieste with the guarantee of the "integrity and independence" of the territory. The office of the Governor was to be exercised by an international civil servant, who was to "be appointed by the Security Council, after consultation with the Governments of Yugoslavia and Italy",[159] in order to serve as the Council's administrative arm and representative in Trieste.[160] The Statute granted the Governor wide powers of control. He had the primary responsibility to supervise the observance of the Statute, including the protection of the basic rights of the inhabitants, and to ensure that public order and security were maintained by the Government of Trieste in accordance with the Statute, the Constitution and the laws of the territory.[161] For

---

[150] See the Statute of the Free Territory of Trieste, Article 8.
[151] See *ibid.*, Article 6.   [152] See *ibid.*, Article 10.   [153] See *ibid.*, Article 13.
[154] See *ibid.*, Article 14.   [155] See *ibid.*, Article 24.   [156] See *ibid.*, Article 30.
[157] The Statute stated that legislative authority should be exercised "by a popular Assembly consisting of a single chamber elected on the basis of proportional representation". See *ibid.*, Article 12.
[158] A Council of Government, formed by the Assembly and responsible to it, was to assume executive powers. See *ibid.*, Article 13.
[159] See *ibid.*, Article 11.
[160] See *ibid.*, Article 17. The Governor was not to be a citizen of Yugoslavia, nor of Italy or the Free Territory. He was supposed to report directly to the Council and was prohibited from receiving instructions from any other authority.
[161] See *ibid.*, Article 17.

that purpose, the Governor was vested with comprehensive veto powers that went beyond the prerogatives of the High Commissioner under the Danzig arrangement. The Governor of Trieste was not only empowered to prevent the entry into force of international treaties or agreements conflicting with the Statute, Constitution or laws of the Free Territory;[162] he could also veto legislation passed by the Trieste Assembly which he considered contrary to the Statute[163] and suspend administrative measures of the Trieste Government[164] – two powers which exceeded the authority of the Danzig Commissioner.[165]

Moreover, the Statute followed the precedent of the Danzig settlement in that it made formal amendments of the governing framework subject to approval by the UN.[166]

2.1.2.2. Trieste – a development of Danzig

Nevertheless, the Statute of Trieste deviated in several respects from the Danzig model. The first important change was that the Trieste regime broke with the passive conception of international authority which had characterised the League's engagement in Danzig. The League's lack of interventionism and the city's subsequent fall under Nazi rule were still fresh in memory when the Statute of Trieste was drafted following World War II. The Statute drew lessons from this experience[167] by providing the UN-appointed executive Governor with active managing powers comparable to "a head of state".[168] The Governor was vested with the authority to initiate legislation in matters affecting the responsibilities of the Security Council under the Statute.[169] The Statute charged him with the appointment of the highest officials of the territory, including the Director of Public Security,[170] members of the judiciary[171] and the Director of the Free Port.[172] Furthermore, the Governor could propose administrative measures to the Council of Government and refer the matter to the Security Council for a decision should the Council of Government refuse to accept the proposal.[173] Finally, in situations of emergency, he

---

[162] See ibid., Article 24 (1).   [163] See ibid., Article 19 (4).   [164] See ibid., Article 20.
[165] The Danzig Commissioner could only veto formal constitutional amendments. See Articles 47–49 of the Constitution of the Free City of Danzig.
[166] See Article 37 of the Statute of the Free Territory of Trieste.
[167] For a similar conclusion, see Korhonen and Gras, International Governance, at 99.
[168] See Ydit, Internationalised Territories, at 253.
[169] See the Statute of the Free Territory of Trieste, Article 19 (1).
[170] See ibid., Article 27.   [171] See ibid., Article 16.
[172] See ibid., Article 18; Annex VIII of the Treaty of Peace with Italy.
[173] See the Statute of the Free Territory of Trieste, Article 20 (2).

could assume control of the security forces and order "appropriate measures" to be taken.[174] These robust powers stood in clear contrast to the mediation and dispute settlement responsibilities of the Danzig High Commissioner.

Drawing from the experiences of World War II, the Statute also placed greater emphasis on the positive guarantee of human rights protection by the acting governing authorities. The Statute expressly vested the Security Council and its Governor with the protection of basic human rights,[175] including religious worship, language, speech and publication, education, assembly and association[176] and civil and political rights.[177]

Finally, the Statute associated the idea of the internationalisation of Trieste more strongly than in the case of Danzig, with the aim of transforming the territory into a communitarian entity with open access to all nations[178] – a feature that would later become the foundation for the proposed functional internationalisation of Jerusalem.[179] The Danzig arrangement was dominated by the objective of granting Poland exclusive economic prerogatives over the Free City. Accordingly, Danzig was in a customs union with Poland. Furthermore, Danzig harbour was primarily open to Poland,[180] while access by third states required a majority vote of the Harbour Board of the Free City. The Statute of Trieste, by contrast, refrained from granting Italy or Yugoslavia special economic privileges over Trieste and made the port and transit facilities "available for use on equal terms by all international trade".[181]

2.1.3.   Responsibilities of the Security Council

The most astonishing feature of the Trieste arrangement, however, was the extensive role that the Security Council itself was supposed to assume in the implementation and supervision of the Statute. The Council was to become the highest supervisory authority and ultimate guarantor of the Territory of Trieste on a permanent basis. This responsibility would have engaged the Council actively in the conduct of the constitutional life of the territory. The Council was obliged to appoint[182] and control the activity of the Governor,[183] to whom it could give

---

[174] See ibid., Article 22 (1).   [175] See ibid., Articles 2 and 7.   [176] See ibid., Article 4.
[177] See ibid., Article 5.   [178] See also Ydit, Internationalised Territories, at 254.
[179] See above Part I, Chapter 1, and below.
[180] See Article 26 of the Treaty of Paris between Poland and the Free City of Danzig.
[181] See Article 1 of the Instrument for the Free Port of Trieste.
[182] See the Statute of the Free Territory of Trieste, Article 11 (1).
[183] See ibid., Article 11 (3), which granted the Council the authority to dismiss the Governor if he "failed to carry out his duties".

instructions.[184] Moreover, in its capacity as "guardian" of Trieste, the Council itself would have exercised direct decision-making authority vis-à-vis the constitutional organs of the territory. Article 19 of the Statute empowered the Council to enact legislation in cases of conflict between the local legislative Assembly and the Governor.[185] Acts adopted by the Governor in the exercise of its "emergency powers" under Statute could be directly appealed to the Council by a petition of the popular Assembly under Article 22 (2) of the Statute.[186] Finally, the Assembly could direct proposals for the amendment of the Statute directly to the Council.[187] These mechanisms were innovative because they gave local authorities unprecedented direct access to the Council and because they challenged the strict separation between a domestic and an international legal order within the framework of a territorial entity that was directly placed under the authority of the UN.[188]

2.1.4. Non-implementation

However, as a result of the emerging tensions between the West and the Soviet Union in 1946–7, this project was never realised. Due to strategic concerns, originating from the beginning of the Cold War and the consolidation of Soviet influence in Eastern Europe, both sides delayed the appointment of the Governor. This in turn blocked the implementation of the Trieste arrangement, because the Governor was charged with the selection of the members of the first provisional government of Trieste and the organisation of the elections for the popular Assembly. The continuing political differences finally led to abandonment of the plan for the internationalisation of Trieste in October 1954.[189] The London Agreement, concluded by Italy, Yugoslavia, the United States and the United Kingdom, divided Trieste along the lines of the military occupation, with Zone A (including Trieste) coming under Italian rule and Zone B falling under Yugoslav authority.

2.1.5. Assessment

Despite its non-realisation, the Trieste arrangement presented one the most interesting models of territorial administration. It placed the

---

[184] See *ibid.*, Article 25.   [185] See *ibid.*, Article 19 (6).
[186] See *ibid.*, Article 22 (2).   [187] See *ibid.*, Article 37.
[188] Kelsen qualified Trieste as "state-like community under the sovereignty of the United Nations". See Kelsen, *Law of the United Nations*, at 832.
[189] For a survey, see Ydit, *Internationalised Territories*, at 268.

undertakings of the League in the Saar and Danzig into a new framework under which the UN would have directly assumed the functions of a state through the organ of the Governor acting as the representative of the Security Council. This model of administration was designed in reaction to and as a development of the League's governing experiences in Danzig. Moreover, it was modern in the sense that it combined the assumption of direct administering powers by the UN with possibilities of legal redress by domestic institutions to the Security Council. The functional division of UN authority among a local representative and the Security Council acting as instance of petition and appeal would have ensured transparency and accountability in UN governance, by making the action of the Governor on the ground subject to checks and balances and collective control exercised by the Council – a feature that would later disappear from the radar screen under the "Special Representative of the Secretary-General (SRSG) model" used in the context of UN governance missions in the 1990s.

One may have some doubts, however, as to whether the Trieste formula would have succeeded as a model of administration, had it been implemented. The Trieste arrangement presented some flaws which call into question its capacity as a long-term solution. It is questionable, whether the Security Council could have fulfilled the direct responsibilities of administration conferred on it by the Statute in its daily practice. Furthermore, being conceived as a permanent framework of governance, the Statute's approach of internationalisation collided with the basic premises of the principle of self-determination. The interests of the inhabitants of Trieste were at the heart of the decision to internationalise Trieste within the confines of its territorial borders. However, the governing framework itself was far from accommodating to modern notions of self-determination. The domestic population had no say in the elaboration of the institutional framework of Trieste,[190] which is astonishing given that the proposed Statute was to be permanent in nature. Even more importantly, the Statute transformed Trieste into a territorial entity that was to be permanently governed by an international institution (the Governor) that enjoyed no democratic accountability vis-à-vis "its" people. One may assume that this deficit would have caused serious challenges to governmental legitimacy as a long-term arrangement.

---

[190] See Hannum, *Autonomy, Sovereignty and Self-Determination*, at 405.

2.2.   United Nations proposals for the internationalisation of Jerusalem

The UN plans for the internationalisation of Jerusalem[191] form the last of the experiments in dispute settlement and neutralisation after World Wars I and II. Unlike their predecessors, the attempts to internationalise Jerusalem were not directly related to the settlement of post-war claims. They originated partly out of the need to fill a power vacuum in Palestine after the termination of the British Mandate of the territory,[192] and partly out of the desire to transform Jerusalem into a common living space for the Jewish and Arab populations of the former Mandate. However, with the outbreak of hostilities in the Arab-Israeli war in May 1948, the plans for the internationalisation of Jerusalem evolved into an instrument to reconcile hard-lined tensions and controversies between both groups.[193] This course of events turned the establishment of an international regime for Jerusalem directly and primarily into an experiment of bilateral dispute settlement and neutralisation.

At the same time, Jerusalem always remained a special case of dispute resolution, because of its strategic importance as a spiritual capital of the Christian, Jewish and Muslim religions. Due to the special status of the city as a strategic site, efforts in internationalisation served a broader communitarian purpose, namely the provision of free access to the "Holy Places".

Both objectives, bilateral dispute settlement and "communitarian neutralisation", received different degrees of attention under the two models of internationalisation promoted by the international community between 1947 and 1950: territorial internationalisation and functional internationalisation. Models of territorial internationalisation placed great emphasis on the resolution and neutralisation of the Jewish-Arab conflict through international governance, whereas proposals of functional internationalisation gave priority to the aim of ensuring equal access to the city.

2.2.1.   Plans for the territorial internationalisation of Jerusalem

The idea of the territorial internationalisation of Jerusalem was expressly raised by the "Partition Resolution" (GA Resolution 181 (II)), which

---

[191] See generally Ydit, *Internationalised Territories*, at 273; Korhonen and Gras, *International Governance*, at 102.

[192] GA Resolution 181 (II) of 29 November 1947 envisaged the termination of the British Mandate and the evacuation of British troops from Palestine by 1 August 1948.

[193] See Ratner, *The New UN Peacekeeping*, at 99.

combined the objective of the partition of Palestine into a Jewish and an Arab state with the concomitant intention to establish the City of Jerusalem "as a *corpus separatum* under a special international regime".[194]

The Trusteeship Council prepared several frameworks of territorial internationalisation between 1947 and 1950, including a "Draft Constitution" for the City of Jerusalem submitted before the outbreak of the Arab-Israeli war in 1948[195] and a revised Draft Statute for the City of Jerusalem completed on 4 April 1950,[196] which mainly introduced additional elements of "democratisation".[197] Both proposals were very similar in terms of their content. They envisaged a long-term internationalisation of Jerusalem under the authority of the Trusteeship Council for a dual purpose:

> to protect and to preserve the unique spiritual and religious interests located
> in the City of the three great monotheistic faiths throughout the world,
> Christian, Jewish and Moslem; to this end to ensure that order and peace,
> and especially religious peace, reign in Jerusalem; and
> to foster co-operation among all the inhabitants of the City in their own
> interests as well as in order to encourage and support the peaceful
> development of the mutual relations between the two Palestinian peoples
> throughout the Holy Land; to promote the security, well-being and any
> constructive measures of development of the residents, having regard to the
> special circumstances and customs of the various peoples and
> communities.[198]

These aims were noble and well intended. But the specific institutional framework established to implement these goals was imperfect. The Statute established institutional checks and balances and some integrative mechanisms in order to guarantee a balanced and peaceful coexistence between the Arab and Jewish population in the city.

---

[194] See UN GA Res. 181 II, sub. C, Part III, in Lapidoth, *The Jerusalem Question*, at 6. The General Assembly outlined the general framework of a Statute for the City of Jerusalem in its resolution and charged the Trusteeship Council with the elaboration and approval of detailed previsions.

[195] See Statute for the City of Jerusalem, Draft prepared by the Trusteeship Council, UN TCOR, 2nd Sess., Third Part, Annex, 4, UN Doc T/118/Rev.2, submitted to the General Assembly on 21 April 1948.

[196] See Statute for the City of Jerusalem, approved by the Trusteeship Council at its 81st meeting, held on 4 April 1950, in GAOR, 5th Sess. (1950), Supp. 9, UN Doc A/1286, 19–27, in Lapidoth, *The Jerusalem Question*, at 117.

[197] GA Res. 303 (IV) of 9 December 1949 requested the Trusteeship Council to complete the preparation of the Statute of Jerusalem, introducing therein "amendments in the direction of its greater democratization".

[198] See para. 3 of the preamble of the Draft Statute for the City of Jerusalem of 4 April 1950.

However, like the Trieste arrangement, the Jerusalem Statute was essentially guided by the idea of reconciling tensions in the city through strong international government and control. The Statute transformed Jerusalem into a demilitarised and neutral territory under strict and hierarchic UN guardianship – a feature which called into question its feasibility as a viable long-term instrument of conflict resolution.

2.2.1.1. Trusteeship in a non-trusteeship context

The weakness of the Jerusalem arrangement was that it instituted a framework of administration that was at odds with the political realities of the time. Under the UN proposal, Jerusalem was to become a long-term "trusteeship territory" under the authority of the UN, although it shared few common features with classic trusteeship territories under Chapter XII (lack of self-government, deficit in "political, economic, social and educational advancement" etc.).[199] The only formal link which connected Jerusalem to the Trusteeship System and the Trusteeship Council was Palestine's capacity as a former mandate. The proposed Trusteeship Council Statute for Jerusalem, however, treated the City essentially as if the Mandate had never ended.[200] The Statute bore strong resemblance to governance devices deployed to administer people not yet ready for self-government or independence. It made the UN the direct source of all authority over Jerusalem, but left little room for local self-government and ownership, which was postulated by both the Jewish and the Arab sides.

2.2.1.2. Centralised governance

The drafters of the Statute placed great emphasis on the idea of neutralising the tensions between the Arab and the Jewish populations through strong and impartial international government. The UN envisaged that it would govern Jerusalem with a "strong hand".[201] The Statute placed the city under the overall authority of the Trusteeship Council and the centralised powers of a UN-appointed governor. Together, these two

---

[199] See also the criticism expressed by Israel, above Part I, Chapter 3.

[200] See also the protest by Israel in the Israeli Memorandum on the Question of Jerusalem submitted to the Trusteeship Council on 26 May 1950, in Lapidoth, *The Jerusalem Question*, 135, at 140. ("Whatever its position in 1947, when it was a 'territory under mandate', Jerusalem no longer falls into any of the categories defined in Article 77, to which any form of international trusteeship may legally be applied.")

[201] See also Ydit, *Internationalised Territories*, at 295 ("quasi complete tutelage which left a very narrow field of autonomy for the local population").

institutions enjoyed wide powers over all branches of government within the city and in the external affairs of Jerusalem.

Acting as the "representative of the United Nations in the City",[202] the Governor of Jerusalem was to become the chief executive authority and the head of the administration in the City, charged with extensive, but largely uncontrolled, powers in fields such as the supervision of religious and charitable bodies,[203] the organisation and direction of the police forces[204] and the assumption of emergency powers in situations in which "*in the opinion of the Governor* the administration was being seriously obstructed by the non-co-operation or interference of persons or groups of persons".[205]

These vast executive powers coincided with wide legislative responsibilities. The Governor held both special veto powers concerning the protection of the different groups in Jerusalem and default legislative authority. The Statute authorised the Governor to reject any bill of the locally elected Legislative Council which he deemed to be "in conflict with the provisions of [the] Statute or ... [would] impede the Administration of the City or inflict undue hardship on any section of the inhabitants of the City".[206] These ambiguous criteria granted the Governor wide discretion to block bills and resolutions. Furthermore, the Statute granted the Governor the authority to initiate legislation,[207] to dissolve the Legislative Council in the event of "a serious political crisis ... in the City"[208] and to legislate himself by order "at any time when there is no Legislative Council"[209] – a regulation which would have easily allowed the Governor to take full control of the city.

Finally, the Governor was vested with foreign affairs powers.[210] The Statute transformed Jerusalem into a separate international entity with limited international legal personality and competencies in the fields of diplomatic protection, treaty-making and diplomatic relations. The Governor of Jerusalem was charged with the protection of the interests of the city and its citizens abroad, and the accreditation of foreign officials in Jerusalem.[211] Moreover, he was authorised to sign international treaties "on behalf of the City" for the achievement of the special

---

[202] See the 1950 Draft Statute, Article 13 (1).   [203] See *ibid.*, Article 13 (3).
[204] See *ibid.*, Article 15.   [205] See *ibid.*, Article 16. Emphasis added.
[206] See *ibid.*, Article 24 (3).   [207] See *ibid.*, Article 24 (2).
[208] See *ibid.*, Article 23 (3).   [209] See *ibid.*, Article 25 (1).
[210] See *ibid.*, Article 37 (1).   [211] See *ibid.*, Article 37 (2) and (4).

objectives of the Statute.[212] These treaties – international agreements, entered into by a representative of the UN on behalf Jerusalem as a separate international entity – were to be ratified either by the local Legislative Council or by the Trusteeship Council itself.[213]

Even the judiciary of Jerusalem was placed under close international scrutiny. The judges of the highest judicial organ in Jerusalem, the Supreme Court, were appointed by the Trusteeship Council which could also remove them from office.[214] The Governor, on the other hand, enjoyed special jurisdiction for the resolution of disputes arising between different religious communities or confessions in connexion with the Holy Places.[215]

2.2.1.3. Inter-community balance

The widely centralised governing structure of the Statute was complemented by special arrangements designed to safeguard a fair and equal balance between the different groups present in the city. The aim of equality between the Arab and Jewish populations and the maintenance of the three principal religions (Christian, Jewish and Muslim) determined the organisation of the entire public life of Jerusalem. The Statute made access and immigration into the city dependent on the "maintenance of equality between the various communities". Arabic and Hebrew were to become the official and working languages of Jerusalem.[216] Candidates for the Legislative Council were to be elected by four electoral colleges: "a Christian college, a Jewish college, a Muslim college and a college ... composed of residents of the City who declare that they do not wish to register with any of the other three colleges".[217] Furthermore, the Statute organised the education and media infrastructure of Jerusalem in line with the principle of inter-community balance. City officials were obliged to "maintain or subsidize and supervise a system of primary and secondary education on an equal basis for all communities in their respective languages and in accordance with their respective cultural traditions".[218] Moreover, representatives of the Christian, Jewish and Muslim religions were given equal rights and opportunities of access to the broadcasting and television facilities of the city.[219]

---

[212] The Statute lists accessions to conventions drawn up by the UN or its specialised agencies as examples. See ibid., Article 37 (5).

[213] See ibid., Article 37 (6).   [214] See ibid., Article 28.

[215] See ibid., Article 38 (3).   [216] See ibid., Article 31.

[217] See ibid., Article 21.   [218] See ibid., Article 32 (3).   [219] See ibid., Article 33 (1).

2.2.1.4. Conceptual deficits

The special administering framework set up by the Statute was supposed to govern the status of Jerusalem for a period of ten years, after which it would be open to review and modification in accordance with the free wishes of the people of the city. But serious doubts arise as to whether it would have proved to be a successful experiment of territorial administration in practice.

2.2.1.4.1. The lack of integrative mechanisms and local consent

The Statute placed great weight on neutralisation and impartial dispute settlement. However, it provided few mechanisms actively to promote meaningful self- and co-governance by Jewish and Arab representatives in Jerusalem or reconciliation between the two groups. Instead of institutionalising inter-group cooperation through communitarian institutions and channels of coordination and exchange, the Statute merely superseded local self-government by international top-down governance. This structure of governance would have made it difficult to turn Jerusalem into a pluralist society and might have even deepened segregation.[220]

This institutional deficit was complicated by the fact that the idea of the fully fledged internationalisation of the city itself enjoyed little acceptance among both sides. The "*corpus separatum*" Statute of the Trusteeship Council was elaborated without participation from domestic actors[221] and against the will of Israel and Jordan. King Abdalla declared that Jerusalem "would be internationalised only over his dead body".[222] Israel, on the other hand, qualified the Statute as "inherently unimplementable", noting that it "would plunge Jerusalem into political suppression and economic decline, while causing grave disturbance of its

---

[220] See also the Israeli Memorandum on the Question of Jerusalem submitted to the Trusteeship Council on 26 May 1950, in Lapidoth, *The Jerusalem Question*, 135, at 136: "The idea that any regime for the protection of religious interests can endure amidst a discontented, aggrieved and turbulent population will be instantly rejected by any serious mind. Religious peace cannot be secured by political oppression. Thus, considerations of justice and of practicability combine to make the will of Jerusalem's population the essential basis for the City's political institutions."

[221] See the Israeli Memorandum on the Question of Jerusalem submitted to the Trusteeship Council on 26 May 1950, in Lapidoth, *The Jerusalem Question*, at 138: "[Jews] would suddenly become subject to the arbitrary enactments of a Constitution that which was neither formulated by them nor evolved out of their experience or consent."

[222] See Ydit, *Internationalised Territories*, at 305.

religious and secular peace".[223] Both reactions show that the Statute was established on a very weak political basis, one which compromised its legitimacy and limited its chances of success.

2.2.1.4.2.   The absence of democratic accountability and judicial review
In addition, the governing framework suffered from a flaw in that it exempted the international rulers of Jerusalem from traditional forms of political accountability and legal control. As an international governing institution, the Governor of Jerusalem was neither formally responsible to the people of Jerusalem, nor subject to the control of domestic actors. The Governor was only "responsible to the Trusteeship Council".[224] Furthermore, the Statute exempted him from the "jurisdiction of the Legislative Council or of the Courts of the City".[225] The only direct form of control envisaged under the Statute was the scrutiny exercised by the Trusteeship Council upon reporting duties of the Governor in specific situations, such as the use of emergency powers by the Governor,[226] the dissolution of the Legislative Council,[227] the vetoing of local legislation[228] or the adoption of legislation by the Governor in the absence of local authorities.[229] Moreover, Article 9 of the Statute granted all persons in Jerusalem a general right to petition, including a right to petition to the Trusteeship Council,[230] although the Statute left open whether this right applied to executive or legislative measures taken by the Governor. This institutional design triggered harsh criticism of the Statute, leading Israel to state that "the Statute itself, with its omnipotent Governor and its artificially constituted Legislative Council, is modelled precisely on the absolutist forms of government which used to be applied in backward regions in days before the elementary principles of self-government began to secure a foothold even in the dependent areas of the world".[231]

2.2.2.   The proposed functional internationalisation of Jerusalem

The proposed functional internationalisation of Jerusalem was far more modest in size and scope than the *corpus separatum* model of the

---

[223] See the Israeli Memorandum on the Question of Jerusalem submitted to the Trusteeship Council on 26 May 1950, in Lapidoth, *The Jerusalem Question*, at 141.
[224] See the 1950 Draft Statute, Article 12 (1).
[225] Emphasis added. See *ibid.*, Article 13 (5).
[226] See *ibid.*, Article 16 (2).   [227] See *ibid.*, Article 23 (3).
[228] See *ibid.*, Article 24 (3).   [229] See *ibid.*, Article 25 (3).   [230] See *ibid.*, Article 9 (2).
[231] See the Israeli Memorandum on the Question of Jerusalem submitted to the Trusteeship Council on 26 May 1950, in Lapidoth, *The Jerusalem Question*, at 138.

Trusteeship Council. It departed from the idea of a territorial governance of Jerusalem by the Trusteeship Council and limited UN control to the "protection of and free access to the Holy Places" by a UN Commissioner appointed by the General Assembly.[232]

The basic proposal was laid down in a Draft Resolution tabled by Sweden in the General Assembly on 5 December 1950.[233] The resolution preserved the divided *status quo* of Jerusalem, noting that pending a final settlement concerning Jerusalem, Israel and Jordan should be allowed to exercise "jurisdiction and control" in the respective parts of the city controlled by them.[234] But the proposal granted the UN special privileges concerning religious buildings and sites. Article 10 of the Resolution empowered the Commissioner to "request the governments in the Jerusalem area to modify, defer or suspend … laws, ordinances regulations and administrative acts" impairing "the protection of and free access to Holy Places" and to "request governments to take … orders or regulations" necessary "for the maintenance of public security and safety" in the area of the Holy Places.[235] The two governments were required to implement these requests ("shall carry into effect") without delay,[236] but remained entitled to refer a matter "for a final decision" to an arbitral tribunal, composed of one arbitrator nominated by the respective government and one arbitrator nominated by the UN Secretary-General.[237]

Like its predecessor, this approach was deeply entrenched in the tradition of strategic neutralisation and bilateral dispute settlement, without devoting great attention to active conflict management. However, the proposal of a functional internationalisation of Jerusalem presented a much more realistic interim solution to the dispute over the city, as it came closer to a commonly agreeable compromise between the conflicting parties. The advantages of this model were highlighted in an official statement by Israel to the Trusteeship Council, which emphasised that:

---

[232] See Article VI (1) of the Draft Resolution.
[233] See the Draft Resolution concerning the future status of Jerusalem, 5 December 1950, UN Doc. A/AC.38.L.68, in Lapidoth, *The Jerusalem Question*, at 149.
[234] See Article IX of the Draft Resolution: "The jurisdiction and control of each part of the Jerusalem area shall be exercised by the States concerned, subject to the powers of the Commissioner with respect to this area and without prejudice to the rights and claims of either party in the ultimate peaceful settlement for the area."
[235] See the Draft Resolution, Article X (1).
[236] See *ibid.*, Article X (2).   [237] See *ibid.*, Article XV (1).

[u]nder a plan elaborated on those lines, the United Nations would exercise full jurisdiction in respect of matters which are the object of international and religious concern; and all this would be achieved without the drastic process of political and economic disintegration envisaged by the [Trusteeship Council] Statute, and without any violence to the democratic principle or to the provisions of the Charter. At the same time, the simplicity of these arrangements and the degree of consent which would be confidently anticipated for them would secure their swift and secure implementation.[238]

The implementation of this proposal would have turned Jerusalem into "the first place in the world where the United Nations would be permanently and directly represented for the purpose of carrying out functions on behalf of the international community".[239] However, the international pressure brought by the Catholic Church and Latin American states pushed the UN General Assembly to vote in favour of a return to a territorial internationalisation approach,[240] which again failed to be adopted as a result of the Soviet block withdrawing its support for the implementation of the Partition Resolution, arguing that it lacked Arab and Jewish consent.[241]

3. Conclusion

A survey of the first experiments in international territorial administration under the auspices of the League of Nations and the UN presents a mixed picture. The founders of a new peace architecture under the Treaty of Versailles and post-World War II peace treaties placed great trust in the concept of internationalisation and territorial administration. International territorial administration was in, in particular, used as a device to solve inter-state disputes over areas of strategic importance in post-conflict settlements. The main idea was that a long-term neutralisation under international supervision would temper nationalist tensions and conflicts among divided populations sharing cultural, historical and social bonds with different territorial entities. But the mandate of international administrators was often over-ambitious and forcefully imposed on local actors. These factors limited the chances of success of international governance missions.

---

[238] See the Israeli Memorandum on the Question of Jerusalem submitted to the Trusteeship Council on 26 May 1950, in Lapidoth, *The Jerusalem Question*, at 144.

[239] *Ibid.*, at 144.

[240] See General Assembly, UN GAOR, 326th Meeting, 15 December 1950, at 684.

[241] See Ydit, *Internationalised Territories*, at 306–7.

3.1. Dichotomies of the first experiments in territorial administration

All the first experiments in territorial administration encountered conceptual tensions concerning the deployment of structures of international administration and the definition of the mandate of international actors. The choice was mostly made in favour of traditional concepts prevailing at the time, such as state-oriented forms of balance of power and dispute settlement or top-down systems of governance. However, international practice incorporated at the same time some important innovations and traces of modernity that reflect or provide guidance to modern experiments in territorial administration.

3.1.1. Bilateralism v. communitarism

The victorious powers did consider peoples' rights in the practice of international post-conflict settlements. The establishment of the administrations in the Saar and Danzig and the plans for the internationalisation of Trieste and Jerusalem marked at least, in part, a victory for Wilsonian ideals of self-determination in the definition of territorial borders and post-war entities. However, the enforcement of these rights remained selective and shaped by bilateral interests. International administration was by no means a universal undertaking. It was restricted to the pacification of areas of strategic importance that formed the subject of long-standing territorial or historical disputes. Furthermore, international territorial administration had a strongly bilateral-oriented focus. The League of Nations and the UN served mainly as organs of neutralisation and dispute settlement. International governing institutions were either created to protect national groups from foreign dominance in a divided territorial enclave or to establish a balance of power and neutral building block between competing actors. The defence and realisation of broader community interests (like access to the Holy Places of Jerusalem) or universal values (human rights, democratisation), however, remained an exception or a by-product of neutralisation.

3.1.2. Long-term internationalisation v. transitional administration

The substantive and temporal mandate of major experiments in territorial administration (Saar, Danzig, Trieste and Jerusalem) was defined in generous and sometimes over-ambitious terms. International actors were supposed to act as guarantors and guardians of territorial entities in the cases of Danzig and Trieste, and were required to assume comprehensive state powers in the cases of the Saar Basin and Jerusalem. Internationalisation was, in each of these cases conceived as a long-term mandate, ranging from a minimum of ten years (Jerusalem) or twenty-five years (Saar), to permanent attempts at neutralisation (Trieste). The actual practice in territorial administration, however, could not quite live up to these hopes and expectations. None of the first experiences in international territorial administration managed to serve as a permanent model of dispute settlement. The most successful undertaking was the League of Nations' governance of the Saar, which ended peacefully with the reintegration of the territory into Germany after the holding of the referendum envisaged in the Treaty of Versailles. The other attempts in internationalisation, on the contrary, were either forcefully terminated (Danzig) or never realised at all (Trieste and Jerusalem).

3.1.3.   Centralised governance v. power-sharing

The model of governance of early undertakings in international territorial administration was shaped by static and power-centred conceptions of the exercise of public authority. The administrations of the Saar and the proposed internationalisation of Jerusalem had absolutist features. They were simple top-down models of governance, superseding domestic structures of administration by largely authoritarian mechanisms of international rule. The governing frameworks of Danzig and Trieste were more balanced in nature. International governing institutions were required to exercise their authority in a relationship of power-sharing with local actors. However, even these formulas of governance were rather intrusive mechanisms of authority, because they were conceived as permanent solutions and did not contain a timetable for a gradual transfer of control to local actors.

Moreover, in each of the four cases, international actors were widely shielded from the jurisdiction and control of domestic authorities. The international governing institutions were both appointed by organs of the League or the UN and exclusively responsible to the entities which established them. This created an accountability gap between international rule and the administered population. Any mechanisms created to institute some form of control upon the initiative of local actors were limited. None of the arrangements gave domestic authorities a comprehensive legal remedy against decisions of international governing institutions. Institutional remedies were either non-binding or very restricted in scope.[242] The Trieste arrangement and the proposed Statute of Jerusalem contained only provisions on a right of petition of local institutions (Trieste) or local actors (Jerusalem), and these mechanisms were clearly borrowed from colonial practice. Furthermore, the right of appeal to the League Council in the case of Danzig was limited to the adjudication of disputes between the Free City and Poland, but did not extend to a right to appeal substantive decisions of the League Commissioner himself. Both mechanisms were novel in the sense that they broke with the state-centred conception of international law, by giving domestic political institutions or private actors a right of access to institutions like the Trusteeship Council (Jerusalem), the Security Council (Trieste) or the Council of the League (Danzig). But the limited scope of judicial review left domestic actors with few authoritative means to challenge the exercise of power by international rulers.

3.2. Lessons

Despite their mistakes and failings, the early experiments in territorial administration were ground-breaking. They dissociated territorial administration from the tradition of foreign-state administration[243] and turned it into a multilateral undertaking. Moreover, they provided some conceptual lessons for the development of international territorial administration. The experiences of Danzig and the Saar made it quite clear that international administering structures are ill-equipped to serve as permanent governance devices, but may provide valuable models of temporary dispute settlement. The non-realisation of the proposed internationalisations of Trieste and Jerusalem provided evidence that undertakings in international territorial administration have limited chances of success if they lack the political backing of the major territorial powers involved in conflict resolution.

---

[242] In the case of the Saar, the governing framework lacked any provision, granting the Council of the League a power to review decisions of the League Commissioner. See Russell, *The International Government of the Saar*, at 238.

[243] See also Russell, *International Government of the Saar*, at 239.

7   From the post-war period to the end of the Cold War: the use of international territorial administration as an *ad hoc* device

Following the non-realisation of the proposed internationalisations of Jerusalem and Trieste, the practice of the UN in the area of international territorial administration changed. The UN refrained from undertaking or designing large-scale and long-term projects of neutralisation *à la* Saar or Danzig. Instead, it adopted a rather pragmatic stance on the exercise of functions of governance and administration outside the context of the Trusteeship System. The organisation assumed tasks of direct territorial administration in the fields of decolonisation and conflict management in situations where a need for multilateral solutions arose. Yet, the UN was neither systematic nor organised along the lines of a coherent institutional model. International territorial administration was mainly used as an *ad hoc* device, deployed and adjusted to meet the needs of the specific situation in which it was practised. This pragmatic approach gave rise to a variety of different forms of engagement, involving many of the Charter's main organs (the Security Council, the General Assembly, the Secretary-General) in distinct capacities.

At the same time, the UN learned some lessons from the previous undertakings in territorial administration. Deviating from the experiences in the cases of Trieste and Jerusalem, the organisation based its engagements, as far as possible, on the consent of local actors involved. Non-consensual undertakings remained the exception, and occurred mostly by accident in situations in which domestic authorities lost control over their territory. Furthermore, UN practice departed from the tradition of conceiving international authority as a permanent model of dispute settlement. The organisation limited its territorial administration missions strictly to temporary and transitional undertakings, which took the form of assistance or governance missions. The degree of administering authority held by UN administrators varied. But generally, the UN was less inclined to take over intrusive and authoritative governing mandates, giving priority to advisory and cooperative models of partnership or governance assistance.[1]

1. Governance assistance missions

Although the major experiments in internationalisation in the cases of Jerusalem and Trieste had failed, the UN came to exercise administering functions soon after these efforts. The organisation established a number of governance assistance missions, in order to facilitate the process of decolonisation and the realisation of self-determination of formerly dependent territories – a tradition that was later expanded in the context of multi-dimensional peacekeeping.

1.1. Post-war decolonisation

The first two undertakings of the UN of this kind were its post-war missions in Libya[2] and Eritrea.[3] Both territories were former Italian colonies whose status had remained unresolved after World War II. Italy had renounced "all right and title" related to these territories in Article 17 of the 1947 Peace Treaty. The agreement provided that the "final disposal of these possessions" should be determined "jointly by the Governments of the U.S.S.R., U.K., U.S.A. and France ('the Four Powers') within one year of the coming into force of the ... Treaty".[4] But when negotiations over the status of the Italian colonies failed after three years of debate,[5] the Four Powers referred the matter to the UN General Assembly in accordance with Annex XI of the Peace Treaty with Italy. The General Assembly recommended Libya's accession to independence in Resolution 289 (IV),[6] while suggesting the establishment of a federation with Ethiopia in the case of Eritrea (Resolution 390 (V)[7]). Furthermore, in both cases, the

---

[1] For a conceptualisation, see Jarat Chopra, *Introducing Peace-Maintenance*, in Politics of Peace-Maintenance (J. Chopra ed., 1998), 1, at 14.
[2] For a detailed analysis, see Adrian Pelt, *Libyan Independence and the United Nations, A Case of Planned Decolomization* (1970).
[3] See generally Eyassu Gayim, *The Eritrean Question* (1993).
[4] See Article 17 (3) of the 1947 Peace Treaty with Italy.
[5] For a full survey, see Gayim, *The Eritrean Question*, at 91–101.
[6] See UN General Assembly Resolution 289 (IV) of 21 November 1949, UN Doc A/1251, p. 10 (1949).
[7] See UN General Assembly Resolution 390, UN GAOR, 5th Sess., Supp. No. 20, p. 20, UN Doc A/1775 (1950).

Assembly decided to establish special UN assistance missions in order to help local authorities to devise a constitution. The subsequent UN operations marked the first two famous direct engagements of the UN in the exercise of self-determination and constitution-framing.[8] They occurred by accident, as a result of the inability of the Four Powers to establish a commonly accepted framework for the future of the two ex-colonies.

1.1.1. The United Nations assistance mission in Libya

The role of the UN in Libya's access to independence was limited, but successful in the sense that it helped local authorities to establish a constitutional system for the newly independent entity.

1.1.1.1. The background

The framework of the UN mission in Libya was largely conditioned by the specific geopolitical circumstances of the territory after World War II. Libya was still under British-French military administration[9] when the UN General Assembly was requested to decide on the future status of the territory on 15 September 1948. There was widespread agreement that Libya should ultimately gain full independence. However, the means through which this goal should be achieved were disputed. Some states, such as India and the Soviet Union, proposed to place Libya under direct UN trusteeship, with a UN-appointed administrator exercising full executive powers in cooperation with a multinational advisory committee.[10] Other countries advocated a collective trusteeship solution, with the United Kingdom, France and Italy acting as temporary administering authorities.[11]

Both proposals were finally rejected. The option of direct UN trusteeship was opposed by France and the United Kingdom, which both had strategic interests in Libya and wanted to remain involved in the process of access to independence. Furthermore, the idea of placing an entire (large and developed) country like Libya for two or more years under direct UN administration was a rather unrealistic option in terms of the limited resources of the UN, as the establishment of a full UN administration would have "raised a host of legal, financial, and administrative questions far beyond the organisational capacity of the United Nations

---

[8] See also Ratner, *The New UN Peacekeeping*, at 116.

[9] See generally, Francis Rennell Rodd, *British Military Administration of Occupied Territories in Africa during the Years 1941–1947* (1948).

[10] For a survey, see Pelt, *Libyan Independence*, at 73 and 77.   [11] *Ibid.*, at 82–4.

as it stood in 1950–1951".[12] The proposal of dividing Libya into three different zones, each administered by a single trustee, met with harsh criticism from Libyan representatives, who protested against the restoration of Italian rule and discarded collective trusteeship as a revival of old colonial rule.[13] The only agreeable solution was a formula which promised Libya fast access to independence and tempered the influence of the administering powers (the United Kingdom and France) in the decision-making process. This compromise was finally adopted by the General Assembly in its Resolution 289 (IV), which recognised that Libya should become "an independent and sovereign State ... as soon as possible and in any case not later than 2 January 1952",[14] while instituting a system of power-sharing between Libyan authorities, the administering powers and the UN.

1.1.1.2. The transitional power-sharing arrangement

Resolution 289 (IV) was one of the most far-reaching decisions of the General Assembly.[15] It determined the future of Libya in a binding manner *vis-à-vis* the Four Powers[16] and created a complex institutional framework for the country's process of transition to independence. The General Assembly granted local representatives of Libya's three main regions (Cyrenaica, Tripolitania and the Fezzan) the right to enact and determine the framework of "a constitution for Libya, including the form of government".[17] But the resolution established at the same time a UN Commissioner for Libya (appointed by the General Assembly) and an advisory Council composed of representatives from ten UN members,[18] who were charged with the task of "assisting the people of Libya in the formulation of the constitution and the establishment of an independent

---

[12] *Ibid.*, at 867.   [13] *Ibid.*, at 80–2.   [14] See paras. 1 and 2 of GA Res. 289 (IV).

[15] India stated at the time of the adoption of the Resolution that the draft resolution "[was] unique in the history of the United Nations". See GAOR, 4th Sess., 1949, 247th Plenary Meeting, 19 November 1949, pp. 271–2.

[16] The Resolution was formally framed as a recommendation. But the Four Powers had agreed in advance "to accept the recommendation of the General Assembly on the disposal of the former Italian colonies" under Annex XI, para. 3 of the Treaty of Peace with Italy. See para. 1 of the preamble of GA Res. 289 (IV).

[17] See para. 3 of GA Res. 289 (IV).

[18] The resolution noted that "the Council shall consist of ten members, namely: One representative nominated by the Government of each of the following countries: Egypt, France, Italy, Pakistan, the United Kingdom of Great Britain and Northern Ireland and of the United States of America; One representative of the people of each of the three regions of Libya and one representative of the minorities in Libya". See para. 6 of GA Res. 289 (IV).

Government".[19] This mandate struck a delicate balance. It preserved the "*pouvoir constituant*" of the Libyan National Assembly, but placed the elaboration of the constitution under the scrutiny of the UN and the multinational Council for Libya.

Moreover, the resolution divided the responsibilities in transitional territorial administration among the UN Commissioner and British and French authorities. The General Assembly charged "the administering Powers *in co-operation with the United Nations Commissioner*" with the organisation and implementation of the process of decolonisation, including the initiation of "all necessary steps for the transfer of power to a duly constituted independent Government", and the administration of "the territories for the purpose of assisting in the establishment of Libyan unity and independence, co-operate in the formation of governmental institutions and co-ordinate their activities to this end".[20] This cooperation arrangement was a compromise, dictated by the factual presence of French and British troops in Libya and reasons of efficiency, saving the UN from the burden of establishing a costly administration structure in the territory.[21] It placed the administering powers under an "obligation to abstain from any governmental or administrative decisions which would run counter to the accomplishment" of Libyan unity and independence.[22]

1.1.1.3. United Nations engagement

The UN Commissioner, Assistant Secretary-General Adrian Pelt, exercised a number of important functions. His main task was to give political and constitutional advice to the Libyan people in the process of accession to independence, which was organised according to a strict timetable. The views expressed by the Commissioner were neither binding on the Libyan people nor on the Council for Libya.[23] But in the exercise of his advisory function, the Commissioner "found himself increasingly called upon to play the part of mediator, even of arbitror", because he provided impartial and unbiased expertise that was backed by the

---

[19] See para. 4 of GA Res. 289 (IV).
[20] Emphasis added. See para. 10 of GA Res. 289 (IV).
[21] See also Pelt, *Libyan Independence*, at 867.   [22] *Ibid.*, at 312.
[23] Resolution 289 (IV) clearly spelled out that "in the discharge of his functions, the United Nations Commissioner [should] consult and be guided by the advice of the members of his Council, it being understood that he may call upon different members to advise him in respect of different regions or different subjects". For an interpretation of this clause, see Pelt, *Libyan Independence*, at 332.

authority of Resolution 289 (IV), which again constituted the only authoritative framework commonly agreed by all parties.[24]

Relying strictly on the mandate of the General Assembly,[25] the Commissioner took the position that it was "neither his nor the United Nations' responsibility, but that of the representatives of the Libyan people, to draft the Constitution".[26] Nevertheless, the Commissioner exercised considerable influence over the process of the drafting of the Libyan Constitution. He protested against the decision by domestic leaders to form a Preparatory National Assembly by nomination rather than by representative elections.[27] Furthermore, he helped to protect Libyan unity and to further the cause of democratisation by suggesting the establishment of a federal form of government with an upper chamber composed of appointed territorial representatives and a lower chamber elected on the basis of ensuring proportional representation.[28] The Commissioner insisted, in particular, that the new Libyan government be subject to a "restricted form of responsibility", in order to avoid autocratic government, on the one hand, and governmental instability, on the other.[29] Finally, the Commissioner arranged economic assistance to Libya[30] and elaborated a programme for the transfer of power from the British and French administering authorities to "the duly constituted Libyan Government" until 24 December 1951, the date of Libya's access to independence.[31]

1.1.1.4. Assessment

Overall, the UN engagement in Libya marked a successful case of "planned decolonisation". As Mr Pelt himself would later state, the UN had good reasons "to be satisfied with its achievement in creating the

---

[24] See Pelt, *Libyan Independence*, at 885. He added that "this in effect meant that on a number of occasions, for want of a better alternative, [the Commissioner's] advice constituted the only acceptable solution. Thus he found, after a time, that he could wield more influence than he had expected at the outset, though this would, of course, have been impossible in the absence of mutual confidence".

[25] See para. 3 of GA Res. 289 (IV).   [26] See Pelt, *Libyan Independence*, at 447.

[27] *Ibid.*, at 466. The Commissioner requested therefore that "the Constitution now under preparation by the National Assembly should be enacted only in a provisional form and require final approval, and if necessary amendment by a parliament to be elected by the Libyan people as a whole".

[28] *Ibid.*, at 485.   [29] *Ibid.*, at 468.

[30] See para. 4 of GA Res. 387 (V) of 17 November 1940 and Pelt, *Libyan Independence*, at 662 *et seq.*

[31] See para. 3 (d) of GA Res. 387 (V) of 17 November 1940 and Pelt, *Libyan Independence*, at 725 *et seq.*

independent and sovereign State of Libya", as the organisation had successfully accomplished the task entrusted to it by the Paris Peace Conference in 1947, "by recognising... the right of the Libyan people to freely determine its future form of government" and by "assisting and advising it in the process of decolonisation and the creation of an independent State,... with the help of its specialised agencies and of the Administering Powers".[32]

The daily administration of the territory was left to the former administering powers, whereas the UN served mainly as a monitoring and advisory institution. This formula proved to work well in practice. It ensured a peaceful period of transition, and led to the emergence of a federal and democratic Constitution for Libya, which ensured stability in Libya for a period of seventeen years, during which the country made significant economic, social and constitutional progress. One may assume that the path towards unity and independence would have taken considerably longer without the UN's engagement and independent expertise.[33]

The key to success was achieving the right balance between determinative UN decision-making and deference to local rule.[34] The goal of Libyan unity and independence was firmly established by the General Assembly and was based on the agreement of the interested powers, who had previously agreed to carry out the terms of the Assembly's recommendation. The decision as to the form of statehood and governance, however, remained with the Libyan people, satisfying claims for free and independent domestic self-determination. Finally, the role of the UN in the implementation of this process through impartial advice and assistance was limited enough to escape the reproach of colonial dominance, and strong enough to reunite local actors and the administering powers in constitution-framing and the ultimate transfer of power to a "duly constituted Libyan Government".

1.1.2. The United Nations engagement in Eritrea

The unresolved status of Eritrea after World War II presented the UN with similar problems as in the case of Libya. The Four Allied Powers charged with the settlement of the future of Eritrea under the

---

[32] See Pelt, *Libyan Independence*, Preface, at xxiv.
[33] See also *ibid.*, at 36. ("It is also probably correct to say that, had not the United Nations been called to Libya's bedside, it would have taken the patient longer to recover from his internal and external ills than it in fact did.")
[34] *Ibid.*, at 883 and 885.

1947 Peace Treaty with Italy examined several status models (Ethiopian administration under multinational supervision,[35] Italian or collective trusteeship[36]), but failed to agree on a commonly acceptable solution which reflected the wishes of the local population. This left the General Assembly with the thorny task of proposing a suitable governing framework for the former Italian colony.[37] The Assembly adopted a different solution from that adopted in the Libyan case. It rejected Eritrean demands for independence and opted instead for a federal model, integrating Eritrea into Ethiopia in its Resolution 390 (V) of 2 December 1950.

This decision distinguished the format of UN involvement fundamentally from the UN mission in Libya. General Assembly Resolution 390 (V) indirectly determined the political status of Eritrea. Furthermore, it curtailed local decision-making power to a strict minimum, by laying down a detailed regulatory framework for the future governing system of Eritrea, which even set out the kind of government and constitution that Eritrea should have. Similarly, the role of the UN Commissioner, established by the General Assembly to assist Eritreans and Ethiopians in devising a constitution, differed from that of its Libyan counterpart. The Commissioner acted as an enforcement organ of the Assembly rather than as an impartial and neutral constitutional advisor.

1.1.2.1.   The federal status decision of the General Assembly
The General Assembly's decision to opt for a "federal solution" rather than granting Eritrea independence was a controversial move. It followed long and intensive debates among UN members over three different status models: independence, trusteeship or integration within Ethiopia. Representatives from Eastern European states and the Soviet block argued that Eritrean independence constituted the only viable solution in the light of the UN Charter principle on self-determination and the aspirations of the Eritrean people.[38] This view was opposed by the major Western powers (United Kingdom, United States, Canada, New Zealand,

---

[35] This idea was favoured by the United Kingdom, which sought to place Eritrea under Ethiopian administration, while establishing a supervisory commission composed of representatives from Italy, Switzerland, a Nordic country and a Moslem country. See Gayim, The Eritrean Question, at 96.

[36] These models were supported by the Soviet Union. See Gayim, The Eritrean Question, at 96-97.

[37] The Four Powers transmitted the question to the UN on 15 September 1948.

[38] The question was debated in the UN by an ad hoc Political Committee from 8 to 25 November 1950. For a full account of the discussions, see Gayim, The Eritrean Question, at 144.

Australia, France, South Africa and Norway), who rejected independence or trusteeship arguing that Eritrea lacked the necessary resources and economic capacities to govern itself and its people – a claim that was reinforced by empirical doubts about the political will of the majority of Eritreans to become an independent entity. The only way to reconcile these conflicting positions and to overcome the deadlock in the Assembly over the issue of Eritrea was the idea of a joint federation between Eritrea and Ethiopia. This proposal was introduced by the United States and soon gained the support of Ethiopia, the United Kingdom and Italy, the countries with the closest ties to Eritrea. When the federal proposal was put to vote, it was adopted by a majority of thirty-eight to fourteen votes (with eight abstentions) in the General Assembly's *ad hoc* political committee,[39] and then approved by the General Assembly by forty-six to ten votes (with four abstentions).[40]

This solution marked an ambiguous compromise.[41] It treated Eritrea substantially as a non-self-governing territory[42] or an entity entitled to internal self-determination, instead of granting it a full right to self-determination,[43] which had been advocated by many states before the adoption of the resolution.[44] Furthermore, the plan to incorporate Eritrea into Ethiopia was adopted without a popular consultation of the will of the domestic population, which was considered to be too immature to choose its political status through a referendum.[45] Instead, the General Assembly itself took on the role of a quasi "*pouvoir constituant*"

---

[39] The Socialist block, El Salvador, Iraq, Pakistan, Syria, Uruguay, Cuba, Guatemala, the Dominican Republic and Saudi Arabia opposed the draft resolution, whereas Chile, India, Columbia, Indonesia, Iran, Israel, Sweden and Afghanistan abstained. See Gayim, *The Eritrean Question*, at 148–9.

[40] Cuba, Czechoslovakia, the Dominican Republic, El Salvador, Guatemala, Pakistan, Poland, the Soviet Union, Ukraine and the Byelorussian Republic voted against the resolution. Israel, Saudi Arabia, Sweden and Uruguay abstained from the vote.

[41] The imposition of a federal status on Eritrea continued to be criticised by the Socialist states as a "flagrant violation of the Charter". See Gayim, *The Eritrean Question*, at 234.

[42] This may be inferred from para. 7 of the preamble of GA Res. 390 (V), which alludes to Article 73 of the UN Charter, by granting "the inhabitants of Eritrea the fullest respect and safeguards for their institutions, traditions, religions and languages, as well as the widest possible measure of self-government".

[43] Eritrea's case for self-determination had a solid legal foundation, as the inhabitants of Eritrea constituted a single, identifiable community, formed by European colonialism. They shared a common language, culture and economic life. See Gayim, *The Eritrean Question*, at 235.

[44] For a survey, see Gayim, *The Eritrean Question*, at 236–8.

[45] The British delegation noted that "in a more developed country it was possible to ascertain public opinion by means of the normal processes of a democratic state", but "Eritrea had not reached that stage of development". See UN Doc. A/AC.38/SR.55, p. 248. For similar state positions, see Gayim, *The Eritrean Question*, at 230 and 442.

and surrogate constitutional legislator, by determining the contours and details of the proposed federal framework in its resolution.[46]

Resolution 390 (V) was one the most far-reaching interferences by the UN into the internal affairs of an ex-colonial territory. It virtually determined the internal organisation of the future federation between Ethiopia and Eritrea. The resolution not only stated that "Eritrea shall constitute an autonomous unit federated with Ethiopia under the sovereignty of the Ethiopian Crown", enjoying "legislative, executive and judicial powers in the field domestic affairs";[47] it contained detailed provisions concerning the jurisdiction of the Federal Government,[48] the composition of the Imperial Federal Council,[49] the nationality of Eritreans,[50] the list of human rights and fundamental liberties to be integrated in the new Constitution[51] and the establishment of a customs union between the two territories.[52] The task of elaborating the Eritrean Constitution was formally conferred on an Eritrean Assembly.[53] But the General Assembly made it clear that the provisions of the future Constitution of Eritrea had to be "based on principles of democratic government" and consistent with the detailed stipulations of Resolution 390 (V).[54] Furthermore, the new governing framework was made subject to the approval of the UN Commissioner.[55]

Both the establishment of strict normative requirements for the Eritrean Constitution and the modalities of the entry into force of the new framework showed very clearly that the "federal solution" was largely imposed on the Eritrean people. Moreover, the way in which the UN dealt with the future of Eritrea was in conflict with the UN Charter[56] and the role of the General Assembly,[57] because it deprived the people of

---

[46] A draft resolution designed to enable Eritreans to choose between independence or a federal option was rejected. See Gayim, *The Eritrean Question*, at 642–3.

[47] See GA Res. 390 (V), paras. 1 and 2.

[48] See *ibid.*, para. 3.   [49] See *ibid.*, para. 5.   [50] See *ibid.*, para. 6.

[51] See *ibid.*, para. 7.   [52] See *ibid.*, para. 4.   [53] See *ibid.*, para. 12.

[54] See *ibid.*, para. 12. ("The Constitution of Eritrea shall be based on principles of democratic government, shall include the guarantees contained in paragraph 7 of the Federal Act, shall be consistent with the provisions of the Federal Act and shall contain provisions adopting and ratifying the Federal Act on behalf of the people of Eritrea.")

[55] See *ibid.*, para. 13. ("The Federal Act and the Constitution of Eritrea shall enter into effect following ratification of the Federal Act by the Emperor of Ethiopia, and following approval by the Commissioner, adoption by the Eritrean Assembly and ratification by the Emperor of Ethiopia of the Eritrean Constitution.")

[56] See also Gayim, *The Eritrean Question*, at 642.

[57] *Ibid.*, at 241. The General Assembly obviously inferred its powers to determine the content of the future Eritrean Constitution from the terms of the 1947 Peace Treaty

Eritrea from the possibility of rejecting its incorporation into Ethiopia, and of freely determining its governing framework.

1.1.2.2. The role of the United Nations Commissioner

The mandate of the UN Commissioner for Eritrea went beyond the role of the UN Commissioner for Libya. The Commissioner, Mr Eduardo Anze Matienzo, was not only supposed to act as an advisor to the Eritrean people, but was also charged with active drafting tasks and powers of control. Resolution 390 (V) vested him with a multi-faceted mandate: to exercise a consultative role in the "organization of an Eritrean administration", to "prepare a draft of the Eritrean Constitution", to "advise and assist the Eritrean Assembly in its consideration of the Constitution" and to approve the Constitution following its ratification of the Assembly.

The Commissioner fulfilled these tasks with strict commitment to the framework set by the General Assembly. Upon arrival in Eritrea, he emphasised that the terms of Resolution 390 (V) were "binding for everyone concerned" even though it had "formally the character of a recommendation".[58] He took the position that neither the Eritrean Assembly, nor the Ethiopian government, nor the Commissioner himself was entitled to deviate from the terms of the resolution.[59] The UN Commissioner consulted representatives of Eritrean political organisations and parties, the Ethiopian government and the United Kingdom as the remaining administering power in his attempts to prepare a broadly acceptable federal framework for Eritrea. But it was the Commissioner himself, who prepared the first draft of the Eritrean Constitution.

The draft Constitution was drafted in strict accord with the recommendations of the General Assembly. It provided for substantial Eritrean legislative and executive autonomy under overall Ethiopian sovereignty.[60] When submitting the proposal to the Eritrean Assembly

---

with Italy. Para. 1 of the preamble of Resolution 390 (V) states: "Whereas by paragraph 3 of Annex XI to the Treaty of Peace with Italy, 1947, the Powers concerned have agreed to accept the recommendation of the General Assembly on the disposal of the former Italian colonies in Africa *and to take appropriate measures for giving effect to it.*" (Emphasis added.)

[58] See Progress Report of the United Nations Commissioner for Eritrea During the Year 1951, UN Doc. A/1959 of 16 November 1951, p. 94.

[59] *Ibid.*, at 94 and 133.

[60] The Constitution established a single national chamber for the Eritrean Assembly, a strong executive and a judiciary with powers to control the constitutionality of laws. The Ethiopian Emperor was vested with the authority to request the reconsideration of laws affecting the interests of the Federation. Furthermore, the human rights catalogue embodied in GA Res. 390 (V) was incorporated in draft.

for consideration, the Commissioner put pressure on the domestic institutions to adopt the instrument without major amendments. He advised
the Assembly "not to discuss the United Nations resolution but to consider the draft Constitution"[61] and to act with "dignity and a sense of
responsibility"[62] in considering it. The Assembly followed this advice and
adopted the instrument. It entered into force in September 1952, after
the Commissioner's formal approval and Ethiopia's ratification.

Following the transfer of power by the British authorities to the newly
established Eritrean institutions, the General Assembly welcomed "the
establishment of the Federation of Eritrea with Ethiopia under the
sovereignty of the Ethiopian Crown" and praised the federal framework
as an "effective and loyal fulfilment of resolution 390 (V)" in its Resolution 617 (VII) of 17 December 1952.[63]

1.1.2.3.   Assessment

The UN assistance mission in Eritrea stood in stark contrast to the UN
engagement in Libya. It had little in common with the approach taken
by the General Assembly in Resolution 289 (IV), which placed trust in local ownership and decision-making power, but maintained international
control and authority over the process of decolonisation through UN expertise and the obligation of the UN Commissioner to cooperate with
the administering powers. The adoption of the federal framework for the
Eritrean people was overshadowed by power politics.[64] It was dictated by
the interests of UN member states to find a quick compromise solution
to the Eritrean problem, satisfactory enough to please the major Western powers and Ethiopia and which guaranteed Eritrea a basic degree
of self-government. But the solution conceived by the General Assembly
was artificial and short-sighted. It fell short of paying adequate tribute
to the principle of self-determination and the necessity to ascertain the
free wishes of the Eritrean people in the determination of the status
of the territory.[65] This shortcoming led to massive uprisings in Eritrea
against Ethiopian domination, which disturbed the federal balance in

---

[61] See UN Doc. A/AC.44/L.9, p. 1. See also Gayim, *The Eritrean Question*, at 157.

[62] See UN Doc A/AC.44/L.8, p. 2. See also Gayim, *The Eritrean Question*, at 158.

[63] See paras. 1 and 2 of GA Res. 617 (VII) of 17 December 1952, UN GAOR, 7th Sess., Supp.
20 (A/2361), Resolutions October–December 1952, at 9.

[64] See also Ratner, *The New UN Peacekeeping*, at 116.

[65] A confidential report by an Eritrean administrator indicated that at the time of the
adoption of the resolution "43% were in favour of union with Ethiopia, 52% (Moslem
League and Liberals) were against union with Ethiopians, and 5% were in favour of the
return of the Italians". See Gayim, *The Eritrean Question*, at 320.

the early stage of its existence and finally resulted in the abolition of the federation through Ethiopia's annexation of Eritrea in 1962. The General Assembly arrangement for the decolonisation of Eritrea was therefore a questionable political compromise, which compromised the UN's' reputation as an impartial and organised actor in dispute resolution and statebuilding.

Technically the operation barely fitted within the framework of traditional governance assistance missions. It amounted essentially to an experiment of the UN in constitution-framing and the forging of a new federal state. The UN Commissioner acted formally only as a guiding and advising force in the drafting process of the Eritrean Constitution. But the main features of this federal framework had long before been incorrigibly set by the multinational bargaining process in the General Assembly, which culminated in the adoption of Resolution 390 (V).

1.2.   Referendum and election assistance

After the two experiments in Libya and Eritrea which were mainly the result of the failure of the Four Powers to solve the status of the Italian colonies, the activism of the UN in the area of governance assistance declined. Peacekeeping operations had either a primarily military mandate or involved the UN in the exercise of broader executive or legislative authority. Furthermore, Cold War tensions and a state-oriented conception of sovereignty prevented the UN from undertaking audacious operations going beyond the traditional role of peacekeepers as truce observers.[66] It took almost three decades before the UN resumed its functions in civil administration. The engagement of the UN was again closely linked to the process of decolonisation. It confronted the organisation's policing and assistance tasks in two territories which had long fought for political self-determination: Namibia and Western Sahara. However, by that time, the policies and priorities of UN assistance had changed. The UN began to see itself more directly as a promoter and protector of people's rights, providing native actors with the necessary capacities and capabilities to hold fair and democratic elections and freely to determine their own status and political future. Moreover, the regulatory authority of the UN was essentially limited to the organisation and management of elections.

[66] See also Ratner, *The New UN Peacekeeping*, at 133.

1.2.1.   The United Nations Transition Assistance Group (UNTAG)

The United Nations Transition Assistance Group in Namibia (UNTAG)[67] marked the first major UN operation with a strong civilian mandate following the end of the Cold War. It was designed to ensure the peaceful decolonisation of Namibia by a transfer of power from the South African government to the people of Namibia. The UN itself held rather limited powers. However, the mission became the experiment of a new school of peacekeeping, expanding the role of the UN from traditional military and security functions to electoral matters, policing tasks and human rights protection.

1.2.1.1.   A difficult birth

The first steps by the UN to become actively involved in the process of decolonisation of Namibia[68] date back to 1978, when five Western members of the Security Council ("the Western Contact Group" composed of Germany, France, Canada, the United Kingdom and the United States) took measures to implement the terms of Security Council Resolution 385, which called for the holding of free elections in Namibia under the auspices of the UN. The former Mandate was at that time still un-lawfully occupied by South Africa, which refused to terminate its presence in the territory despite the revocation of its Mandate by General Assembly Resolution 2145 (XXI) and the confirmation of the illegality of its occupation by Security Council Resolution 276 (1970). The Contact Group managed to reach agreement on a Settlement proposal with South Africa and the South West Africa People's Organisation (SWAPO),[69] which provided a schedule for the exercise of self-determination of the Namibian people and Namibia's gradual transition to independence. The proposal envisaged a number of concrete steps towards the realisation of this goal, including the creation of a UN peacekeeping force (UNTAG) to supervise free and fair elections to a Namibian Constituent Assembly, the formulation and adoption of a Constitution for Namibia by the Constituent Assembly and an obligation on South Africa to release political

---

[67] See generally United Nations, *The Blue Helmets – A Review of United Nations Peacekeeping* (1990), at 341; Virginia Page Fortna, *United Nations Transition Assistance Group*, in The Evolution of UN Peacekeeping: Case Studies and Comparative Analysis (William J. Durch ed., 1993), 353; Chesterman, *You, The People*, at 58–60; Dobbins, *The UN's Role in Nation-Building*, at 29.

[68] For earlier activities of the UN under the auspices of the UN Council for Namibia, see below under (2) "(Co-)governance missions."

[69] SWAPO was recognised by the UN as "the sole and authentic representative of the Namibian people" in General Assembly Res. 31/146.

prisoners and detainees and to repeal all discriminatory or restrictive laws, regulations or administrative measures, which might inhibit the holding of free and fair elections.[70]

The Security Council approved this plan in its Resolution 435 (1978) and decided to establish under its authority "a United Nations Transition Assistance Group... to ensure the early independence of Namibia through free elections under the supervision and control of the United Nations".[71] However, due to South Africa's subsequent reluctance to implement the Settlement proposal and a US-initiated "linkage" of Namibian independence to parallel progress on withdrawal of Cuban troops from Angola,[72] UNTAG was unable to assume its functions for more than ten years. The deadlock was only resolved in 1988, when Angola, South Africa and Cuba signed the trilateral Namibian Accords, which paved the way for the deployment of UNTAG, by providing for "the total withdrawal of Cuban troops from the territory of the People's Republic of Angola"[73] and the departure of "all military forces of the Republic of South Africa" from Namibia.[74]

1.2.1.2. Limited regulatory authority

UNTAG was established in accordance with Security Council Resolution 632 (1989) of 16 February 1989, in which the Council decided "to implement its Resolution 435 (1978) in its original and definitive form to ensure conditions in Namibia which will allow the Namibian people to participate freely and without intimidation in the electoral process under the supervision and control of the United Nations".[75] The authority of UNTAG was rather limited. The mission was supposed to guarantee the freedom and fairness of the elections. However, the Special Representative of the Secretary-General (SRSG), Mr Martti Ahtisaari, enjoyed few regulatory powers to ensure this goal was achieved. Although the elections were to be held under the "supervision and control" of the SRSG,

---

[70] See Report of the Secretary-General concerning the situation in Namibia, UN Doc. S/12827 of 29 August 1978, in Robert C. R. Siekmann, *Basic Documents on United Nations and Related Peace-Keeping Forces* (1989), at 231.

[71] See para. 3 of SC Res. 435 (1978) of 29 September 1978.

[72] On the background, see Stephen M. Hill and Shahin P. Malik, *Peacekeeping and the United Nations* (1996), at 65.

[73] See para. 4 of the Agreement among the People's Republic of Angola, the Republic of Cuba, and the Republic of South Africa of 22 December 1988, UN Doc. A/43/989, in Siekmann, *Basic Documents*, at 233.

[74] See para. 2 of the Agreement.

[75] See para. 2 of SC Res. 632 (1989) of 16 February 1989.

the organisation and conduct of the proceedings remained under the general authority of a South African Administrator-General. The SRSG was confined to satisfy himself "at each stage, level and place... that the conduct and the procedure of the election, including the establishment of the list of candidates, the taking of the poll, the determination of the results of the poll, and the declaration of the results of the election [were] fair and appropriate".[76]

Furthermore, the UN played only a minor role in the elaboration of the Namibian Constitution. A text of "Principles concerning the Constituent Assembly and the Constitution for an independent Namibia" had been prepared by the Contact Group and the major parties to the negotiations before the deployment of UNTAG in July 1982.[77] The task of drawing up and adopting the Constitution, however, was left to the newly elected Constituent Assembly itself.

The only significant regulatory activity of the SRSG was its participation in the drafting of a Code of Conduct for political parties during the election campaign.[78] The Code was negotiated by UNTAG with the leaders of the main political groups. It proved to be a document of "central importance" because it "laid the ground rules for political conduct in a country which had never before enjoyed free and fair elections".[79]

1.2.1.3. A broad mandate, nevertheless
Despite the limited scope of "real powers" held by the SRSG on paper, UNTAG's mandate entailed in practice a significant political engagement. The task of creating a peaceful and neutral environment for the holding of democratic elections involved the UN in a variety of responsibilities that went beyond the traditional framework of peacekeeping. Furthermore, the advice provided by the SRSG became an important instrument of guidance and restraint vis-à-vis the South African Administrator-General.[80]

Perhaps the most difficult task of the UN was to create a political climate that allowed the people of the territory freely to exercise their

---

[76] See Report of the Secretary-General on the implementation of Security Council Resolution 435 (1978), Official Records of the Security Council, 44th Year, Supp. October, November and December 1989, UN Doc, S/20967 of 14 November 1989.
[77] See United Nations, *Blue Helmets*, at 348.
[78] Reprinted in *ibid.*, at 385.   [79] *ibid.*, at 369.
[80] Chopra goes so far to state that "the SRSG exercised a kind of veto authority in the process [of transition to independence] and began to behave as a quasi joint-governor-in-trust". See Chopra, *Peace-Maintenance*, at 46.

will in a neutral climate. Namibia enjoyed little experience in democratic government and had suffered from discriminatory rule and administration for several decades. UNTAG had to eliminate the traces and reminders of this past by ensuring that "the people of the country could feel sufficiently confident, free from intimidation from any quarter, and adequately informed, to exercise a free choice as regards their political future".[81] This process required not only changes to the Namibian public information and broadcasting system,[82] but also the ending of discriminatory laws and practices in the period of transition to independence. UNTAG played an important role in this field. The SRSG was entitled to receive complaints about discriminatory or restrictive measures that might abridge the objective of free and fair elections.[83] Furthermore, UNTAG held consultations with South African officials about the repeal of discriminatory legislation, which resulted in the abolition or amendment of fifty-six laws, including "some of the most conspicuous legal instruments of colonial repression and apartheid".[84] Although the SRSG himself had no direct authority to order the repeal of specific pieces of legislation, his assessments were reported to the Security Council, which demanded shortly before the elections "the immediate repeal of such remaining restrictive and discriminatory laws and regulations as inhibit the holding of free and fair elections",[85] including the elimination of a controversial law (the AG-8 law) which provided for a system of ethnic administration in Namibia.[86]

UNTAG also actively intervened in the organisation of the electoral process. The SRSG negotiated all administrative matters affecting the fairness of the elections with the South African authorities, who were barred from taking electoral decisions without the consent of UNTAG. The SRSG used this authority on a number of occasions, requiring changes in legislation or practice.[87] This activity culminated in the supervision of the elections held in November 1989.[88]

---

[81] Ibid., at 354.   [82] For a survey, see ibid., at 368.
[83] See para. 38 of the Further Report of the Secretary-General concerning the implementation of resolutions 435 (1978) and 439 (1978) concerning the question of Namibia, UN Doc. S/20412 of 23 January 1989, in Siekmann, Basic Documents, 236, at 238.
[84] See United Nations, Blue Helmets, at 376.
[85] See para. 8 of SC Res. 643 (1989) of 31 October 1989.
[86] For a discussion of the "AG-8" controversy, see United Nations, Blue Helmets, at 376–7.
[87] See Chopra, Peace-Maintenance, at 47; Ratner, The New UN Peacekeeping, at 121; United Nations, Blue Helmets, at 369–0.
[88] See Dobbins, The UN's role in Nation-Building, at 40.

Finally, the need to organise the transition of Namibia from an "illegally occupied colony [in]to [a] sovereign and independent State"[89] made it necessary to complement the UN's activities in election supervision and control with a number of additional organisational responsibilities, paving the way for a smooth process of transition. UNTAG was required to monitor the withdrawal and dismantling of the South African military presence in Namibia,[90] and the conduct of the remaining South African police force,[91] in order to eliminate threats of intimidation. Moreover, the UN assisted in the registration and return of refugees[92] and made provision for the peaceful return of former SWAPO forces under UN supervision. This broad range of tasks distinguished UNTAG from previous UN undertakings in the field of decolonisation and turned UNTAG into an early experiment in multi-dimensional peacekeeping.

1.2.1.4. Assessment

UNTAG turned out to be one of the biggest successes of UN-supervised decolonisation. The operation had a cumbersome start due to its strategic instrumentalisation in the Security Council at the height of the Cold War. It was also far from clear that the SRSG would be able successfully to accomplish his mandate with the weak authority provided to him by the Security Council. However, the partnership model envisaged by the Settlement plan operated very efficiently after South Africa had fully committed itself to the realisation of Namibian independence in the Tripartite Agreement of 22 December 1988.[93] The mutual checks and balances between UNTAG and the South African Administrator-General in the organisation of the electoral process produced a satisfactory result.[94] The elections of the Namibian Assembly took place smoothly and non-violently under free and fair conditions, with a 97 per cent turnout.[95] The Constituent Assembly managed quickly to draft the Constitution of an independent and democratic Namibia.[96] UNTAG itself became, as

---

[89] See United Nations, *Blue Helmets*, at 385.
[90] For further details, see United Nations, *Blue Helmets*, at 370.
[91] See United Nations, *Blue Helmets*, at 374.
[92] For a survey, see United Nations, *Blue Helmets*, at 378.
[93] See para. 3 of the Agreement, under which South Africa undertook the obligation to cooperate with the UN.
[94] See on this aspect also Chopra, *Peace-Maintenance*, at 46.
[95] See Ratner, *The New Peacekeeping*, at 120.
[96] Namibia gained independence on 21 March 1990. See generally Eckart Schmidt-Jortzig, *The Constitution of Namibia: An Example of a State Emerging under Close Supervision and World Scrutiny*, German Yearbook of International Law, Vol. 34 (1991), 413.

was later noted by UN Secretary-General Perez de Cuellar, "something far more than its somewhat pedestrian name implied. It... proved the executive ability of the United Nations in successfully managing a complex operation".[97] This experiment marked a positive point of departure for multi-dimensional peacekeeping in the 1990s.[98]

1.2.2.   The United Nations Mission for the Referendum in the Western Sahara (MINURSO)

The United Nations Mission for the Referendum in the Western Sahara (MINURSO)[99] was launched two years after UNTAG. It shares many conceptual parallels with the UN engagement in Namibia. Like UNTAG, MINURSO was essentially a decolonisation mission. The operation was created to bring to an end a long-standing historical dispute between Morocco, Mauritania and the Western Saharan liberation movement POLISARIO (Front for the Liberation of Saguia el Hamra and Rio de Oro) over the status of the former Spanish colony.[100] The UN was formally charged with the conduct, organisation and verification of a referendum over the political future of the indigenous population of Western Sahara, following a scheme (phased troop withdrawal, repatriation of refugees, establishment of a neutral election environment, holding of the referendum) that bears much resemblance to Namibia's transition to independence. However, the continued tensions between the Government of Morocco and POLISARIO over the modalities of the referendum (voter identification, appeal hearings in the process of voter identification, repatriation of refugees etc.) prevented a successful implementation of the Settlement plan[101] initially agreed upon by both parties in 1988. These complications led to the proposal of a new "Peace plan for self-determination of the people of Western Sahara" (the "Peace plan") by the UN in January 2003,[102] which maintained the option of a UN-organised and conducted

---

[97] See Report of the Secretary-General on the Work of the Organization, UN GAOR, 45th Sess., Supp. No. 1, at 2, UN Doc. A/45/1 (1991).

[98] See Dobbins, *UN's Role in Nation-Building*, at 43.

[99] See generally Chopra, *Peace-Maintenance*, at 160–84.

[100] See Thomas M. Franck, *The Stealing of the Sahara*, American Journal of International Law, Vol. 70 (1976), at 694; Yahia H. Zoubir, *The Western Sahara Conflict: A Case Study in Failure of Prenegotiation and Prolongation of Conflict*, California Western International Law Journal, Vol. 26 (1996), 173; Chesterman, *You, The People*, at 68–70.

[101] The Settlement plan is contained in the Report of the Secretary-General on the situation concerning Western Sahara of 18 June 1990, UN Doc. S/21360.

[102] See *Peace plan for self-determination of the people of Western Sahara*, in Report of the Secretary-General on the situation concerning Western Sahara of 23 May 2003, UN Doc S/2003/565, 14–18.

referendum on self-determination,[103] but envisaged the creation of an autonomous Western Sahara Authority for the transitional government of the territory[104] with the assistance of the UN.[105]

1.2.2.1. The historical dispute

The controversy over the status of Western Sahara has its origin in the fact that Spain, the former administering power of the colony, failed to comply with its commitment to organise a referendum on independence before its withdrawal from the territory. The UN General Assembly had first demanded such a move in 1965.[106] Furthermore, the Spanish administration had, in principle, agreed to hold a referendum in 1975 and conducted a population census in preparation of the vote. However, following a joint invasion ("the Green March"[107]) by Morocco and Mauritania, who had claimed legal ties with Western Sahara, Spain ceded its control over the colony to the two countries under the terms of the Madrid Accords of November 1975.[108] This agreement was a clear negation of the 1975 Advisory Opinion of the ICJ (Western Sahara Case),[109] which only one month before had ruled that the legal ties between Western Sahara and the Kingdom of Morocco and the Mauritanian entity were not of such a nature so as to preclude the application of the principles of Resolution 1514 (XV) ("Declaration on the Granting of Independence to Colonial Territories and Peoples"[110]), which states that all non-self-governing territories have the right of self-determination, to the territory.

Both Morocco and Mauritania remained hostile to the idea of the holding of a referendum on self-determination, fearing that the Sahrawi inhabitants of Western Sahara would vote in favour of independence – a

---

[103] See paras. 2 and 4 of the Peace plan.

[104] See ibid., paras. 8–16.   [105] See ibid., paras. 21 and 22.

[106] See GA Res. 2072, UN GAOR, 20th Sess., Supp. No. 14, at 59–60, UN Doc A/6014 (1965).

[107] The "Green March" was an initiative of Morocca, in which 350,000 "volunteers" (civilians and troops) entered Western Sahara, in order to reclaim the territory on historical grounds. See Zoubir, The Western Sahara Conflict, at 176–7.

[108] See Agreement on the Question of Western Sahara, Nov. 14, 1975, between Morocco, Mauritania and Spain, in United Nations, Third Report by the Secretary-General in Pursuance of Resolution 379 (1975) Relating to the Situation concerning Western Sahara, UN SCOR, 30th Sess., UN Doc. S/11880, Annex I (1975).

[109] See ICJ, Western Sahara Case, Advisory Opinion, 16 October 1975, ICJ Rep. 1975, 68. The Court found that there were no valid reasons as to why the rules of decolonisation and self-determination as contained in General Assembly resolution 1514 (XV) should not apply to Western Sahara. More than thirty years after the opinion, the resolution has still not been implemented. See Report of the Secretary-General on the situation concerning Western Sahara of 19 April 2006, UN Doc. S/2006/249, para. 38.

[110] See GA Res. 1514, UN GAOR, 15th Sess., Supp. No. 16, at 66, UN Doc A/4684 (1960).

result predicted by a UN mission of inquiry in October 1975.[111] The reluctance of both entities to ascertain the wishes of the people of Western
Sahara led to violent conflict with POLISARIO, which received support
from Algeria, Libya and Cuba. After three years of conflict, Mauritania renounced all claims to Western Sahara in 1979. But it took until 1988 for
Morocco and POLISARIO to agree to a UN Settlement plan, which called
for a referendum, to be organised and conducted by the UN (MINURSO),
asking Sahrawis to choose between independence and integration into
Morocco. The referendum was supposed to be conducted on the basis
of the census carried out by Spain in 1974 and following a cease-fire
between the two parties. The UN Security Council approved the plan on
29 April 1991 by Resolution 690 (1991) and established MINURSO by the
same resolution.[112]

1.2.2.2.   The role of the United Nations

The mandate of MINURSO under the architecture of both the Settlement
plan and the new Peace plan was very similar to the role of UNTAG in
Namibia. Under both arrangements, the UN was required to act as a
government assistance force with special administering powers in the
organisation and conduct of the self-determination referendum.

1.2.2.2.1.   The Settlement plan – a purported reprise of UNTAG

The Settlement plan entrusted the UN with a number of functions in
the transitional period leading up to the scheduled referendum. Following the entry into force of a cease-fire, MINURSO was mandated to
verify the reduction of Moroccan troops in the territory, to take steps
with the parties to ensure the release of all Western Saharan political prisoners or detainees, to implement the repatriation programme,
to identify and register qualified voters and to ensure a free referendum. The regulatory authority held by the UN in order to implement
these goals was construed more widely than in the case of Namibia.
MINURSO was conceived as a "miniature governance-in-trust" operation,
providing the UN with authority in all matters concerning the referendum.[113] The two parties, the Kingdom of Morocco and Frente POLISARIO,
granted the UN sole and exclusive responsibility for the organisation

---

[111] See Report of the United Nations Mission to Spanish Sahara, UN GAOR, 30th Sess.,
Supp. No. 23, at 66, UN Doc A/10023/Rev. 1 (1975).
[112] See paras. 1 and 4 of SC Res. 690 (1991) of 29 April 1991.
[113] See para. 9 of the Report by the Secretary-General, The Situation Concerning Western
Sahara, UN Doc. S/22464 of 19 April 1991. See also Jarat Chopra, *Breaking the Stalemate*

and conduct of the referendum. This mandate authorised MINURSO to take all legislative and administrative measures necessary to achieve the aim.[114] The UN was therefore entitled to "promulgate and repeal laws in the Western Sahara, maintain law and order independently of local security forces", and arguably also to "assume the role of territorial authority".[115]

But the mission never advanced to this stage in practice. While the UN managed to draw up a draft code of conduct for the referendum by 1994, the implementation of the Settlement plan was obstructed by cease-fire violations and complications in the process of voter identification and registration, caused by the nomadic and tribal structure of the Western Saharan society and strategic disputes initiated by the two parties.[116]

Both sides had, in particular, divergent interests in the definition of the electorate for the referendum. Morocco intended to expand the number of qualified voters as far as possible, by including additional contingents of Moroccans to the list.[117] POLISARIO, on the other hand, wished to restrict voter eligibility essentially to the group of persons registered by the 1974 census, limiting the number of Moroccan voters. Efforts by both sides to advance their cause led to severe controversies with the UN Identification Commission, which delayed the registration process. Moreover, when voter identification was finally completed, the parties continued to take divergent views on the issue of individual voter appeals, the repatriation of refugees and other fundamental aspects of the settlement, which finally led to the plan being put on hold.[118]

1.2.2.2.2.   The Peace plan – an extension of UNTAG

Following the rejection of a draft framework agreement on the status of Western Sahara, which envisaged a devolution of authority to the inhabitants of the territory with final status to be determined by a referendum

---

in *Western Sahara*, International Peacekeeping, Vol. 1 (1994), 310 ("quasi-governor-in trust, responsible for administering-in-transition the last colony of Africa").

[114] See UN Doc. S/21360, para. 58.

[115] See Chopra, *Peace-Maintenance*, at 164.   [116] For a survey, see *ibid.*, at 167–74.

[117] Morocco organised a second and a third "Green March" on 17 September 1991 and 12 January 1998, designed to register Moroccan nationals with the UN identification commission. See Letter dated 8 March 2003 from the Secretary-General of the Frente POLISARIO to the Secretary-General of the United Nations, UN Doc. S/2003/565 of 23 May 2003, p. 41.

[118] See paras. 20–57 of the Report of the Secretary-General on the situation concerning Western Sahara of 20 June 2001, UN Doc. S/2001/613, at 10.

five years later,[119] and a failed initiative by Algeria to grant the UN full territorial authority over Western Sahara for the implementation of the Settlement plan,[120] Personal Envoy James Baker managed to revive the dialogue between Morocco and POLISARIO by drafting the 2003 Peace plan for self-determination for the people of Western Sahara.[121]

The Peace plan maintained the option of a status decision of the residents of Western Sahara. But it made this decision subject to completion of a provisional period of power-sharing between Morocco and a locally elected authority with legislative, executive and judicial authority.[122] The proposal envisaged a division of the main powers of governance within this transitional period between Morocco (foreign relations power[123]), on the one hand, and the future institutions of the Western Saharan Authority (the Chief Executive,[124] the Legislative Assembly[125] and the Supreme Court and lower courts[126]), on the other. Furthermore, the proposal suggested that the UN be vested with exclusive authority "over all matters relating to" the election for the Legislative Assembly and Chief Executive of the Western Sahara Authority[127] and "sole and exclusive" authority to organise and conduct the referendum on self-determination.[128]

In addition, the plan proposed a dispute-settlement function for the UN.[129] Paragraph 21 of the proposal entrusted the organisation with a general assistance role, designed to help the "interested parties, in particular the Western Sahara Authority, in fulfilling their responsibilities under [the] plan".[130] The following paragraph specified that "the Secretary-General shall have the authority to interpret this plan and

---

[119] The proposal is contained in the Report of the Secretary-General on the situation concerning Western Sahara of 20 June 2001, UN Doc. S/2001/613, at 11–12. See also the respective assessments by Morocco, ibid., at 15; Algeria, ibid., at 118; and POLISARIO, ibid., at 20.

[120] See para. 40 of the Report of the Secretary-General on the situation concerning Western Sahara of 23 May 2003, UN Doc S/2003/565, at 8.

[121] See also the observations on the Peace plan by Morocco, UN Doc S/2003/565, at 21–32; and POLISARIO, ibid., at 33–44.

[122] See para. 8 (a) of the Peace plan.   [123] See ibid., paras. 8 and 9.

[124] See ibid., para. 10.   [125] See ibid., para. 11.

[126] See ibid., para. 12.   [127] See ibid., para. 15.   [128] See ibid., paras. 4 and 15.

[129] The Peace plan contained several provisions, which required monitoring. A good example is para. 13 ("All laws, regulations and acts of the Western Sahara Authority shall be consistent with internationally recognized human standards") or para. 18 ("Neither Morocco nor the Western Sahara Authority may unilaterally change or abolish the status of Western Sahara, except for the adoption of such laws as may be necessary to conform to the results of the referendum on final status").

[130] See para. 21 of the Peace plan.

that in the event of any disagreement about the meaning of the plan, the Secretary-General's interpretation shall be binding on the interested parties".[131] These two provisions were intended to reverse the unfortunate framework of the Settlement plan, which left the ownership over each and every step of implementation in the hands of the two parties,[132] making it difficult to achieve substantial progress in the process of decolonisation.[133]

The Security Council endorsed the Peace plan as "an optimum political solution" in Resolution 1495 (2003).[134] But its implementation was once again blocked by a lack of consent of the parties[135] including, in particular, Morocco's continued reluctance to accept a free status decision involving the option of independence (rather than "autonomy within the framework of Moroccan sovereignty").[136] This impasse sparked calls for a disengagement of the UN and recourse to direct negotiations between the parties, in order to accomplish what no UN plan managed to achieve, namely a consensual solution to the question of Western Sahara that provides for the self-determination of the people of the territory.[137]

1.2.2.3. Assessment

MINURSO was established in the spirit of the success of UNTAG, yet it proved to be one of the hardest test cases for the UN in decolonisation.

---

[131] See *ibid.*, para. 22.

[132] See paras. 49 and 50 of UN Doc. S/2003/565.   [133] See para. 47 of UN Doc. S/2001/613.

[134] See para. 1 of SC Res. 1495 (2003) of 31 July 2003, UN Doc. S/RES/1495 (2003).

[135] The Frente POLISARIO supported the implementation of the Peace plan: see Report of the Secretary-General on the situation concerning Western Sahara, 13 October 2005, UN Doc. S/2005/648, para. 2. Morocco reiterated that it would not agree to a referendum that includes the option of independence. See Report of the Secretary-General on the situation concerning Western Sahara of 19 April 2006, UN Doc. S/2006/249, para. 6.

[136] See Reply of the Kingdom of Morocco to Mr Baker's proposal entitled "Peace Plan for Self-Determination of Western Sahara", Annex I of the Report of the Secretary-General on the situation concerning Western Sahara, UN Doc. S/2004/325 of 23 April 2004, pp. 10–11. In 2005, the Government of Morocco "reiterated its readiness to conduct negotiations that would lead to the granting of autonomy to the Territory under Moroccan sovereignty". See Report of the Secretary-General on the situation concerning Western Sahara, 13 October 2005, UN Doc. S/2005/648, para. 2.

[137] See Report of the Secretary-General on the situation concerning Western Sahara of 19 April 2006, UN Doc. S/2006/249, paras. 32–5 and 40. In its Resolution 1754 (2007), the SC called "the parties to enter into negotiations without preconditions in good faith, taking into account the developments of the last months, with a view to achieving a just, lasting and mutually acceptable political solution, which will provide for the self-determination of the people of Western Sahara". See para. 2 of SC Res. 1754 (2007) of 30 April 2007.

The experience of the first stage of the mission (the Settlement plan) indicates that such a mandate can only work effectively with the consent of the actors involved. The lack of cooperation[138] and the "winner-take-all" mentality of both parties have brought international assistance efforts to the edge of failure. The unwillingness of both sides to implement the obligations undertaken under the Settlement plan has led the SRSG to propose to the Security Council in 2002, as one of four options, "to terminate MINURSO, thereby recognising and acknowledging that after more than eleven years and the expenditure of sums of money nearing half a billion dollars, the United Nations is not going to solve the problem of Western Sahara without requiring that one or the other of both of the parties do something that they do not wish to voluntarily agree to do".[139]

The decolonisation process could only be revived through a change in policy by the UN, which broke with its limited role as an enforcement agency responsible for the implementation of the Settlement plan and took on the function of a constructive peace-broker, proposing a series of new arrangements, including the 2003 Peace plan. This plan draws lessons from the failures of the past by granting the UN authoritative dispute-settlement authority in the process of transitional governance pending a status decision. However, it failed again to solve the main policy issue, namely to gain consensus on the holding of a referendum that includes independence as an option – a prerequisite of UN negotiation policy since the 1975 Advisory Opinion of the ICJ.[140]

This dilemma led to a preliminary withdrawal of the UN Secretariat from the negotiation process. Following years of reliance on UN-sponsored plans and continued political deadlock,[141] the Special Envoy recommended that the parties hold direct talks between themselves "without preconditions".[142] The Secretary-General called upon the

---

[138] See para. 42 of the Report of the Secretary-General on the situation concerning Western Sahara of 19 February 2002, UN Doc. S/2002/179, at 7.

[139] See ibid., para. 51, at 8.

[140] See Report of the Secretary-General on the situation concerning Western Sahara of 19 April 2006, UN Doc. S/2006/249, para. 31. ("The United Nations could not endorse a plan that excluded a genuine referendum while claiming to provide for the self-determination of the people of Western Sahara.")

[141] See the Report of the Secretary-General on the situation concerning Western Sahara, UN Doc. S/2004/325 of 23 April 2004, paras. 36–40. See also Report of the Secretary-General on the situation concerning Western Sahara, 13 October 2005, UN.Doc. S/2005/648, paras. 2–3.

[142] See Report of the Secretary-General on the situation concerning Western Sahara of 19 April 2006, UN Doc. S/2006/249, paras. 34–5.

Security Council and its individual member states to help in initiating such negotiations.[143]

1.3. Conclusion

The four major governance assistance missions undertaken by the UN in the period between the end of World War II and the end of the Cold War share many common features. They were all driven by the objective of realising decolonisation-based claims of self-government or self-determination in situations in which the future status of the territory was either uncertain or still subject to a final decision by the people of the territory in question. The UN supported the different processes of decolonisation through assistance missions, which relied strongly on the cooperation and the consent of the different actors involved in the resolution of the status question. This led to different results.

The governance assistance model worked successfully in the cases of Libya and Namibia, because the UN could rely on the support and consent of the various actors involved in the decolonisation process, and because the final outcome of the process, namely independence, was fairly clear. The Western Sahara engagement, by contrast, remained a constant source of struggle and contention, because Morocco and POLISARIO vigorously pursued their disputes over the "determination of the self" entitled to vote in the status referendum, and because different final status models (independence or autonomous integration into Morocco) continued to divide the two parties.

The case of Eritrea falls into a category of its own. Unlike the three other cases, the UN intervened actively in the status decision. Although the UN mission provided mere assistance in the process leading up to the elaboration of the Eritrean Constitution, the General Assembly predetermined the result of this process through the adoption of its federal model, which set down very precise prescriptions concerning the future governing framework of the territory. This model failed relatively quickly, with a lack of necessary support form local actors contributing to its failure.

2.   (Co-)governance missions

The UN also conducted a number of operations between the end of World War II and the beginning of the 1990s in which it exercised full

---

[143] *Ibid*, para. 40.

or shared governing authority over territories. After the high-spirited and ambitious, yet unrealised, visions of UN administration in Trieste and Jerusalem, the UN slipped into the role of governance by accident rather than through its own choosing. In three out of four cases (Congo, Namibia and Somalia), the UN did not take over governing authority according to a preconceived plan, but by an unwanted turn of events, caused by the incapacity of the formal territorial sovereign to exercise this function (Congo, Somalia) or the failure of the controlling state to exercise its governing function in accordance with its international obligations (Namibia). Moreover, the objective of the exercise of governing power by the UN varied. Two undertakings, the UN Temporary Executive Authority in West Irian and the establishment of the UN Council for Namibia, had a decolonisation-oriented background. The other two missions, the UN operation in the Congo and UNOSOM II, resulted from a power vacuum caused by armed conflict.

These divergent settings gave UN authority a different focus in each of the cases. In the cases of Congo and Somalia, the exercise of regulatory functions by the UN was strongly determined by the need to maintain law and order. The assumption of governing authority in the context of West Irian and Namibia, in contrast, was guided by broader considerations of daily administration (UNTEA) or international regulation (Namibia).

This type of intervention was, however, not entirely new. One early precedent may be found in the era of the League of Nations.

2.1.   The Leticia intervention – a precedent of ad hoc UN governance

The League of Nations' administration of Leticia may be counted as the first example of interventionist conflict resolution through ad hoc temporary governance.[144] Unlike the League's experiences in internationalisation in the cases of the Saar, Danzig and Memel, the Leticia engagement was not directly provided for under the Treaty of Versailles, but undertaken immediately in response to a crisis arising between Peru and Columbia in 1932. This spontaneous mode of dispute settlement distinguished the Leticia incident from the other governance and administration missions of the League and brought it more directly within the realm of modern peacekeeping.

---

[144] See generally L. H. Woolsey, *The Leticia Dispute between Columbia and Peru*, American Journal of International Law, Vol. 29 (1935), at 94; Walters, *History of the League of Nations*, Vol. II (1952), 536–40; Ydit, *Internationalised Territories*, at 59–62.

2.1.1. Background

The dispute arose from the fact that a group of armed individuals of Peruvian nationality attacked and invaded the port-town of Leticia in Columbian territory on 1 September 1932 in violation of the terms of a 1922 Columbian-Peruvian boundary treaty which had granted the "Leticia trapezium" on the Amazon river to Columbia. The government of Peru, which had a strategic interest in Leticia due to its access to the Amazon river, first condemned the action, but later acquiesced to the presence of a detachment of the Peruvian army in the city.[145] Columbia brought the case to the attention of the League of Nations, arguing that the action violated the 1922 border treaty, the Kellogg-Briand Pact and the League Covenant and that Columbia had the right to have its sovereignty over the territory restored.[146]

The Council appointed a three-member Committee to investigate the dispute, and the Committee reminded the Peruvian government "that it is the duty of Peru, as a member of the League, to refrain from any intervention by force on Columbian territory and to ensure that all necessary instructions are given to the Peruvian commanders concerned to the effect that the military forces of Peru should take no action beyond the defence of Peruvian territory and should not hinder Columbian authorities from the exercise of full sovereignty and jurisdiction recognised by treaty to belong to Columbia".[147] Furthermore, the Committee proposed the establishment of a League Commission to administer the territory for a period of one year before its handover to Columbia. When this compromise was rejected by Peru, the Council adopted a report under Article 15 (4) of the League Covenant, which condemned the presence of Peruvian forces in Leticia as a violation of the "Covenant of the League of Nations and of the Pact of Paris" and recommended the complete evacuation of the occupied area by Peru.[148] The subsequent negotiations between the two parties led to the adoption of an agreement, signed at Geneva on 25 May 1933 (the Geneva Agreement),[149] by which both sides agreed to the withdrawal of Peruvian

---

[145] See Walters, *History of the League of Nations*, at 536–7.
[146] For the Peruvian argument, see League of Nations, Report of the Council in the dispute between Columbia and Peru, LNOJ, Vol. 14 (1933), 599, at 602.
[147] *Ibid.*, at 604.   [148] *Ibid.*, at 609.
[149] See Agreement between Columbia and Peru relating to the procedure for putting into effect the recommendations proposed by the Council of the League of Nations in the report which it adopted on 18 March 1933, signed at Geneva, 25 May 1933, in LNTS, Vol. 138 (1933), at 253.

forces and transitional administration of Leticia by a League of Nations Commission.

2.1.2. The League's engagement

The Geneva Agreement provided for the immediate evacuation of Leticia by Peru upon the arrival of a League of Nations-appointed governing Commission in the territory. The Commission was initially required to administer the district for one year, during which time direct negotiations between the parties concerning the Leticia dispute were supposed to continue.[150]

The Commission was charged with "the administration of the [evacuated] territory" in "the name of the Government of Columbia",[151] which was also to bear the expenses of the work.[152] The Geneva Agreement granted the Commission wide powers, vesting it with "the right to decide all questions relating to the performance of its mandate".[153] Moreover, the Commission was authorised to command "military forces of its own selection", in order to maintain order in the administered territory.[154]

The League established the Commission on 19 June 1933 as a three-member body, composed of a US, a Brazilian and a Spanish national. It took up its activities four days later, following the departure of Peruvian forces from the city. The Commission assumed the direct administration of the territory with the support of a force of fifty Columbian soldiers placed under its control. It divided its work into three main areas of administration, each of which was assumed by one Commissioner: "maintenance of order and security", "care of public works and public health" and the "examination and payment of claims in respect of property lost by inhabitants" due to the Peruvian attack.[155] In order to emphasise its international and independent authority, the Commission even raised the League's flag and flew it alongside the Columbian flag.

In the meantime, Peru and Columbia held further negotiations about the future of the "Letivia Trapezium", which led to the conclusion of a Treaty of Friendship and Co-operation between the two countries on 24 May 1934[156] that ended the dispute over Leticia through special customs and navigation arrangements concerning the port city.[157] Several

---

[150] See Ydit, *Internationalised Territories*, at 61.   [151] See para. 2 of the Geneva Agreement.
[152] See *ibid.*, para. 5.   [153] See *ibid.*, para. 4.
[154] See *ibid.*, para. 3.   [155] See Woolsey, *The Leticia Dispute*, at 96.
[156] See Protocol of Friendship and Co-operation, 24 May 1934, Columbia-Peru, League of Nations Treaty Series, Vol. 164, at 21.
[157] See Ydit, *Internationalised Territories*, at 61.

weeks later, on 19 June 1934, the Commission terminated its mandate and restored full Columbian authority by turning Leticia over to the Columbian Governor of the Amazonian territory.[158]

2.1.3. Assessment

The League's engagement in Leticia was a short-term administering mission in a small, Columbian outpost on the Amazon River, inhabited only by a few hundred people. Given both the limited scope and length of the mandate, it is no surprise that the operation turned out to be a relatively successful enterprise in transitional administration. The population of the little town increased under the auspices of the League. A hospital, three schools and other useful buildings were erected; not a single incident of violence took place; and the Commission enjoyed the respect, confidence and affection of the inhabitants of Leticia.

The most remarkable feature of the Leticia mission, however, was not its record, but the fact that the technique of international territorial administration contained an element of "managerial" conflict resolution.[159] The League intervened in response to an ongoing crisis and established the Leticia administering mission in order to facilitate the continuing negotiations between Peru and Columbia over the settlement of the Leticia dispute. The deployment of the League's administering Commission therefore directly contributed to the problem-solving process between the two conflicting parties. This constructive use of strategies of territorial administration was unique in the history of the League of Nations, and set an important precedent for the later practice of the UN in territorial governance and statebuilding.

2.2. The United Nations Operation in the Congo (ONUC)

The UN Operation in the Congo (ONUC)[160] marked the first experiment of the UN in conflict-related administration. The mission was established in order to assist the Congolese government in the restoration of order and security after the withdrawal of the Belgian colonial authorities from

---

[158] See Woolsey, *The Leticia Dispute*, at 96.

[159] See in this sense Wilde, *From Danzig to East Timor*, at 588.

[160] See Rosalyn Higgins, *United Nations Peacekeeping 1946–1967*,Vol. III Africa (1980), 1–445; Abi-Saab, *United Nations Operation in the Congo*; United Nations, *United Nations Operation in the Congo*, in Blue Helmets, at 215–59; George Martelli, *Experiment in World Government: An Account of the United Nations Operation in the Congo, 1960–1964* (1966); Derek Bowett, *United Nations Forces* (1964), at 153–254; Ratner, *The New UN Peacekeeping*, at 102–9; Chesterman, *You, The People*, at 83–4; Dobbins, *UN's Role in Nationbuilding*, at 5–27.

the newly independent territory. ONUC was originally conceived as a primarily military operation. However, with the intensification of civil unrest in the Congo, and the threat of secession from the government of the mineral-rich region of Kantanga, it changed in nature to become more of a statebuilding mission, filling the power vacuum caused by instability and lack of control over Congo's centralised institutions. This gave the operation an unprecedented focus. The UN acted as a *de facto* executive authority under the heading of peacekeeping – driven less by its own political will, and more by the realities on the ground.

The new role assumed by ONUC represented a "constitutional change" for the UN itself. The organisation had to depart from some of the very principles on which it had based its action in the past. Instead of acting as a neutral force observing a truce between two conflicting parties, ONUC itself became a player in the internal armed conflict in the Congo, supporting the Congolese central government in its fight against the Belgian-aided Kantanga secession movement. This proactive military activism signalled a change from the UN's neutral pacifism of the past and led ONUC to undertake actions that were not covered by the consent of either of the two warring parties.[161] The role exercised by the UN in the field of policing and civil administration even sparked a Congolese government complaint about an intervention by ONUC in its internal affairs.[162]

2.2.1. The background of ONUC's deployment

Although ONUC was deployed in the context of assisting Congo's access to independence, it constituted all but a decolonisation mission. The operation responded primarily to gap in law and order, caused by the failure of the Belgian colonial powers to provide adequate security and stability guarantees for the immediate aftermath of Congo's independence.

2.2.1.1. Colonial failures

Congo's process of transition from colonial status to independent statehood was poorly organised. The new institutional framework of the country was hastily prepared. The "*Loi fundamentale*", the Constitution for the Congo, was adopted only three months before the date of independence. The main political organs, the President of the Republic and its

---

[161] See Ratner, *The New UN Peacekeeping*, at 103–4.   [162] *Ibid.*, at 107.

Prime Minister, were elected six days before independence,[163] and the rivalries among the Congolese leaders remained unresolved. The Belgian authorities left Congo divided between the nationalist, centrist government and the leaders of the Kantanga movement which sought financial and political autonomy from the central government.[164] The security architecture continued to be fragile and unstable. Belgium hoped to ensure law and order after independence through the Force Publique, the former colonial security force composed of 25,000 soldiers which was to remain under the command of a Belgian Lieutenant-General.[165] This arrangement, however, proved to be insufficient. Shortly after independence, the Belgian commander was dismissed and the force itself fell in disorder. Finally, when tensions between the Congolese government and the secessionist movement in Kantanga increased, Belgium sent troops to the region without the agreement of the central government – a move that was interpreted by the government as an attempt by Belgian authorities to re-establish control over the Congo.[166]

2.2.1.2. United Nations proactivism

After the arrival of Belgian forces in the province of Katanga, the Congolese government asked Dag Hammarskjöld, the acting UN Secretary-General, for military assistance to protect the country against what it called "external aggression" and a "threat to international peace".[167] Hammarskjöld regarded the crisis as a test case for the concept of preventive diplomacy which, in his eyes, could be beneficially deployed "in conflicts which are initially only on the margin or outside the bloc conflicts, but which, unless solved or localised, might widen the bloc conflicts and seriously aggravate them".[168] He used his powers under Article 99 of the UN Charter to bring the matter to the attention of the Security Council. The Council reacted benevolently to this initiative and adopted Resolution 143 (1960) on 14 July 1960, through which it called upon Belgium to withdraw its forces and decided "to authorise the Secretary-General to take the necessary steps, in consultation with

---

[163] See United Nations, Blue Helmets, at 216.
[164] See Hill and Malik, Peacekeeping and the United Nations, at 38.
[165] See United Nations, Blue Helmets, at 217.
[166] See Hill and Malik, Peacekeeping and the United Nations, at 38.
[167] See Telegrams dated 12 and 13 July 1960 from the President and the Prime Minister of the Republic of Congo to the Secretary-General, UN Doc. S/4382 of 13 July 1960, in Siekmann, Basic Documents, at 75.
[168] See Statement in the Annual Report to the General Assembly, UN Doc. A/4390/Add.1, in Abi-Saab, United Nations Operation in the Congo, at 2.

the Government of the Republic of Congo, to provide the Government with such military assistance as might be necessary until, through that Government's efforts with United Nations technical assistance, the national security forces might be able, in the opinion of the Government, to meet fully their tasks".[169]

This authorisation was inventive in the sense that it followed the Secretary-General's strategy of preventive diplomacy through peacekeeping. The UN mission was directly guided by the objective of stemming any further hostilities through intervention. The resolution itself, however, was drafted in rather traditional terms, relying on the classic concepts of assistance and consent.

2.2.2. A new dimension of peacekeeping

Secretary-General Hammarskjöld tried to follow this approach, by defining ONUC's role in the Congo on the basis of well-established principles of peacekeeping. In his first report on the implementation of Resolution 143 (1960), he reiterated that ONUC was to "to be regarded as a temporary security force, present in the Republic of the Congo with the consent of the Government"[170] and that, although it was to assist the Congolese Government in the maintenance of law and order, the UN operation had to remain "separate and distinct from activities by any national authorities" and could not "be used to enforce any specific political solution of pending problems or to influence the political balance decisive to such a solution".[171] But these guidelines were difficult to maintain in practice.

2.2.2.1. A novel function

Under pressure from the dynamics of the civil war in the Congo, ONUC was obliged to assume tasks that deviated from UN peacekeeping or conflict resolution under the auspices of the League of Nations. While ONUC's initial mandate to restore law and order and to facilitate the withdrawal of Belgian troops retained its full validity, the mission was required to transcend the boundaries of traditional peacekeeping. The breakdown of local authority and the division of Congo into four competing armed groups in late 1960 led to a situation in which the UN had to become involved in the ending of a civil war and in statebuilding.

---

[169] See para. 2 of SC Resolution 143 (1960) of 14 July 1960.

[170] See para. 6 of the First report of the Secretary-General on the implementation of Security Council Resolution 143 (1960) of 14 July 1960, UN Doc. S/4389 of 18 July 1960, in Siekmann, *Basic Documents*, at 76.

[171] *Ibid.*, para. 13., at 77.

The role of providing assistance gradually developed into an independent UN mandate, which gave ONUC primary responsibilities. Although the mission had been established to help the Congolese government in the reduction of violence, ONUC came to perform security tasks in the place of local forces.[172] This change in role was reflected in Security Council Resolution 145 (1960), which emphasised that "the complete restoration of law and order in the Republic of Congo would effectively contribute to the maintenance of international peace and security".[173] Furthermore, during a constitutional crisis between September 1960 and September 1961 which was caused by the dismissal of Congolese Prime Minister Lumumba, Congo had no formal legal government. ONUC therefore had to cooperate with *de facto* authorities and "do whatever it could to avert civil war and to protect the civilian population".[174]

Moreover, ONUC itself became increasingly engaged in the process of terminating the civil war – a function that was previously unfamiliar to the UN.[175] ONUC's responsibility for the prevention and termination of the civil war was only reluctantly pronounced by the UN at the beginning of the conflict, when the Security Council urged ONUC "to take immediately all appropriate measures to prevent the occurrence of civil war in the Congo, including arrangements for ceasefires, the halting of all military operations, and *the use of force, if necessary, in the last resort*".[176] This tone changed, however, later in the year. In what was a far-reaching and open statement at the time, the Council declared in its Resolution 169 (1961) that "all secessionist activities against the Republic of Congo are contrary to the Loi fondamentale and Security Council decisions".[177] Consequently, the Council vested ONUC with a Chapter VII-like enforcement

---

[172] See United Nations, *Blue Helmets*, at 226.

[173] See para. 5 of the preamble of SC Res. 145 (1960) of 22 July 1960, in Siekmann, *Basic Documents*, at 78.

[174] United Nations, *Blue Helmets*, at 226.

[175] Bowett still noted in 1964 that "[p]rima facie the United Nations have no power to intervene in a civil war within a state, and it is believed that this remains the position even when a request for assistance has been made to the United Nations by the authorities generally recognized as he lawful government". See Bowett, *United Nations Forces*, at 191.

[176] See para. 1 of SC Res. 161A (1961) of 21 February 1961, in Siekmann, *Basic Documents*, at 81. (Emphasis added.)

[177] See para. 8 of SC Res. 169 (1961) of 24 November 1961, in Siekmann, *Basic Documents*, at 82.

mandate,[178] authorising the Secretary-General "to take vigorous action, including the use of the requisite measure of force, if necessary, for the immediate apprehension, detention pending legal action and/or deportation of all foreign military and paramilitary personnel and political advisers not under United Nations command, and mercenaries".[179]

2.2.2.2. Beyond consent

The deviation from consent-based practices was also reflected in the implementation of the mandate. ONUC undertook a number of actions without the consent of, or even against the will of the Congolese government.

The Secretary-General had made it very clear in his first report that even though the UN force might be regarded as "serving as an arm of the Government for the maintenance of order and protection of life" it was necessarily under the exclusive command of the United Nations ... [and] not under the orders of the Government".[180] ONUC acted along these lines. It usually coordinated its action with the Congolese government, but it retained its operational independence and took the action that it regarded necessary to fulfil its mandate, even if it went against the will of the Congolese authorities. Despite protests by the host government, ONUC assumed authority over formerly Belgian-controlled military bases and airfields and established them as "neutral zones".[181] Furthermore, the UN undertook separate negotiations with the provincial government in Katanga, without consulting the central government.[182] Even more importantly, ONUC deployed its troops freely in the territory, without seeking the consent of either the government or the secessionist movement, and later, restored governmental control in Kantanga against the will of the provincial rulers, who had by then became a major player in Congo's civil war.[183]

The Secretary-General justified ONUC's authority for the undertaking of such actions on the basis of the existing Security-Council resolutions

---

[178] Chapter VII was not expressly invoked by the Council. The exact legal basis remained therefore disputed. For a full analysis, see Abi-Saab, *United Nations Operation in the Congo*, at 103–6.
[179] See para. 4 of SC Res. 169 (1961).
[180] See para. 7 of UN Doc.S/4389, in Siekmann, *Basic Documents*, at 76.
[181] See Bowett, *United Nations Forces*, at 234.
[182] See the protest by Congolese Prime Minister Lumumba, in Higgins, *United Nations Peacekeeping*, Vol. III, at 133.
[183] See Ratner, *The New UN Peacekeeping*, at 104.

242 FROM THE POST-WAR PERIOD TO THE END OF THE COLD WAR

and the necessity to counteract "an international threat to peace".[184] He noted in response to protest against ONUC's action that:

the relationship between the United Nations and the... Congo is not merely a contractual relationship in which the Republic can impose its conditions as host state and thereby determine the circumstances under which the Nations operates. It is rather a relationship governed by mandatory decisions of the Security Council. The consequence of this is that no Government, including the host Government, can by unilateral action determine how measures taken by the Security Council in this context should be carried out.[185]

2.2.2.3. Beyond neutrality

In practice, ONUC's mission conflicted not only with the principle of consent, but also with the traditional requirement of impartiality. The Security Council itself attempted to uphold UN neutrality as far as possible, by stating that "the United Nations Force in the Congo will not be a party to or in any way intervene in or be used to influence the outcome of any internal conflict, constitutional or otherwise".[186] This position corresponded to a widely shared view "that the United Nations has no right to interfere into a purely civil war, which does not of itself constitute a threat to international peace and security" and that it would be even less entitled "to dictate to a people which government it should have, or... whether a part of the people should remain within a particular State".[187] The Secretary-General sought to avoid this kind of criticism by establishing general principles of impartiality, which stressed, inter alia, that the UN force could not be used "on behalf of the Central Government to subdue or to force the provincial government to a specific line of action" and that it would not be deployed "to transport civilian or military representatives, under the authority of the Central Government, to Katanga against the decision of the Katanga provincial government".[188]

---

[184] Para. 5 of SC Res. 145 (1960) made reference "to the maintenance of international peace and security".

[185] See Statement of 8 March 1961, UN Doc. S/4775, reprinted in Bowett, *United Nations Forces*, at 235.

[186] See para. 4 of SC Res. 146 (1960), in Siekmann, *Basic Documents*, at 78.

[187] See Bowett, *United Nations Forces*, at 197–8.

[188] See para. 8 of the Memorandum of the Secretary-General on the implementation of the Security Council resolution of 9 August 1960, operative paragraph 4, UN Doc. S/4417/Add.6 of 12 August 1960, in Siekmann, *Basic Documents*, at 79.

However, it was naive to assume that ONUC could exercise its mandate without taking sides in the conflict.[189] Despite the involvement of Belgium, the dispute in the Congo was essentially of a domestic nature. The UN assistance provided to the Central Government amounted in fact to an overthrow of the Kantangese secession movement. The presence of UN forces did not end with the removal of Belgian troops or other foreign elements in the Congo,[190] but involved armed violence against Kantangese forces.[191] Furthermore, ONUC arrested provincial ministers and assisted in the re-establishment of the authority of the Central Government. These measures radically changed the political climate in the Congo.[192]

2.2.3.   De facto governance by accident

The administering functions exercised by ONUC within the framework of its four-year deployment differed. ONUC was originally established as an assistance force. But it developed, at least partly, into a *de facto* governance mission.

In the first stage of the operation, the assumption of administering authority was closely linked to ONUC's military mandate. The Security Council established ONUC primarily as a military force. Resolution 143 (1960) referred to a civilian mandate, but limited it to the provision of "technical assistance" to the Congolese government.[193] ONUC came to exercise regulatory authority only by accident and in the field in which it was active, namely the maintenance of law and order. Following Prime Minister Lumumba's removal from office, ONUC troops took steps to prevent Lumumba taking political or military countermeasures. UN officials first closed all major airports in the Congo to all but UN traffic on 5 September 1960 to prevent the infiltration of troops loyal to Lumumba.[194] Furthermore, the following day, ONUC temporarily closed down the Leopoldville radio station, on the ground that it had been used as vehicle for the promotion of conflict-inciting speech.[195] Both measures remained controversial.[196] They were officially justified on the basis of

---

[189] See also Ratner, *The New UN Peacekeeping*, at 104–5.
[190] See United Nations, *Blue Helmets*, at 240–1.
[191] See Abi-Saab, *United Nations Operation in the Congo*, at 129–48.
[192] For a critique, see Bowett, *United Nations Forces*, at 198.
[193] See para. 2 of SC Res. 143 (1960).   [194] See Dobbins, *UN's Role in Nationbuilding*, at 22.
[195] See United Nations, *Blue Helmets*, at 228.
[196] See Higgins, *United Nations Peacekeeping*, Vol. III, at 144–8; Abi-Saab, *United Nations Operation in the Congo*, at 59–75.

the maintenance of law and order. But they had a political dimension and were criticised.[197]

At the same time, UN-appointed personnel exercised important advisory functions in Congo's administration.[198] The Secretary-General had soon recognised that the UN must "in the situation now facing the Congo go beyond the time-honoured forms of technical assistance in order to do what is necessary".[199] He therefore decided to establish a special Consultative Group of high-ranking officials[200] which "without being accredited to the [Congolese] ministries... would be *de facto* able to serve, with senior responsibility, at the request of the Government, the various ministries and departments".[201] The members of the group were supposed to undertake "activities on a level of higher administrative responsibility" in a broad range of areas, including agriculture, communications, education, finance, foreign trade, health and public administration.[202] These "consultants" became vital for the functioning of the Government of Congo, "provid[ing] bone and sinew to the Administration in its different branches".[203] The members of the Consultative Group trained Congolose administrators in the management of government and established an organisational structure for domestic ministries. Furthermore, they assisted in the "long-term planning of central economic, educational and social services".[204]

UN authority gained even more exclusivity in the period of the power vacuum in Congo during the constitutional crisis (September 1960–September 1961). At that time, the country was governed only by four rival factions. ONUC did not take on any official government functions, although it exercised extensive policing powers in the absence of the

---

[197] See Abi-Saab, *United Nations Operation in the Congo*, at 60; Bowett, *United Nations Forces*, at 234.

[198] See Morphet, *Organising Civil Administration in Peace-Maintenance*, in Politics of Peace-Maintenance, 41, at 43.

[199] See para. 3 of the Memorandum by the Secretary-General on the Organization of the United Nations Civilian Operation in the Republic of Congo, 11 August 1960, UN SCOR, 15th Year, Supp. for July, August and September 1960, UN Doc. S/4417/Add.5, p. 60, reprinted in Higgins, *United Nations Peacekeeping*, Vol. III, at 77–80.

[200] The status of the Consultative Group was ambiguous. Most of the members of the group "retained their primary affiliation with their specialized UN agencies". See Dobbins, *UN's Role in Nationbuilding*, at 20.

[201] *Ibid.*, para. 7.   [202] *Ibid.*, para. 9.

[203] See First progress report to the Secretary-General from his Special Representative in the Congo, Mr Rajeshwar Dayal, 21 September 1960, UN SCOR, 15th Year, Supp. for July, August and September 1960, UN Doc S/4531 of 21 September 1960, p. 176, at 194.

[204] See Dobbins, *UN's Role in Nationbuilding*, at 20–1.

local central authorities.[205] Furthermore, UN civilian personnel continued their initial "technical assistance" functions,[206] working with "those
Congolese authorities exercising *de facto* control in the provinces or lo-
calities where United Nations Civilian Operations were undertaken".[207]

Finally, after the ending of the Kantangese secession, ONUC's civilian personnel assumed a role in constitution-framing and in the reintegration of the Kantangese services (customs, immigration, civil administration, telecommunications and banking) under centralised rule.[208]
These executive activities complemented the previous responsibilities
undertaken by ONUC in this field, which included the coordination of
Congo's economic policy, the establishment of a Monetary Council serving as Congo's Central Bank and the organisation of foreign assistance
to Congo.[209]

2.2.4. Assessment

ONUC was one of the most complex peacekeeping operations ever conducted by the UN. It marked the first operation in which the UN actively
performed extensive policing powers and civilian administration tasks
in a conflict environment. The mission benefited from a general international consensus on the feasibility of UN involvement.[210] However,
the organisation exercised these functions out of necessity rather than
choice. The Security Council had deployed the mission in the firm conviction that ONUC would act as a neutral "third party" to the conflict.
Yet, with the decline of local capacity, ONUC expanded itself into one
of the main "executive" authorities in the field. The Secretary-General
struggled to bring these new responsibilities in line with the traditional
principles of peacekeeping (consent, neutrality, limitation of the use of
force to self-defence). Both the challenges on the ground and the change
in role of UN actors could only be managed through a constant renewal
and update of ONUC's mandate by the Security Council.

---

[205] See Chopra, *Peace-Maintenance*, at 45.
[206] See generally Memorandum by the Secretary-General on the Organization of the
United Nations Civilian Operation in the Republic of Congo, 11 August 1960, UN
SCOR, 15th Year, Suppl. for July, August and September 1960, UN Doc. S/4417/Add.5,
p. 60.
[207] See Morphet, *Organising Civil Administration*, at 44.
[208] See United Nations, *Blue Helmets*, at 255.
[209] See Ratner, *The New UN Peacekeeping*, at 106–7; United Nations, *Blue Helmets*, at 254.
[210] Different international actors shared an interest in the "democratisation" of Congo.
See Dobbins, *UN's Role in Nationbuilding*, at 9.

In the end, ONUC accomplished its immediate goals by a "trial and error" approach.[211] It achieved its main objective, namely to maintain the territorial integrity of the newly independent Congo and to create some stability based on a balance of power among the competing domestic authorities. This was a success.[212] But it came at a high price, and was overshadowed by losses and failures. In order to accomplish its mission in the Congo, the UN was forced to act inconsistently with some of its own principles. With the death of Dag Hammarskjöld in a plane crash,[213] the UN lost one of its Secretary-Generals during the course of the mission. Finally, the peace and stability brought by ONUC remained an *ad hoc* victory. The UN was primarily preoccupied with the present situation; it did not give extensive thought to the idea of creating sustainable and long-term structures for peace[214] through post-conflict statebuilding, as it would later do in other contexts. By contrast, following the experiences gained in the Congo crisis, the organisation refrained from taking on expansive and costly administering responsibilities in a concrete conflict situation for almost the next three decades.[215]

2.3.   The United Nations Temporary Executive Authority (UNTEA)

The next operation in which the UN again came to exercise direct administering authority had a quite different background. It was a short-term governance engagement in West Irian (West New Guinea) with a clear and well-defined purpose: to prepare the territory for a transfer of authority from Dutch colonial rule to Indonesian administration.[216] Unlike in the case of the Congo, the mandate of the UN was rather easy to

---

[211] See also Chopra, *Peace-Maintenance*, at 45.

[212] See Hill and Malik, *Peacekeeping and the United Nations*, at 40.

[213] See United Nations, *Blue Helmets*, at 245.

[214] UN sources provide several reasons for the non-extension of ONUC's mandate after 1964. See United Nations, *Blue Helmets*, at 259. ("[T]he Secretary-General concluded, a further extension would provide no solution to the Congo's severe difficulties. The time had come when the Congolese Government would have to assume full responsibility for its own security, law and order, and territorial integrity. He believed this was the position of the Congolese Government, since it had not requested a further extension of ONUC".)

[215] See also Dobbins, *UN's Role in Nationbuilding*, at 27.

[216] See generally Rosalyn Higgins, *United Nations Peacekeeping 1946–1967*, Vol. II, Asia (1970), 93–149; Bowett, *United Nations Forces*, at 255–61; Franck, *Nation against Nation*, at 76–82; United Nations, *Blue Helmets*, at 263–77; John Saltford, *United Nations and the Indonesian Takeover of West Papua, 1962–1969: The Anatomy of Betrayal* (2002); Chesterman, *You, The People*, at 65–7; Daniel Gruss, *UNTEA and West New Guinea*, Max Planck Yearbook of United Nations Law, Vol. 9 (2005), 97.

accomplish.[217] The authority of the UN to administer West Irian until its transfer to Indonesia rested on the firm consent of the states involved, expressed in a UN-sponsored agreement concluded in 1962. Furthermore, the UN administration enjoyed "full" executive and legislative authority over the territory for the purpose of the fulfilment of its mandate – a feature which has led some observers to call West Irian the "first U.N. State".[218] The UN concluded its administering responsibilities in the first phase of the mission successfully. Acting as a "buffer" between the Netherlands and Indonesia, the organisation facilitated a smooth transfer of territory. However, it failed to exercise strict scrutiny over the organisation and conduct of the proposed self-determination process after the cession of the territory to Indonesia. This shortcoming turned the West Irian case into one of the less flattering experiences of the UN in the supervision and realisation of claims of self-determination.[219]

2.3.1. Provisional UN authority – a compromise solution over a (post-)colonial status dispute

UNTEA was established in order to solve the long-running dispute between the Netherlands and Indonesia over the status of West Irian. The future of the territory was left open when Indonesia gained independence from the Kingdom of the Netherlands after World War II. Article 2 of the 1949 Draft Charter of Transfer of Sovereignty, an instrument accepted by both parties, stated that "the status quo of the residency of New Guinea shall be maintained with the stipulation that within a year from the date of transfer of sovereignty to the Republic of the United States of Indonesia the question of the political status of New Guinea be determined through negotiations".[220] The framing of this clause was subject to controversy among the two parties. Indonesia claimed title over West Irian, arguing that the provision granted the Netherlands only a provisional right of administration for the one-year period mentioned in the agreement.[221] The Netherlands, on the other hand, defended the position that the clause maintained the *status quo* and Dutch rule over

[217] For a comparison, see Chopra, *Peace-Maintenance*, at 44–5.
[218] See Franck, *Nation against Nation*, at 76.
[219] See also Ratner, *The New UN Peacekeeping*, at 112 and Franck, *Nation against Nation*, at 79 ("What appeared on the surface a triumph for the international system was in fact an arbitrary disposition of people and territory by power politics reminiscent of the 1878 Congress of Berlin").
[220] See Draft Charter of Transfer of Sovereignty, United Nations Treaty Series, Vol. 69, at 206. Article 2 is reprinted in Higgins, *United Nations Peacekeeping*, Vol. II, at 93.
[221] See Higgins, *United Nations Peacekeeping*, Vol. II, at 94.

the territory. The Netherlands government regarded itself, in particular, as the Administering Authority of a non-self-governing territory under Article 73 of the Charter and declared "self-determination for the people of West New Guinea... [as] the sole purpose of its policy".[222]

When the matter was taken to the UN, the Dutch delegation proposed to charge the UN directly with administering responsibilities in the process of decolonisation. In a "Memorandum on the Future and the Development of Netherlands New Guinea",[223] the Netherlands agreed "that its present powers should... be exercised by an organisation or international authority, established by and operating under the United Nations, which would be vested with executive powers and which could gradually take over tasks and responsibilities and thus prepare the population for early self-determination under stable conditions".[224] This new form of administration "under the supervision of the General Assembly" was to be established by an agreement between the UN and the Netherlands.[225] However, the proposal for full UN authority over West Irian until the exercise of self-determination in a UN-led referendum failed to gain sufficient support in the General Assembly, because it ignored the interests and ties of West Irian to Indonesia.[226] Instead, the UN initiated a new round of consultations between the Netherlands and Indonesia, which culminated in the conclusion of an agreement in 1962 (Agreement between the Republic of Indonesia and the Kingdom of the Netherlands concerning West New Guinea[227]), and provided for a transfer of West Irian from the Netherlands to Indonesia through transitional UN rule (Phase 1) and the subsequent option for the native population to freely decide "with the assistance and participation of the United Nations Representative" (Phase 2) whether "they wish[ed] to remain with Indonesia" or whether "they wish[ed] to sever their ties with Indonesia".[228] The Agreement was endorsed by the General Assembly in its Resolution 1752

---

[222] Ibid., at 95.

[223] The Memorandum is reprinted in Higgins, United Nations Peacekeeping, Vol. II, at 96.

[224] See para. 6 c) of the Memorandum.   [225] See para. 8 of the Memorandum.

[226] See, for example, the statement of Liberia: "Knowing... the situation, and the background of the issue here, my delegation is inclined to the opinion that any action taken by this Assembly with regard to West Irian must also consider the long standing claims of Indonesia to this Territory. Any settlement regarding West Irian, we opine, must be made in consultation with Indonesia." See GAOR, 16th Sess., 1054th Plenary Meeting, at 640.

[227] The Agreement was concluded on 15 August 1962. See UNTS, Vol. 437, at 274. See also Higgins, United Nations Peacekeeping, Vol. II, at 101.

[228] See Article XVIII c) of the 1962 Agreement.

(XVII), which authorised the Secretary-General to establish UNTEA and carry out the mandate set out in the agreement.[229]

2.3.2.   Phase 1: the United Nations as government

The main role of the UN in the first stage of the mission was to serve as a provisional ruler, "neutralising" the process of transition of West Irian from Dutch authority to Indonesian culture. The agreement granted the UN wide powers to achieve this goal. West Irian was placed under the exclusive jurisdiction and authority of UNTEA from 1 October 1962 to 1 May 1963. Neither the Netherlands nor Indonesia held sovereignty over the territory during the period of UN administration. Furthermore, the UN administrator enjoyed "full authority under the direction of the Secretary-General to administer the territory for the period of the UNTEA administration".[230] UN authority included the "power to promulgate new laws and regulations or amend them within the spirit and framework of the... Agreement"[231] and the responsibility to "replace, as rapidly as possible, top Netherlands officials... with non-Netherlands, non-Indonesian officials".[232] These features made UN administration comparable to the government of a state[233] – a finding that is further reinforced by the fact that the UN was entitled to fly its own flag,[234] to issue travel documents to Papuans (West Irianese)[235] and to request consular assistance and protection abroad to citizens of the territory.[236]

The powers of the UN were subject to few express limitations. The Agreement obliged UNTEA to "guarantee fully... the rights of free speech, freedom of movement and of assembly of the inhabitants of the area",[237] including, *inter alia*, the "existing rights of the inhabitants" (such as "existing Netherlands commitments in respect of concessions and property rights"[238]) and free movement for civilians of Indonesian and Netherlands nationalities".[239] Moreover, UNTEA was to consult local

---

[229] See GA Res. 1752 (XVII) (1962).   [230] See Article V of the 1962 Agreement.
[231] See *ibid.*, Article XI.   [232] See *ibid.*, Article IX.
[233] See also Higgins, *United Nations Peacekeeping*, Vol. II, at 120 ("administrative, quasi-governmental role").
[234] See Article VI (1) of the 1962 Agreement.
[235] See para. 1 of the Exchange of Letters concerning the Issue of Passports and Consular Protection during the Administration of West New Guinea (West Irian) by the United Nations Temporary Executive Authority, 15 August 1962, UNTS, Vol. 437, at 306.
[236] *ibid.*, at 306.
[237] See Article XXII (1) of the 1962 Agreement.
[238] See *ibid.*, Article XXII.   [239] See *ibid.*, Article XXII (4).

representative Councils "prior to the issuance of new laws and regulations or the amendment of existing laws"[240] and before the appointment
of new representatives to these Councils.[241]

The UN completed its tasks and responsibilities in this phase of the
mission rather successfully. UNTEA acted as a "government-in-trust" of
the territory. The departure of Dutch officials caused a disruption of services. UNTEA helped to maintain basic services and supplies for the local
population. At the same time, the mission ensured the continuing functioning of the administration and judiciary of West Irian. Top officials of
the former colonial power were replaced by UN-appointed personnel.[242]
Judicial vacancies caused by the departure of Dutch personnel from various judiciary organs were filled by judicial officers from Indonesia.[243]
The new UNTEA institutions were instructed "to uphold the rule of law
and the principles of the Charter of the United Nations, to ensure respect for human rights, and to preserve intact, as a public trust, the
rights and liberties of the people of the Territory".[244] Furthermore, UN-
TEA appointed new representatives to the local New Guinea Council and
issued travel documents which were subsequently recognised by other
governments.[245]

The UN administration encountered some problems in day-to-day administration. UNTEA lacked personnel able to translate Dutch records
or capable of communicating in Malay/Indonesian.[246] Moreover, the mission operated under constant pressure from Indonesia. Despite its obligation to protect the rights of assembly and free speech of the native
population, UNTEA banned, *inter alia*, a demonstration aimed at cel-
ebrating the Papuan flag and attempted to prevent pro-independence
propaganda, in order to avoid rivalries with Indonesia.[247]

However, the first phase of the mission was, overall, considered a success by the UN. The organisation managed, in particular, to absorb the
gaps in public administration and services arising from the exodus of
Dutch personnel. The Secretary-General praised the achievements of UN

---

[240] See *ibid.*, Article XI.   [241] See *ibid.*, Article XXIIIt.
[242] See the Report of the Secretary-General on the implementation of UNTEA's duties,
"Organization of the Civilian Administration", in Higgins, *United Nations Peacekeeping*,
Vol. II, 142, at 143.
[243] See United Nations, *Blue Helmets*, at 272.
[244] See the Report, Organization of the Civilian Administration, in Higgins, *United Nations
Peacekeeping*, Vol. II, at 143
[245] *Ibid.*, at 143–4.   [246] See Gruss, *UNTEA and West New Guinea*, at 109.
[247] See Saltford, *United Nations and the Indonesian Takeover of West Papua*, at 50–7; Gruss,
UNTEA and West New Guinea, at 111.

administration, noting that it "had been unique experience, which had once again proved the capacity of the United Nations to undertake a variety of functions provided it receives adequate support from the States Members of the Organisation".[248]

2.3.3.   Phase 2: the self-determination "charade"

The engagement of the UN in the supervision of the exercise of self-determination after the transfer of power to Indonesia on 1 May 1963 was less meritorious.[249] The 1962 agreement vested the UN with advisory and assistance functions in the process of self-determination, which was supposed to "give the people of the territory the opportunity to exercise freedom of choice" after "consultations with the representative councils on procedures and appropriate methods to be followed for ascertaining the freely expressed will of the population".[250] The UN SRSG, Mr Fernando Ortiz-Sanz, suggested the holding of "one man one vote" elections, in order to implement the terms of the agreement. However, Indonesia rejected this advice, and informed the UN that it would not hold a plebiscite but only consult West Irianese representative councils, in order to ascertain the wishes of the people. These councils were neither democratically established nor selected under UN supervision. In August 1969, 1,022 carefully selected representatives "dutifully voted (unanimously)" in favour of continuing Indonesian rule in West Irian.[251] The UN SRSG criticised the voting method applied by Indonesia, which violated the terms of the agreement ("freely expressed will of the population"). But instead of taking a strong stance on the issue, he finally noted that "it can be stated that... an act of free choice has taken place... in accordance with Indonesian practice".[252] The General Assembly subsequently adopted this report in its Resolution 2504 by a clear majority.[253] However, a large number of states abstained from the vote, thereby

---

[248] See the Report Organization of the Civilian Administration, in Higgins, *United Nations Peacekeeping*, Vol. II, at 147.

[249] But see Bowett, *United Nations Forces*, at 261 ("the administration appears to have been a complete success").

[250] See Article XVIII of the 1962 Agreement.

[251] See Report of the Secretary-General regarding the act of self-determination in West Irian, 6 November 1969, UN GAOR, 24th Sess., Annex, Agenda item 98, p. 2, at 20, UN Doc. A/7723.

[252] *Ibid.*

[253] See GA Resolution 2504, adopted by a vote of eighty-four to zero, UN GAOR, 24th Sess., Supp. No. 30, p. 3, UN Doc. A/7630 (1969).

252 FROM THE POST-WAR PERIOD TO THE END OF THE COLD WAR

expressing their criticism about the doubtful means by which the "act of self-determination" had been carried out.[254]

2.3.4. Assessment

UNTEA was a territorial dispute resolution mission of the UN coupled with a decolonisation mandate. Undoubtedly, the operation succeeded in its first function, namely as an instrument of facilitating a smooth transition from Dutch to Indonesian rule. This success resulted from a number of factors: the short duration of the operation (seven months), the largely organisational nature of the mandate and the firm commitment of the Netherlands and Indonesia to the transfer of the territory. However, the 1962 Agreement was flawed in that it left the final stage of decolonisation, namely the act of self-determination, primarily in the hands of Indonesia, which had a manifest interest in its outcome. The decision "against independence" may be partly explained by the fact that the agreement allowed the act to take place at a time when Indonesia had already administered the territory for six years.[255] However, the acquiescence of the UN in this decolonisation procedure, and the limited protest of the organisation against its final result (cynically called the "act of no choice") cast a shade of doubt on the ability of the UN to serve as a credible guarantor of the exercise of claims of self-determination.[256]

2.4. The United Nations Council for Namibia

The UN mission in West Irian was followed by another UN undertaking in decolonisation which was born out of necessity and has been overshadowed by difficulties in enforcement – the administration of Namibia by the UN Council for Namibia.[257] The UN Council for South West Africa (later changed to Namibia in accordance with General Assembly Resolution 2372 (XXII)) was established by the UN General Assembly in 1967 to "[t]o administer South West Africa until independence" after the termination of South Africa's League of Nations Mandate over

---

[254] Thirty states abstained from the vote. See Franck, *Nation against Nation*, at 82; Ratner, *The New UN Peacekeeping*, at 111.

[255] See also Gruss, *UNTEA and West New Guinea*, at 115.

[256] See Saltford, *United Nations and the Indonesian Takeover of West Papua*, at 158–85.

[257] See generally Itsejuwa Sagay, *The Legal Aspects of the Namibian Dispute* (1975), at 262; Dugard, *The South West Africa/Namibia Dispute*, at 409; Issak I. Dore, *Self-Determination of Namibia and the United Nations: Paradigm of a Paradox*, Harvard International Law Journal, Vol. 27 (1986), 159; Herman, *The Legal Status of Namibia*, at 306; Andreas Junius, *Der United Nations Council for Namibia* (1989).

South West Africa by General Assembly Resolution 2145 (XXI),[258] which was later recognised by the Security Council in its Resolutions 264 and 269 (1969) and by the ICJ.[259] The accomplishment of the Council's mandate was severely hampered by the dissociation of *de jure* authority and *de facto* powers. The wide governance powers entrusted to the Council by the General Assembly stood in stark opposition to South Africa's exercise of effective control over the territory. This conflict shaped the entire period of UN administration and distinguished it from later experiments such as UNTAET, in which legal authority coincided with "real powers" of governance over the population of the administered territory.

Although the UN was formally the only lawful holder of public authority in Namibia after South Africa's loss of title over the territory, it was forced to act as a government-in-exile rather than as an effective state authority.[260] The lack of effective control turned UN administration into a unique experiment of territorial governance.[261] The exercise of UN authority remained controversial in conceptual terms and was justified by pragmatic considerations and arguments of exceptionalism. Furthermore, the UN was largely compelled to limit its regulatory activism to the regulation of external relations.[262] The impact of the Council was therefore primarily of a symbolic nature: its establishment demonstrated the will of the UN to take its decolonisation agenda and administering responsibilities over Namibia seriously; and it paved the way for the creation of UNTAG – the assistance mission leading Namibia to independence.[263]

---

[258] General Assembly Resolution 2145, UN GAOR, 21st Sess., Supp. No. 16, p. 2, UN Doc. A/63/16 (1966), adopted by 119 affirmative to two negative votes (South Africa, Portugal), with three abstentions (United Kingdom, France, Malawi).

[259] See on the practice of the Security Council with respect to Namibia, Eckart Klein, *Statusverträge im Völkerrecht* (1980), 487. On the 1971 advisory opinion of the ICJ, see Ralph Zacklin, *The Problem of Namibia in International Law*, Recueil des Cours, Vol. 171 (1981 II), 225, at 288.

[260] Sagay notes that the Council constituted in relation to South Africa "a legitimate government dispossessed of its territory by a foreign power in occupation". See Sagay, *Legal Aspects of the Namibian Dispute*, at 272.

[261] See also Zacklin, *The Problem of Namibia*, at 310 ("the Council for Namibia is unique in United Nations practice").

[262] See Ebere Osieke, *Admission to Membership in International Organizations: The Case of Namibia*, British Yearbook of International Law, Vol. 51 (1980), 189; Henry G. Schermers, *The Namibia Decree in National Courts*, International & Comparative Law Quarterly, Vol. 26 (1977), 81.

[263] See above Chapter 7, 1.2.1.

2.4.1. Virtual governance

Disputes over the feasibility of the creation of a special *de jure* UN administering authority concerning Namibia began at the stage of the establishment of the Council as a subsidiary organ of the General Assembly[264] by GA Resolution 2248 (S–V) of 19 May 1967. Resolution 2248 was adopted by eighty-five votes to two with thirty abstentions. The relatively high number of abstentions reflected the controversies existing in the General Assembly over the creation of the Council. Some states continued to challenge the competence of the Assembly to terminate South Africa's mandate and questioned its authority to endow the Council with full legislative and administering powers concerning Namibia.[265] The majority of states rightly acknowledged that the UN was legally entitled to establish the Council as a governing organ of Namibia even without the express consent of South Africa, because the latter had forfeited its rights over the territory and because the UN represented the only party concerned with authority to act on behalf of the people of Namibia.[266] Nevertheless, countries like Canada, Denmark, the Netherlands and Finland abstained from the vote, arguing that it was politically unwise to establish a governing institution that was barred from exercising any *de facto* authority in Namibia without further cooperation by South Africa.[267]

2.4.1.1. *Exclusive, state-like authority in theory*
Resolution 2248 ignored this criticism. It conceived the post-Mandate relationship between Namibia and the UN as a relationship between "a *de*

---

[264] See para. 2 of GA Res. 2248 ("in the exercise of its powers and in the discharge of its functions the Council shall be responsible to the General Assembly").

[265] The representative of Sweden noted that Resolution 2248 "did not command the broad persuasive support of resolution 2145 (XXI)" and that there was possibly "not a firm basis for further United Nations action". See General Assembly, Official Records, Fifth Special Session, 1518th meeting. For a survey of state practice, see also the Report of the Secretary-General, Compliance of Member States with the United Resolutions and Decisions relating to Namibia, taking into account the Advisory Opinion of the International Court of Justice of 21 June 1971, UN Doc. A/AC.131/37 of 12 March 1975.

[266] In this sense see also the Separate Opinion of Judge Ammoun in the *Namibia case*, ICJ, *Legal Consequences for States of the Continued Presence of South Africa in Namibia (South West Africa)*, ICJ Rep. 1971, p. 70. ("These are powers which it was necessary for the mandatory to exercise until the expiry of the mandate, and they entitle the Council, acting on behalf of the United Nations, to exercise legislative competence and administrative authority in Namibia as well as to represent it diplomatically and exercise diplomatic protection of its nationals.")

[267] The representative of Finland praised Resolution 2248 as "an impressive expression of the convictions of a great majority of the Assembly", but stressed that it could not be effectively carried out. See Zacklin, *The Problem of Namibia*, at 309.

jure government and a territory under its rule".[268] The General Assembly established the Council as an authority-in-trust[269] with full and exclusive legislative and administering powers. The resolution authorised the Council to "promulgate such laws, decrees and administrative regulations as are necessary for the administration of the Territory" until the establishment of a domestic legislative assembly,[270] to take immediate measures, in consultation with the inhabitants, to establish a "constitutional assembly to draw up a constitution on the basis of which elections [would] be held",[271] to maintain law and order[272] and to transfer "all powers to the people of the Territory upon the declaration of independence".[273]

In the discharge of these responsibilities, the Council was supposed to act in a dual capacity – as an organ of the UN, on the one hand, and as the legal administering authority of Namibia, on the other.[274] However, these lofty ambitions were based on a fiction of effective UN authority and control over Namibia. The resolution assumed that the Council would "be based in South West Africa" and that it would be able to "proceed to South West Africa" in order to take "over the administration of the Territory" and to ensure "the withdrawal of South African police and military forces".[275] This objective was to be achieved with the assistance of the Security Council, which was requested by the General Assembly "to take all appropriate measures to enable the United Nations Council for South West Africa to discharge the functions and responsibilities entrusted to it by the General Assembly".[276] However, these plans remained dormant until the revival of dialogue with South Africa in 1978, because of South Africa's declared refusal to withdraw from Namibia[277] and the Security Council's unwillingness to enforce the terms of Resolution 2248 by force.[278]

---

[268] See Sagay, *Legal Aspects of the Namibian Dispute*, at 269.
[269] *Ibid.*, at 269. For a qualification of the Council as an administering authority under Article 81 of the Charter, see Schermers, *The Namibia Decree*, at 85.
[270] See para. 1 b of GA Res. 2248.
[271] See *ibid.*, para. 1 c.
[272] See *ibid.*, para. 1 d.
[273] See *ibid.*, para. 1 e.
[274] See Osieke, *Admission to Membership*, at 193; Zacklin, *The Problem of Namibia*, at 309.
[275] See paras. 1–3 of Part IV of GA Res. 2248.   [276] See *ibid.*, para. 5 of Part IV.
[277] See Dore, *Self-Determination of Namibia*, at 163. See also the Report of the Secretary-General of 3 October 1969 on the Implementation of SC Resolution 269, UN SCOR, Vol. 24, Spec. Supp. No. 2, at 1, UN Doc. S/9463/Add.1 (1969).
[278] The Security Council set South Africa several unsuccessful deadlines for withdrawal. See para. 6 of SC Res. 366 (1975) and para. 12 of SC Res. 385 (1976).

2.4.1.2. Limited governmental capacities in practice

Despite its wide authority on paper, the Council for Namibia was essentially a government without teeth. The lack of effective control over Namibia affected both its regulatory and its representational activity. The most famous legal act of the Council was its Decree No. 1[279] which made the exploitation of Namibian natural resources dependent on the consent and permission of the Council[280] while adding that resources removed without such consent could be seized.[281] The Decree marked, to some extent, a logical corollary of the 1971 *dictum* of the ICJ in the Namibia case, in which the Court had reaffirmed the view that UN members were obliged by UN secondary law to recognise the illegality of South Africa's continued presence in Namibia and the illegality of its acts.[282] But its implementation was compromised by the fact that the Council failed to hold effective control over Namibia. Many major Western industrial nations with mining or other investments in Namibia refused to recognise the validity or binding nature of the Decree, arguing that as a public act of a foreign authority,[283] the Decree could not be enforced because it emanated from an entity which lacked *de facto* control over the territory in question.[284]

This lack of recognition of the decree under municipal law compromised both the implementation of the decree and the authority of the Council for Namibia. Several years after the adoption of the decree, the Council was also forced to admit openly that the possibility of the seizure of illegally exported resources failed to "be an effective remedy in States which do not recognize the power of the General Assembly to revoke the Mandate... or to create a subsidiary organ to administer Namibia pending independence, as well as in those which deny the

---

[279] See Decree No. 1 for the Protection of the Natural Resources of Namibia of 27 September 1974, UN Doc. A/AC.131/33, in ILM, Vol. 13 (1974) 1513.

[280] See para. 1 of Decree No. 1.   [281] See *ibid.*, para. 4.

[282] The Decree was also approved by the General Assembly immediately after its enactment. See GA Res. 3295, UN GAOR, Vol. 29, Supp. No. 31, UN Doc. A/9631 (1974).

[283] The Decree is frequently assimilated to a foreign public law in legal doctrine. See Schermers, *The Namibia Decree*, at 90 ("decree of a foreign government"); Zacklin, *The Problem of Namibia*, at 322 ("decree of a foreign state").

[284] Courts are normally reluctant to apply foreign laws adopted by entities that do not exercise effective authority over their territory. See Schermers, *The Namibia Decree*, at 90; Zacklin, *The Problem of Namibia*, at 322. The enforcement of Decree No. 1 encountered obstacles in the US, the UK, France and the Netherlands because the respective governments did not recognise the Council for Namibia as the *de jure* or the *de facto* administering authority of Namibia. See Dore, *Self-Determination of Namibia*, at 168; Zacklin, *The Problem of Namibia*, at 323–5.

power of the Council to adopt decrees".[285] This obstacle further reduced the effectiveness of Decree No. 1, as the principal importers of Namibian natural resources (the US, the UK, Japan, Belgium, Germany and Switzerland) fell into one of these three categories. The Council therefore adopted a change in strategy, seeking to enforce the decree by political rather than legal means.[286]

The absence of factual UN authority over Namibia caused additional complications in another area of international concern – the conduct of external relations, in particular the admission for membership in international organisations.[287] The most famous example is the Council's request for full membership in the International Labour Organization (ILO) on behalf of Namibia before the country's access to independence. The application raised serious legal concerns, because admission to ILO is reserved for "states" under Article 1 of the ILO Constitution.[288] In a written opinion, the ILO's legal advisor concluded that Namibia could not be admitted as a member of the organisation "until it attains independence".[289] After lengthy discussions, the International Labour Conference rejected this recommendation and admitted Namibia as a member, noting that "until the present illegal occupation of Namibia is terminated, the United Nations Council for Namibia... will be regarded as the Government of Namibia for the purpose of the application of the Constitution of the Organisation".[290] However, the Conference stressed the exceptional nature of the admission. It justified its decision essentially on the basis of the principle *ex injuria jus non oritur*, stating that "[t]he International Labour Organization is not prepared to allow the legitimate rights of the Namibian people to be frustrated by the illegal occupation of South Africa".[291] Moreover, the Conference explained

---

[285] See UN Doc. A/AC/.131/81 of 18 July 1980, para. 16. See also Zacklin, *The Problem of Namibia*, at 325.

[286] The Council organised, *inter alia*, panel hearings on the implementation of the decree. See Zacklin, *The Problem of Namibia*, at 327.

[287] The General Assembly had requested UN specialised agencies to grant Namibia full membership. See GA Res. 32/9E of 4 November 1977. See also Zacklin, *The Problem of Namibia*, at 314.

[288] Article 1 opens ILO membership to "*States* which were Members of the I.L.O. on 1 November 1945" and to "such other *States* as may become Members of the Organization in pursuance of the provisions of paragraphs 3 and 4 of Article I" (emphasis added). See also Zacklin, *The Problem of Namibia*, at 314.

[289] See Opinion Legal Advisor, ILO, 64th Sess., Geneva, June 1978, in Osieke, *Admission to Membership*, at 213.

[290] The text of the resolution is reprinted in Osieke, *Admission to Membership*, at 214.

[291] *Ibid.*, at 214.

the deviation from the requirement of effective control in the case of Namibia by formally stating its belief "that the occupation of Namibia by South Africa" would be terminated "in the near future".[292] Both clarifications served to illustrate the continuing relevance of the effective control criterion under Article 1 of the ILO Constitution and the exceptional character of admission in the case of Namibia.[293]

2.4.2. The record of the Council

The practical record of the Council for Namibia is mixed. The Council adopted only a few measures of "internal" relevance in its capacity as a *de jure* government of Namibia, for example, it initiated measures to abrogate discriminatory laws and practices introduced by South Africa;[294] it launched a comprehensive training and assistance programme for civil servants and other personnel, in order to enhance the future self-administering capacities of the Namibian people.[295] The biggest achievements of the work of the Council, however, lay in the field of external relations. The Council issued passports and travel documents to Namibians in exile, in order to allow them to travel.[296] It acted as a claimant in legal proceedings before courts in the Netherlands to enforce Decree No. 1.[297] The Council managed to realise Namibian membership in the ILO and FAO – even against the opposition of some other members of the organisations.[298] Finally, the Council participated as the "legal administering authority for Namibia" (without the right to vote)

---

[292] *Ibid.*, at 214.   [293] For a discussion, see Osieke, *Admission to Membership*, at 217.

[294] The Council requested the UN Commission for Namibia, in particular, to compile a survey of the existing South African laws and practices. See Sagay, *Legal Aspects of the Namibian Dispute*, at 274.

[295] *Ibid.*, at 274. See also GA Res. 2372 (XXII) of 12 June 1968 and GA Res. 2679 (XXV) of 9 December 1970.

[296] For a survey of the practice of the Council, see Junius, *United Nations Council for Namibia*, at 194.

[297] In 1987, the Council summoned Urenco Nederland, Ultra Centrifuge Nederland (UCN) and the State of the Netherlands to appear in the District Court in The Hague, requesting the Court to prohibit Urenco and UCN from any future execution of enrichment orders concerning uranium originating from Namibia. For a full analysis, see Nico Schrijver, *Permanent Sovereignty over Natural Resources* (1997), at 140.

[298] Namibia's application for membership of the FAO was approved by 112 to four votes, with eleven abstentions. The US delegate explained its opposition to membership, noting that "that a state or nation in the sense meant in Article II of the FAO Constitution is a territory controlled by an internationally recognised government located in the territory that it controls or administers. We [the US] do not consider it wise for the future of this Organisation or other Organisations in the United Nations System to take decisions that create confusion as to the meaning of the concept of state or nation as it relates to membership in United Nations Organisations". The statement is reprinted in Osieke, *Admission to Membership*, at 209.

in various international treaty conferences, including the Vienna Conference on the Succession of States in respect of Treaties[299] and the Third United Nations Conference on the Law of the Sea.[300]

2.4.3.   Assessment

The practice of the Council for Namibia marked a unique case of UN engagement in the administration of territory.[301] The Council was not established by consent, but imposed on South Africa against its will by a resolution of the General Assembly. The fact that the Council was created by a General Assembly resolution (and not by a binding Chapter VII resolution of the Security Council) weakened the authority of the Council. Although a strong case can be made that the General Assembly was legally entitled to establish the Council as the formal administering authority of Namibia,[302] both the Council's existence and its legal acts remained open to legality and legitimacy challenges in state practice. This dilemma could have been avoided had the Council been directly created by a binding Security Council resolution – a practice later adopted in the cases of Eastern Slavonia, Kosovo and East Timor.

The main accomplishment of the Council was its external representation of Namibia, which gave the idea of Namibia's independence a concrete and physical identity on the international plane. But the Council remained a "paper tiger"[303] which failed to realise its "governance" mandate in the strict sense, because it lacked the means to gain effective control over the territory and the people of Namibia.

2.5.   The United Nations Operation in Somalia (UNOSOM II)

The takeover of administering responsibilities by the UN in Somalia[304] shared many parallels with the UN engagement in the Congo. The UN

---

[299] For a full account, see Osieke, *Admission to Membership*, at 201.   [300] *Ibid.*, at 204.
[301] The non-consensual nature of the Council's mandate distinguished it from the classical tradition of peacekeeping. The assumption of administering authority by the UN marked the closest case of direct UN administration under Article 81 of the Charter. See above Part I, Chapter 3.
[302] See Sagay, *Legal Aspects of the Namibian Dispute*, at 268–73.
[303] See also Zacklin, *The Problem of Namibia*, at 319, who notes that the political purpose of the enactment of Decree No. 1 was to "strengthen the claim of the Council for Namibia that it is fulfilling the 'legislative' function conferred upon it by the General Assembly".
[304] See Sean D. Murphy, *Nation-Building: A Look at Somalia*, Tulane Journal of International & Comparative Law, Vol. 3 (1995), at 19; Kelly, *Restoring and Maintaining Order*, at 67–8; Chopra, *Peace-Maintenance*, at 123–60; Chesterman, *You, The People*, at 84–6; Christiane E. Philipp, *Somalia – A Very Special Case*, Max Planck Yearbook of United Nations Law, Vol. 9 (2005), 518–54.

assumed the role of a "surrogate government" in the course of an on-going conflict and without its expressed own intention. Like ONUC, UN-OSOM was pulled into the internal dynamics of the conflict in Somalia and developed from a mere assistance mission into a *de facto* governing authority of parts of the territory. This time, the UN received less crit-icism about its involvement in the internal affairs of the administered state. But the organisation was once again insufficiently prepared to deal with the collapse of domestic authority in course of ongoing hostilities. Instead of learning from the lessons of the Congo, the UN repeated some of its previous mistakes. The Security Council provided UNOSOM with a robust military mandate, but failed to grant it comprehensive civilian authority – a shortcoming that had already compromised the effective-ness of the UN Operation in the Congo.[305] Furthermore, the mission in Somalia illustrated even more clearly than before the lack of a coherent legal framework to deal with complex emergencies. UN peacekeepers were forced to maintain law and order and to carry out detentions and other executive or enforcement measures, without certainty about the legal basis of their action. It was, in particular, unclear whether and to what extent the laws of occupation could be invoked as an authoritative guide of reference, determining the rights and obligations of UNOSOM. Finally, the UN disregarded the lessons of ONUC by terminating its en-gagement in Somalia without a clear strategy. UN military and civilian personnel left the country in a state of disarray after a series of Somali attacks on UNOSOM II forces, leaving no recognised authority in place. These experiences turned UNOSOM into one of the most controversial undertakings in multi-dimensional peacekeeping.

2.5.1.   Background

Somalia formally emerged as a unified state in 1960 after the accession to independence of former British Somaliland and Italian Somalia (for-mer Italian trust territory). The two territories had been administered as separate entities under British and Italian rule. In 1961, they were merged into a common constitutional structure which was modelled on Western standards of parliamentary democracy.[306] This pluralist and

---

[305] See Ratner, *The New UN Peacekeeping*, at 107.

[306] The UN created a Consulative Commission for Integration, in order facilitate the transition. The Commission had an international component and was supposed to assist in the development of Somalia's new laws and institutions. See Philipp, *Somalia – A Very Special Case*, at 521.

multi-party-based constitutional structure was gradually abolished in the 1970s following a military coup by General Siad Barre. The parliamentary Constitution enacted in 1961 was repealed. Public administrators at the regional and local level were replaced by military governors. Powers of government at the central level were vested in a Supreme Revolutionary Council, which took over functions formerly attributed to democratic organs (the President, Council of Minister, National Assembly). Continuing opposition to the Barre regime led to unrest and civil strife in the country throughout the 1980s.

The UN decided to intervene in 1991 after the overthrow of Barre's autocratic government by a coalition of politically fragmented warlords and clan leaders. The UN involvement in Somalia started initially as a humanitarian relief operation. The country had fallen into a state of lawlessness. Famine, the lack of a centralised government and power struggles among competing factions led to a vicious cycle of violence which dragged Somalia into political chaos and a state of anarchy.[307] The Security Council sought to break the dynamics of this process by establishing the United Nations Task Force (UNITAF) – a Chapter VII-based mission designed to create a secure environment for the unimpeded delivery of humanitarian assistance.[308] But it soon became evident that the successful delivery of humanitarian assistance alone would not suffice to address the root causes of the conflict – the grave lack of law and politically viable institutions.[309] This gap should have been closed by UNOSOM II, which was established to maintain law and order in Somalia and to assist the people of Somalia in the implementation of the UN-brokered Addis Ababa Agreement,[310] through which the warring factions expressed their commitment to enhance security through disarmament and to endow a Somali Transitional National Council (TNC) with political responsibilities for a transitional period of two years.[311]

---

[307] For a closer analysis of the symptoms of this cycle, see Chopra, *Peace-Maintenance*, at 139.

[308] SC Res. 794 authorised the mission to use "all necessary means to establish as soon as possible a secure environment for humanitarian relief operations in Somalia".

[309] The absence of functioning state institutions encouraged the "warlord syndrome" which was at the heart of the Somali crisis. See Chopra, *Peace-Maintenance*, at 141.

[310] See para. 8 of SC Res. 814 of 26 March 1993.

[311] Under the Agreement, the TNC was vested with executive and legislative functions for a transitional period of two years (from 27 March 1993). The TNC was to be supplemented by eighteen Regional Councils and ninety-two District Councils. For a survey of the Agreement, see Chopra, *Peace-Maintenance*, at 156.

2.5.2.   An unsatisfactory mandate

The mandate of UNOSOM II, however, was poorly adjusted to the needs of the situation, and contradictory in its conception.[312] The official policy of the UN was to take a strong role in the maintenance of order and security, but to leave the process of political reconstruction and stabilisation primarily in the hands of the Somalis themselves. This approach was clearly expressed in a statement by the Secretary-General, who noted on 3 March 1993, shortly before the establishment of UNOSOM II by the Council:

[T]he political will to achieve security, reconciliation and peace must spring from the Somalis themselves. Even if it is authorised to resort to forceful action in certain circumstances, UNOSOM II cannot and must not be expected to substitute itself for the Somali people. Nor can or should it use its authority to impose one or another system of governmental organisation.[313]

The trust in domestic capacities and the corresponding reluctance of the UN formally to assume political power on its own initiative under the terms of Resolution 814 (1993) led to an asymmetric mandate. UNOSOM II maintained UNITAF's strong Chapter VII-based military enforcement powers. However, it was conceived as a "political gnome" in terms of civilian responsibilities. Resolution 814 construed UNOSOM II's civilian mandate as a governance assistance mission without clearly defined executive or legislative authority.[314] The Security Council merely "request[ed]" the Secretary-General to "assist" the people of Somalia in "the re-establishment of national and regional institutions and civil administration" and in "the restoration and maintenance of peace stability and law and order, including in the investigation ... prosecution of serious violations of international humanitarian law"[315] without granting UNOSOM II any real powers to implement these responsibilities. This weak and minimalist mandate stood in stark contrast to the overall goal of the mission, which was to rehabilitate the political institutions and economy of Somalia[316] and to "create conditions under which the

---

[312] Chopra speaks of "the contradictory logic of consent to enforcement". See *ibid.*, at 154.

[313] See Further Report of the Secretary-General, Submitted in Pursuance of Paragraphs 18 and 19 of Resolution 794 (1992), New York: S/25354, 3 March 1993, para. 92.

[314] It is quite telling that the provisions of UNOSOM II's civilian mandate are not included under the authorisation under Chapter VII in SC Res. 814 (1993).

[315] See paras. 4 b–d of SC Res. 814 (1993).

[316] See the chapeau of para. 4 of SC Res. 814 (1993).

Somali civil society may have a role at every level, in the process of reconciliation".[317]

2.5.3.   From assistance to *de facto* governance

Political disagreement among local leaders in the implementation of the Addis Abbaba accords and the resurgence of violence after the adoption of Resolution 814 forced the UN to deviate from its "hands off approach"[318] in practice. UNOSOM II had to fill the power vacuum created by the absence of a functioning government in the country, the shortage of organised civilian police and the lack of a court system. In order to respond to these challenges, the UN crossed over the limit of providing mere "assistance" and military presence.[319] Both UNITAF and UNOSOM II assumed a number of executive and legislative functions in the place of indigenous institutions. The TNC was formally charged with the exercise of administrative and legislative authority in Somalia under the Addis Ababa Agreement.[320] But the UN exercised these functions until the creation of the TNC, over one year after the conclusion of the Agreement.[321] Before the establishment of the TNC, UNITAF and UNOSOM II acted as the provisional governmental authorities in Somalia,[322] supported by a national "consultative body".[323] The focus of attention was devoted to the re-establishment of the judicial systems in Somalia. UNOSOM II adopted administrative measures to create an independent judiciary[324] and a functioning prison system.[325] Moreover, the Secretary-General's Special Representative to Somalia promulgated the former Somali Penal Code of 1962 as the criminal law in force in Somalia, while adding special *habeas corpus* guarantees derived from international human rights instruments.[326] Later, the UN closed down broadcasting facilities that

---

[317] See para. 4 g of SC Res. 814 (1993).

[318] See also Philipp, *Somalia - A Very Special Case*, at 540.

[319] See Chopra, *Peace-Maintenance*, at 141–2.

[320] See Article 1, Section 4 of the General Agreement signed in Addis Ababa on 8 January 1993, UN Doc. S/25168, Annex II (1993). See also *ibid.*, at 156.

[321] See the Reports of the Secretary-General on the situation in Somalia, Report of 12 November 1993, UN Doc. S/26738, para. 28 and Report of 6 January 1994, UN Doc. S/1994/12, para. 14.

[322] See Hufnagel, *UN-Friedensoperationen*, at 175 and 185. See also Chopra, *Peace-Maintenance*, at 142: "[I]n the absence of an existing infrastructure... the UN had effectively the power of a governor-in-trust."

[323] See Report of the Secretary-General of 12 November 1993, UN Doc. S/26738, para. 28.

[324] See Report of the Secretary-General of 17 August 1993, UN Doc. S/26317, Annex I, paras. 29 *et seq.*

[325] See *ibid.*, paras. 42 *et seq.*   [326] See *ibid.*, paras. 29, 31 and 36.

incited violence against UNOSOM,[327] and it assisted in the drafting of a new constitution for Somalia.[328]

2.5.4. The lack of a legal framework

The harsh divergence between theory and practice in the case of Somalia revealed very clearly the lack of a unified legal framework for the exercise of public authority and regulatory functions by UN missions. Due to the absence of a Security Council-authorised governing mandate, UNOSOM acted on many occasions on uncertain legal ground. Resolution 814 provided general guidelines for the conduct of the mission, but it failed to lay down principles for the treatment of detainees, the trial of war criminals and the relationship between the UN and domestic actors.[329] This legal vacuum created doubts and uncertainties as to the scope and limits of UN authority. In particular, it remained unclear whether UNOSOM was bound to comply with the provisions of the laws of occupation – an obligation recognised by Australian peacekeepers,[330] but denied by the Legal Advisor to the Special Representative of the Secretary-General.[331] Furthermore, disputes arose in the area of detentions. It was debated whether UN forces were entitled to detain Somalis captured during combat operations for purposes of prevention.[332] Finally, doubts were expressed as to whether the enactment of the Somali Penal Code was covered by the authority of the Secretary General's Special Representative to Somalia in the absence of an express delegation of governing authority to the latter under Resolution 814 (1993).[333]

2.5.5. Assessment

The UN engagement in Somalia was in many ways a learning experience for the organisation, not only because of its dramatic ending with open and direct attacks against UN peacekeepers, but also in terms of its legal and institutional design. The creation of UNOSOM II was a well-intended attempt to address the root causes of conflict through the assumption

---

[327] See Kelly, *Restoring and Maintaining Order*, at 88.
[328] See Report of 17 August 1993, paras. 25–9.
[329] See also the critique by Kelly, *Restoring and Maintaining Order*, at 70.
[330] *Ibid.*, at 79.   [331] See Chopra, *Peace-Maintenance*, at 143.
[332] *Ibid.*, at 143. For further discussion, see below Part IV, Chapter 15.
[333] See Report of the Commission of Inquiry Established Pursuant to Security Council Resolution 885 (1993) to Investigate Armed Attacks on UNOSOM II Personnel which Led to Casualties Among Them, UN Doc. S/1994/653 of 1 June 1994. Critical also, Danesh Sarooshi, *The United Nations and the Development of Collective Security* (1999), at 523. For a full discussion, see below Part 4, Chapter 15.

of managerial functions by the UN in fields such as civil reconstruction, refugee return and the restoration of the judiciary, instead of simply re-lieving symptoms through military enforcement action.[334] But the oper-ation suffered from the fact that UNOSOM was unable to remain a mere assistance force, and "unprepared" to assume the role of "statesman".[335] The UN realised only at a late stage of the mission that it needed to fos-ter political authority at the local and regional level. The reluctant law and order policy of the UN decreased the credibility and legitimacy of UNOSOM in the eyes of the Somalis,[336] and sent the message that peace-building in a direct conflict environment may require "a strong hand" and a strong civilian mandate – two strategies that the Secretary-General was unwilling to explore in 1993. These difficulties were compounded by the fact that UNOSOM lacked the support and cooperation of com-peting clan leaders.[337] Taken together, these factors eroded the soil for a lasting political engagement of the UN.

At the same time, the mission illustrated more than any previous UN mission the need for agreement on legal standards guiding the exercise of public authority by UN actors in a situation of conflict or transition. UNSOM was perceived by many Somalis as being "above the law", be-cause it lacked independent oversight which could consider grievances by the local population against the UN.[338] Similarly, the mission failed to recognise clear-cut obligations under human rights law and interna-tional humanitarian law, in particular, in the area of detentions. The Somalia experience marked, in this sense, the tip of the iceberg, which revealed a broader need to identify legal parameters guiding the UN generally in the exercise of public functions.[339]

---

[334] See also Sonia K. Han, *Building A Peace That Lasts: The United Nations and Post-Civil War Peacebuilding*, NYU Journal of International Law and Politics, Vol. 26 (1994), 837, at 862–7.

[335] See Chopra, *Peace-Maintenance*, at 146.

[336] See also Kelly, *Restoring and Maintaining Order*, at 88.

[337] See also the statement of the Representative of Spain at the occasion of the adoption of SC Res. 954 of 4 November 1994: "The Council's decision today to terminate the mandate of UNOSOM II ... cannot be construed as a failure of the United Nations' involvement in Somalia. It is rather evidence that without the effective co-operation of the parties involved any peacekeeping operation will be unable to reach all of its objectives." See UN Doc. S/PV.3447 of 4 November 1997.

[338] See para. 57 of the Comprehensive Report on Lessons from the United Nations Operation in Somalia.

[339] This shortcoming was only partially addressed by the UN in its Bulletin on the Observance by United Nations Forces of Humanitarian Law of 6 August 1999. See United Nations Secretary-General's Bulletin, ST/SGB/1999/13 of 6 August 1999, in ILM, Vol. 38 (1999), at 1656.

8   The systematisation of international governance

Although the UN engagement in Somalia was in many ways a reversion to the traditions and habits of the Cold War experiment in the Congo, the 1990s marked a conceptual turning point in UN practice. The organisation made increasing efforts to eliminate the root causes of conflict through the assumption of administering responsibilities, instead of merely combating the symptoms of violence. The theoretical cornerstone of the new UN agenda was Secretary-General Boutros-Ghali's *Agenda for Peace*,[1] which developed the concept of "post-conflict peace building", arguing that UN interventions require political, economic and social support structures in order to address the causes of conflict and to avoid a relapse into hostilities.[2] This new strategy was subsequently reaffirmed by the *Agenda for Democratisation*,[3] the *Brahimi* Report[4] and the practice of the Security Council which emphasised at the beginning of the new millennium that peacebuilding operations "should focus on fostering sustainable institutions and processes in areas such as sustainable development, the eradication of poverty and inequalities, transparent and

---

[1] See *An Agenda for Peace, Preventive Diplomacy, Peacemaking and Peace-Keeping*, Report of the Secretary-General, UN SCOR, 47th Sess., at 22, UN Doc. S/24111 (1992).

[2] As Boutros-Ghali later put it: "UN operations may now involve nothing less than the reconstruction of an entire society and state. This requires a comprehensive approach, over an extended period. Security is increasingly understood to involve social, economic, political and cultural aspects far beyond its traditional military dimension." See Boutros Boutros-Ghali, *Beyond Peacekeeping*, NYU Journal of International Law and Politics, Vol. 25 (1992), 115.

[3] See Boutros Boutros-Ghali, *An Agenda for Democratisation*, Supplement to Reports A/50/332 and A/51/512 on Democratisation, 17 December 1996, para. 17. ("Democracy within States ... fosters the evolution of the social contract upon which lasting peace can be built. In this way, a culture of democracy is fundamentally a culture of peace.")

[4] The report recommended, *inter alia*, a strengthening of rule of law institutions and the improvement of respect for human rights obligations in post-conflict environments.

accountable governance, the promotion of democracy, respect for human rights and the rule of law and the promotion of a culture of peace and non-violence".[5]

This agenda is reflected in the peacemaking practice of the UN in the 1990s. Peace-maintenance did not stand still at the ideal of the absence of violence ("negative peace") or the restoration of the *status quo ante*. Intervention was more systematically coupled with UN initiatives to reform the internal structure of conflict areas, or the will of the organisation to fill political, economic and legal gaps in post-conflict societies. The organisation began, in particular, to combine its practice in election monitoring with the exercise of governing authority. It conducted four missions within eight years, which encompassed the exercise of public authority *vis-à-vis* the inhabitants of post-conflict territories: UNTAC in Cambodia, UNTAES in Eastern Slavonia, UNMIK in Kosovo and UNTAET in East Timor. Moreover, the international community became involved in the administration of Bosnia – the pioneer experiment in long-term international governance in the 1990s.

The revival of comprehensive and complex formulas of governance and administration marked, to some extent, a return to the past. The transformation of UN administrators into "statesmen" and holders of public authority was accompanied by a sense of trust in robust models of international engagement that is not very different from the tradition of the League of Nations administrations in the Saar and Danzig and the UN experiments in Trieste and Jerusalem. The architecture of the UN mission in Kosovo shared striking parallels with the League's engagement in the Saar, both in terms of the scope of international authority (exclusive powers) and the objective of the mandate, namely provisional administration until the settlement of a status question under the authority of the administering power. The technique of delegation of powers, used by the four Cambodian factions to transfer authority to UNTAC under the Paris Accords,[6] may be traced back to the institutional model of delegation used under the Tangier arrangement,[7] through which the Sultan of Morocco endowed the international administration of Tangier with legislative and executive authority, while maintaining sovereignty over the territory.[8] The objective of the UN mission in Eastern Slavonia,

---

[5] See UN Doc. S/PRST/2001/5 of 20 February 2001.
[6] See Article 6 of the Agreement on the Political Settlement of the Cambodia Conflict.
[7] For an appraisal, see Korhonen and Gras, *International Governance*, at 80.
[8] See Article 5 of the Tangier arrangement.

namely to insulate the territory provisionally from the influence of former parties to a conflict, is comparable to the overall purpose of the League's one-year intervention in Leticia.[9]

Nevertheless, the basic parameters of the exercise of international authority evolved in several respects since the inter-war period and the end of World War II. International territorial administration took on a different face: it was primarily used as a vehicle for problem-solving, combining security and stabilisation agendas with the promotion of liberal democracy and institutional and legal reform in the administered territories. The establishment of UNTAC and UNTAET, and the international administration of Bosnia-Herzegovina were directly determined by the objectives of statebuilding and democratisation. Where considerations of transitional strategic neutralisation continued to remain relevant (such as in the cases of Kosovo and Eastern Slavonia), they were combined at least with elements of liberal reform and reconstruction. Furthermore, the UN did not limit itself to the exercise of executive or supervisory responsibilities, typical of the organisation's decolonisation (Libya, West Irian, West Sahara) and *ad hoc* practice (Congo, Somalia), but engaged in regulatory activism shaping the legal and institutional system of the administered territories along the long-term ideals of constitutional democracy.[10]

The renewed UN commitment to the assumption of governing and administering authority in the 1990s represented, in some ways, a progression. It marked a departure from a short-sighted and symptom relief-oriented concept of intervention; it strengthened the capacities of the UN to act as a "public authority by default" for the benefit of war-torn societies; and it contributed to the multilateralisation and legalisation of post-conflict relations, including a determination of the UN's own powers and responsibilities. However, the practice of the UN remained overshadowed by trials and errors. The UN assumed its function as surrogate governmental authority in the post-Cold War era without internal institutional adjustments, and without drawing lessons from the past. This shortcoming has exposed UN governance missions to various criticisms, such as an autocratic understanding of governance, placing UN authority over local ownership; an over-ambitious belief in the enforcement of liberal international standards; a lack of accountability, caused

---

[9] For an analysis of this aspect of the Leticia arrangement, see also Wilde, *From Danzig to East Timor*, at 588.

[10] This is a clear departure from the Cold War politics of neutrality and non-intervention, which characterised UN peacekeeping for four decades.

by the institutional and conceptual equation of UN governance to traditional peacekeeping; and a lack of institutional preparedness to deal
with comprehensive and long-term processes of statebuilding.

1. The United Nations transitional authority
in Cambodia (UNTAC)

The UN engagement in Cambodia marked the first systematic governance undertaking of the UN in the 1990s.[11] It presented a midway point
between the accidental UN governance experiences of the Cold War period and the comprehensive UN statebuilding missions of the mid- to
late 1990s. UNTAC exercised widespread governmental authority within
the framework and the confines of the institutional system of a state.
The 1991 Paris Accords on the Political Settlement of the Cambodia
conflict gave the UN a transitional co-governance role in the administration of the country, to be exercised in cooperation with the Supreme
National Council – "the unique legitimate body and source of authority in which ... the sovereignty, independence and unity of Cambodia"
resided.[12]

The UN assumed a governance and administration role that went beyond the traditional boundaries of "impasse management"[13] and encompassed broader responsibilities than the mandate of UNTEA. But the
scope of UN engagement did not yet quite reach the depth of the UN
mandates in Kosovo and East Timor. The grant of governmental authority
to UNTAC was linked to a very specific purpose: the creation of a "neutral political environment conducive to free and fair general elections"
within a "period not to exceed eighteen months".[14] This strict time-
limit restricted the exercise of regulatory activities by UNTAC largely to

---

[11] See generally, Ratner, *Cambodia Settlement*, at 1; Ratner, *The New Peacekeeping*, at 132;
Doyle, *UN Peacekeeping in Cambodia*, at 13; Findlay, *Cambodia: The Legacy and Lessons of
UNTAC*, at 3; Fen Osler Hampson, *Nurturing Peace: Why Peace Settlements Succeed or Fail*
(1996), 171; Mari Katayanagi, *Human Rights Functions of United Nations Peacekeeping
Operations* (2002) 101; Criswell, *Durable Consent*, 577; Nhan T. Vu, *The Holding of Free and
Fair Elections in Cambodia: The Achievement of the United Nations Impossible Mission*,
Michigan Journal of International Law, Vol. 16 (1995), 1177; Chesterman, *You, the People*,
at 73–5; Lucy Keller, *UNTAC in Cambodia – from Occupation, Civil War and Genocide to Peace*,
Max Planck Yearbook of United Nations Law, Vol. 9 (2005), 127–78; Dobbins, *UN's Role in
Nation-Building*, at 69–90.
[12] See Article 3 of the Agreement on the Political Settlement of the Cambodia Conflict of
October 23, 1991, in ILM, Vol. 31 (1992), 183.
[13] See Ratner, *Cambodia Settlement*, at 41.
[14] See Article 6 of the Agreement on the Political Settlement of the Cambodia Conflict.

security and electoral matters. Furthermore, the factual dependency on local consent and institutional power-sharing constrained the decision-making power and constructivism of the Special Representative of the Secretary-General. UNTAC therefore turned out to be a "moderate" state-building mission in practice. It encountered two types of criticism – a lack of time and enforcement power to create the conditions for sustainable democratic change and a lack of will on behalf of the UN to assume active responsibilities in the post-election phase.[15]

1.1. A consensual origin

UNTAC was established in response to a "governance problem" in Cambodia after twenty years of civil unrest. After the end of the Pol Pot regime in 1979, through the intervention of Vietnamese troops, Cambodia was split into two political camps: the Vietnam-supported regime of the People's Republic of Kampuchea, which later renamed itself the State of Cambodia, and the resistance's National Government of Cambodia, composed of three factions: the United National Front For an Independent, Neutral, Peaceful and Cooperative Cambodia (FUNCINPEC), led by Prince Sihanouk; the Khmer People's National Liberation Front (KPNLF), a pro-Western movement; and the Party of Democratic Kampuchea, the political wing of the Khmer Rouge.[16] The idea of the creation of UNTAC emerged as a result of the failure of both sides to agree on a commonly accepted single government. The two competing governments were unable to reach agreement on power-sharing structures for the peace process in Cambodia. This deadlock was overcome by a double arrangement negotiated at the Paris Conference. Instead of establishing one single government, the parties agreed to create the Supreme National Council (SNC), composed of all four political factions, which was designed to serve as a quadripartite transitional government until the holding of supervised free elections. At the same time, the SNC delegated in advance "all powers necessary to ensure the implementation" of the Paris Accords to the UN, in order to ensure both viable governance and the creation of a politically neutral climate for the elections.[17]

This formula was a clever tactical move. It avoided the imposition of trusteeship or exclusive international governance – two approaches that were opposed by the Cambodian factions and the Security Council itself.[18] Instead, the Paris Accords built a transitional, mixed

---

[15] See Criswell, *Durable Consent*, at 608.   [16] See Ratner, *The New UN Peacekeeping*, at 142–5.
[17] See Article 6 of the Agreement on the Political Settlement of the Cambodia Settlement.
[18] See Ratner, *Cambodia Settlements*, at 9.

national-international governance structure on the "torso of consent" existing among the local parties. The four factions "invit[ed] the United Nations Security Council to establish [UNTAC] with civilian and military components under the direct responsibility of the Secretary-General" in the Agreement of the Political Settlement of the Cambodia Conflict.[19] The Security Council followed that request by establishing UNTAC as a co-governance mission in Resolution 745 of 28 February 1992,[20] without having to overcome the prohibition of the interference in the domestic affairs of UN members under Article 2(7) of the Charter.[21]

1.2. A balanced statebuilding mandate

In terms of its mandate, UNTAC was the prototype of a statebuilding mission of the 1990s. Its function was to combine the maintenance of security with the promotion of democratic change and individual rights in a socially and politically unstable environment – two objectives which began to gain constant and systematic attention after the end of the Cold War in the practice of UN peace-maintenance. Conceptually, UNTAC was built to a large extent on the success and the strategy of UNTAG in Namibia. However, the UN mission in Cambodia was, from its inception, endowed with a stronger civilian mandate than UNTAG, in order to promote the advancement of the carefully drafted and fragile Cambodian peace settlement.

UNTAC shared governmental authority with domestic institutions. The SNC maintained the right to initiate regulatory measures, but the UN-appointed Special Representative held a significant a degree of control over the exercise of public authority by the SNC. The UN acted, first of all, as a public authority by default, entitled to intervene in the case of a deadlock in the SNC. UNTAC's power to adopt acts concerning the implementation of the peace settlement was expressly stated in Annex 1 of the Agreement on the Political Settlement of the Cambodia Conflict, which authorised the UN Special Representative to act on the basis of automatic transfer of authority in cases where the President of the SNC failed to reach agreement in the Council.[22] Furthermore, the UN Special Representative was empowered to overrule decisions of the Cambodian factions which he considered to be inconsistent with the settlement. UNTAC had to comply with the SNC's "advice" only if the advice was "consistent with the objectives of the...Agreement" as determined by

---

[19] See Article 2 of the Agreement on the Political Settlement of the Cambodia Conflict.
[20] See SC Res. 745 of 28 February 1992.   [21] See also Ratner, *Cambodia Settlements*, at 12.
[22] See Section A, para. 2 (c) and (d) of Annex 1 to the Agreement on the Political Settlement of the Cambodia Conflict.

the head of UNTAC.[23] These two prerogatives vested the UN with a watch-dog function in the regulatory field, which revealed UNTAC's dual capacity: its role as an independent external actor and its function as a governing institution of Cambodia under the institutional framework of the Paris Accords.

UNTAC held even more extensive executive responsibilities. The peace settlement placed all administrative agencies, bodies and offices acting in the politically sensitive fields of "foreign affairs, national defence, finance, public security and information" under "the direct control of UNTAC".[24] The UN administrator was authorised to issue binding directives concerning administrative agencies operating in the above-mentioned fields.[25] Civil police were subordinated to "UNTAC supervision or control".[26] Moreover, the UN Special Representative possessed two important prerogatives *vis-à-vis* "administrative agencies, bodies and agencies of all the Cambodian parties": the right of unrestricted access "to all administrative operations and information"[27]; and the authority to "require the removal of any personnel" of these entities.[28] Only the League of Nations had exercised executive powers of a comparable depth and breadth.[29]

UNTAC's supervisory and executive authority in the field of civil administration was closely linked to additional responsibilities in two other areas which are typical of modern statebuilding missions, namely the organisation of elections and the protection of human rights. The basic framework of these tasks was regulated by the peace settlement. As a guardian and guarantor of democratic transition in Cambodia, UNTAC had full responsibility for the organisation and conduct of elections to a new Cambodian Constituent Assembly,[30] which in turn was to draft and adopt a new Cambodian Constitution and should later transform itself into a legislative Assembly.[31] This electoral mandate was connected to a human rights mandate. The Paris Accords charged UNTAC with the

---

[23] See the Agreement on the Political Settlement of the Cambodia Conflict, Annex 1, para. 2 (a) and (b).
[24] See *ibid.*, Annex 1, Section B, para. 1.
[25] Ibid.   [26] See *ibid.*, Annex 1, Section B, para. 5 (b).
[27] See *ibid.*, Annex 1, Section B, para. 4 (a).   [28] See *ibid.*, Annex 1, Section B, para. 4 (b).
[29] For a discussion of the Saar administration, see above Part B, Chapter I.
[30] See Article 12 of the Agreement on the Political Settlement of the Cambodia Conflict.
[31] The elections were to be held "in accordance with a system of proportional representation on the basis of lists of candidates put forward by political parties". See para. 2 of Annex 3 to the Agreement on the Political Settlement of the Cambodia Conflict.

facilitation of the repatriation of refugees and displaced persons,[32] "the investigation of human rights complaints"[33] and "general human rights oversight during the transitional period",[34] both in order to foster a free and fair environment with respect for freedoms of speech, assembly and movement and equal access to the media for the elections,[35] and to accommodate local actors to the liberal and pluralist foundations of the Cambodia's new constitutional system, which was to contain a declaration of fundamental rights based on modern standards[36] and special human rights enforcement mechanisms[37], in order to overcome "Cambodia's tragic recent history".

Overall, the architecture of the Paris settlement was a well-balanced compromise. It maintained local decision-making power and gave the four factions an incentive to take political responsibilities into their own hands through consensual action.[38] UNTAC, on the other hand, enjoyed the powers necessary to smooth over the process of transition and to avoid the dominance of one Cambodian faction over the other. International human rights obligations and Western standards of governance were not imposed by the UN Special Representative, but were undertaken by the state of Cambodia itself under Part III[39] (Human Rights) and Annex 5[40] (Principles for a New Constitution for Cambodia[41]) of the political settlement. This mechanism of voluntary self-commitment absolved UNTAC formally from the reproach of the imposition of

[32] See Articles 19 and 20 of the Agreement on the Political Settlement of the Cambodia Conflict.

[33] See Section E, para. (c) of Annex 2 to the Agreement on the Political Settlement of the Cambodia Conflict.

[34] See *ibid.*, Section E, para. (b).

[35] See para. 9 of Annex 3 to the Agreement on the Political Settlement of the Cambodia Conflict.

[36] See para. 2 of Annex 5 to the Agreement on the Political Settlement of the Cambodia Conflict.

[37] *Ibid.*

[38] See Section A, para. 2 (a) of Annex 1 to the Agreement on the Political Settlement of the Cambodia Conflict: "The SNC offers advice to UNTAC which will comply with this advice provided there is a consensus among the members of the SNC and provided this advice is consistent with the objectives of the ... Agreement."

[39] See Article 15 of the Agreement on the Political Settlement of the Cambodia Conflict.

[40] See paras. 4 and 5 of Annex 5 which contain the Principles for a New Constitution of Cambodia: "The Constitution will state that Cambodia will follow a system of liberal democracy, in the basis of pluralism ... An independent judiciary will be established, empowered to enforce the rights under the constitution."

[41] For an analysis of the Cambodian Constitution, see Stephen P. Marks, *The New Cambodian Constitution: From Civil Law to a Fragile Democracy*, Columbia Human Rights Law Review, Fall 1994, 45–110.

governance structures[42] – a criticism that was later voiced in relation to UNMIK and UNTAET.

1.3.   "Looking big, acting small" – challenges in implementation

The practical implementation of this mandate, however, proved to be more difficult than anticipated by the drafters of the Paris Accords. The UN Representative of the Secretary-General had to strike a delicate balance between mediation and authoritative action in decision-making. Furthermore, the scope of UNTAC's responsibilities exceeded its operational capacities.

1.3.1.   Cooperation with domestic authorities

The main challenge that UNTAC faced in practical terms was the interaction with local actors. Due to the persistence of rivalries and power struggles among the four Cambodian factions, the country's peace process remained fragile.[43] Each of the four powerful groups had different interests and perceptions as to the implementation of the Paris Accords. UN action that was directed against one of the factions or perceived by them as an assault on its interests met with fierce resistance and triggered complaints of bias.[44] In particular, the Khmer Rouge and the State of Cambodia, the two parties which feared a loss of authority and control, remained opposed to UNTAC's action and viewed the SNC as the only legitimate governing entity[45] – an interpretation that was based on the wording of Article 3 of the Political Settlement ("the unique legitimate body and source of authority"), but failed to take into account the Council's delegation of power to UNTAC under Article 6 of the same agreement.

The lack of cooperation by local factions created regular problems in the monitoring and supervision of domestic institutions. Cambodian officials tried to bypass UNTAC control, by establishing informal and

---

[42] But see the broader socio-cultural critique by Rami Mani, *Conflict Resolution, Justice and the Law: Rebuilding the Rule of Law in the Aftermath of Complex Political Emergencies*, International Peacekeeping, Vol. 5 (1998), 6, at 8, who argues that international legal experts introduced a new legal and social tradition that ignored local customs.

[43] See also Chopra, *Peace-Maintenance*, at 47, who points out that UNTAC "tested the ability of the UN to exercise authority not just independently, but in spite of four intransigent and well-defined factions" each of which had "controlled Phnom Penh at one time or another and so had a historical reference point as a basis of unity and for determining membership".

[44] See Ratner, *The New UN Peacekeeping*, at 158.   [45] *Ibid.*, at 159.

concealed channels of communication.[46] Furthermore, UNTAC administrators met "resistance in providing information or obeying orders at national and local levels of government".[47] The Khmer Rouge denied UNTAC officials access to territory under their control.[48] In other cases, UNTAC initiatives were blocked by contrary action at the domestic level.[49]

UNTAC's standing was further compromised by its particular institutional dispute settlement function. The power-sharing mechanism under Annex 1, which empowered UNTAC to act by way of a transfer of authority from Prince Sihanouk in cases where the SNC failed to agree by consensus, had a negative side-effect. It turned UNTAC into an authority of last resort that was charged with problem-solving in all areas that required unpopular decision-making.[50] These two factors and the lack of experience of the UN in the conduct of modern governance missions[51] hampered UNTAC's determination to impose far-reaching reforms without local consent and led the UN Special Representative to exercise his mandate with caution and restraint.

Mr Yasushi Akashi, the UN administrator, conceived UNTAC essentially as a "custodian of the Paris Accords".[52] He exercised his wide regulatory and executive powers rather reluctantly. In order to avoid public confrontation, Akashi refrained as far as possible from removing public representatives or officials of the four political factions by force. If he decided to remove or reassign personnel, mostly on grounds of corruption, he did so in the form of a simple request, instead of ordering the removal by binding decisions.[53] A similar attitude characterised UNTAC's other activities. UNTAC's human rights component investigated a large number of complaints, but avoided pronouncing sanctions or

---

[46] It is reported that a document by the Cambodian government instructed domestic officials to maintain "the initiative with regard to the storage of documents to prevent control of them by UNTAC". See Dobbins, *The UN's Role in Nation-Building*, at 84.

[47] *Ibid.*, at 83.   [48] *Ibid.*, at 84.

[49] UNTAC introduced a new passport and visa system in order to reduce corruption and cross-border smuggling. This aim of this effort was, however, defeated by the policy of the government which continued to issue its own entry visas. *Ibid.*

[50] For example, UNTAC rejected a proposal by the Khmer Rouge to base the voter registration of Vietnamese settlers on ethnic criteria. The Secretary-General noted that the "extension of the franchise on purely ethnic grounds to persons who were not born in Cambodia would not be consistent with the letter or the spirit of the Paris Agreements". See Third Progress Report of the Secretary-General on the United Nations Transitional Authority in Cambodia, UN Doc. S/25124 (1993), at 8.

[51] See also Findlay, *Cambodia: The Legacy and Lessons of UNTAC*, at 137.

[52] See Ratner, *The New UN Peacekeeping*, at 199.   [53] *Ibid.*, at 176 and 199.

publicly offending human rights violators.[54] Moreover, the UN Special Representative sought to encourage consensual decision-making in the SNC,[55] instead of imposing regulations on the four factions.[56] He overruled local objections to regulatory measures only in electoral matters and in the last period of UNTAC's mission, when the Khmer Rouge boycotted the sessions of the SNC.[57] Although this policy had a stabilising short-term effect, it exposed UNTAC to the criticism of inefficiency.

1.3.2. Capacity gaps

Two other factors compromised the accomplishment of UNTAC's ambitious mandate:[58] a lack of resources and the absence of a reliable judicial system in Cambodia. UNTAC's broad role in governance and administration on paper contrasted with its operational capacities. Because of its limited size, the mission was, in particular, unable to exercise extensive executive control over state agencies in the five major areas of foreign affairs, defence, information, security and finance. UNTAC established local offices in the Cambodian provinces, deployed personnel to Cambodia's ministries and administration[59] and created a border control unit to monitor customs and immigration.[60] However, the "[b]arely 200 UN civil administrators" were hardly able to exercise in-depth control over estimated 140,000 domestic civil servants.[61] The mission decided therefore to focus its activities in civil administration on matters closely related to the elections.[62] This strategy, namely a clear focus on elections, continued to dominate the exercise of public authority by UNTAC.

---

[54] Ibid., at 196 and 201.

[55] During the period of UN administration, the SNC adopted a number of measures, including decisions on the receipt of foreign aid and the definition of foreign forces to be banned from the territory, and the promulgation of domestic penal law. See ibid., at 185.

[56] The UN Secretary-General described the SNC as a forum of dialogue and "focal point of the United Nations relationship Cambodia". See the Report of the Secretary-General on Cambodia of 19 February 1992, UN Doc. S/23613. For a more UN-dominated assessment of the SNC's activities, see Korhonen and Gras, International Governance, at 142.

[57] Ibid., at 185–6.

[58] For a critique of the scope of UNTAC's mandate, see Ken Berry, UNTAC: A Flawed Paradigm/Success, in The United Nations Transitional Authority in Cambodia (UNTAC): Debriefing and Lessons, Report of the 1994 Singapore Conference (1995), at 244.

[59] UNTAC officials held weekly meetings with domestic decision-makers. See Dobbins, The UN's Role in Nation-Building, at 83.

[60] See Doyle, UN Peacekeeping in Cambodia, at 37.

[61] See Dobbins et al., UN's Role in Nation-Building, at 82.

[62] See Ratner, The New UN Peacekeeping, at 173. See also Korhonen and Gras, International Governance, at 139.

Moreover, the absence of a functioning judicial system in Cambodia hampered UN activity in the field of human rights protection and the restoration of the rule of law. Because of the lack of effective domestic institutions, UNTAC itself took active steps to improve the human rights situation. UNTAC encouraged the SNC, *inter alia*, to adopt regulations setting standards for judiciary and criminal proceedings.[63] Acting under Articles 6 and 16 of the Political Settlement, UNTAC elaborated the Transitional Criminal Provisions in Directive No. 93/1,[64] which were subsequently adopted by the SNC,[65] but were criticised as interfering with Cambodian sovereignty.[66] The same Directive established procedures for the prosecution of human rights violations, and vested an UNTAC Special Prosecutor with the authority to arrest and try people for serious human rights violations within the courts of Cambodia.[67] But UNTAC's

---

[63] See Findlay, *Cambodia: The Legacy and Lessons of UNTAC*, at 64.
[64] See Directive No. 93/1 from the Special Representative of the Secretary-General establishing procedures for the Prosecution of persons responsible for Human Rights violations, 6 January 1993. See also United Nations, Third Progress Report of the Secretary-General on UNTAC, UN Doc. S/25154 of 25 January 1993, para. 103.
[65] See Provisions Relating to the Judiciary and Criminal Law and Procedure Applicable in Cambodia During the Transitional Period, adopted by the Supreme National Council by decision of 10 September 1992. The State of Cambodia later adopted its own law on criminal procedure on 29 January 1993. Its relationship to the UNTAC transitional code was unclear. The new law was considered by some as being supplementary to the UNTAC transitional provisions, while others argued that the new Criminal Code was meant to replace the UNTAC transitional law.
[66] See Katayanagi, *Human Rights Functions*, at 116.
[67] Directive No. 93/1 stated: "UNTAC will take the initiative: 1. To prosecute cases involving serious human rights violations; 2. For the purpose of such prosecutions, UNTAC will review investigations carried out by all UNTAC components recommending criminal law prosecutions of serious violations of human rights, particularly of officials, police, or military officers of existing administrative structures. UNTAC shall have discretion as to whether cases are taken up for prosecution or not; 3. UNTAC officers, authorised by the Special Representative of the Secretary-General, will have the powers to issue warrants for the arrest and detention of suspects; take appropriate action for protection of witnesses and other persons deemed by UNTAC to require protection; and prosecute cases before the Cambodian trial courts and, where appropriate, before the appellate courts; 4. UNTAC Civil Police and Military will exercise the powers to make arrests and detain suspects for the purposes of such prosecutions; 5. Duly authorised UNTAC officers will be recognised by the judicial apparatus of all existing administrative structures of Cambodia as having jurisdiction to perform all functions necessary in the fulfillment of their duties, and shall have standing to appear before all courts in Cambodia on behalf of UNTAC. All existing administrative structures within Cambodia shall allow access to and use of courts, court resources and prisons wherein persons arrested under this process shall be held. 6. All relevant provisions of the Provisions Relating to the Judiciary and Criminal Law and Procedure Applicable in Cambodia During the

prosecution efforts were compromised by its lack of enforcement powers and the lack of local courts or their (politically motivated) refusal to conduct proceedings.[68]

1.4. Assessment

UNTAC's track record was mixed.[69] The main achievement of the temporary UN presence in Cambodia was that it laid the political and legal groundwork for the Cambodian elections[70] and some foundations for the country's transition to a new constitutional system. UNTAC's exercise of executive control over domestic agencies limited public corruption and improved the functioning of Cambodia's ministries.[71] UNTAC's Human Rights Component initiated important reforms, both in the sector of criminal procedure and detention, ranging from the elaboration of the Transitional Criminal Provisions to the establishment of a Prisons Control Commission,[72] and technical assistance in the drafting of Cambodia's Constitution.[73] UNTAC's information component facilitated the conditions for freedom of press by removing restrictions on the media.[74] Furthermore, UNTAC managed successfully to organise and conduct the Cambodian elections and repatriated a large number of refugees and displaced persons in accordance with its mandate under the peace settlement. These are considerable achievements, especially in the light of the mission's short eighteen-month presence in Cambodia.

The operation was not, however, free from criticism. Despite the previous undertakings of the UN in Namibia and West Irian, UNTAC was in many ways another *ad hoc* experience of the organisation. UNTAC's mandate was predetermined by the Paris Peace Settlement. But the UN itself had little time for the preparation and planning of the operation. Moreover, the breadth of the mandate exceeded UNTAC's capacities, and had to be narrowed in practice. UNTAC, for example, never fully succeeded

---

Transitional Period, adopted on 10 September 1992, shall be read so as to extend to UNTAC officers all powers necessary for the execution of the tasks and functions referred to in paragraphs 3, 4, and 5 above. In particular, the terms prosecutor shall include duly authorised UNTAC officers and the term 'police' shall include UNTAC Civil Police and Military wherever such terms appear in the said provisions. 7. Any person prosecuted by UNTAC shall be accorded all rights of defense and clue process as are provided in the applicable criminal law referred to in paragraph 6 above." See generally Ratner, *The New UN Peacekeeping*, at 181–2.

[68] See below Part IV, Chapter 16.   [69] See also Keller, *UNTAC in Cambodia*, at 167–9.
[70] See also Dobbins, *UN's Role in Nation-Building*, at 89.
[71] See Ratner, *The New Peacekeeping*, at 177.
[72] For a survey, see Katayanagi, *Human Rights Functions*, at 119.
[73] *Ibid.*, at 120–4.   [74] See Dobbins, *UN's Role in Nation-Building*, at 84.

in establishing a neutral political environment in Cambodia. The UN administration operated successfully in areas which required little co-operation with the four factions, such as the organisation and conduct of the elections or the repatriation of refugees.[75] It failed, however, to disarm the military wings of the conflicting factions, or to reduce the fundamental tensions between the four groups[76] – shortcomings which exposed UNTAC to the criticism of temporary conflict management and political short-sightedness.

This critique was further reinforced by the weak post-conflict engagement of the UN. The organisation did not have a firm or well-defined closure strategy. The elections were virtually regarded by UNTAC as an end in itself, allowing the international community to withdraw from the peace process.[77] This methodology reduced the prospects of lasting democratic reform.

2. The United Nations transitional administration for Eastern Slavonia (UNTAES)

The establishment of the UN Transitional Administration for Eastern Slavonia, Baranja and Western Sirmium (UNTAES)[78] set off a new tradition of Chapter VII-based UN governance missions in the mid-1990s, which formed the political and legal high-water mark of UN territorial administration in terms of authority. UNTAES was a short-lived, two-year project[79] with a very specific goal, namely the peaceful transfer of

---

[75] See Michael W. Doyle and Nishkala Suntharalingam, The UN in Cambodia: Lessons for Complex Peacekeeping, International Peacekeeping, Vol. 1 (1994), at 130.

[76] See Ratner, The New UN Peacekeeping, at 190.

[77] The results of the 1993 elections were accepted by all parties and led to the formation of a coalition government. But Cambodia as a state remained a divided and unstable polity. Four years after the 1993 elections Prime Minister Hun Sen seized political power in a military coup. For a criticism of the lack of an "exit" strategy, see also Chesterman, You, the People, at 224–5; Korhonen and Gras, International Governance, at 137; Susan S. Gibson, The Misplaced Reliance on Free and Fair Elections in Nation-Building: The Role of Constitutional Democracy and the Rule of Law, Houston Journal of International Law, Vol. 21 (1998), 1, at 43. See also below Part IV, Chapter 16.

[78] See generally Derek Boothy, The Political Challenges of Administering Eastern Slavonia, Global Governance, Vol. 10 (2004), 37; Bothe, The Peace Process in Eastern Slavonia, at 6; Johan Schoups, Peacekeeping and Transitional Administration in Eastern Slavonia, in Peacebuilding: A Field Guide (Luc Reychler and Thania Paffenholz eds., 2001), at 389. See also Katayanagi, Human Rights Functions, at 191; Korhonen, Gras and Creutz, International Post-Conflict Situations, 126–31; Chesterman, You, The People, at 70–2; Dobbins, UN's Role in Nation-Building, at 107–27.

[79] The mandate of UNTAES ended on 15 January 1998.

Eastern Slavonia from Serb to Croatian control.[80] The UN acted from the beginning of the mission as the exclusive governing authority in a post-conflict environment, with a multiplicity of daily life functions to be exercised on behalf of Croatia, the formal territorial sovereign,[81] and for the benefit of the Serb-Croatian population of the territory. This experience provided some of the conceptual groundwork for the two major UN governance engagements at the end of the 1990s, UNMIK and UNTAET.

2.1. A dual function

UNTAES had a dual function: a dispute settlement function, encompassing responsibilities for the transfer of territory of Eastern Slavonia, Baranja and Western Sirmium to Croatia (the "reintegration function"), and a "statebuilding function", involving tasks of reconstruction.

The main purpose of the mission was to facilitate the peaceful reintegration of the three regions of the formerly Serb controlled Republika Srpska Krajina into Croatia. All three areas possessed a significant Serbian community and had come under Serbian control in the Yugoslav conflict after Croatia's declaration of independence. After the ending of hostilities, both sides agreed to reintegrate the region into Croatia under the terms of the Basic Agreement on the Region of Eastern Slavonia, Baranja and Western Sirmium (The "Erdut Agreement"),[82] following a transitional period of UN administration, designed to reduce the mutual tensions and the deep-rooted mistrust between the Croatian government and local Serbs.[83] The Security Council accepted a corresponding request from the two parties[84] in its Resolution 1037 (1996),[85]

---

[80] Croatia wished to regain sovereignty over the territory. The Serb side, by contrast, sought a settlement which would accommodate the interests of Serb population.

[81] The Security Council reaffirmed in its Resolution 1037 (1996) "that the territories of Eastern Slavonia, Baranja and Western Sirmium are integral parts of the Republic of Croatia". See para. 2 of the preamble of SC Res. 1037.

[82] See Basic Agreement on the Region of Eastern Slavonia, Baranja and Western Sirmium between Serbia and Croatia of 12 November 1995, UN Doc. S/1995/951, Annex, entered into force on 22 November 1995, reproduced in ILM, Vol. 35 (1996), p. 184.

[83] The parties asked the UN Security Council to establish a Transitional Administration to "govern the region during the transitional period [of 12 months] in the interests of all persons resident in or returning to the region". See para. 1 of the Agreement.

[84] The Council determined "that the situation in Croatia continues to constitute a threat to international peace and security" and expressly invoked Chapter VII in para. 10 of the preamble of SC Res. 1037.

[85] See SC Res. 1037 of 15 January 1996, UN Doc. S/RES/1037.

and established UNTAES under Chapter VII in order to "support the parties in their effort to provide for a peaceful settlement of their disputes, and thus to contribute to achievement of peace in the region as a whole".[86]

It was clear, however, that territorial dispute settlement alone would not suffice to create a peaceful and stable environment for the transition. Large parts of the region's infrastructure were destroyed, and peace efforts in the Serb-controlled areas were compromised by lawlessness and the fear of Croatian military and police action.[87] This geopolitical reality made it necessary to combine transitional administration with the exercise of statebuilding functions, including the re-establishment "of the normal functioning of all public services in the Region",[88] the promotion of the return of refugees and displaced persons,[89] the creation of police forces "to build professionalism among the police and confidence among all ethnic communities",[90] and the restoration of human rights protection, in particular property rights.[91] The Security Council recognised this necessity and vested UNTAES with a strong civilian mandate,[92] including, *inter alia*, the responsibility:

   a. To establish a temporary police force, define its structure and size...and oversee its implementation...
   b. To undertake tasks relating to civil administration...
   c. To undertake tasks relating to the functioning of public services...
   d. To facilitate the return of refugees....
   e. To organise elections, to assist in their conduct, and to certify the results...; and
   f. To monitor the parties' compliance with their commitment, as specified in the Basic Agreement, to respect the highest standards of human rights and fundamental freedoms.[93]

The UN engagement in Eastern Slavonia implied therefore much broader responsibilities than a mere transfer of territory *à la* West Irian. It amounted *de facto* to a combined dispute settlement and statebuilding mission with parallels to UNTEA and UNTAC.

---

[86] See para. 7 of the preamble of SC Res. 1037 (1996).

[87] See the Report of the Secretary-General Pursuant to Security Council Resolution 1025 (1995), UN Doc. S/1995/1028 of 13 December 1995, para. 4.

[88] See para. 4 of the Erdut Agreement.   [89] *Ibid*.

[90] See para. 5 of the Erdut Agreement.   [91] See paras. 7–9 of the Erdut Agreement.

[92] For the recommendation of the Secretary-General, see paras. 15–18 of UN Doc. S/1995/1028.

[93] See paras. 11 and 12 of SC Res. 1037 (1996).

2.2. The institutional design

UNTAES was required to exercise its transitional authority over Eastern Slavonia, Baranja and Western Sirmium as a trustee. This followed from paragraph 2 of the Erdut Agreement, which stated expressly that the Transitional Administration should "govern the Region during the transitional period in the interests of all persons resident in or returning to the Region".[94]

The model of governance adopted by the Security Council in order to implement the parties' request for transitional UN administration was in part a reaction to the difficulties encountered by UNTAC under the power-sharing arrangement of the Paris Accords.[95] The Council refrained from establishing a system of governance under which UNTAES would be obliged to share its powers with domestic institutions such as the Cambodian SNC. Local actors were allowed to participate in the governance and administration through a Transitional Council, to be composed of "one representative each of the Government of Croatia, the local Serb population, the Local Croat population and other minorities".[96] But the decisions of this Council remained purely "advisory in nature".[97] The UN administrator (Jacques Klein) exercised executive and legislative powers[98] in accordance with paragraph 2 of SC Resolution 1037 (1996), which granted the UN Special Representative "the overall authority over the civilian and military components of UNTAES".[99]

This exclusive governance mandate, based on the Erdut Agreement,[100] on the one hand, and a binding Chapter VII Resolution,[101] one the other, created a novel territorial situation for the region of Eastern Slavonia, Baranja and Western Sirmium during the period of international administration. The exercise of public authority did not coincide with ownership over the territory. UNTAES constituted the only legitimate government, whereas Croatia remained the territorial sovereign.[102]

---

[94] See para. 2 of the Erdut Agreement.
[95] See also Katayanagi, *Human Rights Functions*, at 191.
[96] See para. 14 of UN Doc. S/1995/1028.   [97] *Ibid.*
[98] See also para. 17 of UN Doc. S/1995/1028.
[99] See para. 2 of Security Council Resolution 1037. See also para. 14 of UN Doc. S/1995/1028. ("[T]he transitional administrator alone would have executive power and he would not have to obtain the consent of either the [transitional] council or the parties for his decisions.")
[100] See para. 2 of the Erdut Agreement, which fails to impose express limitations on the scope of UN governance ("which shall govern the Region").
[101] See para. 10 of the preamble of SC Res. 1037 (1996) ("acting under Chapter VII of the Charter of the United Nations") and para. 11 of the resolution ("decides").
[102] See para. 2 of the preamble of SC Res. 1037 (1996).

Security Council Resolution 1037 (1996) did not specify in detail, how UNTAES was to exercise its authority.[103] The administration itself opted for a model which was based on "supervision and oversight", rather than "direction and control".[104] Following the recommendation in the Report of the Secretary-General, the UN administrator exercised his authority with the help of "functional implementation committees". The committees were composed of Serb and Croat representatives and led by UNTAET. They enjoyed responsibilities in all sectors of public life, over which UNTAES was responsible for, namely, police, civil administration, public services, education and culture, return of displaced persons, human rights and elections.[105] The main advantage of the technique was that it offered a forum for dialogue and exchange between Serb and Croat representatives on a variety of public issues, such as agricultural and rural issues, property records and public utilities.[106] In addition, UNTAES established regional liaison offices, which followed the work of Serb Executive Councils and assemblies.[107]

The government of the Republic of Croatia was obliged to cooperate fully with the UN administration.[108] When it failed to fulfil its responsibilities, UNTAES reported the matter to the Security Council. The Council reacted promptly and directly in such situations. It even used its Chapter VII powers to compel Croatia to undertake specific measures for the implementation of the Erdut Agreement, such as the removal of administrative and legal obstacles to the return of refugees,[109] the payment of pensions to persons returning to their homes[110] and the elimination of ambiguities in the implementation of a Croatian Amnesty Law.[111]

2.3. Practice

The exercise of public authority by UNTAES did not by any means reach the scope and variety of action undertaken by UNMIK or UNTAET. But the UN administration was successful in accomplishing its main

---

[103] Paragraph 11 (b) of SC Res. 1037 (1996) authorises UNTAET to "undertake tasks relating to civil administration, as set out in paragraph 16 (b) of the Secretary-General's report".

[104] For a detailed survey, see Boothby, *Political Challenges of Administering Eastern Slavonia*, at 41.

[105] See para. 16 (a)–(h) of UN Doc. S/1995/1028.

[106] Boothby notes that "the mutual hostility between Serbs and Croats was at first so high that it was often difficult to get them in the same room and have a meaningful exchange". See Boothby, *Political Challenges of Administering Eastern Slavonia*, at 49.

[107] *Ibid.*, at 41.   [108] See para. 13 of the Erdut Agreement.

[109] See para. 4 of SC Res. 1120 of 14 July 1997, UN. Doc: S/RES/1120.

[110] *Ibid.*   [111] See para. 7 of SC Res. 1120 (1997).

goal, namely to "achieve the peaceful reintegration of the region into the Croatian legal and constitutional system".[112]

Unlike UNTAC, UNTAES managed to establish a relatively stable climate in the region.[113] The military component of the mission neutralised security risks through the successful disarmament of armed groups, which was completed on 20 June 1996. Emerging power vacuums were closed by the establishment of a Transitional Police Force. The outflow of new refugees was largely eliminated. Furthermore, UNTAES provided sufficient stability to help Croatia and the former FRY to "normalise their relations" and to conclude bilateral agreements on key issues, such as the border regime and the restoration of commercial and traffic links.

The exercise of executive and legislative authority remained strongly focused on the process of transition from Serb to Croatian control. The UN administrator abrogated legislation enacted by the local Serb authorities and restored Croatian law by a directive issued on 29 May 1997, which ordered the region's judiciary "to apply Croatian law for all new cases as from 1 June 1997".[114] He instituted a political and institutional framework for the reintegration of civil administration and public services. Moreover, UNTAES negotiated a number of public agreements with the Government of Croatia, in order to provide the local population with reassurances for the post-UNTAES period and comprehensive political and institutional guarantees under Croatian rule.[115]

In other sectors, the impact of the mission remained rather limited. The work of the fifteen Joint Implementation Committees produced mixed results. The common involvement in the decision-making process forced Serbs and Croats to cooperate in the design of government services. Agreement could be reached in some areas, such as economic issues. Other areas, however, such as education and culture, remained

---

[112] See para. 6 of UN Doc. S/1995/1028.
[113] See paras. 5–6 of the Report of the Secretary-General of the United Nations Transitional Administration for Eastern Slavonia, Baranja and Western Sirmum, UN Doc. S/1997/953 of 4 December 1997.
[114] See para. 23 of UN Doc S/1997/953.
[115] Among these agreements are: the Agreement by the Croatian Pension Fund on Pension Services of 29 May 1997; the Declaration on Educational Certificates of 11 March 1997; the Declaration on Minority Education Rights of 6 August 1997; the Joint Statement on Reintegration of the Employment System of 11 September 1997; the Organization of Joint Council of Municipalities of 23 May 1997; and the Declaration on Conditions for Judicial Reintegration of 30 September 1997. For a survey, see para. 7 and Annex I of UN Doc. S/1997/953.

contentious due to divergent views on ethnic rights (language, teaching etc.).[116]

The issue of accountability for perpetrators of war crimes before domestic courts was never fully resolved. UNTAET lacked the means and resources to conduct a comprehensive reform of the domestic judiciary.[117] Its role remained, therefore, essentially confined to general monitoring of local judicial procedures.[118] Moreover, UNTAET had only mixed success in the area of the repatriation of displaced persons.[119] In particular, many Serbs preferred to build their future in Serbia instead of returning to the Danube Region or living under Croat rule.[120]

The mission ended on 15 January 1998, after a peaceful transfer of authority from UNTAES to Croatia, including the holding of municipal and local elections[121] and a gradual devolution of power to Croatia on the basis of a two-phase exit strategy, under which the UN administrator maintained "his authority and ability to intervene and overrule decisions" in the first phase of the devolution of executive responsibilities, before granting Croatia full authority "commensurate with Croatia's demonstrated ability to reassure the Serb population and successfully complete peaceful reintegration".[122]

2.4. Assessment

The UN engagement in Eastern Slavonia illustrated some of the potential strengths of UN territorial administration. Due to the clearly defined purpose of the mission, and the firm consent of the principal parties (Serbia and Croatia) to the transfer of the territory, UNTAES managed to establish itself as a successful interim authority for a post-conflict society that needed international assistance. The UN managed to stabilise the administered region and to reduce ethnic tensions through its neutral and independent authority and its organisational skills in

---

[116] See Dobbins, *The UN's Role in Nation-Building*, at 120–1.

[117] See Boothby, *Political Challenges of Administering Eastern Slavonia*, at 44.

[118] See also para. 16 (b) of the Report of the Secretary-General, UN Doc. S/1995/1028 of 13 December 1995.

[119] For a full discussion, see below Part IV, Chapter 16.

[120] Boothby notes that "several thousand" indigenous Serbs preferred this option. See Boothby, *Political Challenges of Administering Eastern Slavonia*, at 50.

[121] The elections held by the UN administrator to grant the local population legitimate representation in the Croatian political and legal system turned out to be a success, with a high voter turnout and no security incidents or evidence of fraud. The newly formed Independent Democratic Serb Party won an absolute majority in eleven of the twenty-eight municipalities.

[122] See para. 48 of UN.Doc S/1997/487 of 23 June 1997.

conflict management and mediation. The mandate itself was relatively short and concise. It was limited to a few lines in SC Resolution 1037 (1996) and the Erdut Agreement, entrusting UNTEAES mainly with the institutional and administrative aspects of reintegration. This minimalist approach gave UNTAES an advantage. The UN administrator was able to fulfil his tasks successfully, and to adjust his responsibilities to the needs of the situation – a flexibility that allowed him to complete his mission to the satisfaction of the main stakeholders involved in the post-conflict peace process.

Nevertheless, the short and narrow institutional design of the operation also had one downside. Being devised as a quick and technical mission, UNTAES was unable to deal effectively with the more complex, long-term challenges of peacebuilding, such as housing, reconstruction and property issues.[123] This shortcoming made the mission vulnerable to criticism of half-hearted engagement and missed opportunities.

The historical significance of UNTAES goes beyond its actual governance record. The positive experiences in Eastern Slavonia encouraged the UN to apply the UNTAES model in two other cases: Kosovo and East Timor. UNMIK and UNTAET were established according to the same formula, namely as exclusive governance missions created under Chapter VII of the UN Charter. This approach marked a progression in the development of territorial administration, in so far as it brought some institutional consistency in the otherwise rather improvised UN practice. However, the UNTAES role model had, at the same time, some negative implications. It institutionalised one of the shortcomings that would characterise UN governance missions in the years to come: the unwillingness or inability of the UN to conceive its governing responsibility as state-like public authority, requiring institutional checks and balances and mechanisms of accountability.[124]

---

[123] See below Part IV, Chapter 15. Only 9,000 Serbs and 6,000 Croats had returned from and to the Danube region by the end of UNTAES's mandate. Furthermore, UNTAES failed to provide adequate safeguards from institutional discrimination by Croatian authorities. Croatia's 1996 Law on Reconstruction continued to discriminate against ethnic Serbs in reconstruction funding until the year 2000. Moreover, Croatian executive decrees made the right to return conditional on Croatian citizenship. See Government of the Republic of Croatia, Procedures for the individual return of persons who had abandoned the Republic of Croatia, 27 April 1998.

[124] The operation was treated by the UN like an ordinary peacekeeping mission in terms of status and accountability questions. The Security Council simply called "upon the Government of the Republic of Croatia to include UNTAES and the United Nations Liaison Office in Zagreb in the definition of United Nations Peace Forces and Operations in Croatia in the present Status of Forces Agreement with the United

3. Bosnia and Herzegovina: a special case of international administration

The Balkan conflict gave rise to another major challenge in territorial administration in the mid 1990s: the international administration of Bosnia and Herzegovina (BiH) under the Dayton Peace Agreement (DPA).[125]

3.1. The international administration of Bosnia and Herzegovina

The DPA marked an attempt to create peace in BiH through the federal decentralisation of the state and the internationalisation of the country's constitutional system. The international presence in Bosnia became the first long-term governance engagement of the international community following the end of the Cold War. However, this engagement constituted in many respects a special case of international administration.[126] Three aspects deserve special attention here: the deviation of the Bosnian governance experience from the model of direct UN administration,[127] the institutional framework of the DPA[128] and the special administering regime for the City of Mostar.

Nations". See para. 13 of SC Res. 1037 (1996). This construction left local inhabitants with less means of protection and redress against the ruling authorities than people administered under the Trusteeship System – a flaw that was only later partially corrected by UNMIK and UNTAET.

[125] See generally Richard Caplan, *International Authority and Statebuilding: The Case of Bosnia and Herzegovina*, Global Governance, Vol. 10 (2004), 53; Gerald Knaus and Felix Martin, *Travails of the European Raj*, Journal of Democracy, Vol. 14, No. 3 (2003), 60–74; David Chandler, *Bosnia: Faking Democracy After Dayton* (1999). See also Oliver Dörr, *Die Vereinbarungen von Dayton/Ohio*, Archiv des Völkerrechts, Vol. 35 (1997), 129; F. Ni Aolain, *The Fractured Soul of the Dayton Peace Agreement: A Legal Analysis*, Michigan Journal of International Law, Vol. 19 (1997/8), 957; Wolfgang Graf Vitzthum and Marcus Mack, *Multiethnischer Föderalismus in Bosnien-Herzegovina*, in Europäischer Föderalismus (W. Graf Vitzthum ed., 2000), 81; Wolfgang Graf Vitzthum, *Muliethnische Demokratie – Das Beispiel Bosnien-Herzegovina*, in Festschrift für Thomas Oppermann (Claus D. Classen ed., 2001), 87; Joseph Marko, *Fünf Jahre Verfassungsgerichtsbarkeit in Bosnien and Herzegowina: Eine erste Bilanz*, in Der Rechtsstaat vor neuen Herausforderungen – Festschrift für Ludwig Adamovich zum 70. Geburtstag (B.-Ch. Funk *et al.* eds., 2002), 385; Karin Oellers-Frahm, *Restructuring Bosnia-Herzegovina: A Model With Pitfalls*, Max Planck Yearbook of United Nations Law, Vol. 5 (2005), 179–224.

[126] See also para. 39 of SC Res. 1031 (1995) of 15 December 1995, in which the Council recognises "the unique, extraordinary and complex character of the present situation in Bosnia and Herzegovina, requiring an exceptional response".

[127] See generally Thomas D. Grant, *International Guaranteed Constitutive Order, Cyprus and Bosnia as Predicates for a New Non-traditional Actor in the Society of States*, Journal of Transnational Law and Policy, Vol. 8 (1998), 1.

[128] For a critique of the Bosnian model, see A. Pajic, *A Critical Appraisal of Human Rights Provisions of the Dayton Constitution of Bosnia and Herzegovina*, Human Rights Quarterly, Vol. 20 (1998), 125; Robert C. Slye, *The Dayton Peace Agreement: Constitutionalism and*

3.1.1.   The marginalisation of the United Nations

Following the rather ambiguous crisis management of the UN in the Bosnian conflict (Srebrenica) and the leading role of a multinational Contact Group in the conclusion of the Dayton Agreement, the parties to the Agreement[129] granted the UN a limited role in the management of the Bosnian peace process. The parties decided to endow civilian authority to a state-nominated High Representative (OHR) who derived his authority from three sources: the DPA,[130] the Peace Implementation Council (PIC) (a group of states acting on behalf of the international community)[131] and the Security Council.[132]

The wording of the Dayton Agreement itself was rather opaque. Article I, paragraph 2 of Annex 10 suggested that the OHR would act a subsidiary organ of the Security Council rather than as a party-appointed administrator. The clause provided that:

the Parties request the designation of a High Representative, to be appointed consistent with relevant United Nations Security Council resolutions, to facilitate the Parties' own efforts and to mobilize and, as appropriate, coordinate the activities of the organizations involved in the civilian aspects of the peace settlement by carrying out, *as entrusted by a United Nations Security Council resolution*, the tasks set out below (emphasis added).

The Council assumed, however, only nominal functions in practice.[133] The OHR was continuously nominated by the Steering Board of a group

---

Ethnicity, Yale Journal of International Law, Vol. 21 (1996), 459; Edin Sarcevic, *Verfassungsgebung und "konstitutives Volk": Bosnien-Herzegovina zwischen Natur- und Rechtszustand*, Jahrbuch des Öffentlichen Rechts, Vol. 50 (2002), 494.

[129] See *General Framework Agreement for Peace in Bosnia and Herzegovina with Annexes*, Paris, 14 December 1995, initialled in Dayton/Ohio, 21 November 1995, in ILM, Vol. 35 (1996), 75.

[130] See Annex 10 of the DPA.

[131] The PIC acts as the "overall structure supervising peace implementation in BiH". See conclusions of the PIC Conference in London, 4–5 December 1996, in particular, the decisions concerning Co-ordination Structures. The fact that the PIC conceives its role as a task exercised on behalf of the international community follows from the frequent references to this notion in the documents issued by the PIC. See, for example, paras. 3, 4, 19, 28, 31 of the Conclusions of the PIC Conference in London, 8–9 December 1995, and paras. 5 and 6 of the Conclusions of the PIC Conference in Florence, 13–14 June 1996.

[132] See also Dörr, *Vereinbarungen von Dayton/Ohio*, at 137, Laurent Pech, *La Garantie Internationale de la Constitution de Bosnie-Herzégovine*, Revue Française de Droit Constitutionnel, Vol. 42 (2000), 421, at 431.

[133] The administration of Bosnia and Herzegovina represents therefore, in sum, an example of indirect international territorial administration.

of fifty-five governments and international organisations involved in the peace process (the PIC[134]). The Council confined itself to the endorsement of the appointment[135] and to the exercise of a general monitoring function, based on reports submitted by the OHR[136] and the PIC.[137] The UN exercised a mere assistance role in law enforcement and policing through its UN Mission in Bosnia and Herzegovina (UNMIBH).[138]

3.1.2. Institutional engineering

The Dayton Agreement created a contradictory institutional framework for the post-conflict governance of BiH.[139] The new constitutional system of the country, established by Annex 4 of the DPA, was shaped by two conflicting imperatives: the long term-objective of creating a democratic state and a pluralist society after armed conflict and the short-term goal of establishing a stable and peaceful co-existence of the three ethnic groups – Bosnians, Croats and Serbs. The drafters of the Agreement sought to reconcile these ambitions through three main strategies: the creation of a highly decentralised federal state, with ethnically based mechanisms of power-sharing and collective rights for the three ethnic

[134] Following the negotiation of the DPA, a Peace Implementation Conference was held in London on 8–9 December 1995, to "mobilise the international community behind a new start for the people of Bosnia and Herzegovina". The meeting resulted in the establishment of the PIC. See Conclusions of the Peace Implementation Conference held at Lancaster House, London, 8–9 December 1995, reprinted in ILM, Vol. 35 (1996), at 223 et seq. Since the London Conference, the PIC has come together several times at the ministerial level to review progress and define the goals of peace implementation. For the conclusions and declarations of the PIC conferences, see www.ohr.int.

[135] See paras. 26 and 27 of SC Res. 1031 of 15 December 1995, whereby the Security Council, acting under Chapter VII "endorses the establishment of the High Representative" and "confirms that the High Representative is the final authority in theatre regarding interpretation of Annex 10". For a reaffirmation, see SC Res. 1256 (1999), para. 4.

[136] The Security Council requested the Secretary-General to submit reports from the High Representative, in accordance with Annex 10 of the DPA and the conclusions of the London PIC Conference: see para. 32 of SC resolution 1031 of 15 December 1995. The reports of the HR are available at www.ohr.int.

[137] See, for example, UN Doc. S/1995/1029 by which the Conclusions of the PIC Conference in London, 8–9 December 1995, were reported to the Security Council.

[138] For a survey of policing in Bosnia and Herzegovina, see Caplan, International Governance of War-Torn Territories, at 51–5.

[139] For an assessment, see Sarcevic, Verfassungsgebung und "konstitutives Volk", at 494–532. See also Stahn, Die Verfassungsrechtliche Pflicht zur Gleichstellung der drei Ethnischen Volksgruppen in den Bosnischen Teilrepubliken, 663; Carsten Stahn, Föderalismus im Dienste der Friedenssicherung: Bosnien-Herzegowina unter dem Friedensabkommen von Dayton, Jahrbuch des Föderalismus (2002), 388–403; Oellers-Frahm, Restructuring Bosnia-Herzegovina, at 197–204.

groups;[140] the establishment of strong human rights guarantees and mechanisms for their protection; and the institutionalisation of external control.

These three strategies reflect some commonly recognised tendencies in post-conflict governance, including the desire to overcome the dangers of majoritarianism in a transitional society through power arrangements involving the major ethnic and religious groups of the country in the political system of the post-conflict polity, anti-discrimination obligations and return-related property rights. However, the Dayton Agreement overemphasised some of these principles.

3.1.2.1. Ethnic democracy

The main idea behind the Agreement was to secure peace and basic stability in BiH through the territorial division of Bosnia into a federal system with two powerful sub-entities, the Republika Srpska (49 per cent) and the Federation of BiH (51 per cent), and a weak central government, with limited enumerated powers and *Kompetenz-Kompetenz*. This territorial division helped to preserve the territorial unity and integrity of the country and to open a window for reconstruction after conflict. But it was built along the lines of ethnic conflict and failed to reverse the internal division of the Bosnian society.[141]

The continuing struggle in Bosnia for pluralism and viable democracy may be explained by several institutional flaws in the Dayton system. The institutional model of a weak federation was ill-suited to overcome the problem of ethnic fragmentation in BiH. The high degree of decentralisation and the lack of power of the central institutions divided the state into two separate entities, each of them dominated by the majoritarian ethnic group(s). This strict separation hampered national integration.[142] The institutionalisation of ethnicity was further reinforced by the features of the Bosnian constitutional system. The Constitution of

---

[140] See also European Commission for Democracy Through Law, *Opinion on the Constitutional Situation in Bosnia and Herzegovina and the Powers of the High Representative*, 11 March 2005, CDL-AD (2005) 004, para. 45.

[141] See International Crisis Group, *Is Dayton failing?, Bosnia Four Years After the Peace Agreement*, ICG Balkans Report No. 80, 28 October 1999, at www.crisisweb.org.

[142] This is evidenced by the low figures of minority return. See para. 92 of the Third Partial Decision of the Bosnian Constitutional Court in the Izetbegovic-Case, Case No. 5/98, Judgment of 1 July 2000, at www.ustavnisud.ba. See also Pajic, *Critical Appraisal of Human Rights Provisions*, at 134. ("To be very precise, Bosnians and Croats are no constituent peoples in the entity of the Republika Srpska, and in the same way Serbs are denied constituent people status in the Federation.")

BiH granted Bosnians, Croats and Serbs special privileges by defining them as the "constituent peoples" of BiH. The Constitution organised parliamentary representation in accordance with ethnic quotas and reserved the holding of government offices to members of a specific ethnic group.[143] Furthermore, each of the constituent peoples was vested with a power to veto decisions affecting their vital interests in the most important national institutions.[144]

These checks and balances ensured equality among the three ethnic groups and protected them from abuse of majority rule. However, this special protection created obstacles for the development of a commonly accepted political system and a pluralist domestic society.[145] National judges of the Constitutional Court acted as representatives of their constituent group of population rather than as independent personalities.[146] The ethnic requirements for government officeholders and representatives[147] created an incentive for members of the three ethnic groups to congregate in the entity in which their ethnicity forms the majority.[148] Moreover, the focus on the three constituent groups implied a discrimination vis-à-vis the so-called "others", i.e. everybody not identified with one of the three constituent people. Only Serbs, Bosniaks and

---

[143] See the composition of the House of Peoples under Article IV of the BiH Constitution and the composition of the Presidency according to Article V.

[144] See Article IV 3. e of the BiH Constitution (Parliamentary Assembly) and Article V 2. d (Presidency). The European Commission for Democracy Through Law addressed this clause in its *Opinion on the Constitutional Situation in Bosnia and Herzegovina*. It noted: "Under present conditions within BIH, it seems unrealistic to ask for a complete abolition of the vital interest veto. The Commission nevertheless considers that it would be important and urgent to provide a clear definition of the vital interest in the text of the Constitution. This definition... should not be excessively broad but focus on rights of particular importance to the respective peoples, mainly in areas such as language, education and culture." *Ibid.*, para. 33. The Constitutional Court of Bosnia and Herzegovina started to interpret the notion in its Decision No. U 8/04 on the vital interest veto against the Framework Law on Higher Education, 25 June 2004.

[145] See also European Commission for Democracy Through Law, *Opinion on the Constitutional Situation in Bosnia and Herzegovina*, para. 68.

[146] Politically motivated reasonings were in particular advanced by national judges in order to prevent modifications of the constitution and laws of the Republika Srpska or the Federation. See the dissenting votes of Judges Popovic, Zovko, Miljho and Savic in the Third Partial Decision in Case U 5/98 of 1 July 2000.

[147] See, for example, Article IV of the BiH Constitution, which provides that the House of Peoples must be composed of ten representatives from the Federation, "including five Croats and five Bosnians", and five representatives from the RS must be "five Serbs."

[148] See also the criticism by the European Commission for Democracy Through Law, *Opinion on the Constitutional Situation in Bosnia and Herzegovina*, para. 43.

Croats were able to stand for direct election to the Presidency[149] and for the indirect election to the legislative Chamber,[150] the House of Peoples. This exclusion of "others" from public office was found to be incompatible with the equal right to vote and to stand for election under Article 25 of the ICCPR and the right to equality of members of minorities under Article 4 of the Framework Convention for the Protection of National Minorities (Presidency),[151] the right of non-discrimination under Article 3 of the (First) Protocol to the European Convention on Human Rights (ECHR) in conjunction with Article 14 ECHR (House of Peoples)[152] and the prohibition of discrimination under Protocol No. 12 to the ECHR.[153]

The use of ethnic veto powers contributed to a paralysis of the national institutions.[154] The Parliamentary Assembly was, *inter alia*, unable to adopt laws on citizenship, the flag, the national hymn, the policy of direct investment, telecommunications, administrative taxes, common vehicle licence plates or property protection. This impasse could only be overcome through the active intervention of the OHR,[155] who started not only to impose laws and decisions against the will the domestic players, but gradually turned into the central legislative and executive authority in situations of political crisis.

[149] Article V of the Constitution provides: "The Presidency of Bosnia and Herzegovina shall consist of three Members: one Bosniac and one Croat, each directly elected from the territory of the Federation, and one Serb directly elected from the territory of the Republika Srpska." This construction has three problematic implications: it implies that a citizen has to belong to one of the constituent peoples to be elected member of the Presidency; that the choice of candidates is limited to Bosniac and Croat candidates in the Federation and to Serb candidates in the Republika Srspka; and that Bosniacs and Croats can be elected only from the territory of the Federation, while Serbs can only be elected from the Republika Srpska.

[150] Article IV of the Constitution provides: "1. The House of Peoples shall comprise 15 Delegates, two-thirds from the Federation (including five Croats and five Bosniacs) and one-third from the Republika Srpska (five Serbs). The designated Croat and Bosniac Delegates from the Federation shall be selected, respectively, by the Croat and Bosniac Delegates to the House of Peoples of the Federation. Delegates from the Republika Srpska shall be selected by the National Assembly of the Republika Srpska." This means, *inter alia*, that "others" cannot be elected to the House of Peoples and that Serbs can only be elected to the House of Peoples from the Republika Srpska, while Bosniacs and Croats can only be elected from the Federation of Bosnia and Herzegovina.

[151] See European Commission for Democracy Through Law, *Opinion on the Constitutional Situation in Bosnia and Herzegovina*, para. 70.

[152] *Ibid.*, para. 80.

[153] *Ibid.*, para. 102. See also Council of Europe, Parliamentary Assembly, Res. 1513 (2006), para. 10.

[154] See with respect to the vital interest clause also European Commission for Democracy Through Law, *Opinion on the Constitutional Situation in Bosnia and Herzegovina*, para. 31.

[155] For the list of laws and decisions adopted by the OHR, see www.ohr.int.

3.1.2.2. Human rights excess

The strong focus on ethnicity and collective rights in the DPA was countered by the incorporation of comprehensive human rights standards in the BiH constitutional system, including positive obligations on public authorities to take action against discriminatory practices by state or private actors. Article II and Annex I to the BiH Constitution declared the provisions of the ECHR and its Protocols and not less than fifteen other international human rights agreements directly applicable in Bosnia,[156] in addition to a list of human rights and fundamental freedoms enunciated in the Constitution.[157] The Dayton Agreement devoted particular attention to the protection of refugees and displaced persons. Article II (5) of the BiH Constitution and Article 1 of Annex 7 to the DPA granted all refugees and displaced persons the right to "freely return to homes of origin" and obliged the parties to the Agreement to accept these persons in the respective entities. In addition, the parties specifically agreed to repeal discriminatory legislation, suppress incitement of ethnic or religious hostility and acts of retribution by public or private individuals or forces.[158]

The introduction of human rights guarantees was coupled with the establishment of numerous human rights institutions. The architects of the Dayton Agreement entrusted the BiH Constitutional Court[159] and municipal and state courts in both entities with the supervision and enforcement of human rights provisions.[160] Moreover, the agreement attributed separate human rights mandates to specialised institutions such as the Human Rights Chamber,[161] the Ombudsperson,[162] the Commission for Real Property Claims of Displaced Persons and Refugees (CRPC).[163]

---

[156] See Article II ("shall have priority over all other law") and Annex 1, which lists "additional human rights agreements to be applied in Bosnia and Herzegovina".
[157] See Article II. 3 of the BiH Constitution.
[158] See Article I (3) of Annex 7.
[159] See Article 6 of Annex 4 of the DPA.
[160] See generally Karin Oellers-Frahm, *Die Rolle internationaler Gerichte im Friedensprozess in Bosnien und Herzegowina nach dem Abkommen von Dayton*, in Liber amicorum Günther Jaenicke – Zum 85. Geburtstag (Volkmar Götz et al. eds., 1998), 263.
[161] See Article 7 of Annex 6 of the DPA. The Human Rights Chamber had jurisdiction to consider complaints about violations of the ECHR and its Protocols. Applications could be submitted by the Ombudsperson, any natural or legal person or group of persons, and either one of the entities (the Federation of BiH and the Republika Srpska) against either of the entities or against the state itself. The judgments of the Chamber were binding and irrevocable. The Chamber operated until the end of 2003.
[162] See Article 4 of Annex 6 of the DPA.   [163] See Article 7 of Annex 7 of the DP.

This institutionalisation of human rights protection was instrumental for the process of peacebuilding. The establishment of human rights complaint procedures allowed individuals to vindicate disputed rights before impartial expert bodies. The work of the CRPC helped reverse the effects of ethnic cleansing and to improve the degree of return and reconstruction. Finally, the commitment to normative human rights standards embedded BiH more closely in the constitutional tradition of other European states.

However, the approach of the DPA towards the scope and coordination of human rights protection requires some further reflection.[164] The level of human rights obligations imposed by the agreement on domestic institutions was disproportionate to the capacities of the Bosnian judicial system. Domestic courts often had neither the knowledge nor the means to apply the various human rights obligations enshrined in the BiH Constitution in the phase after the cessation of hostilities. Similarly, the proliferation of international(ised) human rights institutions created institutional overlaps, conflicts of jurisdiction and the risk of diverging jurisprudence, especially in the application of the ECHR, among the different institutions. The concurrent jurisdiction of the Constitutional Court and the Human Rights Chamber over human rights violations led to parallel claims and disputes over the hierarchy between these two organs.[165] Both organs agreed that complaints which had been brought

---

[164] For general criticism of the "multitude of international actors involved [under the DPA] and the lack of cohesion between them", see Oellers-Frahm, *Restructuring Bosnia-Herzegovina*, at 219.

[165] Joseph Marko, a former judge of the Constitutional Court of Bosnia and Herzegovina noted: "[I]t can be traced back to human nature that a far-reaching 'co-operative' harmonization of the two Annexes could not be achieved; instead there came into existence a form of 'institutional jealousy', in other words, which organ should have priority over the other? Even before a concrete case was brought before the Court, informal negotiations between the two organs revealed that both sides claimed to be the higher organ and could therefore in effect accept appeals from the other. The Human Rights Chamber was for example of the opinion that they were established as a substitute for the lack of membership of the Council of Europe and the subsequent membership of the ECHR of Bosnia and Herzegovina which would mean that they would be required to check the decisions of the national Constitutional Court. In the other hand, the Constitutional Court presented itself as 'guardian of the Constitution' and thereby as highest organ, decisions of which could not be put into question, provided that Bosnia and Herzegovina does not ratify the ECHR and in doing so subject the entire national system to the supranational jurisdiction of the European Court of Human Rights." See Joseph Marko, *Five Years of Constitutional Jurisprudence in Bosnia and Herzegovina: A First Balance*, European Diversity and Autonomy Papers 7/2004, at 14.

before one organ should be declared inadmissible by the other,[166] but
the duplication of roles provoked proposals for a merger of both institutions in the aftermath of the immediate phase of transition.[167]
Other overlaps in jurisdiction arose in the relationship between the
Commission on Real Property Claims, the Human Rights Chamber and
the Constitutional Court. The Human Rights Chamber refused to address
cases dealt with by the Commission in principle,[168] but assumed a role
in enforcing decisions which had not been properly implemented by
officials of the Bosnian entities.[169] The Constitutional Court adopted a
similar approach. The Court formally refused to hear appeals against
decisions of the Commission.[170] But the Court left a door open for

[166] The Constitutional Court of Bosnia and Herzegovina concluded that the Court and
the Human Rights Chamber enjoy equal legal rank because of the "legal unity" of the
Annexes of the DPA. The Court based its jurisprudence therefore on the principle
that neither of the two bodies has the authority to review the decision of the other.
See Constitutional Court of Bosnia and Herzegovina, Decisions U 7/98, U 8/98 and U
9/98 of 26 February 1999, in Constitutional Court of Bosnia and Herzegovina,
Decisions 1997–1999, at 227, 249, 273.
[167] See Proposal for a Law on the Merger of the Human Rights Chamber and the
Constitutional Court of Bosnia and Herzegovina, 23 October 2001, approved at the
48th Plenary Meeting of the Venice Commission on 19–20 October 2001, at
www.venice.coe.int/docs/2001/CDL-INF (2001)020-e.asp.
[168] See Human Rights Chamber for Bosnia and Herzegovina, Annual Report 1998, at
para. I, at www.gwdg.de/~jvr/hrch/98annrep.html.
[169] Article 12, para. 6 of Annex 7 states the decisions of the Commission are binding.
The Chamber found that the misapplication of the law constitutes a violation of
citizen's rights under the ECHR and the Constitution and laws of Bosnia and
Herzegovina. See, for example, Human Rights Chamber, *Bojkovski v. Bosnia and
Herzegovina and Federation of Bosnia and Herzegovina*, Decision of 6 April 2001, CH/97/73;
Petrovic v. Federation of Bosnia and Herzegovina, Decision of 9 March 2001, CH/00/6142;
Leko v. Federation of Bosnia and Herzegovina, Decision of 9 March 2001, CH/00/6144.
[170] See Constitutional Court of Bosnia and Herzegovina, Decision in case U 21/01, 22 June
2001 ("*Mu. K. v. Commission for Real Property Claims*"). The Court found that it is "not
competent to review decisions of the Commission for Real Property Claims (CRPC) in
order to clarify any legal positions relevant for those decisions". The Court stated: "In
Decisions No. U-7/98, U-8/98 and U-9/98, the Constitutional Court concluded that the
Human Rights Chamber could not be considered as a court in Bosnia and
Herzegovina and that the Constitutional Court was not competent to review the
decisions of the Human Rights Chamber since the Human Rights Chamber exercises
its functions outside the ordinary judicial structure of Bosnia and Herzegovina. In
accordance with such jurisprudence, the Constitutional Court holds that the
Commission is an institution outside the ordinary judicial structure of Bosnia and
Herzegovina" (para. 19). See also the decision in case U 32/01, 22 June 2001 ("*Joint
Stock Company Central Profit Banka Sarajevo v. Commission for Real Property Claims*), where
the Court held "that there is no hierarchical relationship between the bodies
established by Annexes of the Agreement" which were meant to "complement each
other and act in a parallel manner" (para. 17).

judicial review by allowing lower courts and the Constitutional Court to address and clarify matters excluded by the Commission.[171]

These experiences demonstrate that it may, in fact, be in the interests of the efficiency and sustainability of a peace process not to overload a post-conflict society with international standards and institutions in the immediate aftermath of hostilities, but gradually to adjust the scope of international obligations and institutions to the stage of transition of that society and the actual need for internationalisation.

3.1.2.3. External control – too little authority too early, too much too late

It was clear that the framework of the DPA could only be implemented with external control. This is reflected in the composition of the BiH Constitutional Court, which was vested with three international judges, acting in concert with six other domestic judges selected by the two entities (four members selected by the Federation of BiH and two by the Republika Srpska).[172] This composition allowed the Court to adopt decisions against the will of either of the two republics with the affirmative vote of the three international judges.

The specific role and powers of the OHR under the peace settlement, by contrast, remained rather vague. Annex 10 of the DPA endowed the High Representative with a relatively weak coordination mandate, including the duty to "monitor the implementation of the peace settlement", to establish "close contacts with the parties to promote their full compliance with all civilian aspects of the peace settlement" and to "facilitate, as … necessary, the resolution of any difficulties arising in connection with civilian implementation".[173] The agreement failed expressly to grant the OHR binding regulatory powers. Annex 10 confined itself to declare the High Representative "the final authority in theatre regarding interpretation of [the] agreement on the civilian implementation of the peace settlement".[174]

With the increasing blockades by, and lack of inter-entity cooperation between, the central institutions (the Parliamentary Assembly and the Presidency), it soon became evident that the express delineation of powers enumerated in Article II of Annex 10 would not suffice to ensure the implementation of the aims of the DPA. The OHR thus widened its mandate in a mixture of self-arrogation and teleological treaty interpretation, "interpreting" it so as to encompass the power to impose laws

---

[171] See Marko, *Five Years of Constitutional Jurisprudence in Bosnia and Herzegovina*, at 16.
[172] See Article VI (1) of the BiH Constitution.
[173] See Annex 10, Article II (1).   [174] See Annex 10, Article V.

and decisions without or against the will of the domestic institutions – a practice that was subsequently endorsed by the conclusions of the PIC Conference in Bonn (1997),[175] by which the PIC approved the OHR's authority to remove from office those public officials violating legal commitments of the DPA and his power to impose interim legislation in situations where BiH's national institutions failed to do so.[176]

From that time, the OHR acted as a "stand-in legislator" and highest executive authority in BiH, basing its decisions on "its authority" under Annex 10 of the DPA and Article XI of the Bonn Declaration of the PIC. The OHR not only used its powers to decree laws in the case of inaction of the divided institutions of the central state, and to remove elected officials at all levels from office,[177] but also overruled certain provisions of a law adopted by the national parliament, arguing that the law violated the Bosnian Constitution.[178] Moreover, the OHR exercised strong pressure on the two entities by imposing a final and binding arbitration on an Inter-Entity Boundary Line in Sarajevo[179] and by decreeing amendments to the constitutions of both entities[180] following a ruling

[175] The "Conclusions of the Peace Implementing Conference held in Bonn" and the "final authority" of the OHR regarding Annex 10 of the DPA were then approved by the Security Council. The Council 'expresses its support for the conclusions of the Bonn Peace Implementation Conference' (emphasis added) in para. 2 of Res. 1144 of 19 December 1997. For a reaffirmation of the "final authority" of the OHR, see para. 4 of Res. 1256 of 3 August 1999.

[176] In paragraph XI of its conclusions the PIC "welcomes the High Representative's decision to use his final authority in theatre regarding interpretation of the Agreement on the Civilian Implementation of the Peace Settlement . . . by making binding decisions, as he judges necessary, on the following issues: . . . b. interim measures to take effect when parties are unable to reach agreement, which will remain in force until the Presidency or Council of Ministers has adopted a decision consistent with the Peace Agreement on the issue concerned; other measures to ensure implementation of the Peace Agreement throughout Bosnia and Herzegovina and its Entities, as well as the smooth running of the institutions. Such measures may include actions against persons holding public offices or officials who are absent from meetings without good cause or who are found by the High Representative to be in violation of legal commitments made under the Peace Agreement or the terms for its implementation."

[177] For the removals from office and suspensions, see www.ohr.int/decisions/removalsdec.

[178] See Decision on Amending the Law on Filing a Vacant Position of the Member of the Presidency of Bosnia and Herzegovina of 7 August 2000, available at www.ohr.int.

[179] See the Decision imposing Arbitration in Dobrinje I and IV of 5 February 2001, by which the OHR has substituted the Entities agreement to a procedure specified under Annex 5 of the DPA.

[180] See also the Decision establishing interim procedures to protect vital interests of Constituent Peoples and Others, including freedom from Discrimination of 11 January 2001. The substantive role of the OHR in the work of these Commissions is

of the BiH Constitutional Court,[181] by which the Court had declared certain provisions of the entity's Constitution incompatible with the Constitution of BiH, in order to break up the territorial separation and ethnocratic structures in the entities.[182]

This practice raises several concerns. It poses, first, a legitimacy problem.[183] The people of Bosnia were *de facto* subjected to the rule of a foreign actor which derived its authority from a weak bond of local consent expressed by the enactment of the DPA, which was not accountable to the people and whose action was not even closely monitored by the PIC or the Security Council.[184] Executive decisions of the OHR, such as the dismissal of public authorities, including elected domestic officials, were not subject to judicial[185] or quasi-judicial scrutiny.[186] The Constitutional Court of BiH did not examine whether there is "enough justification for

reflected in para. 10 of the decision, which reads: "In the event that the Constitutional Commission concerned fails... to reach an Agreement supported by a majority of the delegates of each of the constituent peoples and Others, the said Commission shall... lodge with the Office of the High Representative an application for the High Representative to resolve the issue finally in a manner as he deems to be appropriate, in accordance with the mandate given to him by the international community."

[181] See on this ruling, Stahn, *Die verfassungsrechtliche Pflicht zur Gleichstellung*, at 679.

[182] In its reasoning, the Court relied in particular on the positive obligations and the strong emphasis on individual rights under Article 2, para. 5 of the Bosnian Constitution and Articles 1 and 2 of Annex 7, in order to strengthen the development of a more integrated and multi-ethnic society.

[183] See also European Commission for Democracy Through Law, *Opinion on the Constitutional Situation in Bosnia and Herzegovina*, para. 100.

[184] Formally, the OHR is accountable to the Peace Implementation Council as the body appointing body. Furthermore, the OHR is under an obligation to report to the UN Secretary-General. But neither of the two bodies have monitored the routine practice of the OHR in a systematic fashion. See also Caplan, *International Authority and Statebuilding: The Case of Bosnia and Herzegovina*, at 62.

[185] See also European Commission for Democracy Through Law, *Opinion on the Constitutional Situation in Bosnia and Herzegovina*, paras. 93 and 96 and Amnesty International, *The apparent lack of accountability of international peace-keeping forces in Kosovo and Bosnia-Herzegovina*, AI Index: EUR 05/002/2004, April 2004, at 18.

[186] The Human Rights Chamber did not exercise jurisdiction over removals from office by the OHR. See Human Rights Chamber, *Dragan Cavic against Bosnia and Herzegovina*, Case No. CH/98/1266, Decision on Admissibility, 18 December 1998, paras. 18–19, where the Chamber found that: "[t]he actions complained of were carried out by the High Representative in the performance of his functions under the General Framework Agreement, as interpreted by the Bonn Peace Implementation Conference. There is no provision for any intervention by the respondent Party (or by any of the other Parties to the General Framework Agreement) in those actions. In addition, the High Representative cannot be said to be acting as, or on behalf of, the State or the Entities when acting in pursuance of his powers. As a result, the actions giving rise to the present application cannot be considered to be within the scope of responsibility of the respondent Party."

the High Representative to enact the legislation instead of leaving it to the democratically elected organs of BiH".[187] Such a *status quo* is difficult to reconcile with principles of due process and democratic control, including Article 3 of the (First) Protocol to the ECHR,[188] in particular, if it is maintained over a period of several consecutive years.

Moreover, the process of gradual empowerment of the OHR in the Dayton process was ambivalent from a policy perspective. The systematic intervention of the OHR in Bosnian politics triggered a "democracy fatigue" among local actors.[189] The reliance on the OHR served as an excuse or incentive for domestic institutions to escape their responsibilities[190] and thus increased the dependency of BiH on the international community, instead of furthering democratic pluralism and progressive self-government.[191]

It does therefore not come as a surprise that in an opinion adopted on 11 March 2005 ("Opinion on the Constitutional Situation in Bosnia and Herzegovina and the Powers of the High Representative"), the European Commission for Democracy through Law called for "a progressive phasing out of the [Bonn] powers [of the OHR] and for the establishment of an advisory panel of independent lawyers" in order to establish control over "decisions directly affecting the rights of individuals".[192]

---

[187] See European Commission for Democracy Through Law, *Opinion on the Constitutional Situation in Bosnia and Herzegovina*, para. 89.

[188] This provision "requires that legislation is adopted by a body elected by the people". For a criticism, see also European Commission for Democracy Through Law, *Opinion on the Constitutional Situation in Bosnia and Herzegovina*, para. 88.

[189] Even the OHR has acknowledged the naissance of a "dependency syndrome". He noted in 2000: "Local parties begin to rely opportunistically on the political intervention of the High Representative, especially when it comes to unpopular measures. They can behave, despite their being in government, as if they are in the opposition and defend their ethno-nationalist goals without the need to compromise." See Wolfgang Petritsch, *Bosnien and Herzegovina fünf Jahre nach Dayton*, Südosteuropa Mitteilungen, Vol. 40 (2000), 301.

[190] Dismissals of government officials by the OHR have often been followed by new appointments which were as critical as the previous ones. See *ibid.*, at 59.

[191] Annual elections since 1996 have not established a balanced multi-ethnic party system, but have strengthened the parameters of ethnic representation. In 2002, representatives of the three main nationalist parties, the SDA (Party of Democratic Action), SDS (Serbian Democratic Party), and the HDZ (Croatian Democratic Community) won the Bosniak, Serb and Croat seats in the three-member Presidency of Bosnia and Herzegovina. At the state level, and in the elections for the Entity parliaments, the HDZ, SDS and SDA were the leading parties in their respective ethnic constituencies.

[192] See European Commission for Democracy Through Law, *Opinion on the Constitutional Situation in Bosnia and Herzegovina*, para. 100.

3.1.3. Assessment

The framework of the Dayton Agreement was crucial for the peace process in Bosnia and Herzegovina. The internationalised structure of the DPA facilitated the implementation of goals of the agreement[193] and laid the foundations for the country's accession to the Council of Europe. However, the features of the Dayton model do not necessarily lend themselves to further replication in other contexts.

The very way in which the foundations for a constitutional democracy were laid is open to criticism. The drafters of the Dayton peace settlement defined the parameters of the Constitution of BiH on the basis of an international agreement that entered into force upon signature, that is, without ratification or popular consent.[194] The Constitution was therefore essentially an international construction (a "Dayton constitution" rather than a "Bosnian Constitution"[195]), which suffered from an initial lack of identification and public acceptance by domestic leaders.

Secondly, the loose federal structure and the strong institutionalisation of ethnicity in the constitutional system of the state and the entities stood in open contrast to the goal of the Dayton process, namely to reverse the consequences of the conflict and to reduce the divisions in society. Moreover, it was contradictory to endow the OHR with weak authority at the beginning of the peace process, and to extend its powers *ex post* from outside. The opposite logic may have been more promising, initially namely to provide a transitional administrator with some teeth and to couple its mandate with a successive devolution of authority increasing over time.[196]

The flagrant deficiencies of BIH constitutional system, namely the weak competencies of the central state, the burdensome decision-making structures at the central level and the ethnically based mechanisms of representation, have driven the country into a "constitutional impasse"[197] which continues to persist more than ten years after Dayton. The remaining traces of the war-torn past can only be overcome by mutual openness to dialogue and comprehensive constitutional reform.[198]

---

[193] See also para. 97.
[194] See also Oellers-Frahm, *Restructuring Bosnia-Herzegovina*, at 194–5.
[195] See Ni Aolain, *The Fractured Soul of the Dayton Peace Agreement*, at 971.
[196] See also below Part IV, Chapter 16.
[197] See Council of Europe, Parliamentary Assembly, Resolution 1513 (2006), *Constitutional reform in Bosnia and Herzegovina*, para. 15.
[198] In March 2006, the six main political parties reached an agreement on constitutional reform. The proposed constitutional amendments provided, *inter alia*, for

3.2. The European Union Administration of the City of Mostar (EUAM)

The internationalisation of Bosnia and Herzegovina under the Dayton Agreement was complemented by another type of administration at the municipal level, namely the European Administration of Mostar (EUAM).[199] The mission was a follow up of the historic experiments in the internationalisation of small entities,[200] but in a new format, namely as the first major joint action of EU member states within the framework of the Common Foreign and Security Policy (CFSP) of the EU.[201]

The EUAM was unique in structure and design. The format of the mission was shaped by the structure of the Dayton Agreement. Mostar became an "area under EU administration",[202] but it remained officially part of the Federation of BiH.[203] The mission was therefore an "administration within an administration", namely an experiment of international governance at the local level, operating under the internationalised structure of the Dayton Agreement.

The influence of the EU was directly reflected in the governing structure of the mission. The EUAM was not only headed by a European Administrator, but shaped by governing principles which are typical of

representation of "others" in the House of Representatives. For a survey, see European Commission for Democracy Through Law, *Preliminary Opinion on the Draft Amendments to the Constitution of Bosnia and Herzegovina*, Opinion 375/2006, 7 April 2006. However, on 26 April 2006 the reform package failed to reach the required two-thirds majority in parliament by two votes. The Council of Europe recommended the drafting and adoption of a new constitution by October 2010. See Resolution 1513, para. 20.

[199] See generally Fabrizio Pagani, *L'Administration de Mostar par l'Union Européenne*, Annuaire français de Droit International (1996), 245; Korhonen, Gras and Creutz, *International Post-Conflict Situations*, at 107–25.

[200] See above Part I, Chapter 1 and Part II, Chapter 6.

[201] See the preamble of the Memorandum of Understanding on the European Administration of Mostar of 5 July 1994, concluded between the Member States of the European Union, Member States of the Western European Union, the Republic of Bosnia and Herzegovina, the Federation of Bosnia and Herzegovina, the Local Administration of Mostar East and the Local Administration of Mostar West and Bosnian Croats. This solution was a compromise dictated by the particularities of the EU CFSP. The parties adopted a Memorandum of Understanding, because the EU lacked the legal capacity to conclude agreements in this field. Furthermore, the document used the words "Member States of the European Union acting within the framework of the Union", in order to disguise the fact that they acted as twelve member states individually. See Korhonen, Gras and Creutz, *International Post-Conflict Situations*, at 112.

[202] See Article 5 of the Memorandum of Understanding on the European Administration of Mostar. An engagement of the EU in Mostar was regarded as a realistic option, due to the early signing of a cease-fire and the small geographic size of the city.

[203] See Article 5 (1) of the MOU.

the framework of the EU governance, such as the "principle of subsidiarity"[204] and mechanisms of consultation,[205] and accountability.[206] These principles gave the mission some traces of modernity, which deviated from the traditional structure of administering missions under the umbrella of the UN.

Nevertheless, the framework of administration stood in contrast to the practical challenges of the mission. The administration was charged with an ambitious mandate, namely to identify "a lasting solution for the administration of the Mostar city municipality" and to restore Mostar as a "single, self-sustaining and multiethnic" city.[207] These objectives conflicted with the operational capacities of the mission and the continuing mistrust and tensions among the different ethnic groups in the city. The mission was therefore obliged to scale down its ambitions and to focus on immediate and short-term-goals, such as reconstruction, security, elections and the establishment of a commonly accepted governing framework for the city.[208]

3.2.1.   Origin

The EUAM was established in order to reverse the ethnic division of Mostar, which was split into a Bosniak-controlled zone in the eastern part of the city and a Croat zone in the western part after the Bosnian conflict.[209] The decision to place the city under EU administration

---

[204] See Article 7 (1) of the MOU.

[205] The EU Administrator was, in particular, obliged to seek the advice of a local Advisory Council and to pay tribute to the "views and wishes of the local parties and population". See Article 7 (1) of the MOU.

[206] An ombudsperson was set up to monitor the EU Administration. See Council of the European Union, Council Decision 94/776/EC of 28 November 1994 appointing an Ombudsman for Mostar for the duration of the European Union administration in Mostar. For a discussion, see Korhonen, Gras and Creutz, *International Post-Conflict Situations*, at 115.

[207] Article 2 of the Memorandum of Understanding on the European Administration of Mostar. See also the report by Hans Koschnick, *The EU Administration of Mostar – a balance after one year*, August 1995, at 9.

[208] The reduced agenda of the mission was summarised in a strategy paper by the EU Administrator, issued in May 1995. The main objective was to establish a single administration, with a central municipal authority acceptable to the population, guaranteed rights for all citizens, a common public service, tax system and police force and guaranteed freedom of movement. See Strategy for the EU Administration of Mostar, 13 May 1995. For a general assessment, see International Crisis Group, *Reunifying Mostar: Opportunities for Progress*, 19 April 2000.

[209] Before the Bosnian conflict, the city had almost an equal share of Muslim, Croats and Serb inhabitants. See Commission on Human Rights, Fourth periodic report by

resulted from a political compromise. During the peace talks leading to the Dayton Agreement, Western negotiators and Bosnian leaders agreed that Mostar should neither be formally divided nor separated from the Federation of BiH. The Croat side remained opposed to the establishment of a UN administration in Mostar.[210] The only way out of the dilemma was a temporary administration of the city under the auspices of the EU. The member states of the EU welcomed this option for two reasons: first, because they could demonstrate that they were able to act in concert under the CFSP introduced by the Treaty of Maastricht; and, secondly, because they saw the reconstruction of Mostar as a symbolic step and blueprint for peacemaking in Bosnia after Dayton more generally.[211]

The formal structures of the administration were laid down in several instruments. The majors of east Mostar and west Mostar and Hans Koschnick, the EU administrator, devised a basic administrative structure for Mostar, which was included as an annex to the DPA.[212] The principles of administration were finalised in a Memorandum of Understanding concluded by EU member states and the Republic of BiH, the Federation of BiH and the Local Administration of Mostar on 5 July 1995 (MOU).[213]

3.2.2. Institutional design

The mission was vested with classical governance powers in order to achieve these goals. The MOU granted the chief EU administrator "the powers necessary to fulfil the aims and principles of the EU Administration...and to administer the Mostar city municipality properly and

---

Special Rapporteur Tadeusz Mazowiecki, UN Doc. E/CN.4/1994/8 of 26 September 1993, para. 12. When the EUAM began to exercise its mandate, Bosniacs and Croats exercised exclusive control in their respective zones.

[210] See Korhonen, Gras and Creutz, *International Post-Conflict Situations*, at 112.

[211] See European Parliament, Committee on Budgetary Control, *Report on Special Report No. 2/96 of the Court of Auditors concerning the accounts of the Administrator and the European Administration, Mostar*, 21 November 1996, Explanatory Statement, para. 1.

[212] See Annex to the Dayton Agreement on Implementing the Federation of Bosnia and Herzegovina: Agreed Principles for the Interim Statute for the City of Mostar, 10 November 1995.

[213] See Memorandum of Understanding on the European Administration of Mostar of 5 July 1994, concluded between the Member States of the European Union, Member States of the Western European Union, the Republic of Bosnia and Herzegovina, the Federation of Bosnia and Herzegovina, the Local Administration of Mostar East and the Local Administration of Mostar West and Bosnian Croats.

efficiently",[214] including regulatory powers[215] and final decision-making authority in the executive field.[216]

Yet, the EU Administrator had to exercise these powers within the domestic realm of the Federation of BiH. The EUAM was expressly bound by the terms of the MOU to comply with domestic law,[217] including the Constitution of the Federation of BiH.[218] Furthermore, the MOU spelled out that domestic courts of the municipality retain full independence, including the power to review "regulations issued by the EU Administrator".[219] The decision-making authority of the EUAM administrator was therefore directly embedded in the institutional structure of the municipality.

At the same time, the EUAM was subjected to direct institutional checks and balances from the beginning of the operation. The EU administration was urged to exercise public authority in cooperation with a local Council, which held advisory powers "on all issues concerning the administration of the Mostar city municipality"[220] and powers of initiation in the legislative field.[221] The MOU obliged the EU administrator, in particular, to "operate in consultation and close collaboration with the local parties"[222] and to apply the "principle of subsidiarity" in its decision-making practice.[223] This concept was obviously intended to encourage the EUAM to defer to domestic decision-making in cases where domestic institutions were capable or better placed to realise specific types of action.

The second innovative feature of the mission was its accountability structure. The EUAM was placed under a double form of supervision: general political control and human rights monitoring.

---

[214] See Article 7 (1) of the MOU.

[215] See Article 10 (3) of the MOU. ("After consultation with the Advisory council and observing Chapter IX, art. 10 of the Constitution, the EU Administrator has the right to introduce different or additional regulations applicable in the area of the EU Administration, if he deems such regulations necessary for the functioning of the Administration or in the interests of the Mostar city municipality.")

[216] See Article 8 of the MOU.

[217] See article 10 (1) of the MOU. ("The laws and regulations of the Federation of Bosnia and Herzegovina will apply in the city of Mostar, in conformity with Chapter IX, art. 10 of the Constitution of the Federation of Bosnia and Herzegovina.")

[218] See Article 7 (2) and Article 10 (3) of the MOU.   [219] See Article 11 (1) of the MOU.

[220] The Advisory Council consisted of five Bosniaks, five Croats and five representatives of other groups. See Article 8 of the Memorandum of Understanding on the European Administration of Mostar.

[221] See Article 10 (2) of the MOU.   [222] See Article 9 (1) of the MOU.

[223] See Article 7 (1) of the MOU. For doubts as to the effectiveness of this principle in practice, see Korhonen, *International Governance in Post-Conflict Situations*, at 520; Korhonen, Gras and Creutz, *International Post-Conflict Situations*, at 114.

The mechanism of political control was rather weak. The EU administrator was appointed by the Council of Ministers of the EU, and thus obliged to report to the Council and to follow its instructions.[224] However, the Council entrusted the practical implementation of the joint action under the CFSP to the rotating Council Presidency and a consultative committee. This meant that the political actors carrying out the concrete supervision of the EU administrator changed every six months.[225]

A more direct and continued form of control was exercised by an EU Ombudsman. The Ombudsman was established by the Council of Ministers in order to monitor the daily work of the EU administration. The Ombudsman was authorised to hear complaints by persons who alleged that "that his/her rights have been violated by a decision of the European Union Administrator based on a Regulation introduced pursuant to Article 10 (3) of the Memorandum of Understanding".[226] Following an examination of the complaint, the Ombudsman could address recommendations to the EU Administrator, or refer the matter to the Council of the EU.[227]

The EU Ombudsman played a limited role in practice. The scope of activity of the institution was hampered by the fact that it was not competent to deal with complaints concerning the conduct of the local administration.[228] Nevertheless, the combined form of political supervision

---

[224] See Article 7 (3) of the MOU.

[225] See also European Parliament, Committee on Budgetary Control, *Report on Special Report No. 2/96 of the Court of Auditors concerning the accounts of the Administrator and the European Administration, Mostar*, 21 November 1996, para. 18.

[226] See para. 3 of Council Decision 94/776/EC. ("Any natural person residing in the European Union administrated area and any legal person operating in that area directly and individually concerned, who claims that his/her rights have been violated by a decision of the European Union Administrator based on a Regulation introduced pursuant to Article 10 (3) of the Memorandum of Understanding may bring that decision to the attention of the European Union Ombudsman for Mostar. The Ombudsman may deal with the matter only if all other legal remedies have been exhausted.".

[227] See para. 4 of Council Decision 94/776/EC. ("The European Union Ombudsman for Mostar may address recommendations concerning claims referred to in paragraph 3 to the European Union Administrator. If, in a serious matter, the Administrator does not agree with the Ombudsman's recommendations, the Ombudsman may refer the matter to the Council of the European Union together with a written comment by the European Union Administrator.")

[228] The EU Ombudsman, Mr Ioannis Voulgaris, received a number of complaints in areas such as employment policy, freedom of movement and housing. See Pagani, *L'Administration de Mostar*, at 249. But he could only make a limited contribution to the broader unification of the city, *inter alia*, as he was not able to respond to requests for concrete assistance. See Korhonen, Gras and Creutz, *International Post-Conflict Situations*, at 115.

and legal monitoring triggered by individuals was remarkable in the sense that it revived a complaint-based accountability tradition, which had fallen into oblivion after the early experiments of the League of Nations and the UN.

3.2.3. Practice

The record of the EUAM was mixed. The mission had some successes in reconstruction, but it failed to achieve overall political reunification.

The main contribution of the EU Administration is that it helped to restore normal life in Mostar.[229] EUAM contributed to rebuilding the infrastructure in the city, via the reconstruction of schools, nurseries and basic public services (transport, telecommunications). The mission played a central role in re-establishing freedom of movement within the city. The EUAM lifted, in particular, restrictions on free movement and restored unlimited access to all parts of the city by 20 February 1996. Furthermore, it managed to establish a joint local police force.

Attempts to foster a long-term political and social transformation of Mostar were less successful.[230] Moves towards the political unification of the city were often blocked by political opposition or a lack of co-operation by local groups. The EU Administrator managed to introduce some regulatory changes, by issuing decrees in a number of areas of public concern (construction permits, conditions of evictions, conduct of elections).[231] However, the regulation of matters concerning the status or the future of the city posed a severe problem in practice. Both the Muslim and the Croat sides failed to agree on the size of the so-called "central zone" – a part of the city which was to be administered within the framework of a unified city administration. When the EU Administrator attempted to break this impasse, by issuing a compromise solution in a decree issued on 7 February 1996, the Croat side reacted with public outrage. Faced with a threat by Croatian representatives to break off relations with the EU, the EU Presidency brokered a new deal, which reversed the decision of the EU Administrator. The new formula

---

[229] See European Parliament, *Report on Special Report No. 2/96*, Explanatory Statement, para. 4.

[230] See also European Parliament, *Report on Special Report No. 2/96*, Explanatory Statement, para. 3. ("Measured by its own ambitious aims, the EUAM has not been an unqualified success...In Mostar, as in the rest of Bosnia, those overtly or covertly seeking to establish or to secure ethnically cleansed areas are still in the ascendant.")

[231] See Korhonen, *International Governance*, at 520.

⁸⁸⁸⁸⁸⁸⁸⁸ok

was then incorporated in the Interim Statute for the City of Mostar – a document published by the EUAM on 20 February 1996.[232]

The EUAM faced further obstacles in the area of the elections, which were to be organised under the umbrella of the EU. First, both sides disagreed over the question of who should be allowed to vote.[233] Then, the Croat side blocked the implementation of the results of the elections held on 30 June 1996, on the ground that twenty-six extra ballots had been in a polling station in Germany. The dispute had to be resolved by the EU Ombudsman,[234] who decided that the elections were valid despite these irregularities.[235]

These two examples demonstrate the fragile status of the EUAM. The EU Administrator was de facto dependent on the consent and cooperation of local actors. The WEU exercised only advisory and observer functions in Mostar. The EU Administrator was therefore not in a position "to enforce his decisions and impose them on the hardliners in the opposing factions".[236]

The mission formally terminated its two-year mandate on 22 July 1996. The EU itself had to acknowledge at the end of the mission that the EUAM had "managed to make only modest progress towards the reunification of the city and the removal of the invisible wall along the demarcation lines".[237] Some of these responsibilities were then passed on to the OHR and the PIC, which assumed general political control after the withdrawal of the EU and the integration of Mostar into the overall structure for peace implementation on Bosnia and Herzegovina.

---

[232] See ICG, Reunifying Mostar, at 9–11.

[233] Croat representatives argued that only current residents in Mostar were authorised to participate in the elections. Bosniaks contended that persons who fled or were evicted from their home during the 1993 conflict were also entitled to vote. This approach was consistent with the Dayton Agreement and later applied in practice.

[234] Article 11 of the Decree on the Conduct of Elections for the City Council of Mostar allowed the Ombudsman to overrule the decision of the election committee if only one of the parties lodged a complaint.

[235] The Ombudsman justified its decision of 6 July 1996 as follows: "[T]he only issue to be considered is that 26 ballot papers more than the number of voters were found in the ballot boxes used in the polling station in Bonn...The distribution of the additional ballots shows clearly that the irregularity should be attributed to material errors committed in the procedure by the Polling Committee rather than to fraudulent intentions...the influence of the additional votes on the returns of the mentioned municipalities, or on those of the City-wide list was clearly negligible, and as such should not be considered."

[236] See European Parliament, Report on Special Report No. 2/96, Explanatory Statement, para. 7.

[237] Ibid., Explanatory Statement, para. 3.

3.2.4. Assessment

The EUAM was a very particular undertaking of territorial administration, which resulted largely from the involvement of EU members in the Dayton Peace talks and the wish of European powers to make a symbolic contribution to peacemaking in Bosnia and Herzegovina.

One of the main achievements of the mission is that it managed to prevent the danger of oppressive international administration by integrating EUAM's authority in the framework of the domestic legal system. Yet, like other experiments, the mission suffered from a lack of preparation and long-term planning. The mandate of the mission was overambitious in design. The EUAM lacked the necessary means (e.g. compliance structure, institutional experience) and timeframe to achieve a fully fledged unification of the city.

The concept of joint action under the CFSP was not an ideal framework for the conduct of a mission of territorial administration. The six-month rotation of the Council Presidency led to a "travelling circus of political responsibility" from one capital to the next.[238] This structure slowed up decision-making and compromised cooperation with the EU Administration. Furthermore, gaps of coordination and a lack of Council support on vital questions, such as the future administrative structure of Mostar, culminated in the resignation of the EU Administrator Koschnick.[239]

These findings left some doubt as to whether the concept of "Joint Action" under the Treaty of Maastricht was indeed the right framework to embark on an experiment of territorial administration in a fragile and ethnically divided environment.

4. The United Nations interim administration in Kosovo (UNMIK)

UNMIK became the hallmark of authoritative and long-term UN post-conflict engagement.[240] By establishing UNMIK, the UN started to fill gaps that the organisation had previously left open in Congo and

---

[238] See also European Parliament, *Report on Special Report No. 2/96*, para.18.

[239] See ICG, *Reunifying Mostar*, at 9.

[240] See generally Tomuschat, *Yugoslavia's Damaged Sovereignty*, at 323; Frowein, *Notstandsverwaltung durch die Vereinten Nationen*, at 43; Bothe and Marauhn, *UN Administration of Kosovo and East Timor*, at 217; Yannis, *Kosovo Under International Administration*, at 11; Yannis, *The UN As Government in Kosovo*, at 67; Marcus G. Brand, *Institution-Building and Human Rights Protection in Kosovo*, Nordic Journal of International Law 70 (2001), 461; Betts, Carlson and Gisvold, *The Post-Conflict Transitional Administration of Kosovo*, at 371; Philipp A. Zygojannis, *Die Staatengemeinschaft und das Kosovo* (2002), 142; Anthony J. Miller, *UNMIK: Lessons From the*

Somalia. Instead of operating in a state of lawlessness, the UN took active steps to restore the applicable law[241] and basic judicial functions in the administered territory.[242] Moreover, the UN assumed full regulatory authority at the very beginning of the mission – a feature that distinguished UNMIK from the OHR in Bosnia. Nevertheless, both the sudden takeover of power as well as the accumulation of responsibilities tested the limits of the UN's capacities. UNMIK's governance practice was marked by "trial and error", especially in the regulatory and administrative field. The organisation was reluctant to conceive its own powers as state-like public authority, subject to independent checks and balances or judicial review. Furthermore, the exercise of the mandate of the administration remained overshadowed by the unresolved status question.[243]

4.1. Origin

The UN's administering role in Kosovo was forced by the turn of events rather than through the organisation's own will. Under the Interim Agreement for Peace and Self-Government in Kosovo ("Rambouillet Agreement") which was submitted to the FRY as a last-minute diplomatic effort before the use of military force, Kosovo was meant to become a democratic self-governing unit of Serbia operating under an OHR-like type of international supervision.[244] The rejection of the framework by the FRY, and the subsequent military intervention by NATO sparked calls for the assumption of post-conflict responsibilities by the UN. This led to the adoption of Resolution 1244, by which the Security Council adopted one of its most complex mandates ever, namely to establish "an interim administration for Kosovo under which the people of Kosovo can enjoy substantial autonomy within the Federal Republic of Yugoslavia, and

---

Early Institution-Building Phase, New England Law Review, Vol. 39 (2004), 9–24; Jürgen Friedrich, *UNMIK in Kosovo: Struggling with Uncertainty*, Max Planck Yearbook of United Nations Law, Vol. 9 (2005), 225–93; Knoll, *From Benchmarking to Final Status?*, at 637.

[241] See Section 3 of UNMIK Regulation No. 1/1999 of 25 July 1999 (*Authority of the Interim Administration in Kosovo*) and UNMIK Regulation No. 24/1999 of 12 December 1999 (*Law Applicable in Kosovo*).

[242] See UNMIK Regulation No. 18/1999 of 10 November 1999 (*Appointment and Removal From Offices and Lay-Judges*) and UNMIK Regulation No. 64/2000 of 15 December 2000 (*Assignment of International Judges/Prosecutors*).

[243] See on this aspect, in particular, Knoll, *From Benchmarking to Final Status?*, at 656–60; Friedrich, *UNMIK in Kosovo*, at 651–4.

[244] See Kosovo Peace Agreement, Rambouillet, February 23, 1999, Chapter 1 and Chapter 5, Article V, in Fred L. Israel (ed.), *Major Peace Treaties of Modern History (1980-2000)*, Vol. VI, at 370.

which will provide transitional administration while establishing and overseeing the development of provisional democratic self-governing to ensure conditions for peaceful and normal life for all inhabitants in Kosovo".[245] The resolution itself, however, presented neither a political solution to the Kosovo conflict, nor a comprehensive peace settlement between Kosovo Albanians and Serbs. It was an *ad hoc* response by the Security Council,[246] designed to stabilise the humanitarian situation in Kosovo, to reverse the effects of ethnic cleansing against Kosovo Albanians and to provide an interim basis for the political settlement of the Kosovo conflict.

4.2.   A tripartite function

UNMIK's mandate bears functional resemblances to the Saar administration and the administration of Bosnia. The mission was vested with a status resolution mandate comparable to the engagement of the League in the Saar,[247] and with a statebuilding mandate similar to the engagement in Bosnia. These two classical functions of international territorial administration were coupled with a third rationale: to reduce the gap between the (il-)legality and the legitimacy of the Kosovo intervention.

4.2.1.   UNMIK and territorial conflict solution

UNMIK's status resolution mandate resulted from the inability of the international community to solve the political dispute with the former FRY over the future status of Kosovo in 1999.[248] Security Resolution 1244 (1999), the founding Charter of Kosovo's transitional political status, was drafted at a moment in time when NATO's humanitarian intervention had barely ended and when Yugoslav troops and police forces were still in Kosovo.[249] The Council refrained from expressly recognising Kosovo's right to self-determination or independence,[250] despite the systematic oppression of Kosovars by the Milosevic regime and the

---

[245] See para. 10 of SC Resolution 1244 (1999).
[246] See also the critique by Yannis, *Kosovo Under International Administration*, at 33 ("another case-by-case response" that "did not address the underlying causes of the conflict and left Kosovo in limbo").
[247] In the case of the Saar, the holding of a referendum and the different status options were regulated by the Treaty of Versailles.
[248] For a discussion, see also Crawford, *Creation of States*, 2nd edn, at 557–60.
[249] For a full account, see Andreas Zimmermann and Carsten Stahn, *Yugoslav Territory, United Nations Trusteeship or Sovereign State? Reflections on the Current and Future Legal Status of Kosovo*, Nordic Journal of International Law, Vol. 70 (2001), 423.
[250] The Council merely mentioned the concepts of "substantial autonomy" and "self-government". See para. 11 of SC Res. 1244 (1999).

proclamation of an independent "Republic of Kosovo" by the Rugova government in 1992.[251] The Council opted instead for a political bargain, which reaffirmed the sovereignty and territorial integrity of the FRY,[252] but abstained from making binding determinations with respect to Kosovo's definitive status. Security Council Resolution 1244 charged UNMIK with the task of "facilitating a political process designed to determine Kosovo's future status, taking into account the Rambouillet accords" and "in a final stage, overseeing the transfer of authority from Kosovo's provisional institutions to institutions under a political settlement".[253] Both the practice of UNMIK[254] and the Secretary-General[255] made it clear that the determinations in Security Council Resolution 1244 did not pre-empt the option of independence.[256] UNMIK, therefore, exercised a genuinely open status resolution mandate,[257] which was to

[251] For a critical analysis, see Gerd Seidel, *A New Dimension of the Right of Self-Determination in Kosovo*, in Kosovo and the International Community: A Legal Assessment (Christian Tomuschat ed., 2002), 203. For a survey of the repression, see Joseph Marko, *Kosovo/a – A Gordian Knot?*, in Gordischer Knoten Kosovo/a: Durschchlagen oder entwirren? (Joseph Marko ed., 1999), 261.

[252] See para. 10 of the preamble of SC Resolution and para. 10 of the operative text. Later, Kosovo became part "of the territory of Serbia and Montenegro", which adhered to the Council of Europe in 2003. See Council of Europe, Parliamentary Assembly, *Protection of human rights in Kosovo*, Report of 6 January 2005, Doc.10393, para. 1.

[253] See para. 11 of SC Res.1244 (1999).

[254] See para. 6 of the preamble of Regulation No. 9/2001 of 15 May 2001 (Constitutional *Framework for Provisional Self-Government in Kosovo*), which refers to the "determination of Kosovo's future status through a process at an appropriate future stage, which shall, in accordance with UNSCR 1244 (1999), take full account of all relevant factors including the will of the people". See generally Carsten Stahn, *Constitution Without a State? Kosovo Under the United Nations Constitutional Framework for Self-Government*, Leiden Journal of International Law, Vol. 14 (2001), 531.

[255] See the Report of the Secretary-General of 20 April 2001, *No Exit Without Strategy: Security Council Decision-making and the Closure or Transition of United Nations Peacekeeping Operations*, UN Doc. S/2001/394 of 20 April 2001, paras. 39 and 40. ("In the case of Kosovo, the mandated benchmark for the exit of UNMIK is tied to determination of the final status...In keeping with the mandate, the operation has begun to devolve increasing autonomy and self-government in Kosovo, while avoiding any actions that would prejudge the outcome on final status.")

[256] The text of Resolution 1244 (1999) itself left room for a variety of scenarios. The general reference of the Council to the sovereignty and territorial integrity of the FRY in the Resolution could be read as an indication that Kosovo should remain part of the FRY, even under the future settlement. Such a narrow reading conflicts, however, with several other considerations, including (1) the express reference to the Rambouillet Agreement in Resolution 1244, which contains an express reference to "a final settlement for Kosovo, on the basis of the will of the people", (2) the fact that the settlement promoted by UNMIK shall only be of a temporary nature under the terms of Annex 1 and 2 to SC Resolution (1244) and (3) legal concerns about the authority of the Council itself to determine the political status of Kosovo.

[257] See also Knoll, *From Benchmnarking to Final Status?*, at 656.

be solved in "full account of all relevant factors including the will of the people".[258]

The status issue influenced the daily practice of the UN. UNMIK was forced "to navigate skilfully between the Scylla of independence and the Charybdis of FRY sovereignty".[259] It operated under continuous pressure from the Kosovo Albanian majority which pushed for a limitation of UN authority and a timetable for independence. At the same time, the UN administration faced opposition from Belgrade, which perceived UNMIK legislation as an encroachment upon its sovereignty and called upon the Serb minority to boycott elections.[260]

The open status question had direct implications for UNMIK's regulatory activity and reconstruction efforts. Kosovo's open status compromised the prospects of political and economic progress. Due to its uncertain political status, Kosovo was unable to "access international financial institutions, integrate into the regional economy or attract...foreign capital" necessary to reduce poverty and foster employment.[261] This *status quo* made it difficult for UNMIK to develop a viable economy under UN administration.

UNMIK was further prevented from adopting any measures that could preclude the choice of status options (independence, association with or re-integration into Serbia and Montenegro).[262] Controversies arose, in particular, in the phase of the adoption of the first UNMIK Regulations that were systematically opposed by the FRY[263] and in the context of the negotiation of the Constitutional Framework for Provisional Self-Government in Kosovo, where issues such as the title of the document,[264] the creation a directly elected President, the potential establishment of a "Constitutional Court", the holding of a referendum and or the stipulation of a "sunset" clause spelling out the time period for provisional self-government proved to be extremely controversial due to the demands of the Kosovo Albanian majority for a constitutional roadmap to independence.[265] The structure of the Constitutional Framework

---

[258] See para. 6 of the preamble of the Constitutional Framework.
[259] See Yannis, *Kosovo Under International Administration*, at 29.   [260] See also *ibid.*, at 28.
[261] See Report of the Special Envoy of the Secretary-General on Kosovo's future status, UN Doc. S/2007/168 of 26 March 2007, para. 9.
[262] See also Handbook on UN Multidimensional Peacekeeping Operations, at 20.
[263] *Ibid.*, at 27.
[264] Kosovo Albanians intended to call the document the "Provisional Constitution of Kosovo".
[265] UNMIK refused, in particular, to accept the adoption of a clause which would provide "the determination of Kosovo's future status in conformity with the express will of

made it clear that UNMIK sought to prevent any unilateral decisions or declarations by the Kosovo Assembly prior to the settlement of the status question.[266]

These tensions became even more apparent in the context of the conduct of status negotiations. Here, UNMIK faced a direct conflict of interest. In its capacity as an international territorial agent, the administration was forced to balance two conflicting objectives, namely the right of the Kosovar people to attain a legal status reflecting their historical, cultural and legal identity, on the one hand, and the preservation of the interests of the "organized international community", on the other.[267] This hybrid position created problems in two areas: the timing of the triggering of status negotiations and the issue of representation in the negotiations.

UNMIK adopted a delicate policy with regard to the start of status talks. Building upon the example of the "benchmark" policy of the PIC in Bosnia and Herzegovina,[268] the mission made the beginning of negotiations contingent upon the fulfilment of certain standards of governance by domestic institutions in Kosovo ("standards before status").[269] This policy sent an ambiguous message. It created the impression that self-government and self-determination are not absolute entitlements, but variables whose realisation depends to a large part on the good will of the members Contact Group. The Kosovo Albanian population interpreted the "benchmark" policy as an attempt by UNMIK to postpone the

---

the people". See generally the Report of the Secretary-General on the United Nations Interim Administration in Kosovo, UN Doc. S/2001/565 of 7 June 2001, para. 22. For a survey, see also Stahn, *Constitution Without a State?*, at 542.

[266] The area of foreign affairs was reserved to UNMIK. Moreover, the SRSG retained the "ultimate authority...for the implementation of UNSCR 1244 (1999)".

[267] See also Knoll, *From Benchmarking to Final Status?*, at 657–60.

[268] The Brussels Declaration of the PIC defined certain standards to measure the performance of domestic institutions in Bosnia. See Declaration of the Peace Implementation Council, Brussels, 24 May 2000, including annexes.

[269] The SRSG laid down eight benchmarks that should be achieved before the discussion of the final status question. The eight benchmarks are: functioning democratic institutions; rule of law (police/judiciary); freedom of movement; returns and integration; economy (legislation, balanced budget, privatisation); respect for property rights (clear title, restitution); dialogue with Belgrade; and the Kosovo Protection Corps (size, compliance with mandate, minority participation). The "standards before status" policy was formulated in a document entitled "Standards for Kosovo", UNMIK/PR/1078 of 10 December 2003. It was later followed by a "Kosovo Standards Implementation Plan" of 31 March 2004. For further discussion, see below Part IV, Chapter 16.

settlement of the status question. This ambiguity led to criticism of the UN administration[270] and a wave of localised violence in 2004.[271]

Paragraph 11 (e) of Resolution 1244 entrusted UNMIK itself with the mandate to facilitate "a political process designed to determine Kosovo's future status". This mandate raised a problem of representation. Controversies arose to what extent UNMIK could act as a mediator between the Kosovar and the Serbian side in status negotiations. Initially, UNMIK adopted a literal reading of the resolution and accepted to assume the role of a broker in the negotiations.[272] This direct involvement was, however, difficult to reconcile with the purported neutrality of the mission and its specific fiduciary responsibilities *vis-à-vis* the territory under administration.[273] The UN Secretary-General therefore decided to entrust a Special UN envoy (Martti Ahtisaari), with the mandate to lead the status talks and to mediate the divergent positions of the Kosovar and the Serb delegation.[274]

The UN Special Envoy held seventeen rounds of direct talks, bilateral negotiations and expert consultations over a period of fourteen months. In the course of the status negotiations, the Kosovar and the Serbian sides restated their divergent positions.[275] Kosovars insisted on full independence; Serbian officials made it clear that they would grant Kosovo substantial autonomy, but would not accept independence.[276] Members of the six-nation Contact Group (the UK, France, Germany, Italy, Russia

---

[270] See the Report of the Head of the DPKO Political Assessment Mission in Kosovo, Ambassador Kai Eide, *The Situation in Kosovo, Report to the Secretary-General of the United Nations*, Summary and Recommendations, UN Doc. S/2004/932, Annex I, Brussels, 15 July 2004, at 13 and 16. ("[W]ell functioning institutions depend on a strong sense of local ownership. Such ownership cannot be achieved if the owners do not know what they own and what they are intended to govern...The 'standards before status' policy is untenable in its present form. It must be replaced by a broader policy where standards implementation takes Kosovo in an orderly way from the present through future status discussions and into a wider regional and European integration process.")

[271] See Knoll, *From Benchmarking to Final Status?*, at 659.   [272] *Ibid.*, at 658.   [273] *Ibid.*

[274] The Security Council endorsed the selection of the UN Special Envoy on 10 November 2005.

[275] See Report of the Secretary-General on the United Nations Interim Administration in Kosovo, UN Doc. S/2006/2007, 1 September 2006, para. 29.

[276] The special status of Kosovo was recognised in the 2003 Constitution of Serbia and Montenegro which defined Serbia and Montenegro as "the state of Montenegro and the state of Serbia which includes the Autonomous Province of Vojvodina and the Autonomous Province of Kosovo and Metohija, the latter currently under international administration in accordance with SC Resolution 1244". The new Serbian Constitution adopted in 2006 reiterated that Kosovo forms part of Serbia.

and the US) stressed that any status settlement must preserve the multi-ethnic character of the territory and must be acceptable to the people of Kosovo.[277] The Guiding Principles of the Contact Group stipulated that there should be "no return of Kosovo to the pre-1999 situation, no partition of Kosovo and no union of Kosovo with any other, or part of another, country".[278]

The irreconcilable positions of the two parties made it impossible to reach a negotiated settlement between the parties by 2007. Due to the impasse in negotiations and the threat of growing social and political unrest in Kosovo, UN Special Envoy Athisaari presented a status proposal (the Comprehensive Proposal for the Kosovo Status Settlement) which attempted to bridge the gap between the different positions through a model supervised independence. The proposal was based on the premise that independence was "the only viable option" for status resolution in light of "Kosovo's history", its contemporary "realities", the need for political stability, economic viability and full responsibility and democratic accountability of Kosovo's institutions of self-government and "the positions of the parties in the negotiation process".[279] However, the exercise of Kosovo's independence was made contingent upon strict conditions: "fulfilment of the obligations set forth in [the] Settlement proposal" and continuing supervision by "international civilian and military presences".[280]

The content of the status settlement was in many ways reminiscent of the Dayton precedent. The proposal regulated the foundations of "Kosovo's future governance" as an independent state in a detailed way.[281] It set out fundamental "principles" and "elements" of a future constitution in a general and mandatory fashion ("The future

---

[277] For a survey, see the record of statements at the 5522nd meeting of the Security Council on 13 September 2006, UN Doc. S/PV.5522.

[278] Ibid., at 18–19. See also the Statement by the Contact Group on the Future of Kosovo, Washington, 31 January 2006. Serbia and Russia have continuously maintained that a solution imposed by the Security Council against the will of Belgrade would be unacceptable. See, for example, the statement of the representative of the Russian Federation at the 5522nd meeting of the Security Council, UN Doc. S/PV.5522, at 10.

[279] See Report of the Special Envoy of the Secretary-General on Kosovo's future status, UN Doc. S/2007/168 of 26 March 2007, paras. 5, 10 and 16.

[280] Ibid., para. 13.

[281] The Special Envoy uses the term "basic framework". See Report of the Special Envoy of the Secretary-General on Kosovo's future status, Annex ("Main Provisions of the Comprehensive Proposal for the Kosovo Status Settlement"), UN Doc. S/2007/168, para. 2. For analysis, see Jean D'Aspremont, Regulating Statehood: The Kosovo Status Settlement, Leiden Journal of International Law, Vol. 20 (2007), 649.

Constitution of Kosovo *shall* include, but not be limited to, the following...),[282] including provisions on the composition and functioning of governmental organs (Kosovo Assembly, President, Government of Kosovo),[283] the judiciary (e.g. Court structure, Constitutional Court),[284] decentralisation,[285] human rights and fundamental freedoms[286] and the protection of rights of communities and their members,[287] as well as provisions on external relations, such as the assumption of a share of external debts of Serbia[288] and the binding force of cooperation agreements and financial obligations undertaken by UNMIK "for and behalf of Kosovo".[289]

The operation and functioning of Kosovo's domestic institutions under the settlement was placed under the "general supervision" of an internationally appointed civilian representative (ICR)[290] who was mandated to act as ultimate supervisory authority until determination by an International Steering Group (comprised of key international stakeholders) that "Kosovo has implemented the terms of [the] Settlement".[291] The powers of the ICR were modelled on those of the OHR and included, *inter alia*: "final authority in Kosovo regarding interpretation of the civilian aspects of [the] Settlement",[292] the authority to annul decisions or laws adopted by Kosovo authorities[293] and the power to sanction or remove public officials whose action the ICR determines to be inconsistent with the settlement.[294] The mandate of the ICR was spelt out in great detail and meant to be scaled down over time.[295] However, the type of supervision was not markedly different from previous UNMIK rule,[296] despite the underlying commitment of the proposal to Kosovo's independence.

---

[282] See Comprehensive Proposal for the Kosovo Status Settlement, Annex I (Constitutional Provisions), preamble.

[283] See Annex I, Articles 3–5.

[284] See Annex I, Article 6 and Annex IV (The justice system).

[285] See Annex III (Decentralisation).   [286] Annex I, Article 2.

[287] See Annex II (The rights of communities and their members).

[288] Annex VI (External debt).

[289] See Article 15.2 of the Comprehensive Proposal for the Kosovo Status Settlement.

[290] See Annex 9, Article 2. The ICR should be appointed by the International Steering Group, following endorsement by the Security Council. See Article 12.1 of the Comprehensive proposal and Article 4 of Annex IX.

[291] See Annex IX, Article 5.2.   [292] See Annex IX, Article 2.1.a.

[293] See Annex 9, Article 2.1.c.   [294] See Annex IX, Article 2.1.d.

[295] See Articles 12.6 and 12.7 of the Comprehensive proposal and Annex IX, Articles 2 and 5. Article 5 of Annex IX mandated the International Steering Group to "establish benchmarks for a periodical review of the mandate of the ICR", with a view to "gradually reducing the scope of the powers of the ICR and the frequency of intervention".

[296] See the broad list of powers enumerated in Article 2 of Annex IX.

The Comprehensive Proposal was intended to form a political settlement determining the future status of Kosovo under Resolution 1244 (1999). This solution would have formalised the separation of Kosovo from Serbia, which started under UNMIK administration. But it failed to get the necessary political support in the Security Council. The Special Envoy "urged" the Council "to endorse [the] Settlement proposal". The Secretary-General submitted it to the Council on 26 March 2007, expressing his full "support" for "both the recommendation made by [the] Special Envoy in his report on Kosovo's future status and the Comprehensive Proposal for the Kosovo Status Settlement".[297] But no agreement could be reached among the P5, in particular due to continuing objections by Russia to the model of "supervised independence".

4.2.2.   UNMIK and statebuilding

The second broader focus of UNMIK was the implementation of its statebuilding mandate. The collapse of Kosovo's political and judicial system after years of repression and conflict, and the persistence of tensions between the Kosovar Albanian Community and the Serb minority, made it necessary to complement the resolution on the future status of Kosovo with a mandate to rebuild a viable political, judicial and economic system in Kosovo.[298] The Security Council authorised UNMIK to perform "basic civilian administrative functions where and as long as required"[299] and to organise and oversee "the development of provisional institutions for democratic and autonomous self-government".[300] This mandate was interpreted by UNMIK in broad terms. Quite to the surprise of and against the protest of the FRY,[301] UNMIK attributed to itself all branches of authority that constitutional theory attributes to a state (executive, legislative and judicial authority) in its Regulation No. 1, which decreed in sweeping terms that "all legislative and executive authority with respect to Kosovo, including the administration of the judiciary,

---

[297] See Letter dated dated 26 March 2007 from the Secretary-General addressed to the President of the Security Council, UN Doc. S/2007/168 of 26 March 2007.

[298] For a recent account of the numerous problems, see European Commission For Democracy Through Law, *Opinion on Human Rights in Kosovo: Possible Establishment of Review Mechanisms*, Opinion No. 280/2004 of 11 October 2004, paras. 32–61. See Council of Europe, Parliamentary Assembly, *Protection of human rights in Kosovo*, para. 29.

[299] See para. 11 (b) of SC Res. 1244 (1999) of 10 June 1999.

[300] See para. 11 (c) of SC Res. 1244 (1999).

[301] See the two memoranda issued by the FRY, First Memorandum, 5 November 1999, Second Memorandum, 6 March 2000. For an analysis, see Tomuschat, *Yugoslavia's Damaged Sovereignty*, at 325–6.

is vested in UNMIK".[302] Furthermore, UNMIK Special Representatives of the Secretary-General (SRSGs) were entitled to appoint or remove public officials, including members of the judiciary, and to revise or revoke all legal texts applicable in Kosovo,[303] with the sole exception of SC Resolution 1244, which constitutes "the only text akin to a basic law or 'constitution' governing UNMIK's action".[304]

Through its lawmaking practice, UNMIK created a novel normative space.[305] UNMIK introduced a novel hierarchy of norms under which previously existing sources of law were superseded or entangled by UN legislation. Moreover, UNMIK decided to adopt legislation in areas which exceeded Kosovo's status as an autonomous province under the 1992 Constitution of the FRY.[306] This practice had a far-reaching effect. It eliminated any substantial ties of authority between Kosovo and the FRY, by dissociating Yugoslavia's formal sovereignty over the territory from UNMIK's international territorial authority.[307] Kosovo and Serbia were "governed in complete separation".[308]

UNMIK faced considerable challenges in the implementation of its mandate. Kosovo was in a state of chaos and disorder after the withdrawal of the FRY troops. Kosovo Albanians and Serbs both had their own local administrations and fought for influence in their mutually controlled areas. Political hard-liners on both sides tried to use the authority vacuum to increase their influence in the respective

---

[302] See para. 1 of UNMIK Regulation No. 1/1999 of 25 July 1999 (*Authority of the Interim Administration in Kosovo*), which was later amended by UNMIK Regulation No. 54/2000.

[303] This follows from UNMIK Regulation No. 2471999, as amended by UNMIK Regulation No. 59/2000, which states that the applicable law in Kosovo shall, in order of precedence, include (1) regulations promulgated by the SRSG and subsidiary instruments, (2) the law in force prior to 22 March 1989 and (3) in case of lacuna and so long as it is not discriminatory and in accordance with internationally recognized human rights standards, the law in force after 22 March 1989.

[304] See also Council of Europe, Parliamentary Assembly, *Protection of human rights in Kosovo*, III. Explanatory Memorandum, para. 6.

[305] See also Knoll, *Beyond the "Mission Civilisatrice"*, at 283.

[306] See with respect to the adoption of provisions in the field of war crimes and crimes against humanity, Michael Bohlander, *The Joint Advisory Council Draft Criminal Code of Kosovo of 13 August 2001: Some Comments on War Crimes, Crimes Against Humanity and Security Council Resolution 1244*, Kosovo Legal Studies, Vol. 3 (2002), 5–6.

[307] Kosovo remained formally under the sovereignty of Serbia and Montenegro, but under the jurisdiction of UNMIK. See also Council of Europe, Parliamentary Assembly, *Protection of human rights in Kosovo*, III. Explanatory Memorandum, para. 4. ("Kosovo is part of the national territory of Serbia and Montenegro. That said, Kosovo no longer falls within the jurisdiction of Serbia and Montenegro, but is instead administered by UNMIK.")

[308] See Report of the Special Envoy of the Secretary-General on Kosovo's future status, UN Doc. S/2007/168 of 26 March 2007, para. 7.

communities. Irregular groups exercised control over economic resources and public buildings. In addition, an estimated 500,000 people were internally displaced within Kosovo.[309]

UNMIK focused on two objectives in order to restore peace and stability. It established law and order in Kosovo and it built functioning institutions involving the local population.[310]

The creation of a transitional system of law and order was not only crucial to fill legal gaps, but also necessary to reverse the past discriminatory practices of the Serbian regime and to restore their belief in the building of a pluralist Kosovo. In order to avoid a legal vacuum in the initial phase of the administration, UNMIK decided that the "laws applicable in Kosovo prior to 24 March 1999" should continue to apply, in so far as they did not conflict with internationally recognised human rights standards, Security Council Resolution 1244 (1999) and subsequent regulations issued by UNMIK. This approach was pragmatic, but problematic[311] because it charged a young and inexperienced judiciary with the difficult task of assessing whether a specific provision of the Kosovo legal system was compatible with the treaty law and case law of the ECHR or the ICCPR.[312] Even the existing courts in Kosovo were supposed to "request clarification from the Special Representative of the Secretary-General" in the absence of legal certainty about the applicable law.[313]

Later, UNMIK went on to reform the legal system from scratch. It repealed discriminatory legislation,[314] appointed lay-judges,[315] created an Ad Hoc Court of Final Appeal and an Ad Hoc Office of the Public Prosecutor,[316] established regional and municipal administrators[317] and

[309] See Strohmeyer, *Making Multilateral Interventions Work*, at 109; Yannis, *Kosovo Under International Administration*, at 25.
[310] Four "pillars" were set up by UNMIK: Pillar I: Police and Justice, under the direct leadership of the United Nations; Pillar II: Civil Administration, under the direct leadership of the United Nations; Pillar III: Democratisation and Institution-Building, led by the OSCE; Pillar IV: Reconstruction and Economic Development, led by the EU.
[311] See Strohmeyer, *Making Multilateral Interventions Work*, at 112. For a discussion, see also Caplan, *International Governance of War-Torn Territories*, at 70–80.
[312] See Section 1 of UNMIK Regulation No. 24/1999 of 12 December 1999 (*Law Applicable in Kosovo*).
[313] See Section 3 of UNMIK Regulation No. 24/1999.
[314] See UNMIK Regulation No. 10/1999 of 13 October 1999 (*Repeal of Discriminatory Legislation Affecting Housing and Rights in Property*).
[315] See UNMIK Regulation No. 18/1999 of 10 November 1999 (*Appointment and Removal from Office of Lay-Judges*).
[316] See UNMIK Regulation No. 5/1999 of 4 September 1999 (*Ad hoc Court of Final Appeal and Ad hoc Office of the Public Prosecutor*).
[317] See UNMIK Regulation No. 14/1999 of 21 October 1999 (*Appointment of Regional and Municipal Administrators*).

designated international judges and prosecutors for service in the judicial system,[318] before cutting back its role to the promulgation of laws such as the Provisional Criminal Code of Kosovo[319] or the Provisional Criminal Procedure Code of Kosovo.[320] However, both legal uncertainty and a lack of institutional knowledge within the judiciary continued to hamper the development of the domestic legal system even half a decade after the establishment of UNMIK.[321]

The second great challenge that UNMIK faced immediately after its establishment was the need to replace the existing self-appointed institutions in Kosovo with legitimate public representatives and to generate public resources, for the running of the state institutions. UNMIK employed a two-stage strategy to accomplish these goals, first creating the basic conditions for economic and political reconstruction, allowing local actors to assume a partnership role in governance; and then devolving daily governing authority to elected representatives of the different local communities, while retaining full power to overrule acts by the local political institutions.

The first phase lasted from June 1999 to October 2000, the date of the first municipal elections in Kosovo. During this period, UNMIK established the foundations for Kosovo's state and institutional systems. The SRSG established a customs system,[322] a currency regime,[323] a Central Fiscal Authority,[324] the Banking and Payments Authority of Kosovo,[325]

---

[318] See UNMIK Regulation No. 64/2000 of 15 December 2000 (*Assignment of International Judges/Prosecutors and/or Change of Venue*).

[319] See UNMIK Regulation No. 25/2003 of 6 July 2003 (*Provisional Criminal Code of Kosovo*).

[320] See UNMIK Regulation No. 26/2003 of 6 July 2003 (*Provisional Criminal Procedure Code of Kosovo*).

[321] See Council of Europe, Parliamentary Assembly, *Protection of human rights in Kosovo*, III. Explanatory Memorandum, para. 29. ("In addition to the problem of 'legal chaos' in identifying, interpreting and applying proper law, Kosovo police, prosecution and judges, already inexperienced, have been faced with the introduction of a legal system quite different from that in which they were trained and previously practiced... As for international judges, whilst in general well appreciated for their experience and ability to deal with politically or ethnically sensitive cases, not all have had the training necessary for the job...[There is] anecdotal evidence of judges applying their own national laws instead of the law applicable in Kosovo and of judges lacking familiarity with European human rights principles.")

[322] See UNMIK Regulation No. 3/1999 of 31 August 1999 (*Establishment of the Customs and other Related Services in Kosovo*).

[323] See UNMIK Regulation No. 4 /1999 of 2 September 1999 (*Currency Permitted to Be Used in Kosovo*).

[324] See UNMIK Regulation No. 16/1999 of 6 November 1999 (*Establishment of the Central Fiscal Authority of Kosovo and Other Related Matters*).

[325] See UNMIK Regulation No. 20/1999 of 15 November 1999 (*Banking and Payments Authority of Kosovo*).

a municipality system,[326] regulation on the degree of self-government of municipalities,[327] a Central Election Commission,[328] a system for the registration and operation of political parties in Kosovo,[329] regulation of the broadcast and print media system in Kosovo[330] and a framework for the creation of liaison offices of foreign governments in Kosovo.[331] Following the example of the Allied reconstruction of Germany after 1945, political self-government was restored in a "bottom-up" fashion, starting at the municipal level and moving progressively towards the central level.

The elections of 28 October 2000, a victory for democratic and moderated forces after the historic changes in Belgrade of 5 October 2000, marked the first political turning point. Despite continuing rivalries among the main political parties,[332] the first locally elected representatives assumed governmental authority at the municipal level.[333] The transfer of administering responsibilities at the central level followed one year later with the enactment of the Constitutional Framework which granted newly established provisional institutions of self-government (the Assembly, the President of Kosovo, the Government and the Courts[334]) direct powers in the legislative, executive and judicial fields.[335]

In the second phase of transitional administration, beginning with the election of the provisional institutions of self-government in 2001,

---

[326] See UNMIK Regulation No. 43/2000 of 27 July 2000 (*On the Number, Names and Boundaries of Municipalities*).

[327] See UNMIK Regulation No. 45/2000 of 14 August 2000 (*On Self-Government of Municipalities in Kosovo*).

[328] See UNMIK Regulation No. 21/2000 (*Establishment of the Central Election Commission*).

[329] See UNMIK Regulation No. 16/2000 (*Registration and Operation of Political Parties in Kosovo*).

[330] See UNMIK Regulation No. 36/2000 of 17 June 2000 (*Licensing and Regulation of Broadcast of Media*) and UNMIK Regulation No. 37/2000 of 17 June 2000 (*Conduct of Print Media in Kosovo*).

[331] See UNMIK Regulation No. 42/2000 of 10 July 2000 (*Establishment and Functioning of Liaison Offices in Kosovo*).

[332] See para. 31 of the Report of the Security Council Mission on the Implementation of Security Council Resolution 1244 (1999), UN Doc. S/2001/600 of 19 June 2001.

[333] Municipal assemblies were elected in October 2000, and again in 2002 and 2004. These assemblies enjoyed autonomy to manage local affairs, including public services, education, urban planning, health care and environmental issues. See Sections 3.1–3.3 of UNMIK Regulation No. 2000/45.

[334] Under Section 9.4.4 of the Constitutional Framework, the Court system comprises: a Supreme Court of Kosovo, District Courts, Municipal Courts and Minor Offences Courts.

[335] For a detailed survey, see UNMIK, *Report to the Human Rights Committee on the Human Rights Situation in Kosovo since 1999*, CCPR/C/UNK/1, 13 March 2006, paras. 38–82.

the UN assumed the role of a guarantor of the surrogate peace settlement embodied in Security Council Resolution 1244 (1999). The transfer of authority to Municipal Assemblies and Provisional Institutions of Self-Government entailed a decentralisation of authority. Nevertheless, UNMIK retained important prerogatives even in this second phase of transitional administration. The Constitutional Framework left crucial areas such as external relations, law enforcement, the protection of minority communities and budgetary control under the direct responsibility of the SRSG. UNMIK maintained its "ultimate authority...for the implementation of UNSCR 1244 (1999)",[336] including the power to supervise the Provisional Institutions of Self-Government, its officials and agencies, and to take "appropriate measures" against actions that "are inconsistent with UNSCR 1244 (1999) or [the] Constitutional Framework"[337] – a power that the SRSG used, at least twice, namely to veto a resolution of the Kosovo Assembly on the "territorial integrity of Kosovo"[338] and to abrogate a "Memorandum of Understanding between the Ministry of Economy and Finance of Kosovo and the Ministry of Economy of Albania".[339]

In this second phase, powers of lawmaking were predominantly exercised by the Kosovo Assembly. UNMIK confined its role essentially to the control and promulgation of legal acts adopted by domestic institutions,[340] the amendment of existing UNMIK Regulations and the assessment of progress in implementation of the "standards for Kosovo".[341] The

[336] See para. 9 of the preamble of the Constitutional Framework.
[337] See Chapter 12 of the Constitutional Framework. It is also worth noting that the Constitutional Framework itself was adopted in the form of a regulation, which implies that it may be unilaterally amended by UNMIK through subsequent regulatory action.
[338] The resolution was adopted by the Kosovo Assembly on 23 May 2002. It was annulled by SRSG Steiner on the same day. For further discussion, see below Part IV, Chapter 13 (2. Treatment of the status question in practice).
[339] In June 2002, the SRSG abrogated a Memorandum for Understanding for economic cooperation and the establishment of a liberal trade agreement between Kosovo and Albania, signed on 30 May 2002 in Prishtina by Kosovo Trade Minister Ali Jakupi and Albanian Economy Minister Ermelinda Meksi. The SRSG justified this move by UNMIK's final authority in the area of external relations. See www.unmikonline.org/press/2002/mon/july/lmm010702.htm.
[340] Under the Constitutional Framework, laws adopted by the Kosovo Assembly must be promulgated by the SRSG through a UNMIK Regulation before they enter into force. See generally on the process of lawmaking, UNMIK, *Report to the Human Rights Committee on the Human Rights Situation in Kosovo since 1999*, CCPR/C/UNK/1, 13 March 2006, paras. 61–5.
[341] See, for example, Report of the Secretary-General on the United Nations Interim Administration Mission in Kosovo, 1 September 2006, Annex 1.

SRSG intervened directly in the legislative process only in exceptional cases.[342]

This overview of mission's practice illustrates that UNMIK was more than an ordinary statebuilding mission: it marked the epitome of a governance mission in which the UN deviated from its classical function as an arbiter of third party interests and became virtually "the government of the state" itself.

4.2.3.   UNMIK and post-conflict responsibility

A third noteworthy feature of the UN engagement in Kosovo is the relationship between the post-conflict responsibilities of the mission and the preceding use of force.[343] There is a link between the creation of UNMIK and the Kosovo intervention. International administering authority was used as a technique to lend credibility to Operation Allied Force, which had been conducted without previous Council authorisation. UNMIK was, at least partly, established in order to validate[344] and implement the goals of the humanitarian intervention.[345] The Council failed

---

[342] The SRSG, for instance, refused to promulgate the Law on Higher Education adopted by the Kosovo Assembly on 25 July 2003. See Knoll, *Beyond the "Mission Civilisatrice"*, at 293.

[343] See generally, Tania Voon, *Closing the Gap Between Legitimacy and Legality of Humanitarian Intervention: Lessons From East Timor and Kosovo*, UCLA Journal of International Law and Foreign Affairs, Vol. 7 (2002), 31.

[344] The prevailing legal opinion on Kosovo continues to maintain that the intervention was illegal under the Charter. See, *inter alia*, Thomas M. Franck, *Recourse to Force: State Action Against Threats and Armed Attacks* (2002), at 180–1, Albrecht Randelzhofer, *On Article 2 (4)*, in B. Simma (ed.), Charter of the United Nations, 2nd edn (2002), 130–2, at para. 56; Yoram Dinstein, *War, Aggression and Self-Defense* (2001), at 270–1, Jonathan I. Charney, *Anticipatory Humanitarian Intervention in Kosovo*, American Journal of International Law, Vol. 93 (1999) 834, at 837; Simon Chesterman, *Just War or Just Peace?: Humanitarian Intervention and International Law* (2001), at 226; Bruno Simma, *NATO, the UN and the Use of Force: Legal Aspects*, European Journal of International Law, Vol. 10 (1999), 1; (1999); Peter Hilpold, *Humanitarian Intervention: Is There a Need for a Legal Reappraisal?*, European Journal of International Law, Vol. 12 (2001), 437, at 461.

[345] Some authorities have gone so far as to regard the exercise of administering functions by UNMIK and KFOR as a formal requirement of the legality of the humanitarian intervention itself, which is said to impose a post-conflict responsibility on the intervening actors ("*Verpflichtung zur Nachsorge*"). See Zygojannis, *Die Staatengemeinschaft und das Kosovo*, at 125 ("Die Verpflichtung des Intervenienten zur Nachsorge als Rechtsfolge durchgeführter humanitärer Intervention"). This reasoning is tempting from a conceptual point of view, but not necessarily the most convincing model to explain the link between the use of force and territorial administration in the specific case of Kosovo. It tends to ignore the fact that civil administration was not carried out by the coalition of states leading the intervention, but under the independent umbrella of the UN.

expressly to endorse the use of force by NATO intervention. But it quietly accepted the outcome of the intervention and supported the new situation by authorising the Kosovo Force (KFOR) and UNMIK to administer Kosovo separately from the rest of Yugoslavia.

4.3. Fostering people's rights

The close relationship between the UN administration and the concept of humanitarian intervention is reflected in UNMIK's design and practice. The mission was focused on the restoration of peoples' rights. The Security Council charged the UN administration with the re-establishment of self-government and substantial autonomy in Kosovo[346] – two group rights which may be viewed as institutional options for the implementation of claims of internal self-determination. The mandate of the mission was drafted in a dynamic fashion, requiring UNMIK to devolve its governing authority progressively to local institutions.[347] Moreover, one of the principal purposes of the UN operation was to reverse the consequences of the ethnic conflict through the promotion of minority returns and human rights protection.[348]

UNMIK's practice reflects this trend. The administration coupled its assumption of authority with the dissociation of Yugoslav authority over the people of Kosovo.[349] It took active steps to limit and reduce the effects of ethnic division. The SRSG created, in particular, a Housing and Property Directorate and a Housing and Property Claims Commission[350] to cope with the large number of property claims and to prevent ethnic segregation.[351] UNMIK established a Code of Conduct and a Temporary Media Commissioner to prevent and reduce ethnic discrimination in print and other media.[352]

Furthermore, the UN administration adopted special measures to protect the Serb minority in Kosovo.[353] It refused to grant Serbs territorial

---

[346] See SC Res. 1244 (1999), paras. 10 and 11.   [347] See *ibid.*, para. 11 d).
[348] See *ibid.*, para. 11 j) and k).   [349] See UNMIK Regulation No. 1/1999.
[350] See UNMIK Regulation No. 23/1999. The Directorate was established to mediate solutions to property claims, whereas the Commission gained the authority to resolve legal disputes over residential property claims. For a full discussion, see below Part IV, Chapter 16.
[351] On the background, see Council of Europe, Parliamentary Assembly, *Protection of human rights in Kosovo*, III. Explanatory Memorandum, para. 23.
[352] See UNMIK Regulations No. 36/2000 and No. 37/2000.
[353] For a full survey, see UNMIK, *Report to the Human Rights Committee on the Human Rights Situation in Kosovo since 1999*, CCPR/C/UNK/1, 13 March 2006, paras. 253–84.

autonomy.[354] But the SRSG launched an Agenda for Coexistence[355] which ensured the delivery of public services to Serbs and provided for minimum self-rule by Serbs in the municipalities.[356] At the same time, the SRSG retained the power to set aside any decision of a municipality that "does not take sufficiently into account the rights and interests of the communities which are not in the majority in the territory of the municipality".[357]

Serbs and other minorities were also granted strong protection under Kosovo's provisional institutional system created by the Constitutional Framework. The document established a self-governing structure at the central level with special privileges and protection for "national communities".[358] Representatives of non-Albanian Kosovo communities obtained a fixed share of twenty seats in the 120-member Kosovo Assembly[359] and two guaranteed seats in the Assembly Presidency.[360] Following the example of the Bosnian Constitution[361] and the Rambouillet Accord,[362] the Constitutional Framework also instituted a "vital interest" procedure,[363] allowing "any member if the Assembly, supported by five additional members" to "submit a motion to the Presidency claiming that [a] law or certain of its provisions violate the vital interests of the Community to which he belongs". Unlike in the Bosnian case, however, and based on the painful lesson learned by the experience under the DPA, the vital interest motion was only vested with a suspensive effect. It could be overruled by a positive vote of the Assembly,[364] unless the

[354] Serb leaders submitted a proposal for a "cantonisation" of Kosovo, which provided for the creation of Serb cantons in rural areas where Serbs would be independent from Kosovo Albanian rule. Ibid., at 49. But this proposal was rejected by the SRSG.
[355] Section 4.3 of UNMIK Regulation No. 45/2000 of 11 August 2000 (Self-Government of Municipalities in Kosovo) placed municipal bodies under a positive obligation "to promote coexistence between their inhabitants and to create appropriate conditions enabling all communities to express, preserve and develop their ethnic, cultural, religious and linguistic identities". The Constitutional Framework extended this positive obligation to the Provisional Institutions of Self-Government at all levels.
[356] See Section 23 of UNMIK Regulation No. 45/2000 of 11 August 2000.
[357] See Section 47 (2) of UNMIK Regulation No. 45/2000.
[358] See Section 4 (3) of the Constitutional Framework.
[359] See Section 9.1.3 (b) of the Constitutional Framework. This provision was inserted in order to grant minority groups public representation even in the case of a boycott of elections.
[360] See Section 9.17 (d) and (e) of the Constitutional Framework.
[361] See Article IV (3) and V (2) of the Constitution of BiH.
[362] See Rambouillet Agreement, Chapter 1, Article II (7)-(9).
[363] See Section 9.1.39 of the Constitutional Framework.
[364] See Section 9.1.41-9.1.42 of the Constitutional Framework.

SRSG decided to protect the interests of the community concerned by
making use of his authority under Section 4 (6) of the Constitutional
Framework to act as the ultimate guardian of the rights of the national
communities.[365]

UNMIK exercised its role as a guardian of inter-ethnic relations on a
number of occasions. The SRSG set aside decisions of municipalities[366]
and opposed a controversial resolution of the Kosovo Assembly on "liberation war of the people of Kosovo for freedom and independence".[367]

4.4. Trials and errors

In spite of the advancement and innovations brought by the practice of
the UN administration in fields such as property protection, institutional
engineering, judicial reform and the rule of law, UNMIK's track record
is far from perfect. The administration encountered criticism, for both
the exercise and the conception of its own public authority.

4.4.1. Benevolent autocracy

UNMIK adopted an autocratic style of governance, in particular, in the
first phase of administration: it acted largely as a government for, but
without the people; it maintained essentially a top-down approach in
the exercise of public authority, which caused discontent among local
political leaders and created local dependencies on the international
authority. The UN administration regulated virtually each and every aspect of public life,[368] ranging from the licensing of security services
in Kosovo[369] to the stamps to be used in domestic courts,[370] although

---

[365] See Section 4 (6) of the Constitutional Framework. ("[T]he SRSG will retain the
authority to intervene as necessary in the exercise of self-government for the purpose
of protecting the rights of Communities and their members.")

[366] See, for example, UNMIK Executive Decision 2004/8 of 8 April 2004, by which the
SRSG set aside provisions in the Municipal Regulation No. 2000/1 of the Municipal
Assembly of Mitrovica of 20 February 2004.

[367] The Resolution was adopted by the Kosovo Assembly on 15 May 2003. The SRSG issued
a declaration stating that the text of the resolution "was divisive and ... against the
reconciliatory spirit enshrined in Security Council Resolution 1244 and the
Constitutional Framework" since it failed to pay respect the rights and interests of all
communities. See Declaration of SRSG Michael Steiner on the Assembly Resolution on
War Values, dated 15 May 2003, at www.kosovo.net/erpkim16may03.html#1.

[368] See generally on UNMIK lawmaking, von Carlowitz, *UNMIK Lawmaking*, 336; Irmscher,
Legal Framework, 353.

[369] See UNMIK Regulation No. 33/2000 of 25 May 2000 (*Licensing of Security Services Providers
in Kosovo and the Regulation of Their Employees*).

[370] See UNMIK Regulation No. 30/2000 of 20 May 2000 (*On Stamps and Headings of Official
Documents of Courts, Prosecutors' Offices and Penal Establishments*).

the UN had little experience in this type of lawmaking and lacked the time and the resources to subject this legislation to expert scrutiny or parliament-like control.[371] This shortcoming led to flaws in the exercise of regulatory authority, and to incompatibilities with international human rights standards (e.g. in the field of "executive detentions").[372]

Moreover, the UN administration failed to grant the domestic population a direct means of petition or redress against acts of UNMIK before domestic courts or UN supervisory bodies. UNMIK faced therefore less institutional control and accountability than the proposed UN governors of Trieste or Jerusalem, although it enjoyed wider powers than its (fictitious) historical precedents. These shortcomings weakened UNMIK's legitimacy as an international public authority and exposed the UN governance framework in Kosovo to a wave of criticism from human rights institutions,[373] the OSCE[374] and legal scholars,[375] which culminated in the adoption of an Opinion by the European Commission for Democracy Through Law on Human Rights in Kosovo in October 2004, highlighting the need for the creation of additional international accountability mechanisms for UNMIK and KFOR,[376] and the subsequent adoption of

[371] UNMIK issued formalised "Guidelines for the Preparation of UNMIK Legislation" only in May 2001. See generally on UNMIK lawmaking procedures, von Carlowitz, *UNMIK Lawmaking*, at 376–7.

[372] For a good survey, see Marshall and Inglis, *Disempowerment of Human Rights-Based Justice*, at 110, 137.

[373] Ombudsperson Institution in Kosovo, *Special Report No. 1 on the Compatibility with recognized international standards of UNMIK Regulation No. 47/2000 on the Status, Privileges and Immunities of KFOR and UNMIK and Their Personnel in Kosovo* (18 August 2000); *Special Report No. 2 on Certain Aspects of UNMIK Regulation No. 24/1999 on the Law Applicable in Kosovo* (27 October 2000); *Special Report No. 3 on the Conformity of Deprivations of Liberty under 'Executive Orders' with Recognized International Standards* (29 June 2001); *Special Report No. 4, Certain Aspects of UNMIK Regulation No. 18/2001 on the Establishment of a Detention Review Commission for Extra-judicial Detentions Based on Executive Orders* (25 August 2001); *Special Report No. 5 on Certain Aspects of UNMIK Regulation No. 17/2001 on the Registration of Contracts for the Sale of Real Property in Specific Geographical Areas of Kosovo* (22 August 2001).

[374] See, for example, OSCE Mission in Kosovo "Review of the Criminal Justice System", 11, available at www.oesce.org/kosovo.

[375] See Frédéric Mégret and Florian Hoffmann, *The UN as a Human Rights Violator? Some Reflections on the United Nations Changing Human Rights Responsibilities*, Human Rights Quarterly, Vol. 25 (2003), 314; Marshall and Inglis, *The Disempowerment of Human Rights-Based Justice*, at 95; Ralph Wilde, *Accountability and International Actors in Bosnia and Herzegovina, Kosovo and East Timor*, ILSA Journal of International and Comparative Law, Vol. 7 (2002), 455; Friedrich, *UNMIK in Kosovo*, at 277–80.

[376] See European Commission For Democracy Through Law, *Opinion on Human Rights in Kosovo: Possible Establishment of Review Mechanisms*, Opinion No. 280/2004 of 11 October 2004, paras. 67–148.

Resolution 1417 (2005) by the Parliamentary Assembly of the Council of Europe in January 2005, which recommended, *inter alia*, the establishment of a Human Rights Court for Kosovo, with "jurisdiction to examine complaints alleging violations of the rights contained in the European Convention on Human Rights and its additional protocols by UNMIK, KFOR and KFOR national contingents and the Provisional Institutions of Self-Government"[377] and the creation of an "Advisory panel/Human Rights Commission consisting of international human rights experts ... charged with scrutinising (draft) UNMIK regulations and subsidiary instruments for compliance with international human rights standards, along with other tasks such as hearing appeals from the UNMIK Claims Office, and addressing to UNMIK opinions on issues, other than individual complaints, brought to its attention by the Ombudsperson [Institution]".[378]

UNMIK responded to some of these recommendations in 2006. The UN administration refused to be subject to binding judicial scrutiny, arguing that such a review would be "problematic from the perspective of the privileges and immunities of UNMIK and its personnel, their possible exposure to liability and the importance of not compromising the discretion of the institutions of the United Nations to interpret the mandate of UNMIK under UNSCR 1244".[379] However, it decided to establish a Human Rights Advisory Panel which was authorised to examine individual complaints concerning alleged violations of human rights by UNMIK and to communicate (non-binding) findings and recommendations to the SRSG.[380]

4.4.2. Dictatorship of virtues

The second criticism that may be voiced in relation to UN administration in Kosovo is that it strictly enforced "its" conceptions of good governance and the rule of law on the territory. Like the drafters of the DPA, UNMIK had a tendency to impose international standards in disregard of the conditions on the ground.[381] The UN administration, in particular, overcharged the judiciary with legal obligations in the first phase of the

[377] See Council of Europe, Parliamentary Assembly, Resolution 1417 (2005), adopted on 25 January 2005, para. 4.
[378] *Ibid.*, para. 5 (v).
[379] See UNMIK, *Report to the Human Rights Committee on the Human Rights Situation in Kosovo since 1999*, CCPR/C/UNK/1, 13 March 2006, para. 132.
[380] See UNMIK Regulation No. 12/2006 of 23 March 2006 (*Establishment of the Human Rights Advisory Panel*). For a full treatment of the accountability dilemma, see below Part IV, Chapter 14.
[381] See also Knoll, *Beyond the "Mission Civilisatrice"*, at 280–3.

mission, without assessing whether the conditions were ripe for such a change.[382] Later, UNMIK used the strict letter and wording of Security Council Resolution 1244 (1999), to impose a transitional regime of democratic governance in the Constitutional Framework that reserved important decision-making powers to the SRSG and institutionalised UN supervised ethnic rights and checks and balances, but was not agreed upon by any of the local actors.[383] UNMIK's regulatory action suffered from a lack of transparency[384] and a tendency of overregulation.[385] The agenda promoted by UNMIK remained therefore sometimes far ahead of the reality of domestic politics.[386]

This normative ambition was coupled with a strong degree of interference in domestic decision-making. The SRG used its prerogatives under SC Resolution 1244 to veto or invalidate a number of domestic acts, ranging from resolutions of the Kosovo Assembly[387] to acts of the executive branch of power and judicial decisions,[388] often with only a few lines of legal reasoning.

---

[382] UNMIK's definition of the applicable law caused objections by local leaders and confusion among local lawyers. For a survey of the difficulties, see Miller, *UNMIK: Lessons From the Early Institution-Building Phase*, at 15–18.

[383] UNMIK hoped to gain the support of the different national communities for the Constitutional Framework. But none of the local actors agreed to the compromise solution that became the final version of the document. See Simon Chesterman, *Kosovo in Limbo: State-Building and "Substantial Autonomy"*, Report, International Peace Academy, August 2001, at 6.

[384] See Council of Europe, Parliamentary Assembly, *Protection of human rights in Kosovo*, III. Explanatory Memorandum, para. 28. See also below Part IV, Chapter 16.

[385] It is symptomatic that the former Legal Counsel, Hans Corell, compared UNMIK and UNTAET to "legislative factories". See Chestermann, *You the People*, at 129.

[386] The Secretary-General acknowledged in September 2006 that "Kosovo Serb participation in the government structures of Kosovo remains marginal, particularly at the central level, and their lack of engagement in political and institutional life an obstacle to the fulfilment of certain standards". See Report of the Secretary-General on the United Nations Interim Administration in Kosovo, 1 September 2006, para. 9.

[387] For a discussion of the annulment of a resolution of the Kosovo Assembly on the territorial integrity of Kosovo of 23 May 2002. See below Part IV, Chapter 13.

[388] On 20 October 2004 UNMIK intervened in the tender process for a mobile phone operator (Mobitel) carried out by the Telecommunication Regulatory Authority (TRA) by Executive Decision 2004/25. When the Prishtina Municipal Court required the TRA to execute the agreement with Mobitel, UNMIK declared the decision of the Court "without legal basis and non-enforceable", since it "disregarded the applicable law in Kosovo as established by the Executive Decision of the SRSG". UNMIK's position was justified as follows: "In issuing the Executive Decision, the SRSG was acting under the authority vested in him pursuant to the UN Security Council mandate under resolution 1244. In making such a determination the SRSG has full authority to issue an Executive Decision which has the force of law and is not subject to any challenges". See UNMIK Press Briefing Notes, 23 March 2005, at www.unmikonline.org/DPI/Transcripts.nsf/0/7BFC995720F089A1C1256FEE00292B97/$FILE/tr230305.pdf.

4.4.3. Lack of control over KFOR

At the same time, the UN administration lacked one form of control, which might have been appropriate in the light of UNMIK's mandate, namely control over the armed forces. The Kosovo Force (KFOR), a NATO-led international force[389] composed of four multinational brigades,[390] was charged by the Security Council with an independent institutional mandate concerning the establishment and maintenance of a secure environment in Kosovo, including public safety and order. SC Resolution 1244 (1999) and Article 8 (2) of UNMIK Regulation No. 2001/19 limited the role of the SRSG in relation to KFOR to mere tasks of coordination. Democratic control over KFOR troops remained therefore entirely in the hands of the governments of the individual troop-contributing states. This system led to a "removal of civilian democratic control [over the armed forces] from the areas of operations" and to a "fragmentation of democratic control over KFOR", which was criticised from an accountability perspective by several institutions,[391] including the High Commissioner for Human Rights of the Council of Europe.[392]

4.5. Assessment

UNMIK was a groundbreaking mission. The strong commitment to the objective of statebuilding marked a conceptual change in the practice of UN administration. The UN did not avoid the assumption of governing responsibilities in a politically fragile environment, as it had done previously in Somalia or in the Congo; it sought comprehensive authority in order to create sustainable peace among the conflicting ethnic groups in Kosovo and to preserve the unity of the territory. This practice indicated a move towards a more problem-solving-oriented agenda of UN territorial administration.

---

[389] The following NATO member states participate in KFOR: Belgium, Bulgaria, Canada, Czech Republic, Denmark, Estonia, France, Germany, Greece, Hungary, Italy, Lithuania, Luxembourg, Norway, Poland, Portugal, Romania, Slovakia, Slovenia, Spain, Turkey, the UK and the US. Non-NATO members are: Argentina, Armenia, Austria, Azerbaijan, Finland, Georgia, Ireland, Morocco, Sweden, Switzerland, Ukraine and United Arab Emirates.

[390] The KFOR brigades act "under the unified command and control" of Commander KFOR from NATO. See SC Resolution 1244, Annex 2, para. 4.

[391] See Amnesty International, *The apparent lack of accountability of international peace-keeping forces in Kosovo and Bosnia-Herzegovina*, AI Index: EUR 05/002/2004, April 2004, at 9–10.

[392] See Council of Europe, Office of the Commissioner for Human Rights, *Kosovo: The Human Rights Situation and the Fate of Persons Displaced from their Homes*, 16 October 2002, 21, paras. 85–6, at 87.

The implementation of the UN's mandate was, however, hampered by several factors. Both the ongoing disputes between Serbs and Kosovo Albanians and UNMIK's duty to respect Yugoslav sovereignty by virtue of SC Resolution 1244 placed the mission in a delicate situation, in which UN administrators were continuously forced to act against the will of local actors. The concomitant lack of public support for UNMIK's policies significantly weakened the accomplishment of the goals of the mandate.[393] Social and political progress was further hampered by Kosovo's uncertain status. UNMIK managed to facilitate the creation of local institutions of self-government, but was unable to develop a viable economy in light of Kosovo's uncertain political status under UN administration. Uncertainty over the future status became "a major obstacle to Kosovo's democratic development, accountability, economic recovery and inter-ethnic reconciliation".[394]

At the organisational level, the UN itself was scarcely prepared to assume its new governing responsibilities. UNMIK displayed, in particular, a contradictory self-understanding of governance. The mission eclipsed the territorial authority of Yugoslavia, in order to strengthen the rights of the people of Kosovo in accordance with SC Resolution 1244 (1999). But instead of establishing a culture of democratic governance and accountability, it essentially replaced FRY rule by a heavy-handed policy, under which the UN itself acted as a quasi-absolutist power.[395] This practice raised doubts about the legitimacy and the limits of authority of international administrations.[396]

Events such as the eruption of ethnic violence against non-Albanian communities and UNMIK in mid-March 2004[397] demonstrated the

[393] See also Friedrich, *UNMIK in Kosovo*, at 292.
[394] See Report of the Special Envoy of the Secretary-General on Kosovo's future status, UN Doc. S/2007/168 of 26 March 2007, paras. 5 and 9.
[395] In 2006, the SRSG was still qualified by UNMIK as the "highest international civilian official in Kosovo" who "enjoys the maximum civilian executive powers envisaged and vested in him by the Security Council in its resolution 1244 (1999), and is the final authority on their interpretation". See UNMIK, *Report to the Human Rights Committee on the Human Rights Situation in Kosovo since 1999*, CCPR/C/UNK/1, 13 March 2006, para. 26.
[396] The Ombudsperson Institution in Kosovo noted that the "the United Nations, the self-proclaimed champion of human rights in the world has by its own actions placed the people of Kosovo under UN control, thereby removing them from the protection of the international human rights regime that formed the justification for UN engagement in Kosovo in the first place". See Ombudsperson Institution in Kosovo, *Second Annual Report 2001-2002*, at 5.
[397] It is reported that as a result of this violence "19 persons died, 954 were injured and 4100 were displaced; 550 houses and 27 churches and monasteries were burned (with 182 houses damaged)". See European Commission For Democracy Through Law, *Opinion on Human Rights in Kosovo: Possible Establishment of Review Mechanisms*, para. 29.

difficulties faced by the mission in the realisation of its "statebuilding" agenda, even half a decade after its creation. Both, the Venice Commission and the Parliamentary Assembly of the Council of Europe identified a range of issues which were of continuing concern by 2004/5, including:

the inability of [internally displaced persons] – predominantly Serbs and members of other minority communities – to return to their homes in safety...; a general lack of security in the province, particularly for members of minority communities...; a consequential lack of freedom of movement; infringements of property rights, caused by the illegal occupation of abandoned property but also by the expropriation of property by the international authorities without adequate remedies;...inadequacy of judicial proceedings, mainly in relation to length of proceedings, procedural fairness and access to courts, which in turn permits the perpetuation of the climate of impunity, along with the continuing existence of a 'parallel' court system operating in the northern part of Kosovo and controlled from Serbia proper; lack of adequate safeguards to ensure the lawfulness of detentions, in particular those by KFOR, for which there is no independent review mechanism; corruption of public officials, including the judiciary; ...and lack of legal certainty, concerning inaccessibility of legal texts, lack of judicial review and absence of an effective remedy for human rights violations.[398]

UNMIK sought to address these shortcomings through its benchmark policy. However, the political developments in Kosovo remained dominated by the overarching problem of the status question.[399]

5.   The United Nations transitional administration in East Timor (UNTAET)

UNTAET, the United Nations Transitional Administration in East Timor,[400] was established a few months after UNMIK. The objective of

---

[398] See Council of Europe, Parliamentary Assembly, *Protection of human rights in Kosovo*, III. Explanatory Memorandum, para. 2. See also European Commission For Democracy Through Law, *Opinion on Human Rights in Kosovo: Possible Establishment of Review Mechanisms*, paras. 27–75.

[399] Report of the Secretary-General on the United Nations Interim Administration Mission in Kosovo, 5 June 2006, UN Doc. S/2006/361, para. 7; Report of the Secretary-General on the United Nations Interim Administration Mission in Kosovo, 1 September 2006, para. 30. In 2006, the UN and the EU began to make plans and preparations for a follow-up mission (e.g. EU engagement in the areas of police and justice), which would take over selected civilian functions from UNMIK in the post-settlement phase. See Report of the Secretary-General on the United Nations Interim Administration Mission in Kosovo, 5 June 2006, para. 21; Report of the Secretary-General on the United Nations Interim Administration Mission in Kosovo, 1 September 2006, para. 28.

[400] See generally Anthony Goldstone, *UNTAET with Hindsight: The Peculiarities of Politics in an Incomplete State*, Global Governance Vol. 10 (2004), 83; Ian Martin and A. Mayer-Rieckh,

the mission differed slightly from UNMIK. The UN engagement was not the result of an ethnic conflict, rather it was designed to settle the consequences of a colonial dispute. UNTAET was created in order to implement the terms of the Agreement of 5 May 1999, through which Indonesia and Portugal had agreed to end their long-standing claims over East Timor through the holding of a UN-monitored referendum, which was to be followed by a period of transitional UN administration in the case of a vote for independence.[401] This clear-cut mandate facilitated the successful accomplishment of the operation, because the objective of the transitional administration was clearly determined from the beginning of the mission, namely to create the conditions for independent statehood. Moreover, as a result of the renunciation of territorial claims by Portugal and Indonesia over East Timor in 1999, UNTAET had one main prerogative: to serve the interests of the people of East Timor.

Yet, UNTAET shared many structural parallels with the interim administration in Kosovo. The decolonisation process was strongly connected to a statebuilding mandate. The UN administration was not only charged with creation of sovereign institutions; it was required to build an entirely new state and judicial system in East Timor on the ashes of the destruction caused by the armed conflict between independence supporters and pro-Indonesian militia forces after the holding of the 1999 referendum. As in the case of Kosovo, the UN had very little time to prepare for this challenge. The organisation transposed the basic features of the Kosovo "governing model" to the circumstances of East Timor. This time, the Security Council endowed the administration directly with the three classical powers of the state ("all legislative and executive authority, including the administration of justice").[402] The SRSG, in turn,

The United Nations and East Timor: From Self-Determination to State-Building, International Peacekeeping, Vol. 12 (2005), 125–45; Michael G. Smith, *Peacekeeping in East Timor: The Path To Independence* (2002); Kondoch, *The United Nations Administration of East Timor*, 245; Mark Rothert, *U.N. Intervention in East Timor*, Columbia Journal of Transnational Law, Vol. 39 (2000), 257; Susannah Linton, *Rising from the Ashes: The Creation of a Viable Criminal Justice System in East Timor*, Melbourne University Law Review, Vol. 25 (2001), 122; Korhonen and Grass, *International Governance*, at 63; Sue Downie, *The United Nations in East Timor: Comparisons with Cambodia*, in Guns and Ballot Boxes: East Timor's Vote for Independence (Damien Kings ed., 2000), 117; Benzing, *Midwifing a New State*, 316; Dobbins, *The UN's Role in Nation-Building*, at 151–78; Korhonen, Gras and Creutz, *International Post-Conflict Situations*, at 151–65; Laura Grenfell, *Legal Pluralism and the Rule of Law in Timor Leste*, Leiden Journal of International Law, Vol. 19 (2006), 305–37.
[401] See Articles 5 and 6 of the Agreement between the Republic of Indonesia and the Portuguese Republic on the Question of East Timor of 5 May 1999, UN Doc. S/1999/513, in Israel, *Major Peace Treaties*, at 634.
[402] See para.1 of SC Resolution 1272 of 25 October 1999, UN Doc. S/RES/1272 (1999).

drew extensively from the experiences of UNMIK in the exercise of its powers. This practice exposed UNTAET to some of the same criticisms as UNMIK, namely that it exercised an autocratic conception of governance and an over-enthusiastic belief in the application of highest international norms and standards to post-conflict territories.[403]

5.1. Historical background

The establishment of UNTAET was largely guided by the will of the international community to end the grave humanitarian crisis which had arisen in East Timor following the population's vote for independence[404] – a situation which was characterised by the Security Council as a threat to international peace and security.[405] Nevertheless, the significance of the mission lies beyond its function of restoring law and order. UNTAET's creation was, at the same time, designed to restore some credibility to the damaged record of the international community in the treatment of decolonisation-based claims of self-determination, following two decades of silent toleration of Indonesia's occupation of East Timor.[406]

Indonesia's sovereignty over East Timor had remained controversial since its armed invasion of the territory on 7 December 1975.[407] The UN

---

[403] See generally Chopra, *UN's Kingdom of East Timor*, at 30; Mégret and Hoffmann, *UN as a Human Rights Violator?*, at 335.

[404] The UN Security Council reacted to the violence on 15 September 1999 by adopting Resolution 1264 (1999), in which the Council determined that the systematic, widespread and flagrant violations of international humanitarian and human rights law constituted a threat to peace and security. Acting under Chapter VII of the UN Charter, the Security Council authorised the establishment of a multinational force under a unified command structure, which became known as the International Force for East Timor (INTERFET). On the legal problems encountered by INTERFET, see Michael Kelly, Timothy McCormack, Paul Muggleton and Bruce Oswald, *Legal aspects of Australia's involvement in the International Force for East Timor*, International Review of the Red Cross, Vol. 83 (2001), 101. Moreover, on 25 October 1999, shortly after the Indonesian People's Consultative Assembly had recognised the results of the referendum and repealed the legislation that declared East Timor to be a province of Indonesia, the Security Council adopted Resolution 1272 creating UNTAET.

[405] See para. 16 of the preamble of SC Resolution 1272 (1999).

[406] See generally Roger S. Clark, *East Timor, Indonesia and the International Community,* Temple International & Comparative Law Journal, Vol. 14 (2000), 75.

[407] The territory was recognised as a non-self-governing territory under Portuguese administration until its armed occupation by Indonesia. Portugal had initially commenced steps in preparation for the decolonisation of East Timor and the realisation of its people's right to self-determination in 1974. However, following a period of civil disorder with conflicting statements from the East Timorese political parties with respect to the future of the territory, ranging from declarations of

condemned the Indonesian invasion of 1975 and rejected Indonesia's claim that the people of East Timor had freely chosen integration with Indonesia as one of the options of the realisation of self-determination. Security Council Resolutions 384[408] and 389[409] reaffirmed the UN's support for East Timor's right to self-determination and called upon the government of Indonesia to "withdraw without further delay all its forces from the territory". Yet, despite its non-recognition of the Indonesian occupation, the UN failed to take further action.

State practice showed a similarly divided picture. Some states recognised Indonesia's sovereignty over East Timor,[410] while others[411] took the view that East Timor continued to be a non-self-governing territory, with Portugal as the administering power. Portugal acknowledged that Indonesia's occupation of East Timor entailed *de facto* limitations on its own powers,[412] but continued to insist on its capacity as administering power. It carried out several initiatives to solve the problem of East Timor, including the 1995 application to the ICJ,[413] in which it tried to challenge the validity of the Timor Gap Treaty concluded between Australia and Indonesia, by claiming the treaty legitimised Indonesia's annexation of East Timor and violated the right to self-determination of

independence to calls for integration with Indonesia, Indonesian armed forces invaded the territory on 7 December 1975. East Timor was formally incorporated as Indonesia's "27th province" on 17 July 1976. Indonesia continued to govern the territory for almost twenty-five years. See generally Toole, *A False Sense of Security*, at 208.

[408] Security Council Resolution 384, UN SCOR, 30th Sess., paras. 1-2, UN Doc.S/RES/384 (1975).

[409] Security Council Resolution 389, UN SCOR, 31st Sess., para. 2, UN Doc. S/RES/389 (1976).

[410] These states include Australia, Bangladesh, India, Iran, Iraq, Jordan, Malaysia, Morocco, Oman, the Philippines, Saudi Arabia, Singapore, Surinam and Thailand.

[411] The member states of the EU, for example, never accepted Indonesia's *de jure* or *de facto* sovereignty over East Timor. See on the position of European states Raymond Goy, *L'Indépendance du Timor Oriental*, Annuaire Français de Droit International (1999), 203, at 212.

[412] For an analysis of the Portuguese position, see M. Clara Maffei, *The Case of East Timor before the International Court of Justice – Some Tentative Comments*, European Journal of International Law, Vol. 4 (1993), 223.

[413] See ICJ, *Case concerning East Timor (Portugal v. Australia)*, Advisory Opinion of 30 June 1995, ICJ Rep. 1995, p. 90. See on this decision Thomas D. Grant, *East Timor, the U.N. System, and Enforcing Non-Recognition in International Law*, Vanderbilt Journal of Transnational Law, Vol. 33 (2000), 273, at 298; Richard Burchill, *The ICJ Decision on the Case Concerning East Timor: The illegal use of force validated*, Journal of Armed Conflict Law, Vol. 2 (1997), 1; Roger S. Clark, *Obligations of Third States in the Face of Illegality – Ruminations Inspired by the Weeramantry Dissent in the Case Concerning East Timor*, in Legal Visions of the 21st Century: Essays in Honour of Judge Christopher Weeramantry (A. Anghie and G. Sturgess eds., 1998), 631–51.

the people of East Timor. However, neither the ICJ nor the international community finally resolved the issue.

Instead, Portugal and Indonesia came to a political compromise which left the issue of the territorial status open.[414] In the Tripartite Agreement of 5 May 1999 between Indonesia, Portugal and the UN,[415] both Indonesia and Portugal agreed to hold a referendum under UN auspices, in which the people of East Timor were to be asked whether they wished to accept autonomy within Indonesia[416] or pursue independence. Portugal agreed to remove East Timor from the list of non-self-governing territories, if the people of East Timor voted in favour of the Indonesian autonomy proposal.[417] Indonesia, on the other hand, affirmed its responsibility to "take the constitutional steps necessary to terminate its links with East Timor, thus restoring under Indonesian law the status held prior to July, 17 1976", if the people of East Timor voted against a status autonomy within Indonesia.[418] In the latter case, both parties also agreed to make "arrangements for a peaceful and orderly transfer of authority in East Timor to the UN, which would be charged with "enabling East Timor to begin a process of transition towards independence".[419]

The UN-administered referendum was held on 30 August 1999. Seventy-eight per cent of the voters rejected the autonomy proposal.[420] The Security Council regarded the outcome of the popular consultation as "an accurate reflection of the views of the East Timorese people",[421] despite intimidations by Indonesian and militia forces. The

---

[414] This is reflected in paras. 5 and 6 of the preamble of the Agreement, in which the parties note the position of the Government of Indonesia, on the one hand, according to which "the proposed special autonomy should be implemented only as an end solution to the question of East Timor and with full recognition of Indonesian sovereignty over East Timor", and acknowledge the position of Portugal, on the other, according to which "an autonomous regime should be transitional, not requiring recognition of Indonesian sovereignty over East Timor or the removal of East Timor from the list of Non-Self-Governing Territories of the General Assembly, pending a final decision on the status of East Timor by the East Timorese people through an act of self-determination under United Nations auspices".

[415] Agreement between the Republic of Indonesia and the Portuguese Republic on the Question of East Timor, 5 May 1999, UN Doc. S/1999/513, including Annexes I–III.

[416] For a survey of the autonomy proposal, see Jean-Marc Sorel, *Timor Oriental: Un resumé de l'histoire du droit international*, Revue Générale de Droit International Public (2000), 37, at 46.

[417] See the Agreement of 5 May 1999, Article 5.

[418] See *ibid.*, Article 6.   [419] See *ibid.*, Article 6.

[420] Ninety-eight per cent of the registered voters went to the polls: 94,388 (21.5 per cent) voted for autonomy and 344,580 (78.5 per cent) voted against. See UN Press Release, GA/9691 of 17 December 1999.

[421] See para. 3 of the preamble of Security Council Resolution 1264.

UN stepped in when pro-Indonesian forces started to reverse the outcome of the referendum through a violent campaign of terror against the East Timorese people with systematic attacks on the civilian population, including murder, torture, rape and forcible deportations of civilians and widespread plunder.[422] The organisation had by then become a trustee of the interests of the people of East Timor[423] as a result of the transfer of authority agreed under the Agreement of 5 May.[424]

5.2. UNTEAT – a reprise of UNMIK

UNTAET's organisational framework was largely modelled on the precedent set in Kosovo. The concrete design of the administration had been left open by the terms of the Agreement of 5 May.[425] UNTAET's specific powers were defined by the Security Council, which endowed UNTEAT with "overall responsibility for the administration of East Timor".[426] As was the case in Kosovo, people's rights were at the heart of the administration's mission. UNTAET had to create the conditions required for East Timorese self-government, and its later independence. This process required a dynamic mandate, involving the empowerment of domestic institutions. The Security Council was well aware of these sensitivities. It incorporated the requirement of a gradual devolution of power unambiguously in the founding instrument of the mission.[427]

---

[422] See Report of the International Commission of Inquiry to the Secretary-General, UN Doc. A/54/726, S/2000/59 (2000). See also the Report on the situation of human rights in East Timor, UN Doc. A/54/660 (1999).

[423] See para. 3 of the preamble of SC Resolution 1272 (1999), in which the Security Council welcomes "the successful conduct of the popular consultation of the East Timorese people of 30 August 1999", through which "the East Timorese people expressed their clear wish to begin a process of transition under the authority of the United Nations towards independence".

[424] UN Security Council Resolution 1272 must be conceived as a direct implementation of Article 6 of the Agreement of 5 May 1999, in which Indonesia and Portugal agreed to transfer the authority over East Timor to the UNs. See the reference to the Agreements of 5 May 1999 in para. 2 of the preamble of Resolution 1272 (1999).

[425] The agreement itself charged the Secretary-General only with the general responsibility to "initiate the procedure enabling East Timor to begin a process of transition towards independence". See Article 6 of the Agreement of 5 May 1999.

[426] See para. 1 of SC Resolution 1272 (1999).

[427] See para. 8 of SC Resolution 1272 (1999), where the Council stresses "the need for UNTEAT to consult and cooperate closely with the East Timorese people in order to carry out its mandate effectively with a view to the development of local democratic institutions, including an independent East Timorese human rights institution, and the transfer to these institutions of its administrative and public service functions".

The general structure of the mission was based on the Kosovo model. The UN established a centralised governing structure, with an SRSG (the "Transitional Administrator") acting as a head of mission. The SRSG exercised his regulatory authority through regulations that were deemed to remain in force "until repealed by the Transitional Administrator or superseded... by rules... issued" by the democratically elected institutions of an independent East Timor.[428] The activity of the administration was monitored by the Department of Peacekeeping Operations (DPKO) and the Office of Legal Affairs of the Secretariat, which reviewed the constitutional elements of the legislation.

UNTAET's practice shared strong resemblances to UNMIK.[429] UNTAET's first regulation defined the law applicable in East Timor. It decided that Indonesian law should continue to apply in East Timor, because it was familiar to local actors.[430] At the same time, the "laws applied in East Timor" were made subject to the observance of internationally recognised human rights standards, such as the two International Covenants or the Convention on the Elimination of All Forms of Racial Discrimination. This move was undertaken in agreement with the East Timorese leadership.[431] But it created the same practical problems as in Kosovo, namely the necessity for all lawyers to interpret domestic rules "through the lens" of a variety of international human rights instruments that were neither widely publicly known in East Timor, nor easily accessible.[432]

Although the situation in East Timor presented fewer security and political difficulties than in Kosovo, due to the absence of ethnic rivalries, UNTAET faced serious challenges in local capacity-building.[433] It had to establish a new administration and democratic institutions, restore public services and revive an economy in just over two years. The administration responded to these tasks by adopting a wide array of legislative measures.[434] It created the conditions for economic recovery and trade

---

[428] See Section 5.2 of UNTAET Regulation No. 1/1999 of 27 November 1999 (*Authority of the Transitional Administration in East Timor*).

[429] The leadership of UNTAET was entrusted to Sergio Vieira de Mello, who had acted as a former head of UNMIK.

[430] Portuguese law had not been applied in East Timor for twenty-five years.

[431] See Beauvais, *Benevolent Despotism*, at 1151.

[432] See generally Hans-Jörg Strohmeyer, *Building a New Judiciary for East Timor, Challenges of a Fledgling Nation*, Criminal Law Forum, Vol. 11 (2000), 259, at 267.

[433] See Dobbins, *The UN's Role in Nation-Building*, at 154–5.

[434] UNTAET failed to target the issue of property protection. The mission adopted one regulation related to this issue. However, it left the bulk of land title legislation open

by establishing a Central Fiscal Authority,[435] a currency system[436] and a provisional tax and customs regime.[437]

The main area of concern, however, was the (re-)establishment of a functioning political and legal system. Following the example of UNMIK, UNTAET decided not to integrate East Timor into its transitional structure, but chose rather to recruit or appoint locals to separate consultative or administrative institutions. Less than two months after the assumption of authority, the SRSG created the National Consultative Council, a joint consultative forum of representatives of the East Timorese people and UNTAET with the power to "make policy recommendations on significant executive and legislative matters".[438] Similar consultative responsibilities were granted to a Transitional Judicial Service Commission[439] and a Public Service Commission, which were designed to oversee the selection and recruitment of members of the East Timorese judiciary and civil service. Direct political authority was only delegated at a later stage, with the creation of village and sub-district development councils,[440] first at a local level, and the subsequent transfer of regulatory authority to a National Council,[441] a Transitional Government[442] and a Council of Ministers[443] in the second phase. UNTAET's methodology was not identical to, but was very close to UNMIK's governing strategy. The mission practiced a top-down approach which gradually evolved into a co-governance system.

to regulation by East Timorese authorities, because of the complex legal problems caused by diverging claims arising from colonial and pre-colonial rule. See Simon Chesterman, *Justice Under International Administration: Kosovo, East Timor and Afghanistan*, International Peace Academy, September 2002, at 9.

[435] See UNTAET Regulation No. 1/2000 of 14 January 2000 (*Central Fiscal Authority of East Timor*).

[436] See UNTAET Regulation No. 2/2000 of 14 January 2000 (*Use of Currencies in East Timor*).

[437] See UNTAET Regulation No. 12/2000 of 8 March 2000 (*Provisional Tax and Customs Regime For East Timor*).

[438] See Section 3 (1) of UNTAET Regulation No. 2/1999 of 2 December 1999 (*Establishment of a National Consultative Council*).

[439] See UNTAET Regulation No. 3/1999 of 3 December 1999 (*Transnational Judicial Service Commission*).

[440] See UNTAET Regulation No. 13/2000 of 10 March 2000 (*Establishment of Village and Sub-District Development Councils For the Distribution of Funds for Development Activities*).

[441] See Section 2 of UNTAET Regulation No. 24/2000 of 14 July 2000 (*Establishment of a National Council*).

[442] See UNTAET Regulation No. 23/2000 of 14 July 2000 (*Establishment of the Cabinet of the Transitional Government in East Timor*).

[443] See UNTAET Regulation No. 28/2001 of 19 September 2001 (*Establishment of the Council of Ministers*).

Particular attention was devoted to the reconstruction of the East Timorese judicial system. When UNTAET arrived in East Timor, most judges, prosecutors and other members of the legal profession had left the country. East Timorese citizens lacked experience, because they had not exercised judicial or prosecutorial functions under Indonesian rule. UNTAET enacted institutional legislation on the organisation of the courts[444] and the prosecutorial system[445] in East Timor. These positions were, as far as possible, filled with East Timorese officials, acting under the assistance of international legal practitioners ("two-track model").[446] Later, the UN administration adopted transitional rules of criminal procedure[447] and a regulation on the establishment of panels with exclusive jurisdiction over serious criminal offences,[448] which granted mixed national/international chambers in the District Court in Dili the authority to prosecute core crimes committed in the entire territory of East Timor between 1 January 1999 and 25 October 1999.[449] Moreover, in a historically unprecedented move, the UN administration created the institutional framework of a Truth and Reconciliation Commission, which upholds the principle of international criminal responsibility for genocide, crimes against humanity and war crimes, while instituting an individual reconciliation procedure with the possibility of amnesty for the commission of less serious crimes.[450] These regulatory measures combined the need for international expertise with the preservation of local ownership.[451]

---

[444] See UNTAET Regulation No. 11/2000 of 6 Match 2000 (*Organization of Courts in East Timor*).

[445] See UNTAET Regulation No. 16/2000 of 16 June 2000 (*Organization of the Public Prosecution Service in East Timor*).

[446] In other cases, UNTAET appointed one local and one international professional, in order to share expertise. See Beauvais, *Benevolent Despotism*, at 1101.

[447] See UNTAET Regulation No. 30/2000 of 25 September 2000 (*Transitional Rules of Criminal Procedure*).

[448] See UNTAET Regulation No. 15/2000 of 6 June 2000 (*Establishment of Panels with Exclusive Jurisdiction over Serious Criminal Offences*).

[449] See Section 2 (3) of UNTAET Regulation No. 15/2000.

[450] See UNTAET Regulation No. 10/2001of 13 July 2001 (*On the Establishment of a Commission for Reception, Truth and Reconciliation in East Timor*). For a survey, see Carsten Stahn, *Accommodating Individual Criminal Responsibility and National Reconciliation: The UN Truth Commission for East Timor*, American Journal of International Law, Vol. 95 (2001), 952.

[451] See generally on the role of mixed national international institutions in international criminal law Daryl A. Mundis, *New Mechanisms for the Enforcement of International Humanitarian Law*, American Journal of International Law, Vol. 96 (2001), 934.

5.3.   Beyond UNMIK

UNTAET departed even further than UNMIK from the traditional notions of state-centred sovereignty and governance. First, it departed from the principle that the exercise of sovereign-like functions is reserved exclusively for states. The UN became the only lawful authority in East Timor ("both state and state builder"[452]) after the transfer of power to the UN under the Agreement of 5 May,[453] and a restatement of this principle by both parties in a meeting of 28 September 1999.[454] Indonesia's official acceptance of the outcome of the August elections,[455] Portugal's confirmation that it would relinquish its legal ties to East Timor[456] and the Council's assertion of authority in SC Resolution 1272 (1999) transformed East Timor into a special international entity placed under the exclusive jurisdiction of the UN,[457] which continued to be listed as a non-self-governing territory under Article 73 (e) of the UN Charter, but with UNTAET as the administering power.[458] The mission therefore exercised core functions such as defence or external affairs directly on behalf of the people of East Timor without interference from any state entity.

The SRSG established an East Timorese Defence Force which acted under "the supreme command, control andadministrative authority" of

---

[452] See James Cotton, *Against the Grain: the East Timor Intervention*, Survival, Vol. 43 (2001), 127, at 139.

[453] See also Traub, *Inventing East Timor*, 74 ("UNTAET is not just helping the new country's government – it is that government").

[454] See para. 25 of the Report of the Secretary-General on the situation in East Timor of 4 October 1999.

[455] When a delegation of Indonesian representatives met UN officials on 20 October 1999 to deliver their acceptance of the August election results, the Secretary-General's Personal Representative for East Timor, Jamsheed Marker, even "informed them that no such formality was required since the UN had never recognised the Indonesian occupation as legitimate". *Ibid.*, at 29.

[456] See Jarat Chopra, *Introductory Note to UNTAET Regulation 13 (2000)*, ILM, Vol. 39 (2000), 936, at 937: "On 20 October 1999, Lisbon's representative in New York, Ambassador Antonio Monteiro, expressed to UN officials that Portugal would relinquish its legal ties to East Timor and consider UNTAET its successor with the passage of the Security Council mandate." See also Chopra, *UN's Kingdom of East Timor*, at 29.

[457] For further discussion, see below Part IV, Chapter 13.

[458] See United Nations, *United Nations and Decolonization*, at www.un.org/Depts/dpi/decolonization: "The current administering powers are France, New Zealand, the United Kingdom and the United States. East Timor is now administered by the United Nations Transitional Administration in East Timor (UNTAET)."

the transitional administrator until the territory's access to independence.[459] UNTAET regulated the conditions governing the conduct of relations between the transitional administration and foreign governments (representation, privileges and immunities).[460] Moreover, the UN exercised treaty-making power on behalf of East Timor. In an exchange of notes constituting an agreement with Australia, UNTAET assumed all rights and obligations under the Timor Gap Treaty previously exercised by Indonesia. UNTAET acted on behalf of East Timor, limiting its contractual obligations "until the date of independence of East Timor".[461] Later, UNTAET concluded a grant agreement with the World Bank's International Development Association, which designated UNTAET and East Timor as each being a "recipient".[462] This illustrated that there are instances in international legal practice which international entities may replace the state in the exercise of traditional fields of public authority.

Secondly, the UN engagement in East Timor deviated more visibly than other missions from the Cold War practice of neutrality and non-interference. The strategic goal of the mission was to create an independent and democratic East Timor under the auspices of the international community – a task which was interpreted by the mission so as to imply a role in the elaboration of the territory's future constitutional system. UNTAET's mandate forced the administration to balance the promotion of Charter-based values like democracy and the rule of law against the free choice of a people freely to determine its own political system. UNTAET solved this conflict by limiting its own role in the process of constitution-making to advice and monitoring. It charged a Constituent Assembly with the preparation of a "Constitution for an independent

---

[459] See UNTAET Regulation No. 1/2001 of 31 January 2001 (*Establishment of a Defence Force for East Timor*).

[460] See UNTAET Regulation No. 31/2001 of 27 September 2000 (*Establishment of Representative Offices of Foreign Governments in East Timor*).

[461] See Exchange of Notes constituting an Agreement between the Government of Australia and the United Nations Transitional Administration in East Timor (UNTAET) concerning the continued Operation of the Treaty between Australia and the Republic of Indonesia on the Zone of Cooperation in an Area between the Indonesian Province of East Timor and Northern Australia of 11 December 1989, entered into force on 10 February 2000, Australian Treaty Series 2000, No. 9.

[462] See Chopra, *UN's Kingdom of East Timor*, at 30. Pursuant to the International Development Association-UNTAET Trust Fund for East Timor Grant Agreement, UNTAET established a system of village and sub-district councils for the allocation of development funds. See Regulation No. 13/2000 of 10 March 2000.

and democratic East Timor"[463] and required this Assembly and constitutional commissions at the district level to consult the Timorese people on the contents of the Constitution.[464] Furthermore, the administration avoided openly excluding parties from the constitutional process[465] that had formerly opposed East Timorese independence.

At the same time, UNTAET kept close track of the developments through two informal, but effective mechanisms. It provided advice to the Constitutional Assembly, and it made its own phasing-out dependent on two conditions: the adoption of the Constitution, and its successful implementation.

The phase of direct UN administration was followed by several post-independence engagements, the first being the United Nations Mission of Support in East Timor (UNMISET),[466] which started its mandate after East Timor's access to independence. UNMIL was an assistance mission with visibly scaled down responsibilities. It was designed to provide assistance to the local administration as well as police and other security institutions in three core areas: public administration (including democratisation and justice), law enforcement and security.[467] In April 2005, UNMISET was replaced by an even smaller mission, the United Nations Office in Timor-Leste (UNOTIL) which was charged advisory functions and knowledge transfer.[468]

5.4. Critique

Despite its numerous accomplishments, UNTAET was not free from criticism. The operation suffered from a flaw that is typical of many other UN missions, namely a lack of preparation. The administration was drawn up hastily by the Secretariat after the holding of the referendum. One

---

[463] See UNTAET Regulation No. 2/2001 of 16 March 2001 (*Election of a Constituent Assembly to Prepare for an Independent and Democratic East Timor*). This decision was justified by the outcome of the 1999 popular consultation and by the need "to protect the inalienable human rights of the people of East Timor". See Section 1 (1) of the regulation.

[464] See Section 2 (4) of UNTAET Regulation No.2/2001 and UNTAET Directive on the Establishment of District Constitutional Commissions, UNTAET/Dir/2001/3 of 30 March 2001.

[465] For a survey, see Chesterman, *You, The People*, at 231–3.

[466] See para. 1 of SC Resolution 410 of 17 May 2002, UN Doc. S/RES/410 (2002). See also paras. 62–103 of the Report of the Secretary-General on the United Nations Transitional Administration in East Timor of 17 April 2002, UN Doc. S/2002/432.

[467] UNMISET provided, *inter alia*, law enforcement functions and helped build the East Timor Police Service.

[468] UNOTIL's mandate is set in paras. 1 and 2 of SC Resolution 1599 of 28 April 2005.

of the main shortcomings of this approach was that the institutional design of the mission was established without genuine involvement or participation of East Timorese representatives in the planning phase.[469] This lack of consultation with local actors weakened the authority of the administering framework in the eyes of the East Timorese leadership and triggered public discontent in the early stages of the operation.

Moreover, the UN repeated one of the conceptual weaknesses of the Kosovo model – the application of an absolutist governing regime after the takeover of authority – which sent the message to the East Timorese that they continued to be the object of external regulation. The UN administration abstained from adopting a clear timetable and framework for the devolution of power. It instituted participatory models of power-sharing and co-governance only when it felt compelled to do so by the increasing pressure and resentment voiced by local political groups.[470] This policy created the unfortunate perception that UNTAET conceived itself as an external *deus ex machina*, bound to act for, but not necessarily with, the people. The failure of the UN administration to adopt its style of governance earlier to the necessities of domestic actors illustrates that the UN itself was still undergoing a learning process when it assumed the administering mandate in East Timor.[471]

The vast amount of legal and institutional reform introduced within the two-year period of UN rule appears to be at odds with the capabilities and pace of transformation of the East Timorese society. UNTAET legislation paved the way for the democratic re-organisation of the territory on the basis of the highest international legal standards. UNTAET Regulation No. 1/1999 required all holders of public offices to apply the entire body of "internationally recognised human rights standards".[472] Furthermore, the UN supported the adoption of a modern, Western-liberal constitution which was built on a complex system of presidential democracy

---

[469] The basic architecture of the mission was drafted by the Secretariat in New York. A proposal by Xanana Gusmao for the future structure of the administration received little support.

[470] A good example is the establishment of representative village and sub-district councils for the disbursement of development funds. This project was rejected twice by UNTAET, because it was viewed by UN administrators as an inadequate surrogate of local elections in a non-neutral and unstable environment. See Beauvais, *Benevolent Despotism*, at 1126.

[471] Even SRSG De Mello noted later that "[t]he question remains open how the UN can exercise fair governance with absolute powers in societies recovering from war and oppression". See Beauvais, *Benevolent Despotism*, at 1101.

[472] See Section 2 of UNTAET Regulation No. 1/1999, which contains a non-exhaustive list of standards ("as reflected, in particular, in . . . ").

and extensive civil liberties and economic and social rights.[473] In the course of reform efforts, little attention was paid to the question as to what extent the local society would be able conform to these standards with its given infrastructure and its material and human resources after the end of the international presence. The SRSG himself pointed at this inconsistency in another context, noting that "[s]omething is not right when UNTAET can cost $692 million and the budget of East Timor is little more than $59 million".[474]

One of the strengths of the mission is that it took concrete steps towards the promotion of justice and reconciliation in the immediate aftermath of the human rights violations in 1999. A Commission of Experts appointed by the Secretary-General in 2005 reaffirmed that the establishment of the Truth Reconciliation Commission[475] and the deployment of the Special Crimes Unit[476] helped to ensure a "notable degree of accountability" in East Timor.[477] However, the efficiency of criminal justice was considerably weakened by the limited jurisdiction of the Special Panels for Serious Crimes. More than 300 arrest warrants issued by the Special Panels remained outstanding and hundreds of indicted persons residing in Indonesia had not been brought to justice[478] when the serious crime process was closed in 2005.[479]

Last, but not least, the UN was not very successful in its disengagement policy. Neither UNMISET, nor UNOTIL managed to secure long-term stability after UNTEAT's departure and East Timor's access to independence. UNTEAT had failed to engage in necessary security sector reform. It left East Timor with a weak system of border control, divided armed forces and a fragile law enforcement system.[480] The local economy declined due to reduced donor funding and assistance. The successor missions

---

[473] See Titles II and III of the Constitution of the Democratic Republic of East Timor, which entered into force on 20 May 2002.
[474] Statement in Beauvais, *Benevolent Despotism*, at 1125.
[475] The Commission submitted its final report to President Gusmao on 31 October 2005 after five years of operation. The report contains more than 200 recommendations related to justice, truth and reconciliation.
[476] The Special Panels for Serious Crimes conducted fifty-five trials involving eighty-seven defendants. Eighty-five persons were convicted.
[477] See Report of the Secretary-General on justice and reconciliation for Timor-Leste, UN Doc. S/2006/580 of 26 July 2006, para. 8.
[478] *Ibid.*, paras. 9 and 35. In total, only two-fifths of the murders committed in 1999 were indicted.
[479] The serious crimes process was concluded on 20 May 2005 in accordance with Security Council Resolution 1543 (2005).
[480] See Korhonen, Gras and Creutz, *International Post-Conflict Situations*, 168.

were not able to close this gap. Six years after UNTEAT's creation, this omission became blatantly evident in the context of the crisis of the East Timorese armed forces[481] which led to a renewed outbreak of violence and the resignation of several members of government (Prime Minister, Minister of Defence, Minister of Interior). At this point, the UN recognised that capacity-building in East Timor required further and enhanced commitment.[482]

5.5. Assessment

UNTAET was both a "learned" and a "learning" experiment of the UN in decolonisation and statebuilding. The organisation managed to complete its decolonisation mandate successfully. East Timor reached its independence after thirty months of transitional UN administration, and become a member of the UN in the same year. This process was visibly facilitated by the UN presence which secured the necessary stability to prepare the territory for statehood. The success of the mission was reinforced by two factors: the acceptance of the option of independence by all interested parties (Portugal, Indonesia and the East Timorese people) and the willingness of the Security Council to assume interim trusteeship authority under Chapter VII of the Charter. Both elements helped the UN pave the way for independence within a relatively short period a time, after almost three decades of inaction.

The record of the UN in the process of statebuilding in East Timor is less convincing. It is overall a success that UNTAET managed to establish a new public administration within in its short mandate. UNTAET'S presence helped the East Timorese society to set up the foundations of a democratic state. The Security Council avoided some of the pitfalls of the past (Cambodia) when it decided to extend the UN's engagement in East Timor to the period after the holding of elections and transfer of authority to domestic institutions in 2002.[483] However, the organisation

---

[481] In mid-March 2006 nearly 600 persons were dismissed from the East Timorese armed forces following complaints about their discriminatory treatment as persons from western districts. These dismissals led to a wave of violence, including attacks on government buildings. President Gusmao requested police and military assistance from the Governments of Australia, New Zealand, Malaysia and Portugal. See Report of the Secretary-General on Timor-Leste pursuant to Security Council resolution 1690 (2006), UN Doc. S/2006/628 of 8 August 2006, paras. 2–23.

[482] The Secretary-General acknowledged in hindsight that "the building of institutions on the basis of fundamental principles of democracy and rule of law is not a simple process that can be completed within a few short years". See UNOTIL Press Release, Timor-Leste: Annam Appeals to Security Council for Renewed UN Action, 13 June 2006.

[483] See SC Resolution 410 of 17 May 2002.

repeated many of the flaws of the UNMIK governing model in East Timor – a factor which may have contributed to the shrinking enthusiasm for authoritative UN governance missions in the more recent past. Moreover, it was short-sighted to assume that UN statebuilding would produce sustainable results in the short term.[484] Domestic institutions were unable to overcome fundamental problems of governance and capacity development in the first years after independence. Socio-economic progress was hampered by a number of factors, including a "lack of a sufficiently developed democratic culture and practices; uneven progress in translating progress in State building into human development, including reduced poverty, inequality and unemployment rates, especially among the youth; inadequate access to formal education and other basic health and social services; highly centralized decision-making systems across all organs of the state; and inadequate formal and informal consultation and communication mechanisms".[485]

The fragile state of the young democracy and the remaining frictions within and between defence and police forces became evident in the context of the constitutional crisis in Spring 2006. These events underscored the need for a continued international engagement in the security sector and the establishment of a new multidimensional UN mission in East Timor.[486]

---

[484] See also the observations in the Report of the Secretary-General on Timor-Leste pursuant to Security Council resolution 1690 (2006), UN Doc. S/2006/628 of 8 August 2006, para. 142.

[485] *Ibid.*, para. 93.   [486] *Ibid.*, paras. 109–137.

9 The "light footprint" and beyond

The turn of the millennium brought a certain shift in strategy. UN administration moved away from comprehensive governance models à la Kosovo or East Timor, and returned to more moderate formulas of international administering authority.

The idea of preserving local capacity and domestic decision-making choices in processes of foreign governance is by no means novel. Practices of deference to local rule were well established in the colonial practice of the nineteenth century. British administrators maintained and used certain local laws and institutional structures for the purpose of the administration of African colonies.[1] This practice continued under the Mandate and Trusteeship Systems.[2] Moreover, on various occasions, the UN itself decided to limit its engagement in the field of territorial administration to forms of governance assistance.

However, it took some time for the principle of "local ownership" to begin to gain ground in contemporary practice. The notion of "local ownership"[3] emerged formally in the context of economic development

---

[1] The principle of indirect rule was, *inter alia*, practised in the protectorate of Northern Nigeria. The UK High Commissioners held executive and legislative powers in the protectorate. But most of the activities of government were undertaken by the emirs and their local administrations, subject to UK approval. Locals were transformed into salaried district heads and became, in effect, agents of the UK authorities, responsible for peacekeeping and tax collection. A dual system of law applied. Islamic law continued to govern with matters affecting the personal status of Muslims, including land disputes, divorce, debt and slave emancipation.

[2] See above Part I, Chapters 2 and 3.

[3] Today, local ownership is associated with a bundle of principles, such as "acknowledging the primacy of people affected in transforming conflict, ... respecting gender and cultural diversity, ... ensuring independence from political agendas, ...

assistance.[4] International organisations such as the OECD promoted the principle of "local ownership" in donor policies in the 1990s. The OECD emphasised that that "the peoples of... countries concerned must remain the 'owners' of their policies and programmes", in order to achieve sustainable development and to avoid the pitfalls of donor dependency.[5] In the field of UN administration, this idea began to gain systematic support and recognition after the experiences of Kosovo and East Timor. Various contemporary policy documents and mission statements contain an express commitment to the idea that domestic stakeholders must maintain primary control over their "own" affairs in various domains of public authority and stages of a mission ("local ownership"[6]).

One of the most striking examples is the role of the UN under the Bonn Agreement on Provisional Arrangements in Afghanistan.[7] Given both the previous UN action vis-à-vis Afghanistan and the breakdown of centralised authority and the scope of destruction caused by years of armed hostilities, it would have been conceivable to place parts of the country under transitional international control. Yet, another path was chosen. Rather than assuming a position of government, the UN merely assumed a role of assistance under the Bonn Agreement.[8] Two years later, the UN was urged to play a similarly limited role in the process of reconstruction of Iraq.[9]

---

building sustainable partnerships". See International Alert, Supporting and Enhancing Community-based Peacebuilding, *Global Issues Policy Notes No. 1* (2002), at www.international-alert.org.

[4] See generally Simon Chesterman, *Ownership in Theory and Practice: Transfer of Authority in UN Statebuilding Operations*, Journal of Intervention and Statebuilding, Vol. 1 (2007), 3–26.

[5] The concept of "local ownership" may be traced back to an OECD document from 1995 entitled "Development Partnership in the new global context". The document is available at www.oecd.org/dataoecd/31/61/2755357.pdf.

[6] The term "local ownership" in itself is a rather general notion. It covers a wide span of deferences to domestic rule, ranging from the maintenance of full decision-making powers by domestic leaders to substantive or geographic limitations on international rule. As a concept, the idea of "local ownership" becomes relevant at different stages of a mission, including planning and design, implementation and post-administration presence.

[7] See Agreement on Provisional Arrangements in Afghanistan Pending the Re-establishment of Permanent Government Institutions (Bonn Agreement), concluded at Bonn, 5 December 2001, UN Doc. S/2001/1154. See also UN SC Res. 1383 of 8 December 2001, UN Doc. S/RES/1383 (2001).

[8] See Annex II and III of the Bonn Agreement.

[9] See para. 8 of SC Res. 1483 (2003) of 22 May 2003 and para. 8 of SC Res. 1511 (2003) of 16 October 2003.

In the following, the UN opted for an assistance-oriented approach in a number of multi-dimensional peace operations, including the cases of Liberia (UNMIL),[10] Democratic Republic of Congo (MONUC)[11] and Ivory Coast (UNOCI).[12] In the aftermath of the 2005 World Summit, the Security Council and the General Assembly reiterated the importance of "national ownership" in the definition of the powers of the UN Peacebuilding Commission and the concept of "responsibility to protect".[13]

This trend towards greater self-restriction and moderation may be explained by several factors. In some cases (Afghanistan, Iraq), the limited role of the UN may be attributed to geopolitical factors, such as the dominance of US interests in international affairs, the changing geopolitical structure after 9/11 and the decline of multilateral frameworks of action in the context of the responses to terrorism and "rogue states".[14]

However, the move towards the preservation of "local ownership" is supported by a changing attitude towards the design and conception of projects of transitional administration. The idea to limit the scope of international involvement in experiments of international administration and to increase the focus on domestic capacity-building and the use of local staff prevailed, in particular, in the context of the international presence in Afghanistan, in which *Brahimi* pleaded for a "light" form of international engagement, arguing that international actors

---

[10] The Security Council established a governance assistance mission (UNMIL), in order to facilitate the implementation of the Ceasefire Agreement, and to assist the new transitional government in the "reestablishment of national authority throughout the country". See para. 3 of SC Res. 1509 of 19 September 2003.

[11] See the mandate of MONUC, as defined by SC Res. 1565 (2004) of 1 October 2004.

[12] See the mandate of UNOCI, as set out in SC Res. 1633 (2005) of 21 October 2005 and the communique of the 40th meeting of the African Union Peace and Security Council.

[13] The preambular paragraphs of GA Res. 60/180 of 30 December 2005 and SC Res. 1645 (2005) of 20 December 2005 affirm "the primary responsibility of national and transitional Governments and authorities of countries emerging from conflict or at risk of relapsing into conflict... in identifying their priorities and strategies for post-conflict peacebuilding, with a view to ensuring national ownership".

[14] See generally Chesterman, *You, the People*, at 249–56; Philippe Sands, *Lawless World: America and the Making and Breaking of Global Rules* (2005); Nico Krisch, *Weak as Constraint, Strong as Tool: The Place of International Law in U.S. Foreign Policy*, in Unilateralism and U.S. Foreign Policy: International Perspectives (David M. Malone and Y. Foong Khong eds., 2003), 41; Nico Krisch, *The Rise and Fall of Collective Security, Terrorism, U.S. Hegemony and the Plight of the Security Council*, in Terrorism as a Challenge for National and International Law: Security versus Liberty? (Christian Walter, Silja Vöneky, Volker Röben and Frank Schorkopf eds., 2003).

gain credibility and influence through recognising Afghan leadership.[15] This proposition coincided with a wider critique of some of the governance models applied by international administrations throughout the 1990s,[16] calls for greater self-restraint in statebuilding[17] and a gradual reconsideration of UN policies by the UN Secretariat.[18]

In the context of Afghanistan and Iraq, the adoption of a lighter "footprint" was further guided by pragmatic considerations. The sheer size of the respective territories did not lend itself to the establishment of centralised international rule. The continuing presence of powerful warlords and/or rival political leaders made it impossible to impose an international legal framework without a broader national consensus.

This practice marks a certain departure from the ambitious governance agenda of some missions of the past decades. Notions such as "local ownership" and "partnership" became official and integral features of UN peacebuilding efforts. However, these principles were not always followed by corresponding practice. In some cases, they were labels, which masked the actual degree of international interference (Democratic Republic of Congo, Ivory Coast). The mandates of the respective missions were drafted in terms of the provision of technical and expert support

---

[15] For a full discussion, see below UNAMA.

[16] Some voices argued that the imposition of external laws and reforms actually undermines the building of democracy. See Knaus and Martin, *Travails of the European Raj*, at 60–74. See also James D. Fearon and David D. Laitin, *Neotrusteeship and the Problem of Weak States*, International Security, Vol. 28 (2004), 5–43.

[17] See Amitai Etzioni, *A Self-restrained Approach to Nation-building by Foreign Powers*, International Affairs, Vol. 80 (2004), 1, at 4 and 17.

[18] This is, *inter alia*, reflected in the Report of the Secretary-General on the rule of law and transitional justice. In this report, the Secretary-General addressed some of the implications of the principle of "local ownership" for international action ("[a]ssessing national needs and capacities", paras. 14–16; "[s]upporting domestic reform constituencies", paras. 17–18; "[e]mbracing integrated and complementary approaches" in the area of the area of the restoration of justice, paras. 23–6). The report also includes a growing recognition by the UN that externally imposed forms of governance may create an artificial gap between international and domestic rulers and pose questions of public legitimacy. In the case of Iraq, where the Secretary-General provided a principled (rather than a strategic) justification for moderate interventionism and "genuine and widespread national ownership", the UN opted for a "light footprint" approach on the basis of two key factors: the need to foster self-government in countries of transition and to assist domestic actors to progressively achieve democratic reform. The Secretary-General noted that past "United Nations experience in various post-conflict environments" revealed that "conducting these critical democratization processes in suboptimal conditions and haste risk[s] fuelling divisions rather than promoting genuine national ownership of, and full legitimacy for,... new constitutional arrangements". See para. 59 of the Report of the Secretary-General of 5 December 2003, UN Doc. S/2003/1149.

to transitional domestic governments. The actual scope of international involvement, however, exceeded the level of technocratic assistance.

1. The United Nations Assistance Mission in Afghanistan (UNAMA)

The UN engagement in Afghanistan[19] differs significantly from the missions in Kosovo and East Timor. The most striking feature of the operation is its normative restraint. The format of the UN engagement was determined by the Afghan leaders themselves. Moreover, the structure of the mission was constructed with the ambition of furthering local solutions to local problems. This approach was not entirely new: this type of assistance was successfully practised by the UN in the 1950s in the context of the decolonisation of Libya.[20] However, the case of Afghanistan deserves special attention because the idea of building capacity through domestic forums was applied here as a structural principle of transitional administration.

1.1. Background

The UN presence in Afghanistan was established for a dual purpose: to consolidate the effects of Operation Enduring Freedom, and to facilitate the long-term political and social reconstruction of the country.

Afghanistan was a shattered and divided country after twenty-three years of conflict and the toppling of the Taliban regime by the US-led military campaign in October 2001.[21] The security situation remained

---

[19] See generally Simon Chesterman, You, The People, 88-92; Walking Softly in Afghanistan: the Future of UN State-Building, Survival, Vol. 44 (2002), 37; Thilo Marauhn, Konfliktbewältigung in Afghanistan zwischen Utopie und Pragmatismus, Archiv des Völkerrechts, Vol. 40 (2002), 480; Neil Kritz, Securing the Rule of Law in Post-Taliban Afghanistan: Promoting a Formal System of Justice, Connecticut Journal of International Law, Vol. 17 (2002), 451; Laura Dickinson, Transitional Justice in Afghanistan: The Promise of Mixed Tribunals, Denver Journal of International Law and Policy, Vol. 31 (2002), 23-42; Mark Drumbl, Rights, Culture and Crime: The Role of Rule of Law for the Women of Afghanistan, Columbia Journal of Transnational Law, Vol. 42 (2004), 349-390; Ebrahim Afsah & Alexandra Hilal Guhr, Afghanistan: Buiding a State to Keep the Peace, Max Planck Yearbook of United Nations Law, Vol. 9 (2005), 373-456; Korhonen, Gras & Creutz, International Post-Conflict Situations, 55-80.

[20] See above Part II, Chapter 7

[21] The process of reconstruction was therefore complicated by the fact that "effective governance in the modern sense... never existed [in the country], even before the war". See Ebrahim Afsah and Alexandra Hilal Guhr, Afghanistan: Building a State to Keep the Peace, Max Planck Yearbook of United Nations Law, Vol. 9 (2005), 376.

tense, due to unsettled political conditions in the south and east of the country and armed hostilities between Pashtun political and tribal leaders.[22] The country suffered from the damages inflicted on its infrastructure and its people over almost a quarter of a century of war. The majority of its population was impoverished and desperate for peace. The UN pursued a two-track approach in order to stabilise the country.

Following some initial steps taken in the Security Council,[23] the organisation invited selected leaders of the existing Afghan factions and representatives from the different provinces to Bonn with the aim of establishing a multi-ethnic and broadly representative Afghan interim administration for the transitional administration of the country.[24] The talks led to the adoption of the Bonn Agreement, which determined the groundwork and the timetable for the process of political unification and reconstruction. The participants of the Conference agreed to nominate an "Interim Authority"[25] and charged it with the organisation of an Emergency Loya Jirga,[26] designed to appoint a more inclusive transitional government (the "Transitional Authority") with the support of all ethnic and religious communities and all segments of society.[27] The Transitional Authority was mandated to "lead Afghanistan until such time as a fully representative government can be elected through free and fair elections to be held no later than two years after the date of

[22] See para. 9 of the Report of the Secretary-General on the situation in Afghanistan and its implications for international peace and security of 18 March 2002, UN Doc. A/56/875-S/2002/278.

[23] Paragraph 3 of SC Res. 1378 (2001) of 14 November 2001 affirmed "that the United Nations should play a central role in supporting the efforts of the Afghan people to establish urgently... a new and transitional administration leading to the formation of a new government". See UN Doc. S/RES/1378 (2001).

[24] For a criticism of the choice of leaders, see Astri Suhrke, Kristian Berg Harpiviken and Arne Strand, *Conflictual Peacebuilding; Afghanistan Two Years After Bonn* (2004), at 63. ("The Bonn meeting was highly unrepresentative, dominated by the Northern Alliance and Pashtuns in exile. The traditional conservative Pashtun society was mostly excluded, as was everybody that had even been remotely associated with the Taliban. No efforts were made to deal with the politically with the defeated regime and its supporters.") For a similar criticism, see Afsah and Guhr, *Afghanistan: Building a State to Keep the Peace*, at 410.

[25] See Section I (2) of the Bonn Agreement. The Interim Authority consisted of an Interim Administration, a Commission for the Convention of the Emergency Loya Jirga and judicial bodies (Supreme Court, lower Courts).

[26] A *Loya Jirga* is traditionally forum of deliberation, which encompasses clan leaders and delegates representing the different political, religious and ethnic groups in Afghan society. Article 110 of the new Constution of Afghanistan defines the *Loya Jirga* as the "highest manifestation of the people of Afghanistan".

[27] See Section IV of the Bonn Agreement.

the emergency *Loya Jirga*."[28] Furthermore, the Agreement requested the UN to support the process of national transition by two measures: the establishment of a UN mandated security force for the maintenance of law and order in Kabul and its surrounding areas[29] (Annex 1), and the creation of a civilian support mission[30] (Annex 2).

The Security Council endorsed the Bonn Agreement[31] and the civilian mission entrusted to the Secretary-General under Annex 2 of the document[32] one day after its adoption. Two weeks later, the Council used its powers under Chapter VII to authorise the establishment of the International Security Assistance Force (ISAF), in order to create a secure environment for the Afghan Interim Authority and the personnel of the UN in Kabul,[33] and later in "areas of Afghanistan outside Kabul and its environs".[34]

1.2.   The choice in favour of a light footprint – a deliberate decision

The overarching feature of the Afghan model of transition is the preservation of control by domestic actors. Afghan authorities maintained "genuine authority" during the different stages of the process of transition.[35]

This principle is reflected in the Bonn Agreement. The opening lines of the Agreement reaffirmed the "national sovereignty and territorial integrity of Afghanistan", as well the "right of the people of Afghanistan to freely determine their own political future in accordance with the principles of Islam, democracy, pluralism and social justice".[36] The agreement defined a general framework and a timetable for the process transition, but left major political and substantive decisions to domestic and genuinely "Afghan" forums, such as the Emergency *Loya Jirga* (grand assembly)[37] (which was convened to select the Transitional Authority), the

---

[28] See Section I, Article 1 (4) of the Bonn Agreement.
[29] See Annex 1 of the Bonn Agreement.   [30] See Annex II of the Bonn Agreement.
[31] See para. 1 of SC Res. 1383 (2001) of 6 December 2001), UN Doc. S/RES/1383 (2001).
[32] See *ibid.*, para. 3 of SC R. 1383 (2001).
[33] See para. 1 of SC Res. 1386 (2001) of 20 December 2001, UN Doc. S/RES/1386 (2001).
[34] See para. 1 of SC Res. 1510 of 13 October 2003, UN Doc. S/RES/1510 (2003).
[35] See Afsah and Guhr, *Afghanistan: Building a State to Keep the Peace*, at 415.
[36] See the preamble of the Bonn Agreement.
[37] The Emergency *Loya Jirga* was held in June 2002. It marked "the first moderately democratic forum in which differences could be aired and women were given the opportunity to participate in building the foundations for future democratic processes". See Afsah and Guhr, *Afghanistan: Building a State to Keep the Peace*, at 423.

Transitional Authority[38] (which named the transitional government) and the Constitutional *Loya Jirga*[39] (which was convened to adopt the new Afghan Constitution).[40]

The role of the UN in the process of administration was limited from the start. The Bonn Agreement merely requested the UN to "monitor and assist in the implementation of all aspects of [the] agreement"[41] through dispute resolution,[42] the investigation of human rights violations[43] and advice to the Interim Authority in establishing a politically neutral environment.[44]

The features of the mission were set out in a Report of the Secretary-General dated 18 March 2002.[45] The report defined three core functions:

(a) Fulfilling the tasks and responsibilities, including those related to human rights, the rule of law and gender issues, entrusted to the United Nations in the Bonn Agreement, which were endorsed by the Security Council in resolution 1383 (2001);

(b) Promoting national reconciliation and rapprochement throughout the country, through the good offices of the Special Representative;

(c) Managing all United Nations humanitarian relief, recovery and reconstruction activities in Afghanistan, under the overall authority of the Special Representative and in coordination with the Interim Authority and the successor administrations of Afghanistan.

This limited mandate did not in any way come close to the broad governing responsibilities assumed by the UN in Eastern Slavonia, Kosovo and East Timor, or the public authority shared by UNTAC in

---

[38] The Transitional Authority was selected by the Emergency *Loya Jirga* in June 2002. For a detailed account of the difficulties and criticisms arising in this context, see Afsah and Guhr, *Afghanistan: Building a State to Keep the Peace*, at 419–22. The Transitional Authority carried out a reform of ministries and adopted legislation in areas such as the media, banking, customs and investment. See Report of Secretrary-General, *The Situation in Afghanistan and its Implications for International Peace and Security*, UN Doc. S/2005/525 of 12 August 2005, para. 5.

[39] The Constitutional *Loya Jirga* adopted the provisions of the new Afghan Constitution on 4 January 2004. For a survey of the work of the *Loya Jirga*, see Afsah and Guhr, *Afghanistan: Building a State to Keep the Peace*, at 427.

[40] This methodology may be explained the fact that the group of Afghan representatives convened in Bonn lacked legitimacy and authority to adopt a true peace settlement. Afsah and Guhr, *Afghanistan: Building a State to Keep the Peace*, at 383–5.

[41] See Article 2 of Annex 2 of the Bonn Agreement.

[42] See *ibid.*, Article 5.   [43] See *ibid.*, Article 6.   [44] See *ibid.*, Article 3.

[45] See Report of the Secretary-General, *The Situation in Aghanistan and its Implications for International Peace and Security*, UN Doc. A/56/875-S/2002/278 of 18 March 2002, para. 97.

Cambodia.[46] The UN did not act as a provisional governance or co-governance institution in Afghanistan. Rather, it merely served as a consultant and mediator in institutional matters[47] and as a preparatory agent in the organisation of elections,[48] without holding final authority over parts of the governmental functions of the Afghan state.[49]

The decision to restrict the scope of public authority exercised by the UN in Afghanistan was a deliberate choice of the organisation, which was sponsored by Lakhdar Brahimi, the UN Special Representative in Afghanistan and the driving force behind the Bonn process.[50] Given the continuing security threats repeatedly emphasised by the Security Council since 2001, and the prevailing governance vacuum in large sections of Afghanistan, the establishment of another governance mission in the style of the 1990s was anything but a remote idea, even within UN circles.[51] But a radically different approach was adopted. Following the experiences of Kosovo and East Timor, where the mission had entailed not only great responsibilities but also heavy personal and financial burdens, the UN Secretariat defended the idea that the organisation should primarily strengthen domestic initiatives and authorities in the Afghan peace process. The Secretary-General officially proposed a "light footprint" approach noting that the United Nations Assistance Mission in Afghanistan (UNAMA) should "aim to bolster Afghan capacity (both official and non-governmental, relying on as limited an international

---

[46] The overall goal of the UN engagement (assistance in the establishment of permanent domestic governing institutions and the holding of elections in a post-conflict environment) bears some resemblance to the role of UNTAC under the Cambodian peace settlement. But the means provided to achieve this end were considerably different from the Cambodia mission.

[47] See Article 5 of Annex 2 of the Bonn Agreement: "If for whatever reason, the Interim Administration or the Special Independent Commission were actively prevented from meeting or unable to reach a decision on a matter related to the convening of the Emergency Loya Jirga, the Special Representative of the Secretary-General shall, taking into account the views expressed in the Interim Administration or in the Special Independent Commission, use his/her good offices with a view to facilitating a resolution to the impasse or a decision."

[48] See Article 3 of Annex 3 of the Bonn Agreement.

[49] It is quite telling that the SRSG was merely entitled to "use his/her good offices" to solve disputes in case of disagreement among local actors. See Article 5 of Annex 2 of the Bonn Agreement. The focus was on "consulation and consent of the local authorities". See also Afsah and Guhr, Afghanistan: Building a State to Keep the Peace, at 417.

[50] Brahimi argued that a large-scale mission was "not necessary and not possible". See Chesterman, Walking Softly in Afghanistan, at 38.

[51] See Chesterman, You, The People, at 89.

presence and on as many Afghan staff as possible, and using common support services where possible, thereby leaving a light expatriate 'footprint'".[52]

Several factors supported this conceptual leap. There were strong political reasons in support of the argument that the local population should take charge of its own affairs. The country had suffered from foreign influence for "far too long" in the past.[53] The peace process itself still rested on weak grounds. It was therefore preferable to consolidate consensus among local leaders, instead of imposing solutions from outside.[54] Furthermore, the decision to reduce the UN footprint and to strengthen local capacity had economic benefits. It avoided the diversion of resources from local actors[55] and prevented the emergence of micro-economic imbalances between international and national administrators – a problem which had caused public disagreement in East Timor.[56] Finally, plans to establish a strong UN presence would have contrasted with the security situation on the ground, the initial limitation of international control to the area of Kabul[57] and the will of the US to maintain operational control in Afghanistan.[58]

1.3. Role and function of UNAMA

The minimalist conception of UN authority is particularly well reflected in the small range of responsibilities assumed by UNAMA. Most of the

---

[52] See para. 98 of the Report of the Secretary-General of 18 March 2002, UN Doc. A/56/875-S/2002/278.

[53] See ibid., para. 120. See also Afsah and Guhr, Afghanistan: Building a State to Keep the Peace, at 381.

[54] See also Chesterman, Walking Softly in Afghanistan, at 38, who rightly notes that a dominant international agenda might have entailed "setting policy (on, say, human rights, democracy, gender, rule of law) in accordance with donor requirements and time-lines, rather than on the basis what is locally feasible".

[55] See para. 129 of the Report of the Secretary-General of 18 March 2002, UN Doc. A/56/875-S/2002/278: "The proposed structure and size of the mission is relatively lean. This is precisely so that the Organization's overhead costs do not consume too much of the overall aid destined for the people of Afghanistan, and so that the presence of too many international staff does not overwhelm the nascent Interim Administration by creating conflicting demands."

[56] See Beauvais, Benevolent Despotism, at 1125–6.

[57] See Chesterman, You, the People, at 174.

[58] Coalition forces, led by the US, retained initial control over international military operations in Afghanistan. Later, they handed over operational command to ISAF (led by NATO) in different stages. See Report of the Secretary-General, The Situation in Afghanistan and its Implications for Peace and Security, UN Doc. S/2006/727, 11 September 2006, para. 38.

core functions exercised by UN administrators in Kosovo or East Timor were carried out by transitional Afghan institutions. The Bonn Agreement itself defined the law applicable in Afghanistan until the adoption of the new Constitution. The agreement obliged the Interim Authority and the Emergency *Loya Jirga* to act in accordance with international human rights and humanitarian law, but limited this obligation to the observance of "international instruments on human rights and international humanitarian law *to which Afghanistan is a party*"[59] – a move which avoided legal uncertainty and confusion caused by the lack of training of local actors.[60]

Domestic interim authorities set up many of the same institutions necessary for the functioning of the state that had been established by UNMIK and UNTAET in Kosovo and East Timor. The Afghan interim administration established a Judicial Reform Commission, which was charged with the reconstruction of the domestic justice system in accordance with Islamic principles, international standards, the rule of law and Afghan legal institutions.[61] Similarly, Afghan interim institutions created a Civil Service Commission,[62] a Human Rights Commission,[63] a Constitutional Commission[64] and a national police force.[65]

UNAMA's role in the process of reconstruction remained quite limited.[66] The mission exercised a primarily advisory and monitoring

---

[59] See Section II, Article 1 and Section V, Article 2 of the Bonn Agreement. Emphasis added.

[60] See also Chesterman, *You, The People*, at 176.

[61] The establishment of the Commission was envisaged by Section 2, Article 2 of the Bonn Agreement. The Commission was created by decree on 21 May 2002. See para. 12 of the Report of the Secretary-General, *The Situation in Afghanistan and its Implications for International Peace and Security* of 11 July 2002, UN Doc. A/56/1000-S/2002/737. The Commission identified priorities in the sector of judicial reform.

[62] The creation of this Commission was foreseen in Section III C, Article 5 of the Bonn Agreement.

[63] The creation of the Human Rights Commission was ordered by way of a Presidential Decree dated 2 June 2002. See Decree of the Presidency of the Interim Administration of Afghanistan on the Establishment of an Afghan Independent Human Rights Commission, dated 6 June 2002. For a survey, see Afsah and Guhr, *Afghanistan: Building a State to Keep the Peace*, at 444–5.

[64] A Constitutional Drafting Commission was appointed in 2002. This Commission was later followed by a Constitutional Review Commission. For a full survey of the constitutional process, see the information on the Constitutional Commission at www.constitution-afg.com.

[65] See para. 30 of the Report of the Secretary-General of 23 July 2003, UN Doc. A/57/850-S/2003/754.

[66] See most recently, Report of the Secretary-General on the situation in Afghanistan and its implications for international peace and security, UN Doc. S/2004/925 of 26 November 2004.

function in justice sector reform,[67] gender issues[68] and human rights issues,[69] with a right to "investigate human rights violations and where necessary, recommend corrective action".[70] Furthermore, the mission assumed increased responsibilities in the area where the classical strengths of UN peacekeeping lie, namely the provision of conditions for free and fair elections. UNAMA drew attention to the need to create a neutral environment for the national elections,[71] encouraging measures such as disarmament, demobilisation and reintegration programmes, the reform of the media system (radio and television and the law governing the press) and the completion of the necessary legal and institutional frameworks for the electoral process in 2004.[72]

In accordance with its mandate, UNAMA played only a limited role in the elaboration of the new Afghan Constitution; the drafting process remained essentially under Afghan "ownership".[73] The preparatory work was undertaken by a domestic Commission (the Constitutional Drafting Commission) which developed a draft text building on elements enshrined in previous Afghan constitutions.[74] This draft was reviewed by a Constitutional Review Commission, which sought expert advice from selected international experts.[75] UNAMA's input was confined to technical assistance. The mission created a Constitutional Commission Support Unit, which coordinated foreign technical assistance and financial support. In December 2003, the draft text prepared by the Constitutional Commission was presented to the Constitutional *Loya Jirga*, which adopted the final document on 4 January 2004.[76]

The Constitution marks an attempt to build a bridge between the future and the past. It is guided by the objective of reconciling secular values, such as respect for democracy and human rights standards, including gender-based equality, with Islamic traditions. Both rationales were expressly embodied in the text. Article 6 requires the Afghan state "to create a prosperous and progressive society based on social justice, protection of human dignity, protection of human rights" and the "realization of democracy". Article 7 of the Constitution commits the state to "abide by the UN Charter", the "Universal Declaration of Human Rights"

---

[67] For a survey, see Chesterman, *You, the People*, at 179–80.

[68] See paras. 43–5 of the Report of the Secretary-General of 23 July 2003.

[69] See *ibid.*, paras. 39–42.   [70] See Annex II, Article 6 of the Bonn Agreement.

[71] See para 63 of the Report of the Secretary-General of 23 July 2003.

[72] See *ibid.*, para. 64.

[73] See Afsah and Guhr, *Afghanistan: Building a State to Keep the Peace*, at 424–5 ("an overwhelmingly 'Afghan' process").

[74] For a full discussion, *ibid.*, at 424–7.   [75] *Ibid.*, at 425.

[76] For a survey, see Report of the Secretary-General of 26 November 2004, paras. 3–10.

and other "international conventions that Afghanistan has signed", such as the ICCPR and the Convention on the Elimination of Discrimination against Women.[77] The Constitution departs, however, from the model of a classic Western democracy by its clear commitment to Islam and Islamic law. The link between law and religion is, *inter alia*, reflected in the recognition of Afghanistan as "an Islamic Republic" (Article 1) and the supremacy clause in Article 3 ("In Afghanistan, no law can be contrary to the beliefs and provisions of the sacred religion of Islam"). The Constitution thus established the foundations of an Islamic democracy whose structures reflect the role of domestic ownership in the constitutional process.[78] The interpretation and settlement of conflicts between individual rights and freedoms and Islamic law was left to domestic constitutional organs, such as the Supreme Court.

Following the holding of parliamentary and provincial council elections in September 2005 and formal completion of the political agenda of the Bonn Agreement,[79] UNAMA assumed tasks of coordination of international assistance (as co-chair of a Joint Coordination and Monitoring Board)[80] and continued to provide technical assistance and support in selected fields, including electoral processes and human rights monitoring.[81]

1.4. Assessment

The model of administration governing the process of transition in Afghanistan was carefully adjusted to the principles of self-determination and local ownership. External interference in civil affairs was restricted to a minimum, both at the stage of the preparation and in implementation of the framework. The organisation did not only actively involve local stakeholders in the drafting of the architecture of the Bonn Agreement, but left them wide decision-making power and discretion in the choice of their future political system.[82] This policy had several positive implications.

---

[77] Article 58 of the Constitution vests a newly established Independent Human Rights Commission with the power to monitor human rights violations.

[78] See Korhonen, Gras and Creutz, *International Post-Conflict Situations*, at 78.

[79] See Report of the Secretary-General, *The Situation in Afghanistan and is Implications for International Peace and Security*, 12 August 2005, paras. 2–20.

[80] See Report of the Secretary-General, *The Situation in Afghanistan and its Implications for International Peace and Security*, UN Doc. S/2006/145 of 7 March 2006, para. 71.

[81] *Ibid.*, para. 58. UNAMA's new mandate was approved by the Security Council in para. 3 of SC Res. 1662 (2006) of 23 March 2006.

[82] This methodology contrasts with practice of the UN in cases like Eritrea and East Timor where the organisation determined the governing framework largely of its own will.

The gradual empowerment of public authorities through a combination of traditional mechanisms of decision-making (*Loya Jirgas*) and subsequent elections increased the legitimacy and trust of local communities in the (transitional) political institutions of the Afghan state.[83] Moreover, the "light footprint" approach helped to adjust the pace and scope of political and legal reform in Afghanistan more closely to the wishes of the Afghan society.[84] The increased focus on local ownership tempered the risk of artificial liberalisation, all too often hastily imposed on transitional societies by moment-based donor requirements.

However, the Afghan model also had some downsides. The Bonn process suffered from an initial lack of political inclusiveness. The group of Afghan leaders who made the basic choices over the timetable and framework of the peace process in Bonn was not necessarily representative of Afghan society as a whole, and excluded, in particular, members of the Taliban.[85]

Secondly, the Afghan experience revealed that a "light footprint" agenda may distort the balance between individual and collective rights in post-conflict situations. The prioritisation of local ownership protected the Afghan state from external interference, but it reduced the scope and pace of individual rights. Initiatives to establish a new justice system in Afghanistan advanced only slowly, due to security challenges, the limited powers of the UN in this field and the need for mutual consultation between the different authorities involved.[86] Domestic authorities failed, in particular, to target law enforcement and justice issues in a timely manner. This led to shortcomings and delays in the institutionalisation

---

[83] It consolidated the principle "that power should be based on popular participation rather than military might" – a standard that supposedly even "the warlords themselves had to acknowledge". See para. 42 of the Report of the Secretary-General on the situation in Afghanistan and its implications for international peace and security of 11 July 2002, UN Doc. A/56/1000-S/2002/737.

[84] Note, however, that the Bonn Agreement set a relatively strict timetable for the holding of elections and the drafting of a new constitution, which has been criticised. See Suhrke, Karpviken and Strand, *Conflictual Peacebuilding*, at 63.

[85] See also International Peace Academy, *The Future of UN-Statebuilding: Strategic and Operational Challenges and the Legacy of Iraq* (2004), at 8.

[86] Progress in domestic justice reform has been very slow. By 2003, the Judicial Reform Commission had rebuilt some courts and started judicial training. However, fundamental issues like the conflict between Islamic principles and secular law remained largely unaddressed. For a criticism, see Suhrke, Karpviken and Strand, *Conflictual Peacebuilding*, at 38; Chesterman, *You, The People*, at 178. See also Report of the Secretary-General, The situation in Afghanistan and its implications for peace and security, UN Doc. S/2006/727, para. 54.

mechanisms of transitional justice[87] and human rights protection more generally.[88]

The continuing gulf between Islamic traditions and principles of Western-liberal democracy[89] became evident in March 2006 when several people were accused of apostasy under Islamic law on the basis of Article 130 of the new Afghan Constitution.[90] Some individuals were forced to leave the country by local leaders. Abdul Rahman, a former aid worker, was charged with the death penalty in connection with his conversion to Christianity,[91] despite the express commitment of the Afghan Constitution to international human rights conventions (e.g. the ICCPR)

---

[87] The Bonn Agreement failed to address the issue of transitional justice partly because some of the leaders united in Bonn were previously involved in armed conflict. See Afsah and Guhr, *Afghanistan: Building a State to Keep the Peace*, at 386. For a long time, UNAMA officials took the position that Afghanistan was not yet ripe to address past human rights violations due to lack of security and political stability. See Suhrke, Karpviken and Strand, *Conflictual Peacebuilding*, at 40. In June 2002, the Afghan Independent Human Rights Commission was vested with the mandate to "undertake national consultations and propose a national strategy for transitional justice and for addressing the abuses of the past". See Annex I, Article 9 of the Decree of the Presidency of the Interim Administration of Afghanistan on the Establishment of an Afghan Independent Human Rights Commission. However, the Commission could only start this work six months after its establishment and lacked means to carry out this mandate effectively. The Commission issued its recommendations in 2005. See Afghanistan Independent Human Rights Commission, *A Call for Justice, A National Consultation on Past Human Rights Violations in Afghanistan*, February 2005, at www.aihrc.org.af.

[88] Two years after the Bonn Agreement, UNAMA was only staffed with one human rights official. See Suhrke, Karpviken and Strand, *Conflictual Peacebuilding*, at 40.

[89] The Afghan Constitution recognises freedom of religion and the Hanafi school of sharia law.

[90] The Hanafi school of Islamic jurisprudence mandates the death penalty for an apostate. State prosecutors relied on Article 130 of the Constitution of Afghanistan which enables prosecutors to bring charges "in accordance with the Hanafi jurisprudence". The text of the Article reads: "In cases under consideration, the courts shall apply provisions of this Constitution as well as other laws. If there is no provision in the Constitution or other laws about a case, the courts shall, in pursuance of Hanafi jurisprudence, and, within the limits set by this Constitution, rule in a way that attains justice in the best manner."

[91] Abdul Rahman was arrested in February 2006 for converting from Islam to Christianity, possibly in connection with a family dispute over the custody of children. The prosecution demanded a death sentence before a primary court in Kabul. These charges attracted widespread international attention in March 2006. On 26 March 2006, the court referred the case back to the prosecution on the basis of technical and legal flaws. Two days later, Rahman was released. See also Report of the Secretary-General, *The Situation in Afghanistan and Its Implications for Peace and Security*, 11 September 2006, paras. 45 and 55.

in Article 7 of the Constitution.[92] These cases highlighted the remaining confusion about the role of international human rights guarantees (protection of freedom of conscience and religion) in constitutional interpretation.[93]

2. The international administration of Iraq

The international engagement in Iraq[94] is a more hybrid case of UN restraint in international administration. The design of the international presence was influenced by the continuing divergences among UN members over the (il)legality of the Iraq intervention and its legal consequences.[95] The UN Secretariat again adopted a "light footprint" agenda. However, the decision to limit the scope of UN involvement in

---

[92] Afghanistan is a party to the ICCPR. The Covenant is binding upon domestic authorities by virtue of Article 7 of the Afghan Constitution.

[93] The charging of a person for religious beliefs conflicts with Article 7 of the Constitution. See Amnesty International, *Afghanistan: Case of Abdul Rahman Underlines Urgent Need for Judicial Reform*, AI Index, ASA 11/008/2006, 22 March 2006, at http://web.amnesty.org/library/print/ENGASA110082006.

[94] See generally International Crisis Group, *Governing Iraq*, ICG Middle East Report No. 17 of 25 August 2003, at 20–5; Rick Kirgis, *Security Council Resolution 1483 on the Rebuilding of Iraq*, ASIL Insights, May 2003; Jordan J. Paust, *The U.S. as Occupying Power over Portions of Iraq and Relevant Responsibilities Under the Laws of War*, ASIL Insights, April 2003; Thomas D. Grant, *How to Reconcile Conflicting Obligations of Occupation and Reform*, ASIL Insights, June 2003; Outti Korhonen, *"Post" As Justification: International Law and Democracy-Building after Iraq*, German Law Journal, Vol. 4 (2003), 709; Rüdiger Wolfrum, *The Attack of September 11, 2001, the Wars Against the Taliban and Iraq: Is There a Need to Reconsider International Law on the Recourse to Force and the Rules in Armed Conflict*, Max Planck Yearbook of United Nations Law, Vol. 7 (2003), 1–78; Rüdiger Wolfrum, *Iraq – from Belligerent Occupation to Iraqi Exercise of Sovereignty: Foreign Power versus International Community Interference*, Max Planck Yearbook of United Nations Law, Vol . 9 (2005), 2–45; Chesterman, *You, The People*, at 92–7; Sassòli, *Legislation and Maintenance of Public Order*, at 661; Fox, *Occupation of Iraq*, at 195; Kaikobad, *Problems of Belligerent Occupation*, 253–64; Bali, *Justice under Occupation*, 431; Andrea Carcano, *End of Occupation in 2004? The Status of the Multinational Force in Iraq after the Transfer of Sovereignty to the Interim Iraqi Government*, Journal of Conflict and Security Law, Vol. 11 (2006), 41–66; Korhonen, Gras and Creutz, *International Post-Conflict Situations*, at 81–106.

[95] For a critical analysis of the intervention, see Rüdiger Wolfrum, *Iraq – A Crisis for our System of Collective Security*, at www.mpil.de/en/Wolfrum/eirak.pdf; Christian Tomuschat, *Iraq – The Demise of International Law*, Die Friedenswarte, Vol. 78 (2003), 141–60; Jochen Abr. Frowein, *Issues of Legitimacy around the Security Council*, in Negotiating for Peace, Liber Amicorum Tono Eitel (Jochen Abr. Frowein et al., eds., 2003), 121, at 125–6; Gerd Seidel, *Quo Vadis Völkerrecht*, Archiv des Völkerrechts, Vol. 41 (2003), 449, at 478–80. Dissenting Christopher Greenwood, *International Law and the Pre-emptive Use of Force: Afghanistan, Al-Qaida, and Iraq*, San Diego International Law Journal, Vol. 4 (2003), 7, 36; Ruth Wedgwood, *The Fall of Saddam Hussein: Security Council Mandates and Pre-emptive Self-Defense*, American Journal of International Law, Vol. 97 (2003), 576, at 582. For a

the process of the reconstruction of Iraq resulted not only from voluntary self-restriction by the organisation itself, but from US pressure to
maintain full and unimpeded operational control over the conduct of
the post-war occupation. Power struggles between members of the US-
led coalition (the "Coalition"), on the one hand, and states supporting
a lead role of the UN in Iraq, on the other, led to the adoption of a
unique compromise arrangement under which the occupying powers
act alongside and in cooperation with a UN assistance mission.[96] This
compromise itself was not free from ambiguities, because it made the
UN a *de facto* accomplice of the Coalition in the post-war occupation
of Iraq, without granting it the necessary teeth and independence to
neutralise and shape the decision-making process.[97] Critics may therefore claim that the UN was in fact bypassed twice in relation to Iraq: in
the decision over the resort to the use of force, and in the process of
post-conflict administration.[98]

Nevertheless, there are some encouraging signs in the international
treatment of governance issues in Iraq after the intervention. All sides,
including the members of the coalition and the UN, agreed on the principle that the multinational administration of Iraq must be transitional
in nature and guided by a swift process of re-empowerment of domestic authorities[99] – a step which reflects an increasing willingness to
recognise local ownership as a necessary corollary of democratic change.

discussion of the implications of the Iraq crisis, see Thomas Franck, *What Happens
Now? The United Nations After Iraq*, American Journal of International Law, Vol. 97 (2003),
607, at 614; Richard Falk, *What Future for the UN Charter System of War Prevention?*,
American Journal of International Law, Vol. 97 (2003), 590, at 594; Jane E. Stromseth,
Law and Force After Iraq: A Transitional Moment, American Journal of International Law,
Vol. 97 (2003), 628, at 633; Carsten Stahn, *Enforcement of the Collective Will After Iraq*,
American Journal of International Law, Vol. 97 (2003), 804.

[96] See para. 8 of SC Res. 1483 (2003) and paras. 1 and 8 of SC Res. 1511 (2003).

[97] See also the critique by former UN High Commissioner for Human Rights, Mary
Robinson, who noted that "it is not healthy for the UN to be playing a secondary role
to an occupation power as it is perceived". See BBC Interview, 20 August 2003.

[98] For calls in favour of stronger involvement of the UN after the transfer of power of
Iraqi authorities, see William Slomanson, *UN Post-Transfer Role in Iraq*, Miskolc Journal
of International Law, Vol. 2 (2005), 83–4.

[99] See the statement of the Secretary-General following the adoption of Resolution 1511
(2003): "Our common objective is to restore peace and stability to a sovereign,
democratic and independent Iraq as quickly as possible." See also para. 3 of the
preamble of SC Res. 1483, in which the Council stresses "the right of the Iraqi people
freely to determine their own political future and control their own resources,
welcoming the commitment of all parties concerned to support the creation of an
environment in which they may do so as soon as possible, and expressing resolve that
the day when Iraqis govern themselves must come quickly".

Furthermore, the Security Council itself determined both the strategic guidelines of the post-conflict administration and the responsibilities of the Coalition in the exercise of their functions.

2.1. Background

The post-war involvement of the UN in Iraq shares some contextual parallels with the UN engagement in Kosovo. The UN presence was established in a moment of crisis of the collective security system, namely in the direct aftermath of an unlawful intervention. The division over the legality of the use of force turned the definition of the role of the UN in the reconstruction of Iraq into a delicate exercise in strategic policy-making. There was strong support for the view that the UN should play a central role in the design of the post-conflict administration, in order to internationalise the process of reconstruction of Iraq and in order to strengthen the damaged authority of the Security Council after Operation Iraqi Freedom. But many Council members, in particular Russia, France and Germany, remained opposed to the idea that a possible UN engagement should be understood as a retroactive validation of the intervention.[100] Due to these visible tensions, the Council exercised caution in the drafting of the post-conflict framework.

SC Resolution 1483 (2003), which was adopted to bridge the gap between the (illegal) recourse to force and the (lawful) post-conflict-presence of US-UK forces in Iraq, avoided any language which could be interpreted as a tacit approval of the use of force. The Security Council took a pragmatic stance on the consequences of the military action and the factual *status quo* created by it. It endorsed the continuing presence of the US and the UK as occupying powers in Iraq[101] and charged them with a provisional administering mandate,[102] without, however, endorsing the use of force leading to the occupation.[103]

---

[100] French President Chirac noted that France would veto any resolution that "would legitimize the military intervention". See "We Will Not Help You to Justify War, Chirac Tells Blair", *The Times* (London), 22 March 2003.

[101] See para. 4 of SC Res. 1483 (2003). See also para. 8, which requests the Secretary-General to appoint a Special Representative for Iraq, charged with reconstruction assistance "in coordination with the Authority".

[102] See para. 4 of SC Res. 1483 (2003), where the Council "calls upon" the US and the UK "to promote the welfare of the Iraqi people through the effective administration of the territory".

[103] Later, the Council went as far as to "authorise" the establishment of "a multinational force under unified command" in Iraq. But it again remained mute on the issue of the (il)legality of the use of force in its substance. See para. 13 of SC Res. 1511 (2003).

The main reasons behind the UN engagement were to close the security gap after the intervention and to foster the re-establishment of Iraqi self-government. These two rationales were spelled out by the Council in its two main legal decisions on the architecture of the interim governing framework, Resolutions 1483 (2003) and 1511 (2003). Both resolutions directly linked the function of the post-war occupation to the right of self-determination of the Iraqi people. Security Council Resolution 1483 (2003) charged the occupying powers expressly with the "creation of conditions in which the Iraqi people can freely determine their own political future". Security Council Resolution 1511 (2002) emphasised "the temporary nature" of the powers of the Coalition Provisional Authority[104] and called upon "the Authority, in this context, to return governing responsibilities and authorities to the people of Iraq as soon as practicable",[105] while reaffirming that "the Iraqi interim administration", composed of the Iraqi Governing Council and its ministers "embodies the sovereignty of the State of Iraq" pending the election of an "internationally recognised, representative government".[106] These few lines made it clear that international administering agents were conceived as trustees of the interests of the Iraqi people, charged with the restoration and establishment of national and local institutions for representative governance.

The need to maintain an international presence in Iraq resulted not only from the governance vacuum arising in the country after the toppling of the Baathist regime, but also from the general collapse of law and order in Iraq caused by the breakdown of vital public and civil services (electricity, clean water, banking system), the dissolution of the domestic law enforcement institutions (police, army), large-scale unemployment and continuing security challenges from insurgency forces (acts of sabotage, attacks on Coalition forces and civilians, abductions). This situation made an immediate withdrawal of the coalition forces impossible, even in the eyes of those who had opposed the use of force,[107] and induced the Council to use its Chapter VII powers to "call upon the Authority",[108] and the later established multinational force,[109] to restore the conditions of stability and security deemed necessary for both "the well-being of the people of Iraq as well as to the ability of all concerned to carry out their work on behalf of the people of Iraq".[110]

---

[104] See *ibid.*, para. 1.   [105] See *ibid.*, para. 6.   [106] See *ibid.*, para. 4.
[107] See International Crisis Group, *Governing Iraq*, at 2.
[108] See para. 4 of SC Res. 1483 (2003).   [109] See para. 13 of SC Res. 1511 (2003).
[110] See para. 3 of the preamble of SC Res. 1511 (2003).

2.2.   The light footprint: a power bargain

The role of the UN in the process of statebuilding was a bone of contention among supporters and opponents of the intervention, and within the Coalition itself. The US was from the beginning of Operation Iraqi Freedom opposed to a central role being given to the UN in post-conflict Iraq. It envisaged a temporary US-led administration, which would govern Iraq until the establishment of an interim Iraqi government, with possible delegations of power to selected Iraqi-led institutions. The US believed that the UN should mainly serve to exercise humanitarian functions.[111] This position contrasted with the views of most members of the EU, Russia, China, and virtually all of the G-77 states, which called for a leading role of the UN in Iraq, including genuine authority over the political transition process.[112] They argued that the UN should be substantially involved in the government of Iraq because of its experience in transitional administration, its function as the institutional embodiment of international legitimacy and the stabilising effect of its presence on the security situation in Iraq. A similar position was taken by the UK, which urged the US to grant the UN political control in Iraq, in order to facilitate international assistance efforts and in order to help to overcome the crisis in transatlantic relations.

The UN itself supported a rather moderate post-conflict engagement in Iraq. In a confidential blueprint prepared in February 2002,[113] the Secretariat proposed a light footprint following the model of Afghanistan.[114] The blueprint envisaged the creation of an assistance mission that would provide guidance and advice on various aspects of post-conflict government (democratic governance, judicial and legal reform, national reconciliation), while leaving the primary responsibility for the determination of the governing framework with the Iraqi people.

---

[111] See Nile Gardiner and David B. Rivkin, *Blueprint for Freedom: Limiting the Role of the United Nations in Post-War Iraq*, Heritage Foundation, Backgrounder No. 1646, 21 April 2003; David E. Sanger and Eric Schmitt, "US Has a Plan to Occupy Iraq, Officials Report", *New York Times*, 11 October 2002. See also "Rice Says U.S. to Have 'Leading' Role in Iraq", *Washington Times*, 5 April 2003.

[112] The former French Foreign Minister Dominique de Villepin argued that the UN "must steer the process and must be at the heart of the reconstruction and administration of Iraq". See Gardiner and Rivkin, *Blueprint for Freedom*.

[113] See "UN Leaders Draw Up Secret Blueprint for Postwar Iraq", *The Times* (London), 5 March 2003.

[114] See also para. 92 of the Report of the Secretary-General pursuant to paragraph 24 of Resolution 1483 (2003) and paragraph 12 of Resolution 1511 (2003) of 5 December 2003, UN Doc. S/2003/1149, which notes that the "United Nations Assistance Mission for Iraq was never envisaged to be a large operation with a complex structure".

Power brokering in the Security Council over broader international support for the coalition[115] led to the adoption of an arrangement which involved three main entities in the post-conflict government of Iraq (the Coalition Provisional Authority, the Iraqi Governing Council and the United Nations Assistance Mission for Iraq (UNAMI)).[116] The scope of UN tasks was extended beyond the area of humanitarian relief to include "a vital role" in "the restoration and establishment of national and local institutions for representative governance".[117] But this "vital role" was *de facto* a light footprint. UNAMI was requested to "work intensively with the Authority, the people of Iraq, and others"[118] to restore governance and to encourage "international efforts to promote legal and judicial reform".[119] The powers of the mission were limited to the level of "assistance to the people of Iraq" and/or "coordination with the Authority".[120] The role of the Iraqi interim administration remained similarly vague. Resolution 1483 (2003) envisaged its creation as "a transitional administration run by Iraqis", but failed to vest it with concrete governing powers and responsibilities.[121]

2.3.   The scope of UN involvement

The details of the tripartite relationship were elaborated by subsequent practice. Two institutions assumed a key role: the Security Council and the CPA. The Security Council determined the broad strategic guidelines of the administration, whereas the Coalition took charge of most of the governing responsibilities on the ground. The post-war administration of Iraq became thereby more or less a replication of UN administration missions with exchanged roles, namely with a multinational coalition of states exercising governing responsibilities under the guidance of the Council.

2.3.1.   The (self-defined) role of the CPA

The Coalition Provisional Authority (CPA) assumed full governmental control in Iraq.[122] Its first regulation, adopted on 16 May 2003 (CPA

---

[115] See Philip Gordon, "Swap Control for Support", *The International Herald Tribune*, 20 August 2003.

[116] UNAMI was established by SC Res. 1500 (2003) of 14 August 2003, UN Doc. S/RES/1500 (2003). See also para. 2 of the Report of the Secretary-General pursuant to paragraph 24 of resolution 1483 (2003), UN Doc. S/2003/715 of 17 July 2003.

[117] See para. 7 of the preamble of SC Res. 1483 (2003).

[118] See para. 8 c) of SC Res. 1483 (2003).   [119] See para. 8 f) of SC Res. 1483 (2003).

[120] See the chapeau of para. 8 of SC Res. 1483 (2003).

[121] See para. 9 of SC Res. 1483 (2003).

[122] For an assessment of the powers of the CPA, see also Kaikobad, *Problems of Belligerent Occupation*, at 254–64.

Regulation No. 1), reads like a reprise of UNMIK's or UNTAET'S authoritative assumption of control. Section 1 (1) of the Regulation reflects more or less the mandate enshrined in SC Resolution 1483 (2003). It provides:

The CPA shall exercise powers of government temporarily in order to provide for the effective administration of Iraq during the period of transitional administration, to restore conditions of security and stability, to create conditions in which the Iraqi people can freely determine their own political future, including by advancing efforts to restore and establish national and local institutions for representative governance and facilitating economic recovery and sustainable reconstruction and development.[123]

Section 1 (2) of the Regulation defined the scope of powers that the coalition can exercise for this purpose. It states:

The CPA is vested with all executive, legislative and judicial authority necessary to achieve its objectives, to be exercised under relevant U.N. Security Council resolutions, including Resolution 1483 (2003) and the laws and usages of war. This authority shall be exercised by the CPA Administrator.[124]

This sweeping accumulation of authority bears more resemblance to the administering framework of the post-surrender occupation of Germany and Japan and/or exclusive UN governance missions than with an ordinary regime of occupation. Neither the Fourth Geneva Convention nor the Hague Rules provides an occupying power with full legislative and judicial power to promote economic, social and institutional change for the purpose of statebuilding. The influence of other actors on the process of governance was limited to a strict minimum. The role of the UN was not even mentioned in Regulation No. 1.

2.3.2.   Corrective action by the Security Council

This far-reaching assertion of authority triggered not only critical statements from Iraqis,[125] but also opposition from other Security Council members. The Council induced the Coalition, in particular, to pay greater tribute to the preservation of local ownership. Resolution 1483 (2003) reminded the members of the Coalition of their obligations as occupying powers, including the responsibility to comply fully "with Geneva Conventions of 1949 and Hague Regulations of 1907".[126] Later,

---

[123] See Section 1 of CPA Regulation No. 1 of 16 May 2003.
[124] See *ibid.*, Section 2. See also ICG Report, *Governing Iraq*, at 10.
[125] Iraqi political leaders criticised the US approach, noting that what the coalition gives the Iraqi interim authority in 2003 is "far less" than what was given to the Iraqi government by the British when they "occupied Iraq in 1920". See ICG Report, at 11.
[126] See para. 5 of SC Res. 1483 (2003).

the Security Council expressly required the CPA to defer powers to local authorities. SC Resolution 1511 (2003) emphasised that the administration of Iraq should be "progressively undertaken by the evolving structures of the Iraqi interim administration".[127] The Coalition was obliged to "return governing responsibilities and authorities to the people of Iraq as soon as practicable" and to "report to the Council on the progress being made".[128] Furthermore, the Security Council invited the Iraqi Governing Council to establish a timetable for the drafting of a new constitution for Iraq and the holding of elections under that constitution.[129]

These requirements were subsequently implemented by an Agreement of 15 November 2003, between the Governing Council and the CPA, which laid down the basic parameters of the future political process in Iraq. The Agreement contained two fundamental decisions. It determined that by 30 June 2004, a new transitional administration would assume full responsibility for governing Iraq from the Coalition Authority, following the adoption of a "fundamental law" regulating the scope and structures of the administration by the Governing Council and the Coalition. In addition, the Agreement specified that the transfer of power should be followed by elections for a constitutional conference to be held by 15 March 2005 and a popular referendum on the constitution.[130]

2.3.3. The role of UNAMI

UNAMI's influence on the governance process in Iraq remained very limited. Contrary to previous UN practice, UN officials emphasised that democracy should evolve from within Iraq and should not be imposed from outside.[131] The mission therefore conceived itself as a complementary assistance mission, designed to empower "to the maximum extent possible... the Iraqi Governing Council and related Iraqi institutions, to ensure Iraqi ownership of key decisions taken in the lead-up to the formation of a fully representative and sovereign Iraqi Government".[132] Furthermore, UNAMI took the view that the future Iraqi constitution "must be wholly produced and owned by the people of Iraq",[133] limiting the role of the UN to the provision of assistance to "an internally driven constitutional process".[134] The only field, in which the mission sought to play a leading role was the area of elections.[135] But this

---

[127] See para. 5 of SC Res. 1511 (2003)   [128] See ibid., para. 6.   [129] See ibid., para. 7.
[130] See paras. 64 and 65 of the Report of the Secretary-General of 5 December 2003, UN Doc. S/2003/1149.
[131] See ibid., para. 2.   [132] Ibid., para. 2.
[133] Ibid., para. 79.   [134] Ibid., para. 80.   [135] Ibid., para. 77.

intention was soon hampered by the growing security risks for the UN in Iraq, caused by events such as the 19 August 2003 attack on the UN headquarters in Baghdad. These changing circumstances restricted the UN engagement even further than anticipated under UNAMI's light footprint approach.[136]

2.4. The practice of the CPA

The governing model of the CPA shared many structural parallels with the practice of the UN in East Timor and in Kosovo. The CPA placed the applicability of Iraqi law under a broad proviso, widely determined by the authority's own functions. Section 2 of CPA Regulation No. 1 determined that the "laws in force in Iraq as of 16 April 2003" shall only "continue to apply in Iraq insofar the[se] laws do not prevent the CPA from exercising its rights and fulfilling its obligations, or conflict with the present or any other Regulation or Order issued by the CPA".

Section 3 of the same regulation established a new hierarchy of norms. It stated:

In carrying out the authority and responsibility vested in the CPA, the Administrator will as necessary, issue Regulations ("instruments that define the institutions and authorities of the CPA") and Orders ("binding instructions issued by the CPA")... Regulations and Orders issued by the Administrator shall take precedence over all other laws and publications to the extent such other laws and publications are inconsistent.[137]

Regulatory acts of the CPA therefore became a primary source of law in Iraq, applicable "until repealed by the Administrator or superseded by legislation issued by democratic institutions of Iraq".[138] The Authority failed, however, to subject its Regulations and Orders to legal limitations other than "Resolution 1483, and the laws and usages of war". Human rights obligations were not explicitly mentioned, although both the U.S. and Iraq are, inter alia, a party to the ICCPR. Moreover, the CPA's definition of the applicable law raised legal concerns because of its uncertainty and its wide conception of the powers of the CPA.[139]

The CPA exercised broad control over public life in Iraq in the period between May 2003 and June 2004.

---

[136] The Secretary-General requested the insertion of a *caveat* into para. 11 of SC Res. 1511 (2003), making UN assistance dependent on the security situation ("as circumstances permit"). *Ibid.*, para. 62.

[137] See Section 3 (1) of CPA Regulation No. 1.   [138] See *ibid.*

[139] For further discussion, see below Part IV, Chapter 15.

In the early days of the occupation, the broad authority of the CPA contrasted with the limited means of the Coalition to restore order. Coalition forces faced considerable problems in the protection of public property (museums, universities, hospitals, government buildings) and facilities (water, electricity). Iraqis engaged in widespread looting of stores and public facilities from hospitals to ministries. The Coalition took some steps to limit this violence.[140] However, some doubts remained whether the Coalition was sufficiently prepared to discharge its obligation under Article 43 of the Hague Regulations ("the occupant... shall take all measures in his power") to "restore and ensure" public order and safety. Coalition forces lacked the necessary means to protect private and public property, including Iraqi cultural property, against looting or destruction. There are even some indications that, in some instances, forces were ordered not to intervene.[141] This omission raised criticisms that the Coalition failed to live up to its responsibilities to preserve civil life and public welfare in the initial phase of the occupation.[142]

One of the first institutional acts of the CPA was the establishment of the Iraqi Governing Council. SC Resolution 1483 (2003) mandated the CPA to support the "formation, by the people of Iraq... of an Iraqi interim administration".[143] The CPA used this authority to establish an Interim Governing Council on 13 July 2003, which was deemed to act as "the principal body of the Iraqi interim administration".[144] However, the mode of establishment and the *modus operandi* of the Governing Council remained ambiguous. The terms of Resolution 1483 appeared to suggest that such an interim authority would be created by way of a democratic procedure ("by the people of Iraq") and upon consultation with the UN. Yet, neither the people of Iraq nor the UN Special Representative was involved by the CPA in the formation of the Council.[145] The CPA created the Council by way of a CPA Regulation and appointed its twenty-five members of the Council. Three months later, the Security Council

---

[140] Coalition forces re-established police stations, judicial services and detention facilities.

[141] See Amnesty International, *Iraq: Looting, Lawlessness and Humanitarian Consequences* (2003) (MDE 14/083/2003).

[142] See Sassòli, *Legislation and Maintenance of Public Order*, at 667–8; Wolfrum, *Iraq – From Belligerent Occupation to Sovereignty*, at 9 and 13; Bali, *Justice under Occupation*, at 452.

[143] See para. 9 of SC Res. 1483 (2003).

[144] See Sections 1 and 2 of CPA Regulation No. 6 of 13 July 2003 (*Governing Council of Iraq*).

[145] For a criticism of this procedure, see Wolfrum, *Iraq – From Belligerent Occupation to Sovereignty*, at 26. ("More intensive consultations with the UN Special Representative ...would have not only been possible but necessary to meet the standards as enshrined in Resolution 1483.")

legitimised the outcome of this process by determining that "the Governing Council and its ministers are the principle bodies of the Iraqi interim administration".[146]

CPA Regulation No. 6 failed to set out in greater detail the role of the Governing Council in the governing structure of the occupation regime. The CPA accorded the Council a consultative role (the CPA "shall consult and coordinate") "in all matters involving the temporary governance of Iraq".[147] However, Regulation No. 6 did not specify the powers of the Council in the lawmaking process (i.e. right to initiate legislation, resolution of conflicts with the CPA). This omission left the CPA some flexibility in the involvement of the Governing Council in regulatory action.

In practice, the Governing Council acted essentially as a random advisory body.[148] The Council was consulted by the CPA in the area of economic reforms.[149] Moreover, the Council had some autonomous powers. It was formally authorised to appoint executive authorities (interim diplomats and ministers), to approve budgets and to propose certain policies. But the CPA retained its executive, legislative and judicial authority under CPA Regulation No. 1 and could veto decisions of the Council.[150] In some instances, the CPA enabled the Council to adopt regulatory measures on the basis of delegated authority. The CPA delegated its powers in specific fields, in order to allow the Council to take specific measures, such as creation of the Iraqi Special Tribunal,[151] the establishment of an Iraqi Property Claims Commission on the basis of the rules stipulated in CPA Regulation No. 8,[152] or the implementation of the de-Ba'atification of the Iraqi society consistent with CPA Order No. 1.[153]

---

[146] See para. 4 of SC Res. 1511 (2003) of 16 October 2003.

[147] See Section 2 of Coalition Provisional Authority Regulation No. 6 (*Governing Council of Iraq*): "In accordance with Resolution 1483, the Governing Council and the CPA shall consult and coordinate on all matters involving the temporary governance of Iraq, including the authorities of the Governing Council."

[148] It is reported that "the Governing Council governed no one. Its 'decisions' were more in the nature of recommendations. While it named technocrat transitional ministers to run Iraq's various ministries, the Governing Council had little or no say in the ministries' day-to-day operations". See Feldman, *What We Owe Iraq*, at 110.

[149] For a survey, see Fox, *Occupation of Iraq*, at 248 and note 285.

[150] See *ibid.*, at 205–6.

[151] See Section 1 (1) of CPA Order No. 48 of 9 December 2003 (*Delegation of Authority Regarding an Iraqi Special Tribunal*).

[152] See Section 1 of CPA Regulation No. 8 (*Delegation of Authority Regarding an Iraq Property Claims Commission*).

[153] See Section 1 (1) of CPA Memorandum No. 7 of 4 November 2003 (*Delegation of Authority under De-Baathification Order No. 1*) and CPA Order No. 1 of 16 May 2003 (*De-Baathification of Iraqi Society*).

Yet the bulk of legal and institutional reform was undertaken by the CPA itself. The CPA dissolved most of the Iraqi military and security institutions, including the Ministry of Defence, the Ministry of Information, the Iraqi Intelligence Service, the Ministry of State for Military Affairs and all entities affiliated with or comprising Saddam Hussein's bodyguards and various military and paramilitary organisations.[154] Emerging gaps in the public sector were filled through the reorganisation of ministries,[155] the creation of new public institutions such as the Council for International Coordination[156] and the Trade Bank,[157] and the establishment of a new Iraqi Army.[158] The Iraqi judiciary, which had been stifled by political interference and corruption in the years of Baath Party rule, was placed under the supervision of a mixed Iraqi-international Judicial Review Committee operating "at the discretion of the Administrator",[159] and was later subjected to the control of the Council of Judges, an independent body charged "with the supervision of the judicial and prosecutorial systems of Iraq".[160] The Baath Party was disestablished by CPA Order No. 1 and its leadership removed from positions of authority in the administration of Iraq and in Iraqi society,[161] under the guidance of a US-appointed De-Ba'athification Council.[162] Moreover, the CPA restored basic freedoms such as the freedom of assembly[163] and the right to travel abroad for academic purposes.[164]

Many acts of legal reform were undertaken in order to bring domestic law into compliance with international human rights standards. The CPA

---

[154] See CPA Orders Nos. 2 and No. 3 of 23 May 2003 (*Dissolution of Entities*).
[155] See Section 2 of CPA Order No. 11 (*Licensing Telecommunications Services and Equipment*). See also CPA Order No. 32 of 4 September 2003 (*Legal Department of the Ministry of Justice*).
[156] See CPA Regulation No. 5 of 18 June 2003 (*Council for International Coordination*).
[157] See CPA Order No. 20 of 17 July 2003 (*Trade Bank of Iraq*).
[158] See CPA Order No. 12 of 7 August 2003 (*Creation of a New Iraqi Army*).
[159] See Section 1 (1) of CPA Order No. 15 of June 2003 (*Establishment of the Judicial Review Committee*). The Committee was charged with the appointment and removal from office of prosecutors and judges. See Section 4 of Order No. 15.
[160] See Section 1 of CPA Order No 35 of 13 September 2003 (*Re-establishment of the Council of Judges*). The creation of the Council was guided by the idea that "a judicial system staffed by capable persons and free and independent from outside influences" is "a key to the establishment of the rule of law". See para. 3 of the preamble of CPA Order No. 35.
[161] See CPA Order No. 1 of 16 May 2003 (*De-Baathification of Iraqi Society*).
[162] See CPA Order No. 5 of 25 May 2003 (*Establishment of the Iraqi De-Baathification Council*).
[163] See CPA Order No. 19 of 9 July 2003 (*Freedom of Assembly*).
[164] See CPA Order No. 8 of 7 June 2003 (*Travelling Abroad for Academic Purposes*).

ordered amendments to the Iraqi Labour Code in order to combat child labour and implement Iraq's obligations two ILO Conventions (ILO Convention No. 138 Concerning Minimum Admission to Employment of 26 June 1973, ILO Convention No. 182 Concerning the Prohibition and Immediate Action for the Elimination of the Worst Forms of Child Labour of 17 June 1999).[165] These measures were complemented by reforms of the Iraqi criminal system, which had been used as a tool of repression by the former regime. The CPA ordered several modifications of the penal system. The CPA prohibited torture[166] and suspended (capital punishment) or amended (kidnapping, rape, damage to public utilities) certain provisions of the 1969 Iraqi Penal Code.[167] Some additions were made to the Iraqi Code of Criminal Procedure, such as the express codification of the obligation of law enforcement agencies "to inform [a] person of his or her right to remain silent and to consult an attorney" in case of arrest.[168] Moreover, the CPA suspended all existing Iraqi prison regulations and issued standards for the management of detention and prison facilities.[169]

Other reforms were undertaken in the economic sector. The goal of the Coalition was to facilitate a "transition from a non-transparent centrally planned economy to a market economy".[170] The transformation required a restructuring of Iraq's economic system in areas such as foreign investment, banking and taxation. The CPA adopted a range of regulatory measures to facilitate these reforms.[171] The CPA amended the Iraqi banking system,[172] including the Iraqi Central Bank,[173] in order to provide stable conditions for reconstruction and to open the Iraqi market for foreign banks. A new foreign investment law was introduced, which allowed foreign investors to acquire ownership over Iraqi companies (including the oil and insurance sector) and to conduct business

---

[165] See CPA Order No. 89 of 5 May 2004 (*Amendments to the Labor Code – Law No. 71 of 1987*).
[166] See CPA Order No. 7 of 9 June 2003 (*Penal Code*).
[167] See Sections 2 and 3 of CPA Order No. 31 of 10 September 2003 (*Modifications of Penal Code and Criminal Proceedings Law*).
[168] *Ibid.*, Section 4.
[169] See CPA Order No. 10 of 8 June 2003 (*Management of Detention and Prison Facilities*) and the corresponding CPA Memorandum No. 2 of 8 June 2003.
[170] See CPA Order No. 39 of 19 September 2003 (*Foreign Investment*).
[171] For a more comprehensive survey, see Fox, *Occupation of Iraq*, at 208–225.
[172] See CPA Order No. 30 of 19 September 2003 (*Bank Law*) and CPA Order No. 94 of 6 June 2004 (*Banking Law of 2004*).
[173] See CPA Order No. 56 of 1 March 2004 (*Central Bank Law*).

on terms no less favourable than domestic enterprises ("national treatment").[174] The Iraqi corporate law[175] and the Iraqi bankruptcy law[176] were amended, in order to stimulate "company foundation and investment"[177] and to prevent "unduly harsh punishments" for financially distressed businesses.[178] Moreover, trading of capital was facilitated by a reform of the Iraqi securities market[179] and the creation of an independent Iraqi Stock Exchange.[180]

These activities of the CPA culminated in its involvement in the brokering of the Iraqi Transitional Administrative Law (TAL).[181] The TAL provided an interim Constitution of Iraq. It determined the system of government in the country for the period from the full transfer of sovereignty by the CPA to the Iraqi Interim Government (30 June 2004[182]) "until the formation of an elected Iraqi government" under a permanent Iraqi constitution.[183] The TAL specified, in particular, that Iraq would operate as a federalist state in this period.[184] This form of decentralisation was actively supported by the CPA. The CPA favoured the option of granting autonomy to the Kurdish people. Moreover, it shaped the new political structure of Iraq by setting out the structure of local government.[185]

The TAL also provided a basis for the continuing application of the acts of the CPA after its dissolution. The law reaffirmed that "[t]he laws, regulations, orders and directives issued by the Coalition Provisional

---

[174] See CPA Order No. 39 of 19 September 2003 (*Foreign Investment*).

[175] See CPA Order No. 64 of 29 February 2004 (*Amendment to the Company Law No. 21 of 1997*).

[176] See CPA Order No. 78 of 19 April 2004 (*Facilitation of Court-Supervised Debt Resolution Procedures*).

[177] See the preamble of CPA Order No. 64.   [178] See the preamble of CPA Order No. 78.

[179] See CPA Order No. 18 of 18 April 2004 (*Interim Law on Securities Markets*).

[180] *Ibid.*, Section 2 (1).

[181] See CPA, *Law of Administration for the State of Iraq for the Transitional Period*, 8 March 2004.

[182] The Security Council assumed that the occupation ended on 30 June 2004. See para. 2 of SC Res. 1546 (2004), where the Council "welcomes that,... by 30 June 2004, the occupation will end and the Coalition Provisional Authority will cease to exist". However, one may take the view that the continuing presence of foreign troops in Iraq after 30 June 2004 marks a case of peacetime occupation (*occupatia pacifica*).

[183] See Article 2 of the TAL. A parallel reference to the powers of an elected National Assembly under Article 59 made it clear that the law was not designed to serve as a permanent constitution.

[184] See Article 4 of the TAL: "The system of government in Iraq shall be republican, federal, democratic and pluralistic, and powers shall be shared between the federal government and the regional governments..."

[185] See CPA Order No. 71 of 6 April 2004 (*Local Government Powers*).

Authority pursuant to its authority under international law shall remain in force until rescinded or amended by legislation duly enacted and having the force of law".[186] CPA legislation therefore continued to apply after the transfer of authority to the Interim Government of Iraq on 28 June 2004, unless abrogated by subsequent domestic legislation.[187]

The practice of the CPA raised a number of legal problems. The multinational nature of the framework of occupation created some confusion about the scope of obligation of the members of the coalition and troop-contributing countries. The different member states of the Coalition were subject to a network of distinct legal obligations. The UK had to consider the possible impact of the ECHR on its decision-making practice in Iraq[188] – a factor which influenced, *inter alia*, the decision of the CPA to suspend the applicability of the death penalty during the period of occupation.[189] US CPA personnel, by contrast, faced the problem of the extraterritorial application of the ICCPR in its practice.[190] Other states shared conflicting understandings about their status as occupying powers.[191] SC Resolution 1483 (2003) itself distinguished the "occupying powers" (the US, the UK) from "other States" in the Authority that "are not occupying powers".[192] This divergence in the recognition and interpretation of legal obligations complicated the work of the Coalition partners.

Secondly, the legal basis for the exercise of some regulatory acts of the CPA remained unclear[193] due to the parallel invocation of the laws of occupation and the principles of Security Council Resolutions.[194] Several regulatory acts, including the measure of economic liberalisation and

---

[186] See Article 26 (c) of the TAL.

[187] This effect was reinforced by the issuance of an order by the CPA which enabled the application of CPA legislation to future Iraqi institutions. See CPA Order No. 100 of 28 June 2004 (*Transition of Laws, Regulations, Orders and Directives Issued by the Coalition Provisional Authority*).

[188] For a more detailed discussion of the extraterritorial application of the Convention, see below Part III, Chapter 11.

[189] See Kelly, *Iraq and the Law of Occupation*, at 134.

[190] For a discussion of the applicability of the ICCPR to US action, see Theodor Schilling, *Is the United States Bound by the Covenant of Civil and Political Rights in Relation to Occupied Territories*, Jean Monnet Paper No. IV (2004), at 17–18, 34–8.

[191] The Kingdom of the Netherlands did not consider itself formally as an occupying power despite sending troops to Iraq. Other states like Australia did not regard themselves as occupants, because they did not exercise control over Iraqi territory. See Kelly, *Iraq and the Law of Occupation*, at 132.

[192] See paras. 13 and 14 of the preamble of SC Res. 1483 (2003).

[193] See below Part IV, Chapter 15.   [194] See above Part I, Chapter 4.

market reform, exceeded the traditional framework of military necessity and orderly administration of territory and went therefore arguably beyond the limits of international law.[195] CPA Order No. 39 on the conditions of privatisation and the formation of the Iraqi Special Tribunal are probably the two most compelling examples of questionable regulatory interventionism. CPA Order No. 39 boldly decreed Iraq's transition from a centrally planned economy (under which all national enterprises were under state ownership) to a market economy. This transformation was not only critical in light of the regulatory limitations of an occupant under the law of occupation, but visibly guided by economic self-interest. When defining the conditions of investment, the CPA allowed, in particular, 100 per cent foreign ownership of key industrial sectors (except oil and mineral extraction and bank and insurance companies). Bids during the privatisation were allegedly restricted to members of the "coalition of the willing".[196] Corresponding contracts with US corporations were negotiated with ownership licences of up to forty years.[197] This practice was difficult to reconcile with the fiduciary nature of occupation authority which seeks to protect the population of the administered territory against favouritism by the occupant.[198]

The Iraqi Special Tribunal was officially qualified as an independent entity[199] and as an Iraqi creation since it was formally established by decree of the Governing Council and later confirmed by the TAL.[200] However, its creation remained in substance a product of the CPA. The CPA issued the text of the Statute (CPA Order No. 48)[201] and retained control over the Council and the enactment of the Statute at the time of its entry into force.[202] The Statute was therefore formally created by a subordinate body of the occupying powers on the basis of delegated

---

[195] See generally Fox, *Occupation of Iraq*, at 282–9; Sassòli, *Legislation and Maintenance of Public Order*, at 678–81, Amnesty International, *Memorandum on Concerns Related to Legislation Introduced by the Coalition Provisional Authority*, AI Index MDE 147180/2003, 4 December 2003. For a detailed analysis, see below Part IV, Chapter 15.

[196] See Boon, *Legislative Reform in Post-Conflict Zones*, at 310.

[197] See Bali, *Justice under Occupation*, at 442–3.

[198] See Boon, *Legislative Reform in Post-Conflict Zones*, at 294 and 310; Bali, *Justice under Occupation*, at 443.

[199] See Article 1 of the Statute of the Special Iraqi Tribunal.

[200] The TAL confirmed CPA Order No. 48, which contained the text of the Statute. The TAL again was promulgated by the Governing Council under the authority of the CPA.

[201] The CPA issued Order No. 48 on 9 December 2003, which was adopted by the Governing Council on 10 September 2003.

[202] The entry into force of the Statute was subject to the signature of CPA Administrator Bremer, who enjoyed veto power over decisions by the Council.

occupation authority,[203] which is traditionally hostile to changes of the judicial structure of the occupied territory and the prosecution of inhabitants for acts committed before the occupation.[204]

Moreover, the Coalition failed to establish mechanisms to ensure impartial and independent investigations of violations of international human rights and humanitarian law committed by the CPA and Coalition forces. CPA officials and Coalition forces personnel were exempted from the jurisdiction of Iraqi courts in civil, criminal and administrative matters.[205] Later, this protection was even extended to cover foreign private actors, such as contractors or sub-contractors of the CPA.[206] The system created an accountability gap for both public and private foreign entities[207] which exceeded previous UN practice.

Finally, the framework of the occupation of Iraq created some legal problems concerning the regulation of the period of transition from the dissolution of the CPA on 30 June 2004 until the formation of an elected Iraqi government.[208] The law of occupation does not provide the occupant with an express title to determine the legal regime governing a caretaker government, which takes over governing responsibility from an occupying power; nor do the rules of occupation expressly authorise an occupying power to extend the validity of its acts beyond the period of occupation by way of legislation. The CPA, however, took active steps to ensure the continued validity and applicability of its acts to Iraqi authorities after 30 June 2004 through the TAL. This methodology was difficult to justify in legal terms (i.e. by way of administering authority derived from a Security Council mandate), since existing Security Council resolutions (including Resolution 1546 (2004) which dealt specifically with the process of transition) failed to mention the TAL and lacked a specific authorisation to that effect.[209]

---

[203] See also Ryan Swift, *Occupational Jurisdiction: A Critical Analysis of the Iraqi Special Tribunal*, New York International Law Review, Vol. 19 (2006), 99, at 120–1. Following election of the Iraqi National Assembly, a revised Statute was adopted in 2005.

[204] See Articles 64 and 70 of the Fourth Geneva Convention.

[205] See Section 2 of CPA Order No. 17 of 27 June 2003 (*Status of the Coalition, Foreign Liaison Missions, Their Personnel and Contractors*).

[206] See Sections 1 (11), 1 (12) and 4 (3) of CPA Order No. 17 of 27 June 2003 (revised).

[207] See also Amnesty International, *Memorandum on Concern Relating to Law and Order*.

[208] See Kelly, *Iraq and the Law of Occupation*, at 160–5.

[209] In its Resolution 1546 (2004), the Council reaffirmed the authorisation of the multinational force under Resolution 1511 (2003) and the authority of the multinational force to "take all necessary measures to contribute to maintenance of security and stability in Iraq". See paras. 9 and 10 of SC Res. 1546 (2004). Moreover, the Council endorsed "the formation of a sovereign Interim Government of Iraq" and

2.5. Assessment

Iraq marked a unique case of international territorial administration. The tasks of the Coalition resembled those of the nationbuilding projects after World War II. However, the format differed considerably. The choice of an internationalised occupation regime as governing model, with three different players (the multinational coalition authority, the Iraqi Governing Council and the UN) acting in concert with each other under the umbrella of Security Council resolutions, was a novelty in international law. This formula departed not only from the classical model of centralised UN administration, but also from the practice of post-surrender occupation after 1945 or the multinational administration of Bosnia and Herzegovina. It is the result of a difficult bargaining process in the Security Council over the scope and legitimacy of occupation authority, different strategic and economic state interests in Iraq and the desire to preserve Iraqi sovereignty and territorial integrity. The merit of the compromise lies in the fact that it managed to facilitate a unified international approach towards the reconstruction of Iraq, which recognised the need to restore Iraqi self-government.

However, the modalities by which this objective was realised were far from perfect. The CPA took over the basic responsibilities and style of governance exercised by previous UN administrations without learning from past lessons.[210] US and UK forces assumed their governing responsibilities on the ground without adequate preparation for a civilian administration mandate. They failed to provide emergency law and order in the immediate aftermath of the intervention. Moreover, they applied a top-down style of administration in the immediate aftermath of the intervention, which did not provide Iraqis with sufficient perspectives for self-rule[211] and had to be refined by the Security Council. The subsequent Council arrangement under Resolutions 1483 (2003) and 1511 (2003) helped to clarify the obligations of the CPA and to strengthen the transfer of authority to domestic actors, but it failed to establish a clear and coherent division of power between the Coalition authority and the UN.

---

the "proposed timetable for Iraq's political transition to democratic government" in paras 1 and 4 of the Resolution. But the Council omitted any reference to the TAL. Any authority for the enactment of the TAL must therefore be derived from SC Res. 1483 (2003) and SC Res. 1511 (2003) which are not explicit on this point.

[210] See also Dobbins, *The UN's Role in Nation-Building*, at 211–12.

[211] See ICG, *Governing Iraq*, at 11.

Finally, the way in which the Coalition dealt with the security problem in Iraq after the transfer of powers and the holding of elections was ambiguous. The continued presence of Coalition troops in Iraq became a pretext for acts of resistance, because it was perceived as an act of foreign domination. Both an increased reliance on Iraqi military personnel and the establishment of a UN police force might have alleviated some of the tensions.[212]

The fragile security situation was aggravated by a lack of national unity. The legal and political reforms undertaken by the CPA failed to prevent the gradual segregation of communities.[213] The exclusion of former Baath Party officials from public office and the army hit mostly members of the Sunni community.[214] In January 2005, Sunnis widely boycotted the elections for the Iraqi Transitional Assembly. The election gave Shiites and Kurds a broad majority in the drafting of the new Iraqi Constitution,[215] which was then subsequently accused by Sunnis as failing adequately to represent their interests. This marginalisation of Sunni interests left the country divided.

3. Multidimensional peace operations after Iraq

The UN engagement in Iraq was followed by a series of other missions with a focus on governance assistance. Three of them will be described briefly here: the UN Mission in Liberia (UNMIL), the UN Mission in the Democratic Republic of the Congo (MONUC) and the UN Operation in Côte d'Ivoire (UNOCI).[216] The common denominator of these missions is that they pursued a non-coercive approach towards statebuilding. The

---

[212] Some of these mistakes could have been avoided, had the Coalition paid greater respect to the lessons learned from previous UN operations. See also Simon Chesterman, Michael Ignatieff and Ramesh Thakur, *Making States Work, From State Failure to State-Building* (2004), at 15. ("Three of the most egregious errors in Iraq – failing to provide for emergency law and order, disbanding the Iraqi army, and blanket de-Baathification – ran counter to lessons from previous operations.")

[213] See generally, International Crisis Group, *The Next Iraqi War? Sectarianism and Civil Conflict*, Middle East Report No. 52, 27 February 2006.

[214] See Korhonen, Gras and Creutz, *International Post-Conflict Situations*, at 98.

[215] They held over 221 of 275 seats in the Iraqi Transitional Assembly.

[216] Other assistance missions are the UN Stabilisation Mission in Haiti (MINUSTAH) and the UN Operation in Burundi (ONUB). MINUSTAH was charged with a classical assistance mandate. The mission was, *inter alia*, mandated to "ensure a secure and stable environment within which the constitutional ad political process in Haiti can take place", "to assist the Transitional Government in monitoring, restructuring and reforming the Haitian National Police, consistent with democratic policing standards", "to support the constitutional and political process under way in Haiti,

UN did not act as a government of territory, but exercised specific functions of assistance or coordination on the basis of a peace settlement and/or a Security Council Resolution. Yet the formal commitment to the preservation of domestic ownership contrasted occasionally with the actual degree of influence exercised by international actors.

3.1. The United Nations Mission in Liberia (UNMIL)

The first operation which deserves some attention in this regard is the UN engagement in Liberia.

3.1.1. Background

UNMIL was created following the resumption of civil war in Liberia at the beginning of the new millennium which led to the resignation of Charles Taylor and the conclusion of the Comprehensive Peace Agreement (the Accra Agreement) by the Liberian factions on 18 August 2003.[217] In the Accra Agreement, the parties requested the UN to deploy a force to Liberia to support the National Transitional Government of Liberia and to assist in the implementation of the agreement.[218] The Security Council established UNMIL by Resolution 1509 (2003) in mid-2003.[219]

3.1.2. Mandate

The option of a UN mission à la Kosovo or East Timor was discussed at the outset of the operation.[220] But the UN refrained from conducting a

---

including through good offices, and foster principles of democratic governance and institutional development", "to assist the Transitional Government in its efforts to organize, monitor and carry out free and fair municipal, parliamentary and presidential elections" and "to assist the Transitional Government in extending State authority throughout Haiti and support good governance at local levels". See para. 7 of SC Res. 1542 (2004) of 30 April 2004. ONUB was created to support the Peace and Reconciliation Agreement for Burundi, signed at Arusha on 28 August 2000. The mission was authorised to provide advice and assistance to the domestic transitional government in areas such as border control, judicial reform, electoral matters and reform of the security sector. In addition, ONUB was mandated to assist the domestic government and authorities in Burundi in "extending State authority and utlities throughout the territory, including civilian police and judicial institutions". See paras. 6 and 7 of SC Res. 1545 (2004) of 21 May 2004.

[217] See Comprehensive Peace Agreement Between the Government of Liberia and the Liberians United for Reconciliation and Democracy (LURD) and the Movement for Democracy in Liberia (MODEL) and Political Parties, Accra 18 August 2003.

[218] See Article XXIX of the Accra Agreement.

[219] See SC Res. 1509 (2003) of 19 September 2003, para. 3 (a)–(i).

[220] See Thalif Deen, "Experts Split on Plan for U.N. Trusteeship of Liberia", at http://ipsnews.net/interna.asp?idnews=19710.

fully fledged governance mission. Instead, it opted once more for a "light footprint" approach. Acting under Chapter VII of the UN Charter, the Security Council granted UNMIL functions of governance assistance in the areas human rights protection, security reform and civil administration. The Council vested the mission, in particular, with the mandate:

> to contribute towards international efforts to protect and promote human rights in Liberia...;[221]
>
> to assist the transitional government of Liberia in monitoring and restructuring the police force of Liberia [and] in the formation of a new and restructured Liberian military;
>
> to assist the transitional Government... in the reestablishment of national authority throughout the country, including the establishment of a functioning administrative structure at both the national and local levels;
>
> to assist the transitional government in conjunction with ECOWAS and other international partners in developing a strategy to consolidate governmental institutions, including a national legal framework and judicial and correctional institutions; [and]
>
> to assist the transitional government, in conjunction with ECOWAS and other international partners, in preparing for national elections.[222]

3.1.3. Practice

The mission started to implement its mandate after the establishment of the National Transitional Government of Liberia in October 2003. Following the wording of SC Resolution 1509 (2003), UNMIL saw its own mission primarily as one of governance assistance.[223] It interpreted its mandate to restore and consolidate state authority in a technical sense. UNMIL facilitated the return of government officials to their respective areas of responsibility[224] and provided transportation assistance to customs and immigration officials, which led to increased revenue collection and improved border control.[225] The mission also exercised advisory and monitoring functions in the area of the rule of the law. UNMIL created, *inter alia*, a civil affairs component and a judicial and corrections

---

[221] Note that the mandate introduced an innovation in UN practice. It included a mainstream human rights clause, which requires the mission to "ensure an adequate human rights presence, capacity and expertise *within UNMIL* to carry out human rights promotion, protection and monitoring activities". See para. 3 (m) of SC Res. 1509 (2003).

[222] See SC Res. 1509 (2003) of 19 September 2003, para. 3 (l)–(s).

[223] See First Progress Report of the Secretary-General on the United Nations Mission in Liberia, UN Doc. S/2003/1175 of 15 December 2003, paras. 35–41.

[224] The work of government and county officials was hampered by a lack of infrastructure and accommodation facilities.

[225] See Eleventh Progress Report of the Secretary-General on the United Nations Mission in Liberia, UN Doc. S/2006/376, 9 June 2006, para. 27.

component, in order to assist the transitional government in strengthening the capacity of the domestic judiciary and to improve the conditions of correctional services.[226]

The core task of the mission was to facilitate the holding of national elections following a two-year transition period stipulated in the Comprehensive Peace Agreement. UNMIL provided classical functions of assistance in this regard. The mission assisted the National Election Commission in finalising draft legislation on electoral reform. UNMIL police forces helped to ensure a secure environment for the presidential and legislative elections which were held on 11 October and 9 November 2005.[227]

After the 2005 elections, the mission developed benchmarks in four different areas (security, governance and the rule of law, economic revitalisation and infrastructure) in order to prepare a gradual drawdown and withdrawal of UNMIL.[228]

3.1.4. Assessment

The most striking feature of the mission is the discrepancy between the interpretation of the mandate and reality on the ground. UNMIL had to exercise state-building tasks in a fragile environment with weak domestic institutions and a poorly developed infrastructure. The transitional government lacked the resources to effectively run or restore its presence throughout the country.[229] This environment could have provided an opportunity for a stronger engagement of the UN. The mission, however, continued to take a low-profile approach in its civilian activities, an approach which created mixed reactions. UN administrator Jacques Klein acknowledged in hindsight that the establishment of a proper UN transitional administration might have facilitated the process of reconstruction.[230]

---

[226] See Ninth Progress Report of the Secretary-General on the United Nations Mission in Liberia, UN Doc. S/2005/764 of 7 December 2005, paras. 45 and 47; Eleventh Progress Report of the Secretary-General on the United Nations Mission in Liberia, paras. 40 and 42.

[227] See Ninth Progess Report of the Secretary-General on the United Nations Mission in Liberia, para. 14.

[228] See Twelfth Progress Report of the Secretary-General on the United Nations Mission in Liberia, UN Doc. S/2006/743, 12 September 2006, para. 72.

[229] See Report by Special Representative Jacques Klein, RFTF Progress Review Meeting, The World Bank, Washington DC, 24 September 2004, at http://66.249.93.104/search?q=cache:EVroYfdDzKsJ:www.humanitarianinfo.org/liberia/infocentre/rimco/doc/SRSG_As%2520Delivered.pdf+Klein+Transitional+Administration+Liberia&hl=en.

[230] See BBC World, Interview with Jacques Klein, 25 June 2005.

3.2. The United Nations Organisation Mission in the Democratic Republic of Congo (MONUC)

The operational history of MONUC confirms the trend towards technical support and assistance in situations of transitional government. The mission was initially established as a military support operation and later endowed with civilian functions of governance assistance, in order to support the work of the transitional Congolese government and to secure the transition towards the holding of democratic elections. This extension of the mandate was labelled as a new type of "partnership". This label, however, downplayed the actual impact of international authority.

3.2.1. Background

MONUC was established in 1999 in order to ensure the implementation of the Lusaka Ceasefire Agreement which was signed by the six warring countries (Democratic Republic of Congo (DRC), Angola, Namibia, Zimbabwe, Rwanda and Uganda) and the Movement for the Liberation of Congo at the end of the "First Congo War".[231] The agreement declared an end to hostilities in the DRC and called for the establishment of a UN mission with peacekeeping and peace-enforcement elements.[232] The Security Council took note of this request and established MONUC by Resolution 1279 (1999).[233]

Following the continuation of violence in the country (the "Second Congo War") leading to the assassination of Laurent Kabila and the establishment of a Government of National Unity and Transition[234] by Congolese parties under the Global and All-Inclusive Agreement signed on 17 December 2002,[235] the UN decided to extend MONUC's mandate. Both the fragile security situation in the DRC and the general weakness of the transitional government and the Congolese state administration made it necessary to vest MONUC with a broader role in governance assistance and a wider range of civilian functions. The Council expanded the mandate of the mission in SC Resolution 1493 (2003) which charged MONUC,

---

[231] Article 1 of the Lusaka Ceasefire Agreement of 10 July 1999.
[232] See Lusaka Ceasefire Agreement, Chapter 8.
[233] See para. 4 of SC Res. 1279 of 30 November 1999.
[234] The Transitional Government took up its functions on 18 July 2003.
[235] The Global and All-Inclusive Agreement was signed by the parties of the Inter-Congolese Dialogue. The agreement envisaged the creation of a transitional government, pending the holding of legislative and presidential elections. It marked the end of the "Second Congo War".

inter alia, with the reform of security forces, the "re-establishment of a State based on the rule of law" and the preparation and holding of elections, throughout the territory of the DRC.[236]

3.2.2.   The "partnership" approach

The wording of the Resolution left open how the mission should implement these daunting objectives. This point was subsequently clarified by the Secretary-General. The Secretary-General proposed to foster co-ordination among MONUC, the Transitional Government and relevant international actors in these areas through the creation of "joint commissions" in three respective fields: "essential legislation (including the post-transitional constitution)", "security sector reform" and "elections".

Formally, the UN did not endeavour to gain authoritative decision-making power through interpretation of a Chapter VII resolution, but opted for self-restraint and "partnership".[237] The Secretary-General emphasised in his report that "MONUC [would] not assume responsibility in those areas, but rather provide support to the overall coordination by assisting such commission, and, at an early stage, by identifying gaps in the international support".[238] But this statement masked an important reality, namely the fact that the UN actually played a role in legislative reform.

3.2.3.   Practice

MONUC provided assistance and support to the transitional government within the framework of the joint commissions proposed by the Secretary-General. Representatives of MONUC participated in the Technical Committee which assisted in the preparation of draft laws on nationality and voter registration and the establishment of the operational framework for elections.[239] Most importantly, the mission chaired the meetings of Joint of Commission on Essential Legislation, which provided advice on the adoption and implementation key legislation,

---

[236] See para. 5 of SC Res. 1493 (2003).

[237] See Third Special Report of the Secretary-General on the United Nations Organisation Mission in the Democratic Republic of Congo, UN Doc. S/2004/650 of 16 August 2004, para. 62.

[238] *Ibid.*, para. 63. This approach was approved by the Security Council in its Resolution 1565 (2004). See para. 7 of SC Res. 1565 (2004) of 1 October 2004.

[239] See Sixteenth Report of the Secretary-General on the United Nations Organisation Mission in the Democratic Republic of the Congo, UN Doc. S/2004/1034, 31 September 2004, para. 35. The electoral law was promulgated on 9 March 2005.

including decentralisation and the post-transition constitution[240] which was adopted by the Congolese National Assembly on 13 May 2005.[241] MONUC also exercised monitoring functions in the area of human rights protection, which included the overseeing of human rights violations during the electoral process, reports on the standards of arrest and detention and recommendation for legislative reform (e.g. the criminalisation of cross-border trafficking of illegal weapons).[242]

3.2.4. Assessment

The most important achievement of the mission was that it managed to facilitate the holding of the first multi-party elections in the DRC (30 July 2006) since the country's access to independence in 1960. The UN itself claimed that these elections were "of an unprecedented scope in United Nations operations".[243] The mission met this challenge successfully with the support of a standby force of the EU (EUFOR RD Congo)[244], which was authorised by the Security Council to provide additional security during the electoral process.[245]

However, the operational record of MONUC remained tainted by the misconduct of UN personnel in the course of the mission. Complaints against abuses by mission personnel led to investigations into allegations of sexual exploitation and abuse in 167 cases.[246] These incidents highlighted the need to reform the framework governing the accountability of peacekeepers.[247]

---

[240] *Ibid.*, para. 36.
[241] See Special Report of the Secretary-General on the elections in the Democratic Republic of the Congo, UN Doc. S/2005/320, 26 May 2005, paras. 4–5.
[242] See Twenty-first report of the Secretary-General on the United Nations Organisation Mission in the Democratic Republic of the Congo, UN Doc. S/2006/390, 13 June 2006, paras. 56–8.
[243] See Twenty-Second Report of the Secretary-General on the United Nations Organisations Mission in the Democratic Republic of the Congo, UN Doc. S/2006/759 of 21 September 2006, para. 81.
[244] EUFOR RD Congo was authorised to provide airport protection in Kinshasa and "to support MONUC to stabilize a situation in case MONUC face[d] serious difficulties in fulfilling its mandate within its existing capabilities". See para. 8 of SC Res. 1671 (2006) of 25 April 2006.
[245] The deployment of EUFOR RD Congo was authorised under Chapter VII of the UN Charter. See paras. 1 and 23 of SC Res. 1671 (2006).
[246] In seventy-eight cases, these allegations were substantiated. See Twentieth Report of the Secretary-General on the United Nations Organisation Mission in the Democratic Republic of Congo, para. 62.
[247] For a full discussion, see below Part IV, Chapter 14.

3.3. The United Nations Operation in Côte d'Ivoire (UNOCI)

The UN engagement in Ivory Coast illustrated some of the downsides of a light footprint agenda. It underscored, in particular, that a governance assistance mandate may fail to provide sufficient stability in cases where transitional domestic institutions lose their constitutional authority.

3.3.1. Background

UNOCI was established in the context of the conflict in Ivory Coast which divided the Ivorian government forces in the south of the country and the rebel group in the north ("*Les Forces Nouvelles*"). In January 2003, the two parties signed a political agreement ("the Linas-Marcoussis Agreement"),[248] which provided for the establishment of a "Government of National Reconciliation" (to be headed by a consensus prime minister) and the holding of presidential elections. The Security Council created UNOCI in February 2004 in order to support the peace process.[249] However, when both sides failed to comply with deadlines for legislative reform and rebel disarmament, hostilities resumed a few months later. The peace process gained a new momentum with the conclusion of the Pretoria Agreement in April 2005, in which domestic political leaders (the President of the Republic, members of the transitional government and representatives of the main political parties) declared "the immediate and final cessation of all hostilities and the end of the war throughout the national territory" as well as their willingness to hold "presidential elections in October 2005 and legislative elections… immediately thereafter".[250] The UN was, in particular, invited to "participate in the organisation of general elections".[251]

However, delays in the implementation of the agreement hampered the accomplishment of this mandate. The postponement of presidential elections caused a broader constitutional crisis in Ivory. Political struggles emerged between the members of the transitional government over the extension of the term of office of the acting President (President Laurent Gbagbo), the selection of the Prime Minister and the future status of the National Assembly.

---

[248] See Linas-Marcoussis Agreement, dated 23 January 2003.
[249] See SC Res. 1528 (2004) of 27 February 2004.
[250] See Pretoria Agreement on the Peace Process in the Côte d'Ivoire, 6 April 2005, preamble and joint declaration of the end of the war.
[251] *Ibid.*, para. 10.

3.3.2. Institutional adjustments

This political impasse led to a stronger engagement of international actors in domestic politics. The Peace and Security Council (PSC) of the African Union (AU) took a leading role in the settlement of the crisis. In October 2005, the PSC decided, *inter alia*, that the acting President should remain in office and that that the signatories to the Pretoria Agreement should appoint "a new Prime Minister acceptable to all Ivorian parties".[252] In addition, the PSC recommended the creation of an International Working Group (IWG) which should "evaluate, monitor and follow-up the peace process" and "make appropriate recommendations to the AU Peace and Security Council and to the UN Security Council".[253] The UN Security Council endorsed both measures in its Resolution 1633 (2005), acting under Chapter VII of the UN Charter.[254] The Security Council also clarified that the IWG should be "co-chaired by the Special Representative of the Secretary-General" (together with the representative of the Chair of the AU) and that the Secretariat of the Working Group would be coordinated by the UN.[255]

The UN and the AU thereby assumed the role of guardians of the proper functioning of the state institutions in Ivory Coast. The Prime Minister remained formally charged to "ensure effective functioning of the Government". However, the IWG was vested with important monitoring and managing powers. SC Resolution 1633 (2005) specified that the IWG should exercise three core functions, namely:

> to verify that the Prime Minister has all the necessary powers and resources to exercise his mandate and to report to the Security Council any hindrance or difficulty which the Prime Minister may face in implementing his tasks and to identify those responsible,[256]
> to consult with all the Ivorian parties... with a view to ensure that the Ivorian institutions function normally until the holding of the elections in Côte d'Ivoire;[257] and
> to draw up as soon as possible a road map, in consultation with the Ivorian parties, with a view to hold free, fair, open and transparent elections.[258]

The IWG took a number of measures to solve the political deadlock, identifying a new roadmap and new timelines for the implementation of

---

[252] See para. 10 of the Communique of the 40th Meeting of the African Union Peace and Security Council, 6 October 2005.
[253] *Ibid.*   [254] See paras. 3–7 of SC Res. 1633 (2005) of 21 October 2005.
[255] *Ibid.*, para. 4.   [256] See *ibid.*, para. 10.
[257] See *ibid.*para. 11.   [258] See *ibid.*para. 13.

the outstanding goals of the peace agreement, including disarmament, demobilisation and reintegration of combatants, the redeployment of state administration, voter identification and election.[259] Moreover, the IWG intervened in the settlement of the constitutional dispute over the status of the National Assembly, whose mandate had expired on 16 December 2005. In a communiqué issued on 15 January 2006, the IWG decided that the mandate of the National Assembly should not be extended and that pending the convening of the Forum for National Dialogue envisaged in SC Resolution 1633 (2005), "all necessary legislation would be initiated by the Council of Ministers and submitted by the Prime Minister to the President for signature".[260]

This decision of the IWG caused violent demonstrations and outrage in some parts of the country. Protesters argued that the Group "had decided to dissolve the National Assembly in contravention of the country's sovereignty".[261] The violence led to an intervention by the President Gbagbo, who signed a decree extending the mandate of the National Assembly on the basis of a recommendation by the domestic Constitutional Council.[262] This move, in return, met strong opposition from the *Forces Nouvelles*[263] and the UN SRSG,[264] who emphasised that the interim arrangement decided by the IWG (under which legislation should be initiated by the Council of Ministers and signed by the President) "is consistent with Security Council resolution 1633 (2005) and *must be respected by all parties*".[265]

A new deadlock arose in 2006 when it became clear that parties were not able to meet the 31 October 2006 deadline for the elections due

[259] See Seventh Progress Report of the Secretary-General on the United Nations Operation in Côte d'Ivoire, UN Doc. S/2006/2 of 3 January 2006, para. 16.
[260] *Ibid.*, para. 15.
[261] See Eighth Report of the Secretary-General on the United Nations Operation in Côte d'Ivoire, UN Doc. S/2006/222 of 11 April 2006, para. 4.
[262] *Ibid.*, para. 7 and 8.
[263] The Presidential decree dated 27 January 2006 was contested by members of the opposition and the *Forces Nouvelles* who argued that the extension of the mandate of the National Assembly was incompatible with the Constitution of Ivory Coast and Security Council Resolution 1633 (2005). *Ibid.*, para. 7.
[264] The SRSG issued a statement "expressing [his] concern about the Presidential decree of 27 January". *Ibid.*, para. 7. In a communiqué issued after the meeting convened by the Prime Minister in February 2006, Ivorian leaders recognised in particular that the findings contained in Security Council Resolution 1633 (2005) are not inconsistent with the Ivorian Constitution. *Ibid.*, para. 11.
[265] Emphasis added. See Seventh Progress Report of the Secretary-General on the United Nations Operation in Côte d'Ivoire, para. 78.

to continuing disagreements about voter identification, disarmament, demobilisation and reintegration. The IWG and the SRSG used this opportunity to seek a clarification of the existing transition arrangements and a reinforcement of the powers of the Prime Minister. The SRSG recommended, in particular, three measures in order to close the existing loopholes and to avoid further stalemate, namely to clarify the precedence of the international "arrangements for the transition period (past and future Security Council resolutions, African Union and ECOWAS decisions, and peace agreements)" over provisions of the Ivorian Constitution and national laws in case of conflict;[266] to specify that the Prime Minister has "the necessary authority over all relevant public offices, as well as the Defence and Security Forces, for all issues pertaining to the implementation of the road map";[267] and to ensure that the UN "High Representative for the elections has the authority to make binding determinations on all issues pertaining to the electoral process".[268] The PSC of the AU[269] and the Security Council[270] recognised the need to adjust the framework for the transitional period to the new realities and implemented the respective recommendations in their subsequent decisions on the situation in Ivory Coast.

---

[266] See Tenth Progress Report of the Secretary-General on the United Nations Operation in Côte d'Ivoire, UN . Doc S/2006/821, 17 October 2006, para. 75.

[267] Ibid.   [268] Ibid., para. 78.

[269] See the Communiqué of the 64th meeting of the PSC, 17 October 2006. The PSC decided on the timing and modalities of a new transition period starting 1 November 2006. In this context, the PSC extended the powers of the Prime Minister. See para. 14 of the Communiqué of the 64th meeting.

[270] The Security Council endorsed the decisions taken by the PSC at its 64th meeting in SC Res. 1721 (2006) of 1 November 2006. In para. 4 of the Resolution, the Security Council "declare[d] that the full implementation of the present resolution, consistent with paragraphs 13 and 14 of the decision of the Peace and Security Council, and of the peace process led by the Prime Minister requires full compliance by all Ivorian parties and that *no legal provisions should be invoked by them to obstruct the process*" (emphasis added). The Council reiterated that "the Prime Minister, for the implementation of [his] mandate ... must have all the necessary powers, and all appropriate financial, material and human resources, as well as full and unfettered authority ... and must be empowered to take all necessary decisions, in all matters, within the Council of Ministers or the Council of Government, by ordinances or decree-laws". See para. 8 of SC Res. 1721 (2006) Moreover, the Council decided that the High Representative for the Elections "shall be the sole authority authorized to arbitrate with a view to preventing or resolving any problems or disputes related to the electoral process". *Ibid.*, para. 22.

These steps facilitated a novel dialogue between President Gbagbo and the *Forces Nouvelles*[271] which culminated in the conclusion of new Agreement with updated institutional arrangement (the Ouagadougou Agreement).[272]

3.3.3. Assessment

The peace process in Ivory Coast demonstrated some of the weaknesses of assistance-based approaches in processes of transitional government. Delays in the implementation of the Ivorian peace accords and, most notably, the postponement of the holding of presidential elections created a constitutional vacuum which hampered progress in government. In this situation, the PSC of the AU and the UN Security Council were forced to abandon their assistance-based agenda and to intervene more actively in the settlement of the unfolding constitutional crisis. This engagement was officially marketed as a novel model of "*partnership* between regional leaders, including the African Union ... and the United Nations" necessary "to secure the parties' continued commitment to fulfil their obligations under the various peace agreements".[273] However, it entailed a strong degree of interference in areas of domestic jurisdiction. The IWG became a "guarantor and impartial arbitrator of the peace process",[274] and exercised these powers to shape the functioning of domestic governing institutions. The PSC of the AU and the Security Council adopted decisions with a direct impact on constitutional politics. They defined the powers of the Prime Minister, the status of the National Assembly or the hierarchy of norms applicable in the process of transition. This regulatory involvement modified the nature of international engagement. Due to continuing stalemate at the domestic level, the UN Security Council and the PSC of the AU gradually assumed some of the functions that were exercised by international administrators in the course of governance missions of the 1990s.

---

[271] See Twelfth Progress Report of the Secretary-General on the United Nations Operation in Côte d'Ivoire, UN Doc S/2007/133, 8 March 2007, paras. 7–18.

[272] The Peace Agreement was signed in Ouagadougou by Laurent Gbagbo and Guillaume Soro on 4 March 2007. See Thirteenth Progress Report of the Secretary-General on the United Nations Operation in Côte d'Ivoire, UN Doc S/2007/275, 14 May 2007, paras. 2–5.

[273] See Eighth Report of the Secretary-General on the United Nations Operation in Côte d'Ivoire, para. 77.

[274] See para. 25 of SC Res. 1721 (2006).

4. The end of the era of comprehensive governance missions?

This survey of recent UN practice seems to indicate that robust governance models are in decline. There is a tendency to encourage the formation of domestic transitional institutions in the aftermath of conflict and to focus international engagement on partnership-based types of support and assistance. However, it would be premature to discard more interventionist forms of engagement from the range of available options. The existing practice shows that technocratic notions such as "capacity-building" or "partnership" tend to mask political realities. There is a need for a broad spectrum of different approaches.[275]

Cases such as Liberia or Ivory Coast illustrate that there are situations in which the collapse of state authority or a constitutional crisis may require managerial or regulatory engagement by international decision-making bodies. It is thus too early to proclaim the end of governance missions in times of a broader recognition of the need for local ownership.[276] The reality appears to be more nuanced. The choice of the respective model is influenced by a number of factors, including the existence of a transitional domestic government, the size of the territory and its legal status.

A light footprint agenda is the obvious choice if statebuilding tasks are to be carried by international actors in the presence of a sufficiently stable and representative transitional government (e.g. a transitional government established pursuant to a peace agreement). However, such an approach is difficult to implement where parties are unable to reach such an initial political consensus or where they fail to implement an agreed process of transition (institutionbuilding, elections) in time (Ivory Coast).

Secondly, geopolitical circumstances play a role. The history of territorial administration tends to show that it is generally easier to place small territorial entities (West Irian, Eastern Slavonia, Kosovo, East Timor) under exclusive UN jurisdiction than entire states. Such considerations may explain, for example, the application of separate formulas in the cases of Kosovo and East Timor, on the one hand, and Afghanistan and Iraq, on the other.

Finally, the status of the territory may gain some importance. The exercise of centralised international authority appears to be easier to

---

[275] The need for diversity was already well established in the era of the League of Nations. See above Part I, Chapter 1.

[276] See also Chesterman, *You, the People*, at 242.

justify in circumstances where territorial administration is designed to realise self-determination based on claims of a people (independence, meaningful self-government). International authority serves in this context as a direct device for the development of local ownership on behalf of the people. The situation is different when international actors assume authority over state entities with an established territorial status (Afghanistan, Iraq).

10   A conceptualisation of the practice

A study of the evolution of transitional administration in the twentieth and early twenty-first centuries confirms that the practice of territorial administration has developed in historical cycles. Throughout this evolution, international territorial administration has taken on different forms and functions.

1.   Models of administration

One may distinguish between at least three different models of governance: direct and indirect models of territorial administration, exclusive and shared forms of authority and governance systems established by consent and by unilateral acts.

1.1.   Direct v. indirect administration

Most engagements in international territorial administration throughout the twentieth century have been direct forms of governance and assistance, in the sense that they were carried out by organs or subsidiary organs of international organisations, or by institutions directly appointed by the latter (direct international territorial administration).

1.1.1.   Forms of direct international territorial administration

The first high tide of the technique of direct international territorial administration was the inter-war period. The League of Nations exercised concrete governing or administering powers over territories placed under its scrutiny. The governing institutions of the three main undertakings in territorial administration at that time, the High Commissioner for Danzig, the Governing Commission for the Saar Territory and the transitional Governing Commission for Leticia, were directly appointed by the League of Nations. The Council of the League of Nations itself served as a monitoring organ for individual petitions in the Saar, and as an instance of appeal against decisions of the High Commissioner in Danzig. Moreover, the PCIJ assumed a strong advisory role concerning disputes in Danzig[1] and a special dispute resolution function in Memel, allowing the Principal Allied Powers to bring disputes concerning the status of Memel for final resolution to the Court.[2]

The UN continued this practice after 1945. The first UN experiments followed the tradition the League. Main organs of the UN were directly charged with supervisory authority or administering powers. The best examples are the cases of Jerusalem and Trieste. The Security Council was supposed to be directly involved in the administration of Trieste, exercising direct regulatory and dispute settlement functions *vis-à-vis* the territory. The Trusteeship Council was charged with various supervisory functions over Jerusalem under the proposed framework of territorial internationalisation, including the investigation of petitions from individuals, the approval of international agreements concluded on behalf of Jerusalem and the appointment of the highest constitutional organs of the city. Later, the General Assembly exercised similar responsibilities in different cases of decolonisation. It appointed UN Commissioners, acting directly under its authority, in the cases of Libya and Eritrea, and it created the Council for Namibia as a General Assembly subsidiary organ[3] to administer former South West Africa.

The peacekeeping practice of the UN brought a shift in methodology. The Security Council and the General Assembly limited their role essentially to the authorisation and monitoring of UN missions and left the concrete implementation of administering responsibilities within the hands of the UN Secretary-General. The Secretary-General again appointed Special Representatives to discharge the civilian administration mandate on the ground. This system instituted a functional division of labour between the Council or the Assembly and the UN Secretariat. In most cases (ONUC, UNTAG, MINURSO, UNOSOM, UNTAC, UNTAES, UNMIK, UNTAET, UNMIK, UNAMA, UNAMI, UNMIL, MONUC, UNOCI), the Security Council played the leading role in the creation of governance or assistance missions, by authorising, establishing or defining the mandate of the UN operation, while leaving the exercise of governing or administrative functions to the Secretary-General, subject to periodical reporting duties. The General Assembly exercised this role in the case

---

[1] See above Part II, Chapter 6.
[2] See Article 13 of the Memel Convention.   [3] See Article 22 of the UN Charter.

of West Irian.[4] Moreover, it endorsed administrations established by the Security Council.[5]

On some occasions,[6] regional organisations exercised powers of governance or governance assistance. The EU exercised direct administering powers in the case of the administration of Mostar.[7] A special power-sharing arrangement emerged in the context of the engagement in Ivory Coast where the UN shared decision-making authority with the AU.[8]

1.1.2. Indirect international territorial administration

Direct forms of international territorial administration may be distinguished from indirect models of administration, which cover cases in which an international legal entity (e.g. a multinational administration or an international institution with independent legal personality) exercises administering authority over a territory with the authorisation, mandate or approval of an international organisation, but without being functionally part of the latter.

The institutional layout of indirect international administration varies from case to case. Two examples are examined here: the administrations of Bosnia and Herzegovina and Iraq. In both cases, international authorities (the OHR, the CPA)[9] assumed direct administering responsibilities over foreign territories with the approval of the Security Council taking the form of an endorsement (Bosnia and Herzegovina) or of a mandate (Iraq). Both entities exercised reporting duties *vis-à-vis* the Council, but remained institutionally independent from the UN.

1.2. Exclusive v. shared forms of authority

A further distinction may be made between exclusive and shared forms of international authority. International practice has used at least three different categories of missions: exclusive governance missions (Saar administration, Leticia, UNTEA, Council for Namibia, UNTAES, UNMIK,

---

[4] The General Assembly established UNTEA and entrusted the Secretary-General with the administering mandate. See GA Res. 1752 (XVII) of 21 September 1962.

[5] See, for example, A/RES/437232 of 1 March 1989 (UNTAG), A/RES/47/41 B of 15 April 1993 (UNOSOM), A/RES/51/153 of 13 June 1997 (UNTEAS), A/RES/53/241 of 28 July 1999 (UNMIK), A/RES/64/246 of 23 December 1999 (UNTAET).

[6] Note that the Security Council authorised the establishment of an African Union Mission to Somalia on 21 February 2007. See para. 4 of SC Res. 1744 (2007) of 21 February 2007.

[7] See above Part II, Chapter 8.

[8] This is reflected in the decision-making practice of the PSC of the AU and the composition of the International Working Group. See above Part II, Chapter 9.

[9] For a discussion of the legal personality of the OHR and the CPA, see below Part IV, Chapter 13.

UNTAET), co-governance missions (Danzig, Trieste, Jerusalem, ONUC, UNTAC, UNOSOM II, Bosnia and Herzegovina) and assistance missions (Memel, Libya, Eritrea, UNTAG, MINURSO, UNAMA, UNAMI, UNMIL, MONUC).[10] It is often difficult to draw a clear borderline between these three types of missions, due to uncertainties and changes in the configuration of the mandate of a mission[11] or discrepancies between *de facto* and *de jure* powers.[12] Examples like Ivory Coast show that an international engagement may, for instance, start as an assistance mission and develop into a surrogate governance mechanism by default. However, one may note one that these three general models were deployed on a repeated basis during the major periods in time studied here.

The distinction began under the Treaty of Versailles. The Treaty vested the Governing Commission of the Saar with almost unlimited authority in the legislative and executive field, including the *Kompetenz-Kompetenz* to interpret its own powers. The legal framework of the City of Danzig, by contrast, was based on a co-governance regime, in order to preserve the city's autonomy and the interests of the German population. Finally, mere assistance mandates were used to resolve the German-Danish dispute over the frontier in Slesvig, the Polish-German border disputes over certain regions in Eastern Prussia and Upper Silesia[13] and the dispute over the status of Memel.

A similar degree of diversity characterised the UN engagements in the field of decolonisation after 1945. The post-war assistance missions in Libya and Eritrea were soon followed by the exclusive governance operation in West Irian and the establishment of the Council for Namibia – another attempt in exclusive governance, undertaken before the return to more modest formulas in the later era of decolonisation in the form of UNTAG and MINURSO.

The greatest variety as between institutional design, however, can be found in the context of statebuilding. While ONUC, the first attempt in

---

[10] For a slightly different classification, see Wolfrum, *International Administration in Post-Conflict Situations*, at 656–63. Wolfrum distinguishes "technical assistance", "States acting under the Authority of the United Nations" and "Direct Administration of Territories".

[11] Sometimes an exclusive governance mission is gradually scaled down to a co-governance mission in practice, and later replaced by an assistance mission. Such a process may, for example, be observed in the case of East Timor, where UNTEAT gradually transferred powers to domestic authorities, before being replaced by an assistance mission (UNMISET).

[12] A good example is the Council for Namibia whose authority remained largely virtual. See above Part II, Chapter, 7.

[13] See Articles 87–94 and 109–114 of the Treaty of Versailles.

UN statebuilding, may be characterised as a co-governance operation, all three types of missions have been established simultaneously over the last decade. UNOSOM II, a co-governance mission by accident, was followed by two deliberate co-governance operations, UNTAC and the framework of the Dayton Agreement, before culminating in the two exclusive governance missions in Kosovo (UNMIK) and East Timor (UNTEAT) and the subsequent deployment of simple assistance models in Afghanistan (UNAMA), Iraq (UNAMI), Liberia (UNMIL) and the Democratic Republic of Congo (MONUC).

1.3.   Creation by consent and/or by unilateral act

Finally, there have been differences in the form of creation of missions of territorial administration. One may distinguish consensual and unilateral administration.[14] The degree of importance attached to the role of consent in international administration varied throughout the twentieth century. Consent was never an absolute precondition to the establishment of mechanisms of territorial administration by international practice, but it has progressively grown into a building block of international territorial arrangements.

International practice indicates that the consent of the territorial state to undertakings in international territorial administration was not perceived as a strict legal prerequisite of the exercise of governing authority in the first half of the twentieth century. If consent was sought, it was primarily regarded as a tool to enhance the acceptability and compliance with international arrangements. This thinking is particularly well reflected in the peace settlements after World Wars I and II. Consent was treated as a mere formality by the drafters of the Treaty of Versailles. The Agreement was negotiated by the US, the UK and France, without substantial German involvement in shaping the text of the treaty.[15] Similar traces of unilateralism characterised peacemaking after World War II. The Potsdam decisions, which laid the groundwork for the post-war administrations of Germany and Japan, were taken by the leaders of the three major victorious powers (the UK, the Soviet Union and the US) without German or Japanese participation.[16]

---

[14] For a discussion, see also Wolfrum, *International Administration in Post-Conflict Situations*, at 660–3.

[15] Germany signed the agreement only reluctantly after an ultimatum set by the Allies.

[16] Neither of the two countries were able to participate in the negotiation process. Furthermore, there were no moderating forces at the Conference table to balance the interests of the victorious powers. See Tomuschat, *How To Make Peace After War*, at 26–7.

The requirement of consent gained visibly more support in the context of international administering arrangements in the era of the UN. Most experiments in territorial administration in the era of the UN were based on some form of consent from the main political forces involved or affected by international administration.

The UN opted, first, for consent-based formulas in the numerous cases in which it decided to establish governance assistance missions, namely in the cases of Libya, Namibia (UNTAG), Western Sahara (MINURSO), Afghanistan (UNAMA), Liberia (UNMIL) and Democratic Republic of Congo (MONUC). In other situations, such as, in particular, the governance missions in 1990s, the UN adopted more robust models of engagement, allowing international administrators to act independently of domestic authorities or against the will of the latter. But even these undertakings remained strongly shaped by the prerogative of consent.

Most international governance missions were established after, or on the basis of, a political settlement contained in an international agreement, which may be rightly viewed as "a request to the organisation to exercise its power in a particular situation".[17] The UN engagements in West Irian (UNTEA) and East Timor (UNTAET) were undertaken to implement the political agreement between a former colonial ruler and the previous or future holder of public authority.[18] The basic structures of UNTAC, UNTAES and the international administration of Bosnia and Herzegovina were laid down by peace settlements (Paris Accords, Erdut Agreement, Dayton Agreement) among formerly warring factions. UNMIK, perhaps the most authoritative governance mission of the 1990s, was formally created under Chapter VII, but following a general political settlement with the FRY (the "G-8 plan for Kosovo").[19]

Straight deviations from the principle of obtaining consent are rare. The UN adopted unilateral strategies of action only in exceptional situations, namely where local authorities were unable to express consent (such as the cases of ONUC, UNOSOM), or where they were genuinely unwilling to do so (Council for Namibia). These experiments proved to be some of the most vulnerable exercises of international authority in practice.

---

[17] See Danesh Sarooshi, *Some Preliminary Remarks on the Conferral by States of Powers on International Organizations*, Jean Monnet Working Paper 4/2003, at 17.

[18] See the Agreement between the Netherlands and Indonesia and the Agreement of 5 May.

[19] See Annex II of SC Res. 1244 (1999).

2.   Functions of international territorial administration

On a functional level, mechanisms of territorial administration have been deployed to address at least four different policy goals: dispute settlement, decolonisation, statebuilding and the legitimation of intervention. These four functions have gradually emerged through practice since the nineteenth century and have repeated themselves over time.[20]

2.1.   The resolution of territorial disputes

Territorial dispute settlement is the oldest function of international territorial administration. It took three different forms: status resolution, neutralisation and facilitation of a transfer of territory.

2.1.1.   Status resolution

Status resolution engagements have occurred in two different formats in the history of territorial administration. International actors were, in at least two cases (Saar administration and UNMIK), directly involved in the resolution of an open status dispute. These engagements may be qualified as status resolution missions in the narrow sense. In a broader range of cases (UNTEA, MINURSO, UNTAET), status resolution was a by-product of decolonisation, involving international administrations merely in the formal organisation (referendum, elections) or the implementation of a status decision.

Status resolution missions have traditionally faced challenging mandates. The accomplishment of the mandate was typically compromised by two factors: uncertainties about the status of the territory and/or ongoing disagreement among the political stakeholders about a proposed status model. These problems have turned status resolution missions into long-term engagements, requiring a wide degree of managerial skills. The practical difficulties in this field are particularly well illustrated by the practice of UNMIK and the Saar administration.[21]The

---

[20] The tradition of neutralisation, for example, which began with the early experiments in Danzig, Trieste and Jerusalem, can be traced up to the more recent experiments in Cambodia and Eastern Slavonia. The status resolution mandate, which UNMIK faced in Kosovo, bears strong resemblance to the finality of the League engagement in the Saar. The roots of contemporary statebuilding go back to earlier engagements such as ONUC.

[21] Similar lessons may be drawn from the UN involvement in the settlement of the question of Western Sahara. See above Part II, Chapter 7.

functioning of the administration was in both cases affected by the fact that the final status of the administered territory remained open until the end of the mission. Both administrations were, in particular, obliged to preserve and reconcile the different interests and privileges of all stakeholders until the final phase of the operation, in order to provide a neutral and equal basis for the status decision. This factor complicated the daily functioning and decision-making of the respective missions.

The record of international practice in this area of involvement is mixed. The Saar administration may be counted as a successful undertaking in dispute resolution. MINURSO and UNTEA, on the contrary, remained rather ambiguous experiences in dispute settlement, suffering partly from a lack of support from stakeholders for a free status decision and partly from the failure of the UN to implement an equitable solution.

2.1.2. Neutralisation

Territorial administration has on several occasions served as a device of neutralisation, namely as an instrument to insulate a disputed territory from the influence of competing entities, in order to reduce tensions between the conflicting actors.

This technique has taken on different forms in practice. In the first half of the twentieth century, territorial administration was, in particular, used as a device of strategic neutralisation. This objective was at the heart of the internationalisation of Danzig. The UN sought to replicate this practice after World War II in Trieste and Jerusalem. The practice in these cases has made it clear that neutralisation rarely provides a permanent solution for territorial dispute. None of the three long-term projects of internationalisation (Danzig, Trieste, Jerusalem) managed to establish itself as a permanent solution.

Subsequently, the technique of neutralisation gained a different focus in practice. Neutralisation progressively developed into a transitional device. Instead of serving as an end of territorial administration in itself, neutralisation gained a supportive function in UN practice. Strategies of internationalisation and neutralisation were used in order to facilitate the realisation of other policy goals, namely to ensure a transfer of territory from one entity to another (West Irian, Eastern Slavonia) or to facilitate a process of statebuilding (Cambodia, Kosovo) or decolonisation (East Timor). In this capacity neutralisation has shown some success in practice.

2.1.3. Transfer of territory

The use of international territorial administration as an instrument to facilitate the peaceful transfer of territory from one state to another marks the least ambitious, yet most successful model of dispute settlement. The UN engagement in West Irian was the first successful undertaking of this kind. The mission provided the necessary administrative groundwork to integrate the territory into Indonesia. This technique was later repeated in Eastern Slavonia, where the UN facilitated the peaceful reintegration of the war-torn Danube region into Croatia. The success of this model of dispute settlement may be explained by two factors: the clarity of the mandate of the respective missions and the degree of political consensus on their respective goals.

2.2. Decolonisation

The administering practice of the UN in the field of decolonisation served principally as a device for the realisation of people's rights. Nevertheless, most of the international engagements in this field had a problem-solving dimension. The UN intervened regularly in cases where colonial powers were unable to reach consensus on the status of the territory. The engagement of the UN in Libya and Eritrea was the result of the inability of the Four Powers (the USSR, the UK, the US and France) to agree on the future of the former Italian colonies. UNTEA and UNTAET were established to resolve the long-standing dispute between the Netherlands and Indonesia over the status of West Irian and East Timor. Finally, the Council for Namibia and UNTAG were created in response to the conflict between South Africa and the international community over the status of Namibia after the termination of South Africa's mandate.

The record of these engagements differs from case to case. The UN assistance mission in Libya was instrumental in the country's access to independence. UNTAG and UNTAET are commonly praised as highlights in territorial administration, although independence was in both cases preceded by over a decade of fruitless UN administration (Namibia) or inaction (East Timor). The UN engagement in relation to Eritrea, by contrast, failed to meet its goals in the long run, due to a lack of support for the status solution adopted by the General Assembly.

2.3. Statebuilding

The idea of using territorial administration as a technique for the (re-)construction of war-torn societies ("statebuilding") emerged essentially in the second half of the twentieth century. Some early League of Nations missions such as the Saar administration encompassed elements of state organisation. However, it was at least two more decades before statebuilding was actively practised by the UN. The four-year UN engagement in the Congo in the 1960s made it clear that military engagements may require further efforts in civilian assistance and administrative support in order to restore security. Yet the necessary political climate to develop reconstruction into a more systematic technique of peacemaking came only in the 1990s, when concepts such as democratic governance, individual criminal responsibility and international human rights protection gained broader international recognition. The changing security architecture in the post-Cold War era facilitated a more systematic engagement of the UN in (post-)conflict territories, as evidenced by the engagements in Cambodia, Kosovo, Afghanistan, Iraq, Liberia and Ivory Coast.

The management of a process of transition from conflict to peace has been a learning process for the UN. The first experiments in Congo and Somalia have made it clear that peacebuilding operations encounter significant obstacles if the respective missions are deployed in the course of an ongoing conflict and not sufficiently equipped to take on tasks of reconstruction. UN operations have shown some promising results in more stable, post-conflict environments. Statebuilding missions from Cambodia to East Timor have to a greater extent managed to remove immediate threats to peace and security in the territories under administration.[22] The existing practice appears to indicate that territorial administration may facilitate the transition from political turmoil, dependence, or ethnic oppression to a more secure and just political environment.[23]

The question to what extent international administration may, in fact, make a lasting contribution to the development of pluralist and democratic structures of society is more difficult to answer, and compromised by repeated drawbacks, such returns toviolence (East Timor,

---

[22] See also David Harland, *Legitimacy and Effectiveness in International Administration*, Global Governance, Vol. 10 (2004), No. 1, at 15.
[23] *Ibid.*

Kosovo, Afghanistan) or the strengthening of radical political forces in elections (Bosnia and Herzegovina).[24] However, exercises in statebuilding have produced some positive results for the creation of conditions for sustainable peace, going beyond the mere staging of elections. UNTAC, the OHR and UNTAES played a key role in the implementation of various civilian aspects of the peace settlements in Cambodia, Bosnia and Herzegovina and Eastern Slavonia. UNMIK and UNTAET have paved the way for judicial reform, democratic institution-building and economic reconstruction in Kosovo and East Timor. UNMIL, MONUC and UNOCI have provided technical support assistance to domestic transitional institutions.

In some instances, projects of territorial administration have been linked to the broader goal of nationbuilding.[25] Historical precedents of such experiments are the post-war occupations of Germany and Japan in which reconstruction coincided with the defence of Western-liberal ideology against totalitarian rule and the rise of communism. Traces of this tradition re-emerged in cases such as Bosnia and Herzegovina and Iraq where international authority was used to instil a new political and economic culture on domestic society.

Such projects are more ambiguous from a conceptual point of view than exercises in statebuilding. The notion of nationbuilding itself is often misplaced. Nationbuilding involves not only the forging of new institutions, but also the creation of a new sense of identity and nationhood.[26] International entities are generally ill-equipped to meet such objectives through the instrument of transitional administration.[27] Fundamental aspects of nationbuilding, such as democratisation or liberalisation, are shaped by the historical and socio-political traditions of a society and require a long-term and genuine commitment by domestic actors in order to become an integral part of the constitutional order of a constituency. The post-war occupations of Germany and Japan were

---

[24] See also Gregory Fox, *International Law and the Entitlement to Democracy After War*, Global Governance, Vol. 9 (2003), 179.

[25] See generally Feldman, *What We Owe Iraq*; Antonio Donini et al., *Nation-Building Unraveled?: Aid, Peace and Justice in Afghanistan* (2004).

[26] See also Wolfrum, *International Administration in Post-Conflict Situations*, at 653–4.

[27] It is illusory to assume that foreign entities could virtually "build" a nation. International administrations may create conditions which are conducive to the formation of a shared sense of identity and community (e.g. through the development of governmental structures for a territory), but they are not in a position to create a sense of identity. See also Bali, *Justice under Occupation*, at 436–437.

successful to a large extent because they were conducted in entities with a shared sense of identity and nationhood.[28]

Modern experiments in this field have encountered significant obstacles. There are at least two cases in which international actors sought to unite different constituencies in a novel communal framework through the imposition of federalist structures (Eritrea, Bosnia and Herzegovina). In both instances, this initiative failed to produce the desired goal of unification. In the case of Iraq, the CPA repeated some of the failures of UK mandatory rule (1920–32) by seeking to create a modern liberal and unified society within a relatively short period of time, without a detailed knowledge of Iraqi society and under constant pressure for withdrawal.[29]

The UN supported processes of nationbuilding in the context of its decolonisation mandate (Namibia, Western Sahara, East Timor). However, the organisation generally avoided defining its responsibilities in the area of peacemaking in terms of nationbuilding. In some cases (e.g. Kosovo), the UN adopted measures which shaped the identity of a territory under administration (e.g. external representation, citizenship). Such measures were, however, primarily tied to functional goals of administration during the period of transition and not aimed at nationbuilding as such.

2.4.   The nexus to intervention

The linkage between territorial administration and the effects of the use of force is a relatively modern phenomenon. It emerged in three contexts: Kosovo, Afghanistan and Iraq. In each of the three cases, international administrations were established in the immediate aftermath of collective enforcement action undertaken without or with doubtful Security Council authorisation. The creation of international administering structures established a link between the use of force and the collective security system in the post-conflict phase.

---

[28] *Ibid.*, at 437.

[29] The UK assumed the role of a mandatory power for Iraq on 5 May 1920. UK administrators endeavoured to create a modern democratic nation from the three former districts of the Ottoman Empire (Basra, Badgad and Mosul). This exercise was a complex and difficult task. Tribal leaders had little trust in the central government. The UK retained control through "air policing". To end its conflict with the Iraqi political elite, the UK recommended Iraq's acceptance as a member of the League of Nations in 1932. The emerging Iraqi state remained fragile and weak. For a survey see, Toby Dodge, *Inventing Iraq: The Failure of Nationbuilding and a History Denied* (2003).

2.4.1. International territorial administration as a validating or mitigating factor of the consequences of collective enforcement action

One may witness a certain tendency to invoke post-conflict engagement as a factor to validate intervention or to respond benevolently to the *status quo* created by it. The treatment of the use of force in the cases of Kosovo, Afghanistan and Iraq appears to indicate that post-conflict engagement may entail different scales of approval and legitimation, which vary according to the intent of the Security Council and the degree of UN engagement: *ex post facto* validation and mitigation.[30]

2.4.1.1. Kosovo: UN administration as ex post facto *validation*
As a political body, the Security Council is, in principle, not called upon to make judicial determinations about the compatibility of the action of UN member states with the UN Charter.[31] However, the Council may endorse unauthorised interventions, if such a finding serves to promote the goals of peace-maintenance in a specific situation. The Council acted in this capacity when it endorsed the ECOMOG interventions in Liberia and Sierra Leone.[32] The legal response to Operation Allied Force comes within this tradition. Both the adoption of Resolution 1244 (1999) and the subsequent creation of UNMIK may be viewed as an implicit validation of the preceding intervention.[33] This validation may be inferred from two factors: the regulatory content of Resolution 1244, which despite its careful drafting did nothing less than re-arrange the status, political structure and legal system of Kosovo in order realise the claim of the people of Kosovo for substantial autonomy and self-government

---

[30] Note that the Report of the High-Level Panel on Threats, Challenges and Changes establishes not only criteria for the authorisation, but also for the endorsement of the use of military force. See *A More Secure World: OurShared Responsibility*, para. 207.

[31] See also Singh and Kilroy, *In The Matter of the Legality of the Occupation of Iraq by UK Armed Forces*, para. 36.

[32] The Council retroactively endorsed ECOMOG's intervention in Liberia, by "commend[ing] the efforts made by the ECOWAS Heads of State and Government to promote peace and normalcy in Liberia" and welcoming the intervention in SC Res. 788 (1992). See Presidential Statement, UN Doc. S/22133 (1991) and SC Res. 788 of 19 November 1992. A similar attitude characterised the UN's reaction to the role played by ECOWAS and ECOMOG in Sierra Leone. The Council acknowledged the "outstanding contribution" of ECOMOG in restoring security and stability in Sierra Leone and established a new UN peacekeeping mission in Sierra Leone cooperating with ECOMOG. See SC Res. 1260 of 20 August 1999 and SC Res. 1270 of 22 October 1999.

[33] See Franck, *Recourse To Force*, at 186; Craig Scott, *Interpreting Intervention*, Canadian Yearbook of International Law, Vol. 39 (2001), 333, at 355.

which was at the heart of the intervention; and the scope of authority assumed by the UN, which transformed the UN, along with KFOR, into a guarantor and manager of the implementation of the goals of the intervention.

2.4.1.2. Afghanistan: UN engagement as acquiescence in the consequences of Operation Enduring Freedom
The reaction to the use of force in Afghanistan was different in nature. The Council had already indicated in the immediate aftermath of the attacks on the World Trade Center and the Pentagon that the acts of 9/11 could give rise claims of self-defence.[34] Yet, some legal uncertainties remained as to whether Operation Enduring Freedom exceeded the parameters of Article 51 and interfered with Security Council responsibilities under Chapter VII, at least in so far as the overthrow of the Taliban regime was concerned.[35] These legal doubts were only removed by the subsequent reaction of the international community to the military operation, which included not only widespread statements by states in support of the intervention,[36] but also an indirect acknowledgment of the effects of the use of force by the Security Council.[37] In particular, the endorsement of the Bonn Agreement and its subsequent establishment of UNAMA may be interpreted as an indication of the Security Council's willingness to accept the consequences of overthrowing the Taliban regime and its intention to restore peace and security through UN participation in statebuilding.

[34] The clearest reference to the right of self-defence may be found in the preamble of SC Resolutions 1368 and 1373, in which the Council reaffirmed the "inherent right of individual and collective self-defense". See para. 3 of the preamble of SC Res. 1368 (2001) of 12 September 2001 and para. 4 of the preamble of SC Res. 1373 (2001) of 28 September 2001.

[35] For a full analysis, see Carsten Stahn, *International Law at a Crossroads? The Impact of September 11*, Zeitschrift für ausländisches öffentliches Recht und Völkerrecht, Vol. 62 (2002), 183, at 229–2. Critical also Jost Delbrück, *The Fight Against Global Terrorism: Self-Defence or Collective Security as Internal Police Action? Some Comments on the International Legal Implications of the "War Against Terrorism"*, German Yearbook of International Law, Vol. 44 (2001), 9, at 21. See also Christian Tomuschat, *Der 11. September 2001 und seine Rechtlichen Folgen*, Europäische Grundrechte Zeitschrift, Vols. 21–3 (2001), 535, at 543.

[36] In particular, many Western countries have openly stated that they regard the US-led military campaign as being "legitimate and in accordance with the terms of the Charter and Security Council Resolution 1368 (2001)". See Security Council, 4414th meeting, 13 November 2001, UN Doc. S/PV.4414 (Resumption 1), at 2.

[37] Note that in its Resolution 1386 (2001) of 20 December 2001, the Security Council established the International Security Assistance Force for Afghanistan, which draws upon the achievements of the military campaign.

2.4.1.3. Iraq: non-validation, but exemption from legal sanction

The reaction of the Council to the Iraq crisis may be interpreted as a case of application of the theory of mitigation.[38] Security Council members refrained from acknowledging the (il)legality of Operation Iraqi Freedom, yet they absolved it from legal sanction because the *status quo* produced by the use of military force required further common action. Faced with growing security gaps in post-war Iraq[39] and the need to restore sovereign and democratic institutions in the territory for the realisation of self-determination,[40] the Council merely decided, as the Secretary-General stated, to "place the interests of the Iraqi people above all other considerations", leaving the continuing controversies over the use of force a matter of the past.[41]

2.4.2. Post-conflict engagement as condition of liberal intervention

Some authorities even go a step further and interpret post-conflict engagements as part of the legal requirements of liberal interventions ("humanitarian intervention", "democratic intervention").[42] Proponents of this approach argue, in particular, that such interventions require states to take sustainable measures to implement the proclaimed goals of the use of force, including efforts to restore basic human rights and democratic governance in the post-intervention phase. The novelty of this approach lies in the fact that it derives certain (post-)conflict responsibilities from the very requirements of intervention, instead of deducing

---

[38] The doctrine of mitigation holds that the international legal system tolerates certain violations of the law as acceptable patterns of conduct that do not necessarily entail legal sanction. For an early statement in this direction, see Oscar Schachter, *International Law in Theory and Practice* (1991), 126. See also Ian Brownlie, *Thoughts on Kind-Hearted Gunmen*, in Humanitarian Intervention and the United Nations (Richard B. Lillich ed., 1973), 139, at 146; Tom Farer, *A paradigm of Legitimate Intervention*, in Enforcing Restraint: Collective Intervention in Internal Conflicts (Lori Fisler Damrosch ed., 1993), 316, at 327; Franck, *Recourse to Force*, at 185–6.

[39] See para. 13 of SC Res. 1511 (2003).   [40] See *ibid.*, paras. 1, 4, 6, 7, 8 and 10.

[41] See Secretary-General, Press Release SG/SM/8945 of 16 October, 2003, at www.un.org/News/Press/docs/2003/sgsm8945.doc.htm. ("[T]he outcome is a clear demonstration of the will of all the members of the Security Council to place the interests of the Iraqi people above all other considerations.")

[42] For arguments in this direction, see Blerim Reka, *UNMIK as International Governance within Post-Conflict Societies*, New Balkan Politics, Issue 7/8, at www.newbalkanpolitics.org.mk/napis.asp?id=17&lang=English, sub II.

such duties from the concept of responsibility for internationally wrongful acts (reparation, compensation).[43]

This argument receives some support from the guidelines on the authorisation of the use of force in the Report of the High-Level Panel on Threats, Challenges and Change, which linked the legitimacy of interventions to their capacity to meet "the threat in question".[44] Nevertheless, the view that post-conflict engagement marks a *conditio sine qua non* of liberal interventions cannot (yet) be said to form part of the applicable *lex lata*. It encounters three major objections. Empirically, no consensus has been reached on the permissibility of humanitarian interventions, and even less on an entitlement to realise normative change by force.[45] Secondly, there are no reliable parameters rationally to limit the scope of post-conflict responsibilities in size and in time.[46] Finally, there is a lack of a corresponding *opinio juris*, expressing a commitment of states to implement humanitarian or democratic principles through international institution- or statebuilding. States and international organisations tend to recognise the feasibility, rather than the obligation to complement the use of military force by social, institutional and legal reconstruction. It is therefore too early to conceive international post-conflict engagement as a fully fledged legal condition of intervention, going beyond its function as a validating or legitimating factor for the recourse to force.[47]

3.   International territorial administration and trusteeship

The concept of trusteeship is a recurring feature in the history of territorial administration. It was invoked by the UN in the aftermath of 1945 in order to justify the proposed territorial internationalisation of Jerusalem.[48] Recent experiments in international territorial

---

[43] See Articles 31 and 36 of the ILC Draft Articles on State Responsibility. For an examination of post-conflict duties under the law of state responsibility, see Katharina Kunzmann, *Reconstructing Iraq and Who Pays: Is There an International Responsibility to Reconstruct a Country Destroyed by War?*, German Law Journal, Vol. 4 (2003), No. 7.

[44] See *A More Secure world: Our Shared Responsibility*, para. 207.

[45] This is evidenced by the continuing controversy over the legality of humanitarian and democratic interventions. For a recent assessment, see Stahn, *Enforcement of the Collective Will*, at 806–13.

[46] Several questions arise in this regard. Is there a positive obligation to rebuild social and political institutions, to eliminate ethnic rivalries or to maintain law and order, maybe even against the will of local actors? When does it end?

[47] See also Zygojannis, *Die Staatengemeinschaft und das Kosovo*, at 130.

[48] See above Part I, Chapter 3 and Part II, Chapter 6.

administration have been compared to modern trusteeships because they bear some resemblance to the classic policy rationale of the trust.[49] This analogy is defendable from a policy perspective. Many of the missions treated here are therefore linked to the ideas of incapacity and need for care and assistance, which are inherent in the concept of the trusteeship.[50] However, only a few of these engagements qualify as trusteeship administrations in the legal sense of the term.[51]

The notion of trusteeship has generally been avoided in contemporary practice. This results partly from the fact that modern administrations differ from the tradition of Mandate administration or Trusteeship administration from which the analogy to trusteeship originally emerged.[52] As a general rule, international administrations have no longer purported to exercise trusteeship over a people or a territory in the proper sense.[53] Instead, they have exercised public authority in trust.

Secondly, the individual missions vary considerably in format. Modern practice encompasses a broad variety of engagements, ranging from pure assistance missions to exclusive governance missions. Only some of these engagements amount to legal trusteeship. The temporary exercise of public authority by foreign actors takes on features of legal trusteeship (e.g. capacity to act on behalf of another entity, fiduciary obligations of the trustee) in cases where the international engagement entails a substantive displacement or substitution of domestic authority.[54] Such a situation has arisen on a number of occasions (e.g. West Irian, Eastern Slavonia, Kosovo, East Timor, Iraq) where international administrators effectively assumed the role of a guardian of foreign interests at the place of domestic actors. This type of administration raised conflicts of interest in terms of representation and accountability which are typical of trusteeship administration and justify an analogy to the institution of the trust.

---

[49] See, for example, Boon, *Legislative Reform in Post-Conflict Zones*, at 294.
[50] See Bain, *Between Anarchy and Society*, at 172. ("A trustee acts on behalf of someone who is thought to be incapable of navigating the choices, dilemmas and responsibilities of ordinary life [...] Thus, trusteeship answers the call of humanity by treating states, and the peoples residing with them, as if they have no will of their own.")
[51] See also Wolfrum, *International Administration in Post-Conflict Situations*, at 694; Michael Bothe and Thilo Marauhn, *The United Nations in Kosovo and East Timor: Problems of a Trusteeship Administration*, International Peacekeeping, Vol. 6 (2000), 152, at 153 *et seq.*
[52] See also above Part I, Conclusions.
[53] See above Part I, Chapter 5.
[54] See also Wolfrum, *International Administration in Post-Conflict Situations*, at 694.

Other missions, by contrast, lack these distinctive features. International actors have acted on numerous occasions in support of or in conjunction with domestic authorities without acquiring authority to replace domestic decision-making processes. These engagements do not qualify as trusteeships in the full sense. Nonetheless, particular aspects of these missions may be theorised on the basis of principles that are reflected in trusteeship relationships. These types of administrations may, in particular, be subject to fiduciary duties (e.g. the duty to act in the best interests of the population of the administered territory) in light of the specific objectives of their deployment.[55] Such responsibilities have typically arisen from the mandate of the respective mission (e.g. protection or restoration of sovereignty, furtherance of domestic capacity, promotion of human rights) or underlying agency relationships.

[55] Ibid.

Part III

The foundations of international territorial administration

[T]he United Nations just as much as any government – and I would say more than any government – cannot easily brush aside legal considerations so that the United Nations itself can be accused of lawlessness
Dag Hammarskjöld, Statement before the UN Advisory Committee,
2 March 1961

Introduction

Due to its historical origins and existing challenges, the project of international administration has been described as an "arrangement of power rather than one of law".[1] This assertion is only partially founded. The deployment and design of such undertakings have been shaped by political and strategic considerations. However, these types of engagements are governed by legal rules and principles which regulate the exercise of public authority. This framework shall be examined in Part III. It addresses the foundations of territorial administration from two different perspectives: legality and legitimacy.

A closer analysis of these two issues shows that treatment of territorial administration has evolved over time. In the early era of the UN Charter, the legality of territorial administration was mainly viewed as a problem of statutory authority. States and legal scholars questioned the legal authority of the UN to exercise functions of public authority in the context of the proposed UN supervision of Trieste envisaged by the Peace Treaty with Italy.[2] Today, the focus of the debate has shifted. The issue is not so much whether the UN may assume tasks of temporary

---

[1] See Bain, *Between Anarchy and Society*, at 153.
[2] See Hans Kelsen, *Law of the United Nations*, at 834.

governance in light of the UN Charter, but rather where the specific limits of the exercise of UN public authority lie and how the existing legal norms may be reconciled with the specific challenges of transitional administration.[3]

Moreover, the very activity of international administration is increasingly perceived as a form of governance which requires further justification from the point of view of public legitimacy.[4] This finding makes it necessary to examine whether and to what extent traditional criteria for the legitimation of public authority apply to the exercise of public authority by international territorial administrations.

[3] See in this sense Bothe and Marauhn, *UN Administration of Kosovo and East Timor*, at 233–40; Tomuschat, *Yugoslavia's Damaged Sovereignty*, at 339–5; Erika De Wet, *Chapter VII Powers of the United Nations Security Council* (2004), at 311–37. For a more cautious approach, see André de Hoogh, *Attribution or Delegation of (Legislative) Power by the Security Council? The case of the United Nations Transitional Administration in East Timor (UNTAET)*, International Peacekeeping, Vol. 7 (2001), 1.

[4] Various works approach the topic of international administration from the angle of legitimacy. See, for example, Caplan, *A New Trusteeship*, at 57–8; Wilde, *Representing International Territorial Administration*, 71; Salamun, *Democratic Governance in International Territorial Administration*, at 128; Bernhard Knoll, *Legitimacy and UN-Administration of Territory*, German Law Journal, Vol. 8, No. 1 (2007), 39.

11 The legality of international territorial administration

The UN Charter does not expressly provide for the conduct of the UN in an executive capacity such as territorial administration outside the framework of the Trusteeship system. Nevertheless, three factors support the claim that the United Nations has statutory authority to administer territories beyond the scope of application of Article 81: the drafting history of the Charter, the institutional practice of the organisation, and the systemic structure of the Charter system.[1]

1. Authority to administer territories under the Charter of the United Nations

The debates at the San Francisco Conference lend support to the view that the UN was intended to possess sufficient personality to exercise jurisdiction and control over territory.[2]

---

[1] Concurring Finn Seyersted, *United Nations Forces in the Law of Peace and Wars* (1966), at 150 and 363; Elihu Lauterpacht, *Contemporary Practice of the United Kingdom in the Field of International Law*, International & Comparative Law Quarterly, Vol, 5 (1956), 405, at 411; Brownlie, *Principles of Public International Law*, at 178–9; Sarooshi, *United Nations and the Development of Collective Security*, at 60; Chesterman, *You, The People*, at 50.

[2] See also Frowein and Krisch, *On Article 41*, at 744, para. 21; Sarooshi, *United Nations and the Development of Collective Security*, at 60; Chesterman, *You, The People*, at 50. For a different view, see the statement of the Australian delegate in the context of the debate over the legality of the adoption of the Statute of Trieste, who noted that "at San Francisco, the question of including in the Charter of the United Nations a general guarantee of territorial was discussed; but as members of the Security Council will know, the proposals for such a guarantee were deliberately rejected". See UN SCOR, 2nd year (1947), No. 1, at 5.

1.1. The drafting history of the UN Charter

Following the practice of the League of Nations in territorial administration, the drafters of the Charter deliberated in 1945 whether it was
necessary to bestow the organisation with the express power to exercise territorial jurisdiction or to guarantee the territorial integrity of
an entity. The Norwegian delegation introduced a proposal expressly
to state that the Security Council may "take over on behalf of the Organisation the administration of any territory of which the continued
administration by the state in possession is found to constitute a threat
to the peace". This proposal was only withdrawn because it was assumed
that such a reference could limit the discretion and field of application
of measures at the disposition of the Council under Chapter VII.[3] The
drafters therefore agreed that "a general provision authorising the Council to make binding decisions and to apply military sanctions constituted
sufficient authority for it to establish cession of jurisdiction, and that
no specific mention of territorial jurisdiction was necessary to enable
the Organisation to assume such jurisdiction".[4]

1.2. Institutional practice

The argument that the UN may exercise legislative, administrative or
judicial functions within the context of territorial administration receives further support from the institutional practice in the cases of
the Permanent Statute for the Free Territory of Trieste and the creation
of the Council for Namibia.[5] Both frameworks were adopted following
extensive discussion over the authority of the UN to exercise territorial
jurisdiction over territories outside Chapter XIII of the UN Charter.

1.2.1. Trieste

Critics of the Trieste arrangement argued that the Security Council could
not assume the functions determined in Annexes VI, VII and VIII of the
Peace Treaty with Italy due to the absence of a "provision in the Charter
that empowers ... the Security Council to exercise the function of the
head of state or statelike community".[6] The Australian delegate voiced
express doubts as whether Article 24 of the Charter would authorise the
Council to exercise the functions assigned to it by the Trieste Statute,

---

[3] See Commission III, Committee 3, Session of 23 May 1945, UNCIO, Vol. XII, 353, at
354–5, UN Doc. 539 III/3/24.
[4] See Seyersted, *United Nations Forces*, at 150
[5] See also Sarooshi, *United Nations and the Development of Collective Security*, at 60–1.
[6] See Kelsen, *Law of the United Nations*, at 834.

noting that "[t]he functions to be assigned to the Council are not necessarily limited to the maintenance of international peace and security" and that "[t]he giving of a categorical guarantee of the integrity and the independence of the Free Territory goes further than is warranted by the purposes and principles of the United Nations".[7]

Proponents of the authority of the Council to exercise territorial powers over Trieste countered these objections by arguing that the assumption of governmental responsibilities over disputed territories is an implied power of the Council which is in accordance with the *telos* of the Charter. A good example is the statement of the delegate of Poland, who noted:

> We do not have any legal qualms about the Security Council accepting the responsibilities it is asked to accept. I know that it may be somewhat difficult to point to a specific phrase in the Charter which would justify the taking over of the functions we are asked to assume. However, I think it would be entirely within the general spirit of the Charter of the United Nations, if it were decided to form a Free Territory under a quasi-international administration. We believe that is only proper that the United Nations, as an Organisation, should be given the responsibility of supervision over its administration. And since it is a matter which involves peace and security, we believe that the Security Council is the logical organ to carry out these functions.[8]

The Secretary-General took the view that the words "primary responsibility for the maintenance of international peace and security" in Article 24 of the Charter, coupled with the phrase, "acts on their behalf", constitutes a sufficiently wide grant of power to justify the exercise of territorial jurisdiction over Trieste, because the UN members had thereby conferred upon the Council "powers commensurate with its responsibility for the maintenance of peace and security".[9] This position was finally

---

[7] See SCOR, 2nd year (1947), No. 3, at 56. See also the statement of the Representatives of Syria on the question of the Statute of Free Territory of Trieste, Repertoire of the Practice of the Security Council, 1946–1951, at 482. For a similar claim, see Kelsen, *Law of the United Nations*, at 833–4: "When the Permanent Statute comes into force, the Council has to exercise – partly directly, partly through the Governor – functions usually conferred upon a head of state, which functions have nothing in common with anything the Council has to do under the Charter, except in case the Organisation itself is established as administering authority of a trust territory under Art. 81. This is the only case where the United Nations is authorised by the Charter to exercise rights of sovereignty over a territory. But the Free Territory of Trieste is certainly not a trust territory."

[8] See SCOR, 2nd year (1947), at 4–19, 44–61. See also Oscar Schachter, British Yearbook of International Law (1948), 96–101.

[9] See statement made by the Secretary-General on 10 January 1947, Repertoire of the Practice of the Security Council, 1946–1951, at 483.

adopted by the majority of the Council[10] and invoked as a validation for the adoption of the Permanent Statute.[11]

1.2.2. Namibia

The second case in which the authority of the UN to assume governmental authority of a territory was openly debated[12] was the establishment of the UN Council for Namibia by General Assembly Resolution 2248 of 19 May 1967 by eighty-five votes to two with thirty abstentions. The large number of abstentions reflects the controversial nature of the decision. Many states abstained simply because they feared that the resolution could not be implemented in practice. But others expressed doubts as to the competence of the General Assembly to confer extensive legislative powers on the Council. The representative of Sweden, for example, considered that Resolution 2248 was flawed because "it did not command the broad persuasive support of resolution 2145 (XXI) and possibly was not a firm basis for further United Nations action".[13]

The majority of states agreed, however, that the General Assembly was entitled to assume governing responsibilities over Namibia on the basis of the implied powers of the organisation. An international study of the various sources of authority of the General Assembly had used the concept of "inherent powers" to justify the capacity of the Assembly to act as administering authority over Namibia, noting that:

[i]n those areas and on those matters where sovereignty is not rested in a member state, the General Assembly, acting as the agent of the international community, may assert the right to enter the legal vacuum and take a binding decision ... Decisions in regard to territory for which the international community has assumed responsibility may be suggested as an example.[14]

---

[10] The representatives of the Soviet Union, the UK, France and the US viewed Article 24 as the basis of the Council's authority.

[11] See Security Council Resolution 16 of 10 January 1947, UN SCOR, 2nd year, Res. and Dec., 1, UN Doc. S/INF/2/Rev. I (II). The resolution was adopted by ten votes to zero with one abstention (Australia).

[12] The authority of the UN to establish UNTEA as a subsidiary body of the General Assembly has not been called into question. For an analysis of the votes, see Higgins, United Nations Peacekeeping 1946–1967, Vol. 2 (1970), at 121.

[13] See GAOR, Fifth Special Session, 1518th meeting. See on the attitude of governments towards Resolution 2248 also the Report by the Secretary-General "Compliance of Member States with the United Nations Resolutions and Decisions relating to Namibia, taking into account the Advisory Opinion of the International Court of Justice of 21 June 1971", UN Doc. A/AC.131/37 of 12 March 1975.

[14] Ibid.

The same line of argument was later adopted by the Secretary-General in his official written statement in the Namibia case, which welcomed the decision of the General Assembly to exercise territorial authority on grounds of functional necessity. The Secretary-General stated:

Decisions taken by the General Assembly concerning the implementation of the collective responsibilities of the United Nations towards the people and territory of Namibia must... be distinguished from other General Assembly resolutions, and from recommendations calling for action within the sovereign authority of states for in the absence of an intervening Sovereign jurisdiction between the General Assembly and the people of the territory of Namibia... no governmental authority exists other than the General Assembly and the Security Council...[15]

This approach was confirmed by the ICJ[16] and legal doctrine.[17]

1.3. Territorial authority and systemic coherence

The argument that the UN is entitled to exercise territorial authority in non-trusteeship territories is in line with the system of the UN Charter. It is neither excluded by the limited legal personality of the organisation, nor by the protection of state sovereignty under the Charter.

1.3.1. Kelsen revisited

The Kelsian theory, according to which "the Organisation is not authorised by the Charter" to assume territorial authority over an entity, "which has not the legal status of a trust territory"[18] because the UN Charter precludes the UN from exercising sovereign powers over its members or any other territory,[19] must be revisited.

---

[15] See ICJ, *Written Statements Namibia case*, ICJ Rep., Vol. 6 (1970), at 802.

[16] In its 1971 advisory opinion in the *Namibia* case, the ICJ did not directly address the legal basis for the establishment of the Council for Namibia. However, the Court observed that "Article 24 of the Charter vests in the Security Council the necessary authority to take action such as that taken in the present case". See ICJ Rep. 1971, p. 52.

[17] Some authors took the view that the creation of the Council could be based on a direct (see Schermers, *Namibia Decree in National Courts*, at 85) or an analogous (see Klein, *Statusverträge im Völkerrecht*, at 303) application of Article 81 of the UN Charter, despite the lack of a trusteeship agreement within the sense of Article 79 of the Charter. Other scholars placed an emphasis on the concept of implied powers and the previous practice adopted by both the League of Nations and the UN in the field of territorial administration. For an invocation of the concept of implied powers, see Sagay, *Legal Aspects of the Namibian Dispute*, at 271. For a different view, see Herman. *Legal Status of Namibia*, at 320 ("uncertain ground")

[18] See Kelsen, *Law of the United Nations*, at 651.

[19] See Kelsen, *Law of the United Nations*, at 834.

The basic starting point of this theory is a noble one. The central claim of Kelsen, namely the contention that a sovereign state or a portion thereof cannot be subjected to a relation of trust, is defendable from a moral point of view.[20] Moreover, there are valid reasons to argue that the UN is not empowered to take on the function of a territorial sovereign under the Charter.[21] But this does not mean that the organisation is not empowered to administer territories.

UN territorial administration has by its very nature been *non-sovereign* governance. The UN has regularly acted as a functional authority.[22] UN administrations were formally carried out in the interests and for the benefit of the inhabitants of the territory, and were limited in purpose and time. This form of transitional administration differs from sovereignty-based forms of authority, which are based on the concept of ownership.[23] It is therefore erroneous to assume that this type of administration conflicts *per se* with the prohibition of the exercise of sovereign territorial powers over a UN member state or a non-trust territory.

The prohibition of trusteeship between equals does not rule out administering practice outside the Trusteeship System. It rather serves as a limit in the exercise of powers of administration. It highlights that the format and scope of such projects must be determined in light of other cardinal principles of the Charter, such as territorial integrity and sovereign equality.[24]

1.3.2.   UN territorial authority and Articles 2 (1) and 2 (7)

It is also not plausible to argue that the performance of functions of territorial administration by the UN is generally incompatible with the protection of sovereignty (Article 2 (1) UN Charter) and the prohibition of interference in the domestic affairs of a state under Article 2 (7) of the Charter. This is evident in cases in which the UN exercises governmental functions on the basis of an agreement with the territorial state. The PCIJ clarified in its *Wimbledon* ruling that the voluntary surrender of sovereign rights by way of an international agreement is not unlawful

---

[20] This point has been made by scholars in the field of international relations. See, for example, Jackson, *Global Covenant*, at 178–9, 294–316.
[21] See in this sense Brownlie, *Principles of Public International Law*, at 167.
[22] For a survey of the practice, see below Part IV, Chapters 13 and 15.
[23] See on this distinction in the context of the UN administration of Namibia, Sagay, *Legal Aspects of the Namibian Dispute*, at 268–9.
[24] See below Chapter 11, 4.2.

per se, but rather a legitimate act by which the contracting state makes use of its sovereign powers.[25] It is therefore relatively well established that international organisations may assume territorial rights by agreement with the territorial sovereign, if this task falls within their general functional mandate.[26]

The Charter even goes a step further. It permits the establishment of mechanisms of transitional administration even without the consent of the territorial state in the context of the maintenance of international peace and security.[27] The second sentence of Article 2 (7) of the Charter allows an interference in "the domestic jurisdiction" of a state against its will, if that state is subject to measures under Chapter VII. This implies that the Security Council may deploy transitional administrations as enforcement measures under Chapter VII without violating the principle of non-intervention.[28]

Moreover, the claim that UN administration infringes upon the sovereignty of a state is not very compelling in substance, since many administrations are typically aimed at creating or restoring sovereign governance in territories where sovereign governance has vanished or is, at least, in transition. This is evident in the case of three major governance missions with a focus on decolonisation (UNTEA, Council for Namibia, UNTEAT). The title of the former territorial sovereign over the administered entity (the Netherlands in the case of West Irian, South Africa in the case of Namibia and Indonesia in the case of East Timor) was in each of these cases disputed before the assumption of UN authority. The UN administrations were created to help non-sovereign entities to gain self-government or independence. A similar *rationale* underlies the practice of UN statebuilding, which is designed to restore viable domestic governance in situations where the political structures and foundations of a polity have been destroyed by armed conflict.

It is contradictory to argue that the exercise of UN governance powers contravenes the protection of sovereignty if it is designed to create or restore the sovereignty of a territorial entity or of a people. It may even be claimed that states have endowed the UN with a subsidiary competence to administer their territories in situations, where their own domestic institutions are unable to perform these functions – a theory which is

---

[25] See PCIJ, *Case of the S.S. Wimbledon*, Ser. A, No. 1 (1923), 23.
[26] See also De Wet, *Direct Administration of Territories by the United Nations*, at 313–15.
[27] See also Sarooshi, *United Nations and the Development of Collective Security*, at 62.
[28] See also Frowein and Krisch, *On Article 41*, at 744, para. 21.

perfectly in accordance with the modern understanding that sovereignty resides in the people and not in the state.[29]

1.3.3.   UN territorial authority and Chapter XIII

Finally, it is misconceived to interpret the provisions on the UN Trusteeship System (Articles 77 and 78 of the UN Charter) as a conclusive set of rules which preclude *e contrario* the exercise of trusteeship authority in any other form than the UN Trusteeship System.

Article 77 (1) of the Charter limits the applicability of the Trusteeship System to three different categories of territories: territory formerly held as mandates under the Mandates System of the League of Nations; territories detached from enemy states as a result of World War II; and territories voluntarily placed under the Trusteeship System by states responsible for their administration. Article 78 of the Charter prohibits the application of the Trusteeship System to states against their will, by stating that "the trusteeship system shall not apply to territories which have become members of the United Nations". However, this does not imply that the UN cannot exercise administering responsibilities in a different capacity than established under the Trusteeship System.

Such a restrictive systematic interpretation of the Charter would stand in contradiction to the concept of implied powers, according to which the UN is deemed to possess the powers necessary to exercise the powers expressly granted to it by the Charter.[30] Moreover, Chapter XII of the Charter was not in any way adopted with the object and purpose of restricting the scope of application of Chapters VI and VII of the Charter. The powers of the Security Council under Chapter VII are wider than the powers of the organisation under the Trusteeship System. Article 77 of the Charter makes administration under the Trusteeship System dependent on the conclusion of a "trusteeship agreement" with the territorial state in the context of Chapter XII. However, it cannot be assumed that the absolute requirement of consent applies equally in the context of Security Council action for the maintenance of international peace and security. The preservation of national sovereignty, which Articles 77 and 78 seek to protect, may be overcome in situations qualifying as a threat

---

[29] See also the preamble of the Charter: "We, the *people* of the United Nations" (emphasis added).

[30] See ICJ, *Reparation for Injuries Suffered in the Service of the United Nations*, ICJ Rep. 1949, 174 *et seq.* and ICJ, *Effect of Awards of Compensation Made by the United Nations Administrative Tribunal*, ICJ Rep. 1954, 47.

to the peace.[31] Article 78 of the Charter may therefore be interpreted as a special reaffirmation of the principle of non-intervention which prevents the application of the trusteeship system to member states of the UN,[32] but which does not prohibit the establishment of transitional UN administrations[33] in such states[34] or in territories which have not yet gained independence.

2. Legal basis in the UN Charter

Despite the strong arguments in support of the capacity of the UN to administer territories, it is difficult to find an express legal basis for the creation of transitional administrations under the UN Charter. Several legal constructions have been invoked in order to justify the establishment of transitional administrations in addition to Article 81, namely the provisions under Chapter VII of the Charter (in particular Articles 41 and 42), the concept of "Chapter VI $1/2$" measures, Article 36 of the Charter and the doctrine of implied powers.

2.1. Security Council action

Article 24 of the UN Charter vests the Security Council with the primary responsibility for the maintenance of international peace and security. The specific powers for the discharge of this duty are laid down in Chapters VI, VII, VIII and XII. Many UN administrations were created in response to a "threat to the peace" within the meaning of Article 39 of the UN Charter, which has been interpreted broadly as to encompass situations of civil strife and grave violations of human rights.[35] This does not, however, mean that all of these missions were established on the same legal basis. Three main cases must be distinguished: the creation of UN administrations as enforcement mechanisms not involving the use

---

[31] See also Hufnagel, UN-Friedensoperationen, at 304.
[32] See Jackson, Global Covenant, at 305 ("independence is a one-way street with no return to dependency status"). See also Gordon, Some Legal Problems with Trusteeship, at 326.
[33] Concurring De Wet, Chapter VII Powers of the United Nations Security Council, at 318. Article 78 is sometimes interpreted as an indication that the Security Council may not impose a permanent form of government on a state. See Terry D. Gill, Legal and Some Political Limitations on the Power of the UN Security Council to Exercise its Enforcement Powers under Chapter VII of the Charter, Netherlands Yearbook of International Law, Vol. 26 (1995), 33, at 74–7.
[34] See also Kondoch, United Nations Administration of East Timor, at 254.
[35] See Jochen Abr. Frowein and Nico Krisch, On Article 39, in Charter of the United Nations (B. Simma ed., 2002), at 722–5, paras. 16–22.

of armed force (Article 41); the deployment of territorial administration missions with a military component (Article 42); and the establishment of transitional administrations as classical peacekeeping missions based on the consent of the host state ("Chapter VI $\frac{1}{2}$").[36] Furthermore, some missions have been qualified as measures under Articles 36 and 40 of the Charter. But these two provisions have largely fallen into oblivion in the light of the growing complexity and dynamics of modern peacekeeping operations.

2.1.1. Chapter VII

The most specific basis for the deployment of transitional administrations under Chapter VII is Article 41 of the UN Charter.

2.1.1.1. Article 41

Article 41 provides the general legal basis for non-military enforcement measures. It reads:

> The Security Council may decide what measures not involving the use of armed force are to be deployed to give effect to its decision, and it may call upon the members of the United Nations to apply such measures. These measures may include complete or partial interruption of economic relations and of rail, sea, air, postal, telegraphic, radio and other means of communication, and the severance of diplomatic relations.

2.1.1.1.1. International territorial administration – a measure within the confines of Article 41

The wording of the provision does not expressly list the establishment of transitional administrations as an example of non-military enforcement. But this does not imply that the possibility to create territorial administrations for the purpose of the maintenance of peace and security does not come within the ambit of Article 41.[37] The Security Council enjoys wide discretion in the choice of response necessary to react to a threat to international peace and security, including the possibility of taking atypical measures, such as the creation of international administering institutions.[38]

---

[36] See also Bothe and Marauhn, *UN Administration of Kosovo and East Timor*, at 231; De Wet, *Direct Administration of Territories by the United Nations*, at 311.

[37] See also European Court of Human Rights, Grand Chamber, *Behrami & Behrami v. France*, Application No. 71412/01; *Saramati v. France, Germany and Norway*, Application No. 78166/01, Decision of 31 May 2007, para. 130.

[38] See also Frowein and Krisch, *On Article 41*, at 744, para 21. Concurring, Kondoch, *UN Administration of East Timor*, at 256; von Carlowitz, *UNMIK Lawmaking*, at 342.

Article 39 grants the Council the general authority to decide "*what measures* shall be taken in accordance with Articles 41 and 42, to maintain or restore international peace and security".[39] This broad formulation confirms that the Council itself is empowered to determine the range of measures necessary and available within the framework of Article 41. The interpretation is further reinforced by the fact that the list of measures enumerated in Article 41 is illustrative and not exhaustive in nature. The drafting history of the Charter, with its withdrawal of the Norwegian proposal for the sole reason of not binding the Council to specific enforcement measures, appears to imply that it was the unstated intent of the framers of Chapter VII to grant the Council the possibility to "take over on behalf of the Organisation the administration of any territory" for the purposes of the maintenance of international peace and security.

2.1.1.1.2. Compatibility of UN governance with the function of the Council under Chapter VII

The capacity of the Council to endow international administrations with transitional governing responsibilities is also compatible with the general role of the Security Council in the Charter system.[40] Within the architecture of the Charter, the Council itself is vested with an executive, rather than a legislative function.[41] Chapter VII grants the Council a police-like guardian function over the maintenance of peace and security,[42] which is complemented by specific decision-making powers.[43]

---

[39] Emphasis added.

[40] See also Simon Chesterman, *Virtual Trusteeship*, in The UN Security Council: From the Cold War to the 21st Century (David M. Malone ed., 2004), at 222.

[41] See ICTY, Appeals Chamber, *Prosecutor v. Tadic*, Decision on the Defence Motion for Interlocutory Appeal on Jurisdiction, Case No. IT-94-1-A, 2 October 1995, para. 34. ("Plainly, the Security Council is not a judicial organ and is not provided with judicial powers (though it may incidentally perform certain quasi-judicial activities such as effecting determinations or findings)".)

[42] See Jochen Abr. Frowein and Nico Krisch, *Introduction to Chapter VII*, in Charter of the United Nations (Bruno Simma ed., 2002), at 705–6, paras. 12–14. The specific role of the Council under the Charter is difficult to qualify in terms of classical constitutional theory. One of the specificities of the Chapter VII system is that the Charter combines the enforcement function of the Council with concrete regulatory powers. The Council is therefore more than a pure law enforcement agency. See De Wet, *Chapter VII Powers of the United Nations Security Council*, at 112. For a discussion, see also Bardo Fassbender, *The United Nations Charter as a Constitution of the International Community*, Columbia Journal of Transnational Law, Vol. 36 (1998), 575.

[43] Frowein and Krisch qualify these powers as "quasi-legislative functions". Frowein and Krisch, *Introduction to Chapter VII*, at 708–9, paras. 21–3.

This specific Charter-given role does not preclude the Council from endowing Chapter VII-established mechanisms with legislative or judicial functions for the maintenance of international peace and security.[44] The fact that a public authority acts as an organ of a specific branch of government (executive, legislative or judicial branch of power) does not necessarily predetermine the form or the content of the legal acts adopted by it. It is quite common in domestic legal systems that executive authorities adopt abstract regulatory acts. Executive authorities may even, in exceptional cases, create judicial institutions.

The same principle must apply in the definition of the powers of the Security Council under Chapter VII. The question of whether an act comes within the scope of application of Article 41 cannot depend on the nature of activity that it regulates (executive, legislative or judicial), but must be judged according to whether it was adopted in the form proscribed by the Charter and within the substantial limits set by Chapter VII. This may be inferred from the Council's own practice in the 1990s, during which the Council used its Chapter VII powers to create quasi-judicial[45] and judicial institutions[46] under Article 41. It is only consequential to argue that the Council is entitled to create UN administrations under Article 41, which exercise legislative, administrative or judicial functions in the administered territory,[47] provided that these mechanisms are necessary to secure peace and stability and transitional

---

[44] See also ICTY, Appeals Chamber, *Prosecutor v. Tadic*, at para. 38. ("The establishment of the International Tribunal by the Security Council does not signify, however, that the Security Council has delegated to it some of its own powers. Nor does it mean, in reverse, that the Security Council was usurping for itself part of a judicial function which does not belong to it but to other organs of the United Nations according to the Charter. The Security Council has resorted to the establishment of a judicial organ in the form of an international criminal tribunal as instrument for the exercise of its own principal function of maintenance of peace and security, i.e. as a measure contributing to the restoration and maintenance of peace in the former Yugoslavia.")

[45] The Council created the UN Compensation Commission for damages arising out of the 1991 Iraq invasion of Kuwait by SC Res. 687 (1991). See para. 16 of SC Res. 687 of 3 April 1991. The Commission was established as a subsidiary body of the Council.

[46] Both UN *ad hoc* tribunals were established under Chapter VII. See SC Res. 827 of 25 May 1993, para. 1 *et seq.* and SC Res. 955 of 8 November 1994, para. 1 *et seq.* Both UN *ad hoc* tribunals confirmed this interpretation in their practice See ICTY, *Prosecutor v. Tadic*, Appeals Chamber, Judgment of 2 October 1995, ILM, Vol. 36 (1996), 32, para. 32; ICTR, *Prosecutor v. Kanyabashi*, Decision on Jurisdiction, Case No. ICTR-96-15-T, 18 June 1997, para. 7.

[47] Concurring Seyersted, *United Nations Forces*, at 363.

in nature.[48] The exercise of legislative or other powers by such Council-created institutions is again subject to the general limitations of the UN.[49]

2.1.1.1.3.   The power to supersede domestic governance structures under Article 41

Finally, it seems safe to argue that the Council is generally even entitled to override structures of domestic government by its powers under Chapter VII. Two arguments support this assumption. First, there is the explicit reference to the power of the Council to "intervene in matters which are essentially within the jurisdiction of any State" by enforcement action under Chapter VII. This reference indicates that Council action may supersede the domestic structures of a state if this necessary to restore international peace and security.

Secondly, the construction of Chapter VII is not jurisdiction oriented, but subject-matter focused. UN members have authorised the Security Council to take the appropriate measures it deems necessary when a situation under Article 39 arises, and have thereby opened their jurisdiction to legal acts adopted by the Council under Chapter VII. This transfer of authority implies that Chapter VII measures may penetrate into the domestic legal order of a state and take precedence over those legal norms which are inconsistent with the objective of international peace and security. Otherwise, the application of Chapter VII would be deprived of any meaningful effect with respect to those states whose internal policies violate of the UN Charter – a result which is hardly consistent with the founding spirit of the Charter, which was precisely a reaction to World War II and the events in Nazi Germany.

The practice of the Security Council confirms this argument. The Council has interpreted Chapter VII as a normative framework which allows the Council to adopt measures which interfere with the domestic affairs and structures of government of a state in cases where the conduct of that entity violates the principles of the UN Charter on a large-scale or systematic basis. This is reflected in the practice of the Council in

---

[48] See generally on the conception of Chapter VII as a framework for short-term measures of peace enforcement, Frowein and Krisch, *Introduction to Chapter VII*, in Charter of the United Nations, paras. 13 and 20.

[49] For a more detailed discussion, see below Part 4, Chapter 15. For a critique of UNTAET's practice, see De Hoogh, *Attribution or Delegation of (Legislative) Power*, at 30–2, who argues that some of UNTAET's legislative acts are questionable because they are not related to peace maintenance in the narrow sense.

the cases of Southern Rhodesia (Zimbabwe)[50] and South Africa,[51] where the Council used sanctions as a means to counter political oppression under the internal domestic system of a polity. This approach was later developed in the practice of the 1990s,[52] where the Council used its authority under Chapter VII to restore democratically legitimated authority after military coup (Haiti[53]) and to charge international institutions with functions of domestic jurisdiction for the purpose of peace-maintenance.[54] Both *ad hoc* tribunals (ICTY, ICTR) were vested with primacy over national jurisdiction. Their creation shows that the Council may override national jurisdiction by temporary international institutions to restore viable peace.

All of these examples indicate that the scope of application of Chapter VII entails responsibilities which make it necessary to fill governance gaps, to replace existing governmental institutions or to shape the internal political organisation of a territorial entity. Such interferences in the internal structure of a territory appear to be permissible under the Charter, providing that the measures of the Council itself are temporary in nature and applied in accordance with the constraints binding the Council under Article 24 (2) of the Charter and general international law.[55]

[50] In 1966, the Council adopted an arms embargo in order to protect the black majority against the new constitutional situation in the territory arising out of the declaration of independence by the white settlers regime. See SC Res. 216 (1965) and Res. 217 (1965).

[51] The Council imposed economic sanctions against South Africa, in order to reverse the oppressive effects of the apartheid regime. See SC Res. 418 (1977).

[52] The Council has on various occasions reacted to purely internal situations by taking enforcement measures under Chapter VII. This practice is by now a firmly established rule, which can no longer be seriously challenged. See Frowein and Krisch, *On Article 39*, at 724, para. 18. For earlier doubts, see Kelsen, *Law of the United Nations*, at 19. ("International peace is to be distinguished from internal peace. Hence it is not the purpose of the United Nations to restore internal peace by interfering in a civil ware within a state.")

[53] See para. 4 of SC Res. 940 of 30 July 1994, by which the Council authorised "Member States to form a multinational force under unified command and control and, in this framework, to use all necessary means to facilitate the departure from Haiti of the military leadership, consistent with Governors Island Agreement, the prompt return of the legitimately elected President and the restoration of the legitimate authorities of the Government of Haiti".

[54] The intervention in Somalia showed that the assumption of public authority by the UN may be a necessary corollary of the conduct of enforcement action – a gap which the UN sought to fill through the creation of UNOSOM II.

[55] It is important to note that the establishment of transitional administrations by the Council under Chapter VII has met few objections in state practice. See also De Wet, *Direct Administration of Territories by the United Nations*, at 337.

2.1.1.1.4. International territorial administration as enforcement action

Some doubts have been expressed as to whether the establishment of international administrations constitutes "enforcement action" within the ambit of Chapter VII. It has, in particular, argued that Article 41 covers only "action or measures... taken against a State or a specific entity", in order to compel the latter "to agree or to adopt specific measures".[56] This narrow conception of Article 41 is, however, based on a misinterpretation of Chapter VII.

It is highly questionable whether measures under Article 41 must be directed against the will of a territorial entity or designed to force a specific state or entity to adopt a certain conduct. Article 2 (7) lends some support to this assumption by speaking of "the application of enforcement measures under Chapter VII" – a notion translated by "*coercition*" in the French text of the Charter. However, it is not explicitly stated that all measures under Chapter VII, including measures under Article 41, must be coercive in the above-mentioned sense. The wording of Article 41 merely states that measures under Article 41 must be employed "to give effect" to a previous Council decision. The language of Article 41 suggests that any measure not involving the use of force, including the establishment of a UN administration, qualifies as a measure under Article 41, as long as it is designed to implement another resolution or determination by the Council,[57] irrespective of whether it is designed to break the will of a specific entity. It would be absurd to require such measures to be specifically intended to force a state or entity to comply with Security Council demands. Otherwise, the Council would be prevented from adopting measures under Article 41 in a governmental vacuum.

In practice, it is not always easy to determine whether a mission was established under Article 41 or under a different basis of authority (e.g. implied powers[58]). The Council itself has regularly refrained from indicating a precise source of authority for the establishment of UN administrations. The Council established some missions following a simple reference to the existence of a threat to international peace and security; in other cases, the Council made explicit reference to Chapter VII.

While no conclusive catalogue of references exists, a number of criteria may be used to distinguish Article 41-based administrations from

---

[56] See De Hoogh, *Attribution or Delegation of (Legislative) Power*, at 23–4.
[57] See also Frowein and Krisch, *On Article 41*, at 739, para. 10, and 740, para. 14.
[58] For a discussion of implied powers as a basis for UN administrations, see De Wet, *Direct Administration of Territories*, at 312–18.

other administrations. All Article 41-based missions must be established on the basis of a decision under Chapter VII. This follows from the wording of the first sentence of Article 41 ("The Security Council may *decide*"[59]). Further guidance may be drawn from a number of substantive criteria, including a determination:

- whether or not the establishment of the administration is related to military enforcement action or to a previous authoritative Council decision (enforcement character of the mission);
- whether or not the creation of the mission exceeds the framework of a pre-established or consent-based contractual arrangement (consent-based or unilateral mode of establishment); and
- whether the decision of the Council is of a regulatory rather than of a purely organisational nature (authoritative nature of the Council's decision).

2.1.1.1.5. Practice under Article 41

Although the Council has so far refrained from invoking Article 41 as an express source of authority for the establishment of a transitional administration, several UN missions may be qualified as cases of action under Article 41: UNTAES, UNMIK and UNTAET.[60] Each of these missions was directly established under a Chapter VII mandate and not only on the basis of a finding as to the existence of a threat to the peace. The mandate was pronounced in the course of an armed conflict or in its immediate aftermath – a factor which brings all three administrations within the realm of enforcement action. Lastly, the decision of the Council in each of the three cases had a regulatory impact going beyond the aspect of mere organisation. The founding instrument of each of the three missions contained an operative paragraph which highlighted the intention of the Council to limit or supersede existing domestic structures of jurisdiction by way of the establishment of a UN transitional administration.[61]

---

[59] Emphasis added.

[60] See also Bothe, *Peace-keeping*, in Charter of the United Nations, at 685, para. 85.

[61] See para. 2 of SC Res. 1037 (1996) ("[A]cting under Chapter VII of the Charter of the United Nations... Requests the Secretary-General to appoint, in consultation with the parties and with the Security Council, a Transitional Administrator, who will have the overall authority over the civilian and military components of UNTAES, and who will exercise the authority given to the Transitional Administrator in the Basic Agreement"); para. 10 of SC Res. 1244 (1999) ("[A]cting... under Chapter VII of the Charter of the United Nations... Authorizes the Secretary-General... to establish an international civil presence in Kosovo in order to provide an interim administration for Kosovo under which the people of Kosovo can enjoy substantial autonomy within

2.1.1.2. Articles 42 and 48

Some administrations contain military components in addition to a civilian administration mandate. SC Resolution 1244, for example, charged a separate international military presence (KFOR) with a range of security tasks (the demilitarisation of the Kosovo Liberation Army, the conduct of border controls, the protection of freedom of movement of the international civil presence and the provisional maintenance of public safety and order),[62] to be undertaken in coordination with UNMIK.[63] Similar arrangements were made under SC Resolution 1272 (1999), with the only difference being that the military component replacing the multinational force conducting the intervention was this time directly integrated into the military component of UNTAET,[64] operating under the authority of the SRSG.[65]

These military contingents deployed in the context of international administrations do not have a legal basis in Article 41, which envisages only non-coercive enforcement measures. The decision to create a Chapter VII-based administration involving a military force therefore requires an additional legal basis. This foundation can be found in Article 42, which authorises the Council to adopt enforcement measures involving the use of armed force.[66] Article 42 applies on its own if the military component is directly part of the transitional administration (such as in the case of East Timor), or in conjunction with Article 48, if the Council authorises a separate organisation or individual states to provide security by military means (Kosovo).[67]

---

the Federal Republic of Yugoslavia"); and paras. 1 and 6 of SC Res. 1272 (1999). Dissenting in relation to UNTAET, see De Hoogh, *Attribution or Delegation of (Legislative) Power*, at 20–6.

[62] See para. 9 of SC Res. 1244 (1999).

[63] Paragraph 6 of SC Res. 1244 (1999) requests the Secretary-General "to instruct his Special Representative to coordinate closely with the international security presence to ensure that both presences operate towards the same goals and in a mutually supportive manner".

[64] See paras. 3 c) and 9 of SC Res. 1272 (1999).

[65] See *ibid.*, para. 6.

[66] See Article 42, second sentence: "Such action may include demonstrations, blockade, and other operations by air, sea, or land forces of Members of the United Nations."

[67] See also Bothe and Marauhn, *UN Administration of Kosovo and East Timor*, at 232. It is widely accepted that Article 42, in conjunction with Article 48, may provide a basis for the authorisation of states to undertake military measures for the maintenance of international peace and security. See De Wet, *Chapter VII Powers of the United Nations Security Council*, at 260–4. See also European Court of Human Rights, *Behrami & Behrami v. France*, Application No. 71412/01, *Saramati v. France, Germany and Norway*, Application No. 78166/01, Decision of 31 May 2007, para. 130.

2.1.1.3. Article 40

Some authorities have viewed UN peace operations as provisional measures under Article 40 of the Charter, which allows the Council to "call upon the parties concerned to comply with such provisional measures as it deems necessary or desirable", in order "to prevent an aggravation of the situation". It has, in particular, been argued that the deployment of ONUC was a provisional measure under Article 40, designed to stabilise the Congo in order to facilitate a peaceful settlement between all factions.[68] But this legal view is problematic. It is questionable whether the deployment of a four-year UN peace operation may be reasonably characterised as a provisional measure.[69] Moreover, ONUC was designed to assist the government of Congo in the fight against the secessionist Katanga government, and was therefore not in accordance with the conditions of Article 40, which requires UN action to be impartial and neutral in nature ("without prejudice to the rights, claims or the position of the parties concerned").[70]

It is even more difficult to bring more recent administrations within the realm of Article 40. Action under Article 40 is conservative in nature. It is meant to preserve the existing *status quo* and to "prevent an aggravation of the situation", that is to "freeze a conflict in place".[71] UN administrations, however, are often dynamic in nature and designed to effect legal change. Furthermore, they aim to establish more than a mere provisional settlement in the context of dispute resolution. Both features speak strongly against a characterisation of UN administrations as provisional measures under Article 40.

2.1.2.   Article 24 and/or Article 39 in conjunction with Article 29 and/or Article 98 of the Charter

The Council has on numerous occasions established UN missions which fall outside the ambit of Articles 41 and 42 and outside the scope of application of consensual dispute settlement under Chapter VI. This type

---

[68] The UN itself viewed the action in Congo as a measure under Article 40. See the statement of former UN Legal Counsel Oscar Schachter under the pseudonym E. M. Miller, *Legal Aspects of the United Nations Action in the Congo*, American Journal of International Law, Vol. 55 (1961), 1, at 2–9. See also Hilaire McCoubrey and Nigel D. White, *The Blue Helmets: Legal Regulation of United Nations Military Operations* (1996), at 53.

[69] For doubts as to the applicability of Article 40 peacekeeping operations, see also Frowein and Krisch, *On Article 40*, in Charter of the United Nations, 732, para. 8.

[70] See also Alexander Orakhelashvili, *The Legal Basis of United Nations Peace-Keeping Operations*, Virginia Journal of International Law, Vol. 43 (2003), 485, at 500.

[71] See Ratner, *The New UN Peacekeeping*, at 58.

of peace-maintenance has been referred to as action under Chapter VI $\frac{1}{2}$ (*Hammarskjöld*), because it is situated between consensual peacetime engagement and Chapter VII.[72] It covers multi-dimensional UN operations, which are formally established under the heading of peace-maintenance, but do not come within the ambit of classical Chapter VII action, because they are built on the consent of the parties and involve peace-implementation, rather than peace-enforcement.

The Security Council has created a number of missions which come within this category. The first example was ONUC, which contained elements of both enforcement and traditional peacekeeping.[73] This practice was later continued in the cases of UNTAG, MINURSO and UNTAC. These three multi-dimensional operations were created under the heading of peace-maintenance, with the consent of the main stakeholders and without any connection to an enforcement mandate.[74]

The engagements in Somalia (UNOSOM II), Afghanistan (UNAMA), Iraq (UNAMI), Liberia (UNMIL), Democratic Republic of Congo (MONUC) and Ivory Coast (ONUCI) fall into a similar category. These missions were established in a Chapter VII context and in connection with military enforcement action. But the underlying Council resolutions fell short of meeting the classical, above-mentioned characteristics of Article 41. The civilian mandates of UNOSOM II and UNAMI were formally drafted in the form of a request to the Secretary-General, without a distinct and independent regulatory determination ("decision") *vis-à-vis* another territorial entity.[75] UNAMA and the civilian components of UNMIL, MONUC and UNOCI were established on the basis of requests contained in the respective peace settlements and without an express intention to supersede domestic structures of jurisdiction.

The Charter appears to grant the Council sufficient authority and flexibility to establish such missions. Article 39 implies that Chapter VII measures may not be taken unless a determination under Article 39 is

---

[72] See also McCoubrey and White, *The Blue Helmets*, at 50.

[73] It is widely suggested that ONUC was neither classical enforcement action under Chapter VII, nor a means of dispute settlement under Chapter VI. See ICJ, *Certain Expenses of the United Nations*, Advisory Opinion of 20 July 1962, ICJ Rep. 1962, 151, at 177. See also McCoubrey and White, *The Blue Helmets*, at 53.

[74] Both UNTAG and UNTAC were established on the basis of consensus-based mandates, without a reference to Chapter VII. See SC Res. 623 (1988) of 23 November 1988, paras. 1–2 and SC Res. 745 (1992) of 28 February 1992. See also De Wet, *Direct Administration of Territories by the United Nations*, at 313.

[75] See paras. 4 and 14 of SC Res. 814 and para. 8 of SC Res. 1483 (2003).

made.[76] However, the Charter does not limit the regulatory powers of the Council to measures under Article 41 or 42.[77] The Council is entitled to establish territorial administrations outside the scope of enforcement action under Article 41 or 42, especially if the assumption of UN administering authority is founded upon the consent of the state concerned.

Several legal constructions may be used to validate this type of action. A textual basis for the deployment of non-Article 41-based administrations can be found in Articles 24 and 39 read in conjunction with Articles 29 and 98 of the Charter. The power to establish a UN administration after a finding of the existence of a threat to peace and security may be inferred from Articles 24 and 39, which can be viewed as establishing a basis of action for measures below the threshold of Article 41. Articles 29 and 98 allow the Council to assign administering functions to the Secretary-General for the implementation of such a decision.[78]

An alternative basis for the establishment of non-Article 41-based UN administrations by the Council may be found in the concept of *implied powers*.[79] The authority to establish such administrations may be viewed as a power necessary for the Council to exercise its primary responsibility for the maintenance of international peace and security under Article 24 of the Charter, namely as a means to secure sustainable peace. This power of the Council receives, in particular, some backing from international practice. Consent-based missions, which were not directly established under Chapter VII, were regularly endorsed by the General Assembly, and did not encounter objections by UN member states.[80]

[76] See Article 39 of the UN Charter ("shall make recommendations, or decide what measures shall be taken in accordance with Articles 41 and 42").
[77] See also Orakhelashvili, *Legal Basis of United Nations Peace-Keeping Operations*, at 493.
[78] This procedure usually involves three steps. The Security Council first entrusts the Secretary-General with the exercise of the administering responsibilities identified in the resolution creating the mission (Article 98), who then appoints a Special Representative of to carry out this mandate. This Special Representative acts as a representative of the Secretary-General but remains responsible to the Security Council. At the same time, the transitional administration constitutes, in institutional terms, a subsidiary organ of the Council (Article 29). See also Paulus, *On Article 29*, in Charter of the United Nations, at 553, para. 48.
[79] See in this sense De Hoogh, *Attribution or Delegation of (Legislative) Power*, at 14. The applicability of the doctrine of implied powers to the interpretation of the Charter has been reaffirmed by the ICJ in the *Reparations* case, where the Court noted that the UN "[o]rganization must be deemed to have those powers, which, though not expressly provided in the Charter, are conferred on it by necessary implication as being essential to the performance of its duties". See ICJ, *Reparation for Injuries in the Service of the United Nations*, Advisory Opinion, ICJ. Rep.1949, at 182.
[80] See De Wet, *Direct Administration of Territories by the United Nations*, at 312–15.

2.1.3.   Chapter VI – Article 36 (1)

Article 36 (1) provides a last option to justify the establishment of UN administrations by the Security Council. This provision is formally enshrined in Chapter VI of the Charter ("Pacific Settlement of Disputes"). It grants the Council the authority to "recommend appropriate procedures or methods of adjustment" of any dispute referred to it that could endanger international peace and security.

Article 36 (1) has, in particular, been invoked as a legal basis for early peacekeeping missions in which the UN acted as a monitoring organ over the implementation of mutually agreed cease-fires and truces. Consensual non-enforcement action was interpreted as an attempt by the Security Council to facilitate a solution to a dispute.[81] This theory was later extended justify the establishment of multi-dimensional peacekeeping operations involving patterns of civil administration. It has been argued that Article 36, as well as Article 38, "could cover the second-generation missions established at the request of the parties".[82] The establishment of ONUC was occasionally qualified "as a method of adjustment of the situation under Article 36 (1)".[83] The same link to dispute settlement could be made in relation to other engagements established in connection with a peace settlement.

Nevertheless, substantial doubt exists as to whether Article 36 (1) provides a solid legal basis for the establishment of UN administrations specifically. The framing of the provision appears to imply that the decision of the Security Council to establish a specific mission is merely a recommendation to the parties which they can freely accept or reject at any time. This assumption is incompatible with the organisational design of UN administrations, which are usually established as fixed-term operations without the possibility of unilateral revocation by domestic actors. Furthermore, Article 36 (1) shares some of the basic features of Article 40 of the Charter. It is essentially based on the idea that the UN intervenes as an impartial and neutral third party which assists in the resolution of the dispute, but which does not itself take an active role in the settlement.[84] This passive understanding of the function of the UN is at odds with the realities of transitional administration, under which UN administrators are frequently charged with managerial

---

[81] See McCoubrey and White, *The Blue Helmets*, at 50.
[82] See Ratner, *The New UN Peacekeeping*, at 58.
[83] See Orakhelashvili, *Legal Basis of United Nations Peace-Keeping Operations*, at 500.
[84] See also Ratner, *The New UN Peacekeeping*, at 57.

responsibilities (e.g. to initiate reforms or shape processes of governance and administration).

2.2. General Assembly action

It is even more difficult to find a clear legal basis for the establishment of UN administrations by the UN General Assembly.[85] The Assembly has created missions of transitional administration in four cases: Libya, Eritrea, West Irian and Namibia. The authority of the Assembly to take such action may be based on different legal foundations, namely Article 11 (2) and/or Article 14 of the Charter, or the doctrine of implied powers.

2.2.1. Articles 11 (2) and 14 of the Charter

The Charter vests the General Assembly with a subsidiary responsibility for the maintenance of international peace and security, which complements the primary responsibility of the Security Council under Article 24 (1). This function of the Assembly is reflected in two provisions. Article 11 (2) empowers the Assembly to issue recommendations to states concerning "questions relating to the maintenance of international peace and security". Article 14 extends this competence to any situation that might impair peace.[86] It states:

Subject to the provisions of Article 12, the General Assembly may recommend measures for the peaceful adjustment of any situation, regardless of origin, which it deems likely to impair the general welfare or friendly relations among nations, including situations resulting from a violation of the present Charter setting forth the Purposes and Principles of the United Nations.

UN members have interpreted these assertions of authority as providing the Assembly with sufficient legal competence to establish peacekeeping operations. The ICJ has reaffirmed this principle in its advisory opinion in the *Certain Expenses* case.[87] The Court noted that Articles 11 (2) and 14 empower the General Assembly to organise, by means of recommendation, peace operations with the consent of the government on whose territory the mission shall be stationed.

---

[85] The Charter indicates that the Assembly has a secondary competence in the field of collective security. However, it fails expressly to grant the Assembly concrete and binding decision-making powers in this area.

[86] The difference between these two provisions is that Article 14 only addresses measures of a peaceful nature ("peaceful adjustment of situations and disputes"), while Article 11 (2) provides a basis for any recommendations.

[87] See ICJ, *Certain Expenses of the United Nations*, ICJ Rep. 1962, 151.

It is widely recognised that the Assembly may create missions which do not interfere with the powers reserved to the Security Council under the second sentence of Article 11 (2).[88] The General Assembly may, in particular, create transitional administration missions of a purely civilian nature, following the examples of the engagements in Libya and Eritrea. Such administrations may be established as subsidiary organs of the Assembly under Article 22 of the Charter.

It is less clear if and to what extent the Charter allows the General Assembly to establish UN administrations with a military component.[89] Such action requires some justification in the light of Article 11 (2), which restricts the authority of the Assembly by precluding it from ordering "action" which falls in the sphere of authority of the Security Council. The mere wording of Article 11 (2) appears to suggest that the establishment of *any* larger peacekeeping operation with a military unit constitutes "action" which ought to be "referred to the Security Council".[90]

Nevertheless, two arguments may be advanced in support of the view that the General Assembly may, in exceptional circumstances, create transitional administrations with a military component. First, the limitation contained in Article 11 (2) may be read in a narrow fashion, namely as a provision which excludes only action expressly attributed to the Council under the Charter VII, such as enforcement action under Articles 41 and 42. This interpretation leaves some leeway for the view that the Assembly may establish missions involving a military contingent

---

[88] The ICJ held in the *Nambia* case "it would not be correct to assume that, because the General Assembly is in principle vested with recommendatory powers, it is debarred from adopting, in specific cases within the framework of its competence, resolutions which make determinations or have operative design". See ICJ, *Advisory Opinion* (1971), at para. 105.

[89] The Assembly assumed this competence in the case of West Irian. The mission in West Irian included a military component, being the United Nations Security Force (UNSF). Moreover, it took control over ONUC in 1960, when the Security Council was unable to deal with the situation as a result of a deadlock between the superpowers. The General Assembly adopted a resolution on 20 September 1960, which reaffirmed that it was "essential for the United Nations to continue to assist the Central Government of the Congo" and requested the Secretary-General to take action to restore law and order.

[90] See Michael Bothe, *Peace-keeping*, in Charter of the United Nations (Bruno Simma ed., 2002), at 685, para. 89. This interpretation receives further support from the organisational practice of the UN, which has increasingly conceived peacekeeping as a type of action which falls into the sphere of competence of the Security Council.

with the consent of the host state.[91] Secondly, it is worth noting that
the limitation imposed by Article 11 (2) does not appear in the text of
Article 14. It is therefore possible to invoke Article 14 as a basis for the
creation of UN administrations by consent.[92]

2.2.2. Implied powers and Uniting for Peace doctrine

Neither Article 11 (2) nor Article 14 of the Charter provides the General Assembly with authority to create UN administrations against or
without the will of the territorial sovereign. Such action comes much
closer to enforcement action under Article 41 or 42 than purely consensual models of administration. It is therefore primarily reserved to the
Security Council[93] and requires a different foundation.

   One possible justification is the doctrine of implied powers. This doctrine has been used in the context of transitional administration in the
Namibia case.[94] The ICJ stated that "the United Nations as a successor to
the League, acting through its competent organs, must be seen above all
as the supervisory institution, competent to pronounce, in that capacity, on the conduct of the mandatory with respect to its international
obligation, and competent to act accordingly".[95] The subsequent assertion of direct administering authority by the General Assembly over the

---

[91] This argument has, in particular, been invoked by the ICJ in its advisory opinion in the
Certain Expenses case, which validated the engagement of the General Assembly in the
Congo. The ICJ noted in the *Certain Expenses* advisory opinion that action within Article
11 (2) means enforcement action specifically entrusted to the Security Council under
Chapter VII. See ICJ, *Certain Expenses of the United Nations*, ICJ Rep. 1962, at 164. See also
Kelsen, *Law of the United Nation*, at 204–5. ("In Article 11, paragraph 2, the term 'action'
can hardly mean 'discussion' and 'recommendation by the General Assembly'... For if
the term 'action' includes 'discussion' and 'recommendation by the General Assembly'
the previous sentence is meaningless....'Action' can only mean 'enforcement action'.
This is the specific function which is reserved to the Security Council.")
[92] This argument has been made in legal doctrine, most notably, in order to justify the
action of the General Assembly in West Irian. See Higgins, *United Nations Peacekeeping
1946–1967*, at 120. See also Bowett, *United Nations Forces*, at 256.
[93] See also Kelly, *Restoring and Maintaining Order*, at 101.
[94] The UN practice in the case of Nambia may interpreted as evidence supporting the
claim that the Assembly may be entitled to exercise governmental authority without
the will of the territorial ruler, namely in cases where there is no territorial sovereign
and where the UN has a special responsibility for the territory concerned. This point
was made by Judge Dillard in the *Namibia* case, who noted that "the exercise of the
power involved no invasion of national sovereignty since it was focused on a territory
and a regime with international status". See ICJ, *Separate Opinion of Judge Dillard*, ICJ
Rep. 1971, at 163. See also Seyersted, *United Nations Forces*, at 150.
[95] See ICJ, *Legal Consequences for States of the Continued Presence of South Africa in Namibia*,
Advisory Opinion of 21 June 1971, paras. 87–116.

territory through the establishment of the Council for Namibia by Resolution 2248 (S–V) may be viewed as a measure necessary for the Assembly
to perform its functions effectively.[96]

Secondly, it may be argued that the General Assembly is entitled to
assume administering powers including control over military forces by
way of an analogous application of the Uniting for Peace Resolution, in
circumstances where "the Security Council, because of lack of unanimity
of the permanent members, fails to exercise its primary responsibility for
the maintenance of international peace and security".[97] One of the main
objects and purposes of the peace-maintenance system of the Charter
is to protect people's rights in situations of emergency. It is therefore
plausible to allow the Assembly to assume territorial authority over a
collapsed state in cases where the Council fails to take action.

2.3.   The Trusteeship Council

The Trusteeship Council is the only organ of the UN which has been expressly vested with the power to administer territories under the Charter.
However, the UN avoided using the Trusteeship System as a framework
for the direct administration of territories.

2.3.1.   Article 81: a marginalised norm

Article 81, which envisages the possibility of the exercise of direct governing powers under Chapter XII of the Charter, has remained a dead
letter in practice.[98] The UN avoided using this provision as a direct basis
for the exercise of direct administering authority under Chapter XII.[99]
Furthermore, the organisation was reluctant to make an express reference to Article 81 in the two cases in which an analogy could have been
drawn: Jerusalem and Namibia.[100]

This practice may be explained by two factors. It was convenient for
the organisation to rely on state-based forms of administration under
the Trusteeship System, due to both the greater experience of former
colonial powers in the management of processes of decolonisation and
the lower budgetary implications for the UN. Secondly, the authority of
the Trusteeship Council did not lend itself particularly well to extension

---

[96] See also Sagay, *Legal Aspects of the Namibian Dispute*, at 258.
[97] See GA Res. 377A, UN GAOR, 5th Sess., Supp. No. 20, at 10, UN Doc. A/1775 (1950).
[98] See Rauschning, *On Article 81*, at 1122, para. 2.
[99] See above Part I, Chapter 3. The UN has instead preferred to appoint states as
administering authorities.
[100] *Ibid.*

LEGALITY OF INTERNATIONAL TERRITORIAL ADMINISTRATION

by way of analogy due to the inapplicability of the Trusteeship System to UN members (Article 78) and its ideological linkage to the process of decolonisation.

2.3.2. No need for reform

Some proposals for a revitalisation of the Trusteeship Council have been formulated in the mid-1990s.[101] It was suggested to endow the Trusteeship Council with responsibilities concerning areas which form part of the common heritage of mankind. Later, the growing number of multidimensional UN peace operations sparked calls for an application of UN governance under Trusteeship Council control to disintegrating states.[102] But the application of Trusteeship Council control over collapsed states is neither realistic, nor politically feasible.[103]

There are various legal and political impediments to reactivation of Trusteeship administration. A revitalisation of the Trusteeship System could not be effected without an amendment of the Charter. Articles 77 (categories of territories which may placed under the Trusteeship System) and 78 (prohibition of the application of the Trusteeship System to UN members) would have to be amended, in order to allow Trusteeship Council control over collapsed states. Secondly, the requirement of

[101] Initiatives by Malta led to a new draft proposal for Article 88 of the Charter, which defined the responsibilities of a renewed Trusteeship Council as follows: "The Trusteeship Council shall hold in sacred trust the Principle of the Common Heritage of Mankind. It shall monitor compliance with this principle in accordance with international law, in Ocean Space, Outer Space, the atmosphere as well as Antarctica and report on any infringement thereof to the General Assembly and/or CCSSD. It shall deliberate on its wider application of matters of common concern affecting comprehensive security and sustainable development and the dignity of human life, and make its recommendations to the authorities and institutions concerned. The Trusteeship Council shall act as the conscience of the United Nations and the guardian for future generations." See Elisabeth Mann Borgese, *Ocean Governance and the United Nations* (1995), at 240. Others have proposed charging the Trusteeship Council with responsibilities over "failed states". See Helman and Ratner, *Saving Failed States*, at 16. This proposal was specifically made in relation to Rwanda and Burundi in 1993. See Kelly, *Restoring and Maintaining Order*, at 103. It has been repeated with regard to Iraq. See Paul Kennedy, *UN Trusteeship Council Could Finally Find a Role in Postwar Iraq*, Daily Yomiuri, May 9 2003, at www.globalpolicy.org/security/issues/iraq/after/2003/0511trusteeshipcouncil.htm.
[102] See Tomuschat, *General Course*, at 122.
[103] For a recent discussion, see Saira Mohamed, *From Keeping Peace to Building Peace: A Proposal for a Revitalized United Nations Trusteeship Council*, Columbia Law Review, Vol. 105 (2005), 809–40. For an application of the idea of trusteeship in the context of Iraq, see Brian Deiwert, *A New Trusteeship for World Peace and Security: Can an Old League of Nations Idea be Applied to a Twenty-first Century Iraq?*, Indiana International & Comparative Law Review, Vol. 14 (2004), 771, at 805.

a trusteeship agreement is problematic in this context. If Trusteeship Council control is supposed to serve as an institution exercising administering authority in situations of emergency where ordinary channels of state control have collapsed, it may not always be possible to conclude such an agreement.[104] Lastly, the composition of the Council would have to be re-determined, since the criteria for membership in the Council under Article 86 of the Charter have become redundant.

Such amendments are difficult to justify in the present situation. The Trusteeship Council has lost its traditional *raison d'être* with the accession to independence or self-government of all of the former trust territories. Moreover, the experience of the 1990s has established that the creation of UN administrations is inextricably linked to a threat or breach of international peace and security, triggering the responsibility of the Security Council or the General Assembly. Since either one of the bodies is typically involved in the direction of peacemaking efforts, it makes sense to charge subsidiary bodies of these two organs with the responsibility for transitional administration.[105] It seems therefore more reasonable to strengthen the traditional system of peace-maintenance "from within", as recommended by the *Brahimi* Report, which suggested that "a dedicated and distinct responsibility centre ... be created within the United Nations System", in order to keep charge of governance missions.[106]

This approach is reflected in recent documents.[107] The High-level plenary meeting of the General Assembly proposed the deletion of Chapter XIII of the Charter in September 2005, noting that the "Trusteeship Council no longer meets and has no remaining functions".[108]

2.4. The Secretary-General

The role of the Secretary-General in the field of territorial administration differs from that of the Security Council, the General Assembly and the Trusteeship Council.

---

[104] See Article 77 (1) (c) of the Charter.

[105] See also Groom, *The Trusteeship Council*, at 172.

[106] See para. 78 of the *Brahimi* Report. See also Chesterman, *You, the People*, at 240, who proposes the establishment of a monitoring mechanism for transitional administrations which follows the precedent of the Sanctions Committee of the Security Council.

[107] See Report of the High-level Panel on Threats, Challenges and Change, *A more secure world: our shared responsibility*, UN Doc. A/59/565 of 2 December 2004, para. 99 (Deletion of Chapter XIII of the Charter).

[108] See para. 176 of GA Resolution 60/1 (World Summit Outcome) of 24 October 2005.

2.4.1. The Charter framework: limited autonomous powers

The Charter conceived the Secretary-General (SG)[109] essentially as an executive organ, with limited regulatory authority in the field of peace-maintenance. This follows from Chapter XV of the Charter, which vests the SG with two responsibilities in the area of maintenance of international peace and security: the power to perform functions entrusted to him by other organs of the UN (General Assembly, Security Council, Economic and Social Council and Trusteeship Council) under Article 98, and the authority to bring to the attention of the Security Council "any matter which in his opinion may threaten the maintenance of international peace and Security" (Article 99). These two provisions indicate that the Secretary-General is not entirely free in its choice of legal action, but dependent upon authorisation of other organs.[110] It is therefore widely agreed that the SG is not empowered to establish peacekeeping operations or territorial administration missions on his own motion,[111] without a delegation of power from the Security Council or the General Assembly, which are vested with the exclusive authority to provide a legal basis for the creation of such operations.[112]

2.4.2. The institutional practice: managerial responsibilities by invention

Although this repartition of competencies remains valid, in principle its limits have been extended by the practice of the UN. The SG has undertaken managerial functions in all aspects of transitional administration, reducing the impact of legal authorisation by the Security Council or the General Assembly to a mere formality. The SG has exercised wide powers in two areas: the negotiation of legal frameworks for transitional administration and their institutional implementation.

[109] See generally Danesh Sarooshi, *The Role of the United Nations Secretary-General in United Nations Peace-Keeping Operations*, Australian Yearbook of International Law, Vol. 20 (1999), at 279.

[110] This restrictive conception of authority contrasts visibly with the active powers of the General Assembly and the Security Council, which were both explicitly authorised to adopt measures for the maintenance of peace and security.

[111] This appears to be the understanding of the SG. The Secretariat refused to establish a peacekeeping force in Iraq in 1991, despite calls for it to do so for the protection of minorities in the country. See Sarooshi, *United Nations and the Development of Collective Security*, at 64.

[112] See Sarooshi, *United Nations and the Development of Collective Security*, at 124; Ratner, *The New UN Peacekeeping*, at 71; Rosalyn Higgins, *A General Assessment of United Nations Peace-Keeping*, in UN Peace-Keeping: Legal Essays (Antonio Cassese ed., 1978), 1, at 7. Dissenting Orakhelashvili, *Legal Basis of United Nations Peace-Keeping Operations*, at 508.

2.4.2.1.   Initiation of frameworks of administration

The Charter fails to provide the UN Secretariat with express authority to facilitate the adoption of peace settlements. Various office-holders have, however, derived such authority from the powers inherent in the office of the SG.[113] This proactive understanding of the terms of office of the SG is typical of the contemporary practice in the field of transitional administration. The UN Secretariat has not only taken a lead role in the negotiation of peace settlements, but has also assumed key responsibilities in the design of UN transitional administrations. The most compelling examples of this practice are the UN engagements in Cambodia, Somalia, East Timor, Kosovo and Afghanistan. The UN SG has in all of these cases shaped the mandate of the UN operation before its formal deployment by the Security Council. Neither Article 97 nor Article 99 of the Charter provides a direct legal basis for this type of action. However, the managerial powers of the SG in the negotiation of peace settlements may be justified by the powers implied in the office of the SG, which are designed to facilitate the political groundwork for the peacemaking efforts of the General Assembly and the Security Council, if necessary through preliminary executive action.[114]

2.4.2.2.   Implementation of UN mandates

The strong managerial functions of the SG are even more evident in the case of the implementation of UN mandates under Article 98 of the Charter. The exercise of delegated powers often requires difficult questions of interpretation, arising from a lack of clarity of the respective authorisation.[115] The SG has used different methodologies to respond to those gaps, ranging from *ex ante* requests for further authorisation,[116]

---

[113] This trend started in the 1950s when Hammarskjöld offered his good offices to act as a mediator in crisis situations. It was later expanded, *inter alia*, by the deployment of fact-finding missions of the SG under Article 99 in Laos and North Borneo and the provisional establishment of two monitoring missions without initial authorisation of the Council, namely the UN Good Offices Mission in Afghanistan and Pakistan (UNGOMAP) and the UN Observer Mission for the Verification of Elections in Nicaragua (ONUVEN). See Ratner, *The New UN Peacekeeping*, at 70.

[114] It is quite telling that the "accumulation of responsibility" by the SG since the 1950s has been tacitly accepted through state practice. See Ratner, *The New UN Peacekeeping*, at 69.

[115] See Sarooshi, *United Nations and the Development of Collective Security*, at 57.

[116] See, for example, the proposals for the adjustment of the mandate of MONUC. See above Part II, Chapter 9.

to informal forms of consultation, mechanisms of *ex post* endorsement and/or cases of unilateral interpretation without consultation.[117]

Article 98 of the Charter appears to imply that that the SG himself is vested with the authority to interpret the nature of powers delegated to him by the Council or the Assembly. Otherwise the SG would be barred from exercising his responsibilities under Article 98 in a useful and effective way.[118] Nevertheless, the SG has, in at least two cases, adopted a very wide conception of his powers by reformulating a mandate[119] entrusted to him by the Security Council, namely in Somalia[120] and in Kosovo.[121]

The only plausible way to justify such far-reaching organisational acts is through an implicit approval by subsequent Security Council action. The mandate of the SG typically includes a duty to report to the Security Council, through which the SG communicates his interpretation of the mandate to the Council. The continued acceptance of this conduct by the Security Council may be viewed as an implicit act of recognition by the Council, indicating its intention to recognise the interpretation given by the SG as an authoritative reflection of the powers delegated under Article 98.[122]

2.5. Other institutional options

Some proposals for institutional reform in the area of UN peacebuilding have been made in the context of the 2005 World Summit. Various bodies have recognised the need to develop new institutional structures in order to address the problems of countries emerging from conflict. However,

---

[117] See Ratner, *The New UN Peacekeeping*, at 71.

[118] See Sarooshi, *United Nations and the Development of Collective Security*, at 57.

[119] Ordinary rules of interpretation suggest that the SG cannot re-invent his mandate through unilateral regulatory action going beyond the initial authorisation.

[120] In 1993, the SG interpreted his mandate under UNOSOM II so as to allow for the promulgation of the Somali Penal Code of 1962 as the criminal law in force in Somalia. This was difficult to reconcile with the language of SC Res. 814. See below Part IV, Chapter 15.

[121] One may have some doubts as to whether the sweeping definition of the SG's powers in Kosovo by UNMIK Regulation No. 1/1999 represented an accurate reflection of the wording of SC Res. 1244. See Section 1 (1): "All legislative and executive authority with respect to Kosovo, including the administration of the judiciary, is vested in UNMIK and is exercised by the Special Representative of the Secretary-General." SC Res. 1244 contained no reference to the exercise of all-embracing legislative, executive and judicial authority by the SRSG. It merely entrusts the SG with the performance of "basic civilian functions". See para. 11 b) of SC Res. 1244.

[122] For a similar line of argument, see Sarooshi, *United Nations and the Deverlopment of Collective Security*, at 57.

the legal framework governing the administration of territory by the UN was widely left aside in the reform process, despite suggestions to the contrary.

2.5.1.   The proposal for a Committee on UN Administration and Governance Assistance

The Dutch Advisory Council on International Affairs proposed the establishment of a novel expert body under Article 29 of the UN Charter with specific expertise in transitional administration. It recommended the creation of a permanent Security Council Committee on UN Administration and Governance Assistance, in order to address the problems posed by "failing states".[123] The report suggested that this committee could "temporarily take over some or all of the state's sovereignty in the name of the international community", as well as "administrative tasks", either by way of consent of the government of the country concerned or on the basis of a Chapter VII mandate.[124]

This proposal would have attenuated some of the antinomies of the current institutional architecture in the field of transitional administration.[125] But it failed to gain broader attention in the reform process due to growing preference for a coordination- and advice-based forum of assistance reflecting "the primary responsibility of national and transitional Governments": the Peacebuilding Commission.[126]

2.5.2.   The mandate of the Peacebuilding Commission

The Peacebuilding Commission lacks direct powers in the field of transitional administration due to its limited mandate and its conception as an "intergovernmental advisory body".[127]

The Commission was established by a concurrent decision of the Security Council and the General Assembly[128] in order to enable the UN to

---

[123] See Advisory Council on International Affairs, *Failing States: A Global Responsibility*, May 2004, at 82.

[124] *Ibid.*, at 83.

[125] The proposal was, *inter alia*, motivated by the insight that a permanent Security Council Committee on UN Administration and Governance Assistance would possess greater legitimacy than the Council to exercise authority over administered territory. *Ibid.*

[126] See para. 9 of the preamble of GA Res. 60/180 of 30 December 2005 (Peacebuilding Commission) and SC Res. 1645 (2005) of 20 December 2005.

[127] See para. 1 of GA Res. 60/180 and SC Res. 1645 (2005).

[128] *Ibid.* ("acting concurrently..., in accordance with Articles 7, 22 and 29 of the Charter of the United Nations").

help "avoid State collapse and the slide to war [and] to assist countries in their transition from war to peace".[129] The main purpose of the Commission is "to bring together all relevant actors to marshal resources and to advise on and propose integrated strategies for post-conflict peacebuilding and recovery".[130] The Commission is therefore primarily a forum of coordination in which various stakeholders can share information and develop and coordinate strategies concerning post-conflict peacebuilding. Its decision-making powers are limited. The Commission may provide "recommendations and information to improve the coordination of all relevant actors within and outside the United Nations".[131] This mandate enables the Commission to draw the attention of the UN and other institutions to the needs of countries in transition and to play a constructive role in developing and coordinating development and assistance strategies for societies in transition following the withdrawal of a UN peacekeeping presence.[132] The Commission might also be requested to provide advice to UN peacekeeping missions and transitional administrations (e.g. upon request of the Security Council or the SG).[133]

However, UN members failed to entrust the Commission with broader "managerial" responsibilities in the area of peacebuilding. The Commission itself is neither authorised to take on administering powers in situations of transitions (as was envisaged in the proposal by the Dutch Advisory Council on International Affairs), nor is it meant to supervise the UN's own activities in peacebuilding on its motion. This limitation is reflected in paragraph 16 of GA Resolution 60/180 and SC Resolution 1645 (2005) which subject action of the Commission to the primary responsibility and initiative of the Security Council, in "post-conflict situations on the agenda of the ... Council."[134]

---

[129] This gap was identified in the Report of the High-level Panel on Threats, Challenges and Change, *A more secure world: our shared responsibility*, para. 261.

[130] See para. 2 (a) of GA Res. 60/180 and SC Res. 1645 (2005).

[131] See *ibid.*, para. 2 (c).

[132] See also Explanatory Note of the Secretary-General on the Peacebuilding Commission, sub. IV.

[133] See para. 12 (a) and (d) of GA Res. 60/180 and SC Res. 1645 (2005). Paragraph 14 invites "all relevant United Nations bodies or other bodies and actors ... to take action on the advice of the Commission, as appropriate and in accordance with their respective mandates".

[134] Paragraph 16 underlines that the Commission shall "provide advice to the Council *at its request*" (emphasis added) in situations where the Council is "actively seized".

3. Authorisation of multinational administrations

A different problem of institutional competence has arisen in the context of the multinational occupation of Iraq. The involvement of the Council in the post-war occupation has raised the question whether the UN is entitled to authorise non-UN bodies to administer territories for the purpose of maintaining peace and security under Chapter VII.

It is well known that the Council has delegated Chapter VII powers to member states[135] and regional organisations[136] for the exercise of enforcement action.[137] Articles 42[138] and 53 (1)[139] of the Charter are drafted in broad enough terms to allow for such a decentralised application of the use of force.[140] The use of "coalitions of the able and willing" to carry out enforcement action[141] has become routine practice in the work of the UN. The situation is, however, slightly different in the context of territorial administration. The Charter contains no explicit reference as to whether the Council may vest states or international organisations with authority to administer territories. Moreover, hardly any institutional practice exists in support of a decentralised exercise of territorial authority under Chapter VII. The question therefore requires some more detailed attention here.

3.1. Authorisation of states to administer territories

The Charter mentions the concept of decentralised territorial administration only within the context of the Trusteeship System. There are, nevertheless, convincing arguments in support of the claim that the Security Council may authorise states to exercise territorial authority by

---

[135] For a survey of the practice, see Frowein and Krisch, *On Article 42*, at 757–8, paras. 21–3.

[136] See generally Christian Walter, *Vereinte Nationen und Regionalorganisationen* (1996), at 260–7; Ugo Villani, *The Security Council's Authorisation of Enforcement Action by Regional Organisations*, Max Planck Yearbook of United Nations Law, Vol. 6 (2002), 55. For a survey of the practice, see Christine Gray, *International Law and the Use of Force* (2000), at 233–6.

[137] For a recent discussion, see De Wet, *Chapter VII Powers of the United Nations Security Council*, at 256–310.

[138] Articles 42 and 48 (1) of the Charter allow the Council to authorise states to carry out military measures. See also Frowein and Krisch, *On Article 42*, at 758, para. 25.

[139] Article 53 (1) states that the Council shall, where appropriate, "utilise regional arrangements or agencies for enforcement action under its authority".

[140] See Sarooshi, *United Nations and the Development of Collective Security*, at 148–9.

[141] See generally, Niels M. Blokker, *Is the Authorisation Authorised? Powers and Practice of the United Nations Security Council to Authorise the Use of Force by Coalitions of the "Able and Willing"*, European Journal of International Law, Vol. 11 (2000), 542.

virtue of Chapter VII, subject to the limits inherent in its own powers and the limits of delegation.[142]

3.1.1. Authority

Some support for this view may be found in Chapter VII of the Charter. It has been noted above that the establishment of transitional administrations may be conceived as a measure under Article 41 of the Charter. This provision itself is not foreign to the idea that "measures not involving the use of armed force" are carried out by states. Article 41 even provides a list of potential measures which may be carried out by states under this provision, namely "demonstrations, blockade, and other operations by air, sea or land forces of Members of the United Nations".[143] The most compelling examples are sanctions imposed under the heading of collective security. There are even some parallels between the role of states under UN-mandated administrations and the UN sanctions regime. Like UN-mandated administration, the implementation of sanctions requires additional regulatory activity by states, including administrative cooperation, executive control or even implementing legislation.[144] It is therefore plausible to argue that the Council may authorise state-based frameworks of territorial administration under Article 41.

Additional authority for decentralised administration under Chapter VII may be derived from a reading of Article 41 in conjunction with Article 48.[145] If Article 41 is recognised as forming a valid legal basis for the creation of frameworks of transitional administration, nothing prevents the Council from conferring the execution of this task on states, in accordance with Article 48 (1).

Moreover, considerations of necessity may require a delegation of territorial authority to states. There are situations in which the authorisation of a multinational administration composed of specific states is the only effective option to maintain peace and security after conflict. It may, for example, be necessary to involve a group of states in temporary reconstruction, because their personnel are present in the conflict territory. Authorisation can, under such circumstances, be a measure

---

[142] See also Crawford, *Creation of States*, 2nd edn (2006), at 563.
[143] See Article 41, second sentence.
[144] See generally on the practice of the sanctions committees, François Alabrune, *La Pratique des Comités des Sanctions du Conseil de Sécurité depuis 1990*, Annuaire Français de Droit International, Vol. 45 (1999), 226.
[145] See also De Wet, *Chapter VII Powers of the United Nations Security Council*, at 315–16.

necessary for the Council to be able to fulfil its functions under Chapter VII.[146]

The competence of the Council to authorise states to administer territories may thus, in sum, be regarded as a power that is not expressly provided for in Article 41, but is consistent with the purpose of that article and necessary to give effect to the Council's authority.

3.1.2. Limits

The authorisation of state-based frameworks of administration under Chapter VII is, however, subject to strict limits.[147] The delegation of territorial authority to states creates significant risks and problems which need to be addressed by adequate safeguards. There is a general danger that states will use powers over foreign territory more directly than UN organs to meet their own national interests rather than to further the overall goals of the organisation. Secondly, the exercise of regulatory authority by states within the framework of territorial administration may have a deeper and more sustainable impact on the population of the administered territory than short and targeted military enforcement action. Finally, the authorisation of states to exercise territorial powers in another territory conflicts with Article 2 (1) of the Charter, which is binding upon the Council according Article 24 (2). This implies that it can only be applied in exceptional circumstances, namely as an *ultima ratio* option exercised under the scrutiny of the Council.

Two limitations apply, in particular: the authorisation of multinational frameworks of administration must be justified by special reasons of functional necessity, i.e. the need to vest states with territorial authority because multinational administration presents the most viable option in the given situation to maintain or restore international peace and security effectively and, secondly, the administration must be conducted under the overall authority and control of the Council.

---

[146] A similar argument is frequently made to justify the competence of the Council to delegate enforcement powers to states. See Sarooshi, *United Nations and the Development of Collective Security*, at 143.

[147] See Sarooshi, *United Nations and the Development of Collective Security*, at 154–5, who argues that the Council must maintain effective authority and control over delegated powers, because its own authority is based on powers delegated to it by UN member states. See also European Court of Human Rights, *Behrami & Behrami v. France*, Application No. 71412/01, *Saramati v. France, Germany and Norway*, Application No. 78166/01, Decision of 31 May 2007, para. 132. ("[D]elegation must be sufficiently limited so as to remain compatible with the degree of centralisation of UNSC collective security constitutionally necessary under the Charter.")

This principle follows from the general limitation on the competence of the Council to delegate its powers under the Charter[148] and Article 41, which requires the Council itself to determine the scope and contours of the Chapter VII measure to be implemented by states under Article 48. The Council must therefore at least define the objectives, powers and obligations of the administration in the resolution and exercise some form of supervision, i.e. through the receipt of periodic reports.[149]

3.2. Authorisation of international organisations to administer territories

The Charter offers even less guidance with respect to a possible delegation of territorial powers to international organisations. Although the Charter gives the Council an express competence to delegate enforcement powers to regional arrangements,[150] it is silent as to whether the Council may use its Chapter VII powers to authorise international organisations to perform other functions for the maintenance of peace and security.

This silence cannot, however, be interpreted as a prohibition of the authorisation of international organisations to assume the administration of territories. From the perspective of law enforcement, it does not make much difference as to whether UN members implement decisions of the Security Council for the maintenance of international peace and security jointly as members of the UN or through the framework of an organisation to which they are members.[151] The idea that mandates of territorial administration are carried out by international organisations rather than by individual states is even closer to the spirit of Chapter VII, which favours multilateralist solutions over unilateralist approaches. It is therefore logical to assume that Article 41 entitles the Council to authorise states to administer territories jointly or through the framework of international organisations. This idea is, at least partially, reflected in Article 48 (2) of the Charter, which states that decisions of the Security Council "shall be carried by the Members of the United Nations directly

---

[148] For a full account, see Sarooshi, *United Nations and the Development of Collective Security*, at 34–5.

[149] See also with respect to delegation of Chapter VII authority to UN member states, *ibid.*, at 155.

[150] See Article 53 (1) of the Charter.

[151] For a similar reasoning, see Sarooshi, *United Nations and the Development of Collective Security*, at 148.

and *through their action in the appropriate international agencies of which they are members*".

3.3. Practice

In its practice, the Council has been reluctant to authorise states or international organisations to exercise governmental authority.[152] It has mainly done so in an indirect way, namely by authorising military forces to exercise specific forms of executive action within the carrying out of their mandates, or by endorsing or approving multinational forms of administration.

3.3.1. Civilian responsibilities as an annex of enforcement action

The UN has charged military forces with the performance of law enforcement and executive functions under a Chapter VII mandate, in particular in the process of the implementation of peace settlements. The two most famous examples are the cases of Bosnia and Herzegovina and of Kosovo.

In 1995, the Council authorised a multinational force of NATO and non-member states (IFOR "Implementation Force", later SFOR "Security Force") to "use all necessary means to effect the implementation of and to ensure compliance" with the Dayton Peace Agreement.[153] This mandate included a number of police and administrative responsibilities related to the military mandate, including assistance in the delivery of humanitarian aid, supervision of the clearing of minefields, the creation of a secure environment for free and fair elections and responsibilities for the protection of civilian populations, refugees and displaced persons.[154]

Four years later, the Council vested the international security presence in Kosovo (KFOR)[155] with substantial NATO participation[156] with similar

---

[152] The Security Council has authorised states and international organisations to achieve peace and security through military enforcement action, including the enforcement of a naval interdiction, the supervision of no-fly zones and the guarantee of the safety of humanitarian convoys. For a survey, see Sarooshi, *United Nations and the Development of Collective Security*, at 167.

[153] See SC Res. 1031 of 15 December 1995, para. 15 *et seq.* See also Articles I 2 (b) and IV 4 (b) of Annex 1A of the Dayton Agreement.

[154] See Article VI, para. 3 of Annex 1 A of the Dayton Peace Agreement.

[155] KFOR derives its mandate from SC Res. 1244, but it "is not a subsidiary organ of the United Nations". See also European Commission for Democracy Through Law, *Opinion on Human Rights in Kosovo*, para. 79.

[156] According to the findings of the ECHR, UNSC 1244 gave rise to the following chain of command: "The UNSC was to retain ultimate authority and control over the security

responsibilities,[157] including the mandate to provide public safety and order until the establishment of UNMIK.[158] Both examples establish that multinational forces have exercised a rudimentary form of civilian responsibilities under a Chapter VII mandate, namely an annex to Chapter VII authorised enforcement action.[159]

In February 2007, the Security Council authorised a peacekeeping mission of the African Union (AMISOM) to perform functions of security and assistance in Somalia.[160] AMISOM was established to close the security vacuum caused by the withdrawal of Ethiopian troops from Somalia.[161] The Council authorised both the mission's establishment by "member States of the African Union" and its mandate ("take all necessary measures ... to carry out the ... mandate") under Chapter VII of the UN Charter.[162] AMISOM's was mandated to "support dialogue and reconciliation in Somalia" through security-related assistance (e.g. protection of domestic institutions, establishment of free movement and safe passage). [163] This precedent indicates that the Council might, at some point, authorise a regional organisation to carry out broader tasks of governance and administration under the umbrella of Chapter VII.

mission and it delegated to NATO ... the power to establish, as well as the operational command, of the international presence, KFOR. NATO fulfilled its command mission via a chain of command ... to COMKFOR, the commander of KFOR." See European Court of Human Rights, *Behrami & Behrami* v. *France*, Application No. 71412/01, *Saramati* v. *France, Germany and Norway*, Application No. 78166/01, Decision of 31 May 2007, para. 135.

[157] See para. 9 of SC Res. 1244 (1999).

[158] See *ibid.*, para. 9 (d).

[159] For a discussion of KFOR's mandate in the areas of detention, see European Court of Human Rights, *Behrami & Behrami* v. *France*, Application No. 71412/01, *Saramati* v. *France, Germany and Norway*, Application No. 78166/01, Decision of 31 May 2007, paras. 123–6.

[160] SC Res. 1744 (2007) of 21 February 2007.

[161] AMSOM was established on the premise that the mission would "evolve into a United Nations operation that will support the long-term stabilization and post-conflict restoration of Somalia". See para. 6 of the preamble of SC Res. 1744 (2007.

[162] See para. 4 of SC Res. 1744 (2007).

[163] See *ibid.* AMISOM was authorised: "(a) To support dialogue and reconciliation in Somalia by assisting with the free movement, safe passage and protection of all those involved with the process referred to in paragraphs 1, 2 and 3; (b) To provide, as appropriate, protection to the Transitional Federal Institutions to help them carry out their functions of government, and security for key infrastructure; (c) To assist, within its capabilities, and in coordination with other parties, with implementation of the National Security and Stabilization Plan, in particular the effective re-establishment and training of all-inclusive Somali security forces; (d) To contribute, as may be requested and within capabilities, to the creation of the necessary security conditions for the provision of humanitarian assistance."

3.3.2. Security Council Resolutions 1483 and 1511 – a quasi-mandate

It is more to difficult to identify cases in which the Council formally authorised multinational administrations to conduct missions of territorial administration under the heading of the collective security system. The US-led administration of Iraq under Resolutions 1483 and 1511 marks a precedent which comes, at least, close to a case of UN-mandated multinational administration. The respective Resolutions explicitly referred to the concept of authorisation in the context of the establishment of the multinational force,[164] but failed to use such language with respect to the system of civil administration.[165] The activity of the CPA in civil administration was therefore not formally "authorised" under the umbrella of the collective security system.[166]

Nevertheless, the Resolutions contained a number of substantive legal determinations which bestowed it with a provisional mandate to administer Iraq. The Council specifically called upon the Authority to "promote the welfare of the Iraqi people through the effective administration of territory".[167] The UN specified the basic rights and obligations of the CPA, including the duty to comply fully with its obligations under international law[168] and the obligation gradually to "return governing responsibilities and authorities to the people of Iraq"[169] – a duty which goes beyond the traditional framework of occupation. Finally, the Council requested that the US and the UK report at regular intervals on their efforts under Resolutions 1483 (2003) and 1511 (2003).[170] All of these factors indicate that the Council charged the CPA effectively with a quasi-mandate to administer Iraq which was meant to be exercised in cooperation with the UN Special Representative.

---

[164] See para. 6 of SC Res. 1511 ("authorises a multinational force under unified command to take all necessary measures to contribute to the maintenance of security and stability in Iraq").

[165] For a different view, see De Wet, *Chapter VII Powers of the United Nations Security Council*, at 315; De Wet, *Direct Administration of Territories by the United Nations*, at 305.

[166] It is deplorable that the multinational administration of Iraq was not based on a clearer Chapter VII mandate, with an express delegation of transitional territorial authority to the UN and the state actors present in the territory. The remaining uncertainty about the delegation of administering authority adds to the general confusion over the interpretation of the terms of Chapter VII resolutions. For a criticism, see Scheffer, *Beyond Occupation Law*, at 859.

[167] See para. 4 of SC Res. 1483 (2003).   [168] See *ibid.*, para. 5.

[169] See para. 6 of SC Res. 1511 (2003).

[170] See para. 24 of SC Res. 1483 (2003) and para. 25 of SC Res. 1511 (2003).

4.   Limits of international authority

International territorial administrations are subject to various legal obligations when they exercise administering powers.[171] Restrictions in the exercise of public authority flow from several sources. A first set of limitations follows from the institutional competences under the Charter itself. UN administrations usually derive their authority from the Security Council or the General Assembly. This implies that their own action must have a general nexus to the maintenance of international peace and security.[172]

Further limitations follow from specific Charter provisions. Article 76 of the Charter contains a minimum bill of rights for the exercise of UN territorial authority. It provides that trusteeship administration must be guided by the objectives of advancing self-government and human rights protection. This obligation is specifically addressed to trusteeship authorities under Chapter XII, including the UN Trusteeship Council. However, the principles enshrined in Article 76 may be applied by way of analogy to missions of territorial administration carried out under the authority of the Security Council, the General Assembly or the Secretary-General. Moreover, the UN as an organisation is bound by the cardinal principles of Articles 1, 2 and 55 of the Charter when it exercises governing responsibilities.

Similar considerations apply to multinational administrations. They may be bound to comply with different types of international standards which apply equally to UN actors and multinational administrations, namely obligations under international customary law, obligations arising under a Chapter VII mandate and obligations flowing from the capacity as territorial ruler (concept of functional duality) and the *acquis* of the local population.

4.1.   The nexus to international peace and security

Following a traditional principle under the law of delegation, no entity can transfer powers which it does not hold itself ("*nemo dat quod non habet*"). If UN administrations have been established by the Security Council and the General Assembly under the heading of peace maintenance, they are bound to act within these boundaries. This requirement places substantial limitations on the exercise of regulatory action. Legal

---

[171] See Irmscher, *Legal Framework*, at 364; Bothe and Marauhn, *UN Administration of Kosovo and East Timor*, at 235.

[172] See also de Hoogh, *Attribution or Delegation of (Legislative) Power*, at 30–1.

acts adopted by UN administrations must present a close connection to the maintenance of international peace and security. Otherwise they exceed the scope of delegated authority.[173]

4.2.   Limits of territorial administration under specific Charter provisions

A UN administration is not an ultimate source of law – as the authority of statehood is considered to be. Rather, it functions within the framework of attributed powers and existing international laws,[174] including a number of principles which set the "constitutional framework" for the exercise of governing powers.

4.2.1.   Article 76

Important guidance may be derived from Articles 76 and 83 (2) of the Charter. Article 76 obliges trusteeship authorities to "promote the political, economic, social, and educational advancement of the inhabitants of the trust territories, and their progressive development towards self-government or independence", and "to encourage respect for human rights and for fundamental freedoms for all without distinction as to race, sex, language, or religion". Article 83 (3) recalls that these guidelines shall also apply to strategic areas administered by the Security Council under Article 83 (1). These two provisions cannot be applied directly to international administrations operating under the umbrella of peace-maintenance. However, they outline key features of trusteeship authority which are of direct relevance to UN governance and co-governance missions.

4.2.1.1.   Article 76 and the purpose of UN territorial administration
Article 76 clarifies that the limits of UN transitional administrators are defined by the rights and obligations of the organisation towards the inhabitants of the administered territory.[175] The explicit reference to

---

[173] For a more detailed study, see below Part IV, Chapter 15. See also de Hoogh, *Attribution or Delegation of (Legislative) Power*, at 31.

[174] See Chopra, *Peace-Maintenance*, at 54 ("the peace-maintenance authority must be accountable itself, and not in some way above the law"), and at 55 ("Consequently, civil officials and military contingents participating in peace-maintenance operations are subject to an interim rule of law, no less than is the local population").

[175] See also Amnesty International, *East Timor: Building a New Country Based in Human Rights*, July 2000: "The responsibility of UNTAET as trustee of the human rights of the East Timorese people requires that UNTAET itself does not violate their human rights."

the promotion of the welfare of the administered population in Article 76 *lit.* b., which complements the notion of the maintenance of peace and security in *lit.* a., makes it clear that UN governance of territories cannot be a strategic end in itself but must be guided by the overall objective of protecting and furthering the interests of the inhabitants of the administered territories.

This general principle has a direct implication for the conduct of administering authorities. It limits the exercise of regulatory authority by UN administrations. Unlike a truly sovereign legislator, UN administrators are not free to legislate in whatever manner and for whatever purpose they choose. They are required to exercise their powers for the benefit of the population. This pre-empts self-dealing and the adoption of legislation which has no connection with the welfare of the population.[176]

4.2.1.2.   Article 76: a "magna charta" of authority-in-trust

Moreover, Article 76 may be read as a mini-charter of rights and obligations of international administrations. Both Article 76 and Article 83 illustrate that an international territorial authority is the servant of both an international and locally supported rule of law in the exercise of its functions.

Article 76 *lit* c. contains more than a mere reiteration of the general principle under Article 55 of the Charter, which vests the UN with the mandate to promote "universal respect for, and observance of, human rights and fundamental freedoms". It lists human rights protection specifically as a guiding principle for the exercise of territorial authority under the trusteeship system. Article 83 extends the obligation to ensure a fair degree of human rights protection to the Security Council. Both the letter (Article 24 (2)) and the spirit of the Charter suggest that a similar standard must apply when the UN exercises the very same functions, but in a different form, namely under the umbrella of peace-maintenance.

The same reasoning applies in relation to Article 76 *lit.* b., which lists the gradual empowerment of the people "towards self-government or

---

[176] See also Boon, *Legislative Reform in Post-Conflict Zones*, at 294. For corresponding jurisprudence of the Israeli Supreme Court in the context of the legislative powers of a military government under Article 43 of the Hague Regulations, see E. Nathan, *The Power of Supervision of the High Court of Justice over Military Government*, in Military Government in the Territories Administered by Israel, 1967–1980: The Legal Aspects, Vol. 1 (M. Shamgar ed., 1982), 109, at 163 *et seq.*

independence" as a requirement of trusteeship administration. The obligation to foster the development of self-rule is an inherent component of any form of people-based territorial administration, and must be applied beyond the direct context of Chapter XII of the Charter,[177] especially in the light of contemporary trends of international law pointing towards the emergence of an internal right of self-determination, the development of a right to political participation[178] and the crystallisation standards of democratic governance.[179]

Article 76 lit. provides thus some support for projects that are designed to provide individuals, minorities or peoples with the help and protection necessary to enable them to manage their own affairs.[180] But it implies, at the same time, that international administrations have a duty to involve local actors progressively in the process of political participation[181] in order to comply with international standards.

4.2.2. The right of self-determination (Article 1(2) of the UN Charter)

The second express limitation on the exercise of governmental powers by UN authorities is the right of self-determination. The principle is enshrined in Articles 1 (2) and 55 of the UN Charter, Article 1 of the two international Covenants and the Friendly Relations Declaration.[182] Self-determination has been recognised as a right under international law on numerous occasions.[183] In inter-state relations, it is generally understood to encompass two components: the right of a people to organise its own state free from foreign oppression (external self-determination) and the right of a people to adequate political representation within the

---

[177] See also Frowein and Krisch, *On Article 41*, at 744, para. 21; Bothe and Marauhn, *UN Administrations of Kosovo and East Timor*, at 236.
[178] See Gregory H. Fox, *The Right to Political Participation*, at 539.
[179] See Franck, *The Emerging Right to Democratic Governance*, at 86. For the proclamation of the right to democracy as a human right, see UN Commission on Human Rights, Res. 1999/57 of 27 April 1999.
[180] See para. 11 of Security Council Res. 1244 (1999) and paras. 2 and 8 of Security Council Res. 1272 (1999).
[181] See also Tomuschat, *Yugoslavia's Damaged Sovereignty*, at 327.
[182] See Principle V of the Declaration on Principles of International Law concerning Friendly Relations and Cooperation among States in accordance with the Charter of the United Nations, GA Res. 2625 (XXV) of 24 October 1970.
[183] See ICJ, Advisory Opinion, *Legal Consequences for States of the Continued Presence of South Africa in Namibia (South West Africa) notwithstanding Security Council Resolution 276 (1970)*, ICJ Rep. 1971, 16, at 31, para. 52; Advisory Opinion, *Western Sahara*, ICJ. Rep. 1975, 12, at 31–3, 68, para. 162.

constitutional structure of its own state (internal self-determination).[184] These principles apply equally in the context of international territorial administration. Self-determination has, however, some distinct characteristics in this field. The first particularity is that it not only serves as a people-state device, but also as a guideline for the conduct of relations between a people and international organisations. Secondly, self-determination is mostly relevant in its form as an "internal" right. It applies as both a defence right (the right of a people to decide on its form of government) and as a participatory right (the entitlement to gradual political empowerment) between a people and its provisional territorial ruler.

4.2.2.1. Applicability to international territorial administrations

It is relatively easy to establish that self-determination not only applies in inter-state relations, but also in the relationship between a people and an international administering authority.[185] This may be inferred from the construction and the *telos* of self-determination.

The right of self-determination is attached to a people. Its scope of application is defined without reference to a specific addressee. The right to organise itself freely and to be free from foreign rule is a right inherent in the people, and is not linked to the concept of external or internal control. This implies that it can be exercised independently of the particular nature of the public ruler.[186] This argument is reinforced by the object and purpose of the right to self-determination. This right is designed to protect and to preserve the freedoms and particular characteristics of this people. A need for protection exists not only in relation to states, but also *vis-à-vis* other international entities exercising control

---

[184] See generally Karl Doehring, *Self-Determination*, in Charter of the United Nations, at 56, para. 32; Allan Rosas, *Internal Self-Determination*, in Modern Law of Self-Determination (C. Tomuschat ed., 1995), 225–52. For discussion, see also Tomuschat, *General Course*, at 258–60.

[185] Concurring in result De Wet, *Chapter VII Powers of the United Nations Security Council*, at 326–37.

[186] Similarly, self-determination might, for example, be invoked against a *de facto* regime. For a more restrictive view, see Kelly, *Iraq and the Law of Occupation*, at 136, who calls into question the applicability of self-determination in situations of occupation in light of "the fact that occupations are not included in the expanded situations of application for the right of self-determination listed in Article 1 (3)" of the ICCPR. ("The States Parties to the present Covenant, *including those having responsibility for the administration of Non-Self-Governing and Trust Territories*, shall promote the realization of the right of self-determination", emphasis added.)

over a people. This reasoning is particularly compelling in the context of territorial administration. Self-determination can be exercised by a people against a foreign state and even against its own state apparatus, if the latter deprives this people of its characteristics and political freedoms.[187] The same standards must apply if international organisations or multinational administrations assume the functions of a state within the framework of transitional administrations.

It is beyond doubt that standards of self-determination apply to UN transitional administrations. This follows from Articles 24 (2), 1 (1) and 55 of the Charter. A similar principle governs multinational administrations. They may be bound to respect the right to self-determination in the exercise of public authority by virtue of international customary law,[188] due to their role as domestic authorities of the territory under administration, or on the basis of an express Security Council mandate, such as in the case of the occupation of Iraq.[189] Moreover, one might even argue that, once acquired, guarantees of self-determination form part of the *acquis* of a people, because they constitute the precondition for the exercise of all other individual human rights.[190]

4.2.2.2.   External v. internal self-determination

The relationship between an international territorial administration and the people of the administered territory is neither purely external, nor purely internal in nature. International governing authorities are usually authorised to administer the territory, either by consent of the host state or by a UN mandate bestowing them with territorial authority. This entitlement distinguishes them from purely external actors. At the

---

[187] This is implied by the savings clause of the Friendly Relations Declaration which states that the principle of territorial integrity and political unity protects States "conducting themselves in compliance with the principle of equal rights and self-determination of peoples... possessed of a government representing the whole people belonging to the territory without distinction as to race, creed or colour".

[188] The ICJ acknowledged in the case of *Portugal v. Australia* that the principle of self-determination has an *erga omnes* character. See ICJ, East Timor (*Portugal v. Australia*), Judgment, ICJ Rep. 1995, 90, at 102, para. 29. For a recognition of self-determination as a norm of *jus cogens*, see Gros Espiell, *Self-Determination and Jus Cogens*, in U.N. Law/Fundamental Rights: Two Topics in International Law (A. Cassese ed., 1979), 167; A. Cassese, *Self-Determination of Peoples: A Legal Reappraisal* (1995), 320.

[189] SC Res. 1483 (2003) emphasised the right of the Iraqi people freely to determine their own political future and mandated the Coalition to realise this objective. See para. 4 of SC Res. 1483 (2003). See also De Wet, *Chapter VII Powers of the United Nations Security Council*, at 335.

[190] For this conception, see GA Res. 637 A (VII) of 12 December 1952.

same time, international authorities are never fully equivalent to domestic governing institutions, because they lack public accountability. They are neither appointed by domestic institutions, nor democratically responsible to the inhabitants of the administered territories. These characteristics place international administrations in a hybrid status, which deviates from the traditional, state-related labels of external or internal self-determination.

It seems fair, however, to transpose the basic principles of self-determination to the relationship between an administered people and an international territorial ruler, in cases where the latter enjoys final authority over all or parts of the internal affairs of the administered entity.

4.2.2.3.   Obligations of international territorial authorities
The law of self-determination contains at least two principles which may be validly applied to the relationship between internal administrators and the people of the administered territory: the freedom of a people freely to decide its form of government and the right of a people to require adequate representation in the process of governance.[191]

4.2.2.3.1.   The prohibition of the imposition of a form of government on a territory
The right to self-determination serves, in part, as a corollary of the principle of non-intervention. It protects a people against the imposition of a form of government from outside.[192] This principle is evident in cases where a people has organised itself within the framework of a state. The right to self-determination grants the people of that state a right freely to decide the form of government that it wishes to adopt. A similar protection may apply in favour of people who have not yet attained statehood. The most popular recognition of this principle is the right of a colonial people to live free from "alien subjugation, domination and exploitation" and to choose its own political system.[193] But there are other cases in which a people may have a right to install or preserve a certain form of government, without being organised in the form of a

---

[191] See generally Doehring, *Self-Determination*, at 56, paras. 32–3.
[192] See also Bowett, *United Nations Forces*, at 197.
[193] See para. 1 of GA Res. 1514 (XV), *Declaration on the Granting of Independence to Colonial Countries and Peoples*. The same passage may be found in Res. 2625 (XXV).

state. It is, in particular, recognised that people under alien domination are protected by the right of self-determination.[194]

The right of a people freely to determine its form of government restricts the scope of authority of international territorial administrations.[195] It precludes them from imposing any permanent form of government on a people against or without its will.[196] This limitation has several practical implications for the conduct of international governing authorities. It forces international administrators to refrain from instituting long-term structures of governance and large-scale constitutional reforms which cannot be reversed by the population of the administered territories after the period of transitional administration.[197] Moreover, self-determination obliges international administrators, in principle, to limit the validity of their legal acts to their period of administration.

4.2.2.3.2.   Self-determination and political participation
The second element of self-determination which plays a role in the context of transitional administrations is the participatory aspect of self-determination. Self-determination is not only a defence right against foreign conduct, but also a participatory right. A people must be in a position to take part in the formation of the political will of its rulers, in order to enjoy *self*-government. This guideline governs the relationship between the majority and the minority within existing states. It finds some support in the savings clause of the Friendly Relations Declaration, which provides that states are entitled to invoke the rightof territorial

---

[194] One example is the right of self-determination of the Palestinian people, which does not have a colonial background. For a recognition of the right of self-determination of the Palestinian people, see most recently ICJ, Advisory Opinion, *Legal Consequences of the Construction of a Wall in the Occupied Palestinan Territory*, 9 July 2004, para. 118. ("[T]he existence of a 'Palestinian people' is no longer in issue.") The Court found that the risk of further alteration to the demographic composition of the Occupied Palestinan Territory "severely impedes the exercise by the Palestinan people of its right to self-determination". See para. 122. Note also that the General Assembly has generally qualified unlawful military occupation as a violation of the right to self-determination. See, for example, paras.1–2 of GA Res. 35/37 of 20 November 1980 ((Afghanistan) and paras. 9–10 of GA Res. 34/22 of 14 November 1979 (Cambodia).

[195] For a discussion, see also Irmscher, *Legal Framework of the Activities of the United Nations Interim Mission in Kosovo*, at 365.

[196] See Gill, Terry. *Legal and Some Political Limitations on the Power of the UN Security Council*, at 75. Against a power of the Security Council to dictate "territorial changes", see also Tomuschat, *Peace Enforcement and Law Enforcement*, at 1750.

[197] See also Irmscher, *Legal Framework of the Activities of the United Nations Interim Mission in Kosovo*, at 365.

integrity provided that they "conduct themselves in compliance with the principle of equal rights and self-determination" and possess "a government representing the whole people belonging to the territory without distinction to race, creed or colour".[198] It is, in particular, widely acknowledged that a people must be granted an opportunity to defend its special characteristics through constitutional arrangements and various forms of political participation in a given state.[199] These arrangements may take the form of autonomy rights, federal structures or institutionalised mechanisms of participatory democracy.[200]

Similar guarantees of internal self-determination apply in the relationship between a people and a territorial ruler within the framework of international administrations. The fact that a people is provisionally subject to foreign rule cannot alone deprive it of its right to self-determination, because self-determination marks the institutional basis for the realisation of all other individual rights. It is therefore justified to claim that a people under transitional administration has a right to meaningful access to government in order to pursue its political, economic, cultural and social development.[201]

The scope of this right must, however, be interpreted in light of the special circumstances of territories in transition. Two factors are relevant in this regard: the security environment and general state of the political system of the territory. The intensity of the obligation must be adjusted to the stage of the mission and the security situation. The development of stable and representative self-government under international administration may require a temporary suspension of participatory rights. The involvement of the local population in

---

[198] See Principle V, para. 7 of GA Res. 2625 (XXV) of 24 October 1979. A similar formula may be found in para. 2 of the Vienna Declaration of the World Conference on Human Rights, see ILM, Vol. 32 (1993), 1663.

[199] See Doehring, *Self-Determination*, at 56–7, paras. 32–4.

[200] In *Reference Re Secession of Quebec* the Supreme Court of Canada held that the notion of a "people" may include a group of population living within an existing state. See Supreme Court of Canada, *Reference Re Secession of Quebec*, 20 August 1998, ILM Vol. 37 (1998), 1340, at para. 124. Groups suffering systematic discrimination from their own government may infer such a right from the penultimate paragraph of Res. 2625 (XXV) on the right to self-determination. The scope of rights attributed to indigenous people and minorities is more ambiguous. See Tomuschat, *General Course on Public International Law*, at 251–3. For a discussion of a "federal right to self-determination", see Otto Kimminich, *A "Federal" Right to Self-Determination?*, in Modern Law of Self-Determination, at 83–100.

[201] For a similar finding with respect to peoples living within an existing federal state structure, see Supreme Court of Canada, *Reference Re Secession of Quebec*, para. 154.

decision-making is typically such a process. In the early stages of a mission, an administration may have legitimate reasons to defer the devolution of authority.[202] The very rationale of representative self-government may require a postponement of the transfer of authority until local leaders have been legitimised through elections. The moment when free and fair elections may be held depends in turn on the general security situation. Participatory self-determination is therefore not a fixed-term parameter, but a variable concept whose scope of application must be assessed in light of the circumstances of the specific situation.[203]

4.2.3.   Territorial integrity and political independence (Articles 2 (1) and 2 (4) of the UN Charter)

Articles 2 (1) and 2 (4) of the Charter incorporate the guarantee of the territorial integrity and political independence of states. Unlike Article 2 (7), this guarantee is not expressly subject to "the application of enforcement measures under Chapter VII". This implies that it serves as a limit on UN action in the field of peace and security.[204] The protection of the territorial integrity and political independence of state entities has direct implications for the exercise of governing functions by international administrations. It limits the authority of the administering power to change the geographic attribution or the title over the administered territory without the consent of the territorial sovereign.[205] Occupying powers are bound to respect this principle by virtue of Article 47 of the IV Geneva Convention. Articles 2 (1) and 2 (4) of the Charter extend this obligation to other international administering authorities.

The duty to respect the territorial integrity and political independence of states entails strict obligations. International administrations must, in particular, observe the distinction between the exercise of territorial jurisdiction and the possession of sovereignty.[206] Subject to the terms of their mandate, they are entitled to exercise jurisdiction and control over the administered territories. This may include a right to agree on

---

[202] It is too simplistic to require that a devolution of authority or the holding of elections should take place "as early as possible" as suggested by Salamun. See Salamun, *Democratic Governance in International Territorial Administration*, at 181–2.

[203] Concurring in result von Carlowitz, *UNMIK Lawmaking*, at 370–1. The extent to which this obligation has been observed in practice is examined below in Part IV, Chapter 15.

[204] See Irmscher, *Legal Framework of the Activities of the United Nations Interim Mission in Kosovo*, at 364.

[205] See also Gill, *Legal and Some Political Limitations on the Power of the UN Security Council*, at 85–6.

[206] See Lauterpacht, *Contemporary Practice*, at 411.

temporary border regimes or other acts of an international character. However, international administrators do not hold the powers of a legitimate sovereign, and are therefore precluded from making unilateral determinations concerning the permanent status of the administered territories. They may not cede the whole or part of the administered territory against the will of the territorial sovereign or the official representatives of the administered territory; nor are they entitled to determine the final political status of the administered entity. Such acts are related to the title over the territory and reserved to the ultimate decision of the legitimate representatives of the territory.

Articles 2 (1) and 2 (4) of the Charter show that states did not generally agree to delegate a power of disposition over territory to the UN by ratifying the Charter.[207] The only international organ which might, under exceptional circumstances, be authorised to certain acts affecting the territorial integrity of a state, is the Security Council. Judge Fitzmaurice denied such a right in his dissenting opinion in the *Namibia* case.[208] He noted:

> Even when acting under Chapter VII of the Charter itself, the Security Council has no power to abrogate or alter territorial rights, whether of sovereignty or administration... The Security Council might, after making the necessary determinations under Article 39... order the occupation of a country or piece of territory in order to restore peace and security, but it could not thereby, or as part of that operation, abrogate or alter territorial rights... It was to keep the peace, not change the world order, that the Security Council was set up.

However, this statement requires further clarification. One may indeed agree that it is beyond the authority of the Council to decree permanent territorial changes or losses of territory as part of a peace settlement.[209] But the prerogatives of peace and security may justify, at least, temporary

---

[207] See also Brownlie, *Principles of Public International Law*, at 163. ("It is doubtful if the United Nations has a 'capacity to convey title', in part because the Organization cannot assume the role of territorial sovereign.")

[208] See ICJ, *Legal Consequences for States of the Continued Presence of South Africa in Namibia notwithstanding Security Council Resolution 276 (1970)*, Dissenting Opinion by Judge Fitzmaurice, ICJ Rep. 1971, 16, at 280–3, 294–5.

[209] See also Tomuschat, *Peace Enforcement and Law Enforcement*, at 1750 and 1768. ("To enjoin a State to cede parts of its territory or to order the disintegration of a State, splitting it up into a number of sucessor States, would constitute a clear *excès de pouvoir*.") This view is supported by the practice of the Council which has so far shown reluctance to impose territorial changes or border adjustments on states or territories. In its Resolution 242 of 22 November 1967, the Council came close to legitimating some of Israel's territorial gains in the 1967 war, because it did not force Israel to withdraw from *all* territories occupied in the 1967 War. See Yehuda Z. Blum,

alterations of jurisdiction over territory against or without the will of a state.[210] The protection of territorial integrity must be balanced against the principle of self-determination and the authority of the Council to take enforcement action interfering with the domestic jurisdiction of states (Article 2 (7)) under Chapter VII.[211] It is, in particular, reasonable to argue that the Council may place a territory under transitional administration without consent of the territorial state, if this constitutes a means of protecting a specific group or people from oppression and subjugation (Kosovo).[212]

4.2.4. Article 1(3) in conjunction with Article 55

Another limitation of transitional administrations may be derived from a reading of Article 1 (3) of the Charter in conjunction with Article 55. Both provisions oblige the UN as an organisation to promote universal respect for, and observance of, human rights and fundamental freedoms. This mandate to promote and encourage respect for human rights was traditionally viewed as an obligation of states to respect human rights ("direct obligation"), while the UN was essentially conceived as an entity

---

Secure Boundaries and Middle East Peace in the Light of International Law and Practice (1971), at 72–4. But the Council placed the responsibility on the parties to adopt a "peaceful and accepted settlement". See para. 3 of SC Res. 242. A similar reticence characterises the Council's reaction to the annexation of Kuwait in 1991, which was not followed by any attempts to punish Iraq through conquest or territorial mutilation for its act of aggression. The measure which comes closest to a territorial settlement under Chapter VII is the establishment of the demarcation line between Iraq and Kuwait in the Final Report of the UN-created Demarcation Commission, which was accepted by the Council as being "final". See SC Res. 833 (1993). Finally, even in the case of Kosovo, which was accompanied by claims of secession, the Council refrained from enforcing permanent territorial changes on the FRY as a result of Belgrade's suppression of Kosovo Albanians. Instead, the Council opted for a model of substantial territorial autonomy, in order to prevent further civil war. In spring 2007, the Security Council failed to "endorse" Comprehensive Proposal for the Kosovo Status Settlement due to objections by Russia.

[210] See Crawford, *Creation of States*, 2nd edn (2006), at 552. See with respect to the demarcation of the boundary between Iraq and Kuwait also Brownlie, *Principles of Public International Law*, at 166.

[211] The guarantee of territorial integrity of a state is not sacrosanct under the Charter. See generally, Jarat Chopra and Thomas G. Weiss, *Sovereignty is No Longer Sacrosanct: Codifying Humanitarian Intervention,* Ethics & International Affairs, Vol. 6 (1994), 95.

[212] Note, however, that on most occasions, less intrusive measures such as minority protection, internal institutional reform, or measures of disarmament, reparation and individual criminal adjudication are at hand and better suited to serve the purpose of peacemaking than territorial segregation. For a particularly wide interpretation of the Council's powers, see Matheson, *United Nations Governance of Post-Conflict Societies*, at 85.

charged with the obligation to assist in the organisation and establishment of a state-centred framework of human rights protection through
the work of its human rights bodies ("indirect obligation").[213] This view
receives further support from the wording of Article 56, which implies
a self-commitment of states "to take joint and separate action in cooperation with the Organisation for the achievement of the purposes set
forth in Article 55".[214]

But the institutional practice of the organisation points in a different direction. The traditional conception of the Charter, according to
which states are the primary addressees of human rights obligations
under Articles 1 (3) and 55 of the Charter is open to challenge in the
context of the exercise of governing powers by the UN. Articles 1 (3) and
55 were drafted on the basis of the assumption that states are the exclusive holders of territorial jurisdiction. This narrow conception does
not make sense in situations where the UN exercises direct administering authority in the field of peace-maintenance. In these cases, the UN
itself is in a position of authority, which places it under the obligation
to ensure human rights protection.

This special role of the organisation must be taken into account in
the assessment of its institutional responsibilities. It is contradictory to
maintain that the UN has a mere indirect obligation to ensure respect
for human rights in circumstances where the organisation directly exercises the function of a state.[215] In such circumstances, the obligation to
promote and encourage respect for human rights turns from an indirect
obligation to assist in the realisation of human rights into a direct obligation to respect these rights. This shift in the scope of responsibility
may be based on the preamble and Article 1 (3) of the Charter, which
make it clear that the protection of human rights is designed to serve
as an objective standard of assessment governing every type of action
taken by the organisation.[216]

---

[213] This classical thinking is particularly well captured in a statement by
Schwarzenberger, who noted in 1964: "In the Charter, a clear distinction is drawn
between the promotion and encouragement for respect of human rights, and the
actual protection of these rights. The first one is entrusted to the United Nations. The
other remains the prerogative of each Member state." See Georg Schwarzenberger,
Power Politics: A Study of World Society (1964), at 462.

[214] See Article 56 of the Charter ("All Members pledge themselves...").

[215] Concurring in result, Mégret and Hoffmann, *UN as a Human Rights Violator?*, at 341.

[216] For a similar argument formulated in the context of reservations to human rights
treaties, see Thomas Giegerich, *Vorbehalte zu Menschenrechtsabkommen: Zulässigkeit,
Gültigkeit und Prüfungskompetenz von Vertragsgremien*, Zeitschrift für ausländisches
öffentliches Recht und Völkerrecht, Vol. 55 (1995), 713, at 743, 772.

4.3.   Limitations arising from the law of occupation

There are a number of other, non-Charter-based rules which impose restrictions on international territorial administrations. One body of law is the law of occupation. It has been noted earlier that the law of occupation is not particularly well suited to serve as a general legal framework for international territorial administrations,[217] since it is primarily designed to balance the competing interests of former parties to a conflict and is unable to address the deeper legality and legitimacy problems of territorial administration.[218] Nevertheless, the rules of the law occupation fulfil two principal functions within the context of international territorial administrations: they may serve as a point of reference for the legal problems arising in the initial phase of the deployment of transitional administrations in the area of order and security;[219] and they may provide some general guidelines for the regulation of the relations between international administrations and the local population in peacetime.[220]

4.3.1.   Applicability to international administrations

The application of the law of occupation to transitional administrations poses a number of legal problems. The first obstacle is the personal scope of application of Hague Rules and the Fourth Geneva Convention. Both treaties are directly applicable only to states. Additional arguments must be advanced to establish they apply equally to multinational administrations or UN administrations. Furthermore, due to its specific focus on specific state interests in an occupant-occupied relationship, the laws of occupation can only be transposed to a limited extent to international civil administrations, which are based on cooperation and gradual power-sharing between the administering power and the inhabitants of the local population.

---

[217] See above Part I, Chapter 4. For a full analysis of the applicability of international humanitarian law to international administrations, see Kolb, Porretto and Vité, *L'Application du Droit International Humanitaire et des Droits de l'Homme aux Organisations Internationales*.

[218] See Robert O. Weiner and Fionnuala Ni Aolain, *Beyond the Laws of War: Peacekeeping in Search of a Legal Framework*, Columbia Human Rights Law Review, Vol. 27 (1996), 293, at 352.

[219] See Sylvain Vité, *L'Applicabilité du Droit International de l'Occupation Militaire aux Actvités des Organisations Internationales*, International Review of the Red Cross, Vol. 86 (2004), 9, at 30. See also Roberts, *What is Military Occupation?*, at 301.

[220] See Irmscher, *Legal Framework of the Activities of the United Nations Interim Mission in Kosovo*, at 387. See also Vité, *L'Applicabilité du Droit International de l'Occupation Militaire*, at 31.

4.3.1.1. Ratione personae

It is relatively well established today that both states and other international entities must abide by and are protected in turn by the principles of international humanitarian law, provided that these rules can be validly transposed to them.[221] This practice is of special significance in the context of the applicability of the law of occupation to international territorial administrations.

4.3.1.1.1. Applicability of humanitarian law to UN forces

There is widespread agreement that UN peacekeepers must observe standards of international humanitarian law, although the UN is not a party to the 1907 Hague and 1949 Geneva Conventions.[222] This position was officially recognised by the UN in the 1999 Secretary General's Bulletin on the Observance by United Nations Forces of International Humanitarian Law, in which the UN conceded that the core rules of the customary law of armed conflict apply to enforcement operations.[223] The same understanding is reflected in Article 28 of the "Model Agreement Between the United Nations and Member States Contributing Personnel and Equipment to United Nations Peacekeeping Operations" which formulates the general principle that any UN "peacekeeping operation shall observe and respect the principles and spirit of the general international conventions applicable to conduct of military personnel", including "the four Geneva

---

[221] See Paolo Benvenuti, The Implementation of International Humanitarian Law in the Framework of UN Peacekeeping, in Law in Humanitarian Crises: How Can International Humanitarian Law Be Made Effective in Armed Conflicts? (1995), 114, at 116.

[222] Marten Zwanenburg, Accountability of Peace Support Operations (2005), at 184–93; Kelly, Restoring and Maintaining Order, at 176; Seyersted, United Nations Forces, at 297–8; Irmscher, Legal Framework of the Activities of the United Nations Interim Mission in Kosovo, at 376. This position has been defended by the Institut de Droit International since the early 1970s. See Institut de Droit International, Resolution, Conditions of Application of Humanitarian Rules of Armed Conflict to Hostilities in which United Nations Forces may be Engaged, Annuaire Institut de Droit International 54 (II) (1971), at 465. ("[T]he humanitarian rules of the law of armed conflict apply to the United Nations as of right, and they must be complied with in all circumstances by United Nations Forces which are engaged in hostilities. The rules referred to in the preceding paragraph include in particular: a. the rules pertaining to the conduct of hostilities in general...; b. the rules contained in the Geneva Conventions of August 12, 1949; c. the rules which aim at protecting civilians and property.")

[223] See UN Secretary's Bulletin on the Observance by United Nations Forces of International Humanitarian Law, Vol. 38 (2000), at 1656. See also SC Res. 1327 of 13 November 2000.

Conventions of 12 August 1949 and their Additional Protocols of 8 June 1977".[224]

4.3.1.1.2. *Closing the gap in the context of occupation*

The principle that UN peace operations are bound to respect international humanitarian law is not strictly limited to the conduct of hostilities. It may be extended to the post-conflict phase, in particular, to situations in which UN actors exercise effective control on foreign territory. Several factors indicate that UN established or UN authorised entities may, in such situations, be obliged to comply with the standards of Section III of the Hague Regulations and the Fourth Geneva Convention.[225]

First, as an actor of international law, the UN is generally bound to observe customary international law.[226] The organisation was founded on the basis of this understanding, and it is reflected in the preamble of the UN Charter, which emphasises the determination of the peoples of the UN "to establish conditions under which justice and respect for the obligations arising from treaties and *other sources of international law* can be maintained".[227] UN actors may therefore be compelled to observe customary standards of the law of occupation within their practice.[228]

Secondly, the fact that the UN enjoys independent legal personality as an actor of international law does not shield it from the applicability of the laws of war. The law of occupation is not directed towards a specific addressee, but is based on the exercise of factual control over

---

[224] See Model Agreement between the United Nations and Member States Contributing Personnel and Equipment to United Nations Peace Operations, Annex to Report of the Secretary-General to the General Assembly, A/64/185 of 23 May 1991.

[225] Concurring Irmscher, *Legal Framework of the Activities of the United Nations Interim Mission in Kosovo*, at 376.

[226] This obligation is, however, subject to derogation by more specific determinations such as Chapter VII. See Article 103 of the Charter.

[227] See the preamble of the UN Charter: "We, the peoples of the United Nations, determined... to establish conditions under which justice and respect for the obligations arising from treaties and *other sources of international law* can be maintained" (emphasis added). See also Article 24 (2).

[228] Note that the binding nature of the Hague Regulations as customary law was reaffirmed by the ICJ in the Nuclear Weapons Advisory Opinion. See ICJ, *Legality of the Threat or Use of Nuclear Weapons*, Advisory Opinion, ICJ Rep. 1996, 256, para. 75.

people.[229] The factual character of occupation is reflected in Article 42 of the Hague Regulations[230] and, in the drafting history,[231] Article 4[232] and Article 47 of the IV Geneva Convention[233]. The ICTY adhered to this position when reaffirming that the rules of international humanitarian law apply even to non-state actors which exercise *de facto* control over a territory.[234] The ICJ reiterated this factual character in the *Case concerning Armed Activities on the Territory of the Congo*.[235] UN forces may, at least, be bound to respect the basic principles and spirit of the rules of occupation when they exercise command and control over a territory.

A similar reasoning applies in relation to multinational forces acting under independent control. These forces cannot escape their responsibilities under the laws of occupation law by acting jointly under the

---

[229] This position is taken by the ICRC Commentary on the Fourth Geneva Convention. See Commentary, (IV) Geneva Convention relative to the protection of Civilian Persons in Time of War (J. Pictet ed., 1958), at 60. See also Benvenisti, *International Law of Occupation*, Preface, at xvi. ("[T]he law of occupation should apply to any case of 'effective control of a power (be it one or more states or an international organization, such as the United Nations) over a territory to which that power has no sovereign title, without the volition of the sovereign of that territory'.")

[230] Territory is considered to be occupied when it is "actually" placed under the authority of a hostile army.

[231] The *travaux préparatoires* of the Fourth Geneva Convention indicate that the conventions are applicable "in cases of occupation of territories in the absence of any state of war". See Report on the Work of the Conference of Government Experts for the Study of the Conventions for the Protection of War Victims, Geneva, 14–26 April 1948, at 8.

[232] See also ICTY, Appeals Chamber, *Prosecutor v. Tadic*, Case No. IT-94-1-A (1999), para. 168. ("Article 4 of Geneva Convention, if interpreted in the light of its object and purpose, is directed to the protection of civilians to the maximum extent possible. It therefore does not make its applicability dependent on formal bonds and purely legal relations. Its primary purpose is to ensure the safeguards afforded by the Convention to those civilians who do not enjoy the diplomatic protection, and correlatively are not subject to the allegiance and control of the State in whose hands they may find themselves. In granting this protection, Article 4 intends to look at the substance of relations, not their legal characterisation as such.") For an elaboration, see also ICTY, Trial Chamber, *Prosecutor v. Naletilic and Martinovic*, Judgment of 31 March 2003, Case No. IT-98-34-T, para. 218.

[233] Article 47 of the Fourth Geneva Convention states that "protected persons who are in occupied territory shall not be deprived, *in any case or in any manner whatsoever, of the benefits of the Convention by any change introduced*, as the result of the occupation of a territory, into the institutions or authorities of the occupied territories and the Occupying Power" (emphasis added).

[234] See ICTY, Appeals Chamber, *Tadic*, para. 168, noting that the Convention "does not make its applicability dependent on formal bonds and purely legal relations".

[235] See ICJ, *Case concerning Armed Armed Activities on the Territory of the Congo*, 19 December 2005, paras. 172–3. The ICJ examined whether "the said authority was *in fact* established and exercised" (emphasis added).

umbrella of the UN or within the framework of a multinational administration rather than individually. They may be obliged to comply with international humanitarian law if they find themselves in a situation of occupation.[236]

4.3.1.2.   Ratione materiae

Additional problems arise, however, from the fact that international territorial administrations do not typically fit within the framework of traditional military occupations.

4.3.1.2.1.   Differences between territorial administrations and classical occupying powers

International territorial administrations usually differ from classical occupying powers in two respects: they are not belligerents or parties to the conflict and they operate in a grey area "between the absence of war and the attainment of peace".[237] This makes it difficult to apply the rules of occupation directly to their conduct.[238]

The application of the Hague Regulations is based on the assumption of the existence of a military occupation in an ongoing conflict and the establishment and exercise of authority by a state over the armed forces of its rival.[239] This follows from the title of the section dealing with occupation ("Military Authority Over the Territory of the Hostile State") and the wording of Article 42 which states that "[t]erritory is occupied when it is actually placed under the authority of the hostile army". These requirements limit the applicability of the Hague law to the exercise of governing responsibilities by international entities in a post-conflict environment.

The Fourth Geneva Convention offers more flexibility. Article 2 of the Convention specifies that the "Convention shall also apply to all cases of partial or total occupation of the territory of a High Contracting Party,

---

[236] See also Benvenisti, *International Law of Occupation*, Preface, at xvi.

[237] See Mégret and Hoffmann, *UN as a Human Rights Violator*, at 331.

[238] See Dinstein, *Legislation under Article 43 of the Hague Regulations*, at 2. See also Irmscher, *Legal Framework of the Activities of the United Nations Interim Mission in Kosovo*, at 383.

[239] In the *Case concerning Armed Activities on the Territory of the Congo*, the ICJ held that "occupation extends only to the territory where such authority has been established and can be exercised". *Ibid.*, para. 172. The Court examined whether the relevant forces "were not only stationed in particular locations" but also "whether they had substituted their own authority for that of" of the territorial sovereign. *Ibid.*, para. 173. See also ICTY, *Prosecutor v. Naletilic and Martinovic*, Case No. IT-98-34-T, para. 218.

even if the said occupation meets with no armed resistance". This statement suggests that the Convention may govern peacetime occupations.
Furthermore, its applicability depends essentially on the factual exercise
of authority over territory. This is, in particular, reflected in Article 4
of the Fourth Geneva Convention, which states that the Convention
shall protect all persons "who at a given moment and in any manner
whatsoever, find themselves, in case of a conflict or occupation, *in the
hands of* a Party to the conflict or Occupying Power of which they are
not nationals".[240] It has therefore been argued in legal doctrine that
the regime of the Convention applies to UN peace operations involving
military forces, such as the UN engagements in Congo, Cambodia and
Somalia.[241]

This theory contrasts, however, with international legal practice. The
UN itself has systematically refrained from regarding itself as a (non-
belligerent) occupying power. State practice appears to be divided. While
Australian peacekeepers considered themselves formally bound by the
laws of the Convention in UN peace operations in Somalia[242] and East
Timor,[243] other states such as the US refused officially to acknowledge the applicability of the Convention.[244] Similar problems arose in
the context of Iraq, where some troop-contributing states such as the
Netherlands refused to recognise their status as occupying powers even

---

[240] Emphasis added. See also ICTY, *Prosecutor* v. *Naletilic and Martinovic*, Case No. IT-98-34-T,
Judgment of 31 March 2003, para. 221.
[241] See Kelly, *Restoring and Maintaining Order*, at 178. Australia stated at the Meeting of the
Contracting Parties to the Geneva Convention in 1998 that "the Fourth Geneva
Convention is a good model to use in peace operations involving deployment without
consent as it is geared to take account of the exigencies of attempting to administer
or restore order in war-like conditions as opposed to a peace time human rights
regime. Australian troops in Somalia found this to be the case when they were
deployed into, and given responsibility for, the Bay province during Operation Restore
Hope in 1993. Following a determination that the Fourth Convention applied to that
intervention, the Australian force relied on the Convention to provide answers to,
and a framework for, many initiatives". See Zwanenburg, *Accountability of Peace Support
Operations*, at 198.
[242] See Kelly, *Restoring and Maintaining Order*, at 17, 29–31, 37.
[243] See Kelly *et al.*, *Legal Aspects of Australia's Involvement in the International Force for East
Timor*, at 104.
[244] For the disputes about the applicability of the laws of occupation in the case of Iraq,
see above Part II, Chapter 9. Critical also Zwanenburg, *Accountability of Peace Support
Operations*, at 198–9, who makes reference to two factors: a 1997 decision of a Belgian
Military Court which refused to recognise the applicability of the Fourth Geneva
Convention to UNOSOM II, and the fact that NATO troop did not consider the laws of
occupation applicable to KFOR.

though they exercised control over Iraqi territory by the presence of their troops.[245]

Moreover, the text of the Fourth Geneva Convention envisages occupation as a short-term measure which shall cease to apply one year after the general close of military operations[246] or, at least, when "most of the governmental and administrative duties carried out at one time by the occupying power ha[ve] been handed over to the authorities of the occupied territory".[247] This restriction limits the formal application of the Convention to long-term administrations such as in Kosovo or consensual co-governance missions.

Finally, it is generally difficult to extend the ambit of the law of occupation from the area of military enforcement to civil administration. UN governance missions and undertakings in civil administration serve different purposes than regimes of military occupation.[248] Such engagements share, in particular, two characteristics which distinguish them from classical military occupations: they are typically pacific in nature (e.g. designed to secure peace through peaceful means) and aimed at the furtherance of the rights of the inhabitants of the territory or established upon their request. These features do not fit well into the traditional scope of application of the law of occupation. The regime of the Fourth Geneva Convention is geared towards military presences. Article 2 (2) of extends the scope of the Convention to occupying powers meeting no "armed resistance". Civilian administrations, by contrast, are typically neither designed nor equipped to overcome "armed resistance".[249] This makes it difficult to bring them directly into the ambit of the law of occupation. Such administrations fail to meet the attributes of "belligerent" occupation in particular if they operate independently of a military presence[250] or with the consent of the territorial state.[251]

---

[245] Kelly, *Iraq and the Law of Occupation*, at 132.

[246] See Article 6 (3) of the IV Geneva Convention.

[247] See Roberts, *What is Military Occupation?*, at 272.

[248] Some missions are not all related to conflict situations. Other operations are situated in a post-conflict environment, but pursue rationales which are different from the maintenance of a balance of power among former belligerents or the preservation of security interests. See above Part II, Chapter 10.

[249] See also Sassòli, *Legislation and Maintenance of Public Order*, at 688–9.

[250] *Ibid.*, at 689–90. Critically also Vité, *L'Applicabilité du Droit International de l'Occupation Militaire*, at 26.

[251] See also Zwanenburg, *Accountability of Peace Support Opetations*, at 196.

4.3.1.2.2. Application of the laws of occupation by way of analogy

It is nevertheless plausible to argue that some provisions of the Hague and the Geneva law may apply by way of analogy to certain territorial administrations.[252] The applicability of the rules of the law of occupation may be dissociated from the status of a party to a conflict or actual engagement in an activity of armed combat.[253] At the heart of the notion of occupation is the idea that foreign actors exercise "some kind of domination or authority over inhabited territory outside the accepted international frontiers of their State and its dependencies" without a formal title to do so.[254] The purpose of the laws of occupation is to provide a supplementary legal regime for such cases, which establishes a minimal normative framework for the maintenance of law and order and the protection of individuals.

The very same type of conflict arises in two situations which occur frequently in the context of transitional administration. These are cases where international authorities assume responsibility for the maintenance of public order and security in a legal vacuum;[255] and cases where they come to exercise an extensive range of public responsibilities within the foreign territory, which are not adequately covered by the original arrangement authorising their engagement. One may argue that some of the limitations of the laws of occupation should apply by way of analogy in both cases.[256]

4.3.1.2.2.a. Power vacuums

The first *lacuna* arises in situations in which international authorities assume *de facto* control over matters of public order and safety in cases where state authorities are absent or have collapsed.[257] This situation

---

[252] For a discussion, see also Sassòli, *Legislation and Maintenance of Public Order*, at 691.

[253] See Kelly, *Restoring and Maintaining Order*, at 178.

[254] See Roberts, *What is Military Occupation?*, at 300.

[255] See Michael J. Kelly, *Legitimacy and the Public Security Function*, in Policing the New World Disorder (R. Oakley, M. Dziedzic and E. Goldberg eds., 1998), at 399. Kelly notes that the law of occupation applies if "the force present is not just passing through, is not engaged in actual combat, and is, in effect, the authority capable of exercising control over the civilian population or if any remaining authority requires the approval or sanction of the force to operate".

[256] This finding is not in contradiction to existing state practice. States have often refused to accept the applicability of the law of occupation, in order to avoid positive obligations for the restoration of order in short situations of transition. But this argument loses its validity if international actors actually exercise exclusive public authority on a longer a term.

[257] For a discussion, see also Sassòli, *Legislation and Maintenance of Public Order*, at 692.

existed, *inter alia*, in Congo, Somalia and in the early phase of the East Timor intervention, when INTERFET took over control over Indonesian militia forces. In each case, UN-deployed military forces exercised control over foreign citizens in the absence of displaced local civil authorities. The protection of domestic actors requires that the standards of the Hague Regulations and the Fourth Geneva Convention apply under such circumstances irrespective of whether the international force is a party to the conflict or involved in armed hostilities. There is, in particular, a need to apply the humanitarian provisions of the Convention, which contain a nucleus of fundamental rights (*"ordre public humanitaire"*[258]) in cases where human rights obligations might be suspended.

The idea that international authorities are obliged to maintain basic standards of the rule of law is a corollary of an expanding concept of intervention. It has been tentatively endorsed by the UN. When drawing its lessons from Somalia, where UN forces encountered widespread criticism for their arbitrary detention practice, the organisation suggested that the Fourth Geneva Convention "could supply adequate guidelines for regulation relations between peacekeeping troops and the local population".[259]

This line of thought applies with equal force to transitional administrations.[260] The obligations under the laws of occupation are, by their very nature, applicable to the military contingents of international administrations. They may also be extended to international civilian authorities that exercise control over public order and safety in cooperation with a military presence. The eighth paragraph of the Preamble to the Fourth Hague Convention of 1907 (the so-called Martens clause), Common Article 3 to the Geneva Conventions and Article 158, paragraph 5 of the Fourth Geneva Convention[261] indicate that the customary standards of the laws of occupation provide a non-derogable framework of protection against the exercise of public authority in situations of emergency. This legal framework may be transposed to international civilian actors

[258] See Robert Kolb, *Ius in Bello: Le Droit International des Conflits Armés* (2003), at 79.
[259] See United Nations, *The Comprehensive Report on Lessons Learned from the United Nations Operation in Somalia (UNOSOM)*, April 19902–March 1995 (1995), at 57.
[260] See also Vité, *L'Applicabilité du Droit International de l'Occupation Militaire*, at 30.
[261] It reads: "The denunciation [of the Convention] shall have effect only in respect of the denouncing Power. It shall in no way impair the obligations which the Parties to the conflict shall remain bound to fulfil by virtue of the principles of the law of nations, as they result from the usages established among civilized peoples, from the laws of humanity and the dictates of public science."

who share responsibilities for public order and security with military entities.[262]

4.3.1.2.2.b.   *Peacetime occupation by default*

Another situation in which the laws of occupation may be applied by analogy is the area of peacetime occupation. In this context, the provisions of the Hague law and the Geneva law may serve as a supplementary body of law which comes into play when international authorities exercise an extensive range of exclusive powers over the citizens of the host territory which are not adequately covered by the original arrangement under which these authorities intervened.[263] The law of occupation provides a minimum level of safeguards for the state and its inhabitants in this situation.

The argument is simple. An international presence is typically not governed by the standards of occupation if its activities are validated by an agreement with the host state or a title to exercise these powers on foreign soil. The laws of occupation are under these circumstances superseded by the provisions of the respective arrangement or title. However, if the international authority exceeds the framework of powers entrusted to it, its presence takes on an "element of extraneous determination contrary to the intentions of the legitimate government" which justifies recourse to the prohibitions of the international law of occupation.

Both the Hague Rules and the Fourth Geneva Convention serve here as a complementary normative framework for the exercise of public authority,[264] triggered by contact with the institutions and inhabitants of the host state.

4.3.2.   Scope of obligations

The scope of obligations of international administrations under the law of occupation varies.

---

[262] Otherwise, military authorities could absolve themselves from responsibility by delegating their executive powers to international civilian authorities. Concurring Vité, *L'Applicabilité du Droit International de l'Occupation Militaire*, at 30.

[263] See von Carlowitz, *UNMK Lawmaking*, at 364. See also Roberts, *What is Military Occupation?*, at 300.

[264] For a similar theory, see Irmscher, *Legal Framework of the Activities of the United Nations Interim Mission in Kosovo*, at 384–5.

4.3.2.1. Power vacuums

If international humanitarian law operates in an emergency situation, it fulfils the function of a substitute body of law for the organisation of relations between international administering bodies and domestic actors. Two kinds of provisions are of relevance in this situation: the humanitarian duties of the intervening power[265] and the fiduciary nature of its authority. According to their *ratio legis*, both sets of rules apply by analogy irrespective of whether the ruling authority is a state entity or an international organisation.

The core of the humanitarian provisions of the law of occupation is enshrined in Part II ("General Protection of Populations Against Certain Consequences of War") and Sections I and III of Part III ("Status and Treatment of Protected Persons") of the Fourth Geneva Convention. In particular, the rights and obligations under Articles 46 and 50 of the Hague Rules and Articles 27–33 and 66–77 of the Fourth Geneva Convention may be considered as a minimum framework of protection against arbitrary conduct by international authorities, especially in the field of the rule of law and detention.[266] These requirements are complemented by provisions governing the protection and use of public property (Article 55 and 56 of the Hague Rules, Article 55 of the Fourth Geneva Convention) and the maintenance of public order (Article 64 of the Fourth Geneva Convention).

Some more caution is required in relation to the applicability of the positive obligations under the law of occupation, including the duty to restore and ensure public order and civil life, as far as possible (Article 43 of the Hague Regulations). The applicability of these obligations has generally been denied by states within the context of peace support operations.[267] Such obligations appear to require a longer-term engagement in order to come into play.

4.3.2.2. Under peacetime occupation

The circumstances are slightly different in the situation of peacetime occupation. The laws of occupation collide here with more specific rights

---

[265] For a discussion, see Vité, *L'Applicabilité du Droit International de l'Occupation Militaire*, at 31.

[266] The applicability of Section II ("Aliens Within the Territory of a Party to the Conflict") of Part III of the Fourth Geneva Convention is not fully excluded, but is less relevant in the context of international territorial administration.

[267] For further reference, see Zwanenburg, *Accountability of Peace Support Operations*, at 198–9.

and obligations under peace arrangements (e.g. provisions under the Paris or Dayton Accords or Security Council Resolutions 1244 (1999) and 1272 (1999)).[268] In this context, the Hague law and the Geneva Convention may provide guidance only in a subsidiary fashion, namely as supplementary legal framework governing exercises of power not provided for under the arrangement legitimating the presence of an international administration.[269]

Some indication can be inferred from the permanent obligations of occupants under Article 6 of the Fourth Geneva Convention which provides that any "Occupying Power shall be bound, for the duration of the occupation, to the extent such Power exercises the function of government in such territory, by the provisions of the following Articles of the... Convention: 1 to 12, 27, 29 to 34, 47, 49, 51, 52, 53, 59, 61 to 77, 143". In cases where the territorial arrangement is silent or lacking, international administrations may be bound to respect core rules of fiduciary territorial administration, such as the principle that administration does not confer title over the territory, or the rule that the occupant may use public property only in a capacity as usufructuary.[270]

Moreover, the framework of the law of occupation may provide useful guidance on the scope of lawmaking powers. Analogies to the Hague and Geneva law may indicate some substantial limitations in the exercise of public authority, such as restrictions in the field of institutional or law reform (Article 43 of the Hague Regulations, Article 47 of the Fourth Geneva Convention) or financial and tax matters (Article 48 and 49 of the Hague Regulations).[271]

4.3.3. Deficiencies

Despite their undeniable merits, the laws of occupation present neither a conclusive, nor an ideal framework for the regulation of international territorial administrations. Some of the prohibitions may be superseded by more specific authorisations pronounced in a treaty arrangement or

---

[268] For a survey of the legal regime of peacetime occupations, see above Part I, Chapter 4.

[269] For a compilation of views, see Irmscher, *Legal Framework of the Activities of the United Nations Interim Mission in Kosovo*, at 380–3.

[270] See, for instance, Article 55 of the Hague Regulations.

[271] For an analysis in relation to UNMIK, see Irmscher, *Legal Framework of the Activities of the United Nations Interim Mission in Kosovo*, at 388. For a more restrictive view, see Vité, *L'Applicabilité du Droit International de l'Occupation Militaire*, at 32. ("D'autres règles, en revanche, posent problème. Les articles articles 48, 49 et 51, relatifs aux prélèvements d'impôts et de taxes, semblent en effet difficilement applicables sans un mandat spécifique en ce sens de la part du Conseil de sécurité.")

a Security Council Resolution.[272] Moreover, in the context of long-term processes of governance or civil administration, the provisions of the law of occupation may be part of the problem rather than part of the solution.[273] The laws of occupation follow a strict top-down approach.[274] They fail, in particular, to deal adequately with the imperative of the gradual devolution of power to domestic actors. It is therefore appropriate to examine the rights and obligations of international administrations from the perspective of a further body of law: international human rights law.

4.4. Universally recognised human rights standards

International human rights law offers, in many ways, a more modern and a more nuanced framework for the conduct of international administrations than international humanitarian law.[275]

The main difference between these bodies of law is that human rights law addresses the limitation and scope of public authority directly from the perspective of individual and group rights, whereas international humanitarian law continues to view public authority, at least partly, through the lens of competing state interests. Human rights law, by contrast, is more origin-neutral, in that it may be directed against domestic authorities and entities acting in the place of domestic authorities. This conceptual difference provides human rights law with a better normative foundation to deal with two phenomena: civil administrations and long-term processes of territorial governance.

The main doctrinal problem is the lack of a unified legal theory which renders human rights guarantees directly applicable to all entities exercising public authority on a given territory. There is a basic assumption that international organisations or multinational administrations may be subject to different treatment than state actors in the exercise of public authority due to their status as independent legal persons and the necessity to preserve the independence and efficient performance of

---

[272] Concurring Vité, L'Applicabilité du Droit International de l'Occupation Militaire, at 32. Obligations arising under the Hague Rules and the Fourth Geneva Convention may be overridden by colliding responsibilities under a Chapter VII mandate pronounced by the Security Council.

[273] For an excellent critique, see Mégret and Hoffmann, UN as a Human Rights Violator?, at 330–2.

[274] See von Carlowitz, UNMIK Lawmaking, at 374.

[275] See also Mégret and Hoffmann, UN as a Human Rights Violator?, at 320; Jan Klabbers, Redemption Song? Human Rights Versus Community-building in East Timor, Leiden Journal of International Law, Vol. 16 (2003), 367–76.

their functions.[276] Moreover, the applicability of international human rights treaty law raises problems on a practical level, since the respective conventions are typically not open to accession by international organisations.

Yet, there is strong evidence that human rights law may and should, in particular, apply to the activity of international administrations.[277] There is, first, a functional argument. If international actors exercise the powers of the state in territories, either exclusively or with final decision-making authority in specific areas, they are public authorities and may in this capacity be bound to comply with specific human rights obligations towards the inhabitants of the administered territory, irrespective of their international legal personality.[278] This argument is particularly persuasive in light of the universal and indivisible nature of fundamental rights and freedoms. If human rights are universal rights inherent in the people and independent of the state, they may be conceived as minimum guarantees of protection applicable to any entity exercising direct public authority towards individuals.

4.4.1. Applicability to international administrations

Human rights obligations may apply to international administrations on the basis of four legal constructions: institutional (self-) commitment, the crystallisation of human rights law as customary law, the concept of functional duality and the applicability of human rights treaty obligations on the basis of the exercise of effective control over territory.

---

[276] The decision of the European Commission for Human Rights in the *Hess* case seems to indicate that joint actions undertaken by a number of states are not subject to the control of the organs of the Convention, if some of the participating states are not party to the Convention. See European Commission on Human Rights, *Hess v. Great Britain*, Application No. 6231/73, Decisions and Reports, Vol. 2, at 72.

[277] See generally Wilde, *International territorial administration and human rights*, at 167; see also Abraham, *The Sins of Saviour*.

[278] See European Commission for Democracy Through Law, *Opinion on Human Rights in Kosovo*, para. 91. ("It is worth underlining at the outset that the main obstacle to setting up a mechanism of review of UNMIK and KFOR is their character as international organizations... Nevertheless, it must be recalled that in Kosovo UNMIK and KFOR carry out tasks which are certainly more similar to those of a State administration than those of an international organization proper. It is unconceivable and incompatible with the principles of democracy, the rule of law and respect for human rights that they could act as State authorities and be exempted from any independent legal review.")

4.4.1.1. Institutional (self-)commitment

The UN has traditionally been inclined to apply human rights obligations to administered territory by way of an express mandate or treaty arrangement.[279]

4.4.1.1.1. Practice

This practice started in the post-war era, when the organisation charged UN-appointed administrators with a mandate to ensure that local actors act in conformity with human rights standards. The Statute of the Free Territory of Trieste, for example, vested the Governor of the Territory with the responsibility to "supervise" the observance of the Statute, including the protection of the basic rights of the inhabitants, and the duty to ensure that public order and security were maintained by the Government of the Territory in accordance with the Statute, the Constitution and the laws of the territory.[280] This treaty arrangement subjected the acts of local authorities to human rights scrutiny.

The Trusteeship proposal for a Statute for the City of Jerusalem was even more explicit. It contained a very detailed catalogue of human rights obligations, modelled after the Universal Declaration on Human Rights.[281] These rights were declared applicable to "all persons" in the territory[282] and were given priority over "any legislation or administrative act".[283] Moreover, the Statute reaffirmed that the Universal Declaration of Human Rights should "be accepted as a standard of achievement for the City",[284] in anticipation of the "proposed United Nations Covenant of Human Rights", which should "enter into force also in the City".[285]

The Agreement between the Republic of Indonesia and the Kingdom of the Netherlands concerning West New Guinea (West Irian) went one step further in the recognition of the applicability of human rights. The arrangement therefore left no doubt that the UN administration itself was the addressee of human rights obligations.[286] It recognised

---

[279] For a discussion, see also De Wet, *Chapter VII Powers of the United Nations Security Council*, at 319–26.

[280] See Article 17 of the Statute of the Free Territory of Trieste.

[281] See Article 9 of the proposed Statute for the City of Jerusalem, adopted by the Trusteeship Council on 4 April 1950.

[282] See *ibid.*, Article 9, paras. 1–14.   [283] See *ibid.*, Article 29, para. 1.

[284] See *ibid.*, Article 9, para. 15.   [285] See *ibid.*, Article 9, para. 16.

[286] But the list of obligations assumed by the UN fell far short of meeting the standards set by the Universal Declaration on Human Rights and the ICCPR.

that the rights acquired by the inhabitants before the transfer of the territory to the UN would continue to apply in relation to UNTEA. UNTEA was expressly bound to guarantee "the rights of free speech, freedom of movement and of assembly of the inhabitants of the area" as well as "existing Netherlands commitments in respect of concessions and property rights".[287]

The technique of institutional (self-)commitment was later revived in the 1990s. The most prominent examples are UNMIK and UNTAET. Both administrations were charged by the Security Council with the mandate to protect and promote human rights.[288] This mandate is expressly enshrined in Section 11 of Security Council Resolution 1244 (1999) which provides that "the main responsibilities of the international civil presence... will include protecting and promoting human rights",[289] including a duty to ensure the "safe and unimpeded return of all refugees and displaced persons".[290] The corresponding obligation of UNTAET may be founded upon paragraph 3 of Security Council Resolution 1272 (1999)[291] which refers to Part IV of the Report of the Secretary-General of 4 October 1999.[292] Similar mandates may be found in Paris Accords[293] and the Dayton Peace Agreement.[294]

In some cases, these general references to human rights law were translated into specific human rights commitments for domestic holders of public authority. One of the best examples is UNMIK, which adopted several regulations with detailed human rights obligations[295]

---

[287] See Article XXII of the Agreement.

[288] SC Res. 1483 (2003) was drafted in more cautious terms. It stated that the Coalition should administer Iraq "in accordance with the Charter of the United Nations". This clause may, however, be read as an implicit reference to Articles 1(3) and 55 of the Charter. See also De Wet, *Chapter VII Powers of the United Nations Security Council*, at 321.

[289] See para. 11 j) of SC Res. 1244 (1999).   [290] See *ibid.*, para. 11 k).

[291] Para. 3 of SC Res. 1272 (1999) provides that "UNTAET shall have the objectives and a structure along the lines set out in part IV of the report of the Secretary-General".

[292] Paragraph 29 h) of the Report of the Secretary-General of 4 October 1999 notes that UNTAET will have the objective to "ensure the establishment and maintenance of the rule of law and to promote and protect human rights". See UN Doc. S/1999/1024, p. 7.

[293] See Articles 16 and 19 of the Agreement on the Political Settlement of the Cambodia Conflict and Annex 1, Section 1.

[294] See Article II of Annex 4 to the Dayton Agreement and Annex 7.

[295] Regulation No. 54/2000 stated that all persons undertaking public authority or holding public office in Kosovo shall observe internationally recognised human rights standards and shall not discriminate against any person on any ground. Regulation No. 59/2000 set out the prohibition on discrimination, abolished capital punishment and clarified lists of texts reflecting internationally recognised human rights standards, including the ECHR, the ICCPR, the Convention on the Elimination of All

and concluded two agreements with the Council of Europe in June 2004 in order to ensure compliance with two Council of Europe Conventions, namely the Framework Convention for the Protection of National Minorities[296] and the Anti-Torture Convention.[297]

Finally, as a result of efforts of the Secretary-General to "mainstream" international human rights standards in all areas of UN involvement, the UN began to incorporate "human rights components" into peacekeeping operations. This is reflected in a Memorandum of Understanding between the High Commissioner for Human Rights and the Department of Peacekeeping Operations,[298] which calls for the establishment of internal monitoring mechanisms under the authority of Special Representatives of the Secretary-General, in order to "ensure a comprehensive approach to human rights, in accordance with international standards".[299]

4.4.1.1.2. Disadvantages

Nevertheless, the technique of self-commitment has some disadvantages. One of its main deficits lies in its imprecision.[300] Security Council mandates or human rights clauses in peace arrangements often leave

Forms of Racial Discrimination and the UN Convention Against Torture and the International Convention on the Rights of the Child. Finally, the Constitutional Framework for Provisional Self Government provided that domestic Provisional Institutions of Self-Government shall "observe and ensure internationally recognized human rights and fundamental freedoms" including those set out in UNMIK Regulation No. 59/2000.

[296] See Agreement between the United Nations Interim Administration in Kosovo (UNMIK) and the Council of Europe on technical arrangements related to the Framework Convention for the Protection of National Minorities, approved by the Committee of Ministers of the Council of Europe at its 890th meeting on 30 June 2004. UNMIK submitted its first report in June 2005. See Report submitted by the United Nations Interim Administration in Kosovo (UNMIK) pursuant to Article 2 (2) of the Agreement between UNMIK and the Council of Europe related to the Framework Convention for the Protection of National Minorities, Doc. ACFC(2005)003, 2 June 2005.

[297] See Agreement between the United Nations Interim Administration in Kosovo (UNMIK) and the Council of Europe on technical arrangements related to the European Convention for the Prevention of Torture and Inhuman or Degrading Treatment or Punishment, approved by the Committee of Ministers of the Council of Europe at its 890th meeting on 30 June 2004.

[298] See Memorandum of Understanding Between the Office of the High Commissioner for Human Rights and the Department of Peacekeeping Operations of 5 November 1999, at www.unhcr.ch/html/menu2/4/mou_dpko.htm.

[299] See Article B (5) of the Memorandum of Understanding.

[300] See also Mégret and Hoffmann, UN as a Human Rights Violator?, at 334.

considerable ambiguity as to the scope of obligations which international territorial administrations are bound to uphold.

Apart from the UNTEA arrangement, early instruments failed to clarify whether these standards applied to the UN itself. The same ambiguity arose in the context of UNMIK and UNTEAT. Both administrations officially reaffirmed the applicability of human rights standards in their first regulations. They noted that "in exercising their functions, all persons undertaking public duties or holding public office [in the respective territories] shall observe international human rights standards",[301] as defined in a vast list of treaties, including the Universal Declaration on Human Rights, the two Covenants and their Protocols and the Convention on the Elimination of All Forms of Racial Discrimination. But the regulations failed expressly to render these obligations applicable to the UN transitional administrations.[302] This failure created confusion about the scope of human rights obligations of UNMIK and UNTEAT[303] in matters such as detention and the reconstruction of the criminal justice system,[304] and ended with a finding of a number of human rights violations by UNMIK in the reports of the OSCE and the Kosovo Ombudsperson.[305]

Moreover, exclusive reliance on the technique of institutional self-commitment sends an unfortunate message in terms of human rights commitment. It creates the impression that human rights standards are implemented at the discretion of the individual administrations, rather than being binding upon them by force of law.[306]

---

[301] See Section 3 of UNMIK Regulation No. 1/1999 and Section 3 of UNTAET Regulation No. 1/1999.

[302] Later, the UN Secretary-General added that the UN administrations themselves would be "guided by internationally recognised standards of human rights". See Report of the Secretary-General on the United Nations Interim Administration in Kosovo, 12 July 1999, UN Doc. S/1999/779, para. 42.

[303] See also Jonathan Morrow and Rachel White, *The United Nations in Transitional East Timor: International Standards and the Reality of Governance*, Australian Yearbook of International Law, Vol. 22 (2002), at 11.

[304] See OSCE, Kosovo, *A Review of the Criminal Justice System*, 1 September 2000–28 February 2001, Section 2, II.

[305] For a full account, see below Part IV, Chapters 14 and 15.

[306] This criticism may, in particular be voiced in relation to Memorandum of Understanding between the DPKO and the High Commissioner for Human Rights, which does not vest human rights components of peacekeeping operations with the power to follow up on human rights violations through judicial or enforcement action, but makes all public statements of human rights components subject to authorisation by the Special Representative of the Secretary-General. See Article C (6)–(9) of the Memorandum of Understanding.

4.4.1.2. Human rights obligations of international administrations under customary law
In addition to their UN or treaty-based mandates, international territorial administrations may be bound to comply with human rights standards recognised by customary international law in relation to persons under their authority or jurisdiction.[307]

International organisations and other non-state actors can affect individual and group rights in the same manner as states. It is therefore reasonable to argue that responsibility under human rights law cannot be strictly linked to the concept of the state, but should be founded upon an impact-based assessment of responsibility, namely "the degree to which actors can impact an individual or group's human rights".[308] This theory is used to establish human rights accountability for organised non-state actors.[309] It applies with equal force to international organisations.

The argument that control entails responsibilities is particularly compelling in the context of territorial administration. The applicability of customary human rights law to international administrations may be founded upon the exercise of territorial authority and control by these entities. Some guidance may, in particular, be derived from the interpretation of the term "jurisdiction" by human rights treaty bodies in the context of the extraterritorial application of human rights conventions.[310] International practice has increasingly linked human rights accountability to the notion of effective control. Various treaty bodies have disassociated the concept of jurisdiction from territorial sovereignty, and linked it to effective control. The Inter-American Commission on Human Rights adopted this reasoning expressly in *Coard et al. v. United States*. It noted:

Given that individual human rights inhere simply by virtue of a person's humanity, each American State is obliged to uphold the protected rights of any person subject to its jurisdiction. While this most commonly refers to persons within a state's territory, it may, under given circumstances, refer to conduct

[307] See also De Wet, *Direct Administration of Territories by the United Nations*, at 320.
[308] See Mégret and Hoffmann, *UN as a Human Rights Violator?*, at 321.
[309] See Steven R. Ratner, *Corporations and Human Rights: A Theory of Legal Responsibility*, Yale Law Journal, Vol. 111 (2001), at 443, 465-472, 509.
[310] For a discussion, see Rick Lawson, *The Concept of Jurisdiction and Extraterritorial Acts of State*, in State, Sovereignty and International Governance (G. Kreijen ed., 2004), 281. See also generally Theodor Meron, *Extraterritoriality of Human Rights Treaties*, American Journal of International Law, Vol. 89 (1995), 78.

with an extraterritorial locus where the person concerned is present in the territory of one state, but subject to the control of another state – usually through the acts of the latter's agents abroad. In principle, the inquiry turns not on the presumed victim's nationality or presence within a particular geographic area, but on whether, under the specific circumstances, the State observed the rights of a person subject to its authority and control.[311]

A very similar approach was adopted by the Human Rights Committee in its General Comment on Article 2, in which the Committee stated that the Covenant applies to persons *"within the power or effective control of a State Party acting outside its territory, regardless of the circumstances in which such power or effective control was obtained, such as forces constituting a national contingent of a State party assigned to an international peace-keeping or peace-enforcement operation".*[312] The ICJ gave additional support to this interpretation, by reaffirming the extraterritorial application of the Covenant in advisory opinion on the *"Legal Consequences of the Construction of a Wall in the Occupied Palestinian Territory".*[313]

The European Court of Human Rights took a slightly more cautious position in relation to the definition of term jurisdiction under Article 1 of the Convention in the *Bankovic* case.[314] The Grand Chamber acknowledged that customary international law and treaty provisions have recognised the extraterritorial exercise of jurisdiction by a state in two instances, namely:

---

[311] See Inter-American Commission on Human Rights, *Coard et al.* v. *United States*, Case No. 10.951, Report No. 109/99 of 29 September 1999, para. 37.

[312] Emphasis added. See Human Rights Committee, *General Comment No. 31 on Article 2 of the Covenant: The Nature of the General Legal Obligation Imposed on States Parties to the Covenant*, UN Doc. CCPR/C/74/CRP.4/Rev.6 of 21 April 2004, para. 10. The Committee stated that: "States Parties are required by article 2, paragraph 1, to respect and to ensure the Covenant rights to all persons who may be within their territory and to all persons subject to their jurisdiction. This means that a State party must respect and ensure the rights laid down in the Covenant to anyone with the power or effective control of that State Party, even if not situated within the territory of the State Party."

[313] The ICJ noted that the "travaux préparatoires of the Covenant confirm the Committee's interpretation of Article 2 of that instrument", since "the drafters of the Covenant did not intend to allow States to escape from their obligations when they exercise jurisdiction outside their national territory". See ICJ, Advisory Opinion, *Legal Consequences of the Construction of a Wall in the Occupied Palestinian Territory*, paras. 109–11.

[314] See European Court of Human Rights, *Bankovic et al.* v. *Belgium, the Czech Republic, Denmark, France, Germany, Greece, Hungary, Iceland, Italy, Luxembourg, the Netherlands, Norway, Poland, Portugal, Spain, Turkey and the United Kingdom*, Decision of 12 December 2001, Appl. No. 52207/99.

when the respondent state, through the effective control of the relevant territory and its inhabitants abroad as a consequence of military occupation or through consent, invitation or acquiescence of the Government of that territory, exercises all or some of the public powers normally to be exercised by that Government (para. 71, recalling the jurisprudence in *Loizidou v. Turkey*[315]); and in cases involving the activities of [a State's] diplomatic or consular agents abroad and on board craft and vessels registered in. or flying the flag of, that State (para. 73).

The Grand Chamber further embraced an "essentially territorial" understanding of the notion of jurisdiction under Article 1 of the Convention. It noted that:

[T]he Convention is a multilateral treaty operating, subject to Article 56 of the Convention, in an essentially regional context and notably in the legal space (*espace juridique*) of the Contracting States ... The Convention was not designed to be applied throughout the world, even in respect of the conduct of Contracting States. Accordingly, the desirability of avoiding a gap or vacuum in human rights' protection has so far been relied on by the Court in favour of establishing jurisdiction only when the territory in question was one that, but for the specific circumstances, would normally be covered by the Convention.[316]

This jurisprudence triggered a vivid debate about the limits of the extraterritorial application of the Convention. The UK courts had to interpret the *Bankovic* jurisprudence in the context of compensation claims arising from the death of six Iraqi civilians by members of the UK armed forces in Iraq between 1 August and 10 November 2003 (*Al-Skeini and others v. Secretary of State for Defence*).[317] The Secretary of State relied on the *Bankovic* jurisprudence to argue that none of the claimant's complaints fell within the territorial scope of the Convention recognised by the Strasbourg jurisprudence.[318] The UK courts ruled that the case of Colonel Mousa, an Iraqi police officer killed when held as a prisoner in

[315] European Court of Human Rights, *Loizidou v. Turkey*, Preliminary Objections, Judgment of 23 March 1995 (*Preliminary Objections*), Ser. A, No. 310.
[316] See para. 80 of the *Bankovic* decision.
[317] See House of Lords, *Opinions of the Lords of Appeal for Judgment in the cause Al Skeini and others v. Secretary of State for Defence*, Judgment of 13 June 2007, 2007 UKHL 26.
[318] This narrow interpretation receives some support from the fact that the doctrine of effective control of an area has so far only been applied within the sphere of states parties to the Convention, namely northern Cyprus and Moldova. See High Court of Justice, Queen's Bench Division, Divisional Court, *Mazin Jumaa Gatteh Al Skeini and Others v. Secretary of State for Defence and the Redress Trust*, Judgment of 14 December 2004, para. 249. For a criticism see Ralph Wilde, *The "Legal Space" or "Espace Juridique" of the European Convention on Human Rights: Is it Relevant to Extraterritorial State Action*, European Human Rights Law Review, Issue 2 (2005), 115, at 123.

a UK military base in Basra, fell within the scope of Article 1 of the Convention. However, they differed in their reasoning. The Queen's Bench Divisional Court justified this result by way of an analogy to the narrow exception in paragraph 73 of the *Bankovic* ruling. It held that "a British military prison, operating in Iraq with the consent of Iraqi sovereign authorities, and containing arrested suspects, falls within the... exception exemplified by embassies, consulates, vessels and aircraft".[319] The Court of Appeal relied on a test, which is more closely based on the exception in paragraph 71 of *Bankovic* ruling. It upheld jurisdiction on the ground that Mr Mousa, from the moment of his arrest, "came within the control and authority of the UK".[320] The opinions of individual law lords in the judgment of the House of Lords again showed a preference for a narrower reading of *Bankovic* in line with the Divisional Court.[321]

The broader interpretation of *Bankovic* receives support from the jurisprudence of the second Chamber of the ECHR in *Issa and Others* v. *Turkey*, which acknowledged that the *"espace juridique"* requirement may even be met in circumstances in which state party exercises "effective overall control of a particular portion of the territory" of a third party.[322] The Court noted that "[a]ccountability in such situations stems from the fact that Article 1 of the Convention cannot be interpreted so as to allow a State party to perpetrate violations of the Convention on the territory of another State, which it could not perpetrate on its own territory".[323]

---

[319] High Court of Justice, Judgment of 14 December 2004, para. 287.

[320] House of Lords, *Opinions of the Lords of Appeal for Judgment in the cause Al Skeini and others* v. *Secretary of State for Defence*, para. 107. The Court of Appeal referred to para. 18 of Resolution 1386, adopted by the Parliamentary Assembly of the Council of Europe on 24 June 2004, in which the Assembly called upon member states to "accept the full applicability of the European Convention on Human Rights to the activities of their forces in Iraq, in so far those forces exercised effective control over the areas in which they operated".

[321] See Opinion of Lord Bingham of Cornhill, para. 25, Opinion of Lord Rodger of Earlsferry, para. 81, Opinion of Lord Brown of Eaton-Under-Heywood, paras. 132 and 150.

[322] The Court noted: "The Court does not exclude the possibility that, as a consequence of the military action, the respondent State could be considered to have exercised, temporarily, effective overall control of a particular portion of the territory of northern Iraq. Accordingly, if there is a sufficient factual basis for holding that, at the relevant time, the victims were within that specific area, it would follow logically that they were within the jurisdiction of Turkey (and not that of Iraq, which is not a Contracting State and clearly does not fall within the legal space (espace juridique) of the Contracting States." See *Issa and Others* v. *Turkey*, para. 74.

[323] See *Issa and Others* v. *Turkey*, para. 71. This argument draws on the views of the Human Rights Committee in *Lopez* v. *Uruguay* (29 July 1981) and *Celiberti de Casariego* v. *Uruguay*

These findings show that there is not unanimous,[324] but considerable support for the proposition that human rights obligations may apply to persons who are under effective control of a state party even if situated on foreign soil. The main bone of contention is the required degree of control and the scope of applicability of respective obligations. The case-law of the Human Rights Committee and the ECHR in *Issa and Others. v. Turkey* suggests that the exercise of effective overall control over foreign territory may suffice to trigger the applicability of human rights treaty law.[325] Following this logic, specific human rights obligations[326] may, for instance, apply extraterritorially in cases where a state agent exercises public authority over part of a foreign territory within the framework of an occupation regime or a Chapter VII established framework of admin-istration.[327] Advocates of a more restrictive approach would concede that human rights obligations may apply extraterritorially in circumstances in which a state exercises institutional authority over certain outposts abroad, such as embassies, consulates or military prisons operated in the territory of another state.[328]

Similar principles may be invoked in relation to the human rights obligations of international organisations under customary law.[329] The applicability of human rights standards to international organisations

((29 July 1981) which invoked Article 5 of the Covenant to justify that "it would be unconscionable to so interpret the responsibility under Article 2 of the Covenant as to permit a State party to perpetrate violations of the Covenant on the territory of another State which it could not perpetrate on its own territory".

[324] The British High Court of Justice acknowledged its uncertainty about the state of the Strasbourg jurisprudence in para. 265 of its Judgment of 14 December 2004. See also the individual opinions of the Law Lords in the respective judgment of the House of Lords.

[325] See *Issa and Others* v. *Turkey*, para. 72.

[326] The scope of applicability would need to be determined in the light of the context of the specific situation. The extraterritorial application of treaty obligations may, *inter alia*, clash with local values and restrictions under the law of occupation. See, for example, House of Lords, *Al-Skeini and others*, Opinion of Lord Rodger of Earlsferry, para. 78 ([The Convention] "is a body of law which may reflect the values of the contracting states, but which most certainly does not reflect those in many other parts of the word"), Opinion of Lord Brown of Eaton-Under-Heywood, para. 129.

[327] This development is in line with the conception of the ECHR as a "living instrument", see Wilde, *The "Legal Space" or "Espace Juridique" of the European Convention on Human Rights*, at 124. For a general discussion, see Dirk Lorenz, *Der Territoriale Anwendungsbereich der Grund- und Menschenrechte: Zugleich ein Beitrag zum Individualschutz in Bewaffneten Konflikten* (2005).

[328] High Court of Justice, Judgment of 14 December 2004, para. 287.

[329] Concurring Irmscher, *Legal Framework of the Activities of the United Nations Interim Mission in Kosovo*, at 370.

cannot be based on the concept of territorial sovereignty, because international entities usually lack permanent ownership or title over territory. But it is possible to consider the criterion of effective control as a nexus triggering the applicability of human rights obligations.[330] The exercise of territorial authority by an international organisation is comparable to the extraterritorial exercise of jurisdiction by states. Both types of engagement involve the exercise of authority over foreign citizens. It is therefore reasonable to treat them according to similar legal parameters.

The controversy over the required degree of control appears to be of limited significance in the area of international territorial administration. International administrations satisfy the threshold of effective control more easily than traditional peacekeeping forces, since their activity involves a significant number of direct points of contact with domestic actors. A distinction must, however, be made on the basis of the type of operation. International administrations are likely to meet the standard of effective control when they hold exclusive of control and decision-making power over the inhabitants of the administered territories within the exercise of their administrative or governmental mandate.[331] Mere assistance engagements, on the contrary, fall typically short of meeting the effective control test.

4.4.1.3. Human rights obligations by virtue of "functional duality"

An alternative concept to explain why international administrations are bound to comply with international human rights obligations is the theory of "functional duality".[332] International administrations may be said to encounter obligations under human rights law, not only because they exercise "effective control" over the territory and are therefore bound by governance obligations as an international actor, but rather because

[330] See also Council of Europe, Parliamentary Assembly, *Protection of Human Rights in Kosovo*, para. 18. ("In certain circumstances, Serbia and Montenegro may be held responsible for human rights violations in Kosovo. This arises from the fact that although Kosovo is 'extra-jurisdictional territory' of Serbia and Montenegro, nevertheless responsibility may arise as a result of actions which establish some form of effective control over certain activities within Kosovo. In particular, the continuing presence of 'parallel structures' in the northern part of Kosovo – including the maintenance of a separate judicial system, administered from within Serbia proper, applicable in practice only to Serbs and applying laws different to those applicable generally in Kosovo – establishes potential responsibility, insofar as the activities of these structures may violate individual rights.")
[331] See also Mégret and Hoffmann, *UN as a Human Rights Violator?*, at 323.
[332] For a full discussion, see below Part IV, Chapter 14.

they act as organs of a state.[333] These obligations have a different foundation from the classical obligations of international law. They are not directly tied to the nature of the international administration as an international legal entity, nor to the degree of factual control, but to the fact that the administration acts in a capacity as a domestic public authority. Under this theory, international administrations may be bound to respect not only self-imposed human rights obligations or standards of customary law applicable to them as international legal actors, but also other international legal norms that are applicable in the territory, due to the fact and to the extent that they perform the functions of a "surrogate" domestic government.[334]

4.4.1.4. Treaty obligations

Last, but not least, international territorial administrations may encounter human rights obligations under treaty law. Treaty obligations may potentially apply in three ways: by accession of transitional administrations to human rights conventions, through succession into previously applicable human rights obligations or by way of the extraterritorial application of human rights treaties to states involved in territorial administration.

4.4.1.4.1. The problem of formal treaty accession

The option of a formal accession to human rights conventions has been discussed in the case of Kosovo. Proposals have been made to extend the jurisdiction of the European Court of Human Rights to UNMIK and KFOR.[335] However, such an approach faces significant obstacles. The jurisdiction *ratione personae* of regional and universal human rights treaties such as the ECHR and the ICCPR is confined to states.[336] An extension of the jurisdiction of these treaty regimes to international administrations

---

[333] See also Ralph Wilde, *The Accountability of International Organizations and the Concept of "Functional Duality"*, in From Government to Governance, Proceedings of the Sixth Hague Joint Conference (Wybo P. Heere ed., 2004), 164, at 168. See Wilde, *International Territorial Administration and Human Rights*, at 171.

[334] With respect to treaty obligations, see below the discussion of "functional succession".

[335] See European Commission for Democracy Through Law, *Opinion on Human Rights in Kosovo*, para. 80.

[336] Article 59 of the ECHR states that the Convention is only open to signature by member states of the Council of Europe. Furthermore, Articles 33 and 34 clarify that applications can only be submitted to the European Court of Human Rights, if they are directed against a member state of the Convention.

would not only require the political will of international organisations such as the UN or NATO to accede to these instruments and to subject themselves to the scrutiny of an independent treaty body, but would also necessitate an amendment of the provisions of these treaties.[337] Such an amendment has been envisaged in the context of the ECHR in order to facilitate the accession of the EU to the Convention.[338] However, formal treaty accession is not necessarily the most appropriate technique to deal with the specific problems arising in the context of international territorial administration. In this context, multiple organisations (UN, NATO, EU) may operate under joint mandate. A treaty amendment, which would bring all of these organisations under the umbrella of the respective human rights conventions and the jurisdiction of their treaties bodies, is cumbersome because it would take a significant amount of time. Moreover, such an approach creates other conflicts of interest. International territorial administration is by its very nature a temporary undertaking. To require international organisations to ratify human rights conventions in the light of the performance of specific and temporary governance functions over territory may "seem to be a disproportionate response", given the "interim nature" of the tasks of international administering authorities and the nature of human rights treaty regimes, which are supposed to apply on a longer-term basis.[339]

4.4.1.4.2. Functional succession

Another concept by which international organisations may be bound to respect treaty law is the principle of functional succession.

The idea of the continuity of legal obligations has a long tradition in the case of a change of government. It was developed by the PCIJ in the *German Settlers* case, where the Court found that private property rights do not cease to exist by virtue of a change of sovereignty, but continue to be binding on the successor regime.[340] Since then, the notion of "acquired rights"[341] has become a core principle of the law of

---

[337] See European Commission for Democracy Through Law, *Opinion on Human Rights in Kosovo*, paras. 81–7.

[338] See Council of Europe, Parliamentary Assembly, *Protection of Human Rights in Kosovo*, sub III., para 35.

[339] *Ibid.*

[340] See PCIJ, *Settlers of German Origin in the Territory Ceded by Germany to Poland*, Ser. B, No. 6 (1923).

[341] They may be defined as rights "which where there no territorial changes, would be protected by the courts in a lawful state". See Lauterpacht, *Succession of States with Respect to Private Law Obligations*, in International Law being the Collected Papers of Hersch Lauterpacht, Vol. 3 (E. Lauterpacht ed., 1977), 121, at 136.

state succession.[342] A similar idea of continuity is reflected in the duty of occupying powers to preserve the law applicable in the administered territory.[343]

This concept has been further developed in the context of human rights treaty law. The Human Rights Committee established the concept of automatic succession into human rights obligations in its practice.[344] The Committee noted in its famous General Comment No. 26 that human rights obligations under the Covenant are attached to the people rather than the state and remain in force in a specific territory despite a change in government or territorial attribution, because they form part of an *acquis* acquired through treaty ratification.[345] This principle may be transposed to the context of territorial administration. If human rights guarantees are not affected by a change in statehood, they must *a fortiori* remain in force in the case of a mere change of effective control, which is typical of territorial administrations, in particular, in the cases of exclusive governance or co-governance missions.

It is difficult to establish how international organisations may be bound to respect human rights instruments to which they are not parties, nor eligible to membership. The obstacle of the lack of treaty membership may, however, be overcome in theory if one introduces a distinction between formal treaty membership and the material obligation to

---

[342] See D. P. O'Connell, *State Succession in Municipal Law and International Law*, Vol. 1 (1967), 237.

[343] Article 43 of the Hague Regulations obliges the occupying power, in principle, to respect the law applicable in the administered territory. See Article 43 of the Hague Regulations ("while respecting, unless absolutely prevented, the laws in force in the country").

[344] See generally Menno T. Kamminga, *State Succession in Respect of Human Rights Treaties*, European Journal of International Law, Vol. 7 (1996), 469; Akbar Rasulov, *Revisiting State Succession to Humanitarian Treaties: Is There a Case for Automaticity?*, European Journal of International Law, Vol. 14 (2003), 141. This concept is an extension of the concept of acquired rights. It not only forbids territorial rulers to deprive domestic actors of certain treaty-based rights, but compels the ruling authorities to abide by human rights guarantees in their relations with the inhabitants of the administered territory.

[345] See Human Rights Committee, *General Comment No. 26*, UN Doc. A/53/40, Annex VII, para. 4. ("The rights enshrined in the Covenant belong to the people living in the territory of the State party. The Human Rights Committee has consistently taken the view, as evidenced by its long-standing practice, that once the people are accorded the protection of the rights of the Covenant, such protection devolves with territory and continues to belong to them, notwithstanding change in Government of the State party, including dismemberment in more than one State or State succession or any subsequent action of the State party designed to divest them of the rights guaranteed by the Covenant.")

comply with the substantial guarantees of treaty law. It may be argued that territorial successors are bound to comply with the substantive guarantees of previously applicable treaty law, irrespective of their status as potential parties to the treaty, because these rights reside in the people.[346]

The obligation of international organisations to respect previously applicable human rights guarantees may be based on the idea of "functional succession".[347] One might argue that international organisations may be obliged to abide by substantive treaty-based standards applicable in the territory[348] and, in particular, with those treaty-based rights which are relevant to their functions as surrogate state authorities, where they assume the classical functions of a state in the place of domestic authorities ("functional succession").

This concept receives some support from international practice. The idea of "functional succession" was applied by a UK court in the context of the determination of the obligations under the 1951 Refugee Convention.[349] Moreover, the Human Rights Committee invoked this concept in its Concluding Observations[350] on the Report by UNMIK on the

---

[346] The idea inherent in the concept of automatic succession is that the rights granted to individuals in a treaty arrangement continue to apply in relation to any new territorial ruler because they are part of the acquired rights of the people and transcend state sovereignty. See also Separate Opinion of Judge Weeramantry, *Application of the Convention on the Prevention and Punishment of the Crime of Genocide (Bosnia Herzegovina v. Yugoslavia)*, Judgment on Preliminary Objections, ICJ Rep. 1996, 595, at 646, 654–5.

[347] The concept of "automatic succession" has predominantly been invoked to establish the continued application of human rights treaties in the context of state succession. The International Law Association qualified this doctrine as customary law in *statu nascendi* in 2002. See International Law Association, *Rapport Final sur la Succession en Matiére de Traités* (2002), at 28. But the rationale behind this principle applies equally to the transitional assumption of territorial authority by international organisations. For a more restrictive view, see De Wet, *Direct Administration of Territories by the United Nations*, at 319.

[348] See also Bothe and Marauhn, *UN Administration of Kosovo and East Timor*, at 237; Irmscher, *Legal Framework of the Activities of the United Nations Interim Mission in Kosovo*, at 371–2.

[349] A UK court held that UNMIK was the "relevant entity" and bound to ensure protection under Article 1 of the 1951 Convention and Protocol relating to the Status of Refugees, because "UNMIK/KFOR [had] lawful authority in and over Kosovo, and … had all the powers and functions of the state transferred to them". See High Court, *Vallaj v. Special Adjudicator*, Queen's Bench Division, 21 December 2000 (Westlaw: 2000 WL 1881268).

[350] See Human Rights Committee, *Concluding Observations on Kosovo (Republic of Serbia)*, 25 July 2006, CCPR/C/UNK/CO/1.

Human Rights Situation in Kosovo since June 1999.[351] In this context, the Committee expressly extended the principle of the continued application of human rights obligations to "changes in the administration of... territory".[352] The Committee stressed that "UNMIK, as well as the [Provisional Institutions of Self-Government], or any future administration in Kosovo, are bound to respect and to ensure to all individuals within the territory of Kosovo and subject to their jurisdiction the rights recognized in the Covenant", recalling both General Comment No. 26 and the general human rights obligation under Security Council Resolution 1244.[353]

This position contrasts, however, with the view of other bodies. In its Opinion on Human Rights in Kosovo, the Venice Commission refused to recognise the applicability of the ECHR and the jurisdiction of the European Court of Human Rights over UNMIK and KFOR solely on the ground that "Serbia and Montenegro [had] ratified the Convention and... [that] UNMIK should be seen as a 'care-taker' for Serbia and Montenegro, having assumed the obligations by Serbia and Montenegro under the European Convention on Human Rights or having succeeded in those obligations".[354] A similar reservation was shared by UNMIK. The UN administration continuously rejected the view that treaties and agreements applicable in the former SFRY or concluded by Serbia and Montenegro are automatically binding on UNMIK.[355] It is therefore doubtful whether

---

[351] See UNMIK, *Report Submitted by UNMIK to the Human Rights Committee on the Human Rights Situation in Kosovo since June 1999*, CCPR/C/UNK/1, 13 March 2006.

[352] Human Rights Committee, *Concluding Observations on Kosovo (Republic of Serbia)*, 25 July 2006, para. 4. ("[O]nce the people are accorded the protection of the rights under the Covenant, such protection devolves with the territory and continues to belong to them, notwithstanding changes in the administration of that territory.")

[353] *Ibid.*

[354] See European Commission for Democracy Through Law, *Opinion on Human Rights in Kosovo*, para. 78. The Commission noted: "Such a theory would not be limited to the Convention, and indeed not to Kosovo. It implies the assertion that all UN interim administrations would have to respect all treaties which the state on whose territory they operate, has concluded and continues to conclude. Such a rule would contradict the need for the UN to establish and implement a mandate which is unrestrained by limitations which are created independently by individual member states or other third parties. Indeed the UN Charter provides that the Security Council may, under Chapter VII, take binding decisions, such as Resolution 1244, and it states in its Article 103 that the obligations of the Charter 'shall prevail' over 'obligations under any other international agreement'."

[355] UNMIK acknowledged to be bound by substantive treaty law only in cases, where it undertook these obligations by way of self-commitment, such in the cases of the Anti-Torture Convention or the Framework Convention on the Protection of National

the principle of functional succession forms already part of the *lex lata* in the field of treaty law.

4.4.1.4.3.   *Extraterritorial application of human rights treaties*

States may be bound by their own treaty obligations when they exercise territorial control within the framework of transitional administrations.[356] This responsibility is easy to establish in cases where states act individually. The case-law on the extraterritorial application of human rights indicates that states parties may be obliged to comply with their treaty obligations when they exercise territorial jurisdiction abroad.[357] Human rights treaty law may, in particular, serve as a limitation for the exercise of public authority in specific areas such as detention, access to justice etc.

Additional difficulties arise, however, in cases where states act within collective bodies. The main question which arises in this context is whether the exercise of authority outside domestic soil establishes a sufficient jurisdictional link to the state to trigger the applicability of human rights obligations.

Minorities. The preambles of both agreements even contained an express disclaimer which specified that the text of the respective "Agreement does not make UNMIK a Party to the... Convention" in question. See para. 6 of the preamble of the Agreement between UNMIK and the Council of Europe on technical arrangements related to the European Convention for the Prevention of Torture and para. 9 of the Agreement between UNMIK and the Council of Europe on technical arrangements related to the Framework Convention for the Protection of National Minorities. In its report to the Human Rights Committee, UNMIK reiterated this position. UNMIK stressed that provisions of international human rights treaties, which were part of the law in force in Kosovo on 22 March 1989, are not automatically binding on UNMIK. It stated: "It must be remembered throughout that the situation of Kosovo under interim administration by UNMIK is *sui generis*. Accordingly, it has been the consistent position of UNMIK that treaties and agreements, to which the State Union of Serbia and Montenegro is a party, are not automatically binding on UNMIK." See UNMIK, *Report Submitted by UNMIK to the Human Rights Committee on the Human Rights Situation in Kosovo since June 1999*, paras. 123–4.

[356] See with respect to KFOR also Amnesty International, *The apparent lack of accountability of international peace-keeping forces in Kosovo and Bosnia-Herzegovina*, AI Index: EUR 05/002/2004, April 2004, at 12. ("In the case of Kosovo, KFOR is present 'through the consent, invitation or acquiescence' of the government of Serbia and Montenegro, and it exercises 'some of the public powers [notably in the realms of defence and public order, including the powers to arrest and detain people] normally exercised by that Government'. Thus, the contracting states can be held accountable... for alleged breaches of ECHR by their troops in Kosovo.")

[357] For a discussion of the case-law, see above "Human rights obligations of international administrations under customary law".

*4.4.1.4.3.a. State obligations within the framework
of multinational administrations*

Some guidelines may be drawn from the case-law of the European Commission of Human Rights in the case of *Hess* v. *the UK*.[358] In this case, Ilse Hess, the wife of former Nazi leader Rudolph Hess filed a complaint before the Commission arguing that the UK violated her husband's rights under Articles 3 and 8 of the Convention by detaining him in the prison of Berlin-Spandau under Allied control in Berlin. The Commission declared the case inadmissible. It argued that the UK lacked jurisdiction under Article 1 of the Convention, because the responsibility for the administration of the prison and the detention of Rudolph Hess fell into the joint competence of the Control Council made up of the Four Powers, the decisions of which could not be attributed to one state individually.

The criteria of assessment deployed by the Commission may be applied in the context of transitional administrations. The Commission based its decision implicitly on the criterion of effective control, by making a distinction between the exercise of joint and divisible authority within the framework of collective decision-making bodies. The Commission found that the decisions of the Control Council were distinct from individual decisions of its members, because they were taken jointly by quadripartite body acting on the basis of unanimity.[359] The *ratio decidendi* of the *Hess* decision is of interest in the context of transitional administrations, because it does not exclude the possible application of human rights obligations to multinational administrations.

The threshold of the exercise of effective control may be met in situations in which several states assume administering responsibilities collectively (e.g. as a joint administration), but where each individual state maintains control over the common decision-making process. The most typical case is a scenario in which a state exercises exclusive control over

[358] See *Ilse Hess.* v. *UK*, Application No. 6231/73, Decision of 28 May 1975, Decisions and Reports, Vol. 2, at 72.

[359] It seems that jurisdiction might have been established if the prison had been run under the sole administration of the UK. The Commission noted: "As the Commission has already decided, a State is under certain circumstances responsible under the Convention for actions of its authorities outside its territory... V. v. Federal Republic of Germany. The Commission is of the opinion that there is, in principle, from a legal point of view, no reason why the acts of British authorities in Berlin should not entail the liability of the United Kingdom under the Convention." See also High Court of Justice, *Mazin Jumaa Gatteh Al Skeini and Others* v. *Secretary of State for Defence*, paras. 138, 252.

a specific part of the territory, for example, in a specific area of administration.[360] It may very well be argued that each individual state remains
bound in these cases by its treaty obligations, if it exercises independent decision-making authority or other forms of exclusive control over
specific parts of collectively administered territory.[361]

4.4.1.4.3.b.   State obligations within the framework of operations conducted by international organisations

The situation is different in circumstances where state entities participate in frameworks of administration conducted by international organisations. A typical example is the exercise of military or civilian functions
by national contingents under the umbrella of NATO or the UN, such as
in the case of KFOR. A question arises as to whether participating troop
contingents continue to be bound by the human rights treaty obligations of their sending states. Both, the jurisprudence of the European
Court of Human Rights and the ILC Draft Articles on the Responsibility
of International Organisations[362] lend support to the view that member
states remain bound by their treaty obligations when acting under the
umbrella of an international organisation.[363] However, two distinctions
must be made in this regard.

First, it must be established whether participating states or the organisation retain effective control over the respective action. Human
rights treaty obligations may continue to apply individually to states
where the role of the organisation is confined to the mere coordination of individual actions of participating states that maintain control

---

[360] See also Amnesty International, *Memorandum on concerns relating to law and order*, sub.
II. ("[C]onsistent with international humanitarian law, Coalition states are also under
the obligation to respect the provisions of the human rights treaties to which they
are a party, as well as those to which Iraq is a party, especially given that these
treaties have been formally incorporated into Iraqi domestic law.") For doubts as to
whether the UK was in "effective control" of Basra and the surrounding areas during
the occupation of Iraq, see House of Lords, *Al-Skeini and others* v. *Secretary of State for
Defence*, Opinion of Lord Rodger of Earlsferry, para. 83.

[361] It is interesting to note in this context that ICRC upheld the principle of member
state responsibility in the context of detention issues in Iraq. See below Part IV,
Chapter 15.

[362] See ILC, Report on the work of its 56th Session (2004), UN GAOR, 59th Sess., Suppl.
No. 10 (A/59/10), at 94–110 (Responsibility of International Organisations).

[363] See European Court of Human Rights, *Bosphorus Hava Yolllari Turizm ve Ticaret Anonim
Sirketi (Bosphorus Airways)* v. *Ireland*, Judgment of 30 June 2005, Application No.
45036/98, paras. 152–4, as well Articles 28 and 29 of the ILC Draft Articles on the
Responsibility of International Organisations.

over their respective contingents and their instructions.[364] However, the responsibility of states may be superseded by a responsibility of an international organisation in cases where the organisation exercises effective control over the operation. This approach is reflected in Article 5 of the ILC's Draft Articles on the Responsibility of International Organisations, which provides that:

The conduct of an organ of a State or of an organ or agent of an international organisation that is placed at the disposal of another international organisation shall be considered under international law an act of the latter organization *if the organisation exercises effective control over that conduct*.[365]

This principle coincides with the practice of the UN, which assumes responsibility for acts of national contingents of a peacekeeping force,[366] except in cases where UN commanders lack effective control.

The question of whether an act may be attributed to a troop contributing country is a factual question, which must be assessed on the basis of the degree of operational control in the individual circumstances. The Grand Chamber of the European Court of Human Rights had to deal with this question in a case concerning member state responsibility for KFOR action in Kosovo (*Behrami & Behrami v. France* and *Saramati v. France, Germany and Norway*). The applicants argued for the retention of individual state accountability on the ground that KFOR troops were directly

---

[364] This occurred, for example, in the case of UNOSOM. UNOSOM operated formally under the control and command of the SRSG. The Italian contingent followed orders from its own government, rather than orders issued by the UN command structure. In such a case, it may be argued that "the Italian contingent was acting as an agent of Italy as such and that any responsibility arising from these acts are to be attributed to Italy and not the UN". See Sarooshi, *Preliminary Remarks on the Conferral by States of Powers of International Organisations*, at 59.

[365] Emphasis added. See ILC Draft Articles on the Responsibility of International Organizations (2004), at 109.

[366] The UN Secretary-General acknowledged that the criterion of effective control is applied by the UN in the context of joint operations. See UN Doc. A/51/389, paras. 17–18, p. 6. ("The international responsibility of the United Nations for combat-related activities of United Nations forces is premised on the assumption that the operation in question is under the exclusive command and control of the United Nations... In joint operations, international responsibility for the conduct of the troops lies where operational command and control is vested according to the arrangements establishing the modalities of cooperation between the State or States providing the troops and the United Nations. In the absence of formal arrangements between the United Nations and the State or States providing troops, responsibility would be determined in each and every case according to the degree of effective control exercised by either party in the conduct of the operation.")

answerable to their national commanders and remained within the exclusive jurisdiction of the respective member state with respect to civil and criminal matters.[367] The Court rejected this claim. It found that NATO retained "effective" command in the relevant operational matters (detention), since national command was under the "direct operational authority of COMKFOR", which "acted at all times as a KFOR officer answerable to NATO through [a] chain of command".[368]

However, not all acts which occur within the course of an operation under "unified command and control" must necessarily be attributed to the entity which holds formal control.[369] UN practice has shown that the chain of operational command may be interrupted by interferences or conflicting orders of domestic contingents in specific matters.[370] In such cases, action may be attributable to domestic contingents or there may even be cases of "shared responsibility",[371] in which certain human rights violations are attributable to an international organisation, whilst others remain within the responsibility of a particular member state.[372]

Secondly, some attention must be devoted to the question of whether the collective decision-making body enjoys independent legal

---

[367] See European Court of Human Rights, *Behrami & Behrami v. France*, Application No. 71412/01, *Saramati v. France, Germany and Norway*, Application No. 78166/01, Decision of 31 May 2007, para. 79. The applicants argued that member state responsibility should be retained since a UK court considered itself competent to examine a case concerning the action of UK KFOR troops in Kosovo. See High Court of Justice, Queen's Bench Division, *Bici v. Ministry of Defence*, Judgment of 7 April 2004, 2004 EWHC 786.

[368] See *Behrami & Behrami v. France*, Application No. 71412/01, *Saramati v. France, Germany and Norway*, Application No. 78166/01, Decision of 31 May 2007, para. 139.

[369] See also European Commission on Democracy Through Law, *Opinion on Human Rights in Kosovo*, para. 79. ("There may ... be difficult intermediate cases, such as when soldiers are acting on the specific orders of their national commanders which are, however, themselves partly in execution of directives issued by KFOR commanders and partly within the exercise of their remaining scope of discretion.")

[370] Lack of effective control was a problem in the context of UNOSOM. See the Report of the Commission of Inquiry in relation to armed attacks on UNOSOM II personnel, UN Doc. S/1994/653, paras. 243–4. ("The Force Commander of UNOSOM II was not in effective control of several national contingents which, in varying degrees, persisted in seeking orders from their home authorities before executing orders of the Forces Command. Many major operations undertaken under the United Nations flag and in the context of UNOSOM's mandate were totally outside the command and control of the United Nations, even though the repercussions impacted crucially on the mission of UNOSOM and the safety of its personnel.")

[371] See Council of Europe, Parliamentary Assembly, *Protection of Human Rights in Kosovo*, sub. III, para. 33.

[372] See expressly in relation to KFOR action, *ibid.*, paras. 33 and 36 (noting that "[w]hilst the European Court of Human Rights may rule that European NATO-member States have responsibilities under the ECHR extending also to their activities of their KFOR contingents, the[se] obligations ... are not relevant to non-European contingents").

personality. The European Court of Human Rights emphasised in several decisions that the contracting parties of the Convention are entitled to transfer competences to autonomous legal entities beyond their individual control.[373] However, the Court set specific limits to the devolution of accountability under the Convention. The Court noted that member states cannot generally exempt themselves from their obligations under the Convention by way of a transfer of authority to international organisations.[374] When dealing with the permissibility of the transfer of competences to the European Space Agency (ESA) and the EU, the Court inquired specifically whether the rights guaranteed by the Convention continue to be recognised by the respective multilateral framework,[375] or whether there are, at least, alternative mechanisms to ensure the level of human rights protection required by the Convention.[376] Moreover, the Court found that a state remains responsible under Article 1 of the Convention for all acts and omissions of its organs, regardless of whether they were a consequence of the necessity to comply with international legal obligations, for example, the implementation of a regulation of the EU (*Bosphorus* v. *Ireland*).[377]

---

[373] See with respect to transfer of powers to the European Communities, European Court of Human Rights, *Denise Matthews* v. *United Kingdom*, Application No. 24833/94 of 18 February 1999.

[374] *Ibid.*, para. 32, where the Court found that "[t]he Convention does not exclude the transfer of competences to international organisations provided that Convention rights continue to be 'secured'". See also Karel Wellens, *Remedies Against International Organizations* (2002), at 214–15; De Wet, *Chapter VII Powers of the United Nations Security Council*, at 380–1. In *Bosphorus* v. *Ireland*, the Court reaffirmed the principle that a state cannot absolve itself from responsibilities under the Convention by transferring functions to an international organisation. The Court noted that such a transfer would be "incompatible with the purpose and object of the Convention" and that a state "is considered to retain Convention liability in respect of treaty commitments subsequent to the entry into force of the Convention". See *Bosphorus* v. *Ireland*, para. 154.

[375] See European Court of Human Rights, *Waite and Kennedy* v. *Germany*, Application No. 26083/94, Judgment of 18 February 1999, para. 67.

[376] In *Waite and Kennedy* v. *Germany*, the Court shared the Commission's view that granting ESA immunity from German jurisdiction was not disproportionate, because of the existence of alternative means of legal process available to the applicants. See *Waite and Kennedy* v. *Germany*, para. 73.

[377] See *Bosphorus* v. *Ireland*, para. 153. The ILC incorporated this jurisprudence in Article 28 of the ILC Draft Articles on the Responsibility of International Organisations, which reads: "A State member of an international organization incurs international responsibility if it circumvents one of its international obligations by providing the organization with competence in relation to that obligation, and the organization commits an act that, if committed by that State, would have constituted a breach of that obligation."

These principles may be transposed to the context of human rights responsibilities within the framework of international administrations. According to these criteria, the separate legal personality of an international organisation is not an absolute shield from member state responsibility. The allocation of responsibility must be made in light of the circumstances of the respective case. Collective responsibility may prevail over individual responsibility in cases where an international administering authority possesses a legal personality distinct from its members and where comparable human rights guarantees apply to this entity, either by virtue of the internal constitution of that entity or by virtue of customary law.[378] This scheme introduces some flexibility into the accountability assessment. The distinct legal status of the collective body may create an alternative forum for accountability which reduces the need to hold member states individually accountable. The absence of independent legal personality, by contrast, increases the necessity to maintain the responsibility of each respective state entity through the extraterritorial application of human rights.

The applicants in *Behrami & Behrami* v. *France* and *Saramati* v. *France, Germany and Norway* relied on the "alternative forum" jurisprudence before the Grand Chamber in order to establish individual member state accountability. They argued that the protection of fundamental rights provided by NATO and KFOR was not "equivalent" to that under the Convention within the meaning of paragraph 155 of the *Bosphorus* judgment, with the consequence that the "presumption of Convention compliance on the part of the respondent States was rebutted".[379] Unfortunately, the Court failed to engage with the substance of this argument.[380] It ruled out subsidiary member state responsibility on the ground that the "impugned acts and omissions of KFOR and UNMIK... did not take place on the territory of those States or by virtue of a decision of their authorities".[381] Moreover, it justified its lack of judicial scrutiny by the

---

[378] Note that states have generally been reluctant to accept liability for acts of international organisations. Article 29 of the ILC Draft Articles on the Responsibility of International Organisations foresees a subsidiary liability of states for wrongful acts of international organisations in two instances: in cases where a member state "has accepted responsibility for that act" and in cases where a state "has led the injured party to rely on its responsibility".

[379] See *Behrami & Behrami* v. *France* and *Saramati* v. *France, Germany and Norway*, paras 80 and 150.

[380] The Court did examine to what extent NATO and KFOR provide substantive and procedural protection of fundamental rights in this operations. The Court mainly attempted to distinguish the case from the *Bosphorus* jurisprudence. *Ibid.*, para. 151.

[381] *Ibid.*, para. 151.

fact that "KFOR was exercising powers lawfully delegated under Chapter VII of the Charter by the UNSC".[382] This reasoning left the delicate question of member state accountability for human rights gaps in peace operations[383] unanswered.

4.4.2. The scope of obligations

When transitional administrations are bound to protect and ensure human rights standards under customary law or treaty law, they face a variety of different obligations. These obligations include, *inter alia*:

- *habeas corpus* and fair trial guarantees in matters of arrest and detention;
- the duty to ensure fundamental freedoms such as the free movement of persons in the territory, freedom of expression and association, freedom of the press, the right of access to the courts and the protection of property;
- the obligation to preserve the independence of the judiciary in the process of state reconstruction; and
- the facilitation of the right of refugees and displaced persons to return to their homes.[384]

In practice, the realisation of these rights and obligations often conflicts with the realities on the ground, which are shaped by security gaps, uncertainties about the applicable domestic law, continuing ethnic or societal divisions, the absence of local law enforcement agencies or the lack of a consolidated human rights culture and judicial practice. International administrations are often incapable of ensuring the full plenitude of treaty-based fundamental human rights.[385] Moreover, they

---

[382] *Ibid.*, para. 152.
[383] The applicants highlighted this dilemma in their submissions. They argued that that it "was disingenuous to accept that KFOR troops were subject to the exclusive control of their [troop-contributing nation] and yet deny that they fell within their jurisdiction". *Ibid.*, para. 77.
[384] An express recognition of this principle may be found in Principles 28 (1) and 29 of the Guiding Principles on Internal Displacement, issued in 1999 by the Representative of the Secretary-General on Internally Displaced Persons. See UN Doc. E.CN.4/1998/53/add.2. For a study in the Bosnian context, see Marcus Cox, *The Right to Return Home: International Intervention and Ethnic Cleansing in Bosnia and Herzegovina*, International & Comparative Law Quarterly, Vol. 47 (1998), 599–631. For a survey of the practice of international administrations, see below Part IV, Chapter 15.
[385] See also, House of Lords, *Al-Skeini and other v. Secretary of State for Defence*, Opinion of Lord Rodger of Earlsferry, para. 78. ("[T]he idea that the United Kingdom was obliged to secure observance of all the rights and freedoms as interpreted by the European Court in the utterly different society of southern Iraq is manifestly absurd.")

must reconcile their obligation to comply with human rights obligations with the duty not to interfere in areas of domestic decision-making. These circumstances may make it necessary to adjust some of the generally applicable standards to the special circumstances prevailing in the context of transitional administration.

Three main factors may restrict the scope of the application of human rights standards: the applicability of more specific provisions under international humanitarian law, the existence of a public emergency justifying derogation from the guarantees of human rights conventions and the derogatory effect of a Chapter VII mandate.

The application of these three limitations has been subject to conflicting interpretations in international legal practice. Both the broad scope of application of international human rights treaties generally and their restrictive derogation regime make it clear that exceptions to the framework of human rights law must be narrowly construed and considered within the context of specific human rights regimes.[386] Yet international administering authorities have shown a tendency to invoke overly broad exceptions from human rights standards, in order to preserve unfettered authority in the exercise of their administering responsibilities.

4.4.2.1.   *International humanitarian law* – lex specialis *to human rights law?* International administering powers have occasionally misinterpreted the relationship between human rights law and international humanitarian law. It has been argued that the rules of international humanitarian law supersede human rights obligations generally in times of armed conflict. This argument was made in the context of the occupation of Iraq. In a letter dated 27 June 2003, Paul Bremer, the chief CPA administrator, stated that:

the only relevant standard applicable to the Coalition's detention practice is the Fourth Geneva Convention of 1948. This Convention takes precedence, as a matter of law, over other human rights conventions.[387]

This claim is misleading. International humanitarian law and human rights law come into operation simultaneously in situations of armed conflict.[388] States are generally obliged to protect the core of

---

[386] See Article 4 of the ICCPR and Article 15 of the ECHR.
[387] See Amnesty International, *Memorandum on concerns relating to law and order*, sub. II 1.
[388] Both areas of law complement each other and ensure minimum standards of treatment for persons involved in armed conflict. See also Human Rights Committee, *General Comment No. 29 on States of Emergencies*, UN Doc. A/56/40, Annex VI of 24 July 2001, para. 3.

non-derogable rights guaranteed under human rights law, and those treaty rights which have not been subject to a formal derogation in accordance with the derogation mechanism provided for under the relevant treaty instrument.[389] In the case of an apparent inconsistency between human rights law and international humanitarian law, some human rights provisions may defer to the more specific provisions of humanitarian law.[390] However, as a general principle, human rights law and international humanitarian law are considered to be complementary and overlapping bodies of law.[391]

The ICJ adopted this position in the *Nuclear Weapons Advisory Opinion*,[392] where the Court observed in relation to rights protected under the ICCPR that "the protection of the International Covenant on Civil and Political Rights does not cease in times of war, except by operation of Article 4 (derogation clause) of the Covenant".[393] This principle was later reaffirmed by the Court in its opinion on the *Legal Consequences of the Construction of a Wall in the Occupied Palestinian Territory*.[394] The Human Rights Committee clarified in its General Comment No. 29 that some rights remain applicable even in a state of emergency. The Committee stated specifically in relation to states of emergency:

---

[389] Under Article 15, para. 1 of the ECHR and Article 4, para. 1 of the ICCPR, human rights obligations continue to apply in principle even in an active state of war.

[390] It is, for example, a well-established rule that in times of armed conflict, the right to life is not violated by the lawful killing of a combatant, although the right to life is normally a non-derogable right. Moreover, in a situation of armed conflict, the right to liberty may be distinct from that applicable in peacetime. In such situations, the standards of human rights law must be interpreted by reference to international humanitarian law as the applicable *lex specialis*.

[391] See also Jochen A. Frowein, *The Relationship between Human Rights Regimes and Regimes of Belligerent Occupation*, Israel Yearbook on Human Rights, Vol. 28 (1998), 1, at 16.

[392] ICJ, *Legality of the Threat or Use of Nuclear Weapons*, Advisory Opinion, ICJ Rep. 1996., p. 226.

[393] *Ibid.*, at para. 25.

[394] See ICJ, *Legal Consequences of the Construction of a Wall in the Occupied Palestinian Territory*, para. 106. ("[T]he Court considers that the protection offered by human rights conventions does not cease in case of armed conflict, save through the effect of provisions for derogation of the kind to be found in Article 4 of the International Covenant on Civil and Political Rights. As regards the relationship between international humanitarian law and human rights law, there are thus three possible situations: some rights may be exclusively matters of international humanitarian law; others may be exclusively matters of human rights law; yet others may be matters of both these branches of international law.")

It is inherent in the protection of [non-derogable] rights that they must be secured by procedural guarantees, including, often judicial guarantees. The provisions of the Covenant relating to procedural safeguards may never be subject to measures that would circumvent the protection of non-derogable rights... Thus, for example, as article 6 is non-derogable in its entirety, any trial leading to the imposition of the death penalty during a state of emergency must conform to the provisions of the Covenant, including all the requirements of articles 14 [fair trial] and 15 [prohibition on retroactive criminal penalties].[395]

This practice indicates that international administrations cannot justify exemptions from fundamental human rights guarantees by merely invoking the applicability of the rules of international humanitarian law. The exclusion of human rights norms is subject to a twofold test. International territorial administrations must establish that a specific human rights obligation is derogable in situations of emergency. Moreover, they should demonstrate that the specific obligation is superseded by a more specific rule or duty under humanitarian law (e.g. an occupant's obligation to respect "the laws in force").[396] This understanding may help avoid the emergence of human rights vacuums, but also mitigate the risk of "human rights imperialism".

4.4.2.2.   Conditions of derogation

There has also been some confusion about the conditions of derogation from human rights obligations.[397] International treaty law sets a high threshold for the suspension of human rights obligations in times of emergency. Some rights must be protected at all times, including, *inter*

---

[395] See Human Rights Committee, General Comment No. 29 of 31 August 2001 (*States of Emergency*), CCPR/C/21/Rev.1/Add.11, para. 15. Later, the Committee added that "fundamental requirements of fair trial must be respected during a state of emergency". See Human Rights Committee, *General Comment No. 29*, para. 16.

[396] See also the methodology applied by the ICJ in the Opinion on the *Legal Consequences of the Construction of a Wall in the Occupied Palestinian Territory*, para. 106. ("In order to answer the question put to it, the Court will have to take into consideration both these branches of international law, namely human rights law and, as *lex specialis*, international humanitarian law.") For a critique, see Kelly, *Iraq and the Law of Occupation*, at 137, who notes that "the ICCPR, as a matter of law... can add nothing to the human rights protections of GC IV and effort would be better directed in ensuring compliance with GC IV rather than engaging in extended debate on this point".

[397] See generally Rosalyn Higgins, *Derogations under Human Rights Treaties*, British Yearbook of International Law, Vol. 48 (1976/77), 281; Jaime Oraá, *Human Rights in States of Emergency in International Law* (1992); Oren Gross, *Once More unto the Breach: The Systematic Failure of Applying the European Convention on Human Rights to Entrenched Emergencies*, Yale Journal of International Law, Vol. 23 (1998), 437.

alia, the right to life, freedom from torture and freedom from inhuman or degrading treatment and punishment or freedom of religion.[398] Others may be restricted, but only "to the extent strictly required by the exigencies of the situation" and following an express declaration of derogation.[399]

This high threshold has not always been observed in practice. UNMIK, for example, qualified the situation in Kosovo still as an "internationally-recognised emergency", two years after the establishment of the mission.[400] UNMIK officials used this explanation to justify executive detentions in Kosovo for security reasons.[401] They noted:

Our position is that the authority for law and order and public safety is vested in the SRSG acting on behalf of the Secretary-General and the Security Council, according to Resolution 1244. Article 15 of the European Convention on Human Rights recognises that there may be exceptions to the conventions principles in certain emergency situations. This is acceptable in European courts. The situation in Kosovo is analogous to emergency situations envisioned in the human rights conventions. We emphasise that UNMIK's mandate was adopted under Chapter VII, which means that the situation calls for extraordinary means and force can be used to carry out the mandate. Any deprivation of liberty by an Executive Order is temporary and extraordinary, and its objective is the effective and impartial administration of justice.[402]

---

[398] See, for example, Article 4 (2) of the ICCPR.   [399] See Article 4 (1) and (3) of the ICCPR.

[400] UNMIK's general legal position is reflected in a paper entitled "Security and the Rule of Law in Kosovo" of 12 January 2000. It describes the position of UNMIK as follows: "Human rights principles should not be viewed as operating to dogmatically bar action that must be taken to address urgent security issues. A number of rights, including the rights to privacy, freedom of expression, freedom of assembly and freedom of movement, are subject to limitations which are 'necessary in a democratic society in the interests of national security or public safety, for the maintenance of public order [and] for the prevention of crime'. Within the framework of human rights, there is flexibility to take the necessary steps to promote public peace and order, even where such steps may constrain individual rights. It should also be noted that both the European Convention on Human Rights and the ICCPR contain a provision on 'public emergency'. This permits states, which are in a declared state of public emergency, to take measures derogating from human rights standards. For instance, it may be noted that a declaration of public emergency was accepted by the European Court of Human Rights in the case of Northern Ireland, where low-intensity, irregular violence was established. It is clear, on its face, that Kosovo falls within this category of a public emergency given the security situation and the need for an international military force to maintain peace and order. Further consideration should, however, be given to how the principles of derogation may apply to the current situation in Kosovo."

[401] For a more detailed discussion, see below Part IV, Chapter 15.

[402] See UNMIK Press Briefing of 2 July 2001, Statement on the Ombudsperson's report.

This justification is questionable. UNMIK made this claim for derogation at a moment where a functioning legal system with domestic courts
and prosecutors had been re-established.[403] It was therefore difficult to
prove that the severe restrictions on the rights guaranteed in Article 5 of
the ECHR and Article 9 of the ICCPR were justified on the basis of strict
necessity[404]. Furthermore, the UN administration had failed publicly to
declare the derogation when defining the law applicable in Kosovo.[405]
Both a measure-related explanation and a norm-specific declaration of
derogation would have been necessary to justify an exception to the
right to liberty and security of person.[406]

4.4.2.3. Human rights exception by virtue of an overriding Chapter VII resolution

Finally, international administrations have adopted very flexible standards of interpretation when determining whether a Chapter VII mandate of the Security Council may be construed as derogation from
human rights obligations. UNMIK representatives argued that Security
Council Resolution 1244 carved out a general security exception in relation to the human rights obligations of international administrators in
Kosovo.[407] This position is untenable in this generalised form.

---

[403] See also Ombudsperson Institution, *Special Report No. 3*, paras. 10, 24 and 29. UNMIK
noted only in general terms that "international human rights standards accept the
need for special measures that, in the wider interests of security, and under
prescribed legal conditions, allow authorities to respond to the findings of
intelligence that are not able to be presented to the court system".

[404] Under Article 15 of the ECHR, emergency measures must be "strictly required by the
exigencies of the situation". Several factors must be examined: the necessity of the
derogations to cope with the threat, the proportionality of the measures, the
duration of the derogation as well as the nature of rights affected and the
circumstances leading to the derogation. See European Court of Human Rights,
Brannigan & McBride v. UK, Ser. A., No. 258-B.

[405] Regulation 2000/59 declared the ECHR and the ICCPR applicable in their entirety. See
Section 1 (3) of Regulation 2000/59.

[406] See also John Cerone, *Minding the Gap: Outlining KFOR Accountability in Post-Conflict
Kosovo*, European Journal of International Law, Vol. 12 (2001), 469.

[407] See UNMIK Press Briefing of 2 July 2001, Statement on the Ombudsperson's report:
"We emphasize that UNMIK's mandate was adopted under Chapter VII, which means
that the situation calls for extraordinary means and force can be used to carry out
the mandate". KFOR also referred to UN SC Res. 1244 as the basis for KFOR authority
to detain persons outside judicial process. KFOR assumed its detention authority
from the authorisation to use "all necessary means" to fulfil its responsibilities and
its mandate to maintain a "safe and secure environment" in Kosovo as long as
"civilian authorities are unable or unwilling to take responsibility for the matter".
This argument is not convincing, as was properly observed by the OSCE: "[A]t the

The Security Council may be entitled to exempt peacekeeping missions from the observance of certain human rights standards under a Chapter VII Resolution, in particular, if these rights are derogable in a state of emergency[408]. The exemption of US peacekeepers from the jurisdiction of the International Criminal Court provides a precedent in which the Council carved out an exception from an international treaty regime under Chapter VII.[409] However, such an exception cannot be inferred from the very general language typically used by the Council in the framing of Chapter VII mandates. A finding by which the Council affirms the existence of a threat to peace in a specific situation does not automatically imply that there is state of emergency in the territory in question.[410] Furthermore, the official policy of the UN is to abide by international human rights instruments and standards within the framework of peacekeeping operations. This principle was reaffirmed in the *Brahimi* Report,[411] which stressed "the essential importance of the United Nations system adhering to and promoting international rights instruments and standards and international humanitarian law in all aspects of its peace and security activities". A derogation from the principle of adherence to human rights standards can only be assumed in exceptional circumstances.[412]

outset of UNMIK's mission, there was a need for a stabilising authority to preserve security, which, from an operational point of view, could have only been provided by KFOR. However, once a regular judicial system was in place, no matter how incipient, KFOR should have gradually adapted its policy regarding detention with a view to phasing it out altogether, and to encourage review of detention issues by regular judicial bodies. A striking example that cuts against KFOR's assertion that its detention authority is justified by the need to preserve a safe and secure climate in a post-conflict territory is... UNTAET... The UN Mission in East Timor has been confronted with a similar security post-conflict environment... and has never claimed nor exercised any detention authority of its own." See OSCE Mission in Kosovo, Department of Human Rights and Rule of Law, Kosovo, *Review of the Criminal Justice System*, September 2001–February 2002, at 47.

[408] See Article 15 of the ECHR and Article of the 4 ICCPR. The right to challenge the lawfulness of a detention before a court is a derogable right.

[409] See most recently para. 6 of SC Res. 1593 of 31 March 2005. For a discussion of the exemptions under SC Res. 1422 (2002), see Carsten Stahn, *The Ambiguities of Security Council Resolution 1422 (2002)*, European Journal of International Law, Vol. 14 (2003), 85, at 98–9.

[410] Dissenting De Wet, *Chapter VII Powers of the United Nations Security Council*, at 322. ("As far as the Security Council is concerned, a determination that the situation in the administered territory constitutes a threat to international peace, would suffice to indicate the existence of a state of emergency.")

[411] See para. 6 of the Report of the Panel on United Nations Peace Operations.

[412] For a parallel argument with respect to derogation from international humanitarian law, see Sassòli, *Legislation and Maintenance of Public Order*, at 681.

Two propositions can be made in this regard. First, there needs to be, at least, a reference in a Chapter VII resolution, which indicates the will of the Council temporarily to supersede the human rights responsibilities of transitional administrations due to considerations of public emergency. Otherwise, the presumption in favour of the applicability of universally recognised human rights standards would continue to apply. Secondly, there is a minimum requirement of transparency. International administrations must publicise this derogation from human rights law. There is even some authority to argue that international administrations should make such a declaration under the relevant international treaty law[413] in an analogous fashion to states,[414] in particular, where they assume the actual powers of a state in their capacity as a surrogate government.

4.5. Territorial administration and democratic governance

International administrations may also be subject to democratic limitations when exercising territorial authority with final decision-making authority.[415] There is not only strong moral support, but also legal authority for the proposition that the legitimacy of public power cannot be founded on norms and institutions alone, but must be established and renewed in a relationship of dialogue between the governing and the governed. This is reflected in the growing number of legal and political instruments that recognise democracy as a universal value, and in the increasing trend towards the universalisation of democracy as a system of government.[416]

The consolidation of the democratic principle as a standard of governance in domestic systems is further complemented by widespread efforts to apply democratic principles to the exercise of public authority at the international level. It is increasingly acknowledged that international entities are subject to basic forms of accountability and responsibility *vis-à-vis* domestic stakeholders the more they exercise direct control

---

[413] See Article 15 (3) of the ECHR and Article 4 (3) of the ICCPR.

[414] See Cerone, *Minding the Gap*, 478, at note 50, who argues that this duty would derive from "the general principle of interpretation that obligations should be construed, where possible, so as to avoid conflicting obligations".

[415] See Salamun, *Democratic Governance in International Territorial Administration*, at 128–87; Bothe and Marauhn, *UN Administration of Kosovo and East Timor*, at 238; Tomuschat, *Yugoslavia's Damaged Sovereignty*, at 326.

[416] See the excellent survey, Commission on Human Rights, *Promotion and Consolidation of Democracy*, UN Doc. E/CN.4/Sub.2/2001/32 of 5 July 2001, paras. 47-78.

over local politics in the era of globalisation.[417] This phenomenon is particularly visible in the debate over the "democratisation" of international institutions such as the EU or the WTO.[418] Both developments converge in the area of international territorial administration. International administering authorities may be bound to comply with democratic principles in two capacities: as transnational entities exercising international public authority and as direct holders of domestic authority.

4.5.1. Applicability of standards of democratic governance to international territorial administrations

The idea that the exercise of governmental authority requires popular consent has a basis in international law.

4.5.1.1. The universalisation of democratic standards

It is inherent in the UN Charter itself. The opening lines of the preamble of the Charter reflect a popular notion of sovereignty by making reference to "the Peoples of the United Nations". Furthermore, the provisions of the trusteeship system (Article 76 (b)) and the concept of self-determination may be understood as early reflections of the underlying democratic foundations of the Charter system. This concept was, three years later, expressed in Article 21 (3) of the Universal Declaration, which stated that the sovereignty of the people is the only legitimate source of governmental authority.[419] The ICCPR went a step further by linking electoral democracy more broadly to the protection of participatory political rights (right to take part in the conduct of public affairs, right to have access to public service) and the rule of law (independence

---

[417] See David Held, *Democracy and the Global Order*, at 267; Susan Marks, *Democracy and International Governance*, in The Legitimacy of International Organizations (J.-M. Coicaud and V. Heiskanen eds., 2001), at 51–2. Sarooshi argues that it is "the inextricable link between domestic public law and the activity of governing that mandates in general terms the application of domestic public law principles to those international organizations that exercise conferred powers of government". See Sarroshi, *International Organizations and their Exercise of Sovereign Powers*, at 91

[418] See, *inter alia*, Giandomenico Majone, *Europe's Democratic Deficit: The Question of Standards*, European Law Journal, Vol. 4 (1998), 5; Andrew Moravcsik, *In Defense of the "Democratic Deficit": Reassessing Legitimacy in the European Union*, Journal of Common Market Studies, Vol. 40 (2002), 803.

[419] The provision reads: "The will of the people shall be the basis of the authority of government, This will shall be expressed in periodic and genuine elections which shall be by universal and equal suffrage and shall be held by secret vote or by equivalent free voting procedures."

of the judiciary, guarantees of due process).[420] Today, these principles enjoy quasi-universal recognition under the heading of the notion of democratic governance.[421] The promotion and protection of democratic standards is not only a core value of the member states of the Council of Europe and the OSCE, but also a founding principle of the fifty-four members of the Commonwealth,[422] the Inter-American system,[423] the newly founded African Union[424] and a constant ingredient of trade arrangements ("democratic clauses")[425] and development policies.[426]

4.5.1.2.   Application to international administrations

Democratic standards may apply to international territorial administrations in at least two ways: by way of the principle of functional duality and by way of a conception of democracy as a human right.

4.5.1.2.1.   Functional duality

International territorial administrations act in specific cases in a dual capacity, namely as independent international entities with separate legal personality, and as functional organs of the territory which they administer.[427] This is, in particular, the case in situations in which international actors exercise exclusive or shared forms of public authority with direct and binding effect on the inhabitants or the institutions of the administered territory. It is plausible to argue that international entities are bound to observe core principles of democratic governance in

---

[420] See Article 25 ICCPR.

[421] See on the emergence the early contributions Franck, *The Emerging Right to Democratic Governance*, Vol. 86 (1992), 46; Fox, *The Right to Political Participation in International Law*, 539.

[422] See Commission on Human Rights, *Promotion and Consolidation of Democracy*, UN Doc. E7CN.4/Sub.2/2001/32 of 5 July 2001, paras. 63–8.

[423] Membership in the Organization of American States is based on democratic standards. See Article 3 of the OAS Charter ("the solidarity of the American States and the high aims which are sought through it require the political organization of those States on the basis of the effective exercise of representative democracy"). Furthermore, OAS member states agreed on a sanctions regime designed to outlaw the non-democratic overturn of democratic governments.

[424] The preamble and Articles 3 and 4 of the Constitutive Act of the African Union make it clear that popular participation and democratic governance are key principles of the Union.

[425] See on the European practice generally Hoffmeister, *Menschenrechts- und Demokratieklauseln*, at 7–117.

[426] See Irving, *The United Nations and Democratic Intervention*, at 49–52.

[427] For a full discussion of the concept of "functional duality", see below Part IV, Chapter 14.

these circumstances. In these cases, the obligation to respect democratic principles derives from the fact that international administrations cross the boundary between the domestic and the international legal order, as they assume the traditional functions of a state in territories under transition.[428] This accumulation of functions justifies the extension of certain elements of democratic theory to international administrations, including the duty to further political participation.[429]

4.5.1.2.2. Democracy as a human right

An additional argument to support the applicability of standards of democratic governance to international administration is the growing recognition of democracy as a human rights entitlement.

Early human rights instruments such as the Universal Declaration on Human Rights reflect a minimalist conception of democracy, based on the requirement of the periodic replacement of rulers following free and fair elections. The ideological divide of the Cold War made it impossible to recognise democracy as a broader right and concept. This limited understanding of democracy was, however, soon overtaken by a growing recognition of the mutual interdependence between democracy and human rights. The ICCPR combined the right to fair and free elections with the broader recognition of political rights, such as the right of political participation and access to public services.[430] Furthermore, regional conventions such as the ECHR[431] or the American Convention on Human Rights[432] began to emphasise the interrelationship between human rights, democracy and the rule of law by recognising that democracy is linked to the existence of a system of government that allows the realisation of human rights. This holistic understanding of democracy[433] culminated in the formal recognition of democratic governance as a human right by the Commission on Human Rights in

---

[428] See also with respect to human rights law more generally, Wilde, *The Accountability of International Organization*, at 168.

[429] Concurring von Carlowitz, *UNMIK Lawmaking*, at 368–9.

[430] See Article 25 of the ICCPR.

[431] See Article 11 of the ECHR.

[432] See Article 29 of the American Convention on Human Rights.

[433] This approach is particularly well captured in an expanded working paper on the promotion and consolidation of democracy of the Commission of Human Rights, which notes: "If the sovereign will of the people is to be reflected in 'the holding of periodic free and fair elections by universal suffrage and by secret ballot', the State must guarantee respect for the human rights and fundamental freedoms of citizens. In order for electors to be able to express their preferences among the various forms of government, it is *sine qua non* that, in particular, the constitution should provide

its Resolutions 1199/57 ("Promotion of the right to democracy")[434] and 2000/47 ("Promoting and consolidating democracy").[435] Referring to the right of self-determination and the protection of democracy as universal values, the Commission observed that a large body of international law and instruments confirm "the right to full participation and other fundamental democratic rights and freedoms inherent in any democratic society".[436] This led the Commission to the definition of a non-exhaustive list of "rights of democratic governance",[437] which was then confirmed by the General Assembly in its Resolution 55/96 ("Promoting and consolidating democracy").[438]

The increasing recognition of democratic governance as a human right entitlement[439] has implications for the definition of the scope of the obligation of international territorial administrations. If democratic governance is qualified as a subjective right, it may form part of an irrevocable *acquis* of the people. International administering authorities may thus be obliged to apply principles of good governance (transparency, accountability) to their own action, and help restore the standards of democratic governance which prevailed before their own assumption of authority in the administered territories.

4.5.2. The scope of obligation

Although it may be acknowledged that standards of democratic governance apply in principle to international territorial administrations,

and offer guarantees for the exercise of 'freedom of association' and 'freedom of expression and opinion'. These fundamental freedoms are, likewise, a prerequisite for 'a pluralistic system of political parties and organizations' which in turn presupposes the existence of 'free, independent and pluralistic media'... [T]he exercise of power in a democratic system must be 'in accordance with the rule of law' which is supported by the 'separation of powers', and, in particular, by the 'independence of the judiciary'. Finally, if democracy is to have the added value of being an effective way to exercise power, good governance must be based on 'transparency and accountability in public administration'." See Commission on Human Rights, *Promotion and Consolidation of Democracy*, UN. Doc E/CN.4/Sub.2/2002/36 of 10 June 2002, para. 12.

[434] See Commission on Human Rights, *Resolution 1999/57* of 27 April 1999, adopted by fifty-one votes to zero, with two abstentions.

[435] See Commission on Human Rights, *Resolution 2000/47* of 25 April 2000, adopted by forty-five votes to zero, with eight abstentions.

[436] See para. 5 of the preamble of Resolution 1999/57.

[437] See para. 2 of Resolution 1999/57 and para. 1 of Resolution 2000/47.

[438] See para. 1 of GA Res. 55/96 of 28 February 2001.

[439] The expanded working paper of the Commission of Human Rights speaks of an "*opinio juris* in the process of the international legitimization of a right to democracy". See Commission on Human Rights, *Promotion and Consolidation of Democracy*, UN. Doc E/CN.4/Sub.2/2002/36 of 10 June 2002, para. 13.

there is some uncertainty as to the precise scope of rights and obligations covered by this duty, in particular in the light of the special factual circumstances prevailing in situations in transition. Both the Commission on Human Rights and the General Assembly adopted a very wide notion of democratic governance, encompassing a range of institutional and human rights components.[440] In its Resolution 1999/57, the Commission on Human Rights linked democracy, *inter alia*, to the following rights and freedoms:

(a) The rights to freedom of opinion and expression, of thought, conscience and religion, and of peaceful association and assembly, (b) The right to freedom to seek, receive and impart information and ideas through media; (c) The rule of law, including legal protection of citizens' rights, interests and personal security, and fairness in the administration of justice and independence of the judiciary; (d) the right of universal and equal suffrage, as well as free voting procedures and periodic and free elections; (e) The right of political participation, including equal opportunity for all citizens to become candidates, (f) Transparent and accountable government institutions; (g) The right of citizens to choose their governmental system through constitutional or other democratic means; (h) The right to equal access to public service in one's own country.[441]

This catalogue cannot be unconditionally transposed to international territorial administrations which often have to deal with the administration of territories in a state of transition.[442] It may be impossible to demand full compliance with standards of democratic governance in the early stage of a mission. The scope of obligations must be determined in the light of the circumstances of the specific situation.[443]

Some general guidelines may, however, be formulated *in abstracto*. Democratic standards cannot be established or restored overnight, even if they were applied in a territory before the establishment of an international territorial administration. At the beginning of a mission, international territorial administrations may encounter an objective duty to ensure and respect the democratic rights and freedoms inherent in a democratic society. This duty may, in particular, oblige the administration to institutionalise checks and balances in the framework of the

---

[440] See para. 1 of Commission on Human Rights Resolution 2000/47 and para. 1 of GA Res. 55/96.

[441] See para. 2 of Resolution 1999/57.

[442] See also Smyrek, *Internationally Administered Territories*, at 217 *et seq.*

[443] Security concerns or inter-group rivalries may, for example, justify the postponement of the holding of elections. Furthermore, both the enjoyment of certain human rights and the degree of institutional checks and balances may be limited in situations of conflict or emergency. See also above "Self-determination and political participation".

mission,[444] to apply principles of state organisation (separation of power, accountability, judicial independence) in the establishment of governing structures and to increase the involvement of local stakeholders in legislative and executive decision-making in accordance with the principle of self-determination and the right to political participation.[445]

Over time, this obligation may then develop into a subjective entitlement to democratic governance, would encompass a right of individuals and peoples to demand of their rulers "a political regime based on the rule of law and separation of powers, in which citizens can periodically elect their leaders and representatives in free and fair elections, on the basis of the interaction between a number of political parties".[446]

---

[444] See also Knaus and Martin, *Travails of the European Raj*, at 73.
[445] Concurring von Carlowitz, *UNMIK Lawmaking*, at 371.
[446] See Commission on Human Rights, *Promotion and Consolidation of Democracy*, UN Doc. E/CN.4/Sub.2/2001/32 of 5 July 2001, para. 81.

12   The legitimacy of international territorial authority

The assumption of public authority by international actors raises not only issues of legality, but also questions of public legitimacy.[1] International territorial administration is a prime example of the exercise of public authority by a non-state entity. This makes it necessary to devote some more thinking to the legitimacy of transitional administrations, and to their role and place in the debate over legitimacy beyond the state more generally.[2]

1. Features of international territorial authority

The authority exercised by international administrations is a special form of authority.[3] It has two dimensions. It bears significant resemblances to state authority,[4] but remains related to an external framework

---

[1] Medieval thought did not distinguish between the legality and the legitimacy of public power. Public authority was considered as legitimate if the ruling power was brought into office by the right procedure, being either by hereditary order or by election, and if that authority was exercised within the boundaries of positive law. This understanding changed with the emerging ideas of democracy and sovereignty of the people in the era of Enlightenment and the consolidation of democratic schools of legitimacy over the twentieth century. Sources for the justification of governance were developed at the national level, namely to legitimise the exercise of authority by a state in relation to its people, and later extended to transnational entities exercising public authority within a multilayered system of governance. For a historical survey of the evolution of legitimacy, see Ian Clark, *Legitimacy in International Society* (2005).

[2] The practice of international territorial administration has received little attention from this angle. See also Korhonen and Gras, *International Governance*, at 150. For a treatment, see Berman, *Intervention in a "Divided World"*, at 758–67.

[3] It differs from classical state authority in the sense that the former is based on sovereignty, whereas the latter is merely founded upon territorial jurisdiction.

[4] Note, however, that international territorial authority is typically a non-sovereign form of authority. See above Part III, Chapter 11.

of reference, namely the legal order under which the international entity is constituted. In particular, this internal dimension of authority is of special interest.[5] This type of authority is exercised either in conjunction with or at the place of domestic organs. Moreover, it has immediate effect on domestic actors. The exercise of legislative, executive and judicial functions by international administrators within the framework of governance missions come very close to replicating the traditional power structures between a state and its people in practice.[6] This substitution raises fundamental questions of legitimacy.

2. Models of legitimation

Although international territorial administrations are frequently involved in the exercise of governmental functions performed by states, traditional strategies of legitimising public authority cannot simply be transferred to international territorial administrations. Democratic concepts of legitimacy which legitimate the authority of a government towards its people do not apply in the same fashion to international administering authorities as they are typically authorised or appointed by a decision of an independent international organisation. Furthermore, democratic procedures may not even provide the most suitable form of legitimacy because a system of pure majority rule and popular or representative democracy is often ill-equipped to address the particular necessities of post-conflict societies.

The legitimation of the exercise of public authority by international administrations must therefore be founded on alternative concepts of legitimacy. Some sources of justification are directly linked to democracy-based concepts of legitimacy. International administrations may derive legitimacy from a discourse-based understanding of governance, involving a gradual involvement of local stakeholders in the decision-making process. Additional legitimation for exercise of public authority may follow from the observance of transparency and accountability in government – two concepts which are inherent in democratic governance. Moreover, the acceptance of international governance may be built on certain comparative advantages that are inherent in the design and

---

[5] Knoll speaks of "domestic legitimacy". See Knoll, *Legitimacy and UN-Administration of Territory*, at 43–4.
[6] International administrations may, in particular, adopt legal acts which directly penetrate into the domestic legal system of territories under administration and create rights and obligations for individuals. See below Part IV, Chapter 15.

functioning of territorial administration. Functionalist criteria such as expertise and impartiality may, for example, be considered as legitimating factors for the exercise of public power, *en lieu* or, at least, as a supplement to democracy-related notions of legitimacy.

Four different models of legitimating international territorial authority will be examined in greater detail here: legitimacy qua consent, utilitarian models of justification, participatory legitimacy structured around constitutive process rules of participation and reasoned dialogue, and functionalist criteria of legitimacy. None of these legitimacy models offer a conclusive justification for the contemporary conceptions of governance within the framework of international territorial administration. Nevertheless, they provide, at least a partial justification for the exercise of governmental authority beyond the state.

2.1. Legitimacy by consent

The idea of consent is the most traditional criterion for the justification of public authority. It goes back to the political theories of Locke,[7] Rousseau,[8] and Kant,[9] who founded the legitimacy of government on the assumption of a social contract between the governed with the governor. Consent is one of the core foundations of the obligations of states under international law[10] and it is of direct relevance in the area of territorial administration.

2.1.1. Delegation of authority

The most classical justification for the exercise of public authority by international entities is the argument of delegation of authority by the territorial sovereign. States are generally free to grant parts of their authority or jurisdiction to another entity, which may act on their behalf. International territorial authority may be viewed as delegated state authority. It may, in particular, be argued that states consent to the exercise of public authority by international entities by acceding to a multilateral treaty arrangement (e.g. a peace treaty) or the constitutive document of an international organisation (UN Charter, NATO Treaty), which allows this type of undertaking. The legitimacy of international

---

[7] See John Locke, *Two Treatises on Government* (1690) (Peter Laslett ed., 1988), at 230–1.

[8] See Jean Jacques Roussseu, *Du Contrat Social* (1762) (Union Générale D'Editions, 1963).

[9] See Immanuel Kant, *Metaphysik der Sitten, Das Öffentliche Recht* (1748), §§ 43–9 (Wilhelm Weischedel ed., 1968).

[10] See generally on "common consent" as the "basis the Law of Nations", Oppenheim, *International Law*, Vol. I (1947), at 16–20.

territorial authority derives thus from a process of delegation of powers, by which a state agrees to accept and implement specific international decisions.

This voluntarist model of legitimacy is at the heart of the justification of the institutional powers of international organisations, generally. The argument of general consent explains, in particular, why certain projects of governance are legitimate even though they are established against the will of the ruling government of the host state. But this type of consent provides a rather formal and weak source of justification for the internal dimension of authority exercised within the framework territorial administration. It is, in particular, ill-equipped to justify the authority of international entities to make decisions that bind the inhabitants of the administered territories. Voluntarism does not sufficiently take into account the increasing disaggregation of the state into sub-state actors for whom general state consent may have little legitimating effect. General state consent may provide a sufficient justification for the exercise of public authority in cases where this consent only has direct implications for the state as an international entity. However, it is problematic in cases such as international territorial administration where the decisions directly affect private actors. This model of legitimacy equates states' consent to the consent of the governed. This equation is justifiable from a strictly legal point of view,[11] but may be criticised from a legitimacy perspective, because it assumes the will of the governed, even in the absence of explicit popular consent. Projects of administration which are aimed at determining the status or condition of the inhabitants of the territory require consent by the governed in order to gain legitimacy.

Furthermore, the model of delegation of powers does not offer a justification for all types of international administrations. Given the drafting history of Chapter VII, it may be argued that states vested the Security Council with the power to exercise powers of governance within a state for the purpose of peace-maintenance.[12] However, such a delegation is less clear in the case of the General Assembly.[13] Moreover, some administering authorities were established without a UN mandate (OHR, CPA)

---

[11] The government is traditionally the organ which obliges states in their external relations. This approach is reflected by court practice. See Elihu Lauterpacht, *The Development of the Law of International Organizations by the Decisions of International Tribunals*, Recueil des Cours, Vol. 152 (1976, IV), 377, at 459–60.

[12] See Sarooshi, *The United Nations and the Development of Collective Security*, at 16–19.

[13] See above Part III, Chapter 11.

and later endorsed by the Security Council. Such administrations are merely built on implied international consent.

2.1.2.   Case-specific consent

Alternatively, it may be argued that the consent given to the establishment of a specific international territorial administration may legitimate the public authority exercised by it. As has been shown in Part II,[14] most administrations were indeed established on the basis of some form of case-specific consent, expressed either in an agreement or by an acceptance of the takeover of governmental functions by the UN. Nevertheless, this variation of the consent theory suffers equally from shortcomings.

There is, first of all, a problem of representation. Internationally expressed state consent often rests on weak grounds domestically in situations of transition. International law ties powers of representation to factual parameters, such as effective control[15] or the presumed continuity of sovereign statehood.[16] This approach may raise legitimacy conflicts in cases where a government maintains the power to represent a state entity externally, but lacks recognition and representativity internally. The government of the FRY, for example, could hardly be said to be an adequate representative of the will of the people of Kosovo when agreeing to the terms of SC Resolution 1244 in 1999, which (other than the Rambouillet Accord) does not expressly provide for the holding of a referendum on independence. Similarly, one may equally have doubts as to whether the anticipated consent by Indonesia to the establishment of a UN mission in the Accords of 5 May 1999 may be viewed as an adequate reflection of the consent of the East Timorese people to the creation of UNTAET. The weakness in both cases is that international law equates the consent of a government to the consent of its people, regardless

---

[14] See above Part II, Chapter 10.

[15] See Thomas M. Franck, *Postmodern Tribalism and the Right to Secession*, in Peoples and Minorities in International Law (C. Brölmann, R. Lefeber, M. Zieck eds, 1993), at 24. ("The requirement that a state, to be eligible for recognition, be in *effective control of a defined territory and population is a requisite of customary international law*.") For a discussion of effectiveness as a criteria for statehood, see also Crawford, *Creation of States*, 2nd edn (2006), at 55–61.

[16] Jennings and Watt note: "Mere territorial changes, whether by increase or by diminution do not, as long as the identity of the State is preserved, affect the continuity of its existence or the obligations of its treaties. Changes in the government or the internal polity of a State do not as a rule affect its position in international law." See *Oppenheim's International Law* (1996), at 146.

of the representative nature of the authority of that state over these individuals.

Moreover, in the numerous cases in which an international administration is established on the basis of a Chapter VII resolution of the Security Council, the argument of specific consent is very difficult to make. The authority of the legal obligation primarily derives in this case from the effect of the Council's decision, which does not require state consent.[17]

2.2. Alternatives to consent

Four different concepts may provide further guidance: emergency-related arguments, utilitarian models of legitimacy, process-oriented conceptions of legitimacy and functionalist considerations.

2.2.1.   The emergency situation argument

Deviations from traditional governance have been justified by emergency-related arguments. International administrations deployed in conflict and post-conflict situations have to operate in a different political setting than peacetime governments.[18] These circumstances have been used to justify some of the particularities of international territorial authority. It has, in particular, been argued that internationalised governance models and centralist forms of authority are permissible exceptions to the rule of local ownership because they are better placed than ordinary forms of government to address scenarios of domestic turmoil and transition.

This claim has been presented in different variations. UNMIK invoked the "emergency" situation in Kosovo in order to justify the maintenance of international authority[19] and derogations from human rights standards to its conduct.[20] UNTAET pointed to a lack of stability and

[17] The contractual arrangement, which precedes the exercise of the power, may be rightly qualified as a request to the Council to exercise its powers. See Danesh Sarooshi, Preliminary Remarks on the Conferral by States of Powers of International Organizations, British Yearbook of International Law, Vol. 74 (2003), at 17–18.
[18] The experience of the UN in post-conflict settings has revealed that "legislative frameworks often show ... signs of neglect and distortion, contain discriminatory elements and rarely reflect the requirements of international human rights and criminal law standards". See the Report of the Secretary-General, The Rule of Law and Transitional Justice in Conflict and Post-conflict Societies, para. 27. In this context, "emergency laws and executive decrees are often the order of the day". Ibid., para. 27.
[19] See UNMIK Press Briefing of 2 July 2001, Statement on the Ombudsperson's report, above Chapter 11, 4.4.2.3.
[20] Ibid., above Chapter 11, 4.4.2.2.

preparedness of local actors in order to defer a transfer governing powers to local institutions.[21] Finally, members of the CPA referred to the lack of security and rule of law in Iraq in order to take control of the detention system and detain persons for imperative reasons of security.[22]

The plea for commissarial state reconstruction and a concentration of power in the hands of a few in situations of emergency finds some support in legal theory and practice. Theorists like Carl Schmitt have criticised the concept of the "minimal state" (*Minimalstaat*) on the ground that liberal democracy requires a rational, secularised environment in order to function.[23] The idea of a centralisation of power within situations of emergency is also common in constitutional theory, which tends to support a concentration of authority in the hands of the executive in situations of emergency.[24]

But the emergency argument is subject to abuse and is ambivalent from the perspective of legitimacy. The fact that a territory under international administration is in a state of exception does not mean that international administration *per se* can be construed as an exceptional governance paradigm, which is subject to exceptionalist rules and double standards in governance. International administrations serve, to some extent, as a model for domestic authorities in situations of emergency. The establishment of a political and judicial system, based on institutional pluralism, human rights protection and the rule of law, is usually the very purpose of international statebuilding and ought to be at the forefront of international engagement. There is, in particular, a point in time in every mission at which the maintenance of autocratic rule on the basis of emergency powers becomes a contradiction in itself, because it runs counter to the mandate of international territorial administration.

Secondly, international governance is in all situations the best option to address emergency scenarios. A strong international presence, indeed,

---

[21] See the statement by former UNTAET SRSG De Mello in Beauvais, *Benevolent Despotism*, at 1120.

[22] See below Part IV, Chapter 15.

[23] This argument is, in particular, developed in Schmitt's theory of emergency powers. See generally Oren Gross, *The Normless and Exceptionless Exception: Carl Schmitt's Theory of Emergency Powers and the "Norm-Exception" Dichotomy*, Cardazo Law Review, Vol. 21 (2000), 1820.

[24] Note also that the framework of the laws of occupation fails to place administering powers under an obligation to further the establishment of democratic structures of governance. See also J. M. Mossner, *Military Government*, Encyclopedia of Public International Law, Vol. 3 (1997), at 391.

may be required in a concrete governance vacuum.[25] However, in other situations the externalisation of authority may be counterproductive. The UN itself has recognised that robust international governance may be less effective than support for "local ownership, local leadership and a local constituency for reform".[26]

2.2.2.   Governance for the greatest benefit of the people – the utilitarian argument

A different justification for international authority may be drawn from utilitarian models of legitimacy. Utilitarian doctrines focus on the needs of a society and provide legitimation to the form of government which is best suited to serve goals of that society in a given situation.[27] This argument was originally used as a justification for democratic government by eighteenth-century utilitarians such as Bentham and Mill, who viewed democracy as a means of maximising the realisation of individual's interests rather than as an end in itself.[28] In the context of territorial administration, this claim has some force as a counter-argument against purely majoritarian rule in the context of societies in transition. International administration may be justified as a form of government which is likely to secure the interest of the greatest number of persons in a process of transition.[29]

There may be compelling reasons to postpone the holding of democratic elections in the immediate aftermath of conflict or after a transfer of authority.[30] Newly autonomous or divided societies often still lack the political infrastructure for democratic pluralism and multi-party government because the structure of the society is dominated by specific

---

[25] See the Report of the Secretary-General, *The Rule of Law and Transitional Justice in Conflict and Post-conflict Societies*, para. 27.

[26] *Ibid.*, para. 17.

[27] Utilitarist doctrines generally look at governmental authority from the angle of maximising general welfare and happiness. For a survey, see Herbert L. Hart, *"Utilitarism and Natural Rights"*, in Essays in Jurisprudence and Philosophy (1983), at 181.

[28] See Diane F. Orentlicher, *Separating Anxiety: International Responses to Ethno-Separatist Claims*, Yale Journal of International Law, Vol. 23 (1998), 1, 53-54.

[29] For a qualification of utilitarism as a criterion of legitimacy, see also Thomas M. Franck, *Fairness in International Law and Institutions* (1995), at 7, 22, 25, 26.

[30] See also the Report of the Secretary-General, *The Rule of Law and Transitional Justice in Conflict and Post-conflict Societies,* para. 22. ("Recent experience has demonstrated that holding elections without adequate political and security preparation and disengaging too soon can undermine, rather than facilitate the process of building the rule of law.")

national elites or alliances built in the course of conflict.[31] The holding of general elections may be a zero sum game under such circumstances. It may result in a "winner-takes-all" scenario or in a "majority dictatorship". There must first be some institutional diversity and competition among different political forces for democracy to work. In many cases, such a climate can be built or restored only through the presence and regulatory involvement of external powers and affirmative action in favour of specific groups.

Secondly, there is a need to provide special mechanisms of "minority protection" in situations of transition, through power-sharing arrangements at the institutional level and proportional restrictions of liberal rights. The very process of liberalisation presents new opportunities for increased ethnic mobilisation and abuses of power. Conflicts of identity may continue and may destabilise the political climate.

One principal forum in which such conflicts unfold is the media. Instead of fostering a balance of views that limits the spread of hatred, the media may become a source for the incitement of hatred and the vindication of ethno-national identities. Such practices occurred in the context of the genocide in Rwanda and in the process of reconstruction of Kosovo.[32] Governing authorities may be compelled to impose a greater level of control over the media in post-conflict societies than in the context of stabilised social orders.

Moreover, premature democratisation may destabilise a society in the short term.[33] The establishment of pluralism may require the

---

[31] See Samuel H. Barnes, *The Contribution of Democracy to Rebuilding Postconflict Societies*, American Journal of International Law, Vol. 95 (2001), 86, at 88.

[32] See Laura R. Palmer, *A Very Clear and Present Danger: Hate Speech, Media Reform, and Post-Conflict Democratization in Kosovo*, Yale Journal of International Law, Vol. 26 (2001), 179.

[33] See the Report of the Secretary-General, *The Rule of Law and Transitional Justice in Conflict and Post-conflict Societies*, para. 22. See also Boutros Boutros-Ghali, *An Agenda For Democratization*, para. 16. ("This is not to say that democracy is without detractors ... [T]he charge is made that there can be no democracy in times of trouble or war, that democracy itself leads to disorder, that democracy diminishes efficiency, that democracy violates minority and community rights, and that democracy must wait until development is fully achieved.") Note also that the usual claim according to which the features of liberal democracy promote international peace cannot be transposed to the context of domestic conflicts among ethnic groups. Even proponents of the liberal state theory admit that "[n]o systematic evidence exists ... to demonstrate that liberal democracy has an equally pacific effect on internal ethnic strife". See Anne-Marie Slaughter, *Pushing the Limits of the Liberal Peace: Ethnic Conflict and the "Ideal Polity"*, in International Law and Ethnic Conflict (D. Wippman ed., 1998), 128, at 143.

establishment of an institutional framework which protects populations against the power of national elites to secure their interests. This lesson has led to the adoption of several variations to the liberal democracy theory in divided societies, such as Lijphart's elite-based consociational approach[34] or integrationalist models of power-sharing,[35] which propose to foster political reconstruction in situations of transition through special power-sharing and autonomy arrangements for conflicting social groups.

These findings are of direct relevance to the legitimation of international authority. Both the procedural and the socio-political concerns regarding instant majority rule in situations of transition indicate that the finality of providing a society with a stable and integrative long-term legal order may constitute a legitimating factor for the provisional internationalisation of governance. A conceptual justification for derogation from domestic authority may be found in the benefit of the society as a whole. International authorities may, in some cases, be better placed than domestic authorities to take charge of majority and minority interests alike.

However, such a justification of the coercive side of international administration continues to suffer from a paradox. A utilitarian vision of government tends to shut its eyes to the organisational aspects of the relations between the rulers and its people in the exercise of public authority (e.g. accountability and identification among the governors and governed). Moreover, it fails provide an answer to the deeper question as to what extent international actors should be involved in domestic decision-making processes at all and what comparators they should use in making utilitarian assessments.[36]

---

[34] Under the consociational approach, elites directly represent the various societal segments and act to forge political ties at the centre. Lijphart suggests that consociation encompasses four basic principles: a broad-based coalition executive; minority veto; proportionality in the allocation of public funds and civil service positions; and group autonomy. See Arend Lijphart, *Democracy in Plural Societies* (1977), 25. Nordlinger argues that "elites alone can initiate, work out and implement conflict regulating practices, therefore they alone can make direct and positive contributions to conflict regulating outcomes". See Eric Nordlinger, *Conflict Regulation in Divided Societies* (1972), 73.

[35] Critics of the consociational approach argue that the reliance on elite accommodation institutionalizes ethnicity. They argue that the likelihood of violent conflict is reduced more effectively by institutions and practices that create incentives for the formation of coalitions and that encourage intra-group competition rather than inter-group competition. See Donald Horowitz, *Ethnic Groups in Conflict* (1985), 14.

[36] See also Knoll, *Beyond the "Mission Civilisatrice"*, at 281–3.

2.2.3.   Participatory legitimacy

Another alternative to classical rules of governmental legitimacy may be found in participatory models of legitimacy. Participatory theories seek to justify authority through rules of participation and reasoned dialogue within a polity. They operate on the assumption that the legitimacy of government rests not so much on the normative order of a system, but rather on democratic discourse and the process of decision-making.[37] The main postulate of this model of legitimacy is that the acceptance of governmental decisions derives from the interaction of a variety of actors in the decision-making process and the internalisation of these decisions in the institutional practice of the respective polity.

This view has particular importance in the context of the governmental legitimacy of international territorial administrations. A process-based understanding of legitimacy presents a viable alternative to traditional democratic models of legitimacy, because it builds on similar parameters of legitimation (accountability, transparency), without relying strictly on popular consent in the choice of the rulers. One core idea of participatory legitimacy, in particular, applies directly to transitional administration: the legitimation of authority through the involvement of stakeholders in the decision-making process.

Public participation may occur in several forms. It can simply mean the representation of local actors in the public institutions of an internationally administered territory, but it can also take the form of citizen participation in the deliberative processes of a polity. Both methods of participation have served as sources of legitimacy in the area of international territorial administration.[38] These forms of participation create legitimacy through process. They make a tripartite contribution to the legitimation of international authority: they increase transparency, they institutionalise accountability and they add to the dispersion of power.

---

[37] For a detailed discussion of Habermas' discursive theory and the concept of deliberative democracy, see Jürgen Habermas, *Between Facts and Norms: Contributions to a Discourse Theory of Law and Democracy* (William Rehg trans., 1996), at 118.

[38] The first approach dates back to colonial practice and the UN Trusteeship System and has been practised by the UN in the context of direct territorial administration since the engagement in West Irian in the 1960s. The second one, power-sharing among local and international actors in decision-making, has become an integral part of modern governance missions (Kosovo, East Timor, Iraq). It is typically applied in the process of a gradual devolution of authority to domestic actors, with varying degrees of participation ranging from advisory functions in decision-making to veto powers or a full control over governmental affairs. For a full discussion, see below Part IV, Chapter 16.

2.2.4.   Functionalist criteria of legitimacy

Lastly, the acceptability of acts of public authorities may be founded upon functionalist criteria. Functionalist factors of legitimation are typically used to legitimise the authority and impact of specialised international decision-making bodies (e.g. WTO, ILO, WHO etc.) on domestic legal systems. They are also relevant in the context of territorial administration. Two criteria of legitimacy shall be discussed here, in particular: expertise and neutrality.

2.2.4.1.   Expertise

Expert legitimacy has a long-standing tradition as an alternative to democratic decision-making.[39] It is based on the assumption that decision-makers with special knowledge should be charged with regulatory or administering powers, because they are the most qualified organs to make a well-informed and reasonable judgments. This approach enjoys, in particular, widespread popularity in the scientific and technical fields,[40] and it is an integral part of environmental decision-making.[41]

There are, however, some doubts as to whether this line of justification may be extended from the technical field to the exercise of territorial authority. International administrators cannot be said to possess more political expertise than local actors about the management of the public affairs of administered territory, nor are they necessarily more qualified to make political (value) judgments than domestic authorities.

There are some selected fields in which expertise may provide a special source of legitimacy for international actors, including, *inter alia*, international criminal adjudication, human rights protection, election monitoring and specific aspects of reconstruction (de-mining, refugee return). Transitional justice and human rights protection, in particular, may be considered as areas, in which there is often an urgent need for additional assistance and expertise.[42] There are frequently normative gaps in the domestic law of a society in transition. Moreover, the domestic judiciary may require training. These gaps may be addressed by

---

[39] See Bodansky, *Legitimacy of International Governance*, at 620.

[40] The Agreement on the Application of Sanitary or Phytosanitary Measures, for example, relies on the findings of expert bodies such as the Codex Alimentarius Commission and the International Office of Epizootics, when defining international standards relating to food safety or animal health. See Annex A, para. 3 of the Agreement.

[41] The International Panel on Climate Change is, for example, one of the organs which has become famous for its expertise in the area of climate change.

[42] See the Report of the Secretary-General, *The Rule of Law and Transitional Justice in Conflict and Post-conflict Societies*, para. 27.

a provisional internationalisation of the judiciary and administration of a post-conflict territory, which may include measures such as the appointment of international judges or international prosecutors following the examples of Kosovo or East Timor, the establishment of international(ised) human rights bodies (e.g. ombudspersons, human rights complaint mechanisms, property commissions) or the internationalisation of the police apparatus.[43]

Moreover, valuable expert assistance may be provided by specific international actors which have developed specialised skills in statebuilding. These include regional organisations and NGOs that have developed special expertise in the conduct and monitoring of free and fair elections, refugee return, de-mining and technical assistance.[44]

However, expert knowledge is only a provisional justification for the internationalisation of public authority. Its justificatory effect is limited in time. Expert legitimacy loses its compellingness with the progress of domestic capacity-building in the administered territory and the concurrent emergence of local expertise.[45]

2.2.4.2.   Independence and neutrality

A further functionalist justification for the deployment of international administering structures lies in potential independence and neutrality of international decision-makers.

The mandate of international administrators is often related to conflict resolution or conflict management, be it in the context of territorial dispute resolution, decolonisation or statebuilding. International authorities may enjoy special legitimacy in these situations, not necessarily because of their superior technical knowledge but rather because of their status as independent decision-making powers.[46]

---

[43] Ibid., para. 30.

[44] NGOs have been called upon to perform state-type functions in areas like health care, the re-establishment of water and sanitation systems and in the agricultural and environmental sector in the Balkans. Moreover, they have been actively involved in election monitoring since the 1990s. This process has culminated in the establishment of formal registration systems for NGOs by UNMIK and the High Representative in Bosnia and Herzegovina. See UNMIK Regulation No. 22/1999 of 15 November 1999. For a detailed survey, see Stahn, NGOs and International Peacekeeping, at 397.

[45] See also the Report of the Secretary-General, The Rule of Law and Transitional Justice in Conflict and Post-conflict Societies, para.17.

[46] See also ibid., para. 27. ("National judicial police and corrections systems have typically been stripped of the human, financial and material sources necessary for their proper functioning. They also often lack legitimacy, having been transformed by conflict and abuse into instruments of repression.")

The legitimacy of authority is based on a reciprocal relationship. International authorities are bestowed with governing functions because they are presumed to be more detached from local conflict and politics than domestic actors. This distance may provide them with a better ability to analyse the causes of conflict and neutralise its sources. At the same time, the special status of international authorities may enhance the chances of compliance with public authority. Domestic actors are more likely to accept the authority and decisions of entities which are by their very nature able to balance conflicting interests.

The neutrality and even-handedness associated with international entities may, in particular, explain the use of international administering structures in cases such as the Saar, Leticia, West Irian, Eastern Slavonia and Mostar. However, the virtues of neutrality and impartiality vanish in cases where international institutions become "the government of the state" and run the internal affairs of a territory. In this situation, the "foreign interests", which need to be reconciled by the administration, become more closely intertwined with the self-interests of the administration. This may trigger a conflict of interest in which the requirement of neutrality collides with the responsibilities of the administration as an internal organ of the territory under administration.

Conclusion

A survey of the foundations of international territorial administration shows that this project poses a number of conceptual challenges, which require fresh thinking in terms of law and theory.

Today, there are hardly any doubts that international administrations may be lawfully established under the umbrella of peace-maintenance of the UN Charter. Moreover, it is widely recognised that international administrations face substantive obligations in the exercise of public authority. However, there are still contrasting views about the applicable sources of law and the scope of legal obligations.[47] This uncertainty does not result from a lack of legal norms, but from a lack of consistency and a certain misperception of the nature of international territorial authority. The legal framework of international administrations has been predominantly viewed through the lens of the institutional law of international organisations and the legal regime applicable in traditional

---

[47] Note that the law in this area has been largely applied and shaped by practice. The individualised vision of the respective engagements may have contributed to divergent and sometimes conflicting interpretations of the nature and scope of legal obligations.

peacekeeping operations. Accordingly, the obligations of modern missions have been primarily derived from the UN Charter, the underlying mandate or self-commitment.

This vision is unsatisfactory. Contemporary developments in international law suggest that additional guidance may be derived from at least three other sources, namely the law of occupation, human rights law and the right to democratic governance. These norms may be applied with certain adjustments or by way of analogy to the exercise of public authority by international actors. In some situations, the law applicable to international administrations may be assessed in light of theories which govern the relationship between individuals and states.

A similar tendency may be observed in the area of legitimacy. International territorial administration has only recently been perceived as a special type of governance which requires attention from the angle of public legitimacy. Some of the traditional models of legitimacy, such as procedural rule-of-law principles (fairness, transparency), institutional checks and balances and mechanisms of public participation may be used to justify the exercise of territorial authority by international actors. But neither the classical state-centred models of legitimacy, nor the global governance schools of justification offer an entirely satisfactory explanation of some of the specific features and pitfalls of international territorial authority fully. This makes it necessary to devote new attention to the justification of public authority in such types of engagements. The way in which specific status and governance problems have been handled in existing practice is now examined in Part IV.

Part IV

A typology of legal problems arising within the context of international territorial administration

Acts by... international authorities were often passed in the name of... States under supervision. Such a situation amounts to a sort of functional duality: an authority of one legal system intervenes in another legal system, thus making its functions dual

Constitutional Court of Bosnia and Herzegovina, Case No. U/9/00 (2000)

Introduction

Under classical international law, the domestic and the international legal orders are portrayed as separate legal orders.[1] International law is conceived as a body of law applicable to various subjects of international law, while municipal law is regarded as the law which applies within a state and between the citizens and institutions of that entity.[2] This strict separation is blurred in the context of international territorial administration.[3] Transitional administrations operate at the edge of the

---

[1] See Georg Schwarzenberger, *International Law*, Vol. 1 (1957), at 67. This statement is particularly well reflected in the judgment of the PCIJ regarding Certain German Interests in Polish Upper Silesia, where the Court found that "[f]rom the standpoint of international law and of the Court... municipal laws are merely facts which express the will and constitute the activities of States, in the same manner as do legal decisions or administrative matters". See PCIJ, *German Interests in Polish Upper Silesia* (1926), Ser. A., No. 7, at 19.

[2] See also the conceptualisation of the "dualist" doctrine by Brownlie, *Principles of Public International Law*, at 32.

[3] Knoll goes so far to argue that the "normative environment of a 'perfectly' internationalized territory resembles a monist model in which municipal and international law form part of a unitary normative system". See Knoll, *Beyond the Mission Civilisatrice*, at 280.

traditional law of international organisations and domestic law. They may be subject to two legal orders when administering territories: the internal legal order of the international legal person or entity which created them and the domestic legal order of the administered territory.

This particularity poses a number of conceptual challenges for international law. Four issues merit special attention in this regard: the legal status of the administered territory, the status of international entities as administering powers, the nature and scope of international lawmaking and the obligations of the administering powers *vis-à-vis* the people of the territory.

13   The legal status of the administered territory

The international administration of territories raises different legal questions related to the status of the administered territory. The establishment of an international administration may affect the status of the administered territory itself. Moreover, the assumption of territorial authority by an international administration may have an impact on relations between the administered territory and other entities.

1.   Status concepts

Territories under international administration do not fit easily within traditional status models. There is often dissociation between sovereignty and government. International administrations typically assume powers of government and administration over the administered territory without acquiring ownership or title over the territory. This distinguishes international administration from territorial sovereignty.[1] The scope of authority assumed by international administrations varies from case to case. It may range from mere coordination and assistance in specific sectors of public authority, to the exercise of exclusive jurisdiction.

1.1.   Notions developed in legal doctrine

Legal scholars recognised quite early on that the phenomenon of international territorial administration raises status questions which require further specification. International territorial administration has, in particular, been rightly distinguished from historical models of foreign

---

[1] See generally on sovereignty and ownership Brownlie, *Principles of Public International Law*, at 106.

administration within the framework of protectorates and condominia,[2] and from administration within the framework of the Mandate and the Trusteeship Systems.[3] However, most of the alternative classifications developed in legal doctrine suffer from conceptual problems. Some of them are too narrow, because they have been developed in response to very specific types of administration. Others are impractical, because they are too vague and imprecise in scope.

1.1.1.   Narrow status concepts

Guggenheim limited his conceptualisation of the paradigm to "subjects of international law created by international treaties".[4] This understanding captures the early practice of free cities and free territories established by treaty, but fails to address the status of territories placed under administration by virtue of a UN resolution.

Others scholars have used the notion of "internationally guaranteed statehood" in order to describe the status of territories which are subject to "external intervention in internal constitutive processes over an extended period".[5] This categorisation addresses the generic features of two administrations: the engagement of the League of Nations in Danzig and the international administration of Bosnia and Herzegovina.[6] But it does not cover the status of territories which are placed under less or more comprehensive supervision than legal guarantee.

1.1.2.   Vague status notions

Other status notions lack precision and clarity. The most prominent example is the concept of "internationalised territories". This concept has been applied to a diversity of cases of territorial administration,

---

[2] See above Part I, Introduction.   [3] See above Part I, Conclusion.
[4] See Paul Guggenheim, *Traité de Droit International Public*, Vol. I (1953), at 216–35 ("Les états créés par traité international").
[5] The particular status of the respective territory is linked to specific features of state organisation. The distinct features of "internationally guaranteed statehood" include, *inter alia*, "the nesting of constitutive instruments with international treaties", "the permeation of the domestic order by external processes of authority", the existence of "[b]alancing mechanisms to foster comity between … constituent ethnic groups" and an "external guarantee of state form". See Grant, *Internationally Guaranteed Constitutional Order*, at 51–2.
[6] See Article 103 of the Treaty of Versaillles: "This constitution shall be placed under the guarantee of the League of Nations." The EU, France, Germany, the Russian Federation, the UK and the US "witnessed" the Dayton Agreement. Article I (2) of Annex 10 specified that the OHR should be "appointed consistent with relevant United Nations Security Council Resolutions".

ranging from the first internationally administered Free Cities to the latest UN administrations in Kosovo and East Timor.[7]

Ydit adopted a rather narrow understanding in his fundamental work on the topic. He defined internationalised territories as "populated areas established for an unlimited duration as special State entities in which supreme sovereignty is vested in (or *de facto* exercised by) a group of States or in the organised international community", where "[t]he local element... is restricted in its sovereign powers by the provisions of an International Statute (Charter, Constitution, etc.) imposed upon it by the Powers holding supreme sovereignty over the territory". This understanding is misleading because it makes internationalisation dependent on the transfer of "sovereignty" to an international authority[8] and it limits the notion of "internationalised territories" to permanently internationalised territories.[9]

Others commentators have defended a broader conception of the notion of "internationalised territories". Internationalised territories have sometimes been defined as "autonomous entities under a form of international protection, supervision or guarantee".[10] This categorisation does not offer much practical guidance because it fails to explain the different status options and types of authority adopted in practice. A similar criticism applies to earlier attempts of definition, such as the proposal to define internationalised territories as a "special category of

---

[7] This concept is the most established notion used to characterise territories under international administration. See Brownlie, *Principles of Public International Law*, at 60; Benzing, *Midwifing a New State*, at 318, Crawford, *Creation of States*, 2nd edn (2006), at 233–41.

[8] The history of international administration from the Mandate System to modern governance missions seems to reveal a different understanding, namely the inappropriateness of the application of the concept of sovereignty to the exercise of public authority by international administrations. The characteristic of territorial internationalisation is the "de-sovereignisation" of a territory. It is therefore more convincing to conceive the exercise of administering powers over an internationalised territory as a form of non-sovereign international governance. See also Ferenc A. Vali, *Servitudes of International Law* (1958), at 282. ([I]n all these cases of administration of foreign territories it is not possible to speak of a cession, the transfer of territorial sovereignty.")

[9] Ydit refers to areas with a "permanent status or at least a status unlimited in time". See Ydit, *Internationalised Territories*, at 20. This limitation presents a selective picture of the practice of internationalisation. Ydit's definition places, in particular, undue emphasis on the period up to the 1960s where international practice was generally receptive to the idea of permanent internationalisation. But it ignores the more recent practice in which international administration has regularly been transitional in nature.

[10] See Crawford, *Creation of States*, at 160.

international persons" which "habitually exhibit severe limitations of their sovereignty" and which can be "classified under the heading of Non-Sovereign Entities with Limited International Personality".[11] Such a definition leaves significant uncertainty about the form of internationalisation and the precise territorial status of the administered entity.[12]

Lastly, a third group of scholars has tried to distinguish territories under international administration from other territorial entities by way of their communitarian form of administration. Verdross used the term "*Staatengemeinschaftsgebiete*" in his 1959 treatise on public international law, in order to distinguish territories under multiple jurisdiction as distinct from condominiums and co-imperiums. A similar notion was later employed by Verzijl, who qualified the League-administered Saar Territory (1920–35) and the UN-governed West Irian (1962–3) as "territor[ies] under the government of the international community". He wrote:

It is possible that a particular portion of the surface of the earth is occasionally placed under the territorial sovereignty or government, not of one or more individual States but under that of the international society of States as a whole, either legally linked in such organizations as the League of Nations or the United Nations, or, hypothetically, even not so linked, but conceived as a kind of mythical all-embracing international Person, the *societas generis humani*.[13]

These attempts of definition are useful in the sense that they underline the special nature and finality of international territorial administration. However, they do not offer substantial guidance for the conceptualisation of the existing international practice.

1.2.   A re-conceptualisation

These conceptual deficiencies make it worthwhile to revisit the existing status notions and to suggest alternative models of classification.

1.2.1.   Territories of international concern

It is, in particular, necessary to draw a general distinction between internationalised and non-internationalised territories. The notion of

---

[11] See Verzijl, *International Law in Historical Perspective*, Part II, at 305.
[12] It is therefore no surprise that some authorities have expressed doubts as to whether the notion of "internationalised territories" has a proper meaning in legal terms at all. The imprecision of the notion of "internationalised territory" led Crawford to conclude in 1979 that "there appears to be no legal – as distinct from political – concept of 'internationalized territory'". See Crawford, *Creation of States*, 1st edn, at 160–1, and 2nd edn (2006), at 233.
[13] See J. H. W. Verzijl, *International Law in Historical Perspective*, Part III (State Territory) (1970), at 473. Verzijl mentions expressly the League's governance of the Saar Territory and UNTEA's supervision of West Irian.

internationalisation may be ascribed to entities which are either re-moved from domestic jurisdiction by the exercise of international au-thority (territorial internationalisation) or placed under the partial con-trol of international administering authorities which act as partners of local authorities in the exercise of specific governing functions (func-tional internationalisation).[14] Some territories fall short of meeting this threshold. The typical cases are those territories in which international actors perform merely tasks of governance assistance or coordination (e.g. Libya, Eritrea, Afghanistan, Liberia), or where international control is weak (e.g. Memel, Western Sahara). The territorial status of these en-tities is not as such affected by the exercise of international authority: following a notion proposed by Hannum, they may simply be referred to as "territories of international concern".[15]

1.2.2. Internationalised entities

Internationalised entities may be further divided into different sub-categories. One may distinguish at least three forms of territorial arrangements: frameworks of administration, under which domestic sovereignty and territorial jurisdiction coincide; arrangements under which the holders of territorial sovereignty and territorial jurisdiction diverge; and situations in which international administrations assume territorial jurisdiction over a territory independent of the control of any other state entity.

These three scenarios are different in substance. They deserve a further terminological differentiation. A tripartite distinction may be made be-tween "internationalised states", "internationalised territories" and "in-ternational territories".[16]

Territories which fall into the first category remain associated with tra-ditional statehood and do not require a distinct status label. The state entities themselves bear traces of internationalisation. They may be re-ferred to as "internationalised states". The notion of international(ised) territories, on the other hand, may be further subdivided in order to distinguish territories of the second and third category.

---

[14] See above Part I, Chapter 1.

[15] See Hannum, *Autonomy, Sovereignty and Self-Determination*, at 383.

[16] Within his examination of "legal persons", Brownlie uses the broader notions of "political entities legally proximate to states" and "UN administrations of territories immediately prior to independence" in order to characterise Danzig and Trieste, on the one hand, and UNTAG and UNTAET, on the other. See Brownlie, *Principles of Public International Law*, at 59–60. These categorisations are, however, of little practical use, because they fail to offer precise criteria for distinction.

Territories which enjoy separate legal personality and in which one or several functions of domestic jurisdiction are exercised by an international institution that administers or governs the territory on behalf of the international community, or by a collectivity of states, may be qualified as internationalised territories *stricto sensu* – a label which highlights the dissociation of jurisdiction and sovereignty.

Lastly, territorial entities which are under the jurisdiction of an international authority and are disconnected from any territorial sovereign enjoy an independent international status. They may be directly qualified as international territories.

1.2.2.1. Internationalised states

Internationalised states may be defined as state entities which are subject to international control and institutionalised power-sharing arrangements within their internal domestic system, while domestic authorities maintain territorial sovereignty and jurisdiction. These requirements are, in particular, met by co-governance missions, which assume governing functions alongside local institutions within the legal system of the administered territory, without replacing or superseding the responsibilities of domestic authorities as the principal territorial ruler.[17]

The typical examples of internationalised statehood are Cambodia[18] and Bosnia and Herzegovina.[19] Both entities were partially

---

[17] The mere exercise of public authority within the framework of a peacekeeping mission, by contrast, does not *per se* suffice to trigger an internationalisation of the legal status of a state. One of the basic features of internationalised statehood is the institutional internationalisation of the domestic legal structure of that state. This feature is lacking in situations in which international authorities replace domestic authority in the exercise of public authorities, because the domestic authority is unable to act due to a collapse of authority, or an emergency situation.

[18] The Paris Peace settlements provided UNTAC with governing responsibilities in specific areas of public authority and veto powers over domestic laws. But domestic authorities retained both territorial sovereignty and jurisdiction over their internal affairs. The agreement itself declared expressly that the Supreme National Council (SNC) represented the "unique legitimate body and source of authority, in which ... the sovereignty, independence and unity of Cambodia are enshrined". See Article 3 of the Agreement on the Political Settlement of the Cambodia Conflict. The power to initiate legislation remained with domestic authorities. Moreover, UNTAC exercised its responsibilities formally only upon a basis of delegation by the SNC. See Article 6 of the Agreement on the Political Settlement of the Cambodia Conflict.

[19] One of the principal objectives of the agreement was to preserve the status of Bosnia and Herzegovina as a sovereign state. See Article X of the Dayton Peace Agreement.

internationalised by way of a peace agreement, but preserved their status as sovereign states and holders of territorial jurisdiction.[20]

1.2.2.2. Internationalised territories

"Internationalised territories" form a separate category of territories. They encompass territorial entities which enjoy some attributes of legal personality as a territory, while remaining attached to the territorial sovereignty of a specific state.

The trademark of "internationalised territories" is the dissociation of sovereignty and jurisdiction. "Internationalised territories" are placed under two layers of public power: the jurisdiction of an international(ised) administration and the sovereignty of the territorial state. The actual governing powers (jurisdiction) lie with ruling authorities of the territorial entity, whereas the territorial sovereign retains the formal title over the latter.

This disjunction of jurisdiction and sovereignty typically arises in cases where the public authority of a territorial state is replaced and superseded by the functional authority of an international institution that administers or governs the territory, either exclusively or in cooperation with domestic authorities of the territory.

The cases in which such a situation has emerged in the context of international territorial administration have been described above in Parts I and II of this book. Classical examples in the era of the League of Nations are the Saar Territory and Leticia.[21] These cases were later followed by the UN administrations in Eastern Slavonia and Kosovo.[22] All of these territories were administered as autonomous territorial entities by the

---

[20] It is more difficult to determine whether the multinational administration of Iraq can be characterised as a case of "internationalised statehood". The Security Council vested the CPA with a quasi-mandate to administer Iraq for the welfare of the Iraqi people. However, one element speaks against the application of the concept of internationalised statehood: the fact that the Iraqi legal system was not internationalised as such, but was temporarily replaced by a governing framework authorising the exercise of foreign authority on Iraqi soil. The CPA continued to rely on occupation authority in its own practice. See above Part II, Chapter 9.

[21] The situation of Danzig was special. Danzig was neither part of Germany, nor part of Poland. But Germany had ceded all rights with regard to the territory to the Principal Allied Powers. The relationship between Danzig and Poland was regulated by an Agreement between the Allied Powers and Poland.

[22] See also Council of Europe, Parliamentary Assembly, Protection of human rights in Kosovo, para. 1. ("Kosovo is part of Serbia and Montenegro... As a result of United Nations Security Council Resolution 1244 (1999), however, Kosovo is administered by the international community.") See also para. 33. ("UNMIK is a UN-mandated mission under the control of the SRSG. Having exclusive jurisdiction in Kosovo, it bears both

League of Nations or the UN, while remaining linked to a territorial sovereign (Germany,[23] Colombia,[24] Croatia,[25] Yugoslavia),[26] which was either deprived of or substantially limited in its exercise of jurisdiction over the territory.

1.2.2.3. International territories

Finally, international organisations have exercised jurisdiction over territory in respect of which no state held territorial sovereignty.[27] This category of international administration is the most unusual type of governance in terms of legal status. The respective territories are neither *terra nullius*, nor attached to any territorial sovereign. They are truly "international territories". The control over these entities lies with an administering entity which exercises its powers on the basis of an international arrangement related to the territory.

Precedents of this type of internationalisation may be found in the post-war practice of the UN. The Statutes of Trieste and Jerusalem contained an express clause which provided that the territorial integrity of both cities was to be ensured by the UN.[28] Later, situations of complete territorial internationalisation arose in several contexts.

The first case was the UN administration of West Irian. The Kingdom of the Netherlands had formally relinquished its sovereignty over the

the negative and positive obligations of human rights protection. This exclusive jurisdiction also implies that ratification of conventions, including the ECHR, by Serbia and Montenegro is not relevant to the obligations of UNMIK.")

[23] Germany renounced only its "government" over the Saar Territory under Article 49 of the Treaty of Versailles. Sovereignty was suspended until the holding of the referendum. But the territory remained linked to Germany as a state entity. See also Hannum, *Autonomy, Sovereignty and Self-Determination*, at 391 ("Formal or residual sovereignty ... remained with Germany"). The French rights within the Saar Territory constituted "special public rights exercised within foreign territory". See Vali, *Servitudes of International Law*, at 280.

[24] Leticia remained under Columbian sovereignty, while the League undertook the "administration of the territory". See above Part II, Chapter 7.

[25] See paragraph 2 of the preamble of SC Res. 1037 (1996), which notes that the Eastern Slavonian region comes within the territorial sovereignty of Croatia.

[26] The preamble of SC Res. 1244 reaffirms the "commitment of all Member States to the sovereignty and territorial integrity of the Federal Republic of Yugoslavia". Paragraph 10 of the Resolution speaks of "substantial autonomy within the Federal Republic of Yugoslavia".

[27] See also Brownlie, *Principles of Public International Law*, at 107–8.

[28] See Article 6 of the *corpus separatum* proposal for Jerusalem. ("The territorial integrity of the City ... shall be assured by the United Nations.") See also Article 2 of the Permanent Statute for Trieste, which charged the Security Council with the responsibility of ensuring the integrity and independence of the Trieste Territory.

territory during the period of UN administration. Indonesia acquired its sovereign rights upon the transfer of the territory by the UN.[29] In the meantime, between October 1962 and May 1963, UNTEA administered West Irian as an "international territory" under the exclusive jurisdiction of the UN.

Later on, the UN exercised independent administering authority in two other situations: Namibia and East Timor. Nambia came under the direct responsibility of the UN after the termination of the Mandate of South West Africa by Resolution 2145 (XXI). South Africa no longer held territorial rights over Namibia, neither by virtue of military conquest, nor on the basis of Chapter XI of the Charter. The territory was therefore under the sole and exclusive authority of the UN during the period of administration by the Council for Namibia.[30]

A similar situation existed in East Timor. The UN administration exercised governing authority independently of any competing territorial sovereign in period leading to independence.[31] East Timor constituted a non-self-governing territory under the full legal authority of the UN[32] after the adoption of Security Council Resolution 1272 (1999) and the assumption of control by UNTAET.[33] UNTAET was both the administering power and the only legitimate government of the territory.[34]

---

[29] See Article XIV of the Agreement between the Republic of Indonesia and the Netherlands of 15 August 1962.

[30] See also Brownlie, *Principles of Public International Law*, at 108.

[31] Some confusion may arise from the fact that the Security Council reaffirmed "respect for the sovereignty and territorial integrity of Indonesia" in para. 12 of the preamble of SC Res. 1272. However, since the UN had always refrained from recognising the legality of the integration of East Timor into Indonesia, this reference cannot be interpreted as a recognition of the sovereignty of Indonesia over East Timor but must be conceived as an affirmation of the obligation of UN authorities to respect the existing territorial border between East Timor and West Timor.

[32] Portugal confirmed on 20 October 1999 that it would relinquish its legal ties to East Timor. See Jarat Chopra, *Introductory Note to UNTAET Regulation 13 (2000)*, ILM, Vol. 39 (2000), p. 936, at 937: "On 20 October 1999, Lisbon's representative in New York, Ambassador Antonio Monteiro, expressed to UN officials that Portugal would relinquish its legal ties to East Timor and consider UNTAET its successor with the passage of the Security Council mandate."

[33] See UN, *The United Nations and Decolonization*, at www.un.org/Depts/dpi/decolonization: "The current administering powers are France, New Zealand, the United Kingdom and the United States. East Timor is now administered by the United Nations Transitional Administration in East Timor (UNTAET)."

[34] Chopra takes the view that "Resolution 1272... became the instrument for bestowing sovereignty over East Timor to the UN, even though it did not explicitly use the word." See Chopra, *United Nations Kingdom of East Timor*, at 29.

2.　Treatment of the status question in international practice

The internationalisation of a territory raises a number of legal problems related to the status of administered territory. Three questions are of special interest here: the authority of international administrations to take status decisions related to the territory, the legal personality of the territory under administration and the external legal representation of the territory.

International actors have approached these questions with pragmatism. The UN itself has generally acted as a functional ruler rather than as a territorial sovereign in relation to status questions. Internationalised territories and international territories were typically not fully equated with states in their relations with other entities, but were treated as legal entities with similar rights and duties.

2.1.　Status decisions

International territorial administration raises different authority problems related to the status of the territory under administration. Two issues must be distinguished: the right of international administrations to make determinations affecting the legal status of the administered territory and their authority to exercise rights relating to ownership over the territory.

International organs may be entitled to adopt decisions which affect the status of a territory, including decisions in relation to the territorial internationalisation of an entity. However, international organs are not generally entitled to exercise rights of ownership and title over territories or to impose permanent status changes. These powers remain with the territorial sovereign, or ultimately with the inhabitants of the territory.[35]

This basic distinction is, *inter alia*, reflected in the Handbook on UN Multidimensional Peaceeping Operations.[36] It was, generally, observed in international legal practice. International territorial administrations

---

[35] See also the discussion above in Part III, Chapter 11 on the limits of territorial administration arising from the right to self-determination and territorial integrity.

[36] See also Handbook on UN Multidimensional Peacekeeping Operations, at 20. ("In exercising authority, the SRSG needs to be aware of the provisional status of the UN peacekeeping operation. This implies that all activities and obligations should be undertaken in a manner that does not prejudice the final settlement (if not clearly defined in the mandate.")

have usually conceived their authority in functional terms and refrained from making final determinations concerning the title over territory.[37] However, there are some cases in which UN status decisions relating to internationalisation have been questioned.

2.1.1. UN status determinations

International administering entities made status determinations in only a few situations. In most cases, the policy decision concerning internationalisation was determined by way of an agreement (Saar,[38] Danzig,[39] Leticia,[40] Trieste,[41] West Irian,[42] Cambodia,[43] Bosnia and Herzegovina,[44] Eastern Slavonia,[45] East Timor[46]), which established the foundation for the internationalisation of a state system or for the assumption of international jurisdiction over a territory. Controversies over the decision-making authority of international actors arose only in instances in which status determinations were essentially taken by the UN, namely in the cases of Eritrea, Jerusalem, Namibia and Kosovo.

The core issue in all of these four cases was not so much a question of institutional authority,[47] but rather the nature of the status decision

---

[37] Article 2 of the Memorandum of Understanding on the European Administration of Mostar is exemplary in this regard. It provides that the "EU Administration will not prejudice permanent arrangements concerning the status of Mostar".

[38] See Articles 49 and 50 of the Treaty of Versailles, including Annex.

[39] See Articles 100–8 of the Treaty of Versailles.

[40] See Agreement Between Columbia and Peru Relating to the Procedure for Putting Into Effect the Recommendations Proposed by the Council of the League of Nations in the Report which it adopted on 18 March 1933.

[41] See Article 21 of the Peace Treaty with Italy and Annex.

[42] See Agreement between the Republic of Indonesia and the Kingdom of the Netherlands Concerning West New Guinea of 15 August 1962.

[43] See Agreement on the Political Settlement of the Cambodia Conflict of 23 October 1991.

[44] See Peace Agreement between Bosnia and Herzegovina, Croatia and the Federal Republic of Yugoslavia.

[45] See the Basic Agreement on the Region of Eastern Slavonia, Baranja and West Sirmium of 12 November 1995.

[46] See Agreement of 5 May 1999 between the Republic of Indonesia and the Kingdom of the Netherlands.

[47] It has been noted earlier that the Security Council may be entitled to alter rights of territorial jurisdiction on a provisional basis, should this be necessary for the maintenance of peace and security. See above Part III, Chapter 11. Even the General Assembly may be entitled make status determinations. The fact that the General Assembly is, in principle, vested with recommendatory powers does not prevent it from adopting resolutions or determinations with an operative design in specific

itself. A distinction must be made in this regard between "pre-emptive" and "enabling" status determinations.[48]

Status decisions which determine the rights of the inhabitants of the territory in an authoritative manner without local consent ("pre-emptive status decisions") are critical. They pre-empt people's rights and stand in contrast to the lack of "sovereign" ownership of international administrations over administered territory.

Status decisions which introduce temporary changes in legal status in order to enable people to exercise territorial rights ("enabling status decisions") are less problematic. They may be justified, even if they impose restrictions on the sovereignty of the territorial state. The acceptability of such decisions can be founded on two grounds: the contribution of the status change to the realisation of people-centred rights ("protective aim") and its provisional character ("limited effect").

2.1.1.1.   Pre-emptive status determinations

The cases of Eritrea and Jerusalem fall into the first category. The UN acted in both situations in a "pre-emptive" capacity.

2.1.1.1.1.   Eritrea

In the case of Eritrea, the General Assembly enjoyed decision-making authority in relation to the territory by virtue of the Peace Treaty with Italy, which provided that in the absence of agreement on the disposal of Italy's colonial possession the General Assembly should make a status recommendation, by which the four Powers agreed to abide.[49] The Assembly was thus empowered to make a status decision regarding the territory.[50] However, the solution adopted by the General Assembly in its "federal status resolution" (GA Resolution 390 (V)) was questionable

---

cases. See ICJ, *Legal Consequences for States of the Continued Presence of South Africa in Namibia*, Advisory Opinion, ICJ Rep. 1971, 16, at 50.

[48] See generally on the limited capacity of the UN to dispose territory, Brownlie, *Principles of Public International Law*, at 163.

[49] See Annex XI of the Peace Treaty with Italy, where the Four Powers noted that in the absence of agreement on the disposal of Italy's colonial possessions "the matter shall be referred to the General Assembly of the United Nations for a recommendation, and the four Powers agree to accept the recommendation and to take the appropriate measures to give effect to it".

[50] See also Brownlie, *Principles of Public International Law*, at 164, who speaks of delegated authority.

in legal terms. By placing Eritrea into a federation with Ethiopia, the Assembly determined the constitutional status of the Eritrean people without a free and genuine consideration of the will of the people.[51] This disregard of people's rights was difficult to reconcile with the principles of the UN Charter.[52]

2.1.1.1.2. Jerusalem

A similar criticism may be voiced in relation to the decision of the General Assembly to internationalise Jerusalem by the terms of Resolution 181 (II) (the "Partition Resolution").[53] Here again, it was not so much the entitlement of the General Assembly to act which was in doubt, but rather the "quasi-constitutive" nature of the decision itself.[54] The Assembly was entitled to make status findings concerning Palestine on the basis of its status as a successor to the League of Nations as a supervisory power over mandates.[55] However, the status decision taken may be questioned from a legal perspective[56] because it was designed to change the status of Jerusalem without further popular consultation.

---

[51] See also Gayim, *The Eritrean Question*, at 241.

[52] States advanced questionable arguments in order to justify the decision not to consult the inhabitants of the territory in the determination of their political status through referendum. They argued the local "inhabitants were backward" or unable to make "a wiser choice than the General Assembly of the United Nations". See UN Doc. A/AC.38/SR.39, at 236, and UN Doc. A/AC.38/SR.49, at 309.

[53] Paragraph 3 of Part I of GA Res. 181 (II) determined that "Independent Arab Jewish States and the Special International Regime for the City of Jerusalem ... shall come into existence in Palestine two months after the evacuation of the armed forces of the mandatory Power has been completed, but in any case not later than 1 October 1948".

[54] See also the criticism raised by Israeli representatives, above Part I, Chapter 1.

[55] This argument has been made in the context of Namibia. See ICJ, *International Status of South West Africa*, Advisory Opinion, ICJ Rep. 1950, 128, at 136–7. The Court argued that the General Assembly succeeded to League of Nations supervisory functions under Article 10 of the Charter.

[56] See also Brownlie, *Principles of Public International Law*, at 163–4. ("It is doubtful if the United Nations has a 'capacity to convey title', in part because the Organization cannot assume the role of territorial sovereign: in spite of the principle of implied powers the Organization is not a state and the General Assembly only has a power of recommendation. Thus, the resolution of 1947 containing a partition plan for Palestine was probably *ultra vires*, and, if was not, was not binding on member states in any case.")

2.1.1.2.   Enabling status determinations

In the cases of Namibia and Kosovo, the UN took "enabling status decisions". These determinations are easier to justify from a legal perspective.

2.1.1.2.1.   Namibia

The General Assembly changed the status of South West Africa by terminating the mandate status of the territory and by assuming administering authority. Namibia became, as the Assembly itself put it, "a territory having international status".[57] This status determination may be defended on two grounds. First, the Assembly was entitled to terminate mandates in its capacity as the proper supervisory authority over mandates.[58] Secondly, the determination of the Assembly pursued a legitimate objective. The UN assumed jurisdiction with the express aim of enabling the people of Namibia to exercise their status rights, namely to decide on the independence of the territory in accordance with the wishes of the people. This "enabling" character justified the primary act of disposition by the Assembly.[59]

---

[57] See GA Res. 2145 (XXI).

[58] See, for example, Sagay, *Legal Aspects of the Namibian Dispute*, at 256. Any doubts as to the binding force of the revocation were removed by the subsequent validation of the decision by SC Res. 264 (1969). See para. 1 of SC Res. 264 (1969) of 20 March 1969, by which the Security Council gave its express imprimatur to the revocation of the mandate.

[59] Note, however, that the UN also made determinations regarding the boundaries of Namibia. South Africa and Namibia shared different opinions as to whether Walvis Bay and the off-shore islands of Namibia formed part of the former mandate. Both the Security Council and the General Assembly took the view that Walvis Bay belongs to Nambia. See para. 1 of SC Res. 432 of 27 July 1978, in which the Council reaffirmed that Walvis Bay should be re-integrated into the territory of Namibia. See also GA Res. 32/9 D of 4 November 1997, in which the General Assembly declared that Walvis is an integral part of Namibia. But the statement of the General Assembly was contested by the Representative of the Netherlands who took the view that the finding of the Assembly was non-binding. See Statement, Netherlands Yearbook of International Law 1978, at 322. The new Constitution of Namibia defined the national territory in 1990 as "the whole of the territory recognized by the international community through the organs of the United Nations" including "the enclave and the port of Walvis Bay, as well as the off-shore islands of Namibia". See Article 1 of the Constitution of Namibia. The dispute was finally solved by the Treaty between the Government of the Republic of South Africa and the Government of the Republic of Namibia with Respect to Walvis Bay and the Off-Shore Islands, in ILM 1994, 1526, at 1528. The Treaty provided that "Walvis Bay shall be incorporated/integrated into the Republic of Namibia on 1 March 1994". For an analysis, see Andreas Zimmermann, *Staatennachfolge in völkerrechtliche Verträge* (2000), at 472–6.

2.1.1.2.2. Kosovo

The removal of Yugoslav jurisdiction over Kosovo by Security Council Resolution 1244 (1999) may be defended on similar grounds. The decision of the Security Council to grant Kosovo substantial autonomy as a legal entity may be justified in the light of the Chapter VII powers of the Council and the rationale of the Council's action. The Security Council made the status arrangement for the purpose of the maintenance of international peace and security,[60] and more specifically, in order to enable the people of Kosovo to enjoy substantial autonomy and rights of self-government.[61] At the same time, the Council refrained from settling status claims definitively, by leaving the settlement of Kosovo's final status open to further resolution.[62]

2.1.2. Exercise of administering authority

International authorities have generally shown restraint when dealing with status questions in their administering practice. Where international administrators exercised extensive regulatory authority in the respective territory, they typically limited the validity of their regulatory acts to the period of international administration[63] and focused their action on the regulation of the modalities of status decisions. The

---

[60] This authority is inherent in the decision-making power of the Council under Chapter VII. See above Part III, Chapter 11.

[61] See para. 10 of SC Res. 1244 (1999).

[62] See para. 11 e) and f) of SC Res. 1244 (1999). ("Facilitating a political process designed to determine Kosovo's future status, taking into account the Rambouillet accords (S/1999/648); In a final stage, overseeing the transfer of authority from Kosovo's provisional institutions to institutions established under a political settlement.") It is a different question whether the Council would be authorised to impose a final status settlement. Such a proposition meets serious objections in light of the various Charter-based limitations to the powers of the Council (e.g. principle of self-determination). See above Part III, Chapter 11, 4.2.3.

[63] The practice of the UN administrations in Kosovo and East Timor is exemplary in this regard. Both administrations expressly limited the validity of their regulatory acts, by providing that their regulations would remain in force until repealed by UNMIK/UNTAET or superseded by acts adopted by domestic institutions after the end of the administration. See Section 4 of UNMIK Regulation No. 1/1999 and Section 4 of UNTAET Regulation No. 1/1999. The same principle was adopted by the CPA in Iraq. See Section 3 of CPA Regulation No. 1 ("Regulations and Orders will remain in force until repealed by the Administrators or superseded by legislation issued by democratic institutions of Iraq").

final status decision was either determined by an international arrangement,[64] or left in the hands of the local population.[65]

[64] In the two cases where the UN was charged with a transfer of territory, namely in West Irian and Eastern Slavonia, the final goal of UN administration was predetermined by the parties concerned. Article II of the Agreement between the Republic of Indonesia and the Kingdom of the Netherlands explicitly obliged UNTEA "to transfer the administration to Indonesia" after completion of its mandate. See Articles II and XII of the Agreement of 15 August 1962. The Erdut Agreement between Serbia and Croatia limited UN administration *ab initio* to a transitional period (see 1 of the Erdut Agreement) during which the territories of Eastern Slavonia, Baranja and Western Sirmium were "integral parts of the Republic of Croatia". See para. 2 of the preamble of SC Res. 1037 (1996). The UN only enjoyed discretion to determine the timing of its own mandate. See para. XII of the Agreement of 15 August 1962. ("The United Nations Administrator will have discretion to transfer all or part of the administration to Indonesia at any time after the first phase of the UNTEA administration. The UNTEA's authority will cease at the moment of transfer of full administrative control to Indonesia.") Article 1 of the Erdut Agreement allowed an extension of the transitional period "if so requested by one of the parties".

[65] The administration of the Saar Territory is exemplary in this regard. The Treaty of Versailles stipulated in sweeping terms that the "League of Nations shall decide on the sovereignty under which the territory is to be placed". See Article 35 of the Annex to Article 50 of the Treaty of Versailles. However, the treaty specified at the same time that the League should base its decision on "the wishes of the inhabitants [of the territory] as expressed by the voting" on the final status of the Saar Territory – a requirement which excluded any discretion on the part of the League. The Treaty of Versailles also made detailed provision in relation to the legal regime governing the implications of the three status choices. It stated: "(a) If for the whole or part of the territory, the League of Nations decided in favour of the maintenance of the regime established by the present Treaty and this Annex, Germany hereby agrees to make such renunciation of her sovereignty in favour of the League of Nations as the latter shall deem necessary. It will be the duty of the League of Nations to take appropriate steps to adapt the regime definitively adopted to the permanent welfare of the territory and the general interest; (b) If, for the whole or part of the territory, the League of Nations decides in favour of union with France, Germany hereby agrees to cede France in accordance with the decision of the League of Nations, all rights and title over the territory specified by the League; (c) If, for the whole or part of the territory, the League of Nations decides in favour of union with Germany, it will be the duty of the League of Nations to cause the German Government to be re-established in the government of the territory specified by the League." A similar solution was adopted in the case of Western Sahara. The UN maintained organisational control over the conduct of the status decision under the 2003 Peace plan for self-determination. But the status decision itself remained within the authority of the people of the territory. See above Part II, Chapter 7. A similar principle was applied in case of Kosovo. SC Res. 1244 gave UNMIK the responsibility to facilitate "a political process designed to determine Kosovo's future status, taking into account the Rambouillet accords". See para. 11 (e) of SC Res. 1244 (1999). The Resolution left no doubt that this political settlement would have to be built on the input of the main stakeholders involved in the process, namely the FRY and the people of Kosovo. The reference to the Rambouillet Accords points towards the holding of a popular

However, international administrations enjoyed some control over the timing and conditions of the status decision.[66] The exercise of these powers has been to open to criticism.

In some cases (West Irian, Namibia, Western Sahara), the timing of the status decision was problematic. The most compelling example is the case of West Irian where holding of the act of self-determination after the transfer of the territory under Indonesian rule significantly affected the method and outcome of the status decision itself. The postponement of the status decision compromised its genuineness ("status delayed, status denied").[67]

Further problems have arisen in the management of status policies.[68] UNMIK's practice is the best example. The mission centred decision-making authority on its own institutions. Through its lawmaking practice, UNMIK extinguished the competencies and powers of the former FRY over Kosovo to an extent that "one [was] left to wonder whether anything short of independence [was] still an option".[69] At the same time, the mission linked the holding of negotiations over Kosovo's final status to the observance of substantive standards by domestic

consultation as envisaged in Article I, paragraph 3 of Chapter 8 of the Rambouillet Accords. The preamble of the Constitutional Framework restated the language of Chapter 8 of the Rambouillet Accords by providing for the "determination of Kosovo's future status through a process at an appropriate stage, which shall... take full account of all the relevant factors, including the will of the people". The requirement of FRY involvement may be inferred from the reaffirmation of Yugoslavia's territorial integrity under SC Res. 1244, and Annex 1 and 2 of SC Res. 1244.

[66] In the context of decolonisation missions, UN administrators exercised some control over the planning and timing of access to independence. The General Assembly gave some general directions to the Council for Nambia. GA Res. 228 (S-V) provided that: "South West Africa shall become independent on a date to be fixed in accordance with the wishes of the people and that the Council shall do all in its power to enable independence to be attained by June 1968." In the case of East Timor, the status decision was made by the East Timorese people through its vote on independence before the assumption of authority by the UN. However, UNTEAT enjoyed control over the process of access to independence. Neither the Agreement of 5 May 1999, nor SC Res. 1272 (1999) envisaged a concrete date for independence. This left the primary responsibility for the timing of elections with UNTAET.

[67] See above Part II, Chapter 7.

[68] See Knoll, *From Bemchmarking to Final Status*, at 658-9. One of the criticisms is that such policies create "phantom states", which are built on externally-driven politics of Western elites rather than the country's popular will. See Chandler, *Empire in Denial*.

[69] See Bohlander, *Some Comments on War Crimes, Crimes Against Humanity and Security Council Resolution 1244*, at 6. Bohlander notes that "[t]his is at odds with the objective of UNMIK as an interim administration and with the general attitude in UN SC Resolution 1244, which still appears to envisage the future of Kosovo as a more or less autonomous province of Serbia and the FRY". *Ibid.*, at 5.

institutions, without defining status goals or options *before* the definition of standards.[70] In this way, UNMIK assumed the role of an arbiter over status questions *vis-à-vis* the formal territorial sovereign and domestic institutions.

The exercise of these powers has sparked fierce opposition. Tensions emerged openly in two instances: the drafting process of the Constitutional Framework for Provisional Self-Government in Kosovo and the border arrangement with Macedonia.

In the first case, UNMIK took a pragmatic stance in order to preserve the "*status quo*". It simply refused to include any reference to status options in the document, although Kosovo Albanians had pushed for an express recognition of the option of independence.[71] In the second case, UNMIK intervened in favour of the formal sovereign. The SRSG vetoed a resolution of the Kosovo Assembly on the "protection of the territorial integrity of Kosovo" which declared a border agreement between the former FRY and Macedonia of 21 January 2001 null and void, because it allegedly transferred 2,500 hectares of land from Kosovo to Macedonia without the consent of the people of Kosovo and its institutions.[72] UNMK had initially opposed the border arrangement since it had not been sufficiently consulted by FRY authorities, but later came to support it. When the Kosovo Assembly dealt with the issue, the SRSG invalidated the resolution on the ground that the Assembly lacked the necessary legislative competences in the field of "territorial integrity" under Chapter 5 of the Constitutional Framework.[73] UNMIK upheld thereby the formal construction of Resolution 1244. But it conceded implicitly that the FRY could dispose over parts of Kosovo without the consent of Kosovo's institutions.[74]

[70] See also the discussion below Part IV, Chapter 16.

[71] The UN linked the Constitutional Framework exclusively with the status of Kosovo under UN administration, without settling issues of external self-determination or independent statehood.

[72] The resolution was adopted on 23 May 2002. The Assembly argued that the people of Kosovo were not consulted on the issue and that the borders of Kosovo could not be changed without the consent of the people of Kosovo.

[73] The Security Council later endorsed the decision of the SRSG by way of a Presidential Statement. See SC, Presidential Statement, S/PRST/2002/16 of 24 May 2002. ("The Security Council deplores the adoption by the Assembly of Kosovo, in its session of 23 May 2002, of a 'resolution on the protection of the territorial integrity of Kosovo'. It concurs with the Special Representative of the Secretary-General that such resolutions and decisions by the Assembly on matters which do not fall within its field of competence are null and void.")

[74] For a critique, see Bernhard Knoll, *UN Imperium: Horizontal and Vertical Transfer of Effective Control and the Concept of Residual Sovereignty*, in "Internationalised Territories",

This practice highlighted that UNMIK navigated on a thin line between status resolution and status denial.[75]

2.2. Legal personality of the territory

The legal personality of the territory under international administration varies according to the type of administration.[76] Where international administrations exercise authority within internationalised states, the legal status of the territory is clear. The state continues to exist as the main legal entity on the international level. The international administration, on the other hand, may enjoy separate legal personality as an international institution.[77]

A status problem arises, however, in the case of international and internationalised territories. In these cases, it is often difficult to determine whether and to what extent the respective territories enjoy separate legal personality in their capacity as territorial entities under international administration.

The legal regime of internationalised and international territories is governed by a multiplicity of sources, including the law applicable to the governing entity (i.e. the law of international organisations) and the legal instruments governing the territory.[78] The practice in international territorial administration suggests that both internationalised and international territories may enjoy autonomous legal personality, independently of a link to a state entity. It is widely accepted that territorial entities other than sovereign states may enjoy legal personality. Oppenheim made this point in relation to territorial entities "under the suzerainty or under the protectorate of another state" and in relation to "member-States of a... federal State".[79] The ICJ took this position in

---

Austrian Review of International and European Law, Vol. 7 (2002), 3; Knoll, *Legitimacy and UN-Administration of Territory*, at 46.

[75] See also Williams, *The Road to Resolving the Conflict Over Kosovo's Final Status*, at 418–9.

[76] For further discussion concerning international legal personality of international organisations and organs, see Finn Seyersted, *International Personality of International Organizations*, Indian Journal of International Law, Vol. 4 (1964), 15; Manuel Rama-Montaldo, *International Legal Personality and Implied Powers of International Organizations*, British Yearbook of International Law, Vol. 44 (1970), 111.

[77] The OHR, for example, enjoyed legal personality as a legal person created by Annex 10 of the Dayton Agreement. Moreover, it may be argued that the Coalition Provisional Authority enjoyed independent legal personality as a civilian institution in Iraq. See below.

[78] See with respect to "internationalised territories" also Benzing, *Midwifing a New State*, at 319 and 321.

[79] See Oppenheim, *International Law*, Vol. I, 8th edn (1955), 119.

the *Western Sahara* case, where the Court acknowledged that the "Mauritanian entity" could enjoy legal rights as an entity independent of statehood.[80] Similarly, the Court clarified in *Reparations for Injuries* that international organisations may possess international legal personality, distinct from that of their members, allowing them to carry their functions on the international plane ("functional legal personality").[81] These principles may be applied to territories under international administrations. They may enjoy functional legal personality, including the capacity to exercise rights and obligations on the international level.[82]

A historical precedent may be found in trust or mandate territories which unlike colonies enjoyed a separate juridical status. The status of trust or mandate territories was determined by the legal provisions of the Mandate System and the Trusteeship System and the agreements concluded under these regimes.[83] The legal personality of internationalised and international territories may be derived from two sources: either by way of status provisions in a treaty arrangement or by way of UN act.

2.2.1. Legal personality by way of agreement

Legal instruments rarely contain explicit references to the legal personality of the administered territories. Partial legal personality may, however, be inferred from specific status features recognised by international agreements and/or from specific functions attributed to the administering authorities.

The Treaty of Versailles, for example, contained implicit statutory recognitions of the legal personality of the Saar Territory and the Free City of Danzig.

The Treaty granted the League's Governing Commission in the Saar "all the powers of government" formerly belonging to Germany,

---

[80] See ICJ, *Western Sahara*, Advisory Opinion, ICJ Rep. 1975, 12, at 63.

[81] See generally ICJ, *Reparations of Injuries*, ICJ Rep. 1949, 174. The Court emphasised in particular: "Whereas a State possesses the totality of international rights and duties recognised by international law, the rights and duties of an entity such as the Organization must depend upon its purposes and functions as specified or implied in its constituent documents and developed in practice." See ICJ Rep. 1949, at 180. In its advisory opinion on the *Legality of the Use of Nuclear Weapons*, the ICJ reaffirmed that "international organizations ... are invested by the States which create them with powers, the limits of which are a function of the common interests whose promotion those States entrust to them". See ICJ, Advisiory Opinion, Legality *of the Threat or Use of Nuclear Weapons*, ICJ Rep. 1996, 66, at 78.

[82] See also Knoll, *From Benchmarking to Final Status*, at 649–51.

[83] See Gordon, *Legal Problems with Trusteeship*, at 339.

including powers over foreign relations.[84] Both this clause and the reference that the League should decide on the status of the territory in the light of the referendum with three different status options [85] made it clear that the Saar Territory was in fact transformed into an autonomous legal entity under League administration, with the capacity to be the subject of rights and obligations, independent of Germany and France.

The terms of the agreement were more ambiguous in relation to Danzig.[86] The Treaty declared Danzig a "Free City" placed "under the protection of the League of Nations",[87] but charged Poland with "the conduct of the foreign relations of the Free City of Danzig".[88] The independent legal status of Danzig was, in particular, evidenced by the reference to Danzig's own nationality[89] and the indication that the relations between Danzig and Poland were to be regulated by an additional "Treaty" between the two entities.[90]

The clearest recognition of the international legal personality of a territory under international administration may be found in the Peace Treaty with Italy. The Treaty defined the Free Territory of Trieste as an "independent" entity[91] with the power to sign treaties, exequaturs and consular commissions.[92] Moreover, the Allied and Associated Powers and Italy expressly recognised Trieste as being a separate legal entity by a formal recognition clause.[93]

Other treaty arrangements in the era of the UN were more ambivalent. The Dutch-Indonesian agreement on West Irian contains no specific findings relating to the status of the territory under UN administration. Only the references to the "full" administering "authority" of the UN Administrator[94] and to the flying of the flag of the UN[95] may be interpreted as indications of the separate legal status of the territory under

---

[84] See Treaty of Versailles, Section IV, Annex, Article 19.   [85] See *ibid.*, Article 35.
[86] The Permanent Court of International Justice later expressly clarified that Danzig was bound by, and had the benefit "of the ordinary rules governing relations between States". See PCIJ, *Treatment of Polish Nationals in Danzig*, Ser. A/B, No. 44 (1932), 23–4.
[87] See Article 100 of the Treaty of Versailles.   [88] See *ibid.*, Article 104.
[89] See *ibid.*, Article 105. It provided that "[o]n the coming into force of the... Treaty [of Versailles] German nationals ordinarily resident in the territory... will ipso facto lose their German nationality in order to become nationals of the Free City of Danzig".
[90] See *ibid.*, Article 104.
[91] Articles 21 and 22 of the Peace Treaty with Italy and Article 2 of Annex VI (Permanent Statute).
[92] See Article 24 of the Peace Treaty with Italy.
[93] According to Article 21, paragraph 1 of the Peace Treaty, the "Free Territory of Trieste is recognized by the Allied and Associated Powers and Italy".
[94] See Article V of the Agreement.   [95] See *ibid.*, Article VI.

UN administration. The Agreement between Indonesia and Portugal of 5 May 1999 was even less explicit in relation to the status of East Timor after the vote on independence. It stated merely that "the Governments of Indonesia and Portugal and the Secretary-General shall agree on arrangements for a peaceful and orderly transfer of authority in East Timor to the United Nations" in order to enable "East Timor to begin a process of transition towards independence"[96] – a formulation which does not in itself suffice to establish functional legal personality.

2.2.2.   Legal personality and UN acts

There are a number of other cases of territorial administration in which the legal personality of territories under international administration was directly linked to UN acts. Two situations must be distinguished in this regard. UN acts may recognise that a territory under international administration enjoys independent legal personality as a territorial entity, or they may entrust international administrations with the power to represent the territory internationally as a legal entity. In the latter case, international legal personality results from the assumption of territorial jurisdiction by the UN. The legal personality of the administered territory is functional in nature: it is a corollary of the mandate of an international administering authority. Moreover, it is derived from the "objective" legal personality of the UN itself.[97]

2.2.2.1.   Recognition of legal personality by UN acts
The Trusteeship Council Proposal for the Statute of the City of Jerusalem, adopted on 4 April 1950 upon request by the General Assembly, made explicit findings in relation to the independent legal status of Jerusalem as a "Special International Regime" and its capacity to act on an international level. The proposal defined Jerusalem as a "*corpus separatum* under the administration of the United Nations"[98] which enjoys territorial integrity.[99] These status determinations were complemented by detailed provisions on citizenship[100] and foreign affairs power.[101] It is therefore

---

[96] See Article 6 of the Agreement of 5 May 1999.

[97] In the *Reparation for Injuries* case, the ICJ clarified that "fifty States, representing the vast majority of the members of the international community, had the power, in conformity with international law, to bring into being an entity possessing objective legal personality, and not merely personality recognized by them alone, together with capacity to bring claims". See ICJ Rep. (1949) 174, at 184–5.

[98] See Article 1 of the Trusteeship Council Proposal.   [99] See *ibid.*, Article 6.

[100] See *ibid.*, Article 11.   [101] See *ibid.*, Article 37.

beyond doubt that the drafters of the Statute intended to recognise Jerusalem's legal personality as a territorial entity by the adoption of the Statute.

Similarly, the UN recognised the independent legal character of Namibia in the aftermath of the revocation of the Mandate over South West Africa. The UN General Assembly reaffirmed "the territorial integrity" of Namibia and the right of its people to freedom and independence in Resolution 2248 (S-V), which established the Council for Namibia.[102] In a later resolution the General Assembly recognised "the Territory's established international status".[103] Similar conclusions may be drawn from the practice of the Security Council. The Council requested "all States to refrain from any relations – diplomatic, consular or otherwise – with South Africa implying recognition of the authority of the South African Government over the territory of Namibia", and called upon "all states maintaining such relations to terminate existing diplomatic and consular representation as far as they extend to Namibia".[104]

2.2.2.2.   Functional legal personality derived from the mandate of UN administrations

Functional legal personality may also flow from the mandate of UN administrations. A UN resolution may bestow international administering authorities with the authority to establish relations with other subjects of international law in relation to the administered territory, either expressly or implicitly. This mandate enables the administering authorities to exercise external relations power on behalf the territory, which in turn gains an identity as a legal entity on the international level.[105] Legal personality is therefore not directly attached to the territory as a legal entity, but is linked to the status and the responsibilities of the international administering organs and confined to affairs which are directly connected to the mandate of the international administration.

2.2.2.2.1.   Express mandate

The international capacity to act was explicitly provided for by a UN resolution in the case of Namibia. Resolution 2248 (S-V) contained a general reference to the power of the Council for Namibia to administer the

[102] See para. 5 of the preamble of GA Res. 2248 (S-V).
[103] See para. 11 of GA Res. 2372 (XXII).   [104] See paras. 1 and 3 of SC Res. 283 (1970).
[105] If legal personality is inferred from a binding Chapter VII mandate, it may not even require a separate (explicit or implicit) recognition by third states.

territory until independence.[106] In a following resolution, the General Assembly set out the functions which the Council should exercise in relation to Namibia. It specifically requested that the Council "represent Namibia to ensure that the rights and interests of Namibia are protected, as appropriate, in all intergovernmental and non-governmental organisations, bodies and conferences".[107] This mandate confirmed the authority of the Council to act internationally on behalf of Namibia as an international entity.

2.2.2.2.2. Implied powers

The facts were slightly different in the cases of Kosovo and East Timor. The power to represent the territory externally was not expressly mentioned in the founding resolutions of UNTAET and UNMIK. The entitlement to act on an international level can therefore only be based on an implied power,[108] namely the necessity to perform functions of external representation for the implementation of the respective governance mandates.

UNTAET's capacity to enter into relations with other actors may be inferred from the interplay between Security Council Resolution 1272 (1999) and the Report of the Secretary-General on the Situation in East Timor of 4 October 1999.[109] Paragraph 4 of the Resolution 1272 contained a very general authorisation clause which empowered "UNTAET to take all necessary measures to fulfil its mandate".[110] Paragraph 35 of the Secretary General's Report made specific mention of UNTAET's power to "conclude such international agreements with states and international organisations as may be necessary for the carrying out of the functions of UNTAET in East Timor". Paragraph 1 of the Resolution defined UNTAET's mandate "in accordance with the report of the Secretary-General".[111] One may therefore infer that UNTAET was endowed with the powers necessary to enter into relations with other entities, even though this power was not explicitly specified in the text of Resolution 1272.

The situation was more ambiguous in the case of Kosovo. Both the preamble and paragraph 10 of Security Council Resolution 1244 (1999)

---

[106] See para. 1 of GA Resolution 2248 (S-V).

[107] See GA Res. A/RES/32/9 of 11 November 1977.

[108] See generally on "implied powers" within the framework international organisations Brownlie, *Principles of Public International Law*, at 657.

[109] See Report of the Secretary-General on the Situation in East Timor, 4 October 1999, para. 35, UN Doc. S/1999/1024.

[110] See para. 4 of SC Res. 1272 of 25 October 1999.   [111] See *ibid.*, para. 1.

emphasised that Kosovo continued to form part of the FRY. Moreover, as in Resolution 1272 (1999), Security Council Resolution 1244 failed to make any specific reference to the international legal personality of the territory or the foreign relations power of the UN administration. UNMIK's capacity to entertain external relations could therefore only be derived from an implied power[112] necessary to fulfil UNMIK's general mandate to "provide an interim administration for Kosovo under which the people of Kosovo can enjoy substantial autonomy"[113] and to perform "basic civilian administrative functions where ... required" to that extent.[114] This interpretation was later confirmed by the Constitutional Framework for Provisional Self-Government which provided that the SRSG remains exclusively responsible for "concluding agreements with states and international organisations in all matters within the scope of UNSCR 1244 (1999)".[115]

The partial international personality of both territories is further reaffirmed by the treaty-making practice of the UN administrations. The case of East Timor is particularly noteworthy in this sense. In an exchange of notes constituting an agreement with Australia, UNTAET assumed all rights and obligations under the Timor Gap Treaty previously exercised by Indonesia. UNTAET acted on behalf of East Timor, limiting its contractual obligations "until the date of independence of East Timor".[116] Furthermore, UNTAET concluded a grant agreement with the World Bank's International Development Association (IDA), which designated both UNTAET and East Timor as a "recipient".[117] The application of IDA's Articles

---

[112] See also the letter dated 31 August 2005 from the SRSG to the Deputy Prime Minister of Macedonia, appended to the Interim Free Trade Agreement between the UNMIK and the Government of Macedonia (UNMIK/FTA/2005/1) where it is noted: "UNMIK was established with a mandate to provide interim administration for Kosovo. Where appropriate and necessary to fulfil its mandate, UNMIK may develop arrangements with relevant states and international organizations in order to establish a proper legal basis for achieving objectives of mutual interst. In areas falling within the competencies of the Provisional Institutions of Self-Government (PISG), UNMIK acts on behalf of the PISG."

[113] See para. 10 of SC Res. 1244 (1999). [114] See ibid., para. 11 (b).

[115] See Chapter 8, para. 8 (m) of the Constitutional Framework.

[116] See Exchange of Notes constituting an Agreement between the Government of Australia and the United Nations Transitional Administration in East Timor (UNTAET) concerning the continued Operation of the Treaty between Australia and the Republic of Indonesia on the Zone of Cooperation in an Area between the Indonesian Province of East Timor and Northern Australia of 11 December 1989, entered into force on 10 February 2000.

[117] Pursuant to the International Development Association-UNTAET Trust Fund for East Timor Grant Agreement, UNTAET established a system of village and sub-district

of Agreement for the provision of funds was extended to a territory under UN administration. Both agreements serve as an illustration of the functional legal personalisation of East Timor by virtue of UNTAET's mandate.

A similar practice was applied in the case of Kosovo. UNMIK acted as a recipient of IDA grants provided for the benefit of Kosovo.[118] Later, UNMIK concluded Free Trade Agreements with Albania[119] and Macedonia[120] and a Framework Agreement with the European Investment Bank "[a]cting on behalf of the Provisional Institutions of Self-Government in Kosovo".[121] UNMIK's treaty-making capacity was reaffirmed by the Venice Commission[122] and expressly recognised by the Council of Europe.[123]

2.2.3. Legal personality of the OHR and the CPA

A different legal personality problem arose in the cases of the administration of Bosnia and Herzegovina and Iraq. In both cases, the status of the territory as a state entity remained unaffected by the establishment of the international administrations. However, it was less clear whether the OHR and the CPA itself enjoyed separate legal personality as governing institutions.

Unlike in the cases of UNMIK and UNTAET, it is difficult to argue that the Council granted the OHR or the CPA with international legal personality by way of a Chapter VII mandate. The Council did not establish

---

councils for the allocation of development funds. See UNTAET Regulation No. 2000/13 of 10 March 2000.

[118] See Knoll, *From Benchmarking to Final Status*, at 647.

[119] See Free Trade Agreement between the United Nations Interim Mission in Kosovo on behalf of the Provisional Institutions of Self-Government in Kosovo and the Council of Ministers of the Republic of Albania, dated 4 July 2003, UNMIK/FTA/2003/1.

[120] See Interim Free Trade Agreement between the United Nations Interim Mission in Kosovo on behalf of the Provisional Institutions of Self-Government in Kosovo and the Government of FYROM, dated 31 August 2005, UNMIK/FTA/2005/1.

[121] See Framework Agreement between UNMIK, Acting for and on behalf of the Provisional Institutions of Self-Government in Kosovo and [European Investment Bank], Governing the Bank's Activities in Kosovo, dated 3 May 2005.

[122] See European Commission for Democracy Through Law, *Opinion on Human Rights in Kosovo*, para. 68.

[123] Both Agreements between UNMIK and the Council of Europe make reference to SC Res. 1244 (1999), which established "the authority of UNMIK, as the international civil presence, to provide an interim administration for Kosovo". See also Council of Europe, Parliamentary Assembly, *Protection of Human Rights in Kosovo*, sub. III, para. 33. ("Whatever its precise status as a subject of international law, UNMIK has been able to engage in relations and sign agreements with various actors, including the Council of Europe.")

either of these two institutions itself. The OHR was envisaged under Annex 10 of the Dayton Peace Accord and was created by the Peace Implementation Council.[124] The CPA was created by "the United States, the United Kingdom and [their] Coalition partners".[125] The Council merely recognised the existence of both institutions.[126]

However, there is some support for the view that the OHR and the CPA institutions enjoyed international legal personality.[127] The Dayton Agreement recognised the status of the OHR as a legal person under the laws of Bosnia and Herzegovina.[128] The OHR enjoyed formal institutional independence from the individual member states of the Peace Implementation Council. It was "made up of diplomats seconded by the governments of the PIC countries, international experts hired directly, and national staff from Bosnia and Herzegovina".[129] Moreover, the OHR was charged with specific functions in its international capacity under Annex 10 of the Dayton Agreement, such as the coordination "of the activities of the organisations and agencies involved in the civilian aspects of the peace settlement", the participation "in meetings of donor organisations, particularly on issues of rehabilitation and reconstruction", and reporting obligations vis-à-vis "the United Nations, European

---

[124] According to information from the OHR, the PIC is comprised of "55 countries and agencies that support the peace process in many different ways – by assisting it financially, providing troops for SFOR, or directly running operations in Bosnia and Herzegovina". See the information of the OHR, at www.ohr.int/ohr-info/gen-info/#pic.

[125] This view was expressed in a letter submitted to the President of the United Nations Security Council by the Permanent Representatives of the United States and the United Kingdom. It stated that "the United States, the United Kingdom and the Coalition partners, acting under existing command and control arrangements through the Commander of Coalition Forces, have created the Coalition Provisional Authority, which included the Office of Reconstruction and Humanitarian Assistance, to exercise powers of government temporarily, and as necessary, especially to provide security, to allow the delivery of humanitarian aid, and to eliminate weapons of mass destruction." See Letter dated 8 May 2003.

[126] SC Res. 1483 of 22 May recognised the responsibilities of the US and the UK as "occupying powers", and it noted the existence of the "authority". See para. 13 of the preamble of SC Res. 1483 (2003).

[127] For an affirmation of the international legal personality of the OHR, see Constitutional Court of Bosnia and Herzegovina, Case No. U 9/00, para. 5.

[128] Article III, para. 3 of Annex 10 states: "The High Representative shall enjoy, under the laws of Bosnia and Herzegovina, such legal capacity as may be necessary for the exercise of his or her functions, including the capacity to contract and to acquire and dispose of real and personal property." The office also enjoyed the status of a diplomatic mission to Bosnia and Herzegovina under Annex 10 of the Dayton Peace Agreement. See Article III, para. 4 of Annex 10 of the DPA.

[129] See the information of the OHR, at www.ohr.int/ohr-info/gen-info/#pic.

Union, United States, Russian Federation, and other interested governments, parties, and organisations".[130] These functions were recognised by the parties to the Dayton Peace Agreement, the member states of the Peace Implementation Council and the Security Council.

The situation is more complicated in the case of the CPA. The Letter of 8 May by the Representatives of the UK and the US to the President of the Security Council left it unclear as to whether the CPA constitutes a mere association of the two states composing it or an organisation with a separate legal identity.[131] The practice of the armed forces in Iraq indicates that the US and the UK acted quite independently of each other in the conduct of military activities, because they assumed control over different zones in Iraq.[132] However, there is some support for the view that the CPA constituted, at least, a jointly acting international institution in the exercise of some civilian responsibilities. Statements by the US and the UK indicate that both sides considered the CPA as an entity distinct from the UK and the US.[133]

The US army took the view that the CPA was not a US federal agency, but a "multi-national coalition that exercises powers of government temporarily in order to provide for the effective administration of Iraq".[134] When faced with protests by the Turkcell Consortium against the issuance of licences for mobile telecommunications in Iraq by the CPA, the US Army Legal Services Agency stressed the institutional independence of the CPA. It stated that:

[130] See Articles I and II of Annex 10.

[131] The letter referred to "[t]he United States, the United Kingdom and Coalition Partners, working through the Coalition Provisional Authority". See para. 3 of the Letter of 8 May 2003.

[132] See High Court of Justice, *Mazin Jumaa Gatteh al Skeini & Others* v. *Secretary of State for Defence*, para. 41. ("During the relevant period the coalition forces consisted of six divisions that were under the overall command of US generals. Four were US divisions and two were multinational. Each division was given responsibility for a particular geographical area in Iraq. The United Kingdom was given command of the multi-national division (south East) (MND) (SE) which comprised the provinces of Al Basrah, Maysan, Thi Qar and Al Muthanna and is an area approximately twice the size of Wales with a total population of about 4.6 million. During the relevant period, the total number of Coalition troops deployed in MND (SE) was about 14,500 of which about 8,150 were UK forces ... ")

[133] For a discussion, see L. Elaine Halchin, CRS Report for Congress, *The Coalition Provisional Authority: Origin, Characteristics and Institutional Authorities*, 29 April 2004, at www.fas.org/man/crs/RL32370.pdf. 1.

[134] See Department of the Army, US Army Legal Services Agency, Protest of Turkcell Consortium, B-293048, 21 October 2003, 2–4, text reprinted in Halchin, *Coalition Provisional Authority*, at 8.

the [General Accounting Office] does not have jurisdiction over this protest because CPA is not a Federal agency. The CPA is an organization comprised of members of a coalition of countries ... CPA is analogous to an organization such as NATO's Stabilization Force (SFOR) in Bosnia and Herzegovina. Like NATO and SFOR, CPA is composed of an *international* coalition.[135]

A similar approach was taken by the UK. When questioned by the House of Commons about the legal personality of the CPA, the UK government cited Security Council Resolution 1483 (2003) and CPA Regulation No.1 as the basis of authority of the CPA.[136] Later, a UK court ruled that the "CPA was not a subordinate organ or authority of the United Kingdom".[137]

This methodology is reflected in the working practice of the CPA. The CPA was staffed by various nationalities from Coalition countries. The US enjoyed formal decision-making power, but the decision-making process of the CPA was collective in nature.[138] Furthermore, contracts concluded with the Authority were not regarded as agreements with individual governments, but as agreements entered into with the CPA.[139]

One may therefore argue that the CPA possessed an identity of its own as an international administering institution in specific areas of common action,[140] which complemented the accountability of individual

---

[135] Text reprinted in Halchin, *Coalition Provisional Authority*, at 8.

[136] See *House of Commons Hansard Written Answers for 10 February 2004 (pt 3)*, at www.publications.parliament.uk/pa/cm200304/cmhansrd/vo040210/text/40210w03.htm. ("As noted in Security Council Resolution 1483 of 22 May 2003, the Coalition Provisional Authority (CPA) was established to exercise the specific authorities, responsibilities and obligations under international law of the occupying powers. The authority of the CPA is set out in CPA Regulation No. 1.".

[137] See High Court of Justice, *Mazin Jumaa Gatteh al Skeini & Others v. Secretary of State for Defence*, para. 20.

[138] The UK was represented in the CPA through a UK special representative. This special representative and his office "sought to influence CPA policy and decisions". See High Court of Justice, *Mazin Jumaa Gatteh al Skeini & Others v. Secretary of State for Defence*, para. 20.

[139] See the statement of the former Administrator of the Office of the Federal Procurement Policy on 20 January 2004: "The CPA is not the United States government ... Accordingly, if one enters into a contractual relationship with the CPA, one is not entering into a contractual relationship with the United States. The rights available and remedies available to parties contracting with the United States will not be available in a contractual relationship with the CPA." Text reprinted in Halchin, *Coalition Provisional Authority*, at 17.

[140] See also Wolfrum, *Iraq – From Belligerent Occupation to Sovereignty*, at 21. ("The CPA thus constituted an institution of its own, based upon international humanitarian law, in particular article 43 of the Hague Regulations, and on a respective agreement between the United States and the United Kingdom.")

members of the coalition for action undertaken under their effective control.[141] This legal identity followed primarily from the recognition of the powers of the CPA by the members of the Coalition. It received further backing from the acknowledgment of the mandate of the CPA by the Security Council,[142] including specific capacities, such as the CPA's right to administer the Development Fund for Iraq.[143]

2.3.   External representation

The international legal status of an entity under international administration is often reflected in further acts and practices. Five elements deserve to be studied in greater detail in this context: the issuance of passports and travel documents by the governing authorities of international(ised) territories; the exercise of diplomatic protection by territories under international administration; the relations between internationally administered territories and foreign state entities; the exercise of treaty-making power by international territorial administrations; and the representation of internationally administered territories in international conferences and organisations.

2.3.1.   The issuance of passports and travel documents by international administrations

Passports and travel documents are concrete embodiments of a separate legal identity. They were used as means of identifying the territorial identity of citizens of territories under international administration in the era of the League of Nations and in the practice of UN administration.

The earliest examples of territory-based identification of citizenship in the practice of territorial administration are the legal regimes of Danzig and the Saar Territory. The Free City of Danzig enjoyed the right to issue its own passports by virtue of Article 104, paragraph 6 of the Treaty of Versailles. The authorities of the Free City issued and renewed Danzig

---

[141] The finding that the CPA enjoyed legal personality in certain areas does not imply that member states of the CPA were automatically exempted from accountability for action falling within the general scope of authority of the Coalition. The case of Iraq is an example of "shared responsibility". It may, in particular, be argued that individual states remained accountable for acts in their specific zone of administration. See above Part III, Chapter 11. For the theory of a joint liability of the US and the UK for violations of international law by the CPA, see Wolfrum, *Iraq – From Belligerent Occupation to Sovereignty*, at 21.

[142] See paras. 4 and 8 of SC Res. 1483 (2003).   [143] See *ibid.*, para. 13.

passports, independently of Polish citizenship.[144] The same principle applied in relation to the granting of visas. Foreigners were allowed to enter Danzig without a Polish visa, unless the government of Danzig desired such a visa.[145] Both practices underlined the autonomous character of the Free City.

Citizens of the Saar Territory also enjoyed a separate identity during the fifteen-year period of League administration. Although Saar residents retained German citizenship, passports were issued by the authorities of the Saar administration to "inhabitants of the Saar".[146]

The UN used a different technique in situations where it held exclusive administering authority over a territory. It introduced travel documents in order to allow inhabitants of territories to travel in and out of the territory. This approach was guided by pragmatic considerations. The introduction of travel documents underscored the functional nature of mobility arrangements and avoided controversies about the legal status of the territory because it does not allude to statehood.[147]

The first instance where the UN resorted to this technique was the case of West Irian. The UN provided local inhabitants with independent documents of identification on the basis of a Note dated 15 August 1962, by which Indonesia and the Netherlands confirmed that "UNTEA shall have the authority to issue travel documents to Papuans (West Irianese) applying therefore without prejudice to their right to apply for Indonesian passports instead".[148]

The Council for Namibia took similar steps in relation to the inhabitants of the former South West Africa. This time, the Security Council requested the Council for Namibia to make proposals for the issuance of special "passports and visas for Namibians" and for travel to Namibia.[149] The Council followed that request, and issued travel documents for Namibians through the UN Institute for Namibia. It also concluded agreements with Zambia and Uganda for the issue of UN

---

[144] See Mason, *The Danzig Dilemma*, at 113.

[145] See Ydit, *Internationalised Territories*, at 200.

[146] See Hannum, *Autonomy, Sovereignty and Self-Determination*, at 392.

[147] This factor was, in particular, a decisive criterion for the introduction of travel documents in Kosovo.

[148] See Note dated 15 August 1962 From the Representative of Indonesia and the Representatives of the Netherlands, Addressed to the Acting Secretary-General, Concerning the Issue of Passports and Consular Protection During the Administration of West New Guinea (West Irian) by the United Nations Temporary Executive Authority (UNTEA), reprinted in Higgins, *United Nations Peacekeeping*, Vol. II, at 108.

[149] See para. 10 of SC Res. 283 (1970).

travel and identity documents to Namibians residing in these countries, while holding similar consultations with officials from Kenya, Tanzania and Ethiopia.[150]

This tradition was later taken up by UNMIK, which issued separate travel documents for people born in Kosovo, or whose parents were born in Kosovo, or who have been residing in Kosovo for at least five years.[151] They were accepted by a large number of third states, including UN member states, for visa purposes.

2.3.2. Diplomatic protection

Another indication of the independent legal status of a territory is the power of the governing entities to exercise diplomatic protection on behalf of the citizens of a territory. This power is traditionally exercised by the territorial state. However, if a territory is under international administration, the right to diplomatic protection may be attributed to the administering authorities of the respective territory.[152] International administrations may be better placed than state authorities to exercise functions of diplomatic protection if they exercise exclusive governing authority over the citizens of the territory. Powers of diplomatic protection have therefore been divested from the state and transferred to the governing authorities of the administered territory on a number of occasions.

2.3.2.1. *Diplomatic protection under the Treaty of Versailles*
The Treaty of Versailles provided different regimes for the exercise of diplomatic protection. The external relations of Danzig remained within the traditional scheme of state representation. Poland assumed the protection of Danzig citizens in foreign countries as a part of its foreign relation power over Danzig.[153]

---

[150] See generally Jacob F. Engers, *The United Nations Travel and Identity documents for Namibians*, American Journal of International Law, Vol. 65 (1971), at 571.

[151] See Section 1 of Regulation No 18/2000 on Travel Documents of 29 March 2000 and Section 3 of Regulation No. 13/2000 on the Central Civil Registry of 17 March 2000.

[152] See also Handbook on UN Multidemsional Peacekeeping Operations, at 21. ("During the period of interm or transitional administration, the political role of the SRSG becomes more prominent as she or he becomes a political advocate in and for the area... Internationally, the SRSG serves as a 'diplomatic' representative of the country, territory or province being administered vis-à-vis the Security Council, the international community and donor organisations.")

[153] See Mason, *The Danzig Dilemma*, at 111.

The drafters of the Versailles Treaty envisaged a different solution for the Saar Territory. The Treaty vested the Governing Commission of the League of Nations itself with "the duty to ensure... the protection abroad of the interests of the inhabitants of the... Saar Basin".[154] However, the Governing Commission of the League decided to delegate this authority to France, contrary to the express wording of the Treaty.

2.3.2.2.   The practice of the United Nations

The UN adopted different approaches in its practice. In West Irian, the UN administration held the right to request the exercise of diplomatic protection for the benefit of the inhabitants of the territory. But the exercise of diplomatic protection itself was carried out through state channels, clearly for reasons of practicality. The Agreement dated 15 August 1962 provided that "[t]he Governments of Indonesia and of the Netherlands shall at the request of the Secretary-General furnish consular assistance and protection abroad to Papuans (West Irianese) carrying... travel documents..., it being for the person concerned to determine to which consular authority he should apply".[155]

In two other cases, UN representatives were directly charged with the exercise of diplomatic protection. The first example is the proposed territorial internationalisation of Jerusalem. The draft Statute of the City of Jerusalem provided for a fully international protection regime. The UN Governor, the main "representative of the United Nations in the City", was directly vested with the authority to "ensure by means of special international agreements, or otherwise, the protection abroad of the interests of the City and of its citizens".[156]

The second example is the case of Namibia. South Africa had lost its right to represent citizens of Namibia through diplomatic or consular relations.[157] The Council for Namibia held the authority to "represent [Namibia] diplomatically and exercise diplomatic protection of its nationals" by virtue of its power to administer the territory.[158]

The UN instruments relating to the UN administrations in Kosovo and East Timor did not specifically refer to the right of diplomatic protection. One may argue, however, that this power was implicit in their respective

---

[154] See Treaty of Versailles, Annex, Article 21.
[155] See Note dated 15 August 1962, in Higgins, *United Nations Peacekeeping*, Vol. II, at 108.
[156] See Article 37, para. 2 of the Trusteeship Council Proposal.
[157] See para. 3 of SC Res. 283 (1970).
[158] See paras. 1 (a) and (d) of GA Res. 2248 (S-V). See also ICJ, *Namibia case*, Separate Opinion Judge Ammoun, ICJ Rep. 1971, at 70.

mandates. Both administrations were endowed with full legislative and executive powers over the citizens of the territories. This power implies the authority to exercise the rights necessary for the protection of the individuals placed under their supervision.

Two arguments support this assumption. In 1949, the ICJ recognised in the *Reparations for Injuries* case that the UN is empowered to exercise diplomatic protection with regard to its own staff.[159] This jurisprudence applies *a fortiori* to the situations in Kosovo and East Timor, where the UN holds not only administrative authority over persons in the same way as an employer, but also exclusive governing authority.[160] Moreover, the Constitutional Framework for Provisional Self-Government expressly clarified that UNMIK maintains "powers and responsibilities of an international nature in the legal field" and authority over "external relations, including with states and international organisations, as may be necessary for the implementation of [its] mandate".[161] These references serve as an indication that the power to exercise diplomatic protection resided with UNMIK in the case of Kosovo.

2.3.3. The establishment of relations with state entities

The governance of territories under international administration may require the establishment of formal ties with other actors. Different models of representation have been applied in legal practice to meet this challenge. Traditionally, the relations between the administered territory and other entities have been conducted through the diplomatic channels of a state. This approach was adopted in the cases of Danzig[162] and West Irian.[163] However, in other situations, the governing authorities of the administered territory entertained direct relations with foreign entities. These arrangements are of special interest in light of the status of territories under international administration. Three examples may be found in the practice of the UN.

---

[159] See ICJ, *Reparations for Injuries*, 174, at 184. ("Upon examination of the character of the functions entrusted to the Organization and of the nature of the missions of its agents, it becomes clear that the capacity of the Organization to exercise a measure of functional protection of agents arises by necessary intendment out of the Charter.")

[160] See Zimmermann and Stahn, *Legal Status of Kosovo*, at 450.

[161] See Constitutional Framework for Provisional Self-Government in Kosovo, Chapter 8.1.

[162] See Mason, *The Danzig Dilemma*, at 98. The only exception is the fact that Danzig nationals were attached to Polish consulates. They were charged with matters especially affecting the interests of the citizens of Danzig, but were responsible to Polish officials.

[163] See Note dated 15 August 1962, in Higgins, *United Nations Peacekeeping*, Vol. II, at 108.

The broadest accumulation of foreign relations power is reflected in the Trusteeship proposal for the territorial internationalisation of Jerusalem. This instrument granted the UN-appointed Governor of Jerusalem the authority to "accredit" representatives of foreign states in Jerusalem and to assign representatives of the City to foreign states "for the protection of the interests of the City and its citizens".[164] This double authority would have allowed the Governor to establish diplomatic ties with state entities inside and outside of Jerusalem.

In Kosovo and East Timor, the power to institutionalise relations with other states was not expressly provided for by the Security Council. However, both UN administrations found this authority to be inherent in their respective mandates, and established relations with foreign officials in the administered territory.[165]

UNTAET institutionalised its relationship with foreign states through the establishment of Representative Offices of foreign governments in East Timor under Regulation No. 31/2000. The functions of these offices were largely identical to those of a diplomatic mission under the Vienna Convention on Diplomatic Relations of 18 April 1961.[166] The Representative Offices were designed to represent and conduct the relations of a foreign government with the transitional administration, to protect the interests of this government and its nationals in East Timor and to negotiate with the transitional administration.[167] Moreover, the Representative Office and its staff enjoyed far-reaching immunities under the framework of the Regulation. Section 16 of Regulation No. 31/2000 granted members of the representative staff the immunities from jurisdiction and legal process granted to diplomats under Article 31 of the Vienna Convention on Diplomatic Relations.[168] Section 19 of the

---

[164] See Article 37, paras. 3 and 4 of the Trusteeship Council Proposal.

[165] See UNTAET Regulation No. 31/2000 of 27 September 2000 on the Establishment of Representatives of Foreign Governments in East Timor. The Regulation was adopted pursuant to the "authority... under United Nations Security Council resolution 1272 (1999)" and on the basis of UNTAET Regulation No. 1/1999. See paras. 2 and 3 of the preamble of UNTAET Regulation No. 31/2000 of 27 September 2000. See also UNMIK Regulation No. 42/2000 of 10 July on the Establishment and Functioning of Liaison Offices in Kosovo, which was based on UNMIK's authority under SC Res. 1244 (1999). For doubts as to authority of UNMIK and UNTAET to establish "diplomatic relations", see Ruffert, *Administration of Kosovo and East Timor*, at 630.

[166] See Vienna Convention on Diplomatic Relations, UNTS, Vol. 500, p. 95.

[167] See Section 3 (1) of UNTAET Regulation No. 31/2000. See also Article 3 of the Vienna Convention on Diplomatic Relations.

[168] The wording of Section 16 of UNTAET Regulation No. 31/2000 and Article 31 of the Vienna Convention on Diplomatic Relations is almost identical.

Regulation added that "the premises and assets of a Representative Office shall be immune from search, seizure or any other form of interference, whether by legislative, judicial or executive action".[169] This far-reaching assimilation of East Timor's foreign relations to inter-state relations was visibly shaped by the special legal status of the territory, which was neither independent nor under the sovereignty of any other state.[170]

UNMIK adopted a slightly more cautious approach due to its continued territorial link to the FRY. It established liaison offices for foreign governments.[171] The status of these liaison offices was modelled after the provisions concerning embassies under the Vienna Convention on Diplomatic Relations. Their role was strictly functional, namely to facilitate "contacts between the international civil and security presences in Kosovo and governments that contribute to the fulfilment of the mandate given to these presences".[172]

2.3.4.   Treaty-making power

Treaty-making power is a common feature of territories under international administration.[173] Nevertheless, two problems arise in this regard. The existence of (partial) legal personality alone does not confer territorial entities with treaty-making power.[174] Internationally administered entities therefore require a separate legal basis to conclude treaties or

---

[169] This provision is even more specific than Article 22 of the Vienna Convention on Diplomatic Relations.

[170] The concept of "Representative Offices of foreign governments" was applied "until the establishment of an independent East Timor". See para. 5 of the preamble of UNTAET Regulation No. 2000/31.

[171] UNMIK Regulation No. 42/2000 of 10 July on the Establishment and Functioning of Liaison Offices in Kosovo.

[172] See para. 3 of the preamble of UNMIK Regulation No. 42/2000. Section 2 of the Regulation provided that liaison offices may perform the following functions: "(a) Conducting the Relations of the Government concerned with the international civil presence and with the international security presence, and with interim institutions as established by the international civil presence in order to contribute to the fulfilment of the mandate given to the international civil and security presences under the resolution; (b) Protecting in Kosovo the interests of the Government concerned and of its nationals, including corporate entities, within the limits permitted by international law ... "

[173] In international practice, it is not unusual that non-state entities may become parties to international treaties. Some conventions are expressly open to Mandate or Trusteeship territories. For a survey, see the respective study of the UN, UN Doc. A/CN.4/281, in Yearbook of the International Law Commission, 1974, Vol. II, at 7.

[174] See Brownlie, *Principles of Public International Law*, at 651.

to be represented in international organisations. Secondly, the authority of international administering authorities is usually limited to the period of administration. International administrators are not allowed to engage the territory beyond the end of their own mandates. This limitation may require alternative solutions to treaty accession.

Both problems have been approached in a pragmatic fashion by international legal practice. Long-term experiments in territorial administration were in many ways equated to state entities in their constitutive treaty arrangements. The mandate of short-term missions, by contrast, was usually framed in more restrictive terms and open to *ad hoc* solutions.

2.3.4.1. Early treaty arrangements
Early treaty arrangements contained clear rules on the treaty-making powers of territories under international administration. They bestowed the international(ised) territory either directly or indirectly with treating-making power.

The Free City of Danzig enjoyed indirect treating-making capacity. Article 6 of the Treaty between Poland and the Free City of Danzig instituted an institutional division of authority between both entities. The Free City was empowered to initiate treaty negotiations with powers other than Poland. But the agreements were formally negotiated and concluded by Poland, acting on behalf of Danzig.[175] The agreements were then binding on Danzig, unless they were detrimental to the interests of the Free City.[176]

Both the Permanent Statute of the Free City of Trieste and the Trusteeship Council Proposal for a Statute for the City of Jerusalem went a step further. They granted representatives of the respective entities direct treaty-making power. The Statute of the Free City of Trieste limited the treaty-making capacity of the territory to specific types of agreements. It provided that "[t]he Free Territory may be or become a party to international conventions... provided that the aim of such conventions... is to settle economic, technical, cultural, social or health questions".[177] The Statute for the City of Jerusalem contained an even wider authorisation. It empowered the Governor to "sign treaties" on behalf of the City

---

[175] See Article 6 of the Treaty between Poland and the Free City of Danzig of 9 November 1920. For further details of treaty-making, see Mason, *The Danzig Dilemma*, at 100.

[176] In this case, the High Commissioner of the League had the right to veto the agreement. See Mason, *The Danzig Dilemma*, at 102.

[177] See Article 24, para. 3 of the Statute of the Free Territory of Trieste.

"which are consistent with [the] Statute", and obliged him "to adhere to the provisions or any international conventions... drawn up by the United Nations or by the specialised agencies... which may be appropriate to the particular circumstances of the City, or would conduce to the achievement of the special objectives set out in the preamble to [the] Statute".[178]

The general openness of these arrangements towards the treaty-making capacity of the governing authorities of the administered territories may be explained by the fact that all of the three entities were supposed to be internationalised permanently or for a substantial period of time. Moreover, the long-term effects of treaty regimes on the inhabitants of the respective territories were validated by requirements of ratification (Jerusalem[179]) or domestic consent (Danzig,[180] Trieste[181]).

2.3.4.2.   UN practice

A different approach was later taken in the era of UN peace-maintenance. In many cases, treaty-making power was not expressly provided for by way of agreement (UNTEA, UNTAES), nor directly mentioned in UN mandates (UNMIK). UN administrations developed alternative strategies of self-obligation. Treaty provisions were declared applicable to the administered territory for the duration of UN administration, without formal accession.[182] Moreover, UN administrations implied treaty-making powers from their general mandates. However, this authority was only used on selected occasions.

The practice of UNTAET is a good example. The mission interpreted its powers widely, by implying treaty-making authority from its mandate under Security Council Resolution 1272 (1999), read in conjunction with the Report of the Secretary-General on the Situation in East Timor of

---

[178] See Article 37, para. 5 of the Trusteeship Council Proposal.

[179] See *ibid*. ("Such treaties or international undertakings entered into by the Governor shall be submitted for ratification to the Legislative Council.")

[180] In cases where the interests of the Free City were opposed to those of Poland, the treaty did not need to be ratified by Danzig.

[181] Under the Statute of Trieste, a representative of the Council of Government had to sign the treaty, in addition to the Governor. See Article 24, para. 2 of Statute of Trieste.

[182] This technique allowed an increase in the international law "friendliness" of the legal system of administered territories, without irreversibly committing the territories to the institutional machinery of international treaty-bodies. See Section 1 (3) of UNMIK Regulation No. 24/1999 and Section 2 of UNTAET Regulation No. 1/1999.

4 October 1999.[183] Nevertheless, the UN administration displayed caution in the exercise of the powers. The grant agreement with the International Development Association (IDA) for the Trust Fund for East Timor[184] was directly related to the mandate of UNTEAT. It regulated the allocation of development funds by the World Bank to East Timor for the purposes of the implementation of Security Council Resolution 1272 (1999). The Exchange of Notes constituting an Agreement between the Government of Australia and the UN Transitional Administration in East Timor concerning the Continued Operation of the Timor Gap Treaty[185] was limited to the duration of UN administration. Moreover, the entry into force of the Timor Sea Arrangement, which was initialled by Australian and East Timorese Cabinet ministers on 5 July 2001, was deferred until the approval, signature and ratification of the Treaty by the elected Government of East Timor.[186]

UNMIK adopted a similar policy. It limited its treaty-making power to functional arrangements. UNMIK concluded international agreements in the field of free trade and economic cooperation[187] as well as agreements with other third parties on the repatriation of Kosovars,[188] acting on behalf of UN-administered Kosovo. In its two Agreements with the Council of Europe, UNMIK included a clause which reaffirmed that "the present Agreement ... is without prejudice to the future status of Kosovo to be determined in accordance with Security Council Resolution 1244

---

[183] It is going too far to say that "the signature and ratification of treaties is beyond the mandates of UNMIK and UNTAET", as proposed by Ruffert, *Administration of Kosovo and East Timor*, at 630. Although the respective mandates could have been formulated more clearly, treaty-making capacity can be implied from the exclusive governing powers of both administrations.

[184] See IDA-UNTAET, Trust Fund for the East Timor Grant Agreement of 21 February 2000. See on this issue Chopra, *United Nation's Kingdom of East Timor*, at 30.

[185] See also Gillian Triggs, *Legal and Commercial Risks of Investment in the Timor Gap*, Melbourne Journal of International Law, Vol. 1 (2000), 99, at 100.

[186] See Report of the Secretary-General on the United Nations Transitional Administration in East Timor of 24 July 2001, para. 12.

[187] See the Free Trade Agreements with Albania (UNMIK/FTA/2003/1) and Macedonia (UNMIK/FTA/2005/1). Moreover, on 9 June 2006, UNMIK signed, on behalf of Kosovo, the Multilateral Agreement on the Establishment of the European Common Aviation Area. See Report of the Secretary-General on the United Nations Interim Administration Mission in Kosovo, 1 September 2006, para. 27.

[188] UNMIK concluded a Memorandum of Understanding with Germany, Switzerland and Sweden in order to avoid the forced return of individuals in need of international protection. In 2005, UNMIK began to accept limited numbers of Ashkali and Egyptian citizens based on an "Agreed Note" with Germany dated April 2005. See UNMIK, *Report to the Human Rights Committee on the Human Rights Situation in Kosovo since 1999*, CCPR/C/UNK/1, 13 March 2006, para. 113.

(1999)".[189] The Free Trade Agreement with Macedonia was placed under an express proviso which limited the validity the agreement to "the date of the expiration of UNMIK's mandate [pursuant] to a decision of the UN Security Council".[190] Furthermore, obligations incurred in or by means of international financial agreements concluded by UNMIK on behalf of the Provisional Institutions of Self-Government (PISG) were declared to be "binding upon the PISG" only.[191]

The cautious treaty-making policy of both administrations was visibly dominated by two considerations: the transitional nature of UN authority, and the attempt of both administrations not to bypass domestic decision-making power through long-term international arrangements affecting the future status of the territory.

In some instances, however, UNMIK's external relations practice gave rise to legal dispute. In January 2006, the Supreme Court of Kosovo refused to give effect to transfer arrangements made by UNMIK under the Provisional Code of Criminal Procedure.[192] UNMIK had made arrangements for the transfer of two Kosovo residents to the UK and Switzerland in the form of a Memorandum of Understanding with a representative of the UK and an Exchange of Letters with the Swiss Liaison Office in Kosovo.[193] The Supreme Court reviewed the respective arrangements and concluded that they would not meet the requirements of "international agreements" within the meaning the Provisional Code of Criminal

---

[189] See para. 7 of the preamble of the Agreement between UNMIK and the Council of Europe on technical arrangements related to the European Convention for the Prevention of Torture and para. 9 of the preamble of the Agreement between UNMIK and the Council of Europe on technical arrangements related to the Framework Convention for the Protection of National Minorities.

[190] See Article 40 of the Interim Free Trade Agreement with Macedonia and the Letter of the SRSG dated 31 August 2005 appended to the Agreement.

[191] Article 5 of the Law on International Financial Agreements (Law No. 2004/14) contained a clause which extended liability to "any successor government or authority exercising administrative powers with respect to Kosovo". UNMIK replaced this wording by a new Article 5 which states: "Upon completion of the mandate of UNMIK under UNSC resolution 1244 (1999) pursuant to a decision of the Security Council of the United Nations, information on all outstanding obligations under agreements to be resolved in accordance with general principles of International Law, shall be duly brought to the attention of the Security Council." See UNMIK Regulation No. 30/2004 of 9 August 2004 (*On the Promulgation of the Law on International Financial Agreements adopted by the Assembly of Kosovo*).

[192] See Article 533 of UNMIK Regulation No. 26 (2003) of 6 July 2003 (*Provisional Criminal Procedure Code of Kosovo*).

[193] See Rebecca Everly, *Reviewing Governmental Acts of the United Nations in Kosovo*, German Law Journal, Vol. 8 (2007), No. 1.

Procedure.[194] The Court motivated this decision by concerns over the capacity of representation of the respective state agents and doubts over the treaty-making powers of UNMIK.[195]

2.3.5. Representation in international conferences and organisations

The special legal status of territories under international administration has raised additional problems of external representation, which have been resolved on a case-by-case basis. One such case is the representation of international(ised) territories in international conferences and organisations.

This issue has given rise to a variety of legal disputes. Some arrangements, such as the Permanent Statute of Trieste made explicit provision for the participation of international(ised) territories in international organisations.[196] Legal problems arose, however, when this question was not addressed by status instruments. The two most notorious examples are the cases of Danzig and Namibia. They led to various power struggles and status disputes, which were solved on an *ad hoc* basis by international decision-making bodies.

2.3.5.1. *Danzig*

The Treaty of Versailles and the Treaty of Paris between Poland and the Free City of Danzig remained silent on the question of the extent to which Danzig was entitled to participate in international conferences and international organisations. Both questions had to be decided by the League of Nations.

The principles governing Danzig's participation in international conferences were determined by the League's High Commissioner for Danzig. The issue of whether Danzig was entitled to separate representation was a matter of division of power between Poland and Danzig. The High Commissioner adopted a compromise solution. In a Decision of 24 August 1922, the Commissioner found that Danzig was not entitled to

---

[194] See Supreme Court of Kosovo, *Decision on Petition for Transfer of Luan Goci and Bashkim Berisha*, Pn-Kr 333/05 of 30 January 2006.

[195] For a more full account, see Everly, *Reviewing Governmental Acts of the United Nations in Kosovo*, sub. IV.

[196] See Article 24 of the Permanent Statute of Trieste. ("The Free Territory may... become a member of international organizations provided that the aim of such conventions or organizations is to settle economic, technical, cultural, social or health questions.") Trieste was thereby empowered to apply for membership in UN specialised agencies.

separate voting at international conferences in the light of Poland's external affairs power, but affirmed Danzig's right to send delegates to international conferences which affected Danzig's economic interests[197] – a right which was, however, later disregarded by Poland in practice.[198]

The matter of Danzig's participation in international organisations arose in the context of Danzig's application for membership of the ILO. This question was decided by an advisory opinion of the PCIJ.[199] In its decision, the Court found that the status of the Free City did not exclude the possibility of Danzig membership in international organisations as such.[200] However, the Court decided that "the Free City of Danzig could not participate in the work of the Labour Organisation until some arrangement had been made assuring in advance that no objection could be made by the Polish Government to any action which the Free City might desire to take as a Member of Organisation".

2.3.5.2. Namibia

Very similar questions arose in the context of the representation of Namibia under the regime of the UN Council for Namibia. Namibia was a territory with an international status *sui generis* at that time. It was unclear how it should be treated in status terms. The UN General Assembly formulated a dual recommendation concerning the treatment of Namibia in international organisations and conferences, in order to enable the Council of Namibia to fulfil its mandate. It requested "all intergovernmental and non-governmental organisations, bodies and conferences to ensure that the rights and interests of Namibia are protected, and to invite the United Nations Council for Namibia to participate in their work, in its capacity as the Legal Administering Authority for Namibia".[201] Furthermore, the Assembly recommended that "all specialised agencies and other organisations and conferences within the United Nations system . . . grant full membership to the United Nations

---

[197] See LNOJ, March 1923, at 257–9.
[198] Poland prevented Danzig's participation at the Berne Railway Conference in 1923 and the World Postal Conference in Stockholm in 1924. See Mason, *The Danzig Dilemma*, at 105–6.
[199] See PCIJ, Advisory Opinion, *Free City of Danzig and International Labour Organization*, Ser. B., No. 18, at 14–16.
[200] The PCIJ decided that "the fact that the conduct of the foreign relations of the Free City is entrusted to the Polish Government" would not *per se* "constitute an obstacle to the Free City becoming a member on the Labour Organization", if an arrangement to that effect "were concluded between Poland and the Free City of Danzig".
[201] See para. 5 of GA Res. A/RES/32/9 of 4 November 1977.

Council for Namibia so that it may participate in that capacity as the legal Administering Authority for Namibia in the work of those agencies, organisations and conferences".[202]

These requests were partly implemented in international practice. The UN Council for Namibia was allowed to participate in various conferences. Moreover, Namibia was admitted as a full member in the FAO and the ILO. [203] This deviation from traditional admission practices was disputed in both cases,[204] but justified by the recognition of the Council as the Government of Namibia for purposes of membership in the respective organisations.

3. Conclusion

Territories under international administration are subject to individualised regimes in terms of legal status. There is neither one status model, nor one common legal framework, but rather a diversity of status regimes. Each case of territorial administration is special in its own way. Nevertheless, there are some common principles which characterise the status of international(ised) territories.

Territorial entities that remained under the plenary sovereignty and jurisdiction of a state have generally been treated like traditional state entities in terms of legal status and external representation because state actors continue to act as territorial representatives and rulers. Special rules, however, have applied to international(ised) territories. Although these territories have typically not been treated as full subjects of international law, they have occasionally enjoyed a separate legal identity as a territory under international jurisdiction. In this context, they have been subject to *sui generis* rules, which took into account their special status as non-state entities, while equating them to states or other international actors for functional purposes.

Internationalised and international territories have also enjoyed international legal personality, either by virtue of status arrangements or as a result of the mandate of international administering authorities. In these cases, governmental authority was usually not linked to the traditional concept of territorial sovereignty, but tied to the concept of limited international legal personality. Consequently, the authority of international administering authorities was limited to the respective

---

[202] See para. 3 of GA Res. A/RES/32/9 of 4 November 1977.
[203] See above Part II, Chapter 8.   [204] See Osieke, *Admission to Membership*, at 209 and 213.

administering mandate and did not encompass independent powers of disposal of territories, or lawmaking power beyond the period of international administration.

International authorities have also been empowered to exercise external relations functions in international(ised) territories. Where they did so, they often used symbols of external representation which are comparable with, but not identical to, traditional state-based forms of representation. One example is the issuance of travel documents to citizens of territories under international administration. These documents differ from passports in the sense that they personify the special legal status of the administered territory in international relations, however, without alluding to statehood. They introduced a distinct form of citizenship, linking the people of the territory to the territory under international administration for the purpose of free movement.

A further example is the establishment of Representative Offices of foreign states in internationally administered territories. The creation of such offices institutionalised quasi-diplomatic relations between the administered territory and foreign states. However, the model of representation remained distinct from formal diplomatic missions used in inter-state relations.

Finally, international(ised) territories in many respects enjoyed the rights and fulfilled the duties of international persons. In some cases, territories under international administrations were even fully equated to states, despite their separate identity as non-state entities. Both the League of Nations and the UN have been charged with the exercise of diplomatic protection, because of their governing powers and jurisdiction over the administered territory. Moreover, Namibia gained state-like membership in international organisations while it was placed under the administration of the Council for Namibia. Both cases illustrate that territories under international jurisdiction may enjoy features of international legal personality independently of their recognition as states.

14 The status of international administering authorities

The status of international territorial authorities varies from case to case. Some international administrations are comparable to traditional peacekeeping missions. Other administrations, however, come much closer to classical state authorities within the exercise of administering powers. This creates difficulties in two areas: the scope of application of privileges and immunities and the accountability of international territorial administrations.[1]

The practice of international administration requires new thinking in the area of the law of immunity and the treatment of the accountability of international organisations more generally.[2] Two arguments shall be developed in greater detail here. There is compelling evidence that the principle of functional immunity, which is largely based on operational necessity, cannot be applied to international administrations which exercise powers of government. An absolute standard of jurisdictional immunity collides in such cases with the governmental and human rights responsibilities of the international administration towards the inhabitants of the administered territory.

---

[1] See also generally Chesterman, *You, The People*, at 126–53; Wilde, *Accountability and International Actors*, at 455; Frederick Rawski, *To Waive or Not to Waive: Immunity and Accountability in U.N. Peacekeeping Operations*, Connecticut Journal of International Law, Vol. 18 (2002), 103, Carla Bongiorno, *A Culture of Impunity: Applying International Human Rights Law to the United Nations in East Timor*, Columbia Human Rights Law Review, Vol. 33 (2002), 623.

[2] State-centred models of immunity and accountability cannot simply be transposed to international administrations, because "the legislative, executive and judicial division of powers which is largely followed in most municipal systems" does not automatically apply "to the international setting nor, more specifically, to the setting of an international organisation, such as the United Nations". See also ICTY, *Tadic*, Appeal on Jurisdiction, 2 October 1995, para. 43.

Secondly, the development of international governance mechanisms creates a need for greater diversity in institutional accountability.[3] A distinction may be made in relation to the type of international administration. Traditional forms of accountability based on intra-institutional control or international monitoring are acceptable in the context of governance assistance missions. The exercise of governmental authority with direct powers over individuals, by contrast, requires basic forms of responsibility towards domestic or quasi-domestic actors.

1.   The conceptual move: from external to internal responsibility

International organisations typically perform functions which are international in nature and detached from the domestic legal order of states. Accordingly, they are primarily treated as subjects of international law with responsibilities *vis-à-vis* states and other international actors under classical international law.[4] It is, in particular, increasingly recognised that international organisations may encounter responsibility on the international plane for acts of their own organs or agents,[5] including their subsidiary bodies, and for the conduct of organs or agents of a state or of another international organisation that are placed at the disposal of the organisation.[6]

However, this formal vision of responsibility does not address some of the specific problems arising in the context of international territorial administration. It requires further differentiation in situations where international organisations assume state-like responsibilities towards the citizens of a territory. In these cases, international organisations may enact laws and regulations which are directly applicable in the domestic legal order. It is therefore artificial to treat them as purely "external" actors that are "distinct and ... 'above' the local" legal order.[7] International actors may even be part and parcel of an internationally

---

[3] For a discussion, see also Chesterman, *You, The People*, at 145–53; Caplan, *International Governance of War-Torn Territories*, at 195–211.

[4] See Brownlie, *Principles of Public International Law*, at 655–6.

[5] See Draft Article 4, para. 1 of the proposed ILC Draft Articles on the Responsibility of International Organisations: "The conduct of an organ or agent of an international organisation in the performance of functions of that organ or agent shall be considered as an act of that organization *under international law* whatever the position the organ or agent holds in respect of the organisation" (emphasis added).

[6] See Draft Article 5 of the proposed ILC Draft Articles on the Responsibility of International Organisations.

[7] See Wilde, *Accountability and International Actors*, at 458.

supervised municipal order. In these circumstances, the classical international responsibility *vis-à-vis* other subjects of international law may be complemented by additional "internal" obligations *vis-à-vis* the inhabitants of the administered territory.[8]

The assumption of "internal" responsibilities has direct implications for the conception of immunity and accountability within the framework of transitional administrations. The traditional conception of immunity as a shield against undue state interference in the fulfilment of the function of a mission becomes blurred, because there is, as was stated by the Ombudsperson Institution in Kosovo, "no need for a government to be protected against itself".[9] Moreover, the exercise of public acts *vis-à-vis* the local population creates an organisational obligation to establish mechanisms of accountability accessible to the domestic population.

2. International administrations and privileges and immunities

International actors typically enjoy privileges and immunities in the exercise of public functions on foreign soil. These protections flow either from UN instruments or special Status of Forces Agreements. They serve to protect international organisations and national contingents of peacekeeping missions from interference by the government of the territory in which they operate. The same architecture was applied to UN administrations. They were primarily treated as an extended form of peacekeeping in relation to the scope of privileges and immunity, instead of being conceived as a governance device, subject to institutional accountability and individual human rights protection.

2.1. Sources of privileges and immunities

The general immunity of the UN and its personnel is laid down in Article 105 of the UN Charter and in the UN Convention on Privileges and Immunities of 13 February 1946 ("the General Convention").[10]

---

[8] See also European Commission for Democracy Through Law, *Opinion on Human Rights in Kosovo*, para. 94. ("[E]ven though UNMIK regulations are inspired by human rights standards and designed to respect them, this does not rule out the possibility that in practice a regulation may breach individual rights. The need for an effective and independent remedy in such cases therefore remains, irrespective of the undoubtedly high quality of the internal mechanisms of control of human rights compatibility.")

[9] See Ombudsperson Institution in Kosovo, *Special Report No. 1*, para. 23.

[10] See Convention on the Privileges and Immunities of the United Nations of 13 February 1946, UNTS, Vol. 1, at 15.

Article 105 of the Charter states that "[t]he organisation shall enjoy in the territory of each of its members such privileges and immunities as are necessary for the fulfilment of its purposes". The General Convention defines the scope of protection. Article II, Section 2 of the Convention establishes an absolute immunity standard concerning action against the UN as an organisation. It exempts the UN from any type of legal proceedings before domestic courts by providing that that "the United Nations... shall enjoy immunity from any form of legal process except insofar as in any particular case it has expressly waived its immunity".[11] Article V, Section 18 of the Convention grants UN officials immunity from legal processes "in respect of words spoken or written and all acts performed by them in their official capacity".[12] Moreover, the Secretary-General and all Under-Secretary-Generals and Assistant Secretaries enjoy diplomatic privileges and immunities in addition to functional immunities.[13] The immunities "of any official" can be waived by the UN Secretary-General, but only under strict conditions, namely where "in [the] opinion" of the Secretary-General, "the immunity would impede the course of justice" and where "it can be waived without prejudice to the interests of the United Nations".[14]

Both the immunity of the UN as a legal person and the functional immunity of its staff are based on two main rationales: the aim of protecting the UN against any form of unjustified claims and law suits before biased domestic courts in the exercise of its functions, and the goal of ensuring a uniform application of UN legal acts in various domestic legal systems.[15]

This framework grants UN missions wide immunity in legal practice. The jurisdictional immunity of the UN as a legal person generally exempts UN bodies from civil and criminal suits and claims of individuals before domestic courts. The head of the mission, a Special Representative of the Secretary-General, typically enjoys diplomatic immunity. Furthermore, acts of the civilian staff of UN missions are only subject to domestic jurisdiction if they are performed in an "unofficial capacity"[16] – a

---

[11] See Article II, Section of the General Convention.
[12] See ibid., Article V, Section 18.
[13] See ibid., Article V, Section 19.   [14] See ibid., Article V, Section 20.
[15] See Charles H. Brower, *International Immunities: Some Dissident Views on the Role of Municipal Courts*, Virginia Journal of International Law, Vol. 41 (2000), 1, at 35.
[16] See Secretary-General, *A Comprehensive Strategy to Eliminate Future Sexual Exploitation and Abuse in United Nations Peacekeeping Operations*, UN Doc. A/59/710 of 24 March 2005, para. 86 ("If staff or experts on mission commit criminal acts in their duty station and the

finding that can be made in a national court, but only on the basis of "the most compelling reasons".[17]

Military personnel are not covered by the protection of the 1946 Convention. Nevertheless, military components of peacekeeping operations usually enjoy complete immunity from the criminal jurisdiction of the host state and immunity for official acts by virtue of a status of mission agreement concluded between the UN and the host state[18] – two jurisdictional immunities which are again designed to protect members of peacekeeping forces against unilateral interferences by the "host" state.

2.2.   Privileges and immunities in the practice of territorial administration

Few attempts have been made to adjust the traditional, peacekeeping-based model of jurisdictional immunity to the reality of UN governance. Generally, the UN authorities did not pierce the veil between the institutional immunity of the UN as an international organisation and the role of the UN as a governing authority of a territorial entity.[19] On

host State seeks to prosecute, the Secretary-General will make a determination as to whether the acts in question were performed in the course of official duties. If the acts were not performed in the course of official duties, the Secretary-General will inform the local authorities that no functional immunity exists.")

[17] See ICJ, *Difference Relating to Immunity From Legal Process of a Special Rapporteur of the Commission on Human Rights*, Advisory Opinion of 29 April 1999, paras. 50, 60–1. ("When national courts are seized of a case in which the immunity of a United Nations agent is in issue, they should immediately be notified of any finding by the Secretary-General concerning that immunity. That finding, and its documentary expression, creates a presumption which can only be set aside for the most compelling reasons and is thus to be given the greatest weight by national courts.")

[18] Paragraph 47 (b) of the Model Status-of-Forces agreement provides that the troop contributing state has criminal and disciplinary jurisdiction over military members of the contingent. See paras. 47 (b) and 49 of the Model Status-of-Forces Agreement for UN Peacekeeping Operations, UN Doc. A/45/594 of 9 October 1990, reprinted in Dieter Fleck (ed.), *The Law of Visiting Forces* (2001), at 603. See also Bothe, *Peacekeeping*, in Simma, Charter of the United Nations, at 693, para. 119.

[19] A similar tendency may be observed in the case of the OHR in Bosnia and Herzegovina. The privileges and immunities of the OHR were provided in Annex 10 of the Dayton Agreement. See Article III, para. 4 of Annex 10 of the Dayton Agreement, which reads: "The Parties shall accord the office of the High Representative and its premises, archives, and other property the same privileges and immunities as are enjoyed by a diplomatic mission and its premises, archives, and other property under the Vienna Convention on Diplomatic Relations. a. The Parties shall accord the High Representative and professional members of his or her staff and their families the same privileges and immunities as are enjoyed by diplomatic agents and their families under the Vienna Convention on Diplomatic Relations; b. The Parties shall accord other members of the High Representative staff and their families the same privileges

some occasions, the UN simply applied the jurisdictional immunities of the General Convention[20] to missions of civil administration.[21] On other occasions, the UN extended the framework of existing Status of Forces Agreements to grant UN administration jurisdictional immunities.[22]

The most notorious example of a sweeping immunity regime is UN-MIK Regulation No 47/2000 on the Status, Privileges and Immunities of KFOR and UNMIK and their personnel. It transposed the absolute jurisdictional immunity standard contained in Article 2 of the 1946 Convention to UNMIK and KFOR, making it very difficult, if not impossible, for individuals to defend their rights against these authorities.[23] Section 3 of Regulation No. 2000/47 provided that:

> 3.1. UNMIK, its property, funds and assets shall be immune from any legal process.
> 3.2. The Special Representative of the Secretary-General, the Principal Deputy, and the four Deputy Special Representatives of the Secretary-General, the Police

and immunities as are enjoyed by members of the administrative and technical staff and their families under the Vienna Convention on Diplomatic Relations." This regime was not adjusted when the OHR started to exercise direct administering powers in line with the Bonn Declaration of the PIC. See above Part II, Chapter 8.

[20] The General Convention covers the privileges and immunities of UN officials. Moreover, civilian police and military observers enjoy the status and the privileges and immunities of experts on mission under the General Convention. See Secretary-General, *A Comprehensive Strategy to Eliminate Future Sexual Exploitation and Abuse in United Nations Peacekeeping Operation*, UN Doc. A/59/710 of 24 March 2005, para. 18.

[21] A typical example is Article XXVI of the Agreement Between the Republic of Indonesia and the Kingdom of the Netherlands concerning West New Guinea, by which Indonesia and the Netherlands agreed to apply the provisions of the Convention on the Privileges and Immunities to "United Nations property funds, assets and officials" and, in particular, "the United Nations Administrator" and "the United Nations Representative". See also Article 27 of Agreement on the Settlement of the Cambodian Settlement, which states: "The Signatories shall provide their full cooperation to the United Nations to ensure the implementation of its mandate, including by the privileges and immunities, and by facilitating the freedom of movement and communication within and through their respective territories." For a discussion of problems arising in the context of the immunity regime of the UN truth commission in Guatemala, see Christian Tomuschat, *Between National and International Law: Guatemala's Historical Clarification Commission*, in Liber amicorum Günther Jaenicke – Zum 85. Geburtstag (V. Götz, P- Selmer and R. Wolfrum, ed. 1998), 991, at 1002-1004.

[22] See para. 13 of SC Res. 1037 (1996) in relation to UNTAES.

[23] For a critique see also OSCE Mission in Kosovo, Department of Human Rights and the Rule of Law, *Review of the Criminal Justice System, September 2001 – February 2002*, at 38. ("The immunity established under UNMIK Regulation 2000/47 ensures that regardless, of the character and consequences of the activities or decisions undertaken by UNMIK in its official capacity, courts cannot review the legality of these activities or decisions, nor can they receive and adjudicate private claims against them.")

      Commissioner, and other high-ranking officials as may be decided from time
to time by the Special Representative of the Secretary-General, shall be
immune from local jurisdiction in respect of any civil or criminal act
performed or committed by them in the territory of Kosovo.

3.3.   UNMIK personnel, including locally recruited personnel, shall be immune
from legal process in respect of words spoken and all acts performed by them
in their official capacity.

A similar immunity regime applied to KFOR, which was equally declared
to "be immune from any legal process".[24] Following traditional state
practice, Section 2 (4) of the Regulation gave exclusive jurisdiction over
disputes with KFOR to "the respective sending States".

When Regulation 2000/47 was discussed in the Security Council in
August 2000, this approach was justified by UN officials with "one major
concern in mind", namely "to protect the personnel of these various
organizations as needed in the local courts".[25]

The conceptual weakness of this immunity regime is that it deviates
from the concept of individualised immunity embodied in the constitutional system of democratic states where immunity is usually conferred
upon persons who act as members of the government or members of
parliaments. By granting immunity to the institutions of UNMIK and
KFOR itself, Regulation No. 2000/47 left individuals largely without a
remedy against acts taken by UNMIK or KFOR.[26]

The UN Administration in East Timor did not quite follow this example. While a Status of Forces Agreement (SOFA) concluded between
Australia and Indonesia[27] established that INTERFET, its property, funds,
assets and members were to enjoy immunity from Indonesian criminal and civil jurisdiction,[28] UNTAET and Indonesia did not enter into

---

[24] Section 2 (1) of Regulation 2000/47 states that "KFOR, its property, funds and assets
shall be immune from any legal process".

[25] See Security Council, 55th Year, 4190th meeting, 24 August 2000, UN Doc. S/PV.4190, at
19.

[26] Section 7 of UNMIK Regulation 47/2000 provided merely for a liability regime before a
Claims Commission. Problems have also emerged in relation to the personal
immunity of UNMIK and KFOR employees from arrest and criminal prosecution. The
OSCE observed that few of the serious criminal charges brought against international
employees were properly investigated and criticised this shortcoming in harsh terms.
See OSCE, *Review of the Criminal Justice System, September 2001–February 2002*, at 42

[27] The Agreement was negotiated by Australia as the lead nation of INTERFET. New
Zealand, however, took the view that the SOFA was a bilateral issue between Australia
and Indonesia, because it not recognise that Indonesia had sovereign rights over East
Timor.

[28] See Kelly, McCormack, Muggleton and Oswald, *Legal Aspects of Australia's Involvement in
the International Force for East Timor*, at 137.

a similar arrangement.[29] UNTAET refrained, in particular, from adopting a regulation based on the terms of UNMIK Regulation No. 47/2000. Nevertheless, UNTAET officials indicated that the provisions of the 1946 Convention applied fully to UN staff.[30] Furthermore, the absence of clear provisions created considerable confusion and ambiguity about the issue of UN immunity in East Timorese courts. Several regulations specified that executive decisions taken by the UN administration could be challenged before "the competent judicial authorities in East Timor".[31] However, it was not fully clear in which forums such claims could be made, and under which circumstances UNTAET legal acts gave rise to institutional or individual accountability.[32] Practice reports suggest that UNTAET enjoyed *de facto* a high degree of immunity.[33]

The CPA in Iraq largely followed the patterns of UNMIK. The CPA avoided any significant degree of accountability by removing the jurisdiction of the Iraqi courts over any Coalition personnel in relation to both civil and criminal matters in CPA Memorandum No. 3 and CPA Order No. 17.[34] The legal position of the CPA was expressed in a public notice of the CPA Administrator of 26 June 2003 as follows:

In accordance with international law, the CPA, Coalition Forces and the military and civilian personnel accompanying them, are not subject to local law or the jurisdiction of local courts. With regard to criminal, civil or administrative or other legal process, they will remain subject to the exclusive jurisdiction of the

---

[29] *Ibid.*, at 118.   [30] See Rawski, *To Waive or Not to Waive*, at 118.

[31] An identical clause was contained in UNTAET Regulations No. 17/2000 and No 19/2000. It reads: "Pending the establishment of adequate judicial procedures for administrative matters, a person or legal entity may challenge a decision of the Deputy Transitional Administrator to uphold the original decision adverse to their interests with the competent judicial authorities in East Timor. In any court proceeding arising out of or in connection with the present regulation against UNTAET or a servant of UNTAET, the court shall apply the same substantive norms as would be applicable under the procedures for administrative matters." See Sections 6 (4) and 6 (5) of UNTEAT Regulation No. 17/2000 of 8 June 2000 and Sections 8.4 and 8.5 of UNTEAT Regulation No. 2000/19 of 30 June 2000.

[32] The best example is a case in which the UN Transitional Administrator in East Timor was found personally liable by the Dili District Court to pay damages in a claim for illegal detention, on the ground that he had adopted an executive order (demanding the release of the claimant), which – in the eyes of the Court – violated UNTAET's own regulations (declaring the more liberal Indonesian Criminal Code applicable). See the case of Takeshi Kashiwagi, as reported by Bongiorno, *A Culture of Impunity*, at 666 and 674–8.

[33] See Amnesty International, *East Timor: Justice Past, Present and Future*, Report of 27 July 2001, AI-Index ASA 57/001/2001.

[34] See Section 2 of CPA Order No. 17 of 26 June 2003.

State contributing them to the Coalition. A mechanism exists for this immunity and jurisdiction to be waived by the State contributing personnel to the Coalition at their discretion.[35]

Accordingly, Section 2 (1) of CPA Order No. 17 declared that the "CPA, Coalition Forces and Foreign Liaison Mission, their property, funds and assets shall be immune from Iraqi Legal process". Section 2 (4) added that "[a]ll Coalition personnel shall be subject to the exclusive jurisdiction of their Parent States, and ... shall be immune from local criminal, civil, and administrative jurisdiction and from any form of arrest or detention other than by persons acting on behalf of their Parent States". This measure reduced mechanisms of redress to military internal investigation, while excluding impartial and independent review of human rights violations by civilian personnel. A similar regime was applied to private contractors of the CPA, i.e. "non-Iraqi legal entities or individuals not normally resident in Iraq ... supplying goods or services in Iraq under a Contract" with the CPA.[36] They were granted immunity "from Iraqi legal process with respect to acts performed by them pursuant to the terms and conditions of a Contract or any sub-contract thereto".[37]

2.3.   A critique of existing approaches

This pragmatic and purely functionalist vision of authority is subject to challenge within the framework of the exercise of direct administering powers by international actors.

2.3.1.   Institutional immunity

It is problematic to grant an organisation or a multinational entity absolute immunity from civil, criminal and administration proceedings in situations in which the same organisation or entity exercises the role of a provisional government of a territory.

There is, first, a constitutional argument. Every modern system of governance is built upon lawmaking, administration and adjudication. If international institutions assume functions and powers which are usually those of a state, they require similar checks and balances and, in particular, the protection of persons affected by the activities of these

---

[35] See Office of the Administrator of the Coalition Provisional Authority, Public Notice Regarding the Status of Coalition, Foreign Liaison and Contracting Personnel, 26 June 2003.

[36] See Section 1 (11) of CPA Order No. 17.   [37] See CPA Order No. 17, Section 4 (3).

institutions.[38] A blanket release of governing institutions from administrative, civil or criminal responsibility contravenes the very precepts of the rule of law and democratic governance,[39] which form the very basis and objective of many international administrations.[40]

Secondly, in a modern immunity doctrine it is not the person, but rather the act of a person which is exempted from the jurisdiction of national courts. Immunity is not granted because the defendant in legal proceedings is a subject of international law and therefore supposed to be beyond the jurisdictional reach of a court, but rather because the act in question is performed by a "foreign" actor in the course of its official functions. This argument raises doubts about the feasibility of an absolute immunity standard for an organisation or an entity which is in charge of the exercise of territorial authority.

Finally, international human rights law places limits on the principle of "functional necessity" which provides a justification for the immunity of international organisations.[41] The jurisdictional immunity of international administrators conflicts, in particular, with the right

[38] See also OSCE Mission in Kosovo, Department of Human Rights and the Rule of Law, *Review of the Criminal Justice System, September 2001–February 2002*, at 38.

[39] See also paras. 23, 24 and 27 of Special Report No. 1 on the Compatibility with recognised international standards of UNMIK Regulation No. 2000/47 of 26 April 2001 by the Ombudsperson Institution of Kosovo: "The main purpose of granting immunity to international organizations is to protect them against the unilateral interference by the individual government of the state in which they are located, a legitimate objective to ensure the effective operation of such organization. The rationale for classical grants of immunity, however, does not apply to the circumstances prevailing in Kosovo, where the interim civilian administration in fact acts as a surrogate state. It follows that the underlying purpose of a grant of immunity does not apply as there is no need for a government to be protected against itself... [N]o democratic state operating under the rule of law accords itself total immunity from any administrative, civil or criminal responsibility. Such blanket lack of accountability paves the way for the impunity of the state... [T]he precept of the rule of law is that the executive and legislative authorities are bound by the law and not above it... [T]he actions and operations of these two branches of government must be subject to oversight of the judiciary, as the arbiter of legality in a democratic society... UNMIK Regulation 2000/47 contravenes all of these principles... [T]he law must protect the individual against arbitrary exercises of governmental authority, inter alia, through the articulation of clear standards for the exercise of governmental authority and the provision of adequate control by independent legislative and/or judicial authorities over the exercise of powers by the executive. None of these forms of protection obtain in the instant Regulation."

[40] Paragraph 29 h) of the Report of the Secretary-General of 4 October 1999 noted expressly that UNTAET had the obligation to "ensure the establishment and maintenance of the rule of law and to promote and protect human rights". See UN Doc. S/1999/1024, p. 7.

[41] For a critique of functional immunity in the light of human rights standards, see Michael Singer, *Jurisdictional Immunity of International Organizations: Human Rights and*

of individuals of access to court under Article 14, paragraph 1 of the ICCPR,[42] Article 6, paragraph 1 of the ECHR[43] and Article 10 of the Universal Declaration of Human Rights.[44] The ICJ recognised the tension between functional immunity and individual rights in the context of disputes between the UN and its employees in the *Effects of Award Case*, in which the Court found that it would "hardly be consistent with the expressed aim of the Charter to promote freedom and justice for individuals... that [the UN] should afford no judicial or arbitral remedy to its own staff for the settlement of any disputes which may arise between it and them".[45]

This argument has been developed further in subsequent domestic and international human rights practice. National courts have linked the granting of immunity for international organisations to the availability of alternative forums of redress.[46] Furthermore, human rights treaty bodies have acknowledged that immunity of international organisations from the jurisdiction of national courts may conflict with the duty of the host state to provide access to court. In particular, the jurisprudence of Strasbourg organs under Article 6 of the ECHR has made

---

Functional Necessity Concerns, Virginia Journal of International Law, Vol. 36 (1995), 53. In some cases national courts have denied immunities to international organisations for acts which fall outside their functional capacities. See generally August Reinisch, *International Organizations Before National Courts* (2000), at 212.

[42] Article 14, para. 1 of the ICCPR provides that: "[a]ll persons are equal before the courts and tribunals. In the determination of any criminal charge against him, or of his rights and obligations in a suit of law, everyone shall be entitled to a fair and public hearing by a competent, independent and impartial tribunal established by law."

[43] Article 6, para. 1 of the ECHR states: "In the determination of his civil rights and obligations or of any criminal charge against him, everyone is entitled to a fair public hearing within reasonable time by an independent and impartial tribunal established by law."

[44] Article 10 of the Universal Declaration of Human Rights reads: "Everyone is entitled in full equality to a fair and public hearing by an independent and impartial tribunal, in the determination of his rights and obligations and of any criminal charge against him."

[45] See ICJ, *Effect of Awards of Compensation Made by the United Nations Administrative Tribunal*, ICJ Rep. 1954, 47, at 57.

[46] See, for example, the French Cour de Cassation, Rapport annuel (1995), 418. ("Les immunités de juridiction des organisations internationales... ont, pour conséquence, lorsque n'est pas organisé au sein de chaque organisation un mode de règlement arbitral ou juridictionnel des litiges, de créer un déni de justice.") See also Swiss Supreme Court, *Groupement d'Entreprises Fougerolle et consorts c./CERN*, 1ère Cour civile du tribunal fédéral suisse, 21 September 1992. For further examples, see August Reinisch and Ulf Andreas Weber, *In the Shadow of Waite and Kennedy: The Jurisdictional Immunity of International Organizations, the Individual's Right of Access to the Courts and Administrative Tribunals as Alternative Means of Dispute Settlement*, International Organizations Law Review, Vol. 1 (2004), 59, at 72, 80–2.

it clear that the jurisdictional immunity of international organisations may run counter to right of access to court in situations in which there are no alternative forums of accountability under which individuals may seek redress. This argument has been developed in two cases before the European Commission of Human Rights concerning the immunity of the European Space Agency (ESA) from German jurisdiction *(K. Beer and P. Regan* v. *Germany, R. Waite and T. Kennedy* v. *Germany*[47]), in which the Commission found that "the legal impediment to bringing litigation before the German Courts, namely the immunity of the European Space Agency from German jurisdiction [was] only permissible under the Convention if there [was] an equivalent legal protection".[48] Contrary to its earlier jurisprudence,[49] the Commission considered a possible violation of Article 6 (1) of the Convention by the German grant of immunity and stated that any limitation on the right of access to court would have "to pursue a legitimate aim and [that there had to be] a reasonable relationship of proportionality between the means employed and the aim sought to be achieved".[50]

This approach was then adopted by the European Court of Human Rights, which examined whether the immunity granted to ESA was proportionate in the light of Article 6 (1) of the ECHR.[51] The

---

[47] See *Beer and Regan*, European Commission of Human Rights, Application No. 28934/95, 2 December 1997; *Waite and Kennedy*, Application No. 26083/94, 2 December 1997. The Commission recalled that: "States may transfer to international organizations competences ... and may also grant these organizations immunity from jurisdiction ... provided that within that organization fundamental rights will receive an equivalent protection." See *Waite and Kennedy*, Report, para. 73.

[48] See *Waite and Kennedy*, Report, 2 December 1997, para. 79.

[49] In its *Spaans* v. *The Netherlands* decision, the Commission had to deal with an application in which the applicant claimed that the immunity of the Iran-US Claims Tribunal violated his right of access to court. The Commission declared the application inadmissible. It found: "Because of the immunity enjoyed by the Tribunal, the administrative decisions of the Tribunal are not acts which occur within the jurisdiction of the Netherlands within the meaning of Article 1 of the Convention and therefore do not engage the responsibility of the Netherlands under the Convention." See European Commission of Human Rights, Application No. 12516/86 of 12 Dec. 1988, *Ary Spaans* v. *The Netherlands*, Decisions and Reports, Vol. 58, p. 119, at 122.

[50] However, the Commission concluded that while the applicants "did not ... receive a legal protection within the European Space Agency which could be regarded as equivalent to the jurisdiction of the German labour courts", it could not "apply the test of proportionality in such a way as to enforce an international organization to be a party to domestic litigation on a question of employment governed by domestic law". See para. 80.

[51] See European Court of Human Rights, *Beer and Regan*, Application No. 28934/95, 18 February 1999, [1999] ECHR 6; *Waite and Kennedy*, Application No. 26083, 18 February 1999, [1999] ECHR 6.

Court acknowledged, in particular that "a material factor in determining whether granting... immunity from... jurisdiction is permissible is whether the applicants had available to them reasonable alternative means to protect effectively their rights under the Convention".[52] This test was reaffirmed in by subsequent case-law.[53]

Later, the contradiction between the necessities of functional immunity and human rights standards was expressly recognised in the context of international administration. Both the OSCE Mission in Kosovo[54] and the Ombudsperson Institution in Kosovo[55] criticised the far-reaching immunities of UNMIK and KFOR. The Ombudsperson Institution found that

[52] See European Court of Human Rights, Judgment of 18 February 1999 in the case of *Waite and Kennedy v. Germany*, Application No. 26083/94, para. 59 *et seq.*, at para. 68. The Court shared the Commission's view that granting ESA immunity from German jurisdiction was not disproportionate, in particular, because of the alternative means of legal process available to the applicants. See para 73 of the judgment.

[53] See *Fogarty v. United Kingdom*, Application No. 37112/97, Judgment of 21 November 2001, para. 33, where the Court noted that an immunity limitation "will not be compatible with Article 6 §1 if it does not pursue a legitimate aim and if there is no reasonable relationship of proportionality between the means employed and the aim sought to be achieved".

[54] See OSCE, *Review of the Criminal Justice System, September 2001–February 2002*, at 38–42. Referring to Article of the 6 ECHR, the OSCE notes: "As the provisions on UNMIK and KFOR immunity strip individuals of basic rights, such as the right to an effective legal remedy, OSCE has concerns with the court's inaction in limiting the extent of immunity." *Ibid.*, at 39.

[55] See Ombudsperson Institution, *Special Report No. 1 on the Compatibility with Recognized International Standards of UNMIK Regulation No 47/2000 of 26 April 2001*, paras. 52 *et seq.* See also Ombudsperson Institution in Kosovo, Report, Registration No. 122/01, *Elife Murseli against The United Nations Missions in Kosovo*, 10 December 2001, paras. 39–49, in which the Ombudsperson found the non-execution of a final judgment of the Municipal Court of Kacanik by UNMIK constitutes a violation of Article 6 of the ECHR. The Ombudsperson noted: "The European Court of Human Rights has consistently held that it would not be consistent with the rule of law in a democratic society or with the basic principle underlying para. 1 of Article 6 of the Convention if a State could remove from the jurisdiction of the courts a whole range of civil claims or confer immunities from civil liability on large groups or categories of persons... The Ombudsperson... recalls... that any limitations applied may not 'restrict or reduce the access left to the individual in such a way or to such an extent that the very essence of the right is impaired'. And, as with regard to other rights guaranteed under the Convention, any limitation on the right to a court will not be compatible with Article 6 if it does not pursue a legitimate aim or if there is not a reasonable degree of proportionality between the means employed and the aim sought to be achieved' (see, *inter alia*, Waite and Kennedy v. Germany judgment of 18 February 1999; Fayed judgment of August 25, 1994)... In considering whether the limitation on the applicant's access to court pursued a legitimate aim, the Ombudsperson recalls that the international legal concept of sovereign immunity developed out of the principle that one State shall not be subject to the jurisdiction of another State, in the interests of comity and good relations between States. The Ombudsperson further recalls that

the wholesale removal of UNMIK and KFOR from the jurisdiction of the domestic courts violated several provisions of the ECHR, namely Article 6 of the ECHR, in that individuals had no adequate judicial forum to raise civil claims against UNMIK and KFOR; Article 1 of Protocol 1, in that KFOR and UNMIK could occupy or damage property without compensating the owners;[56] Article 8, in that KFOR and UNMIK were allowed to deprive individuals of access to their homes;[57] and Article 15, in that KFOR and UNMIK limited these and other rights beyond the standard of strict necessity.[58] In 2005, this criticism was reiterated by the Parliamentary Assembly of the Council of Europe, which noted "a general insufficiency of legal remedies against UNMIK in the peculiar and unique legal and political context of Kosovo" in its report on the "Protection of Human Rights in Kosovo".[59]

In the Bosnian context, the same type of argument was applied to the practice of the UN International Police Task Force (UN-IPTF), established under Annex 11 to the Dayton Peace Accords. The Venice Commission invoked the *Waite and Kennedy* jurisprudence of the ECHR in order to criticise the lack of adequate remedies of Bosnian police officers against decertification decisions by UN-IPTF.[60] The Commission relied on the idea of substitution of authority in order to justify the need for greater "transparency and accountability of transitional territorial administration by international organisations". It held that:

the UN- IPTF has carried out tasks which are certainly more similar to those of a State administration than those of an international organisation proper. It is inconceivable and incompatible with the principles of democracy, the rule of law and respect for human rights that it could act or have acted as a State authority and at the same time be exempted from any independent legal review.[61]

UNMIK acts as a surrogate state in Kosovo and not as a State requiring protection against the jurisdiction of a different state, in the sense of the doctrine of sovereign immunity... The Ombudsperson further recalls that UNMIK Regulation 2000/47 confers immunity on individual UNMIK employees for their acts performed in an official capacity and on the property and assets of UNMIK as an institution, neither of which is at issue in the judgment of the Municipal Court in Kacanik... The Ombudsperson, therefore, concludes that there has been a violation of the right to a court guaranteed under Article 6 of the European Convention on Human Rights."

[56] See Ombudsperson Institution, *Special Report No. 1*, paras. 29 et seq .

[57] See *ibid.*, para. 45 *et seq.*   [58] See *ibid.*, paras. 18 *et seq.* and 82.

[59] See Council of Europe, Parliamentary Assembly, *Protection of Human Rights in Kosovo*, para. 15.

[60] See European Commission for Democracy Through Law, *Opinion on a Possible Solution to the Issue of Decertification of Police Officers in Bosnia and Herzegovina*, Opinion No. 326/2004 of 24 October 2005, CDL-AD (2005) 024, para. 41.

[61] *Ibid.*, para. 51.

2.3.2.   Individual immunity from criminal jurisdiction

International administration also raises accountability problems concerning the criminal accountability of military and civilian personnel.[62] UN peacekeeping personnel have been involved in acts of sexual exploitation and abuse of local civilians in a number of operations, ranging "from those in Bosnia and Herzegovina and Kosovo... to Cambodia and Timor-Leste in the early and late 1999s to... the Democratic Republic of Congo in 2004".[63] Such crimes visibly exceed the ambit of functional immunities attributed to peacekeepers. The existing enforcement system devised by the General Convention and the Model-Status-of Force Agreement needs to be revisited, in order to avoid accountability gaps in the context of transitional administration.

2.3.2.1.   Immunities of UN staff members and experts on mission
A particular *lacuna* exists in relation to UN officials and members of civilian police forces, who are considered as experts on mission. The regime of the General Convention fails to address specific accountability problems raised in the context of UN governance missions and statebuilding engagements in war-torn societies.[64] The Convention operates on the assumption that UN staff and experts on mission may be prosecuted by domestic courts of the host state for acts that were not performed in the course of official duties. But this enforcement model does not function properly in situations in which the UN operates in a territory in which there is effectively no functioning or reliable domestic legal system[65] or where the UN itself exercises exclusive jurisdiction over a justice system. In these situations, accountability before domestic courts may not be an option due the lack of capacity, fairness or independence of the domestic system.[66]

---

[62] See generally Geert-Jan Alexander Knoops, *The Prosecution and Defense of Peacekeepers under International Criminal Law* (2004).

[63] See UN Report, *A Comprehensive Strategy to Eliminate Future Sexual Exploitation and Abuse in United Nations Peacekeeping Operation*, UN Doc. A/59/710 of 24 March 2005, para. 3.

[64] *Ibid.*, paras. 87–90.   [65] *Ibid.*, para. 87.

[66] In some cases, the principle of host state jurisdiction is compromised by the fact that a domestic legal system does not yet exist, or does not offer sufficient guarantees in order to ensure a fair trial. In other cases, such as Kosovo and East Timor, where international actors exercised strict scrutiny over the process of judicial reconstruction, it may not be feasible to entrust domestic courts of territories under international administration with jurisdiction over crimes committed by UN personnel, because the domestic judiciary does not yet enjoy a sufficient degree of institutional independence from the international administration itself, in order to guarantee a free and independent judicial process.

International actors must devise alternative institutional mechanisms in order to ensure an effective prosecution of peacekeepers in these specific situations. Two specific proposals of reform have been made in relation to the practice of UN peaekeeping in the UN report on a "*comprehensive strategy to eliminate future sexual exploitation and abuse in United Nations peacekeeping operations*", namely the creation of a new international convention that would subject UN personnel not only to the jurisdiction of the host state, but also to the jurisdiction of all states parties to the Convention;[67] and the provision of additional judicial assistance to the host state in order to enable the latter "to ensure that criminal proceedings against United Nations personnel satisf[y] international human rights standards" in the specific situation.[68] However, these proposals are not entirely satisfactory because they do not offer a guarantee that UN peacekeeping personnel would indeed be held accountable by a national jurisdiction.[69]

It is preferable to think about an alternative institutional model, namely the creation of an independent judicial institution to try specific crimes committed by UN and Associated Personnel by the UN itself, either within the context of the rule of law mandate of a specific mission (*ad hoc* model) or within the framework of the UN system more generally (permanent model).[70] Such a solution would not only reduce the accountability gaps in the context of traditional peacekeeping missions, but would also avoid the specific problems and conflicts of interests encountered in relation to the accountability of UN personnel within the framework of UN administrations.

2.3.2.2.   Immunity of military personnel of troop-contributing countries
There is also a need to strengthen the accountability framework of military personnel of troop-contributing states. Members of national contingents are typically exempted from the criminal jurisdiction of the host

---

[67] See UN Report, *A Comprehensive Strategy to Eliminate Future Sexual Exploitation and Abuse in United Nations Peacekeeping Operation*, para. 89.

[68] *Ibid.*, para. 89.

[69] A special convention on the adjudication of specified crimes committed by UN and associated personnel would "apply only to the parties to the convention". It would not offer a guarantee that UN peacekeeping personnel would be prosecuted by other jurisdictions than the host state. The problem of the second option is that it "would be seen as instituting two standards of justice: one for local inhabitants and one for international officials". *Ibid.*, para. 89.

[70] Note that the UN has already created an administrative tribunal to resolve disputes concerning its staff.

state. They enjoy privileges and immunities through two types of agreements: a SOFA with the host country, which accords exclusive criminal jurisdiction to the troop-contributing state in the case of military personnel,[71] and a Troop Contribution Agreement between the UN and the sending state, which specifies that peacekeeping personnel shall enjoy the privileges and immunities accorded in the SOFA[72] and be tried for criminal offences by the sending state.[73]

This system of accountability is subject to review from two angles: its scope of application and its transparency. The current system appears to be based on the assumption that contributing states are the only ("exclusive") authorities able to prosecute their own peacekeepers in cases of war crimes.[74] This narrow conception of accountability is problematic, because it unduly excludes the jurisdiction of third states.[75] Secondly, the existing structure is weak in design, because it relies on responsibility of the sending state to try crimes committed by peacekeepers without instituting procedures to verify compliance.[76] UN

---

[71] The UN usually concludes a Status-of-Mission Agreement (SOMA) with the host country, currently based on a 1990 model SOFA. Paragraph 47 (b) of the SOMA provides: "Military members of the military component of the United Nations peace-keeping operation shall be subject to the exclusive jurisdiction of their respective participating States in respect of any criminal offences which may be committed by them in [host country/territory]." See Model Status-of-Forces Agreement for Peacekeeping Operations, UN Doc. A/45/594 of October 9, 1990, in Fleck, Law of Visiting Forces, at 603 et seq.

[72] See para. 5 of the Model Agreement between the United Nations and Member States Contributing Personnel and Equipment to United Nations Peace-Keeping Operations, UN Doc. A/46/185 of 23 May 1991, reprinted in Fleck, Law of Visiting Forces, at 615: "Accordingly, the military and/or civilian personnel provided by [the participating state] shall enjoy the privileges and immunities, rights and facilities and comply with the obligations provided for in the status agreement."

[73] See para. 25 of the Model Contribution Agreement: "[The participating state] agrees to exercise jurisdiction with respect to crimes or offences which may be committed by its military personnel serving with [the UN peacekeeping operation]. [The participating state] shall keep the Head of Mission informed regarding the outcome of such exercise of jurisdiction."

[74] See also Article 4 of the Bulletin on the Observance by United Nations Forces of Humanitarian Law of 6 August 1999 which provides that "[i]n case of violations of international humanitarian law, members of the military personnel of a United Nations force are subject to prosecution in their national courts".

[75] The agreements concluded within the framework of peacekeeping missions are only binding upon their parties, namely the UN, the host state, and the troop-contributing states. A state that is neither a party to the SOFA nor to the Contribution Agreement cannot be bound by them. It is therefore difficult to see how the existing agreements could prevail over possible universal jurisdiction of third states.

[76] See also the statement of the Ombudsman in Bosnia and Herzegovina, Frank Orton, who pointed to the need for accountability and prompt and thorough investigations

experts have therefore rightly called for a strengthening of the obligations of the troop-contributing state under the UN Model Memorandum of Understanding, requiring the latter to forward allegations of criminal conduct to its national prosecutorial authorities, and to inform the Secretary-General about the progress and outcome of these measures.[77]

2.3.3. Towards a restriction of procedural immunities in the context of international territorial administration

In future missions, additional efforts must be made to restrict the scope of procedural immunities of international governing entities. There is a clear trend towards the crystallisation of democracy-linked and human rights-based restrictions on procedural immunities under international law. Two principles may be formulated more generally.

First, there is growing consensus that a continued and wholesale exemption of an international entity from any form of legal process is untenable in cases where the organisation exercises full powers of government over a territory.[78] An absolute immunity standard undercuts both the fundamental protection of any individual against arbitrary exercises of governmental authority and the most basic principles of the rule of law, which require that "the executive and legislative authorities are bound by the law and... not above it".[79] The possibility of a

of human rights violations by peacekeepers in Bosnia. He noted in February 2003: "It is important quickly to find out in a trustworthy way, if these allegations are exaggerated or even incorrect and thereby unnecessarily creating tension and unfounded hostility towards SFOR; or if there is any real substance behind them. Even if the Dayton Agreement offers immunity and impunity to SFPR personnel in certain situations, this personnel should reasonably nevertheless in fact be subject to general accepted legal principles... Allegations on improper behaviour should therefore be checked as swiftly and properly and due sanctions should be imposes, if there is proper cause." See www.ohro.ba/articles/press.php?id=179.

[77] See UN Report, *A Comprehensive Strategy to Eliminate Future Sexual Exploitation and Abuse in United Nations Peacekeeping Operation*, paras. 79–83.

[78] See Ombudsperson Institution, *Special Report No. 1*, para. 84; European Commission for Democracy Through Law, Opinion on Human Rights on Kosovo, para. 95. ("[T]he Commission wishes to underline that while it was reasonable to expect and accept that UNMIK's and KFOR's accountability was limited in the initial phases of the interim administration, such accountability has nowadays, in the Commission's opinion become essential.") See also Abraham, *The Sins of Saviour*, at 1336.

[79] See Ombudsperson Institution, *Special Report No. 1*, para. 24 and para. 63. ("In this light and in connection with the general discussion of immunity, the Ombudsperson considers that UNMIK's conferral of immunity from any civil liability on all KFOR and UNMIK personnel constitutes a procedural bar preventing individuals from bringing potential civil claims before a Court. This grant of immunity is therefore incompatible with Article 6 of the European convention on Human Rights.")

waiver of immunity by the organisation alone does not suffice to justify an absolute immunity regime in such cases, because waivers of immunity are typically subject to the exclusive discretion of the respective organisations and are exempted from any meaningful form of outside scrutiny.[80]

Moreover, the option to pursue a claim before a court in a different jurisdiction (e.g. the courts in the jurisdiction of a sending state), which is typical in the context of military operations cannot justify the removal of the entire group of governmental agents from the jurisdiction of the territory within which they are operating, because redress before foreign courts places unjustifiably high burdens (travel costs, translation costs, court fees etc) on local inhabitants in the realisation of justice.[81]

A clearer distinction must be drawn in the future between classical peacekeeping operations and missions of civil administration. The traditional rule, according to which foreign actors remain subject to the primary jurisdiction of the troop-contributing state,[82] maintains its validity in relation to criminal responsibility[83] and activities through which forces act as agents of foreign states. But the exclusive jurisdiction of the sending state is open to challenge in relation to the exercise of public authority by civil authorities over foreign territories[84] and in relation to executive acts performed by military personnel as a substitute to local institutions or in cooperation with international administrations.[85]

Secondly, international administrations may be under an obligation to provide alternative forums for accountability more generally where they institute functional immunities for authorities which exercise governmental authority in relation to individuals. Norms of international human rights law and the right of access to court, in particular,[86] restrict

---

[80] See also Ombudsperson Institution, *Special Report No. 1*, para. 26.

[81] See *ibid.*, paras. 66–7.

[82] See Articles 47 (b) and 49 of the Model Status-Of-Forces Agreement.

[83] See also UN Report, *A Comprehensive Strategy to Eliminate Future Sexual Exploitation and Abuse in United Nations Peacekeeping Operation*, UN Doc. A/59/710 of 24 March 2005, paras. 78–83.

[84] A typical example in which these two different fields of responsibility have been confused is Public Notice Regarding the Status of Coalition, Foreign Liaison and Contractor Personnel of 26 June 2003.

[85] In these contexts, local actors must be put in a position to have access to locally available forums to claim damages, such as claims commissions.

[86] See also European Court of Human Rights, *Golder*, para. 34, where the Court noted that "in civil matters one can scarcely conceive of the rule of law without there being a possibility of access to courts". See also the early statement by the European Commission of Human Rights in the case of *Dyer* v. *United Kingdom*: "Were Article 6 (1)

the principle of functional necessity that justifies organisational immunity.[87] The right of access to court may oblige international entities to create surrogate mechanisms of control (e.g. independent quasi-judicial or administrative bodies)[88] in fields in which claims of individuals before domestic courts are frustrated by jurisdictional immunities.[89]

3.   International administrations and institutional accountability

The establishment of a right balance between the functional independence of administrators, on the one hand, and the principle of institutional accountability, on the other, is one of the unresolved challenges of territorial administration. Several models of accountability were practised throughout the course of twentieth century, ranging from colonial-based types of supervision to functionalist conceptions of accountability. Today, these conceptions of institutional accountability conflict increasingly with calls for a people-centred and rule of law-based conception of international territorial authority. It is therefore necessary to adjust the existing accountability approaches to contemporary conceptions of governance, and to develop alternative strategies which strengthen the ability of individuals to seek redress against acts of international administering authorities.

3.1. Approaches in international practice

International and foreign authorities have traditionally been subject to loose forms of accountability and control in the exercise of territorial authority. The supervisory mechanisms were primarily political in nature and/or limited to intra-institutional control. Independent judicial review remained an exception.

---

to be interpreted as enabling a State party to remove the jurisdiction of the courts to determine certain classes of civil claims or to confer immunities from liability on certain groups in respect of their actions, without any possibility of control by the Convention organs, there would exist no protection against the danger of arbitrary power." European Commission of Human Rights, Application No. 10475/83, *Graham Dyer* v. *United Kingdom*, 9 October 1984, Decisions and Reports, Vol. 39, p. 246, at 252.

[87] See also Rawski, *To Waive or Not to Waive*, at 124–6.

[88] For a survey, see Bongiorno, *A Culture of Impunity*, at 683; Rawski, *To Waive or Not to Waive*, at 127–30.

[89] Such an argument is in line with the argument made by the ICJ in the *Effect of Awards* Opinion, ICJ Rep. 1954, 47, at 57.

3.1.1.   The post-colonial tradition: political control upon the initiative of local actors

The Mandate System and the Trusteeship System are prime examples of this tradition. They continued the accountability tradition under UK colonial practice, by placing administering authorities under explicit reporting duties and by instituting a petition procedure for the inhabitants of the administered territories. However, international scrutiny remained weak in substance, because the findings of the respective supervisory bodies were discretionary in nature and could not be directly enforced against the administering authorities by the petitioners themselves. The Permanent Mandates Commission, for example, on several occasions expressly refused to consider itself as a judicial authority.[90] Even the decisions of the Trusteeship Council were not directly binding on the administering powers.[91]

The institutional framework of transitional administrations after World Wars I and II was designed in a similar fashion. Domestic actors were given access to international supervisory bodies through various petition systems. But the control of international administrations remained essentially confined to political scrutiny exercised by intra-organisational organs (Council of the League of Nations, Security Council, Trusteeship Council).

Inhabitants of the Saar Territory were authorised to make petitions to the Council of the League of Nations in relation to governmental practices of the League's Governing Commission. However, the Council did not have the power to annul decisions of the Commission. The only sanction was the publicity of the findings of the Council.[92] The situation was slightly different in the case of Danzig. Both the League Council and the PCIJ exercised judicial functions under the governing framework of Danzig.[93] Yet this control was selective in the sense that it extended only to disputes between Danzig and Poland, without covering disputes between the inhabitants of Danzig and the League itself. The Trieste arrangement and the proposed Statute of Jerusalem returned again to an accountability model based on reporting duties of international administrators and a petition system.

---

[90] See above Part I, Chapter 2.   [91] See above Part I, Chapter 3.
[92] See above Part II, Chapter 6.   [93] See above Part II, Chapter 6.

3.1.2.   The peacekeeping tradition: international authority as an act of good will for the benefit of the local actors

The institutional experiences of this early tradition vanished in the context of the subsequent UN practice. UN administration was simply treated as an alternative form of peacekeeping, under which international administrators were largely shielded from extra-organisational forms of accountability and control. The UN did not revive the tradition of petitions by local actors, nor did it invent new accountability models for undertakings in international governance. It transposed the structural framework of peacekeeping missions to the exercise of territorial authority.

This is reflected in the institutional design of UN missions. The governance architecture of UN missions was modelled on the typical framework of institutional balance within international organisations. Organisational principles such as efficiency, centralisation of power and coordination prevailed over checks and balances flowing from the separation of different branches of government. No institutions were set up to independently review the action of the UN transitional administration.[94] Supervision was primarily exercised by the UN Secretariat itself or through reports by the UN mission to the Security Council or the General Assembly.[95]

UNTEA, UNTAC and UNTAES were conceived as expanded forms of peacekeeping which remained primarily dominated by intra-institutional scrutiny and exempted from extraneous control. This technique was then transposed to the UN missions in Kosovo and East Timor.[96] Although both administrations exercised governmental functions, they were not formally or legally accountable to the local population. Moreover, UNMIK and UNTAET both remained the "final arbiter" over the lawfulness of their own legislation. It was generally accepted

---

[94] The creation of the Human Rights Advisory Panel by UNMIK Regulation No. 12/2006 marks a step in the right direction. However, even this forum was criticised by the Human Rights Committee as lacking "the necessary independence and authority". See Human Rights Committee, *Concluding Observations on Kosovo (Republic of Serbia)*, CCPR/C/UNK/CO/1 of 25 July 2006, para. 10. For a parallel finding in the context of the UN Truth Commission in Guatemala, see Tomuschat, *Guatemala's Historical Clarification Commission*, at 1007.

[95] UNTAES, UNMIK and UNTAET were requested to report to the Security Council in regular intervals. See para. 4 of SC Res. 1037 (1996), para. 20 of SC Res. 1244 (1999) and para. 18 of SC Res. 1272 (1999).

[96] UNMIK and UNTAET were essentially conceived as acts of good will for the benefit of the local actors. See also Beauvais, *Benevolent Despotism*, at 1169.

that the UN Secretariat would supervise the adoption of legislative acts elaborated by the SRSG.[97] However, no other institutional checks and balances or forms of extra-organisational legal control were envisaged by the Security Council. UNMIK, in particular, refused to subject its legislation to review by the domestic judicial system[98] and envisaged only internal mechanisms, such as the "Human Rights Oversight Committee" as forums of review.[99] The Human Rights Advisory Panel, with jurisdiction to receive and examine complaints against UNMIK, was only established in 2006.[100]

The main independent institutional control in both cases was exercised by an Ombudsman institution, created by the transitional administrations. The powers of the respective Ombudspersons were, however, limited in scope. The Ombudsperson Institution in Kosovo had a broad mandate to address human rights violations and abuses of power (including by UNMIK), but few means to enhance compliance with its recommendations.[101] The same was true of the East Timorese Ombudsperson,

---

[97] The UN Legal Counsel pointed out that the UN Secretariat tried to assist UNMIK "in particular by reviewing the constitutional elements of the legislations, i.e. that the regulations conform to the Charter of the United Nations, to the mandates given to UNMIK by the Security Council and also respect internationally recognised standards, in particular in the field of human rights". See Hans Corell, *The Role of the United Nations in Peacekeeping – Recent Developments from a Legal Perspective*, Address of 1 December 2000 at the Conference: National Security Law in a Changing World, The Tenth Annual Review of the Field, at 7, available at www.un.org.

[98] This may be derived from Section 4 of the Regulation No. 1/1999 which stated that UNMIK Regulations "shall remain in force until repealed by UNMIK or superseded by such rules as are subsequently issued by the institutions established under a political settlement, as provided for in United Nations Security Council resolution 1244 (1999)". Note also that Section 9.4.11 of the Constitutional Framework exempted UNMIK regulations from the jurisdiction of the Special Chamber of the Supreme Court on Constitutional Framework Matters. The jurisdiction of the Court was limited to the control of acts adopted by the Provisional Institutions of Self-Government. The SRSG, however, did not form part of this group of institutions defined in Chapter 1.5 of the Constitutional Framework.

[99] The Committee was established in June 2002 and charged with "considering and agreeing on actions and policies to enhance human rights protection in Kosovo and ensuring that the actions and policies of all UNMIK Pillars and Offices are in compliance with international human rights standards" and to "make recommendations to the SRSG". This mechanism was criticised for a lack of independence by the Venice Commission. See European Commission for Democracy Through Law, *Opinion on Human Rights in Kosovo*, para. 100

[100] See UNMIK Regulation No. 12/2006 of 23 March 2006 (*On the Establishment of the Human Rights Advisory Panel*).

[101] The Ombudsperson Institution was authorised to "provide advice and make recommendations to any person or entity concerning the compatibility of domestic

who could investigate complaints filed against UNTAET and the Transitional Cabinet, but operated in a legal grey zone.[102] As a result, the accountability of UNMIK and UNTAET was *de facto* limited to their legitimacy in the eyes of local stakeholders and interested third parties[103] and their effectiveness in responding to the needs and interests of the local population.

3.1.3. Judicial control: the exception

Judicial control over the acts of international administering authorities has remained the exception.[104] International and domestic authorities were conceived as parallel, rather than mutually entangled, layers of authority. There have been some cases in which the UN itself allowed for the review of administrative acts of UN administrations or UN-created institutions. But the UN was reluctant to create special judicial bodies to review the legality of the acts of its administering bodies.[105] Domestic courts of the administered territory have only on rare occasions filled the gap by judicially reviewing the legality of acts of UN administrators. Where they have done so, the respective administrations have tended to criticise this exercise of review.[106]

3.1.3.1. *Review of executive authority*
The UN has generally refrained from setting up independent tribunals to review the exercise of governmental authority by UN administrations. Neither the UN nor UN administrations have introduced special courts

laws and *regulations* with recognised international standards" – but *a contrario* was not entitled to invalidate UNMIK legislation. See Section 3 of UNMIK Regulation No. 38/2000. The Parliamentary Assembly of the Council of Europe recommended a strengthening of the powers of the Ombudsperson Institution, by "requiring the Special Representative of the Secretary-General of the United Nations... to give final responses to its recommendations within a reasonable time, with any refusal to accept such recommendations being properly justified". See para. 5 (iv) of Re. 1417 (2005).

[102] The East Timorese Ombudsperson faced considerable difficulties in practice. UNTAET drafted a regulation on the powers of the ombudsperson, but that regulation was not adopted. The lack of a clear framework hampered the functioning of the institution. See generally Bongiorno, *A Culture of Impunity*, at 685.

[103] One example is the OSCE, which took on the role of reviewing UNMIK Regulations in the light of international human rights conventions.

[104] For a survey of case-law with respect to UNMIK, see Everly, *Reviewing Governmental Acts of the United Nations in Kosovo*, sub. IV.

[105] The "Human Rights Advisory Panel" created by UNMIK on 23 March 2006 is a non-judicial body.

[106] See Everly, *Reviewing Governmental Acts of the United Nations in Kosovo*, sub. V.

to control the exercise of executive authority by UN transitional administrations, although such an approach has been suggested in the context of Kosovo.[107] If any form of control was exercised, it was either performed by domestic courts or carried out in a decentralised fashion, namely through the establishment of specialised institutions designed to supervise the action of UN created administering bodies.

3.1.3.1.1. The absence of review

The review of administering decisions of international authorities was a non-issue in many instances. The acts of UN administrators were on some occasions simply declared final and binding on domestic actors. A typical example is the case of Cambodia. Section B of Annex 1 to the Paris Settlements placed "all administrative agencies, bodies and offices acting in the field of foreign affairs, national defence, finance, public security and information" under "the direct control of UNTAC", which was authorised to exercise this control "as necessary to ensure strict neutrality". The SRSG enjoyed unfettered authority in the exercise of these powers under the terms of Annex 1 to the Paris Settlements. The SRSG himself was required to "determine what is necessary" and was empowered to issue directives to domestic administrative agencies which were declared binding on all Cambodian parties.[108] Moreover, other administrative agencies, bodies and offices which could directly influence the outcome of elections were placed under direct supervision or control of UNTAC and bound to "comply with any guidance provided by it".[109]

On other occasions, UN administrations limited administrative control over their own acts by excluding domestic control in their own legislation or by introducing non-reviewable or quasi non-reviewable forms of administrative discretion. In Kosovo, for example, parts of the executive branch of power were exempted from the jurisdiction of the national courts. In many areas which did not fall in the sphere of competence of the municipalities, attempts to seek justice in the courts were frustrated by UNMIK's claim of immunity.[110] The temporary removal of a person from a location for the prevention of a threat to public

---

[107] For proposals concerning the establishment of a Human Rights Court in Kosovo with power to annul decisions and acts of UNMIK and KFOR, see European Commission for Law Through Democracy, Opinion on Human Rights, paras. 101–12; Council of Europe, Parliamentary Assembly, Resolution 1417 (2005), para. 4.

[108] See Section B.1 of Annex 1 to the Paris Accords.   [109] See ibid.

[110] For an example, see the suspension of the operations of the newspaper Dita by UNMIK before the creation of the Kosovo Media Appeals Board. The Board was not competent to deal with this claim, because its authority was limited exclusively to

peace and order under Regulation No. 2/1999 was exempted from judicial scrutiny.[111] UNMIK Regulation No. 26/1999 failed to provide a mechanism which would allow a detainee to challenge the lawfulness of an order for continued detention during the period covered by the Regulation. In other areas, judicial review was restricted,[112] or severely hampered by the wide discretion given to the SRSG or UNMIK in administrative application procedures,[113] making it basically impossible to exercise any form of judicial control over the decision. Moreover, UNMIK invoked immunity in administrative proceedings[114] and occasionally refused to enforce

appeals against decisions of the TMC. Nonetheless, the Board added an *obiter dictum* in para. 55 of the *Dita* Decision: "The Board observes, however, that the present proceedings are deeply coloured by earlier events, and that the Applicant continues to be sincerely concerned by the apparent lack of any forum in which to pursue a challenge to the earlier closure." See *Beqaj and Dita* v. *Temporary Media Commissioner*, p. 14.

[111] See *a contrario* UNMIK Regulation No. 62/2000, which provided expressly for a review of an exclusion order, while emphasising in Section 6 (2) that "[n]othing in the present regulation shall affect the power of the relevant law enforcement authorities to temporarily remove a person from a location or prevent access by a person to a location in accordance with UNMIK Regulation No. 1999/2".

[112] Section 48 of UNMIK Regulation No. 21/1999 on Bank Licensing and Regulation, for instance, stated that "[i]n any proceeding in any court, arbitration court or administrative body in any jurisdiction brought against the Banking and Payments Authority of Kosovo for any action taken in its capacity as supervisor or receiver, or against any of its officials, employees or agents: (a) The sole question before the court or body in determining whether a defendant acted unlawfully, wrongfully or negligently shall be whether a defendant exceeded clear authority or acted in an arbitrary or capricious manner in light of all the facts and circumstances, the provisions and intent of the present regulation, rules, orders and applicable law; (b) No actual or former official, employee, or agent of the Banking and Payment Authority shall be liable for damages or otherwise liable for acts or omissions performed in good faith in the course of his or her duties." A similar provision is also contained in Section 66 of UNMIK Regulation No. 20/1999 on the Banking and Payments Authority of Kosovo.

[113] See below Part IV, Chapter 15.

[114] For an illustration, see the case of a Kosovo Albanian woman who challenged an administrative act issued by Kacanik Municipality and by the former UNMIK Department of Education and Science. The applicant challenged the conditions and procedure of the examination process for the position as a pre-school principal before the Municipal Court in Kacanik. UNMIK invoked immunity from legal process before the Court. On 1 March 2001, Legal Counsel for UNMIK DES sent a letter to the Kacanik Municipal Court, stating in part: "[The Director of Kacanik MDE] is currently employed as the Director of Directorate of the Department of Education and Science, in UNMIK's Interim Administration. He is therefore, immune from legal process in respect of words spoken and all acts performed by him in his official capacity. The immunity of UNMIK personnel is established in section 3 of UNMIK Regulation No. 2000/47 of 18 August 2000 on the Status, Privileges and Immunities of KFOR and

judgments by domestic courts which challenged UNMIK administrative acts.[115]

A similar approach was taken by the OHR. The High Representative was reluctant to accept the exercise of judicial review by domestic courts. Following some initial case-law of the Bosnian Human Rights Chamber,[116] the OHR repeatedly argued that certain executive decisions were

UNMIK and Their Personnel in Kosovo." The Kacanik Municipal Court rejected this claim in a judgment of 12 March 2001 and accepted the applicant's claim as a whole and as completely founded. The relevant provisions of the judgment read as follows: "'The claim by Mrs. Elife Murseli from Doganaj – Kacanik, is hereby accepted as being completely founded, thus annulling the decision on 29.11.2001 on the selection of the Director of PEC 'Agimi' in Kacanik as unfair and unlawful. The respondent party, the Municipal Department of Education in Kacanik is obliged to select the best candidate on the basis of the open competition, in which the applicant and two other candidates applied, within 15 days from the entry into force of this decision, under the threat of forcible execution. The Municipal Court in Kacanik further found that it was competent to proceed and decide on the applicant's case as it related to a violation of the rights of the applicant, and did not fall within the scope of privileges and immunities of UNMIK in the sense of UNMIK Regulation 2000/47." See Ombudsperson Institution in Kosovo, Report, Registration No. 122/01, *Elife Murseli against The United Nations Missions in Kosovo*, 10 December 2001, paras. 14–15.

[115] When Mrs. Elife sought to enforce the judgment of the Municipal Court of Kacanik of 12 March 2001, Legal Counsel for UNMIK DES sent a letter to the Kacanik Municipal Court stating, in part: "[T]he UNMIK Department of Education and Science established the Kosovo-wide School Director Selection Commission, administered the selection process and hired the School Directors, its employees... , all of which was done within the applicable UNMIK regulations. This selection process is not open to judicial review except in so far as there are irregularities. The present action is against the Kacanik Municipal Directorate of Education, an element of the Municipality of Kacanik. The Municipality of Kacanik, a local self-government organized pursuant to UNMIK Regulation No. 2000/45, has no authority to select and hire the staff of the UNMIK Department of Education and Science. The 12 March 2001 decision of the Kacanik Municipal Court orders the Municipality to reselect the School Director of the 'Agimi' Pre-Primary School, an action that the Municipality of Kacanik has no authority to do. The order seeks to enforce an action that is solely within the jurisdiction of UNMIK. Please be informed that any action taken by the Municipality of Kacanik would be without validity and unenforceable against UNMIK or the Department of Education and Science Without in anyway [sic] involving itself in the case, UNMIK is presenting this letter for the Court's consideration and without prejudice to the privileges and immunities enjoyed by UNMIK under UNMIK Regulation No. 2000/47." The consequence of the position adopted by UNMIK was that the Court decision could not be enforced. See OSCE, *Review of the Criminal Justice System, September 2001–February 2002*, at 39. The Ombudsperson Institution in Kosovo qualified UNMIK's non-execution of the judgment as a violation of Article 6 of the ECHR. See Ombudsperson Institution in Kosovo, *Elife Murseli against The United Nations Missions in Kosovo*, paras. 37–49.

[116] See Human Rights Chamber, *Adnan Suljanovic, Edita Cisic and Adam Lelic v. Bosnia and Herzegovina and the Republika Srpska*, Decision of 14 May 1998, Cases Nos. CH/98/230

not subject to review, because they were adopted in the exercise of his "international mandate". In some cases, the OHR even introduced a specific clause into his decisions, in order to prevent the exercise of judicial review.[117]

3.1.3.1.2. Mechanisms of direct review

Mechanisms of direct review of executive authority are rare in UN practice. Some examples may be found in UNTAET's practice. The UN laid down in several regulations that executive decisions taken by organs of the administration could be challenged before domestic courts. An identical clause may be found in UNTAET Regulations No. 17/2000 and No. 19/2000. It reads:

> Pending the establishment of adequate judicial procedures for administrative matters, a person or legal entity may challenge a decision of the Deputy Transitional Administrator to uphold the original decision adverse to their interests with the competent judicial authorities in East Timor. In any court proceeding arising out of or in connection with the present regulation against UNTAET or a servant of UNTAET, the court shall apply the same substantive norms as would be applicable under the procedures for administrative matters.[118]

Similarly, UNTAET Regulation No. 10/2000 provided for a review of decisions taken by the UNTAET procurement policy body before a court of competent jurisdiction.[119] These two examples show that UNTAET made some efforts to pierce the veil between international and domestic authority.

and 231, Decisions and Reports January–June 1998, p. 171. The Chamber found that the application was inadmissible, since acts of international institutions are not imputable to the Bosnian State institutions. The Chamber held: "It is beyond doubt that the actions of neither the High Representative nor the IPTF are subject to any review in relation to the carrying out of their functions under the General Framework Agreement. For this to be the case, the General Framework Agreement would have to provide specifically for any such review." *Ibid.*, para. 39.

[117] See OHR, Order Blocking All Bank Accounts of, held by and/or in the name of Milovan Marijanovic of 9 February 2004. The order stated: "For the avoidance of doubt, it is hereby specifically declared and provided that the provisions of the Order contained herein are... laid down by the High Representative pursuant to his international mandate and are not therefore justiciable by the Courts of Bosnia and Herzegovina or its Entities or elsewhere, whether in respect of the Banking Agencies or otherwise, and no proceedings may be brought in respect of duties carried out thereunder before any court whatsoever at any time thereafter." See OHR, Decisions Relating to Individuals Indicted for War Crimes in the Former Yugoslavia, at http://ohr.int/decisions/war-crimes-decs/default.asp?content_id=31814.

[118] See Section 6 (4) and (5) of UNTEAT Regulation No. 17/2000 of 8 June 2000 and Section 8 (4) and (5) of UNTEAT Regulation No. 19/2000 of 30 June 2000.

[119] See Section 42 of UNTEAT Regulation No. 10/2000 of 6 March 2000.

There is also at least one reported case in which domestic courts exercised judicial review over UNTAET executive action (the *Kashiwagi* case).[120] Takeshi Kashiwagi, a Japanese human rights activist was arrested by UN civilian police on the instruction of the Dili Distict Court and detained in custody on the basis of untenable defamation charges under Indonesian law applicable under UNTAET Regulation No. 1/1999 and the Transitional Rules of Criminal Procedure.[121] The UN Transitional Administrator ordered the immediate release of Kashiwagi by an executive order, which stated that defamation "is of a non-criminal nature in East Timor" and should not form the basis of arrests.[122] When Kashiwagi filed a civil compensation claim for illegal detention against the members of the East Timorese judiciary and the SRSG before the Dili District Court, the court examined the legality of UNTAET's executive order[123] and declared it unlawful.[124]

3.1.3.1.3.   Mechanism of indirect review

In other instances, the UN allowed judicial or quasi-judicial supervisory bodies to review the acts of UN established administering institutions ("indirect review"). These bodies have occasionally carried out an incidental review of the legality of acts of UN administrations.

UNMIK introduced review procedures against acts of UN-established administrative agencies in several areas (licensing of pharmaceutical products,[125] registration of businesses,[126] tax administration[127]). The most famous example is the Kosovo Media Appeals Board. This Board was established by UNMIK Regulation No. 36/2000 on the Licensing and

---

[120] For a full account of this case, see Bongiorno, *A Culture of Impunity*, at 666–76; Megan A. Fairlie, *Affirming Brahimi: East Timor Makes the Case for a Model Criminal Code*, American University International Law Review, Vol. 18 (2003), 1059, at 1088.

[121] See UNTAET Regulation No. 30/2000.

[122] See UNTAET Executive Order No. 2/2000 (*On the Decriminalization of Defamation*), UNTAET/ORD/2000/2 (2000). See generally Bongiorno, *A Culture of Impunity*, at 669.

[123] The court asserted jurisdiction over the case although the defendants had argued that the claim should not be heard before a domestic forum because it challenged an executive act taken on behalf of UNTAET.

[124] For a critique of this ruling, see below Part III, Chapter 15.

[125] UNMIK Regulation No. 52/2000 allowed judicial review of decisions of the Pharmaceutical Appeals Board. See Section 13 of UNMIK Regulation No. 52/2000 of 2 September 2000 (*On the Import, Manufacture, Sale and Distribution of Pharmaceutical Products, including Narcotic Drugs and Psychotropic Substances*).

[126] See Section 4 (4) of UNMIK Regulation No 8/2000 of 29 February 2000 (*On the Provisional Regulation of Businesses in Kosovo*).

[127] See the appeals procedures under Section 7 of UNMIK Regulation No 20/2000 of 12 April 2000 (*On Tax Administration and Procedures*) and Section 9 (5) of UNMIK Regulation No. 23/2003 of 25 June 2003 (*On Excise Taxes on Tobacco Products in Kosovo*).

Regulation of the Broadcast Media in Kosovo, in order to uphold, modify or rescind decisions of the Temporary Media Commissioner (TMC) – the entity responsible for the "implementation of a temporary regulatory regime for all media in Kosovo".[128] The Board was designed as "an independent body" with the authority to "hear and decide on appeals by a person or entity against any of the following decisions by the Temporary Media Commissioner: a) refusal to issue a broadcast licence; or b) the conditions attached to a broadcast licence; or c) sanctions imposed by the Temporary Media Commissioner".[129] The practice of the Board deserves special attention from the perspective of accountability, because it served not only as a means of reviewing decisions of the TMC, but also as an instrument of incidental control over the content of UNMIK Regulations.

This is illustrated by the decision of the Board in the case of *Belul Beqaj & the Newspaper Dita* v. *the Temporary Media Commissioner* (TMC).[130] In this case, the Board found that the conditions justifying the imposition of sanctions against the media under Regulation No. 2000/37[131] did not satisfy the procedural guarantees required by internationally recognised human rights. The Media Appeals Board acknowledged that it is in principle "not competent to review the legality or 'constitutionality' of Regulations promulgated by the Special Representative of the Secretary-General" in the light of Sections 1 and 4 of UNMIK Regulation No. 1/1999 on the Authority of the Interim Administration in Kosovo.[132] It did examine, however, whether the procedural guarantees provided under Regulation No. 37/2000 before the imposition of sanctions were in accordance with the requirements of Article 6 of the ECHR.[133]

---

[128] The TMC was established by the SGSR on 17 June 2000 by UNMIK Regulation No. 36/2000. See Section 1.1 of the Regulation.

[129] Section 4 (2) of UNMIK Regulation No. 2000/36.

[130] See Media Appeals Board, Kosovo, *Beqaj & Dita* v. *Temporary Media Commissioner*, Decision of 16 Sept. 2000, available at www.osce.org/kosovo.

[131] UNMIK Regulation No. 37/2000 on the Conduct of Print Media in Kosovo provides that the TMC may impose sanctions "on owners, operators, publishers, editors-in-chief... who operate in violation of the applicable law...". Section 4 (1) of Regulation No. 37/2000 states that "owners, operators, publishers and editors shall refrain from publishing personal details of any person, including name, address or place of work, if the publication of such details would pose a serious threat to the life, safety or security of any such person through vigilante violence or otherwise".

[132] Kosovo Media Appeals Board, *Beqaj & Dita* v. *Temporary Media Commissioner*, para. 55.

[133] The Board observed that UNMIK Regulation No. 37/2000 provides very little guidance on the procedure to be followed by the TMC in determining the existence of a violation and imposing a sanction, providing merely for a "reasonable opportunity to

A similar mechanism of indirect judicial review was later introduced by the Constitutional Framework for Provisional Self-Government in Kosovo. The Constitutional Framework authorised a Special Chamber of the Kosovo Supreme Court to review the decisions of the Kosovo Trust Agency (KTA) – an independent agency established by UNMIK Regulation No. 2001/12.[134] The Special Chamber was vested with primary jurisdiction to hear challenges to the decisions of the KTA in the exercise of its powers of administration, liquidation and privatisation of Socially and Publicly Owned Enterprises,[135] including claims concerning creditor and ownership rights and entitlements by individuals to the proceeds of privatisation.[136]

The Special Chamber used this power to review the conformity of a provision of UNMIK Regulation No. 13/2003 (*On the Transformation of the Right to Use Socially-Owned Immovable Property*) with international human rights standards in the context of a complaint against a decision of the Kosovo Trust Agency.[137] In this case, Serb employees alleged that they were subject to discrimination in the distribution of the proceeds from the privatisation of a socially owned enterprise (*Termosistem*), but could not provide "documentary evidence of the alleged discrimination" as

---

reply prior to the imposition of any sanction". See Section 2 (3) of Regulation No. 37/2000. It criticised the procedural framework of the Regulation on the ground that the principle of equality of arms requires not only that decisions be taken by an impartial and independent tribunal, but also that parties to proceedings be given an opportunity to present their case, and to know and to "comment on all evidence adduced or observations filed with a view to influencing the court's decision". See para. 63 of the *Dita* decision. The Board concluded that: "Regulation 2000/37 does not permit the TMC to be the independent and impartial tribunal which is required by international human rights standards whenever civil rights and obligations or criminal charges are determined." See para. 67 of the *Dita* decision. Moreover, it recommended in a footnote that "the Regulation [be] amended to ensure a fair hearing from the start". See *Dita* decision, at note 13.

[134] See Sections 1 and 4 of UNMIK Regulation No. 13/2002 of 13 June 2002 (*On the Establishment of a Special Chamber of the Supreme Court of Kosovo on Kosovo Trust Agency Related Matters*).

[135] Section 4 (1) of the Regulation states that the Special Chamber shall, *inter alia*, have jurisdiction over "[c]hallenges to decisions or other actions of the Agency undertaken pursuant to Regulation No. 2002/12, including the imposition of fines as provided in section 27 of Regulation No. 2002/12".

[136] It is reported that the Special Chamber registered ninety-five claims pursuant to UNMIK Regulation No. 2002/13 and 156 claims from individuals by June 2004. See UNMIK, Pillar I, Police and Justice, Presentation Paper, June 2004, at 16.

[137] See Special Chamber of the Supreme Court of Kosovo on Kosovo Trust Agency Matters, *Terrosistem case*, SCEL 04-0001, 9 June 2004. For a full account, see Everly, *Reviewing Governmental Acts of the United Nations in Kosovo*, sub. IV.

required under Section 10 (5) (b) of UNMIK Regulation No. 13/2003.[138] The Special Chamber disregarded this requirement and allowed the applicants to prove their discrimination by non-documentary evidence in light of relevant international human rights standards on discrimination.[139]

3.1.3.2. Review of legislative authority

It is more difficult to identify cases in which judicial authorities exercised control over legislative acts of international administrations. The PCIJ served as an entity of last resort to settle disputes between Danzig and Poland.[140] In that capacity, the PCIJ examined the "Consistency of Certain Danzig Legislative Decrees with the Constitution of the Free City".[141] Furthermore, some foreign courts examined the legal value of Decree No. 1 of the Council for Namibia.[142] However, there is hardly any practice of domestic courts exercising judicial review over acts of international administrators.

This lack of review may be explained by several factors. In some cases, it has been argued that public acts of international entities do not come within the jurisdiction of domestic courts, because they do not stem from a public authority of the territory under international administration.[143] Acts of Security Council-established administrations have been said to benefit from the presumption of legality attached to Chapter VII

---

[138] See Section 10 of UNMIK Regulation No. 13/2003 of 9 May 2003.

[139] This principle was later applied in the Anti-Discrimination Law of the Assembly of Kosovo, which was promulgated by UNMIK Regulation No. 32/2004 of 20 August 2004 and allowed proof of discrimination by other means than documentary evidence.

[140] See above Part II, Chapter 6.

[141] The PCIJ found that several legislative decrees passed by the Danzig Government were incompatible with the rule of law and the principles of *nullum crimen sine lege* and *nulla poena sine lege*. See PCIJ, *Consistency of certain Danzig Legislative Decrees with the Constitution of the Free City*, Ser. A/B 65 (1935), at 57.

[142] For a survey, see Schermers, *The Namibia Decree in National Courts*, at 93–6.

[143] This argument relies on the conception that public acts of international entities are part of a legal order that is distinct and separate from the municipal legal order. German courts explicitly invoked this argument in the context the occupation of Germany after 1945, arguing that the acts of the Allied powers were not reviewable due to the international character of their authority and the international legal nature of their acts. See Badischer Staatsgerichtshof, Judgment of 27 November 1948, Archiv des öffentlichen Rechts (1949), at 486: "Stellt die Anordnung über den Arbeitseinsatz ... somit ihrer äußeren Form nach badisches Recht, ihrem materiellem Gehalt nach aber Recht der französischen Militärregierung dar, so ist sie einer Nachprüfung durch den Staatsgerichtshof entzogen. Maßstab für eine solche Nachprüfung könnte nur die Badische Verfassung sein ... Die Badische Verfassung

Resolutions of the Security Council.[144] Finally, in other cases, the scope of judicial review has been reduced by the fact that international administrations such as UNMIK,[145] UNTAET[146] and the CPA[147] defined their law as the "supreme law of the land", taking precedence over domestic laws and regulations.

Judicial review has been exercised on only a few occasions. Domestic courts relied on the doctrine of *ultra vires* to deny application to certain decrees of the Saar administration.[148] Moreover, in what might be called a Bosnian version of the US Supreme Court's *Marbury* v. *Madison* decision,[149] the Constitutional Court of Bosnia and Herzegovina relied on the concept of "functional duality"[150] in order to allow constitutional review of legislative acts of the OHR – an approach which deserves to be reviewed in greater detail here.

Deviating from the jurisprudence of the Bosnian Human Rights Chamber (*Dragan Cavic* v. *Bosnia and Herzegovina*), which had argued that "the High Representative cannot be said to be acting as, or on behalf of, the

---

kann aber nicht den Maßstab für die Gültigkeit von Besatzungsrecht abgeben. Dieses letztere bemißt sich allein nach völkerrechtlichen Gesichtspunkten und auf einer völkerrechtlichen Ebene, die dem Staatsgerichtshof verwehrt ist". See also Badischer Staatsgerichtshof, Judgment of 15 January 1949, Archiv des öffentlichen Rechts (1949), 477, at 478: "Anstelle der deutschen Regierung, doch nicht als Stellvertreter, sondern kraft unmittelbar aus dem Völkerrecht fließenden eigenen Rechts übte die Besatzungsmacht vorübergehend die volle deutsche Staatsgewalt und damit auch das Recht der Gesetzgebung aus." For a survey of the German practice, see Albrecht, *Randelzhofer, Untersuchung über die Möglichkeiten des Rechtsschutzes der Einwohner Berlins gegen Akte der Alliierten*, Die Verwaltung 19 (1986), 14; Horst Freitag, *Rechtschutz der Einwohner Berlins gegen hoheitliche Akte der Besatzungsbehörden gemäß Art. 6 Abs. 1 EMRK* (1989), 24.

[144] For such an argument, see De Wet, *Direct Administration of Territories by the United Nations*, at 337.

[145] See UNMIK Regulations No. 24/1999 of 15 November 1999 and No. 59/2000 of 27 October 2000.

[146] See UNTAET Regulation No. 1/1999 of 27 November 1999.

[147] See CPA Regulation No. 1 of 16 May 2003.   [148] See above Part II, Chapter 6.

[149] In *Marbury* v. *Madison* (1803) the US Supreme Court held that it was competent to declare acts of Congress, and by implication acts of the President, unconstitutional if they exceeded the powers granted by the Constitution. The Supreme Court thereby assumed its role as arbiter of the Constitution.

[150] See also Ralph Wilde, *The Complex Role of the Legal Adviser When International Organisations Administer Territory*, Proceedings of the American Society of International Law, Vol. 95 (2001), 251, at 254–5; Wilde, *International Territorial administration and human rights*, at 169–72; Wilde, *The Accountability of International Organizations and the Concept of "Functional Duality"*, 164, at 167. For a discussion, see also Knoll, *Beyond the "Mission Civilisatrice"*, at 295–8.

State or the Entities when acting in pursuance of his powers",[151] the Court held that the OHR acts both as a national organ of BiH and as an international authority when adopting decisions in the form of national law of BiH.[152] The Court noted that:

the legal role of the High Representative, as agent of the international community is not unprecedented... Pertinent examples are the mandates under the regime of the League of Nations and, in some respects, Germany and Austria after the Second World War. Though recognised as sovereign, the States concerned were placed under international supervision, and foreign authorities acted in these States, on behalf of the international community, substituting themselves for the domestic authorities. Acts by such international authorities were often passed in the name of the States under supervision. Such situation amounts to a sort of functional duality: an authority of one legal system intervenes in another legal system, thus making its functions dual.[153]

The Court drew a clear distinction between two capacities: the international authority of the OHR and its function as a domestic governmental authority. The Court held that as a national organ of the state of BiH, it was not authorised to determine whether the OHR had exceeded his mandate under Annex 10 of the DPA. However, the Court considered itself competent to examine whether acts of the OHR are in conformity with the Constitution of BiH.[154] The judgment relied essentially

---

[151] See Human Rights Chamber for Bosnia and Herzegovina, *Dragan Cavic* v. *Bosnia and Herzegovina*, Case No. CH/98/1266, Decision of 18 December 1998. In this case, the Chamber had to review a removal from office of an elected member of the National Assembly of the Republika Srpska by the OHR. The Chamber declared the application inadmissible, arguing that the OHR did not act as an agent of Bosnian state institutions. The Chamber stated: "The actions complained of were carried out by the High Representative in the performance of his functions under the General Framework Agreement, as interpreted by the Bonn Peace Implementation Conference. There is no provision for any intervention by the respondent Party (or by any of the other Parties to the General Framework Agreement) in those actions. In addition, the High Representative cannot be said to be acting as, or on behalf of, the State or the Entities when acting in pursuance of his powers. As a result, the actions giving rise to the present application cannot be considered to be within the scope of responsibility of the respondent Party" (emphasis added). *Ibid.*, para. 19.

[152] The same idea was expressed by some authors with reference to the authority of the Allied powers in Germany after 1945. They argued that the occupying powers exercised both military and public authority in Germany. See Grewe, *Ein Besatzungsstatut für Deutschland*, at 82. See on the fiduciary character of the occupation of Germany, Jennings, *Government in Commission*, at 112 *et seq.*

[153] See para. 5 of the judgment.

[154] The Court declared in conclusion: "The competence of the Constitutional Court to examine the conformity with the Constitution of the Law on State Border Service enacted by the High Representative acting as an institution of Bosnia and

on Scelle's idea of "role splitting" (*dédoublement fonctionnel*) in order to establish a right to judicial review. The Court acknowledged the separate legal personality of the OHR as an international legal person, while at the same time stressing that the OHR operates in some cases, such as lawmaking, as an agent of the state of Bosnia and Herzegovina, namely as a representative of the local authorities. The Court held that when imposing the "Law on the State Border Service" of Bosnia and Herzegovina:

the High Representative . . . intervened in the legal order of Bosnia and Herzegovina substituting himself for the national authorities. In this respect, he therefore acts as an authority of Bosnia and Herzegovina and the law which he enacted is in the nature of a national law and must be regarded as a law of Bosnia and Herzegovina.

The Court took the view that the decisive criterion in determining the legal nature of the legislation adopted by the OHR was not the legal personality of its author, but the content of the adopted legislation.[155] The main consequence arising from the decision of the BiH Constitutional Court was that henceforth a distinction had to be drawn between the normative and the interpretative powers of the HR. The OHR remained in principle the final arbiter over the interpretation of Annex 10 of the DPA and acts issued in this capacity.[156] However, Annex 10 ceased to be a source of final and unlimited decision-making power in the exercise of governmental authority within the domestic realm.[157] The judgment made it clear that legislative acts adopted by the OHR in its capacity

Herzegovina is thus based on Article VI.3.a of the Constitution. Consequently, the request is admissible."

[155] This is clearly expressed in para. 6 of the judgment, which reads: "the fact that the Law on State Border Service was enacted by the High Representative and not by the Parliamentary Assembly does not change its legal status, either in form – since the Law was published as such in the Official Gazette of Bosnia and Herzegovina on 26 January 2000 – or in substance, since, whether or not it is in conformity with the Constitution, it relates to a field falling within the legislative competence of the Parliamentary Assembly according to Article IV.4 (a) of the Constitution." See on this approach also Pech, *Garantie Iinternationale de la Constitution de Bosnie*, at 435.

[156] See para. 5 of the judgment, where the Court notes that the powers of the HR under Annex 10 of the DPA, the relevant resolutions of the Security Council and the Bonn Declaration of the PIC are not subject to its review.

[157] The principle of judicial review over legislative acts of the OHR was reaffirmed in a number of subsequent decisions. See Constitutional Court of Bosnia and Herzegovina, Decision U 16/00 of 2 February 2001 and Decision U 25/00 of 23 March 2001, para. 22 and tenor, in which the Court declared the decision Amending the Law on Travel Documents of Bosnia and Herzegovina in conformity with the Constitution of Bosnia and Herzegovina. ("The Court is not competent to review the powers vested in the

as a legal agent of Bosnia and Herzegovina and within the Bosnian legal order share the same legal nature as acts adopted by the national institutions. Accordingly, they are subject to judicial review under the Constitution of BiH and the legal guarantees of the ECHR, which enjoy "priority over all other law" in Bosnia and Herzegovina.[158]

The jurisprudence of the Bosnian Constitutional Court remained within narrow confines. The Court reviewed a number of other acts adopted by the OHR, including legislative amendments to property privatisation and travel documents.[159] However, the Court was reluctant to declare acts adopted by the OHR to be *ultra vires*. It did not find any legislative decision of the OHR to be in violation of the Constitution of Bosnia and Herzegovina. One of the judges of the Court noted that "the entire system was based upon the tacit consensus between the Court and the High Representative that the Court in exercising its power to review all legislative acts whomever they will emanate from will always confirm the merits of his legislation".[160] Furthermore, in an unfortunate move,[161] the Court failed to extend its power of review to executive acts adopted by the OHR (e.g. dismissals of individuals from public office[162]), although this would have been possible under the doctrine of "functional duality".[163] Nevertheless, the general approach taken by the

High Representative under Annex 10 to the Dayton Peace Agreement or to review the exercise of those powers. However, the Court may review the constitutionality of laws or amendments thereto, proclaimed by the High Representative in the place of the Parliamentary Assembly of Bosnia and Herzegovina.") See also Decision U 26/01 of 28 September 2001, paras. 13–14, by which the Court declared the Law on the Court of Bosnia and Herzegovina in conformity with the Constitution of Bosnia and Herzegovina.

[158] See Article II. 2 of the Bosnian Constitution.

[159] See Constitutional Court of Bosnia and Herzegovina, Decision U 16/00 of 2 February 2001 and Decision U 25/00 of 23 March 2001.

[160] See Marko, *Five Years of Constitutional Jurisprudence in Bosnia and Herzegovina*.

[161] See Constitutional Court of Bosnia and Herzegovina, Decision U 37/01 of 2 November 2001. ("Decisions of the High Representative to remove public officials from office are not 'judgments' for the purpose of Article VI.3 (b) of the Constitution of Bosnia and Herzegovina, and the Constitutional Court is therefore not competent to review such decisions.")

[162] The Bosnian Human Rights Chamber denied such a possibility of review in the *Cavic* case. See Human Rights Chamber for Bosnia and Herzegovina, *Dragan Cavic v. Bosnia and Herzegovina*, Case No. CH/98/1266, Decision of 18 December 1998, paras. 17–21.

[163] The Court could have argued that executive decisions of the OHR are potentially subject to scrutiny, where the OHR intervenes in the legal system of Bosnia and Herzegovina, by acting as a "substitute" for domestic executive authorities. See also in relation to Decision U 37/01 Marko, *Five Years of Constitutional Jurisprudence in Bosnia and Herzegovina*. ("The Constitutional Court could have simply accepted on the basis

Court was a milestone in the history of international territorial administration because it provided a conceptual basis for the exercise of internal forms of control within systems of international administration.[164]

3.2. A re-conceptualisation

The current accountability architecture of international administrations requires new thinking. Territorial administration by international actors seriously affects the political and social environment of the people of the administered territories. It is not enough to justify the current institutional structures by the functional and temporarily limited nature of international territorial administration.[165] There is a need for greater diversity in institutional accountability of international governance mechanisms. Traditional forms of intra-institutional control or international monitoring are sufficient in the context of governance assistance missions. Direct forms of responsibility towards domestic or quasi-domestic actors must, however, be increased in the context of governance missions, where international administrations exercise direct and exclusive governmental powers over individuals of the administered territory. This is not a new postulate,[166] but a lesson learned from the Mandate and the Trusteeship Systems and the experiments in territorial administration in the inter-war period.

A variety of practices may serve as a source of inspiration for a strengthening of accountability procedures. They include the institutionalisation of complaint procedures triggered by local institutions, the creation of independent ombudspersons to deal with individual complaints against human rights violations, the establishment of claims commissions to allow recovery for damages suffered from acts of international administrations, the establishment of independent administrative supervisory bodies to review acts adopted by internationally

---

of the theory of functional dualism that the High Representative 'substituted' either the management board of the public enterprise or even the High Court of the Federation of Bosnia and Herzegovina.")

[164] See also Wilde, *The Complex Role of the Legal Adviser When International Organizations Administer Territory*, at 255–6.

[165] See also Wilde, *Accountability and International Actor*, at 458–61.

[166] See in this sense Resolution 1384 of the Parliamentary Assembly of the Council of Europe, 26 June 2004, para. 13. ("The scope of OHR is such that, to all intents and purposes, it constitutes the supreme institution vested with power in Bosnia and Herzegovina. In this connection, the assembly considers it irreconcilable with democratic principles that the OHR should be able to take enforceable decisions without being accountable for them or obliged to justify their validity and without there being as legal remedy.")

established agencies and, last but not least, judicial review by domestic courts of acts carried out by international administrators in their capacity as public organs of the territory under international administration ("functional duality"), as well as potential review by international courts and tribunals.

3.2.1. Intra-institutional control

Intra-institutional forms of control of transitional administration through reporting and monitoring mechanisms remain an essential part of the organisational structure of UN administrations. They are necessary to ensure regular interaction between the mission and the author of the mandate (Security Council, General Assembly) on the progress and accomplishment of the goals of the operation. Nevertheless, the current format of internal review fails to establish an effective mechanism of accountability.[167] It suffers from two shortcomings. First, the content of the reports is exclusively shaped by the input of the respective international administrators. This precludes domestic actors from presenting their views and criticisms directly to UN supervisory organs. Secondly, reports from the mission to main organs only provide limited forums of control, because the respective administrations enjoy a considerable degree of institutional credibility and confidence in their capacity as subsidiary bodies of the principal UN organs.[168] These close institutional links distinguish the reporting system under the umbrella of peace-maintenance from the questionnaire system under the Trusteeship System, where the administering powers were institutionally independent from the Trusteeship Council.

The current architecture needs to be revisited in circumstances where UN administrations act as governance or co-governance missions. Some structural features of League of Nations administration or Trusteeship System administration could be transposed to territorial administration under the heading of peace-maintenance in order to increase the level of local input in intra-institutional review.[169] One option to strengthen the existing system would be to allow local institutions to present their views in an annex, or as a response to the report filed by UN administrators to the UN Secretariat, the General Assembly or the Security Council. This

---

[167] See also Mortimer, *International Administration of War-Torn Societies*, at 13. ("The Council does not have any mechanism, and its members seldom have much appetite, for scrutinising the conduct of an administration in detail.")

[168] See also Chesterman, *You, the People*, at 152.

[169] See also Caplan, *International Authority and Statebuilding: The Case of Bosnia and Herzegovina*, at 62.

technique would not only give local actors an opportunity to present their views independently, but it may help to ease political tensions between the UN administration and domestic forces.

Furthermore, accountability structures could be enhanced through the establishment of mediated complaint procedures in the context of peace-maintenance. In some situations the political institutions of the administered territories might be expressly authorised by future UN resolutions to address communications or petitions to supervisory bodies of UN administrations following the practice under Article 87, paragraph 1 (b) of the UN Charter or the complaint procedures under the Trieste Statute and the Jerusalem Statute.[170] Such a move would establish a more direct and institutionalised form of intra-institutional control, without overloading UN political bodies with individual communications.

In other situations, independent monitoring institutions could be authorised to address UN political bodies independently of UN administrators. This approach was adopted by the EU in the context of the administration of Mostar, where the EU Ombudsperson[171] was entitled to make recommendations to the EU administrator and refer matters to the EU Council in cases of disagreement with the administrator.[172] Such a model of independently triggered intra-institutional control may be of particular value in cases where the political context is still unstable or domestic institutions are non-operational or biased.

3.2.2. Expert control and independent external scrutiny

Traditional forms of intra-institutional monitoring and control of transitional administrations need to be complemented more systematically by mechanisms of expert control and independent external scrutiny.[173] There are a number of institutional mechanisms which could be used to improve accountability in international practice.

---

[170] See also Chesterman, *You, the People*, at 152.

[171] See EU Council Decision 94/776/EC of 28 November 1994 on the appointment of an Ombudsman for Mostar for the duration of the European Union administration in Mostar.

[172] See para. 4 of Council Decision 94/776/EC.

[173] Note that such a suggestion was made in the context of the dispute over the decertification of Bosnian police officers by UN-IPTF. The Venice Commission recommended "that the Security Council set up a review body of (three) independent experts, entrusted with reviewing the approximately 150 decertification cases which have been challenged before the domestic courts". See *Opinion on a Possible Solution to the Issue of Decertification of Police Officers in Bosnia and Herzegovina*, para. 56.

3.2.2.1. International monitoring bodies

One way to enhance accountability which would be consistent with recent UN practice under Chapter VII is to charge UN-created, but institutionally independent transitional administration committees with monitoring and supervisory functions in relation to the action of UN administrations.

3.2.2.1.1. Transitional administration committees

Within its own practice the Security Council has, on several occasions, established committees to monitor the implementation of Chapter VII resolutions that require prolonged interaction with other entities. For example, the Council has created sanctions committees to supervise the implementation of economic sanctions. These committees have examined reports of the Secretary-General on the implementation of sanctions; they were authorised to make recommendations to states on improving the efficacy of sanctions; and they were empowered to report violations of sanctions to the Council and make these violations known publicly.[174] Similarly, the Council established a Counter-Terrorism Committee to ensure the effective implementation of state obligations under Security Council Resolution 1373 (2001).[175]

As has been recently suggested in legal doctrine,[176] a similar model of control could be used to monitor the action of Chapter VII-established UN administrations. Instead of exercising general political control over UN administrations, the Council could charge specialised expert committees with the supervision of the exercise of territorial authority by UN transitional administrations. These expert committees may not only fill the gap left by the lack of monitoring bodies such as the Permanent Mandates Commission or the Trusteeship Council in the context of peace maintenance, but may also help replace the tradition of internal UN control through independent expert scrutiny. Moreover, such committees would allow the Council to keep track of the functioning of UN administration and intervene as supervisory body in the administration upon the initiative of domestic actors. Building on the practice of Sanction Committees, expert committees could be charged with different tasks, including:

---

[174] See generally on the work of Sanctions Committees, Andreas Paulus, *On Article 29*, in Simma, Charter of the United Nations, at 548–50.

[175] See SC Res. 1373 (2001) of 28 September 2001.

[176] See Chesterman, *You, the People*, at 152, 240. See also De Wet, *Direct Administration of Territories by the United Nations*, at 339, who proposes the "creation of a standing committee responsible for the overseeing of United Nations-authorized civil administrations".

- the examination of reports by UN administrators;
- the identification of shortcomings in the governing practice of UN administrations in light of human rights law and principles of good governance;
- the reporting and publication of violations of such standards to the Security Council and UN member states;
- the formulation of recommendations to UN administering bodies; and
- the examination of complaints by local institutions.

The establishment of such committees would be a natural corollary of the extension of administering responsibilities of the UN in the name of peace-maintenance over the last decade.

It could even be envisaged that transitional administration committees could act as monitoring bodies over individual human rights violations.[177] The inhabitants of territories under international administrations are typically barred from filing individual complaints against public acts of UN administrations before human rights treaty bodies such as the European Court of Human Rights, the Inter-American Commission on Human Rights or Human Rights Committees because the jurisdiction of these treaty bodies is limited to the investigation of human rights abuses committed by states parties.[178] The conduct of international organisations can only be examined indirectly, namely through the assessment of the responsibility of states for acts undertaken within the framework of international organisations to which they are party, or alternatively through reports submitted by these organisations to human rights bodies on a voluntary basis.[179]

The establishment of transitional administration committees would help to reduce this gap. Transitional administration committees may be vested with a right to review individual human rights violations in particular cases where the UN exercises exclusive authority over territories and where no other forums for review of the conduct of transitional administrations exist. The recognition of an individualised complaint procedure before transitional administration committees would bridge the gap between the normative obligation of the UN to respect universally

---

[177] Institutionalised expert control should be accessible to private actors, where the action of UN territorial administrators directly affects the exercise of individual rights of freedoms. Similar calls have been raised in the context of work of the counter-terrorism of the Security Council.

[178] See Article 48, para. 1 of the ICCPR, Article 59 of the ECHR and Article 74 of the American Convention of Human Rights.

[179] UNMIK accepted the submission of reports to the Human Rights Committee on a voluntary basis. Moreover, in 2005 UNMIK started to submit reports under the Framework Convention on the Protection of National Minorities.

recognised human rights norms and the lack of access of the inhabitants of internationally administered territories to international treaty bodies under existing human rights treaties.[180] This type of expert review enjoys two potential advantages over review procedures. It would concentrate powers of review on an international expert body that is easily accessible and sufficiently specialised to deal with the problem of a specific transitional administration, and, secondly, it is a more pragmatic solution than the extension of the jurisdiction of international treaty bodies to transitional administrations.[181]

3.2.2.1.2. Scrutiny by the Peacebuilding Commission

Alternatively, some functions of supervision might be entrusted to the Peacebuilding Commission.[182]

The mandate of the Commission could be extended so as to include not only advisory functions *vis-à-vis* states in transition, but also a role in supervising UN administrations and identifying best practices for UN and other international administrations.[183] The Commission would thus perform a dual role: a classical intergovernmental mandate, encompassing functions of coordination and assistance, and an institutional role in the UN system itself, including monitoring and supervision of transitional administrations. The Commission could, in particular, benefit from the direct input from "the country under consideration" and other experts and stakeholders, when exercising these functions.[184] Such an approach would, at least partially, fill the gap left by the

---

[180] See also Jens Marten, *Menschenrechtsschutz in Internationalen Mandatsgebieten und ihre Strukturellen Widersprüche am Beispiel des Kosovo*, Humanitäres Völkerrecht, Vol. 3 (2004), 144, at 150.

[181] This option remains rather theoretical in the light of the continuing limitation of membership of major human rights treaty instruments to states. For further discussion, see below 3.2.4, Judicial review by independent international courts.

[182] For a survey of options concerning the mandate of the proposed Peacebuilding Commission, see Report of the High-level Panel on Threats, Challenges and Change, *A More Secure World: Our Shared Responsibility*, paras. 261–5; paras. 98–101 of the Outcome Document of the High-level Plenary Meeting of the Gerneral Assembly in September 2005.

[183] The Outcome Document states that the Commission may address recommendations to "relevant bodies and actors, including international financial institutions". See para. 99 of the Outcome Document. This wording might allow the Commission to make recommendations to UN peacekeeping missions and transitional administrations.

[184] See para. 100 of the Outcome Document, which specifies that "country-specific meetings of the Commission *should* include" representation from domestic and regional actors.

non-applicability of the accountability regime under the Trusteeship System to transitional administration.[185]

3.2.2.1.3. Ombudsperson control
Access to independent ombudspersons institutions may provide an alternative forum for review. The exercise of monitoring functions by ombudsperson institutions is an established model of individualised control over the exercise of international territorial authority today.[186] Ombudspersons were traditionally established as a mechanism of control over executive authority in domestic systems.[187] However, they have gradually gained recognition as supervisory bodies in the international legal field[188] and in the area of the exercise of international public authority more specifically. Ombudspersons have been established as individual complaint mechanisms in the context of the administrations of Bosnia and Herzegovina,[189] in Kosovo,[190] in East Timor[191] and in Iraq.[192] They enjoy particular prominence in the transitional administrations field because they provide an individualised and flexible forum for human

[185] For a discussion, see above Part I, Chapter 3 and Part III, Chapter 11.
[186] For a survey, see Lina C. Reif, *Building Democratic Institutions: The Role of National Human Rights Institutions in Good Governance and Human Rights Protection*, Harvard Human Rights Journal, Vol. 13 (2000), 1.
[187] The first ombudsperson was established in Sweden in 1809, in order to control the executive. For a survey, see Zwanenburg, *Accountability of Peace Support Operations*, at 294–9.
[188] The most prominent examples are the World Bank Inspection Panel and the European Ombudsman.
[189] See Annex 6, Chapter II, Part B of the Dayton Peace Agreement. The mandate of the Human Rights Ombudsman is described in Article V, para. 1 as follows: "The Ombudsman may investigate, either on his or her own initiative or in response to an allegation by any Party or person, non-governmental organisation, or group of individuals claiming to be victims of a violation by any Party or acting on behalf of alleged victims who are deceased or missing, alleged or apparent violations of human rights with the scope of paragraph 2 of Annex II." The Ombudsman was authorised to publish its findings in a report. In case of non-compliance by the respective party, the Ombudsman was entitled to forward its conclusions and recommendations to the OHR or to initiate proceedings before the Human Rights Chamber. See Article V, para. 7 of Annex 6 to the Dayton Peace Agreement.
[190] See UNMIK Regulation No. 2000/28 on the Establishment of the Ombudsperson Institution in Kosovo of 30 June 2000. Section 4 (1) of the Regulation authorises the Ombudsperson to "receive complaints, monitor, investigate, offer good offices, take preventive steps, make recommendations and advise on matters relating to his or her functions".
[191] The Ombudsperson in East Timor was appointed in September 2001. See generally Chestermann, *You, The People*, at 149.
[192] See CPA Order No. 98 of 27 June 2004 (*Iraqi Ombudsman for Penal and Detention Matters*).

rights complaints and independent scrutiny, which identifies flaws in international governance, without combining them with directly legally binding sanctions for the respective administration. This recommendatory type of review accords very well with the cooperation-based nature of international relations. It has even been praised as a new accountability mechanism for peace support operations more generally.[193]

In practice, ombudspersons have been charged with a variety of operational mandates. The Human Rights Ombudsperson in Bosnia and Herzegovina was vested with broad investigative powers over alleged human rights violations by individuals. However, its work was restricted by two features which do not lend themselves to further generalisation: the limitation of its jurisdiction to violations of the Parties to Annex VI[194] ("The Republic of Bosnia and Herzegovina, the Federation of Bosnia and Herzegovina and the Republika Srpska"[195]), without inclusion of monitoring powers over the action of the OHR; and the competing overlaps of authority between the Ombudsperson and the Human Rights Chamber.[196]

The mandate of Ombudsperson Institution in Kosovo under UNMIK Regulation No. 2000/38[197] was construed in different terms. The Regulation granted the Ombudsperson "jurisdiction to receive and investigate complaints from any person or entity in Kosovo concerning human rights violations and actions constituting an abuse of authority by the interim civil administration or any emerging central or local institution".[198] This definition of authority marked an innovation in that it subjected international and domestic holders of public power to comparable scrutiny and supervision in the exercise of governmental powers. However, the "Kosovo model" suffered from two shortcomings which compromised its capacity as a precedent for accountability structures

---

[193] See Zwanenburg, *Accountability of Peace Support Operations*, at 310–12.

[194] See Article V, para. 2 of Annex 6 to the Dayton Peace Agreement.

[195] See the definition of the "Parties" in the opening line of Annex 6.

[196] See Annex 6, Chapter II, Part C.

[197] Note that the jurisdiction of the Ombudsperson Institution in Kosovo was amended by UNMIK Regulation No. 6/2006 of 16 February 2006 (*On the Ombudsperson Institution in Kosovo*) following the establishment of the Human Rights Advisory Panel. Section 3 (1) of UNMIK Regulation No. 6/2006 vests the Ombudsperson Institution with the authority to "receive and investigate complaints ... concerning violations of international human rights standards as incorporated in the applicable law and acts ... which constitute *an abuse of authority by the Kosovo institutions*" (emphasis added). Cases involving UNMIK can only be dealt with following the conclusion of a "bilateral agreement" with the SRSG. *Ibid.*, Section 3 (4).

[198] See Section 3 (1) of UNMIK Regulation No. 2000/38.

in further experiments in territorial administration. The findings of the Ombudsperson were mere recommendations, which did not entail further follow-up requirements for UNMIK. The administration's record of "accepting and acting upon the Ombudsperson's recommendations" remained "disappointing".[199] The powers of ombudsperson could have been reinforced by measures, such as a right to require the SRSG to "give final responses to recommendations within a reasonable time" or the power to demand "justification" from UNMIK for non-compliance.[200]

Secondly, the jurisdiction of the Ombudsperson did not extend to complaints against KFOR. Section 3 (4) of UNMIK Regulation No. 2000/38 made the exercise of jurisdiction over "cases involving the international security presence" dependent on the conclusion of a separate "agreement" between the Ombudsperson and "the Commander of the Kosovo Forces".[201] No such agreement has yet been concluded. This lack of jurisdiction left accountability gaps in relation to violations of international human rights law by KFOR and triggered calls for additional mechanisms, such as the establishment of a separate "NATO Ombudsman" with jurisdiction over complaints against the conduct of troop contributing states[202] or the creation of a KFOR Review Board.[203]

The Ombudsperson models used in East Timor and Iraq were even less sensitive to the idea of establishing comprehensive expert control over human rights violations by international administering authorities. In July 2001, UNTEAT announced that it had established an independent Ombudsperson Office to address complaints against UNTEAT and the East Timorese Transitional Cabinet.[204] The Ombudsperson was supposed to hear and monitor human rights infractions independently of any official or governmental authority.[205] However, UNTAET failed to define the mandate of the Ombudsperson formally in the terms of a specific Regulation and it did not provide the office with sufficient institutional support to carry out its functions effectively. Therefore, the impact of the East Timorese Ombudsperson remained very limited in practice.[206]

---

[199] See Council of Europe, Parliamentary Assembly, *Protection of Human Rights in Kosovo*, para. 44.

[200] See *ibid.*, para. 45.   [201] See Section 3 (4) of UNMIK Regulation No. 2000/38.

[202] See Zwanenburg, *Accountability of Peace Support Operations*, at 311.

[203] See European Commission for Democracy Through Law, *Opinion on Human Rights in Kosovo*, paras. 125–33.

[204] See *Welcome to the Ombudsperson of East Timor*, Tais Timor, July 2001, at 5, at www.gov.easttimor.org/news/Tais_Timor/2001070128/Eng_Tais-Final.pdf.

[205] See Bongiorno, *A Culture of Impunity*, at 685.

[206] See Chestermann, *You, The People*, at 149–50.

The Iraqi Ombudsperson was vested with a specialised mandate. CPA Order No. 98 limited the role of Ombudsman to the investigation of complaints in penal and detention matters. Individuals were only authorised to file complaints concerning the conduct of a "detaining authority",[207] that is "Iraqi, Multinational Force or contracted personnel employed, engaged in, supervising or commanding, criminal or security custody in Iraq with respect to persons held in such custody for any period".[208] This definition excluded remedies against the governmental acts of the CPA as a civilian authority more generally. Moreover, the order specifically excluded the investigation of conduct which had taken place prior to 27 June 2004 – a condition which exempted from independent scrutiny the detention practice during the core period of US-UK occupation, including the incidents in the Abu Ghraib prison.

These different experiences indicate that international practice has not yet developed a common scheme for ombudsperson control in cases of international administration. Future experiments in territorial administration should draw to a larger extent from the Kosovo precedent, if ombudsperson control is to serve as a meaningful accountability model and as a device to counter the lack of institutional checks and balances on international actors in the exercise of territorial authority. It is, in particular, of paramount importance that ombudspersons be vested with independent investigative powers, the capacity to subject critical acts by international administrations to further justification and the possibility of bringing their findings to the attention of supervisory bodies of international administrations.[209]

Secondly, there is a more general reservation towards the consideration of ombudsperson control as a solution to the accountability problem in international territorial administration. Access to ombudspersons is not sufficient in all circumstances. Ombudsperson institutions are generally well-suited to address "individual complaints of maladministration", but they do not normally provide recommendations on legislative or policy initiatives.[210] Moreover, in some situations, the mere identification and publication of human rights violations by international administrations is simply not enough. Individuals may, in particular,

---

[207] See Section 4.1 of CPA Order No. 98.   [208] See *ibid.*, Section 1 (1).

[209] UNMIK is again a good example in this regard. It has either taken considerable time to implement recommendations of the Ombudsperson Institution in Kosovo, or has not acted at all.

[210] See also Council of Europe, Parliamentary Assembly, *Protection of Human Rights in Kosovo*, para. 47.

suffer material harm from the action of international administrations. In such cases, effective human rights protection requires alternative accountability forums through which individuals may seek direct legal redress.

3.2.2.1.4. Independent advisory panels

An additional institutional option to enhance accountability at the level of the respective administration is the establishment of independent advisory panels. The particular merit of such panels is that they may contain more explicit commitments to transparency and compliance than ombudsperson models, and may thus enhance the effectiveness of international review.

Different proposals have been made in the case of Kosovo. The Venice Commission recommended the establishment of an UNMIK Advisory Panel and a KFOR Advisory Board in order to reinforce the scope of protection of individual against decisions or acts by the respective institutions. The Commission invited UNMIK to subject itself to the scrutiny of an independent panel of experts with decision-making power over individual human rights complaints and appropriate means of redress, and to commit itself to carry out the findings of this body (except in cases where "exceptional" reasons prevent the administration from doing so).[211] Moreover, the Commission recommended the establishment of

---

[211] See European Commission for Democracy Through Law, *Opinion on Human Rights in Kosovo*, paras. 118–23. ("This panel would be set up by an UNMIK Regulation. It would be composed of three (six/nine, depending on the workload) independent international experts with demonstrated experience in human rights (particularly the European System). The members of the Advisory Panel would be formally appointed by the SRSG upon the proposal of the President of the European Court of Human Rights ... The Advisory Panel would have advisory functions. Nevertheless, in the regulation setting it up, UNMIK would commit itself to accepting its findings, except if the SRSG personally determines that extraordinary reasons exist that do no not make this possible. This would mean that that UNMIK should commit itself to the following: a) If the finding of a violation concerns a general act or regulation, UNMIK should take the appropriate legal action (e.g. repeal or amend the regulation); b) If the finding concerns an individual case, UNMIK should provide appropriate redress (ranging from public recognition of the violation, to *restitutio in integrum*, and to possible compensation). In this respect, the Commission considers that that the UNMIK regulation setting up the Advisory Panel should also explicitly provide for the possibility of applicants to seek appropriate individual measures from UNMIK, following the Panel's finding of human rights breaches in their own case; c) Should UNMIK, in exceptional cases, disagree with the findings of the Advisory Panel, it should give reasons for such disagreement.")

an independent Advisory Board by KFOR,[212] which would be competent to "review all cases of allegations of serious human rights violations by KFOR troops", including "complaints against house searches and physical mistreatment of persons",[213] while leaving KFOR the right not to communicate to the detainee or to the public certain pieces of sensitive information.[214] The Commission recommended that these panels be created in addition to the Ombudsperson Institution.[215]

A slightly different proposal was formulated by the Parliamentary Assembly of the Council of Europe in its Resolution 1417 (2005) on the "Protection of Human Rights in Kosovo".[216] The Assembly supported the creation of an Advisory Panel, but recommended a clear division of responsibilities between the panel and Ombudsperson Institution in Kosovo, in order to "avoid creating a system of multiple and overlapping human rights protection mechanisms".[217] The Assembly suggested that the ombudsperson should remain the primary organ to deal with individual human rights complaints, while recommending that the Advisory panel be "charged with scrutinising (draft) UNMIK Regulations and subsidiary instruments for compliance with international human rights standards, along with other tasks such as hearing appeals from the UNMIK Claims Office, and addressing to UNMIK opinion on issues, *other than individual complaints*".[218]

UNMIK's response to these proposals remained half-hearted. UNMIK created a human rights advisory panel with jurisdiction to examine human rights violations by UNMIK in March 2006.[219] However, the

---

[212] *Ibid.*, para. 175. ("As regards KFOR, and in particular the power to detain, an embryonic form of review procedure already exists requiring that any decision on extending detention beyond an initial period of 72 hours must be made upon a request by the Legal Advisor. It seems advisable to strengthen the role of the Legal Adviser, by adding two independent lawyers to his review functions, who should not be members of the military and not within the chain of command or within the administrative hierarchy. Their inclusion would institutionally ensure that the KFOR Commander receives independent advice and would therefore reassure the public (in Kosovo and beyond) that proper human rights standards are applied by KFOR.")

[213] *Ibid.*, para. 166.   [214] *Ibid.* para. 165.

[215] The Commission favoured the creation of the panel to examine individual complaints "in cases where the Ombudsperson has found human rights breaches, without his/her report resulting in UNMIK recognizing its responsibility for the human rights violation". See European Commission for Democracy Through Law, *Opinion on Human Rights in Kosovo*, para. 115.

[216] See Council of Europe, Parliamentary Assembly, *Protection of Human Rights in Kosovo*, paras. 45–6.

[217] See *ibid.*, para. 46.   [218] See para. 5 (v) of Res. 1417 (2005). Emphasis added.

[219] See UNMIK Regulation No. 12/2006 of 23 March 2006 (*On the Establishment of the Human Rights Advisory Panel*).

mechanism established under UNMIK Regulation No. 12/2006 fell short of meeting standards of independent review. The SRSG retained control over the appointment of the members of the panel.[220] Moreover, the implementation of findings and recommendations was left in the "exclusive authority and discretion" of UNMIK.[221] The Human Rights Committee expressed concern regarding this type of review of UNMIK action, noting that the "Human Rights Advisory Panel established under UNMIK Regulation 2006/12... lacks the necessary independence and authority".[222]

3.2.2.2. Claims commissions

The exercise of independent control by ombudspersons or advisory panel must go hand in hand with the creation of forums to seek redress for human rights violations. The UN has officially recognised that violations of international obligations by its organs or agents within the framework of peacekeeping missions entail the international responsibility of the UN and liability in compensation.[223] This function has traditionally been fulfilled by claims commissions.[224] Claims commissions have been created by the UN, or by both the UN and the host state in the context of peacekeeping operations as a response to the host state's lack of jurisdiction over compensation claims for damage suffered from acts of a UN force. The Model Status of Forces Agreement provides an example in this regard. It envisages the creation of a standing claims commission to settle compensation claims against the UN or its members in relation to disputes over which local courts have no jurisdiction due to the immunity of the UN or its members.[225]

---

[220] The members of the panel were appointed by the SRSG, upon the proposal of the President of the European Court of Human Rights. See Section 5 of UNMIK Regulation No. 12/2006.

[221] See Section 17 (3) of UNMIK Regulation No. 12/2006.

[222] See Concluding Observations of the Human Rights Committee, Kosovo (Republic of Serbia), 87th Sess., Geneva, 10–28 July 2006, CCPR/C/UNK/CO/1 of 25 July 2006, para. 10.

[223] See the statement by the UN Legal Counsel in a letter of 3 February 2004. ("As a subsidiary organ of the United Nations, an act of a peacekeeping force is, in principle, imputable to the Organization, and if committed in violation of an international obligation entails the international responsibility of the Organization and its liability in compensation.") See ILC, Report of its 56th Session (2004), at 112. For a survey of UN practice, see Zwanenburg, *Accountability of Peace Support Operations*, at 89–93.

[224] See Bothe, *Peace-Keeping*, in Simma, Charter of the United Nations, at 694, para. 123.

[225] See Article 51 of the UN Model Status of Forces Agreement. The Commission is supposed to be composed of one member appointed by the Secretary-General, one member appointed by the government of the host state and one chairman appointed conjointly by both sides.

This mode of dispute settlement is not only relevant to military enforcement action. It must also be applied in the context of civilian administration.[226] The establishment of claims commissions provides citizens of administered territories with a pragmatic device to recover damage (property loss or other harm) suffered from the actions of the UN or members of a UN force. This approach has been adopted by UNMIK. UNMIK Regulation No. 2000/47 contains a dispute settlement mechanism which provides that:

> third party claims for property loss or damage and for personal injury, illness or death arising from or directly attributed to KFOR, UNMIK or their respective personnel and which do not arise from "operational necessity" of either international presence, shall be settled by Claims Commissions established by KFOR and UNMIK, in the manner to be provided for.[227]

This formula is visibly modelled on the claims commission regime envisaged by Article 51 of the UN Model Status of Forces Agreement. This regime must, however, be more closely adjusted to the particularities of peacetime administration. Two elements of this dispute settlement formula are open to criticism in the context of international administration: the potential ability to invoke the concept of "operational necessity" as a bar to compensation claims and the lack of institutional independence and procedural fairness of the respective claims commissions from the international administrations. Both factors have been openly criticised by the Ombudsperson Institution in Kosovo[228] and the OSCE.[229]

First, to regard "operational necessity" as a ground for excluding compensation *per se* creates an overly broad exception from the requirement of liability and reparation.[230] The concept of "operational necessity"[231]

---

[226] See also Bongiorno, *A Culture of Impunity*, at 683; Abraham, *The Sins of the Saviour*, at 1337.

[227] See Section 7 of UNMIK Regulation No. 47/2000.

[228] See Ombudsperson Institution in Kosovo, *Special Report No. 1*, paras. 41–2.

[229] See OSCE Mission in Kosovo, Department of Human Rights and Rule of Law, *Property Rights in Kosovo 2002–2003*, at 45–6. ("[KFOR's Standard Operating Procedure 3023 for Claims in Kosovo] has the advantage of being more concise than the former 'draft' Claims Policy... However, the [Standard Operating Procedure] has no legally binding force on the [Troop Contributing Nations], the legal basis on which both claims and appeals will be adjudicated remain imprecise, and KFOR's immunity from claims on the grounds of 'operational necessity' remains unaffected as well as undefined.")

[230] See also Zwanenburg, *Accountability of Peace Support Operations*, at 289–90.

[231] Operational necessity may potentially exclude compensation for damage resulting from actions taken by a mission in the course of an operation conducted in accordance with the mandate. *Ibid.*, at 289.

is broader than the concept of military necessity typically used in the context of armed hostilities. Even military necessity does not in all cases justify a blanket exemption from responsibility under international humanitarian law.[232] Moreover, "operational necessity" can hardly be invoked as a ground for excluding compensation under human rights law, because the failure to pay compensation for the actual taking of property "is incompatible with obligations set forth under both Article of the Additional Protocol [No. 1 to the ECHR] and Article 15 of the Convention itself".[233]

Secondly, the discretion of UNMIK and KFOR under UNMIK Regulation No. 2000/47 in relation to the appointment and composition of the potential claims commissions ("established by KFOR and UNMIK, in the manner to be provided for") is problematic in light of the right to an independent and impartial tribunal established by law under Article 6 of the ECHR and Article 14 of the ICCPR. The Regulation permits that those entities whose potential liability is subject to scrutiny and review by the Commission "are also charged with the establishment and operation of the organs of that review". The evident link between "the authority charged with the establishment and administration of the 'tribunal' at issue" and the "potential defendants in the cases falling within that tribunal's jurisdiction" is too close to meet the requirement of independence and impartiality.[234]

Furthermore, the existing mechanisms have been criticised for procedural inadequacies. Proceedings against UNMIK provided no opportunity for individuals to be heard and to be represented by legal counsel, and no genuine possibility to appeal decisions of first instance.[235] KFOR's

---

[232] See also Ombudsperson Institution in Kosovo, *Special Report No. 1*, para. 42. ("The Ombudsperson considers that the additional requirement, even during wartime, of 'military' necessity for the appropriation of property implies a much stricter standard than does the 'operational' necessity provided for in Section 7 of UNMIK Regulation 2000/47. The Ombudsperson therefore considers that by permitting UNMIK and KFOR to invoke 'operational necessity' to preclude any review of allegations that their actions caused harm that could fall within the category of grave breaches of Geneva Convention IV, Section 7 of UNMIK Regulation 2000/47 fails to meet any reasonable standard of proportionality.")

[233] See also Ombudsperson Institution in Kosovo, *Special Report No. 1*, para. 43.

[234] See also *ibid.*, para. 75.

[235] See the criticism by the European Commission for Democracy Through Law, *Opinion on Human Rights in Kosovo*, para. 61. ("The only appeal possible against this internal first instance decision is the sending of a 'memorandum' to the UNMIK Director of Administration.") See also Council of Europe, Parliamentary Assembly, *Protection of Human Rights in Kosovo*, para. 23.

claims system allowed an appeal for claims against the KFOR Headquarters in Pristina before the Kosovo Claims Appeals Commission (KCAC), but failed to subject individual KFOR contingents to this system.[236]

These shortcomings should be corrected in future practice. An exemption of liability should, if at all, only be made in relation to damage caused by "combat or combat related activities",[237] but not in relation to harm suffered from ordinary operations of a military presence or civilian activities of a transitional administration. Moreover, additional measures must be taken in order to ensure that claims commissions act as independent institutions. The independence and impartiality of such Commissions could be significantly enhanced in four ways, namely by the regulation of the law and functioning of the commission in a resolution of a collective UN decision-making body (Security Council, General Assembly) rather than by the head of the transitional administration itself; by the appointment of independent expert members to the commission, so as to avoid direct conflicts of interest with the administration;[238] through the attribution of investigative powers to the commission;[239] and by "strengthening the standing of applicants and/or their legal representatives and providing for an effective right of appeal".[240]

3.2.3.   Domestic forums of accountability

Where international actors pierce the veil between international to domestic authority by exercising exclusive governing powers or final executive or legislative authority on behalf of and in the interest of local actors, they may be subject to an additional layer of accountability, namely scrutiny and control by domestic judicial authorities. The extent to which this form of control may be exercised in practice depends largely on the factual and circumstantial parameters of each situation,

---

[236] Some states, such as the US, France, Sweden and the Russian Federation, did not participate in the appeals regime of the KCAC. For a criticism, see European Commission for Democracy Through Law, *Opinion on Human Rights in Kosovo*, para. 6; Council of Europe, Parliamentary Assembly, *Protection of Human Rights in Kosovo*, para. 23.

[237] See Article VI, para. 1 of Annex 1 A to the Dayton Peace Agreement.

[238] It is critical that claims under UNMIK Regulation No. 2000/47 are heard by a panel of three UNMIK members, and only subject to review by the UNMIK Director of Administration. See also Caplan, *International Governance of War-Torn Territories*, at 209–10.

[239] See also the proposal for a central UN claims commission by Zwanenburg, *Accountability of Peace Support Operations*, at 288–9.

[240] See Council of Europe, Parliamentary Assembly, Res. 1417 (2005), para. 5 (vii) (c).

such as the scope and nature of authority of international actors, the availability and reliability of domestic forums of control and the stage of advancement of the specific mission. Nevertheless, two general rules can be formulated.

International administrations may be under an institutional obligation progressively to develop local forums for review of executive and legislative authority as part of their statebuilding or governance mandate. This obligation to decentralise authority may, in particular, oblige international administrations to subject internationally created domestic institutions to independent local review, or to create mixed national-international forums of review in situations of transition.

Moreover, in situations where international administrations substitute domestic authorities in a circumscribed and defined domestic legal order, they may be subject to judicial review by local courts in the exercise of lawmaking powers more generally.[241] Two legal concepts may be invoked to support this type of control from a legal point of view: the concept of "functional duality" and the doctrine of "*ultra vires*".

3.2.3.1.   Decentralised and mixed national-international forms accountability
International administrations face a specific accountability dilemma in post-conflict settings. They are, on the one hand, obliged to restore local capacity and create a viable and independent domestic judiciary, which may potentially review the action of all holders of public authority, including international institutions. This mandate often conflicts, however, with a capacity or reliability gap of domestic judicial institutions.[242]

These conflicting responsibilities can be reconciled in several ways. International administrations may, first, gradually "localise" domestic

---

[241] For a more cautious approach towards the option of judicial review by domestic courts in the Bosnian context, see Human Rights Chamber for Bosnia and Herzegovina, *Suljanovic, Cisic and Lelic* v. *Bosnia and Herzegovina and the Republika Srpska*, para. 39; *Cavic* v. *Bosnia and Herzegovina*, para. 19. See also the findings of the Venice Commission with respect to the exercise of control by domestic Bosnian courts over the decertification of police officers by UN-IPTF, *Opinion on a Possible Solution to the Issue of Decertification of Police Officers in Bosnia and Herzegovina*, 24 October 2005, para. 35. ("Bosnian courts, even if formally competent to review the decisions of domestic authorities implementing UN-IPTF decisions on denial of certification, have no competence to annul such decisions and order that new ones should be taken, as they have no power to ignore or reverse the IPTF recommendations on decertification.")

[242] Domestic institutions may not yet be sufficiently impartial or experienced to ensure independent and effective judicial review in accordance with international standards; or there may be no functioning justice system at all.

judicial control over executive action by empowering local courts and institutions to review the action of domestic authorities, including institutions created by transitional administrations. This approach allows the administration to maintain general control over the territory in the initial phase of engagement, while encouraging it gradually to hand over control to domestic institutions as required by its mandate.

A second approach which may help international administrations to comply with their institutional responsibility to institute independent forums of review is the provisional internationalisation of domestic courts. International judges may be appointed to domestic institutions in order to enhance the perceived objectivity, impartiality and fairness of the national judiciary, and to allow a balanced review of the regulatory action of international administrations.[243]

So far this approach has been used predominantly by international administrations for the adjudication of serious crimes in a post-conflict setting. UNMIK appointed international judges and prosecutors to the courts in Kosovo to ensure that war crimes trials are conducted in a neutral and independent environment, in accordance with international fair trial guarantees.[244] Similar measures have been taken in Bosnia and Herzegovina and East Timor, with the creation of a Special Chamber in the State Court of Bosnia and Herzegovina[245] and the establishment of

---

[243] The need for this type of internationalisation was set out by UNMK Regulation No. 34/2001 in the context of Kosovo. The preamble of the Regulation states that "the continued presence of security threats may undermine the independence and impartiality of the judiciary and impede the ability of the judiciary to properly prosecute crimes, which gravely undermine the peace process and the full establishment of the rule of law in Kosovo".

[244] UNMIK Regulation No. 2000/6 allowed the appointment of international judges and prosecutors to courts in the district of Mitrovica. UNMIK Regulation No. 2000/34 extended this regime to other courts, including the Supreme Court. Subsequently, the role of international judges and prosecutors was regulated by UNMIK Regulation No. 2000/64, which provides as follows: "At any stage in the criminal proceedings, the Department of Judicial Affairs, on the basis of [a petition from the competent prosecutor, the accused or the defence counsel] or on its own motion, may submit a recommendation to the Special Representative of the Secretary-General for the assignment of international judges/prosecutors and/or a change of venue if it determines that this is necessary to ensure the independence and impartiality of the judiciary or the proper administration of justice." It is reported that in June 2004, international judges were involved in ninety-two cases, including appeals of judgments, trials in district courts and decisions on detentions. See UNMIK, Pillar I, Police and Justice, Presentation Paper, June 2004, at 15.

[245] See Report of the Secretary-General, *The Rule of Law and Transitional Justice in Conflict and Post-conflict Societies*, UN Doc. S/2004/616 of 3 August 2004, para. 38.

the panels with exclusive jurisdiction over serious criminal offences in East Timor.[246]

This technique could be extended to the review of the exercise of public authority in territories under international administration more generally. Rather than relying on purely external mechanisms of control, international decision-makers could endow specialised mixed national-international courts of domestic jurisdictions with the authority to exercise independent review over specific types of regulatory action, including regulatory action by transitional administrations in international(ised) territories. This approach has been taken by the internationalised Constitutional Court of Bosnia and Herzegovina, which interpreted its mandate under Annex IV of the Dayton Agreement as an entitlement to watch over the constitutionality of any legislative act in Bosnia.[247] Wider and systematic use of internationalised domestic courts as forums of independent review would help reduce the existing lack of reviewability of acts adopted by international administrators, while mobilising to the extent possible expertise resident in the country.

Two lessons must, however, be learned from existing practice.[248] It is crucial to the success of a process of internationalisation of the judiciary that the role and competences of international judges be clearly defined. Otherwise, their authority is likely to be challenged and called into question by domestic actors or the international administration itself. Secondly, international judges must be sufficiently independent from the executive in the exercise of their functions, and, in particular, from supervision by international administrations themselves.[249] This institutional independence is not only a *conditio sine qua non* of their impartiality, but also a legal requirement under the fair trial guarantees of international human rights law.

3.2.3.2. Judicial control

Finally, domestic institutions may claim powers of judicial review over acts of international administrations in specific situations. Two different

---

[246] See UNTAET Regulation No. 15/2000 of 6 June 2000 (*On the establishment of Panels with Exclusive Jurisdiction over Serious Criminal Offences*).

[247] See Constitutional Court of Bosnia and Herzegovina, Case No. 9/00 of 3 November 2000.

[248] See John Cerone and Clive Baldwin, *Explaining and Evaluating the UNMIK Court System*, in, Internationalized Criminal Courts and Tribunals (Cessare P. R Romano, André Nollkaemper and J. K. Kleffner eds., 2004), at 55–6.

[249] See also below Part IV, Chapter 15 on the independence of the judiciary.

bases must be distinguished: domestic review of acts which fall within the jurisdiction of the domestic legal system and domestic control over acts which exceed the competences of the international administration.

3.2.3.2.1. Functional duality

Domestic courts may invoke the reasoning of the Constitutional Court of Bosnia and Herzegovina in the case on the "Law on the State Border Service", in order to exercise control over acts adopted by administering authorities in their capacity as representatives of domestic authorities. The concept of "functional duality" has ramifications beyond the Bosnian context. It can be used as a model for judicial review in cases where international administrations act not only as independent "external" legal authorities, but as "internal" decision-making powers exercising authority within the realm of domestic jurisdiction.[250]

The concept of "functional duality" may be developed into a more systematic tool to overcome the artificial conception of international administrators as extraneous actors in the exercise of international territorial authority, without compromising their status as separate legal persons or independent actors on the international plane. The general idea behind the "functional duality" doctrine is that domestic courts should base their conception of jurisdiction on the legal nature of acts of international administrations, that is their form and content, rather than refraining from exercising jurisdiction due to the separate international identity of the authority from which these acts emanate.[251] Competent domestic courts may argue that they are entitled to exercise review over legislative and executive acts of international administrations which intervene in the domestic legal system and "substitute" decisions regularly taken by national institutions (parliament, administrative agencies etc.). This functionalist approach may help to build a bridge between the domestic and the international legal order, which converge in the context of territorial administration.

3.2.3.2.1.a. Criteria

Nevertheless, the applicability of the concept of "functional duality" is subject to certain substantive criteria. These are: (1) intervention in the domestic legal system; (2) substitution of domestic authorities;

---

[250] See also Knoll, *Beyond the "Mission Civilisatrice"*, at 303.

[251] See also Wilde, *Accountability of International Organizations and the Concept of "Functional Duality"*, at 168.

(3) power of review by the domestic institution; and (4) the existence of internal(ised) norms of review.

The domestic legal order must be distinguishable from the legal order under which the administration is established. There must, in particular, be a separate framework of law against which the acts of international administrators may be tested.[252] Otherwise, international action remains self-referential. A situation of "functional duality" will most likely exist in situations where international administrations operate within the framework of an existing domestic system, or where they shape the normative parameters of an existing domestic legal order through their own legislation.

Secondly, the act which is subject to review must have been adopted by international administrators in their capacity as domestic authority or as a substitute for domestic organs.[253] Two criteria may serve as references in this regard: the substantive content of the act and its form of enactment. Acts of international administrations must, first of all, address a subject matter that directly affects the institutions or inhabitants of the administered territory. Otherwise, the act will lack the necessary substitutive effect upon which the doctrine of "functional duality" is built. Moreover, additional guidance may be derived from the way in which the act was adopted. The case for domestic review is particularly compelling in cases where international administrations exercise their regulatory powers formally in the position of a trustee, namely on behalf of and in the interest of local actors.[254]

Thirdly, the domestic court which intends to exercise judicial scrutiny must be empowered under the law of the territory under administration to exercise judicial review over the specific type of legal act (law, executive decision) which is adopted by the international administration as a substitute for domestic authorities.[255] This follows from the very nature of the doctrine of "functional duality". This doctrine cannot give

---

[252] This distinction is inherent in the concept of "functional *duality*".

[253] See also the discussion below Part IV, Chapter 15.

[254] See para. 5 of the decision of the Constitutional Court of Bosnia and Herzegovina.

[255] The Constitutional Court of Bosnia and Hezegovina used this argument in its decision in the case U/37/01. The Court found in this case that "[d]ecisions of the High Representative to remove public officials from office are not 'judgments' for the purpose of Article VI.3 (b) of the Constitution of Bosnia and Herzegovina, and the Constitutional Court is therefore not competent to review such decisions". Moreover, the Court held that it could not "review a decision of the High Representative to remove a public official under Article VI.3 (a) Constitution of Bosnia and Herzegovina". See Constitutional Court of Bosnia and Herzegovina, Case U 37/01 of 2 November 2001, Conclusion.

domestic courts more powers than they enjoy under their own domestic system.

Finally, the scope of judicial review is limited. It is tied to the law applicable in the domestic system. Domestic courts may not necessarily be entitled to review whether a specific act was adopted in accordance with the legal order of the institution which established the administration.[256] They are only called upon to assess whether the act is in conformity with law applicable at the domestic realm. Subject to the specific hierarchy of norms applicable in the territory, courts of the administered territory might, *inter alia*, review whether the act is compatible with general domestic law applicable in the administered territory (e.g. constitutional provisions), with norms and standards declared applicable by the international administration[257] or with international legal standards that form part of the domestic legal order.

3.2.3.2.1.b. Scope of application

The criteria of the "functional duality" doctrine are most likely to be met in the context of internationalised states, where international actors exercise governing powers within the framework of an existing and well defined municipal system. Such conditions existed, in particular, in Cambodia and Bosnia and Herzegovina, including the Municipality of the City of Mostar,[258] where international administrators acted as public authorities within an internationalised constitutional system determined by multilateral treaty arrangements.[259]

However, the applicability of the principle of "functional duality" is not confined to these cases. The concept may also be applied in situations where international authorities shape the contours and structures

---

[256] See *ibid.*, para. 6. This argument appears to explain why the Venice Commission held in its opinion on decertification that Bosnian courts are not competent to review or reverse decertification decisions by UN-ITPF. See *Opinion on a Possible Solution to the Issue of Decertification of Police Officers in Bosnia and Herzegovina*, 24 October 2005, paras. 35 and 61.

[257] See, for example, the UN Regulations on the law applicable in Kosovo and East Timor.

[258] Article 8 of the Memorandum of Understanding on the European Union Administration of Mostar provided that that the "EU Administrator will apply the Constitution of the Federation of Bosnia and Herzegovina in conformity with Chapter IX, Article 10 this Constitution". Article 11 of the Memorandum of Understanding added that: "Courts set up in the Mostar city municipality in conformity with the Constitution, will rest fully independent in performing their adjudicative tasks on the basis of the applicable law, including regulations issues by the EU Administrator."

[259] See Annex IV of the Dayton Peace Agreement and Annex 1 of the Agreement on the Political Settlement of the Cambodian Conflict.

of a domestic system through their regulatory activity. In this context, "functional duality" may serve to ensure compliance by international administrations with the norms and standards that have been declared applicable by them as public authorities acting within the territory under administration. Domestic courts may hold that international administrations are not exempted from, but are required to comply with general governmental and human rights standards declared applicable to the territory as a whole in cases where international authorities act as domestic or surrogate domestic authorities. In these cases, the "constitutional" parameters of the domestic legal system are defined by specific international legal acts which define the norms applicable in the territory. "Functional duality" ensures that both the acts of domestic authorities and individual acts taken by international administrators as a public authority of the territory under administration are, in principle, subject to objective standards of governance in the exercise of domestic authority.

This variation of "functional duality" may come to apply in scenarios like Kosovo and East Timor, where UN administrations determined both the normative system of the respective territories and their identity as an independent legal entity on the international plane. In both situations, domestic courts could have invoked the concept of "functional duality" in order to determine whether specific regulatory acts of the UN administrations or public agencies created by them are in conformity with the law applicable in Kosovo and East Timor.[260]

Finally, the concept of "functional duality" may be invoked to exercise control over acts of specific multinational administrations provided that these entities enjoy a legal personality separate from the states composing them and exercise general executive and lawmaking functions on behalf of local actors. The CPA may serve as a typical example.[261] The Authority enjoyed not only a separate legal identity as multinational administering institution,[262] but exercised a governance mandate which encompassed the responsibility to promote the "welfare of the Iraqi people through the effective administration of the territory".[263] The concept

---

[260] See Section 1 (3) of UNMIK Regulation No. 24/1999, as amended by UNMIK Regulation No. 59/2000 and Sections 2 and 3 of UNTAET Regulation No.1/1999.

[261] Concurring De Wet, *Direct Administration of Territories by the United Nations*, at 331.

[262] The CPA was different from a bilateral state authority exercising occupying powers on foreign soil. For a discussion of the legal personality of the CPA, see above Part IV, Chapter 13.

[263] See para. 4 of SC Res. 1483 (2003).

of "functional duality" could have been used in this context to examine whether acts carried by the authority in the exercise of regulatory authority on behalf domestic institutions[264] were consistent with the substantive law applicable in Iraq at the time of the administration.[265]

3.2.3.2.2. Ultra vires *control*

The second legal concept which may be invoked by domestic courts to assert control over the regulatory activity of international administrations is the argument of *ultra vires* action.[266] This doctrine was, *inter alia*, used in the 1920s to control the acts of the Saar administration. It must, however, be applied with some caution in the context of contemporary frameworks of administration.

The exercise of judicial review by domestic courts over *ultra vires* acts of international administrations is a schismatic concept. There is some merit in the claim that domestic courts may refuse legal acts which exceed the competences of international administrations and which come within the ambit of domestic jurisdiction.[267] However, the assessment of the legality of the acts of international administrations may require domestic courts to review whether these acts are compatible with the internal legal order of the organisation that established the administration.[268] This type of review may be incompatible with the institutional structures and international checks and balances of that organisation or exclusive interrogatory powers attributed to that organisation under a specific treaty arrangement. The question as to whether domestic courts may declare an act of an international administration *ultra vires* and inapplicable in the domestic system must therefore be determined

---

[264] See Section 1 (2) of CPA Order No. 1.

[265] See on the definition of the applicable law by the CPA, Section 2 of CPA Regulation No. 1.

[266] See generally on *ultra vires* acts of international organisations, R. Y. Jennings, *Nullity and Effectiveness in International Law*, in Cambridge Essays in International Law – Essays in Honour of Lord McNair (1965), 72; Felice Morgenstern, *Legality in International Organizations*, British Yearbook of International Law, Vol. 48 (1976–7), 241; Ebere Osieke, *Ultra Vires Acts in International Organizations – The Experience of the I.L.O.*, British Yearbook of International Law, Vol. 48 (1976–7), 259. See also Niels Blokker, *Beyond "Dili": On the Powers and Practice of International Organizations*, in State, Sovereignty and International Governance (G. Kreijen ed., 2004), 299.

[267] See generally, Erika de Wet and André Nollkaemper, *Review of the Security Decisions by National Courts*, German Yearbook of International Law, Vol. 45 (2002), at 166–202.

[268] Note that this type of control was excluded by the Constitutional Court of Bosnia and Herzegovina in its conception of "functional duality".

individually in each case, depending on the institutional design of the administration.

3.2.3.2.2.a. The problematic case: Review of acts of Chapter VII-based administrations

The exercise of *ultra vires* control over acts adopted by Chapter VII–based administrations is not excluded *per se*, but it may pose legal problems. Difficulties arise in particular, in cases where review by domestic courts entails an implicit finding on the legality of Chapter VII action.[269]

There is, first, an issue of powers of interpretation. The normative acts of transitional administrations are regularly adopted for the implementation of a Chapter VII-based mandate. The power to interpret the scope of Chapter VII mandates belongs primarily to UN organs themselves, namely transitional administrations charged with their implementation, or the Security Council. Domestic courts are not directly called upon to decide disputes about the ambit of a Chapter VII mandate. The final say as to whether an act adopted by a transitional administration comes within the scope of the mandate must, in principle, remain with the Council itself, which acts as a direct supervisory body.

Furthermore, it is controversial whether, or under which circumstances domestic courts are authorised to review the compatibility of a Chapter VII resolution with the UN Charter itself.[270] Domestic review of the compatibility of Security Council resolutions with principles of

---

[269] The question as to what extent states may exercise judicial review over Chapter VII Resolutions of the Security Council has not yet been resolved. Some states have raised the issue at the open Council meeting convened on 10 July 2002 concerning the adoption of SC Resolution 1422 (2002). The Representative of Jordan stated that the Council would "edge itself toward acting *ultra vires* – that is, beyond its authority under the UN Charter" if it considered "the adoption of a draft resolution on the ICC falling under Chapter VII". The Permanent Representative of Canada emphasised at the same meeting that the "adoption of the resolutions currently circulating could place Canada and, we expect, others in the unprecedented position of having to examine the legality of a Security Council resolution". For a discussion of the different views held in legal doctrine, see generally Delbrück, *On Article 25*, in Simma, Charter of the United Nations, 459, paras. 17 and 18. In favour of review, De Wet, *Chapter VII Powers of the United Nations Security Council*, at 375–82; Derek Bowett, *The Impact of Security Council Decisions on Dispute Settlement Procedures*, European Journal of International Law, Vol. 5 (1994), 89, at 95; Karl Doehring, *Unlawful Resolutions of the Security Council and their Legal Consequences*, Max Planck Yearbook of United Nations Law, Vol. 1 (1997), 91, at 98.

[270] Against such a power of review, see Delbrück, *On Article 25*, in Simma, Charter of the United Nations, 459, para. 18. For a general discussion, see de Wet, *Chapter VII Powers of the United Nations Security Council*, at 376–7.

international law, including those mentioned in Article 24, paragraph 2 of the Charter, conflicts with Article 25, which declares Chapter VII resolutions binding on UN member States[271], Article 103, which has been interpreted so as to give obligations of states under Chapter VII of the Charter priority over other treated-based commitments[272], and the discretionary nature powers of the Council under Article 39 of the Charter.[273] Although a power of review may potentially be asserted in cases of the violation of *jus cogens*, this right has been disputed in content and scope.[274]

Last but not least, domestic review is complicated by the fact that Chapter VII Resolutions may be said to benefit from a presumption of

---

[271] The formulation under Article 25 of the Charter, according to which members agree "to accept and carry out the decisions of the Security Council in accordance with the present Charter" has been subject to different interpretations . See Delbrück, *On Article 25*, in Simma, Charter of the United Nations, 455, para. 6.

[272] Article 103 of the Charter does not directly state that a Chapter VII decision of the Council prevails over any other inconsistent treaty provision. However, the obligation of UN Member states under Article 25 of the Charter to "accept and carry out decisions of the Security Council" is an "obligation under the Charter" within the meaning of Article 103. UN member states are therefore bound by Article 103 to give obligations arising from binding Chapter VII resolutions of the Council priority over any other commitments. See Rudolf Bernhardt, *On Article 103*, in Simma, Charter of the United Nations, 1120, at para. 10. This view was taken by the Security Council in its Resolution 670 (1990) in which the Council expressly recalled the "provisions of Article 103 of the Charter", and then went on to decide "that all States, *notwithstanding the existence of any rights or obligations conferred or imposed by any international agreement* or any contract entered into or any license or permit granted before the date of the present resolution, shall deny permission to any aircraft to take off from their territory if the aircraft would carry any cargo to or from Iraq or Kuwait other than food in humanitarian circumstances" (emphasis added). See the preamble and para. 3 of SC Res. 670 (1990) of 25 September 1990, UN Doc. S/RES/670 (1990). The same reasoning underlies the practice of the Council in the *Lockerbie* case, in which the Council decided that Libya must surrender the persons charged with the terrorist action against Pan Am flight 103 to the UK and the US despite the applicability of the Montreal Convention for the Suppression of Unlawful Acts against the Safety of Civil Aviation of 23 September 1971, which is based on the principle *aut dedere aut judicare*. The ICJ accepted this view in its two Orders of 14 April 1992. See ICJ, *Case Concerning Questions of Interpretation and Application of the 1971 Montreal Convention arising from the Aerial Incident at Lockerbie (Libya v. United Kingdom)*, ICJ Rep. 1992, p. 16, at para. 39.

[273] One of the main legality questions under UN Charter law in the field of territorial administration is whether an individual act of a Chapter VII established administration comes within the ambit of the maintenance of international peace and security. This finding is, however, closely linked to the Council's discretionary determination of a breach of the peace under Chapter VII, and may therefore not necessarily be open to judicial review by domestic courts.

[274] See A. Mark Weisburd, *International Law and the Problem of Evil*, Vanderbilt Journal of Transnational Law, Vol. 34 (2001), 237, at 238–41.

legality under the Charter system[275], which would have to be reversed by domestic courts.

3.2.3.2.2.b.   Options for review

The case for the exercise of judicial review is easier to make in two other contexts, namely territorial administration carried out under the auspices of the General Assembly and the review of the acts of occupying powers.

3.2.3.2.2.b(1)   Transitional administrations created by the General Assembly

The doctrine of *ultra vires* is of some use in the context of the exercise of territorial authority by administering entities created by the General Assembly. Domestic courts may use arguments of *ultra vires* in order to deny giving effect to regulatory acts adopted by international administrations. The reasoning is simple. International administrations established by the General Assembly are generally subsidiary organs of the Assembly. Since the Assembly itself cannot, in principle, make decisions which are binding on UN member states, the administrations established by it are not empowered to adopt legal acts which bind member states without their consent.

This argument was advanced in the debate over the legal implications of Decree No. 1 of the UN Council for Namibia on UN member states.[276] A similar argument can be invoked in relation to laws and regulations adopted by other subsidiary bodies of the General Assembly. Domestic courts may seek to dispute the binding nature of such acts in the legal order of the territory under administration on the ground that they exceed the authority of the General Assembly under the legal order of the UN.

---

[275] See De Wet, *Direct Administration of Territories*, at 337, who highlights the problems of judicial review by domestic courts, noting that "[i]n the absence of protest by a significant number of Member States at a very early stage after the adoption of the measures for civil (co-)administration, the legality of these measures becomes very difficult to dispute".

[276] The decree was enacted by the UN Council for Namibia on 27 September 1967, in order to protect the natural resources of Namibia against exploitation. Both the form of the decision ("Decree") and its mandatory language ("No person or entity... may", "Any permission, concession or licence... is null, void and of no force or effect", "Any... vehicle... shall also be subject") indicated that the Decree was meant to be a binding decision with direct applicability within UN member states. See paras. 1–3 of Decree No. 1. But this view was contested on the ground that "the Assembly cannot confer on a subsidiary organ powers greater than those possessed by itself". See Zacklin, *The Problem of Namibia in International Law*, at 320.

However, there are limits to this principle. The ICJ pointed out in its 1971 Advisory Opinion that specific regulatory acts of the General Assembly may have greater authority than a mere recommendation.[277] The powers of an Assembly-created administering authority may therefore, in special circumstances, include authoritative decision-making power. Moreover, the invocation of the limited decision-making authority *vis-à-vis* UN member states loses its compellingness if the territory under administration is detached from any state entity and temporarily placed under the exclusive jurisdiction of the UN. Decisions of UN-administering authority may be authoritative for the legal system of the administered territory, because the territory is directly subject to the "legal order of the United Nations", in which the resolutions of the General Assembly are binding.[278]

3.2.3.2.2.b(2)   Acts of occupying powers

Judicial review of *ultra vires* acts also has a certain tradition in the context of belligerent occupation. Municipal courts have invalidated acts of a belligerent occupant which exceeded military necessity. Examples of judicial review and invalidation of acts of occupying powers by domestic courts may be found in the practice of the occupations of Norway, Greece and Belgium during World War II.[279] Similar positions have been voiced in legal doctrine. Some authors have argued that domestic courts are generally entitled to declare acts of belligerent occupants invalid where they exceed the powers attributed to occupying powers under international treaty law.[280] Other scholars recognise the option of *ultra vires* control in cases where "evidence of illegality under conventional law is clear-cut and incontrovertible", while denying it in cases where "the evidence concerning a given ordinance or order is clouded by doubt,

---

[277] See ICJ Rep. 1971, 58.

[278] See also the argument made by Zacklin on the effect of Decree No. 1 within the domestic system of Namibia. ("It must be concluded, therefore, that at least as so far as the internal order of the United Nations is concerned, for the great majority of member States who consider the Mandate to be validly terminated and recognize the Council to be the legal administering authority for Namibia, Decree No. 1 forms part of the municipal law of Namibia. Within the legal orders of these member States, Decree No. 1 may be regarded as being assimilated to decrees of foreign States.") See Zacklin, *The Problem of Namibia in International Law*, at 321.

[279] For a survey, see Morgenstern, *Validity of the Acts of the Belligerent Occupant*, at 306–7; Romulus A. Picciotti, *Legal Problems of Occupied Nations after the Termination of Occupation*, Military Law Review, Vol. 33 (1966), 25, at 52.

[280] See Morgenstern, *Validity of the Acts of the Belligerent Occupant*, at 309.

that is, for instance, when questions of necessity are raised".[281] This practice indicates that the review of *ultra vires* acts by domestic courts enjoys some, albeit not unanimous recognition[282] under the law of occupation, especially in the historical tradition of the first half of the twentieth century.

This recognition of judicial review has, however, only a limited impact within the context of international territorial administrations.[283] The framework of modern administrations is increasingly based on UN mandates and treaty arrangements, which vest international authorities with a multiplicity of tasks and governance powers. In this setting, international administrations enjoy greater flexibility to shape the legal identity of the domestic system. The laws of occupation play only a subsidiary role in this context. They are often not officially invoked at all,[284] or are interwoven with other legal regimes.[285] These structural changes make it difficult to transpose the rationale of judicial review under law of occupation to the exercise of public authority within the framework of contemporary territorial administrations.[286] Nevertheless, domestic courts may have an opportunity to exercise this type of judicial review in cases in which multinational administrations act on the traditional basis of occupation law.

3.2.4. Judicial review by independent international courts

Finally, international administrations may be subject to judicial review by international courts. Both, the Venice Commission and the Parliamentary Assembly of the Council of Europe have recommended the

---

[281] See von Glahn, *The Occupation of Enemy Territory*, at 110.

[282] See the practice of German courts in the context of the Allied Occupation after 1945 as discussed above Part I, Chapter 4. See also the examples given by Piccioti, *Legal Problems of Occupied Nations after the Termination of Occupation*, at 52–3.

[283] This type of judicial review is inextricably linked to the structure and context of classical occupation regimes. It makes sense in the specific context of Section III of the Hague Regulations and the Fourth Geneva Convention which provide only a limited entitlement to exercise public authority over foreign territories and rely, in principle, on the continuing operation of domestic courts.

[284] See generally on the decline of the laws of occupation in post-war practice above Part I, Chapter 4.

[285] The most evident examples are the post-war administrations of Germany and Japan, where the concept of occupation was mixed with the implications of surrender, and the recent US-UK-led administration of Iraq, where the framework of the law of occupation was complemented by the governance principles of the Security Council. See above Part I, Chapter 4.

[286] The case for *ultra vires* review becomes weaker the more the model of administration deviates substantially from the classical structure of the law of occupation.

establishment of judicial control over the action of UNMIK and KFOR in Kosovo as a practical and rapid alternative to the extension of jurisdiction of the European Court of Human Rights to both entities. The Commission proposed the creation of a special Human Rights Court for Kosovo to "deal with complaints about violations of the ECHR and its Protocols by UNMIK, the Provisional Institutions of Self-Government and possibly NATO (including NATO member States)".[287] This initiative was taken up by the Parliamentary Assembly of the Council of Europe, which recommended in its Resolution 1417 (2005)[288] that UNMIK and KFOR/NATO "commence work, in co-operation with the Council of Europe, towards establishing a human rights court for Kosovo with... the power to annul decisions or acts of UNMIK and KFOR and to award appropriate redress or compensation".[289]

The creation of such a body would mark a novelty in the conception of the accountability of international administrations.[290] It would close jurisdictional gaps left open by mechanisms such as the Human Rights Chamber for Bosnia and Herzegovina[291] and the European Court of Human Rights.[292] Moreover, it would extend the scrutiny of UNMIK and KFOR beyond internal and advisory types of review which provide only short-term solutions to accountability deficits.

However, the likelihood that such a special jurisdiction will be established in the near future is quite limited. Universal and regional international organisations are generally not inclined to subject themselves to the jurisdiction of an independent judicial body with binding decision-making power. Furthermore, in many situations, it will simply not be feasible to create a mission-specific human rights court due to the short and limited duration of the mandate of the respective administration.

---

[287] See European Commission for Democracy Through Law, *Opinion on Human Rights in Kosovo*, para. 104.

[288] See para. 5 of Res. 1417 (2005) on the Protection of Human Rights in Kosovo.

[289] For an explanation, see para. 52 of the Report of the Parliamentary Assembly of the Council of Europe on the protection of human rights in Kosovo.

[290] This proposal is novel, because it would grant "a (quasi-) international court... jurisdiction over an international organisation to which it does not belong". See European Commission for Democracy Through Law, *Opinion on Human Rights in Kosovo*, para. 104.

[291] The Human Rights Chamber in Bosnia and Herzegovina lacked the authority to review action by international governing authorities.

[292] The European Court of Human Rights lacks the power to annul decisions and acts by national authorities.

15 The exercise of regulatory authority within the framework of international administrations

The exercise of lawmaking powers by international organisations is mostly discussed in the context of the secondary law of the EU and Chapter VII Resolutions of the Security Council.[1] In this context, it is frequently overlooked that the exercise of regulatory authority by international entities has an established tradition in one field of international practice, namely international territorial administration.

International administrations have exercised a broad range of lawmaking powers, including executive and legislative authority throughout the twentieth century.[2] This phenomenon deserves attention from a legal perspective, because it deviates from the traditional structures of the international legal system.[3] International administrations may adopt regulatory acts which are binding and directly applicable to both the internal legal order of the organisation which created them, and to the legal order of the territory which is placed under international control. This direct penetration of such legal acts into the domestic legal system of territory under administration ("direct applicability") is innovative in a dual sense. It breaks with the conception that the regulatory powers of international organisations apply exclusively within

---

[1] See generally on the exercise of lawmaking powers by international organisations, José E. Alvarez, *International Organisations as Law-Makers* (2005). Frequently cited examples of Security Council "lawmaking" are SC Res. 1540 of 28 April 2004 (*Non-proliferation of weapons of mass destruction*) and SC Res. 1373 of 28 September 2001 (*Threats to international Peace and Security by Terrorist Acts*).

[2] For an analysis of lawmaking by international administrations, see generally von Carlowitz, *UNMIK Lawmaking*, at 336; von Carlowitz, *Crossing the Boundary from the International to the Domestic Legal Realm: UNMIK Lawmaking and Property Rights in Kosovo*, Global Governance, Vol. 10 (2004), 307; Boon, *Legislative Reform in Post-Conflict Zones*, at 306–18;

[3] See also Ruffert, *Administration of Kosovo and East Timor*, at 624; Knoll, *Beyond the "Mission Civilisatrice"*, at 280–6.

the confines of their own legal order, namely *vis-à-vis* their own organs and member states.[4] Moreover, it deviates from the classical dualist tradition according to which international regulatory acts require domestic implementation, in order to be directly applicable in the domestic realm.[5]

This form of international lawmaking has its origins in the era of the League of Nations. The PCIJ opened a conceptual door by developing the concept of direct invokability ("direct effect"[6]) of international treaty norms in the context of litigation concerning the railway system of the Free City of Danzig (*Jurisdiction of the Courts of Danzig*)[7] – over three decades before the famous jurisprudence of the ECJ in *Van Gend en Loos*.[8] The decrees issued by the Governing Commission in the Saar in the 1920s count among the first lawmaking acts by international administrations which enjoyed direct applicability in the domestic system of the territories under administration. They were later followed by decrees enacted by the UN Council for Namibia in the 1970s. In the last two decades, this practice has reached new heights, with the adoption of a vast amount of laws and decisions by the OHR in Bosnia and Herzegovina, the systematic issuance of regulations by UNMIK and UNTAET and the wide decision-making practice of the CPA in Iraq. Today, this power

---

[4] See generally Brownlie, *Principles of Public International Law*, at 658–9.
[5] Even the Security Council has been reluctant to vest its subsidiary bodies with the power to directly implement measures in territories. See with respect to sanctions committees, De Wet, *Chapter VII Powers of the United Nations Security Council*, at 252.
[6] This concept has been developed in the context of the invokability of international norms by individuals. Direct effect means that a provision can create rights which individuals may rely on before domestic courts.
[7] The PCIJ had to examine the effect of the Danzig-Polish Agreement of 22 October 1921 in the context of the establishment of conditions of service of Danzig citizens in Polish Railways. Poland had not implemented the agreement. The PCIJ noted that while there was "a well-established principle of international law that [international agreements] cannot as such, create direct rights and obligations for private individuals", that did not necessarily exclude the "adoption by the parties of some definite rules creating individuals rights and obligations enforceable by the national courts". The Court argued that the creation of direct rights and obligations could be assumed if "[t]he wording and general tenor" of the treaty establish that it was the "intention of the Contracting Parties" to do so, thereby creating a "special legal regime". See PCIJ, *Jurisdiction of Courts of Danzig*, PCIJ Ser. B, No. 15 (1928), at 17–18.
[8] See ECJ, *Van Gend en Loos v. Nederlandse Administratie der Belastingen*, Case 26/62 (1963), ECR 1. The Court found, *inter alia*, that a provision of Community law may be directly effective, if it is clear and precise, unconditional and capable of producing rights for individuals.

is even a distinctive feature of UN practice in the area of transitional administration.[9]

This chapter addresses the conceptual and legal implications of law-making by international administrations in two fields: lawmaking and constitution-framing.

1.   Lawmaking by international administrations

International administrations have been engaged in the exercise of reg-ulatory powers on various occasions over the last few decades. Inter-national administrations have exercised lawmaking powers not only in the cases of Bosnia and Herzegovina,[10] Eastern Slavonia,[11] Kosovo,[12] East Timor[13] and Iraq,[14] but also in the earlier experiments in the Saar, Namibia,[15] Cambodia[16] and Somalia.[17] However, international practice

---

[9] The lawmaking powers of UN administrations are recognised in the Handbook on UN Multidimensional Peacekeeping Operations. The Handbook notes: "Vested with legislative authority, the SRSG is responsible for building up a legal and regulatory framework. [T]he mission prepares legislation for promulgation by the SRSG, which may be subsequently published in an official gazette. The mission may also interpret local laws, assess their compliance with international laws and human rights standards and principles, and modify them as appropriate. The SRSG may exceptionally use executive orders and decrees to promote the rule of law, including provisions for the deployment of international judges and prosecutors" (at 21).

[10] The OHR in Bosnia adopted a wide range of laws and executive decisions. For a survey, see the list of OHR decisions at www.ohr.int.

[11] The UNTAES administrator abrogated legislation enacted by the local Serb authorities and restored Croatian law by a Directive issued on 29 May 1997. See para. 23 of the Report of the Secretary-General on the United Nations Transitional Administration for Eastern Slavonia, Baranja and Western Sirmium, UN. Doc S/1997/953 of 4 December 1997.

[12] UNMIK exercised legislative and executive authority on the basis of Regulation No. 1/1999.

[13] See UNTAET Regulation No. 1/1999 by which the SRSG assumed all legislative and executive authority.

[14] The CPA has issued directly applicable regulations and orders affecting all aspects of civil administration. For a full list, see www.cpa-iraq.org.

[15] The Council of Nambia issued, *inter alia*, Decree No.1 for the Protection of the Natural Resources of Namibia of 27 September 1974 on the basis of its mandate under Res. 2248 (S-V).

[16] UNTAC elaborated, *inter alia*, Transitional Criminal Provisions for Cambodia in its Directive No. 93/1. See UN Third Progress Report of the Secretary-General on UNTAC, UN Doc. S725154 of 25 January 1993, para. 103.

[17] The UN Special Representative in Somalia declared that the former Somali Penal Code of 1962 was the criminal law in force in Somalia. For a critique, see Sarooshi, *United Nations and the Development of Collective Security*, at 63.

has not yet provided fully satisfactory answers to the conceptual and legal implications of the exercise of lawmaking powers by international administrations. Lawmaking has been largely handled in an *ad hoc* fashion by international administrations, with each mission being to some extent a pioneering experiment of its own. Moreover, the analysis undertaken in legal doctrine has so far remained focused on individual cases, without presenting the problems of international lawmaking in a more structured way.[18] It is therefore necessary to revisit the formal and the substantive aspects of international lawmaking.

1.1. Institutional diversity

International administrations have exercised regulatory authority in a variety of frameworks and contexts. Some administrations exercised their powers expressly within the domestic structure of a territory or state. For example, UNTAC exercised regulatory authority under the constitutional structure of Cambodia, according to a power-sharing procedure specified in the Paris Accords.[19] Similarly, the EUAM was bound to act within the confines of the constitutional structure of the Federation of Bosnia and Herzegovina.[20] Other administrations like UNOSOM, UNTAES, UNMIK and UNTAET enjoyed regulatory authority by virtue of an independent Chapter VII mandate, without being integrated into the structure of a particular domestic system. Moreover, in their practice, international administrations adopted different approaches in their form of action. UNTAES exercised mostly executive authority. UNMIK, UNTAET and the CPA, by contrast, adopted a wide range of general and abstract ("legislative") acts by way of Regulations or Orders.

1.2. The legal nature of regulatory acts of international administrations

This diversity is reflected in the discussion about the legal nature of regulatory acts of transitional administrations in legal doctrine.

---

[18] For an assessment of UNMIK's regulatory practice, see von Carlowitz, *UNMIK Lawmaking*, at 371.

[19] See Article 6 of the Paris Accords.

[20] The EUAM exercised regulatory powers on the basis of precise governing instructions laid down in a Memorandum of Understanding between the Member States of the European Union, the Republic of Bosnia and Herzegovina, the Federation of Bosnia and Herzegovina and the Local Administration of Mostar. See Articles 7 (1), 8 and 10 of the Memorandum of Understanding on the European Union Administration of Mostar of 5 July 1994.

1.2.1. The "sui generis" argument

The phenomenon of lawmaking by international administrations has usually been addressed from a very specific angle, namely the immediate environment of the individual mission in which it was practiced.[21] Acts of international administrations have, in particular, been presented as *sui generis* acts, which do not fit within the established parameters of international law. The best known example is Decree No. 1 of the Council for Namibia. The decree was widely described as a unique legal Act. Some authors equated the decree to the public law of a foreign state for purposes of recognition in municipal courts.[22] Other authorities characterised it as a legal instrument *sui generis*.[23] Even the UN itself did not provide a conclusive answer. The UN Commissioner for Namibia himself qualified Decree No. 1 as a "new and strange concept".[24]

This tendency continued in the 1990s. UNMIK and UNTAET regulations were presented as a special type of legislation, which is so new and unique that "we are faced with a special impact of Public International Law on specific territories".[25] Later, this argument was repeated in the context of CPA regulations.[26] It also recurred in different form in the context of the Comprehensive Proposal for the Kosovo Status Settlement.[27]

1.2.2. A new theorisation

The "*sui generis*" methodology is unsatisfactory from an analytical perspective. It fails to address the underlying problems of legal classification. It is true that public acts of international administrations do not

---

[21] This topic has rarely been addressed in legal doctrine. For a discussion in the context of UNMIK and UNTAET, see, however, Ruffert, *Administration of Kosovo and East Timor*, at 622–4; Bothe and Marauhn, *UN Administration of Kosovo and East Timor*, at 228–9; von Carlowitz, *UNMIK Lawmaking*, at 374–7.

[22] See Schermers, *The Namibia Decree in Domestic Courts*, at 90.

[23] See Zacklin, *The Problem of Namibia in International Law*, at 321.

[24] See *Report of the United Nations Commissioner for Namibia on the implementation of Decree No. 1*, UN Doc. A/AC.131/81 of 18 July 1980.

[25] See Ruffert, *Administration of Kosovo and East Timor*, at 624. Knoll speaks of a "sui generis, loosely configured political system" in the context of Kosovo. See Knoll, *Beyond the Beyond the "Mission Civilisatrice"*, at 284.

[26] See De Wet, *Direct Administration of Territories by the United Nations*, at 331, who notes that CPA Regulations have a "*sui generis* international character".

[27] In this context, the UN Envoy defended the adoption of the proposed constitutional settlement by the Security Council on the ground that "Kosovo is a unique case that demands a unique solution". See Report of the Special Envoy of the Secretary-General on Kosovo's future status, para. 15.

fit into a broad one-size-fits-all scheme. However, not all missions are so special and distinct from each other that their legal measures must be qualified as *sui generis* acts.[28] There is a need for further differentiation. The character of the acts of international administrations may be determined on the basis of two criteria: the quality of the author of the act and the nature of the act itself.

1.2.2.1. Regulatory acts as international acts

Regulatory acts of international administrations are typically international acts which form part of the internal legal order of the organisation or the legal person that established the respective administration. In that context, they derive their international character as public acts from the quality of their author. Regulations adopted by UNMIK and UNTAET within the course of their administration are, for instance, formally international legal Acts of subsidiary organs of the Security Council within the meaning of Article 29 of the UN Charter.[29] The decrees of the Council for Namibia were international legal Acts adopted by a subsidiary organ of the General Assembly.[30] Further, Regulations of the US Administrator in Iraq[31] may be viewed as international public acts of the CPA as an international legal person.[32] This international nature distinguishes regulatory acts of international administrations from internal laws and regulations adopted by states.

1.2.2.2. Regulatory acts of international administrations as domestic acts

At the same time, not all acts of international administrations are exclusively international in nature. International governance or co-governance missions may act in a dual function when exercising regulatory authority, namely as international authorities, on the one hand,

---

[28] The repeated invocation of the *sui generis* argument almost raises the suspicion that the exceptional character of acts of international administrations has been used in practice as a pretext to distinguish and exclude these acts from the realm of domestic law.

[29] See previously Stahn, *UN Administrations in Kosovo and East Timor*, at 146.

[30] See Schermers, *The Namibia Decree in Domestic Courts*, at 89.

[31] The CPA introduced a distinction between "Regulations" and "Orders". It defined "Regulations" as "instruments that define the institutions and authorities of the Coalition Provisional Authority". "Orders", on the other hand, were defined as "binding instructions or directives to the Iraqi people that create public consequences or have a direct bearing on the way Iraqis are regulated, including ... Iraqi law".

[32] A similar reasoning applies in relation to the Acts of the OHR in Bosnia and Herzegovina.

and as internationally appointed representatives of national institutions during the interim period of administration, on the other.[33] Regulatory acts of these international administrations may therefore be both: acts of an international character and domestic acts of the territory under international administration.[34] They acquire domestic character when they become part of the internal legal system of the administered territory.[35]

Several criteria may be used to determine whether a regulatory Act shall form part of the domestic legal order. The form of the Act may give some indication. The fact that an Act is qualified as a decree, as a regulation or an order rather than as a resolution may signal that this act is designed to regulate the relations between subjects of law at the domestic level. Further guidance may be drawn from the content of the act. Factors such as the use of clear and precise terms, the regulation of unconditional obligations and the stipulations of rights or obligations for the inhabitants or institutions of the administered territory provide evidence that the respective legal shall be directly effective at the domestic level.[36] Last, but not least, additional clarification may be derived from the regulatory intention of the author of the act. One may assume that a legal act is supposed to produce effects at the domestic level if it is adopted by international authorities on behalf of or in cooperation with domestic institutions.

1.2.3. Justification of direct applicability

The direct applicability of acts of international administrations requires a specific explanation.[37] Acts of international institutions, including secondary acts of international organisations, are only in exceptional circumstances directly applicable in the domestic legal order of states. The Security Council, for instance, usually leaves the implementation its

---

[33] See above Part IV, Chapter 14. See specifically in relation to the UN Council for Namibia, Schermers, *The Namibia Decree in Domestic Courts*, at 89; Osieke, *Admission to Membership in International Organizations*, at 193.

[34] See also Bothe and Marauhn, *UN Administration of Kosovo and East Timor*, at 229.

[35] This means also that a potential presumption of legality attached to Security Council Resolutions ceases to apply. Accordingly, there may be room for judicial review.

[36] See also criteria used by the ECJ in *Van Gend en Loos*, Judgment of 5 February 1963.

[37] For an analysis of problems arising in Kosovo, see Michael Bohlander, *The Direct Application of International Law in Kosovo*, Kosovo Legal Studies, Vol. 1(2001/1), 7–13.

own decisions to UN member states, even in the context of Chapter VII measures that are directly targeted at individuals.[38] The ECJ has developed the concept of the direct applicability of EU law in the sphere of the domestic legal order of EU member states, after clarifying that the "European Community constitutes a new legal order of international law for the benefit of which states have limited their sovereign rights ... and the subjects of which comprise not only Member States, but also their nationals".[39]

The direct applicability of the acts of international administrations may be explained in a different way. It follows from the fact that international administrations act not only as intergovernmental agents, but also as surrogate or complementary domestic authorities in the very process of lawmaking. A legal act which penetrates into the domestic legal system is therefore not a foreign act in the proper sense, but a legal act of the administration, which is duly authorised to regulate on the domestic plane.

The authority of the administration to adopt directly applicable legal acts may be founded on two sources: a corresponding transfer of authority to the administration in a treaty arrangement, by which the territorial sovereign agreed to share part of its jurisdiction over the territory with an international administration; or an opening of the legal order of the territory by way of an authoritative UN Resolution. Both models have been used in international practice.[40]

The direct applicability of legal acts adopted by the SRSG in Cambodia, decisions of the OHR and UNTAET Regulations may be explained by virtue of implicit stipulations to that effect in the respective peace settlement agreements, namely Annex 1 of the Agreement on the Political Settlement of the Cambodia Conflict,[41] Articles II and V of Annex 10 to

---

[38] The Council has, in particular, refrained from granting UN sanctions committees the power to implement directly Chapter VII decisions of the Council. See also De Wet, *Direct Administration of Territories by the United Nations*, at 331–2.

[39] See ECJ, *van Gend & Loos*, Judgment of 5 February 1963, para. 10. The Court added: "Independently of the legislation of Member States, Community law therefore not only imposes obligations on individuals but is also intended to confer upon them rights which become part of their heritage. These rights arise not only where they are expressly granted by the Treaty, but also by reason of obligations which the Treaty imposes in a clearly defined way upon individuals as well as upon the Member States and upon the institutions of the Community."

[40] See also De Wet, *Direct Administration of Territories by the United Nations*, at 331; Bothe and Marauhn, *UN Administration of Kosovo and East Timor*, at 255.

[41] See Section A, para. 2 (c) and (d) of Annex 1.

the Dayton Agreement[42] and the Agreement of 5 May,[43] as implemented by the UN in Security Council Resolution 1272.

The direct applicability of UNMIK and CPA legislation, by contrast, may be founded upon the second construction. Security Council Resolutions 1244 (1999) and 1483 (2003) may be interpreted as legal instruments which opened the legal order of the territories so as to allow for a direct application of the regulatory Acts of the respective administrations.[44] It has been established earlier that the Council is empowered to administer territories or to authorise states to administer territories under Chapter VII of the Charter.[45] This power includes the authority to vest international administrations with the capacity to adopt legal acts that enjoy direct applicability in the administered territory.[46] A similar construction may explain the direct applicability of Decree No. 1 in Namibia, which contained concrete prohibitions concerning mining, processing and selling of natural resources within the territorial limits of Namibia.[47]

Both constructions have the same legal effect. The existing municipal law and the "newly" created law of international administrations form a unity in these cases. They constitute the domestic order of the territory under international administration.[48]

1.3. General authority problems

It is widely accepted that international administrations may exercise lawmaking powers. However, there are divergent conceptions about the scope of regulatory authority to be exercised by international administrators. Both, the post-war administrations of Germany and Japan

---

[42] See, in particular, Article II d., whereby the parties granted the OHR the authority to facilitate "the resolution of any difficulties arising in connection with civilian implementation", as well as Article V, which endowed the OHR with "final authority" to interpret Annex 10.

[43] See Article 6 of the Agreement of 5 May 1999.

[44] Concurring De Wet, *Direct Administration of Territories by the United Nations*, at 331. See with respect to Kosovo also Knoll, *Beyond the "Mission Civilisatrice"*, at 277 ("Resolution 1244 (1999) 'vertically opened' Kosovo's normative space").

[45] See above Part III, Chapter 11. See also Sarooshi, *United Nations and the Development of Collective Security*, at 63 ([T]he Security Council can delegate the power of internal governance to the SG, but it must do so in express terms").

[46] *Ibid.*, at 332.

[47] See para. 1 of Decree No. 1.

[48] See also Ruffert, *Administration of Kosovo and East Timor*, at 623 ("Consequently, UN-legislation and municipal legal provisions are complementing each other"). See Bothe and Marauhn, *UN Administration of Kosovo and East Timor*, at 229.

after 1945 and governance missions of the 1990s (OHR, UNMIK, UNTAET) adopted an interventionist approach towards territorial administration. This broad conception of international territorial authority is subject to increasing doubts in contemporary thinking.[49]

The existing practice has posed problems in this respect. International administrations have not always been attentive to the limits of the organisation's institutional mandate in the exercise of regulatory authority. Moreover, they have on several occasions failed to accord their own regulatory policies to the general legal culture of the territory under administration, and have even been accused of violating international standards in specific areas of law.

1.3.1. General limits of lawmaking by transitional administrations

The practice of modern governance missions (UNTAES, UNMIK, UNTAET) has raised concerns regarding the limits of lawmaking powers of international administrations under the institutional law of the UN.

1.3.1.1.   UN administrations and the link to international peace and security

It is clear from the institutional law of the UN that Acts of UN administrations, especially regulations by Chapter VII-established administrations, must be related to the objectives of peace-maintenance.[50] These limits have been interpreted in an extensive fashion in UN practice. UN administrations have adopted a number of regulations which are only very loosely connected to the goals of international peace and security. Both UNMIK and UNTAET have, for example, enacted legislation concerning the introduction of new currencies,[51] the creation of central fiscal authorities,[52] the registration of vehicles,[53] and the regulation of road traffic[54] in the administered territories. These acts stand in contrast to

---

[49] There are inherent limits to the regulatory authority of international administrations. See above Part III, Chapter 11.

[50] Since the authority of the Security Council is tied to the maintenance of international peace and security, the same principle applies à fortiori to the exercise of regulatory authority by Chapter VII-established administrations. See also Frowein and Krisch, Introduction to Chapter VII, in Simma, Charter of the United Nations (2002), at 713, para. 33.

[51] See, for example, UNTAET Regulation No. 7/2000. See also UNMIK Regulation No. 1999/4 on the Currency to Be used in Kosovo which caused protests by Belgrade and Moscow as an act encroaching on the sovereignty of the FRY.

[52] See, for example, UNTAET Regulation No. 1/2000.

[53] See, for example, UNTAET Regulation No. 6/2001.

[54] See, for example, UNTAET Regulation No. 8/2001.

other acts which have a direct connection to peace and security, such as regulations concerning issues of defence, the return of displaced persons or questions of institutional and judicial reconstruction. It is at least questionable whether they have a sufficient nexus to Chapter VII and may thus be justified on the basis of the model of delegated authority.[55]

The heading peacebuilding may justify a variety of legislative and executive acts within the domestic realm, including measures which are not linked to peace and security, such as measures to restore the infrastructure of the administered territory in various sectors (elections,[56] post and telecommunication,[57] labour and employment,[58] transport,[59] civil security,[60] agriculture[61] and trade and industry[62]). However, as subsidiary bodies of the Security Council or the General Assembly, UN administrations do not have an unqualified right to determine the scope of the nexus to peace and security.[63]

In future UN missions, a clearer distinction should be drawn between acts of institutional and organisational reconstruction in these areas and substantive and long-term changes of the law.[64] Attempts to re-activate domestic capacity-building through the establishment of procedures in institutions may be defended under a wide conception of the objective of peace-maintenance. Matters of substantive legal reform, on the other

---

[55] See de Hoogh, *Attribution or Delegation of (Legislative) Power by the Security Council?*, at 31. Concurring von Leopold, *UNMIK Lawmaking*, at 344. ([I]t is doubtful, whether all aspects of UNMIK's regulatory efforts had a sufficiently strong linkage to international security interests that would warrant automatic justification through Chapter VII.")

[56] See, for example, UNMIK Regulation No. 21/2000 of 18 April 2000 (*On the Establishment of the Central Election Commission*).

[57] See, for example, UNMIK Regulation No. 13/2000 of 21 April 2000 (*On the Establishment of the Administrative Department of Post and Telecommunications*).

[58] See, for example, UNMIK Regulation No. 24/2000 of 21 April 2000 (*On the Establishment of the Administrative Department of Labour and Employment*).

[59] See, for example, UNMIK Regulation No. 25/2000 of 21 April 2000 (*On the Establishment of the Administrative Department of Labour Transport and Infrastructure*).

[60] See, for example, UNMIK Regulation No. 61/2000 of 9 November 2000 (*On the Establishment of the Administrative Department of Civil Security and Emergency Preparedness*).

[61] See, for example, UNMIK Regulation No. 27/2000 of 28 April 2000 (*On the Establishment of the Administrative Department of Agriculture, Forestry and Rural Development*).

[62] See, for example, UNMIK Regulation No. 63/2000 of 7 December 2000 (*On the Establishment of the Administrative Department of Trade and Industry*).

[63] See also Frowein and Krisch, *Introduction to Chapter VII*, in Simma, Charter of the United Nations (2002), at 713, para. 33.

[64] International organisations are mandated to act within the framework of the powers attributed to them. Acts which go beyond their functional personality are *ultra vires*. See Reinisch and Weber, *In the Shadow of Waite and Kennedy*, at 63.

hand, which have a long-term impact on the socio-economic system, should be supported by additional domestic consent.

1.3.1.2. Limits arising from the mandate of international administrations

UN administrations and multinational administrations must consider regulatory limits imposed by their respective mandates, and possibly by the laws of occupation. The line between permissible legal interpretation and unlawful (self-)arrogation of authority is often delicate and hard to determine, in particular, in cases in which the mandate is unclear.[65] In such situations, the scope of regulatory authority of transitional administration must be determined by way of an interpretation of the respective mandate. This interpretation is subject to certain rules.[66] Generally, an interpretation of the mandate must be in line with the wording of the text of the authorisation or treaty arrangement containing the mandate.[67] Furthermore, in cases where a specific interpretation of a UN mandate touches upon issues of domestic jurisdiction, one may return to the old maxim of the *Lotus* case,[68] according to which limitations of sovereignty cannot be assumed lightly.[69] The limitations under the laws of occupation may provide some residual guidelines in this regard.[70] Additional inferences may be drawn from the context of the mandate (e.g. explanatory reports by the Secretary-General)[71] or subsequent practice by the Security Council or the parties to the respective agreement.[72]

1.3.1.3. Authority disputes

Authority problems have arisen in four situations: Somalia, Bosnia and Herzegovina, Kosovo and Iraq.

---

[65] See generally Jochen Abr. Frowein, *Unilateral Interpretation of Security Council Resolutions: a Threat to Collective Security?*, in Liber Amicorum Günther Jaenicke – zum 85. Geburtstag (V. Götz, P. Selmer, R. Wolfrum eds., 1998), 97–112.

[66] Some guidance may be derived from the rules of interpretation contained in Articles 31 and 32 of the Vienna Convention on the Law of Treaties, which serve also as a starting point for the interpretation of Chapter VII Resolutions. See Frowein and Krisch, *Introduction to Chapter VII*, in Simma, Charter of the United Nations (2002), at 713, para. 34. See also Michael C. Wood, *The Interpretation of Security Council Resolutions*, Max Planck Yearbook of United Nations Law, Vol. 2 (1998), 85.

[67] See Article 31, para.12 of the Vienna Convention on the Law of Treaties.

[68] See PCIJ, *Lotus*, Ser. A, No.9 (1927), 19.

[69] See generally in the context of Chapter VII Resolutions, Frowein and Krisch, *Introduction to Chapter VII*, at 713, para. 35.

[70] See also von Carlowitz, *UNMIK Lawmaking*, at 374.

[71] See Frowein and Krisch, *Introduction to Chapter VII*, para. 34.

[72] See Article 31, para. 3 (b) of the Vienna Convention on the Law of Treaties. See also Frowein and Krisch, *Introduction to Chapter VII*, para. 34.

1.3.1.3.1. UNOSOM

Security Council Resolution 814 contained a rather vague mandate, which authorised the Secretary-General to "direct the Force Commander of UNOSOM II to assume responsibility for the consolidation, expansion and maintenance of a secure environment throughout Somalia". This mandate may, at best, be construed as encompassing a delegation of executive authority. But it did not authorise UNOSOM to exercise legislative authority generally, or to introduce the former Somali Penal Code of 1962 as the criminal law applicable in the territory. Such a power was neither expressly mentioned in the Resolution, nor necessarily implied by UNOSOM'S mandate.[73] The general promulgation of a criminal code is therefore difficult to justify in light of rules of interpretation of Chapter VII Resolutions. Moreover, it contrasted with the principle of the continued application of penal laws under Article 64, paragraph 1 of Fourth Geneva Convention which might serve as a residual guideline of interpretation.[74]

1.3.1.3.2. OHR

Similar problems also emerged in the case of the Dayton Peace Agreement. The wording of Annex 10 of the Agreement only provided the OHR with very general powers of supervision (to "[m]onitor the implementation of the peace settlement")[75] and dispute resolution (to "[f]acilitate, as the High Representative judges necessary, the resolution of any difficulties arising in connection with civilian implementation"),[76] without specifically attributing any regulatory powers to the OHR. The decision of the Peace Implementation Council and the OHR to infer this authority from the final authority clause in Article V of Annex 10[77] is, at least, arguable in legal terms. Under the Agreement, the final authority of the OHR was linked to "theatre regarding the *interpretation* of [the] Agreement on the civilian implementation of the peace settlement".[78] This clause granted the OHR the authority to interpret its existing powers under the Agreement. But it did not, strictly speaking, grant the OHR the authority to imply all powers necessary to ensure the civilian

---

[73] Even the UN Commission of Inquiry noted in its 1994 Report that "the promulgation of the Somali Penal Code of 1962 as the criminal law in force in Somalia by the Special Representative of the Secretary-General was capable of being interpreted by the USC/SNA as an overstepping of the UNOSOM II mandate". See UN Doc. S/1994/653, p. 17.

[74] See above Part III, Chapter 11.

[75] See Article II, para. 1 a. of Annex 10.   [76] See Article II, para. 1 d. of Annex 10

[77] See above Part II, Chapter 8.   [78] Emphasis added.

implementation of the peace settlement. The assumption of direct executive and legislative powers by the OHR essentially marked a constructive
adjustment of the law to factual necessity, which received some backing
by subsequent international practice, but comes very close to a *de facto*
amendment of the Dayton Agreement.

1.3.1.3.3.   UNMIK

UNMIK's mandate was also drafted in ambiguous terms. UNMIK's legislative authority over Kosovo was not directly mentioned in the terms of Security Council Resolution 1244 (1999). This omission weakened UNMIK's
claim for regulatory authority in the legislative field. UNMIK derived its
legislative powers from an extensive interpretation of Resolution 1244
in Regulation No. 1/1999, which was backed by key Western powers and
was not contradicted by the Council itself.[79] However, the ambiguity in
the law has given rise to criticisms. It has been argued that some of the
regulatory acts adopted by UNMIK in the field of private law violated
the administration's duties under the "freezing clause" of the Hague
Regulations, because they modified the law applicable in the territory
in a substantive way.[80] This reproach was, in particular, formulated in
relation to the introduction of the UN Convention for the Sales of Goods
by UNMIK Regulation No. 2000/64,[81] the adoption of a framework of foreign investment by UNMIK Regulation No. 2001/3[82] and the creation of a
uniform regime for pledges over movable property by UNMIK Regulation
No. 2001/5.[83]

1.3.1.3.4.   CPA

Finally, uncertainties as to the scope of regulatory authority of international administrations have arisen in the context of the powers of the
CPA. Security Council Resolution 1483 (2003) entrusted the CPA with
broader responsibilities in the field of statebuilding, but failed to clarify
how legal contradictions between the "quasi-mandate" of the CPA under
UN law and the existing limitations under the laws of occupation could

---

[79] See Yannis, *The UN as Government in Kosovo*, at 70.
[80] See Irmscher, *Legal Framework of the Activities of the United Nations Interim Mission in Kosovo*, at 393–4.
[81] See UNMIK Regulation No. 68/2000 on Contracts for the Sale of Goods of 29 November 2000. The Regulation superseded the previously applicable law. See Section 1 (2) of Regulation No. 2000/68.
[82] See UNMIK Regulation No. 3/2001 on Foreign Investment in Kosovo of 12 January 2001.
[83] See UNMIK Regulation No. 5/2001 on Pledges of 7 February 2001.

be reconciled. The CPA adopted a practical stance on this issue. It solved the apparent contradiction inherent in the parallel application of SC Resolutions and the laws of occupation by citing a dual foundation for its regulations and orders: "relevant U.N. Security Council resolutions, including Resolution 1483 (2003)" and "the laws and usages of war".[84]

This double invocation of UN law and the laws of occupation approach allowed the CPA to pick and choose the legal regime which was most favourable to it in the particular case, and in particular to invoke exceptions from its obligations under international humanitarian law in the exercise of its administering functions. But this approach remained critical from a point of view of legal interpretation. One has to bend and stretch the language of the relevant SC Resolutions in order to imply from their wording an express indication of the Council's will to supersede the framework of the law of occupation in a general fashion. Two factors speak against such an assumption: the fact that the Council reaffirmed the continued application of the law of occupation to the CPA[85] and the fact that the Council failed to link the statebuilding tasks of the CPA to specific regulatory powers in the field,[86] such as is usually done in peacekeeping mandates through an authorisation to take "all necessary measures to fulfil [this] mandate".[87]

This leaves some doubts as to whether all of the regulatory acts adopted by the CPA had sufficient authority under international law. Some acts were at the edge of the regulatory discretion of occupying powers, but could be justified by an extensive interpretation of the existing law or by the necessity to maintain public order. These acts include: the increase of sentences for kidnapping, rape and offences involving damage to public infrastructure under CPA Order No. 1;[88] the

---

[84] See, for example, the preamble of CPA Order No. 2 on the Dissolution of Entities of 23 May 2003.

[85] See para. 13 of the preamble of SC Res. 1483 (2003) and para. 1 of SC Res. 1511 (2003).

[86] See para. 4 of SC Res.1483 (2003) ("calls upon").

[87] See, for example, para. 4 of SC Resolution 1272 (1999).

[88] See CPA Order No. 31 of 14 July 2003 (*Modifications of Penal Code and Criminal Proceedings Law*). This modification of existing Iraqi law was introduced in order to enhance security and stability for the Iraqi population and the CPA. See paras. 2 and 3 of the preamble of CPA Order No. 31. It may therefore be justified on the basis of Article 64, para. 1 ("penal laws ... may be repealed or suspended by the Occupying Power in cases where they constitute a threat to its security") or Article 64, para. 2 of the Fourth Geneva Convention. ("The Occupying Power may ... subject the population of the occupied territory to provisions which are essential to enable the Occupying Power to fulfil its obligations under the ... Convention, to maintain orderly government the territory, and to ensure the security of the Occupying Power.")

establishment of the Iraqi Civil Defense Corps;[89] the creation of Code of Military Discipline for the New Iraqi Army;[90] the introduction of provisions on the confiscation of property used in or resulting from crime involving the theft of natural resources or state property or damage of utility infrastructure;[91] the restriction of media activity under CPA Order No. 14;[92] and the establishment of the Trade Bank of Iraq and adoption of the Central Bank Law.[93]

Some other regulatory measures are doubtful in light of the limitations under the laws of occupation. One may have doubts as to whether the lawmaking practice of the CPA in the field of economic liberalisation fits under the umbrella of occupation authority.[94] The CPA adopted at least three regulatory acts which went beyond the restoration of basic conditions for public order. CPA Order No. 39 replaced the existing Iraqi law on foreign investment with new legislation which specified the terms and procedures for making foreign investments,[95] in order to "attract new foreign investment in Iraq".[96] CPA Order No. 74 introduced a

[89] See CPA Order No. 28 of 3 September 2003 (*Establishment of the Iraqi Civil Defense Corps*). This order may be justified by considerations of public order.

[90] See CPA Order No. 23 of 7 August 2003 (*Creation of a Code of Military Discipline for the New Iraqi Army*). See, in particular, para. 4 of the preamble. ("Acknowledging the need to ensure that the New Iraqi Army has a system of discipline to maintain order.")

[91] See CPA Order No. 25 of 31 August 2003 (*Confiscation of Property used in or resulting from certain crimes*).

[92] CPA Order No. 14 placed sweeping restrictions on the right of freedom of expression and the role of the media. It prohibited media organisations from publishing or broadcasting original or re-broadcasted, reprinted or re-syndicated material that "advocates the return to power of the Iraqi Ba'ath Party or makes statement that purport to be on behalf of the Iraqi Ba'ath party". See CPA Order No. 14 of 10 June 2003 (*Prohibited Media Activity*). This restriction may be linked to Article 53, para. 2 of the Laws and Customs of War on Land (Hague IV), which authorises occupying powers to seize "all appliances ... adapted for the transmission of news ... even if they belong to private individuals". Paragraph 2 of the preamble of CPA Order No. 14 makes this link. ("Noting the extensive specific authority granted to the CPA under the laws and usages of war for control of all appliances, whether on land, at sea, or in the air, adapted for the transmission of information, whether State or privately owned.")

[93] These acts may still be conceived as being measures necessary to "maintain the orderly government of the territory" in accordance with Article 64, para. 2 of the Fourth Geneva Convention.

[94] For a different view, see Kelly, *Iraq and the Law of Occupation*, at 160. ("[I]f the CPA worked with UN Special Representatives and one or more of the international financial institutions, such as the IMF or the World Bank, and the Interim Iraqi Authority, any type of economic restructuring would be permitted and would be under a Chapter VII mandate, which is binding on member states.")

[95] See CPA Order No. 39 of 19 September 2003 (*Foreign Investment*).

[96] See Section 2 of CPA Order No. 39.

new interim law on securities markets,[97] "recognising that some of the regulations concerning securities markets under the prior regime are not well-suited to a modern, efficient, transparent and independently regulated securities market".[98] Further, CPA Order No. 83 amended Iraqi Copyright Law No. 3 of 1971, in order to "ensure that Iraqi copyright law meets current internationally-recognised standards of protection and, and to incorporate the modern standards of the World Trade Organisation into Iraqi law".[99]

These measures introduced substantive changes in the domestic economic law of Iraq which were not directly linked to the regulatory objectives mentioned in Article 64, paragraph 2 of the Fourth Geneva Convention, but guided by long-term goals of economic reconstruction. Such measures are typically left to domestic authorities under the spirit of the laws of occupation. Secondly, all three orders were officially "marketed" as measures necessary to promote significant change to the Iraqi economic systems and the people of Iraq,[100] but were, at least partly, shaped by subjacent economic interests of the occupying powers. This is, in particular, evident in the case of CPA Order No. 39, which opened the gates for US corporations to assume key roles in the reconstruction of the Iraqi infrastructure.[101]

Moreover, some of the acts adopted against former members of the Ba'ath Party were controversial in legal terms. CPA Order No. 1 instituted blanket restrictions on access to employment in the public sector for former members of the Ba'ath Party[102] which were difficult to reconcile with the right of citizens to hold public office under Article 25 of

---

[97] See CPA Order No. 74 of 18 April 2004 (*Interim Law on Securities Markets*).

[98] See para. 5 of the preamble of CPA Order No. 74.

[99] See Section 1 of CPA Order No. 83.

[100] See para. 3 of the preamble of CPA Order No. 39 ("Acknowledging the Governing Council's desire to bring about significant change to the Iraqi economic system"), para. 3 of the preamble of CPA Order No. 74 ("Acknowledging the Governing Council's desire to bring about significant change to the Iraqi economic system as necessary to improve the condition of the people of Iraq") and para. 3 of the preamble of CPA Order No. 83 ("Acknowledging the Governing Council's desire to bring about significant change to the Iraqi intellectual property system as necessary to improve the economic condition of the people of Iraq").

[101] These decisions are problematic in light of the law of occupation because they are difficult to reverse by domestic authorities and are therefore likely to a have a long-term impact on Iraqi society. See Bali, *Justice under Occupation*, at 442–3.

[102] See Section 1 (2) of CPA Order No. 1 of 16 May 2003 (*De-Ba'athification of Iraqi Society*), which bans Ba'ath party members who had held the ranks of Regional Command Member, Branch Member, Section Member and Group Member, from future employment in the public sector.

the ICCPR.[103] Even more critical was CPA Order No. 30, which followed the precedent of the elimination of pension rights of Japanese officials after 1945, by adding that "Public Service Employees who lost their civil service positions as a result of the implementation of CPA Order No. 1 ... are not entitled to retirement benefits".[104] This practice is hardly compatible with the occupant's duty to respect minimum property rights.[105]

Thirdly, it is questionable whether the law of occupation provides an occupying power with sufficient legal authority to establish the legal framework and the rules of operation of a Property Claims Commission, as envisaged in CPA Regulation No. 12.[106] Both the Hague Regulations and the Fourth Geneva Convention oblige occupying powers to protect property rights.[107] Nevertheless, they do not expressly authorise occupying powers to implement general mechanisms for property restitution and compensation, including claims concerning confiscations and seizures carried out by former regimes.[108] Such decisions should be reserved to the decision of elected representatives of the administered territory.

---

[103] Article 25 reads: "Every citizen shall have the right and the opportunity, without any of the distinctions mentioned in article 2 and without unreasonable restrictions: (a) To take part in the conduct of public affairs, directly or through freely chosen representatives; (b) To vote and to be elected at genuine periodic elections which shall be by universal and equal suffrage and shall be held by secret ballot, guaranteeing the free expression of the will of the electors; (c) To have access, on general terms of equality, to public service in his country."

[104] See Section 5 of CPA Order No. 30 of 8 September 2003 (*Reform of Salaries and Employment Conditions of State Employees*).

[105] See above Part I, Chapter 4.

[106] See CPA Regulation No. 12 of 23 June 2004 (*Iraqi Property Claims Commission*).

[107] See Articles 46 and 56 of the Laws and Customs of War on Land and Article 53 of the Fourth Geneva Convention.

[108] CPA Regulation No. 12 created a property claims system which regulates not only the status of claims arising during the period of occupation, but also claims arising "between July 17, 1968 and April 9, 2003". See Article 9 of Regulation No. 12. It is doubtful whether the enactment of such far-reaching regulatory mechanisms with direct implications for property holders is indeed covered by authority "under the laws and usages of war, and consistent with relevant U.N. Security Council resolutions", as proclaimed by the CPA. The rationale given in paras. 3 and 4 of the preamble of Regulation No. 8 (*Delegation of Authority Regarding an Iraq Property Claims Commission*) is quite weak ("Recognising that as a result of ... Ba'athist policies, many individuals have conflicting claims to the same real property, resulting in instability, and occasional violence"). Kelly justifies the measures on the basis of a broad understanding of the term "public order and safety" in Article 43 of the Hague Regulations, based on the French translation of the text ("*l'ordre et la vie publique*"). See Kelly, *Iraq and the Law of Occupation*, at 147.

Finally, in two other critical cases, the CPA delegated "its" authority under "the laws and usages of war" and "relevant U.N. Security Council Resolutions" to the Iraqi Governing Council, in order to enable the latter to adopt regulatory acts. In CPA Order No. 48, the Coalition authorised the Governing Council "to establish [the] Iraqi Special Tribunal to try Iraqi national or residents accused of genocide, crimes against humanity, war crimes or violations of certain Iraqi laws, by promulgating [the] Statute [of the Iraqi Special Tribunal], the proposed provisions of which have been discussed extensively between the Governing Council an the CPA".[109] Similarly, the CPA delegated authority to the Governing Council in order to facilitate the establishment of the "Iraq Commission on Public Integrity as an independent body responsible for enforcing anti-corruption laws and public service standards".[110] Both delegations of authority were obviously undertaken with the aim of underlining the independence of the two institutions from the occupying powers. Nevertheless, both institutions rested on weak legal foundations, because they formally derived their authority from the law of occupation which operates on the principle of the continuity of domestic ownership over courts[111] and public institutions.[112]

1.3.1.3.5.   Lessons learned

At least two lessons may be learned from these four examples. First, it is essential for the credibility and success of transitional administrations that their authority be clearly defined in the UN Resolutions or contractual arrangements which form the constitutive instruments of the administration. Experience shows that it is ambiguous to leave the determination of competences and authority widely to the (self-)interpretation of international administrations. These powers have all too often been interpreted in an excessive fashion, making regulatory acts of international administrations open to challenges by domestic actors.[113]

Secondly, it must be examined more closely to what extent international actors are entitled to take decisions on behalf of local actors in the

---

[109] See Section 1 of CPA Order No. 48 of 9 December 2003 (*Delegation of authority Regarding an Iraqi Special Tribunal*).

[110] See Section 1 of CPA Order No. 55 of 27 January 2004 (*Delegation of Authority Regarding the Iraq Commission on Public Integrity*).

[111] See Article 64, para. 1 of the Fourth Geneva Convention.

[112] See *ibid.*, Articles 47 and 54.

[113] Such interpretations weaken the legitimacy of international administrations and may ultimately deepen the divisions within vulnerable and unstable political environments.

period of administration. International actors may legitimately counter governmental vacuums by addressing technical and security aspects of reconstruction, such as law enforcement, border control, monetary questions and institution-building. However, there are some core areas of statebuilding which should be left to domestic regulation.

1.3.2.   Definition of the applicable law

Further regulatory problems have arisen in the context of the definition of the applicable law. UNMIK, UNTAET and the CPA have used their normative powers not only to abrogate the existing law, but also to place the administered territories under a new legal order. All three administrations have deployed a similar methodology. They introduced a new hierarchy of norms in the territory under international administration, granting international acts ("Regulations" and "Directives" in the case of UNMIK and UNTAET, "Regulations" and "Orders" in the case of the CPA) precedence over all others law applicable in the territory.[114] They then defined the applicable law in the territory with reference to this new hierarchy of norms and/or a catalogue of applicable standards of international treaty law.[115] This methodology has raised various problems, both from the angle of authority and legal certainty.

1.3.2.1.   UNMIK

UNMIK Regulation No. 24/1999 (as amended by UNMIK Regulation No. 59/ 2000) defined four sources of law applicable in Kosovo: (1) Regulations promulgated by the SRSG; (2) the law in force in Kosovo on 22 March 1989; (3) the law applied in Kosovo between 22 March 1989 and 12 December 1999 (the date Regulation 1999/24 came into force), provided that it is not discriminatory; and (4) internationally recognised human rights standards. However, the relationship between these different bodies of law within the legal system of Kosovo remained unclear.[116]

The scope of applicable domestic law was defined in a contradictory way.[117] Section 3 of UNMIK Regulation No. 1/1999 of 25 July 1999 allowed for a broad application of laws applicable in Kosovo "prior to

---

[114] See Sections 2 and 3 of UNMIK Regulation No. 1/1999, as amended by Section 1 of UNMIK Regulation No. 25/1999 and UNMIK Regulation No. 54/2000, Sections 2 and 3 of UNTAET Regulation No. 1 and Sections 2 and 3 of CPA Regulation No. 1.

[115] *Ibid.* The CPA, by contrast, did not make reference to human rights standards.

[116] See also Knoll, *Beyond the "Mission Civilisatrice"*, at 284.

[117] See also Bohlander, *The Direct Application of International Law in Kosovo*, at 9.

24 March 1999", including FRY laws enacted after 22 March 1989. UNMIK Regulation No. 24/1999, by contrast, introduced a subsidiarity clause, which made it clear that "the law in force in Kosovo on 22 March 1989" should remain the primary source of applicable domestic law and that laws enacted "after 22 March 1989" should only apply as "an exception".[118] The relationship between these two Regulations had to be resolved through the enactment of additional UNMIK Regulations which repealed Section 3 of UNMIK Regulation No. 1999/1.[119]

Later, the hierarchy between the other sources of law remained unclear.[120] Section 1 (1) of Regulation No. 59/2000 stated that regulations "shall take precedence" over the 1989 law, while adding that the law in force in Kosovo after 22 March 1989 must comply with the internationally recognised human rights standards listed in Section 1 (3) of the Regulation. But the Regulation failed to specify whether human rights law takes precedence over domestic laws or UNMIK regulations. Section 1 (3) of Regulation No. 59/2000 merely stated that "in exercising their functions, all persons undertaking public duties or holding public office in Kosovo shall observe internationally recognised human rights standards" as defined in the Regulation.[121] The SRSG was forced to set out the meaning of Section 1 (3) in a letter to the Belgrade Bar Association, confirming that human rights law takes precedence over the provisions of the domestic law.[122]

This shortcoming was critical, because it gave rise to doubts as to the applicable law. In one case (the *Trajkovic* case), a district court composed of international and local judges even went so far as to hold crimes

---

[118] Section 2 of UNMIK Regulation No. 1999/24 stated: "If a court of competent jurisdiction or a body or person required to implement a provision of the law, determines that a subject matter or situation is not covered by the laws set out in section 1 of the present regulation [i.e. the law in force in Kosovo on 22 March 1989] but is covered by another law in force in Kosovo after 22 March 1989 which is not discriminatory and which complies with section 3 of the present regulation, the court, body or person shall, as an exception, apply that law."

[119] See Section 1 of UNMIK Regulation No. 25/1999 of 12 December 1999 (*Amending UNMIK Regulation No. 1999/1 on the Authority of the Interim Administration in Kosovo*).

[120] See also the analysis of the Ombudsperson Institution in Special Report No. 2, para. 9 *et seq.*

[121] See also the critical remarks by the Ombudsperson Institution noting that international human rights obligations "do not only attach to public officials in their official capacities, but to the institutions on behalf of whom they exercise their public functions". However, neither UNMIK Regulation No. 59/2000 nor any other law codifies this principle of state responsibility. See para. 11 of Special Report No. 2.

[122] See OSCE, *The Criminal Justice System in Kosovo* (February–July 2000), at 15.

against humanity prohibited under customary international law directly applicable in the context of domestic proceedings, although the international human rights standards referred to in UNMIK Regulation No. 24/1999 could not be used as a basis for establishing criminal liability.[123] A greater degree of legal clarity was only established in 2001 by the enactment of the Constitutional Framework for Provisional Self-Government, which stated that the "Provisional Institutions of Self-Government shall observe and ensure the internationally recognised human rights and fundamental freedoms" set forth in Chapter 3 of the document.[124]

However, legal certainty about applicable law in Kosovo continued. In 2004, the Kosovo Supreme Court was still forced to clarify a fundamental issue such as the hierarchy of norms between an UNMIK administrative direction and a domestic law.[125] In a case concerning the enforcement of a fine imposed by the Temporary Media Commissioner against the local newspaper Bota Sot (*Bota Sot* case), the Pristina District Court refused to apply UNMIK Administrative Direction No. 8/2003[126] on the ground of its alleged incompatibility with the Kosovo Law on Regular Courts.[127] The District Court argued that a law applicable in Kosovo must take precedence over an administrative direction which constitutes only a subsidiary source of law. The Supreme Court, however, followed the interpretation of UNMIK, according to which administrative directions prevail over other law applicable in Kosovo.

---

[123] See District Court Gjilan, *Case against Momcillo Trajkovic*, Judgment of 6 March 2001, Docket No. P Nr. 68/2000. The judgment is reproduced in part by Bohlander in Kosovo Legal Studies, Vol. 1 (2001), 7–8. See also the critical comment by Bohlander, *Direct Application of International Criminal Law*, at 8–12. On appeal, the Office of the Public Prosecutor of Kosovo pleaded for a reversal of the conviction for crimes against humanity. See Office of the Public Prosecutor of Kosovo, *Opinion on Appeals of Conviction of Momcillo Trajkovic*, 30 November 2001, p. 74, at www.ridi.org/adi/documents/trajkovicopp.pdf.

[124] Chapter 9.4.11 of the Constitutional Framework authorised the Special Chamber of the Supreme Court to examine whether "any law adopted by the Assembly is incompatible with this Constitutional Framework, *including the international legal instruments specified in Chapter 3 on Human Rights*" (emphasis added).

[125] See Supreme Court of Kosovo, *Bota Sot* case, AC 37/2004 of 20 August 2004. For a full account, see Everly, *Reviewing Governmental Acts of the United Nations in Kosovo*, sub. IV.

[126] See UNMIK Administrative Direction No. 8/2003 of 8 April 2003 (*Implementing UNMIK Regulation No. 2000/36 on the Licensing and Regulation of the Broadcast Media in Kosovo and UNMIK Regulation No. 2000/37 on the Conduct of Print Media in Kosovo*).

[127] See District Court of Pristina, *Bota Sot* case, E No. 1/2004 of 16 July 2004.

The operation of the legal system was further complicated by a number of practical obstacles.[128] When adopting new laws or regulations, UNMIK and the Provisional Institutions of Self-Government failed to indicate in clear terms which formerly applicable laws or provisions were replaced by the new legislation.[129] A number of legal documents issued by UNMIK were only promulgated in English. Furthermore, the transparency of the lawmaking process was compromised by the fact that many UNMIK documents entered into force directly upon promulgation, leaving domestic courts and interested parties little time to take note of changes in the law and to adjust their practice accordingly.[130] These factors created additional problems in identifying, interpreting and applying the proper law in Kosovo.

1.3.2.2.   UNTAET

UNTAET's definition of the applicable law was, in at least one aspect, clearer than UNMIK's legislation. It implied from the beginning of the mission that domestic authorities must act in conformity with the international human rights standards declared applicable by UNTAET.[131]

---

[128] The Parliamentary Assembly of the Council of Europe recommended that UNMIK improve the state of legal certainty by: "a. ensuring that UNMIK regulations state clearly which, if any, previous instruments they revoke or amend, and if amended, how so; ensuring that all legal instruments are published and disseminated to all concerned parties promptly and effectively, including by efficient use of information technology, with simultaneous high-quality translation into all official languages; c. allowing for an appropriate vacation legis following the promulgation of all legal instruments; d. accompanying the future promulgation of new legal instruments by appropriate training of all public officials concerned, in particular those working within the judicial system and law enforcement agencies, to prepare them for the entry into force of such documents." See para. 5 of Res. 1417 (2005).

[129] See also Human Rights Committee, *Concluding Observations Kosovo (Republic of Serbia)*, 25 July 2006, para. 8.

[130] See Council of Europe, Parliamentary Assembly, *Protection of Human Rights in Kosovo*, para. 28.

[131] Section 2 of UNTAET Regulation No. 1/1999 repeated the equivocal formula contained in UNMIK Regulation No. 59/2000 by providing that "all persons undertaking public duties or holding public office in East Timor shall observe internationally recognized human rights standards" listed in the Regulation. But Section 3 (1) of Regulation No. 1/1999 provided some more clarity by stating that: "[u]ntil replaced by UNTAET regulations or subsequent legislation of democratically established institutions of East Timor, the laws applied in East Timor prior to 5 October 1999 shall apply in East Timor insofar as they do not conflict with the standards referred to in section 2, the fulfilment of the mandate given to UNTEAT under United Nations Security Resolution 1272 (1999), or the present or any other regulation and directive issued by the

However, a fundamental dispute arose in the aftermath of the UN presence as to whether Portuguese law or Indonesian law was the domestic law applicable under UNTAET Regulation No. 1/1999, in the light of status of East Timor prior to the UN administration.[132] Section 3 (1) of the Regulation reads:

Until replaced by UNTAET regulations or subsequent legislation of democratically established institutions of East Timor, the laws applied in East Timor prior to 25 October 1999 shall apply in East Timor insofar as they do not conflict with the standards referred to in section 2, the fulfilment of the mandate given to UNTAET under United Nations Security Council resolution 1272 (1999), or the present or any other regulation and directive issued by the Transitional Administrator.

During the period of the UN administration it was understood that the expression "the laws applied in East Timor prior to 25 October 1999" in Regulation No. 1/1999 meant Indonesian law.[133] This understanding was obviously guided by practical concerns[134] and reflected in the practice of the UNTAET Serious Crimes Panels established under UNTAET Regulation No. 2000/15. But this interpretation was later challenged by the newly restored East Timorese Court of Appeal,[135] which found in a

Transitional Administrator." It follows therefore directly from the wording of the Regulation that all domestic laws must comply with UNTEAT regulations and the human rights standards declared applicable in East Timor by Section 2 of Regulation No. 1999/1.

[132] See generally Sylvia de Bertodano, *East Timor – Justice Denied*, Journal of International Criminal Justice, Vol. 2 (2004), 910.

[133] Courts in East Timor applied Indonesian law as the subsidiary law of East Timor.

[134] UNTAET's former Legal Advisor noted in 2001: "By Regulation No. 1999/1, UNTAET had, in effect, decided that the laws which applied in East Timor prior to the adoption of Security Council Resolution 1272 (i.e. the Indonesian laws) would apply mutatis mutandis, in so far as they were consistent with internationally recognized human rights standards, and in so far as they did not conflict with the mandate given to the mission by the Security Council, or with any other subsequent regulation promulgated by the mission. The decision was made solely for practical reasons: first, to avoid a legal vacuum in the initial phase of the transitional administration, and second to avoid a situation in which local lawyers, virtually all of whom had obtained their law degree at domestic universities, had to be introduced to an entirely foreign legal system." See Hans-Jörg Strohmeyer, *Policing the Peace: Post-Conflict Judicial Reconstruction in East Timor*, University of South Wales Law Journal, Vol. 24 (2001), 171, at 173-174.

[135] UNTAET Regulation No. 1/1999 is still relevant under East Timorese law following to the attainment of independence, because Section 165 of the Constitution of the Democratic Republic of Timor-Leste provides that "the laws and regulations in force in East Timor shall continue to be applicable to all matters except to the extent that they are inconsistent with the Constitution or the principles contained therein".

decision of 15 July 2003 that only Portuguese law was in force in East Timor on 24 October 1999.[136]

The Court held:

[T]here are abundant legal arguments ruling out the interpretation that the "the laws applied in East Timor prior to 25 October 1999" would be Indonesian law. East Timor was a Portuguese colony when it was invaded and occupied militarily by Indonesia in December 1975. As that invasion and occupation constituted a violation of international law, the United Nations never recognised that military occupation and, over the whole period of occupation, kept on classifying East Timor as a non-autonomous territory of Portugal. The Timorese people did not accept the military occupation by Indonesia and fought for 24 years until they got rid of it and saw their independence recognised by the international community. Therefore, from a legal viewpoint, the Indonesian administration, as well as Indonesian law, has never been validly in force in the territory of East Timor ...

In issuing Regulation 1999/1, UNTAET could not ignore that the Indonesian administration, as well as Indonesian law, has never been validly in force in the territory of East Timor, because the Indonesian occupation was in breach of international law ... [I]f UNTAET really wanted to apply Indonesian law in East Timor, it would have said so explicitly; and if it did not do so, it was because UNTAET did not want to subject to Indonesian law the territory and the people they had just liberated from the Indonesian yoke and were now under UN administration.

The Court concluded that, in accordance with international law, the reference to the "laws applied in East Timor prior to 25 October 1999" could only mean Portuguese law. The Court based this conclusion on the argument that Portugal had been "recognised by the international community, by the United Nations Security Council and by the East Timorese people as the administering Power of East Timor during the period between December 1975 and 25 October 1999", and that "Portugal itself, in turn [had] continued to assume clearly its responsibilities as the administering Power".[137]

---

[136] See Court of Appeal, *Prosecutor* v. *Armando Dos Santos*, Case No. 16/2001, Decision of 15 July 2003, at http://jsmp.minihub.org.

[137] The Court noted that in "its article 293, the Portuguese Constitution itself kept on affirming that 'Portugal remains bound by her responsibilities under international law to promote and guarantee the right to self-determination and the independence of East Timor' and that 'the President of the Republic and the Government (of Portugal) have the power to take all necessary action for achieving [these] objectives". Moreover, the Court made reference to a US decision rendered by the Columbia District Court on 10 September 2001 which had found in a civil case that Portuguese torts law continued to apply in East Timor under UNTAET Regulation No. 1999/1. See

The reasoning of the Court of Appeal is open to challenge in legal terms. The fact that UNTAET did not expressly mention Indonesian law in Regulation No. 1/1999 does not mean that it did not refer to it. UNTAET's legislative intent was obviously to declare Indonesian law applicable to East Timor. This follows from a close reading of the text. UNTAET referred to a number of Indonesian laws in Section 3 (2) of the Regulation and declared them inapplicable.[138] Furthermore, in Section 3 (3) of the Regulation, UNTAET abolished the death penalty in East Timor – a punishment which is provided in Section 340 of the Indonesian Penal Code, but is not included in Portuguese law. Any final doubts were removed by references to Indonesian law as the applicable law in later UNTAET Regulations.[139]

Moreover, the fact alone that the Indonesian occupation in 1975 was unlawful[140] did not rule out the possibility that Indonesian law could be applied on an interim basis as the applicable law by the UN administration. Even though Indonesia's presence in East Timor was not recognised as lawful, Indonesian law was applied *de facto* by East Timorese courts. The applicability of Indonesian law was even implicitly recognised by the UN, Portugal and Indonesia in Article 11 of the Agreement of 5 May 1999, which provided that "Indonesian laws in force upon the date of entry into force of this agreement... shall remain in force in SARET [Special Autonomous Region of East Timor]" in the case of a vote in favour of integration into Indonesia. One may therefore very well argue that UNTEAT had the authority to treat Indonesian law as the law applicable

---

US District Court for the District of Columbia, *Jane Doe* v. *Major General Johny Lumintang*, Civil Action No. 00-674, Judgment of 4 October 2001, at http://etan.org.news/2001a/10lumjudg.htm. The US Court qualified the Indonesian invasion as a violation of international law. Then, it noted: "To date, UNTAET has not passed any regulations addressing the torts of assault, battery and intentional infliction of emotional stress. Therefore, the law of Portugal with respect to these torts continues to apply in East Timor."

[138] They include the Law on Anti-Subversion, the Law Social Organisations, the Law on National Security, the Law on Mobilisation and Demobilisation and the Law on Defence and Security.

[139] For example, Section 53 (2) of UNTAET Regulation No. 2000/30 states: "The present regulation takes precedence over Indonesian laws on criminal procedure; provided, however, that any point of criminal procedure which is not specified in the present regulation shall be governed by applicable law as provided in Section 3 of Regulation 1999/1."

[140] It should be noted that the East Timor Parliament passed a Law on the Juridical Regime of Real Estate on 10 March 2003, the preamble of which calls the Indonesian occupation "illegal" ("illegal occupation of the Maubere Motherland by foreign powers").

under its administering mandate, even if it was for functional purposes only.[141]

The decision of the Court of Appeal in *Armando Dos Santos* had far-reaching implications for the entire judicial system.[142] It caused confusion about the applicable law in East Timor and called into question previous convictions pronounced by the Special Crimes Panels on the basis of Indonesian law. The judgment was followed by another decision of the Court of Appeal which also decided in favour of the applicability of Portuguese law as the subsidiary law in East Timor,[143] while the Special Panel for Serious Crimes maintained its jurisprudence.[144]

The difficulties of the East Timorese judiciary in interpreting and applying the legal regime of Regulation No. 1/1999 were further evidenced by the ruling of the Dili District Court in the *Kashiwagi* case.[145] In that case, the Court qualified an executive order issued by UNMIK as an arbitrary interference in the judicial process, without recognising that this order had been issued to supersede Indonesian law which contravened human rights standards.[146] Moreover, the Court found that UNTAET could not set aside law applicable under UNTAET Regulation No. 1/1999 by way of an executive decision, although Section 3 of UNTAET Regulation No. 1/1999 made the applicable law subject to "any other regulation and directive issued by the Transitional Administrator".[147]

---

[141] See also para. 7 of the Dissenting Opinion by Judge Jacinta Correira da Costa in *The Prosecutor* v. *Augustinho da Costa*, Case No. 3/2003 of 18 July 2003, at http://jsmp.minihub.org; Special Panel for Serious Crimes, *Prosecutor* v. *Joao Sarmento Domingos Mendonca*, Case No. 18a/2001, Decision on the defense motion for the Court to order the Public Prosecutor to amend the indictment, 24 July 2003, at 10–13, at http://jsmp.minihub.org.

[142] See De Bertodano, *East Timor – Justice Denied*, at 922. ("The result is that the whole structure of law in East Timor has been thrown into a state of uncertainty.")

[143] See Court of Appeal, *The Prosecutor* v. *Augustinho da Costa*, Case No. 3/2003 of 18 July 2003.

[144] Special Panel for Serious Crimes, *Prosecutor* v. *Joao Sarmento Domingos Mendonca*, Case No. 18a/2001, Decision on the defense motion for the Court to order the Public Prosecutor to amend the indictment, 24 July 2003, at 10–13.

[145] For further references regarding this case, see above Part IV, Chapter 14.

[146] The argument of arbitrary conduct is difficult to maintain, if one takes into account that UNTAET intervened to supersede criminal provision which contravened international human rights standards. One may argue that UNTAET did not require an express legal basis to act, because Section 3 (1) of Regulation No. 1/1999 stated that the applicable laws shall continue to apply "only in so far as they do not conflict" with international standards.

[147] The Court argued that Regulations prevail over executive orders under the hierarchy of norms applicable in East Timor.

1.3.2.3.   CPA

The determination of the applicable law by the CPA in Iraq raised a general authority problem. It is questionable whether an entity which formally qualifies as an occupying power, may make such general determinations as those contained in Section 2 of CPA Regulation No. 1, which stated that the "laws in force in Iraq as of April 16, 2003, shall continue to apply in Iraq, insofar as the laws do not prevent the CPA from exercising its rights and fulfilling its obligations, *or conflict with the present or any other Regulation or Order issued by the CPA*".[148]

This broad replacement of domestic law by CPA-established law is hardly in line with the traditional role and function of an occupying power envisaged by the Geneva law. The Fourth Geneva Convention operates on the principle that an occupant may set aside domestic law in specific cases (security, discharge of duties under the Convention, maintenance of the orderly government of the territory).[149] CPA Regulation No. 1 departed from this rule, because it allowed the CPA to abrogate domestic law where deemed appropriate by the authority. This move from circumscribed powers to a general entitlement to modify the law exceeded the classical framework of the laws of occupation.

1.3.2.4.   Lessons learned

International administrations may be authorised and entitled to modify the applicable law in the territory under administration. However, some of the methodologies deployed in international practice need to be revisited. A clearer distinction should be drawn between the different juridical frameworks under which choices of law reform are made. Large-scale modifications of the existing law, including changes in the hierarchy of norms and the incorporation of entirely new treaty systems into the domestic realm, should, if at all, only be introduced on the basis of a clear Security Council mandate or with domestic consent. Occupation-based frameworks, on the contrary, do not lend themselves to generalised solutions. They should avoid following the model applied by the CPA, which simply transposed UNMIK's and UNTAET's authoritative law reform approach to the multinational administration of Iraq, without paying adequate attention to the compatibility of such a methodology with the status as occupying powers.

---

[148] See Section 2 of CPA Regulation No. 1 of 16 May 2003.
[149] See above Part 1, Chapter 4.

Furthermore, in all three cases (Kosovo, East Timor, Iraq), the respective administrations rushed immediately into new solutions in the definition of the applicable law. This approach is questionable from a policy perspective. Except in the case of obvious injustices (e.g. ethnic discrimination) or gaps in the law, the introduction of new legal norms and structures does not offer quick answers to societal divisions. Experiences such as the *"Trajkovic"* judgment, the *Kashiwagi* case and the *Armando Dos Santos* ruling in East Timor suggest that it may be better to concentrate legal reform on the building of reliable domestic institutions before decreeing vast changes in the applicable law. Moreover, international administrations should consider whether targeted law reform of specific sectors (e.g. the criminal justice system) may produce better results than a wholesale reform of the applicable law in the territory.

1.3.3.   Judicial policy choices

Caution in the exercise of regulatory authority must go hand in hand with sensitivity towards the preservation of local cultures and traditions.

1.3.3.1.   Restraint in the import of foreign traditions
UNMIK's lawmaking practice set a rather questionable precedent in this regard. Kosovo's legal system stands in the tradition of continental civil law, including civil law legislation in the field of obligations,[150] property law[151] and civil procedure.[152] UNMIK deviated from this tradition by introducing a number of legislative acts which were evidently based on common law principles. UNMIK introduced the UN Convention on the International Sale of Goods into domestic law, without harmonising this legislation with the existing domestic law.[153] Furthermore, UNMIK adopted new legislation on business organisations and pledges which was based on common law concepts.[154]

The UN administration applied a similar methodology in the field of administrative law. UNMIK's regulatory practice in this area was shaped by wide administrative discretion – a feature typical of common law jurisdictions. The UN legislation in the field of public law granted, in

---

[150] See FRY Official Gazette 78/29.   [151] See FRY Official Gazette 80/6.
[152] See FRY Official Gazette 77/4.
[153] See UNMIK Regulation No. 68/2000 (*On Contracts for the Sale of Goods*).
[154] UNMIK legislation introduced the term "collateral" in the context of pledges and mortgages – a notion which caused confusion among local lawyers. See Centre for Applied Studies in International Negotiations (CASIN), *Administration and Governance in Kosovo: Lessons Learned and Lessons to be Learned*, January 2003, at 15.

particular, a wide degree of discretion to the SRSG or UNMIK in administrative application procedures,[155] which made it difficult to exercise judicial control over executive decisions.[156]

This legislative policy may be explained by the need to develop a rapid and controlled response to the gaps in domestic law. However, it resulted in a rather curious mixture of common law and civil law elements, which should not necessarily be reproduced in other contexts.[157]

It is questionable whether the development of a standard UN Criminal Code and a standard UN Administrative Code[158] could serve as a useful model to address legal vacuums and problems of UN lawmaking in societies in transition.[159] Such codes may, at best, help establish an "emergency" set of rules governing the relations between local actors and

---

[155] See also Section 2 (4) of UNMIK Regulation No. 16/2000 (*On the Registration and Operation of Political Parties in Kosovo*), which reads: "The minimum number of registered supporters required for a valid application for registration shall be 4,000. The Special Representative of the Secretary-General may, in his sole discretion, grant a political party exemption from the requirement of the minimum number of registered supporters (e.g. if such political party represents a relatively small ethnic community in Kosovo)."

[156] UNMIK Regulation No. 8/2000 (*On the Registrations of Businesses in Kosovo*) and UNMIK Regulation No. 33/2000 (*On Licensing of Security Services Providers in Kosovo*) illustrate this practice. Section 4 of Regulation No. 8/2000 listed a number of concrete grounds upon which applications for the registration of businesses may be rejected; however, it then added a general clause which permits the rejection of an application on "any other legitimate reason pertaining to public peace and order which the Special Representative of the Secretary-General deems sufficient". UNMIK Regulation No. 16/2000, which introduced a registration and licensing requirement for "any business providing security services in Kosovo", contained a broad clause on the refusal, suspension or revocation of security service licences and weapon permits, which stated that "[t]he [UNMIK] Department or the [UNMIK Police] Commissioner may, in their sole discretion, refuse to issue a License or permit to an applicant. The reason for the decision shall be communicated to the applicant". See Section 4 (1) lit. d) of UNMIK Regulation No. 16/2000. Section 5 (1) of Regulation No. 7/2001 on the Authorization of Possession of Weapons in Kosovo went even further by providing that "[t]he UNMIK Police Commissioner may, in his or her sole discretion, refuse to issue a Weapon Authorization Card to an applicant. No reason for refusal need be given to the applicant". See Regulation No. 7/2001 of 21 February 2001.

[157] See also Council of Europe, Parliamentary Assembly, *Protection of Human Rights in Kosovo*, para. 29.

[158] Such an approach is suggested by the *Report of the Panel on United Nations Peace Operations* (Brahimi Report), UN Doc. A/55/305-S/2000/809, 21 August 2000, paras. 80–3.

[159] See also the criticism voiced in the Report of the Secretary-General on the implementation of the report of the Panel on United Nations peace operations of 20 October 2000, UN Doc. A/55/502, para. 31. ("The group doubted whether it would be practical, or even desirable given the diversity of country specific legal traditions, for the Secretariat to elaborate a model criminal code, whether worldwide, regional, or civil or common-law based, for use by future transitional administration missions.")

UN administrations or military contingents. But they are ill-equipped to serve as generally applicable frameworks of law in a post-conflict society because they fail to address the particularities and culture differences which are inherent in any domestic system.[160] Previous practice appears to suggest that international administrations should encourage domestic institution-building and empower local authorities to make lawmaking choices instead of parachuting preconceived "package" solutions into the domestic legal system.[161]

1.3.3.2. Towards a fundamental questions doctrine in international territorial administration

One may also have doubts whether the grand strategic decisions of a post-conflict society, including decisions in relation to the prosecution of past atrocities and property restitution, should ultimately be made by a decision of international administrations, such as in Kosovo and East Timor, where UN administrators determined the essential features of criminal adjudication,[162] restitution[163] and reconciliation[164] by way of legislation.

The very process of lawmaking by international administrations bears structural ambiguities. In a democratic domestic setting, the process of lawmaking is shaped by a balancing of interests through the

---

[160] It is over-simplistic to claim that "where no law exists, a UN 'off the shelf' criminal law and criminal procedure is essential in any peace maintanance arsenal". But see Mark Plunkett, *Reestablishing Law and Order in Peace Maintenance*, in The Politics of Peace Maintenance (J. Chopra ed., 1998), 61, at 69. It is quite telling that even supporters of a Model Code of Criminal Justice for scenarios of transition are divided over its contents. While some advocates favour a merely criminal law and procedure-based approach, others support a complementary role for human rights standards. See Fairlie, *Affirming Brahimi*, at 1097–8.

[161] Less critical CASIN, *Administration and Governance in Kosovo: Lessons Learned and Lessons to be Learned*, at 18.

[162] See UNMIK Regulation No. 64/2000 (*On assignment of International Judges/Prosecutors and/or change of venue*), 15 December 2000; UNTAET Regulation No. 15/2000 (*Establishment of Panels with Exclusive Jurisdiction over Serious Criminal Offences*), 6 June 2000; UNTAET Regulation No. 16/2000 (*Organisation of the Public Prosecution Service in East Timor*), 6 June 2000.

[163] See UNMIK Regulation No. 23/1999 (*On the Establishment of the Housing and Property Directorate and the Housing and Property Claims Commission*), Section 2 (7) and UNMIK Regulation No. 60/2000 (*On Residential Property Claims and the Rules of Procedure and Evidence of the Housing and Property Directorate and the Housing and Property Claims Commission*), Section 3.1.

[164] See UNTAET Regulation No. 10/2001 (*Establishment of a Commission for Reception, Truth and Reconciliation in East Timor*), 13 July 2001. For a survey, see Stahn, *Accommodating Individual Criminal Responsibility and National Reconciliation*, at 952.

involvement of competing political forces and branches of government in the decision-making process. This balance of power is frequently distorted in the framework of international governance missions due to the concentration of authority on international authorities. Substantive decisions are regularly drafted and designed at the international level. Even participatory models of decision-making, involving mechanisms of consultation, power-sharing or devolution of authority[165] do not automatically restore full and representative local "ownership" over the process of lawmaking. Problems of representation arise where international administrations choose the very domestic leaders that participate in domestic decision-making bodies[166] or where domestic institutions are constituted after non-inclusive elections. Moreover, there is often a "structural inequality" between the domestic constituency and the *apparatus* of the administration in the immediate aftermath of conflict. The process of decision-making itself remains largely driven by the preferences and choices of international administrations, because international actors have the technical and legal know-how and the infrastructure to initiate measures of law reform.

International administrations have addressed these problems in a very formal manner, by limiting the scope of application of UN regulations until they are repealed by domestic institutions at the end of the period of administration.[167] Reality is, however, far more subtle. International legislation usually gains recognition and acceptance through institutional routine and practice under transitional administration. If one takes local ownership seriously, the hard question is whether transitional administration should be entitled at all to adopt legal acts with a long-term, and possibly irreversible, impact on the domestic population, such as the introduction of a liberal market economy in territories under transition or changes in criminal law and criminal procedure which lead to final convictions.[168]

---

[165] See below Chapter 16.

[166] For a criticism of the choice of leaders involved in the negotiation of the Bonn Agreement by the UN, see Suhrke, Karpviken and Strand, *Conflictual Peacebuildin*, at 63.

[167] See Section 4 of UNMIK Regulation No. 1/1999 and Section 4 of UNTAET Regulation No. 1/1999.

[168] See also Boutros Boutros-Ghali, *Agenda for Democratization*, Supplement to Reports A/50/332 and A/51/512 on Democratization, 17 December 1996, para. 10. ("While democracy can and should be assimilated by all cultures and traditions, it is not for the United Nations to offer a model of democratisation or democracy or to promote democracy in a specific case. Indeed, to do so could be counter-productive to the process of democratisation which, in order to take root and to flourish, must derive

As a general rule, international administrators should primarily seek to persuade domestic holders of public authority of the necessity and desirability of certain market reform and rule of law agendas, instead of decreeing such measures by way of international legislation.[169]

A key to success in statebuilding may lie in institution-building rather than in general lawmaking. This point was made clear by Paris, who recommended a strategy of "Institutionalization before Liberalisation" in international peacebuilding, noting that:

[w]hat is needed, in the immediate post-conflict period is not quick elections, democratic ferment, or economic 'shock therapy' but a more controlled and gradual approach to liberalization, combined with the immediate building of governmental institutions that can manage these political and economic reforms.[170]

The preservation of local ownership requires that fundamental decisions, which affect the domestic identity, the architecture of the local legal system or market liberalisation are taken by representative domestic institutions and administered by them. International administrations should therefore prioritise the establishment of domestic structures and local security, police and judicial institutions in their regulatory conduct. Furthermore, they should see their own role in law and market reform primarily as advisory, or balancing in nature. Far-reaching reforms of the political and economic system should not be imposed by international administrations in the immediate post-conflict phase, but managed by newly established domestic institutions or mixed national-international organs, acting in concert with international administrations.[171]

from the society itself. Each society must be able to choose the form, pace and character of its democratisation process. Imposition of foreign models not only contravenes the Charter principle of non-intervention in internal affairs, it may also generate resentment among both the Government and the public, which may in turn feed internal forces inimical to democratisation and to the idea of democracy.")

[169] See also Oellers-Frahm, *Restructuring Bosnia-Herzegovina*, at 224.

[170] According to Paris, this strategy has six components: awaiting conditions ripe for elections, creating electoral systems that foster moderation, promoting good civil society, controlling hate speech, adopting conflict-reducing economic policies and rebuilding effective state institutions. See Paris, *At War's End*, at 188.

[171] Such a call for moderation is in line with recent acknowledgments in the UN practice and contemporary academic thinking. See the Report of the Secretary-General on the rule of law and transitional justice in conflict and post-conflict societies, which acknowledges that "ultimately, no rule of law reform, justice reconstruction, or transitional justice initiative imposed from the outside can hope to be successful or sustainable" while emphasizing that "[t]he role of the United

A practical way to implement this policy in practice was highlighted by the Memorandum of Understanding on the EU Administration of Mostar, which obliged the EUAM to exercise its authority in conformity with the "overall principle of subsidiarity", taking "due account of the views and wishes of the local parties and population".[172] This principle merits further attention in other contexts. It would compel international administrations to examine *ex ante* whether the policy goals of lawmaking may be achieved in an equivalent or a more effective fashion through regulatory action by domestic institutions.[173]

1.4. Regulatory problems in specific fields

Additional lessons may be learned from the lawmaking practice in specific areas.

1.4.1. Property issues

It is widely accepted today that the solution of housing and property issues plays a crucial role in (post-)conflict situations.[174] International

---

Nations and the international community should be solidarity, not substitution". See also David Chandler, *Imposing the "Rule of Law": The Lessons of BiH for Peacebuilding in Iraq*, International Peacekeeping, Vol. 11 (2004), 3–4. For a call for moderation with respect to peacebuilding under the laws of occupation, see also Dinstein, *Legislation under Article 43 of the Hague Regulations*, at 12.

[172] See Article 7 (1) of the Memorandum of Understanding on the EU Administration of Mostar. For further disscussion, see above Part II, Chapter 8.

[173] It is occasionally even suggested that the role of international administrators should be limited entirely to the exercise of executive functions. Such a proposal, however, tends to misconstrue the problem. The fundamental legitimacy challenges of the exercise of regulatory authority by international actors do not arise from the form of the underlying act (e.g. law or executive decree), but from its impact on domestic policy choices. It is therefore more logical to confine the boundaries of regulatory action in terms of their subject matter.

[174] See Commission on Human Rights, Sub-Commission on the Promotion and Protection of Human Rights, Economic, Social and Cultural Rights: The Return of Refugees' or Displaced Persons' Property, UN Doc. E/CN.4/Sub.2/2002/17 of 12 June 2002, paras. 9–11, 14, 22–4. Housing and property restitution is essential to secure the safe return of refugees and displaced persons to their homes and places of origin. Moreover, fair housing and property legislation may temper the underlying causes of conflict, by eliminating the effects of conflict-related displacement, ethnic cleansing, or discriminatory expropriation or confiscation. The right of refugees and displaced persons to return to their homes is therefore increasingly recognised as a human right. Article 25 of the Universal Declaration of Human Rights and Article 11, para. 1 of the International Covenant on Economic, Social and Cultural Rights guarantee the right to adequate housing. Article 17, para. 1 of the ICCPR protects individuals from arbitrary or unlawful interference with their home. Furthermore, several UN Resolutions have recognised the right of refugees and displaced persons to return not

administrations have applied various models in practice in order to deal with this challenge.[175] Regulatory policies have ranged from moderate approaches to interventionist forms of engagement in property issues. Some of the internationally created dispute settlement mechanisms have produced encouraging results. But international frameworks have generally failed to reconcile international solutions with parallel responsibilities at the domestic level. Moreover, they have occasionally been over-ambitious, by imposing a return to the pre-conflict situation.

1.4.1.1. Different methodologies

UNTAES and UNTAET have shown modest recommitment to housing and property issues. This policy has been criticised as half-hearted and short-sighted from a human rights perspective.[176]

1.4.1.1.1. Too little?

UNTAET took a pragmatic stance on issues of return, by facilitating the transport of refugees to their preferred destination. But it failed to provide systematic incentives for refugee return and/or to establish a formal dispute settlement body to manage housing or property claims. This "hands-off approach" left a legal vacuum in which housing and property remained subject to competing claims, secondary occupation and forceful evictions.[177]

UNTAET intervened more extensively in the management of property restitution and reconstruction. The UN administration was directly

only to their country of orgin, but their "homes of origin". See the GA Resolution on International Co-operation to Avert New Flows of Refugees, UN Doc. A/RES/35/124 of 11 December 1980 ("right of refugees to return to their homesin their homeland"). See also para. 4 of SC Res. 361 (1974) of 30 August 1974, in which the Council urged the parties to "permit persons who wish to do so to return to their homes in safety". See also para. 7 of SC Res. 752 (1992) of 15 May 1992, in which the Council expressed its support to efforts "to assist the voluntary return of displaced persons to their homes". This approach was later confirmed by Article 1, para. 1 of Annex 7 of the Dayton Peace Agreement, which recognised the rights of refugees and displaced persons to return to their "homes of origin".

[175] For a detailed discussion, see also Caplan, *International Governance of War-Torn Territories*, at 68–85.

[176] For a critique of the approach taken by UNTEAS, see Jelena Smoljan, *International Administration and Socio-economic Policy: UNTAES and the Regulation of Housing and Property Issues*, at www.sgir.org/conference2004/papers/Smoljan%20%20International%20 administrations%20and%20socio-economic%20policy.pdf.

[177] See Daniel Fitzpatrick, *Land-policy in Post-Conflict Circumstances: Some Lessons from East Timor*, New Issues in Refugeee Research Working Paper No. 58, p. 4, at www.unhcr.ch/cgi-bin/texis/vtx/home.

charged with the facilitation of the "return of refugees and displaced persons to their homes of origin" under Article 4 of the Basic Agreement of 12 November 1995.[178] Furthermore, Articles 8 and 9 of this Agreement set a basic legal framework for property restitution and compensation.[179] UNTAES regulated the technical aspects of return, property repossession and reconstruction in an Agreement on Operational Procedures of Return,[180] which established mechanisms for the registration and processing of returns, an agency to facilitate the sale of property ("Land Bank") for persons who did not wish to move back to the Danube region[181] and general administrative arrangements for return. But UNTAES failed to settle two fundamental issues, namely the abolition of discriminatory Croatian property legislation[182] and the establishment of effective mechanisms of property recovery. Croatian policies discouraged Serbs from other parts of Croatia from returning to their homes.[183] The adjudication of property issues remained in the hands of the local administration and was hampered by ethnic differences.[184] These omissions resulted in the continued emigration of ethnic Serbs from the region[185]

---

[178] Article 4 reads: "The Transitional Administration shall ensure the possibility for the return of refugees and displaced persons to their homes of origin. All persons who have left the region or who have come to the Region with previous permanent residence in Croatia shall enjoy the same rights as all other residents in the Region."

[179] Article 8 provides that "[a]ll persons have the right to have restored to them any property that was taken from them by unlawful acts or that they were forced to abandon and to just compensation for property that cannot be restored to them". Article 9 reads: "The right to recover property, to receive compensation for property that cannot be returned, and to receive assistance in reconstruction of damaged property shall be equally available to all persons without regard to ethnicity."

[180] See Agreement of the Joint Working Group on Operational Procedures for Return, April 1997. The Agreement was signed by representatives of the Government of Croatia, UNTEAS and UNHCR in April 1997.

[181] The Land Bank purchased over 1,000 houses from Serb citizens who preferred to sell their property instead of returning to Croatia.

[182] The Croatian reconstruction programme contained discriminatory clauses. Funding for reconstruction did not pay adequate compensation to Serb citizens who had lost occupancy rights in former socially-owned property. Furthermore, the Croatian "Procedures for Individual Return of Persons who had abandoned the Republic of Croatia" discriminated against Serbs. The Croatian rules excluded Serbs residing in Croatia from the benefit of the procedure and made the return of Serbs residing in the FRY or Bosnia and Herzegovina dependent on the acquisition of Croatian citizenship.

[183] See Dobbins et al., *The UN's Role in Nation-Building*, at 118.   [184] *Ibid.*, at 119.

[185] It is reported that "[i]n 1999, the total Serbian population was only 51,000, down from a prewar total of 70,000 and a peak of 127,000 in 1995 when Serbs from Krajina and Western Slavonia sought refuge in the region". *Ibid.*, at 120.

and exposed UNTAET to the criticism of symptom-oriented conflict management in the area of property and housing issues.[186]

1.4.1.1.2. Too much?

The international community applied a diametrically opposed methodology in the cases of Bosnia and Herzegovina, Kosovo and Iraq. International actors regulated the framework and conditions of return and property restitution in great detail. Moreover, the resolution of property disputes was in each of the three cases entrusted to international(ised) property commissions, which were mandated to handle mass claims in a final and binding fashion for local authorities.[187]

The Dayton Agreement determined the formal parameters of property regulation and return in a detailed fashion in its Annex 7,[188] which stated that "[a]ll refugees and displaced persons have the right freely to return to their homes of origin ... [and] to have restored to them property of which they were deprived in the course of hostilities since 1991 and to be compensated for any property that cannot be restored to them".[189] Property claims were filed before an internationalised Commission on Real Property Claims of Refugees and Displaced Persons (CRPC),[190] which was vested with final decision-making authority[191] and authorised to "receive and decide any claims for real property in Bosnia and Herzegovina, where the property has not voluntarily been sold or otherwise transferred since April 1, 1992, and where the claimant does not now enjoy possession of that property".[192] Annex 7 specified even substantive guidelines for the handling of property claims by the Commission,[193]

---

[186] For a more favoroubble assessment, see Caplan, *International Governance of War-Torn Territories*, at 78–9, who qualifies UNTEAS as "a qualified success" in relation to return of refugees and displaced persons.

[187] See generally Leopold von Carlowitz, *Settling Property Issues in Complex Peace Operations: The CRPC in Bosnia and Herzegovina and the HPD/CC in Kosovo*, Leiden Journal of International Law, Vol. 17 (2004), 599.

[188] See generally Rhodri C. Williams, *Post-Conflict Property Restitution and Refugee Return in Bosnia and Herzegovina: Implications for International Standard-Setting and Practice*, NYU Journal of International Law & Politics, Vol. 37 (2005), 441.

[189] See Article 1, para. 1 of Annex 7.

[190] The Commission consisted of nine nembers, four of whom were appointed by the Federation, two by the Republika Srspka and the remaining three by the President of the European Court of Human Rights. See Article 9, para. 1 of Annex 7. See generally Hans van Houtte, *The Property Claims Commission in Bosnia and Herzegovina – A New Path to Restore Real Estate Rights in Post-War Societies*, in International Law: Theory and Practice, Essays in Honour of Eric Suy (K. Wellens ed., 1998), 552.

[191] See Article 12, para. 7 of Annex 7.   [192] See *ibid.*, Article 11.

[193] See *ibid.*, Article 12.

including the mandate "not [to] recognize as valid any illegal property transaction, including any transfer that was made under duress, in exchange for exit permission or documents, or that was otherwise in connection with ethnic cleansing".[194] The Commission processed property claims in a fast-track procedure which relied on available documentary evidence and a presumption that wartime transfers of property were involuntary and made under duress.[195]

UNMIK followed a similar pattern.[196] Rather than relying on municipal courts,[197] UNMIK decided to create a quasi-judicial body outside the domestic judicial system to deal with the massive property problems in Kosovo after the conflict.[198] On 15 November 1999, UNMIK established a Housing and Property Directorate (HPD) and an internationalised Housing and Property Claims Commission (HPCC)[199] by way of Regulation.[200] The Directorate served an administrative organ which mediated solutions in property disputes. The Commission acted as a quasi-judicial organ with exclusive jurisdiction over the majority of property disputes,[201] following detailed rules regulated by UNMIK.[202] The Commission was charged with the most controversial cases of residential property claims,

---

[194] See *ibid.*, Article 12, para. 3.

[195] See Commission for Real Property Claims of Displaced Persons and Refugees, *End of Mandate Report (1996–2003)*, at 3.

[196] See generally, OSCE Mission in Kosovo, Department of Human Rights and Rule of Law, *Property Rights in Kosovo 2002–2003*.

[197] Domestic courts were competent to deal with property issues under the law in force in Kosovo in 1989. But due to ethnic tensions and a breakdown of the court system in Kosovo, there was no domestic mechanism to resolve property and housing disputes in a fair and equitable manner. See von Carlowitz, *Crossing the Boundary from the International to the Domestic Legal Realm*, at 309.

[198] After 1989, Kosovo Albanians had lost their occupancy rights to socially owned properties as a result of discriminatory property laws imposed by the government in Belgrade. Furthermore, during the war and even after the arrival of UNMIK and KFOR, many properties have been destroyed and or abandoned. In many cases, this property was then illegally occupied. See generally Council of Europe, Parliamentary Assembly, *Protection of Human Rights in Kosovo*, para. 23.

[199] The Commission was initially composed of two international members and one local member.

[200] See UNMIK Regulation No. 23/1999 of 15 November 1999 (*On the Establishment of the Housing and Property Directorate and the Housing and Property Claims Commission*).

[201] The Commission was designed to resolve disputes over residential property in a legally binding fashion. It was authorised to issue binding and enforceable decisions, which were "not subject to review by any other judicial or administrative authority in Kosovo". See Section 2 (7) of UNMIK Regulation No. 23/1999 and Section 3 (1) of UNMIK Regulation No. 60/2000.

[202] See UNMIK Regulation No. 60/2000 of 31 October 2000 (*On residential property claims and the Rules of Procedure and Evidence of the Housing and Property Directorate and the Housing and Property Claims Commission*).

including claims for restitution of property lost through discrimination and claims by refugees who had lost their homes and wished to return or transfer their property.[203] It was authorised to decide claims on the basis of written submissions, including documentary evidence.[204]

The Iraqi Property Claims Commission established by CPA Regulation No. 12 falls within the same tradition, but with a slightly different focus from the institutions in Bosnia and Iraq. The Iraqi Commission is composed of domestic members and principally designed to resolve claims concerning the unlawful confiscation, seizure or expropriation of real property by the former governments of Iraq between 19 July 1968 and 9 April 2003, including "any taking that was due to the owner's or possessor's opposition to the former governments of Iraq, or their ethnicity, religion, or sect, or for purposes of ethnic cleansing".[205] The mandate of the Commission is therefore to a lesser extent geared towards the management of return of displaced persons than in the cases of the CRPC in Bosnia or the HPCC in Kosovo. But both the mode of establishment and the functioning of the Commission share significant parallels with the two precedents on the Balkans. The Commission was created on the basis of international authority. Moreover, it is construed as a mass claims mechanism, which acts as a substitute to domestic courts[206] in the adjudication of claims "involving immovable property, assets affixed to immovable property, easements or servitudes on property or land or other interests in real property" defined in the regulation.[207]

This proliferation of internationally created forums for the settlement of housing and property disputes generally marks a step in the right direction. The allocation of property and land to displaced persons and people who have been unlawfully deprived of their rights by a former regime is essential to facilitate returns and to restore security in post-conflict areas. First records confirm that the CRPC in Bosnia and the HPCC have worked relatively successfully.[208] The CRPC adopted over

---

[203] See Sections 2–6 of UNMIK Regulation No. 60/2000. UNMIK Regulation No. 23/1999 removed three categories of claims from the jurisdiction of the regular courts: those related to property rights lost due to discrimination or acquired through informal transactions between 24 March 1989 and 12 June 1999 and those related to property rights removed by illegal occupation.

[204] See Section 19 (1) of UNMK Regulation No. 60/2000. Section 19 (2) of the Regulation expressly prevents any party from giving oral evidence or argument before the Commission, unless it is invited to do so by the Commission.

[205] See Article 9 of CPA Regulation No. 9.

[206] Like the HPCC in Kosovo, the Iraqi Commission enjoys "exclusive jurisdiction".

[207] See Article 11 lit. c. of CPA Regulation No. 12.

[208] The CRPC in Bosnia officially completed its work on 31 December 2003. The HPCC in Kosovo accepted claims until 1 July 2003. It seeks to complete its mandate by 2005.

300,000 final and binding decisions during the course of eight years. The resolution of this caseload facilitated the return of thousands of refugees or displaced persons to their pre-war homes[209] through a procedure which might have taken more than a hundred years if conducted in traditional legal proceedings.[210] The HDP/HPCC received 29,000 claims until the expiry date for the filing of claims on 1 July 2003 and managed to resolve nearly 16,000 claims by February 2004.[211] This effort helped reverse some of consequences of ethnic discrimination and mass flight in Kosovo.[212]

Nevertheless, the way in which international actors approached property settlement in the three cases raises some concerns. All three mechanisms are regulated in an authoritative and detailed fashion, which leaves little room for flexibility and domestic adjustments. For example, both UNMIK and CPA legislation imposed a "straightjacket" on domestic societies by fixing strict and short deadlines for the filing of property claims before the Commissions.[213] Although guided by 'good intentions',[214] this emphasis on quick dispute resolution carries risks because it may set an unrealistic and internationally engineered timetable for property resolution which is difficult to meet in practice.[215]

Furthermore, the regulation of property settlements in the early phase of the post-conflict environment by international actors may create problems of representation. The criteria and conditions of post-conflict settlement were in all three situations decided by leaders of the former parties to the conflict (Bosnia), or international authorities (Kosovo,

---

[209] Until 31 May 2003, almost a million returns were registered. A comparison between the number of minority returns and the number of property repossessions suggests that the return of property was an influential factor in facilitating minority returns. See Commission for Real Property Claims of Displaced Persons and Refugees, *End of Mandate Report (1996–2003)*, at 28–9.

[210] See *ibid.*, at 3 and 36.

[211] See von Carlowitz, *Settling Property Issues in Complex Peace Operations*, at 611–12.

[212] However, many members of minority groups have only returned to sell their property. See HPD/HPCC, Quarterly Report January–March 2003, para. 11.

[213] Section 3 (2) of UNMIK Regulation No. 60/2000 determined that property claims under the Regulation must be "submitted to the Directorate before 1 December 2001". CPA Regulation No. 12 sets binding delays for the filing of property claims before the Commission (30 June 2005). See Article 11 lit. a. of CPA Regulation No. 12. Moreover, the Regulation stipulates that Iraqi courts shall deal with claims filed after that date according to the "principles included in [the] Statute" of the CPA. See Article 11 lit. b. of CPA Regulation No. 12.

[214] This agenda was obviously guided by the intention to foster the quick implementation of internationally funded donor programmes. See Commission for Real Property Claims of Displaced Persons and Refugees, *End of Mandate Report (1996–2003)*, at 4.

[215] See on the backlogs in the context of Kosovo, OSCE, *Property Rights in Kosovo 2002–2003*, at 29, 31–3.

Iraq), rather than by elected officials of the post-conflict societies them-selves.[216] This style of decision-making may create a friction between the ambitious standards of international actors and the will of local author-ities – a phenomenon which has become all too apparent in Bosnia and Kosovo.[217]

1.4.1.2. Lessons learned
Some further practical lessons may be learned from the practice of the CRPC and the HDCC.

1.4.1.2.1. The problem of exclusiveness
The experience of both Commissions shows, first of all, that property claims mechanisms should not necessarily be conceived as exclusive fo-rums for the resolution of housing and property claims in a post-conflict situation.

Mass claims bodies can process a large volume of property claims. However, not all claims lend themselves to resolution by a property com-mission relying on documentary or summary evidence. For example, a finding that a transfer of property was made under duress in a specific situation may require further evidence and litigation than typically al-lowed in a fast-track administrative procedure. These cases were there-fore later removed from the jurisdiction of the CRPC and transferred to domestic courts in Bosnia and Herzegovina by the Law on Implemen-tation of the Decisions of the Commission for Real Property Claims of Displaced Persons and Refugees.[218]

Furthermore, domestic courts may assume jurisdiction in areas which do not fall into within the competences of property commissions. In

---

216 Critically also towards the Bosnian case, David Chandler, *Imposing the "Rule of law": The Lesson of BiH for Peacebuilding in Iraq*, at 11.

217 This tension was obvious in the cases of Bosnia and Kosovo. In its final report the CRPC notes under "lessons learned" that "the settlements found in Annex 7 of the Dayton Peace Agreement faced their greatest challenges at the local level". See Commission for Real Property Claims of Displaced Persons and Refugees, *End of Mandate Report (1996–2003)*, at 37. For a survey of the problems of implementing Annex 7 in Bosnia, see von Carlowitz, *Settling Property Issues in Complex Peace Operations*, at 603–4.

218 See Article 13 of the Law on Implementation of the Decisions of the Commission for Real Property Claims of Displaced Persons and Refugees, imposed by the OHR on 27 October 1999. See Commission for Real Property Claims of Displaced Persons and Refugees, *End of Mandate Report (1996–2003)*, at 3. To attribute such types of claims immediately to alternative forums of adjudication may prevent such problems in future operations. See also the recommendation made by the Commission for Real Property Claims of Displaced Persons and Refugees, *ibid.*, at 38.

Kosovo, local courts decided to take on property cases which, in their view, fell outside the categories of exclusive jurisdiction of the property commissions.[219] This created problems of coordination between the HPD/HPCC and domestic courts.[220] Judicial forums may also take on a fundamental role in the enforcement of decisions of property commissions. The Human Rights Chamber assumed this function in the Bosnian context.[221] The OHR specified in the Decision on the Law on Implementation of the Decisions of the CRPR that "decisions of the Commissions ... carry the force of legal evidence that may be used in administrative, judicial or other legal proceedings".[222] When claimants addressed the Chamber, the latter qualified the failure to implement a binding decision of the CRPC as a violation of the law, giving rise to compensation[223] – an approach which might be repeated in other contexts.

---

[219] Soon after the adoption of UNMIK Regulation No. 23/1999, property claims triggered conflicts of jurisdiction between the Commission and local courts in Kosovo. See OSCE, The Impending Property Crisis in Kosovo, Report of 25 September 2000, at 2, available at www.oesce.org/kosovo. The Commission was not able to begin hearing claims until the promulgation of Regulation No. 60/2000 of 31 October 2000. Since no effective mechanism existed to deal with the majority of property claims, complaints were lodged with the local courts. These courts exercised jurisdiction. See Jean Christian Cady and Nicholas Booth, *Internationalized Courts in Kosovo: An UNMIK Perspective*, in Internationalized Criminal Courts and Tribunals (Cesare P. R. Romano, André Nollkaemper and Jann Kleffner eds., 2004), 59, at 72.

[220] UNMIK circulated an instruction to domestic courts, requiring them to suspend proceedings concerning property issues until the HPD/HPCC had either dealt with the claim or rejected it for lack of jurisdiction. However, this instruction did not solve the problem, because courts were not always aware of the fact that a claim was pending before the HPD/HPCC. See also OSCE, *Property Rights in Kosovo 2002-2003*, at 33.

[221] See Timothy Cornell and Lance Salisbury, *The Importance of Civil Law in the Transition To Peace: Lessons From the Human Rights Chamber for Bosnia and Herzegovina*, Cornell Journal of International Law, Vol. 35 (2002), 389, at 409.

[222] See Article 2 of the Law on Implementation of the Decisions of the Commission for Real Property Claims of Displaced Persons and Refugees, imposed by the OHR on 27 October 1999.

[223] The Human Rights Chamber held that the failure to take actions to remedy interference with property rights may itself constitute an unlawful interference by the government. See *Blentic v. Republic Srspska*, Decision of 5 November 1997, CH/96/17, para. 25. See also Human Rights Chamber, *Petrovic v. Federation of Bosnia and Herzegovina*, Decision of 9 March 2001, Case No. CH/00/6142, para. 49. ("[T]he Chamber recalls that the CRPC has issued a decision confirming Mr. Petrovic's right to repossess the house. The applicants have been unable to regain possession of the house in full due to the failure of the authorities of the Federation to deal effectively, in accordance with Federation Law, with Mr. Petrovic's request for the enforcement of the CRPC decision. The applicants have only repossessed one part of the house. However, according to the CRPC decision Mr. Petrovic has the right to repossess the whole house. It follows that the result of the inaction of the Federation is that the applicants cannot regain possession of the whole house and that there is an ongoing interference with the applicants' right to respect for their home.")

In future contexts, it may be advisable to conceive domestic courts and mass claims commissions as mutually reinforcing institutions. These two mechanisms may positively complement each other, provided that the mutual responsibilities are clear and provided that both entities cooperate and consult each other on competing claims so as to avoid parallel proceedings and risks of forum shopping.[224]

1.4.1.2.2.   The problem of enforcement

Issues of enforcement deserve immediate attention in peace-building frameworks. Annex 7 failed to provide the CRPC with enforcement power, leaving the responsibility for implementing CRPC essentially with domestic authorities. This shortcoming led to an enforcement gap[225] and public distrust in the functioning of the CRPC, which was only overcome by the imposition of new property laws in the two entities by the OHR, which obliged municipal authorities to enforce CRPC decisions[226] and the removal from office of public officials who refused to implement property legislation or otherwise blocked minority returns.[227] UNMIK, on the contrary, avoided some of these problems, by declaring HPD/HPCC decisions directly enforceable in Regulation No. 2000/60.[228] This experience indicates that the efficiency of the work of property commissions may be enhanced, if enforcement obligations are directly addressed in the mandate of the commission or in domestic implementing legislation.[229]

1.4.1.2.3.   The conflation of restitution and return

Finally, it is critical to view mass claims mechanisms primarily as an instrument to foster minority return.[230] Both UNMIK and the OHR regarded the property commissions essentially as a medium to reverse the

---

[224] See also Commission for Real Property Claims of Displaced Persons and Refugees, *End of Mandate Report (1996–2003)*, at 38. For a survey of the rather confusing framework in Kosovo, see also OSCE, *Property Rights in Kosovo 2002–2003*, at 32–5.

[225] See Commission for Real Property Claims of Displaced Persons and Refugees, *End of Mandate Report (1996–2003)*, at 7. See also Council of Europe, Parliamentary Assembly, *Protection of Human Rights in Kosovo*, para 23. ("Enforcement of HPD/CC decision is often impeded by security concerns, such as evicted illegal occupiers threatening bailiffs or returning owners or destroying the property being vacated.")

[226] See Articles 3 and 4 of the Law on Implementation of the Decisions of the Commission for Real Property Claims of Displaced Persons and Refugees, imposed by the OHR on 27 October 1999.

[227] See von Carlowitz, *Settling Property Issues in Complex Peace Operations*, at 604.

[228] See Sections 12 (6) and 13 (4) of Regulation No. 2000/60.

[229] For general concerns regarding the effectiveness of the HPD/CC, see Council of Europe, Parliamentary Assembly, *Protection of Human Rights in Kosovo*, para 23.

[230] For a discussion, see also Caplan, *International Governance of War-Torn Territories*, at 81–5.

consequences of conflict and segregation in order to restore the *status quo ante* before the outbreak of hostilities.[231] Consequently, both Commissions privileged property repossession over compensation in order to reinforce minority returns. There was, in particular, a widespread understanding that granting compensation to refugees and displaced persons would undermine the aim of the restoration of a multi-ethnic society "because it could persuade claimants to seek relocation in an area where they belonged to the majority group or to stay abroad".[232] The option of compensation remained largely a dead letter in practice.[233]

This conflation of property issues and return raises concerns.[234] Refugees and displaced must have an option to choose either restitution or return. This point was made clear by Annex 7 of the Dayton Agreement, which stated that compensation may be granted "in lieu of" property return.[235] To prioritise the option of return over compensation is problematic because it may "lead to *de facto* restriction of the freedom of movement of minority return candidates and their freedom to choose their residence".[236] It is, in particular, questionable whether displaced persons can be prevented from relocating elsewhere after reclaiming their property.[237]

---

[231] In Kosovo, the SRSG noted that UNMIK's "priority is to support returns to the places of orgin" and that the "concept of relocation ... will not be endorsed by UNMIK". See UNMIK, *The Right to Sustainable Return: Concept Paper*, May 2002, at 2. See generally on problems concerning the link between property rights and return in Kosovo, OSCE, *Property Rights in Kosovo 2002–2003*, at 65.

[232] See Commission for Real Property Claims of Displaced Persons and Refugees, *End of Mandate Report (1996–2003)*, at 3.

[233] In Bosnia, 25 per cent of the claimants opted for compensation. But no compensation fund was established. Commission for Real Property Claims of Displaced Persons and Refugees, *End of Mandate Report (1996–2003)*, Annex B ("Annex 7 Compensation Fund Unrealized"). Similar problems arose in Kosovo. See von Carlowitz, *Settling Property Issues in Complex Peace Operations*, at 612.

[234] See also Williams, *Post-Conflict Property Restitution and Refugee Return in Bosnia and Herzegovina*, at 543.

[235] Note that Article 4 of the Erdut Agreement mentioned only the option of the return of refugees and displaced persons "to their homes of origin".

[236] See Report by Alvaro Gil-Robles, Commisioner for Human Rights, *Kosovo: The Human Rights Situation and the Fate of Persons Displaced From Their Homes*, para. 26.

[237] UNMIK prioritised return to the place of origin on the basis of its mandate under SC Res. 1244. See UNMIK, Report *to the Human Rights Committee on the Human Rights Situation in Kosovo since 1999*, CCPR/C/UNK/1, 13 March 2006, para. 99. ("[A]lthough UNMIK understands the possibility that displaced persons might not prefer to the same place in Kosovo from where they were compelled to leave, in order to sustain the long-term goal of promoting a multi-ethnic society in Kosovo and to avoid politicising the plight of thousands of displaced persons, the priority remains to support returns to the place of origin.")

Problems of this type have arisen in the context of minority returns in Bosnia and Herzegovina and Kosovo. The OHR imposed a controversial "two-year rule" which made the right to buy an apartment "which was proclaimed abandoned" in the territory the federation dependent on the requirement of two years of residence after repossession.[238] This clause was introduced with the express intention to counter "the practice of some displaced persons of buying and selling their apartments without returning"[239] and made restitution dependent on return.[240]

A similar problem arose in Kosovo, where many claimants from minority groups resold their property after return in order to resettle in an area where they belonged to the majority.[241] UNMIK intended to end this practice by adopting Regulation No. 2001/17 which subjected the (re-)sale of residential property located in minority community to prior approval by the SRSG.[242] But this legislation encountered strong legal objections. It was criticised by the Ombudsperson Institution as violating recognised international standards (including Articles 8, 14 and 18 of the ECHR and Article 1 of the Additional Protocol to the Convention),[243] because it deprived displaced persons of their private property by prohibiting its alienation on ethnic grounds.[244]

---

[238] Article 8 a of the Federation Apartment Purchase Law provided that "[t]he occupancy right holder to an apartment which was proclaimed as abandoned by special regulations applied at the territory of [the Federation] during the period from 30 April 1991 to 4 April 1998 shall require the right to purchase the apartment in compliance with the provisions of this Law upon the expiry of a two year deadline after his or her reinstatement in the apartment".

[239] See OHR Press Release, Decisions on Federal Property Laws, 2 July 1999, at www.ohr.int/decisions/plipdec/default.asp?content_id=170.

[240] This two-year rule was abandoned in July 2001 and replaced by new legislation in both entities in order to ensure that refugees and displaced persons could "return and purchase the apartments to which they [had] occupancy rights without being discriminated against". See OHR, Press Release, High Representative Amends Entity Laws on Privatisation of Socially-Owned Apartments, 17 July 2001, at www.ohr.int//ohr-dept/presso/pressr/default.asp?content_id=4495. For a discussion, see Williams, *Post-Conflict Property Restitution and Refugee Return in Bosnia and Herzegovina*, at 515–23.

[241] See von Carlowitz, *Settling Property Issues in Complex Peace Operations*, at 613.

[242] See Section 1.2 of UNMIK Regulation No. 2001/17 of 22 August 2001 (*On the Registration of Contracts for the Sale of Real Property in Specific Geographical Areas of Kosovo*).

[243] See Ombudsperson Institution in Kosovo, *Special Report No. 5* (*On Certain Aspects of Regulation No. 2001/17 on the Registration of Contracts for the Sale of Real Property in Specific Geographical Areas of Kosovo*), para. 53.

[244] The Regulation used vague criteria to justify the prohibition, such as "security concerns arising from the sale of minority-owned property" or "evidence of an existing pattern of systematic sales of minority-owned property at prices which are

Such practices are problematic. A strict conditioning of property rights on return may not only institute new discriminations, but also severely curtail the protection of property as a legal right. In future contexts, the options of compensation and/or property resale should not be categorically discarded by property settlements.[245] It should, in particular, be ensured that displaced persons maintain a "choice to settle in a location other than one's previous place of residence".[246]

1.4.2.   Detentions

Some of the most critical examples of lawmaking by international administrations have occurred in the field of detentions. International administrations have been progressively involved in the apprehension and detention of criminals due to their increasing assumption of law and order functions within the framework of multidimensional peacekeeping operations. But they have adopted doubtful legal practices from a human rights perspective.[247]

International administrations have invoked questionable bases of authority in order to justify law enforcement measures. Moreover, they have failed to observe *habeas corpus* guarantees by carrying out preventive detentions and or by authorising detentions without judicial review. These problems have emerged in a range of cases.

1.4.2.1.   UNTAC

UNTAC decided to enact legislation in order to arrest, detain and prosecute persons engaged in violence disturbing the preparation and holding

unrealistic". Moreover it pursued a questionable policy goal. See Ombudsperson Institution in Kosovo, *Special Report No. 5*, para. 16. ("[T]he prohibition of the sale of residential property located in an ethnic minority community by a member of an ethnic minority to a member of an ethnic majority contravenes any of the principles underlying the notion of a 'democratic society' in Europe.")

[245] See also von Carlowitz, *Settling Property Issues in Complex Peace Operations*, at 613.

[246] See Alvaro Gil-Robles, Commisioner for Human Rights, *Kosovo: The Human Rights Situation and the Fate of Persons Displaced From Their Homes*, para. 26. This approach was later also defended by the OHR. See OHR, *A New Strategic Direction: Proposed Ways Ahead for Property Law Implementation in Time of Decreasing IC Resources*, 12 September 2002, para. 1, at http://ohr.int/plip/key-doc/default.asp?content_id=27904. ("Return of property is essential to the creation of durable solutions for refugees and displaced persons. This can take the form of either accrual return to the property or sale of the property in order to finance one's own local integration elsewhere, through purchase or rental of a home that does not belong to someone else.")

[247] For a critical appraisal of KFOR's and SFOR's practice, see Amnesty International, *The Apparent Lack of Accountability of International Peace-keeping Forces in Kosovo and Bosnia-Herzegovina*, April 2004, AI Index: EUR 05/002/2004, at 20-6.

of free and fair elections in Cambodia pre-election political violence.[248] In a directive issued in January 1993 (Directive No. 93/1) the SRSG authorised UNTAC officers "to issue warrants for the arrest and detention of suspects; ... and prosecute cases before the Cambodian trial courts and, where appropriate, before the appellate courts".[249] This decision to endow UNTAC police with investigative powers marked an innovation in the practice of peace-maintenance. But it remained controversial in legal terms. The establishment of UNTAC's Special Prosecutor's Office was criticised as exceeding UNTAC's mandate under the Paris Settlements. Local municipal courts refused to try Khmer Rouge and State of Cambodia officials after UNTAC arrests, arguing that these proceedings fell outside their jurisdiction.[250]

UNTAC's response to political violence remained largely improvised. UNTAC carried out several arrests. But the UN administration was unable to try these people because Cambodia's domestic judiciary lacked the independence and training to prosecute the perpetrators under the newly adopted provisions of UNTAC's sponsored Transitional Code of Criminal Justice.[251] The absence of fair and independent local courts led to an absurd situation. UNTAC suspended the applicability of its own Transitional Criminal Provisions[252] in order to detain SOC officials beyond forty-eight hours without judicial review. The UN Special Representative

---

[248] This decision was a response to increasing political violence in Cambodia in November and December 1992, which included murder, grenade attacks and other forms of political harassment.

[249] For the text of the Directive, see above Part II, Chapter 8.

[250] See Katayanagi, *Human Rights Functions of United Nations Peacekeeping Operations*, at 116. This legality dispute came even before the Security Council, which endorsed the decision of the SRSG, by "[d]emand[ing] that all Cambodian parties take the necessary measures to put an end to all acts of violence and to all threats and intimidation committed on political or ethnic grounds, and urg[ing] all those parties to cooperate with the UNTAC Special Prosecutor's Office in investigations of such acts". See SC Res. 810 (1993).

[251] The "Provisions Relating To The Judiciary And Criminal Law And Procedure Applicable In Cambodia During The Transitional Period" were adopted by the Supreme National Council on 10 September 1992.

[252] Article 13 of the Provisions Relating to the Judiciary and Criminal Law and Procedure Applicable in Cambodia During the Transitional Period provided that "[n]o one may be detained more than 48 hours without being brought before a judge, following charges filed by a Prosecutor. In the event that it is impossible to abide by this time limit due to prevailing transportation conditions in the region, the time may be extended to the extent strictly necessary to bring the detainee before a judge by the most rapid means available". Directive No. 93/1 declared "all relevant Provisions Relating to the Judiciary and Criminal Law and Procedure Applicable in Cambodia" applicable to UNTAC officers.

adopted a second directive (Directive No. 93/2) which provided that UN-
TAC prosecutors were not bound by the standards of the Transitional
Criminal Provisions until the establishment of independent courts.[253]
This Directive was not only contradictory to UNTAC's own human rights
policy, but also critical in terms of international fair trial standards because it denied suspects the right to judicial review of decisions relating
to detentions.[254]

1.4.2.2.   UNOSOM II

UNOSOM II faced similar legality challenges in Somalia. UN officials
claimed that suspects could be detained "when the public authorities
[had] reasonable grounds to believe that the detainee represents a threat
to public order". But UNOSOM failed to provide a legal basis for its practice of "preventive detentions. There was, as Kelly, an Australian army
major, put it, "no indication as to what the detainees could be charged
with, under what law, or which forum would hear the charges".[255] Moreover, the determination of the length of detention which was said to be
"temporary" or limited to "a reasonable period of time" remained within
the discretion of the UN authorities. These legal gaps were later criticised by the Commission of Inquiry to Investigate Armed Attacks on
UNOSOM II, which noted in its report:

UNOSOM II faced a human rights dilemma when it had to detain people in
executing its mandate. In the absence of courts, detentions came to be seen as
arbitrary, exposed UNOSOM to criticism and had to be stopped ... If the United
Nations operates in a country [that is without a government] ... , it necessarily
has to bear responsibility for at least some of the basic state concerns traditionally appertaining to a government.[256]

---

[253] Directive No. 93/2 of 3 February 1993 authorised the continued detention of suspects
in UNTAC custody without judicial review until a competent court was identified to
deal with these cases.

[254] UNTAC officials hoped to solve the matter as promptly as possible. But reportedly, no
such court was identified until the termination of UNTAC's mandate in September
1993. See Basil Fernando, *The System of Trial under the Vietnamese-Khmer Model
(1981–1993)*, at www.ahrchk.net/pub/mainfile.php/cambodia_judiciary/114/. Critical also
Katayanagi, *Human Rights Functions of United Nations Peacekeeping Operations*, at 116.

[255] See Kelly, *Restoring and Maintaining Order*, at 83.

[256] See *Report of the Commission of Inquiry Established Pursuant to Security Council Resolution
885 (1993) to Investigate Armed Attacks on UNOSOM II Personnel which Led to Casualties
Among Them*, UN Doc. S/1994/653 of 1 June 1994, paras. 251–3.

1.4.2.3. UNMIK and KFOR

UNMIK repeated questionable detention practices in its own lawmaking practice.[257] The SRSG adopted several regulations, which failed to comply with *habeas corpus* guarantees enshrined in the ECHR and the ICCPR, by placing security interests over individual rights protection. UNMIK Regulation No. 2/1999 authorised the temporary detention or restriction on the freedom of movement of individuals who may pose a "threat to public peace and order".[258] UNMIK used this Regulation to carry out preventive detentions of individuals, arguing that these persons posed a "threat" to "a safe and secure environment" or to "public safety and order".[259] This practice was difficult to reconcile with the standards of the ECHR.[260] Under Article 5, paragraph 1 of the ECHR, a threat to public order constitutes only a sufficient ground to justify the detention of a person, if there is a concrete suspicion that the person will commit an offence.[261] A "preventive detention" for general security purposes is not allowed under Article 5, paragraph 1.[262]

Moreover, the SRSG issued a number of Executive Orders extending detention periods without providing the detainee or his or her legal counsel with information about the grounds for the continued detention, and without giving the detainee the opportunity to challenge the lawfulness of the detention.[263] This practice was doubtful in the light

---

[257] For a criticism, see also Chesterman, *You, The People*, at 115–18, Caplan, *International Governance of War-Torn Territories*, at 64–5.

[258] See Section 2 of UNMIK Regulation No. 2/1999. According to Section 1 (2) of the Regulation such a threat to public peace and order may be posed by any act that jeopardises the rule of law, the human rights of individuals, public and private property and the unimpeded functioning of public institutions.

[259] The imprecise wording of the Regulation caused problems in practice. The Regulation was also used to carry out evictions of illegally used public property. See von Carlowitz, *Crossing the Boundary from the International to the Domestic Realm*, at 310.

[260] See also Ombudsperson Institution, *Special Report No. 3 on the Conformity of Deprivations of Liberty under "Executive Orders" with Recognised International Standards* of 29 June 2001, para. 10.

[261] See Article 5 (1) lit. c. which states: "No one shall be deprived of his liberty save in the following cases ... c) the lawful arrest or detention of a person effected for the purpose of bringing him before the competent legal authority on reasonable suspicion that of having committed an offence or when it is reasonably considered necessary to prevent his committing an offence or fleeing after having done so."

[262] See ECHR, *Jecius v. Lithuania*, Application No. 34578/97, 31 July 2000. See also on the case-law Frowein and Peukert, *Europäische Menschenrechtskonvention* (1996), Article 5, at 111.

[263] See generally Abraham, *The Sins of the Savior*. On UNMIK's position, see UNMIK News, *UNMIK Refutes Allegations of Judicial Bias and Lack of Strategy*, 25 June 2001, at www.unmikonline.org/pub/news/nl98.html.

of international human rights standards. Article 5, paragraph 3 of the ECHR and Article 9, paragraph 3 of the ICCPR require that anyone who has been arrested or detained must be brought promptly before a judge in order to determine the lawfulness of the arrest or the detention. In addition, Article 5, paragraph 4 of the ECHR and Article 9, paragraph 4 of the ICCPR demand that all persons who have been deprived of their liberty by arrest or detention be entitled to take proceedings by which the lawfulness of their detention may be decided speedily by a court. National authorities are therefore under an obligation to provide a forum by which the lawfulness of a detention may be challenged during the entire period of pre-trial detention. This includes, *inter alia*, the duty to secure a periodic review of the detention order within short intervals.[264]

The preventive detentions carried out by UNMIK and the absence of sufficient judicial control over deprivations of liberty were criticised by the OSCE[265] and by the Ombudsperson Institution, which issued a Special Report which qualified UNMIK's executive detentions as violations of the ECHR.[266] UNMIK responded to this criticism by creating a Detention Review Commission to review extra-judicial detentions based on executive orders.[267] The Commission was vested with authority to make final decisions on the legality of administrative detentions by UNMIK.[268] But it continued to fall short of meeting the requirements of a "Court in the sense of para. 4 of Article 5 ECHR",[269] because it was composed of "three international members appointed by the Special Representative

---

[264] See European Court of Human Rights, Judgment of 25 October 1989, *Bezicheri*, Ser. A, No. 164, para. 24 *et seq*. The UN Body of Principles for the Protection of All Persons under Any Form of Detention or Imprisonment also provide for a right to a review of continued detention by a court or other authority at reasonable intervals. See Principles 11 (3) and 39.

[265] See OSCE Review of the Criminal Justice System, *September 2001–February 2002*, at 45. See also OSCE, Report No. 6, *Extension of Custody Time Limits and the Rights of Detainees: The Unlawfulness of Regulation 1999/26*, 29 April 2000, available at www.osce.org/kosovo. See also Amnesty International, *Federal Republic of Yugoslavia (Kosovo), Amnesty International's Recommendations to UNMIK on the judicial system*, February 2000, available at www.amnesty.org.

[266] See Ombudsperson Institution on Kosovo, *Special Report No. 3 on the Conformity of Deprivations of Liberty under "Executive Orders" with Recognized International Standards*, paras. 25, 29.

[267] See UNMIK Regulation No. 2001/18 on the Establishment of a Detention Review Commission for Extra-Judicial Detentions Based on Executive Orders of 25 August 2001.

[268] See Sections 6 and 7 of UNMIK Regulation No. 18/2001.

[269] See Ombudsperson Institution in Kosovo, *Special Report No 4, Certain Aspects of UNMIK Regulation No. 2001/18 on the Establishment of a Detention Review Commission for Extra-Judicial Detentions Based on Executive Orders*, para. 18. See also OSCE Report, *Review*

of the Secretary-General"[270] and was thus under substantial control of the executive.[271] This deficit set off calls for a further reform of UNMIK's accountability structure,[272] including the option of judicial review over UNMIK Acts.[273]

Similar problems arose in connection with detentions carried out by KFOR. The Commander of KFOR (COMKFOR) interpreted paragraphs 7 and 9 of Security Council Resolution 1244 as a title to carry out arrests and detentions without judicial review.[274] COMKFOR introduced a KFOR Detention Directive on 9 October 2001 (COMFOR Directive 42), which allowed KFOR to detain persons subject to the control of a Detention Review Panel designated by COMKFOR and chaired by the legal advisory body of KFOR. The Directive contained a number of safeguards against unlawful detention. KFOR detention was conceived as an option of last resort, to be carried in cases where persons "constitute a threat to KFOR or a safe environment in Kosovo and [where] civilian authorities are

---

of the Criminal Justice System, September 2001–February 2002, at 37. ("[T]he Commission established under UNMIK Regulation 2001/18 could not be considered a tribunal in the meaning of Article 6 ECHR and in the meaning of Principle 5 of the Basic Principles on the Independence of the Judiciary.")

[270] See Section 2 (1) of UNMIK Regulation No. 18/2001.

[271] See Ombudsperson Institution in Kosovo, *Special Report No. 4*, para. 17. ("The Regulation thus substitutes a 'Commission' under substantial control of the executive whose act is being contested for a 'court' whose independence, impartiality and full jurisdiction has never been questioned.")

[272] See OSCE Report, Kosovo, *Review of the Criminal Justice System*, March 2002–April 2003, at 31–3. UNTAET paid greater respect to the observance of human rights standards in the area of detentions. The regulatory framework of UNTAET was largely based on the ICCPR. UNTAET Regulation No. 30/2000 on Transitional Rules of Criminal Procedure contained detailed regulations of the procedures to be followed at all stages of criminal proceedings. Pre-trial detention was allowed only for crimes carrying a sentence of over one year. See Section 12 a. 1 of UNTAET Regulation No. 11/2000, as amended by UNTAET Regulation No. 14/2000. Furthermore, Section 20 (9) of Regulation No. 30/2000 provided that an investigating judge shall review the detention of a suspect every thirty days. In addition, Section 47 of the Regulation introduced a special *habeas corpus* procedure, allowing the challenge of unlawful arrest or detention.

[273] See Commission for Democracy Through Law, *Opinion on Human Rights in Kosovo*, paras. 92–132; Council of Europe, Parliamentary Assembly, Resolution 1417 (2005), para. 5.

[274] SC Res. 1244 (1999) authorised UN member states and relevant international organisations "to establish the international security presence in Kosovo ... with all necessary means to fulfil its responsibilities under paragraph 9". Paragrraph 9 (c) charged the security presence with "establishing a secure environment in which refugees and displaced persons can return home in safety, the international civil presence can operate, a transitional administration can be established, and humanitarian aid can be delivered".

unable or unwilling to take responsibility for the matter".[275] Further-more, KFOR committed itself generally to respect relevant international human rights standards, *inter alia*, by prohibiting arbitrary detention, requiring that detainees be informed of the reasons for detention in their own language, granting detainees access to a legal representative and allowing them to make submissions on their detention.[276]

However, KFOR's executive detentions remained based on military au-thority[277] and fell short of meeting the standards of Article 5 of the ECHR and Article 9 of the ICCPR, even five years after the adoption of Security Council Resolution 1244 (1999) and despite the establishment of civilian police force in Kosovo.[278] This practice generated criticisms and calls for a revision of the KFOR Detention Directive. The Parliamen-tary Assembly of the Council of Europe recommended, in particular, two changes in order to enhance compliance with *habeas corpus* standards, namely to "remov[e] the qualification 'every effort will be made' from the requirement to comply with all relevant human rights standards" under the Directive, and to "reinforc[e] the authority and independence of the Detention Review Panel by involving it in all detention decisions of the Commander of KFOR" and by "ensuring that it composed exclu-sively by independent lawyers".[279]

1.4.2.4. INTERFET

An emergency solution to deal with detentions in the aftermath of con-flict was adopted in the case of East Timor. INTERFET, the UNTAET prede-cessor force deployed under Security Council Resolution 1264 (1999), was faced with a large number of crimes, including serious offences such as violent assault, rape and murder, without being vested with an adequate legal mechanism to deal with arrests and detentions. The Status of Forces Agreement with Indonesia authorised INTERFET to arrest and detain per-sons, but required that the detainees be handed over to the Indonesian

---

[275] See Section 4 of COMKFOR Directive 42.
[276] Section 7 of the Directive stated that "[n]o one shall be subjected to arbitrary detention". Sections 3 (f) and 7 (z) stressed that KFOR detention "will be as open to the appropriate bodies of the international community as possible" and "that detention facilities will establish and publish an independent inspection mechanism".
[277] Section 2 (e) of Directive 42 stated expressly that "[i]t must be noted that this authority to detain is a military decision, not a judicial one".
[278] For a criticism, see Amnesty International, *Serbia and Montenegro (Kosovo): The Legacy of past human rights abuses*, 1 April 2004, AI Index: EUR 70/009/2004, at 10–11; OSCE Mission in Kosovo. *Kosovo: Review of the Criminal Justice System*, March 2002–April 2003, at 33.
[279] See para. 6 of SC Res. 1417 (2005).

police.[280] This mechanism was unsatisfactory because the civilian legal and administrative order in East Timor had collapsed. Detainees were promptly released by the Indonesian police after being taken into custody. INTERFET therefore established a temporary detention centre (Detention Management Unit, DMU) on 21 October 1999, which served as an interim legal mechanism to deal with persons suspected of having committed serious criminal offences pending the re-establishment of a civil judiciary.[281] Individuals taken in custody by INTERFET were held in the Detention Centre and granted an initial hearing within twenty-four hours. Furthermore, the detention order was to be reviewed within ninety-six hours by the Reviewing Authority of the DMU, which could extend the detention indefinitely.[282]

The conduct of trials was reserved to UNTAET. A Detainee Ordinance declared Indonesian law as the criminal law applicable in East Timor, while suspending all provisions of Indonesian law that were incompatible with the DMU's own provisions on detention and arrest.[283] In the absence of any other legal basis for the establishment of an interim arrest and detention mechanism, which would under normal circumstances fall within the exclusive competence of the local authorities, the creation of the DMU and the Detainee Ordinance were based on the framework of the Fourth Geneva Convention.

1.4.2.5.   CPA

The practice in Iraq revived the critique of the detention policy in a territory under foreign administration.[284] In accordance with Article 29 of the Fourth Geneva Convention, the US and the UK retained legal responsibility for detainees under their custody.[285] But the CPA defined the general framework governing detention. It set out standards for detention in two memoranda: CPA Memorandum No. 2 (Management of Detention and Prison Facilities) and CPA Memorandum No. 3 (Criminal Procedures).

---

[280] See Kelly, McCormack, Muggleton and Oswald, *Legal Aspects of Australia's Involvement in the International Force for East Timor*, at 130.

[281] See Report of the Secretary-General of 4 October 1999, para. 13. For a full account, see Kelly, McCormack, Muggleton and Oswald, *Legal Aspects of Australia's Involvement in the International Force for East Timor*, at 131 *et seq.*

[282] See also Strohmeyer, *Collapse and Reconstruction of a Judicial System*, at 51, note 22.

[283] For a discussion of the Ordinance, see Kelly, McCormack, Muggleton and Oswald, *Legal Aspects of Australia's Involvement in the International Force for East Timor*, at 133.

[284] For an examination of the detention practice by the CPA in light of the security challenges in Iraq, see Kelly, *Iraq and the Law of Occupation*, at 153–4.

[285] Article 29 of the Fourth Geneva Convention provides for the responsibility of the party to the conflict "in whose hands protected persons may be". *Ibid.*, at 153.

This regulatory framework was modelled on the regime of the Fourth Geneva Convention.[286] It was meant to be consistent with detention obligations under international humanitarian law. But it contained a number of shortcomings from a human rights perspective, which exposed it to criticism.[287] The most critical points were: length of detention, lack of judicial review of detention and limited access to the outside world.

CPA Memorandum No. 3 created a two-track system for detention. It provided that "criminal detainees" (that is, persons who are suspected of having committed criminal acts) should be handed over to Iraqi authorities "as soon as reasonably practicable".[288] But members of the coalition remained entitled to detain persons held as "security detainees" (that is, persons who were considered to pose a threat in the context of an ongoing armed conflict) in light of the mandate set out Security Council Resolution 1546, which allowed the Multinational Force to resort to "internment where this is necessary for imperative reasons of security".[289] CPA Memorandum No. 3 set out the conditions of arrest and detention of "security internees", including a right to review of detention of persons held for longer than seventy-two hours.[290]

This regime created different regimes of detention. Suspects held within detention facilities controlled by the Iraqi Ministry of Justice came within the scope of application of the Iraqi Code of Criminal Procedure, according to which detentions had to be reviewed by an examining judge within twenty-four hours after arrest.[291] Suspects held by Coalition forces, by contrast, were initially only entitled to review by a military lawyer.[292]

---

[286] Section 7 (1) of CPA Memorandum No. 3 stated that the "operation, condition and standards of any internment facility established by Coalition forces shall be in accordance with Section IV of the Fourth Geneva Convention".

[287] See Amnesty International, *Beyond Abu Ghraib: Detention and Torture in Iraq*, 6 March 2006, AI Index: MDE 14/001/2006, at http://web.amnesty.org/library/index/engmde140012006.

[288] See Section 5 (1) of CPA Memorandum No. 3.

[289] See *ibid.*, Section 6 (1).   [290] *Ibid.*

[291] See Article 123 of the Iraqi Code of Criminal Procedure.

[292] This system deviates from Principle 11 of the UN Body of Principles for the Protection of All Persons under Any Form of Detention or Imprisonment, which specifies that "a person shall not be kept in detention without being given an opportunity to be heard promptly by a judicial or other authority". A military lawyer is not necessarily an "other authority" within the meaning of UN Principles, whose "status and tenure should afford the strongest possible guarantees of competence, impartiality and independence". See Amnesty International, *Memorandum on concerns relating to law and order*, sub. 4.2.

Moreover, CPA Memorandum No. 3 allowed the possibility of indefinite detention of certain "security detainees". The Memorandum provided that persons who are placed in internment after 30 June 2004 "must be either released from internment or transferred to the Iraqi criminal jurisdiction not later than 18 months from the date of induction".[293] But it did not extend these obligations to detainees placed in internment before the handover of power to the Iraqi authorities on 30 June 2004. This framework left room for an indefinite detention of "security detainees" captured under the period of occupation until 30 June 2004. An administrative review board (the Combined Review and Release Board), comprising representatives from Iraqi ministries and members of the Multinational Force, was created in order to review the conditions for release or continued detention.[294] However, a large number of persons were held for a longer period of time without being charged or tried and without a possibility to challenge their detention before a judicial authority.[295]

This practice was severely criticised by UN bodies. The UN Secretary-General recalled in a report to the Security Council that "prolonged detention without access to lawyers and courts is prohibited under international law, including during states of emergency".[296] UNAMI expressed concerns regarding the "mass arrests carried out during security and military operations" and stressed the "urgent need to provide remedy to lengthy internment for reasons of security without adequate judicial oversight"[297].

Further difficulties arose in the context of access rights of detainees. CPA Memorandum No. 3 referred to Section 4 of the Fourth Geneva Convention, which contains some basic provisions concerning contact with relatives and legal counsel.[298] But according to guidelines issued by the US military, "security detainees" were not entitled to receive visits

---

[293] See Section 6 (5) of CPA Memorandum No. 3.
[294] This mechanism was criticised by UNAMI as establishing "exceptional procedures ... which are in violation of Iraqi emergency law, criminal law and international standards governing the protection of civilians under the law". See UNAMI, *Human Rights Report, 1 July–31 August 2005*, September 2005, para. 6, at www.uniraq.org/documents/HR%20Report%20Sep%20Oct%2005%20EN.PDF.
[295] See Amnesty International, *Beyond Abu Ghraib: Detention and Torture in Iraq*, sub. "Without charge or trial – detention by the Multinational Force".
[296] See para. 2 of the Report of the Secretary-General pursuant to paragraph 30 of Resolution 1546 (2004), UN Doc. S/2005/373 of 7 June 2005.
[297] See UNAMI, *Human Rights Report, 1 July–31 August 2005*, September 2005, para. 6.
[298] See Article 116 of the Fourth Geneva Convention.

by relatives or legal counsel during the first sixty days of internment.[299] Access to official delegates of the ICRC could be denied "for reasons of imperative military necessity", as provided for in Article 143 of the Fourth Geneva Convention.[300] A stricter application of the right of detainees to access to counsel and to communicate with the outside world[301] might have helped prevent some of the atrocities in detention facilities such as the Abu Ghraib Prison Centre.[302]

1.4.2.6. Lessons learned

The practice of UNTAC, UNOSOM, UNMIK, KFOR and the CPA makes it clear that international administrations must devote greater attention to a fair and independent implementation of the conditions of arrest and detention specified in international treaty law and the UN Body of Principles, even when operating in an unstable (post-)conflict environment.

Some of the detention problems encountered by international administration may be addressed by a stronger proceduralisation of *habeas corpus* rights in frameworks of transitional administration, including increased access to judicial review. A clearer distinction must, in particular, be drawn between military and civilian responsibilities. "Internal" systems of review, such as review mechanisms carried out by military lawyers or inspection authorities created by armed forces, may be

---

[299] See Amnesty International, *Beyond Abu Ghraib: Detention and Torture in Iraq*, sub. "Visits by relatives", "Visits by legal counsel".

[300] See Section 6 (8) of CPA Memorandum No. 3. It is reported that US authorities invoked "military necessity" in January 2004 to the ICRC access to eight internees held in Abu Ghraib. See Amnesty International, *Beyond Abu Ghraib: Detention and Torture in Iraq*, sub. "Visits by monitoring bodies".

[301] See Principle 15 of the UN Body of Principles.

[302] It is quite telling that the CPA reinforced the standard of review of detentions in Iraq after the Abu Ghraib scandal. On 27 June 2004, the CPA created an Ombudsman for Penal and Detention Matters by CPA Order No. 98 of 27 June 2004 and a Joint Detainee Committee by CPA Order No. 99. The Joint Committee is a political body, designed to ensure that "operations comport with applicable law and human rights standards". Section 2 of CPA Order No. 99 states the Committee shall be composed of representatives of the Multinational Force in Iraq, the Iraqi Interim Government and states exercising custody over detainees. Its responsibilities include "[e]stablishing criteria for the detention of individuals, including the basis for release or transfer to Iraqi jurisdiction or custody", "[m]onitoring and if necessary proposing standards and safeguards for the conditions and rights of detainees, including processes for determining initial detention decisions and reviewing such decisions" and "[c]onsidering issues relating to the prosecution of criminal detainees and proposing investigative, evidentiary or other measures that will enhance successful prosecution". See Section 3 of CPA Order No. 99.

acceptable in the immediate context of military operations where no other judicial authorities are available, such as in the context of INTER-FET.[303] However, stricter requirements apply when international operations pass from the phase of military enforcement action to the stage of civil administration. In this situation, international administrations are required to ensure that all suspects have access to an independent judicial authority after arrest and to review the lawfulness and necessity of their detention.

Existing practice offers at least two valid institutional models to address this obligation. International administrations may confer functions of judicial review to domestic or international(ised) courts,[304] or they may create special detention "panels composed of international judges to review ... the lawfulness of detentions of individuals" – as recommended in Special Report No. 3 of the Ombudsperson Institution in Kosovo.[305]

1.4.3. Independence of the judiciary

The UN engagements in Kosovo and East Timor indicate that international administrations may make a valid contribution to the restoration of basic judicial functions in (post-)conflict societies.[306] However, international administrations must adjust their regulatory policies more closely to the principle of the impartiality and independence of the judicial bodies, as required by Article 6 (1) of the ECHR, Article 14 (1) ICCPR and the UN Basic Principles on the Independence of the Judiciary.[307]

---

[303] This topic might deserve further attention in the context of the development of Rules of Engagement for United Nations Peacekeeping Operations by the UN Department of Peacekeeping Operations. See also Chesterman, *You, The People*, at 121–2.

[304] See also OSCE Report, *Review of the Criminal Justice System*, September 2001–February 2002, at 43. ("OSCE recommends the amendment of UNMIK Regulation 2000/47, to allow local courts to review and decide on ... administrative actions or decisions of the UNMIK authorities.")

[305] The Ombudsperson recommended that the SRSG "should, no later than 20 July 2001, convene one or more panels composed of international judges to review, on an urgent basis, the lawfulness of detentions of individuals currently deprived of their liberty under Executive orders or any other form of executive instruction, decree or other decision, such review to conform with the requirements of Article 5 of the European Convention on Human Rights".

[306] See generally Strohmeyer, *Collapse and Reconstruction of a Judicial System*, at 60; Chesterman, *You, the People*, at 181.

[307] See Basic Principles on the Independence of the Judiciary, adopted by the 7th UN Congress on the Prevention of Crime and the Treatment of Offenders, held in Milan in August–September 1985 and endorsed by GA Res. 40/32 of 29 November 1985 and GA Res. 40/146 of 13 December 1985.

1.4.3.1.   (Mis-)conceptions of judicial independence in legal practice

The very task of judicial reconstruction creates a conflict of interest for transitional administrations. International administrators are, on the one hand, charged with the de-politicisation and reform of the local judiciary, which requires involvement in and supervision of the judiciary. At the same time, they are required to respect basic notions of the rule of law in the exercise of their mandate, including the independence of the judiciary.[308] This balance has not always been kept in practice.

1.4.3.1.1.   UNMIK

UNMIK displayed a curious understanding of the independence of the judiciary. It inserted a clause in its Regulation No. 24/1999 on the Law Applicable in Kosovo, which encouraged courts in Kosovo to "request clarification from the Special Representative of the Secretary-General in connection with implementation of the present regulation".[309] This provision has been of some use in light of the confusion over the hierarchy of norms and the applicable law under UNMIK Regulations.[310] But it carried an ambiguous undertone. It suggested that courts in Kosovo could seek advice on the interpretation of the law applicable in Kosovo "in the exercise of their functions". Such a conflation of authority is critical from a systemic point of view. It runs counter to the separation of powers and the independence of the judiciary, and is somewhat reminiscent of the political practice of former socialist countries, where the executive controlled the interpretation of the law.[311]

Further problems arose in the context of the appointment and removal of judges and prosecutors from office.[312] International judges were formally employed as UNMIK civil employees by the administration, with short terms of office.[313] This employment policy created an appearance

---

[308] For an analysis, see also Carsten Stahn, *Justice Under Transitional Administration: Contours and Critique of a Paradigm*, Houston Journal of International Law, Vol. 27, No. 2 (2005), 312.

[309] See Section 2 of UNMIK Regulation No. 24/1999 of 12 December 1999 (*On the Law Applicable in Kosovo*).

[310] See above 1.3.2, Definition of the applicable law.

[311] For a critique, see Frowein, *Notstandsverwaltung von Gebieten durch die Vereinten Nationen*, at 43.

[312] See generally Michael E. Hartmann, *International Judges and Prosecutors in Kosovo*, United States Institute of Peace, Special Report No. 112 (2003), at www.usip.org/pubs/specialreports/sr112.pdf.

[313] This role of supervision was even reflected in UNMIK's job descriptions, which noted that international judges and prosecutors act "under the overall supervision of the Deputy Special Representative of the Secretary-General for Police and Justice and the Director of the Department of Judicial Affairs".

of undue executive inference[314] because it gave UNMIK direct control over the extension of contracts. One of the implications of UNMIK's policy was that non-extension of contracts could be used as a means of holding judges accountable for specific conduct undertaken within the term of their offices[315] – a result which is difficult to reconcile with the independence of the judiciary.[316]

The procedure for the removal from office was based on rather vague criteria, leaving UNMIK a wide margin of discretion.[317] National and international judges and prosecutors could be removed from office for such indeterminate grounds as "serious misconduct" or "failure in the

---

[314] The European Commission on Human Rights established strict guidelines in judicial independence in its case-law. It noted that it is irrelevant whether actual bias has occurred because even the appearance of outside pressure may compromise judicial independence. See European Commission on Human Rights, *B Company v. The Netherlands*, 19 May 1994. See also OSCE Report, *Review of the Criminal Justice System*, September 2001–February 2002, at 27.

[315] See OSCE Report, *Review of the Criminal Justice System*, September 2001–February 2002, at 25; *Review of the Criminal Justice System*, March 2002–April 2003, at 28.

[316] UNMIK tried to justify its control over the appointment and assignment of international prosecutors and judges by the temporary nature of their deployment. UN officials invoked a rather curious justification in defence of UNMIK's policy, noting that: "[a]dministrative independence and security of tenure are essential for the justice system which UNMIK must build for Kosovo's future, but the [international judges and prosecutors] are not part of that future. They are a special force for intervention to enable UNMIK to administer impartial justice at this early phase, when the local judiciary is too weak to be able to withstand the societal pressures on it in the aftermath of the conflict. Their appointment and deployment is therefore highly tactical, and must be under the United Nations' direct control (while remaining quite independent of the local judiciary, who play a major role in the administration of the Kosovo justice system). They are in Kosovo, like all UNMIK international staff, only for a short time, to help build a new society in Kosovo, and then to leave." See Jean Christian Cady and Nicholas Booth, *Internationalized Courts in Kosovo: An UNMIK Perspective*, in Internationalized Criminal Courts and Tribunals, at 76. This distinction between strategic appointment and functional independence is artificial. When acting in their judicial capacity as judges, international judges are as much part of the judiciary as domestic judges. It is discriminatory to devise a system based on double standards. Moreover, it is especially important in unstable post-conflict situations that the public can have full confidence in the individual judge making his or her judgment impartially and without having to consider negative consequences for his or her position. Last, but not least, it is difficult to argue that a judge "who goes through a re-appointment process every six months of every year, with no information on the process and the criteria of that re-appointment" can be considered as independent. See also OSCE Report, *Review of the Criminal Justice System*, September 2001–February 2002, at 34.

[317] Note that local judges in Kosovo were appointed by the SRSG, following recommendations by the Kosovo Judicial and Prosecutorial Council (KJPC) established by UNMIK Regulation No. 8/2001 of 6 April 2001. The SRSG was entitled to remove local judges and prosecutors from office without prior consultation of the KJPC.

due execution of office".[318] Furthermore, local judges and prosecutors could not be reappointed by UNMIK for reasons of moral integrity or discriminatory practices – criteria that normally warrant disciplinary measures.[319]

Finally, UNMIK introduced a questionable case management policy for the assignment of cases to international judges under UNMIK Regulation No. 64/2000. International judges were not assigned to a case by a roster system built on neutral pre-established criteria, but by way of approval of the SRSG.[320] This policy is critical in light of the principle of judicial independence, which seeks to protect independence against any doubts of extraneous influence.[321]

1.4.3.1.2. CPA

The CPA repeated many of these pitfalls in its practice. CPA Order No. 13 tied the appointment of judges of the Central Criminal Court of Iraq to one-year contracts approved by the CPA.[322] Furthermore, the Order granted the CPA an undue possibility of influence over the judiciary by providing the Chief CPA Administrator with the possibility to refer cases to court.[323] Additional difficulties emerged in the context of the establishment of the Iraqi Special Tribunal.[324] The Statute granted non-Iraqi nationals a rather obscure right to act "as observers to the Trial Chambers and to the Appeals Chambers", including the possibility to monitor the "protection by the Tribunal of general due process of law

---

[318] The persons concerned did not even have to be heard by the SGSR before their removal from office.

[319] See Section 6 (1) of UNMIK Regulation No. 8/2001. See also OSCE Report, *Review of the Criminal Justice System*, September 2001–February 2002, at 33.

[320] Under Regulation No. 64/2000, the SRSG maintains the right to determine both, the ultimate decision on assignment of international judges to the proceedings, and the particular officials assigned to a case.

[321] See also OSCE Report, *Review of the Criminal Justice System*, September 2001–February 2002, at 28–9 on the assignment of judges under Regulation No. 64/2000. ("Although intended to eliminate the appearance of actual bias in sensitive ethnic or political cases, the Regulation actually established a parallel mechanism of judicial assignments, whose dependence on … the SRSG is not consistent with the standards of institutional independence set forth in the relevant international instruments.") For a criticism of UNMIK Regulation No. 8/2001, see *ibid.*, at 33–4.

[322] See Amnesty International, *Memorandum on concerns relating to law and order*, AI Index 14/157/2003, July 2003, sub. 7.

[323] See CPA Order No. 13, Section 19.

[324] See Statute of the Iraqi Special Tribunal, 10 December 2003, at www.cpa-iraq.org/human_rights/Statute.htm, Article 5.

standards".[325] This type of supervision conflicts with the principle of the independence of judges, which seeks to protect judges from non-judicial oversight in the exercise of their judicial functions.

1.4.3.2. Lessons learned

International administrations must pay greater respect to judicial independence in their practice. The restoration of public confidence in the independent work and functioning of the domestic judiciary is one of the core functions of judicial reconstruction. This endeavour can only succeed if international administrations themselves refrain from exercising undue political control over court proceedings by interfering in pending proceedings or "advising" domestic courts on the applicable law. Such practices are counterproductive. Overstated executive control runs counter to the very essence of sustainable judicial reconstruction because it undermines the independence and credibility of domestic institutions. Moreover, it creates the impression that the work of the judiciary remains driven by politics rather than by law.

The existing record may be improved by a stronger decentralisation of administrative control over the judiciary. Two types of measures may make a positive difference. First, the process of appointment of international prosecutors and judges and the procedure of renewal of their contracts may be entrusted to independent institutions. Judges and prosecutors might be selected from an internationally established roster of judges and placed under the administrative supervision of institutions which are independent from the international administration. This function might be exercised by regional organisations in the immediate post-conflict phase, and could be assumed by domestic institutions at a later stage.[326]

Secondly, the assignment of judges to cases should be effected on the basis of a general, random-based procedure which prevents individual and politicised assignments.[327] This safeguard is necessary in order to ensure that judicial proceedings maintain the appearance of independent adjudication in their routine functioning.

---

[325] See ibid., Article 6 lit. b. of the Statute.

[326] See also OSCE, Review of the Criminal Justice System, September 2001–February 2002, at 43.

[327] Ibid., at 43. See also Principle 14 of the Basic Principles on the Independence of the Judiciary which states that the assignment of cases to judges is a matter of internal judicial administration.

1.5. Conclusions

The experiences in territorial administration from Cambodia to Iraq establish very clearly that the regulatory practice of international administration is often imperfect. Mistakes have frequently been repeated, be it by the same or different legal entities. Problems emerged typically due to shortcomings in preparation, misconceptions about the necessary degree of authority of transitional administrators or a lack of commitment to the observance of international legal standards. At least three lessons may be learned from the existing practice.

Lawmaking by international administrations can only succeed if it is sensitive to domestic particularities. This applies in relation to both the degree of authority exercised by international actors and the law created by them. In this context, less may sometimes be more. A focus on strong local ownership and domestic institution-building from the beginning may enhance sustainability in the long term. Moreover, some moderation in enactment of international legal standards may increase the chances of internalisation. International administrations may provide a better service to societies in transition by facilitating a domestic dialogue over universal values (democracy, human rights, gender equality) rather than predetermining domestic choices.[328]

Secondly, if international actors undertake efforts in judicial reconstruction, they must do so in keeping with *habeas corpus* guarantees and the requirements of judicial independence. To apply double standards in a process of transitional administration is not only incompatible with the role and function of international administrators, but is damaging to the process of state-building as such. It sets the domestic judiciary on the wrong track from its very start and it undermines the authority of transitional authorities as well as the willingness of the domestic population to respect the law.

Finally, international practice suggests that the action of international transitional authorities must itself be subject to some form of scrutiny in order to avoid abuse. This may be achieved in three ways: through inter-institutional checks and balances, resulting from the participation of domestic actors in the process of lawmaking, through the creation of special independent institutions to monitor the exercise regulatory authority by international administrations and through judicial review by domestic courts.

---

[328] This criticism has, in particular, been in the context of the constitutional process in East Timor. See Chesterman, *You, The People*, at 141–2.

2. Involvement in constitution-making

Constitution-making is a more severe form of intervention in the domestic legal system than other forms of regulatory action. Constitutions are usually permanent or even partly immutable frameworks of governance[329] which shape the very foundations of a polity. International administrations only enjoy limited authority to intervene in the process of domestic constitution-making.

2.1. General parameters

International administering authorities cannot act as a *pouvoir constituant* on behalf of a people.[330] The notion of sovereign equality, the right of self-determination and the principle of democratic governance require that domestic actors maintain substantial ownership and control over the process and substance of constitution-framing.[331] International administrations must, in particular, leave the final decision in relation to the adoption of the constitutional structure of the society in transition to the inhabitants of the territory or their elected representatives. The imposition of permanent constitutional structures on a domestic society conflicts not only with principles of policy,[332] but also with established standards of international law.[333]

---

[329] Constitutions establish a higher-rank group of norms, defining the relationship between the bearers of public authority and the members of the given community in a binding manner for both the governors and the governed. Typically, these legal rules enjoy comprehensive validity, while being conceived for an indefinite period of time. See the criteria of the "ideal type" of a constitution, established by Fassbender, *The United Nations Charter as Constitution of the International Community*, at 569–70; Bardo Fassbender, *UN Security Council Reform and the Right to Veto – A Constitutional Perspective* (1998), at 94–5.

[330] See also the ICJ's dictum in the *Reparation for Injuries* case, according to which the UN is not a "super-State". See ICJ, *Reparation for Injuries Suffered in the Service of the United Nations*, Advisory Opinion, ICJ Rep. 1949, 170, at 179.

[331] See also Chestermann, *You, the People*, at 211 and 212.

[332] There is some evidence that "imported constitutions" are less sustainable than locally designed frameworks. See Chesterman, *You, The People*, at 213.

[333] Existing states maintain the right to decide about their constitutional structure by virtue of the principle of sovereign equality. The right of self-determination incorporates the right of a society to determine its own system of government. Even groups within a state enjoy some protection against foreign subordination on the basis of the right to self-determination (self-government, autonomy rights) or minority rights (cultural, religious, linguistic rights). See Article 27 of the ICCPR. See also Council of Europe, *Framework Convention for the Protection of National Minorities*, 1 November 1995, CETS No. 157. The involvement of domestically elected officials in the process of constitution-making is a corollary of the right to democratic governance. See above Part III, Chapter 11.

2.2.   International practice

The practice of international administrations has had a significant impact on constitution-making.[334] The extent to which international actors have intervened in processes of constitution-making varies from case to case. At least two general models of involvement may be distinguished: a partial internationalisation of constitution-making and imposed constitutionalism.[335] In both capacities, international actors have either shaped the process or determined the outcome of constitution-making. In particular, this last type of action is difficult to reconcile with contemporary understandings of popular sovereignty and self-determination, which imply a role of the population in the determination of status or the legislative process.[336]

2.2.1.   Partial internationalisation of constitution-making

Typically, international actors have assumed roles of governance assistance in the area of constitution-framing. The UN Commissioner for Libya, for example, was asked "to assist the people of Libya in the formulation of their constitution and the establishment of an independent government".[337] A similar approach was later adopted in the cases of Namibia,[338] East Timor,[339] Afghanistan,[340] Democratic Republic of Congo[341] and Iraq.[342] It has thus become common to label the role of

---

[334] See generally Philipp Dann and Zaid Al-Ali, *The Internationalized Pouvoir Constituant – Constitution-Making Under External Influence in Iraq, Sudan and East Timor*, Max Planck Yearbook of United Nations Law, Vol. 10 (2006), 423–63; Arnim von Bogdandy *et al.*, *State-Building, Nation-Building and Constitutional Politics of Post-Conflict-Situations*, Max Planck Yearbook of United Nations Law, Vol. 9 (2005), 579; Noah Feldman, *Imposed Constitutionalism*, Connecticut Law Review, Vol. 37 (2004/5), 857; Madhavi Sunder, *Enlightened Constitutionalism*, Connecticut Law Review, Vol. 37 (2004/5), 891.

[335] Dann and Al-Ali distinguish three categories of external influence: "total, partial and marginal degrees of influence". *Ibid.*, *The Internationalized Pouvoir Constituant*, at 428–9.

[336] See also Salamun, *Democratic Governance in International Territorial Administration*, at 139–47.

[337] See above Part II, Chapter 7.

[338] See above Part II, Chapter 7.

[339] Paragraph 29 (e) of the Report of the Secretary-General dated 4 October 1999 contained a clause which mandated UNTAET "to assist the East Timorese in the development of a Constitution". For the practice, see above Part II, Chapter 8.

[340] In keeping with the "light footprint" approach, UNAMA created a Constitutional Commission Support Unit. See above Part II, Chapter 9.

[341] On the respective mandate, see above Part II, Chapter 9 (MONUC).

[342] Para. 7 (a) (iii) of SC Res. 1546 requested UNAMI and the SRSG to "play a leading role to ... promote national dialogue and consensus-building on the drafting of a national constitution by the people of Iraq". It is reported that the President of the Iraqi

international administrations in the terms of technocratic advice and assistance.

Such an approach is deceptive. It tends to hide some of the complexities and antinomies of these types of engagement.[343] International entities have influenced constitutionals processes in various forms.

In some cases, international administrations have exercised influence on the procedure of constitution-making and thereby shaped the conditions of the constitutional discourse. In East Timor, for example, UNTAET determined the process and organisation of the constitution-making through regulation.[344] This regulation had an impact on consensus-building. UNTAET decreed that the members of the Constituent Assembly be elected on the basis of the principle of proportional representation, a choice made in order to reduce the influence of the majority party (FRETILIN) and to empower minority groups.[345] In the context of Iraq and Afghanistan, international actors influenced the constitutional discourse through factual pressure or negative choices, for example, through accepting the exclusion of certain groups (the Taliban in Afghanistan, the Sunni in Iraq) from the drafting process. Such choices were partly motivated by self-interest.[346]

On other occasions, international actors have influenced constitutional processes by favouring or supporting certain value-choices. In the case of Namibia, a group of five lead nations supported the elaboration of the Constitution of Namibia under close UN supervision. Five Western members of the Security Council (Canada, France, Germany, the UK and the US) established a catalogue of "Principles concerning the Constituent Assembly and the Constitution for an independent Namibia".[347]

Parliament invited the UN to provide technical assistance to promote national dialogue. See Dann and Al-Ali, *The Internationalized Pouvoir Constituant*, at 453, note 92.

[343] This discrepancy is also very well illustrated by the practice in the case of Ivory Coast, where the IWG and the PSC of the AU virtually determined a new interim constitutional regime, although UNOCI was formally vested with an assistance mandate. See above Part II, Chapter 9.

[344] See UNTAET Regulation No. 2/2001 of 16 March 2001 (*On the Election of a Constituent Assembly to Prepare a Constitution for an Independent and Democratic East Timor*).

[345] See Benzing, *Midwifing a New State*, at 364–5.

[346] US support for Sunni participation dropped when it became clear that their inclusion would prolong the drafting process of Iraqi Constitution. See International Crisis Group, *Unmaking Iraq: A Constitutional Process Gone Awry*, Briefing, 26 September 2005, at www.crisisgroup.org/home/index.cfm?l=1&id=3703.

[347] See UN Doc. S/15287 of 12 July 1982. See generally on the framing of the Constitution of Namibia, Schmidt-Jortzig, *The Constitution of Namibia*, at 413.

In other instances, the Security Council or other bodies endorsed or guaranteed domestic Constitutions after their adoption.[348]

The most problematic cases are those in which international actors intervene directly in the constitutional debate. UNTAET enjoyed this power in East Timor. UNTAET Regulation No. 2/2001 vested the administration with the power to make recommendations regarding the drafting process itself.[349] UNTEAT exercised this power with restraint.[350] The US, by contrast, intervened more forcefully in the context of constitution-making in Iraq. The CPA did not enjoy a formal say in the elaboration of "the permanent Constitution of Iraq"[351] but it played an active part in the drafting of an Iraqi Interim Constitution (the TAL). The CPA determined not only the composition of the body that established the TAL (the Iraqi Governing Council), but influenced the timing and content of some of its provisions (e.g. the bill of rights catalogue).[352] Moreover, the US intervened to its favour in the subsequent drafting process of the Iraqi Constitution. It successfully prevented the adoption of a clause in the final draft the Iraqi Constitution which would have facilitated the exercise of jurisdiction by Iraqi courts over US troops.[353] This practice was critical in a double sense. It revealed the negative dimension of self-interest in state-building projects and conflicted with the legal authority of the occupying powers which lacked authorisation to determine the constitutional foundations of future Iraq.[354]

---

[348] The Paris Accords were endorsed by the Security Council in its Resolution 718 of 31 October 1991. Similarly, the Constitution of Bosnia and Herzegovina was endorsed by the Security Council as part of the Council's endorsement of the Dayton Accords. The Draft Constitution of Danzig was submitted to the Council of the League of Nations for final approval. See Ydit, *Internationalised territories*, at 190.

[349] See Section 2 (5) of UNTAET Regulation No. 2/2001. ("The Constitutent Assembly will also consider such draft regulations as may be referred to it by the Transitional Administrator. In such circumstance, an affirmative vote of a simple majority of the Constituent Assembly would constitute the endorsement of such draft regulation.")

[350] See Benzing, *Midwifing a New State*, at 365.

[351] See Article 60 of the Law of Administration for the State of Iraq for the Transitional Period ("The National Assembly shall write a draft of the permanent Constitution of Iraq"). Article 61 (b) clarifies that the "draft permanent Constitution shall be presented to the Iraqi people for approval in a general referendum to be held no later than 15 October 2005".

[352] See Dann and Al-Ali, *The Internationalized Pouvoir Constituant*, at 436.

[353] This clause provided that [a]ll individuals shall have the right to enjoy all the rights mentioned in the international treaties and agreements concerned with human rights that Iraq has ratified. *Ibid.*, at 459.

[354] Neither SC Res. 1483 nor SC Res. 1511 authorised the CPA to intervene in the drafting of the temporary or final Iraqi constitution. See above Part II, Chapter 9.

2.2.2. Imposed constitutionalism

In some instances, international authorities have gone a step further and designed or enforced constitutional structures on domestic societies. This type of action was typically taken in two circumstances: to fulfil a specific historical mandate and to overcome a political deadlock among international or domestic stakeholders.

2.2.2.1. Exceptional historical mandates

The imposition of constitutional frameworks has a certain tradition in post-war practice. The German Basic Law was enacted under the authority of the Allied Powers. The Basic Law was approved by the military governors of the three zones in a letter of 12 May 1949[355] and promulgated simultaneously with the Occupation Statute[356] prepared unilaterally by the occupying powers.[357]

The UN exercised similar prerogatives in the early phase of the organisation. Different UN organs adopted constitutional documents by way of resolution. The Security Council adopted the Statute of Trieste on 10 January 1947.[358] The Trusteeship Council elaborated the "Statute for the City of Jerusalem" in April 1948.[359] Both documents were akin to a constitution to the extent that they were designed to determine the future status of the two territories. The General Assembly determined the federal framework for Eritrea by General Assembly Resolution 390 (V). This Resolution determined not only the political status of Eritrea, but also the country's type of government and constitution without ascertaining the will of its inhabitants.[360]

---

[355] See Letter of Approval of the Basic Law of 12 May 1949, in Litchfield, *Governing Postwar Germany*, Appendix J, at 577.

[356] See Occupation Statute of 8/11 April 1949 defining the powers to be retained by the occupation authorities, in *ibid.*, Appendix L, at 616.

[357] The Occupation Statute granted the German Federal state and the Länder "full legislative, executive and judicial powers", but maintained the power of the military governors to ensure the fulfilment of the basic purpose of the occupation. The Letter of Approval of the Basic Law stated that "the powers vested in the Federation by the Basic Law, as well as the powers exercised by Lander and local Governments, are subject to the provisions of the Occupation Statute". See para. 2 of the Letter of Approval of the Basic Law.

[358] See on the legal debate over the powers of Security Council to adopt the Statute, Repertoire of the Practice of the Security Council, 1946–1951, at 482.

[359] See Trusteeship Council Resolution 34 (II) (1948); [Draft] Statute of Jerusalem, UN Doc. T/118 rev. 2 of 21 April 1948.

[360] See Gayim, *The Eritrean Question*, at 241. ("[T]he Charter contains no provision under which the General Assembly can federate a colony with an independent country without the consent of its inhabitants.")

These practices are difficult to reconcile with modern standards of democracy and self-determination. However, they were dictated by special historical circumstances. In each of these instances, the UN acted on the basis of historical mandates entrusted to it. The Security Council and the General Assembly intervened, in order to discharge the statutory responsibilities of the Allied Powers under the 1947 Peace Treaties (Trieste, Eritrea).[361] The Trusteeship Council acted in the exercise of the organisation's responsibilities under the Mandate System (Jerusalem). All three cases were thus rather exceptional in nature.

2.2.2.2.   Modern examples of imposed constitutionalism

Modern peace-maintenance operations have shown a greater degree of deference to local ownership. However, there are at least three situations in modern practice in which documents of a constitutional character were actually or tentatively imposed on domestic societies, namely the constitutional system of Bosnia and Herzegovina, the Constitutional Framework for Provisional Self-Government in Kosovo and the Comprehensive Proposal for the Kosovo Status Settlement.

2.2.2.2.1.   Bosnia and Herzegovina

The Bosnian case is the most compelling example of imposed constitutionalism. The Constitution of Bosnia and Herzegovina under the DPA was not approved by way of a referendum, but enacted in the form of an international agreement among the warring factions, following peace negotiations under international auspices. It is thus a document built on executive consent rather than the actual will of Bosnian society.[362]

Later, the OHR used its powers to amend of the constitution of the Bosnian entities. The OHR intervened in order to implement the ruling of the Constitutional Court of Bosnia and Herzegovina on the rights of the three constituent peoples under the Bosnian Constitution ("the Constituent People's Decision"),[363] in which the Court had ordered amendments to the Constitutions of the two Bosnian entities, including a removal of all references to sovereignty and self-determination of the Bosnian-Serb people in the Constitution of the Republika Srpska

---

[361] See above Part II, Chapters 6 and 7.
[362] See also Dann and Al-Ali, *The Internationalized Pouvoir Constituant*, at 429.
[363] See Constitutional Court of Bosnia and Herzegovina, Decision U 5/98, Partial Decision No. III of 1 July 2000.

and the guarantee of equal participatory rights for representatives of the three constituent people in the constitutional structure of both entities.[364]

The OHR created two constitutional commissions by a Decision of 11 January 2001,[365] in order to facilitate the necessary constitutional amendments. The deliberations of the two Commissions led to proposals for constitutional amendments, which were approved by representatives of several political parties in both entities in the Mrakovica-Sarajevo Agreement on the Implementation of the Constituent People's Decision.[366] However, when the parliamentary institutions in both entities failed to adopt the terms of the agreement,[367] the OHR imposed the constitutional changes by way of decisions amending the Constitutions of both entities.[368] The imposition of the new constitutional arrangements entailed significant implications for the political structure of both entities. The OHR justified its intervention by the need to ensure that "resistance by nationalist opposition parties ... does not prevent the amendments from taking effect".[369] The OHR noted:

In order to overcome the obstructionist tactics of opposition parties in the Federation, in particularly the Croat Democratic Union and the Party of Democratic Action, which prevented the amendments securing a two-thirds majority in the Federation House of Representatives, the High Representative has issued a Decision promulgating amendments in the Federation. In the [Republika Srpska], the High Representative has issued a decision correcting a small number of technical shortcomings. These decisions fully harmonise the amendments with the Mrakovica-Sarajevo Agreement.[370]

---

[364] For a full discussion, see Stahn, *Verfassungsrechtliche Pflicht zur Gleichstellung*, at 679–97.

[365] See OHR, *Decision establishing interim procedures to protect vital interests of Constituent Peoples and Others, including freedom from Discrimination*, 11 January 2001.

[366] The agreement was fully signed by three political parties – the Social-Democratic Party, the Party for BiH and the New Croat Initiative – and signed with two reservations by another four parties – the Party for Democratic Progress, the Serb Democratic Party, the Serb Independent Social-Democrats and the Republika Srpska Socialist Party. See OHR Press Release, Process of Constitutional Change in Bosnia and Herzegovina's Entities is Completed, 19 April 2002.

[367] The amendments did not receive the required two-thirds majority in the House of Representatives of the Federation. The National Assembly of the Republika Srpska adopted corrections which deviated from the terms of the Mrakovica-Sarajevo Agreement. See OHR Press Release, 19 April 2002.

[368] See OHR Decision on Constitutional Amendments in the Federation, 19 April 2002; Decision on Constitutional Amendments in Republika Srpska, 19 April 2002; Decision Amending the Constitution of the Federation of Bosnia and Herzegovina, 7 October 2002; Decision Amending the Constitution of Republika Srpska, 7 October 2002.

[369] See OHR Press Release, 19 April 2002.   [370] See OHR Press Release, 19 April 2002.

The decision of the OHR to impose the constitutional changes in both entities receives some support from the fact that the OHR acted in an enforcement capacity, namely as an organ implementing a binding ruling of the Constitutional Court. Nevertheless, the methodology used by the OHR remained open to challenge. The OHR *de facto* decreed an "an addendum to the Dayton Agreement" without the necessary backing of the parliamentary institutions of the two entities.[371]

2.2.2.2.2. The adoption of the Constitutional Framework for Self-Government in Kosovo

The enactment of the Constitutional Framework for Provisional Self-Government by UNMIK in Kosovo marks the second example, where a constitutional structure was imposed on a post-conflict society in modern practice.[372] The Constitutional Framework determined the institutional structure and the powers of Kosovo's political organs under UN administration. It was elaborated by a Joint Working Group composed of UNMIK and the Kosovo political leaders[373] but promulgated by UNMIK in Regulation No. 9/2001, since domestic leaders were unable to reach agreement on fundamental issues.[374]

The document itself did not create a constitution in the classical sense of the term,[375] but instead a set of organisational principles that defined the functioning and status of Kosovo as a territory under international administration.[376] It would therefore be incorrect to say that UNMIK deprived the inhabitants of Kosovo of the right to determine their own

---

[371] See also Chandler, *Imposing the "Rule of Law"*, at 6–7.

[372] See UNMIK Regulation No. 9/2001 of 15 May 2001 (*On A Constitutional Framework for Provisional Self-Government in Kosovo*).

[373] It was elaborated by a Joint Working Group, composed of representatives of the three major Kosovo Albanian political parties (the Democratic League of Kosovo, the Alliance for the Future of Kosovo and the Democratic Party of Kosovo), a Kosovo Serb member, a Bosniac member representing Kosovo's other minorities, a representative of civil society and an independent expert, as well as seven international members.

[374] In an attempt to allude to statehood, Kosovo Albanians wanted to call the document a "temporary" or an "interim" Constitution. See Report of the Secretary-General on the United Nations Interim Administration in Kosovo of 7 June 2001, para. 3.

[375] The Constitutional Framework was neither conceived for an indefinite period of time, nor did it enjoy comprehensive validity. For a full discussion, see Stahn, *Constitution Without a State?*, at 543–8.

[376] Article 1 of the document defined Kosovo "as an *entity under interim international administration*, which with its people, has *unique* historical, *legal*, cultural and linguistic *attributes*" (emphasis added). The functional character of the Constitutional Framework was reflected in the definition of Kosovo as "an undivided territory throughout which the Provisional Institutions of Self-Government ... shall exercise their responsibilities". See Chapter 1.2 of the Constitutional Framework. The

political status or constitutional system, by enacting the Constitutional Framework. The document rather filled the existing *status quo* defined by Security Council Resolution 1244 (1999) ("substantial autonomy", "meaningful self-government") with concrete legal substance.

However, the way, in which the framework was put into force, displayed a rather a curious understanding of democracy and public legitimacy. None of the local actors agreed to the compromise solution that became the final version of the document. The foundations for provisional self-government in Kosovo were thus determined by virtue of a genuinely undemocratic procedure.

2.2.2.2.3. The Comprehensive Proposal for the Kosovo Status Settlement

The Comprehensive Proposal for the Kosovo Status Settlement, which was recommended for adoption by the Security Council by the UN Special Envoy and the Secretary-General in March 2007, followed a similar logic. UN Special Envoy Ahtisaari downplayed the scope and impact of the status settlement in his report. He stressed that the settlement "builds upon the positions of the parties in the negotiating process".[377] He noted further that the settlement was not meant to "prescribe a complete constitution", but designed to identify "key elements" that should form part of such a document.[378] However, the status settlement was in essence an international document[379] which defined all of the future constitutional foundations of an independent Kosovo.

The main text of the status proposal set out the basic framework of Kosovo's governance system, including its status as a "multi-ethnic society", governing itself "democratically and with full respect for the rule of law".[380] Annex I (Constitutional Provisions) went even a step further. It established a list of "principles and elements" of a "future Constitution of Kosovo" which were mandatory for the *pouvoir constituant*.[381] Some aspects of the future constitutional democracy were defined "in perpetuity". Article 10 of Annex I guaranteed rights of members of

---

document was not intended to "prejudge a final political settlement for Kosovo". See Report of the Secretary-General on the United Nations Interim Administration in Kosovo of 7 June 2001, UN Doc. S/2001/565, para. 20. See also para. 2 of the preamble of the Constitutional Framework ("pending a final settlement").

[377] See Report of the Special Envoy of the Secretary-General on Kosovo's future status, para. 16.

[378] See *ibid.*, Annex, para. 2.

[379] See *ibid.*, paras. 1 and 16 ("my Settlement proposal").

[380] See Article 1.1. of the Comprehensive Proposal.

[381] See Article 1.3 of the Comprehensive Proposal and the introductory clause of Annex I.

minority groups in any future constitutional amendment procedure. The rights and fundamental freedoms set out in Article 2 of Annex I were exempted from any possible future amendment by state organs.[382] The final clauses of the proposal specified that the provisions of the "settlement" were to serve as a surrogate Constitution in the absence of the enactment of a constitution by the Kosovo Assembly at the end of the transition period.[383]

The status proposal was thus an international constitutional settlement *per excellence* in anything but its title.

---

[382] Article 10.2 of Annex I reads: "No amendment to the Constitution may diminish any of the rights and freedoms referred to in Article 2 of this Annex".
[383] See Article 15.1. d of the Comprehensive proposal.

16 The relationship with domestic actors

International territorial administration entails conflicting duties. International actors are usually entrusted with transitional authority on the basis of the assumption that they are able to fill gaps or perform functions that domestic authorities are unable or unwilling to exercise. In that capacity, they may be forced to resist to political pressure from domestic leaders or to adopt measures which run counter to the prevailing public opinion in the territory under administration. At the same time, they are bound to exercise their powers for the benefit of the inhabitants of the administered territory and to "do themselves out of a job".[1]

The tension between institutional independence and the duty to transfer authority and/or to complete the administering mandate increases with the temporal progression of the mission. In fact, part of the success of comprehensive governance missions depends on how transitional administrations manage to handle this responsibility. If they hold on to power for too long, the operation may fail because international authority is subject to growing resentment by domestic actors. If international actors terminate their engagement too early or without a sustainable exit strategy, the progress achieved throughout the mission may be reversed by the return to previous power structures.

---

[1] See also Report of the International Commission on Intervention and State Sovereignty, *The Responsibility to Protect*, para. 5.31. Today, it is acknowledged by the UN that "[t]he success of an interim or transitional administration is ultimately determined by its effectiveness in devolving the powers held by the UN to local authorities". See Handbook on UN Multidimensional Peacekeeping Operations, at 21.

The way in which these responsibilities were handled has not always succeeded in practice. The concepts of self-determination and self-government have become more constant features of mandates of international administration. However, numerous problems have arisen in the interaction between international and domestic authorities and in the management of withdrawal/closure strategies.[2]

1.   From the rule of territory to rule for the people

One may observe a certain progress if one analyses the relationship between international actors and domestic actors from a long-term perspective.

At the time of the League of Nations, self-determination was essentially understood as a concept to prevent the recurrence of inter-state conflict and to support the sovereign state as the basic guarantor of human rights. In cases such as Danzig or Memel, and later Trieste, self-determination was acknowledged in the process of determination of territorial borders, but not institutionalised as a participatory right.[3] People were treated as objects of peacemaking rather than as holders of subjective rights.

This perception changed in the context of the decolonisation and peacekeeping practice of the UN. The process of gaining access to independence, self-government and democratisation itself received more and more international attention. The UN took on responsibilities in the organisation of domestic elections. The UN engagement in decolonisation led to a broader recognition that "[i]t is for the people to determine the destiny of the territory and not the territory the destiny of the people".[4] The participation of domestic actors became an integral part of the governing mandate of international territorial administrations. In 1968, the General Assembly mandated the Council for Namibia expressly to "administer South West Africa until independence, *with the maximum possible participation of the people of the Territory*".[5] Later, the conception of territorial governance as a process of participation and gradual self-empowerment of domestic actors gained some ground in the context of the statebuilding missions of the 1990s, with the adoption of dynamic

---

[2] For a discussion, see also Chestermann, *You, The People*, at 128 and 204.
[3] See Ydit, *Internationalised Territories*, at 252.
[4] See Separate Opinion of Judge Dillard, *Western Sahara Case*, ICJ Rep. 1975, 12, 122.
[5] See para. 1 (a) of GA Res. 2248.

mandates in cases such as Kosovo,[6] East Timor[7] and Iraq,[8] and a growing consensus on the need to strengthen "local ownership" in the process of peacebuilding.[9]

2. Techniques of realising self-government and political participation

The dynamic nature of authority, geared towards the progressive development of domestic self-government, distinguishes authority within the framework of transitional administrations from governmental powers within the environment of a stabilised constitutional system. The management of gradual (self-)empowerment of domestic actors is a delicate task. The transfer of authority to a local legislature or municipal institutions is usually tied to the holding of elections. The holding of such elections requires a peaceful and neutral environment in the first place.[10]

The conflicts which may emerge in relation to the delegation of authority and the maintenance of neutrality were vividly described by former UNTAET SRSG De Mello, who noted with respect to East Timorese participation:

The involvement of local leaders is a prerequisite for stability and sustainability of the UN administration. But in the absence of elections, on what basis are leaders to be chosen? Difficulties arose not only in the choice of local representatives but also in the delegation of authority to them. The more powers conferred on local representatives, the closer power is to the people and thus the more legitimate the nature of the administration. But conferring power on non-elected local representatives can also have the undesired effect of furthering a particular party. The inclination of the UN is thus to be cautious about delegating power in the interest of avoiding furthering any particular party.[11]

---

[6] See para. 10 ("provide transitional administration while establishing and overseeing the development of provisional democratic self-governing institutions") and para. 11 of SC Res. 1244 (1999).

[7] See para. 8 of SC Res. 1272 (1999).

[8] See para. 4 of the preamble and para. 4 of SC Res. 1483 (2003) and para. 6 of SC Res. 1511 (2003), where the Council called upon the CPA "to return governing responsibilities and authorities to the people of Iraq as soon as practicable".

[9] Secretary-General, *The Rule of Law and Transitional Justice in Conflict and Post-conflict Societies*, para. 17.

[10] Citizens, particularly minorities, are highly vulnerable in the transitional period and must be protected adequately. Moreover, international control may be necessary to ensure the neutrality of the judicial system and to minimise the risks of corruption and clientelism.

[11] See De Mello, in Beauvais, *Benevolent Despotism*, at 1120.

International administrations typically apply a three-stage procedure in order to foster the gradual development of self-government within statebuilding missions. First, they create integrated forums of consultation and co-governance in order to involve domestic actors in the process of decision-making. In a second stage, international administrations transfer selected decision-making powers to domestic authorities. Finally, domestic institutions resume full control over their internal affairs after the holding of national elections and the adoption of the constitutional framework for the polity.

This general methodology has become institutional wisdom in the practice of territorial administration since the reconstruction of Germany after 1945. But the techniques of consultation, devolution of authority and elections have not been applied consistently within the framework of statebuilding missions. Both the timing and the degree of the devolution of authority have varied, as well as the "exit strategies". Furthermore, individual governance strategies were not always well adjusted to the challenges of the specific situation.

2.1. Consultation

The development of structures of cooperation and power-sharing between international and domestic actors has a long tradition in international administration. It was used as a technique to balance domestic ownership against international control in the context of internationalisations, such as the International Zone of Tangier[12] or the Free City of Danzig.[13] Later, consultative governance became a structural feature of peacebuilding missions.[14]

In some cases, cooperation between domestic and international actors was expressly provided for in treaty arrangements.[15] In other cases, international administrations instituted mechanisms of cooperation which,

---

[12] The Tangier Administration was based on a fictive delegation of authority by the Sultan to the international administration. See above Part I, Chapter 1.

[13] See on the division of power between the local legislature (*Volkstag*) and the League Commissioner, above Part II, Chapter 6.

[14] For a discussion, see also Chestermann, *You, the People*, at 128–45.

[15] See, for example, Article XI of the Agreement Between the Republic of Indonesia and the Kingdom of the Netherlands Concerning West New Guinea. ("The representative councils will be consulted prior to the issuance of new laws and regulations or the amendment of existing laws.") See also Annex 1 to the Agreement on the Political Settlement of the Cambodia Settlement. ("The SNC offers advice to UNTAC which will comply with this advice provided there is consensus among the members of the SNC and provided this advice is consistent with the objectives of the present agreement.")

in practice, were not directly regulated in their mandates. UNTAET, for example, decided to establish Joint Implementation Committees in its practice to cooperate with Serb and Croat actors, although this was not directly foreseen in the Erdut Agreement or Security Council Resolution 1037 (1996).[16]

Furthermore, UNMIK invented structures of cooperative governance which were not mentioned in Security Council Resolution 1244 (1999).[17] The SRSG established a joint administrative structure which gave local representatives a share in the provisional administrative management of Kosovo.[18] The Kosovo Transitional Council (KTC), a common institution of representations of the different political parties and ethnic groups in Kosovo, was charged with a consultative role in the decision-making process.[19] Moreover, an Interim Administrative Council (IAC), composed equally of members appointed by UNMIK and local representatives,[20] was vested with the power to recommend the adoption of new legislation or amendments to the existing legal framework.[21] Although the powers of the joint administrative bodies were rather limited, the early participation of local actors in the decision-making process at the central level served an important function. It contributed to the dissolution of the Albanian "shadow" government, elected under the proclaimed Constitution of the "Republic of Kosovo"[22] and set the groundwork for the establishment of the provisional institutions of self-government.[23]

---

[16] Consultation was only expressly provided for in the context of the appointment of the Transitional Administrator. See para. 2 of SC Res. 1037 (1996).

[17] See para. 11 of SC Res. 1244 (1999).

[18] The role of the Joint Interim Administrative Structure (JIAS) and its component bodies were defined in UNMIK Regulation No. 1/2000. The JIAS consisted of the Office of the SRSG, Kosovo-wide advisory organs representing Kosovo's institutions and central administrative departments responsible for administration, service delivery and revenue collection.

[19] See Section 2 (1) of UNMIK Regulation No. 1/2000.   [20] See *ibid.*, Section 4.

[21] The SRSG, however, maintained the authority to reject such proposals. See *ibid.*, Section 6 (2).

[22] Regulation No. 1/2000 provided that the parallel political institutions of the Albanian community, be they executive, legislative or judicial such as the Provisional Government of Kosovo or the Presidency of the Republic of Kosovo should "cease to exist" by 31 January 2000. See *ibid.*, Section 1 b).

[23] The JIAS ended with the establishment of domestic executive authorities at the central level in accordance with UNMIK Regulation No 19/2001 on the Executive Branch of the Provisional Institutions of Self-Government. The JIAS administrative departments became Ministries of the Provisional Institutions of Self-Government. See UNMIK, Report *to the Human Rights Committee on the Human Rights Situation in Kosovo since 1999*, CCPR/C/UNK/1, 13 March 2006, paras. 38–43.

In recent cases, the Security Council directly integrated the objective of power-sharing and cooperation in the mandate of transitional administrations. In Security Council Resolution 1272 (1999), the Council expressly stressed "the need for UNTAET to consult and cooperate closely with the East Timorese people in order to carry out its mandate effectively with a view to the development of local democratic institutions".[24] Following some criticism by domestic actors that UNTAET had failed to take due account of the views of the local population,[25] the SRSG used its authority to create the National Council and the Cabinet of the Transitional Government in East Timor. The Cabinet, a special administering body comparable to a national government, was vested with powers of recommendation in the approval and promulgation of regulation[26] and was charged with the supervision of the East Timor Administration.[27] The National Council, a body entirely composed of East Timorese,[28] was authorised by the SRSG "to act as a forum for all legislative matters related to the exercise of the legislative authority of the Transitional Administrator"[29] – a function which included the authority to recommend the adoption of new draft legislation and the amendment of existing regulations.[30]

Finally, in the case of Iraq, the Security Council expressly called upon the CPA to cooperate with the Iraqi Governing Council in the exercise of its administering functions.[31] This mandate was implemented by the CPA in CPA Regulation No. 6, which stated that "the Governing Council and the CPA shall consult and coordinate on all matters involving the temporary governance of Iraq, including the authorities of the Governing Council".[32]

---

[24] See para. 8 of SC Res. 1272 (1999).

[25] For a survey of the problems in East Timor, see Caplan, *International Governance of War-Torn Territories*, at 96–7.

[26] See Section 4 d) of UNTAET Regulation No. 23/2000 of 14 July 2000 (*On the Establishment of the Cabinet of the Transitional Government in East Timor*).

[27] See *ibid.*, Section 4 b).

[28] The National Council consisted of thirty-six members representing the thirteen districts of East Timor, different political parties, civic organisations and religious groups.

[29] See Section 1 (1) of UNTAET Regulation No. 2000/24 of 14 July 2000 (*On the Establishment of a National Council*).

[30] See Section 2 (1) a) of UNTAET Regulation No. 24/2000.

[31] See paras. 4–6 of SC Res. 1511 (2003).   [32] See Section 2 of CPA Regulation No. 6.

2.2.   Restoration of domestic authority, including devolution of authority

The restoration of domestic authority, including the process of devolution of authority to domestic institutions has been a gradual learning process for international administrations.

2.2.1.   Advantages of a bottom-up methodology

International administrations typically use a "bottom-up" approach in statebuilding, starting with the restoration of the authority at the municipal level and gradually moving up to transfers of authority to central institutions.[33] This strategy is particularly well equipped to address the challenges of international administration in a post-conflict environment. In this context, institution-building must often start at the local level because it is uncertain whether officials at the central level are sufficiently accepted and recognised to represent local communities and implement decisions negotiated with international administrations.[34] Furthermore, a swift transfer of authority to centralised institutions may be premature in a post-conflict environment because the domestic society still lacks the political culture or the necessary party system after conflict. Reconstruction from the bottom-up offers a balanced solution because it reconciles the need for the maintenance of centralised control over domestic affairs in the early post-conflict phase with the obligation to restore domestic capacity.[35] Moreover, it offers practical advantages because it leaves the settlement of the big policy questions to a later stage of the mission where security and domestic-institution-building are more advanced.[36]

---

[33] The Allied powers used this technique in the context of the post-war administration of Germany. They revived German administrative institutions at the municipal level, before restoring domestic authority at the state level. See Elmar Plischke, *History of the Allied High Commission for Germany: Its Establishment, Structure and Procedures* (1951), at 1. In Somalia, UNOSOM II failed to rebuild the internal structures of a functioning state. But it did at least put in place fifty-two (of a possible ninety-two) district councils, and eight regional councils (of a possible eighteen). Similarly, EUAM established an advisory council, which replaced the traditional municipal assembly.

[34] See *The Comprehensive Report on Lessons Learned from United Nations Operation in Somalia* (UNOSOM), April 1992–March 1995, para. 35.

[35] See also the two-phase exit strategy adopted by UNTAET, Report of the Secretary-General of 23 June 1997, UN Doc. S/1997/487, para. 48.

[36] See also Chesterman, *You the People*, at 209–10.

2.2.2. Practice

Difficulties have arisen in the implementation of bottom-up approaches and the process of the devolution of authority more generally.

In the case of Somalia, the UN may have underestimated some of virtues of bottom-up reconstruction. UNOSOM initially focused its peace negotiations on clan leaders. Misjudgements regarding the authority or legitimacy of various categories of leaders led to setbacks in the process of political reconstruction. The mission recognised the merits of local-level initiatives only gradually.[37] This deficit was later acknowledged in the Comprehensive Report on Lessons Learned from UNOSOM, which emphasised that "a stronger and more consistent commitment to local and regional peace-initiatives and institution-building would have been more productive".[38]

The statebuilding experience in Bosnia and Herzegovina followed a very different logic. The architecture of the Dayton Agreement was built on the assumption that domestic central and local institutions would be able and willing to exercise governance functions under the umbrella of the internationalised constitutional structure established by the Agreement. The Agreement therefore left all central decision-making powers from the beginning of the mission within the hands of domestic institutions. When it became evident that the model of ethnic power-sharing provided in the agreement did not function effectively in practice and that domestic authorities were unwilling to implement the structural principles of the Dayton Agreement, the OHR took control by executive and legislative decision-making. This gradual move from local ownership to a top-down methodology caused frustration among domestic actors.[39]

UNMIK and UNTAET followed a different approach. They applied a strategy of gradual domestic empowerment, with an emphasis on the establishment of structures at the local level before a final transfer of authority to elected officials at the central level.

---

[37] UNOSOM assisted in the establishment of fifty-two district councils and eight regional councils.

[38] See *The Comprehensive Report on Lessons Learned from United Nations Operation in Somalia* (UNOSOM), April 1992–March 1995, para. 37. ("Over time, it became clear that UNOSOM's only successful reconciliation initiatives took place at those levels. Likewise, the only examples of revival of functional governmental structures occurred at the local level. Under these circumstances, a bottom-up approach to reconciliation and state revival held greater promise of tangible and enduring results.")

[39] For a criticism, see also Perrit, *Structures and Standards for Political Trusteeship*, at 469; Chesterman, *You the People*, at 143. ("[H]anding over power prematurely can be highly destabilizing – not least when it has to be taken back.")

UNMIK facilitated the development of local structures of self-government from the early phase of the mission. The SRSG autho-rised municipalities to regulate and manage a substantial share of public affairs under their own responsibility, including areas such as urban and rural planning, primary and secondary education, health care or tourism.[40] However, UNMIK remained reluctant to give up its final decision-making authority. The UN administration retained over-all supervision powers over the municipalities[41] and all provisional institutions of self-government, including the authority to take "ap-propriate measures whenever their actions are inconsistent with UN-SCR 1244 (1999) or th[e] Constitutional Framework".[42] These limita-tions in the devolution of authority have led to discontent among local actors and feelings of resentment towards of UNMIK's presence in Kosovo.[43]

The UN learned some lessons from these experiences in the case of East Timor. UNTAET created not only an advisory forum at the national level in its Regulation No. 2/1999,[44] but also transferred the first au-tonomous decision-making powers to Village Councils and Sub-District Councils created to administer the development funds granted to UNTAET by the World Bank.[45] Moreover, the Security Council spelled out a more explicit obligation to transfer authority[46] and a clearer sta-tus agenda ("process of transition... towards independence")[47] in the mandate of Resolution 1272 (1999).

---

[40] See UNMIK Regulation No. 45/2000 of 11 August 2000 (*On Self-Government of Municipalities in Kosovo*).
[41] The Special Representative of Secretary-General remained empowered to "set aside any decision of a municipality", which he considered "to be in conflict" with these rules or which did "not sufficiently take into account the rights and interests" of the minority communities living in the municipality. See Section 47 (2) of UNMIK Regulation No. 45/2000.
[42] UNMIK transferred some responsibilities to new domestic ministries in 2004 and 2005. See UNMIK Regulations No. 50/2004 and No. 53/2005. For a survey, see UNMIK, *Report to the Human Rights Committee on the Human Rights Situation in Kosovo since 1999*, CCPR/C/UNK/1, 13 March 2006, paras. 71–2.
[43] See Perrit, *Structures and Standards for Political Trusteeship*, at 468.
[44] See UNTAET Regulation No. 2/1999 of 2 December 1999 (*On the Establishment of a National Consultative Council*).
[45] See UNTAET Regulation No. 13/2000 of 10 March 2000 (*On the Establishment of Village and Sub-District Developmeent Councils for the Disbursement of Funds for Development Activities*). See Sections 7 (1), 7 (2), 11 (1) and 11 (2) of the Regulation.
[46] See para. 8 of SC Res. 1272 (1999), which mentions the "transfer... of [UNTAET's] administrative and public service functions to local institutions".
[47] See para. 3 of the preamble of SC Res. 1272 (1999).

2.3. Disengagement and beyond

International administration is a multi-stage process. A targeted disengagement policy[48] and a follow-up strategy may be as important as the
main phase of administration.[49]

In practice, free and fair elections at the central level[50] or the holding of a popular consultation[51] have often been seen as the endpoint of
a mission. Both procedures are crucial, since they help establish representative government institutions and enable domestic actors to adopt
or validate new constitutional structures of a given polity. Nevertheless,
the staging of elections alone does not suffice to guarantee a successful
outcome of the mission. Some additional considerations must be borne
in mind.

First, it is important that elections are rightly timed. Examples like
the US engagement in Iraq illustrate that it is tempting to call for early
elections in order to lend legitimacy to provisional political authorities,
processes and institutions. However, the experience of the 1996 elections
in Bosnia and Herzegovina[52] has shown that holding elections in the
immediate post-conflict can undermine, rather than facilitate the overall
goal of a mission. The staging of elections prior to the establishment of
adequate security conditions and a neutral political environment may,
in particular, exclude key groups from participating in the elections,
radicalise political dialogue or simply consolidate the power structures
and divisions pre-dating the creation of the administration.[53]

Secondly, elections do not *per se* suffice to manage successful transitions. Both, the restoration of democratic governance in post-conflict societies and the realisation to self-government in processes of external or

---

[48] The term "exit" strategy, which is frequently used in this context, is ambiguous. It
appears to suggest that the respective administration seeks to divest itself from the
problem at the end of mission, instead of addressing the continuing needs of the
society of the administered territory.

[49] This is not only a practical necessity driven by budgetary considerations, but a key
factor for the success of territorial administration. See also Caplan, *International
Governance of War-Torn Territories*, at 212–26.

[50] The holding of elections was provided for in the cases of UNTAG, UNTAC, UNTAES and
UNTAET.

[51] A status decision was foreseen in the cases of the Saar, West Irian, Western Sahara and
Kosovo.

[52] The elections were held several months after the conclusion of the Dayton Agreement.
For an insightful discussion, see Chesterman, *You, the People*, at 207–8.

[53] See also Secretary-General, *The rule of law and transitional justice in conflict and
post-conflict societies*, para. 22.

internal self-determination require the development of a broader demo-cratic culture which cannot emerge without a long-term strategy.

The lack of commitment to or implementation of sustainable comple-tion and follow-up strategies by transitional administrations has been one of the major causes for the failures of international administration. Two types of mistake have been made in practice. Transitional admin-istrations have ended their mandates without a clear strategy or they have failed to consolidate the achievements of transitional administra-tion through post-election engagement.

The UN engagements in West Irian and Somalia were rightly criticised for their "exit without strategy". The causes for that shortcoming differ in nature. In the case of West Irian, the UN administration showed a lack of commitment to the maintenance of international standards in the implementation of the 'act of self-determination' in West Irian. This was partly caused by flaws in the 1962 Agreement between Indonesia and the Netherlands, which provided for the holding of an "act of free choice" *after* the transfer of the territory to Indonesia and left the method of consultation undetermined.[54] But the UN itself shared a bur-den in the deplorable outcome of the process because it merely acted as a "rubber-stamp" of Indonesian policies in the assessment of the will of the people of West Irian.[55]

In Somalia, it was essentially a lack of planning and local support that led to non-completion of the mandate.[56] UNSOM II had neither the adequate mandate, nor sufficient resources and backing by domestic political forces to carry out a fully fledged statebuilding mission in a conflict-area like Somalia. The mission was therefore forced to "exit" without achieving its main goals.

In other cases, the UN administrations had clear guidelines for the closure of the operation, but failed to develop a strategy to secure the

---

[54] The Agreement referred to an "act of free choice", without clearly spelling out the procedures and methods to be followed. Article 18 (a) allowed the use of collective consultations of local West Irian Councils. Article 18 (c) referred to the participation of "all adults, male and female, not foreign nationals".

[55] Instead of pushing for maintenance of international standards, as provided for in Article 18 (c) of the Agreement Between Indonesia and the Kingdom of the Netherlands ("to be carried out in accordance with international practice"), the UN quietly acquiesced in the results of a "sham" consultation, conducted "in accordance with Indonesian practice". See the report of Ortiz Sanz, the SRSG in West Irian, UN Doc. A/7723 of 6 November 1969, Annex I, para. 253. See above Part II, Chapter 7.

[56] See *The Comprehensive Report on Lessons Learned from United Nations Operation in Somalia,* April 1992–March 1995, paras. 10–39.

process of transition through post-election assistance. The main example is UNTAC. The UN administration was rather successful in staging free and fair elections. But the narrow focus on the holding of fair and free elections alone did not suffice to solve the complex problems of democratic transition.[57] Cambodia's lack of democratic experience led to a return to pre-UNTAC policies. Some of the very laws and regulations that had been enacted by the UN administration were reversed.[58] Moreover, the country fell back into political instability "despite free and fair elections, a written constitution, $1.9 billion spent on UNTAC, and millions more in foreign aid".[59]

These experiences have led to a shift in policy in UN administration in the mid- and late 1990s. UN administrations have made increased efforts to avoid premature withdrawal following elections. In 1997, the Security Council extended UNTAES's mandate against the will of the government of Croatia after the holding of elections,[60] following warnings that a precipitate transfer of authority from UNTEAS to Croatia could lead to a mass exodus of Serbs. The SRSG justified the continued international engagement with the "risk that the termination of UNTAES might be seen in retrospect as having been premature".[61]

In 2001, the UN Secretary-General revisited the general UN practice in the closure of peace operations and recommended a more sustainable methodology in a report entitled "No exit without strategy".[62] The report suggested, *inter alia*, a follow-up mission to UNTAET, "in order to ensure that independence is successful and viable".[63] This recommendation was implemented by Security Council Resolution 1410 (2002).[64]

---

[57] See also Chesermann, *You, The People*, at 225.

[58] On UNTAC's Code of Criminal Procedure, see above Part II, Chapter 8 and Part IV, Chapter 15. See also generally Gibson, *The Misplaced Reliance on Free and Fair Elections in Nation-Building*, at 45.

[59] *Ibid.*, at 44.

[60] Croatia held the position that UNTAES' mandate ended with the holding of elections. See Report of the Secretary-General on the Situation in Croatia, UN Doc. S/1997/487 of 23 June 1987, para. 54.

[61] See Report of the Secretary-General on the United Nations Transitional Administration for Eastern Slavonia, Baranja and Western Sirmium, UN Doc. S/1997/953 of 4 December 1997, para. 36.

[62] See Secretary-General, *No Exit Without Strategy: Security Council Decision-making and the Closure or Transition of United Nations Peacekeeping Operations*, UN Doc. S/2001/394 of 20 April 2001.

[63] *Ibid.*, para. 42.

[64] This resolution established the UN Mission of Support in East Timor in order to "provide assistance to core administrative structures critical to the viability and stability of East Timor" and "to contribute to the maintenance of the external and internal security of East Timor". See para. 2 of SC Res. 1410 (2002) of 17 May 2002.

UNMIK even went a step further by introducing the benchmark strat-egy ("standards before status").[65] This strategy followed policy recom-mendations by the DPKO which suggested that that the "progressive disengagement" of UN peacekeepers should be "measured against es-tablished and quantifiable benchmarks".[66] This approach received the blessing of the Security Council[67] and became UNMIK's "core political project".[68] However, it created its own problems.[69]

UNMIK's benchmark strategy was ultimately guided by the laudable idea of enhancing sustainability through domestic implementation of certain standards prior to a possible status change. But the use of condi-tionality policies had some adverse side-effects. The approach deepened the gap between "external" and "domestic" perceptions of democracy, governance and human rights in Kosovo. The standards were essentially steered and assessed by outside actors (UNMIK, Contact Group). This led to a wider perception among the Albanian leadership that implemen-tation of the standards is "simply a test to be passed in order to move on to the next stage", rather than a desirable societal goal in itself.[70] Moreover, the policy failed to provide a proper incentive for the inter-nalisation of standards, since it did not link implementation to a "status vision" or concrete status options. In these circumstances, conditional-ity was perceived as a hindrance rather than a gateway towards a status solution.[71]

2.4. Lessons learned

Two lessons may be learned from these experiences. First, it is not enough to endow an international administration with the power to stage elections or popular consultations in order to realise a sustainable self-government or self-determination. It must be sufficiently clear at the outset of the mission what shall follow after elections.[72] Otherwise,

---

[65] This approach relied on the assumption that substantial autonomy within the meaning of SC Res. 1244 cannot be achieved with the prior existence of reliable domestic institutions. See above Part II, Chapter 8.

[66] See Handbook on UN Multidimensonal Peacekeeping Operations, at 43.

[67] The Security Council expressed its support for the "standards for Kosovo" policy. See Press Release SC/7951 of 12 December 2003, at www.un.org/News/Press/docs/2003/sc7951.doc.htm.

[68] See Press Release SC/7999, atwww.un.org/News/Press/docs/2004/sc7999.doc.htm.

[69] See Report of the Secretary-General on the United Nations Interim Administration Mission in Kosovo of 23 May 2005, UN Doc. S/2005/335, Annex I.

[70] Ibid., para. 14.

[71] See Friedrich, UNMIK in Kosovo, at 292.

[72] See Report of the International Commission on Intervention and State Sovereignty, The Responsibility to Protect, para. 5.12. See also Chestermann, You the People, at 205.

international administration may simply lead to a return to previous customs and power configurations which triggered the need for administration in the first place.

Secondly, it is not sufficient to postulate that there should be "no exit without strategy". Strategies for the devolution of authority by international administrations to domestic actors must be identified at the outset of the mission.[73] Two main models have emerged in practice: substantive and temporal triggers (elections plus representative government) for the devolution of authority.

The first approach may be of some value in processes of self-determination, where the consolidation of certain minimum standards of governance and protection may facilitate access to a novel territorial status. However, such policies must be defined in a way which ensures continued domestic identification with the underlying conditionality requirements. The relevant standards should be determined in consultation with local actors and should remain realistically attainable by domestic institutions (e.g. by a limitation to specific areas of priority).[74] Otherwise local actors will lose the willingness to implement such standards and may, ultimately, fail to develop a sense of responsibility for the management of "their" affairs. Moreover, the relevant status goals should be sufficiently defined to provide incentives for domestic compliance.[75]

A time-based trigger for the devolution of power may have advantages in the context of the reconstruction of existing nation-states.[76] In such instances, the goal of the mission (e.g. restoration of domestic capacity and functioning state services) is usually clear at start of the mission. Furthermore, tasks of administration are carried out under the residual sovereignty of domestic institutions. These two considerations may support the use of temporal triggers (e.g. target dates) for the devolution of power.

---

[73] See also Perrit, *Structures and Standards for Politcal Trusteeship*, at 468 ("the trustee must clearly define triggers for devolution of power to local institutions").

[74] See also Friedrich, *UNMIK in Kosovo*, at 284 and 292.

[75] See also the discussion above Part IV, Chapter 13.

[76] See, for example, para. 7 of SC Res. 1511 (2003), which "[i]nvites the Governing Council to provide to the Security Council, for its review, no later than 15 December 2003, in cooperation with the Authority... a timetable and programme for the drafting of a new constitution for Iraq and for the holding of democratic elections under that constitution".

Part V

International territorial administration at the verge of the 21st century: achievements, challenges and lessons learned

Wer will was Lebendigs erkennen und beschreiben,
Sucht erst den Geist heraus zu treiben,
Dann hat er die Teile in seiner Hand,
Fehlt, leider! Nur das geistige Band.

> Johann Wolfgang von Goethe,
> Faust, Studierzimmer*

Introduction

International territorial administration has seen an unprecedented re-vival over the last decade.[1] It is rightly praised as a tool of dispute settlement and conflict resolution.[2] Initiatives such as the concept of responsibility to protect suggest that international administration will remain one of the instruments of foreign policy in the twenty-first century. At the same time, some of the very notions underlying this project have become open to challenge. Arguments like elevation to civilisation and trusteeship, which have been recurring features of the practice of administration under the Mandate and Trusteeship Systems, are subject to review.[3] Some of the techniques used in this context (e.g. the imposition of normative standards, the lack of accountability of international administrators) are increasingly questioned in the light

---

* "Who'll know aught living and describe it well, Seeks first the spirit to expel. He then has the component parts in hand, But lacks, alas! the spirit's band", Johann Wolfgang von Goethe, Faust, Faust's Study.
[1] For an analysis of the "contradictions" of transitional administration, see also Chesterman, *You, The People*, at 238–48.
[2] See Bothe and Marauhn, *UN Administration of Kosovo and East Timor*, at 242.
[3] See Mortimer, *International Administration of War-Torn Societies*, at 12.

of a people-centred vision of governance and a growing recognition of domestic ownership.

Moreover, there is still a lack of institutional culture. The planning and operation of international administrations has remained dictated by improvisation and case-by-case approaches. Projects of administration were carried out under many different headings, namely under the auspices of three different UN organs (the Trusteeship Council, the General Assembly and the Security Council), the authority of the EU (Mostar) or the leadership of coalitions of states acting with Security Council endorsement (Bosnia and Herzegovina, Iraq). In many cases, little time was spent considering the appropriateness of the governance model or the techniques required to ensure long-term stability. A process of review of the policies of international territorial administration has only started recently.[4]

---

[4] Some preliminary reflections are included in paras. 76–83 of the *Report of the Panel on United Nations Peace Operation*. Some further lessons are drawn in Secretary-General, *The Rule of Law and Transitional Justice in Conflict and Ppost-conflict Societies*, paras. 14–37. See also UN DPKO, Best Practices Unit, *Handbook on Multidimensional Peacekeeping Operations*, December 2003.

17 Strong on concept, imperfect in practice: international territorial administration as a policy device

The Report of the Panel on UN Peace Operations stressed one of the main dilemmas of the future management of international administration. It noted that the Secretariat may either "assume that transitional administration is a transitory responsibility, not prepare for additional missions and do badly if it is once again flung into the breach, or... prepare well and be asked to undertake them more often because it is well prepared".[1]

1. On the record – a response to some criticisms

Existing practice leaves few doubts that the UN should follow the second route. UN and international administrations have passed through different historical cycles and trials and errors in the exercise of mandates of territorial administration. Yet these imperfections do not call into question the validity and merits of the concept of international territorial administration as such.

1.1. International territorial administration and (ir-)relevance

The history of international territorial administration itself provides compelling testimony that there is a continuing "niche" for international administration in practice.[2] International actors have exercised territorial authority in various forms and variations throughout much of the twentieth century. It is, in particular, important to keep in mind that international administration has historically fulfilled not only one, but four different functions, namely to facilitate a transfer of

---

[1] See *Brahimi* Report, para. 78.
[2] See also Mortimer, *International Administration of War-Torn Societies*, at 10.

territory; to manage the realisation of claims of decolonisation and self-determination; to restore authority in a governance vacuum; and to implement the policy objectives of intervention.[3] There is a great chance that further engagements of international administration will be needed in order to realise these operational objectives over the coming decades. The long-term experience of the UN in the areas of peacekeeping and decolonisation, including its expertise in the organisation and holding of elections, make it rather likely that that functions of administration will be entrusted to UN operations in these fields in the future. International administration remains, in particular, one of the institutional techniques to foster statebuilding.

The exercise of direct territorial authority by UN actors will certainly not be "the rule". However, the concept of international territorial administration itself, with its different forms and variations of the exercise of public authority by international actors, remains one of the primary options to institutionalise processes of peacemaking and to restore political authority. The main difficulties appear to be the choice of the model of administration and the timing of the individual mission. Both early and recent practice suggests that in some cases engagements with modest, but targeted international input (governance assistance missions, partial institutional internationalisation) may have advantages over intrusive governance missions. In other situations, however, the assumption of centralised authority by international actors may be the only feasible option to restore stability and security in the short term and to avoid a relapse into conflict. This is particularly so where domestic authorities are unable or unwilling to assume these responsibilities on their own due to the absence of local institutions or a political deadlock in government.[4]

The case for the exercise of functions of territorial administration by international entities receives further support by the changing nature of intervention.[5] The establishment of structures of civil administration is often a necessary corollary of military operations. The experiences in UN peacebuilding throughout the 1990s have shown that the

---

[3] See above Part II, Chapter 10.

[4] See also Chesterman, Ignatieff and Thakur, *Making States Work*, at 15.

[5] See the Report of the United National High Level Panel on Threats, Challenges and Change, *A More Secure World: Our Shared Responsibility*, para. 201. The Report stated, *inter alia*, that the Security Council should inquire before the authorisation or endorsement of the use of force whether an intervention is likely to be successful, and whether the consequences of that action are not likely to be worse than the consequences of inaction. See para. 207.

restoration of a conflict-neutral or democratic environment after conflict cannot be undertaken by military contingents alone,[6] but requires the presence of civilian support structures. Moreover, the institutional challenges of post-conflict reconstruction cannot be managed by a simple application of principles of the law of occupation or trusteeship administration. Statebuilding requires more elaborate arrangements addressing the goals, responsibilities and limits of authority of international actors in the exercise of public authority. Consensual peace settlements or UN mandates defining the role of international actors appear to offer the best technique for establishing targeted and case-specific arrangements for the process of peacemaking.

1.2. International territorial administration and (in-)efficiency

The record of international territorial administrations is mixed.[7] However, this is no pretext to argue that it has failed as a technique.[8] It is, in particular, inaccurate to claim that undertakings in international territorial administration should not be pursued in the future because they are allegedly less economical or efficient than other forms administration.[9]

Internationalised frameworks of governance have faced this type of criticism since the beginning of the twentieth century.[10] This claim has been repeated recently in the form of an argument to counter calls for the involvement of a stronger international presence in Iraq.[11] It is unfounded in substance. It is generally difficult to compare the

---

[6] See also Secretary-General, *Rule of Law and Transitional Justice in Conflict and Post-conflict Societies*, para. 28.

[7] For a discussion of ways to enhance the "effectiveness" of transitional administration, see also Caplan, *International Governance of War-Torn Territories*, at 230–50.

[8] A recent study concludes that post-conflict intervention is one of the most cost-effective options to avoid civil war. See Paul Collier and Anke Hoeffler, *The Challenge of Reducing the Global Incidence of Civil War*, Centre for the Study of African Economics, Oxford University, Copenhagen Challenge Paper, 23 April 2004, 22.

[9] But see the arguments advanced against UN administration in Iraq, by Gardiner and Rivkin, *Blueprint for Freedom*.

[10] Critics have invoked a lack of "efficiency" of international administering structures in order to justify their opposition to the exercise of direct administering powers by the League under the Mandate System. See above Part I, Chapter II. For a general critique of democratic statebuilding, see Jack Snyder, *From Voting to Violence: Democratization and National Conflict* (2000), at 16, 316.

[11] US policy-makers rejected stronger UN involvement in territorial administration on the basis of the assumption, that UN statebuilding produced mixed results "because of UN incompetence, rather than due to the inherent contradictions in building democracy". See Chesterman, Igatieff and Thakur, *Making States Work*, at 15.

"efficiency" rate of international administrations with the record of domestic or multinational administrations.[12] Furthermore, a recent comparative study of UN and US experiments in statebuilding comes to a contrary result. The study notes that "UN-led nation-building missions tend to be smaller than American, ... to have more circumspectly defined objectives ... and to enjoy a higher success rate than U.S. led efforts".[13] It is even contended that the costs of UN administration are "modest" in comparison with the costs of some contemporary US operations.[14]

Secondly, one may observe that some international administrations have produced encouraging results.[15] The Saar administration was celebrated by the League of Nations as an "undeniable success".[16] The League completed its short-term administration of Leticia successfully. The settlement of the Namibia dispute took several decades, but was a success in the end, not only for the people of the territory, but also for the UN. Finally, UNTAET managed its governing and decolonisation mandate comparatively well.[17]

In other cases, international territorial administration was partially successful, to the extent that international administrations did not meet all, but some of the goals of the mission. Here again, it is difficult to criticise international administration as being "flawed" or "inefficient", because it met some its principal objectives, namely to remove the threat to international peace or to facilitate a process of territorial transition. The League's engagement in Danzig falls within this category. The League ultimately failed in its mandate to "freeze" the status of Danzig, but moderated tensions between Poland and the citizens of Danzig on an interim basis through its peaceful dispute settlement.[18] This experiment

---

[12] The best example is the administration of Iraq. The CPA was viewed by Iraqis as an occupying force, rather than as a truly international administration. See also IPA, *The Future of UN-Statebuilding: Strategic and Operational Challenges and the Legacy of Iraq* (2004), at 4. This factor compromised the realisation of the goals of the mission.

[13] See also Dobbins, *The UN's Role in Nation-Building*, at 244.

[14] Ibid., at xxxvi. ("At present the United States is spending some \$.4.5 billion per month to support its military operations in Iraq. This is more than the United Nations spends to run all 17 of its current peacekeeping missions for a year.")

[15] Ibid., at xxxvi. ("The UN success rate among missions studied – seven out of eight societies left peaceful, six out of eight left democratic – substantiates the view that nation-building can be an effective means of terminating conflicts, insuring against their reoccurrence, and promoting democracy.")

[16] See Secretariat of the League of Nations, *The Aims Methods and Activity of the League of Nations* (1935), 121, at 125.

[17] See above Part II, Chapter 8.   [18] See above Part II, Chapter 6.

was followed by other missions with a mixed record. UNTEA was unsuccessful in its attempts to ensure a free act of self-determination in West Irian, but managed to facilitate a swift and secure transfer of the territory to Indonesia in the first phase of the administration.[19] UNTAC failed to establish a stable political environment in the long term, but succeeded in its short-term goals, namely the staging of elections and the repatriation of refugees.[20] EUAM succeeded as a short-term undertaking.[21] Finally, UNTAES marked a "historic milestone in the peaceful reintegration" of territory,[22] although it lacked the means to establish a fully multi-ethnic environment in Eastern Slavonia.[23] Last, but not least, the widely criticised international presences in Bosnia and Herzegovina and Kosovo deserve credit for the fact that they have facilitated peace and stability and have managed to consolidate a status, which is more favourable than the *status quo ante*.

It is thus fair to say that undertakings in international administration have succeeded to a wider degree,[24] in the sense that they have accomplished at least part of their goals and have facilitated a process of transition to peace.[25] The only true exceptions are ONUC and UNO-SOM II, which faced difficulties due to the fact that they operated in a direct conflict environment. These findings support the view that the potential success of a mission depends not so much on its basic rationale or on the general competence of international administrators, but rather on other external factors such as the size of the territory, the degree of local support and consent to the mission and the complexity of the mandate.

1.3. International territorial administration and UN involvement

It is difficult to conceive a future for territorial administration without substantial involvement of the UN. The existing UN system is imperfect.

---

[19] See above Part II, Chapter 7. See also Korhonen and Gras, *International Governance in Post-Conflict Situations*, at 116.

[20] This may be explained by the fact that UNTAC did not depend on the cooperation of the four factions in these areas. See Doyle and Suntharalingam, *The UN in Cambodia: Lessons for Complex Peacekeeping*, 130.

[21] See above Part II, Chapter 8.

[22] See also Korhonen and Gras, *International Governance in Post-Conflict Situations*, at 50.

[23] See Boothby, *Political Challenges of Administering Eastern Slavonia*, at 49.

[24] Concurring Harland, *Legitimacy and Effectiveness in International Administration*, at 15.

[25] Note, in particular, that Namibia, Cambodia, Bosnia and Herzegovina, Eastern Slavonia, East Timor and Kosovo are at peace today. See also Dobbins, *The UN's Role in Nation-Building*, at xxv.

It still lacks a fully developed and coherent structure to deal with challenges of territorial administration outside the context of the Trusteeship System. There has been an (over-)excessive tendency to advocate and practice institutional diversity. Each mission became to some extent a pioneering experiment of its own which had to start from scratch.[26] However, the UN remains the best and the "least illegitimate of all outside actors" to take on tasks of international administration.[27]

Past experience has shown that the UN organs are typically involved in crisis management of this kind. Following the expanding interpretation of the notion of international peace and security in the 1990s, it is difficult, if not impossible, to leave aside the Security Council in situations which typically lend themselves to the creation of international administrations. The Council has been regularly called upon to create and frame the mandate of international territorial administrations acting directly under the umbrella of the UN. Furthermore, in cases of indirect territorial administration, the Council endorsed or supported peace settlements which contain components of international administrations.

There are also few viable institutional alternatives to the UN. The UN Secretariat has gained significant institutional knowledge and experience in the management of transitional administrations over the last five decades. This expertise is an invaluable asset. Regional organisations have started to assume a role in this field. They played a key role in two sectors: security arrangements[28] and technical assistance, including election monitoring and human rights monitoring.[29] NATO has a played a key role in the Balkans and Afghanistan. The EU has contributed police officers to peace operations and participated in UNMIK's Pillar structure. The PSC of the AU has assumed a role of crisis management in Ivory Coast.[30] AMISOM was established by the AU to help avoid a security vacuum in Somalia.[31] However, none of these organisations

---

[26] See also Mortimer, *International Administration of War-Torn Societies*, at 10.

[27] See also Harland, *Legitimacy and Effectiveness in International Administration*, at 17.

[28] The African Union is about to develop a regional force. For a survey, see Caplan, *International Governance of War-Torn Territories*, at 236–44.

[29] The OSCE monitored the human rights and rule of law practice of UNMIK. The Council of Europe assisted in the appointment of human rights officials under the Dayton Agreement.

[30] See above Part II, Chapter 9.

[31] The communiqué of the PSC of 19 January 2007 stated that the AU shall deploy AMISOM for a period of six months. The mission was then authorised by UN SC Res. 1744 (2007).

has managed to develop the same expertise and institutional knowledge as the UN in the field of territorial administration. The EU administration of Mostar remained the only case in which a regional organisation assumed plenary powers of administration over a territory itself. In that case, the EU acknowledged that it lacked a formal organisational structure to undertake missions of this type.[32]

Multinational administrations are not necessarily a valuable alternative to UN administrations. The experience of the Dayton Agreement, with an international administrator acting upon a gradual extension of authority by a loose assembly of interested states, does not lend itself to further repetition in other contexts, neither in design nor in record. A similar conclusion must be drawn from the practice of the CPA, which repeated many of the mistakes and misconceptions of UN missions.[33] In addition, there is a broader point of principle, which weighs in favour of UN-based engagements: the legality dimension. It is widely accepted today that that legal framework of the UN Charter allows the establishment of international administrations for the purposes of peace-maintenance.[34] The creation of an administration on the basis of the will of a "coalition of able and willing" is likely to lack such legal backing and institutionalised form of international support.[35] Such engagements are therefore more vulnerable to criticism.

It is less clear which organ within the UN is best equipped to establish and monitor international administrations. From a point of view of efficiency, the answer is quite obvious. The Security Council is the most effective organ to address the challenges of international territorial administration. The General Assembly is competent to create UN administrations; however, it is too "large and unwieldy" to monitor the daily functioning of UN administrations.[36] The mechanism of the Trusteeship Council is ill-suited, because its entire functioning and structure would have to be redesigned in order to allow UN administrations to exercise territorial authority over UN member states or part of their territories through UN-established sub-entities.[37]

---

[32] See above Part II, Chapter 8.
[33] See also Chesterman, Igatieff and Thakur, *Making States Work*, at 15. ("Three of the most egregious errors in Iraq – failing to provide for emergency law and order, disbanding the Iraqi army, and blanket de-Baathification – ran counter to lessons from previous operations.")
[34] See above Part III, Chapter 11.
[35] See also Harland, *Legitimacy and Effectiveness in International Administration*, at 17.
[36] See also Helman and Ratner, *Saving Failed States*, at 18.
[37] See above Part III, Chapter 11.

At the same time, the Security Council is not an ideal body to take on tasks of transitional administration. The legitimacy of the Council is increasingly called into question.[38] The composition of the Council does not reflect the post-Cold War reality.[39] The Council is selective in its choice of engagement. International administration has often remained focused on territories which have been on the agenda of the UN for decades (Namibia, Cambodia, East Timor) or which attracted the immediate attention of European powers or the US (Bosnia and Herzegovina, Eastern Slavonia, Kosovo, Afghanistan, Iraq).[40] Moreover, the Council is neither an expert body for territorial administration, nor do inhabitants of administered territories enjoy a possibility to address individual communications to the Council. The General Assembly, by contrast, enjoys greater political legitimacy due to the fact that it accommodates a broader spectrum of states' interests. Even the Trusteeship Council offered a more balanced institutional framework for territorial administration than the Security Council, because its functioning was geared towards direct interaction with representatives of the territories under administration and exempted from the scope of application of the veto.[41]

These structural tensions deserve broader attention if territorial administration is developed into a more systematic device of peace-maintenance in the future. Taking into account the current institutional structure of the UN and the practice of the 1990s, it is feasible to maintain the Security Council-SRSG model as the basic structure for future administrations, while refining its functioning.[42]

Two types of measures may enhance the existing *status quo*. UN administration would, first of all, benefit from a reform of the composition and working method of the Council more generally. The enlargement of membership in the Council and the introduction of a transparency requirement for the exercise of the veto[43] would reduce the risk of

---

[38] See generally, Sean D. Murphy, *The Security Council, Legitimacy, and the Concept of Collective Security after the Cold War*, Columbia Journal of Transnational Law, Vol. 32 (1994), 201; David D. Caron, *The Legitimacy of the Collective Authority of the Security Council*, American Journal of International Law, Vol. 87 (1993), 552. For a recent critique, see also Wilde, *Representing International Territorial Administration*, at 95; Ayoob, *Third World Perspectives on Humanitarian Intervention*, at 110–15.

[39] See Report of the High Level Panel on Threats, Challenges and Change, *A More Secure World: Our Shared Responsibility*, para. 245–8.

[40] Territories such as Palestine and Chechnya have been kept off the Council's agenda. For a criticism, see Korhonen and Gras, *International Governance*, at 527.

[41] See above Part I, Chapter 3.   [42] See also Chesterman, *You, The People*, at 3.

[43] See Report of the High Level Panel on Threats, Challenges and Change, *A More Secure World: Our Shared Responsibility*, paras. 249–55.

selectivity in the deployment of transitional administrations[44] and provide greater institutional legitimacy to authoritative choices, such as the creation of robust or long-term missions which, inevitably, have a considerable impact on the internal structure of the administered territory.

Secondly, the capacity of the UN to monitor the exercise of the mandate and daily functioning of UN missions may be strengthened by the creation of an additional, specialised subsidiary body of the Council (transitional administration committee),[45] which could take on tasks of supervision and investigate complaints by domestic actors following the example of the petition regime under the Trusteeship System.[46] This body should be composed of independent experts, including members of the administered territory. This dualist structure would introduce an additional layer of expert control and accountability in UN administration, while leaving general political oversight with the Council.

2. Lessons learned

The administering practice of territorial administrations has been characterised by trials and errors. Several lessons may be learned from the previous practice.

2.1. The transitional nature of international territorial authority

The most general conclusion, which may be drawn from past experiences, is that international territorial administration must remain limited in their duration. None of the attempts to internationalise territories on a longer-term basis (Danzig, Trieste, Jerusalem) succeeded in practice. Any attempt to repeat such experiments today would conflict with structural principles of international law, including self-determination and democratic governance.[47]

2.2. The role of domestic support

Secondly, previous missions have shown that the degree of domestic support is an important factor for the success of an international administration. Domestic consent is not strictly necessary for the establishment

---

[44] The cases of Kosovo, on the one hand, and Iraq on the other, illustrate that strong international engagements are particularly likely to occur in situations in which the establishment of international authority coincides with the strategic interests of the major powers, including the permanent members of the Security Council.

[45] See Report of the High Level Panel on Threats, *Challenges and Change, A More Secure World: Our Shared Responsibility*, paras. 261–5.

[46] See above Part IV, Chapter 14.   [47] See above Part III, Chapter 11.

of an international administration.[48] However, the identification of domestic actors with the basic goals of the mission is essential for its success. This is illustrated by international practice.[49]

Missions which were built on fragile consent have rarely succeeded in the long run. The proposed internationalisations of Trieste and Jerusalem were not even implemented due to a lack of commitment by the main political stakeholders involved. Eritrea's imposed federal structure broke apart soon after its adoption and ended in 1962 when Ethiopia annexed the territory.[50] The UN's engagement in Congo was severely compromised by the lack of cooperation by local parties outside the central government's control and failed to restore stability after ONUC's departure.[51] UNOSOM II failed in its attempt to pursue statebuilding against the interests of warlords in Somalia – an experience which led the UN Commission of Inquiry to conclude that UN "peacekeeping forces should not enter a conflict area if there is no political will among the parties towards reconciliation".[52] The model of ethnic federalism drawn up by the architects of the Dayton Agreement encountered severe opposition in practice because it lacked the necessary political support by the organs and institutions of the two entities. Even a relatively promising mission like UNMIK, which was initially welcomed by Kosovo Albanians as an instrument of liberation from political oppression, faced a growing degree of hostility due to a lack of identification of local parties with UNMIK's status policy.[53]

International territorial administrations have generally produced more sustainable results in contexts where their engagement was backed by basic domestic consent from the outset of the mission. Assistance missions like the UN engagement in Libya and UNTAG succeeded because their deployment enjoyed full support by domestic actors.[54] UNTAET's statebuilding policy in East Timor was facilitated by the fact that there

---

[48] Several administrations (ONUC, Council for Namibia, UNSOM) have been created without the express consent of the territorial state.

[49] See with respect to the administration of the Saar, Knudson, *History of the League of Nations*, at 180. ("This experiment in international government serves to show the inadvisability of detaching a large and compact national group from its country of origin and placing it under a rule contrary to the desires of the inhabitants.")

[50] See above Part II, Chapter 7. See also Ratner, *The New UN Peacekeeping*, at 116.

[51] See above Part II, Chapter 7. Ratner, *The New UN Peacekeeping*, at 108.

[52] See the *Comprehensive Report on Lessons Learned From the United Nations Operation in Somalia (UNOSOM)*, April 1992–March 1995, para.87.

[53] See above Part II, Chapter 8.

[54] See in relation to the Libyan case also Pelt, *Libyan Independence and the United Nations*, at 881.

was a consensus on the goals of the mission due to the holding of the referendum in August 1999. Finally, statebuilding in Afghanistan owes substantial part of its progress to the fact that the general agenda of political reconstruction was agreed upon by Afghan leaders in the Bonn Agreement.

One of the lessons to be learned in this context is that formal consent alone is not enough to ensure sustainable peacemaking through international administration. The mixed results of the operations in Cambodia and Bosnia and Herzegovina show that prior agreement at the negotiation table is not necessarily a guarantee for the success of international administration, even if that consent is reflected in the formal conclusion of a peace agreement before the mission. The chances of success of a mission appear to depend essentially on the degree of support from the inhabitants of the territory for the underlying objective of agreement and the corresponding goals of the mission. The political consent expressed by a certain "elite" may provide a provisional basis for statebuilding and international engagement, but it should not constitute the "ultimate basis" for the creation and design of a domestic polity.[55]

2.3. Institutional design of the mission

One of the main challenges of international territorial administration is the design of the mission. There is a need for a variety of models. International territorial administration may require strong international authority in some contexts, and a "light footprint" in other situations.

The choice of the appropriate model depends on a number of factors. One important correlation has been identified by Doyle, who has rightly argued that the choice of the respective governing models is essentially determined by two criteria: the level of local hostility and the potential for local capacity-building in light of factional capabilities.[56]

---

[55] See also Oellers-Frahm, *Restructuring Bosnia-Herzegovina*, at 218, note 99.

[56] He notes: "There thus appears to be a relation between the depth of hostility and the number and character of the factions, on the one hand, and the extent of effective authority needed to build peace, on the other. There is a functional progression from ONUSAL's monitoring/assisting, to UNTAC's 'administrative control', to UNTAES's 'executive authority', to a Brcko-style sovereign 'supervision'. Authority greater than monitoring/facilitating would have been redundant in El Salvador; authority less than supervisory and sovereign in Brcko would be insufficient." See Michael W. Doyle, *Strategy and Transitional Authority*, in Ending Civil Wars (Stephen John Stedman, Donald Rothchild and Elizabeth M. Cousens eds., 2002), 71, at 85. See also Michael W. Doyle and Nicholas Sambanis, *International Peacebuilding: A Theoretical and Quantitative Analysis*, American Political Science Review, No. 94 (2000), 779–801.

But there are additional criteria. The size of the administered territory obviously plays a decisive role. It is striking that both the League of Nations and the UN have undertaken exclusive governance missions in relatively small territories (Saar Territory, District of Leticia, West Irian, Eastern Slavonia, Kosovo, East Timor). Tasks of decolonisation and state-building in entire countries (Libya, Eritrea, Cambodia, Bosnia and Herzegovina, Somalia, Afghanistan, Iraq) have generally been carried within the format of cooperative models of co-governance or governance assistance. This methodology may be explained by two factors: the sheer lack of operational capacity of the UN to administer large-scale territories on its own and the difficulty of imposing intrusive forms of governance on sovereign states.

Last, but not least, a "light footprint" approach may not always be the ideal method to ensure the implementation of the goals of the mission.[57] Substantial local ownership favours the general internalisation of change and reform. But it may be retrogressive in that it slows down reform in specific sectors where quick and effective conflict resolution may be needed, such human rights protection or property restitution.[58] It is therefore necessary to strike a balance between the benefits of "managerial" international involvement (e.g. expertise, swift reform and assistance) and the necessity of local ownership in each of the sectors of public authority.

2.4. Clarification of the legal framework

International administrations must exercise their authority within a sufficiently clear legal framework. This clarification is necessary for two reasons: to enable international administrations to assess the limits of their powers and responsibilities and to protect domestic actors from possible abuses of authority.

Contemporary practice suggests international operations are subject to different bodies of law within the course of a mission. The experiences of UNOSOM and INTERFET have shown that the provisions of the Fourth Geneva Convention may provide a useful body of law for the exercise of policing functions and other tasks of public authority in the initial emergency phase of a mission. Until now, these provisions have been applied on a selective basis, without a clear-cut recognition of their

---

[57] See also Chesterman, You, The People, at 242.
[58] See the Afghan experience, above Part II, Chapter 9.

applicability to UN military contingents.[59] Future operations should show a more systematic and open commitment to these standards.

Furthermore, there is a need to define the legal framework governing the exercise of public authority by civil administrations at the outset of a mission. The disputes about the powers of the OHR under Annex 10 of the Dayton Agreement[60] and the human obligations of UNMIK under Security Council Resolution 1244 (1999)[61] have illustrated that conflicting interpretations of rights and obligations may cause frictions between the administration and domestic actors. The core rights and responsibilities of international administrations should therefore not be left to interpretation through subsequent practice, but clarified in the mandate of the mission.

The respective treaty arrangement or the UN Resolution, which regulates the functioning of the mission, should specify that international administrations operate within a legal framework in which the exercise of public authority is subject to internationally accepted legal standards. Fundamental principles such self-determination and democratic governance should serve as the basic framework of reference for all authorities undertaking civilian function within the context of a UN mission. It is, in particular, important to note that security and order can only be restored jointly with respect for law and human rights in any post-conflict environment.[62] Future mandates should therefore identify clear human rights standards from the start of the mission.[63] Moreover, it should be borne in mind that international administrations may not only be subject to the legal order of the UN, but also part of the constitutional order of the territory under administration.

It seems, by contrast, less promising to mix different legal regimes such as belligerent occupation and UN administration under the umbrella of one framework without determining their mutual relationship. A fusion of different legal frameworks such as in the case of Iraq may cause doubts about the scope of authority and the legality of regulatory

---

[59] See above Part III, Chapter 11.
[60] See above Part IV, Chapter 14.   [61] See above Part III, Chapter 11.
[62] For instance, law enforcement agencies cannot operate in a legal vacuum or in the absence of a judicial system. Judicial or administering authorities, in turn, cannot function without a secure environment in the first place. UNSOM was stymied by this vicious circle. See *The Comprehensive Report on Lessons Learned from United Nations Operation in Somalia*, para. 33.
[63] See also David Marshall and Shelley Inglis, *The Disempowerment of Human Rights-Based Justice*, at 144.

acts adopted by international administrations, which may have damaging repercussions in the post-administration phase.[64]

2.5.   Framing of the mandate

The mandate of an administration is the key to its success. Experience shows that mandates need specific ingredients and features in order to succeed in practice.

There must, first of all, be a balance between precision and flexibility. The mandate of an international territorial administration should be clear in relation to its objective, but flexible in means. This balance is crucial for the conduct of the mission. The overall goal of the engagement must be well-planned and clearly defined in advance.[65] At the same time, the mandate must allow a sufficient degree of operational flexibility in order to enable the administration to perform its functions effectively. This lesson may be learned from ONUC's experience in Congo, where the narrow framing of the mandate compelled the Secretary-General to invent new strategies and doctrines and of his own making in order to justify ONUC's practice in the field.[66]

Secondly, the mandate should outline the general responsibilities and competencies of the administration. In cases where international administrations assume direct functions of governance, it is important to create institutional checks and balances or even a system of division of power with domestic institutions from the early stages of the mission.[67] Such a system of division of authority is necessary to prevent autocratic decision-making structures which are hard to reconcile with the very principles of democratic governance. Historical examples may be found in earlier experiments of transitional administration, such as the administration of Danzig, the proposed framework for Trieste and the EU administration of Mostar.[68]

Furthermore, where international administrations perform tasks of statebuilding, particular emphasis should be placed on the early reconstruction of an independent and impartial judiciary, either through internationalisation or institution-building and training.[69] The existence

---

[64] See above Part IV, Chapter 15.
[65] See also para. 56 of the *Brahimi* Report, in which the Panel recommends the adoption of "clear, credible and achievable mandates".
[66] See above Part II, Chapter 7.
[67] See also Marshall and Inglis, *Human Rights in Transition*, at 144.
[68] Concurring Korhonen, Gras and Creutz, *International Post-Conflict Situations*, at 262.
[69] See also Marshall and Inglis, *Human Rights in Transition*, at 144–5.

of an independent court system is necessary in order to ensure judicial control over detentions by law enforcement agencies, to provide a check on the exercise of public authority and to give people a quickly available remedy against regulatory action.[70]

Thirdly, the mandate should outline mechanisms to involve domestic actors in the process of administration.[71] This may be done in several ways. A mandate may, first of all, institute procedures of consultation which give domestic actors an advisory or even an initiative role in the process of decision-making. Such procedures ensure transparency, co-operative governance and a division of labour. They are, in particular, indispensable in the field of lawmaking. Moreover, in cases where international administrations hold exclusive powers over specific branches of power, such consultative procedures should be complemented by triggers for the devolution of authority.[72]

Last, but not least, the mandate should contain a general timeframe. In many cases, it is unrealistic to set a precise deadline for the termination of a mission because its completion is dependent on a specific event (elections) or procedure (referendum), the date of which cannot be determined in advance. But the mission itself should be established for a limited period of time, with a possibility of an extension of the mandate,[73] in order to allow some flexibility in the management of the operation, while avoiding the ambivalent impression of an open-ended international presence.

2.6. Exercise of authority

The way in which international administrations exercise their authority in practice is at least as important for the success of the mission as the planning and framing of the mandate. The existing record highlights the need to revisit some of the approaches taken in the past.

There is a need to reflect on the choice of means and methodologies by which international administration is carried out, in particular, in the field of statebuilding and decolonisation. International territorial administration has imported a broad range of "foreign" and "liberal" ideas,

---

[70] See also the points made by the Secretary-General, *The Rule of Law and Transitional Justice in Conflict and Post-conflict Societies*, paras. 30 and 35.

[71] See also the priorities identified by the Report of the International Commission on Intervention and State Sovereignty, *The Responsibility to Protect*, para. 5.30.

[72] The process of devolution of authority itself may be tied to time limits or to the fulfilment of specific substantive criteria. See above Part IV, Chapter 16.

[73] See also Korhonen, Gras and Creutz, *International Post-Conflict Situations*, at 263.

such as the adoption of democratic and secular forms of government, the rule of law, political pluralism and gender equality. This process is to some extent a corollary of the broad support for these principles at the universal level. However, some more time should be spent to reflect about the timing and internalisation of these choices.

It is not enough for international administrations to take control over territory while using their "own experience and national background" as a model for institution-building and statebuilding in the territory under administration.[74] International administrators should inquire, in the first place, whether the process and period of transitional administration marks the most appropriate and best moment in time to realise change and reform of a domestic constituency. The first and foremost task of international actors should be one of "persuasion", namely to convince domestic constituencies of the advantages of democracy- and rule of law-based norms and institutions.[75]

Secondly, international administrations should consider more closely whether such choices should be made by the domestic authorities of the territories under international administration themselves.[76] A closer examination shows that it may often be better and more effective to leave lawmaking projects with a long-term impact to domestic authorities. Domestic authorities are usually better placed to make grand strategy choices because they enjoy greater institutional legitimacy. Furthermore, international engagement may be more sustainable if it is undertaken in the form of expert advice or long-term governance assistance. Regulatory action should therefore focus on institution-building and matters which require immediate attention in a (post-)conflict situation.[77]

Quick and effective decision-making may be needed in some fields such as human rights protection, criminal adjudication and property resolution. The experiences in Bosnia and Herzegovina, Kosovo, East Timor indicate that international administrations may play an important role in this area by creating internationalised expert bodies, such as internationalised court chambers as well specialised human rights bodies

---

[74] See also Wilde, *Accountability of International Organizations and the Concept of Functional Duality*, Discussion, at 172.

[75] For a similar conclusion, see Oellers-Frahm, *Restructuring Bosnia-Herzegovina*, at 222.

[76] See also the conclusion drawn by the Secretary-General, *The Rule of Law and Transitional Justice in Conflict and Post-conflict Societies*, para. 15. Some guidance may be drawn from the structural "principle of subsidiarity" which was embodied in the framework of the EUAM.

[77] See above Part IV, Chapter 15.

and property commissions. However, the mandates of these institutions should be coordinated and planned more carefully so as to avoid overlapping responsibilities and conflicts of jurisdiction with other domestic entities.

Finally, international administrations must revisit their own status as holders of public authority.[78] International administrations have never been, and will probably never be, subject to the same degree of accountability and checks and balances as democratically elected institutions. This is due to their international status and the exceptional political circumstances under which they must operate. But some changes in conception are indispensable.

International administrations must acknowledge that they are bound to respect international human rights standards when they act as holders of public authority. They cannot pretend to be "guardians of human rights protection" while placing themselves above the law.[79] Further efforts must be made to bring international administrators into the realm of the law when they act as alleged enforces of universal values. Dismissals of domestic leaders, for instance, should not be dominated by political considerations, but based on legal criteria. International administrations should also revisit their of claim absolute immunity for acts performed in their capacity as governmental authority of territories under administration. Absolute immunities are a contradiction in cases where international actors act as part and parcel of an (internationally supervised) municipal order and are highly questionable in legal terms.[80]

2.7. Enhancing sustainability

The record of territorial administration may be improved by a better planning of the timing, phasing out and consolidation of the results of a mission. In practice, public attention has all too often moved on to a different focus after a mission achieved its first tangible results.[81] International territorial administration should be conceived more distinctly as a multi-staged process which may require different forms and

---

[78] It is sometimes even claimed that that an internationally administered territory must be a "showcase of accountability and participatory government". See Mortimer, *International Administration of War-Torn Societies*, at 13.

[79] See also the implicit acknowledgment by the Secretary-General, *Rule of Law and Transitional Justice in Conflict and Post-conflict Societies*, para. 33.

[80] See above Part IV, Chapter 14.

[81] See also Report of the High-level Panel on Threats, Challenges and Change, *A More Secure World: Our Shared Responsibility*, para. 225.

designs of international engagement within the course of one mission. Experience has shown that a mission may require a governance mandate at the beginning, a supervisory role in the period of transition up to the holding of central elections and a "governance assistance" approach or some other form of continued support (phase-out mission) after the completion of the short-term goals of a mission.

18 International territorial administration and normative change in the international legal order

International territorial administration is not only an accumulation of individual undertakings in governance and administration from Versailles to Iraq, but also part of a process of transformation of the international legal order as such.

In this context, international administration has revealed the conflicting sides of normative change: it is rooted in a cosmopolitan tradition of thought to the extent that it seeks to create conditions for a stable and humane universal order, in which state interests are balanced against certain communitarian interests and fundamental human rights and freedoms. But it has at the same time created new forms of dependencies and novel contradictions which undermine its cause.[1]

This dichotomy is reflected in three areas: the treatment of the principle of the neutrality, the conception of state sovereignty and the vision of the role of international administration.

1. International territorial administration and neutrality *vis-à-vis* the internal realm of a constituency

International territorial administration marks one of the areas in which international institutions have penetrated the domestic sphere of societies, which was traditionally outside the scope of international law. This practice was motivated by ideological and humanitarian considerations and the will to do "good". To end autocratic rule and to foster "good governance" has become part of the vocabulary of progress in

---

[1] See also above Part I, Conclusion.

international law.[2] But it has also caused tensions and antinomies, in particular in the areas of state- or nationbuilding.

1.1. The classical principle of neutrality

At the beginning of the twentieth century, governmental authority was essentially conceived as an instrument to achieve peaceful balance and cooperation among states. This understanding is reflected in a classical *dictum* by Oppenheim, who noted in 1905:

[t]he Law of Nations prescribes no rules as regards the kind of head a State may have. Every State is naturally, independent regarding this point, possessing the faculty of adopting any Constitution according to its discretion.[3]

This conception endured in the inter-war period.[4] The Mandate System endowed the League of Nations with the power to supervise the development and governance of mandated territories, but it did not change the classical perception of the immunity of the interior of a state. The degree of control of the League varied according to the level of "advancement" of mandate peoples. Moreover, the internal system of sovereign European states remained absolved from scrutiny.[5]

After World War II, the drafters of the UN Charter continued to view concepts such as democracy and human rights essentially through the lens of the preservation of sovereignty and political independence of nations and the consolidation of the state as the basic guarantor of human rights.[6] The continuing commitment to the concept of neutrality is reflected in Articles 2 (7) and 2 (1) as well as in Article 4 of the Charter, which makes membership in the organisation exclusively dependent on the peace-loving character of a state, without requiring a commitment to democracy by the entity seeking membership.

---

[2] McNair made this point in the inter-war period. He noted that "progress of international law is intimately connected with the victory everywhere of constitutional government over autocratic government, or what is the same thing, of democracy over autocracy". See Oppenheim, *International Law*, 4th edn, Vol. I (1928), at 100–1.

[3] See Oppenheim, *International Law*, Vol. I (1905), at 403.

[4] McNair continued to maintain the principle of constitutional neutrality in the 4th edition of Oppenheim's treatise in 1928: "In consequence of its internal independence and territorial supremacy, a State can adopt any constitution it likes, arrange its administration in a way it thinks fit, enact such laws as it pleases." See Oppenheim, *International Law*, 4th edn, Vol. I, at 250.

[5] See above Part I, Chapter 2.

[6] See also Boutros Boutros-Ghali, *Agenda for Democratization*, para. 27.

This general understanding prevailed during the Cold War and in the first era of peacekeeping.[7] The UN presented itself as an organisation which is "universal and impartial" by design.[8] However, this clear-cut vision has been blurred over the years, and in particular, in the past two decades.

1.2. From neutrality to the agenda for democratisation

The practice of the Security Council made it clear that the principle of non-intervention in internal affairs does not shield large-scale violations of human rights from the scrutiny of the international community.[9] This practice has led to a gradual decline of the principle of neutrality towards the internal organisation of a polity. The proactive engagement towards democratisation and liberalisation reached a new quality in the statebuilding practice of the 1990s. When taking over the administration of territory, the UN and other actors began to manage domestic politics themselves,[10] and to foster popular participation and democratic reforms. In cases such as Cambodia, Bosnia and Herzegovina, Kosovo, East Timor and Iraq, international administrations actively shaped liberal and democratic values in domestic polities under the label of "good governance".

Former Secretary-General Boutros Boutros-Ghali expressed the new self-understanding and policy-approach of in its "Agenda for Democratisation".[11] This practice marks a deviation from the principle of neutrality towards the internal organisation of a constituency. The UN continued to rely on neutrality and deference to domestic will in its policy documents.[12] However, in its peacekeeping practice, it actively promoted

---

[7] Note that there have been a few exceptions to the principle of neutrality towards in the practice of the UN, such as SC Resolution 4 of 29 April 1946 and SC Resolution 7 of 26 June 1946 concerning the Franco regime in Spain. See Tomuschat, *Yugoslavia's Damaged Sovereignty* at 337.

[8] See also Boutros-Ghali, *Agenda for Democratisation*, para. 10.

[9] See also Report of the High-level Panel on Threats, Challenges and Change, *A More Secure World: Our Shared Responsibility*, paras. 199–200. The Security Council even authorised the use of military force to return elected regimes to power twice, namely in the case of Haiti in 1994 and in Sierra Leone in 1998.

[10] SC Res. 1244 may be viewed as an act through which the Security Council "has ventured to decide on the internal structures of the system of governance of a state". See Tomuschat, *Yugoslavia's Damaged Sovereignty*, at 333.

[11] See Boutros Boutros-Ghali, *Agenda for Democratisation*, Supplement to Reports A/50/332 and A/51/512 on Democratisation, 17 December 1996.

[12] See Handbook on UN Multidimensional Peacekeeping Operations, at 20 ("the SRSG must ensure that the exercise of administrative authority does not adversely affect any political agreements reached with the parties").

"the universalisation of democracy" as a *leitmotiv* of international action.[13]

1.3. The other side of interference

This move is widely regarded as a progressive development, but it has also raised novel concerns. The activity of international administration has occasionally instituted a new form of tutelage in which technocratic concepts were used and enforced domestically to satisfy the concerns of Western elites and donors.[14] Some of the administrations which were established to foster democracy and pluralism placed their visions over those of domestic constituencies.[15] This externalisation of domestic politics has compromised part of the credibility and success of the respective missions. Statebuilding projects which were meant to bring lasting peace and stability through economic assistance, international security arrangements and rule of law reform have not produced the desired effect. In some cases, the quick and rigid focus on democratisation and liberalisation has been part of the problem. In particular, the engagements in Bosnia and Herzegovina and Iraq have shown that the gap between external pressure and domestic internalisation may foster societal frictions or weaken the authority of a newly established domestic leadership.

Moreover, the interference in the domestic realm has led to a shift of perception of the UN. The UN itself seems to have lost part of its image as a benevolent and impartial actor. The organisation was traditionally perceived as a promoter of human rights. The engagement of international territorial administration and peacekeeping has revealed a less flattering side, namely the fact that the UN and its staff may be human rights violators.[16]

2. International territorial administration and the theorisation of state sovereignty

The hybrid effect of normative change is further reflected in the treatment of the concept of state sovereignty. The practice of international territorial administration has opened new perspectives on the

---

[13] See Commission on Human Rights, *Promotion and consolidation of democracy*, UN Doc. E/CN.4/Sub.2/2001/32 of 5 July 2001, para. 33.

[14] See, in particular, Chandler, *Empire in Denial*).

[15] See above Part IV, Chapter 15.   [16] See above Part IV, Chapters 14 and 15.

theorisation of sovereignty.[17] It has, in particular, challenged the state-centred vision of territorial authority and governance.[18] But this transformation has gone hand in hand with the institution of restrictions for societies aspiring to self-rule and independence.

2.1. The disaggregation of sovereignty

The practice of international territorial administration is difficult to explain on the basis of an exclusively state-centred vision of sovereignty.[19] The experiments in this field have made it clear that international law is at least partially a framework for the organisation of peoples' rights and individual rights.

2.1.1. Sovereignty and the protection of peoples' interests

Some of the international engagements were guided by the idea that sovereign authority exists for the benefit of peoples and individuals, rather than for the interest of "the sovereign's sovereignty".[20]

This understanding is partially rooted in the architecture of Versailles. The practice of the League instituted not only new mechanisms for the protection of national minorities, but has also been viewed as a new form of "international government of peoples".[21] The move towards a people-centred vision of sovereignty is reflected in the decolonisation practice of the UN. The missions in Libya, Eritrea, West Irian and Namibia were undertaken on the understanding that self-determination is an expression of people's sovereignty, which requires international protection irrespective of the recognition of statehood. In the 1990s, international actors took it on themselves to organise societies in a manner that purports to promote the functioning of domestic institutions and the realisation of the rights of individuals. In doing so, the UN balanced the prerogatives of state sovereignty more directly against the rationales of

---

[17] For a survey of different meanings of sovereignty (domestic sovereignty, interdependence sovereignty, international legal sovereignty, Westphalian sovereignty), see Stephen D. Krasner, *Sovereignty: Organized Hypocrisy* (1999), 9–25.

[18] International law itself has traditionally been conceived of as a framework for the organisation of inter-state relations. See Oppenheim, *International Law*, Vol. I, 6th edn (1947), at 19. ("[T]he Law of Nations is primarily a law for the international conduct of States, and not of their citizens. As a rule, the subjects of the rights and duties arising from the Law of Nations are States solely and exclusively.")

[19] For a full analysis, see also Smyrek, *Internationally Administered Territories?*.

[20] See also the Report of the International Commission on Intervention and State Sovereignty, *The Responsibility to Protect*, para. 2.12.

[21] See Knudson, *History of the League of Nations*, at 177–8.

international peace and security ("to save succeeding generations from the scourge of war") and the mission to protect the interests and welfare of people within states ("We, the peoples of the United Nations"). This practice supports the view that territorial sovereignty is essentially a means to safeguard the interests of the people of a territory.

2.1.2.   The empowerment of non-state entities

International administration has further led to a certain empowerment of non-state entities.[22] Classical legal doctrine associated territorial powers with the notions of statehood and state sovereignty.[23] The practice of international territorial administration established an exception to the traditional conception of the state as the exclusive holder of territorial rights. The concept of territorial jurisdiction has been dissociated from the state. International organisations have come to exercise jurisdiction over territory flowing from functional international arrangements related to the objectives of dispute settlement, decolonisation and peacemaking, while the exercise of sovereign ownership and title over territory remained vested in state entities.

In some instances, this exercise of jurisdiction has been accompanied by the assumption of powers in the international sphere. Territories under international administration were not simply treated as a dependent or subordinate territory of a sovereign state. Some administered territories have assumed international legal personality *qua* international administration.[24] The UN has even entered into agreements with other states on behalf of administered entities or represented them in international organisations.[25] Territories have thus gained recognition as legal entities on the international plane.

2.2.   *Sovereignty and conditions for self-rule and independence*

However, this practice has also revealed the contradictions of sovereignty-related conflict management. Domestic capacity-building

---

[22] Historically, state sovereignty was perceived as the classical gate of admission to international relations. See Michael R. Fowler and Julie M. Bunk, *Law, Power and the Sovereign State: The Evolution and Application of the Concept of Sovereignty* (1995), at 12. The practice of international territorial administration reverses this picture. It is in line with contemporary developments, which accord non-sovereign entities significant space in the conduct of external relations.

[23] See Oppenheim, *International* Law, Vol. I, 6th edn (1947), at 255. ("Independence and territorial... supremacy are not rights, but recognised and therefore protected qualities of States as International Persons.")

[24] See above Part IV, Chapter 13.   [25] *Ibid.*

and access to status was coupled with the introduction of normative qualifiers or restrictions in governance and independence.

The rationale or status practice of some governance missions was based on the premise that an entity needs to satisfy certain preconditions before qualifying for self-governance or independence. Sovereignty was thus treated as a flexible attribute that is contingent on different forms of external control ("earned sovereignty").[26]

Three different examples have been identified in doctrine: a scenario in which the territorial entity acquires increasing authority and functions over a specified period of time prior to the determination of final status ("phased sovereignty");[27] a situation in which the respective entity is required to meet substantive benchmarks before it may acquire increased status rights ("conditional sovereignty");[28] and an approach whereby a sovereign entity is subject to limitations in the exercise of sovereign authority and functions, such as continued international administrative and/or military presence ("constrained sovereignty").[29]

All three variations have occurred in different forms in the context of international administration. In the case of Western Sahara (Peace Plan) and East Timor, access to independence was linked to a gradual transfer of authority from a ruling entity (Morocco, UNTAET) to a people prior to the realisation of a status option. The case of Kosovo comes within the second category. Bosnia and Herzegovina and Iraq are a typical example of "constrained sovereignty".

The idea of using "earned sovereignty" as a conflict management technique is guided by laudable intentions, namely the aim of reducing the risk of destabilisation associated with immediate independence through a gradual realisation of self-determination and access to independence.[30] However, the modalities of this concept require further fine-tuning.[31]

---

[26] This understanding stands in contrast to the classical conception under which sovereign statehood was understood as a static concept, namely as a status which either exists or not. See Michael Scharf, *Earned Sovereignty: Juridical Underpinnings*, Denver Journal of International Law & Policy, Vol. 31 (2003), at 375. For an examination, see Williams and Pecci, *Earned Sovereignty: Bridging the Gap Between Sovereignty and Self-Determination*, at 10–40; Williams, *Earned Sovereignty: The Road to Resolving the Coinflict over Kosovo's Final Status*, at 388–90.

[27] See Williams and Pecci, *Earned Sovereignty: Bridging the Gap Between Sovereignty and Self-Determination*, at 20.

[28] *Ibid.*, at 21.   [29] *Ibid.*, at 23.   [30] *Ibid.*, at 38–40.

[31] A "standard-based" approach may be considered in sectors, where the assumption of local control requires a minimum degree of political stability and institutional reliability (security, law enforcement etc.). However, such standards should be

In cases such as Kosovo and Bosnia and Herzegovina, conditionality has not served as a mechanism to empower domestic constituencies, but as a tool to restrict powers of self-government. Benchmarks were defined in broad terms and without clear parameters of evaluation. The respective standards were set by international actors (Contact Group, UNMIK, OHR) and assessed by them. This methodology turned conditionality policies into an instrument of control and domination, which limited progressive self-government and conflict resolution.[32]

The "earned sovereignty" approach suffers therefore from a paradox. It purports to secure stability, by linking the attainment of formal legal sovereignty to changes or transformation in the internal constituency of a territory. However, it may easily produce the contrary effect. The strife for formal sovereignty may actually create a weak society, in which legal equality comes at the price of a loss of political autonomy and self-government.[33]

3. International territorial administration and the theorisation of governance

The contemporary dilemmas of international territorial administration are further epitomised in its theorisation of as a governance issue.

3.1. International territorial administration and communitarism

International territorial administration may be conceived of as a special form of governance beyond the state, which advocates a community-based conception of world order.[34] Although individual engagements have remained driven by underlying state interests, they have pursued certain communitarian goals which do not only concern the territorial state or its neighbouring states, but the international community as a whole (e.g. the ending of mass atrocities, the restoration of peace and security or the realisation of self-determination). To the extent that

---

identified in consultation with domestic actors and, as far as possible, be detached from unclear policy rationales (e.g. open status questions) in order to avoid that they are implemented by local actors merely to achieve short-term political objectives or to satisfy the agenda of the international community. See above Part IV, Chapter 16.

[32] See also Knoll, *From Benchmarking to Final Status*, at 641–3.

[33] See also Robert Keohane, *Political Authority after Intervention: Gradations in Sovereignty*, in Humanitarian Intervention: Ethical, Legal and Political Dilemmas (J. L. Holzgrefe and R. O. Keohane eds., 2003), 276, 277.

[34] See above Introduction before Part I.

territorial administration fosters these objectives, it is an expression of a set of commonly shared values.

International territorial administration may even be viewed as a genuine form of international executive authority.[35] It marks not only one of the few areas in international law in which international authorities have exercised direct regulatory authority within the domestic jurisdiction of states,[36] but a field of public authority in which international authorities have replaced the state as the main executive agent on the international plane.[37]

It has served as a default mechanism for the substitution of state authority in two situations: in cases of a governance vacuum ("public authority by default") caused by the incapacity of domestic actors (Congo, Somalia) or a loss of authority over the territory (Namibia); and in situations where international organisations were deemed to be better placed than states or domestic organs to perform specific functions ("public authority by comparative advantage"), such as territorial dispute resolution (Eastern Slavonia), decolonisation (West Irian) or certain tasks of statebuilding (Cambodia, Kosovo, East Timor). International territorial administration thereby ideally gives a certain meaning to the concept of a "shared" conception of responsibility.[38]

---

[35] The idea that constitutional governance requires a strict separation among executive, legislative and judicial powers goes back to Montesquieu, who argued that a balance among the three powers is necessary in order to create a stable governmental system. Although the concept of the division of international authority into separate branches of government and their mutual separation (trias politica) has so far been mostly invoked in the context of the process of constitutionalisation of the EU, it applies also, to some extent, to the international legal order more broadly, which bears traces of a legislative, judicial and executive branch of authority. For a full account, see Tomuschat, International Law as the Constitution of Mankind, at 44; Tomuschat, General Course on Public International Law, at 305 ("legislative function"), 358 ("executive function"), 390 ("settlement of disputes"). For a conceptualisation of global administrative law, see Nico Krisch and Benedict Kingsbury, Global Governance and Global Administrative Law in the International Legal Order, European Journal of International Law, Vol. 17 (2006), 1–13; Kingsbury, Krisch and Stewart, The Emergence of Global Administrative Law, at 15.

[36] International administering authorities have exercised public authority within the realm of the jurisdiction of the territory under international administration. This fact distinguishes the action of transitional administrations from international administrative law enacted by inter-governmental organisations. See above Part IV, Chapter 15.

[37] States are traditionally the main holders of the executive power within the international legal order. See Tomuschat, International Law as the Constitution of Mankind, at 46.

[38] Sovereignty is increasingly associated with a third dimension of responsibility, namely a wider responsibility towards the international community ("communitarian

3.2. From territoriality to functionality: towards a common pool of governance obligations

However, the way in which this type of public authority has been exercised requires serious reconsideration. States and international institutions have been treated by fundamentally different standards in the exercise of governmental functions.[39] This conception stands to be corrected. There is, in particular, a need to move from a sovereignty-based understanding of governmental responsibility (linked to traditional concepts of citizenship, territorial sovereignty etc.) towards an impact- and people-centred conception of governance, tying responsibility to the effective exercise of control over people.[40] International administering authorities should observe some of the same standards of governance that apply in the relationship between a state and its people.

3.2.1. The origin-neutral application of governance obligations

Contemporary jurisprudence and practice lend support to the assumption that international law imposes a pool of governance obligations on entities exercising effective control over territory, irrespective of whether they are organised in the form of a state, a group of states, or an international organisation.[41]

Traces of an origin-neutral application of international legal obligations may be found in international human rights law where concepts such as the automatic succession into human rights treaties[42] or the extraterritorial application of human rights[43] are gaining ground. Both concepts tie responsibility to the effective exercise of control over people. Similar tendencies may be observed in the context of the law of

---

responsibility"), including foreign populations 'that are in jeopardy or under serious threat". See Report of the International Commission on Intervention and State Sovereignty, *The Responsibility to Protect*, para. 2.31. See also Report of the High-level Panel on Threats, Challenges and Change, *A More Secure World: Our Shared Responsibility*, para. 2.

[39] See above Part IV, Chapter 14.

[40] See also Mégret and Hoffmann, *The UN as a Human Rights Violator?*, at 342.

[41] See also Marshall and Inglis, *Human Rights in Transition*, at 144.

[42] See Human Rights Committee, *General Comment No. 26*, UN Doc. A/53/40, Annex VII, para. 4.

[43] See Human Rights Committee, *General Comment No. 31 on Article 2 of the Covenant: The Nature of the General Legal Obligation Imposed on States Parties to the Covenant*, UN Doc. CCPR/C/74/CRP.4/Rev.6 of 21 April 2004, para. 10.

occupation where obligations of the occupying powers are increasingly based on the exercise of factual control over people.[44]

Such arguments apply with particular force in the context of the administration of territories by international entities. In such instances, a state party or an international organisation should not be allowed to commit violations of the law, which it could not perpetrate on its own territory or under the umbrella of its institutional law.[45]

3.2.2. A legal framework for cosmopolitan governance

International territorial administrations may be deemed to be subject to three types obligations in relation to the exercise of public authority over foreign territory: a substantive limitation, which obliges all territorial authorities to respect a common set of governance obligations; a functional limitation, which adjusts the scope of responsibilities encountered by a territorial ruler to the degree of control exercised by the latter over the administered population; and a temporal limitation, which restricts the duration of the exercise of public authority over foreign territory.

3.2.2.1. The material limitation of public authority

The building block of a cosmopolitan theory of territorial governance is the assumption that an administering authority is subject to the control of authority through law. The normative basis for the exercise of such control may be derived from a crystallising set of universal governing obligations that apply to all international territorial rulers, i.e. international norms that enjoy universal application because they are non-derogable in nature (*jus cogens*), or part of international customary law. This group of norms includes the guarantee of self-determination and customary obligations arising from the law of occupation, universally recognised human rights standards (in particular non-derogable human rights) and the right to political participation.

These rules are complemented by treaty law applicable to the administered territory. International rulers may be bound to respect two types of treaty obligations: obligations related to the territorial entity itself

---

[44] This position is taken by the ICRC Commentary on the Fourth Geneva Convention. See Commentary, (IV) Geneva Convention relative to the protection of Civilian Persons in Time of War (J. Pictet ed., 1958), at 60. See also Benvenisti, *International Law of Occupation*, Preface, at xvi; ICTY, Appeals Chamber, *Tadic*, para. 168.

[45] See most recently European Court of Human Rights, *Issa and Others v. Turkey*, para. 71.

(boundaries etc.) and obligations attached to inherent rights of the people. The assumption of provisional territorial authority by international institutions is in many cases equivalent to a change in government, in which treaty obligations remain in force. It is only consequential to argue that international territorial authorities should respect these obligations in such circumstances.

3.2.2.2. The functional limitation of public authority
However, the scope of obligations must be adjusted to circumstances of the specific situation. The extent to which an administering power is bound to comply with governance obligations varies from case to case. The scale of obligations depends on the degree of authority and the functions exercised by international transitional authorities.[46] A distinction may be made between exclusive and co-governance authorities, on the one hand, and entities involved in governance assistance, on the other.

International administering bodies which exercise final decision-making power over whole or parts of the public affairs of a territory are subject to strict scrutiny. International governance obligations serve in this instance as limitations on public authority. This means that international authorities may be directly bound to comply with governance standards arising from customary law or treaty law due to the fact that they exercise ultimate public authority over a territory as a substitute for domestic authorities.

Actors involved in governing assistance, in contrast, may be held by a different standard tailored to their function. Assistance missions typically fail to meet the threshold of domestic governmental agents because they do not exercise exclusive and direct decision-making power over the local populations. Thus, international governance obligations apply here in a different fashion, namely in the form of an institutional obligation to promote and encourage respect for human standards and the rule of law.

3.2.2.3. The temporal limitation of public authority
The exercise of territorial authority by international actors is further tied to a time factor. International authorities should generally minimise the period of time in which they exercise authority without or against the will of the domestic population. This follows from a people-based

---

[46] For a parallel suggestion, see the three-tier system of allocation of human rights responsibility proposed by Mégret and Hoffman, *UN as a Human Rights Violator*, at 342.

understanding of sovereignty and modern standards of self-determination and political participation.

Moreover, there is a correlation between the length of the exercise of public authority by international actors and the scope of responsibility undertaken. The case for an origin-neutral application of governance standards increases with the duration of the exercise of governmental powers. Deviations from traditional governance obligations become less acceptable the longer international actors exercise direct public authority over people.

This cosmopolitan approach to territorial governance, built on a tripartite limitation of public authority, may ensure a more fair and balanced exercise of international territorial authority in the twenty-first century.

Bibliography

I. SELECTED TREATIES AND AGREEMENTS

Agreed Principles for the Interim Statute for the City of Mostar, Annex to the Dayton Agreement on Implementing the Federation of Bosnia and Herzegovina (10 November 1995).

Agreement between Columbia and Peru Relating to the Procedure for Putting into Effect the Recommendations Proposed by the Council of the League of Nations (25 May 1933), 138 LNTS 251.

Agreement between the Republic of Indonesia and the Kingdom of the Netherlands Concerning West New Guinea (West Irian) (15 August 1962), 437 UNTS 274.

Agreement between the United Nations Interim Administration in Kosovo (UNMIK) and the Council of Europe on Technical Arrangements Related to the Framework Convention for the Protection of National Minorities, approved by the Committee of Ministers of the Council of Europe at its 890th meeting on 30 June 2004.

Agreement between the United Nations Interim Administration in Kosovo (UNMIK) and the Council of Europe on Technical Arrangements Related to the European Convention for the Prevention of Torture and Inhuman or Degrading Treatment or Punishment, approved by the Committee of Ministers of the Council of Europe at its 890th meeting on 30 June 2004.

Agreement on a Comprehensive Political Settlement of the Cambodia Conflict (23 October 1991), 31 ILM 183.

Agreement on Provisional Arrangements in Afghanistan Pending the Re-establishment of Permanent Government Institutions (Bonn Agreement) (5 December 2001), UN Doc. S/2001/1154.

Agreement on the Question of East Timor, Indonesia-Portugal (5 May 1999), UN Doc. S/1999/513, Annex III.

Agreement on the Question of Western Sahara between Morocco, Mauritania and Spain (14 November 1975).

Basic Agreement on the Region of Eastern Slavonia, Baranja and Western Sirmium between Serbia and Croatia (12 November 1995), UN Doc. S/1995/951, Annex, 35 ILM 189 (Erdut Agreement).

Comprehensive Peace Agreement Between the Government of Liberia and the Liberians United for Reconciliation and Democracy (LURD) and the Movement for Democracy in Liberia (MODEL) and Political Parties, Accra 18 August 2003.

Convention Concerning Upper Silesia (15 March 1922).

Convention Concerning the Territory of Memel, France-Italy-Japan-Lithuania-United Kingdom (8 May 1924), 29 LNTS 87.

Convention on the Privileges and Immunities of the United Nations (13 February 1946), 1 UNTS 15.

Declaration regarding the Defeat of Germany and the Assumption of Supreme Authority by Allied Powers, Soviet Union-United Kingdom-United States-Provisional Government of the French Republic, done at Berlin, 5 June 1945.

Exchange of Letters concerning the Issue of Passports and Consular Protection during the Administration of West New Guinea (West Irian) by the United Nations Temporary Executive Authority (15 August 1962), 437 UNTS 306.

Exchange of Notes constituting an Agreement between the Government of Australia and the United Nations Transitional Administration in East Timor (UNTAET) concerning the continued Operation of the Treaty between Australia and the Republic of Indonesia on the Zone of Cooperation in an Area between the Indonesian Province of East Timor and Northern Australia of 11 December 1989, entered into force on 10 February 2000.

Framework Agreement between UNMIK, Acting for and on behalf of the Provisional Institutions of Self-Government in Kosovo and [European Investment Bank], Governing the Bank's Activities in Kosovo (3 May 2005).

Free Trade Agreement between the United Nations Interim Mission in Kosovo on behalf of the Provisional Institutions of Self-Government in Kosovo and the Council of Ministers of the Republic of Albania (4 July 2003), UNMIK/FTA/2003/1.

General Act of the Berlin West Africa Conference (26 February 1885).

General Agreement (Somalia), Addis Ababa (8 January 1993), UN Doc. S/25168.

General Framework Agreement for Peace in Bosnia and Herzegovina with Annexes, Paris, 14 December 1995, initialled in Dayton/Ohio, 21 November 1995, 35 ILM 75.

Interim Agreement for Peace and Self-Government in Kosovo (Rambouilllet Accord), Rambouillet Accord (23 February 1999).

Interim Free Trade Agreement between the United Nations Interim Mission in Kosovo on behalf of the Provisional Institutions of Self-Government in Kosovo and the Government of FYROM (31 August 2005), UNMIK/FTA/2005/1.

Linas-Marcoussis Agreement (23 January 2003).

Lusaka Ceasefire Agreement (10 July 1999).

Memorandum of Understanding on the European Administration of Mostar, concluded between the Member States of the European Union, Member States of the Western European Union, the Republic of Bosnia and Herzegovina, the Federation of Bosnia and Herzegovina, the Local Administration of Mostar East and the Local Administration of Mostar West and Bosnian Croats (5 July 1994).

Military Technical Agreement between the International Security Force (KFOR) and the Governments of the Federal Republic of Yugoslavia and the Republic of Serbia (9 June 1999).

Model Agreement between the United Nations and Member States Contributing Personnel and Equipment to United Nations Peace Operations, Annex to Report of the Secretary-General to the General Assembly, UN Doc. A/64/185 (23 May 1991).

Potsdam Declaration, Soviet Union-United Kingdom-United States, Berlin (2 August 1945).

Pretoria Agreement on the Peace Process in the Côte d'Ivoire (6 April 2005).

Treaty between the Government of the Republic of South Africa and the Government of the Republic of Namibia with Respect to Walvis Bay and the Off-Shore Islands, 33 ILM 1526.

Treaty of Peace, Versailles (28 June 1919).

Treaty of Peace with Italy, Paris (10 February 1947), 19 UNTS 126.

Treaty of Peace with Japan, San Francisco (8 September 1951), 135 UNTS 45.

UNTAES Agreement of the Joint Working Group on Operational Procedures for Return, signed by representatives of the Government of Croatia, UNTEAS and UNHCR (April 1997).

UNTAET-IDA: Trust Fund for the East Timor Grant Agreement (21 February 2000).

II. SELECTED STATUTES

Comprehensive Proposal for the Kosovo Status Settlement (26 March 2007).

Constitution of the Free City of Cracow (5 May 1815).

Constitution of the Free City of Danzig (30 May 1833).

Constitution of Bosnia and Herzegovina, Annex 4 to the General Framework Agreement for Peace in Bosnia and Herzegovina (14 December 1995).

Constitutional Charter, signed by the Commission of the Consuls in Crete (1 September 1896).

Constitutional Framework for Provisional Self-Government in Kosovo, UNMIK Regulation No. 9/2001 (15 May 2001).

Law of Administration for the State of Iraq for the Transitional Period (8 March 2004).

Memel Statute, Annex I to the Convention on Transitory Provision concerning Memel (8 May 1924), 29 LNTS 95.

Occupation Statute, promulgated by military governors and commanders in chief of the Western Zones of Germany (12 May 1949).

Permanent Statute of the Free Territory of Trieste, Annex to Treaty of Peace with Italy (10 February 1947).

Statute for the City of Jerusalem, Draft prepared by the Trusteeship Council (21 April 1948), Draft approved by the Trusteeship Council (4 April 1950), UN. Doc A/1286.

Statute of the International Zone of Tangier (18 December 1923), 28 LNTS 542.

Statute of the Iraqi Special Tribunal (10 December 2003).

III. SELECTED LEAGUE OF NATIONS AND UNITED
NATIONS DOCUMENTS

A Comprehensive Strategy to Eliminate Future Sexual Exploitation and Abuse in United Nations Peacekeeping Operations, UN Doc. A/59/710 (24 March 2005).

An Agenda for Peace, Preventive Diplomacy, Peacemaking and Peace-Keeping, Report of the Secretary-General, UN Doc. A/47/277-S/24111 (17 June 1992).

An Agenda for Democratization, UN Doc. A/51/761 (20 December 1996).

Bulletin on the Observance by United Nations Forces of Humanitarian Law, ST/SGB/1999 (6 August 1999), 38 ILM 1656.

Commission on Human Rights. *Promotion and Consolidation of Democracy*, UN Doc. E/CN.4/Sub.2/2001/32 (5 July 2001).

Commission on Human Rights. Report of the UN Commissioner for Human Rights and Follow-Up to the World Conference on Human Rights, *The Present Situation of Human Rights in Iraq*, Annex II, Submission from the United States of America, UN Doc. E/CN.4/2005/4 (9 June 2004).

Commission on Human Rights, Sub-Commission on the Promotion and Protection of Human Rights. *Economic, Social and Cultural Rights: The Return of Refugees' or Displaced Persons' Property*, UN Doc. E/CN.4/Sub.2/2002/17 (12 June 2002).

Council for Namibia. *Decree No. 1 for the Protection of the Natural Resources of Namibia*, UN Doc. A/AC.131/33 (27 September 1974), 13 ILM 1513.

DPKO. *Handbook on United Nations Multidimensional Peacekeeping Operations*, Peacekeeping Best Practices Unit (December 2003).

DPKO. Political Assessment Mission in Kosovo, *The Situation in Kosovo, Report to the Secretary-General of the United Nations*, Summary and Recommendations, UN Doc. S/2004/932, Annex I, Brussels (15 July 2004).

General Assembly Resolution 181 (II) on the Future Government of Palestine of 29 November 1947 ("Partition Resolution").

General Assembly Resolution 289 (IV) of 21 November 1949 (*Libya*).

General Assembly Resolution 390 (V) of 2 December 1950 (*Eritrea*).

General Assembly Resolution 1752 (XVII) of 21 September 1962 (*UNTEA*).

General Assembly Resolution 2248 (S-V) of 19 May 1967 (*Council for Namibia*).

General Assembly Resolution 55/96 of 28 February 2001 (*Promoting and Consolidating Democracy*).

General Assembly Resolution 60/1 of 24 October 2005 (*2005 World Summit Outcome*).

General Assembly Resolution 60/180 of 30 December 2005 (*Peacebuilding Commission*).

High Level Panel on Threats, Challenges and Change. *A More Secure World: Our Shared Responsibility*, UN Doc A/59/565 (2 December 2004).

Human Rights Committee. *General Comment No. 29 on States of Emergencies*, UN Doc. A/56/40, Annex VI (24 July 2001).

Human Rights Committee. *General Comment No. 31 on Article 2 of the Covenant: The Nature of the General Legal Obligation Imposed on States Parties to the Covenant*, UN Doc. CCPR/C/74/CRP.4/Rev.6 (21 April 2004).

International Law Commission. *Responsibility of International Organizations,* Report on the work of its 56th Session (2004), UN GAOR, 59th Sess., Suppl. No. 10 (A/59/10).

League of Nations. *The Aims, Methods and Activity in the League of Nations* (Geneva, League of Nations, 1935).

League of Nations. *The Mandates System, Origin – Principles – Application* (Geneva, League of Nations, 1945).

Letter from the Permanent Representatives of the UK and the US addressed to the President of the Security Council, UN Doc. S/2003/538 (8 May 2003).

No Exit Without Strategy: Security Council Decision-making and the Closure or Ttransition of United Nations Peacekeeping Operations, UN Doc. S/2001/394 20 (April 2001).

Peace Plan for Self-determination of the People of Western Sahara, in Report of the Secretary-General on the situation concerning Western Sahara, UN Doc. S/2003/565 (23 May 2003).

Permanent Mandates Commission. *The Interpretation of that Part of Article 22 of the Covenant Which Relates to the Well-Being and Development of the Peoples of Mandated Territories,* LON Doc. C.648 M.237 1925 VI. (1925).

Permanent Mandates Commission. *The Welfare and Development of the Natives in Mandated Territories,* Annexes to the Minutes of the Third Session, LON Doc. A.19 (Annexes) 1923 VI (1923).

Principles Concerning the Constituent Assembly and the Constitution for an Independent Namibia, UN Doc. S/15287 (12 July 1982).

Report of the Commission of Inquiry Established Pursuant to Security Council Resolution 885 (1993) to Investigate Armed Attacks on UNOSOM II Personnel which Led to Casualties Among Them, UN Doc. S/1994/653 (1 June 1994).

Report of the Panel on United Nations Peace Operations (Brahimi Report), UN Doc. A/55/305, S/2000/809 (21 August 2000).

Report of the Special Envoy of the Secretary-General on Kosovo's future status, UN Doc. S/2007/168 (26 March 2007).

Report of the Secretary-General on the Implementation of the Report of the Panel on United Nations Peace Operations, UN Doc. A/55/502 (20 October 2000).

Report of the Secretary-General, *In Larger Freedom: Towards Development, Security and Human Rights for All,* UN Doc. A/59/2005 (21 March 2005).

Report of the Secretary-General. *The rule of law and transitional justice in conflict and post-conflict societies,* UN Doc. S/2004/616 (23 August 2004).

Report of the Secretary-General on the Situation in East Timor, UN Doc. S/1999/1024 (4 October 1999).

Report of the Secretary-General Regarding the Act of Self-determination in West Irian, UN GAOR, 24th Sess., Annex, Agenda item 98, p. 2, at 20, UN Doc. A/7723 (6 November 1969).

Report of the United Nations Commissioner for Namibia on the Implementation of Decree No. 1, UN Doc. A/AC.131/81 (18 July 1980).

Security Council Resolution 16 of 10 January 1947 (*Trieste*).

Security Council Resolution 143 of 14 July 1960 (*ONUC*).

Security Council Resolution 632 of 16 February 1989 (*UNTAG*).

Security Council Resolution 690 of 29 April 1991 (*MINURSO*).

Security Council Resolution 745 of 28 February 1992 (*UNTAC*).

Security Council Resolution 814 of 26 March 1993 (*UNOSOM II*).

Security Council Resolution 1037 of 15 January 1996 (*UNTAES*).

Security Council Resolution 1244 of 10 June 1999 (*UNMIK, KFOR*).

Security Council Resolution 1272 of 25 October 1999 (*UNTAET*).

Security Council Resolution 1383 of 6 December 2001 (*UNAMA*).

Security Council Resolution 1483 of 22 May 2003 (*CPA*).

Security Council Resolution 1493 of 28 July 2003 (*MONUC*).

Security Council Resolution 1509 of 19 September 2003 (*UNMIL*).

Security Council Resolution 1633 of 21 October 2005 (*Ivory Coast*).

Security Council Resolution 1645 of 20 December 2005 (*Peacebuilding Commission*).

United Nations. *United Nations and Decolonization*, at www.un.org/Depts/dpi/decolonization.

United Nations. *UNTAG, Historical Background*, at www.un.org/Depts/dpko/commission/untagS.htm.

UNMIK Executive Decision 2004/8 (8 April 2004).

UNMIK. *Report to the Human Rights Committee on the Human Rights Situation in Kosovo since 1999*, CCPR/C/UNK/1 (13 March 2006).

UNMIK. *Report Submitted Pursuant to Article 2.2 of the Agreement Between UNMIK and the Council of Europe Related to the Framework Convention for the Protection of National Minorities* (2 June 2005).

UNMIK. *Standards for Kosovo*, Press Release, UNMIK/PR/1078 (10 December 2003).

UNMIK. *Kosovo Standards Implementation Plan* (31 March 2004)

UNTAC Directive No. 93/1 establishing procedures for the Prosecution of persons responsible for Human Rights Violations (6 January 1993).

UNTAC Directive No. 93/2 (3 February 1993).

IV. SELECTED OTHER DOCUMENTS

Advisory Council on International Affairs & the Advisory

Committee on Issues of Public International Law, The Netherlands. *Failing States: A Global Responsibility*, No. 35, May 2004.

Amnesty International, *East Timor: Justice Past, Present and Future*, AI-Index ASA 57/001/2001 (27 July 2001).

Amnesty International, Federal Republic of Yugoslavia (Kosovo). *Amnesty International's Recommendations to UNMIK on the Judicial System* (February 2000).

Amnesty International. *Memorandum on Concerns Related to Legislation Introduced by the Coalition Provisional Authority*, AI Index MDE 147180/2003 (4 December 2003).

Amnesty International. *Memorandum on Concerns Relating to Law and Order*, AI Index 14/157/2003 (July 2003).

Amnesty International. *The Apparent Lack of Accountability of International Peace-keeping Forces in Kosovo and Bosnia-Herzegovina*, AI Index: EUR 05/002/2004 (April 2004).

Amnesty International. *Beyond Abu Ghraib: Detention and Torture in Iraq*, AI Index: MDE 14/001/2006 (6 March 2006).

Centre for Applied Studies in International Negotiations. *Administration and Governance in Kosovo: Lessons Learned and Lessons to be Learned* (January 2003).

COMKFOR Detention Directive 42 (9 October 2001).

Commission for Real Property Claims of Displaced Persons and Refugees. *End of Mandate Report (1996–2003)*.

Council of Europe, Office of the Commissioner for Human Rights, Kosovo. *The Human Rights Situation and the Fate of Persons Displaced from their Homes* (16 October 2002).

Council of Europe. *Protection of Human Rights in Kosovo*, Resolution 1417 (2005) (25 January 2005).

European Commission For Democracy Through Law. *Proposal for a Law on the Merger of the Human Rights Chamber and the Constitutional Court of Bosnia and Herzegovina* (23 October 2001).

European Commission For Democracy Through Law. *Opinion on Human Rights in Kosovo: Possible Establishment of Review Mechanisms*, Opinion No. 280/2004 (11 October 2004).

European Commission for Democracy Through Law. *Opinion on the Constitutional Situation in Bosnia and Herzegovina and the Powers of the High Representative* (11 March 2005).

European Commission for Democracy Through Law. *Opinion on a Possible Solution to the Issue of Decertification of Police Officers in Bosnia and Herzegovina*, Opinion No. 326/2004 (24 October 2005).

European Commission for Democracy Through Law. *Preliminary Opinion on the Draft Amendments to the Constitution of Bosnia and Herzegovina*, Opinion No. 375/2006 (7 April 2006).

European Parliament, Committee on Budgetary Control. *Report on Special Report No. 2/96 of the Court of Auditors concerning the accounts of the Administrator and the European Administration, Mostar* (21 November 1996).

High-Level Workshop on State-Building and Strengthening of Civilian Administration in Post-Conflict Societies and Failed States, New York. *Government Out of a Box – Some Ideas for Developing a Tool Box for Peace-Building* (21 June 2004).

Humanitarian Law Centre. *Analysis of UNMIK Regulations Affecting the Return of Displaced Persons to Kosovo*, at www.hic.org.yu.

Institut de Droit International. *Conditions of Application of Humanitarian Rules of Armed Conflict to Hostilities in which United Nations Forces May be Engaged*, Annuaire de l'Institut de Droit International, Vol. 54 (1971-II), 465.

International Commission on Intervention and State Sovereignty. *The Responsibility to Protect* (Ottawa,: International Development Research Centre, 2001).

International Crisis Group. *Is Dayton failing? Bosnia Four Years After the Peace Agreement*, ICG Balkans Report No. 80 (28 October 1999).

International Crisis Group. *Reunifying Mostar: Opportunities for Progress* (19 April 2000).

International Crisis Group. *Governing Iraq*, ICG Middle East Report No. 17 (25 August 2003).

International Crisis Group. *Unmaking Iraq: A Constitutional Process Gone Awry*, Briefing (26 September 2005).

International Peace Academy. *The Future of UN-Statebuilding: Strategic and Operational Challenges and the Legacy of Iraq* (New York, IPA, 2004).

Koschnick, Hans. *The EU Administration of Mostar – A Balance After One Year* (August 1995).

OHR. Decision establishing interim procedures to protect vital interests of Constituent Peoples and Others, including freedom from Discrimination (11 January 2001).

OHR. Decision Amending the Constitution of the Federation of Bosnia and Herzegovina (7 October 2002).

OHR. Decision imposing Arbitration in Dobrinje I and IV (5 February 2001).

OHR. Decision on Constitutional Amendments in the Federation (19 April 2002).

OHR. Decision on Constitutional Amendments in Republika Srpska (19 April 2002).

OHR. Decision Amending the Constitution of Republika Srpska (7 October 2002).

Ombudsperson Institution in Kosovo. *Special Report No. 1 on the Compatibility with Recognized International Standards of UNMIK Regulation No 47/2000 on the Status, Privileges and Immunities of KFOR and UNMIK and Their Personnel in Kosovo* (18 August 2000).

Ombudsperson Institution in Kosovo. *Special Report No. 2 on Certain Aspects of UNMIK Regulation No. 24/1999 on the Law Applicable in Kosovo* (27 October 2000).

Ombudsperson Institution in Kosovo. *Special Report No. 3 on the Conformity of Deprivations of Liberty under "Executive Orders" with Recognized International Standards* (29 June 2001).

Ombudsperson Institution in Kosovo. *Special Report No. 5 on Certain Aspects of UNMIK Regulation No. 17/2001 on the Registration of Contracts for the Sale of Real Property in Specific Geographical Areas of Kosovo* (22 August 2001).

Ombudsperson Institution in Kosovo. *Special Report No 4, Certain Aspects of UNMIK Regulation No. 18/2001 on the Establishment of a Detention Review Commission for Extra-judicial Detentions Based on Executive Orders* (25 August 2001).

Opinion of the Lord Chancellor and the Law Officers of the Crown, March 1945, Public Record Office FO 371/50759 (U1949).

OSCE, Mission in Kosovo. Report No. 6, *Extension of Custody Time Limits and the Rights of Detainees: The Unlawfulness of Regulation 1999/26* (29 April 2000).

OSCE, Mission in Kosovo. *Review of the Criminal Justice System* (February–July 2000).

OSCE, Mission in Kosovo. *The Impending Property Crisis in Kosovo* (25 September 2000).
OSCE, Mission in Kosovo. *Review of the Criminal Justice System* (September 2001–February 2002).
UNTAC Directive No. 93/1 establishing procedures for the Prosecution of persons responsible for Human Rights violations (6 January 1993).

V. BOOKS AND ARTICLES

Abi-Saab, Georges. *The United Nations Operation in the Congo 1960–1964* (Oxford, Oxford University Press, 1978).
Abraham, Elizabeth. *The Sins of Saviour: Holding the United Nations Accountable to International Human Rights Standards for Executive Order Detentions in its Mission in Kosovo*, American University Law Review, Vol. 52 (2003), 1291.
Afsah, Ebrahim and Guhr, Alexandra Hilal. *Afghanistan: Building a State to Keep the Peace*, Max Planck Yearbook of United Nations Law, Vol. 9 (2005), 373.
Alabrune, François. *La Pratique des Comités des Sanctions du Conseil de Sécurité depuis 1990*, Annuaire Français de Droit International, Vol. 45 (1999), 226.
Allot, Philip. *Eunomia: New Order for a New World* (Oxford, Oxford University Press, 2001).
Alvarez, Alejandro. *The New International Law*, Grotius Society Transactions, Vol. 15 (1930), 35.
Alvarez, José E. *International Organisations as Law-Makers* (Oxford, Oxford University Press, 2005).
Ando, Nisuke. *Surrender, Occupation, and Private Property in International Law: An Evaluation of U.S. Practice in Japan* (Oxford, Clarendon Press, 1991).
Anghie, Anthony. *Imperialism, Sovereignty and the Making of International Law* (Cambridge, Cambridge University Press, 2005).
Anghie, Anthony. *Colonialism and the Birth of International Institutions: Sovereignty, Economy, and the Mandate System of the League of Nations*, NYU Journal of International Law & Politics, Vol. 34 (2002), 513.
Anghie, Anthony. *Finding the Peripheries: Sovereignty and Colonialism in Nineteenth-Century International Law*, Harvard International Law Journal, Vol. 40 (1999), 1.
Anghie, Anthony. *Globalization and its Discontents: International Institutions and the Colonial Origins of Law and Development*, at www.nyulawglobal.org/documents/Anthony_Anghie.pdf.
Arangio-Ruiz, Gaetano. *On the Security Council's "Law-Making"*, Rivista di Diritto Internazionale, Vol. 83 (2000), 609.
Archibugi, Daniele. *Immanuel Kant, Cosmopolitan Law and Peace*, European Journal of International Relations, Vol. 1 (1995), 429.
Aspen Institute, *Honoring Human Rights Under International Mandates: Lessons from Bosnia, Kosovo and East Timor* (Alice H. Henkin ed., The Aspen Institute, 2003).
Aston, Jurij Daniel. *Die Bekämpfung abstrakter Gefahren für den Weltfrieden durch legislative Maßnahmen des Sicherheitsrats – Resolution 1373 (2001) im Kontext,*

Zeitschrift für ausländisches öffentliches Recht und Völkerrecht, Vol. 62 (2002), 257.

Ayoob, Mohammed. *Third World Perspectives on Humanitarian Intervention and International Administration*, Global Governance, Vol. 10 (2004), 99.

Aznar-Goméz, Mariano J. *Some Paradoxes on Human Rights Protection in Kosovo*, in Pierre-Marie Dupuy, Bardo Fassbender, Malcolm N. Shaw and Karl-Peter Sommermann eds., Völkerrecht als Werteordnung, Festschrift für Christian Tomuschat (N. P. Engel, 2006), 15.

Bain, William. *Between Anarchy and Society: Trusteeship and the Obligations of Power* (Oxford, Oxford University Press, 2003).

Bali, Asli U. *Justice under Occupation: Rule of Law and the Ethics of Nation-Building in Iraq*, Yale Journal of International Law, Vol. 30 (2005), 431.

Barkawi Tarak and Laffey, Mark. *The Imperial Peace: Democracy, Force and Globalization*, European Journal of International Relations, Vol. 5 (1999), 403.

Barnes, Samuel H. *The Contribution of Democracy to Rebuilding Postconflict Societies*, American Journal of International Law, Vol. 95 (2001), 86.

Bass, Gary. *Jus Post Bellum*, Philosophy & Public Affairs, Vol. 32 (2004) 384–412.

Bathurst, Maurice Edward and Simpson, John Liddle. *Germany and the North Atlantic Community: A Legal Survey* (London, Stevens, 1956).

Baxter, Richard R. *The Law of International Waterways* (Cambridge MA, Harvard University Press, 1964).

Beauvais, Joel C. *Benevolent Despotism: A Critique of UN State-Building in East Timor*, New York Journal of International Law and Politics, Vol. 33 (2001), 1101.

Beck, Raimund. *Die Internationalisierung von Territorien* (Hamburg, Kohlhammer, 1962).

Bederman, David J. *Globalism and International Law: Values and Choices*, Halle Occasional Paper (2001).

Bentwich, Norman. *The Mandates System* (London, Longmans, 1930).

Benvenisti, Eyal. *The Security Council and the Law on Occupation: Resolution 1483 on Iraq in Historical Perspective*, Israel Defense Forces Law Review, Vol. 1 (2003) 23.

Benvenisti, Eyal. *The International Law of Occupation* (Princeton NJ, Princeton University Press, 1993).

Benvenuti, Paolo, *Implementation of International Humanitarian Law in the Framework of UN Peacekeeping*, in European Commission, Law in Humanitarian Crises: How Can International Humanitarian Law Be Made Effective in Armed Conflicts? (Luxembourg, Office for Official Publications of the European Communities, 1995), 114.

Benzing, Markus. *Midwifing a New State: The United Nations in East Timor*, Max Planck Yearbook of United Nations Law, Vol. 9 (2005), 316.

Berman, Nathaniel. *Intervention in a "Divided World": Axes of Legitimacy*, European Journal of International Law, Vol. 17 (2006), 743.

Berry, Ken. *UNTAC: A Flawed Paradigm/Success*, in The United Nations Transitional Authority in Cambodia (UNTAC): Debriefing and Lessons, Report of the 1994 Singapore Conference (1995), 244.

Betts, Wendy S., Carlson Scott N. and Gisvold, Gregory. *The Post-Conflict Transitional Administration of Kosovo and the Lessons-Learned in Efforts to establish a Judiciary and Rule of Law*, Michigan Journal of International Law, Vol. 22 (2001), 372.

Bhuta, Nehal. *The Antinomies of Transformative Occupation*, European Journal of International Law, Vol. 16 (2005), 721.

Bienen, Derk, Rittberger, Volker and Wagner, Wolfgang. *Democracy in the United Nations System: Cosmopolitan and Communitarian Principles*, in Daniele Archibugi et al. eds., Re-Imagining Political Community: Studies in Cosmopolitan Democracy (Stanford, Stanford University Press, 1998), 287.

Bisschop, Willem. R. *The Saar Controversy* (London, Sweet & Maxwell, 1924).

Blokker, Niels. *Beyond "Dili": On the Powers and Practice of International Organizations*, in G. Kreijen ed., State, Sovereignty and International Governance (Oxford, Oxford University Press, 2004), 299.

Blokker, Niels M. *Is the Authorisation Authorised? Powers and Practice of the United Nations Security Council to Authorise the Use of Force by Coalitions of the "Able and Willing"*, European Journal of International Law, Vol. 11 (2000), 542.

Blum, Yehuda Z. *Secure Boundaries and Middle East Peace in the Light of International Law and Practice* (Jerusalem, The Hebrew University of Jerusalem Faculty of Law Press, 1971).

Bodansky, Daniel. *The Legitimacy of International Governance: A Coming Challenge for International Environmental Law*, American Journal of International Law, Vol. 93 (1999), 596.

Bogdandy, Arnim von et al. *State-Building, Nation-Building and Constitutional Politics of Post-Conflict-Situations*, Max Planck Yearbook of United Nations Law, Vol. 9 (2005), 579.

Bohlander, Michael. *The Joint Advisory Council Draft Criminal Code of Kosovo of 13 August 2001: Some Comments on War Crimes, Crimes Against Humanity and Security Council Resolution 1244*, Kosovo Legal Studies, Vol. 3 (2002), 5–6.

Bohlander, Michael. *The Direct Application of International Law in Kosovo*, Kosovo Legal Studies, Vol. 1 (2001), 7.

Bohman, James. *The Public Spheres of the World Citizen*, in James Bohman and Matthias Lutz-Bachmann eds., Perpetual Peace: Essays on Kant's Cosmopolitan Ideal (Cambridge MA, MIT, 1997), 179.

Bongiorno, Carla. *A Culture of Impunity: Applying International Human Rights Law to the United Nations in East Timor*, Columbia Human Rights Law Review, Vol. 33 (2002), 623.

Boon, Kristen. *Legislative Reform in Post-Conflict Zones: Jus Post Bellum and the Contemporary Occupant's Law-Making Powers*, McGill Law Journal, Vol. 50 (2005), 285.

Boothy, Derek. *The Political Challenges of Administering Eastern Slavonia*, Global Governance, Vol. 10 (2004), 37.

Borgese, Elisabeth Mann. *Ocean Governance and the United Nations* (Halifax, N. S. Centre for Foreign Policy Studies Dalhousie University, 1995).

Bothe, Michael. *Peace-keeping*, in Bruno Simma ed., Charter of the United
Nations (Oxford, Oxford University Press, 2002), 660.

Bothe, Michael. *Belligerent Occupation*, Max Planck Encyclopedia of Public
International Law, Vol. III (1997), at 765.

Bothe, Michael. *Occupation After Armistice*, in Encyclopedia of Public
International Law, Vol. III (1997), 761.

Bothe, Michael. *The Peace Process in Eastern Slavonia*, in International
Peacekeeping, December 1995/January 1996, at 6, and *The New Mission in
Eastern Slavonia*, at 11.

Bothe, Michael and Marauhn, Thilo. *UN Administration of Kosovo and East Timor:
Concept, Legality and Limitations of Security Council Mandated Trusteeship
Administration*, in Christian Tomuschat ed., Kosovo and the International
Community (The Hague, New York, Kluwer Law International, 2002), 217.

Bothe, Michael and Marauhn, Thilo. *The United Nations in Kosovo and East Timor:
Problems of a Trusteeship Administration*, International Peacekeeping, Vol. 6
(2000), 152.

Boutros-Ghali, Boutros. *Beyond Peacekeeping*, NYU Journal of International Law
and Politics, Vol. 25 (1992), 115.

Bowett, Derek. *The Impact of Security Council Decisions on Dispute Settlement
Procedures*, European Journal of International Law, Vol. 5 (1994), 89.

Bowett Derek. *United Nations Forces* (London, Stevens, 1964).

Brand, Marcus, G. *Institution-Building and Human Rights Protection in Kosovo*,
Nordic Journal of International Law, Vol. 70 (2001), 46.

(British) War Office. *The Law of War on Land*, Part III of the Manual of Military
Law (1958).

Brower, Charles H. *International Immunities: Some Dissident Views on the Role of
Municipal Courts*, Virginia Journal of International Law, Vol. 41 (2000), 1.

Brownlie, Ian. *Principles of Public International Law* (Oxford, Clarendon Press,
1979).

Brownlie, Ian. *Thoughts on Kind-Hearted Gunmen*, in Richard B. Lillich ed.,
Humanitarian Intervention and the United Nations (Charlottesville,
University Press of Virginia, 1973), 139.

Bull, Hedley. *The Anarchical Society* (London, Macmillan Press, 1977).

Burchill, Richard. *The ICJ Decision on the Case Concerning East Timor: The Illegal Use
of Force Validated*, Journal of Armed Conflict Law, Vol. 2 (1997), 1.

Cady, Jean Christian and Booth, Nicholas. *Internationalized Courts in Kosovo: An
UNMIK Perspective*, in Cesare P. R. Romano, André Nollkaemper and Jann
Kleffner eds., Internationalized Criminal Courts and Tribunals (Oxford,
Oxford University Press, 2004), 59.

Caillier, C. A. *Le Problème de Trieste et de son Territoire Libre*, in Questions
d'Histoire Diplomatique (Montreux, Gauguin & Laubscher Press, 1956).

Caplan, Richard. *International Governance of War-Torn Territories* (Oxford, Oxford
University Press, 2005).

Caplan, Richard. *International Authority and Statebuilding: The Case of Bosnia and
Herzegovina*, Global Governance, Vol. 10 (2004), 53.

Caplan, Richard. *A New Trusteeship? The International Administration of War-torn Territories*, Adelphi Paper 341 (Oxford, Oxford University Press, 2002).

Carcano, Andrea. *End of Occupation in 2004? The Status of the Multinational Force in Iraq after the Transfer of Sovereignty to the Interim Iraqi Government*, Journal of Conflict and Security Law, Vol. 11 (2006), 41.

Caron, David D. *The Legitimacy of the Collective Authority of the Security Council*, American Journal of International Law, Vol. 87 (1993), 552.

Cassese, Antonio. *Self-Determination of Peoples: A Legal Reappraisal* (Cambridge, Cambridge University Press, 1995).

Cassese, Antonio. *Remarks on Scelle's Doctrine of "Role Splitting" (Dédoublement Fonctionnel) in International Law*, European Journal of International Law, Vol. 1 (1990), 210.

Cerone, John. *Minding the Gap: Outlining KFOR Accountability in Post-Conflict Kosovo*, European Journal of International Law, Vol. 12 (2001), 469.

Cerone, John and Baldwin, Clive. *Explaining and Evaluating the UNMIK Court System*, in Cesare P. R. Romano, André Nollkaemper and Jann Kleffner eds., Internationalized Criminal Courts (Oxford, Oxford University Press, 2004).

Chandler, David. *Empire in Denial: The Politics of State-building* (London, Pluto Press Ltd, 2006).

Chandler, David. *Imposing the "Rule of Law": The Lessons of BiH for Peacebuilding in Iraq*, International Peacekeeping, Vol. 11 (2004), 3–4.

Chandler, David. *Bosnia: Faking Democracy After Dayton* (London, Pluto Press Ltd, 1999).

Charney, Jonathan I. *Anticipatory Humanitarian Intervention in Kosovo*, American Journal of International Law, Vol. 93 (1999), 834.

Charney, Jonathan. *Is International Law Threatened by Multiple International Tribunals?*, Recueil des Cours, Vol. 271 (1998), 101.

Charnovitz, Steve. *WTO Cosmopolitics*, NYU Journal of International Law and Politics, Vol. 34 (2002), 299.

Chesterman, Simon. *Ownership in Theory and Practice: Transfer of Authority in UN Statebuilding Operations*, Journal of Intervention and Statebuilding, Vol. 1 (2007), 3–26.

Chesterman, Simon. *Virtual Trusteeship*, in David M. Malone ed., The UN Security Council: From the Cold War to the 21st Century (London, Lynne Rienner, 2004), 219–33.

Chesterman, Simon. *You, the People: The United Nations, Transitional Administration and State-Building* (Oxford, Oxford University Press, 2004).

Chesterman, Simon. *Justice Under International Administration: Kosovo, East Timor and Afghanistan*, Report, International Peace Academy, September 2002.

Chesterman, Simon. *Walking Softly in Afghanistan: The Future of UN Statebuilding*, Survival, Vol. 44 (2002), 37–46.

Chesterman, Simon. *Just War or Just Peace?: Humanitarian Intervention and International Law* (Oxford, Oxford University Press, 2001).

Chesterman, Simon. *Kosovo in Limbo: State-Building and "Substantial Autonomy"*, Report, International Peace Academy, August 2001.

Chesterman, Simon, Ignatieff, Michael and Thahur, Ramesh. *Making States Work, From State Failure to State-Building* (Tokyo, United Nations University Press, 2004).

Chomsky, Noam. *The New Military Humanism: Lessons From Kosovo* (Monroe ME, Common Courage Press, 1999).

Chopra, Jarat. *The UN's Kingdom of East Timor*, Survival, Vol. 42 (2000), 27.

Chopra, Jarat. *Peace Maintenance: The Evolution of International Political Authority* (London, Routledge Press, 1999).

Chopra, Jarat. *Introducing Peace-Maintenance*, in J. Chopra ed., Politics of Peace-Maintenance (Boulder CO, Lynne Rienner Publishers, 1998).

Chopra, Jarat. *Breaking the Stalemate in Western Sahara*, International Peacekeeping, Vol. 1 (1994), 303.

Chopra, Jarat and Weiss, Thomas G. *Sovereignty is No Longer Sacrosanct: Codifying Humanitarian Intervention*, Ethics & International Affairs, Vol. 6 (1994), 95.

Chowdhuri, Ramendra N. *International Mandates and Trusteeship Systems: A Comparative Study* (The Hague, M. Nijhoff, 1955).

Clark, Ian. *Legitimacy in International Society* (Oxford University Press, 2005).

Clark, Roger S. *East Timor, Indonesia and the International Community*, Temple International & Comparative Law Journal, Vol. 14 (2000), 75.

Clark, Roger S. *Obligations of Third States in the Face of Illegality – Ruminations Inspired by the Weeramantry Dissent in the Case Concerning East Timor*, in A. Anghie and G. Sturgess eds., Legal Visions of the 21st Century: Essays in Honour of Judge Christopher Weeramantry (The Hague, Kluwer, 1998), 63.

Claude, Inis L. *Swords into Plowshares: The Problems and Progress of International Organization* (New York, Random House, 1964).

Collier, Paul and Hoeffler, Anke. *The Challenge of Reducing the Global Incidence of Civil War*, Centre for the Study of African Economics, Oxford University, Copenhagen Challenge Paper, 23 April 2004.

Corbett, Percy Ellwood. *What is the League of Nations*, British Yearbook of International Law, Vol. 5 (1924), 119.

Corell, Hans. *The Role of the United Nations in Peacekeeping – Recent Developments from a Legal Perspective*, Address of 1 December 2000, at www.un.org.

Cornell Timothy and Salisbury, Lance. *The Importance of Civil Law in the Transition To Peace: Lessons From the Human Rights Chamber for Bosnia and Herzegovina*, Cornell Journal of International Law, Vol. 35 (2002), 389.

Cotton, James. *Against the Grain: The East Timor Intervention*, Survival, Vol. 43 (2001), 127.

Coursier, Henri. *Le Statut International de la Sarre* (Paris, Editions A. Pedone, 1925).

Covell, Charles. *Kant and the Law of Peace* (Basingstoke, Macmillan Press, 1998).

Cox, Marcus. *The Right to Return Home: International Intervention and Ethnic Cleansing in Bosnia and Herzegovina*, International & Comparative Law Quarterly, Vol. 47 (1998), 599.

Crawford, James. *Creation of States in International Law*, 2nd edn (Oxford, Clarendon Press, 2006).

Criswell, Dianne M. *Durable Consent and a Strong International Peacekeeping Plan: The Success of UNTAET in Light of the Lessons Learned in Cambodia*, Pacific Rim Law and Policy Journal, Vol. 11 (2002), 577.

Cromer, Evelyn B. *Modern Egypt* (London, Macmillan, 1916).

Czerapowicz, John V. *International Territorial Authority: Leticia and West New Guinea* (Ann Arbor, University of Michigan Press, 1975).

Dahl, Robert A. *Can International Organizations Be Democratic? A Sceptic's View*, in Ian Shapiro and Casioano Hacker-Cordón eds., Democracy's Edges (Cambridge, Cambridge University Press, 1999).

Dann, Philipp and Al-Ali, Zaid. *The Internationalized Pouvoir Constituant – Constitution-Making Under External Influence in Iraq, Sudan and East Timor*, Max Planck Yearbook of United Nations Law, Vol. 10 (2006), 423.

D'Aspremont, Jean, *Regulating Statehood: The Kosovo Status Settlement*, Leiden Journal at International Law, vol. 20 (2007), 649.

David, Christopher. *Russian and Chinese Opposition to NATO, Peacekeeping Operation in Kosovo* (2002), 1, at www.usna.edu/NATAC/Papers/tableo4.

De Bertodano, Sylvia. *East Timor – Justice Denied*, Journal of International Criminal Justice, Vol. 2 (2004), 910.

De Hoogh, André. *Attribution or Delegation of (Legislative) Power by the Security Council? The Case of the United Nations Transitional Administration in East Timor (UNTAET)*, International Peacekeeping, Vol. 7 (2001), 1.

De Lannoy, Charles. *Le Règlement de la Question de Dantzig*, Revue de Droit International et de Législation Comparée (1921), 452.

De Vitoria, Franciscus. *De Indis, Relectiones Prior* (1557), in J. B. Scott ed., The Classics of International Law (1917).

De Wet, Erika. *Chapter VII Powers of the United Nations Security Council* (Oxford, Hart Press, 2004).

De Wet, Erika. *The Direct Administration of Territories by the United Nations and its Member States in the Post Cold War Era: Legal Bases and Implications for National Law*, Max Planck Yearbook of United Nations Law, Vol. 8 (2004), 291.

De Wet Erika and Nollkaemper, André. *Review of the Security Decisions by National Courts*, German Yearbook of International Law, Vol. 45 (2002), 166.

Deen, Thalif. Experts Split on Plan for U.N. Trusteeship of Liberia, at http://ipsnews.net/interna.asp?idnews=19710.

Deiwert, Brian. *A New Trusteeship for World Peace and Security: Can an Old League of Nations Idea be Applied to a Twenty-first Century Iraq?*, Indiana International & Comparative Law Review, Vol. 14 (2004), 771.

Delbez, Louis. *Le Concept d'Internationalisation*, Révue Générale de Droit International Public, Vol. 38 (1967), 5.

Delbrück, Jost. *Exercising Public Authority Beyond the State: Transnational Democracy and/or Alternative Legitimation Strategies*, Indiana Journal of Global Legal Studies, Vol. 10 (2003), 29.

Delbrück, Jost. *Prospects for a "World Internal law"?: Legal Developments in a Changing International System*, Indiana Journal of Global Legal Studies, Vol. 9 (2002), 401.

Delbrück, Jost. *The Fight Against Global Terrorism: Self-Defence or Collective Security as Internal Police Action? Some Comments on the International Legal Implications of the "War Against Terrorism"*, German Yearbook of International Law, Vol. 44 (2001), 9.

Dickinson, Laura. *Transitional Justice in Afghanistan: The Promise of Mixed Tribunals*, Denver Journal of International Law and Policy, Vol. 31 (2002), 23.

Dimier, Veronique. *On Good Colonial Government: Lessons from the League of Nations*, Global Society, Vol. 18, No. 3 (2004), 279.

Dinstein, Yoram. *Legislation under Article 43 of the Hague Regulations: Belligerent Occupation and Peacebuilding*, Program on Humanitarian Policy and Conflict Research, Harvard University, Occasional Paper Series, Fall 2004, No. 1.

Dinstein, Yoram. *War, Aggression and Self-Defense* (Cambridge, Cambridge University Press, 2001).

Dinstein, Yoram. *International Law of Belligerent Occupation and Human Rights*, Israel Yearbook of Human Rights, Vol. 1 (1978), 104.

Dodge, Toby. *Inventing Iraq: The Failure of Nationbuilding and a History Denied* (New York, Columbia University Press, 2003).

Doehring, Karl. *Self-Determination*, in Bruno Simma ed., Charter of the United Nations (Oxford, Oxford University Press, 2002), 48.

Doehring, Karl. *Peace Settlements After World War II*, in Encyclopedia of Public International Law, Vol. III (1997), 931.

Doehring, Karl. *Unlawful Resolutions of the Security Council and their Legal Consequences*, Max Planck Yearbook of United Nations Law, Vol. 1 (1997), 91.

Donini, Antonio et al., *Nation-Building Unraveled?: Aid, Peace and Justice in Afghanistan* (Bloomfield CT, Kumarian Press, 2004).

Dore, Issak I. *Self-Determination of Namibia and the United Nations: Paradigm of a Paradox*, Harvard International Law Journal, Vol. 27 (1986), 159.

Dore, Isaak I. *The International Mandate System and Namibia* (Boulder CO, Westview Press, 1985).

Dörr, Oliver. *Die Vereinbarungen von Dayton/Ohio*, Archiv des Völkerrechts, Vol. 35 (1997), 129.

Dobbins, James. *The UN's Role in Nation-Building: From Congo to Iraq* (Santa Monica CA, Rand Corporation, 2005).

Downie, Sue. *The United Nations in East Timor: Comparisons with Cambodia*, in Damien Kings ed., Guns and Ballot Boxes: East Timor's Vote for Independence (Victoria, Monash University, Monash Asia Initiative, 2000), 117.

Doyle, Michael W. *Strategy and Transitional Authority*, in Stephen John Stedman, Donald Rothchild and Elizabeth M. Cousens eds., Ending Civil Wars (Boulder CO, Lynne Rienner Press, 2002), 71.

Doyle, Michael W. *UN Peacekeeping in Cambodia: UNTAC's Civil Mandate* (Boulder CO, Lynne Rienner Press, 1995).

Doyle, Michael W. and Sambanis, Nicholas. *International Peacebuilding: A Theoretical and Quantitative Analysis*, American Political Science Review, Vol. 94 (2000), 779.

Doyle, Michael W. and Suntharalingam, Nishkala. *The UN in Cambodia: Lessons for Complex Peacekeeping*, International Peacekeeping, Vol. 1 (1994), 130.

Dreiwert, Brian. *A New Trusteeship for World Peace and Security: Can an Old League of Nations Idea Be Applied to a Twenty-First Century Iraq?*, Indiana International and Comparative Law Review, Vol. 14 (2004), 771.

Drumbl, Mark. *Rights, Culture and Crime: The Role of Rule of Law for the Women of Afghanistan*, Columbia Journal of Transnational Law, Vol. 42 (2004), 349–90.

Dugard, John. *The South West Africa/Namibia Dispute* (Berkley, University of California Press, 1973).

Durch, William J. *UN Temporary Executive Authority*, in William J. Durch ed., The Evolution of UN Peacekeeping (New York, St Martin's Press, 1994), 285.

Durch, William J. *United Nations Mission for the Referendum in the Western Sahara*, in William J. Durch ed., The Evolution of UN Peacekeeping (New York, St Martin's Press, 1994), 406.

Dutowski, Jean Stanislaw. *Occupation de la Crète 1897–1909* (Paris, Editions A. Pedone, 1952).

El Erian, Abdalla. *Condominium and Related Situations in International Law* (Cairo, Foud I University Press, 1952).

Engers, Jacob F. *The United Nations Travel and Identity Documents for Namibians*, American Journal of International Law, Vol. 65 (1971), 571.

Escarra, Jean. *Le Régime des Concessions Étrangères en Chine*, Recueil des Cours, Vol. 27 (1929-II), 1–146.

Espiell, Gros. *Self-Determination and Jus Cogens*, in A. Cassese ed., U.N. Law/Fundamental Rights: Two Topics in International Law (Alphen aan den Rijn, Sijrhoff & Noordhoff, 1979), 167.

Esty, Daniel C. *The World Trade Organization's Legitimacy Crisis*, World Trade Review, Vol. 1 (2002), 7.

Etzioni, Amitai. *A Self-restrained Approach to Nation-building by Foreign Powers*, International Affairs, Vol. 80 (2004), 1.

Evans, Gareth. *The Responsibility to Protect and the Duty to Prevent*, American Society of International Law Proceedings, Vol. 98 (2004), 77.

Everly, Rebecca. *Reviewing Governmental Acts of the United Nations in Kosovo*, German Law Journal, Vol. 8 (2007), No. 1.

Fairlie, Megan A. *Affirming Brahimi: East Timor Makes the Case for a Model Criminal Code*, American University International Law Review, Vol. 18 (2003), 1059.

Falk, Richard. *What Future for the UN Charter System of War Prevention?*, American Journal of International Law, Vol. 97 (2003), 590.

Farer, Tom. *A Paradigm of Legitimate Intervention*, in Lori Fisler Damrosch ed., Enforcing Restraint: Collective Intervention in Internal Conflicts (New York, Council on Foreign Relations Press, 1993), 316.

Fassbender, Bardo. *The United Nations Charter as a Constitution of the International Community*, Columbia Journal of Transnational Law, Vol. 36 (1998), 575.

Fassbender, Bardo. *UN Security Council Reform and the Right to Veto – A Constitutional Perspective* (The Hague, Kluwer Law International, 1998).

Favoreu, Louis, *La Cour Constitutionelle de Bosnie-Herzégovine*, Mélanges P. Gélard (Paris, Montchrestien, 2000), 273.

Fearon, James D. and Laitin, David D. *Neotrusteeship and the Problem of Weak States*, International Security, Vol. 28 (2004), 5.

Feinberg, Nathan. *La Juridiction de la Cour Permanente de Justice Internationale dans le Système des Mandats* (Paris, Rousseau, 1930).

Feldman, Noah. *Imposed Constitutionalism*, Connecticut Law Review, Vol. 37 (2004/5), 857.

Feldman, Noah. *What We Owe Iraq: War and the Ethics of Nation-Building* (Princeton NJ, Princeton University Press, 2004).

Fernando, Basil. *The System of Trial under the Vietnamese-Khmer Model (1981–1993)*, at www.ahrchk.net/pub/mainfile.php/cambodia_judiciary/114/.

Fidler, David P. *The Return of the Standard of Civilization*, Chicago Journal of International Law, Vol. 2 (2001), 137.

Findlay, Trevor. *Cambodia: The Legacy and Lessons of UNTAC* (Oxford, Oxford University Press, 1995).

Fitzpatrick, Daniel. *Land-policy in Post-Conflict Circumstances: Some Lessons from East Timor*, New Issues in Refugee Research, Working Paper No. 58, p. 4, at www.unhcr.ch/cgi-bin/texis/vtx/home.

Fleck, Dieter ed. *The Law of Visiting Forces* (Oxford, Oxford University Press, 2001).

Fortna, Virginia Page. *United Nations Transition Assistance Group*, in William J. Durch ed., The Evolution of UN Peacekeeping: Case Studies and Comparative Analysis (New York, St Martin's Press, 1993).

Fowler, Michael R. and Bunk, Julie M. *Law, Power and the Sovereign State: The Evolution and Application of the Concept of Sovereignty* (Pennsylvania State University Press, 1995).

Fox, Gregory H. *International Law and the Entitlement to Democracy After War*, Global Governance, Vol. 9 (2003), 179.

Fox, Gregory H. *The Occupation of Iraq*, Georgetown Journal of International Law, Vol. 36 (2005), 195.

Fox, Gregory H. *The Right to Political Participation in International Law*, Yale Journal of International Law, Vol. 17 (1992), 539.

Fox, Gregory H. and Nolte, Georg. *Intolerant Democracies*, Harvard International Law Journal, Vol. 36 (1995), 1.

Fraenkel, Ernst. *Military Occupation and the Rule of Law* (London, Oxford University Press, 1944).

Franck, Thomas M. *What Happens Now? The United Nations After Iraq*, American Journal of International Law, Vol. 97 (2003), 607.

Franck, Thomas M. *Recourse to Force: State Action Against Threats and Armed Attacks* (Cambridge, Cambridge University Press, 2002).

Franck, Thomas M. *Fairness in International Law and Institutions* (Oxford, Oxford University Press, 1998).

Franck, Thomas M. *Postmodern Tribalism and the Right to Secession*, in C. Brölmann, R. Lefeber and M. Zieck eds., Peoples and Minorities in International Law (Dordecht, Nijhoff Press, 1993).

Franck, Thomas M. *The Emerging Right to Democratic Governance*, American Journal of International Law, Vol. 86 (1992), 91.

Franck, Thomas M. *Nation Against Nation: What Happened to the U.N. Dream and What the U.S. Can Do About It* (New York, Oxford University Press, 1985).

Franck, Thomas M. *The Stealing of the Sahara*, American Journal of International Law, Vol. 70 (1976), 694.

Freitag, Horst. *Rechtschutz der Einwohner Berlins gegen hoheitliche Akte der Besatzungsbehörden gemäß Art. 6 Abs. 1 EMRK* (1989), 24.

Friedmann, Wolfgang Gaston. *The Allied Military Government of Germany* (London, Stevens Press, 1947).

Friedrich, Jürgen. *UNMIK in Kosovo: Struggling with Uncertainty*, Max Planck Yearbook of United Nations Law, Vol. 9 (2005), 225.

Frowein, Jochen Abr. *Issues of Legitimacy around the Security Council*, in Jochen Abr. Frowein *et al.* eds., Negotiating for Peace, Liber Amicorum Tono Eitel (Berlin, 2003), 121.

Frowein, Jochen Abr. *Die Notstandsverwaltung von Gebieten durch die Vereinten Nationen*, in H.-W. Arndt *et al.* eds., Völkerrecht und Deutsches Recht, Festschrift für Walter Rudolf (Geburtstag, Beck, München, 2001), 43.

Frowein, Jochen Abr. *Konstitutionalisierung des Völkerrechts*, in Völkerrecht und Internationales Privatrecht in einem sich Globalisierenden Internationalen System – Auswirkungen der Entstaatlichung Ttransnationaler Rechtsbeziehungen (2000), 427.

Frowein, Jochen Abr. *The Relationship between Human Rights Regimes and Regimes of Belligerent Occupation*, Israel Yearbook on Human Rights, Vol. 28 (1998), 1.

Frowein, Jochen Abr. *Unilateral Interpretation of Security Council Resolutions: A Threat to Collective Security?*, in V. Götz, P. Selmer, R. Wolfrum eds., Liber Amicorum Günther Jaenicke – zum 85. Geburtstag (1998), 97.

Frowein, Jochen Abr. and Krisch, Nico. *Introduction to Chapter VII*, in Bruno Simma ed., Charter of the United Nations (Oxford, Oxford University Press, 2002), 702.

Fukuyama, Francis, *State-Building: Governance and World Order in the 21st Century* (Ithaca NY, Cornell University Press, 2004).

Gann, L. H. and Duignan, Peter. *Rulers of Belgian Africa, 1884–1914* (Princeton NJ, Princeton University Press, 1979).

García, Thierry. *La Mission d'Administration Intérimaire des Nations Unies au Kosovo*, Revue Génerale de Droit International Public, Vol. 104 (2000), 61.

Gardiner, Nile and Rivkin, David B. *Blueprint for Freedom: Limiting the Role of the United Nations in Post-War Iraq*, Heritage Foundation, Backgrounder No. 1646, 21 April 2003.

Gayim, Eyassu. *The Eritrean Question* (Uppsala, Iustus Forlag Press, 1993).

Gerna, Christine. *Universal Democracy: an International Legal Right or a Pipe Dream of the West?*, NYU Journal of International Law and Policy, Vol. 27 (1995), 289.

Gerson, Allan. *Trustee Occupant: The Legal Status of Israel's Presence in the West Bank*, Harvard International Law Journal, Vol. 14 (1973), 1.

Gibson, Susan S. *The Misplaced Reliance on Free and Fair Elections in Nation-Building: The Role of Constitutional Democracy and the Rule of Law*, Houston Journal of International Law, Vol. 21 (1998), 1.

Giegerich, Thomas. *Vorbehalte zu Menschenrechtsabkommen: Zulässigkeit, Gültigkeit und Prüfungskompetenz von Vertragsgremien*, Zeitschrift für ausländisches öffentliches Recht und Völkerrecht, Vol. 55 (1995), 713.

Gill, Terry. *Legal and Some Political Limitations on the Power of the UN Security Council to Exercise its Enforcement Powers under Chapter VII of the Charter*, Netherlands Yearbook of International Law, Vol. 26 (1995), 33.

Goldstone, Anthony. *UNTAET with Hindsight: The Peculiarities of Politics in an Incomplete State*, Global Governance Vol. 10 (2004), 83.

Gong, Gerrit W. *The Standard of "Civilization" in International Society* (Oxford, Oxford University Press, 1984).

Goodrich Leland M. and Hambro, Edvard. *Charter of the United Nations: Commentary and Documents* (London, Stevens Press, 1949).

Gordan, Ruth. *Saving Failed States: Sometimes a Neo-colonialist Notion*, American University Journal of International Law & Policy, Vol. 12 (1997), 903.

Gordon, Ruth. *Some Legal Problems with Trusteeship*, Cornell International Law Journal, Vol. 28 (1995), 301.

Goy, Raymond. *L'Indépendance du Timor Oriental*, Annuaire Français de Droit International (1999), 203.

Grant, Thomas D. *Iraq: How to Reconcile Conflicting Obligations of Occupation and Reform*, ASIL Insights, June 2003.

Grant, Thomas D. *East Timor, the U.N. System, and Enforcing Non-Recognition in International Law*, Vanderbilt Journal of Transnational Law, Vol. 33 (2000), 273.

Grant, Thomas D. *Extending Decolonization: How the United Nations Might Have Addressed Kosovo*, Georgia Journal of International and Comparative Law, Vol. 28 (1999), 9.

Grant, Thomas D. *International Guaranteed Constitutive Order, Cyprus and Bosnia as Predicates for a New Non-traditional Actor in the Society of States*, Journal of Transnational Law and Policy, Vol. 8 (1998), 1.

Gray, Christine. *International Law and the Use of Force* (Oxford, Oxford University Press, 2000).

Greenwood, Christopher. *International Law and the Pre-emptive Use of Force: Afghanistan, Al-Qaida, and Iraq*, San Diego International Law Journal, Vol. 4 (2003), 7.

Greenwood, Christopher. *The Administration of Occupied Territories*, in E. Playfair ed., International Law and the Administration of Occupied Territories (Oxford, Clarendon Press, 1992), 243.

Grenfell, Laura. *Legal Pluralism and the Rule of Law in Timor Leste*, Leiden Journal of International Law, Vol. 19 (2006), 305.

Grewe, Wilhelm W. *Ein Besatzungsstatut für Deutschland* (Stuttgart, Kohler, 1948).

Grimm, Dieter. *Does Europe Need a Constitution*, in P. Gowan and P. Anderson eds., The Question of Europe (London, Verso, 1997).

Groom, Arthur J. R. *The Trusteeship Council: A Successful Demise*, in P. Taylor and A. J. R. Groom eds., The United Nations at the Millennium (London, Continuum, 2000), 142.

Gross, Oren. *The Normless and Exceptionless Exception: Carl Schmitt's Theory of Emergency Powers and the "Norm-Exception" Dichotomy*, Cardazo Law Review, Vol. 21 (2000), 1820.

Gross, Oren. *Once More unto the Breach: The Systematic Failure of Applying the European Convention on Human Rights to Entrenched Emergencies*, Yale Journal of International Law, Vol. 23 (1998), 437.

Grossman Claudio and Bradlow, Daniel D. *Are We Being Propelled Towards a People-Centered Transnational Legal Order?*, American University Journal of International Law and Policy, Vol. 9 (1993), 1.

Grotius, Hugo. *De Jure Belli Ac Pacis* (1625), Francis W. Kelsey trans. (Oxford, Clarendon Press, 1925).

Gruss, Daniel. *UNTEA and West New Guinea*, Max Planck Yearbook of United Nations Law, Vol. 9 (2005), 97.

Guggenheim, Paul. *Traité de Droit International Public*, Vol. I (Geneva, Libr. de L'universite, 1953).

Habermas, Jürgen. *Between Facts and Norms: Contributions to a Discourse Theory of Law and Democracy*, William Rehg trans. (Albany, State University of New York, 1996).

Hajnal Henri. *Le Droit du Danube International* (La Haye, Nijhoff, 1929).

Halchin, L. Elaine. CRS Report for Congress, *The Coalition Provisional Authority: Origin, Characteristics and Institutional Authorities*, 29 April 2004, at www.fas.org/man/crs/RL32370.pdf. 1.

Hall, Duncan Hessel. *Mandates, Dependencies and Trusteeship* (London, Stevens, 1948).

Hampson, Fen Osler. *Making Peace Agreements Work: The Implementation and Enforcement of Peace Agreements between Sovereigns and Intermediate Sovereigns*, Cornell Journal of International Law, Vol. 30 (1997), 701.

Hampson, Fen Osler. *Nurturing Peace: Why Peace Settlements Succeed or Fail* (Washington DC, United States Institute of Peace, 1996).

Han, Sonia K. *Building A Peace That Lasts: The United Nations and Post-Civil War Peacebuilding*, NYU Journal of International Law and Politics, Vol. 26 (1994), 837.

Hannum, Hurst. *Autonomy, Sovereignty and Self-Determination* (Philadelphia PA, University of Pennsylvania Press, 1996).

Harland, David. *Legitimacy and Effectiveness in International Administration*, Global Governance, Vol. 10 (2004), No. 1, January–March 2004.

Harris, Norman Dwight. *Intervention and Colonization in Africa* (Boston, Houghton Mifflin Company, 1914).

Hart, Herbert L. A. *Utilitarism and Natural Rights*, in Hart, Herbert L. A., Essays in Jurisprudence and Philosophy (Oxford, Clarendon Press, 1983), 181.

Hartmann, Michael E. *International Judges and Prosecutors in Kosovo*, United States Institute of Peace, Special Report No. 112 (2003), at www.usip.org/pubs/specialreports/sr112.pdf.

Hatschek, Julius. *Das Völkerrecht als System völkerrechtlich bedeutsamer Staatsakte* (Leipzig, Deichert, 1923).

Held, David. *Democracy and the Global Order: From the Modern State to Cosmopolitan Governance* (Stanford, CA, Stanford University Press, 1995).

Helman, Gerald B. and Ratner, Steven R. *Saving Failed States*, Foreign Policy No. 89 (1992–3), 3.

Herdegen, Matthias and Thürer, Daniel. *Der Wegfall effektiver Staatsgewalt im Völkerrecht: "The Failed State"*, Berichte der Deutschen Gesellschaft für Völkerrecht, Vol. 34 (1996), 9.

Herman, Lawrence L. *The Legal Status of Namibia and of the United Nations Council for Namibia*, Canadian Yearbook of International Law, Vol. 13 (1975), 306.

Hertel, Wolfram. *Supranationalität als Verfassungsprinzip* (Berlin, Tubingen, 1999).

Heyland, Karl L. *Die Rechtsstellung der besetzten Rheinlande nach dem Versailler Friedensvertrag und dem Rheinlandsabkommen* (Stuttgart, Kohlhammer, 1923).

Higgins, Rosalyn. *Derogations under Human Rights Treaties*, British Yearbook of International Law, Vol. 48 (1976/7), 281.

Higgins, Rosalyn. *United Nations Peacekeeping 1946–1967*, Vol. III, Africa (London, Oxford University Press, 1980).

Higgins, Rosalyn. *United Nations Peacekeping 1946–1967*, Documents and Commentary, Vol. II, Asia (London, Oxford University Press, 1970).

Hill, Stephen M. and Malik, Shahin P. *Peacekeeping and the United Nations* (Aldershot, Dartmouth, 1996).

Hilpold, Peter. *Humanitarian Intervention: Is There a Need for a Legal Reappraisal?*, European Journal of International Law, Vol. 12 (2001), 437.

Hirsch, Günther. *EG: Kein Staat, aber eine Verfassung?*, Neue Juristische Wochenschrift (2000), 46.

Hoffmeister, Frank. *Menschenrechts- und Demokratieklauseln in den Vertraglichen Außenbeziehungen der Europäischen Gemeinschaft* (Berlin, Springer, 1998).

Hooker, M. B. *Legal Pluralism: An Introduction to Colonial and Neo-Colonial Laws* (Oxford, Clarendon Press, 1975).

Horowitz, Donald L. *Ethnic Groups in Conflict* (Berkeley, University of California Press, 1985).

Hudson, Manley. *The Prospect for International Law in the Twentieth-Century*, Cornell Law Quarterly, Vol. 10 (1925), 419.

Hufnagel, Frank-Erich. *UN-Friedensoperationen der Zweiten Generation. Vom Puffer zur Neuen Treuhand* (Berlin, Duncker und Humblot, 1996).

Ignatieff, Michael. *Empire Lite: Nation Building in Bosnia, Kosovo and Afghanistan* (London, Vintage, 2003).

Irmscher, Tobias H. *The Legal Framework for the Activities of the United Nations Interim Mission in Kosovo: The Charter, Human Rights, and the Law of Occupation*, German Yearbook of International Law, Vol. 44 (2001), 353.

Irving, Karl J. *The United Nations and Democratic Intervention: Is Swords into Ballot Boxes Enough?*, Denver Journal of International Law and Policy, Vol. 25 (1996), 41.

Israel, Fred L. (ed.). *Major Peace Treaties of Modern History* (1980–2000) (New York, Chelsea House Press, 2000).

Jackson, Robert Houghwont. *The Global Covenant* (Oxford, Oxford University Press, 2000).

Jennings, Robert Y. *Nullity and Effectiveness in International Law*, in Cambridge Essays in International Law – Essays in Honour of Lord McNair (London, Steven & Sons, 1965), 72.

Jennings, Robert Y. *Government in Commission*, British Yearbook of International Law, Vol. 23 (1946), 112.

Johnstone, Ian. *UN Peace-Building: Consent, Coercion and the Crisis of State Failure*, From Territorial Sovereignty to Human Security (Canadian Council on International Law, 2000), 186.

Junius, Andreas. *Der United Nations Council for Namibia* (Frankfurt Am Main, Lang, 1989).

Kaikobad, Kaiyan Homi. *Problems of Belligerent Occupation: The Scope of Powers Exercised by the Coalition Provisional Authority in Iraq, April/May 2003–June 2004*, International & Comparative Law Quarterly, Vol. 54 (2005), 253.

Kamanda, Alfred M. *A Study of the Legal Status of Protectorates in Public International Law* (Ambilly-Annemasse, Les Presses de Savoie, 1961).

Kamminga, Menno T. *State Succession in Respect of Human Rights Treaties*, European Journal of International Law, Vol. 7 (1996), 469.

Kant, Immanuel. *Metaphysik der Sitten, Das Öffentliche Recht* (1748), §§43-49, Wilhelm Weischedel ed., (1968).

Kant, Immanuel. *Perpetual Peace* (London, Sweet & Maxwell, 1927), Third Definitive Article for Perpetual Peace.

Katayanagi, Mari. *Human Rights Functions of United Nations Peacekeeping Operations* (The Hague, Nijhoff 2002).

Keller, Lucy. *UNTAC in Cambodia – From Occupation, Civil War and Genocide to Peace*, Max Planck Yearbook of United Nations Law, Vol. 9 (2005), 127.

Kelly, Michael. *Iraq and the Law of Occupation: New Tests For an Old Law*, Yearbook of International Humanitarian Law, Vol. 6 (2003), 128.

Kelly, Michael, McCormack, Timothy, Muggleton, Paul and Oswald, Bruce. *Legal Aspects of Australia's Involvement in the International Force for East Timor*, International Review of the Red Cross, Vol. 841 (2001), 101.

Kelly, Michael J. *Restoring and Maintaining Order in Complex Peace Operations* (The Hague, Kluwer Law International, 1999).

Kelly, Michael J. *Legitimacy and the Public Security Function*, in R. Oakley, M. Dziedzic and E. Goldberg eds., Policing the New World Disorder (Washington DC, National Defence University Press, US Government Printing Office, 1998).

Kelsen, Hans. *The Law of the United Nations: A Critical Appraisal of Its Fundamental Problems* (1964; New Jersey, Lawbook Exchange LTI Union, 2000).

Kelsen, Hans. *The Legal Status of Germany According to the Declaration of Berlin*, American Journal of International Law, Vol. 39 (1945), 518.

Kelsen, Hans. *The International Legal Status of Germany to be Established Immediately Upon Termination of the War*, American Journal of International Law, Vol. 38 (1944), 692.

Kennedy, David. *The Dark Sides of Virtue: Reassessing International Humanitarianism* (Princeton NJ, Princeton University Press, 2004).

Kennedy, David. *The Disciplines of International Law and Policy*, Leiden Journal of International Law, Vol. 12 (1999), 9.

Kennedy, Paul. *UN Trusteeship Council Could Finally Find a Role in Postwar Iraq*, Daily Yomiuri, 9 May 2003, at www.globalpolicy.org/security/issues/iraq/after/2003/0511trusteeshipcouncil.htm.

Keohane, Robert Owen. *Political Authority after Intervention: Gradations in Sovereignty*, in J. L. Holzgrefe and R. O. Keohane eds., Humanitarian Intervention: Ethical, Legal and Political Dilemmas (Cambridge, Cambridge University Press, 2003), 276.

Keohane, Robert Owen and Nye, Joseph S., Jr. *The Club Model of Multilateral Cooperation and Problems of Democratic Legitimacy*, in Roger Porter *et al.* eds., Efficiency, Equity and Legitimacy: The Multilateral Trading System at the Millennium (Center for Business, Harvard University, Brookings Institution, 2001), 264.

Kimminich, Otto. *A "Federal" Right to Self-Determination?*, in C. Tomuschat ed., Modern Law of Self-Determination (Dordrecht, Nijhoff, 1993).

Kingsbury, Benedict. *The International Legal Order*, in Peter Cane and Mark Tushnet eds., Oxford Handbook of Legal Studies (Oxford, Oxford University Press, 2003), 271.

Kingsbury, Benedict. *Is the Proliferation of International Courts and Tribunals a Systemic Problem?*, NYU Journal of International Law and Politics, Vol. 31 (1999), 679.

Kingsbury, Benedict. *A Grotian Tradition of Theory and Practice?: Grotius, Law and Moral Scepticism in the Thought of Hedley Bull*, Quinnipiac Law Review, Vol. 17 (1997), 3.

Kingsbury, Benedict, Krisch, Nico and Stewart, Richard. *The Emergence of Global Administrative Law*, Law & Contemporary Problems, Vol. 68 (2005), 15.

Kingsbury, Benedict and Roberts, Adam. *Introduction: Grotian Thought in International Relations*, in Hedley Bull *et al.* eds., Hugo Grotius and International Relations (Oxford, Clarendon Press, 1990), 51.

Kirgis, Frederic L. *Security Council Resolution 1483 on the Rebuilding of Iraq*, ASIL Insight, May 2003.

Kirgis, Frederic L. *International Organizations in Their Legal Setting* (St Paul Minn., West Publ. Co., 1993).

Klabbers, Jan. *Redemption Song? Human Rights Versus Community-building in East Timor*, Leiden Journal of International Law, Vol. 16 (2003), 367.

Klein, Eckard. *Namibia*, in Encyclopedia of Public International Law, Vol. 3 (Amsterdam, North Holland Press, 1997).

Klein, Eckart. *Statusverträge im Völkerrecht* (Berlin, Springer, 1980).

Knaus, Gerald and Martin, Felix. *Travails of the European Raj*, Journal of Democracy, Vol. 14, No. 3 (2003), 60.

Knoll, Bernhard. *Legitimacy and UN-Administration of Territory*, German Law Journal, Vol. 8, No. 1 (2007), 39.

Knoll, Bernhard. *Beyond the "Mission Civilisatrice": The Specific Properties of a Normative Order within an "Internationalized" Territory*, Leiden Journal of International Law, Vol. 19 (2006), 275.

Knoll, Bernhard. *From Benchmarking to Final Status? Kosovo and the Problem of an International Administration's Open-Ended Mandate*, European Journal of International Law, Vol. 16 (2005), 637.

Knoll, Bernhard. *UN Imperium: Horizontal and Vertical Transfer of Effective Control and the Concept of Residual Sovereignty*, in "Internationalised Territories", Austrian Review of International and European Law, Vol. 7 (2002), 3.

Knudson, John L. *A History of the League of Nations* (Atlanta, TE Smith & Co, 1938).

Koh, Harald. *Transnational Public Law Litigation*, Yale Law Journal, Vol. 100 (1991), 2372.

Kolb, Robert. *Does Article 103 of the Charter of the United Nations Apply to Decisions or also to Authorizations Adopted by the Security Council?*, Zeitschrift für ausländisches öffentliches Recht und Völkerrecht, Vol. 64 (2004), 21.

Kolb, Robert. *Ius in Bello: Le Droit International des Conflits Armés* (Bale, Helbing & Lichtenhahn, 2003).

Kolb, Robert, Porretto, Gabriele and Vité, Silvain. *L'Application du Droit International Humanitaire et des Droits de l'Homme aux Organisations Internationales: Forces de Paix et Administrations Civiles Transitoires* (Bruxelles, Bruylant, 2005).

Kondoch, Boris. *The United Nations Administration of East Timor*, Journal of Conflict and Security Law, Vol. 6 (2001), 245.

Korhonen, Outi. *International Governance in Post-Conflict Situations*, Leiden Journal of International Law, Vol. 14 (2001), 495.

Korhonen, Outi. *"Post" As Justification: International Law and Democracy-Building after Iraq*, German Law Journal, Vol. 4 (2003), 709.

Korhonen, Outi and Gras, Jutta. *International Governance in Post-Conflict Situations* (Helsinki, University of Helsinki, Faculty of Law, 2001).

Korhonen, Outi, Gras, Jutta and Creutz, Katja. *International Post-Conflict Situations: New Challenges for Co-Operative Governance*, Erik Castrén Institute Research Reports 18, Helsinki, 2006.

Korman, Sharon. *Right of Conquest* (Oxford, Clarendon Press, 1996).

Krajewski, Markus. *Democratic Legitimacy and Constitutional Perspectives of WTO Law*, Journal of World Trade, Vol. 35 (2001), 167.

Krasner, Stephen D. *Sovereignty: Organized Hypocrisy* (Princeton NJ, Princeton University Press, 1999).

Krisch, N. and Kingsbury, B. *Global Governance and Global Administrative Law in the International Legal Order*, European Journal of International Law, Vol. 17 (2006), 1.

Krisch, Nico. *The Rise and Fall of Collective Security, Terrorism, U.S. Hegemony and the Plight of the Security Council*, in Christian Walter, Silja Vöneky, Volker Röben and Frank Schorkopf eds., Terrorism as a Challenge for National and International Law: Security versus Liberty? (Berlin, Springer, 2004), at edoc.mpil.de/conference-on-terrorism/index.cfm.

Krisch, Nico. *Weak as Constraint, Strong as Tool: The Place of International Law in U.S. Foreign Policy*, in David M. Malone and Y. Foong Khong eds., Unilateralism and U.S. Foreign Policy: International Perspectives (Boulder, Lynne Rienner, 2003), 41.

Kritz, Neil. *Securing the Rule of Law in Post-Taliban Afghanistan: Promoting a Formal System of Justice*, Connecticut Journal of International Law, Vol. 17 (2002), 451.

Kunzmann, Katharina. *Reconstructing Iraq and Who Pays: Is There an International Responsibility to Reconstruct a Country Destroyed by War?*, German Law Journal, Vol. 4 (2003), No. 7.

Lagrange, Evelyne. *La Mission Intérimaire des Nations Unies au Kosovo, Nouvel Essai d'Administration Directe d'un Territoire*, Annuaire Française de Droit International, Vol. XLV (1999), 335.

Lakshiminarayan, Chetlur. *Analysis of the Principles and System of International Trusteeship in the Charter* (Geneva, Impr. Populaires, 1951).

Lapidoth, Ruth. *The Jerusalem Question and Its Resolution: Selected Documents* (Dordrecht, Nijhoff, 1994).

Laurent, Pech. *La Garantie Internationale de la Constitution de Bosnie-Herzégovine*, Revue Française de Droit Constitutionnel, Vol. 42 (2000), 421.

Lauterpacht, Elihu. *The Development of the Law of International Organizations by the Decisions of International Tribunals*, Recueil des Cours, Vol. 152 (1976, IV).

Lauterpacht, Elihu. *Contemporary Practice of the United Kingdom in the Field of International Law*, International & Comparative Law Quarterly, Vol. 5 (1956), 405.

Lauterpacht, Hersch. *Succession of States with Respect to Private Law Obligations*, in E. Lauterpacht ed., International Law being the Collected Papers of Hersch Lauterpacht, Vol. 3 (Cambridge, Cambridge University Press, 1977), 121.

Lauterpacht, Hersch. *The "Grotian Tradition" in International Law*, British Yearbook of International Law, Vol. 23 (1946), 1.

Lawson, Richard. *The Concept of Jurisdiction and Extraterritorial Acts of State*, in G. Kreijen ed., State, Sovereignty and International Governance (Oxford, Oxford University Press, 2004), 281.

Leprette Jacques, *Le Statut International de Trieste* (Paris, Pedone, 1948).

Levesque, Geneviéve. *La Situation Internationale de Dantzig* (Paris, Pedone, 1924).

Lewis, Malcolm L. *The Free City of Danzig*, British Yearbook of International Law, Vol. V (1924), 89.

Lijphart, Arend. *Democracy in Plural Societies* (Newhaven CT, Yale University Press, 1977).

Lindley, Mark F. *The Acquisition and Government of Backward Territory in International Law* (New York, Negro University Press, 1926).

Linton, Susannah. *Rising from the Ashes: The Creation of a Viable Criminal Justice System in East Timor*, Melbourne University Law Review, Vol. 25 (2001), 122.

Litchfield, Edward H. *Governing Postwar Germany* (Ithaca NY, Cornell University Press, 1953).

Locke, John. *Two Treatises of Government* (1690), Peter Laslett ed. (Cambridge, Cambridge University Press 1988).

Lorenz, Dirk. *Der Territoriale Anwendungsbereich der Grund- und Menschenrechte: Zugleich ein Beitrag zum Individualschutz in Bewaffneten Konflikten* (Berlin, Berliner Wissenschaftsverlag, 2005).

Luckau, Alma. *The German Delegation at the Paris Peace Conference* (New York, Columbia University Press, 1941).

Lugard, Frederick. *The Dual Mandate in British Tropical Africa* (London, Frank Cass Publishers, 1922).

Maffei, M. Clara. *The Case of East Timor before the International Court of Justice – Some Tentative Comments*, European Journal of International Law, Vol. 4 (1993), 223.

Majone, Giandomenico. *Europe's Democratic Deficit: The Question of Standards*, European Law Journal, Vol. 4 (1998), 5.

Makowski, Julijan. *La Situation Juridique de la Ville Libre de Dantzig*, Revue Générale de Droit International Public, Vol. 30 (1923), 169.

Mani, Rami. *Conflict Resolution, Justice and the Law: Rebuilding the Rule of Law in the Aftermath of Complex Political Emergencies*, International Peacekeeping, Vol. 5 (1998), 6.

Marauhn, Thilo. *Konfliktbewältigung in Afghanistan zwischen Utopie und Pragmatismus*, Archiv des Völkerrechts, Vol. 40 (2002), 480.

Marazzi, Alessandro. *I Territori Internazionalizzati* (Torino, Giappichelli, 1959).

Marko, Joseph. *Five Years of Constitutional Jurisprudence in Bosnia and Herzegovina: A First Balance*, European Diversity and Autonomy Papers 7/2004, at 14.

Marko, Joseph. *Fünf Jahre Verfassungsgerichtsbarkeit in Bosnien and Herzegowina: Eine erste Bilanz*, in B.-Ch. Funk *et al.* eds., Der Rechtsstaat vor neuen Herausforderungen – Festschrift für Ludwig Adamovich zum 70. Geburtstag (Wien, Verlag Österreich, 2002), 385.

Marko, Joseph. *Kosovo/a – A Gordian Knot?*, in Joseph Marko ed., Gordischer Knoten Kosovo/a: Durrchschlagen oder entwirren ? (Baden-Baden, Verlagsgesellschaft, 1999), 261.

Marks, Stephen P. *The New Cambodian Constitution: From Civil Law to a Fragile Democracy*, Columbia Human Rights Law Review, Fall (1994), 45.

Marks, Susan. *Democracy and International Governance*, in J.-M. Coicaud and V. Heiskanen eds., The Legitimacy of International Organizations (Tokyo, The United Nations University Press, 2001), 51.

Marshall, David and Inglis, Shelley. *Human Rights in Transition: The Disempowerment of Human Rights-Based Justice in the United Nations Mission in Kosovo*, Harvard Environmental Law Review, Vol. 16 (2003), 95.

Martelli, George. *Experiment in World Government: An Account of the United Nations Operation in the Congo, 1960–1964* (London, Johnston Publications, 1966).

Marten, Jens. *Menschenrechtsschutz in Internationalen Mandatsgebieten und ihre Strukturellen Widersprüche am Beispiel des Kosovo*, Humanitäres Völkerrecht, Vol. 3 (2004), 144.

Martin, Edwin M. *The Allied Occupation of Japan* (New York, American Institute of Pacific Relations, 1948).

Martin, Ian and Mayer-Rieckh, A. *The United Nations and East Timor: From Self-Determination to State-Building*, International Peacekeeping, Vol. 12 (2005), 125.

Mason, John B. *The Danzig Dilemma* (Stanford CA, Stanford University Press, 1945).

Matheson, Michael J. *United Nations Governance of Postconflict Societies*, American Journal of International Law, Vol. 95 (2001), 76.

McCoubrey, Hilaire and White, Nigel D. *The Blue Helmets: Legal Regulation of United Nations Military Operations* (Aldershot, Dartmouth, 1996).

McDougal, Myres S., Lasswell, Harold D. and Reisman, W. Michael, *The World Constitutive Process of Authoritative Decision*, in M. S. McDougal and W. M. Reisman eds., International Law Essays: A Supplement to International Law in Contemporary Practice (Mineola NY, Foundation Press, 1981), 191.

McNair, Arnold Duncan and Watts, Arthur D. *The Legal Effects of War* (Cambridge, Cambridge University Press, 1966).

Matz, Nele. *Civilization and the Mandate System under the League of Nations as Origin of Trusteeship*, Max Planck Yearbook of United Nations Law, Vol. 9 (2005), 47.

Mégret, Frédéric and Hoffmann, Florian. *The UN as a Human Rights Violator? Some Reflections on the United Nations Changing Human Rights Responsibilities*, Human Rights Quarterly, Vol. 25 (2003), 314.

Meron, Theodor. *Extraterritoriality of Human Rights Treaties*, American Journal of International Law, Vol. 89 (1995), 78.

Metha, Uday Singh. *Liberalism and Empire: A Study in Nineteenth Century British Liberal Thought* (Chicago, University of Chicago Press, 1999).

Miller, Anthony J. *UNMIK: Lessons From the Early Institution-Building Phase*, New England Law Review, Vol. 39 (2004), 9.

Miller, David Hunter. *The Drafting of the Covenant*, Vol. II (New York, G.P. Putnam's Sons, 1928).

Mohamed, Saira. *From Keeping Peace to Building Peace: A Proposal for a Revitalized United Nations Trusteeship Council*, Columbia Law Review, Vol. 105 (2005), 809.

Montgomery, John D. *Forced to Be Free* (Chicago, Chicago University Press, 1957).

Moravcsik, Andrew. *In Defense of the "Democratic Deficit": Reassessing Legitimacy in the European Union*, Journal of Common Market Studies, Vol. 40 (2002), 803.

Morgenstern, Felice. *Legality in International Organizations*, British Yearbook of International Law, Vol. 48 (1976–7), 241.

Morgenstern, Felice. *Validity of the Acts of the Belligerent Occupant*, British Yearbook of International Law, Vol. 28 (1951), 297.

Morlok, Martin. *Grundfragen einer Verfassung auf Europäischer Ebene*, in P. Häberle ed., Staat und Verfassung in Europa (Baden-Baden, Nomos Verlagsgesellschaft, 2000), 73.

Morphet, Sally. *Organising Civil Administration in Peace-Maintenance*, in Politics of Peace-Maintenance (Boulder CO, Lynne Rienner Publishers, 1998), 41.

Morrow Jonathan and White, Rachel. *The United Nations in Transitional East Timor: International Standards and the Reality of Governance*, Australian Yearbook of International Law, Vol. 22 (2002), 11.

Morrow, Ian F. D. *The International Status of the Free City of Danzig*, British Yearbook of International Law, Vol. 18 (1937), 114.

Morrow, Jan F. D. *The Peace Settlement in the German-Polish Borderlands* (London, Oxford University Press, 1936).

Mortimer, Edward. *International Administration of War-Torn Societies*, Global Governance, Vol. 10 (2004), 7.

Mosler, Hermann. *The International Society as a Legal Community* (Alphen Aan Den Rijn, Sijthoff, Noordhoff, 1980).

Mossner, J. M. *Military Government*, in Encyclopedia of Public International Law, Vol. 3 (1997), 391.

Müllerson, Rein. *Ordering Anarchy, International Law in International Society* (The Hague, Nijhoff, 2000).

Münch, Fritz. *Saar Territory*, in Rudolf Bernhardt ed., Encyclopedia of Public International Law, Vol. IV (2000), 271.

Mundis, Daryl A. *New Mechanisms for the Enforcement of International Humanitarian Law*, American Journal of International Law, Vol. 96 (2001), 934.

Murphy, Sean D. *Nation-Building: A Look at Somalia*, Tulane Journal of International & Comparative Law, Vol. 3 (1995), 19.

Murphy, Sean D. *The Security Council, Legitimacy, and the Concept of Collective Security after the Cold War*, Columbia Journal of Transnational Law, Vol. 32 (1994), 201.

Nathan, E. *The Power of Supervision of the High Court of Justice over Military Government*, in Meir Shamgar ed., Military Government in the Territories Administered by Israel, 1967–1980: The Legal Aspects (Jerusalem, The Harry Sacher Institute for Legislative Research and Comparative Law, 1982), 109.

Ni Aolain, F. *The Fractured Soul of the Dayton Peace Agreement: A Legal Analysis*, Michigan Journal of International Law, Vol. 19 (1997/8), 957.

Nolte, Georg. *Eingreifen auf Einladung* (Berlin, Springer, 1999).

Nordlinger, Eric. *Conflict Regulation in Divided Societies* (Cambridge MA, Harvard University, 1972).

Nye, Joseph S. and Donahue, John D. eds. *Governance in a Globalizing World* (Washington DC, The Brookings Institution, 2000).

O'Connell, Daniel P. *State Succession in Municipal Law and International Law*, Vol. 1 (Cambridge, Cambridge University Press, 1967), 237.

Oellers-Frahm, Karin. *Die Rolle Internationaler Gerichte im Friedensprozess in Bosnien und Herzegowina nach dem Abkommen von Dayton*, in Volkmar Götz et al. eds., Liber Amicorum Günther Jaenicke – Zum 85. Geburtstag (1998), 263.

Oellers-Frahm, Karin. *Restructuring Bosnia-Herzegovina: A Model With Pitfalls*, Max Planck Yearbook of United Nations Law, Vol. 5 (2005), 179.

Oeter, Stefan. *Die Internationalen "Protektorate" in Bosnien-Herzegowina und im Kosovo – Entwicklung und Rechtliche Folgeprobleme der UN-Friedensregime*, in Horst Fischer *et al.* eds., Krisensicherung und Humanitärer Schutz – Crisis Management and Humanitarian Protection, Festschrift für Dieter Fleck (Berlin, Berliner Wissenschafts-Verlag, 2004), 427.

Oeter, Stefan. *International Law and the General Systems Theory*, German Yearbook of International Law, Vol. 44 (2001), 72.

Oppenheim, Lassa. *International Law: A Treatise*, 6th edn, Vol. I (1947), Vol. II (1944), ed. H. Lauterpacht (London, New York, Toronto, Lomgmans, Green and Co.).

Oppenheim, Lassa. *Le Caractère Essentiel de la Societé des Nations*, Revue Générale de Droit International Public, Vol. 24 (1919), 234.

Oraá, Jaime. *Human Rights in States of Emergency in International Law* (Oxford, Clarendon Press, 1992).

Orakhelashvili, Alexander. *The Legal Basis of United Nations Peace-Keeping Operations*, Virginia Journal of International Law, Vol. 43 (2003), 485.

Orend, Brian. *The Morality of War* (Toronto, Broadview Press, 2006).

Orend, Brian. *Justice After War*, Ethics & International Affairs, Vol. 16 (2002), 43.

Orend, Brian. *Jus Post Bellum*, Journal of Social Philosophy, Vol. 31 (2000), 117.

Orend, Brian. *War and International Justice, A Kantian Perspective* (Waterloo, Wilfried Laurier University Press, 2000).

Orentlicher, Diane F. *Separating Anxiety: International Responses to Ethno-Separatist Claims*, Yale Journal of International Law, Vol. 23 (1998), 1.

Osieke, Ebere. *Admission to Membership in International Organizations: The Case of Namibia*, British Yearbook of International Law, Vol. 51 (1980), 189.

Osieke, Ebere. *Ultra Vires Acts in International Organizations – The Experience of the I.L.O.*, British Yearbook of International Law, Vol. 48 (1976–7), 259.

Ottolenghi, Michael. *The Stars and Stripes in Al-Fardo Square: The Implications for International Law of Belligerent Occupation*, Fordham Law Review, Vol. 72 (2004), 2177.

Pagani, Fabrizio. *L'Administration de Mostar par l'Union Européenne*, Annuaire Français de Droit International (1996), 234.

Pajic, A. *A Critical Appraisal of Human Rights Provisions of the Dayton Constitution of Bosnia and Herzegovina*, Human Rights Quarterly, Vol. 20 (1998), 125.

Palmer, Laura R. *A Very Clear and Present Danger: Hate Speech, Media Reform, and Post-Conflict Democratization in Kosovo*, Yale Journal of International Law, Vol. 26 (2001), 179.

Paris, Roland. *At War's End: Building Peace After Civil Conflict* (Cambridge, Cambridge University Press, 2004).

Paris, Roland. *Peacebuilding and the Limits of Liberal Internationalism*, International Security, Vol. 22 (1997), 54.

Parker, Tom. *The Ultimate Intervention: Revitalising the UN Trusteeship Council for the 21st Century* (Brussels, Report Centre for European and Asian Studies, 2003).

Paulus, Andreas L. *Die Internationale Gemeinschaft im Völkerrecht* (Munich, Beck, 2001).

Paust, Jordan J. *The U.S. as Occupying Power over Portions of Iraq and Relevant Responsibilities under the Laws of War*, ASIL Insight, April 2003, at www.asil.org.

Paust, Jordan. *Use of Armed Force against Terrorists in Afghanistan, Iraq and Beyond*, Cornell Journal of International Law, Vol. 35 (2002), 533.

Pech, Laurent. *La Garantie Internationale de la Constitution de Bosnie-Herzégovine*, Revue Française de Droit Constitutionnel, Vol. 42 (2000), 421.

Pelt, Adrian. *Libyan Independence and the United Nations, A Case of Planned Decolomization* (New Haven, CT, Yale University Press for the Carnegie Endowment for International Peace, 1970).

Pernice, Ingolf. *Multilevel Constitutionalism and the Treaty of Amsterdam: European Constitution-Making Revisited?*, Common Market Law Review, Vol. 36 (1999), 703.

Perrit, Henry H. *Structures and Standards for Political Trusteeship*, UCLA Journal of International Law and Foreign Affairs, Vol. 8 (2003), 385.

Peters, Anne. *There is Nothing more Practical than a Good Theory: An Overview of Contemporary Approaches to International Law*, German Yearbook of International Law, Vol. 44 (2001), 25.

Petrisch, Wolfgang. *Bosnien and Herzegovina fünf Jahre nach Dayton*, Südosteuropa Mitteilungen, Vol. 40 (2000), 301.

Pfeuffer, Rudolf. *Die Völkerrechtliche Stellung der Freien Stadt Danzig* (Danzig, Kafemann Press, 1921).

Philipp, Christiane, *Somalia – A Very Special Case*, Max Planck Yearbook of United Nations Law, Vol. 9 (2005), 518–54.

Picciotti, Romulus A. *Legal Problems of Occupied Nations after the Termination of Occupation*, Military Law Review, Vol. 33 (1966), 25.

Pictet, Jean S. *Commentary, IV Geneva Convention* (Geneva, International Committee of the Red Cross, 1958).

Pirenne, Jacques and Vauthier, Maurice E. A. *La Législation et l'Administration Allemandes en Belgique* (Paris, Presses Univ. de France, 1925).

Plischke, Elmar. *History of the Allied High Commission for Germany: Its Establishment, Structure and Procedures* (Historical Division, Office of the Executive Secretary, Office of the US High Commissioner for Germany, 1951).

Plunkett, Mark. *Reestablishing Law and Order in Peace Maintenance*, in J. Chopra ed., The Politics of Peace Maintenance (Boulder CO, Lynne Rienner Publishers, 1998), 61.

Pomerance, Michla. *Methods of Self-Determination and the Argument of "Primitiveness"*, Canadian Yearbook of International Law, Vol. 12 (1974), 38.

Potter, Pitman B. *Legal Bases and Character of Military Occupation in Germany and Japan*, American Journal of International Law, Vol. 43 (1949), 323.

Rama-Montaldo, Manuel. *International Legal Personality and Implied Powers of International Organizations*, British Yearbook of International Law, Vol. 44 (1970), 111.

Randelzhofer, Albrecht. *On Article 2 (4)*, in B. Simma ed., Charter of the United Nations (Oxford, Oxford University Press, 2002), 114.

Randelzhofer, Albrecht. *Souveränität und Rechtsstaat: Anforderungen an eine Europäische Verfassung*, in H. Noske ed., Der Rechtsstaat am Ende? (München, Olzog Verlag, 1995), 123.

Randelzhofer, Albrecht. *Untersuchung über die Möglichkeiten des Rechtsschutzes der Einwohner Berlins gegen Akte der Alliierten*, Die Verwaltung 19 (1986), 14.

Rasulov Akbar. *Revisiting State Succession to Humanitarian Treaties: Is There a Case for Automaticity?*, European Journal of International Law, Vol. 14 (2003), 141.

Ratner, Steven R. *Foreign Occupation and International Territorial Administration, The Challenges of Convergence*, European Journal of International Law, Vol. 15 (2005), 695.

Ratner, Steven R. *Corporations and Human Rights: A Theory of Legal Responsibility*, Yale Law Journal, Vol. 111 (2001), 443.

Ratner, Steven R. *The New UN Peacekeeping: Building Peace in Lands of Conflict After the Cold War* (New York, St Martin's Press, 1995).

Ratner, Steven R. *The Cambodia Settlement Agreements*, American Journal of International Law, Vol. 87 (1993), 1.

Rauschning, Dietrich. *United Nations Trusteeship System*, in Encyclopedia of Public International Law, Vol. IV (2000), at 1193.

Rauschning, Dietrich, *Mandates*, in Encyclopaedia of Public International Law, Vol. III (1997), 280.

Raustiala, Kal. *Sovereignty and Multilateralism*, Chicago Journal of International Law, Vol. 1 (2000), 401.

Rawski, Frederick. *To Waive or Not to Waive: Immunity and Accountability in U.N. Peacekeeping Operations*, Connecticut Journal of International Law, Vol. 18 (2002), 103.

Reif, Lina C. *Building Democratic Institutions: The Role of National Human Rights Institutions in Good Governance and Human Rights Protection*, Harvard Human Rights Journal, Vol. 13 (2000), 1.

Reinisch, August. *Governance Without Accountability*, German Yearbook of International Law, Vol. 44 (2001), 270.

Reinisch, August. *International Organizations Before National Courts* (Cambridge, Cambridge University Press, 2000).

Reinisch, August and Weber, Ulf Andreas. *In the Shadow of Waite and Kennedy: The Jurisdictional Immunity of International Organizations, the Individual's Right of Access to the Courts and Administrative Tribunals as Alternative Means of Dispute Settlement*, International Organizations Law Review, Vol. 1 (2004), 59.

Reisman, Michael. *Stopping Wars and Making Peace: Reflections on the Ideology and Practice of Conflict Termination in Contemporary World Politics*, Tulane Journal of International and Comparative Law, Vol. 6 (1998), 5.

Reisman, Michael. *Why Regime Change is (Almost Always) a Bad Idea*, American Journal of International Law. Vol. 98 (2004), 516–25.

Reka, Blerim. *UNMIK as International Governance within Post-Conflict Societies*, New Balkan Politics, Issue 7/8, at www.newbalkanpolitics.org.mk/napis.asp?id=17&lang=English.

Ress, Georg. *On Article 107*, in B. Simma ed., Charter of the United Nations (Oxford, Oxford University Press, 2002), 1330.

Rheinstein, Max. *The Legal Status of Occupied Germany*, Michigan Law Review, Vol. 47 (1948), 23.

Richardson, Henry J. *Failed States, Self-Determination and Preventive Diplomacy: Colonialist Nostalgia and Democratic Expectations*, Temple International & Comparative Law Journal, Vol. 10 (1996), 1.

Richmond, Oliver P. *The Globalization of Responses to Conflict and the Peacebuilding Consensus*, Cooperation and Conflict, Vol. 39 (2004), 129.

Roberts, Adam. *The End of Occupation: Iraq 2004*, International & Comparative Law Quarterly, Vol. 54 (2005), 27.

Roberts, Adam. *Transformative Military Occupation: Applying the Laws of War and Human Rights*, American Journal of International Law, Vol. 100 (2006), 580.

Roberts, Adam. *The So-Called "Right" of Humanitarian Intervention*, Yearbook of International Humanitarian Law, Vol. 3 (2000), 3.

Roberts, Adam. *What is Military Occupation?*, British Yearbook of International Law, Vol. 55 (1984), 249.

Rodd, Francis Rennell. *British Military Administration of Occupied Territories in Africa during the Years 1941–1947* (London, Her Majesty's Stationery Office, 1948).

Rosas, Allan. *Internal Self-Determination*, in C. Tomuschat ed., Modern Law of Self-Determination (Dordrecht, Nijhoff, 1995), 225.

Rosenau, James N., Czempiel, Ernst-Otto and Smith, Steve. *Governance without Government: Order and Change in World Politics* (Cambridge, Cambridge University Press, 1992).

Rothert, Mark. *U.N. Intervention in East Timor*, Columbia Journal of Transnational Law, Vol. 39 (2000), 257.

Rouard De Cord, Emile. *Modifications du Statut de Tanger* (Paris, Pedone, 1928).

Roussseu, Jean Jacques. *Du Contrat Social* (1762) (Paris, Union Générale D'Editions, 1963).

Ruffert, Matthias. *The Administration of Kosovo and East Timor by the International Community*, International & Comparative Law Quarterly, Vol. 50 (2001), 555.

Russell, Frank M. *The International Government of the Saar* (Berkely, University of California Press, 1926).

Russell, Ruth B. and Muther, Jeanette E. *A History of the United Nations Charter: The Role of the United States 1940–1945* (Washington DC, Brookings Institution, 1958).

Sagay, Itsejuwa. *The Legal Aspects of the Namibian Dispute* (Ile-Ife, University of Ife Press, 1975).

Salamun, Michaela. *Democratic Governance in International Territorial Administration: Institutional Prerequisites for Democratic Governance in the Constitutional Documents of Territories Administered by International Organisations* (Baden-Baden, Nomos, 2005).

Saltford, John. *United Nations and the Indonesian Takeover of West Papua, 1962–1969: The Anatomy of Betrayal* (London and New York, Routledge, 2002).

Sands, Philippe. *Lawless World: America and the Making and Breaking of Global Rules* (London, Penguin Allen Lane, 2005).

Sands, Philippe. *Turtles and Torturers: The Transformation of International Law*, NYU Journal of International Law and Policy, Vol. 33 (2001), 527.

Sarcevic, Edin. *Verfassungsgebung und "konstitutives Volk": Bosnien-Herzegovina zwischen Natur- und Rechtszustand*, Jahrbuch des Öffentlichen Rechts, Vol. 50 (2002), 494.

Sarooshi, Danesh. *Preliminary Remarks on the Conferral by States of Powers of International Organizations*, British Yearbook of International Law, Vol. 74 (2003), 291.

Sarooshi, Danesh. *The Role of the United Nations Secretary-General in United Nations Peace-Keeping Operations*, Australian Yearbook of International Law, Vol. 20 (1999), 279.

Sarooshi, Danesh. *The United Nations and the Development of Collective Security* (Oxford, Oxford University Press, 1999).

Sassòli, Marco. *Legislation and Maintenance of Public Order and Civil Life by Occupying Powers*, European Journal of International Law, Vol. 16 (2005), 661.

Sayre, Francis Bowes. *Experiments in International Administration* (New York, Harper, 1944).

Scelle, Georges. *Précis de Droit des Gens. Principes et Systématique, Première Partie* (Paris, Recueil Sirey, 1932).

Schachter, Oscar. *International Law in Theory and Practice* (Dordrecht, Nijhoff, 1991).

Schachter, Oscar, under the pseudonym E. M. Miller, *Legal Aspects of the United Nations Action in the Congo*, American Journal of International Law, Vol. 55 (1961), 1.

Scharf, Michael. *Earned Sovereignty: Juridical Underpinnings*, Denver Journal of International Law & Policy, Vol. 31 (2003), 373.

Scheffer, David, *Beyond Occupation Law*, American Journal of International Law, Vol. 97 (2003), 842.

Schermers, Henry G. *The Namibia Decree in National Courts*, International & Comparative Law Quarterly, Vol. 26 (1977), 81.

Schilling, Theodor. *Is the United States Bound by the Covenant of Civil and Political Rights in Relation to Occupied Territories*, Jean Monnet Paper No. IV, 2004.

Schmalenbach, Kirsten, *Die Haftung Internationaler Organisationen im Rahmen von friedenssichernden Maßnahmen und Territorialverwaltungen* (Frankfurt am Main, Lang, 2004).

Schmidt-Jortzig, Eckart. *The Constitution of Namibia: An Example of a State Emerging under Close Supervision and World Scrutiny*, German Yearbook of International Law, Vol. 34 (1991), 413.

Schoups, Johan. *Peacekeeping and Transitional Administration in Eastern Slavonia*, in Luc Reychler and Thania Paffenholz eds., Peacebuilding: A Field Guide (Boulder CO, Lynne Rienner Publishers USA, 2001), 389.

Schrijver, Nico. *Permanent Sovereignty over Natural Resources* (Cambridge, Cambridge University Press, 1997).

Schücking, Walther and Wehberg, Hans. *Die Satzung des Völkerbundes* (Berlin, Vahlen, 1931).

Schwarzenberger, Georg. *Power Politics: A Study of World Society* (London, Stevens, 1964).

Schwarzenberger, Georg. *International Law*, Vol. 1 (London, Stevens, 1957).

Schwarz-Liebermann von Wahlendorf, Hans Albrecht. *Vormundschaft und Treuhand des Römischen und Englischen Privatrechts in ihrer Anwendbarkeit auf Völkerrechtlicher Ebene* (Tübingen, Mohr, 1951).

Schweisfurth, Theodor. *Germany, Occupation After World War II*, Encyclopedia of Public International Law, 582.

Scott, Craig. *Interpreting Intervention*, Canadian Yearbook of International Law, Vol. 39 (2001), 333–69.

Seidel, Gerd. *A New Dimension of the Right of Self-Determination in Kosovo*, in C. Tomuschat ed., Kosovo and the International Community: A Legal Assessment (The Hague, Martinus Nijhoff, 2002), 203.

Seidel, Gerd. *Quo Vadis Völkerrecht*, Archiv des Völkerrechts, Vol. 41 (2003), 449.

Seyersted, Finn. *United Nations Forces in the Law of Peace and War* (Leyden, Sijthoff, 1966).

Seyerstedt, Finn. *International Personality of International Organizations*, Indian Journal of International Law, Vol. 4 (1964), 15.

Siekmann, Robert C. R. *Basic Documents on United Nations and Related Peace-Keeping Forces* (Dordrecht, Nijhoff, 1989).

Simma, Bruno. *NATO, the UN and the Use of Force: Legal Aspects*, European Journal of International Law, Vol. 10 (1999), 1.

Simma, Bruno. *From Bilateralism to Community Interest in International Law*, Recueil des Cours, Vol. 250 (1994), 219.

Singer, Michael. *Jurisdictional Immunity of International Organizations: Human Rights and Functional Necessity Concerns*, Virginia Journal of International Law, Vol. 36 (1995), 53.

Singh, Rabinder and Kilroy, Charlotte. *In The Matter of the Legality of the Occupation of Iraq by UK Armed Forces*, An Opinion Given to the Campaign for Nuclear Disarmament, 23 July 2003.

Slaughter, Anne-Marie. *International Law and International Relations*, Recueil des Cours, Vol. 285 (2000), 13.

Slaughter, Anne-Marie. *Pushing the Limits of the Liberal Peace: Ethnic Conflict and the "Ideal Polity"*, in D. Wippman ed., International Law and Ethnic Conflict (New York, Cornell University, 1998), 128.

Slomanson, William. *UN Post-Transfer Role in Iraq*, Miskolc Journal of International Law, Vol. 2 (2005), 83.

Slye, Robert C. *The Dayton Peace Agreement: Constitutionalism and Ethnicity*, Yale Journal of International Law, Vol. 21 (1996), 459.

Smith, Michael G., *Peacekeeping in East Timor: The Path To Independence* (Boulder CO, Lynne Rienners, 2002).

Smyrek, Daniel. *Internationally Administered Territories – International Protectorates? An Analysis of Sovereignty over Internationally Administered Territories with Special Reference to the Legal Status of Post-War Kosovo* (Berlin, Duncker & Humblot, 2006).

Smuts, Jan. *The League of Nations: A Practical Suggestion* (1918), in D. H. Miller, *The Drafting of the Covenant*, Vol. II (New York, G.P. Putnam's Sons, 1928).

Snow, Alpheus H. *The Question of Aborigines in the Law and Practice of Nations* (New York, Putnam, 1919).

Snyder, Jack. *From Voting to Violence: Democratization and National Conflict* (New York, W. Norton & Company Limited, 2000).

Sorel, Jean-Marc. *Timor Oriental: Un Resumé de l'Histoire du Droit International*, Revue Générale de Droit International Public (2000), 37.

Stahn, Carsten. *Responsibility to Protect: Political Rhetoric or Emerging Legal Norm*, American Journal of International Law, Vol. 101 (2007), 99.

Stahn, Carsten. *Jus Ad Bellum, Jus in Bello ... Jus Post Bellum: Rethinking the Conception of the Law of Armed Force*, European Journal of International Law, Vol. 17 (2006), 921.

Stahn, Carsten. *Governance Beyond the State: Issues of Legitimacy in International Territorial Administration*, International Organizations Law Review, Vol. 1 (2005), 9.

Stahn, Carsten. *Justice Under Transitional Administration: Contours and Critique of a Paradigm*, Houston Journal of International Law, Vol. 27 (2005), 312.

Stahn, Carsten. *Nicaragua is Dead, Long Live Nicaragua*, in C. Walter, S. Vöneky, V. Röben and F. Schorkopf eds., Terrorism as a Challenge for National and International Law: Security versus Liberty (Berlin, Springer, 2004), 827.

Stahn, Carsten. *Enforcement of the Collective Will After Iraq*, American Journal of International Law, Vol. 97 (2003), 804.

Stahn, Carsten. *The Ambiguities of Security Council Resolution 1422 (2002)*, European Journal of International Law, Vol. 14 (2003), 85.

Stahn, Carsten. *Föderalismus im Dienste der Friedenssicherung: Bosnien-Herzegowina unter dem Friedensabkommen von Dayton*, Jahrbuch des Föderalismus (Baden-Baden, Nomos 2002), 388.

Stahn, Carsten. *International Law at a Crossroads? The Impact of September 11*, Zeitschrift für Ausländisches Öffentliches Recht und Völkerrecht, Vol. 62 (2002), 183.

Stahn, Carsten. *Accommodating Individual Criminal Responsibility and National Reconciliation: The UN Truth Commission for East Timor*, American Journal of International Law, Vol. 95 (2001), 952.

Stahn, Carsten. *Constitution Without a State? Kosovo Under the United Nations Constitutional Framework for Self-Government*, Leiden Journal of International Law, Vol. 14 (2001), 531.

Stahn, Carsten, *International Territorial Administration in the Former Yugoslavia: Origins, Developments and Challenges Ahead*, Zeitschrift für ausländisches öffentliches Recht und Völkerrecht, Vol. 61 (2001), 108.

Stahn, Carsten. *NGOs and International Peacekeeping – Issues, Prospects and Lessons Learned*, Zeitschrift für Ausländisches Öffentliches Recht und Völkerrecht, Vol. 61 (2001), 379.

Stahn, Carsten. *The United Nations Transitional Administrations in Kosovo and East Timor: A First Analysis*, Max Planck Yearbook of United Nations Law, Vol. 5 (2001), 105.

Stahn, Carsten. *Die Verfassungsrechtliche Pflicht zur Gleichstellung der drei Ethnischen Volksgruppen in den Bosnischen Teilrepubliken – Neue Hoffnung für das Friedensmodell von Dayton*, Zeitschrift für Ausländisches Öffentliches Recht und Völkerrecht, Vol. 60 (2000), 663.

Stoyanovski, Jacob. *La Théorie Générale des Mandats Internationaux* (Paris, Presses Univ. de France, 1925).

Stromeyer, Hans-Jörg. *Collapse and Reconstruction of a Judicial System: The United Nations Missions in Kosovo and in East Timor*, American Journal of International Law, Vol. 95 (2001), 46.

Strohmeyer, Hans-Jörg., *Making Multilateral Interventions Work: The U.N. and the Creation of Transitional Justice Systems in Kosovo and East Timor*, Fletcher Forum of World Affairs, Vol. 25 (2001), 107.

Strohmeyer, Hans-Jörg. *Policing the Peace: Post-Conflict Judicial Reconstruction in East Timor*, University of South Wales Law Journal, Vol. 24 (2001), 171.

Strohmeyer, Hans-Jörg. *Building a New Judiciary for East Timor, Challenges of a Fledgling Nation*, Criminal Law Forum, Vol. 11 (2000), 259.

Stromseth, Jane E. *Law and Force After Iraq: A Transitional Moment*, American Journal of International Law, Vol. 97 (2003), 628.

Stuart, Graham H. *The International City of Tangier* (Stanford, Stanford University Press, 1955).

Suhrke, Astri, Harpiviken, Kristian Berg and Strand, Arne. *Conflictual Peacebuilding; Afghanistan Two Years After Bonn*, CMI Report R 2004: 4, Bergen, Chr. Michelsen Institute, 2004.

Suksi, Markku. *Constitutional Options for Self-determination: What Works?*, Paper prepared for the UNA-USA/IAI Conference on "Kosovo's final status", Rome, 12–14 December 1999, at www.unausa.org/issues/kosovo.

Sunder, Madhavi. *Enlightened Constitutionalism*, Connecticut Law Review, Vol. 37 (2004/5), 891.

Swift, Ryan. *Occupational Jurisdiction: A Critical Analysis of the Iraqi Special Tribunal*, New York International Law Review, Vol. 19 (2006), 99.

Szasz, Paul. *The Security Council Starts Legislating*, American Journal of International Law, Vol. 96 (2002), 901.

Talmon, Stefan. *The Security Council as World Legislature*, American Journal of International Law, Vol. 99 (2005), 175.

Téson, Fernando R. *The Kantian Theory of International Law*, Columbia Law Review, Vol. 92 (1992), 53.

Teubner, Gunter (ed.). *Global Law without a State* (Aldershot, Dartmouth, 1997).

Thomas, Chantal. *Constitutional Change and International Government*, Hastings Law Journal, Vol. 52 (2000), 1, 41.

Thullen, George. *Problems of the Trusteeship System* (Geneva, Droz, 1964).

Thürer, Daniel. *Der zerfallene Staat und das Völkerrecht*, Die Friedens-Warte, Vol. 74 (1999), 275.

Tomuschat, Christian. *Iraq – The Demise of International Law*, Die Friedenswarte, Vol. 78 (2003), 141.

Tomuschat, Christian. *Peace Enforcement and Law Enforcement: Two Separate Chapters of International Law?*, in Studi di Diritto Internazionale in Onore di Geatano Arangio-Ruiz, Vol. 3 (Napoli, Editoriale Scientifica, 2003), 1745–69.

Tomuschat, Christian. *Yugoslavia's Damaged Sovereignty over the Province of Kosovo*, in Gerard Kreijen *et al.* eds., State, Sovereignty and International Governance (Oxford, Oxford University Press, 2002), 323.

Tomuschat, Christian. *Der 11. September 2001 und seine Rechtlichen Folgen*, Europäische Grundrechte Zeitschrift, Vols. 21–3 (2001), 535.

Tomuschat, Christian. *General Course on Public International Law*, Recueil des Cours, Vol. 281 (1999), 13.

Tomuschat, Christian. *Between National and International Law: Guatemala's Historical Clarification Commission*, in V. Götz, P. Selmer and R. Wolfrum eds., Liber Amicorum Günther Jaenicke – zum 85. Geburtstag (1998), 991.

Tomuschat, Christian. *Die Kapitulation: Wirkung und Nachwirkung aus völkerrechtlicher Sicht*, in R. Schröder ed., 8. Mai 1945 – Befreiung oder Kapitulation (Berlin, Arno Spitz Verlag, 1997), 21.

Tomuschat, Christian. *How To Make Peace After War – The Potsdam Agreement of 1945 Revisited*, Die Friedenswarte, Vol. 72 (1997), 11.

Tomuschat, Christian. *International Law and the Constitution of Mankind*, in International Law on the Eve of the Twenty-first Century (New York, United Nations, United Nations Publications, 1997), 37.

Tomuschat, Christian. *Die Internationale Gemeinschaft*, Archiv des Völkerrechts, Vol. 33 (1995), 1.

Tomuschat, Christian. *Obligations Arising for States Without or Against Their Will*, Recueil des Cours, Vol. 241 (1993), 195.

Tomuschat, Christian. *Solidarity Rights* (Development, Peace, Environment, Humanitarian Assistance), in Encyclopaedia of Public International Law, Vol. IV (1992), 460.

Toole, Jennifer. *A False Sense of Security: Lessons Learned from the United Nations Organization and Conduct Mission in East Timor*, American University International Law Review, Vol. 16 (2000), 199.

Toussaint, Charmian Edwards. *The Trusteeship System of the United Nations* (London, Stevens, 1956).

Traub, James. *Inventing East Timor*, Foreign Affairs, July/August (2000), 74.

Triggs, Gillian. *Legal and Commercial Risks of Investment in the Timor Gap*, Melbourne Journal of International Law, Vol. 1 (2000), 99.

Villani, Ugo. *The Security Council's Authorisation of Enforcement Action by Regional Organisations*, Max Planck Yearbook of United Nations Law, Vol. 6 (2002), 55.

Vali, Ferenc A. *Servitudes of International Law* (London, Stevens, 1958).

van Houtte, Hans. *The Property Claims Commission in Bosnia and Herzegovina – A New Path to Restore Real Estate Rights in Post-War Societies*, in K. Wellens ed., International Law: Theory and Practice, Essays in Honour of Eric Suy (The Hague, Nijhoff, 1998), 552.

Verdross, Alfred and Zemanek, Karl. *Völkerrecht*, 4th edn (Wien, Springer, 1959).

Verzijl, Jan Hendrik Willem. *International Law in Historical Perspective*, Part III (State Territory) (Leyden, Stjthoff, 1970).

Verzijl, Jan Hendrik Willem. *International Law in Historical Perspective*, Part II (International Persons) (Leyden, Stjthoff, 1969).

Virally, Michel. *L'Administration Internationale de L'Allemagne* (Baden-Baden, Regie Autonome des Publ. Officielles, 1948).

Vité, Sylvain. *L'Applicabilité du Droit International de l'Occupation Militaire aux Actvités des Organisations Internationales*, International Review of the Red Cross, Vol. 86 (2004), 9.

Vitzhum, Wolfgang Graf. *Multiethnische Demokratie – Das Beispiel Bosnien-Herzegovina*, in Claus Dieter Classen *et al.*, eds., In Einem Vereinten Europa dem Frieden der Welt zu dienen ..., Festschrift für Thomas Oppermann (Berlin, Duncker & Humblot, 2001), 87.

Vitzthum, Wolfgang Graf and Mack, Marcus. *Multiethnischer Föderalismus in Bosnien-Herzegovina*, in W. Graf Vitzthum ed., Europäischer Föderalismus: Supranationaler, Subnationaler und Multiethischer Föderalismus in Europa, Tübinger Schriften zum Staats- und Verwaltungsrecht, Band 57 (Berlin, Duncker & Humblot, 2000), 81.

von Carlowitz, Leopold. *Crossing the Boundary from the International to the Domestic Legal Realm: UNMIK Lawmaking and Property Rights in Kosovo*, Global Governance, Vol. 10 (2004), 307.

von Carlowitz, Leopold. *Settling Property Issues in Complex Peace Operations: The CRPC in Bosnia and Herzegovina and the HPD/CC in Kosovo*, Leiden Journal of International Law, Vol. 17 (2004), 599.

von Carlowitz, Leopold. *UNMIK Lawmaking between Effective Peace Support and Internal Self-Determination*, Archiv des Völkerrechts, Vol. 41 (2003), 336.

Von Glahn, Gerhard. *Law Among Nations: An Introduction to Public International Law*, 5th edn (New York, MacMillan, 1986).

Von Glahn, Gerhard. *The Occupation of Enemy Territory* (Minneapolis, University of Minnesota Press, 1957).

von Heinegg, Wolff Heintschel. *Factors in War to Peace Transitions*, Harvard Journal of Law and Public Policy, Vol. 27 (2004), 843.

von Laun, Kurt. *The Legal Status of Germany*, American Journal of International Law, Vol. 45 (1951), 274.

Voon, Tania. *Closing the Gap Between Legitimacy and Legality of Humanitarian Intervention: Lessons From East Timor and Kosovo*, UCLA Journal of International Law and Foreign Affairs, Vol. 7 (2002), 31.

Voos, Sandra. *Die Schule von New Haven – Darstellung und Kritik einer amerikanischen Völkerrechtslehre* (Berlin, Duncker und Humblot, 2000).

Vu, Nhan T. *The Holding of Free and Fair Elections in Cambodia: The Achievement of the United Nations Impossible Mission*, Michigan Journal of International Law, Vol. 16 (1995), 1177.

Walter, Christian. *Vereinte Nationen und Regionalorganisationen* (Heidelberg, Springer, 1996).

Walters, Francis P. *A History of the League of Nations* (London, Oxford University Press, 1952).

Wedgwood, Ruth. *The Fall of Saddam Hussein: Security Council Mandates and Pre-emptive Self-Defense*, American Journal of International Law, Vol. 97 (2003), 576.

Weeramantry, Christopher G. *Nauru: Environmental Damage under International Trusteeship* (Melbourne, Oxford University Press, 1992).

Wehberg, Hans. *Theory and Practice of International Policing* (London, Constable, 1935).

Weiner, Robert O. and Aolain, Fionnuala Ni. *Beyond the Laws of War: Peacekeeping in Search of a Legal Framework*, Columbia Human Rights Law Review, Vol. 27 (1996), 293.

Weisburd, A. Mark. *International Law and the Problem of Evil*, Vanderbilt Journal of Transnational Law, Vol. 34 (2001), 237.

White, Nigel D. and Klaasen, Dirk (eds.), *The UN, Human Rights and Post-Conflict Situations* (Manchester, Manchester University Press, 2005).

Wight, Marin. *International Theory: The Three Traditions*, ed. by Gabriele Wight and Brian Porter (Leicester, Leicester University Press, 1991).

Wight, Martin. *An Anatomy of International Thought*, Revue of International Studies, Vol. 13 (1987), 221.

Wilde, Ralph. *International Territorial Administration* (Oxford, Oxford University Press, 2008).

Wilde, Ralph. *International Territorial Administration and Human Rights*, in Nigel D. White and Dirk Klaasen eds., The UN, Human Rights and Post-conflict Situations (Manchester, Manchester University Press, 2005), 149.

Wilde, Ralph. *The "Legal Space" or "Espace Juridique" of the European Convention on Human Rights: Is it Relevant to Extraterritorial State Action*, European Human Rights Law Review, Issue 2 (2005), 115.

Wilde, Ralph. *The Accountability of International Organizations and the Concept of "Functional Duality"*, in Wybo P. Heere ed., From Government to Governance, Proceedings of the Sixth Hague Joint Conference, 2004.

Wilde, Ralph. *Representing International Territorial Administration: A Critique of Some Approaches*, European Journal of International Law, Vol. 15 (2004), 71.

Wilde, Ralph. *Taxonomies of International Peacekeeping: An Alternative Narrative*, ILSA Journal of International & Comparative Law, Vol. 9 (2003), 391.

Wilde, Ralph. *The United Nations as Government: The Tensions of an Ambivalent Role*, American Society of International Law, Vol. 97 (2003), 212.

Wilde, Ralph. *Accountability and International Actors in Bosnia and Herzegovina, Kosovo and East Timor*, ILSA Journal of International and Comparative Law, Vol. 7 (2002), 455.

Wilde, Ralph. *From Danzig to East Timor and Beyond: The Role of International Territorial Administration*, American Journal of International Law, Vol. 95 (2001), 583.

Wilde, Ralph. *The Complex Role of the Legal Adviser When International Organisations Administer Territory*, Proceedings of the American Society of International Law, Vol. 95 (2001), 251.

Wilde, Ralph. *From Bosnia to Kosovo and East Timor: The Changing Role of the United Nations in the Administration of Territory*, ILSA Journal of International & Comparative Law, Vol. 6 (2000), 467.

Wilde, Ralph. *Quis Custodiet Ipsos Custodes? Why and How UNHCR Governance of "Development" Refugee Camps Should be Subject to International Human Rights Law*, Yale Human Rights and Development Law Journal, Vol. 1 (1998), 107.

Williams, Paul R. *Earned Sovereignty: The Road to Resolving the Conflict Over Kosovo's Final Status*, Denver Journal of International Law and Policy, Vol. 31 (2003), 387.

Williams, Paul R. and Pecci, Francesca J. *Earned Sovereignty: Bridging the Gap between Sovereignty and Self-Determination*, Stanford Journal of International Law, Vol. 40 (2004), 347.

Williams, Rhodri C. *Post-Conflict Property Restitution and Refugee Return in Bosnia and Herzegovina: Implications for International Standard-Setting and Practice*, NYU Journal of International Law and Politics, Vol. 37 (2005), 441.

Wilson, Sir Arnold. *The Laws of War in Occupied Territory*, Transactions of the Grotius Society, Vol. 18 (1933).

Wolfrum, Rüdiger. *International Administration in Post-Conflict Situations by the United Nations and Other International Actors*, Max Planck Yearbook of United Nations Law, Vol. 9 (2005), 649.

Wolfrum, Rüdiger. *Iraq – From Belligerent Occupation to Iraqi Exercise of Sovereignty: Foreign Power versus International Community Interference*, Max Planck Yearbook of United Nations Law, Vol. 9 (2005), 1.

Wolfrum, Rüdiger. *The Attack of September 11, 2001, the Wars Against the Taliban and Iraq: Is There a Need to Reconsider International Law on the Recourse to Force and the Rules in Armed Conflict*, Max Planck Yearbook of United Nations Law, Vol. 7 (2003), 1.

Wolfrum, Rüdiger. *Internationalisation*, in Encyclopedia of Public International Law, Vol. II (1995), 1395.

Wolfrum, Rüdiger. *Die Internationalisierung Staatsfreier Räume* (Berlin, Springer, 1984).

Wolfrum, Rüdiger. *Iraq – A Crisis for Our System of Collective Security*, at www.mpil.de/en/Wolfrum/eirak.pdf.

Wood, Michael C. *The Interpretation of Security Council Resolutions*, Max Planck Yearbook of United Nations Law, Vol. 2 (1998), 85.

Woolsey, L. H. *The Leticia Dispute Between Columbia and Peru*, American Journal of International Law, Vol. 27 (1933), 317, Vol. 29 (1935), 94.

Wright, Quincy. *The Status of Germany and the Peace Proclamation*, American Journal of International Law, Vol. 46 (1952), 307.

Wright, Quincy. *Mandates under the League of Nations* (Chicago, University of Chicago Press, 1930).

Wright, Quincy. *Some Recent Cases on the Status of Mandated Areas*, American Journal of International Law, Vol. 20 (1926), 768.

Yannis, Alexandros. *The UN as Government in Kosovo*, Global Governance, Vol. 10 (2004), 67.

Yannis, Alexandros. *The Concept of Suspended Sovereignty in International Law*, European Journal of International Law, Vol. 13 (2002), 1037–52.

Yannis, Alexandros. *Kosovo under International Administration: An Unfinished Conflict* (Athens: ELIAMEP & PSIS, 2001).

Ydit, Méir. *Internationalised Territories: From the "Free City of Cracow" to the "Free City of Berlin"* (Leyden, Sythoff, 1961).

Zacklin, Ralph. *The Problem of Namibia in International Law*, Recueil des Cours, Vol. 171 (1981 II), 225.

Zaum, Dominik. *The Sovereignty Paradox: The Norms and Politics of International Statebuilding* (Oxford, Oxford University Press, 2007).

Zimmermann, Andreas. *Staatennachfolge in völkerrechtliche Verträge* (Heidelberg, Springer, 2000).

Zimmermann, Andreas and Stahn, Carsten. *Yugoslav Territory, United Nations Trusteeship or Sovereign State? Reflections on the Current and Future Legal Status of Kosovo*, Nordic Journal of International Law, Vol. 70 (2001), 423.

Zoubir, Yahia H. *The Western Sahara Conflict: A Case Study in Failure of Prenegotiation and Prolongation of Conflict*, California Western International Law Journal, Vol. 26 (1996), 173.

Zwanenburg, Marten. *Accountability of Peace Support Operations* (Leiden and Boston: Martinus Nijhoff Publishers, 2005).

Zwanenburg, Marten. *Existentialism in Iraq: Security Council Resolution 1483 and the Law of Occupation*, International Review of the Red Cross, Vol. 86 (2004) 745.

Zygojannis, Philipp A. *Die Staatengemeinschaft und das Kosovo* (Berlin, Duncker & Humblot, 2002).

Index

accountability *see* institutional
    accountability
Accra Agreement 382, 384
Afghanistan
  Bonn Agreement 349, 353–4, 355, 358,
      360, 743
  Constitutional *Loya Jirga* 355, 359
  Constitutional Review Commission 359
  Emergency *Loya Jirga* 354, 358
  human rights and 358, 359–60, 361,
      362–3
  Interim Authority 353, 354, 358
  Islamic law 360, 362
  Joint Coordination and Monitoring
      Board 360
  Judicial Reform Commission 358
  new Constitution 358, 359–60
  Operation Enduring Freedom 352, 408
  Taliban, exclusion of 361, 709
  Transitional Authority 353–4, 355
  UN Assistance Mission in Afghanistan
      (UNAMA) 23, 24, 35, 352, 399, 408
    assessment 360–3
    background 352–3
    consent 400, 743
    constitution-framing 359–60, 708, 709
    International Security Assistance
        Force (ISAF) 354
    "light footprint" agenda 17, 351,
        356–7, 361
    limited mandate 355–6
    local ownership 360, 361
    Report of the Secretary General 355
    role and function 357–60
African Union (AU)
  Peace and Security Council (PSC) 389,
      391, 392, 397, 738
  peacekeeping mission (AMISOM) 452,
      738
Agenda for Democratisation 266

Ahtisaari, Martti 221, 314
Akashi, Yasushi 275
Albanian Control Commission 56–7, 58–9
AMISOM 452, 738
Anghie, Anthony 48n
Angola (UNAVEM II) 149
annexation
  prohibition 150
Antarctica 65
applicable law *see* definition of applicable
    law
assistance missions 9, 17
  see also governance assistance missions

Barre, Siad 261
Bentham, Jeremy 524
Berlin West Africa Conference (1884–5)
    74–5, 89
bilateralism 47, 174, 183, 187, 195, 197,
    202, 204
Bonn Agreement on Provisional
    Arrangements in Afghanistan 349,
    353–4, 355, 358, 360, 361, 743
Bosnia and Herzegovina
  Dayton Peace Agreement (DPA) 69, 287,
      399, 400, 451, 739
    assessment 300
    authority of OHR 288, 657, 724, 745
    compensation for lost property 688
    Constitutional Court 633
    ethnic democracy 290
    ethnic federalism 742
    external control 296–9
    human rights 293–6, 482
    institutional framework 289–90, 291
    property issues 681, 688
  EU administration of City of Mostar
      (EUAM) 62, 301–2, 397, 739
    accountability structure 304
    assessment 308, 737

Common Foreign and Security Policy
    (CFSP) 301, 303, 305, 308
    elections 307
    EU Ombudsman 305–6, 617, 621
    exercise of regulatory powers 648, 678
    institutional checks and balances 304
    institutional design 303–6
    mandate 746
    Memorandum of Understanding
        (MOU) 303–4, 678
    origin 302–3
    political control 305–6
    political unification attempt 206–7
    practice 306–7
imposed constitutionalism 712–14
international administration 268, 287
    assessment 300, 737, 743, 753, 754
    Commission for Real Property Claims
        of Displaced Persons and Refugees
        (CRPC) 70, 293, 295–6, 681–2, 683–4,
        685, 686, 687–9
    Constitutional Court 633, 634
    constrained sovereignty 757, 758
    Dayton Peace Agreement see Dayton
        Peace Agreement
    elections 291–2, 726
    ethnic democracy 290–2
    exercise of regulatory powers 647
    external control 296–9
    functional internationalisation 69–70
    Human Rights Chamber 70, 293, 686
    human rights guarantees 70, 293–6,
        482
    institutional engineering 289–99
    marginalisation of UN 288–9
    Ombudsperson Institution 70, 293,
        622
    Peace Implementation Council (PIC)
        288, 289
    property issues 70, 293, 295–6, 681–2,
        683–4, 685, 686, 687
    reconstruction of legal system 69–70
    restoration of domestic authority 724
    Special Chamber 632
    statebuilding and democratisation
        268, 724
internationalised statehood 540–1
Office of the High Representative (OHR)
    45, 288–9, 296–9, 397, 520
    authority dispute 657–8
    Dayton Peace Agreement 288, 657,
        724, 745
    direct applicability of legal acts 646,
        652
    immunities 583n, 605–6
    imposed constitutionalism 712–14
    judicial review of acts 611–15

legal personality 560–2
    mandate 69–70, 296–7
    property issues 686, 687–9
    restoration of domestic authority 724
    sources of authority 288
Boutros-Ghali, Boutros 266, 753
Brahimi, Lakhdar 356
Brahimi Report 3, 266, 350–1
Bremer, Paul 504
British Cameroons 107, 109
British Empire 93
Burke, Edmund 89

Cambodia
    Cambodian Peace Accords 68–9
    delegation of power 267
    functional internationalisation 68–9, 71
    internationalised statehood 540–1
    Paris Accords 1991 278, 400, 482
        delegation of powers 267
        power-sharing arrangements 282,
            648
        transitional government 270–1
        UN co-governance role 269, 272–3
    power vacuum 13
    power-sharing 68–9
    self-commitment to human rights 273–4
    Supreme National Council (SNC) 68,
        269, 270, 271, 274, 275, 276
    UN Transitional Authority in Cambodia
        (UNTAC) 23, 24, 35, 267, 269–70
        assessment 278–9, 737, 743, 753
        capacity gaps 276–8
        as co-governance operation 399
        consensual origin 270–1
        cooperation with domestic authorities
            274–6
        criticisms 270, 278–9
        detentions 690–2
        direct applicability of legal acts 652
        elections 272, 728
        executive responsibilities 272–3
        exercise of regulatory powers 647,
            648, 652
        governance and administration role
            269–70
        governmental authority 271–2
        human rights mandate 272–3, 275–6,
            277
        judicial system 275, 276–7
        lack of resources 276–7
        nature of mandate 271–4
        peace settlement 271–2
        power-sharing mechanism 275
        Special Representative of the
            Secretary-General (SRSG) 270, 271,
            272, 273, 275, 276, 603, 652, 691–2

Cambodia (*cont.*)
  statebuilding and democratisation 9,
    149, 268, 271–4
  time limit 269–70
  UNTAG compared 271
capacity-building 17, 350, 393
  Afghanistan 352, 356–7
  Liberia 384
  sovereignty and 756–7
Chamberlain, Joseph 74*n*
Chopra, Jarat 44
Churchill, Winston 93
claims commissions 597*n*, 615, 627–30
co-governance/co-administration
    operations 17, 159, 232–4, 398–9
  see also Cambodia; Congo; Leticia; West
    Irian
colonialism 74–5, 157–8, 348
  dual mandate 19, 89, 156*n*
  respect for local tradition 151–2
  see also decolonisation
Committee on UN Administration and
    Governance Assistance, proposed
    445
communitarisation of international law
    31–2, 38
communitarism 172, 187, 192, 195, 204,
    758–9
condominiums 48
Congo
  UN Mission in the Democratic Republic
    of Congo (MONUC) 23, 24, 71, 350,
    381–2, 399
  assessment 387
  background 385–6
  complexity 12
  consent 400
  elections 387
  Government of National Unity and
    Transition 385
  human rights monitoring 387
  Joint Commission on Essential
    Legislation 386–7
  Lusaka Ceasefire Agreement 385
  misconduct of UN personnel 387
  "partnership" approach 385, 386
  practice 386–7
  Technical Committee 386
  Transitional Government 386
  UN Operation in Congo (ONUC) 8, 23, 24,
    35, 148, 233, 236–7, 268, 400, 737
  abandonment of neutrality 242–3
  acting without consent 241–2
  advisory functions 244
  Article 40, UN Charter 432
  assessment 245–6, 742
  background 237–9

  civilian mandate 243, 245
  as co-governance operation 399
  colonial failures 237–8
  constitutional crisis and 244–5
  as *de facto* governance mission 243–5
  framing of mandate 746
  military mandate 243
  overthrow of Kantangese secession
    movement 243, 245
  policing powers 244–5
  power vacuum 13
  security tasks 240
  termination of civil war 240–1
  UN proactivism 238–9
  UNOSOM II compared 259–60, 266
Congress of Vienna 7
  Final Declaration 53
constitution-making 707
  general parameters 707
  imposed constitutionalism 711
  Bosnia and Herzegovina 712–14
  exceptional historical mandates 711–12
  Kosovo 274, 714–16
  modern examples 712–16
  international practice 708–16
  partial internationalisation 708–10
Convention on the Law of the Sea 32
corporal punishment
  abolition 109
cosmopolitanism 36–40
  basic premise 37–8
  intellectual roots 36–7
  legal framework for cosmopolitan
    governance 761–3
  statism and 38
  World Law 40
Côte d'Ivoire *see* Ivory Coast
Cracow
  Free City of Cracow 7, 53
  multinational administration 53–4
  territorial internationalisation 7, 53–4
Crete
  Board of Ambassadors 55
  de facto governance 7, 54–6
  military occupation 7, 54–6, 58
  multinational administration 7, 54–6, 58
  territorial internationalisation 7, 54–6
  zones of occupation 55–6
Croatia *see* Eastern Slavonia

Danzig xvii, xxi, 7, 14, 23, 35, 71, 78,
    173–4, 204, 205
  assessment 182–5, 736
  autonomy over internal affairs 176
  co-governance 398
  complexity 11–12
  Constitution 175–6, 180, 184

Council of the League of Nations 178, 206
diplomatic protection 566
direct model of intervention 395–6
dispute settlement 599, 610
establishment of relations with state entities 568
governing framework 175–8
High Commissioner 175–6, 178, 181, 184, 395, 396
internationalisation 174–5, 180
League of Nations functions
    appeals to 178, 183–4, 206, 396
    dispute settlement 178–9, 183–4
    mediation mechanisms 180
    protective function 180–1
legal personality 554–5
mandate 746
Nazi government 181, 184–5
neutralisation 174, 177, 183, 402
passports, issuance 564–5
PCIJ advisory opinions 179, 184, 396
railway system 646
reparation 60
representation in international conferences and organisations 575–6
sovereignty 177, 182
special Polish rights 177
Treaty of Paris 177, 179
Treaty of Versailles 174, 175–8, 179, 180, 183, 398
    diplomatic protection 566
treaty-making power 571
Trieste model compared 189, 191–2
Dayton Peace Agreement (DPA) see Bosnia and Herzegovina
de Cuellar, Perez 225
De Mello, Sergio Vieira 719
debellatio doctrine 120n, 125, 134–7, 138
    decline 141
Declaration by the United Nations on National Independence 92–3
decolonisation 13, 14–15, 49, 403
    Trusteeship System 92, 94
    see also East Timor; Eritrea; Libya; Namibia; Somalia; West Irian; Western Sahara
definition of applicable law 664, 672–3
    CPA 672
    UNMIK 664–7
    UNTAET 667–71
democratic governance 510–11
    applicability of standards 511–14
    application of standards to international administrations 512–14
    constitution-framing and 707
    democracy as a human right 513–14

functional duality 512–13
scope of obligation 514–16
universalisation of democratic standards 511–12
Democratic Republic of Congo see Congo
democratisation 9, 19, 27, 753–4
    premature 525–6
detentions 690, 700–1
    Cambodia 690–2
    East Timor 696–7
    Fourth Geneva Convention 698, 699, 700
    habeas corpus 690, 700
    Iraq 697–700
    judicial review 700
    Kosovo 507–8, 693–6
    "security detainees" 699–700
    Somalia 260, 692
diplomatic immunity see immunities
diplomatic protection 566
    Treaty of Versailles 566–7
    United Nations practice 567–8
dispute resolution xxi, 33–5, 160, 162–3, 401–3
    claims commissions 597n, 615, 627–30
    development of international law and 162
    League of Nations 70–1
    see also Danzig; Leticia; Memel; Saar Territory
    neutralisation see neutralisation
    post-war see Jerusalem; Trieste
    post-World War II 61–2
    resolution of territorial disputes 401–3
    status dispute resolution 401–2
    territorial disputes 13–14, 401–3
    transfer of territory 403, 550n
    Treaty of Versailles 59–61
    World Trade Organization 30
domestic support
    role 741–3
Doyle, Michael 743
dual mandate 19, 89, 156n

East Timor
    constitutional crisis 2006 346, 347
    International Force for East Timor (INTERFET) 696–7, 701
    Timor Gap Treaty 335
    Tripartite Agreement 336
    UN Mission of Support in East Timor (UNMISET) 343, 345
    UN Office in Timor-Leste (UNOTIL) 343, 345
    UN Transitional Administration in East Timor (UNTAET) 2, 10–11, 15, 17, 23, 24, 63, 149, 259, 267, 332–4, 355, 356, 393, 399, 400

East Timor (cont.)
applicable law, definition of 667–71,
672, 673, 697
assessment 346–7, 736, 737, 742–3, 753
co-governance system 340
constitution-framing 342–3, 708, 709,
710
Council of Ministers 339
criticism 343–6
democratisation 268, 344–5
Department of Peacekeeping
Operations (DPKO) 338
detentions 696–7, 701
diplomatic protection 567
direct applicability of legal Acts 646,
652
direct review of executive authority
606–7
East Timorese Defence 341–2
emergency situation argument 522–3
establishment of relations with state
entities 569–70
exercise of regulatory powers 647,
648, 649, 650
historical background 334–7
human rights standards 338, 344, 482,
667
immunities 585–6
imposition of liberal governance
structures 274
judicial system 339, 340
legal and institutional change 344
legal personality 556, 558–60
mandate 269
National Council 339
Ombudsperson 623
people's rights 337
phased sovereignty 757
power vacuum 13
restoration of domestic authority 724,
725
serious criminal offences jurisdiction
633, 668–9, 671
Special Panels for Serious Crimes 345
Special Representative of the
Secretary-General (SRSG) 334, 338,
339, 341–2, 345, 396
statebuilding 268, 346–7
strategic goal 342
territorial internationalisation 543
as "third generation" operation 16
Transitional Administrator 338
Transitional Government 339
treaty-making power 572–3
trials 697
Truth and Reconciliation Commission
345

UNMIK and 333–4, 337–40, 347
UNTAES and 280, 283, 285, 286
Eastern Slavonia
Erdut Agreement 280, 282, 283, 286, 400
UN Transitional Administration for
Eastern Slavonia (UNTAES) 10, 11,
14, 23, 35, 63, 71, 149, 259, 267,
279–80, 355, 393, 400
accountability for perpetrators of war
crimes 285
assessment 285–6, 737
civilian mandate 281
dual function 280–1
exclusive governance mandate 282,
397–8
exercise of regulatory powers 647, 648
functional implementation
committees 283
human rights protection 281, 482
institutional design 282–3
internationalised territory 541–2
Joint Implementation committees
284–5
Leticia intervention compared 267–8
military mandate 284
objective 279–80
practice 283–5
property issues 679–81
Security Council Resolution 1037 280,
282, 283, 286
statebuilding functions 281
status dispute resolution 401
transfer of territory 550n
transitional strategic neutralisation
268, 402
UNMIK and 280, 283, 286
UNTAET and 280, 283, 285, 286
El Salvador (ONUSAL) 149
elections
assistance 219
Bosnia and Herzegovina 291–2, 726
Mostar 307
Cambodia 272, 728
Congo 387
disengagement and beyond 726–7, 728,
729
Iraq 381
Ivory Coast 388, 390–1
Liberia 384
emergency operations xviii, 522–4
Erdut Agreement 280, 282, 283, 286, 400
Eritrea, governance assistance mission 71,
148, 208–9, 213–14, 232, 398
assessment 218–19, 742
draft Constitution 217–18
federal status decision 208, 214–17
imposed constitutionalism 711, 712

local decision-making power 214
status determination 546–7
UN Commissioner 214, 217–18
European Commission for Democracy
    Through Law on Human Rights in
    Kosovo 327
European Convention on Human Rights
    (ECHR) 293, 294, 299, 319, 495, 608
access to courts 589, 629
compensation for lost property 629
CPA and 377
detentions 508, 693, 694, 696
immunities 589–92
judicial independence 701
judicial review 614
jurisdiction *ratione personae* 491–2
non-discrimination right 292
violations 644
European Union
    administration of Mostar *see* Bosnia and
        Herzegovina
    direct applicability of laws 652
    EUFOR RD Congo 387
    UNMIK and 738
exclusive governance missions 397–9
exit strategies 717, 720, 726n
    "exit without strategy" 727
    "no exit without strategy" 728, 730
    UNMIK 311n
    UNTAES 285

fiduciary authority
    Mandate System 74, 89–90, 155
    post-war occupation 127, 155
    Trusteeship System 151, 155
Final Act of the Congress of Vienna 7
Fourth Geneva Convention
    application 744–5
    continued application of penal laws 657
    detentions 698, 699, 700
    post-surrender occupation 141
    post-war occupation 117–19, 120–2, 348,
        471–2
    property rights 662
Framework Convention for the Protection
    of National Minorities 292
Free City model 53, 58, 537
    see also Cracow; Danzig
functional duality
    democratic governance 512–13
    domestic courts 634
        criteria 634–6
        scope of application 636–8
    human rights 490–1
functional internationalisation 50, 51, 64
    Antarctica 65
    Bosnia and Herzegovina 69–70

Cambodia 68–9, 71
International Settlement of Shanghai 7,
    65–6
Jerusalem 67–8, 201–3
Memel 66–7, 71
modern examples 68–70
Outer Space 65
patterns 64–5
Spitzbergen 65
territories under domestic jurisdiction
    65–70
waterways 64–5
see also internationalisation
functions of international territorial
    administration 401
    decolonisation 403
    nexus to intervention 406
        mitigation of consequences of action
            409
        post-conflict engagement 409–10
        validation of consequences of action
            407–8
    statebuilding *see* statebuilding
    territorial dispute resolution 401
        neutralisation 402
        status dispute resolution 401–2
        transfer of territory 403
fundamental questions doctrine 675–8

Gbagbo, Laurent 388, 390, 392
General Assembly xviii, 39, 98, 109, 111,
    739, 740
    legal basis for actions 436
        Articles 11 (2) and 14, UN Charter
            436–8
        implied powers 438–9
        transitional administrations with
            military component 437–8
        Uniting for Peace doctrine 439
    maintenance of peace and security 436
    petition system 107–9
    recommendations 436
Germany, post-surrender occupation 25,
    39, 49, 55–6, 62–3, 125–6, 399
    Allied Control Council 130–2, 156n
    assumption of supreme authority 128
    authority of military governors 131–2
    Basic Law 711
    challenges of Allied control 126–33
    de-nazification and re-education 126,
        128, 129, 130
    debellatio doctrine 120n, 125, 134–7
    decentralisation of political structure
        129
    Declaration of Berlin 127–8
    demilitarisation 128
    fiduciary authority 127

Germany, post-surrender occupation (*cont.*)
  Hague Regulations, applicability 134–7
  humanitarian occupation 136
  imposed constitutionalism 711
  indirect territorial administration 156n
  interventionist occupation 136
  Japanese occupation compared 138–9
  judicial system 129, 130
  justification for Allied occupation 132–8
  legal issues 132–8
  legal status of Germany under
    occupation 132–4
  loss of sovereignty 133
  nationbuilding 405
  Occupation Statute 711
  persistence of German Reich post-1945
    133–4
  political and economic reconstruction
    126, 127, 128, 129, 140
  position of Germany in 1945 127, 132
  Potsdam Declaration 127, 128–9, 130,
    132, 138, 139
  preparation for 126–7
  status of occupying powers 137–8
  sui generis regime of occupation 134
  theories of exception 132
  trusteeship occupation 136
  Virally's "international administration"
    135–6
globalisation 17–18, 20
governance assistance missions 71, 159,
    208, 232
  criticism 268–9
  election assistance 219
    see also elections
  peacekeeping and 208
  post-war decolonisation *see* Eritrea; Libya
  referendum assistance 219
    see also Western Sahara
  see also assistance missions; governance
    missions
governance issues 17–22, 758
  communitarism 758–9
  functional approach 760–3
  justification of governance 25–6
  legal framework for cosmopolitan
    governance 761–3
  limitation of public authority
    functional 762
    material 761–2
    temporal 762–3
  Mandate System 79–83, 88
  origin-neutral application of governance
    obligations 760–1
governance missions 17, 21
  exclusive 397–9
    see also governance assistance missions

Grotius, Hugo 33
  rationalism 38, 39
  waterways 64–5
Guggenheim, Paul 536

habeas corpus 690, 700
  see also detentions
Hague Regulations Respecting Laws and
    Customs of War 1907
  freezing clause 658
  post-war occupation 116–17, 119, 129,
    134–7, 139–40, 144, 471
  property rights 662
Haiti (ONUVEH) 149
Hammarskjöld, Dag 147, 238, 239, 246,
    413, 443n
*Handbook on United Nations Multidimensional
    Peacekeeping Operations* 1–2, 44
Helman, Gerald B. 159–60
High-level Panel on Threats, Challenges
    and Change
  Report 3, 27–8, 410
High-level Plenary Meeting of the General
    Assembly, September 2005
  Outcome Document 3
Hitler, Adolf 164, 181
human rights xviii, 9, 27, 479–80
  Afghanistan 358, 359–60, 361, 362–3
  applicability to international
    administrations 480–503
  Bosnia and Herzegovina 70, 293–6,
    482
  Cambodia 272–4, 275–6, 277
  customary law obligations 485–90
  derogation from obligations 506–8
  doctrinal problem 479–80
  East Timor 338, 344, 482
  Eastern Slavonia 281
  functional duality 490–1
  institutional commitment 481–4
  institutionalisation 32
  Iraq 374–5
  Jerusalem 481
  jurisdiction 485–90
  Kosovo 328, 482, 498–500, 502–3
  lack of unified legal theory 479–80
  peacekeeping operations 483
  political participation 152
  scope of obligations 503–4
    conditions of derogation 506–8
    exception by virtue of overwhelming
      Chapter VII resolution 508–10
    relationship between human rights
      law and humanitarian law 504–6
  security exceptions 506–10
  self-commitment to human rights
    273–4, 481–4

Cambodia 273–4
disadvantages 483–4
treaty obligations 491
extraterritorial application 496–503
formal accession 491–2
functional accession 492–6
operations of international
organisations 498–503
state obligations within framework of
multinational administrations
497–8
Trieste 192, 481
Universal Declaration of Human Rights
152, 589
West Irian 481–2
see also European Convention on Human
Rights; International Covenant on
Civil and Political Rights (ICCPR)
humanitarian assistance 136, 261, 409
humanitarian occupation 136

Identification Commission 228
immunities 581
East Timor 585–6
future restriction of procedural
immunities 596–7
individual immunity from criminal
jurisdiction 593
military personnel of
troop-contributing countries 594–6
UN staff members and experts on
mission 593–4
institutional immunity 587–92
Iraq 586–7
Kosovo 584–5, 591–2
military personnel 583, 594–6
in practice of territorial administration
583–7
sources 581–3
institutional accountability
claims commissions 597n, 615, 627–30
design of UN missions 600, 743–4
domestic forums of accountability 630–1
decentralised and mixed
national–international forums
accountability 631–3
functional duality 634–8
judicial control 633
ultra vires control 638–43
expert control and independent
external scrutiny 617
claims commissions 597n, 615, 627–30
independent advisory panels 625–7
international monitoring bodies 618
Ombudsperson control 621–5
scrutiny by Peacebuilding
Commission 620–1

transitional administration
committees 618–20
functional duality 634
criteria 634–6
scope of application 636–8
independent advisory panels 625–7
international monitoring bodies
618
intra-institutional control 616–17
judicial review 84–5, 114, 602
absence of review 603–6
domestic institutions 633
by independent international courts
643–4
mechanism of indirect review 607–10
mechanisms of direct review 606–7
post-war occupation 138
review of executive authority 602–3
review of legislative authority 610–15
Mandate System 83–6, 599, 615
annual report to League Council
83–4
judicial supervision 84–5
petition system 85–6
Ombudsperson see Ombudsperson
peacekeeping tradition 600–2
petition system 599
Mandate System 85–6
Saar Territory 170, 396, 599
Trieste 193, 194, 206, 599
Trusteeship System 107–9
post-colonial tradition 599
scrutiny by Peacebuilding Commission
620–1
transitional administration committees
618–20
Trusteeship System 106–10, 599,
615
petition system 107–9
questionnaire system 616
ultra vires control 638–9
acts of occupying powers 642–3
domestic courts 638–43
options for review 641
review of acts of Chapter VII-based
administrations 639–41
transitional administrations created
by General Assembly 641–2
institutional design of mission 600,
743–4
INTERFET see East Timor
International Bill of Rights xviii
International Commission on Intervention
and State Sovereignty
"Responsibility to Protect" 27
International Control Commission 57
International Court of Justice 30

International Covenant on Civil and
    Political Rights (ICCPR) 152, 319,
    360, 362, 505
  access to courts 589, 629
  CPA and 371, 377
  democratic governance 511–12, 513
  detentions 508, 693, 694, 696
  elections 292, 513
  immunities 589
  judicial independence 701
  jurisdiction *ratione personae* 491
  public office 661–2
International Criminal Court 30
International Danube Commission 65
International Development Association
    573
International Labour Organization (ILO)
    257–8
International Olympic Committee 30
International Sea-Bed Authority 32, 62
International Telegraphic Union 56
international territorial administration
  aim 48
  authority, exercising 747–9
  communitarism 758–9
  condominiums 48
  as conflict management device 23–5, 62–4
  consent and 399–400
  definition 43–5
  development of international legal
      system and 29
    executive function of the
        international community 29–33
    legal theory 33–40
  direct 395–7
  as dispute resolution device 59
    aftermath of World War II 61–2
    Treaty of Versailles 59–61
  domestic support, role 741–3
  efficiency 735–7
  functions *see* functions of international
      territorial administration
  "generations" 15–17
  globalisation and 17–18, 20
  governance issues 17–22, 758–63
  indirect 397
  institutional design of mission 600,
      743–4
  legal framework, clarification 744–6
  legality *see* legality of international
      territorial administration
  mandate 32
    framing 746–7
  meaning 2–3
  modernity and 6–12
  multi-functionalism 12–15
  neutrality and 751–4

peacemaking and 22, 49
  justification of governance and 25–6
  post-conflict administration 26–9
  sustainability of peace 22–5
practice 159–61
problem-solving approach 22, 24, 35–6
progression and 15–17
protectorates and protected states 45–8
relevance 733–5
self-interest 48, 156*n*
strategic liberalisation 18
sustainability, enhancing 749–50
territorial internationalisation and
    52–64
theorisation of state sovereignty 754–8
trusteeship and 410–12
UN involvement and 737–41
unilateral actions 400
utilitarian considerations 48, 524–6
International Tribunal for the Law of the
    Sea 30
International Zone of Tangier 7, 57–8
internationalisation xviii, 50–1
  self-interest and 54
  see also functional internationalisation;
      territorial internationalisation
Iraq
  Coalition Provisional Authority (CPA) 45,
      145, 146, 397, 453, 520, 739
    applicable law, definition of 672, 673
    authority dispute 658–63
    banking system 375
    corrective action by Security Council
        369–70
    delegation of authority to Iraqi
        Governing Council 663
    detentions 697–700
    direct applicability of legislation 646,
        653
    economic reforms 375–6
    emergency situation argument 523
    exercise of regulatory powers 647,
        648, 649, 650, 658–63
    functional duality 637–8
    human rights violations 379
    immunities 586–7
    international human rights standards
        374–5
    judicial independence 704–5
    legal basis for exercise of regulatory
        acts 377–8
    legal personality 560–4
    legal problems for member states 377
    new hierarchy of norms 371
    practice 371–9
    Property Claims Commission 373, 662
    property issues 683, 684

regulatory acts 371
"security detainees" 699–700
self-defined role 368–9
supremacy of law 611
constitution-framing 370, 709, 710
constrained sovereignty 757
de-Ba'atification 373, 374, 381, 661–2
detentions 697–700
economic reforms 375–6
elections 381
illegality of Operation Iraqi Freedom
    409
Interim Governing Council 372–3
international human rights standards
    374–5
Iraq Commission on Public Integrity 663
Iraq Transitional Assembly elections 381
Iraqi Governing Council 372, 663
    delegation of authority to 663
Iraqi Property Claims Commission 683,
    684
Iraqi Special Tribunal 373, 378–9, 663
judiciary 374
Kurdish people 376, 381
lack of national unity 381
Mandate 85
new Constitution 370, 376, 381, 708, 710
Ombudsperson 624
Operation Iraqi Freedom 144, 409
post-war occupation 142–6
    interim administration 144
    legal problems 379
    Operation Iraqi Freedom 144
    UK and US as occupying powers 143,
        144
    US control 364
Security Council Resolution 1483 143–6,
    366, 369, 377, 453, 653, 658, 659
Security Council Resolution 1511 366,
    370, 453
Shiites 381
statebuilding 405–6
Sunnis, exclusion of 381, 709
Transitional Administrative Law (TAL)
    376–7, 378, 379
UN Assistance Mission in Iraq (UNAMI)
    xix, 2, 23, 350, 364, 399, 409
    background 365–6
    constitution-framing 370, 709
    "light footprint" agenda 351, 363–4,
        367–8
    local ownership 369
    mass arrests and detentions 699
    role 370–1
    scope of UN involvement 368–71
    Security Council resolutions 143–6,
        366, 369, 370, 377, 453

Israel 61–2
    title claim over Jerusalem 61
    see also Jerusalem
Ivory Coast
    UN Operation in Côte d'Ivoire (UNOCI) 2,
        23, 350, 381–2, 388, 393, 398
    African Union (AU) Peace and Security
        Council (PSC) 389, 391, 392, 397, 738
    assessment 392
    background 388
    constitutional crisis 388, 389
    elections 388, 390–1
    Forces Nouvelles 388, 390, 392
    Forum for National Dialogue 390
    Government of National
        Reconciliation 388
    institutional adjustments 389–92
    International Working Group (IWG)
        389–90, 391
    Linas–Marcoussis Agreement 388
    National Assembly 390
    Ouagadougou Agreement 392
    "partnership" approach 392
    Special Representative of the
        Secretary-General (SRSG) 390, 391,
        396
    UN Security Council 388, 389, 391,
        392

Japan, post-surrender occupation 25, 39,
    49, 125–6, 138, 399
    ambiguities of US reformism 139–40
    German occupation compared 138–9
    Hague Regulations 139–40
    Initial Post Surrender Policy for Japan
        139
    nationbuilding 405
    pension rights 140, 662
    Potsdam Declaration 139
    Supreme Commander for the Allied
        Powers (SCAP) 139, 140
Jerusalem xvii, xviii, 8, 71, 92, 99–102, 187,
    204–5, 207
    absence of democratic accountability
        and judicial review 201
    bilateralism 204
    centralised governance 197–9, 205–6
    communitarian purpose 192, 195, 204
    complaints procedure 617
    conceptual deficits 200
    diplomatic protection 567
    direct model of administration 396
    Draft Constitution 196
    establishment of relations with state
        entities 569
    functional internationalisation 67–8,
        201–3

Jerusalem (*cont.*)
  Governor of Jerusalem 198, 201
  Holy Places 67–8, 195, 202, 204
  human rights obligations 481
  imposed constitutionalism 711,
    712
  inter-community balance 199
  judiciary 199
  lack of integrative mechanisms and
    local consent 200–1
  legal personality 556–7
  neutralisation 402
  Partition Resolution 195–6
  petitions 201, 206, 396
  power-sharing 205–6
  pre-emptive status determination 547
  Statute for the City of Jerusalem 98,
    99–102, 196–201, 711
  territorial integrity 542
  territorial internationalisation 61–2, 67,
    68, 195–201
  treaty-making power 571–2
  Trusteeship Council functions 99–102,
    196, 197–8, 199, 201, 202–3, 206,
    396, 439
  trusteeship in a non-trusteeship context
    197
  see also Palestine
Jordan
  title claim over Jerusalem 61–2
judicial independence 701, 705
  appointment of judges 702–3, 705
  assignment of judges to cases 704, 705
  CPA 704–5
  misconceptions 702–5
  UNMIK 702–4
judicial review 84–5, 114, 602
  absence of review 603–6
  detentions 700
  domestic institutions 633
  by independent international courts
    643–4
  mechanism of indirect review 607–10
  mechanisms of direct review 606–7
  post-war occupation 138
  review of executive authority 602–3
  review of legislative authority
    610–15

Kabila, Laurent 385
Kant, Immanuel 37, 519
Kashiwagi, Takeshi 607
Kelsen, Hans 41, 102, 133*n*, 419–20
Khmer Rouge 270, 274, 275
Klein, Jacques 282, 384
Knoll, Bernhard 533*n*
Koschnick, Hans 303, 308

Kosovo, UN Interim Administration in
    Kosovo (UNMIK) xix, 2, 10–11, 14, 15,
    23, 24, 35, 63, 71, 149, 259, 267,
    308–9, 355, 356, 393, 399
  applicable law, definition of 664–7, 672,
    673
  assessment 330–2, 742, 753
  authority dispute 658
  as benevolent autocracy 326–8
  claims commission 628–30
  Comprehensive Proposal for the Kosovo
    Status Settlement 315, 317, 715–16
  conditional sovereignty 757, 758
  Constitutional Framework for
    Provisional Self-Government 312–13,
    321, 322, 325–6, 329, 609, 714–15,
    725
  criticism 327
  detentions 507–8, 693–6
  dictatorship of virtues 328–9
  diplomatic protection 567–8
  direct applicability of legislation 646,
    653, 666
  disengagement 729
  emergency situation argument 522–4
  establishment of relations with state
    entities 569, 570
  European Union and 738
  as *ex post facto* validation of intervention
    407–8
  exercise of regulatory powers 647, 648,
    649, 650
  FRY sovereignty 311, 312, 318, 331
  Housing and Property Claims
    Commission (HPCC) 682–3, 684,
    687–8, 689
  Housing and Property Directorate (HPD)
    682
  Human Rights Advisory Panel 328, 601
  Human Rights Court, proposed 328,
    603, 644
  human rights protection 328, 482,
    498–500, 502–3, 665
  immunities 584–5, 591–2, 603–4
  imposed constitutionalism 274, 714–16
  independent advisory panel 625–7
  indirect judicial review 607–10, 611
  institutional change 320–3
  internationalised territory 541–2
  judicial independence 702–4
  judicial policy choices 673–4
  Kosovo Force (KFOR) 324, 328, 431
    accountability 327, 499–500
    civilian functions 451–2, 498
    Commander (COMKFOR) 695
    detentions 332, 695–6
    lack of control over 330

proposed advisory panel 26, 625
protection of fundamental rights
    502–3
Kosovo Media Appeals Board 607–9
lack of public support 331
legal personality 558–10
legal system 319–20, 328–9
mandate 269
media control 607–9
minority rights protection 324–6
Ombudsperson Institution 622–3,
    628
Operation Allied Force 323, 407
origin 309–10
people's rights, fostering 324–6
post-conflict responsibility 323–4
privilege and immunities 584–5
property issues 682–3, 684, 687–8, 689
Provisional Institutions of
    Self-Government 322, 328, 667
restoration of domestic authority 724–5
restraint in import of foreign traditions
    673–4
Saar administration compared 267
Security Council Resolution 309–10, 311,
    322, 745
Special Chamber of the Supreme Court
    609–10
Special Representative of the
    Secretary-General (SRSG) 318, 320–1,
    322–3, 324, 325, 326, 396, 604, 665,
    693, 704
statebuilding 317–23, 332
status issue 310–17, 401–2, 549, 551–3
Temporary Media Commissions (TMC)
    608
territorial conflict solution 310–17
as "third generation" operation 16, 17
transitional strategic neutralisation 268,
    402
travel documents, issuance 566
treaty-making power 573–5
tripartite function 310–24
UN Special Envoy 314
UNTAES and 280, 283, 286
UNTAET and 333–4, 337–40, 347
war crimes trials 632

lawmaking by international
    administrations 645, 647–8, 706
authority disputes 656, 663–4
    CPA 658–63
    OHR 657–8
    UNMIK 658
    UNOSOM 657
definition of applicable law 664, 672–3
    CPA 672

UNMIK 664–7
UNTAET 667–71
detentions 690, 700–1
    CPA 697–700
    INTERFET 696–7
    UNMIK and KFOR 693–6
    UNOSOM II 692
    UNTAC 690–2
direct applicability 645–6
    justification 651–4
direct effect 646–7
institutional diversity 648
judicial independence 701, 705
    appointment of judges 702–3, 705
    assignment of judges to cases 704, 705
    CPA 704–5
    misconceptions 702–5
    removal from office 703–4
    UNMIK 702–4
judicial policy choices 673
    fundamental questions doctrine 675–8
    restraint in import of foreign
        traditions 673–5
legal nature of regulatory acts 648
    justification of direct applicability
        651–4
    regulatory acts as domestic acts 650–1
    regulatory acts as international acts
        650–1
    sui generis argument 649–50
limits
    authority disputes 656–63
    mandate of international
        administrations 656
    UN administration and link to
        international peace and security
        654–6
property issues 678–9
    Bosnia and Herzegovina 293, 295–6,
        681–2, 683–4, 685, 686, 687
    conflation of restitution and return
        687–90
    CPA 683
    enforcement problem 687
    exclusiveness problem 685–7
    UNMIK 682–3, 684, 687–8, 689
    UNTAES 679–81
League of Nations xvii, xxii, 1, 7–8, 14, 16,
    38, 52, 59
Covenant 23
direct international territorial
    administration 395–6
dispute settlement 70–1
    see also Danzig; Leticia; Memel; Saar
    Territory
International Zone of Tangier 7, 57–8
legal personality 8

League of Nations (*cont.*)
  Mandate System *see* Mandate System of
    the League of Nations
  peacemaking 23
  Saar Territory *see* Saar Territory
  "sacred trust of civilisation" 74, 94, 113,
    151
legal personality 553–4
  CPA 560–4
  Danzig 554–5
  East Timor 556, 558–60
  express mandate 557–8
  functional 557–60
  implied powers 558–60
  Jerusalem 556–7
  Kosovo 558–10
  League of Nations 8
  Namibia 557–8
  OHR 560–2
  partial legal personality 112–13, 554, 570
  recognition by UN acts 556–7
  Trieste 555
  UN acts and 556–60
  by way of agreement 554–6
  West Irian 555–6
legal status of administered territory 535,
    577–8
  diplomatic protection 566
    Treaty of Versailles 566–7
    United Nations practice 567–8
  establishment of relations with state
    entities 568–70
  exercise of administering authority
    549–53
  external representation 564–77
  international territories 542–3
  internationalised entities 539–43
  internationalised states 540–1
  internationalised territories 536–7,
    541–2
  internationally guaranteed statehood
    536
  Kosovo 310–17, 401–2, 549, 551–3
  legal personality 553–4
    CPA 560–4
    express mandate 557–8
    functional 557–60
    implied powers 558–60
    OHR 560–2
    partial legal personality 112–13, 554,
      570
    recognition by UN acts 556–7
    UN acts and 556–60
    by way of agreement 554–6
  Mandate System 86
    location of sovereignty 86–8
    nature of authority 89–91

  suspended sovereignty 87
    trust concept 89–91
  narrow status concepts 536
  notions from legal doctrine 535–6
  passports, issuance 564–5
  representation in international
    conferences and organisations
    575
    Danzig 575–6
    Namibia 576–7
  status concepts 535–43
  status decisions 544–53
    timing 551
  status resolution missions 401–2
  territories of international concern
    538–9
  travel documents, issuance 565–6
  treaty-making power 570–1
    early treaty arrangements 571–2
    UN practice 572–5
  Trusteeship System 111
    partial legal personality 112–13
    sovereignty 112, 150
    trusteeship authority 113–14
  UN status determinations 545–6
    enabling determinations 548–9
    Eritrea 546–7
    Jerusalem 547
    Kosovo 548
    Namibia 548
    pre-emptive determination 546–7
  vague status notions 536–8
legal theory
  dispute settlement 33–5
  international territorial administration
    and 33–40
  Memel 66
  problem-solving approach 22, 24,
    35–6
legality of international territorial
    administration 22
  Article 1 (3) in conjunction with Article
    55 465–6
  Articles 2 (1) and 2 (4) 463–5
  authorisation to administer territories
    authority of states 448–9
    civilian responsibilities as annex of
      enforcement action 451–2
    international organisations 450–1
    limits on state-based frameworks
      449–50
    practice 451–3
    quasi-mandate 453
    SC Resolutions 1483 and 1511 453
    states 447–50
  democratic governance 510–11
    applicability of standards 511–14

application of standards to
  international administrations
  512–14
constitution-framing and 707
democracy as a human right 513–14
functional duality 512–13
scope of obligation 514–16
universalisation of democratic
  standards 511–12
General Assembly 436
  Articles 11 (2) and 14, UN Charter
    436–8
  implied powers 438–9
  legal basis in the UN Charter 436–9
  transitional administrations with
    military component 437–8
  Uniting for Peace doctrine 439
human rights 479–80
  applicability 480–503
  customary law obligations 485–90
  derogation from obligations 506–8
  exception by virtue of overwhelming
    Chapter VII resolution 508–10
  extraterritorial application of human
    rights treaties 496–503
  formal treaty accession 491–2
  "functional duality" theory 490–1
  functional succession to treaty
    obligations 492–6
  institutional commitment 481–4
  jurisdiction 485–90
  operations of international
    organisations 498–503
  relationship between human rights
    law and international
    humanitarian law 504–6
  scope of obligations 503–10
  self-commitment to human rights
    273–4, 481–4
  state obligations within framework of
    multinational administrations
    497–8
  treaty obligations 491–503
legal basis in the UN Charter 423
  General Assembly action 436–9
  Secretary-General 441–4
  Security Council action 423–36
  Trusteeship Council 439–41
limits of international authority 454
  Articles 76, under 455
  nexus to international peace and
    security 454–5
occupation law 467
  applicability to international
    administrations 467–76
  application by way of analogy 474
  deficiencies 478–9

humanitarian law applicable to UN
  forces 468–9
peacetime occupation 477–8
peacetime occupation by default 476
power vacuums 474–6, 477
ratione materiae 471
ratione personae 468
scope of obligations 476–8
territorial administrations and
  classical occupying powers
  compared 471–3
Secretary-General, legal basis in the UN
  Charter 441–4
Security Council 406, 423–4
  Article 40 432
  Article 41 424–30
  Articles 24 and/or 39 in conjunction
    with Articles 29 and/or 98 432–4
  Articles 42 and 48 431
  Chapter VI, Article 36 (1) 435–6
  Chapter VII 424–32
  compatibility of UN governance with
    function of Security Council 425–7
  enforcement action 429–30
  implied powers 434
  legal basis in the UN Charter 423–36
  peacekeeping 435–6
  power to supersede domestic
    governance structures 427–8
  practice under Article 41 430
  sanctions 428
self-determination right 457–8
  applicability 458–9
  constitution-framing and 707
  external self-determination 459–60
  internal self-determination 35, 152–3,
    459–60
  obligations of international territorial
    authorities 460
  political participation and 461–3
  prohibition on imposition of form of
    government 460–1
territorial authority under UN Charter
  415
  Article 2 (1) and 420–2
  Article 2 (7) and 420–2
  Chapter XIII and 416, 422–3
  drafting history of Charter 416
  institutional practice 416–19
  Namibia 418–19
  prohibition of interference and 420–2
  protection of sovereignty and 420–2
  systemic coherence and 419–23
  Trieste 413, 416–18
territorial integrity and political
  independence guarantee 463–5
Trusteeship Council 439–41

legitimacy of international territorial
    authority 22, 517
  emergency situation argument 522–4
  features of international territorial
      authority 517–18
  functionalist criteria 528
    expertise 528–9
    independence and neutrality 529–30
  legitimacy by consent 519
    case-specific consent 521–2
    delegation of authority 519–21
  models of legitimation 518–30
  participatory legitimacy 527
  utilitarian argument 48, 524–6
Leticia 7, 14, 23, 63, 71, 78, 233
  assessment 236, 736
  background 234–5
  direct model of intervention 395
  Geneva Agreement 234–5
  Governing Commission 235, 236, 395
  internationalised territory 541–2
  investigation Committee 234
  League's engagement 235–6
  Treaty of Friendship and Co-operation
      235
  UNTAES compared 267–8
Liberia
  Comprehensive Peace Agreement (Accra
      Agreement) 382, 384
  National Election Commission 384
  National Transitional Government of
      Liberia 382, 383
  UN Mission in Liberia (UNMIL) 23, 24,
      71, 350, 381–2, 393, 399
    assessment 384, 742
    background 382
    capacity-building 384
    consent 400
    elections 384
    governance assistance role 383
    "light footprint" agenda 383
    mandate 382–3
    police forces 384
    practice 383–4
Libya, governance assistance mission 71,
    148, 208–9, 232, 268, 398
  assessment 212–13
  background 209–10
  consent 400, 742
  constitution-framing 210–11, 212, 213,
      708
  Council for Libya 211
  deference to local rule 210, 213
  as planned decolonisation 212–13
  self-determination 213
  transitional power-sharing arrangement
      210–11
  UN Commissioner 211–13

"light footprint" agenda 2, 17, 393, 744
  Afghanistan 17, 351, 356–7, 361
  balance of individual and collective
      rights and 361
  Iraq 351
  Liberia 383
Linas–Marcoussis Agreement 388
Lithuania 66, 185
  see also Memel
Lloyd George, David 77
local ownership 348–9, 350, 351, 364, 393
  Afghanistan 360, 361
  Iraq 369
Locke, John 519
London Ambassadorial Conference 1913 56
Lugard, Frederick 80, 156n

McArthur, General Douglas 139
McNair, Lord Arnold Duncan 88, 113,
    114
Mandate System of the League of Nations
    25, 49, 155–8, 752
  A-Mandates 76, 82n, 86, 88
  Article 22 of the League Covenant 73
    drafting history 76–8
    promotion of well-being 81–3
    reporting system 83
    "sacred trust of civilisation" 74, 94,
        113, 151
    sovereignty and 87–8
    trusteeship concept 89–91
    "tutelage" of peoples 79–80, 94, 151
  B-Mandates 76, 82n, 88
  challenges 78–91
  choice of indirect administration 76–8
  C-Mandates 76, 82n, 88
  economic development 80, 84
  fiduciary authority 74, 89–90, 155
  governance issues 79–83, 88
  institutional accountability 83–6, 599,
      615
    annual report to League Council 83–4
    judicial supervision 84–5
    petition system 85–6
  international territorial administration
      distinguished 156–8
  judicial supervision 84–5
  native customs and institutions 81–2,
      152
  objectives 73–4
  origin 74–6
  Permanent Court 84–5
  Permanent Mandate Commission
    accountability issues 83–4
    governance issues 80–1, 82
    petition system 85–6
    reporting system 83
    supervision 84

petition system 85–6
sovereignty and 86–8
status issues 86
  location of sovereignty 86–8
  nature of authority 89–91
  suspended sovereignty 87
  trust concept 89–91
Tanganyika 80–1
trust concept 89–91
Memel 8, 23, 35, 78
  functional internationalisation 66–7, 71
  League of Nations' engagement 185–7
    Commission of Experts 186
    draft Statute 186
    as guarantor of Memel settlement
      186–7
    Memel Convention 186–7
    port administration 187
  Lithuanian sovereignty 186
  neutralisation 185
  PCIJ dispute resolution function 187, 396
  Treaty of Versailles 66, 185
Mill, John Stuart 524
minimal state 523
MINURSO see Western Sahara
mitigation theory 409
Model Status of Forces Agreement 627
models of administration
  creation by consent and/or by unilateral
    act 399–400
  direct 395–7
  exclusive forms of authority 397–9
  indirect 397
  shared forms of authority 397–9
models of involvement 159–60
Montesquieu 759n
MONUC see Congo
Morocco
  French Protectorate 57
  International Zone of Tangier 7,
    57–8
Mostar see Bosnia and Herzegovina
Mosul 71
multinational state administration see
  territorial internationalisation

Namibia
  Constituent Assembly 222, 224
  constitution-framing 222, 224, 708, 709
  de jure UN authority 92
  legal personality 557
    express mandate 557–8
  participation of domestic actors 718
  South Africa
    continued occupation 256, 259
    Mandate over Namibia 92, 104–6, 220,
      252–3
    Namibian Accords 221

status determination 548
SWAPO 220, 224
territorial internationalisation 543
Trusteeship System and 103–6
UN Council for Namibia 9, 11, 14–15, 64,
    71, 219, 252–4, 398, 400
  application for ILO membership 257–8
  assessment 259, 742
  as authority-in-trust 255
  criticism of establishment of 418–19
  Decree No. 1 256–7
  diplomatic protection 567
  direct applicability of decrees 646, 653
  disputes over 254
  dual role 255
  exclusive, state-like authority 254–5,
    397
  exercise of regulatory powers 647,
    649, 650
  limited governmental capacities 256–8
  record 258–9
  representation in international
    conferences and organisations
    576–7
  review of legislative authority 610
  travel documents, issuance 565–6
  virtual governance 254–8
UN Transition Assistance Group (UNTAG)
    9, 71, 220, 232, 233, 253, 398
  assessment 224–5
  broad mandate 222–4
  consent 400
  constitution-framing 222, 224, 708
  electoral process, organisation 223
  limited regulatory authority 221–2
  MINURSO compared 225, 227–30
  Namibian Accords 221
  Special Representative of the
    Secretary-General (SRSG) 221–2, 223,
    396
  transition process 224
  UNTAC compared 271
nationbuilding see statebuilding
NATO 451, 738
natural resources
  internationalisation 32
Nauru 63, 110
neutralisation 204, 402
  Danzig 174, 177, 183, 402
  Eastern Slavonia 268, 402
  Jerusalem 402
  Kosovo 268, 402
  Memel 185
  post-war experiments 187–203
  Saar Territory 169–70, 173
  as transitional device 402
  Treaty of Versailles 173
  Trieste 189–90, 205, 402

neutrality 751–2
  classical principle 752–3
    decline 753
    exceptions 753n
New Guinea 107
New Haven School 34

occupation law
  applicability to international
    administrations 467–76
  application by way of analogy 474
  caretaker governments 379
  deficiencies 478–9
  humanitarian law applicable to UN
    forces 468–9
  legality of international administration
    and 467–79
  peacetime occupation 477–8
    by default 476
  postliminium 122
  power vacuums 474–6, 477
  ratione materiae 471
  ratione personae 468
  scope of obligations 476–8
  Somalia 260
  territorial administrations and classical
    occupying powers compared 471–3
  uti possidetis 122
  see also Crete; post-war occupation
Ombudsperson 601–2, 621–5
  Bosnia and Herzegovina 70, 293, 622
    Mostar 305–6, 617, 621
  East Timor 623
  Iraq 624
  Kosovo 622–3, 628
ONUC see Congo
Operation Enduring Freedom 352, 408
Oppenheim, Lassa 752
Organisational Statute of Albania 56–7
Ottoman Empire 55, 56
Ouagadougou Agreement 392
Outer Space 65

Palestine 62
  draft trusteeship agreement 98
  Mandate 84, 195, 197
  Special Committee on Palestine 100
  UK Mandate 92
  see also Jerusalem
Paris, Roland 677
Paris Accords on the Political Settlement
  of Cambodia 1991 see Cambodia
Paris Peace Treaty Conference 189,
  213
"partnership" approach 351, 393
  Ivory Coast 392
  MONUC 385, 386

passports
  issue by international administrations
    564–5
Peace and Security Council (PSC) of the
    African Union (AU) 389, 391, 392,
    397, 738
Peacebuilding Commission xix, 3
  mandate 445–6
peacekeeping 12, 147–54, 219, 266–7, 396
  changing conception of trusteeship
    150–1
  collapsed states 148–9
  conceptual developments 149–54
  conflict resolution 24
  governance assistance missions and 208
  human rights components 483
  internal armed conflicts 148–9
  internal self-determination and 152–3
  international territorial administration
    and 1–2, 9, 16, 24, 49
  legal basis for actions 435–6
  multi-dimensional 1–2, 9, 12, 147, 208
  neutrality and non-intervention 148
  statebuilding and 149
  UN as neutral buffer 148
  Uniting for Peace doctrine 439
peacemaking 22, 39, 49, 266–7, 734–5
  conflict resolution 23–5
  Germany and Japan 39
  justification of governance and 25–6
  League of Nations 23
  new normative underpinning of
    territorial governance 151–4
  post-conflict administration 26–9
  sustainability of peace 22–5
Pelt, Adrian 43, 211, 212–13
Permanent Court of International Justice
    (PCIJ) 84
  advisory opinions, Danzig 179, 184, 396
  direct invokability 646
  dispute resolution function, Memel 187,
    396
Permanent Mandate Commission see
    Mandate System of the League of
    Nations
petition system 599
  Jerusalem 201, 206, 396
  Mandate System 85–6
  Saar Territory 170, 396, 599
  Trieste 193, 194, 206, 599
  Trusteeship Council 107–9, 201
  UN Charter 107–9
positivism 34
post-conflict administration
  as corollary of intervention 26–9
  occupation see post-war occupation
  "responsibility to protect" 27–9

post-conflict engagement 409–10
post-surrender occupation 125–6
  Fourth Geneva Convention 141
  see also Germany; Japan
post-war occupation 25–6, 115
  as administrative device 116–17
  armistice occupations 123–5
  consent-based occupations 123–5
  debellatio doctrine 120*n*, 125, 134–7, 138
    decline 141
  demise of concept of occupation in
    legal practice 141–2
  fiduciary authority 127, 155
  Fourth Geneva Convention 117–19,
    120–2, 141, 348
    post-surrender occupations 141
  Hague Regulations Respecting Laws and
    Customs of War 1907 116–17, 119,
    129, 134–7, 139–40, 144, 471
  humanitarian occupation 136
  international territorial administration
    distinguished 155
  interventionist occupation 136
  Iraq 142–6
    interim administration 144
    legal problems 379
    Operation Iraqi Freedom 144
    Security Council Resolution 1483
      (2003) 143–6
    UK and US as occupying powers 143,
      144
    US control 364
  judicial review powers 138
  limitations of occupation authority
    119–23
  multilateralism 142
  post-surrender occupation 125–6
    Fourth Geneva Convention 141
    see also Germany; Japan
  protection of civilians 118
  rationale of laws of occupation 116–19
  treaty-based occupation 123–5
  trusteeship occupation 117–18, 136
  zones of occupation 55–6
  see also occupation law
Potsdam Conference 188, 399
Potsdam Declaration 127, 128–9, 130, 132,
  138, 139
power vacuums 13, 474–6, 477
Pretoria Agreement 389
Principal Allied Powers 86, 87
property issues 678–9
  Bosnia and Herzegovina 293, 295–6,
    681–2, 683–4, 685, 686, 687
  CPA 683
  enforcement problem 687
  exclusiveness problem 685–7

UNMIK 682–3, 684, 687–8, 689
UNTAES 679–81
protected states 45–8
  historical context 47–8
  meaning 45–6
  treaty basis 47
protectorates 45–8
  historical context 47–8
  meaning 46
  takeover of foreign relations 47
  treaty basis 47

Rahman, Abdul 362
rationalism 36
  Grotian 38, 39
Ratner, Steven R. 159–60
realism 36, 38
referendum assistance 219
  see also Western Sahara
relationship with domestic actors 717–18
  see also self-determination;
    self-government
Report of the High-level Panel on Threats,
  Challenges and Change 3, 27–8, 410
"responsibility to protect" 27–9, 350
river commissions 64–5
Rousseau, Jean-Jacques 519
Rwanda-Urundi 107, 109

Saar Territory xvii, xxi, 7, 11, 14, 23, 35, 71,
  78, 163–73, 204, 205, 206
  Advisory Council 167, 168
  assessment 171–3, 736
  background 163–4
  balancing German and French interests
    164, 165–7
  diplomatic protection 567
  direct model of administration 395–6
  exercise of regulatory powers 647
  Governing Commission 172, 395, 398
    consultation 167–8
    criticism 173
    duties 168
    educational policies 166–7
    lack of accountability 173
    neutralising function 169–70, 173
    powers 165, 166, 167
    status 166
  Hitler and 164
  as internationalised territory 541–2
  limited scope of people's rights 167–9
  monitoring function of League Council
    170–1
  passports, issuance 564, 565
  petitions and memorials 170, 396, 599
  referendum 14*n*, 205
  reparation 60

Saar Territory (cont.)
  sovereignty 172
  status dispute resolution 401–2, 550n
  Treaty of Versailles 163–4, 398
    civil liberties 168
    diplomatic protection 567
    ultra vires doctrine 611
    UNMIK compared 267
"sacred trust of civilisation" 74, 94, 113,
    151
sanctions 428, 448, 618
Sayre, Francis Bowes 59n, 78
Scelle, Georges 613
Schmitt, Carl 523
seabed 32
Secretary-General
  fact-finding missions 443n
  implementation of UN mandates 443–4
  initiation of frameworks of
    administration 443
  institutional practice 396, 442–4
  legal basis for territorial
    administrations 441–4
  limited autonomous powers 442
  managerial functions 442–4
  special representatives see Special
    Representative of the
    Secretary-General (SRSG) model
Security Council xvii, xviii, 30, 39, 98, 738,
    739, 740
  authority xviii
  Committee on UN Administration and
    Governance Assistance, proposed
    445
  criticism 740
  discretionary powers xviii
  implementation of decisions 651–2
  legal basis for actions 406, 423–4
    Article 40 432
    Article 41 424–30
    Articles 24 and/or 39 in conjunction
      with Articles 29 and/or 98 432–4
    Articles 42 and 48 431
    Chapter VI, Article 36 (1) 435–6
    Chapter VII 424–32
    compatibility of UN governance with
      function of Security Council 425–7
    enforcement action 429–30
    implied powers 434
    peacekeeping 435–6
    power to supersede domestic
      governance structures 427–8
    practice under Article 41 430
    sanctions 428
  legitimacy 740
  peacebuilding operations 266–7
  Resolution 1037 280, 282, 283, 286

Resolution 1244 653
Resolution 1272 653
Resolution 1483 143–6, 366, 369, 377,
    453, 653, 658, 659
Resolution 1511 366, 370, 453
Trieste 192–3, 194, 206, 396, 413, 416–18
unauthorised interventions 407–8
Western Contact Group 220
see also UN Charter
self-determination
  applicability to international territorial
    administrations 458–9
  concept 718–19
  constitution-framing and 707
  external 459–60
  internal 35, 152–3, 459–60
  League of Nations era 718
  Libya 213
  obligations of international territorial
    authorities 460
  peacekeeping and 152–3
  political participation and 461–3
  prohibition on imposition of form of
    government 460–1
  right 20, 25, 27, 35, 457–63
  West Irian 247, 248, 251–2
self-government xviii, 19–20, 94
  techniques of realising 719–20
    consultation 720–2
    disengagement and beyond 726–9
    elections 726–7, 728
    exit strategies 727, 728, 730
    restoration of domestic authority
      723–5
self-interest 48, 54, 156, 524–6, 709
Shanghai
  International Settlement 7, 65–6
Sihanouk, Prince 275
Smuts, Jan 75, 77
Somalia
  Addis Ababa Agreement 261, 263
  AMISOM 452, 738
  Barre regime 261
  military coup 261
  Transitional National Council (TNC) 261,
    263
  UN Operation in Somalia (UNOSOM II)
    9–10, 12, 23, 24, 35, 149, 233,
    259–60, 268, 400
    assessment 264–5, 737, 742
    authority dispute 657
    background 260–1
    civilian mandate 262–3
    as co-governance operation 399
    de facto governance 263–4
    detentions 260, 692
    exercise of regulatory powers 647, 648

"exit without strategy" 727
judicial systems 263
lack of legal framework 264
laws of occupation and 260
military mandate 260
nature of mandate 262–3
power vacuum 13
restoration of domestic authority 724
termination of engagement 260
UNOC compared 259–60, 266
United Nations Task Force (UNITAF) 261,
    262, 263
South Africa
Mandate over Namibia 92, 104–6, 220,
    252–3
South West Africa see Namibia
South West Africa People's Organisation
    (SWAPO) 220, 224
sovereignty
"conditional sovereignty" 757, 758
conditions for self-rule and
    independence and 756–8
constitution-framing and 707
"constrained sovereignty" 757
disaggregation 755–6
"earned sovereignty" 757, 758
empowerment of non-state entities 756
functionalist understanding 33
Mandate System and 86–8
"phased sovereignty" 757
protection of people's interests and
    755–6
theorisation of state sovereignty 35,
    754–8
Special Committee on Palestine 100
Special Representative of the
    Secretary-General (SRSG) model 194,
    221–2, 223, 396
Cambodia 270, 271, 272, 273, 275, 276,
    603, 652, 691–2, 740
diplomatic immunity 582
East Timor 334, 338, 339, 341–2, 345, 396
Ivory Coast 390, 391, 396
Kosovo 318, 320–1, 322–3, 324, 325, 326,
    396, 604, 665, 693, 704
Namibia 221–2, 223, 396
Spitzbergen 65
"standards of civilisation" 19
statebuilding 12–13, 49, 268, 404–6
Cambodia 268, 271–4
East Timor 268, 346–7
Eastern Slavonia 281
Iraq 406
Kosovo 317–23, 332
peacekeeping and 149
post-war Germany and Japan 405
self-interest and 48

status of administered territory see legal
    status of administered territory
status of international administering
    authorities 579–80
immunities see immunities
internal responsibilities 580–1
privileges 581
Statute of Tangier 58
Statute of Trieste see Trieste
Stoyanovski, Jacob 88
strategic liberalisation 18
surrogate state 21

Tanganyika 107, 108
Mandate 80–1
Tangier
arrangement 267
multinational administration 7, 57–8
territorial internationalisation 7, 57–8
Taylor, Charles 382
territorial internationalisation 50, 51
aftermath of World War II 61–2
Albanian Control Commission 56–7, 58–9
concept of "international(ised)
    territories" 51–2
Cracow 7, 53–4
de facto governance of Crete 7, 54–6
institutionalisation of territorial
    administration as conflict
    management device 62–4
international territorial administration
    and 52–64
International Zone of Tangier 7, 57–8
Jerusalem 61–2, 67, 68, 195–201
multinational state administration 53–9,
    62–3
post-war eras 59–62
see also internationalisation
Togoland 107, 109
transfer of territory 403, 550n
travel documents
issue by international administrations
    565–6
Treaty of Paris 177, 179
Treaty of Versailles 1, 7, 38, 49, 59–61
Danzig 174, 175–8, 179, 180, 183, 398
diplomatic protection 566–7
dispute resolution 59–61
exclusive forms of authority 398
Hitler and 164, 420–2
Memel 66, 185
neutralisation 173
Saar Territory 163–4, 168, 398
shared forms of authority 398
treaty-making power 570–1
early treaty arrangements 571–2
UN practice 572–5

Trieste 204, 205, 206, 207, 413
  assessment 193–4
  authority of Governor 191–2, 193, 194
  bilateralism and 204
  communitarian objective 192, 204
  complaints procedure 617
  Danzig model compared 189, 191–2
  governing framework of Statute 189–92
  guarantee of observance of Statute by
      Governor 190–1
  historical context 188–9
  human rights protection 192, 481
  imposed constitutionalism 711, 712
  legal personality 555
  mandate 746
  neutralising function of Trieste
      settlement 189–90, 205, 402
  non-implementation 193
  petitions 193, 194, 206, 599
  representation in international
      conferences and organisations 575
  Security Council responsibilities 192–3,
      194, 206, 396, 413, 416–18
  Statute of Trieste xvii, 8, 35, 61, 71, 72,
      187, 188–94, 711
  territorial integrity 542
trusteeship 197, 410–12
  Mandate System and 89–91
  in non-trusteeship context 197
  post-war occupation 117–18, 136
  prohibition 420
Trusteeship Council xvii, 78, 98, 739, 740
  composition 110–11
  Jerusalem 99–102, 196, 197–8, 199, 201,
      202–3, 206, 396, 439
  legal basis for territorial
      administrations 439–41
  petition system 107–9, 201
  revitalisation proposals 440–1
Trusteeship System xvii, xxi, 25, 49, 91, 92,
      155–8, 447, 511
  Article 81, UN Charter 95–6
      drafting and construction 96–8
      practice under 99–106
  Articles 77 and 78, UN Charter 422–3
  authority 113–14
  concept of trusteeship 197, 410–12
  consent requirement 422
  Declaration by the United Nations on
      National Independence 92–3
  decolonisation 92, 94
  fiduciary authority 151, 155
  genesis 92–3
  institutional accountability 106–10, 599,
      615
      petition system 107–9
      questionnaire system 616

institutional diversity 110–11
international territorial administration
    and 96–114, 156–8
  Jerusalem 197
  limitation 422–3
  Namibia 103–6
  Nauruan independence 110
  petition system 107–9, 201
  questionnaire system 616
  revitalisation proposals 440–1
  sovereignty and 422
  status issues 111
      partial legal personality 112–13
      sovereignty 112, 150
      trusteeship authority 113–14
  Statute for Jerusalem 98, 99–102
  supervision under Article 87 109
  trusteeship agreement 422
  visiting missions 98, 108, 109, 111

ultra vires control 638–9
  acts of occupying powers 642–3
  domestic courts 638–43
  options for review 641
  review of acts of Chapter VII-based
      administrations 639–41
  transitional administrations created by
      General Assembly 641–2

UN Charter xviii, 8, 39
  annexation 150
  Article 1 (2) 457–63
  Article 1 (3) 465–6
  Article 2 (1) 420–2, 463–5, 752
  Article 2 (4) 463–5
  Article 2 (7) 420–2, 752
  Article 4 752
  Article 10 109
  Article 11 (2) 436–8
  Article 14 436–8
  Article 24 416–17
  Article 55 465–6
  Article 73 94
  Article 76 455–7
  Article 78 150
  Article 81 95–6, 439–40
      drafting and construction 96–8
      practice under 99–106
  Article 87 109
  Article 98 432–4, 442, 444
  Article 99 442
  Article 105 582
  Chapter VI, Article 36 (1) 435–6
  Chapter VII xviii, 39–40, 286, 383, 386,
      416
      Article, enforcement action 429–30
      Article 40 432

Article 41 424–30, 448
Articles 24 and/or 39 in conjunction
    with Articles 29 and/or 98 432–4
Articles 42 and 48 431
authority of states to administer
    territories 448–9
compatibility of UN governance with
    function of Security Council 425–7
drafting history 520
legal basis for territorial
    administrations 424–32
Security Council action 424–32
security exceptions and 508–10
Chapter XI 93–4
Chapter XII 93, 94, 96
Chapter XIII, territorial authority and
    416, 422–3
Chapters VI and VII 150
drafting history 416, 425
    Article 81 96–8
    Chapter VII 520
General Assembly see General Assembly
legal basis for territorial
    administrations 423
    General Assembly action 436–9
    Secretary-General 441–4
    Security Council action 423–36
    Trusteeship Council 439–41
monitoring compliance 107
petition system 107–9
Secretary-General see Secretary-General
Security Council see Security Council
territorial authority 415
    Article 2 (1) and 420–2
    Article 2 (7) and 420–2
    Chapter XIII and 416, 422–3
    drafting history of Charter 416
    institutional practice 416–19
    Namibia 418–19
    prohibition of interference and 420–2
    protection of sovereignty and 420–2
    systemic coherence and 419–23
    Trieste 413, 416–18
trusteeship see Trusteeship System
UNAMA see Afghanistan
UNAMI see Iraq
United Nations 52, 59, 62, 737–41
    diplomatic protection 567–8
    misconduct of personnel 387
    public authority by default 268
    status determinations 545–6
        enabling determinations 548–9
        Eritrea 546–7
        Jerusalem 547
        Kosovo 548
        Namibia 548
        pre-emptive determination 546–7

treaty-making power 572–5
see also General Assembly;
    Secretary-General; Security Council;
    UN Charter
United Nations Task Force (UNITAF) 261,
    262
Uniting for Peace doctrine 439
Universal Declaration of Human Rights
    152, 589
Universal Postal Union 30, 56
UNMIK see Kosovo
UNMIL see Liberia
UNOSOM II see Somalia
UNTAC see Cambodia
UNTAES see Eastern Slavonia
UNTAET see East Timor
UNTAG see Namibia
UNTEA see West Irian
Upper Silesia 70

Verzijl, Jan Hendrik Willem 538
Vilna 71
Virally, Michel 135–6

war crimes 285, 632
waterways
    international administration 64–5
West Irian
    decolonisation 15, 246–52, 398
    establishment of relations with state
        entities 568
    legal personality 555–6
    UN Temporary Executive Authority
        (UNTEA) 9, 11, 14, 15, 35, 64, 71,
        233, 246–7, 268, 269, 393, 400, 737
        consent 400
        "exit without strategy" 727
        human rights obligations 481–2
        provisional UN authority 247–9
        self-determination 247, 248, 251–2
        status dispute resolution 401, 402
        territorial internationalisation 542–3
        transfer of territory 550n
        travel documents, issuance 565
        UN as government 249–51, 396–7
Western Contact Group 220
Western Sahara, UN Mission for the
    Referendum in Western Sahara
    (MINURSO) 9, 14–15, 71, 149, 219,
    225, 268, 398
    assessment 230–2
    draft code of conduct 228
    historical dispute 225, 226–7
    mandate 227
    Peace plan 228–30
    phased sovereignty 757
    role of UN 227–30

Settlement plan 227–8, 231
status dispute resolution 401, 402
UN Identification Commission 228
UNTAG compared 225, 227–30
voter identification and registration 227,
    228
Western Samoa 109
Wilde, Ralph 11
William von Wied 57

Wilson, Woodrow 74, 75, 77
World Law 40
World Trade Organization 30
Wright, Quincy 136

Yalta Conference 1945 93
Ydit, Méir 537

zones of occupation model 55–6

CAMBRIDGE STUDIES IN INTERNATIONAL AND COMPARATIVE LAW

Books in the series

The Law and Practice of International Territorial Administration: Versailles to Iraq and Beyond Carsten Stahn

United Nations Sanctions and the Rule of Law Jeremy Farrall

National Law in WTO Law: Effectiveness and Good Governance in the World Trading System Sharif Bhuiyan

The Threat of Force in International Law Nikolas Stürchler

Indigenous Rights and United Nations Standards Alexandra Xanthaki

International Refugee Law and Socio-Economic Rights Michelle Foster

The Protection of Cultural Property in Armed Conflict Roger O'Keefe

Interpretation and Revision of International Boundary Decisions Kaiyan Homi Kaikobad

Multinationals and Corporate Social Responsibility: Limitations and Opportunities in International Law Jennifer A. Zerk

Judiciaries within Europe: A Comparative Review John Bell

Law in Times of Crisis: Emergency Powers in Theory and Practice Oren Gross and Fionnuala Ní Aoláin

Vessel-Source Marine Pollution: The Law and Politics of International Regulation Alan Tan

Enforcing Obligations Erga Omnes in International Law Christian J. Tams

Non-Governmental Organisations in International Law Anna-Karin Lindblom

Democracy, Minorities and International Law Steven Wheatley

Prosecuting International Crimes: Selectivity and the International Law Regime Robert Cryer

Compensation for Personal Injury in English, German and Italian Law: A Comparative Outline Basil Markesinis, Michael Coester, Guido Alpa, Augustus Ullstein

Dispute Settlement in the UN Convention on the Law of the Sea Natalie Klein

The International Protection of Internally Displaced Persons Catherine Phuong

Imperialism, Sovereignty and the Making of International Law Antony Anghie

Necessity, Proportionality and the Use of Force by States Judith Gardam

International Legal Argument in the Permanent Court of International Justice: The Rise of the International Judiciary Ole Spiermann

Great Powers and Outlaw States: Unequal Sovereigns in the International Legal Order Gerry Simpson

Local Remedies in International Law C. F. Amerasinghe

Reading Humanitarian Intervention: Human Rights and the Use of Force in International Law Anne Orford

Conflict of Norms in Public International Law: How WTO Law Relates to Other Rules of Law Joost Pauwelyn

Transboundary Damage in International Law Hanqin Xue

European Criminal Procedures Edited by Mireille Delmas-Marty and John Spencer

The Accountability of Armed Opposition Groups in International Law Liesbeth Zegveld

Sharing Transboundary Resources: International Law and Optimal Resource Use Eyal Benvenisti

International Human Rights and Humanitarian Law René Provost

Remedies Against International Organisations Karel Wellens

Diversity and Self-Determination in International Law Karen Knop

The Law of Internal Armed Conflict Lindsay Moir

International Commercial Arbitration and African States: Practice, Participation and Institutional Development Amazu A. Asouzu

The Enforceability of Promises in European Contract Law James Gordley

International Law in Antiquity David J. Bederman

Money Laundering: A New International Law Enforcement Model Guy Stessens

Good Faith in European Contract Law Reinhard Zimmermann and Simon Whittaker

On Civil Procedure J. A. Jolowicz

Trusts A Comparative Study Maurizio Lupoi

The Right to Property in Commonwealth Constitutions Tom Allen

International Organizations Before National Courts August Reinisch

The Changing International Law of High Seas Fisheries Francisco Orrego Vicuña

Trade and the Environment: A Comparative Study of EC and US Law Damien Geradin

Unjust Enrichment: A Study of Private Law and Public Values Hanoch Dagan

Religious Liberty and International Law in Europe Malcolm D. Evans

Ethics and Authority in International Law Alfred P. Rubin

Sovereignty Over Natural Resources: Balancing Rights and Duties Nico Schrijver

The Polar Regions and the Development of International Law Donald R. Rothwell

Fragmentation and the International Relations of Micro-States: Self-determination and Statehood Jorri Duursma

Principles of the Institutional Law of International Organizations C. F. Amerasinghe